R. Gupta's®

POPULAR MASTER GUIDE



# BSNL

Bharat Sanchar Nigam Ltd.

# Junior Accounts Officers [ JAO ]

## Recruitment Examination

*by*

RPH Editorial Board

RAMESH PUBLISHING HOUSE, NEW DELHI

**_Published by_**
O.P. Gupta *for* Ramesh Publishing House

**_Admin. Office_**
12-H, New Daryaganj Road, Opp. Officers' Mess,
New Delhi-110002 ✆ 23275224, 23245124

**E-mail:** info@rameshpublishinghouse.com
**For Online Shopping:** www.rameshpublishinghouse.com

**_Showroom_**
- Balaji Market, Nai Sarak, Delhi-6 ✆ 23253720, 23282525
- 4457, Nai Sarak, Delhi-6, ✆ 23918938



**Book Code: R-1198**

**ISBN: 978-81-7812-903-7**

**Price: ₹ 540**

**Printed at: Deepak Offset, Delhi**

# CONTENTS

# PAPER-II

---

# Scheme of Online Competitive Exam for Direct Recruitment of Junior Accounts Officers in BSNL

The Direct Recruitment of Junior Accounts Officers will be conducted on the following scheme of examination.

**Scheme**: There would be two subjects with one paper in each subject as under:

## SUBJECT-I : GENERAL ENGLISH & GENERAL APTITUDE/AWARENESS

**PAPER-1: General English & General Aptitude/Awareness: 3 hours**

(a) **General English:** 100 marks (Short Answer/Objective type)

(b) **General Aptitude/Awareness:** 50 marks (Objective type)

## SUBJECT-II : FINANCIAL & COMMERCIAL ACCOUNTS

**PAPER-2: Financial Management/Cost Accounting/Tax & Commercial Law: 3 hrs. : 300 marks (Objective type)**

**Note:** (a) In the General aptitude/Awareness Test, special attention will be paid to assess the candidate's capacity for general awareness. The standard of paper in General Awareness test will be such as may be expected of a Post-Graduate.

(b) The standard of the paper in Commerce Subjects, Taxation & Commercial Laws will be that of Commerce Post-Graduate Degree Examination of an Indian University.

Previous Paper (Solved)

# BSNL–Junior Accounts Officers (JAO) Online Exam, 2017*

## PAPER-I

**1.** Meaning of "Chicken feed":
A. A very small money
B. A huge money
C. Food for thought
D. None of these

**2.** Meaning of "Cost an Arm and a Leg":
A. Scene in battle field
B. War hero
C. Very expensive
D. Very Cheap

**3.** Meaning of "Fly by night":
A. Cat's eye B. Night journey
C. A bird busy in night D. Swindler

**4.** Synonym of Exhort:
A. Weak plea B. To urge strongly
C. Beg D. Borrow

**5.** Antonym of Blunt:
A. Lazy B. Easy
C. Sharp D. Speedy

**6.** Antonym of Brave:
A. Give B. Achieve
C. Gain D. Cowardly

**7.** Synonym of Abjure:
A. Happy B. To give
C. To take back D. Sorry

**8.** Synonym of Abrogate:
A. Create B. Abolish
C. Run D. Fascinate

**9.** Unfortunately, he ______ a lot of money to the bank.
A. owed B. borrowed
C. deposited D. lent

**10.** I ______ the apartment all day yesterday.
A. cleaned up B. clear
C. washed out D. None of these

**11.** Choose the word spelt correctly:
A. Macsculine B. Masculine
C. Maxculine D. Massculine

**12.** Choose the word spelt correctly:
A. Begininng B. Begining
C. Beignning D. Beginning

**13.** Choose the word spelt correctly:
A. Ambulance B. Ambulence
C. Ambulancs D. Ambalence

**14.** Choose the word spelt correctly:
A. Criticael B. Criticice
C. Criticise D. Criticese

**15.** Choose the word spelt correctly:
A. Substential B. Substandial
C. Substantial D. Substendial

**16.** Synonym of Botch:
A. Clumsy effort B. Positive effort
C. Blessing D. Mild

**17.** Synonym of Brusque:
A. Enjoy B. Polite
C. Speed D. Curt

**18.** Synonym of Chagrin:
A. Delight B. Vexation
C. Levy D. Give up

**19.** Synonym of Congruent:
A. Salute
B. Of different shape
C. Of the same shape
D. Dispose

* Online exam held on 05-11-2017.

**20.** Synonym of Copious:
A. Plenty B. Less
C. Good D. Discourage

**21.** Synonym of Debilitate:
A. To discourage B. Neat and clean
C. To strengthen D. To weaken

**22.** Synonym of Deluge:
A. Flood B. Dry
C. Less D. None of these

**23.** Synonym of Fetter:
A. Shackle B. Free
C. Strength D. Fat

**24.** Synonym of Gist:
A. Good B. Elaborate
C. Essence D. Bad

**25.** Synonym of Innate:
A. To borrow
B. To smell something
C. To run
D. Existing since birth

**26.** Synonym of Limpid:
A. Enjoy B. Cloudy
C. Clear D. Sorrow

**27.** Synonym of Maul:
A. Rough B. Smooth handling
C. Not handling D. A shop

**28.** Synonym of Vie:
A. Compete B. Withdraw
C. Lazy D. Enjoy

**29.** Antonym of Wince:
A. Quail B. Blench
C. Cringe D. Advance

**30.** Antonym of Vigorous:
A. Substitute B. Dull
C. Alternative D. Speed

**31.** Antonym of Segregate:
A. Split B. Different
C. Integrate D. Separate

**32.** Antonym of Triumph:
A. Gain B. Win
C. Victory D. Defeat

**33.** Antonym of Wax:
A. Wane B. Win
C. Victory D. Gain

**34.** Antonym of Attic:
A. Cellar B. Cockloft
C. Garret D. Loft

**35.** Antonym of Swerve:
A. Move B. Deviate
C. Sharply D. Straight

**36.** Antonym of Suavity:
A. Urbanity B. Rude
C. Polish D. Soft

**37.** Antonym of Slur:
A. Rap B. Hit
C. Praise D. Blur

**38.** Antonym of Pungent:
A. Sweet B. Salty
C. Sour D. Bitter

**39.** Antonym of Progeny:
A. Kids B. Parent
C. Offspring D. Lineage

**40.** Antonym of Cavil:
A. Finding fault B. Carp
C. Criticize D. Appreciate

**41.** Antonym of Array:
A. Marshall B. One
C. Pattern D. Design

**42.** Antonym of Annex:
A. Affix B. Attach
C. Base D. Add

**43.** Antonym of Throwback:
A. Gift B. Birthright
C. Estate D. None of these

**44.** I was delighted ______her answer.
A. at B. on
C. for D. in

**45.** I have no doubt______it.
A. upon B. at
C. on D. about

**46.** I assure you______your safety.
A. off B. of
C. from D. with

**47.** He competed ________ me for the prize.
A. of  B. off
C. to  D. with

**48.** He is_______difficulties.
A. in  B. on
C. from  D. with

**49.** He is true__________his words.
A. with  B. to
C. on  D. for

**50.** The fan is_________my head.
A. with  B. on
C. to  D. above

**51.** You can see the house _________ the trees.
A. to  B. among
C. on  D. with

**52.** Do you want to speak_________me?
A. to  B. with
C. above  D. over

**53.** I have not________from him so far.
A. seen  B. hear
C. heard  D. listen

**54.** We_______ there three days ago.
A. gone  B. go
C. will go  D. went

**55.** _________he really a thief?
A. is or was  B. are
C. were  D. None of these

**56.** They__________ very happy seeing you here.
A. shall  B. will be
C. will  D. were be

**57.** We_________there if you_______us the address at the right time.
A. should reach; had told
B. would have reached; tell
C. would have reached; had told
D. have reached; will tell

**58.** Older Woman =
A. Matron  B. Patron
C. Synonyms  D. None of these

**59.** Choose the correct sentence.
A. The police is come
B. The police is coming
C. The police coming
D. The police are coming

**60.** Choose the correct sentence.
A. The house is not big enough
B. The house is not enough big
C. The house are not big enough
D. The house are not enough big

**61.** Choose the correct sentence.
A. There is seven girl in the class.
B. There is seven girls in the class.
C. There are seven girl in the class.
D. There are seven girls in the class.

**62.** I ______a letter to the Principal yesterday.
A. write  B. mailed
C. forward  D. have signed

**63.** Antonym of affectation.
A. Behaviour  B. Artificial
C. Simplicity  D. Pretence

**64.** Meaning of "Soft-soap:"
A. Inspire  B. Adamant
C. Suffuse  D. Gentle urging

**65.** Antonym of mayhem.
A. Havoc  B. Peace
C. Chaos  D. Continuous

**66.** Antonym of regression:
A. Progress  B. Reversion
C. Backward  D. Static

**67.** Antonym of tempestuous:
A. Sedate  B. Stormy
C. Violent  D. None of these

**68.** Antonym of unhinge:
A. Mentally Unstable  B. Sane
C. Unsettled  D. None of these

**69.** Antonym of titillate:
A. Excite  B. Stimulate
C. Repulse  D. None of these

**70.** Antonym of transfix:
A. Motionless  B. Petrify
C. Paralyse  D. Animate

**71.** Antonym of succinct:
A. Circumlocutory  B. Clear
C. Concise  D. None of these

**72.** We ________ at the party.
A. enjoyed ourself  B. enjoyed ourselves
C. played with  D. None of these

**73.** Choose the correctly spelt word.
A. Obnaxious B. Obnoxious
C. Obnexious D. Obnaxeous

**74.** Choose the correctly spelt word.
A. Redeculos B. Rediculos
C. Ridiculous D. Redicilos

**75.** Choose the correctly spelt word.
A. Uneficetion B. Unefication
C. Unefecation D. Unification

**76.** Choose the correctly spelt word.
A. Atmosphere B. Atmasphere
C. Atmosphare D. Atmesphere

**77.** Choose the correctly spelt word.
A. Oppositt B. Oposite
C. Opposite D. Oppusite

**78.** Choose the correctly spelt word.
A. Circumfurence B. Circumferrence
C. Circumferance D. Circumference

**79.** Choose the correctly spelt word.
A. Waitres B. Waitress
C. Waittress D. None of these

**80.** Choose the correctly spelt word.
A. Expectition B. Expactation
C. Expectation D. Expection

**81.** Choose the correctly spelt word.
A. Anemation B. Animation
C. Animetion D. None of these

**82.** Choose the correctly spelt word.
A. Moneylender B. Moneylander
C. Monilender D. Monieslander

**83.** Choose the correctly spelt word.
A. Anixoas B. Anxeous
C. Anxioes D. Anxious

**84.** Choose the correctly spelt word.
A. Bornfire B. Bonefide
C. Bonfire D. Benfire

**85.** Choose the correctly spelt word.
A. Delivary B. Delivery
C. Delvery D. Deliverry

**86.** Choose the correctly spelt word.
A. Chalenge B. Challange
C. Challenge D. Chellenge

**87.** Choose the correctly spelt word.
A. Borrowinng B. Borrawing
C. Borowing D. Borrowing

**88.** Choose the correctly spelt word.
A. Composure B. Composare
C. Composhare D. Commposure

**89.** Choose the correctly spelt word.
A. Permenant B. Permanent
C. Permanant D. None of these

**90.** Choose the correctly spelt word.
A. Recommendetion B. Recommandation
C. Recommendation D. Recomendation

**91.** Synonym of Ape:
A. Yearly B. Imitate
C. Comments D. Fellow

**92.** Synonym of Profane:
A. Religious B. Poor
C. Rich D. Irreligious

**93.** Out of norm:
A. Eccentric B. Bibliophile
C. Sematic D. Asocial

**94.** Choose the correct sentence.
A. The person which works here is from USA
B. The person that works here is from USA
C. The person who works here is from USA
D. The person whose works here is from USA

**95.** Choose the correct sentence.
A. You must to call him immediately
B. You must call him immediately
C. You to call him immediately
D. You must called him immediately

**96.** Choose the correct sentence.
A. When I arrived, I will call you.
B. When I will arrive, I will call you.
C. When I arrive, I will call you.
D. When I arrive, I called you.

**97.** Study of disease:
A. Telepathic B. Apathy
C. Incongruous D. Pathology

**98.** Pertaining to the science of linguistics.
A. Philological B. Bibliophile
C. Sematic D. Epitome

**99.** Antonym of Abject:
A. Noble B. Pitiful
C. Despicable D. None of above

**100.** Antonym of Accentuate:
A. Stress B. De-Emphasise
C. Highlight D. Underline

**101.** The reports of the Comptroller and Auditor-General, in relation to audit of accounts of a Government company or a corporation referred to in section 19, shall be submitted to the ________.
A. Parliament
B. Public
C. Government or Governments concerned
D. CMD of the respective Company

**102.** What is VPN?
A. Virtual Personal Network
B. Virtual Private Network
C. Virtual Protected Network
D. Valued Premium Network

**103.** The Airline that has added ATRs in its fleet recently is:
A. Indigo B. Air India
C. Jet Airways D. SpiceJet

**104.** One Commodity Exchange that launched Options on Gold Futures is:
A. NCX B. SEBI
C. BCX D. MCX

**105.** What number should be added to each term of ratio 2 : 5 to make it 3 : 4?
A. 6 B. 5
C. 7 D. 8

**106.** Vice President of India is elected by:
A. Members of Lok Sabha, Rajya Sabha and State Assemblies
B. Members of Lok Sabha and State Assemblies
C. Elected Members of Lok Sabha and Rajya Sabha
D. Members of State Assemblies

**107.** Secretary General of UN is:
A. Joseph Blatter B. David Morgan
C. Ban-ki-Moon D. Antonio Guterres

**108.** What is the tenure of Secretary General of UN?
A. 3 years ( renewable-traditionally limited to 2 years)
B. 5 years ( renewable-traditionally limited to 5 years)
C. 5 years ( renewable-traditionally limited to 2 years)
D. 3 years

**109.** Two Insurance companies proposing merger are:
A. Max Life and HDFC Life
B. Max Life and Bajaj Alliance
C. HDFC and Bajaj Alliance
D. None of these

**110.** Mariyappan Thangavelu became India's ________ ever gold medalist at the Paralympic Games:
A. First B. Third
C. Second D. Fourth

**111.** Gulf Countries recently cut off ties with ________, another Gulf Country.
A. Saudi Arabia B. Bahrain
C. Qatar D. Egypt

**112.** ICIS =
A. India Computer Information System
B. India Code Information Scheme
C. Indian Computer Information System
D. India Code Information System

**113.** MANAK =
A. Measures for Augmenting National Aspirations and Knowledge
B. Million Minds Augmenting National Aspirations and Knowledge
C. Manpower Augmenting National Aspirations and Knowledge
D. None of these

**114.** SAMPADA =
A. Related to Agro-Marine produce Processing
B. Marginal farmers' Scheme
C. Small Savings Scheme
D. None of these

**115.** Kidambi Srikanth won Denmark Open by defeating ________.
A. Lee Hyun I  B. Lee Hyun II
C. Lee Ping  D. Lee Zen

**116.** The Airport that is closed every year on a particular date and time for allowing the procession of Deity is:
A. Kochi  B. Mumbai
C. Trivandrum  D. Madurai

**117.** The author of Book "The Coalition Years 1996-2012":
A. Navy Kapadia  B. Rajdeep Sardesai
C. Pranab Mukherjee D. None of these

**118.** The author of book "Democracy's XI—The Great Indian Cricket Story:
A. Rajdeep Sardesai  B. Sachin Tendulkar
C. Navy Kapadia  D. None of these

**119.** TRAI =
A. Telecom Regulatory Authority of India
B. Telecommunication Regulatory Authority of India
C. Telecom Regulatory Agency of India
D. None of these

**120.** Chief Justice of India is:
A. Justice T.S. Thakur
B. Justice Jagdish Singh Khehar
C. Justice Dipak Misra
D. H.L. Dattu

**121.** CPIO:
A. Chief Public Information Officer
B. Central Public Information Officer
C. Central Public Inquiry Officer
D. Chief Public Inquiry Officer

**122.** Line A(4, 3) and B(–2, 1) is internally bisected at point C. Coordinates of bisector will be:
A. 1, 2  B. –2, 3
C. 2, 4  D. 4, 3

**123.** Distance between the points (2, –2) and (–1, 2) will be:
A. 3 units  B. 4 units
C. 5 units  D. 2 units

**124.** A trader allows a discount of 10% on the marked price and still makes a profit of 17% on the cost price. What would have been the % of profit had he sold at market price?
A. 27%  B. 18.7%
C. 30%  D. 33%

**125.** Consider function $y = 2x^2 - x$. It has a stationary point at:
A. $x = 1$  B. $x = 1/2$
C. $x = 2$  D. $x = 1/4$

**126.** Since people are sensitive about disclosure of personal information to strangers, asking them in around about and indirect way ensures collection of the best data:
A. always  B. never
C. most of the time  D. some of the times

**127.** Complex tabulation is resorted to when:
A. A number of aspects/attributes/features need to be presented together
B. 'protecting' Information is a priority
C. Readers are found to be too gullible.
D. Both, 'protecting' Information is a priority and Readers are found to be too gullible.

**128.** Histograms are useful to present:
A. ungrouped data
B. only grouped data
C. only raw data
D. both grouped and ungrouped data

**129.** A pie chart is suitable for pictorial presentation of data divided into:
A. over lapping classes
B. simple additive subgroups
C. percentage components
D. raw data

**130.** Some bags of wheat weighed 90, 95, 97, 93, 95 kgs. The average was reported to be 94 kgs. Later on it was reported that actual content of the first bag was 99 kg which was misrecorded as 90 kg. So the average weight of those bags should be:
A. 95.8  B. 96.5
C. 94.5  D. 95

**131.** Decision in GST Council to be taken by ________ majority
A. 50%  B. 75%
C. 90%  D. 100%

**132.** IBBI =
A. Insolvency and Bankruptcy Board of India
B. Insolvency and Bankruptcy Bureau of India
C. Investment and Banking Board of India
D. Insurance and Bankruptcy Board of India

**133.** RCM =
A. Reserve Cost Mechanism
B. Reverse Cost Management
C. Recycled Core Mechanism
D. Reverse Charge Mechanism

**134.** NEET =
A. National Engineering Eligibility Test
B. National Entrance Cum Eligibility Test
C. National Eligibility Cum Entrance Test
D. National Entrance and Eligibility Test

**135.** BSNL has customer base of ______ as on 31st October, 2016.
A. 148.13 million B. 109.26 million
C. 113.13 million D. 216.17 million

**136.** FTTH =
A. Food to Home B. Fibre to Home
C. Facility to Home D. None of these

**137.** Find the "odd-one out" from NPCC, HPL, CIL and NBCC:
A. CIL B. NPCC
C. HPL D. NBCC

**138.** Mitakshara School does not exist in the States of:
A. Gujarat and Maharashtra
B. Delhi and Haryana
C. Tamil Nadu and Kerala
D. West Bengal and Assam

**139.** What is WMA?
A. Wide Management Area
B. World Management Association
C. Ways and Means Advance
D. None of these

**140.** What is ASBA?
A. Applications Supported by Blocked Amount
B. Applications Supported by Bank Amount
C. Applications Sanctioned by Bank Agreement
D. Applications Supported by Bulk Amount

**141.** The first tea garden in the world to secure Elephant Friendly Certificate is:
A. Lisa Mills Tea farms
B. Bodosa Tea farms
C. John Tea Farms
D. None of these

**142.** Who is the PM of New Zealand?
A. Jacinda Ardern B. Bill English
C. Winston Peters D. Mcmillan

**143.** The country with highest ranking in the Ease of Doing Business Ranking-2017 is:
A. Singapore B. USA
C. New Zealand D. Denmark

**144.** India's first UNESCO World Heritage City is:
A. Chennai B. Kolkata
C. Delhi D. Ahmedabad

**145.** Assange is linked with:
A. WikiLeads B. WikiLinks
C. WikiLeaks D. WifiLeads

**146.** Battle of Buxar took place in the year.
A. 1684 B. 1674
C. 1864 D. 1764

**147.** In how many ways can be letters of the TUESDAY be arranged?
A. 5040 B. 4040
C. 6040 D. 7040

**148.** As production increases from 6000 to 8000, the total cost of production rises from ₹ 33,000 to ₹ 40,000. Assuming linear relationship between output and costs, estimate the total cost for production of 10,000 units:
A. ₹ 47,000 B. ₹ 55,000
C. ₹ 50,000 D. ₹ 45,000

**149.** Perimeter of a right angled triangle is 30 cms. Its hypotenuse is 13 cms. Find the other sides:
A. 7, 5 cms B. 5, 12 cms
C. 12, 7 cms D. 9, 5 cms.

**150.** Diagonal of a 20 feet high solid right circular cylinder is 8 feet. Its total surface area will be _______.
A. 300 sq. feet B. 299.98 sq. feet
C. 301.71 sq. feet D. 301 sq. feet

# PAPER-II

**151.** When the total of Trial Balance does not tally the difference is taken as:

A. Suspense Account
B. Profit and Loss Account
C. Error Account
D. Difference Account

**152.** Current Liabilities are obligations to be settled in _______.

A. Immediately B. Long period
C. Short period D. None of these

**153.** XY Ltd. sells its products on credit basis and its customers are associated with 2% credit risk. Its annual turnover is expected at ₹ 10,00,000 if credit is extended. If no credit is allowed the sales would be 70% thereon. Compute net profit on credit sales assuming cost of capital is 15% p.a. and variable cost 75% of sales, credit period is 30 days. Cost of administration is 2% of credit sales.

A. ₹ 2,50,000 B. ₹ 2,75,000
C. ₹ 2,52,500 D. ₹ 2,47,500

**154.** Greenways Ltd. issued 10,000 shares @ ₹ 100 to the public under the terms: ₹ 20 on application; ₹ 30 on allotment; ₹ 25 on First Call; ₹ 25 on Final Call. All moneys upto Allotment were duly received. But a shareholder holding 500 shares did not pay the first call amount due. Another shareholder who was allotted 250 shares paid them up in full. Show how 'calls-in-advance' will be shown in the Balance-Sheet.

A.

| Liabilities | (in ₹) | Assets | (in ₹) |
|---|---|---|---|
| | | Calls in Advance (250 × 50) = 12,500 | |

B.

| Liabilities | (in ₹) | Assets | (in ₹) |
|---|---|---|---|
| Current Liabilities<br>Calls in Advance ₹ 12,500 | | | |

C.

| Liabilities | (in ₹) | Assets | (in ₹) |
|---|---|---|---|
| Issued and Subscribed capital<br>*Less:* Calls in Advance ₹ 12,500 | | | |

D. None of these

**155.** On 30th June, 2017, the Balance-Sheet of Good Luck Ltd. stood as follows:

| Liabilities | (in ₹) | Assets | (in ₹) |
|---|---|---|---|
| Equity Share capital | 20,00,000 | Sundry Assets | 28,00,000 |
| Redeemable Preference Shares Capital | 8,00,000 | Bank Balance | 10,00,000 |
| P&L Account | 6,00,000 | | |
| Sundry Creditors | 4,00,000 | | |
| | 38,00,000 | | 38,00,000 |

On the above date, the preference shares had to be redeemed. For this purpose, 4,00,000 equity shares of ₹ 100 each were issued at ₹ 110. The company also issued 8% debentures totalling ₹ 2,60,000. The shares and debentures were immediately subscribed and paid for. The preference shares were duly redeemed. You are required to calculate the amount to be shown in the Balance Sheet after redemption under "Bank balance".

A. ₹ 10,20,000 B. ₹ 12,40,000
C. ₹ 10,40,000 D. ₹ 14,20,000

**156.** EF Ltd. issued 1,000, 10% Debentures of ₹ 100 each at a discount of 6%. The Debentures are repayable by annual drawings at the end of each year from the first year onwards at the rate of ₹ 20,000 per year. Ascertain the discount amount to be written off at the end of Fourth Year under Fluctuating Instalment Method.

A. ₹ 400 B. ₹ 800
C. ₹ 6,000 D. ₹ 1,200

**157.** Mr. X, an industrialist (SME Category) decided to convert his firm into a limited company from 1 June, 2016. He obtained the Certificate of Incorporation on 1 October, 2016 and the Certificate of Commencement of Business on 1 December, 2016. His accounts were to be closed on 31 March, 2017. There were 30 employees in the firm on 1 June, 2016 and 20 more employees were appointed on 1 October, 2016. Ascertain the weighted time ratio.

A. 1 : 3 B. 1 : 4
C. 1 : 5 D. 2 : 5

**158.** "Fictitious Assets" are to be shown on the assets side of the Balance Sheet under the Heading:
A. Miscellaneous Expenditure
B. Current Assets
C. Investments
D. Fixed Assets

**159.** Shree Ltd. has a credit balance on P&L Account of ₹ 6,00,000 on 1.4.2016 and net profit for the year is ₹ 60,00,000. The following decisions were taken regarding provisions, reserves and dividends.
(*i*) General Reserve ₹ 7,00,000
(*ii*) Investment Allowance ₹ 7,00,000
(*iii*) Provision for Taxation @ 50%
(*iv*) Dividend Equalisation Fund A/c 4,00,000
(*v*) Dividend on 10% Preference Shares of ₹ 40,00,000
(*vi*) Dividend on 15% on 6,00,000 equity shares of ₹ 10 each fully paid tax

Compute the Balance to be carried forward to the Balance Sheet as on 31.3.2017.
A. ₹ 3,30,000 B. ₹ 5,30,000
C. ₹ 5,00,000 D. ₹ 3,70,000

**160.** The Directors of a public limited company have decided to write off Goodwill appearing ₹ 50,000 at the beginning of the year 2016-17. How will you treat this?
A. ₹ 50,000 should be shown separately in P&L Account.
B. Credit P & L Account by ₹ 50,000
C. Debit P & L Appropriation Account by ₹ 50,000
D. Show in Balance Sheet under Assets ₹ 50,000

**161.** Profit on sale of machinery comes under:
A. Investing activity
B. Financing activity
C. Operating activity
D. None of these

**162.** Which of the following is NOT a characteristic of cash-equivalents?
A. Highly liquid
B. Long-term
C. Readily convertible into cash
D. None of these

**163.** You are required to calculate cash inflow from debtors from the following data:

| | in ₹ |
|---|---|
| Total sales | 10,00,000 |
| Cash sales | 4,00,000 |
| Opening Debtors | 1,00,000 |
| Closing Debtors | 1,60,000 |
| Sales Returns | 40,000 |

A. ₹ 5,00,000 B. ₹ 4,00,000
C. ₹ 4,40,000 D. ₹ 4,60,000

**164.** Compute Net Profit Before Tax:

| **Particulars** | **Balance** | |
|---|---|---|
| | **Opening** | **Closing** |
| P&L Account | 90,000 | 1,10,000 |
| General Reserve | 50,000 | 60,000 |
| Provision for Depreciation Plant | 80,000 | 90,000 |
| Outstanding Expenses | 10,000 | 4,000 |
| Goodwill | 50,000 | 30,000 |
| Sundry Debtors | 1,20,000 | 1,00,000 |

An item of plant costing ₹ 1,00,000 having book value of ₹ 80,000 was sold for ₹ 90,000 during the year.
A. ₹ 25,000 B. ₹ 30,000
C. ₹ 20,000 D. ₹ 22,000

**165.** Anil sells an article to Prakash at 10% profit. Prakash sells it back to Anil at a loss of 10%. The transaction gives:
A. Loss to Anil
B. Profit to Anil
C. There is no loss or gain
D. Prakash makes profit

**166.** In relation to a company, investors are least concerned with:
A. Profitability B. Short term liquidity
C. Solvency D. Future share price

**167.** Which one of the following can be treated as capital expenditure?

A. Acquisition of land, building, machinery etc.

B. Amount spent on modification of asset

C. Expenses incurred for right to carry on a business

D. All of these

**168.** As per accrual concept which one is NOT true:

A. Revenue – expenditure = profit

B. Revenue – profit = expenditure

C. Sales + gross profit = revenue

D. Revenue = profit + expenditure

**169.** Which of the following provide framework and accounting policies so that the financial statements of different periods are comparable?

A. Business standards

B. Accounting standards

C. Market standards

D. None of these

**170.** What is the journal entry for goods purchased on credit?

A. Purchases Dr.
  To Creditor's A/c

B. Creditor's Dr.
  To Purchases A/c

C. Purchases Dr.
  To Debtor's A/c

D. Debtor's Dr.
  To Purchases A/c

**171.** Which one of the following is NOT correct about Fund Flow Statement?

A. Records inflows and outflows of cash only

B. It is based on Cash Accounting System

C. It measures changes in working capital

D. It is based on Accrual accounting system

**172.** Journal entry to be passed when goods are returned under "sale on approval basis" is:

A. Sales A/c Dr.
  To Debtors A/c

B. Purchases A/c Dr.
  To Debtors A/c

C. Debtors A/c Dr.
  To Sales A/c

D. None of these

**173.** XY Ltd. has a policy of maintaining a minimum cash balance of ₹ 45,000. The Standard Deviation of company's daily net cash ₹ 1,000. The transaction cost is ₹ 90 per transaction. The interest rate is 0.2% daily. Compute the upper limit as per Miler Orr Model:

A. ₹ 41,500 B. ₹ 49,500

C. ₹ 43,500 D. ₹ 47,500

**174.** Which of the following statement is correct?

A. Default costs are caused due to failure of customers to pay on time.

B. Financial costs to support credit sales are referred to as collection costs

C. Business firms should not opt for relaxation of credit standards as they cause increase in collection costs, amount of bad debts and financial costs.

D. Receivables management involves a trade-off between costs and benefits or receivable.

**175.** Which of the following statement is NOT TRUE?

A. Cash discount increases the average collection period.

B. The increase in credit period increases average investment in receivables.

C. The credit term "3/10 net 30" implies that the customer is entitled to 3% cash discount only when he pays within 10 days after the beginning of credit period, though the credit period is 30 days.

D. Financial costs of investment in debtors are determined with reference to Cash Cost of Sales.

**176.** AB Ltd. purchased assets for ₹ 4,80,000 from X & Co. payable in fully paid shares of ₹ 100 each at a premium of 20%. Which of the following is the correct Journal Entry in the Books of AB Ltd.

A. X & Co. A/c : Dr. 4,80,000
  To Share Capital A/c : 4,80,000

B. X & Co. A/c : Dr. 4,80,000
  To Share Capital A/c : 4,00,000
  To Share Premium A/c : 80,000

C. Share Capital A/c : Dr. 4,00,000
Share Premium A/c : 80,000
To X & Co. A/c : 4,80,000

D. X & Co. A/c : Dr. 5,60,000
To Share Capital A/c : 4,80,000
To Share Premium A/c : 80,000

**177.** The articles of association of Good Luck Ltd. provide for the following:

(*i*) That 10% of profit of each year shall be transferred to Reserve Fund;

(*ii*) That an amount equal to 10% of equity dividend shall be set aside for bonus to staff;

(*iii*) That the balance available for distribution shall be applied:

(*a*) In paying 7% on Cumulative Preference Shares,

(*b*) In paying 7% on Equity shares

(*c*) One-third of the balance available as additional dividend on preference shares and two-thirds as additional equity dividend.

A further condition was also imposed by the Articles, namely, the balance carried forward shall not be reduced by the provisions under (*ii*), (*iii*) (*b*) or (*iii*) (*c*) below a sum equal to 6% of the preference capital.

The company has issued 52,000 7% cumulative particularly preference shares of ₹ 100 each fully paid. The profit for the year 2016-17 was ₹ 28,85,978 and the balance brought forward from the previous year was ₹ 3,14,349. Provide ₹ 12, 54,600 for taxation before making other appropriations. Ignore corporate dividend tax. Balance c/fd to Balance Sheet will be:

A. ₹ 3,28,680 B. ₹ 3,60,580
C. ₹ 3,18,580 D. ₹ 3,65,680

**178.** From the following particulars, calculate the cash flows from investing activities:

| Particulars | Purchases (in ₹) | Sales (in ₹) |
|---|---|---|
| Investments | 6,00,000 | 4,00,000 |
| Goodwill | 3,00,000 | - |
| Machinery | 13,00,000 | 4,20,000 |
| Patents | - | 2,00,000 |

Dividend received on shares held on investment ₹ 60,000. Interest received on debentures held as investments ₹ 80,000. A building purchased for investment purposes (out of surplus funds) was let out and rent proceeds received thereby ₹ 2,40,000.

A. ₹ 8,00,000 B. ₹ 80,000
C. ₹ 6,00,000 D. ₹ 12,00,000

**179.** Trading Account does not:

A. Compare the sales with the cost of those sales
B. Calculate gross profit
C. Show the effect of return on capital
D. Include the cost of goods sold

**180.** Net current asset is equivalent to:

A. Fixed asset + current assets – current liabilities
B. Current liabilities – current assets
C. Stock + debtors + cash
D. Working capital

**181.** In net profit ratio the denominator is:

A. Net purchase
B. Credit sales
C. Net sales
D. Cost of goods sold

**182.** Unpaid calls are shown in the balance sheet of a company:

A. By adding it to share capital
B. By deducting it from called up share capital
C. Under current liabilities
D. Under current assets

**183.** Interest cost incurred during construction phase or before the asset is put to use is accounted under:

A. Repair
B. Maintenance
C. Capital asset
D. Cost of acquisition

**184.** Which concept satisfy valuation criteria?

A. Going concern, Realisation, Cost
B. Going concern, Cost, Dual aspect
C. Cost, Dual aspect, Conservatism
D. Realisation, Conservatism, Going concern

**185.** An asset was purchased for ₹ 5,00,000 with down payment of ₹ 2,00,000 and bills accepted for ₹ 3,00,000. The effect on total asset of the company will be:

A. Assets increased by 3,00,000 and liabilities decreased by 3,00,000
B. Assets decreased by 3,00,000 and liabilities increased by 3,00,000
C. Assets increased by 5,00,000 and liabilities decreased by 3,00,000
D. Assets increased by 3,00,000 and liabilities increased by 3,00,000

**186.** Historical cost concept requires the valuation of an asset at:

A. Original cost
B. Replacement value
C. Net realizable value
D. Market value

**187.**

| **Particulars** | **As on Dec. 31, 2011 (In ₹)** | **As on Dec. 31, 2012 (In ₹)** |
|---|---|---|
| Pre paid Salary | 20,000 | 35,000 |
| Unpaid Salary | 50,000 | 20,000 |

Salary paid during 2012 amounted to ₹ 2,40,000. Amount to be shown under 'Salaries' in I & E A/c for the year ending December 31, 2012 will be:

A. ₹ 3,10,000 B. ₹ 2,55,000
C. ₹ 1,95,000 D. ₹ 1,70,000

**188.** C was admitted into a Partnership firm for 5 years where A & B were already partners. C paid a premium of ₹ 2,40,000. After 36 months, the partnership firm was dissolved due to misconduct of B. The amount of refund to Mr. C is:

A. ₹ 1,44,000 B. ₹ 96,000
C. ₹ 2,40,000 D. None of these

**189.** A Building was purchased for ₹ 48,00,000 on 14/5/2012. Down payment of ₹ 30,00,000 was made and the balance was to be paid on 14/4/2013. What is the amount on which depreciation on the building was to be charged as at 31/3/2013?

A. ₹ 18,00,000 B. ₹ 30,00,000
C. ₹ 48,00,000 D. ₹ 24,00,000

**190.** Net Working Capital is equal to:

A. Excess of current assets over current liabilities
B. Excess of current liabilities over current assets
C. Total current assets
D. None of these

**191.** Arithmetical accuracy of basic entries, ledger posting & balancing is ensured by:

A. Cash Flow Statement
B. Profit & Loss Account
C. Trial Balance
D. Balance Sheet

**192.** Great Pvt. Ltd. bought machinery for ₹ 1,00,000 on 01.01.2013 and spent ₹ 10,000 on its installation. The life of the machinery is estimated to be 5 years & estimated scrap value at the end of period will be ₹ 5,000. The amount of annual depreciation as per straight line method will be:

A. ₹ 20,000 B. ₹ 21,000
C. ₹ 19,000 D. ₹ 22,000

**193.** A sells goods to B for ₹ 20,000. A draws a bill on B who accepts the same to pay the amount after 2 months. Here, B is:

A. Endorsee B. Drawer
C. Payee D. Drawee

**194.** The payment side of Cash Book is overcast by ₹ 7000. If the starting point of the BRS is the Overdraft Balance as per Pass Book, then what is to be done to reach to Overdraft Balance of Cash Book?

A. Add ₹ 7,000 B. Less ₹ 7,000
C. Add ₹ 13,000 D. Less ₹ 3,500

**195.** If a bill of exchange dated 8th January is issued for 2 months after date, the date of maturity will be:

A. 8th March B. 11th March
C. 15th March D. 11th April

**196.** ______ method of depreciation takes into account the element of interest on capital outlay and sees to write off the asset and the interest cost over the life of asset.

A. Sinking fund
B. Annuity
C. Straight line
D. Written down value

**197.** A Machine was purchased on 1st July, 2010 for ₹ 14,000 and an amount of ₹ 1000 was spent on its installation. The rate of depreciation is 10% p.a. every year. The books are closed on 31st December. Find the value of Machinery as on 31st December, 2011 after following Diminishing Balance method of depreciation.

A. ₹ 13,500 B. ₹ 12,150
C. ₹ 13,575 D. ₹ 12,825

**198.** Which of the following is TRUE?

A. Two mutually exclusive projects (L & M) have been evaluated. Project L has an NPV of ₹ 2 lakh and an IRR of 15 per cent; Project M has NPV of and has an IRR of 17 per cent. Since Project M has higher IRR, it should be selected.
B. Two competing projects have the following NPVs: Project A + ₹ 10 lakhs (with an initial outlay of ₹ 30 lakhs and Project B + ₹ 9 lakhs (with an initial outlay of ₹ 27.5 lakhs). The company should opt for Project A as it has higher NPV.
C. The cost of capital for new projects is 16%. Two competing projects (P&Q) have IRR 15% and 13% respectively. Since IRR of project P is higher, it should be selected.
D. A project requires an initial investment of ₹ 50 lakhs. The estimated profit after tax for years 1-5 are: ₹ 6 lakhs, ₹ 7 lakhs, ₹ 7 lakhs, ₹ 14 lakhs and ₹ 18 lakhs, the accounting rate of return is 18%.

**199.** Z Ltd. has ₹ 30,00,000 lakhs available for investment in capital projects. It has the option of making investment in Projects A, B, C and D. Each project is entirely indepenent and has a useful life of 5 years. The expected present value of cash flows from the projects are as follows:

| Projects | Initial Outlay (in ₹) | Present value of Cash flows (in ₹) |
|---|---|---|
| A | 8,00,000 | 10,00,000 |
| B | 15,00,000 | 19,00,000 |
| C | 7,00,000 | 14,00,000 |
| D | 13,00,000 | 20,00,000 |

Considering capital rationing, which combination of projects will be preferable?

A. Combination of A + B + C
B. Combination of A + D
C. Combination of A + C + D
D. Combination of B + D

**200.** Calculate NPV of Certainty Equivalent of cash flows for the following information:

| Year | Proposal X | | Proposal Y | |
|---|---|---|---|---|
| | CFAT | CE | CFAT | CE |
| 0 | (35,000) | 1 | (25,000) | 1 |
| 1 | 18,000 | 0.8 | 10,000 | 0.9 |
| 2 | 20,000 | 0.7 | 16,000 | 0.8 |
| 3 | 15,000 | 0.6 | 18,000 | 0.7 |
| 4 | 15,000 | 0.5 | 20,000 | 0.4 |

Firm's cost of capital : 12 per cent

Borrowing Rate : Risk free : 7%

NPV for proposals : X & Y

A. X = ₹ 6,372; Y = ₹ 10,657
B. X = ₹ 4,652; Y = ₹ 9,997
C. X = ₹ 5,722; Y = ₹ 10,957
D. X = ₹ 3,752; Y = ₹ 10,975

**201.** Z Ltd. requires 5,000 units of a certain item per year. The Purchase Price per unit is ₹ 20. The Carrying Cost of inventory is 20% of the unit cost and the cost per order is ₹ 400. Compute the total cost of ordering and cost of carrying inventory when 5 orders of equal size are placed.

A. ₹ 3,500
B. ₹ 2,500
C. ₹ 3,000
D. ₹ 4,000

**202.** Which of the following statement is NOT correct?
A. The primary function of financial intermediaries is to convert direct securities into indirect securities.
B. The two key financial markets are money market and capital market.
C. Money market is a market for long term funds having maturity of more than one year.
D. Organisation, underwriting and distribution are three services provided by the New issue market.

**203.** PQ Ltd. has been issued equity share which, are priced currently at ₹ 108. The investor's required rate of return is 12% and the dividend grows at 8% per year. Compute the current dividend declared by the company:
A. ₹ 5 B. ₹ 4
C. ₹ 4.50 D. ₹ 5.50

**204.** The cash outgoings of XY Ltd. are estimated to be ₹ 4,00,000 p.a. spread evenly throughout the year. The money on deposit earns 10% p.a. The switching cost per transaction is ₹ 120. Calculate the optimum amount to be transferred. Use Bau Mol Model:
A. ₹ 30,000 B. ₹ 32,000
C. ₹ 33,333 D. ₹ 31,000

**205.** Equity Share Capital: ₹ 1,50,000; 10% Pref. Share Capital: ₹ 1,00,000; Reserve and Surplus : ₹ 5,00,000; Net Profit after Tax: ₹ 2,10,000. Return on Equity will be:
A. 28% B. 20%
C. 25% D. 30%

**206.** Margin of safety is calculated as:
A. Actual sales + Break even point sales
B. Actual production – Break even point sales
C. Actual sales / Break even point sales
D. Actual sales – Break even point sales

**207.** Angle of incidence is the angle where:
A. The total cost intersects the total sales
B. Variable cost intersects fixed cost
C. Fixed cost intersects total cost
D. Variable cost intersects total Cost

**208.** If selling price per unit increases and other variables remain constant, the operating break-even point in units will:
A. increase B. decrease
C. constant D. None of these

**209.** Limitations of Break-even analysis:
A. non-linear cost behaviour
B. presence of competition
C. static concept
D. capital not considered

**210.** Determine contribution if Fixed cost is ₹ 75000 and loss is ₹ 30000:
A. ₹ 45000 B. ₹ 105000
C. ₹ 75000 D. ₹ 30000

**211.** Determine P/V Ratio when Sales ₹ 80,000 and variable cost ₹ 60,000:
A. 0.1 B. 0.4
C. 0.3 D. 0.25

**212.** What is margin of safety if sales is ₹ 50,000 and BEP is ₹ 30,000:
A. ₹ 30,000 B. ₹ 20,000
C. ₹ 80,000 D. ₹ 50,000

**213.** Material cost ₹ 10, sales price ₹ 30, labour ₹ 5, Electricity ₹ 5, fixed cost ₹ 3000. The BEP will be:
A. 300 B. 3000
C. 30 D. 1000

**214.** Other valuable remain constant, if selling price decreases, the BEP will:
A. Constant B. Increase
C. Decrease D. None of these

**215.** Fixed assets in the business is for:
A. Converting to cash
B. Generating revenue
C. Resale
D. None of these

**216.** According to which concept the closing stock is credited to trading account?
A. Cost B. Realisation
C. Going concern D. Matching

**217.** Any change in the capital account of the proprietor may occur due to:
A. Profit earned B. Loss incurred
C. Capital introduced D. All of these

**218.** For computing the value of equity shares by yield method, it is essential to know:
A. Normal Rate of Return
B. Net Assets
C. Expected Rate of Return
D. Capital employed

**219.** Calculate the value of Goodwill of a company on the basis of 2 years' purchase of weighted average profit for the last 3 years.

| | | |
|---|---|---|
| 2014 | : | ₹ 50,000 |
| 2015 | : | ₹ 35,000 |
| 2016 | : | ₹ 25,000 |

The weights assigned to each year are:

| | | |
|---|---|---|
| 2014 | : | 1 |
| 2015 | : | 2 |
| 2016 | : | 3 |

Further information:
(*i*) On 1.10.2015, a repair in respect of machinery was ₹ 2,500 which was charged to revenue. This is to be capitalised for goodwill calculation subject to the depreciation of 10% p.a. on reducing balance method.
(*ii*) The closing stock for the year 2014 was overvalued by ₹ 1,500.
(*iii*) To cover the management cost, ₹ 2,000 should be made for goodwill valuation.
A. ₹ 62,881　B. ₹ 52,188
C. ₹ 61,818　D. ₹ 63,881

**220.** Variable cost ₹ 10, sale price ₹ 20. Total fixed cost ₹ 10,000. BEP will be:
A. 2000 units　B. 10000 units
C. 100 units　D. 1000 units

**221.** Which one is used to test long-term liquidity?
A. Interest coverage ratio
B. Stock turnover ratio
C. Operating ratio
D. Current ratio

**222.** Which of the following is a budget according to function?
A. Fixed budget
B. Operating budget
C. Flexible budget
D. Long term budget

**223.** A bond has 3 years remaining until maturity. It has a par value of ₹ 1000. The coupon interest rate on bond is 10%. Compute the yield to Maturity (YTM) at current market price of ₹ 900.
A. 14.63%　B. 12.03%
C. 13.63%　D. 14.03%

**224.** Greenways Ltd. issued 10,000 shares @ ₹ 100 to the public under the terms:
₹ 20 on application
₹ 30 on allotment;
₹ 25 on First Call
₹ 25 on Final Call
All money upto Allotment were duly received. But a shareholder holding 500 shares did not pay the first call amount due. Another shareholder who was allotted 250 shares paid them up in full.

How "Calls-in-arrears" will be shown in the Balance Sheet?
A. (₹ 500 ₹ 25): ₹ 12,500 will be shown on the Assets side of the Balance-sheet.
B. ₹ 12,500 is to be shown as deducted from the issued and subscribed capital on the Liabilities side of the Balance-sheet.
C. ₹ 12,500 is not to be shown in the Balance-sheet.
D. None of these

**225.** From the following data, ascertain the amount of Fresh issue of Shares:

| | | |
|---|---|---|
| Redeemable Preference Shares | : | ₹ 1,60,000 |
| Premium on redemption | : | 5% |
| Divisible Profits available | : | ₹ 30,000 |
| General Reserve Balance | : | ₹ 13,000 |
| Securities Premium A/c | : | ₹ 8,000 |

Fresh issue is to be made at a discount of 10%.
A. ₹ 65,000　B. ₹ 2,11,000
C. ₹ 1,47,000　D. ₹ 1,30,000

**226.** The term "acquisition of business" refers to:
A. purchase of business of sole trading concern or partnership firm by an existing company

B. conversion of sole trading concern or partnership firm into a limited company
C. both purchase of business of sole trading concern or partnership firm by an existing company and conversion of sole trading concern or partnership firm into a limited company
D. the purchase of business of one limited company by another limited company.

**227.** Mr. X, an industrialist (SME Category) decided to convert his firm into a limited company from 1 June, 2016. He obtained the Certificate of Incorporation on 1 October, 2016 and the Certificate of Commencement of Business on 1 December, 2016. His accounts were to be closed on 31 March, 2017. Time Ratio is:

A. 1 : 3 B. 2 : 3
C. 1 : 1 D. 1 : 2

**228.** Mr. VR and Mr. ST, partners of a firm agreed to sell their firm to a limited company on 1 April, 2016. It was incorporated on 1 July, 2016. It got Certificate of Commencement of Business on 1 August, 2016. Final Accounts were prepared on 31 March, 2017. It was found that the sales were uniform upto the date of incorporation but went up by 100% on an average thereafter. Compute the weighted sales ratio.

A. 2 : 3 B. 1 : 2
C. 1 : 5 D. 1 : 6

**229.** Which of the following statement is NOT TRUE?

A. In other than Joint Stock Company forms of business concerns, the Final Accounts of such entities are split into two sections: Trading A/c and Profit and Loss A/c.
B. In Company Accounts, a BOLD Line is drawn between P & L A/c and P & L Appropriation A/c.
C. Items that are to be shown in Trading and P & L A/c are called "above line" items.
D. Items that are to be shown in and P & L Appropriation A/c are called "below line" items.

**230.** Balance of profit in P & L Appropriation A/c has to be carried to the Balance Sheet and shown under the heading:

A. Share capital
B. Reserves and surplus
C. Provisions
D. Miscellaneous Expenditure

**231.** A product is sold at ₹ 100 the variable cost is ₹ 80 and Fixed cost is ₹ 5000. What will be the break even point in units:

A. 250 B. 500
C. 600 D. 225

**232.** Degree of solvency of two firms are compared by:

A. Net worth
B. Tangible net worth
C. Asset ratio
D. Solvency ratio

**233.** Financial leverage means:

A. High degree of solvency
B. Low bank finance
C. Use of more debt capital
D. None of these

**234.** Which of the following accounts is a non-current liability?

A. Share capital
B. Bank loan
C. Retained earnings
D. Trade payables

**235.** ABC company has current liabilities ₹ 30,000 and total liability ₹ 80,000 and current asset ₹ 50,000 and total asset ₹ 1,50,000. Equity of ABC company is:

A. ₹ 70,000 B. ₹ 90,000
C. ₹ 1,10,000 D. ₹ 95,000

**236.** Which of the following accounts in a current liability?

A. Tax payable B. Inventories
C. Bank deposits D. Fixed assets

**237.** Price per share is ₹ 60 and earning per share is ₹ 7. The P/E Ratio will be:

A. 8.57 times B. 7.85 times
C. 8.75 times D. 8.00 times

**238.** Net income available to stock holder is ₹ 1.25 lacs and total assets are ₹ 10.96 lacs. The return on common equity will be:
A. 11.04% B. 11.4%
C. 111.4% D. 111.04%

**239.** The market value of a listed company is not shown on its balance sheets because:
A. Market value is not known till balance sheet date
B. Market value changes over time
C. Shares are generally a small portion of the company
D. None of these

**240.** Which of the following is a short term liquidity ratio?
A. Cash ratio B. Quick ratio
C. Inventory ratio D. All of these

**241.** The gross profit is unchanged but net profit margin declined over the same period. This could happen if:
A. Cost of goods sold increased relative to sale
B. Sales increased relative to expense
C. Increase in tax rate
D. Dividends were decreased

**242.** Net profit signifies:
A. Operational profitability
B. Liquidity position
C. Solvency
D. Profit for lenders

**243.** Working capital turnover measures the relationship of working capital with ______.
A. Fixed assets B. Sales
C. Purchases D. Stock

**244.** Return on shareholders investments calculates ________.
A. All reserves
B. Preference of equity capitals
C. All appropriations
D. All of these

**245.** If total cost of 100 units are ₹ 4000 and cost of 105 units are ₹ 4100, then the variable cost per unit is:
A. ₹ 20 B. ₹ 200
C. ₹ 60 D. ₹ 65

**246.** Fixed assets ₹ 6,00,000, current assets ₹ 4,00,000, capital ₹ 5,00,000, fixed liabilities ₹ 2,50,000, current liabilities ₹ 2,50,000. The solvency ratio will be:
A. 20% B. 30%
C. 40% D. 50%

**247.** P/E ratio is calculated by dividing market price per equity by ________.
A. Current assets B. Earning per share
C. Current liabilities D. Liquid assets

**248.** Acid test ratio is quick current assets divided by ________.
A. Total assets B. Current assets
C. Total liabilities D. Current liabilities

**249.** Average stock level = ?
A. 1/2 (Maximum stock level – Minimum stock level)
B. (Maximum stock level + Minimum stock level)
C. 1/2 (Maximum stock level + Minimum stock level)
D. 1/4 (Minimum stock level + Maximum stock level)

**250.** Which of the following is not a reason(s) of depreciation of a fixed asset?
A. Passage of time
B. Proper maintenance
C. Obsolescence
D. Usage

**251.** When the prices of raw material constantly decreasing, LIFO method of raw materials issue:
A. Results in lower cost of production
B. Results in higher cost of production
C. Does not affect the cost of production
D. All the statements are incorrect

**252.** Which of the following items is not an item of direct expense?
A. Hire charges for special machines that is used in relation to a specific job
B. Architect's fees
C. Payment of royalty for using technology
D. General travelling expense

**253.** Re-intended to be used over the prolonged period before becoming unusable or obsolete and the store having a significant disposal value. This type of stores falls under which Category?

A. CS B. LTAS
C. NCS D. None of these

**254.** Mr. A wants to know the present value of ₹ 5,000 to be received 5 years from now, assuming 10% rate of interest. Compute the present value.

A. ₹ 4,000 B. ₹ 5,500
C. ₹ 4,500 D. ₹ 3,105

**255.** If the frequency of compounding is more than 1, relationship between annual effective rate of interest and annual nominal rate of interest will be:

A. Effective Rate = Nominal Rate
B. Effective Rate < Nominal Rate
C. Effective Rate > Nominal Rate
D. None of these

**256.** Compute the present value of a perpetuity of ₹ 1,000 year if the discount rate is 10%.

A. ₹ 100 B. ₹ 10,000
C. ₹ 1,00,000 D. None of these

**257.** Which of the following terms of issue of debentures (including terms of redemption) is not possible?

A. Issue of debentures at Par, redeemable at Discount
B. Issue of debentures at Par, redeemable at Premium
C. Issue of debentures at Discount, redeemable at Premium
D. Issue of debentures at Premium, redeemable at Premium

**258.** Own debentures mean:

A. Debentures owned by the directors exclusively
B. Debentures purchased for immediate consideration
C. Debentures purchased for investment
D. None of these

**259.** XY Ltd. took over the assets and liabilities of ₹ 25,00,000 and ₹ 2,50,000 of PQ Ltd. XY Ltd. paid the purchase consideration of ₹ 24,00,000 by issuing debentures of ₹ 100 each at a premium of 20%. Determine which of the following option is correct:

A. Goodwill : ₹ 1,50,000
B. Capital Reserve: ₹ 1,50,000
C. Goodwill : ₹ 8,00,000
D. Capital Reserve: ₹ 8,00,000

**260.** LM Ltd. issued ₹ 5,00,000, 12% debentures of ₹ 100 each at a premium of 20%. The Net effective rate of interest on debentures will be:

A. 15% B. 13%
C. 10% D. 12%

**261.** RS Ltd. redeemed 4,800 15% debentures of ₹ 100 each which were issued at ₹ 110 by converting them into equity shares of ₹ 10 each issued at a discount of 4%. Compute the number of equity shares to be issued:

A. 1,10,000 equity shares
B. 52,800 equity shares
C. 55,000 equity shares
D. 48,000 equity shares

**262.** GH Ltd. purchased its own 500 debentures of the face value of ₹ 50,000 from the open market for immediate cancellation at ₹ 85 which of the following is the effect of cancellation of Debentures?

A. Loss : ₹ 5,000 B. Profit : ₹ 5,000
C. Loss : ₹ 7,500 D. Profit : ₹ 7,500

**263.** XY Ltd. issued 10,000 shares of ₹ 10 each at ₹ 12 (at a premium of ₹ 2 per share) payable as follows: ₹ 2 on application; ₹ 3 on allotment; ₹ 7 on First Call and the Final Call (including Premium). Correct Journal Entry for Receipt of Call Money will be: Journal Entry for Discount will be:

A. Bank A/c Dr. 70,000
  To Share Allotment A/c 50,000
  To Securities Premium A/c 20,000

B. Bank A/c Dr. 70,000
  To First Call and the Final Call A/c 70,000

C. Bank A/c Dr. 70,000
  To First Call and the Final Call A/c 50,000
  To Securities Premium A/c 20,000

D. None of these

**264.** Which of the following is a non-cash operating activities?
A. Issue of Bonus Share
B. Depreciation on fixed assets
C. Issuance of Equity Shares on cash
D. Increase in inventories

**265.** Which of the following is true?
A. Value of a bond is dependent solely on the interest payment it provides.
B. Bond value will differ from its poor value, even though yield to maturity–coupon rate.
C. For a bond, yield to maturity is always equal to coupon rate.
D. If coupon rate = Required rate, the value of bond is equal to its par value.

**266.** SR Ltd. currently pays ₹ 3 per share as annual dividend. Assuming 10% required rate of return on shares, compute the value of shares: Annual rate of growth, 5% to infinity:
A. ₹ 53 B. ₹ 70
C. ₹ 63 D. ₹ 66

**267.** Best Ltd. purchased a machine for ₹ 2,50,000 which is likely to give the following cash flow. Cash Flow after Taxes (CFAT).

| Year | CFAT |
|---|---|
| 1 | 50,000 |
| 2 | 60,000 |
| 3 | 70,000 |
| 4 | 75,000 |
| 5 | 65,000 |
| 6 | 1,00,000 |

Compute Pay-Back Period:
A. 4.13 years B. 3 years
C. 4 years D. 3.93 years

**268.** X Ltd. plans to purchase a machine for ₹ 4,00,000 which is likely to yield the following returns in the next 3 years.

| Year | CFAT |
|---|---|
| 1 | 1,50,000 |
| 2 | 1,80,000 |
| 3 | 1,60,000 |

Compute the NPV of the proposal at the required rate of interest 10% and 12%.
A. 11.78% B. 10.96%
C. 10.78% D. 11.04%

**269.** A firm is considering to buy one of the following two mutually exclusive investment projects:

**Project S:** Buy a machine that requires an initial investment outlay of ₹ 2,00,000 and with generate CFAT of ₹ 60,000 per year for 5 years.

**Project W:** Buy a machine that requires an initial investment outlay of ₹ 2,50,000 and with generate CFAT of ₹ 54,000 per year for 8 years.

Assume 10% as cost of capital. Determine the Equivalent Annual Net Present Value (EANPV) of both the Projects.
A. S: ₹ 7,140: W: ₹ 7,514
B. S: ₹ 7,243: W: ₹ 7,440
C. S: ₹ 7,243: W: ₹ 7,140
D. S: ₹ 7,140: W: ₹ 7,243

**270.** A company requires an initial investment of ₹ 2,00,000. The estimated net cash flow after tax but before depreciation is as follows:

| Year | Net Cash Inflow (In ₹) |
|---|---|
| 1 | 35,000 |
| 2 | 35,000 |
| 3 | 35,000 |
| 4 | 35,000 |
| 5 | 35,000 |
| 6 | 40,000 |
| 7 | 50,000 |
| 8 | 75,000 |
| 9 | 50,000 |
| 10 | 20,000 |

Calculate NPV (Net Present Value) of cash inflows (using 10% as discount factor).
A. ₹ 45,805 B. ₹ 44,508
C. ₹ 44,805 D. ₹ 46,508

**271.** From the following information, compute the P.I. (Profitability Index) of the two projects:

| | **Project A** | **Project B** |
|---|---|---|
| Total present value | ₹ 54,238 | ₹ 84,940 |
| Cost of investment | ₹ 60,000 | ₹ 82,000 |

A. Project A: 0.9039; Project B: 1.0358
B. Project A: 1.0358; Project B: 0.9039
C. Project A: 0.9039; Project B: 1.358
D. Project A: 0.9039; Project B: 1.538

**272.** AB Ltd. provides the following information:

| | |
|---|---|
| Sales | ₹ 37,50,000 |
| Variable Cost | ₹ 21,00,000 |
| Fixed Cost | ₹ 3,00,000 |
| Debt | ₹ 22,50,000 |
| Rate of Debt | 9% |
| Equity Capital | ₹ 27,50,000 |

ROI (Return on Investment) will be:
A. 27% B. 25%
C. 28% D. 25.5%

**273.** Compute EPS (Earnings per share) from the following data:

Total Funds to be raised = ₹ 5,00,000; 50% to be raised through shares and 50% by Debt cost of Debt 10%; Tax rate 50%; Equity shares of ₹ 10 each to be issued at 10% premium; Expected EBIT ₹ 2,00,000.
A. 3.5 B. 5
C. 6.5 D. 4.5

**274.** From the following data, compute the decrease/increase in duration of Operating Cycle:

| **Particulars** | **Year 2015** | **Year 2016** |
|---|---|---|
| Raw Materials | 20 | 27 |
| W.I.P. | 14 | 20 |
| Finished Goods | 21 | 25 |
| Purchases | 96 | 135 |
| Cost of Goods sold | 180 | 200 |
| Sales | 140 | 180 |
| Debtors | 32 | 40 |
| Creditors | 16 | 21 |

Given: 1 year : 365 days
A. Decrease 21 days B. Increase 20 days
C. Decrease 20 days D. Increase 21 days

**275.** XYZ Ltd. issued 2,50,000 shares of ₹ 100 each at a premium of 20%. The whole issue was underwritten by Mr. A. In addition, there is a firm underwriting of 30,000 shares by Mr. A. Applications for 2,00,000 shares were received by the company in all. Calculate the liability of Mr. A. (in number of shares).
A. 170000 B. 80000
C. 220000 D. 20000

**276.** Excellent Ltd. made an issue of 60,000 shares which were underwriting as under:

| | |
|---|---|
| A | 30,000 shares |
| B | 18,000 shares |
| C | 12,000 shares |

In addition, there was "Firm" underwriting as under:

| | |
|---|---|
| A | 3,000 shares |
| B | 1,500 shares |
| C | 4,500 shares |

The total subscriptions including firm under writing were for ₹ 45,600 shares. The following 'Marked Forms' were included in the subscriptions.

| | |
|---|---|
| A | 9,000 shares |
| B | 13,500 shares |
| C | 5,100 shares |

Compute the total liability of each underwriter, if the benefit of firm underwriting applications are not given to individual underwriters by treating them as Unmarked forms:
A. A-21000, B-4500, C-6900
B. A-12000, B-900, C-3300
C. A-14357, B-1500, C-7543
D. A-11357, B-900, C-3043

**277.** To appropriate the profits of the company:
(*i*) To transfer ₹ 3,15,000 to General Reserve
(*ii*) To pay ₹ 42,500 as ex-gratia bonus to the employees of the company

(*iii*) To declare dividend at 5% on equity shares

(*iv*) To transfer ₹ 22,500 to staff gratuity reserve

(*v*) To transfer ₹ 25,000 to Development Rebate Reserve

(*vi*) To transfer ₹ 45,000 to Deferred Taxation Reserve.

The company's capital consisted of 50,000 equity shares of ₹ 10 each fully paid for the year ending 31.3.2017, the directors transferred ₹ 20,000 to Debenture Redemption Fund A/c. Compute the Balance to be carried forward to the Balance Sheet.

A. ₹ 6,07,700
B. ₹ 6,02,700
C. ₹ 6,07,200
D. ₹ 6,02,200

**278.** Shree Ltd. has a credit balance on P & L A/c of ₹ 6,00,000 on 1.4.2016 and net profit for the year is ₹ 60,00,000. The following decisions were taken regarding provisions, reserves and dividends:

(*i*) General Reserve ₹ 7,00,000

(*ii*) Investment Allowance ₹ 7,00,000

(*iii*) Provision for Taxation @ 50%

(*iv*) Dividend Equalisation Fund A/c ₹ 4,00,000

(*v*) Dividend on 10% Preference Shares of ₹ 40,00,000

(*vi*) Dividend on 15% on 6,00,000 equity shares of ₹ 10 each fully paid.

Compute Net profit after tax (to be carried forward to P & L Appropriation A/c)

A. ₹ 6,00,000
B. ₹ 23,00,000
C. ₹ 30,00,000
D. ₹ 20,00,000

**279.** Which of the following is an example of sources of funds?

A. Decrease in share capital
B. Decrease in long-term liabilities
C. Increase in fixed assets
D. Increase in long-term liabilities

**280.** X Ltd. has part of its Share Capital in 5,000 12% Redeemable Preference Shares of ₹ 100 each. The General Reserve of the Company shows a credit balance of ₹ 6,00,000. The directors decided to utilize 70% of the Reserve in Redeeming Preference Shares and the balance is to be met from the proceeds of the fresh issue of sufficient number of equity shares of ₹ 10 each. No. of fresh issue of shares will be:

A. 14000 B. 6000
C. 3000 D. 8000

**281.** Under income Tax Act, who is empowered to issue Zero Coupon Bonds?

A. All NBFCs
B. All Scheduled Banks
C. All Trusts
D. All State Governments

**282.** ERM under Internal Audit is:

A. Enterprise Risk Manual
B. Enterprise Resource Management
C. Enterprise Resource Manual
D. Enterprise Risk Management

**283.** Surcharge in case of a domestic company if the income exceeds ₹ 10 crore.

A. 12% B. 10%
C. 5% D. 7%

**284.** GST Council has been created:

A. As per Article 279A of the amended Constitution
B. As per Article 280A of the amended Constitution
C. As per Article 281A of the amended Constitution
D. As per Article 282A of the amended Constitution

**285.** The amount of deduction in respect of salary paid to its own members in case of PFAOP is:

A. Without any limit B. 1,50,000
C. Nil D. None of these

**286.** As per the Companies Act, 2013, which one of the following is not allowed for the companies to buy-back its shares:

A. Its free reserves

B. The securities premium account
C. The proceeds of specified securities like employees' stock option
D. The proceeds of an earlier issue of the same kind of shares

**287.** Form for Cancellation of Registration under GST is:
A. GST REG-16 B. GST REG-17
C. GST REG-18 D. GST REG-19

**288.** Under GST CIN stands for:
A. Challan Identification Number
B. Computer Identification Number
C. Cost Identification Number
D. None of these

**289.** What is E-FPB under GST?
A. Electronic Focus Point Bank
B. Electronic Fund Payment Bank
C. Electronic Focal Point Bank
D. Electronic Focal Point Branch

**290.** In terms of GST what is RNR?
A. Rate of Non-Revenue
B. Revenue Natural Rate
C. Revenue Neutral Rate
D. Rate Neutral Revenue

**291.** As per the Payment of Wages Act 1936, when the wages of terminated employee is to be paid?
A. Before the expiry of the 7th day from the date of termination of employment
B. Before 7th of subsequent month of termination of employment
C. Before the expiry of the 2nd day from the date of termination of employment
D. None of these

**292.** Which one of the following is TRUE about GST?
A. GST applies to imports
B. The final consumer will bear only the GST charged by the last dealer in the supply chain with set-off benefits at all the previous stages
C. It covers petrol
D. It covers entertainment taxes earlier levied by local bodies

**293.** Section ____ of the Companies Act which deals with Corporate Social Responsibility.
A. 138 B. 136
C. 137 D. 135

**294.** Which one of the following is True in respect of issue of Shares at discount as per Companies Act 2013?
A. Shares can be issued at discount not exceeding 25%
B. As per Sec 79, shares can be issued at discount with some conditions.
C. Shares other than sweat shares cannot be issued at discount
D. None of these

**295.** SPICe =
A. Simple Protocol for Incorporating Company Electronically
B. Simplified Pro-forma for Incorporating Company Electronically
C. Simplified Protocol for Indian Company Electronically
D. Simplified Proforma for Indian Company Electronically

**296.** Form used for obtaining DIN is:
A. DIR 5 B. DIR 2
C. DIR 4 D. DIR 3

**297.** According to Securities and Exchange Board of India, 1992, Amended Section-49 (VI) is applicable to:
A. Top 100 companies by market capitalisation
B. Top 200 companies by market capitalisation
C. Top 300 companies by market capitalisation
D. Top 400 companies by market capitalisation

**298.** The following loss is not allowed to carry forward:
A. House property loss
B. Loss from running and maintaining of race camels
C. Loss under the head—Income from other source
D. None of these

**299.** Income on which equalization levy is charged is:

A. Not an income under IT Act, 1961
B. Not chargeable under income tax
C. Chargeable under income tax
D. None of these

**300.** The due date for remittance of Provident Fund is:

A. 21st of the subsequent month
B. 7th of the subsequent month
C. 15th of the subsequent month
D. 24th of the subsequent month

# ANSWERS

## PAPER-I

| 1 | 2 | 3 | 4 | 5 | 6 | 7 | 8 | 9 | 10 |
|---|---|---|---|---|---|---|---|---|---|
| A | C | D | B | C | D | C | B | A | A |
| **11** | **12** | **13** | **14** | **15** | **16** | **17** | **18** | **19** | **20** |
| B | D | A | C | C | A | D | B | C | A |
| **21** | **22** | **23** | **24** | **25** | **26** | **27** | **28** | **29** | **30** |
| D | A | A | C | D | C | A | A | D | B |
| **31** | **32** | **33** | **34** | **35** | **36** | **37** | **38** | **39** | **40** |
| C | D | A | A | D | B | C | A | B | D |
| **41** | **42** | **43** | **44** | **45** | **46** | **47** | **48** | **49** | **50** |
| B | C | A | A | D | B | D | A | B | D |
| **51** | **52** | **53** | **54** | **55** | **56** | **57** | **58** | **59** | **60** |
| B | A | C | D | A | B | C | A | D | A |
| **61** | **62** | **63** | **64** | **65** | **66** | **67** | **68** | **69** | **70** |
| D | B | C | D | B | A | A | B | C | D |
| **71** | **72** | **73** | **74** | **75** | **76** | **77** | **78** | **79** | **80** |
| A | B | B | C | D | A | C | D | B | C |
| **81** | **82** | **83** | **84** | **85** | **86** | **87** | **88** | **89** | **90** |
| B | A | D | C | B | C | D | A | B | C |
| **91** | **92** | **93** | **94** | **95** | **96** | **97** | **98** | **99** | **100** |
| B | D | A | C | B | C | D | A | A | B |
| **101** | **102** | **103** | **104** | **105** | **106** | **107** | **108** | **109** | **110** |
| C | B | A | D | C | C | D | C | A | B |
| **111** | **112** | **113** | **114** | **115** | **116** | **117** | **118** | **119** | **120** |
| C | D | B | A | B | C | C | A | A | C |
| **121** | **122** | **123** | **124** | **125** | **126** | **127** | **128** | **129** | **130** |
| B | A | C | C | D | C | A | B | C | A |
| **131** | **132** | **133** | **134** | **135** | **136** | **137** | **138** | **139** | **140** |
| B | A | D | C | B | B | A | D | C | A |
| **141** | **142** | **143** | **144** | **145** | **146** | **147** | **148** | **149** | **150** |
| B | A | C | D | C | D | A | A | B | * |

# PAPER-II

| 151 | 152 | 153 | 154 | 155 | 156 | 157 | 158 | 159 | 160 |
|---|---|---|---|---|---|---|---|---|---|
| A | C | D | B | * | B | D | A | * | A |
| 161 | 162 | 163 | 164 | 165 | 166 | 167 | 168 | 169 | 170 |
| C | B | A | B | B | B | D | C | B | A |
| 171 | 172 | 173 | 174 | 175 | 176 | 177 | 178 | 179 | 180 |
| A | A | B | D | A | B | C | A | C | D |
| 181 | 182 | 183 | 184 | 185 | 186 | 187 | 188 | 189 | 190 |
| C | B | D | A | D | A | C | B | C | A |
| 191 | 192 | 193 | 194 | 195 | 196 | 197 | 198 | 199 | 200 |
| C | B | D | A | B | B | D | B | C | D |
| 201 | 202 | 203 | 204 | 205 | 206 | 207 | 208 | 209 | 210 |
| D | C | B | D | * | D | A | B | C | A |
| 211 | 212 | 213 | 214 | 215 | 216 | 217 | 218 | 219 | 220 |
| D | B | A | B | B | D | D | * | A | D |
| 221 | 222 | 223 | 224 | 225 | 226 | 227 | 228 | 229 | 230 |
| A | B | D | B | D | C | B | D | B | B |
| 231 | 232 | 233 | 234 | 235 | 236 | 237 | 238 | 239 | 240 |
| A | D | C | B | A | A | A | B | D | B |
| 241 | 242 | 243 | 244 | 245 | 246 | 247 | 248 | 249 | 250 |
| C | A | B | D | A | D | B | D | C | B |
| 251 | 252 | 253 | 254 | 255 | 256 | 257 | 258 | 259 | 260 |
| A | D | C | D | C | B | A | C | A | C |
| 261 | 262 | 263 | 264 | 265 | 266 | 267 | 268 | 269 | 270 |
| C | D | D | B | D | C | D | D | C | C |
| 271 | 272 | 273 | 274 | 275 | 276 | 277 | 278 | 279 | 280 |
| A | A | A | B | B | C | * | C | D | D |
| 281 | 282 | 283 | 284 | 285 | 286 | 287 | 288 | 289 | 290 |
| B | D | A | A | C | D | A | A | D | C |
| 291 | 292 | 293 | 294 | 295 | 296 | 297 | 298 | 299 | 300 |
| C | B | D | C | B | D | * | C | C | C |

## Previous Paper (Solved)

# BSNL–Junior Accounts Officers (JAO) Exam, 2015*

## PAPER-I

***Choose one right answer from the four options given for each of the questions.***

### SECTION-I

**Directions (Qs. 1 to 5):** *What is the meaning of the following phrases?*

**1.** *Buy a pig in a poke*
A. To buy something without seeing it
B. To buy something after examining it
C. To transport the pigs
D. None of the above

**2.** *Bring down the house*
A. Braking the house
B. House entering ceremony
D. To become anger
D. To get the audience laugh loudly

**3.** *Break a leg*
A. Hitting the enemy
B. Good luck
C. Dance till you tire
D. Body blow

**4.** *Bulls into a china shop*
A. A Clumsy person who deals roughly
B. A silent person
C. To overwork yourself mentally
D. None of the above

**5.** *Raise an eyebrow*
A. To surprise  B. To kill
C. To cry  D. To wake up

**6.** "CPI inflation will stay at closer to 5% in 2015 as reduction in fiscal deficit, sustained deceleration in rural wages and lower global commodity prices will contain inflationary pressures... ." What is the meaning of Deceleration in this statement?
A. Decrease  B. Increase
D. Static  D. Confused

**7.** "Renewing the focus on a key issue in a rancorous election campaign in Queenslands State".

What is the meaning of rancorous in the above statement?
A. Encouraging  B. Assuring
C. Bitter  D. Lukewarm

**Directions (Qs. 8 to 12):** *From the following passage, find the synonym of the words underlined.*

**Lost and found: a tale of luck and equipoise**
Let me share an experience we had recently as a family that taught us how to think rationally and with equanimity while under stress. We had gone to my in-laws' place in Hyderabad during the Dushera holidays. Two suitcases with clothes, a kindle reader and the customary work laptop were in tow. For our return journey we were dropped at the Kucheguda railway station to head back to Bangalore. As we had reached the station a tad early, we settled down with our luggage on a bench on the platform. When the train came we moved the luggage to our seats. I always look forward to train journeys so that I can read books uninterruptedly. I started a book, so did my husband. An hour and some 40 pages later, my husband's phone rang. I could hear my husband's side of the conversation and see his expressions.

* Exam held on 22-02-2015

His expression was turning <u>quizzical</u>. The call was from RPF who found the laptop and other sundry items which we had left in Kacheguda. We had a situation to deal with......

**8.** Equipoise
A. Imbalance B. Balance
C. Effort D. Initiatives

**9.** Equanimity
A. Stable B. Unstable
C. Worry D. None of the above

**10.** Tow
A. Line B. Platform
D. Carrier D. Disorder

**11.** Uninterruptedly
A. With break B. Happily
C. Continuously D. Deeply

**12.** Quizzical
A. Puzzlement B. Sadly
C. Hurriedly D. Sceptical

**Directions (Qs. 13 to 22):** *Fill the blanks with suitable pronouns in the following sentences.*

**13.** Sachin and ............ were present.
A. me B. I
C. mine D. None of the above

**14.** It was ............ who wrote the letter to you.
A. me B. I
C. mine D. None of the above

**15.** Let you and ............ decide what we could do.
A. me B. I
C. mine D. None of the above

**16.** Can you strike the ball as well as ............ strike?
A. they B. them
C. their D. whom

**17.** ............ hardly knows what to do.
A. One B. They
C. We D. None of the above

**18.** We always appreciate the people ............ speak the truth.
A. who B. that
C. A or B D. when

**19.** Listen to ............ I say.
A. which B. that
C. what D. when

**20.** Sachin is the very man ............ all the cricketer want to follow.
A. what B. that
D. whom D. who

**21.** Say ............ you would like best.
A. what B. which
D. that D. None of the above

**22.** For the work I need such a person ............ she is.
A. whom B. what
C. that D. as

**Directions (Qs. 23 to 32):** *Use suitable prepositions in the following sentences.*

**23.** I agreed ............ his proposal.
A. on B. for
D. in D. to

**24.** She goes ............ school ............ foot.
A. to, on B. for, on
D. to, with D. to, in

**25.** We came ............ car.
A. in B. by
C. on D. with

**26.** He has been singing ............ 8 o'clock.
A. since B. from
C. before D. by

**27.** I prefer hockey ............ cricket.
A. over B. to
C. than D. for

**28.** I kept her ............ falling.
A. from B. by
C. before D. after

**29.** Yamuna Express way which connects Delhi ............ Agra may be closed for traffic on Sunday.
A. and B. with
C. to D. through

**30.** We are praying ............ his speedy recovery.
A. on B. to
C. for D. by

**31.** Exercise your right ............ freedom.
A. to B. for
C. on D. at

**32.** This is the book I was telling you ............ .
A. on B. for
C. to D. about

**Directions (Qs. 33 to 37):** *Read the following material and fill in the blanks with suitable words.*

The Executive Engineer ........... (33) tender from the eligible ........... (34) for the work detailed in the table below, as per the Standard Tender Documents. The ........... (34) may ........... (35) tenders for the work given in the table through e-procurement portal of the Government of India viz., www.eproc.gov.in. The ........... (34) are advised to note the ........... (36) criteria specified in the ........... (37) to qualify for the award of the contract and go through the general conditions for eligible ........... (34) and technical qualification criteria given in the e-portal.

**33.** A. calls B. invites
C. asks D. directs

**34.** A. applicants B. proposers
C. tenderers D. Indian citizens

**35.** A. file B. send
C. apply D. submit

**36.** A. maximum B. minimum
C. exact D. specified

**37.** A. guidelines B. instructions
C. advice D. cautions

**Directions (Qs. 38 to 50):** *Choose suitable Antonyms.*

**38.** Ample
A. Plenty B. Scanty
C. Big D. Dislike

**39.** Absolute
A. Limited B. Full
C. Complete D. None of the above

**40.** Diligent
A. Secure B. Infirm
C. Idle D. Intelligent

**41.** Inherit
A. Bequeath B. Decrease
C. Increase D. Excess

**42.** Entrance
A. Gate B. Start
C. Begin D. Exit

**43.** Fatigue
A. Tired B. Sorrow
C. Refresh D. Exhausted

**44.** Gather
A. Scatter B. Get
C. Collect D. Collate

**45.** Intricate
A. Sample B. Single
C. Simple D. Suppliment

**46.** Pursue
A. Avoid B. Carry on
C. Proceed D. Go with

**47.** Rejoice
A. Happy B. Join
C. Joice D. Lament

**48.** Sacred
A. Profane B. Neat
C. Clean D. Divine

**49.** Town
A. Urban B. Big area
C. Country D. Colony

**50.** Frugal
A. Small B. Low key
C. Extravagant D. Poor

**Directions (Qs. 51 to 55):** *Fill in the blanks with suitable articles.*

**51.** One should take ........... milk.
A. a B. an
C. the D. No articles needed

**52.** It is surely ........... good news.
A. a B. an
C. the D. No articles needed

**53.** ............ dog is ............ faithful animal.

A. A, the B. An, the

D. The, an D. The, a

**54.** The speaker's talk touched ........... artist in him.

A. a B. an

D. the D. No articles needed

**55.** She left for Mumbai by ............ air.

A. a B. an

D. the D. No articles needed

**Directions (Qs. 56 to 65):** *Choose correct meaning of the following words.*

**56.** Acronym

A. Angry

B. Fighting with enemy

C. Useless

D. A word made up of the initials of other words

**57.** Adage

A. Adopt

B. Additional

C. Traditional saying

D. Tour

**58.** Audacious

A. Weak B. Sorrow

C. Sink D. Daring

**59.** Capricious

A. Eagerness B. Adamant

C. Unpredictable D. Disaster

**60.** Cognate

A. Allied by blood B. Collect

C. Designate D. Support

**61.** Enigmatic

A. Hugeness B. Invigorate

C. Puzzling D. Underdeveloped

**62.** Irrevocable

A. Unalterable B. Alterable

C. Cancel D. Returnable

**63.** Maverick

A. Rebel B. Friend

C. Close D. Flashy

**64.** Onerous

A. Ownership B. Light

D. Fast D. Burdensome

**65.** Veneer

A. Strong cover B. Thin cover

C. Big cover D. Small layer

**Directions (Qs. 66 to 70):** *Read the following passage and select the correct meaning of the underlined words.*

The risk-neutral valuation principle states that a derivative can be valued by (a) calculating the expected payoff on the assumption that the expected return from the underlying asset equals the risk-free interest rate and (b) discounting the expected payoff at the risk free interest rate. When interest rates are constant, risk-neutral valuation provides a well-defined and unambiguous valuation tool. When interest rates are stochastic, it is less clear-cut. Here, the theoretical underpinnings of risk-neutral valuation when interest rates are stochastic are explained. Martingales and measures are critical to a full understanding of risk-free neutral valuation.

**66.** Derivative

A. Original

B. Imagine

C. Having a value that depends on an underlying asset

D. Having a value that depends on an underlying liability

**67.** Underpinnings

A. Foundations B. Top structure

C. Pin Badge D. Cylinder

**68.** Stochastic

A. Absolutely

B. Random

C. Total population

D. None of the above

**69.** Martingales

A. Marginal angles

B. Coast patrolling

C. Zero-drift stochastic process

D. None of the above

**70.** Underlying
A. Explicit B. Oral
C. Direct D. Implicit

**Directions (Qs. 71 to 75):** *In the following sentences, use the correct conjunctions.*

**71.** He is ........... intelligent ........... hard working, that is why he could not progress.
A. not, and B. either, or
C. very, but D. neither, nor

**72.** He has ........... gone to the cinema ........... to his friend's house.
A. either, or B. not, either
C. neither, nor D. None of the above

**73.** ........... Kohli's fighting century, India lost the match.
A. Despite B. Although
C. But D. As

**74.** ........... the Investigators confirmed that the Minister's statement was recorded, they remained silent over when exactly they approached him.
A. Despite B. Although
C. But D. As

**75.** ........... leaving the accused offered the victim a drink that was laced with sedative.
A. Before B. When
C. As D. Due to

**76.** Who lives a lonely, austere life?
A. Extrovert B. Egoist
C. Ambivert D. Ascetic

**77.** Who is more interested in the welfare of others than his own?
A. Altruist B. Introvert
D. Egotist D. Ambivert

**78.** Who hates marriage?
A. Introvert B. Egotist
D. Ascetic D. Misogamist

**79.** Who is incredibly conceited?
A. Egotist B. Extrovert
D. Misogamist D. Ambivert

**80.** Keenness of mind is
A. Perspicacity B. Peace
C. Clear D. Capacity

**Directions (Qs. 81 to 90):** *Choose the correct indirect speech.*

**81.** She said to me, "The train will arrive at 10 am".
A. She told me that the train will arrive at 10 am.
B. She told me that the train would arrive at 10 am.
C. She explained me that the train would arrive at 10 am.
D. She said me that the train would arrive at 10 am.

**82.** He said to his friend, "Please wait for me".
A. He requested his friend to wait for him.
B. He asked his friend to wait for him.
C. He told his friend to wait for him.
D. He ordered his friend to wait for him.

**83.** Rahul said to me, "Do not walk so fast".
A. Rahul told do not to walk so fast.
B. Rahul said me not to walk so fast.
D. Rahul told me not to walk so fast.
D. Rahul asked to me not to walk so fast.

**84.** He said to his servant "Clean the room".
A. He requested his servant to clean the room.
B. He said his servant to clean the room.
C. He told his servant to clean the room.
D. He ordered his servant to clean the room.

**85.** They asked me, "What are you doing"?
A. They asked me what I am doing.
B. They asked me what I was doing.
C. They said me what I was doing.
D. They said me what I am doing.

**86.** She said to her brother, "What you have described is interesting".
A. She told her brother what he has described was interesting.
B. She said to her brother what he had described was interesting.
D. She said her brother what he has described was interesting.
D. She told her brother what he had described was interesting.

**87.** He said "Oh! I have qualified".
A. He said with joy he had qualified.
B. He told with joy he had qualified.
D. He exclaimed with joy he had qualified.
D. He danced with joy that he had qualified.

**88.** "Why he absents himself from class is not understandable easily" the teacher said.
A. The teacher said why he absented himself from class was not understandable.
B. The teacher wondered why he absented himself from class was not understandable.
C. The teacher said why he absented himself from class is not understandable.
D. The teacher surprised why he absented himself from class was not understandable.

**89.** One player said to the other, "Let us play in another ground".
A. One player suggested to the other that they should play in another ground.
B. One player told to the other that they should play in another ground.
D. One player called to the other that they should play in another ground.
D. One player suggested to the other that they will play in another ground.

**90.** I said to them, "Where have you been?"
A. I questioned them where they had been.
B. I asked them where they have been.
C. I asked them where they had been.
D. I talked to them where they had been.

**Directions (Qs. 91 to 100):** *Fill in the blanks with suitable words.*

**91.** Logistics and staffing firms are now .......... in villages for delivery boys.
A. scouting B. seeing
D. visiting D. None of the above

**92.** The Minister has .......... the Union Home Ministry with a demand for ₹ 65,000 crore to install instant police system.
A. stumped B. surprised
D. asked D. approached

**93.** Amazon .......... into movie business.
A. enters B. forays
C. moves D. gets

**94.** Lafarge India plans to .......... the 14% stake it sold to Barings.
A. buy B. buy-back
C. get back D. None of the above

**95.** The CBI Court is .......... the validity of a closure report filed by the CBI.
A. hearing B. examining
C. verifying D. None of the above

**96.** Women employees .......... 27% less than men: Monster study.
A. earn B. get
C. receive D. take

**97.** Pace of Chinese economy .......... to 24 year nadir.
A. increases B. slows
C. grows D. goes

**98.** Sensex .......... 523 points on hopes of fresh reform measures.
A. vaults B. drops
C. goes D. dumps

**99.** EU .......... ban on Indian Mangoes.
A. lifts B. cancels
C. raises D. None of the above

**100.** Vikram Pandit & others .......... ₹ 250 crores in Bitcoin firm.
A. puts B. pumps
C. invest D. None of the above

## SECTION-II

**101.** Complete the sequence: 11 80 22 33 40: Delhi, Bangaluru, Mumbai Kolkata, .......?
A. Chennai B. Ranchi
C. Jaipur D. Hyderabad

**102.** Who holds the record of hitting second fastest ODI century?
A. AB de Villiers B. Corey Anderson
C. Shahid Afridi D. Sachin Tendulkar

**103.** Who is the Chief Justice of India?
A. Justice Sathasivam
B. Justice Verma
C. Justice H.L. Dattu
D. Justice R.M. Lodha

**104.** The ratio of present age of mother to her daughter is 5 : 3. Ten years hence, the ratio will be 3 : 2. Find their present ages.
A. 50, 30 B. 45, 27
C. 35, 21 D. 40, 24

**105.** Find modulus of $(3 + 4i)(15 + 12i)$:
A. 65 B. 60
C. 55 D. 70

**106.** Consider $\left(\sqrt{3}+\sqrt{2}\right)\left(\sqrt{3}-\sqrt{2}\right)=3-2=1$

Here, rationalising factor for $\left(\sqrt{3}+\sqrt{2}\right)$ is:
A. 1 B. 3
C. $\left(\sqrt{3}-\sqrt{2}\right)$ D. 2

**107.** Who is the present Censor Board Chief?
A. Leela Simon
B. Pahlaj Nihalani
C. S.Ve. Sekar
D. Dr. Chandra Prakash Dwivedi

**108.** The Indian word added in the 9th edition of Oxford English Dictionary is:
A. Papad B. Catamaran
C. Jelabi D. Achar

**109.** If $\sqrt{5}+x=3\sqrt{5}$, then value of $x$ is:
A. $2\sqrt{5}$ B. 2
C. 5 D. $\sqrt{2}$

**110.** What is FCTC?
A. Framework Convention on Tuberculosis Control
B. Framework Convention on Tobacco Control
C. Fundamental Convention on Tobacco Control
D. Functional Convention on Tuberculosis Control

**111.** Solve simultaneously:
$x + y - 3 = 0$ and $4x - 5y + 6 = 0$
A. 3, 6 B. 4, 1
C. 1, –5 D. 1, 2

**112.** International Yoga Day falls on
A. 21 June B. 20 June
C. 21 July D. 20 July

**113.** Which one of the following is a perishable inventory?
A. Chair
B. A seat in a commercial air-line
C. Computer
D. None of the above

**114.** What is WMA?
A. Ways and Means Advance
B. World Management Association
C. Wide Management Area
D. None of the above

**115.** The first Minister of a State Cabinet who went on to become Supreme Court Judge is
A. Justice Gopalakrishna Gokhale
B. Justice V.R. Krishna Iyer
C. Justice Ramaswamy
D. Justice Soumitra Sen

**116.** GRN = ?
A. Goods Received Note
B. Goods Returned Notice
C. Gross Rate Number
D. Government Rated Note

**117.** What comes in place of "?" mark?

| ? | T | T | F | F |
|---|---|---|---|---|
| S | S | E | N | T |
| E | T | T | F | F |
| S | S | E | N | T |

A. E B. O
D. F D. S

**118.** What is ASBA?
A. Applications Supported by Blocked Amount
B. Applications Supported by Bank Amount
C. Applications Sanctioned by Bank Agreement
D. Applications Supported by Bulk Amount

**119.** What is the meaning of underlined word in the following sentence?

Year 2015 will be crucial as <u>shale oil</u> firms begin to feel the pinch of low prices.

A. Rock
B. Favourable
C. Oil extracted from oil shale by heating
D. None of the above

**120.** What is OECD?
A. Organization for Economic and Collaboration and Development
B. Organization for Economic Cooperation and Development
C. Operation for Economic and Collaboration and Development
D. Organization for Entrepreneurs Cooperation and Development

**121.** Ratnagiri Gas & Power Ltd. as earlier known as
A. Gabhol B. Dabhol
C. Cabhol D. Fabhol

**122.** What is XBRL?
A. Extendable Business Reporting Language
B. Extensible Business Reporting Language
C. X-rayed Business Reporting Loop
D. X-rayed Business Related Licensing

**123.** While working on a word file Key F5 denotes
A. Find and Replace
B. Spelling and Grammar
D. Renaming
D. Help Menu

**124.** We have a group of 8 men and 7 women. We are asked to form a sub-committee of 3 men and 4 women out of them. In how many ways this sub-committee can be formed?
A. 4 B. 1960
C. 672 D. 11640

**125.** A car covered 200 kms, for first 50 kms, it moved at 50 kmph, second at 40 kmph, third at 25 kmph and lastly at 20 kmph. Its average speed (kmph) was:
A. 35 Approx. B. 30 Approx.
C. 20 Approx. D. 39 Approx.

**126.** What is next in the sequence:
4, 16, 36, 64, ?
A. 81 B. 121
C. 144 D. 100

**127.** Match: passw@rd87676*476login987565 with any one of the four options:
A. passw@rd87676*476login887565
B. passw@rd87576*476login987565
C. passw@rd87676*476login987565
D. passw@rd87676*476logon987565

**128.** Who is the vice-chairman of NITI Aayog?
A. PM of India B. Arun Jaitley
C. Arvind Panagariya D. Bagwati

**129.** Who among the following are prefixing "CMA" before their names?
A. Members of the Institute of Cost Accountants of India
B. Members of the Institute of Chartered Accountants of India
C. Members of the Institute of Company Secretaries of India
D. Members of the Institute of CIMA

**130.** Alibaba is linked to
A. Jack Ka B. Jack Ma
C. Marc Jack D. Marc Ma

**131.** As per the latest estimate, India has ............ per cent of the tiger population in the world.
A. 50 B. 60
C. 70 D. 80

**132.** IMF estimates India to grow at .......... in 2015.
A. 7.2% B. 6.8%
C. 5.8% D. 6.3%

**133.** The number of bank accounts opened under PMJDY from 23rd to 29th August 2014, as stated in the Guinness Book of World Records is
A. 11.50 crore B. 1.81 crore
C. 7.5 crore D. 9 crore

**134.** What is H1N1?
A. Ebola B. Swine flu
D. Viral disease D. None of the above

**135.** Who among the following persons has won "Fields Trophy"?
A. Milkha Singh
B. P.T. Usha
C. Manjul Bhargava
D. Dr. Chandrasekar

**136.** Which one of the following is an example of "Target Costing"?
A. Alto K10
B. Nano
D. Hyundai $i10$
D. Nissan Micra

**137.** The latest draft guidelines released by TRAI is
A. On Tariff
B. On spectrum prices
C. On monthly rentals on landline connections
D. On Mobile Number Portability

**138.** Where is Hyderabad House located?
A. Chennai  B. Hyderabad
D. New Delhi  D. Aurangabad

**139.** A recent study indicated that 60% of all businesses use BSNL landline connections. From the binomial probability distribution table, the probability that exactly four businesses will have a BSNL landline connection in a random selection of six businesses is:
A. 0.276  B. 0.137
C. 0.311  D. 0.600

**140.** How many playing 11 can be formed out of 16 probable's in a camp?
A. 1200  B. 4368
C. 3684  D. 7643

**141.** Cost function for '$x$' units of output is:
$C_{(x)} = x\left[\frac{x^2}{100}+200\right]$, the marginal cost at $x$ = 10 will be:
A. 200  B. 300
C. 230  D. 270

**142.** Newspapers, magazines, radio, television are all sources of
A. primary data
B. authentic information
C. propaganda of vested interests
D. secondary information

**143.** Simple tables are used when
A. presenter has nothing to hide.
B. study does not have much substance.
C. data collected is very deficient.
D. very few simple and straight forward features are to be emphasised.

**144.** The selling price of 12 oranges is equal to the cost price of 20 apples. Find the profit percentage:
A. $66\frac{2}{3}\%$  B. 50%
C. $33\frac{1}{3}\%$  D. 75%

**145.** Arithmetic mean of first 10 natural numbers is:
A. 5.5  B. 5
C. 4.8  D. 4.5

**146.** Correct empirical relationship between mean, median and mode is:
A. mean = 3 mode – median
B. mean – median = 3(mode – median)
C. 3 (median – mode) = mean
D. mean – mode = 3 (mean – median)

**147.** A trade designed to reduce risk is:
A. Hedge  B. Pledge
C. Guarantee  D. Warranty

**148.** Zero coupon bonds created by selling the coupons on Treasury bonds separately from the principal are:
A. Treasury Bonds  B. Delta bonds
C. Zebra bonds  D. Strip bonds

**149.** What is NINJA?
A. A person with a poor credit risk
B. A person with a healthy credit risk
C. A person with no credit risk
D. None of the above

**150.** What NITI stands for in NITI Aayog?
A. National Institution for Transforming India
B. National Institute for Transforming India
D. National Initiative for Transforming India
D. National Inclusive for Transforming India

# PAPER-II

**Directions:** *Choose one right answer from the 4 options given under each of the questions:*

1. One of the differences between Partnership and LLP is that:
   A. Restriction on maximum number of partners in case of Partnership firm and no such restrictions for LLP
   B. No restriction on maximum number of partners in case of Partnership firm and restrictions on number of partners for LLP
   C. No partner is liable for legal compliance in case of partnership and in case of LLP all partners are liable for legal compliance
   D. Partnership is created by law whereas LLP is created by agreement.

2. The penalties for avoiding any payments under the Payment of Gratuity Act may extend to ............. months or with fine which may extend to ₹ .............
   A. 7 months ; ₹ 15,000
   B. 6 months ; ₹ 20,000
   C. 6 months ; ₹ 10,000
   D. 7 months ; ₹ 10,000

3. The Payment of Gratuity Act was enacted in the year:
   A. 1972 B. 1872
   C. 1927 D. 1947

4. Gratuity is payable to an employee after he/she has rendered continuous service for not less than ............. years on his/her date of resignation
   A. 7 B. 8
   C. 5 D. 1

5. What is Contract?
   A. Offer + Acceptance
   B. Offer + Acceptance – Enforceability
   C. Offer + Acceptance + Enforceability
   D. Offer – Acceptance + Enforceability

6. Withdrawal from ATM is an emplace of ............. contract
   A. Express B. Implied
   C. Illegal D. Void

7. In which one of the following land mark cases, the agreement with a Minor was declared as void ab initio?
   A. Mobiribibi Vs Dharmodas Ghosh
   B. Jager Nath Singh Vs Lalita Prasad
   C. Raghava Chariah Vs Srinivasa
   D. Fernandez Vs Gonsalves

8. The amount of Gratuity payable for a monthly rated employee is
   A. Last drawn monthly wages × (15/30) × No of completed years of service
   B. Last drawn monthly wages × (15/26) × No of completed years of service
   C. Last drawn monthly wages × (15/31) × No of completed years of service
   D. Average of last 10 months wages × (15/26) × No of completed years of service

9. Which one of the following transactions is considered as wagering?
   A. Chit Fund
   B. Contract of Insurance
   C. Share market transactions
   D. Prize competition in a game of skill having a prize money of ₹ 12,500

10. Which one of the following is not a characteristic of Partnership?
    A. Mutual agency
    B. Limited liability
    C. Restriction on transfer of interest
    D. Agreement between persons

11. In an Electric Company, original cost of an asset: ₹ 3,00,000; Present Cost of replacement: ₹ 5,00,000; Amount spent on replacement: ₹ 5,75,000. The amount charged to revenue is:
    A. ₹ 3,00,000 B. ₹ 5,00,000
    C. ₹ 5,50,000 D. ₹ 2,50,000

**12.** Which one of the following is true above Agreement by a Minor?
A. Agreement by minor is void ab initio.
B. Agreement by minor is valid in law
C. Agreement by minor can be ratified on attaining majority
D. Agreement beneficial to minor is not valid

**13.** An agreement induced by coercion is .........
A. voidable B. void
C. illegal D. None of the above

**14** Mr. A agrees to Purchase from Mr. B, 18 carat gold, thinking to be pure gold. State the validity of contract.
A. Contract is valid between A & B
B. Contract is void between A & B
C. Contract is voidable at the option of A but not B
D. Contract is voidable at the option of B but not A

**15.** Effect of "Fraud" under Contract Act is:
A. Contract is voidable at the option of aggrieved party
B. Contract is ab initio void
C. Contract is valid
D. None of the above

**16.** Which one of the following is an example of contingent contract?
A. Insurance
B. Contract for purchase of land
C. Contract for sale of goods
D. None of the above

**17.** A Transporter refuses to deliver up certain goods to the consignee, except upon the payment of an illegal charge for carriage. The consignee pays the sum charged in order to obtain the goods. Is the consignee is entitled to recover the charge that was illegally charged by the Transporter?
A. Yes
B. No
C. May be yes may be no
D. Information is not sufficient to find an answer

**18.** Returning the benefits to the owner in order to place the parties in the same position as they occupied before the agreement is called
A. Restitution B. Estoppel
C. Coercion D. Remission

**19.** .............. damages are not proportionate in the actual pecuniary loss sustained by the aggrieved party.
A. Exemplary damages
B. Nominal damages
C. Liquidated damages
D. Special damages

**20.** Neo Ltd made sales of ₹ 30 lakhs for the year 2014 and its corresponding debtors was ₹ 4,90,000. Calculate the debtors turnover in terms of days.
A. 60 days B. 45 days
C. 41 days D. 37 days

**21.** A company's shares with a face value of ₹ 10 each and quoted at ₹ 50 each in the stock market. Current rate of dividend is 50% and expected rate of growth is 5% p.a. A steady growth is expected. What is the cost of equity capital of the company?
A. 11% B. 12%
C. 14% D. 15%

**22.** Expand ELGI
A. Estimate, Learn, Grow, Implement
B. Estimate, Learn, Group, Improve
C. Estimate, Learn, Group, Implement
D. Evolve, Learn, Group, Implement

**23.** Expand IFRS
A. International Financial Reporting Systems
B. International Financial Reporting Standards
C. Indian Financial Reporting System
D. International Forecast Reporting Standards

**24.** In case of a sub-division of share capital, the total number of shares will ............... .
A. decrease
B. decrease proportionately
C. increase
D. not change

**25.** Divisible profits do not include .............. .
A. Revaluation Reserve
B. General Reserve
C. Dividend Equalization Reserve
D. P & L A/c balance

**26.** The maximum tolerable lot in any case shall not exceed:
A. 50 shares  B. 100 shares
C. 500 shares  D. No limit

**27.** For issue of "Sweat Equity Shares", the listed companies should follow the guidelines issued by:
A. The Companies Act
B. The Securities and Exchange Board of India
C. Both A and B of the above
D. Controller of Equity Shares (CES)

**28.** Which of the following statement is TRUE:
A. Capital Reserve is that amount which is available for dividend.
B. Capital Reserve cannot be used during life-time of the company.
C. Capital Reserve must be created out of the profits made on forfeited shares.
D. Capital Reserve cannot be used to write off capital losses.

**29.** Which of the following statement is NOT TRUE (relating to the issue of Bonus Shares)?
A. Issue of Bonus Shares is not a dividend
B. The issue of Bonus Shares constitutes a Source of fund to the company
C. It is a free share of stock given to current share holders in a company .
D. It represents no economic event.

**30.** Which of the following statement is NOT TRUE?
A. A company can purchase its own shares from share premium money.
B. No buyback shall be made out of the proceeds of earlier issues.
C. Capital Redemption Reserve cannot be used to issue fully paid Bonus Shares.
D. Securities Premium Account can be used to write off premium payable or to purchase of own shares by a company.

**31.** 'Floating charge' becomes crystallized when:
A. a company ceases to function/goes into liquidation.
B. an official receiver is appointed.
C. a company fails to pay interest/principal amount.
D. All of the above

**32.** Which of the following statement is TRUE relating to Depositories?
A. Depositories holds fund in account .
B. It transfers securities between accounts on the instructions of accountholders.
C. It facilitates transfer without having to handle money.
D. It facilitates safekeeping of money and not shares.

**33.** ABC Ltd. forfeited 100 shares of ₹ 10 each, originally issued at a premium of ₹ 2 per share. The shareholder paid ₹ 4 per share on application but did not pay the allotment money of ₹ 4 per share (including premium) and call of ₹ 4 per share. The shares are subsequently re-issued at ₹ 11 per share as fully paid-up.

Amount transferred to Capital Reserve Account will be:
A. ₹ 500  B. ₹ 400
C. ₹ 600  D. ₹ 550

**34.** VR Ltd. has made a Public Issue of 2000 shares, 6% Preference Shares of ₹ 100 each at a discount of 8% for providing funds for redemption of Preference Shares.

Which of the following amount would be considered as "Proceeds of fresh issue"?
A. ₹ 2,60,000  B. ₹ 2,16,000
C. ₹ 2,84,000  D. ₹ 1,84,000

**35.** A Ltd. has a share capital of ₹ 5,00,000 Equity Shares of ₹ 10 each. Market value is ₹ 25 per share. The company decides to make a rights issue to the existing shareholders in proportion of one right share of ₹ 10 at a premium of ₹ 3 per share for every five shares held.

Compute the value of "Rights".

A. ₹ 2.00 B. ₹ 2.50

C. ₹ 5.00 B. ₹ 7.00

**36.** MV Ltd. issued ₹ 1 0,00,000 12% Debentures of ₹ 100 each at a premium of 20%. The Net Effective Rate of Interest will be:

A. 12% B. 13.33%

C. 20% D. 10%

**37.** PQR Ltd. purchased assets of ₹ 4,50,000 and took over liabilities of ₹ 40,000 at an agreed value of ₹ 4,05,000 of ST Ltd. PQR Ltd. issued debentures of ₹ 100 each at 10% discount in full satisfaction of the purchase price. Determine the value of Goodwill or Capital Reserve.

A. Goodwill ₹ 5,000

B. Capital Reserve ₹ 45,000

C. Capital Reserve ₹ 5,000

D. Goodwill ₹ 45,000

**38.** SR Ltd. issued 8,000 12% Debentures of ₹ 50 each payable at a discount of 10% repayable after 5 years at a premium of 10%. The loss on issue of debenture to be written off every year will be:

A. ₹ 80,000 B. ₹ 16,000

C. ₹ 15,000 D. ₹ 8,000

**39.** RV Ltd. redeemed 5,000 12% Debentures of ₹ 100 each, which were issued at a discount of 10% by converting them into Equity Shares of ₹ 10 each at per Number of equity shares to be issued:

A. 50,000 B. 45,000

C. 55,000 D. 60,000

**40.** A company has outstanding 12% Debentures of ₹ 5,00,000 on 1st January 2013. The company pays interest on 30th June and 31st December. It purchased debentures of ₹ 50,000 for cancellation on 1st May 2013 at ₹ 102 cum-interest. On September 1, 2014, it further purchased for redemption debentures of ₹ 1,00,000 at ₹ 95 ex-interest. Profit on cancellation on September 1 will be:

A. ₹ 1,000 B. ₹ 10,000

C. ₹ 7,500 D. ₹ 5,000

**41.** From the following particulars, calculate the value of each equity share from the view point of Minority Holdings:

(*i*) Share Capital: 1,20,000 equity shares of ₹ 10 each fully paid

(*ii*) Profit (after deduction of tax) for last 3 years: ₹ 2,70,000; ₹ 3,60,000; ₹ 3,42,000 respectively

(*iii*) Dividend paid for the last 3 years: 12%, 17%, 16%

(*iv*) Normal Rate of Return: 12%

A. ₹ 17.00 B. ₹ 22.50

C. ₹ 14.50 D. ₹ 12.50

**42.** X Ltd. has earnings per share of ₹ 70 and is quoted at ₹ 630.

Y Ltd. which is a similar firm has earnings per share of ₹ 60.

What should be the value of share of Y Ltd.?

A. ₹ 420 B. ₹ 540

C. ₹ 570 D. ₹ 600

**43.** TDS on interest on debentures is:

A. Current Assets

B. Reserve

C. Current Liability

D. Appropriation

**44.** Balance of profit in P & L Appropriation Account has to be carried to the Balance-sheet under the heading:

A. Shares Capital

B. Reserves & Surplus

C. Provision

D. Miscellaneous Expenditure

**45.** Unclaimed dividend is to be shown in the Balance-sheet under the heading?

A. Current Assets

B. Provision

C. Current Liabilities

D. Miscellaneous Expenditure

**46.** M/s. Lakshmi Ltd. has been paying a dividend at 20% on capital of ₹ 40 lakh for many years. Its average profit after tax were ₹ 12 lakh. In 2013-14, it earned a profit of ₹ 10 lakh.

Find to be transferred to General Reserve as required by law, will be:

A. ₹ 1 lakh  B. ₹ 4 lakhs
C. ₹ 2 lakhs  D. ₹ 5 lakhs

**47.** Z Ltd. has been suffering heavy losses in the past. So, it has decided to go for reconstruction by reducing 22,000 equity shares of ₹ 100 each into ₹ 50 each so as to write off accumulated losses of ₹ 10,70,000. The amount of Balance in Capital Reduction A/c will be:

A. ₹ 20,000  B. ₹ 30,000
C. ₹ 32,000  D. ₹ 38,000

**48.** Which of the following statement is TRUE?

A. It is voluntary to create DRR A/c equivalent to 50% of the paid-up value of debenture issue.
B. The balance in the Sinking Fund A/c and Sinking Fund Investments A/c will not be same, they will differ.
C. In case of financial institutions, profits on sale of sinking fund investments are not capital but operating profits.
D. Interest is always calculated on the closing balance of the nominal value of investments.

**49.** Rent received by a Company (whose main business is real estate) is classified as:

A. cash equivalent
B. financing activity
C. operating activity
D. investing activity

**50.** From the following particulars, calculate cash inflow from debtors:

| | | |
|---|---|---|
| Total Sales | : | ₹ 10,00,000 |
| Cash Sales | : | 40% of total sales |
| Opening Debtors | : | ₹ 1,00,000 |
| Closing Debtors | : | ₹ 1,60,000 |
| Sales Returns | : | ₹ 40,000 |

A. ₹ 5,00,000  B. ₹ 2,50,000
C. ₹ 7,50,000  D. ₹ 5,50,000

**51.** Calculate cash outflow to creditors from the following particulars:

| | | |
|---|---|---|
| Total Purchases | : | ₹ 3,60,000 |
| Cash Purchases | : | 50% of credit purchases |
| Opening Creditors | : | ₹ 10,000 |
| Closing Creditors | : | ₹ 40,000 |
| Purchase Returns | : | ₹ 50,000 |
| Discount (received) | : | ₹ 20,000 |

A. ₹ 70,000  B. ₹ 1,40,000
C. ₹ 60,000  D. ₹ 1,20,000

**52.** MN Ltd. made a profit of ₹ 1,20,000 after charging depreciation of ₹ 20,000 on assets and a transfer to General Reserve of ₹ 30,000. The Goodwill written off was ₹ 7,000 and the gain on sale of machineries was ₹ 3,000. Changes in the value of current assets and current liabilities at the end of the year were:
Debtors showed an increase of ₹ 6,000
Creditors an increase of ₹ 10,000
Pre-paid expenses an increase of ₹ 200
Bills receivable a decrease of ₹ 3,000
Bills payable a decrease of ₹ 4,000
Outstanding expenses a decrease of ₹ 2,000
Ascertain Net Cash from Operating Activities:

A. ₹ 1,54,800  B. ₹ 1,64,800
C. ₹ 1,74,800  D. ₹ 1,84,800

**53.** During the year a company had the following balances:

Investments at the beginning of the period: ₹ 92,000.

Investments at the end of the period: ₹ 60,000.

During the year, the company sold 60% of its investments held in the beginning of the period at the profit of ₹ 20,000.

Cash flow from Investing Activities will be:

A. ₹ 26,000  B. ₹ 36,000
C. ₹ 42,000  D. ₹ 52,000

**54.** EF & Co. had plant and machinery whose written-down value on April 1, 2013 was ₹ 15,00,000 and March 31, 2014 was ₹ 18,00,000. Depreciation for the year was ₹ 60,000. At the beginning of the year a plant was sold for ₹ 40,000 which had a written down value of ₹ 32,000.

Compute the Net Cash Flow from Investing Activities:

A. ₹ 3,52,000 B. ₹ 3,92,000
C. ₹ 3,82,000 D. ₹ 3,62,000

**55.** Calculate Cash Flow from Financial Activities following based on following information:

| Particulars | March 31, 2013 (in ₹) | March 31, 2014 (in ₹) |
|---|---|---|
| Equity Share Capital | 12,00,000 | 16,00,000 |
| 9% Debentures | 4,00,000 | 2,00,000 |
| Security Premium | 1,00,000 | 1,50,000 |

Additional information: Interest paid on Debentures: ₹ 36,000.

A. ₹ 1,07,000 B. ₹ 2,14,000
C. ₹ 1,57,000 D. ₹ 2,54,000

**56.** From the following figures, compute the Net Cash Flow from Financial Activities:

| Particulars | March 31, 2013 (in ₹) | March 31, 2014 (in ₹) |
|---|---|---|
| Equity Share Capital | 16,00,000 | 24,00,000 |
| 10% Debentures | 3,00,00 | — |
| 10% Debentures | — | 6,00,000 |

Additional information:

(*i*) Interest paid on Debentures : ₹ 30,000
(*ii*) Dividend paid : ₹ 80,000
(*iii*) During the year 2013-14, the company issued Bonus Shares in the ratio of 2 : 1 by capitalizing the reserve

A. ₹ 9,90,000 B. ₹ 1,95,000
C. ₹ 2,90,000 D. ₹ 1,90,000

**57.** Payments on capitalized research and development costs are cash flows from ..........

A. Financing activities
B. Investing activities
C. Operating activities
D. Innovation activities

**58.** Which of the following is NOT a source of Application of Fund?

A. Purchase of Fixed Assets
B. Payment of Dividend
C. Depreciation
D. Re-payment of Long-term Loans

**59.** Which of the following statement is TRUE, relating to "Fund Flow"?

A. Contains both opening and closing cash
B. Changes in working capital
C. Net result is increase/decrease in cash
D. Changes in cash and cash equivalent

**60.** One important object of an Audit is the detection and prevention of "errors". Which of the following type of error is due to the cumulative effect of more than one error?

A. Errors of Omission
B. Errors of Commission
C. Errors of Principle
D. Compensating errors

**61.** Which of the following statement is NOT TRUE (relating to Interim Audit)?

A. Interim Audit means continuous audit.
B. Interim Audit means an audit up to a definite date.
C. Interim Audit enables the company to declare Interim Dividend.
D. Auditor's report is to be submitted immediately after the completion of Interim Audit.

**62.** Which of the following is the main purpose for insisting "Working Papers"?

A. It serves as supporting evidence to Auditor's Report.
B. It is a defence against charge of negligence.
C. Any item omitted to have seen in the previous year can be given top priority and verified in the current year.
D. All of the above

**63.** As per the Section 138 of the Companies Act 2013, who among the following can be appointed as Internal Auditor?

A. Chartered Accountant
B. Cost Accountant
C. Company Secretary
D. Chartered accountant or a cost accountant, or such other professional as may be decided by the Board

**64.** Which of the following is an essential document for "vouching" when a customer returns the goods?

A. Returns Outward Book
B. Purchases Book
C. Credit Note
D. Sales Book

**65.** Vouching the Impersonal Ledger is vital because its irregularity affects:
A. Trading and Profit & Loss A/c
B. Balance sheet
C. Both A and B of the above
D. Neither A nor B of the above

**66.** Which of the following account should be examined properly by an auditor in order to verify "Reserve & Surplus" that appears in the Balance-sheet?
A. Profit & Loss Appropriation A/c
B. Profit & Loss A/c
C. Trading A/c
D. Balance-sheet itself

**67.** In case of a Joint Stock Company, an auditor should verify the share capital by referring to:
A. The Memorandum and Articles of Association
B. Minutes Book
C. Register of Members and Cash Book
D. All of the above

**68.** Which of the following is a "contingent liability" to be shown as a footnote of the Balance-sheet?
A. Uncalled share capital
B. Damages receivable in any legal action taken for infringement of copyright, patents, etc.
C. Claim for money from a previous endorser of a bill receivable discounted but might be dishonoured.
D. Arrears of dividend on Cumulative Preference Shares.

**69.** When checking transmission of shares due to death or insolvency of the shareholders, the vital document/s to be verified:
A. Succession Certificate
B. Directors Minutes approving the transmission
C. Order of insolvency issued by the Court
D. All of the above

**70.** In case, when an auditor is appointed by the Central Government, he has to act an agent of :
A. the shareholders
B. the Central Government
C. Board of Directors
D. None of the above

**71.** Which of the following statement is TRUE?
A. Provision is created to strengthen the financial position of the company.
B. Provision can be utilized for distributing dividends.
C. Provision is a charge against profits.
D. None of the above

**72.** Which of the following statements relating to Specific Reserve is TRUE?
A. Specific Reserve can be distributed if necessary.
B. Specific Reserve is a charge on the profits.
C. Specific Reserves are shown on the liability side of the Balance-sheet alongwith the connected items.
D. An audit need not scrutinize Specific Reserve, as it is created for unascertained loss.

**73.** Which of the following is NOT an essential item to be verified before certifying the Statutory Report (Auditor's Report) as correct?
A. Shares allotted by the company.
B. Cash received in respect of such shares allotted.
C. The receipts and payments of the company.
D. Relevant court proceedings.

**74.** The basic objective of Financial Management is:
A. profit maximization
B. maximization of shareholder's wealth
C. maximization of sales
D. ensuring financial discipline

**75.** The goal of wealth maximization takes into consideration:
A. risk related to uncertainty of returns
B. timing of expected returns
C. amount of returns expected
D. All of the above

**76.** Economic Value Added (EVA) is equal to:
A. After tax operating profit + the cost of funds used.
B. Before tax operating profit – the cost of funds used.
C. After tax operating profit – the cost of funds used.
D. None of the above

**77.** Finance function involves:
A. procurement and effective utilization of funds
B. procurement of assets
C. expenditure of funds
D. safe custody of funds

**78.** The fundamental difference between Finance and Accounting relates to:
A. accounting methods
B. the treatment of funds
C. fiscal policies
D. structure of organization

**79.** Apart from economics and accounting "Finance" draws support from:
A. marketing
B. production
C. quantitative methods
D. All of the above

**80.** The functions of the 'controller' in the "Organisation of Financial Management Functions" are mainly related to:
A. accounting and auditing
B. financing activities of the firm
C. Both A and B of the above
D. None of the above

**81.** The Capitalization Rate determines:
A. the decision relating to dividend policy
B. the management of working capital
C. the time and risk preferences of the owners or suppliers of capital.
D. All of the above

**82.** The primary principle that applies in financial management is:
A. analysis of final accounts
B. marginal analysis
C. corporate governance
D. control of costs

**83.** Which of the following is an "Irrelevant Cash Outflow" in relation to asset selection decisions?
A. Cost of the investment
B. Variable labour expenses
C. Existing Fixed overhead expenses
D. Marginal taxes

**84.** Which of the following is the main technical flaw of Profit/earning per share maximization decision criterion?
A. ambiguity B. timing of benefits
C. quality of benefits D. All of the above

**85.** It is necessary to convert cash flows that result in different time periods to a common point in time. Which of the following technique is most useful to do this?
A. compounding
B. discounting
C. Both A and B of the above
D. None of the above

**86.** X Ltd. is contemplating to buy a machine for ₹ 70,000 which is expected to result in the following Cash Flows After Tax (CFAT). Determine the pay-back period accurately.

| Year | CFAT (in ₹) |
|---|---|
| 1 | 15,000 |
| 2 | 12,000 |
| 3 | 18,000 |
| 4 | 16,000 |
| 5 | 13,000 |
| 6 | 20,000 |

A. 4.69 years B. 4.09 years
C. 4.39 years D. 5.02 years

**87.** The project Y has initial investment of ₹ 80,000 and it earns ₹ 32,000 for four years. What is the NAV of the project? (P.V. of Annuity of ₹ 1 @ 10% for 4 years = 3.17)
A. ₹ 21,440 B. ₹ 18,740
C. ₹ 20,740 C. ₹ 19,440

**88.** In the case of independent investment projects, if the NPV of the project is zero, Internal Rate of Return (IRR) is equal to:
A. Estimated cash outflows
B. Cost of capital
C. Profitability Index (PI)
D. ARR (Average Rate of Return)

**89.** The cost of capital for new projects is 15%. Two competing projects (A & B) have IRRs of 13% and 14% respectively. Which project is to be selected?
A. A
B. B
C. Both A and B of the above
D. None of the above

**90.** In case of mutually exclusive investment proposals, which of the following methods is based on total yield/earnings/NPV?
A. IRR (Internal Rate of Return)
B. PI (Profitability Index)
C. NPV (Net Present Value)
D. None of the above

**91.** Which method is an appropriate measure in divisible projects selection under capital rationing:
A. Equivalent annual NPV
B. IRR
C. Present Value Index
D. All of the above

**92.** The return after the pay-off period is not considered in case of:
A. URR method
B. Pay back method
C. Present value index method
D. Discounted cash flow method

**93.** Depreciation is included in costs in case of:
A. Accounting Rate of Return method
B. Pay back method
C. Present value index method
D. None of the above

**94.** Which of the following is an Internal source of long-term financing?
A. Equity capital
B. Leasing and Hire-purchase finance
C. Venture Capital Financing
D. Retained earnings

**95.** Which of the following is the main component of "financial system"?
A. financial assets/instruments/security
B. financial intermediaries/institutions
C. financial markets
D. All of the above

**96.** Under the "green shoe option", the amount of shares that could be over allotted with the public issue will be:
A. 20% of the issue size
B. upto 10% of the public issue
C. upto 15% of the issue size
D. 25% of the issue size

**97.** Which of the following is a Liability-related Covenants (Negative) relating to features of Term Loans?
A. Reduction in debt-equity ratio by issue of additional capital.
B. Restriction on creation of further charge on asset.
C. Ban on sale of fixed assets without the lenders approval.
D. Maintenance of working capital position in terms of a minimum current ratio.

**98.** Which of the following is an innovative debt instrument as a source of long-term funds?
A. Deep Discount Bond (DDB)
B. Secured Premium Notes (SPNs)
C. Floating Rate Bonds (FRBs)
D. All of the above

**99.** Which of the following instruments is similar in nature to call options?
A. Debentures
B. Warrants
C. Redeemable Preference Shares
D. Bonus Shares

**100.** The measure of liquidity which is not very useful for comparing the performance of different firms but at the same time useful for internal control is:

A. Net working capital
B. Stock Turnover Ratio
C. Net Profit Ratio
D. Capital Turnover Ratio

**101.** To determine an appropriate financing-mix, which of the following is a high profit (low cost)—high rate (no net working capital) approach?
A. Conservative Approach
B. Hedging Approach
C. A Trade-off between the above two approaches
D. All of the above

**102.** The 'Operating Cycle' means:
A. the accounting period of business.
B. the period for which net working capital has been locked.
C. the time gap between the sales and their actual realization in cash.
D. the time gap between purchase of raw materials and sales.

**103.** Which of the following techniques is used as an important control techniques to assess the performance of inventory management?
A. Inventory Turnover Ratio
B. EOQ Model
C. ABC System
D. All of the above

**104.** Which one of the following is NOT a Primary Motive for maintaining "cash balances"?
A. Competition Motive
B. Compensating Motive
C. Speculative Motive
D. Transaction Motive

**105.** Which of the following is TRUE relating to "Management of cash and marketable securities" (working capital management)?
A. Baumol's model takes into account all motives of a holding cash.
B. Miller and Orr model assumes that cash balances randomly fluctuate between an upper bound and lower bound.
C. Olger's model is based on the use of a simple linear programming model
D. All of the above statements

**106.** Roy & Co. furnishes the following information: Accounts receivable collection period at present (reduced to) 3 days; credit sales ₹ 365 lakhs a year (billed on a continuous basis); the firms' opportunity cost of funds is 15%; cost of lock-box system is ₹ 50,000.

What will be the Net Savings/Net Loss?
A. Net Savings ₹ 5,000
B. Net Loss ₹ 5,000
C. Net Savings ₹ 25,000
D. Net Loss ₹ 25,000

**107.** The term "Credit Standard" refers to:
A. the standard rate of interest extended to creditors
B. the standard period for which credit has been granted
C. the basic criteria for extension of credit to its customers
D. the term under which a firm sells goods on credit to the customers.

**108.** The trade-off with reference to credit standards covers:
A. the collection cost
B. cost of investment in debtors
C. bad debts and level of sales
D. All of the above

**109.** In which of the following area "the Management of receivables" involves crucial decision?
A. Credit policies
B. Credit terms
C. Collection policies
D. All of the above

**110.** In the term "4/10 net 30"—the numeral 30 implies (denotes):
A. the maximum period for which credit is available
B. the rate of interest
C. the rate of trade discount allowed
D. the time after which cash discount is allowed

**111.** Compute the average age of receivables from the following particulars:

| | | |
|---|---|---|
| Gross Sales | : | ₹ 80,000 |
| Cash Sales | : | ₹ 30,000 |
| Accounts receivable on December 1, 2014 | : | ₹ 12,000 |
| Accounts receivable on December 31, 2014 | : | ₹ 8,000 |

A. 1.2 months B. 1.8 months
C. 2.4 months D. 2.2 months

**112.** Which of the following is the key decision area in "inventory management"?
A. Classification problem
B. Order quantity problem
C. Safety stock
D. All of the above

**113.** Which of the following is an indirect form of working capitals financing provided by banks?
A. Cash credit/OD
B. Letter of credit
C. Bills purchased/discounted
D. Working capital term loan

**114.** A company raises Preference Share Capital of ₹ 1,00,000 by issue of 10% Preference Shares of ₹ 10 each.

Compute the cost of Preference Share Capital if they are issued at 10% discount.
A. 9.09% B. 10%
C. 11.11% D. 9.99%

**115.** The value of optionally Convertible Debentures (CDs) depends upon the factor:
A. conversion value
B. straight debentures value
C. option value
D. All of the above

**116.** Which of the following statement is TRUE?
A. "Sale and lease back" is an indirect form of leasing.
B. The mandatory for the lessor to transfer ownership to the lessee in the case of financial leases.
C. Lease rents are higher in case of financial leases.
D. Lease period is higher for operating leases

**117.** Under which of the following "Basis of Accounting", revenues are recognized on cash basis while accrual basis is adopted for expenses?
A. Cash basis of accounting
B. Hybrid basis of accounting
C. Accrual basis of accounting
D. Matching concept

**118.** Which of the following is a source document for Return Inward Book?
A. Debit Note issued to creditors
B. Inward Invoice received from the creditors
C. Debit Note received from creditors
D. Credit Note received from creditors

**119.** Revenue Profits are shown as:
A. Fictitious assets in the Balance-sheet
B. Footnote in the Balance-sheet
C. Reserves & Surplus in the Balance-sheet
D. Appropriation of profit in P & L Appropriation A/c

**120.** Accounting Standard AS-9 deals with:
A. Cash flow statement
B. Depreciation accounting
C. Accounting for fixed assets
D. Revenue recognition

**121.** AS-1 requires certain enterprises to prepare a statement disclosing information as to revenue, assets and capital expenditure for each product or geographical area—which is known as:
A. Cash flow statement
B. Times Series
C. Segment Report
D. Trend Ratios

**Directions (Qs. 122 to 126):** *From the following information answer Questions.*

Particulars:

| | | |
|---|---|---|
| Stock Velocity | : | 6 |
| Gross Profit Margin | : | 20% |
| Capital Turnover Ratio | : | 2 |
| Fixed Assets Turnover Ratio | : | 4 |
| Debt Collection Period | : | 2 months |
| Creditors Payment Period | : | 73 days |
| Debt Collection Period | : | 2 months |

| | | |
|---|---|---|
| Gross Profit | : | ₹ 3,00,000 |
| Excess and closing stock over opening stock | : | ₹ 25,000 |

**122.** Calculate Sales:
A. ₹ 12,00,000 B. ₹ 15,00,000
C. ₹ 18,00,000 D. ₹ 20,00,000

**123.** Ascertain cost of goods sold:
A. ₹ 12,00,000 B. ₹ 13,00,000
C. ₹ 14,00,000 D. ₹ 15,00,000

**124.** Calculate Closing Stock:
A. ₹ 1,72,250 B. ₹ 2,02,500
C. ₹ 2,12,500 D. ₹ 1,92,250

**125.** Compute Capital:
A. ₹ 10,00,000 B. ₹ 15,00,000
C. ₹ 3,00,000 D. ₹ 7,50,000

**126.** Calculate Fixed Assets:
A. ₹ 3,75,000 B. ₹ 3,70,000
C. ₹ 3,55,000 D. ₹ 3,15,000

**127.**

| | | |
|---|---|---|
| Fixed Costs | : | ₹ 15,000 |
| Selling Price/Unit | : | ₹ 500 |
| Variable cost/unit | : | ₹ 9 |

What will be the New B.E.P. when variable cost increases by 10%?
A. 2,941 units B. 2,500 units
C. 2,750 units D. 2,841 units

**128.** From the following particulars, calculate the New Selling Price per unit if the B.E.P. is to be brought down to 4,000 units?

| | | |
|---|---|---|
| Variables cost per unit | : | ₹ 60 |
| Fixed expenses | : | ₹ 2,00,000 |
| Selling price per unit | : | ₹ 100 |

A. ₹ 110 B. ₹ 90
C. ₹ 80 D. ₹ 120

**129.** The P/V ratio of a firm is 50% and the Margin of safety is 40%. Compute the Net Profit if Sales is ₹ 5,00,000.
A. ₹ 1,50,000 B. ₹ 1,00,000
C. ₹ 50,000 D. ₹ 1,20,000

**130.**

| | | |
|---|---|---|
| Total Sales | : | ₹ 3,60,000 |
| Selling price per unit | : | ₹ 100 |
| Variables cost per unit | : | ₹ 50 |
| Fixed costs | : | ₹ 1,00,000 |

If the selling price is reduced to ₹ 90 per unit, the margin of safety is reduced by:
A. ₹ 50,000 B. ₹ 66,000
C. ₹ 61,000 D. ₹ 1,50,000

**131.**

| | | |
|---|---|---|
| Selling price per unit | : | ₹ 25 |
| Direct Material cost per unit | : | ₹ 8 |
| Direct Labour cost per unit | : | ₹ 5 |
| Fixed overheads | : | ₹ 24,000 |
| Variables Overheads | : | 60% on Direct Labour |
| Trade discount | : | 4% |

If sales are above 20% above break-even volume, compute the Net Profit.
A. ₹ 6,800 B. ₹ 4,800
C. ₹ 5,800 D. ₹ 5,000

**Directions (Qs. 132 to 134):** *From the following data answer Questions.*

| | | |
|---|---|---|
| Sales | : | ₹ 75 lakhs |
| Variable costs | : | ₹ 42 lakhs |
| Fixed costs | : | ₹ 6 lakhs |
| The firm has borrowed | : | ₹ 45 lakhs @ 9% interest |
| Equity Capital | : | ₹ 55 lakhs |

**132.** Compute Operating Leverage:
A. 1.25 B. 1.22
C. 1.35 D. 1.32

**133.** Compute Financial Leverage:
A. 1.28 B. 1.38
C. 1.18 D. 1.08

**134.** Calculate Combined Leverage:
A. 1.14 B. 1.24
C. 1.34 D. 1.44

**135.** OPC means:
A. Open Personal Computer
B. One Person Company
C. Open Professional Computer
D. One Process Configuration

**136.** Formation of Companies with Charitable Objectives is covered under Sec .......... of the Companies Act, 2013:
A. 25 B. 14
C. 8 D. 27

**137.** What is the minimum number of meeting of the Board of Directors of the Company to be conducted in a year as per the provisions of Companies Act, 2013:

A. 5 B. 6
C. 2 D. 4

**138.** Form to be filed by the resigning Director of a company is

A. DIR 11 B. DIR 12
C. DIR 13 D. DIR 14

**139.** What is NFRA as given in Companies Act 2013?

A. National Financial Reporting Agency
B. Non-Financial Reporting Authority
C. National Financial Reporting Authority
D. National Financial Related Authority

**140.** The first Annual General Meeting of a Company be held within ............... months from the date of closing of the first financial year of the Company.

A. 9 months B. 18 months
C. 4 months D. 6 months

**141.** The requisite quorum for AGM of a Company with 2700 members is

A. 12 B. 05
C. 15 D. 27

**142.** Calculate the adjusted average profit after adjusting the effect of the following errors, if the profit before discovering error was ₹ 10,000:

(*i*) Payment of rent ₹ 1,250 debited to landlord's personal account.
(*ii*) A cash purchase of ₹ 1,050 not posted in the ledger.

A. ₹ 7,700 B. ₹ 12,300
C. ₹ 9,800 D. ₹ 8,950

**143.** Of the following ledger balances, which account has credit balance?

A. Purchases B. Discount allowed
C. Bills payable D. Cash at bank

**144.** Show the necessary adjustments in Trading A/c and Balance-sheet from the following information:

| | | |
|---|---|---|
| 31.12.2014 | Value of Goods still with customers sold on sale or return basis, treated as sales | ₹ 1,20,000 |
| | G.P. on cost = 25% | |

A. Cost of stock with customers: ₹ 90,000
B. Cost of stock with customers: ₹ 96,000
C. Cost of stock with customers: ₹ 30,000
D. Cost of stock with customers: ₹ 1,50,000

**145.** Mr. X has ₹ 5,00,000 to the credit of his capital account on January 1, 2014. His drawings during the year amounted to ₹ 70,000. Charge interest on capital at 5% p.a. and ₹ 4,300 on drawings. Net profit for the year after all adjustments was ₹ 1,24,000. What would be the capital at the end of the year?

A. ₹ 6,24,000 B. ₹ 3,76,600
C. ₹ 5,74,700 D. ₹ 5,79,900

**146.** From the following particulars, ascertain the amount of provision for doubtful debts to be debited to Profit & Loss A/c.

| | | |
|---|---|---|
| Opening Provision for Doubtful Debts | : | ₹ 24,000 |
| Closing Sundry Debtors | : | ₹ 4,20,000 |
| Bad Debts yet to be written off | : | ₹ 20,000 |

Provide for Doubtful Debts @ 10% on debtors.

A. ₹ 39,000 B. ₹ 39,600
C. ₹ 36,600 D. ₹ 36,000

**147.** Analysis of financial statements based on data from year to year and not one date or period of time is referred to as:

A. External Analysis
B. Internal Analysis
C. Vertical Analysis
D. Horizontal Analysis

**148.** While preparing a Common Size Income Statement, which of the following items is to be taken as Base in general?

A. Total amount of all items
B. Net Sales

C. Net Profits
D. Gross Profit

**149.** Calculation of percentage relationship that each item bears to the same item in the base year is known as ....................
A. Common Size Statements
B. Time Series
C. Trend Percentages
D. Trend Ratios

**150.** Which of the following is NOT an appropriation of profit, in the preparation of P & L Appropriation A/c?
A. Provision for tax
B. Amount transferred to General Reserve A/c
C. Amount transferred to Dividend Equalization Reserve
D. Amount of dividend proposed and distributed

# ANSWERS

## PAPER-I

| 1 | 2 | 3 | 4 | 5 | 6 | 7 | 8 | 9 | 10 |
|---|---|---|---|---|---|---|---|---|---|
| A | D | B | A | A | A | C | B | A | A |
| **11** | **12** | **13** | **14** | **15** | **16** | **17** | **18** | **19** | **20** |
| C | A | B | B | A | A | A | C | C | C |
| **21** | **22** | **23** | **24** | **25** | **26** | **27** | **28** | **29** | **30** |
| B | D | D | A | B | A | B | A | B | C |
| **31** | **32** | **33** | **34** | **35** | **36** | **37** | **38** | **39** | **40** |
| A | D | B | C | D | B | B | B | A | C |
| **41** | **42** | **43** | **44** | **45** | **46** | **47** | **48** | **49** | **50** |
| A | D | C | A | C | A | D | A | C | C |
| **51** | **52** | **53** | **54** | **55** | **56** | **57** | **58** | **59** | **60** |
| D | D | D | C | D | D | C | D | C | A |
| **61** | **62** | **63** | **64** | **65** | **66** | **67** | **68** | **69** | **70** |
| C | A | A | D | B | C | A | B | C | D |
| **71** | **72** | **73** | **74** | **75** | **76** | **77** | **78** | **79** | **80** |
| D | A | A | B | A | D | A | D | A | A |
| **81** | **82** | **83** | **84** | **85** | **86** | **87** | **88** | **89** | **90** |
| B | A | C | D | B | D | C | A | A | C |
| **91** | **92** | **93** | **94** | **95** | **96** | **97** | **98** | **99** | **100** |
| A | A | B | B | B | A | B | A | A | C |
| **101** | **102** | **103** | **104** | **105** | **106** | **107** | **108** | **109** | **110** |
| D | B | C | A | A | C | B | A | A | B |
| **111** | **112** | **113** | **114** | **115** | **116** | **117** | **118** | **119** | **120** |
| D | A | B | A | B | A | * | A | C | B |
| **121** | **122** | **123** | **124** | **125** | **126** | **127** | **128** | **129** | **130** |
| B | B | A | B | B | D | C | C | A | B |

| 131 | 132 | 133 | 134 | 135 | 136 | 137 | 138 | 139 | 140 |
|---|---|---|---|---|---|---|---|---|---|
| C | D | B | B | C | B | D | C | C | B |
| **141** | **142** | **143** | **144** | **145** | **146** | **147** | **148** | **149** | **150** |
| C | D | D | A | A | D | A | D | A | A |

## PAPER-II

| 1 | 2 | 3 | 4 | 5 | 6 | 7 | 8 | 9 | 10 |
|---|---|---|---|---|---|---|---|---|---|
| A | C | A | C | C | B | A | B | D | B |
| **11** | **12** | **13** | **14** | **15** | **16** | **17** | **18** | **19** | **20** |
| B | A | A | A | A | A | A | A | A | A |
| **21** | **22** | **23** | **24** | **25** | **26** | **27** | **28** | **29** | **30** |
| D | C | B | C | A | B | C | C | B | C |
| **31** | **32** | **33** | **34** | **35** | **36** | **37** | **38** | **39** | **40** |
| D | B | B | D | A | D | C | B | B | D |
| **41** | **42** | **43** | **44** | **45** | **46** | **47** | **48** | **49** | **50** |
| D | B | C | B | C | A | C | C | C | A |
| **51** | **52** | **53** | **54** | **55** | **56** | **57** | **58** | **59** | **60** |
| B | C | D | A | B | * | B | C | B | D |
| **61** | **62** | **63** | **64** | **65** | **66** | **67** | **68** | **69** | **70** |
| A | D | D | C | C | A | D | D | D | A |
| **71** | **72** | **73** | **74** | **75** | **76** | **77** | **78** | **79** | **80** |
| C | B | D | B | D | C | A | B | D | A |
| **81** | **82** | **83** | **84** | **85** | **86** | **87** | **88** | **89** | **90** |
| C | B | C | D | C | A | A | B | D | C |
| **91** | **92** | **93** | **94** | **95** | **96** | **97** | **98** | **99** | **100** |
| C | B | A | D | D | C | A | D | B | A |
| **101** | **102** | **103** | **104** | **105** | **106** | **107** | **108** | **109** | **110** |
| B | C | D | A | B | B | C | D | D | A |
| **111** | **112** | **113** | **114** | **115** | **116** | **117** | **118** | **119** | **120** |
| C | D | B | C | D | A | B | C | C | D |
| **121** | **122** | **123** | **124** | **125** | **126** | **127** | **128** | **129** | **130** |
| C | B | A | C | D | A | * | A | B | C |
| **131** | **132** | **133** | **134** | **135** | **136** | **137** | **138** | **139** | **140** |
| B | B | C | D | B | C | D | A | C | A |
| **141** | **142** | **143** | **144** | **145** | **146** | **147** | **148** | **149** | **150** |
| C | A | C | B | C | D | D | B | C | A |

# English

# 1 Spelling Errors

The most common errors in English are of spellings of words. Even the most learned men are sometimes confused about the correct spellings of some words. One must keep and use a dictionary religiously. Never ignore and let pass a new word casually.

A number of question to test your knowledge of spellings are compiled here. Try to solve as many as you can.

## Multiple Choice Questions

**Directions:** *Find the correctly spelt word out of the four options in each question.*

**1.** A. Accompalish B. Ackmplesh C. Acomplush D. Accomplish

**2.** A. Acommodation B. Acomodation C. Accomodation D. Accommodation

**3.** A. Astonished B. Astronished C. Astoneshed D. Asstonished

**4.** A. Benefeted B. Benefitted C. Benifited D. Benefited

**5.** A. Belligerent B. Beligirent C. Belligarant D. Belligerrent

**6.** A. Chancelery B. Chancellery C. Chancellary D. Chancelary

**7.** A. Discriminate B. Discremineta C. Discrimenate D. Discriminat

**8.** A. Damage B. Dammage C. Damaige D. Dammege

**9.** A. Efficiant B. Effecient C. Efficient D. Eficient

**10.** A. Extravagant B. Extreragent C. Extreregant D. Extravegent

**11.** A. Efflorascence B. Eflorescene C. Efflorescence D. Efflorescence

**12.** A. Equinimity B. Equanimmity C. Equannimity D. Equanimity

**13.** A. Farmament B. Farmement C. Fermament D. Fremament

**14.** A. Grieff B. Grief C. Grieef D. Grrief

**15.** A. Guarantee B. Garuntee C. Guaruntee D. Gaurantee

**16.** A. Hypocritical B. Hypocretical C. Hypocriticel D. Hypocirticel

**17.** A. Humurous B. Humorous C. Humoreus D. Humorrous

**18.** A. Itenerary B. Itinarery C. Itinarary D. Itinerary

**19.** A. Indipenseble B. Indispansible C. Indispensable D. Indipensable

**20.** A. Imprecticability B. Impracticebility
C. Impracticibility D. Impracticability

**21.** A. Incradulous B. Incredulous
C. Incridulous D. Incredalous

**22.** A. Juddicious B. Judiceous
C. Judicious D. Judiceus

**23.** A. Kleptomonia B. Kleptemonia
C. Kleptomania D. Klaptomania

**24.** A. Lackdaisical B. Lackadaisical
C. Lckadaisicle D. Lackadisical

**25.** A. Licentious B. Licontious
C. Licenttious D. Licientious

**26.** A. Meddicine B. Medicine
C. Medicene D. Medicinne

**27.** A. Meritricious B. Merefrecious
C. Meretricious D. Merritricious

**28.** A. Missunderstood B. Miesunderstood
C. Misunderstood D. Misunderstod

**29.** A. Occurad B. Occurred
C. Ocurred D. Occured

**30.** A. Osttentatious B. Ostentetious
C. Ostentatious D. Ostenttatious

**31.** A. Obnosious B. Obnoxeous
C. Obnoxious D. Obnoseous

**32.** A. Omenous B. Ominous
C. Ommineous D. Omineous

**33.** A. Pecification B. Pacification
C. Pecifacation D. Pecefication

**34.** A. Prograssive B. Progressive
C. Progresive D. Prograsive

**35.** A. Pasiveness B. Passiveness
C. Passeveniss D. Passivines

**36.** A. Polyendry B. Poliendry
C. Pollyendry D. Polyandry

**37.** A. Puerille B. Puerrile
C. Puerile D. Purrile

**38.** A. Pesanger B. Passenger
C. Pessenger D. Pasanger

**39.** A. Querrelsome B. Quarrelsame
C. Quarrelsome D. Querralsome

**40.** A. Rigourous B. Rigerous
C. Rigorous D. Regerous

**41.** A. Survellance B. Surveilance
C. Surveillance D. Survaillance

**42.** A. Schedule B. Schdule
C. Schedale D. Schedeule

**43.** A. Sepalchrle B. Sepalchral
C. Sepulchrle D. Sepulchral

**44.** A. Sympathetic B. Smypathetic
C. Sympothetic D. Sympethetic

**45.** A. Sincerely B. Sencerely
C. Sincerelly D. Sincerrely

**46.** A. Satellite B. Sattellite
C. Satelite D. Sattelite

**47.** A. Teracherous B. Treacherous
C. Treacheraus D. Treachereans

**48.** A. Uncivilized B. Uncevilized
C. Uncivillized D. Uncevelized

**49.** A. Vainglorious B. Vaniglorious
C. Vaniglerious D. Vaingloreus

**50.** A. Vulnarable B. Valnerable
C. Velnerable D. Vulnerable

## ANSWERS

| 1 | 2 | 3 | 4 | 5 | 6 | 7 | 8 | 9 | 10 |
|---|---|---|---|---|---|---|---|---|---|
| D | D | A | B | A | C | A | A | C | A |
| 11 | 12 | 13 | 14 | 15 | 16 | 17 | 18 | 19 | 20 |
| D | D | C | B | A | A | B | D | C | D |
| 21 | 22 | 23 | 24 | 25 | 26 | 27 | 28 | 29 | 30 |
| B | C | C | B | A | B | C | C | B | C |
| 31 | 32 | 33 | 34 | 35 | 36 | 37 | 38 | 39 | 40 |
| C | B | B | B | B | D | C | B | C | C |
| 41 | 42 | 43 | 44 | 45 | 46 | 47 | 48 | 49 | 50 |
| C | A | D | A | A | A | B | A | A | D |

# 2 Spotting Errors

*The most common errors in English are of spellings, grammar and usage of words. By regular practice, the errors can be easily spotted and minimised.*

## Common Errors with Nouns and Noun-Phrases

| Incorrect | Correct |
|---|---|
| 1. I have bought new *furnitures.* | I have bought new *furniture.* |
| 2. The wages of sin *are* death. | The wages of sin *is* death. |
| 3. She told these *news* to her mother. | She told her mother this *news.* |
| 4. He took *troubles* to do his work. | He took *trouble* (or pains) over his work. |
| 5. The *cattles* were grazing. | The *cattle* were grazing. |
| 6. He showered *many abuses* on me. | He showered *much abuse* on me. |
| 7. I spent the holidays with my *family members.* | I spent the holidays with my *family.* |
| 8. There is no *place* in this compartment. | There is no *room* in this compartment. |
| 9. Write this new *poetry* in your *copy.* | Write this new *poem* in your *note-book.* |
| 10. He took *insult* at this. | He took *offence* at this. |
| 11. Put your *sign* here. | Put your *signatures* here. |
| 12. She is my *cousin sister.* | She is my *cousin.* |
| 13. *Sunil's* my *neighbour's* house was burgled. | *Sunil* my *neighbour's* house was burgled. |
| 14. I lost a *ten-rupees* note. | I lost *a ten-rupee* note. |
| 15. Road closed for *repair.* | Road closed for *repairs.* |
| 16. His house is out of *repairs.* | His house is out of *repair.* |
| 17. What is the *reason* of an earthquake? | What is the *cause* of an earthquake? |
| 18. This building is made of *stones.* | This building is made of *stone.* |
| 19. I disapprove of *these kinds* of games. | I disapprove of *this kind* of games. |
| 20. Veena's and Sheela's father is ill. | Veena and Sheela's father is ill. |
| 21. His *son-in-laws* are doctors. | His *sons-in-law* are doctors. |
| 22. *Alms* is given to the *poor.* | *Alms* are given to the poor. |
| 23. He always keeps his words. | He always keeps his *word.* |
| 24. I carried the *luggages.* | I carried the *luggage.* |
| 25. *Two-third* of the work is left. | *Two-thirds* of the work is left. |

## Common Errors with Pronouns

| Incorrect | Correct |
|---|---|
| 1. Both did not go. | Neither went. |
| 2. We all did not go. | None of us went. |
| 3. Each of these boys play. | Each of these boys plays. |
| 4. Whoever does best he will get a prize. | Whoever does best will get a prize. |
| 5. One should not waste his time. | A man should not waste his time. |
| 6. I and she are sisters. | She and I are sisters. |
| 7. He is wiser than me. | He is wiser than I. |
| 8. Between you and I, Anil is not to be trusted. | Between you and me, Anil is not to be trusted. |
| 9. Nobody was there but I. | Nobody was there but me. |
| 10. Who is there ? It is me. | Who is there ? It is I. |
| 11. Only he and me can use this card. | Only he and I can use this card. |
| 12. Let you and I go now. | Let you and me go now. |
| 13. Everyone got one's pay. | Everyone got his pay. |
| 14. Everyone is frightened when they see a tiger. | Everyone is frightened when he sees a tiger. |
| 15. These two friends are fond of one another. | These two friends are fond of each other. |
| 16. I did not like him coming at that hour. | I did not like his coming at that hour. |
| 17. Who do you think I met? | Whom do you think I met? |
| 18. You should avail this opportunity. | You should avail yourself this opportunity. |
| 19. When you have read these books, please return the same to me. | When you have read the books, please return them to me. |
| 20. They that are humble need fear no fall. | Those that are humble need fear no fall. |

## Common Errors with Adjectives

| Incorrect | Correct |
|---|---|
| 1. These all oranges are good. | All these oranges are good. |
| 2. He held the book in the both hands. | He held the book in both hands. |
| 3. Both men have not come. | Neither man has come. |
| 4. That man should do some or other work. | That man should do some work or other. |
| 5. He is elder than I. | He is older than I. |
| 6. Shakespeare is greater than any other poets. | Shakespeare is greater than any other poet. |
| 7. He is a coward man. | He is a cowardly man. |
| 8. Many villagers cannot write his own name. | Many villagers cannot write their own name. |
| 9. Each of us loves our home. | Each of us loves his home. |
| 10. Much efforts bring their reward. | Much effort brings its reward. |
| 11. He found hundred rupees. | He found a hundred rupees. |
| 12. He had leave of four days. | He had four days leave. |

| Incorrect | Correct |
|---|---|
| 13. This is a worth seeing sight. | This is a sight worth seeing. |
| 14. He will spend his future life here. | He will spend the rest of his life here. |
| 15. There is a best teacher in that class. | There is a very good teacher in that class. |
| 16. Of the two plans this is the best. | Of the two plans this is the better. |
| 17. He is becoming strong every day. | He is becoming stronger every day. |
| 18. He is worst than I. | He is worse than I. |
| 19. Jaipur is hot than Delhi. | Jaipur is hotter than Delhi. |
| 20. In our library the number of books is less. | In our library the number of books is small. |

## Common Errors with Verbs

| Incorrect | Correct |
|---|---|
| 1. He asked had we taken our luggage. | He asked if we had taken our luggage. |
| 2. She asked what are you doing. | She asked what we were doing. |
| 3. Rama asked to Anil why he is angry. | Rama asked Anil why he was angry. |
| 4. He does not care for his money. | He does not take care of his money. |
| 5. He does not care for his work. | He takes no care over his work. |
| 6. No one cared for him after his mother died. | No one took care of him after his mother died. |
| 7. He got angry before I said a word. | He got angry before I had said a word. |
| 8. I met a man who was my tutor 20 years ago. | I met a man who had been my tutor twenty years ago. |
| 9. I had been for walking yesterday. | I went for a walk yesterday. |
| 10. If I shall do this I shall be wrong. | If I do this I shall be wrong. |
| 11. I have left trekking. | I have given up trekking. |
| 12. I came to know as to how he did this. | I learnt how he did this. |
| 13. I came to know why he was sad. | I found out why he was sad. |
| 14. He knows to swim. | He knows how to swim. |
| 15. The criminal's head was cut. | The criminal's head was cut off. |
| 16. I said to him to go. | I told him to go. |
| 17. I told the teacher to excuse me. | I asked the teacher to excuse me. |
| 18. He is troubling me. | He is giving me trouble. |
| 19. I have got a hurt on my leg. | I have hurt my leg. |
| 20. She gave a speech. | She made a speech. |

## Common Errors in Subject-Verb Agreement

| Incorrect | Correct |
|---|---|
| 1. The owners of this factory *is* very rich. | The owners of this factory *are* very rich. |
| 2. The pleasures of nature that one can experience at Shimla *is* beyond description. | The pleasures of nature that one can experience at Shimla *are* beyond description. |

| Incorrect | Correct |
|---|---|
| 3. There *is* no street lights in our colony. | There *are* no street lights in our colony. |
| 4. He and I *am* entrusted with the job. | He and I *are* entrusted with the job. |
| 5. Rice and curry *are* his favourite dish. | Rice and curry *is* his favourite dish. |
| 6. The honour and glory of our country *are* at stake. | The honour and glory of our country *is* at stake. |
| 7. Time and tide *waits* for none. | Time and tide *wait* for none. |
| 8. All the passengers with the driver *was* killed. | All the passengers, with the driver, *were* killed. |
| 9. The teacher, with her students, *were* going out. | The teacher, with her students, *was* going out. |
| 10. I as well as they *am* tired. | I as well as they *are* tired. |
| 11. Not only the soldiers but their captain also *were* captured. | Not only the soldiers but their captain also *was* captured. |
| 12. Neither you nor I *were* selected. | Neither you nor I *was* selected. |
| 13. Either of these two applicants *are* fit for the job but neither want to accept it. | Either of these two applicants *is* fit for the job but neither wants to accept it. |
| 14. One of these students are sure to stand first. | One of these students *is* sure to stand first. |
| 15. Everyone of these workers want a raise. | Everyone of these workers wants a raise. |
| 16. None of these letters has been answered so far. | None of these letters *have* been answered so far. |
| 17. None of the girls were present at the party. | None of the girls *was* present at the party. |
| 18. Many a battle were fought on Indian soil. | Many a battle *was* fought on Indian soil. |
| 19. A lot of work remain to be done. | A lot of work *remains* to be done. |
| 20. The majority of these girls likes music. | The majority of these girls *like* music. |

## Common Errors in the Use of Modals/Auxiliary Verbs

| Incorrect | Correct |
|---|---|
| 1. When I shall see him I shall tell him this. | When I *see* him, I shall tell him this. |
| 2. If I should do wrong, he would punish me. | If I *did* wrong, he would punish me. |
| 3. Until he will have confessed his fault, he will be kept in prison. | Until he *has* confessed his fault, he will be kept in prison. |
| 4. She will obey me. | She *shall* obey me. |
| 5. You would work hard. | You *should* work hard. |
| 6. You shall find him in the garden. | You *will* find him in the garden. |
| 7. He must have died of exposure, but we cannot be certain. | He *might* have died of exposure, but we cannot be certain. |
| 8. You might not show disrespect to your elders. | You *must* not show disrespect to your elders. |
| 9. You may take exercise in order to maintain good health. | You *must* take exercise in order to maintain good health. |
| 10. He must be a crook for all we know. | He *may* be a crook for all we know. |

## Common Errors in the Use of Adverbs

| Incorrect | Correct |
|---|---|
| 1. He is very much angry. | He is *very* angry. |
| 2. She was very good enough to help me. | She was *good enough* to help me. |
| 3. She runs much fast. | She runs *very* fast. |
| 4. She runs very faster than Seema. | She runs *much* faster than Seema. |
| 5. It is bitter cold today. | It is *bitterly* cold today. |
| 6. He is a much learned man. | He is a very learned man. |
| 7. She is thinking very hardly. | She is thinking very hard. |
| 8. To tell in brief the film was boring. | *In short* the film was boring. |
| 9. He told the story in details. | He told the story *in detail.* |
| 10. I did it anyhow. | I *managed to do* it somehow. |
| 11. Aeroplanes reach Europe soon. | Aeroplanes reach Europe quickly. |
| 12. Before long there were dinosaurs on the earth. | *Long ago,* there were dinosaurs on the earth. |
| 13. This book is too interesting. | This book is *very* interesting. |
| 14. He lives miserly. | He lives in *a miserly* way. |
| 15. Just I had gone when she came. | I had just gone when she came. |
| 16. He sings good. | He sings *well.* |
| 17. He sings good than I. | He sings *better* than I. |
| 18. Really speaking it is cold. | *As a matter of fact* it is cold. |
| 19. He is enough tall to reach the ceiling. | He is *tall enough* to reach the ceiling. |
| 20. He went directly to his college. | He went *direct* to his college. |

## Common Errors in the Use of Conjunctions

| Incorrect | Correct |
|---|---|
| 1. As he is fat so he runs slowly. | As he is fat *he* runs slowly. |
| 2. If he is fat then he will run slowly. | If he is fat, he will run slowly. |
| 3. Though he is fat still he runs fast. | Though he is fat, *he runs* fast. |
| 4. *As* I pulled the trigger at the sametime he shook my arm. | As I pulled the trigger, he shook my arm. |
| 5. No sooner I had spoken than he left. | No sooner *had* I spoken than he left. |
| 6. Not only he will go, but also he will stay there. | Not only *will he* go, but he *will also* stay there. |
| 7. Neither he comes nor he writes. | Neither *does he* come nor *does he* write. |
| 8. Scarcely he entered the room than the telephone rang. | Scarcely *had* he entered the room *when the* telephone rang. |
| 9. Hardly she had left the house than it began to rain. | Hardly *had she* left the house *when* it began to rain. |
| 10. He is the fastest runner and he comes last. | He is the fastest runner *but* he comes last. |
| 11. She is as innocent as if she looks. | She is as innocent as she looks. |
| 12. Until he does not try he must be punished. | He must be punished unless he tries. |
| 13. I want to know as to why you are late. | I want to know why you are late. |

| Incorrect | Correct |
|---|---|
| 14. I am fond of Chinese food as for example sweet and sour prawns. | I am fond of Chinese food, for example, sweet and sour prawns. |
| 15. He was angry therefore I ran away. | He was angry so I ran away. |
| 16. I was trying to work, at that time he was disturbing me. | While I was trying to work, he was disturbing me. |
| 17. Supposing if he is late, what will happen? | Supposing he is late (or if he is late) what will happen? |
| 18. He asked me that why I was late. | He asked me why I was late. |
| 19. Let us catch a taxi lest we should not get late. | Let us catch a taxi lest we should get late. |
| 20. She dresses herself like the teacher does. | She dresses herself as the teacher does. |
| 21. Wait while I come. | Wait *until* (or *till)* I come. |
| 22. Until, there is corruption in India, there can be little progress. | *As long* as there is corruption in India there can be little progress. |
| 23. I have never told a lie nor cheated anybody. | I have never told a lie *nor have I* cheated anybody. |
| 24. Both Mohan as well as Arun are responsible for this action. | Both Mohan *and* Arun are responsible for this action. |
| 25. Hindus and Muslims both are to blame for the riots. | *Both Hindus* and Muslims are to blame for the riots. |

## Common Errors in the Use of Prepositions

| Incorrect | Correct |
|---|---|
| 1. I will not listen him. | I will not listen *to* him. |
| 2. Copy this word by word. | Copy this word *for* word. |
| 3. He enquired from her where she lived. | He enquired *of* her where she lived. |
| 4. Sign here with ink. | Sign here *in* ink. |
| 5. Has she come in train or by foot? | Has she come *by* train or *on* foot? |
| 6. She said this at his face. | She said this *to* his face. |
| 7. Open the book on page one. | Open the book *at* page one. |
| 8. I was invited for lunch. | I was *invited to* lunch. |
| 9. I am ill since three months. | I have been *ill for* three months. |
| 10. This paper is inferior than that. | This paper is inferior *to* that. |
| 11. This resembles to that. | This *resembles* that. |
| 12. My brother is superior than you in strength. | My brother is superior *to* you in strength. |
| 13. He wrote me. | He wrote *to* me. |
| 14. I shall explain them this. | I shall explain this *to* them. |
| 15. Send this letter on my address. | Send this letter *to* my address. |
| 16. He suggested me this. | He suggested this *to* me. |
| 17. He goes *on his* work. | He goes *to his* work. |
| 18. He *reached to* Nagpur. | He *reached* Nagpur. |
| 19. He told *to me* to go. | He told *me* to go. |
| 20. The term begins *from* July 1st. | The term begins *on* July 1st. |

## Miscellaneous Errors

| Incorrect | Correct |
|---|---|
| 1. Many *homes* are lying vacant. | Many *houses* are lying vacant. |
| 2. It is cool in the *shadow* of the tree. | It is cool in the *shade* of the tree. |
| 3. She *keeps* good health. | She *enjoys* good health. |
| 4. My leg is *paining*. | *I am feeling pain* in my leg. |
| 5. *See* this word in the dictionary. | *Look up* this word in the dictionary. |
| 6. The train will arrive *just now.* | The train will arrive *shortly.* |
| 7. They are *pulling* on well. | They are *getting* on well. |
| 8. The river has *over flown* its bank. | The river has *over flown* its banks. |
| 9. He was appointed *on* the post. | He was appointed *to* the post. |
| 10. Last but not *the least,* we have to discuss the problem of over population. | Last but not *least,* we have to discuss the problem of over population. |
| 11. *Cities* after *cities* fell. | *City* after *city* fell. |
| 12. What is the use Munir going there? | What is the use of Munir going there? |
| 13. He *did many mischief.* | He *made much mischief.* |
| 14. It is exact five *in* my watch. | It is exact five *by* my watch. |
| 15. I will dine with them on *next Sunday.* | I will dine with them *Sunday next.* |
| 16. Misfortunes when faced bravely and *manly* become less troublesome. | Misfortunes when faced bravely and *manfully* become less troublesome. |
| 17. I am *laid down* with fever. | I am *laid up* with fever. |
| 18. Hc is habituated to smoking. | He is *addicted* to smoking. |
| 19. *According to my opinion* he is right. | *In my opinion* (or according *to me)* he is right. |
| 20. Could you please *open* this knot? | Could you please *untie* this knot? |

# Multiple Choice Questions

**Directions:** *In this section, each sentence has three parts, indicated by (A), (B) and (C). Read each sentence to find out whether there is an error. If you find an error in any one of the parts (A, B, C), indicate your response by marking the letter related to that part. If a sentence has no error, indicate this by marking '(D)' which stands for "No error". Errors may belong to grammar, usage or idiom. Ignore errors of punctuation, if any.*

**1.** (A) Beware of/(B) a fair-weather friend/(C) who is neither a friend in need nor a friend indeed/ (D) No error.

**2.** (A) Copernicus proved/(B) that Earth/(C) moves round the Sun./(D) No error.

**3.** (A) Seldom we have been treated/(B) in such a rude manner/(C) by the police personnel./(D) No error.

**4.** (A) Some men are born great,/(B) some achieve greatness/(C) and some had greatness thrust on them./(D) No error.

**5.** (A) The property/(B) was divided/(C) among the two brothers./(D) No error.

**6.** (A) I am quite certain/(B) that the lady is not only greedy/(C) but miserly./(D) No error.

**7.** (A) The aircraft overloaded/(B) there was something wrong of the battery/(C) and the engine was making a queer noise/(D) No error.

**8.** (A) A thorough inquiry of the misappropriation of funds/(B) is now imperative/(C) to bring the guilty to book/(D) No error.

**9.** (A) The brilliant success in the examination/(B) as well as his record in sports/(C) deserves high praise/(D) No error.

**10.** (A) While travelling by a train/(B) on a cold winter night/(C) an argument rose between two passengers in our compartment/(D) No error.

**11.** (A) I cannot find/(B) where has he gone/(C) though I have tried may best/(D) No error.

**12.** (A) If I was/(B) the Prime Minister of India/(C) I would work wonders/(D) No error.

**13.** (A) Amit's severe bout of flu/(B) debilitated him so much/(C) that he was too tired to do for work for a week./(D) No error.

**14.** (A) This is the crux of the entire problem;/(B) everything centres on/(C) it being resolved./(D) No error.

**15.** (A) One of the major aims of the Air Force/(B) was the complete demolition of all means of transportation/(C) by the bombing of rail lines and terminals./(D) No error.

**16.** (A) His strong voice cut over/(B) the hum of conversation/(C) like a knife through butter./(D) No error.

**17.** (A) Even though they weren't expecting us/(B) they managed to knock up/(C) a marvellous meal./(D) No error.

**18.** (A) The celebrated singer was/(B) surrounded by the usual crowd/(C) of lackeys and hanger-ons./(D) No error.

**19.** (A) If it weren't/(B) for you,/(C) I wouldn't be alive today./(D) No error.

**20.** (A) He looked like a lion/(B) baulked from/(C) its prey./(D) No error.

**21.** (A) Widespread flooding/(B) is effecting/(C) large areas of the villages./(D) No error.

**22.** (A) She regards/(B) negotiating prices with customers/(C) as her special preserve./(D) No error.

**23.** (A) Often in political campaigns, a point is reached at which/(B) the candidates take out their gloves./(C) and start slugging with bare fists./(D) No error.

**24.** (A) If we really set to/(B) we can get the whole house/(C) cleaned in an afternoon./(D) No error.

**25.** (A) Pieces of rock plummeted/(B) down the mountainside/(C) in the ground below./(D) No error.

**26.** (A) Since the two parties each won/(B) the same number of seats,/(C) the minority party holds the balance of power./(D) No error.

**27.** (A) It's arrogant for you/(B) to assume you'll/(C)win every time./(D) No error.

**28.** (A) We've paid for our travel and accommodation,/(B) so we need only to take/(C) some pocket-money with us./(D) No error.

**29.** (A) There's no evidence to show/(B) that information technology secrets are more/(C) vulnerable in India than Britain or the US./(D) No error.

**30.** (A) It is shameful that hunting/(B) is still considered sport/(C) by some unscrupulous people in the civilized world./(D) No error.

**31.** (A) The Prime Minister's good looks won him/(B)the election but he has still to prove/(C) that he's not a just pretty face./(D) No error.

**32.** (A) The two books are the same/(B) except for the fact that this/(C) has an answer in the back./(D) No error.

**33.** (A) He estimated his income tax bill/(B) by extrapolation over figures/(C) submitted in previous years./(D) No error.

**34.** (A) The modern office block/(B) sticks out like a sore thumb/(C) among the old buildings in the area./(D) No error.

**35.** (A) I will try to put over/(B) some feelers to gauge/(C) people's reactions to our proposal./(D) No error.

**36.** (A) A major contribution of Mathura sculptors/(B)of that period were the creation and popularization/(C) of the Buddha's image in human form./(D) No error.

**37.** (A) Amit has been deceiving Mona/(B) for many years but she/(C) has not still tumbled to it./(D) No error.

**38.** (A) Mahavira was an advocate of nonviolence and vegetarianism,/(B) who revived and reorganized the Jain doctrine/(C) and established rules for their monastic order. (D) No error.

**39.** (A) Microwaves are the principle carriers/(B) of television, telephone and data transmissions/(C)between stations on earth and between the earth and satellites./(D) No error.

**40.** (A) An unit is an abstract idea,/(B) defined either by reference to/(C) a randomly chosen material standard or to a natural phenomenon./(D) No error.

**41.** (A) With the crisis deepening,/(B) the critics sense an opportunity/(C) about putting in place a more radical strategy./(D) No error.

**42.** (A) The salesman gave us/(B) a big spiel about why/(C) we should buy his product./(D) No error.

**43.** (A) I will need several weeks/(B) to invent the lie of the land before/(C) I can make any decision about the future of the business./(D) No error.

**44.** (A) You should be cautious/(B) and make a few discrete enquiries about/(C) the firm before you sign anything./(D) No error.

**45.** (A) Your husband doesn't/(B) believe that you are older/(C) than I./(D) No error.

**46.** (A) We are meeting today afternoon/(B) to discuss the matter/(C) and reach a compromise./(D) No error.

**47.** (A) Either Ram or/(B) you is responsible/(C) for this action./(D) No error.

**48.** (A) The student flatly denied/(B) that he had copied/(C) in the examination hall./(D) No error.

**49.** (A) By the time you arrive tomorrow/(B) I have finished/(C) my work./(D) No error.

**50.** (A) The speaker stressed repeatedly on/(B) the importance of improving/(C) the condition of the slums./(D) No error.

**51.** (A) The captain with the members of his team/(B) are returning/(C) after a fortnight./(D) No error.

**52.** (A) After returning from/(B) an all-India tour/(C) I had to describe about it/(D) No error.

**53.** (A) The teacher asked his students/(B) if they had gone through/(C) either of the three chapters included in the prescribed text./(D) No error.

**54.** (A) Although they are living in the country/(B) since they were married/(C) they are now moving to the town./(D) No error.

**55.** (A) Do you know/(B) how old were you/(C) when you came here?/(D) No error.

## ANSWERS

| 1 | 2 | 3 | 4 | 5 | 6 | 7 | 8 | 9 | 10 |
|---|---|---|---|---|---|---|---|---|---|
| D | B | A | C | C | C | B | A | D | C |
| 11 | 12 | 13 | 14 | 15 | 16 | 17 | 18 | 19 | 20 |
| B | A | C | C | B | A | A | C | C | C |
| 21 | 22 | 23 | 24 | 25 | 26 | 27 | 28 | 29 | 30 |
| C | A | A | A | C | A | A | B | D | B |
| 31 | 32 | 33 | 34 | 35 | 36 | 37 | 38 | 39 | 40 |
| C | C | C | D | A | B | C | C | A | A |
| 41 | 42 | 43 | 44 | 45 | 46 | 47 | 48 | 49 | 50 |
| C | D | D | D | C | A | B | D | B | A |
| 51 | 52 | 53 | 54 | 55 | | | | | |
| B | C | C | B | D | | | | | |

# 3 Articles

## Definite and Indefinite Articles

(*i*) 'A' and 'an' are Indefinite Articles.
(*ii*) 'The' is Definite Article.
(*iii*) 'A' and 'an' modify a noun in a general way.
(*iv*) 'The' particularises it. *e.g.*,
Mohan has **a pen.**
**The pen** which you gave me was expensive.

## Vowel and Consonant Sounds

(*i*) 'A' is used before words starting with the sound of a consonant.
(*ii*) 'An' is used before a vowel sound (vowels a, e, i, o, u) *e.g.*,
a book, a cat, a useful thing, a European girl, a university,
but an FDR, an MA, an honest boy, an hour, an owl, an egg, an umbrella, etc.

## Use of Articles 'A' and 'An'

**A** cat mews. (*i.e.*, every cat)
**The cat** of my neighbour mews day and night.
(*i.e*:, a particular cat)
He gave me **an** egg. (Here 'an' means 'one')

## Use of Article 'The'

1. 'The' is used before names of rivers, mountains, seas, oceans:
   The Himalayas, the Ganga, the Yamuna, the Bay of Bengal, the Indian Ocean, the Nile, the English Channel, *etc.*
2. Names of newspapers and magazines:
   The Times of India, the Tribune, The Sun, *etc.*
3. Names of the famous and holy books:
   The Guru Granth Sahib, The Gita, The Ramayana, *etc.*
4. Names of creations of nature:
   the sun, the earth, the moon, the sky, *etc.*
5. While using Adjectives as Nouns:
   **The poor** should be helped by **the rich.**
6. Sometimes with the Comparative Degree:
   **The more** you think, **the more** you worry.
7. With the Superlative Degree:
   She is **the most intelligent** girl in our school.
8. Before the imaginary lines and directions:
   The Latitude, The Equator, the east, the west, etc.
9. Before the names of musical instruments:
   the violin, the piano, the flute, etc.
10. While using a Proper Noun as a Common Noun:
    Mohan is **the Sachin** of our team.

## Omission of Article 'The'

1. Before some Nouns used to convey general sense, articles are not used but are used to particularise them:
   Man is mortal.
2. Before Proper Nouns:
   Rakesh is an intelligent boy.
3. With Abstract Noun:
   Childhood is the prime time of one's life.
   The childhood of Sohan was full of sorrow.
4. With Material Nouns:
   Milk is an essential food.
   The milk of the cow is sweet.

5. Usually no article is used before names of diseases:
   Cancer is a fatal disease.
   However, when we talk about a disease figuratively, we use an article before its name, *e.g.* Corruption is a cancer.
6. Names of games and language:
   I like football.
   I can speak Punjabi, Hindi and English.
7. Gold is a precious metal.

   **NOTE:** As you must have noted above, the definite article 'the' has been used where a noun is particularised.

## Double Use of Article 'The'

Read the following sentences carefully to understand this :

1. The poet and novelist has been honoured.
   (The same person is the poet as well as novelist)
2. The poet and the novelist have been honoured.
   (The poet and the novelist are two different persons).
3. I have a black and white dog.
   (that is, one dog)
4. I have a black and a white dog.
   (that is, two dogs)

# Multiple Choice Questions

**Directions :** *Fill in the blanks with suitable articles. Mark 'D' if no article required.*

**1.** Do you know ........ boy in white?
A. a B. an
C. the D. No article

**2.** She is ........ girl I am looking for.
A. a B. an
C. the D. No article

**3.** Have you read ........ Mahabharat?
A. a B. an
C. the D. No article

**4.** ........rich are not always happy.
A. A B. An
C. The D. No article

**5.** Oranges are sold by ........ dozen.
A. a B. an
C. the D. No article

**6.** Milk is sold by ........ litre.
A. a B. an
C. the D. No article

**7.** ........ Amazon is the longest river in the world.
A. A B. An
C. The D. No article

**8.** ........ higher you climb, the colder it gets.
A. A B. An
C. The D. No article

**9.** She is ........ untidy girl.
A. a B. an
C. the D. No article

**10.** I am ........ M.A. is English.
A. a B. an
C. the D. No article

**11.** I have already spent ........ few rupees I had.
A. a B. an
C. the D. No article

**12.** ........ English are very hard-working.
A. A B. An
C. The D. No article

**13.** April is the fourth month of ........ year.
A. a B. an
C. the D. No article

**14.** Rice is sold by ........ kilogram
A. a B. an
C. the D. No article

**15.** She is ........ best of the three girls.
A. a B. an
C. the D. No article

**16.** ........ man in the car is a friend of mine.
A. A B. An
C. The D. No article

**17.** Brevity is ........ soul of wit.
A. a B. an
C. the D. No article

**18.** ........ thing of beauty is a joy for ever.
A. A B. An
C. The D. No article

**19.** ........ little learning is a dangerous thing.
A. A B. An
C. The D. No article

**20.** ........ best sauce for food is hunger.
A. A B. An
C. The D. No article

**21.** Birds of ........ feather flock together.
A. a B. an
C. the D. No article

**22.** He makes ........ living by begging.
A. a B. an
C. the D. No article

**23.** It is ........ pity that he died so young.
A. a B. an
C. the D. No article

**24.** What ........ nuisance it is?
A. a B. an
C. the D. No article

**25.** Delhi is ........ London of India.
A. a B. an
C. the D. No article

**26.** Where is ........ will, there is a way.
A. a B. an
C. the D. No article

**27.** Her father is ........ physician and surgeon.
A. a B. an
C. the D. No article

**28.** This will benefit ........ poor.
A. a B. an
C. the D. No article

**29.** ........bird in hand is better than two in a bush.
A. A B. An
C. The D. No article

**30.** As he is hard-working, he will win ........ prize.
A. a B. an
C. the D. No article

**31.** ........ water of this well is dirty.
A. A B. An
C. The D. No article

**32.** Only ........ wearer knows where the shoe pinches.
A. a B. an
C. the D. No article

**33.** ........ action will be taken against you.
A. A B. An
C. The D. No article

**34.** ........ sun rises in the east.
A. A B. An
C. The D. No article

**35.** She was promoted to ........ highest post.
A. a B. an
C. the D. No article

**36.** Did you see ........ Taj Mahal?
A. a B. an
C. the D. No article

**37.** He is ........ one-eyed man.
A. a B. an
C. the D. No article

**38.** This is ........ useful book.
A. a B. an
C. the D. No article

**39.** Cloth is sold by ........ metre.
A. a B. an
C. the D. No article

**40.** The sun sets in ........ west.
A. a B. an
C. the D. No article

**41.** Amar bought......umbrella yesterday.
A. a B. an
C. the D. No article

**42.** Surinder is ...... honest boy.
A. a B. an
C. the D. No article

**43.** She wrote ...... book in French.
A. a B. an
C. the D. No article

**44.** ...... lion roars.
A. A B. An
C. The D. No article

**45.** ..... apple a day keeps the doctor away.

A. A  B. An
C. The  D. No article

**46.** John bought ...... car yesterday.

A. a  B. an
C. the  D. No article

**47.** His father is ..... engineer in the U.S.A.

A. a  B. an
C. the  D. No article

**48.** It is hard for ..... owl to fly during the day times.

A. a  B. an
C. the  D. No article

**49.** She had ..... rimmed hat.

A. a  B. an
C. the  D. No article

**50.** My uncle is ..... heart specialist.

A. a  B. an
C. the  D. No article

**51.** He looks as foolish as ........ ass.

A. a  B. an
C. the  D. No article

**52.** Did you go to ........ prison to visit him?

A. a  B. an
C. the  D. No article

**53.** I found ........ one-rupee note in the market.

A. a  B. an
C. the  D. No article

**54.** It is a pleasure to meet such ........ efficient man.

A. a  B. an
C. the  D. No article

**55.** The Sanyasi lived in a cave in ........ Himalayas.

A. a  B. an
C. the  D. No article

**56.** There is ........ union in our factory.

A. a  B. an
C. the  D. No article

**57.** He hit his wife on the head with ....... umbrella.

A. a  B. an
C. the  D. No article

**58.** I caught him by ........ collar.

A. a  B. an
C. the  D. No article

**59.** Child is ........ father of man.

A. a  B. an
C. the  D. No article

**60.** He gazed at ....... moon for two hours.

A. a  B. an
C. the  D. No article

# ANSWERS

| 1 | 2 | 3 | 4 | 5 | 6 | 7 | 8 | 9 | 10 |
|---|---|---|---|---|---|---|---|---|---|
| C | C | C | C | C | C | C | C | B | B |
| **11** | **12** | **13** | **14** | **15** | **16** | **17** | **18** | **19** | **20** |
| C | C | C | C | C | C | C | A | A | C |
| **21** | **22** | **23** | **24** | **25** | **26** | **27** | **28** | **29** | **30** |
| A | A | A | A | C | A | A | C | A | A |
| **31** | **32** | **33** | **34** | **35** | **36** | **37** | **38** | **39** | **40** |
| C | C | B | C | C | C | A | A | C | C |
| **41** | **42** | **43** | **44** | **45** | **46** | **47** | **48** | **49** | **50** |
| B | B | A | A | B | A | B | B | A | A |
| **51** | **52** | **53** | **54** | **55** | **56** | **57** | **58** | **59** | **60** |
| B | C | A | B | C | A | B | C | C | C |

# 4 Prepositions

A Preposition is a word that comes before a Pronoun or a Noun and expresses the relationship between Noun or Pronoun and some part of the remaining sentence.

(*a*) He is busy **with** his work.
(*b*) The boy jumped **into** the river.
(*c*) The birds are chirping **in** the trees.

In these sentences the words **with, into** and **in** show the relationship between the verbs **busy, jumped** and **chirping** with the nouns **work, river** and **trees** respectively.

## Position of the Preposition

**A.** A Preposition usually precedes its object.

(*i*) He laughs **at** the poor.
(*ii*) He is angry **with** you.
(*iii*) She agrees **with** me.

**B.** In the case of Relative Pronouns it comes after the subject.

(*i*) This is the boy whom I was looking **for**.
(*ii*) That is the pen whose mention I was making **of**.

**C.** In the following cases, the Preposition comes after its object.

(*i*) Where is the boy you were complaining **against**?
(*ii*) What things are there you are looking **for**?
(*iii*) Who is there, you are waiting **for**?

## Omission of the Prepositon

In many cases when the sentences contain Nouns of Time or Place, the Prepositions **from, in** and **for** are often omitted.

(*i*) He walked many kilometres.
(*ii*) He came to see me last year.
(*iii*) As I could not find my puppy anywhere, I looked here and there.

Prepositions are small words that show the relationship between one word and another. Prepositions in the following sentences show the position of the paper in relation to the desk, the book, hand and the door.

The paper is **on** the desk.
The paper is **under** the book.
The paper is **in** his hand.
The paper is **by** the door.

## Common Prepositions

| | | |
|---|---|---|
| about | at | by |
| in | onto | toward |
| above | before | concerning |
| inside | out | under |
| across | behind | despite |
| into | over | until |
| after | below | down |
| like | since | up |
| against | beneath | during |
| near | through | upon |
| along | beside | except |
| of | throughout | with |
| amid | between | for |
| off | till | within |
| among | beyond | from |
| on | to | without |

# Multiple Choice Questions

**Directions:** *Select the most appropriate preposition from the given alternatives to fill in the blanks and make the sentence meaningfully complete.*

**1.** Don't try to be an advocate ..... these criminals.
A. for B. with
C. across D. in

**2.** The audience admired him ..... his sweet voice.
A. to B. on
C. for D. at

**3.** I want to check your bag ..... fake currency notes.
A. to B. for
C. upon D. on

**4.** The dew drops clung .... the blades of grass.
A. for B. on
C. to D. in

**5.** The thief was chased ..... by the police.
A. on B. after
C. into D. at

**6.** Please carry this bag ..... my room.
A. on B. for
C. to D. in

**7.** A lorry bumped ..... a car.
A. on B. over
C. into D. to

**8.** They were begging ..... food.
A. for B. on
C. to D. after

**9.** She always boasts ..... her wealth.
A. of B. for
C. on D. after

**10.** She banged ..... the door violently.
A. for B. to
C. on D. down

**11.** I applied ..... the post of a clerk.
A. for B. on
C. in D. to

**12.** I applied ..... the Principal for the post of a teacher.
A. to B. on
C. with D. for

**13.** I begged ..... him not to divulge the secret.
A. for B. of
C. with D. to

**14.** You had better borrow a pen ..... Rakesh.
A. over B. into
C. from D. by

**15.** I baked a cake ..... the guests.
A. to B. for
C. on D. of

**16.** She is confident ..... (her) success.
A. with B. on
C. of D. for

**17.** The doctor will cure you ..... malaria.
A. of B. with
C. for D. from

**18.** This law is common ..... all.
A. to B. upon
C. over D. at

**19.** She was condemned ..... her bad hand writing.
A. on B. for
C. into D. of

**20.** In summer there will be a great demand ..... desert cooler.
A. on B. with
C. for D. of

**21.** We shall wait ..... you.
A. on B. for
C. towards D. after

**22.** Tom displayed his injury ..... all his friends.
A. for B. upon
C. to D. at

**23.** She distributed the sweets ..... the two brothers.
A. among B. between
C. for D. in

**24.** Please distribute these apples ..... all.
A. among B. to
C. for D. at

**25.** It rarely happened that he defended ..... an innocent person.
A. against B. for
C. upon D. at

**26.** The parents were disappointed ..... the performance of their son.
A. on B. with
C. at D. of

**27.** Common salt dissolves ..... water.
A. for B. in
C. with D. by

**28.** This medicare is free ..... sugar.
A. on B. to
C. from D. of

**29.** The manager granted leave ..... the clerk.
A. to B. on
C. into D. for

**30.** The air was heavy ..... aroma of perfumes.
A. on B. with
C. into D. from

**31.** She had a quick glance ..... the magazine.
A. at B. from
C. into D. to

**32.** The climate of Kashmir is favourable ..... me.
A. with B. in
C. to D. for

**33.** They hate you ..... your poverty.
A. for B. on
C. in D. of

**34.** He is eligible ..... this post.
A. for B. to
C. with D. at

**35.** The smoke was emerging ..... down the foot of the hill.
A. on B. to
C. from D. at

**36.** The criminal managed to escape ..... the prison.
A. upon B. from
C. with D. of

**37.** You should educate your friends ..... the benefits of living in villages.
A. on B. towards
C. upon D. in

**38.** She made a lot of efforts ..... win the match.
A. for B. to
C. upon D. at

**39.** The new inspector will enquire ..... the murder case.
A. on B. for
C. into D. at

**40.** The retired soldiers were exempted ..... all taxes.
A. from B. to
C. on D. of

**41.** She was adept ..... journalism.
A. at B. on
C. with D. in

**42.** She is afraid ..... snakes.
A. on B. to
C. of D. with

**43.** I agree ..... your proposal.
A. for B. on
C. to D. with

**44.** The children were amazed ..... so big a python.
A. at B. on
C. in D. with

**45.** She was anxious ..... the final match.
A. about B. on
C. with D. for

**46.** He apologized ..... his being late.
A. towards B. for
C. on D. as

**47.** The children were amused ..... his jokes.
A. for B. to
C. at D. on

**48.** She is angry ..... you.
A. to B. with
C. on D. for

**49.** She is angry ..... your teasing remark.
A. at B. in
C. for D. with

**50.** A big patch of land was allocated ..... the refugees.
A. to B. for
C. in D. upon

# ANSWERS

| 1 | 2 | 3 | 4 | 5 | 6 | 7 | 8 | 9 | 10 |
|---|---|---|---|---|---|---|---|---|---|
| A | C | B | C | B | C | C | A | A | C |
| **11** | **12** | **13** | **14** | **15** | **16** | **17** | **18** | **19** | **20** |
| A | A | B | C | B | C | A | A | B | C |
| **21** | **22** | **23** | **24** | **25** | **26** | **27** | **28** | **29** | **30** |
| B | C | B | A | A | C | B | C | A | B |
| **31** | **32** | **33** | **34** | **35** | **36** | **37** | **38** | **39** | **40** |
| A | C | A | A | C | B | A | B | C | A |
| **41** | **42** | **43** | **44** | **45** | **46** | **47** | **48** | **49** | **50** |
| A | C | C | A | A | B | C | B | A | A |

❑❑❑

# 5 Synonyms & Antonyms

*There are thousands of words in English language. No one can remember their meanings easily but with regular practice one can memorise most of them. A number of words with their Synonyms and Antonyms are compiled here. Try to learn as many as you can and answer the questions thereafter.*

| *Words* | *Synonyms* | *Antonyms* |
|---|---|---|
| **Abandon** | Cease, Forsake | Continue |
| **Abhor** | Hate, Loathe, Detest | Like, Love |
| **Abiding** | Enduring, Durable | Fleeting |
| **Able** | Proficient, Competent | Incompetent, Unfit |
| **Ability** | Skill, Power | Disability, Inability |
| **Abortive** | Fruitless, Futile | Fruitful, Successful |
| **Abolish** | Destroy, Undo | Restore, Revive |
| **Abridge** | Shorten, Curtail | Lengthen, Expand |
| **Absolve** | Forgive, Pardon, Excuse | Condemn |
| **Accelerate** | Hasten | Retard |
| **Accord** | Agreement, Harmony | Discord, Disagreement |
| **Accumulate** | Collect, Store, Amass | Distribute, Scatter |
| **Adamant** | Hard, Inflexible | Flexible |
| **Adversity** | Misfortune, Distress | Prosperity |
| **Adept** | Expert, Skilful | Inexpert, Unskillful |
| **Aggravate** | Heighten, Intensify | Quell, Suppress |
| **Agile** | Nimble | Clumsy, Undeft |
| **Alert** | Vigilant | Heedless |
| **Allay** | Calm, Soothe, Assuage | Arouse |
| **Ameliorate** | Improve, Advance, Amend | Worsen, Deteriorate |
| **Ambiguous** | Vague, Unclear | Clear |
| **Amiable** | Lovable, Agreeable | Disagreeable |
| **Annihilate** | Destroy | Create |
| **Arduous** | Hard, Strenuous | Easy |

| *Words* | *Synonyms* | *Antonyms* |
|---|---|---|
| **Attacks** | Assault | Defend |
| **Audacity** | Boldness | Cowardice |
| **Auspicious** | Favourable, Propitious, Lucky | Ominous, Inauspicious, Unlucky |
| **Austere** | Harsh, Severe, Rigorous | Easy-going |
| **Authentic** | True, Genuine | Spurious, False |
| **Avarice** | Greed | Generosity |
| **Averse** | Unwilling, Loath, Disinclined | Willing, Inclined |
| **Aversion** | Hostility, Hatred | Affinity, Liking |
| **Base** | Low, Mean, Ignoble | Noble, Exalted |
| **Boisterous** | Noisy, Stormy | Calm, Quiet |
| **Brave** | Courageous, Daring, Bold, Plucky | Cowardly, Dastardly, Timid |
| **Brief** | Short, Concise, Laconic | Lengthy, Diffuse |
| **Bright** | Vivid, Radiant | Dull, Dark |
| **Brutal** | Savage, Cruel | Humane, Kindly |
| **Callous** | Hard, Cruel, Indifferent | Soft, Tender, Concerned |
| **Cautious** | Careful, Wary | Rash, Reckless, Foolhardy |
| **Censure (*n*)** | Blame, Condemnation | Praise |
| **Censure (*vb*)** | Blame, Condemn | Praise, Commend |
| **Circumscribed** | Restricted, Confined, Limited | Unconfined, Unrestricted |
| **Civil** | Polite, Courteous, Gracious, Urbane | Rude, Uncivil, Impolite, Ungracious |
| **Coerce** | Compel, Force | Volunteer |
| **Compassionate** | Pitiful, Sympathetic, Merciful | Unsympathetic, Merciless, Cruel |
| **Compress** | Condense, Abbreviate | Expand, Lengthen |
| **Conspicuous** | Noticeable, Manifest | Inconspicuous |
| **Constant** | Steady, Steadfast, Uniform | Inconstant, Variable |
| **Cordial** | Friendly, Warm, Hearty | Cold, Unfriendly |
| **Covert** | Hidden, Secret | Overt, Open |
| **Cruel** | Savage, Ruthless, Vicious | Kind, Gentle, Benevolent |
| **Cursory** | Rapid, Superficial | Thorough, Exhaustive, Intensive |
| **Credible** | Believable, Probable, Plausible | Incredible, Unbelievable, Fantastic |
| **Crafty** | Cunning, Sly | Artless, Simple, Ingenuous |
| **Costly** | Expensive, Dear | Cheap, Inexpensive |
| **Confidence** | Trust, Reliance | Distrust, Doubt |
| **Death** | Decease, Demise | Existence, Life |
| **Dearth** | Scarcity, Lack, Want, Paucity, Shortage | Plenty, Abundance |
| **Decay** | Dissolution, Decline, Decomposition, Disintegration | Regeneration |

| Words | Synonyms | Antonyms |
|---|---|---|
| **Deference** | Respect, Reverence | Disrespect, Irreverence |
| **Deficient** | Lacking, Inadequate | Complete, Sufficient |
| **Desolate** | Lonely, Deserted | Crowded, Occupied |
| **Destitute** | Wanting, Needy | Rich, Affluent |
| **Diligence** | Industry, Perseverance | Idleness |
| **Disgrace** | Dishonour, Discredit | Honour, Credit |
| **Dwindle** | Decrease, Shrink | Grow, Increase |
| **Earthly** | Terrestrial, Mundane | Celestial, Heavenly, Unearthly |
| **Eligible** | Qualified, Suitable | Ineligible, Unsuitable |
| **Emancipate** | Liberate, Free | Enslave |
| **Excited** | Impassioned, Stimulated | Composed, Cool, Impassive |
| **Extraordinary** | Uncommon, Remarkable, Marvellous | Commonplace, Ordinary |
| **Extravagant** | Lavish, Prodigal, Wastrel, Spendthrift | Thrifty, Economical, Frugal |
| **Fabricate** | Construct, Make | Destroy |
| **Fabulous** | Fictitious, Mythical | Actual, Real |
| **False** | Untrue, Mendacious | True, Genuine |
| **Famous** | Well-known, Renowned | Obscure, Unknown |
| **Fantastic** | Fanciful, Imaginative, Visionary | Practical, Down to earth |
| **Fearful** | Nervous, Anxious, Afraid, Scared | Fearless, Dauntless |
| **Felicity** | Happiness | Sorrow |
| **Gaiety** | Joyousness, Hilarity | Mourning, Dullness |
| **Garrulous** | Talkative, Loquacious | Taciturn, Silent, Reserved |
| **Generous** | Liberal, Magnanimous | Stingy, Miserly |
| **Gigantic** | Huge, Colossal | Minute, Small |
| **Graphic** | Vivid, Pictorial, Meaningful | Vague |
| **Guest** | Visitor | Host |
| **Guile** | Fraud, Trickery | Artlessness, Ingenuousness |
| **Gratitude** | Gratefulness | Ingratitude, Ungratefulness |
| **Gratuitous** | Voluntary, Spontaneous, Unwarranted | Involuntary, Forced |
| **Hamper** | Hinder, Obstruct | Facilitate, Ease |
| **Haughty** | Arrogant, Proud | Humble, Modest |
| **Hazardous** | Dangerous, Perilous | Safe, Secure Protected |
| **Headstrong** | Obstinate, Stubborn | Weak-willed, Flexible |

| Words | Synonyms | Antonyms |
|---|---|---|
| **Hope** | Belief, Conviction, Expectation | Despair, Hopelessness |
| **Improvident** | Prodigal, Carelessness | Provident, Economical |
| **Incessant** | Unceasing, Continuous | Discontinuous |
| **Indolent** | Slothful, Lethargic | Active, Energetic |
| **Joy** | Delight, Pleasure | Sadness, Gloom |
| **Jolly** | Jovial, Merry | Gloomy, Sad |
| **Judicious** | Discreet, Prudent | Indiscreet, Injudicious |
| **Knowledge** | Enlightenment, Learning | Ignorance, Stupidity |
| **Laborious** | Industrious, Assiduous | Slothful, Lazy |
| **Laxity** | Slackness, Looseness | Firmness |
| **Lenient** | Mild, Forbearing | Strict, Stern |
| **Lethal** | Deadly, Fatal, Mortal | Life-giving, Vital, Vivifying |
| **Liberal** | Generous, Tolerant | Intolerant, Illiberal |
| **Liberty** | Freedom, Independence | Slavery, Bondage |
| **Lively** | Animated, Active | Dull, Listless |
| **Loyal** | Faithful, Devoted | Treacherous, Disloyal, Unfaithful |
| **Lucky** | Fortunate | Unlucky, Unfortunate |
| **Lucrative** | Profitable | Unprofitable |
| **Magnanimous** | Generous, Largehearted | Ungenerous, Stingy |
| **Malady** | Illness, Ailment | Health |
| **Manifest** | Noticeable, Obvious | Obscure, Puzzling |
| **Meagre** | Small | Plentiful, Large |
| **Mean** | Low, Abject | Noble, Exalted |
| **Mendacious** | False, Untruthful | Truthful |
| **Misery** | Sorrow, Distress | Happiness, Joy |
| **Morbid** | Sick, Diseased | Healthy |
| **Mournful** | Sorrowful, Sad | Joyful, Happy |
| **Negligent** | Careless, Heedless | Careful |
| **Notorious** | Infamous, Disreputable | Reputable |
| **Obedient** | Submissive, Compliant, Docile | Disobedient, Recalcitrant, Wayward |
| **Obsolete** | Antiquated, Out-of-Date | Current, Modern |
| **Opportune** | Timely, Seasonable | Inopportune |
| **Opulence** | Wealth, Riches | Penury, Poverty |
| **Onerous** | Heavy, Burdensome | Light, Easy |
| **Palatable** | Tasty, Delicious | Unpalatable |
| **Pathetic** | Touching | Joyous, Cheery |
| **Persuade** | Urge, Induce | Dissuade |
| **Praise** *(vb)* | Applaud, Eulogise | Condemn |

| Words | Synonyms | Antonyms |
|---|---|---|
| **Praise (*n*)** | Applause, Eulogy | Condemnation |
| **Precarious** | Risky, Uncertain | Safe, Certain |
| **Pretence** | Pretext, Excuse | Candour, Frankness |
| **Propagate** | Breed, Circulate | Terminate, Restrict |
| **Quaint** | Odd, Singular | Usual, Ordinary |
| **Quell** | Suppress, Subdue | Agitate, Arouse |
| **Rare** | Uncommon, Scarce | Common, Ordinary |
| **Refined** | Polished, Elegant | Crude, Coarse |
| **Remote** | Distant | Near, Close |
| **Renown** | Fame, Reputation | Infamy, Notoriety |
| **Rigid** | Stiff, Unyielding | Flexible, Yielding |
| **Remorseful** | Regretful, Repentant | Unrepentant |
| **Rebellion** | Revolt, Mutiny, Insurgency | Loyalty |
| **Scared** | Holy, Consecrated | Profane, Unholy |
| **Sane** | Sensible, Sound | Insane |
| **Scold** | Chide, Rebuke | Praise |
| **Serious** | Grave, Earnest | Frivolous |
| **Shy** | Bashful | Bold, Impudent |
| **Simple** | Plain, Artless | Complex, Cunning, Shrewd |
| **Solitary** | Single, Lonely, Secluded | Numerous, Multitude |
| **Shallow** | Superficial | Deep |
| **Solace** | Comfort, Relief | Discomfort, Grief |
| **Spurious** | Sham, False | Genuine, Authentic |
| **Stagnant** | Still, Motionless | Moving |
| **Surplus** | Excess | Deficit, Shortage |
| **Tame** | Gentle, Mild, Domesticated | Savage, Wild |
| **Teacher** | Instructor, Educator | Student, Pupil |
| **Tedious** | Wearisome, Monotonous | Agreeable, Lively |
| **Temporal** | Worldly, Secular | Spiritual |
| **Temperate** | Moderate | Immoderate, Intemperate |
| **Tortuous** | Winding, Circuitous | Straight, Direct |
| **Tough** | Hard, Strong | Tender, Soft, Flexible |
| **Transient** | Temporary, Fleeting | Lasting, Durable. Permanent |
| **Trusworthy** | Reliable | Unreliable, Untrustworthy |
| **Tranquil** | Calm | Agitated |
| **Ugly** | Unsightly, Repulsive | Beautiful, Attractive |
| **Useful** | Advantageous, Serviceable | Useless |
| **Vehemence** | Passion, Force | Apathy, Indifference |

| Words | Synonyms | Antonyms |
|---|---|---|
| **Vindictive** | Revengeful | Forgiving |
| **Wholesome** | Healthy | Unwholesome, Morbid, Unhealthy, Diseased |
| **Wicked** | Evil, Impious | Pious, Good |
| **Wise** | Sagacious, Erudite | Foolish, Stupid |
| **Wrath** | Anger, Fury, Rage | Love, Peace, Calm |
| **Wreck** | Ruin, Destroy | Create, Construct |
| **Yield** | Surrender, Submit | Resist, Revolt |
| **Yielding** | Submissive, Supple | Inflexible, Intractable |
| **Yoke** | Oppression, Bondage | Freedom |
| **Zeal** | Passion, Fervour | Apathy, Indifference |
| **Zest** | Relish, Enthusiasm | Distaste, Disrelish |

# Multiple Choice Questions

**Directions (Qs. 1 to 50):** *In the following questions choose the word which best expresses the MEANING of the given word.*

1. TEPID
   A. Hot B. Warm
   C. Cold D. Boiling
2. MAYHEM
   A. Jubilation B. Havoc
   C. Excitement D. Defeat
3. TIMID
   A. Fast B. Slow
   C. Medium D. Shy
4. CANTANKEROUS
   A. Quarrelsome B. Rash
   C. Disrespectful D. Noisy
5. PRECARIOUS
   A. Cautious B. Critical
   C. Perilous D. Brittle
6. TACITURNITY
   A. Dumbness B. Changeableness
   C. Hesitation D. Reserve
7. INEBRIATE
   A. Dreamy B. Stupefied
   C. Unsteady D. Drunken
8. HARBINGER
   A. Massenger B. Steward
   C. Forerunner D. Pilot
9. INTIMIDATE
   A. To hint B. Frighten
   C. Bluff D. Harass
10. IRONIC
    A. Inflexible
    B. Bitter
    C. Good-natured
    D. Disguisedly sarcastic
11. STRINGENT
    A. Tense B. Stringy
    C. Strict D. Causing to shrink
12. ECSTATIC
    A. Animated B. Bewildered
    C. Enraptured D. Willful
13. COMMENSURATE
    A. Measurable B. Proportionate
    C. Beginning D. Appropriate
14. DESTITUTION
    A. Humility B. Moderation
    C. Poverty D. Beggary

**15.** ASCEND
A. Leap B. Grow
C. Deviate D. Mount

**16.** UNCOUTH
A. Ungraceful B. Rough
C. Slovenly D. Dirty

**17.** LYNCH
A. Hang B. Madden
C. Killed D. Shoot

**18.** LAUD
A. Lord B. Eulogy
C. Praise D. Extolled

**19.** CORRESPONDENCE
A. Agreements B. Contracts
C. Documents D. Letters

**20.** VENUE
A. Place B. Agenda
C. Time D. Duration

**21.** STERILE
A. Barren B. Arid
C. Childless D. Dry

**22.** SYNOPSIS
A. Index B. Mixture
C. Summary D. Puzzle

**23.** GERMANE
A. Responsible B. Logical
C. Possible D. Relevant

**24.** PONDER
A. Think B. Evaluate
C. Anticipate D. Increase

**25.** CANNY
A. Obstinate B. Handsome
C. Clever D. Stout

**26.** ABUNDANT
A. Ripe B. Cheap
C. Plenty D. Absent

**27.** CONSEQUENCES
A. Results B. Conclusions
C. Difficulties D. Applications

**28.** SHIVER
A. Shake B. Rock
C. Tremble D. Move

**29.** DILIGENT
A. Progressive B. Brilliant
C. Inventive D. Hard-working

**30.** DISTANT
A. Far B. Removed
C. Reserved D. Separate

**31.** FORAY
A. Excursion B. Contest
C. Ranger D. Intuition

**32.** FRUGALITY
A. Foolishness B. Extremity
C. Enthusiasm D. Economy

**33.** GARNISH
A. Paint B. Garner
C. Adorn D. Abuse

**34.** VIGOUR
A. Strength B. Boldness
C. Warmth D. Enthusiasm

**35.** CANDID
A. Apparent B. Explicit
C. Frank D. Bright

**36.** BRIEF
A. Limited B. Small
C. Little D. Short

**37.** GARRULITY
A. Credulity B. Senility
C. Loquaciousness D. Speciousness

**38.** FURORE
A. Excitement B. Worry
C. Flux D. Anteroom

**39.** NEUTRAL
A. Unbiased B. Non-aligned
C. Undecided D. Indifferent

**40.** LAMENT
A. Complain B. Comment
C. Condone D. Console

**41.** ADVERSITY
A. Failure B. Helplessness
C. Misfortune D. Crisis

**42.** TURN UP
A. Land up B. Show up
C. Crop up D. Come up

**43.** DEIFY
A. Flatter B. Challenge
C. Worship D. Face

**44.** ERROR
A. Misadventure B. Misgiving
C. Ambiguity D. Blunder

**45.** SHALLOW
A. Artificial B. Superficial
C. Foolish D. Worthless

**46.** MASSACRE
A. Murder B. Stab
C. Assassinate D. Slaughter

**47.** COMBAT
A. Conflict B. Quarrel
C. Feud D. Fight

**48.** VORACIOUS
A. Wild B. Hungry
C. Angry D. Quick

**49.** IMPROMPTU
A. Offhand B. Unimportant
C. Unreal D. Effective

**50.** RABBLE
A. Mob B. Noise
C. Roar D. Rubbish

**Directions (Qs. 51 to 100):** *In the following questions choose the word which is the exact OPPOSITE of the given words.*

**51.** STRINGENT
A. General B. Vehement
C. Lenient D. Magnanimous

**52.** FLIMSY
A. Frail B. Filthy
C. Firm D. Flippant

**53.** BUSY
A. Occupied B. Engrossed
C. Relaxed D. Engaged

**54.** ADAPTABLE
A. Adoptable B. Flexible
C. Yielding D. Rigid

**55.** LOVE
A. Villainy B. Hatred
C. Compulsion D. Force

**56.** BALANCE
A. Disbalance B. Misbalance
C. Debalance D. Imbalance

**57.** RELINQUISH
A. Abdicate B. Renounce
C. Possess D. Deny

**58.** MOUNTAIN
A. Plain B. Plateau
C. Precipice D. Valley

**59.** FICKLE
A. Courageous B. Sincere
C. Steadfast D. Humble

**60.** PERENNIAL
A. Frequent B. Regular
C. Lasting D. Rare

**61.** RARELY
A. Hardly B. Definitely
C. Frequently D. Periodically

**62.** STARTLED
A. Amused B. Relaxed
C. Endless D. Astonished

**63.** ADHERENT
A. Detractor B. Enemy
C. Alien D. Rival

**64.** QUIESCENT
A. Indifferent B. Troublesome
C. Weak D. Unconcerned

**65.** CONDENSE
A. Expand B. Distribute
C. Interpret D. Lengthen

**66.** BENIGN
A. Malevolent B. Soft
C. Friendly D. Unwise

**67.** OBSCURE
A. Implicit B. Obnoxious
C. Explicit D. Pedantic

**68.** HYPOCRITICAL
A. Gentle B. Sincere
C. Amiable D. Dependable

**69.** EVASIVE
A. Free B. Honest
C. Liberal D. Frank

**70.** INDUSTRIOUS
A. Indifferent B. Indolent
C. Casual D. Passive

**71.** EXTRICATE
A. Manifest B. Palpable
C. Release D. Entangle

**72.** LUCID
A. Glory B. Noisy
C. Obscure D. Distinct

**73.** INSIPID
A. Tasty B. Stupid
C. Discreet D. Feast

**74.** OBEYING
A. Ordering B. Following
C. Refusing D. Contradicting

**75.** VICTORIOUS
A. Defeated B. Annexed
C. Destroyed D. Vanquished

**76.** COMMISSIONED
A. Started B. Closed
C. Finished D. Terminated

**77.** VANITY
A. Pride B. Humility
C. Conceit D. Ostentious

**78.** ZENITH
A. Acme B. Top
C. Nadir D. Pinnacle

**79.** TANGIBLE
A. Ethereal B. Concrete
C. Actual D. Solid

**80.** REPRESS
A. Inhibit B. Liberate
C. Curb D. Quell

**81.** EPILOGUE
A. Dialogue B. Prelude
C. Post script D. Epigram

**82.** FRAUDULENT
A. Candid B. Direct
C. Forthright D. Genuine

**83.** LOQUACIOUS
A. Reticent B. Talkative
C. Garrulous D. Verbose

**84.** NIGGARDLY
A. Frugal B. Thrifty
C. Stingy D. Generous

**85.** PERTINENT
A. Irrational B. Irregular
C. Insistent D. Irrelevant

**86.** FAINT-HEARTED
A. Warm-hearted B. Full-blooded
C. Hot-blooded D. Stout-hearted

**87.** VIOLENT
A. Humble B. Harmless
C. Gentle D. Tame

**88.** STATIONARY
A. Active B. Mobile
C. Rapid D. Busy

**89.** HONORARY
A. Dishonourable B. Reputed
C. Paid D. Official

**90.** COMMON
A. Rare B. Small
C. Petty D. Poor

**91.** REPEL
A. Attend B. Concentrate
C. Continue D. Attract

**92.** ARTIFICIAL
A. Red B. Natural
C. Truthful D. Solid

**93.** CAPACIOUS
A. Limited B. Caring
C. Foolish D. Changeable

**94.** PROVOCATION
A. Vocation B. Pacification
C. Peace D. Destruction

**95.** METICULOUS
A. Mutual B. Shaggy
C. Meretricious D. Slovenly

**96.** ABLE
A. Disable B. Inable
C. Unable D. Enable

**97.** COMFORT
A. Uncomfort B. Miscomfort
C. Discomfort D. None of these

**98.** GAIN
A. Loose B. Fall
C. Lost D. Lose

**99.** SYNTHETIC
A. Affable B. Natural
C. Plastic D. Cosmetic

**100.** ACQUITTED
A. Freed B. Burdened
C. Convicted D. Entrusted

# ANSWERS

| 1 | 2 | 3 | 4 | 5 | 6 | 7 | 8 | 9 | 10 |
|---|---|---|---|---|---|---|---|---|---|
| B | B | D | A | B | D | D | C | B | D |
| **11** | **12** | **13** | **14** | **15** | **16** | **17** | **18** | **19** | **20** |
| C | C | B | C | D | A | C | C | D | A |
| **21** | **22** | **23** | **24** | **25** | **26** | **27** | **28** | **29** | **30** |
| A | C | D | A | C | C | A | C | D | A |
| **31** | **32** | **33** | **34** | **35** | **36** | **37** | **38** | **39** | **40** |
| A | D | C | A | C | D | C | A | A | A |
| **41** | **42** | **43** | **44** | **45** | **46** | **47** | **48** | **49** | **50** |
| C | B | C | D | B | D | D | B | A | A |
| **51** | **52** | **53** | **54** | **55** | **56** | **57** | **58** | **59** | **60** |
| C | C | C | D | B | D | C | D | C | D |
| **61** | **62** | **63** | **64** | **65** | **66** | **67** | **68** | **69** | **70** |
| D | B | B | A | C | A | C | B | B | B |
| **71** | **72** | **73** | **74** | **75** | **76** | **77** | **78** | **79** | **80** |
| D | C | A | A | A | D | B | C | A | B |
| **81** | **82** | **83** | **84** | **85** | **86** | **87** | **88** | **89** | **90** |
| B | D | B | D | D | D | C | B | C | A |
| **91** | **92** | **93** | **94** | **95** | **96** | **97** | **98** | **99** | **100** |
| D | B | A | B | D | C | C | D | B | C |

# 6 One Word Substitutions

*There are many words in English language which can be perfectly used for a number of words. These words help in expressing ideas in a short and correct manner for the right occasion. Such words not only enhance the vocabulary but also enable you to economise in the use of words to a great extent. Try to learn as many as you can.*

## Denoting Numbers

- A collection of poems — *anthology*
- A number of merchant ships protected by warships (in war-time) — *convoy*
- A number of stars grouped together — *constellation*
- A number of hired applauders, *i.e.* persons paid to clap — *claque*
- A number of people at church — *congregation*
- A number of people gathered together for some common purpose — *gathering, assembly, society*
- A group of people who get together to work for some cause of common interest — *coterie*
- A number of workmen, prisoners, thieves — *gang*
- A number of sheep — *flock*
- A number of geese — *gaggle*
- A number of leopards — *leap*
- A number of lions, monkeys — *pride, troop*
- A number of herrings, mackerel — *shoal*
- A number of fish taken in a net — *catch, haul*
- A number of whales, porpoises — *school, gam*
- A number of oxen or horses (two or more) harnessed together — *team*
- A number of ships, cars, buses — *fleet*

## Denoting Places

- A place where bees are kept — *apiary*
- A place where birds are kept — *aviary*
- A place where fishes are kept — *aquarium*
- A dwelling-place of an animal underground — *burrow*
- A squirrel's home — *drey*
- A nest of a bird of prey — *eyrie, aerie*

- A place where spirituous liquors are produced *distillery*
- A place where clothes are washed and ironed *laundry*
- A place where Government records are kept *archives*
- A place where treasures of art, curiosities, etc. are preserved or exhibited *museum*
- A place where fruit trees are grown *orchard*

## Pertaining to the Literary Sphere

- A work whose writer is unknown *anonymous*
- A record of one's life written by oneself *autobiography*
- The history of the life of a person *biography*
- The heading or short description of a newspaper article, chapter of a book etc. *caption*
- A humorous play, having a happy ending *comedy*
- A list of books in a library *catalogue, bibliography*
- A book in which the events of each day are recorded *diary*
- A books containing the words of a language with their definitions, in alphabetical order *dictionary*
- A book of names and addresses *directory*
- A short speech by a player at the end of a play *epilogue*
- A brief summary of a book *epitome*
- A book containing information on all branches of knowledge *encyclopedia*
- To remove the offensive portions of a book *expurgate*
- A speech delivered without earlier preparation *extempore*
- A noisy or vehement speech intended to excite passions *harangue*
- A written account, usually in book form of the interesting and memorable experiences of one's life *memoirs*
- A note to help the memory *memorandum*
- A declaration of plans and promises put forward by a candidate for election, political party or a sovereign *manifesto*
- A short speech by a player at the beginning of a play *prologue*
- Literary theft, or passing off an author's original work as one's own *plagiarism*
- Speaking aloud to oneself *soliloquy*
- A play with a sad or tragic end *tragedy*

## Pertaining to Religion

- One who believes that man can have no knowledge of God but only of natural phenomena *agnostic*
- One who renounces his religious vows or forsakes his religious principles *apostate*
- One who does not believe in existence of God *atheist*
- One intolerantly devoted to a particular creed *bigot*
- To utter profane language against God or anything holy *blaspheme*
- A breaker of church images *iconoclast*
- Worship of images or idols *idiolatory*

| | |
|---|---|
| ❑ One who believes in God | *theist* |
| ❑ One who believes in only one God | *monotheist* |
| ❑ One who believes in many Gods | *polytheist* |

## Pertaining to Government

| | |
|---|---|
| ❑ To give up a throne or other office of dignity | *abdicate* |
| ❑ Absence of government | *anarchy* |
| ❑ Government by Sovereign of uncontrolled authority | *autocracy, despotism* |
| ❑ Government by departments of states | *bureaucracy* |
| ❑ Government of the people, for the people and by the people | *democracy* |
| ❑ Government by the nobility | *aristocracy* |
| ❑ The right of self-government | *autonomy* |
| ❑ Government by a few | *oligarchy* |
| ❑ Government by the wealthy | *plutocracy* |
| ❑ Government by divine guidance | *theocracy* |
| ❑ To decide a political question by the direct vote of the whole electorate | *referendum* |
| ❑ Sweeping governmental change | *revolution* |
| ❑ The science of government | *politics* |

## Pertaining tr Professions

| | |
|---|---|
| ❑ One who attends to the diseases of the eye | *oculist* |
| ❑ One who tests eyesight and sells spectacles | *optician* |
| ❑ One who attends to the teeth | *dentist* |
| ❑ One skilled in the care of hands and feet | *chiropodist* |
| ❑ A physician who assists women at child-birth | *obstetrician* |
| ❑ One who drives a motorcar | *chauffeur* |
| ❑ One who makes or sells candles | *chandler* |
| ❑ One who preserves the skins of animals and mounts them so as to resemble the living animals | *taxidermist* |
| ❑ One who compiles a dictionary | *lexicographer* |
| ❑ One who writes books | *author* |
| ❑ One skilled in the treatment of diseases of animals | *veterinarian* |
| ❑ A tradesman who manages funerals | *undertaker* |
| ❑ One who draws up contracts and lends money on interest | *scrivener* |
| ❑ One who lends money and keeps goods as security | *pawnbroker* |
| ❑ A teacher who travels from place to place to give instruction. | *peripatetic* |
| ❑ One who travels from place to place selling miscellaneous articles | *hawker, pedlar* |
| ❑ One who collects postage stamps | *philatelist* |
| ❑ One who lends money at exorbitant interest | *usurer* |
| ❑ One who takes care of a building | *janitor* |
| ❑ One who sells sweets and pastries | *confectioner* |
| ❑ One who works in a coalmine | *collier* |
| ❑ One who flies an aeroplane | *pilot, aviator* |

- ❑ One who studies rocks and soils — *geologist*
- ❑ One who shoes horses — *farrier*
- ❑ A professional rider in horses races — *jockey*
- ❑ One who deals in silks, cotton, woollen, and linen goods — *mercer*
- ❑ One who deals in wines — *vintner*
- ❑ One who deals in fish — *fishmonger*
- ❑ One who deals in iron and hardware — *ironmonger*
- ❑ One who sells fruits, vegetables, etc. from a barrow — *costermonger*
- ❑ One who sets type in a printing office — *compositor*

## Pertaining to Medicine

- ❑ A substance which destroys or weakens germs — *antiseptic*
- ❑ Any medicine which produces insensibility — *anaesthetic*
- ❑ A medicine to counteract poison — *antidote*
- ❑ Want or poorness of blood — *anaemia*
- ❑ A medicine which alleviates pain — *anodyne*
- ❑ To cut off a person's body a part which is infected — *amputate*
- ❑ One who is recovering from illness — *convalescent*
- ❑ To be able to tell the nature of disease by its symptoms — *diagnose*
- ❑ A disease affecting many persons at the same place and time — *epidemic*
- ❑ A disease confined to a particular district or place — *endemic*
- ❑ To disinfect by smoke — *fumigate*
- ❑ Free or exempt from infection — *immune*
- ❑ A person who is sick — *invalid*
- ❑ A cure for all diseases — *panacea*
- ❑ A disease widely epidemic — *pandemic*
- ❑ Confinement to one place to avoid spread of infection — *quarantine*

## Pertaining to Characteristics and Actions

- ❑ One who devotes his life to the welfare and interests of other people — *altruist*
- ❑ One who can use both hands with equal ease — *ambidexterous*
- ❑ One who fishes with a rod — *angler*
- ❑ One who kills secretly or by surprise — *assassin*
- ❑ A person who collects things belonging to ancient times — *antiquary*
- ❑ One who is always finding faults — *censorious*
- ❑ One living at the same time as another — *contemporary*
- ❑ One who sneers at the aims and beliefs of his fellowmen — *cynic*
- ❑ One who delights in speaking about oneself — *egotist*
- ❑ One who exalts his own opinion — *egoist*
- ❑ One who dies for a noble cause — *martyr*
- ❑ One who retires from society to live a solitary life — *recluse, hermit*
- ❑ One who maliciously sets fire to buildings — *incendiary*

- One who is banished from his home or his country *exile*
- One who takes refuge in a foreign country *refugee, alien*
- One who runs away from justice or the law *fugitive*
- One who walks in his sleep *somnambulist*
- One who looks on the bright side of things *optimist*
- One who looks on the dark side of things *pessimist*
- A hater of mankind *misanthropist*
- One who knows everything *omniscient*
- One who is all powerful *omnipotent*
- One who is present everywhere *omnipresent*
- One who devotes his service or wealth for the love of mankind *philanthropist*
- One new to anything *novice, tyro, neophyte*
- One who engages in any pursuit for the love of it, and not for gain *amateur*
- One who journeys to a holy place *pilgrim*
- A leader of the people who can sway his followers by his oratory *demagogue*
- One who has special skill in judging art, music, tastes, etc. *connoisseur*
- One whose reasoning is clever yet false *sophist*
- One who makes a display of his learning *pedant*
- One who is indifferent to pain or pleasure *stoic*
- One who loves his country and serves it devotedly *patriot*
- One devoted to the pleasures of eating and drinking *epicure*
- One who poses to be what he is not *hypocrite, impostor*
- One who foretells events *prophet*
- One who pretends to know a great deal about everything *mountebank, charlatan, quack*
- One versed in many languages *linguist*
- One who cannot pay one's debts *insolvent*
- One who takes over after another in office or employment *successor*
- One who has been before another in office or employment *predecessor*
- One who is opposed to intellectual progress *obscurant*
- One who abstains from alcoholic drinks *teetotaller*
- One who hides away on a ship to obtain a free passage *stowaway*
- One who spends very little *miser*
- One who spends too much *spendthrift*

## Pertaining to War

- An unprovoked attack by an enemy *aggression*
- Shells, bombs, military stores *ammunition*
- A place where naval or military weapons are made or stored *ordnance*
- An agreement between belligerents to stop fighting *armistice*
- A general pardon of offenders *amnesty*
- To reduce to nothing *annihilate*
- Nations carrying on warfare *belligerents*

- To surround a place with the intention of capturing — *besiege*
- To camp in the open air without tents or covering — *bivouac*
- To seize for military use — *commandeer*
- A person who is forced by law to become a soldier — *conscript*
- An order prohibiting ships to leave the ports — *embargo*
- A number of firearms being discharged continuously — *fusillade*
- To make an examination or preliminary survey of enemy territory for military objectives — *reconnoitre*

## Pertaining to Marriage and Children

- One who marries a second wife or husband while the legal spouse is alive — *bigamist*
- One vowed to a single or unmarried life — *celibate*
- One engaged to be married — *fiancé, fiancee*
- A child whose parents are dead — *orphan*
- A hater of marriage — *misogamist*
- One who has more than two wives at a time — *polygamist*

## Pertaining to Death

- Dead and decaying flesh (esp. of animals) — *carrion*
- A monument set up for persons who are buried elsewhere — *cenotaph*
- To preserve a dead body from putrefaction — *embalm*
- Words inscribed on a tomb — *epitaph*
- An examination of dead body — *postmortem, autopsy*
- An account in the newspaper of the funeral of one deceased — *obituary*
- The property left to someone by a will — *legacy*
- Occurring after death — *posthumous*
- The act of killing a human being — *homicide*
- Murder of a new born child — *infanticide*
- Murder of a brother — *fratricide*
- Murder of a sister — *sororicide*
- Murder of a mother — *matricide*
- Murder of a father — *patricide*
- Murder of a parent — *parricide*
- Murder of a king — *regicide*

## Pertaining to Sciences and Arts

- The study of all heavenly bodies and the earth in relation to them — *astronomy*
- The science of land management — *agronomics*
- The study of mankind — *anthropology*
- The study of physical life or living matter — *biology*
- The study of plants — *botany*
- The art of beautiful handwriting — *calligraphy*

- The science which deals with the varieties of human race *ethnology*
- The study of the origin and history of words *etymology*
- The study of coins *numismatics*
- The study of human face *physiognomy*
- The art of making fireworks *pyrotechnics*
- The study of birds *ornithology*
- The study of languages *philology*
- At home equally on land or in water *amphibious*
- The inside of a nut *kernel*
- The central or innermost part of fruit *core*
- The animals of a certain region *fauna*
- The plants and vegetation of a certain region *flora*
- Absence of rain for a long time *drought*
- To supply land with water by artificial means *irrigate*
- One who studies plant and animal life *naturalist*
- A cud-chewing animal, *e.g.* the cow *ruminant*
- A gnawing animal, *e.g.* the rat *rodent*
- A four-footed animal *quadruped*
- Animals which carry their young in a pouch, *e.g.* kangaroo *marsupials*
- Soil composed largely of decayed vegetable matter *humus*
- A preparation for killing insects *insecticide*
- A plant or animal growing on another *parasite*
- Living for many years *perennial*

## Miscellaneous

- Loud enough to be heard *audible*
- Not distinct enough to be heard *inaudible*
- Fit for food *edible*
- Unfit for human consumption *inedible*
- Fit to be chosen or selected *eligible*
- Not having the qualities for being chosen *ineligible*
- Writing that is easy to read *legible*
- Writing that is difficult to decipher *illegible*
- Able to read *literate*
- Unable to read *illiterate*
- Born of married parents *legitimate*
- Born of unmarried parents *illegitimate*
- To send back a person to his own country *repatriate*
- To banish from one's country *expatriate*
- To move from one country to another *migrate*
- One who leaves his country to settle in another *emigrant*
- One who comes into a foreign country to settle there *immigrant*

- ❑ Incapable of being redeemed from evil, *i.e.* beyond correction — *incorrigible*
- ❑ That which cannot be rubbed out or blotted out — *ineffaceable, indelible*
- ❑ That which cannot be conquered — *invincible*
- ❑ Incapable of making errors — *infallible*
- ❑ That which cannot be avoided or prevented — *inevitable*
- ❑ Incapable of being burnt — *incombustible*
- ❑ That which easily catches fire — *inflammable, flammable*
- ❑ That which cannot be seen — *invisible*
- ❑ Living for ever — *immortal*
- ❑ Increase the gravity of an offence — *aggravate*
- ❑ Ordinary or commonplace remark — *platitude*
- ❑ That which cannot be satisfied — *insatiable*
- ❑ That which cannot be repaired — *irreparable*
- ❑ That which cannot be imitated — *inimitable*
- ❑ Persons (or efforts) that cannot be wearied — *indefatigable*
- ❑ One who eats too much — *glutton*
- ❑ To destroy completely — *annihilate*
- ❑ A statement open to more than one interpretation — *ambiguous*
- ❑ A round about way of speaking — *circumlocution*
- ❑ Cautious observation of events, etc. — *circumspection*
- ❑ That which cannot be hurt — *invulnerable*

## Multiple Choice Questions

**Directions:** *Below are given some statements each of which is capable of being expressed by one word only. Each statement is followed by four such words of which only one is correct. Out of the given alternatives A, B, C and D choose the correct word which very closely fits each definition.*

**1.** A set of papers giving information about a person or event:

A. editorial B. agenda
C. dossier D. clippings

**2.** List and explanations of technical, difficult, etc. terms:

A. preface B. glossary
C. bibliography D. appendix

**3.** One who pays too much care to his clothes and personal appearance:

A. conscious B. dandy
C. cynosure D. leer

**4.** A child born after death of father:

A. effeminate B. immature
C. fatherless D. posthumous

**5.** A person who is hard to please:

A. insensible B. hypocrite
C. egoist D. fastidious

**6.** Complete failure in something attempted:

A. fiasco B. vain
C. falsies D. flop

**7.** A word which can be interpreted in any way:

A. confusing B. misnomer
C. ambiguous D. precise

**8.** A group of persons united by common interests:

A. society B. class
C. clique D. coterie

9. A person who is inexperienced and easily deceived:
A. fool B. immature
C. blackhorn D. greenhorn

10. Instruction by question and answer:
A. interrogatory B. catechism
C. bulletin D. alibi

11. Record of events by someone with first hand knowledge:
A. novice B. report
C. memoir D. itinerary

12. A mode of talk familiar to a particular group or profession:
A. jargon B. colloquial
C. slang D. abuses

13. Person who is crazy:
A. lackadaisical B. tarter
C. scrupulous D. loony

14. A person who readily believes others:
A. hasty B. immature
C. credulous D. credible

15. One who eats human flesh:
A. beast B. cannibal
C. maneater D. carnivorous

16. Intentional destruction of racial groups:
A. genocide B. homicide
C. fratricide D. communal riot

17. One with weakness of mind caused by old age:
A. dastard B. dotard
C. fop D. philanderer

18. Study of insects:
A. zoology B. philology
C. entomology D. etymology

19. A critical judge of any art particularly fine arts:
A. connoisseur B. veteran
C. philistine D. dilettante

20. One who introduces items of an entertainment:
A. consort B. compere
C. director D. introducer

21. A combination of business firms:
A. enterprise B. franchise
C. cartel D. autonomous

22. Freeing of suppressed emotions:
A. catastrophe B. catharsis
C. epilogue D. chagrin

23. One who believes in the power of fate:
A. optimist B. pessimist
C. fearful D. fatalist

24. The murder of brother:
A. genocide B. homicide
C. salvage D. fratricide

25. Additional to proper payment:
A. premium B. overtime
C. ex-gratia D. fringe

26. A person or thing used to tempt somebody into a position of danger:
A. decoy B. provocateur
C. jinx D. scapegoat

27. Custom of having more than one husband at the same time:
A. polygamy B. polyandry
C. bigamy D. sexagenary

28. A person of refined taste in food and drink:
A. emeritus B. epicure
C. glutton D. gourmand

29. A tombstone inscription:
A. epithet B. encomium
C. epistle D. epitaph

30. An office which has no work but high salary:
A. fortuitous B. gratuitous
C. sinecure D. ceremonial

31. One who is indifferent to pains and pleasure of life:
A. stoic B. metaphysical
C. pessimist D. sceptic

32. List of names of persons showing duties to be performed by each in turn:
A. notice B. bulletin
C. roster D. agenda

33. Long angry speech of criticism or accusation:
A. track record B. tirade
C. taut D. outburst

34. One who is in favour of never drinking alcoholic drinks:
A. idealist B. uxorious
C. teetotaller D. unalcoholic

**35.** Trying to win favour by flattery and charm:
A. smarmy B. shrewish
C. toady D. loquacious

**36.** A decision on which one cannot go back:
A. incorrigible B. irrevocable
C. rigid D. invulnerable

**37.** The science that studies the varieties of human race:
A. phrenology B. physiology
C. sociology D. ethnology

**38.** A person who hates women:
A. philogynist B. philatelist
C. misogamist D. misogynist

**39.** A group of people in a particular grade in an organisation:
A. colleague B. staff
C. echelon D. commission

**40.** Honourably discharged from service:
A. emeritus B. latitudinarian
C. infallible D. meritorious

**41.** One who does not believe in the existence of God:
A. atheist B. altruist
C. agnostic D. flippant

**42.** The large money paid for an early retirement:
A. goldmine B. golden handshake
C. gratuity D. lion's share

**43.** A hater of learning and knowledge:
A. misologist B. misogynist
C. philologist D. philanthropist

**44.** One who lives and acts for the welfare of others:
A. misanthrope B. credulous
C. altruist D. gregarious

**45.** Mental weariness for want of occupation:
A. desperate B. depression
C. fatigue D. ennui

**46.** That which makes it difficult to recognise the presence in real of somebody or something:
A. cover B. mask
C. make-up D. camouflage

**47.** To bear a hand in one's new business:
A. partnership B. interfere
C. assist D. join

**48.** One who renounces the world and practices self-discipline in order to attain salvation:
A. devotee B. ascetic
C. theist D. parsimonious

**49.** A place where gambling is practiced:
A. hotel B. motel
C. casino D. stadium

**50.** A sad song is a:
A. dirge B. elegy
C. ditty D. knell

## ANSWERS

| 1 | 2 | 3 | 4 | 5 | 6 | 7 | 8 | 9 | 10 |
|---|---|---|---|---|---|---|---|---|---|
| C | B | B | D | D | A | C | C | D | B |
| **11** | **12** | **13** | **14** | **15** | **16** | **17** | **18** | **19** | **20** |
| C | A | D | C | B | A | B | C | A | B |
| **21** | **22** | **23** | **24** | **25** | **26** | **27** | **28** | **29** | **30** |
| C | B | D | D | D | A | B | B | D | C |
| **31** | **32** | **33** | **34** | **35** | **36** | **37** | **38** | **39** | **40** |
| A | C | B | C | A | B | D | D | C | A |
| **41** | **42** | **43** | **44** | **45** | **46** | **47** | **48** | **49** | **50** |
| A | B | A | C | D | D | C | B | C | A |

# 7 Idioms and Phrases

- An idiom is a group of words established by usage as having a meaning different from the individual words.
- A phrase is a small group of words standing together as an idiomatic expression.

Learn and practise as may as you can.

## Idioms and Idiomatic Phrases

- **ABC** (basic principles)
  She does not know the ABC of photography.
- **At one's beck and call** (ready to obey)
  He had a dozen men at his beck and call.
- **At sixes and sevens** (in disorder)
  The drawing room articles were lying at sixes and sevens on the floor.
- **A wet blanket** (a discouraging person)
  Don't allow Rakesh to accompany you to the hunting trip because he is a wet blanket.
- **A big gun** (an important person)
  Mr Smith is a big gun in our city.
- **At a stone's throw** (at a short distance from)
  My school is at a stone's throw from my house.
- **A man of word** (a person who keeps his promise)
  Mr Sharma is a man of word.
- **A man of a few words** (a remarkable person)
  Gandhiji was a man of a few words.
- **At arm's length** (to keep away)
  We should always keep bad boys at arm's length
- **A bolt from the blue** (a sudden and unexpected event)
  The news of my friend's death came to me like a bolt from the blue.
- **A man of letters** (a scholar)
  Radha Krishnan was a man of letters.
- **A hard nut to crack.** (a puzzling problem)
  To get a win over American basket ball team is a hard nut to crack for India.
- **A yeoman's service** (service which is beneficial to the human beings)
  He did yeoman's service through his life.
- **A snake in the grass** (a hidden foe)
  Beware of him because he seems to be a snake in the grass.
- **Acid test** (hard test)
  The election will be an acid test for the ruling party.
- **A wolf in sheep's clothing** (a hypocrite)
  You should not keep company with him because he is a wolf in sheep's clothing.
- **At the eleventh hour** (at the last moment)
  The war was about to start but fortunately at the eleventh hour a messenger came to the PM with a message of peace.
- **A great card** (an important person)
  Mr Sood is a great card in the ministry of finance.
- **A fool of the first water** (one completely foolish)
  Being a fool of the first water he could not solve even the simplest sum.
- **A bone of contention** (to be the cause of quarrel)
  Kashmir is the bone of contention between India and Pakistan.
- **A green hand** (not very much experienced)
  We shall pay a little to a green hand.
- **All in all** (completely)
  Rajesh is all in all in this office.
- **A bed of roses** (a comfort)
  Life is not a bed of roses.

- **An apple of discord** (to be the cause of)
Kashmir is an apple of discord between India and Pakistan.
- **A white elephant** (of no use)
This sort of glib talker always proves a white elephant in the end.
- **A red letter day** (An important day)
15th August is a red letter day for the Indians.
- **By hook or by crook** (by any means fair or foul)
- **Black sheep** (a traitor)
Later on Mr XYZ proved a black sheep.
- **By dint of** (by means of)
By dint of hard work, she earned a lot of money.
- **Break ones back** (to work hard to get something)
He broke his back to earn his livelihood.
- **Break the back of** (accomplish the hardest part of a certain job)
There is nothing to be worried about as we've already broken the back of the problem.
- **Beat about the bush** (to go on talking on some worthless topic)
Stop this beating about the bush, come to the main task.
- **Beyond one's means** (beyond one's budget)
He is living beyond his means, therefore, he is sure to get ruined.
- **Cut loose** (Keep away)
India should cut loose from bad politics.
- **Chips of the same block** (having the same taste)
They are the chips of the same block.
- **Cut-throat competition** (a stiff competition)
There is a cut-throat competition among the publishers in the market.
- **Come what may** (no matter what happens)
I'll do it come what may.
- **Drop someone a line** (send a letter, etc.)
Please drop me a line of your well-being.
- **Dull the edge of** (reduce the intensity of)
Take this pill and it will dull the edge of pain.
- **From hand to mouth** (without any saving)
The poor factory worker is living from hand to mouth.
- **Fair and square** (clean)
One must be fair and square in one's dealing.
- **Hard of hearing** (somewhat deaf)
She is a bit hard of hearing.
- **In the good books of** (be good in one's mind)
Jack is in the good books of his teachers.
- **In black and white** (in written)
Don't give him anything in black and white.
- **In cold blood** (mercilessly)
The old woman was murdered in cold blood.
- **In a crack** (all of a sudden or rapidly)
The thief left the place in a crack.
- **In full swing** (in full force)
The studies of the students are going on in full swing.
- **In the twinkling of an eye** (quickly)
The monkey ate up grams in the twinkling of an eye.
- **Keep the ball rolling** (to maintain the progress of some activity)
After the death of his father he had to take the charge of his office to keep the ball rolling.
- **Neck and neck** (even)
There is a neck and neck fight between the two boxers.
- **Once in a blue moon** (seldom)
She visits her brother once in a blue moon.
- **Slow and steady** (slowly but continually)
Slow and steady wins the race.
- **To cut a sorry figure** (present oneself in a bad way)
She cut a sorry figure on the stage.
- **To give a red carpet reception** (to give a warm welcome)
The PM was given a red carpet reception in America.
- **To dance one's tune** (to follow someone submissively)
He always dances to his brother's tune.
- **To turn a deaf ear to** (to disregard)
She turned a deaf ear to her parents' advice.

- **To call a spade a spade** (to speak the truth)
  Gandhiji always called a spade a spade.
- **To bring to book** (to scold)
  The naughty boy was brought to book by the teacher.
- **To cut short** (to reduce)
  Smoking will cut short your life.
  He wants to get money by hook or by crook.
- **To grease the palm of** (to bribe)
  Rohit greased the palm of the clerk and got the file moved.
- **Through thick and thin.** (under all circumstances)
  We'll stand by you through thick and thin.
- **To die by inches** (to die a painful death)
  The old man died by inches.
- **To eat one's words** (to retract one's statement)
  You'll have to eat your words because you have spoken without thinking.
- **To burn the midnight oil** (to work hard)
  You'll have to burn the midnight oil if you want to get good marks.
- **To poke one's nose into** (to meddle with)
  It is bad to poke your nose into others' affair.
- **To fall flat** (to have no effect)
  His father's advice fell flat on him.
- **To make a clean breast of** (to confess)
  He made a clean breast of his involvement in the bomb blast.
- **To get the better of** (overcome)
  Anger got the better of him.
- **To break somebody's back** (to give too much work to him to do)
  She broke his back by giving him so much hard work to do.
- **Throw cold water on** (to discourage)
  She tried to throw cold water on his plan but he was well-determined.
- **The long and short of** (in brief)
  The long and short of his lecture is that we should live like brothers.
- **To burn one's fingers** (to get oneself in trouble)
  You have burnt your fingers by speaking against him.
- **To turn over a new leaf** (to change the course of life)
  He has turned over a new leaf in his life.
- **To have one's own axe to grind** (to have vested interest)
  He has his own axe to grind in this matter.
- **To take to one's heels** (to run away)
  The thief took to his heels as soon as he saw the policeman.
- **To move heaven and earth** (to make too much effort)
  The young man moved heaven and earth to find a job.
- **To be caught red handed** (to be caught at the time of committing a crime)
  The clerk was caught red handed when he was accepting bribe from Mr ABC.
- **To receive with open arms** (to give a warm welcome)
  The new president of the club was received with open arms by the members.
- **To be born with a silver spoon in one's mouth** (to be born in a rich family)
  Mr. J. L. Nehru was born with a silver spoon in his mouth.
- **To come to light** (to be known)
  A new disease has recently come to light.
- **To be the apple of one's eye** (be very dear)
  He is the apple of his parent's eye.
- **To make fun of** (laugh at)
  The children made fun of the waiter in the hotel.
- **To let the cat out of the bag** (to divulge secret)
  It was Sohan who let the cat out of the bag by telling the real matter.
- **To open a new chapter** (to start some habit, etc.
  By drinking, you've opened a new chapter in your life.
- **To make the flesh creep** (to terrify)
  The story made my flesh creep.
- **To lose ground** (to retreat)
  After fighting for some time the Pakistani army began to lose ground.

✦ **To bring to book** (to punish)
The student was brought to book by the teacher.

✦ **To show a clean pair of heels** (to run away)
The thief showed a clean pair of heels as soon as he saw the policeman approaching.

✦ **To gain ground** (to be established)
He gained ground in India in a few years.

✦ **To get wind of** (to get information)
I got wind of his secret plans.

✦ **Under a cloud** (be in trouble or in a state of disgrace or suspicion)
His company seemed to be under a cloud as it had no funds to pay the wages to the workers.

## Verbal Phrases

✦ **Act upon** (to follow)
I acted upon my father's advice.

✦ **Act upto** (to perform within limits)
He acted upto his conscience.

✦ **Act beyond** (to perform crossing limits)
We should not act beyond our capacity.

✦ **Act for** (to perform in place of someone else)
The vice principal acted for the principal.

✦ **Back up** (to make a queue)
The vehicles began to back up.

✦ **Back down** (withdraw claim in the presence of opposition)
The leader backed down from his previous statement.

✦ **Back off** (draw back some plan or action)
They backed off from building a flyover.

✦ **Back out** (withdraw from a promise, etc.)
The government backed out of its promise.

✦ **Break down** (stop working) My car broke down on the highway.

✦ **Break into** (enter in certain premises by breaking the door, etc.)
Last night a thief broke into my neighbour's.

✦ **Break off** (stop all of a sudden)
She broke off and began to think over about her/his hand.

✦ **Break out** (spread)
Cholera has broken out in the town.

✦ **Break out of** (escape from)
A prisoner broke out of the prison last night.

✦ **Break up** (disperse)
The cloud of fog began to break up as the sun rose.

✦ **Break something up** (Cause something to break into small pieces)
She broke up the chocolate to distribute it among the girls.

✦ **Break with** (Cut off connection after quarrelling with someone)
He has broken with his brother.

✦ **Call on** (pay a visit to somebody)
I'll call on Mohan's today.

✦ **Call out** (to start)
The workers have called out a strike.

✦ **Call off** (to stop the strike etc.)
The workers have called off the strike.

✦ **Call at** (to visit someone's house)
I called at his house yesterday.

✦ **Call in** (send for)
Please call in the doctor.

✦ **Carry on** (continue)
Please carry on your work.

✦ **Carry something out** (perform a task)
Our company is carrying out a big deal with a foreign company.

✦ **Carry something over** (postpone)
The fancy dress competition had to be carried over till Monday)

✦ **Carry someone off** (kill somebody)
Cancer carried her off on the day of her 20th birthday.

✦ **Come of age** (get established)
As our company has come of age, so, there is no problem in selling our goods.

✦ **Come of** (belong to)
She comes of a royal family.

✦ **Come over** (surmount)
We at last came over all our problems.

✦ **Come off** (to take place)
The marriage of my brother comes off in the next month.

✦ **Come round** (agree)
At last he came round to my views.

✦ **Come under** (fall in the category of)
All these animals come under the same species.

✦ **Come down with** (suffer from)
She came down with whopping cough.

✦ **Come from** (be the nature of)
She came from London.

✦ **Come about** (happen)
The explosion came about when the worker struck the match to light a cigarette.

✦ **Cut off** (die)
The princess was cut off in the prime of her life.

✦ **Cut down** (reduce)
The prices of consumer goods should be cut down.

✦ **Cut someone out** (exclude someone)
His father cut him out of his will.

✦ **Fall in**
She fell in love with the prince.

✦ **Fall down** (fail)
The deal fell down for lack of transparency.

✦ **Fall out** (quarrel)
She fell out with his elder brother.

✦ **Fall through** (fail)
The project fell through for lack of funds.

✦ **Get away** (escape)
She got away with her life.

✦ **Get by** (to accomplish something with great difficulty)
She is not rich. She has just enough to get by.

✦ **Get on** (perform)
How are you getting on with your studies?

✦ **Get out** (become known)
The news got out that the PM was paying a visit to Russia.

✦ **Get over** (overcome)
At last I got over all obstacles.

✦ **Get up** (rise)
When do you get up in the morning?

✦ **Give up** (stop)
He gave up smoking.

✦ **Give out** (emit)
Garlic gives out a pungent smell.

✦ **Give in** (collapse)
The bridge gave in under the heavy load.

✦ **Give away** (distribute)
The Principal gave away the prizes.

✦ **Give out** (announce)
It was given out that the President of India would visit the place soon.

✦ **Go off** (explode)
The gun went off suddenly.

✦ **Go on** (continue)
She went on about how she flew the aeroplane.

✦ **Go through** (examine)
I'll go through this book later on.

✦ **Go up** (be built)
The construction of the house is going up.

✦ **Grind on** (continue for a long time in a tedious way)
The discussion over political issues ground on.

✦ **Grind something out** (produce something a tedious way)
She will grind some more short stories.

✦ **Look out** (be careful)
Look out! there is a snake.

✦ **Look down upon** (hate)
We should not look down upon the poor.

✦ **Look at** (watch)
Look at the blackboard.

✦ **Look after** (take care of)
We ought to look after our old parents.

✦ **Look into** (investigate)
The new police inspector will look into the matter.

✦ **Look up** (rise)
The prices of consumer goods are looking up.

✦ **Look back** (think of the past)
It made her feel disolate when she looked back on things of the past.

✦ **Make up** (to fulfil)
I'll make up my deficiency in Mathematics.

✦ **Make out** (understand)
I could not make out what she said.

✦ **Make up one' mind** (to resolve)
I have made up my mind to settle in the USA.

✦ **Make off** (leave hurriedly)
She made off without informing anybody.

✦ **Make something over** (transfer)
She should make her property over to her sons.

✦ **Make over** (hand over)
He made over the charge of the file to Mr Robert.

✦ **Pull back** (retreat)
The government has pulled back from its previous policy.

✦ **Pull something down** (demolish)
The authorities concerned pulled down a few building which were illegally built on government land.

✦ **Pull out** (pluck)
The child pulled out a few petals of the flower.

✦ **Pull through** (recover)
The patient will pull through.

✦ **Push on** (continue a journey)
It was getting darker but we pushed on.

✦ **Push at** (exert force)
He pushed at the bell, but it did not ring.

✦ **Push for** (demand persistently)
The workers have been pushing for the installation of new machines for five years.

✦ **Put out** (extinguish)
She put out the light.

✦ **Put on** (wear)
He put on an overcoat.

✦ **Put off** (postpone)
The plan had to be put off.

✦ **Put by** (spare something for future)
We must put by some money for future.

✦ **Put up with** (stay)
Your aunt is out of town for a couple of days, you may put up with us till she comes.

✦ **Put something down** (record something)
She put a new idea down on the paper.

✦ **Take after** (resemble)
He takes after his father.

✦ **Take off** (remove)
He took off his shoes.

✦ **Take something out** (obtain)
You may take out some money from Rohit if you want to purchase this car.

✦ **Take to** (fall into the habit of)
He took to gambling.

✦ **Turn something down** (reject something)
The judge turned down his appeal.

✦ **Turn on** (attack)
The thief turned on him with a knife.

## Multiple Choice Questions

**Directions:** *Some idioms/phrases are given below with their probable meanings. Select the options with their correct meanings.*

1. **Carry out**
   A. To take from one place to another
   B. To continue
   C. To obey
   D. To make efforts

2. **In the same boat**
   A. A worn out choice
   B. Indifferent
   C. In identical circumstances
   D. Carry off

3. **In one's good book**
   A. A costly book
   B. A priceless treasure

C. In one's favour
D. An enchanting beauty

**4. Keep a straight face**
A. To do make up
B. To change clothes
C. Assume responsibility
D. To remain serious

**5. To be above board**
A. To have a good height
B. To be honest in any business deal
C. To have no debts
D. To try to be beautiful

**6. On the face of it**
A. To agree
B. From an action
C. More than enough
D. Apparently

**7. Let the bygones be bygones**
A. In one's favour
B. To pretend
C. To forget the past
D. Other choice

**8. To split hairs**
A. Major distinctions
B. Hair with two ends
C. To make minute distinction
D. Without distinction

**9. Bread and butter**
A. Both bread and butter
B. Something essential
C. Livelihood
D. Relevant things

**10. To bell the cat**
A. To catch a cat and tie a bell round its neck
B. To make an effort
C. To be quick
D. To face a risk

**11. Hard and fast**
A. Strict
B. Solid
C. Fast moving
D. Some hard surface

**12. Part and parcel**
A. The part of a parcel
B. An essential part
C. A missing parcel
D. Some part of a machine sent by parcel

**13. Null and void**
A. Something invalid
B. Something that can be avoided
C. Something that can be nullified
D. Something evil

**14. To make clean breast of**
A. To gain prominence
B. To praise oneself
C. To confess without reserve
D. To destroy before it blooms

**15. Trump card**
A. A powerful means of achieving an object
B. Resourcefulness
C. The best gamble to attain success
D. None of these

**16. Tall talk**
A. A discussion continued for a long time
B. A high sounding talk
C. A meaningful talk
D. A useless talk

**17. Small talk**
A. Gossip
B. A discussion carried on for a long time
C. A brief discussion
D. None of these

**18. Throw out of gear**
A. To replace
B. Hinder, disturb
C. To decide
D. Take up tune

**19. To and fro**
A. Back and forth
B. Puzzled
C. Amazed
D. Reprove

**20. To bell the cat**
A. To do an easy job
B. To be indifferent to
C. To undertake a difficult job
D. To clarify

**21. To be under cloud**
A. Puzzle
B. Enjoy the favour
C. Talk thoughtlessly
D. To be under suspicion

**22. A labour of love**
A. A tragic end
B. A funny thing
C. Not fruitful
D. Work done without payment

**23. Follow suit**

A. Follow an example B. Wear a new dress
C. Irrelevant D. A gay person

**24. Foul play**

A. Bad intentions
B. A play not well acted
C. A play not liked by the audience
D. None of these

**25. To pick holes**

A. To find some reason to quarrel
B. To destroy something
C. To criticise someone
D. To cut some part of an item

**26. To smell a rat**

A. To see signs of plague epidemic
B. To get bad smell of a dead rat
C. To suspect foul dealings
D. To be in a bad mood

**27. To put a spoke in one's wheel**

A. To encourage
B. Act without restraint
C. Risk something
D. To obstruct one's progress

**28. To pull one's leg**

A. To give up B. Take care of
C. To befool D. To know

**29. To play with fire**

A. Grasp the truth
B. To handle something dangerous
C. To ridicule
D. To flee away

**30. To reckon with**

A. Take up time
B. Make an inventory
C. To deal with
D. Submit to punishment

**31. To run short**

A. Talk until one is tired at
B. Apply to oneself
C. To get rid of
D. To have or be too little

**32. A man of letters**

A. A postman B. A learned man
C. A hypocrite D. An ignorant man

**33. A maiden speech**

A. A speech made in the parliament
B. A speech made before unmarried girls
C. A speech made by a political leader
D. A speech made for the first time

**34. Order of the day**

A. An order passed on a particular day
B. A current law
C. Something common or general
D. None of these

**35. To end in smoke**

A. To make completely understand
B. To ruin oneself
C. To excite great applause
D. None of these

**36. To give vent to**

A. To allow to flow forth
B. To prove a failure
C. To amass wealth
D. To evade

**37. To eat humble pie**

A. To apologise or confess
B. To order
C. To flatter
D. To get rid of

**38. A black sheep**

A. An unlucky person
B. A negro
C. An ugly person
D. None of these

**39. To catch a tartar**

A. To trap wanted criminal with great difficulty
B. To catch a dangerous person
C. To meet with disaster
D. To deal with a person who is more than one's watch

**40. Sit on fence**

A. To remain neutral
B. To show contempt
C. To enjoy the surroundings.
D. To become fond of

**41. Pay off old scores**

A. To repay the debt
B. To have revenge
C. To invite
D. Secretly

**42. Turn turtle**
A. To cheat
B. To be lopsided
C. To frustrate
D. To dance to the tune

**43. Wash one's hands of**
A. To refuse　B. To assist
C. To abuse　D. To refuse to be

**44. Under duress**
A. Under compulsion
B. Willing
C. To elicit information
D. To demand

**45. To turn the tables**
A. To ruin someone
B. To turn the situation to one's own side
C. To reverse the situation
D. To move from one point to another

**46. On the cards**
A. Possibly　B. Probably
C. Openly　D. Likely

**47. To leave someone in the lurch**
A. To come to compromise with someone
B. Constant source of annoyance to someone
C. To put someone at ease
D. To desert someone in his difficulties

**48. To play second fiddle**
A. To be happy, cheerful and healthy
B. To reduce importance of one's senior
C. To support the role and view of another person
D. To do back seat driving

**49. To yearn for**
A. To weep for
B. To remember
C. To admire
D. To long for intensely

**50. Call off**
A. To finish　B. To withdraw
C. To postpone　D. To cry

# ANSWERS

| 1 | 2 | 3 | 4 | 5 | 6 | 7 | 8 | 9 | 10 |
|---|---|---|---|---|---|---|---|---|---|
| C | C | C | D | B | D | C | C | C | D |
| 11 | 12 | 13 | 14 | 15 | 16 | 17 | 18 | 19 | 20 |
| A | B | A | C | C | B | A | B | A | C |
| 21 | 22 | 23 | 24 | 25 | 26 | 27 | 28 | 29 | 30 |
| D | D | A | A | C | C | D | C | B | C |
| 31 | 32 | 33 | 34 | 35 | 36 | 37 | 38 | 39 | 40 |
| D | B | D | C | D | A | A | D | B | A |
| 41 | 42 | 43 | 44 | 45 | 46 | 47 | 48 | 49 | 50 |
| B | B | D | A | C | D | D | C | D | B |

❑❑❑

# 8 Narration

## Direct and Indirect Narration/Speech

The exact words spoken by the speaker are known as Direct Speech.

The words spoken by somebody and expressed by someone else with some modification are known as Indirect Speech.

(*a*) Ram says to me, "You do not help me."

(*b*) Ram tells me that I do not help him.

The sentence (*a*) shows the words spoken by Ram. So, it is a sentence of Direct Speech.

The sentence (*b*) shows the words spoken by Ram and expressed by someone else with certain modification. So, it is a sentence of Indirect Speech.

The following points should be noted while changing Direct Speech into Indirect speech:

1. The verb outside the inverted commas is called the Reporting Verb.
2. The verb or sentence inside the inverted commas is called the Reported Speech.
3. If the Reporting verb is in the Present or Future Tense, there is no change in the tense in the Reported Speech.
4. If the Reporting Verb is in the Past Tense, the Tense in the Reported Speech is changed.
5. The Reporting verb may be in any Tense, in it the Pronouns are changed as under:
   (*i*) First Person according to Subject
   (*ii*) Second Person according to Object
   (*iii*) Third Person, No change.
6. If the Reporting verb is in the Past Tense the Adverb will change as under in the Indirect Speech.

| ***Direct*** | ***Indirect*** |
|---|---|
| now | then |
| here | there |
| after | before |
| today | that day |
| yesterday | the previous day |
| these | those |
| tomorrow | the next day |
| last week | the previous week |
| this | that |

7. Adjectives/Determiners are changed as under:

| ***Direct*** | ***Indirect*** |
|---|---|
| this | that |
| these | those |

### Rules for Change of Tense

| Reporting Verb | Reporting Speech | Change of Tense |
|---|---|---|
| Present Tense | Any Tense | No change |
| Future Tense | Any Tense | No change |
| Past Tense | Present/Future Tense | Change into corresponding Past Tense |
| Past Tense | Past Indefinite Tense | Change into Past Perfect Tense |
| Past Tense | Past Continuous Tense | Change into Past Perfect Continuous Tense |
| Past Tense | Past Perfect/Perfect Continuous Tense | No change |
| Past Tense | Universal Truth | No change |
| Past Tense | Proverb | No change |

## Transformation of Speech Based on Special Rules

### 1. Rule Related to Interrogative Sentence

- If the answer of an interrogative sentence is possible in yes-no manner.

  **Illustration.**

  Dhoni said to Sachin, "Will you help me?"

  Dhoni asked Sachin whether he would help him.

  (**Note :** The answer of R.S. is possible in yes-no manner)

  **Rule of Transformation from Direct to Indirect speech**

  **Step I** : Change R.V. into ask.

  **Step II** : In place of comma use 'if/whether'.

  **Step III** : Change interrogative sentence into assertive sentence.

- If the answer of an interrogative sentence is not possible in yes-no manner.

  **Illustration:**

  Sachin said to Dhoni, "What do you want?"

  Sachin asked Dhoni what he wanted.

  (**Note :** Only in Step II, you have to avoid comma and inverted comma and rest will be same as mentioned above).

### 2. Rule related to Imperative Sentence

- Imperative sentence is a sentence which shows Order/Advice/Request

  **Illustration:**

  My teacher said to me, "Go there".

  My teacher ordered me to go there.

  **Rule of Transformation from Direct to Indirect Speech**

  **Step I** : Change R.V. as per meaning/sense of R.S. into order/request/advise.

  **Step II** : In place of comma, use 'to'.

  **Step III** : Rest portion will be same.

### 3. Rule related to Optative Sentence

- Optative sentence is a sentence which expresses the feeling of bless/curse/pray/wish.

  **Illustration:**

  Mother said to me, "May you live long!"

  Mother blessed me that I might live long.

  **Rule of Transformation from Direct to Indirect Speech**

  **Step I** : Change R.V. as per meaning/sense of R.S. into bless/curse/pray/wish.

  **Step II** : In place of comma, use 'that'.

  **Step III** : Change optative sentence into assertive sentence.

### 4. Rule related to Exclamatory Sentence

- Exclamatory sentence is a sentence which takes note of exclamatory (!) mark in that sentence showing inner feeling.

  **Illustration:**

  She said, "Alas! I am ruined".

  She exclaimed with sorrow that she was ruined.

  **Rule of Transformation from Direct to Indirect Speech**

  **Step I** : Change R.V. as per meaning/sense of R.S. into exclaim/exclaims/exclaimed/will or shall exclaim + joy/sorrow/anger/surprise/applause/contempt.

  **Step II** : Change comma into that.

  **Step III** : Change note of exclamation (!) into full stop (.)

  **Step IV** : Change exclamatory sentence into assertive sentence.

## Universal, Historical truth, etc.

If the Reported Speech expresses a Universal or Historical or Habitual truth, its Tense will not change.

1. The teacher said to the students, "The sun rises in the east."

   The teacher told the students that the sun rises in the east.

2. My father said to me, "The First Battle of Panipat was fought in 1526."

   My father told me that the First Battle of Panipat was fought in 1526.

# Multiple Choice Questions

**Directions (Qs. 1 to 13):** *Select the correct Indirect Speech for the following sentences:*

**1.** I said to him, "I shall help you."
A. I told him that I can help him.
B. I told him that I would help him.
C. I told him that I will help him.
D. I told him that I shall be helping him.

**2.** My Teacher said to me, "The earth revolves round the sun."
A. My teacher told me that the earth revolves round the sun.
B. My teacher told me that the earth revolve round the sun.
C. My teacher told me that the earth had been revolving round the sun.
D. My teacher told me that the earth has been revolving round the sun.

**3.** I said to my friend, "My father daily goes for a walk."
A. I told my friend that my father daily goes for a walk.
B. I told my friend that my father daily went for a walk.
C. I told my friend that my father has to go for a walk.
D. I told my friend that my father had gone for a walk.

**4.** He said to me, "May God bless you!"
A. He requested that God can bless me.
B. He prayed that God can bless me.
C. He prayed that God might bless me.
D. He prayed that God will bless me.

**5.** The patient said, "Thank you, doctor."
A. The patient thanked the doctor.
B. The patient requested the doctor with thanks.
C. The patient told the doctor thanks.
D. The patient suggested the doctor thanks.

**6.** Satish said, "No, I shall not talk to him."
A. Satish told that he should not talk to him.
B. Satish suggested that he would not have talked to him.
C. Satish exclaimed with sorrow that he would not talk with him.
D. Satish refused to talk to him.

**7.** The child said, "What a lovely place!"
A. The child exclaimed with sorrow that it was a lovely place.
B. The child thought that the place was lovely.
C. The child exclaimed with joy that the place was very lovely.
D. The child suggested that the place was lovely.

**8.** He said, "What a fool I have been!"
A. He told himself with sorrow that he was a fool.
B. He confessed with regret that he had been a great fool.
C. He said himself a fool.
D. He suggested that he could be a fool.

**9.** He said, "Alas! I am ruined."
A. He told me that he had been ruined.
B. He exclaimed with joy that he had been ruined.
C. He exclaimed with sorrow that he was ruined.
D. He told me that he should not be ruined.

**10.** The accused said, "I am not guilty."
A. The accused exclaimed with sorrow that I am not guilty.
B. The accused exclaimed with joy that he was not guilty.
C. The accused stated that he was not guilty.
D. The accused told me that he has not been guilty.

**11.** My teacher said, "The earth is round".
A. My teacher said that the earth was round.
B. My teacher says that the earth is round.
C. My teacher said that the earth is round.
D. My teacher ordered that the earth is round.

**12.** He said, "What a place it is!"
A. He said that it was a very fine place.
B. He said that is a very fine place.
C. He said that the place is fine.
D. He exclaimed with joy/surprise that it was a very fine place.

**13.** Ria said, "Shall I thread the needle?"
A. Ria asked if she should thread the needle.
B. Ria asked if she shall thread the needle.
C. Ria ordered if she should thread the needle.
D. Ria says that if she would thread the needle.

**Directions (Qs. 14 to 33):** *Pick out the correct alternative that completes the incomplete sentence which is changed into Indirect Narration.*

**14.** She said to me, "I shall see you as soon as I get time."
She told me:
A. that she will see me as soon as she will get time.
B. that she would see me as soon as she would get time.
C. she would see me whenever she got time.
D. that she would see me whenever she gets time.

**15.** My secretary said to me, "Your plane will leave if you do not go at once."
My secretary told me that:
A. her plane would leave if she did not go at that time.
B. her plane would leave if I do not go at once.
C. my plane would leave if I did not go at that very time.
D. my plane will leave if I did not go at that time.

**16.** My mother said to me, "Don't quarrel among yourselves".
My mother:
A. forbade me to quarrel among ourselves.
B. asked me not to quarrel among ourselves.
C. asked me that not to quarrel among ourselves.
D. asked me to quarrel not among ourselves.

**17.** Her father said to her mother, "Excuse the daughter."
Her father:
A. requested her mother to excuse the daughter.
B. asked her mother to excuse the daughter.
C. asked her mother to have excused the daughter.
D. asked her mother to have been excused.

**18.** He said to his friend, "Wait here till father comes."
He requested his friend:
A. to wait here till father had come.
B. that to wait there till his friend came.
C. to wait there till father came.
D. to wait here until his friend came.

**19.** She said to her maid, "Run and catch the thief."
She ordered her maid:
A. ran and catch the thief.
B. that to run and to catch the thief.
C. ran and caught the thief.
D. to run and catch the thief.

**20.** Anita said to Sunita, "What are you doing?"
Anita asked Sunita:
A. what she will be doing.
B. that what she is doing.
C. that what she was doing.
D. what she was doing.

**21.** She said to me, "Are you meeting me today?"
She enquired of me:
A. whether I am meeting her that day.
B. whether I was meeting her today.
C. whether I was meeting her that day.
D. I was meeting her that day.

**22.** Nitish said to me, "When did you buy this pen?"
Nitish asked me:
A. when I was to buy that pen.
B. when I would buy that pen.
C. when I had bought that pen.
D. when I was buying that pen.

**23.** She said to me, "Are you going to market?"
She enquired of me:
A. I am going to market.
B. I was going to market.
C. if I was going to market.
D. if I had been going to the market.

**24.** Damini said, "Why did not you change your clothes?"
Damini asked me:
A. why I had not changed my clothes.
B. why I did not change my clothes.
C. why I would not change my clothes.
D. why I have not been changing my clothes.

**25.** Umesh said to me, "Have you read that novel?"
Umesh asked me:
A. if he was reading that novel.
B. if he had read that novel.
C. if I had read that novel.
D. if I was reading that novel.

**26.** She said to me, "I shall forgive you."
She told me:
A. that she will forgive me.
B. that she was going to forgive me.
C. that she will not forgive me.
D. that she would forgive me.

**27.** I said to her, "It was very hot last night."
I told her:
A. that it had been very hot the previous night.
B. that it was very hot the previous night.
C. that it has been very hot the last night.
D. that it had been very hot this night.

**28.** She said to me, "I thank you for the help you have given."
She:
A. told me that she thanked me for the help I had given.
B. thanked me for the help I have given.
C. thanked to me for the help I have given.
D. thanked me for the help I had given.

**29.** Mohini said to me, "Trust in God."
Mohini advised me:
A. that I should trust in God.
B. should trust in God.
C. trusted in God.
D. to trust in God.

**30.** I said to him, "Let us go to school."
I told him:
A. we would go to school.
B. we shall go to school.
C. that we would go to school.
D. that we should go to school.

**31.** Rajni said, "May God bless you?"
Rajni:
A. exclaimed with wish that God might bless me.
B. expressed a wish that God might bless me.
C. asked God to bless me.
D. shouted with joy to bless me.

**32.** My mother said me, "Do not have so many friends."
My mother forbade me:
A. to have so many friends.
B. not to have so many friends.
C. to have been so many friends.
D. to possess so many friends.

**33.** Ram said, "Pay attention to me."
Ram asked:
A. pay attention to him.
B. paid attention to him.
C. having paid attention to him.
D. to pay attention to him.

**Directions (Qs. 34 to 50):** *In questions below, the sentences have been given in Direct/Indirect Speech. Out of the four alternatives suggested select the one which best expresses the given sentence in Indirect/Direct Speech.*

**34.** She said that her brother was getting married
A. She said, "Her brother is getting married."
B. She told, "My brother is getting married"
C. She said, "My brother is getting married".
D. She said, "My brother was married".

**35.** "Please don't go away", she said.
A. She said to please her and not go away.
B. She told me to go away.
C. She begged me not to go away.
D. She begged that I not go away.

**36.** "If you don't keep quiet I shall shoot you", he said to her in a calm voice.
A. He warned her to shoot if she didn't keep quiet calmly.
B. He said calmly that I shall shoot you if you don't be quiet.
C. He warned her calmly that he would shoot her if she didn't keep quiet.
D. Calmly he warned her that be quiet or else he will have to shoot her.

**37.** I told him that he was not working hard.
A. I said to him, "You are not working hard."
B. I told him, "You are not working hard."
C. I said, "You are not working hard."
D. I said to him, "He is not working hard."

**38.** She said that she would finish the work the next day.
A. She said, "I will finish the work the next day."
B. She said, "I will finish the work tomorrow."
C. She said, "You will finish the work tomorrow."
D. She said, "I finished the work."

**39.** She said to him, "Why don't you go today?"
A. She asked him why he did not go that day.
B. She said to him that why he don't go today.
C. She asked him not to go today.
D. She asked him why he did not go today.

**40.** "Are you alone, my son?" asked a soft voice close behind me.
A. A soft voice asked that what I was doing there alone.
B. A soft voice said to me are you alone son.
C. A soft voice from my back asked if I was alone.
D. A soft voice behind me asked if I was alone.

**41.** My cousin said, "My room-mate had snored throughout the night."
A. My cousin said that her room-mate snored throughout the night.
B. My cousin told me that her room-mate snored throughout the night.
C. My cousin complained to me that her room-mate is snoring throughout the night.
D. My cousin felt that her room-mate may be snoring throughout the night.

**42.** He asked Rama if he needed his help then.
A. He said to Rama, "Do you need my help?"
B. He told Rama, "Tell me if you need help."
C. He asked Rama, "Do I need your help?"
D. He said to Rama, "Do you need my help now?"

**43.** Nita ordered her servant to bring her a cup of tea.
A. Nita told her servant, "Bring a cup of tea."
B. Nita said, "Bring me a cup of tea."
C. Nita said to her servant, "Bring me a cup of tea."
D. Nita said to her servant, "Bring her that cup of tea."

**44.** He exclaimed with joy that India had won the Sahara Cup.
A. He said, "India has won the Sahara Cup."
B. He said, "India won the Sahara Cup."
C. He said, "How! India will win the Sahara Cup."
D. He said, "Hurrah! India has won the Sahara Cup."

**45.** The boy said, "Who dare call you a thief?"
A. The boy enquired who dared call him a thief.
B. The boy asked who called him a thief.
C. The boy told that who dared call him a thief.
D. The boy wondered who dared call a thief.

**46.** The little girl said to her mother, "Did the sun rise in the East?
A. The little girl said to her mother that the sun rose in the East.
B. The little girl asked her mother if the sun rose in the East.
C. The little girl said to her mother if the sun rises in the East.
D. The little girl asked her mother if the sun is in the East.

**47.** Dhruv said that he was sick and tired of working for that Company.

A. Dhruv said, "I am sick and tired of working for this Company."

B. Dhruv said, "He was tired of that Company."

C. Dhruv said to me, "I am sick and tired of working for this Company."

D. Dhruv said, "I will be tired of working for that Company."

**48.** He said to his father, "Please increase my pocket-money."

A. He told his father, please increase the pocket-money.

B. He pleaded his father to please increase my pocket-money.

C. He requested his father to increase his pocket-money.

D. He asked his father increase his pocket-money.

**49.** She said to her friend, "I know where is everyone."

A. She told that she knew where was everyone.

B. She told her friend that she knew where was everyone.

C. She told her friend she knew where is everyone

D. She told her friend that she knows where was everyone.

**50.** His father ordered him to go to his room and study.

A. His father said, "Go to your room and study."

B. His father said to him, "Go and study in your room."

C. His father shouted, "Go right now to your study room."

D. His father said firmly, "Go and study in your room."

## ANSWERS

| 1 | 2 | 3 | 4 | 5 | 6 | 7 | 8 | 9 | 10 |
|---|---|---|---|---|---|---|---|---|---|
| B | A | A | C | A | D | C | B | C | C |
| **11** | **12** | **13** | **14** | **15** | **16** | **17** | **18** | **19** | **20** |
| C | D | A | B | C | A | B | C | D | D |
| **21** | **22** | **23** | **24** | **25** | **26** | **27** | **28** | **29** | **30** |
| C | C | C | A | C | D | A | A | A | D |
| **31** | **32** | **33** | **34** | **35** | **36** | **37** | **38** | **39** | **40** |
| B | A | D | C | C | C | A | B | A | D |
| **41** | **42** | **43** | **44** | **45** | **46** | **47** | **48** | **49** | **50** |
| A | D | C | B | A | B | A | C | B | A |

❑❑❑

# 9 Voice

A sentence in active voice focuses on the person or thing doing the action. A sentence in passive voice focuses on the person or thing affected by the action.

*e.g.,*

The idol was built. (Active voice)
Someone built the idol. (Passive voice)

## Transformation of Voice

- Voice and Tense are closely associated with each other.
- Tense plays an important role while transforming the voice.

On the basis of following points, voice can be transformed from active to passive voice.

## The Present Indefinite Tense

**Active voice:** Subject + $V_1$ + Object

**Passive voice:** Subject + is, am, are + $V_3$ + by + Object

1. **Active voice:** He sings sweet songs.
   **Passive voice:** Sweet songs are sung by him.
2. **Active voice:** She does not cause any hindrance in my work.
   **Passive voice:** No hindrance in my work is caused by her.
3. **Active voice:** Do they love their country?
   **Passive voice:** Is their country loved by them?

## The Present Continuous Tense

**Active voice:** Subject + is/am/are + $V_1$ + ing + Object.

**Passive voice:** Subject + is/am/are + being + $V_3$ + by + Object.

1. **Active voice:** She is cooking food.
   **Passive voice:** Food is being cooked by her.
2. **Active voice:** Rita is not knitting a sweater.
   **Passive voice:** A sweater is not being knitted by Rita.
3. **Active voice:** Is Meena baking a cake?
   **Passive voice:** Is a cake being baked by Meena?

## The Present Perfect Tense

**Active voice:** Subject + has/have + $V_3$ + Object.

**Passive voice:** Subject + has/have + been + $V_3$ + by + Object.

1. **Active voice:** I have written an essay.
   **Passive voice:** An essay has been written by me.
2. **Active voice:** They have not whitewashed the fence.
   **Passive voice:** The fence has not been whitewashed by them.
3. **Active voice:** Have you cut the cake?
   **Passive voice:** Has the cake been cut by you?

## The Past Indefinite Tense

**Active voice:** Subject + $V_2$ + Object

**Passive voice:** Subject + was/were + $V_3$ + by + Object

1. **Active voice:** He composed a new song.
   **Passive voice:** A new song was composed by him.
2. **Active voice:** He did not operate the computer.
   **Passive voice:** The computer was not operated by him.
3. **Active voice:** Did she catch a fish?
   **Passive voice:** Was a fish caught by her?

## The Past Continuous Tense

**Active voice:** Subject + was/were + $V_1$ + ing + Object
**Passive voice:** Subject + was/were + being + $V_3$ + by + Object

1. **Active voice:** The farmers were ploughing the fields.
   **Passive voice:** The fields were being ploughed by the farmers.
2. **Active voice:** He was not administering the new drug to the patient.
   **Passive voice:** The new drug was not being administered to the patient by him.
3. **Active voice:** Was she sewing a dress?
   **Passive voice:** Was a dress being sewn by her?

## The Past Perfect Tense

**Active voice:** Subject + had + $V_3$ + Object.
**Passive voice:** Subject + had + been + $V_3$ + by + Object

1. **Active voice:** He had issued me an import licence.
   **Passive voice:** I had been issued an import licence.
2. **Active voice:** We had not visited the Taj.
   **Passive voice:** The Taj had not been visited by us.
3. **Active voice:** Who had taught you English?
   **Passive voice:** By whom had you been taught English?

## The Future Indefinite Tense

**Active voice:** Subject + will/shall + $V_1$ + Object.
**Passive voice:** Subject + will/shall + be + $V_3$ + by + Object.

1. **Active voice:** He will remove the dust from the shelf.
   **Passive voice:** The dust from the shelf will be removed by him.
2. **Active voice:** He will not open the main gate.
   **Passive voice:** The main gate will not be opened by him.
3. **Active voice:** Will you help us?
   **Passive voice:** Shall we be helped by you?

## The Future Perfect Tense

**Active voice:** Subject + will/shall + have + $V_3$ + Object.
**Passive voice:** Subject + will/shall + have + been + $V_3$ + by + Object.

1. **Active voice:** They will have sold their house by then.
   **Passive voice:** Their house will have been sold by them by then.
2. **Active voice:** He will not have informed the police about it.
   **Passive voice:** The police will not have been informed about it by him.
3. **Active voice:** Will they have accepted the deal?
   **Passive voice:** Will the deal have been accepted by them?

## Imperative Sentences

1. **Active voice:** Open the window.
   **Passive voice:** You are ordered to open the window.

   ***Or***

   Let the window be opened.
2. **Active voice:** Please/kindly open the window.
   **Passive voice:** You are requested to open the window.
3. **Active voice:** Never make a noise.
   **Passive voice:** A noise should never be made.

## Infinitives

1. **Active voice:** It is time to open the shop.
   **Passive voice:** It is time for the shop to be opened.
2. **Active voice:** He begged the officer to forgive him.
   **Passive voice:** He begged the officer to be forgiven.
3. **Active voice:** He has to break the door.
   **Passive voice:** The door has to be broken by him.

## Prepositional Verb

1. **Active voice:** She laughed at the beggar.
   **Passive voice:** The beggar was laughed at by her.
2. **Active voice:** He listened to the news.
   **Passive voice:** The news was listened to by him.
3. **Active voice:** They called in the doctor.
   **Passive voice:** The doctor was called in by them.

## Double Object

1. **Active voice:** He gave me a pen.
   **Passive voice:** A pen was given to me by him.
   ***Or***
   I was given a pen by him.
2. **Active voice:** She told us a story.
   **Passive voice:** A story was told (to) us by her.
   ***Or***
   We were told a story by her.

## Use of Preposition other than 'by'

1. **Active voice:** The jug contains juice.
   **Passive voice:** Juice is contained in the jug.
2. **Active voice:** The audience thronged the hall.
   **Passive voice:** The hall was thronged with the audience.
3. **Active voice:** I know her.
   **Passive voice:** She is known to me.

## Quasi Passive Verbs

1. **Active voice:** Quinine tastes bitter.
   **Passive voice:** Quinine is bitter when tasted.
   ***Or***
   Quinine is bitter when it is tasted.
2. **Active voice:** Sugar is sweet (to taste).
   **Passive voice:** Sugar is sweet when tasted.
   ***Or***
   Sugar is sweet when it is tasted.

## Implied Sentences

1. **Active voice:** The driver drove the bus.
   **Passive voice:** The bus was driven.
2. **Active voice:** Someone read the news.
   **Passive voice:** The news was read.
3. **Active voice:** They say work is worship.
   **Passive voice:** It is said that work is worship.

# Multiple Choice Questions

**Directions (Qs. 1 to 20):** *In the following questions, a sentence has been given in Active/Passive Voice. Out of the four alternatives suggested, select the one that Best Expresses the same sentence in Passive/Active Voice.*

1. Circumstances will oblige me to go.
   A. I will oblige the circumstances and go.
   B. I shall be obliged to go by the circumstances.
   C. Under the circumstances, I should go.
   D. I shall be obliged by the circumstances to go.
2. We waste much time on trifles.
   A. Much time was wasted on trifles.
   B. Much time will be wasted on trifles.
   C. Much time is wasted by us on trifles.
   D. Much time is wasted on trifles.
3. Mohan gave the beggar an old shirt.
   A. An old shirt was given to Mohan by the beggar.
   B. An old shirt was given to the beggar by Mohan
   C. The begger was gave an old shirt by Mohan.
   D. An old shirt was gave to the beggar by Mohan.
4. They have made him a king.
   A. A king has been made by him.
   B. He was made a king by them.
   C. They have been made kings by him.
   D. He has been made a king by them.

**5.** Who taught you English?
A. By whom English was taught to you?
B. By whom you were taught English?
C. By whom was English taught to you?
D. By whom are you taught English?

**6.** Was he knocking at the door?
A. Was the door being knocked at by him?
B. Was the door being knocked by him?
C. Was the door knocked by him?
D. Was the door knocking at him?

**7.** What was Rani doing?
A. What was done by Rani?
B. What was Rani being done?
C. What was being done by Rani?
D. What was being doing Rani?

**8.** Why were you wasting your time?
A. Why was your time being wasted?
B. Why was your time being wasted by you?
C. Why was your time wasted by you?
D. Why was your time wasted?

**9.** She has laid out a small garden.
A. A small garden has been laid by her.
B. A small garden has laid her.
C. A small garden being laid by her.
D. A small garden has been laid out by her.

**10.** She had already solved all the sums.
A. All the sums had already been solved by her.
B. All the sums have already been solved by her.
C. All the sums have been solved by her.
D. All the sums are solved by her.

**11.** He will have posted the letter.
A. The letter has been posted by him.
B. The letter will be posted by him.
C. The letter will have been posted by him.
D. The letter is posted by him.

**12.** They will have sold all the books by 4 P.M.
A. All the books will be sold by 4 P.M.
B. All the books will have been sold by 4 P.M.
C. All the books were being sold by 4 P.M.
D. All the books must be sold by 4 P.M.

**13.** Do you speak English?
A. Is English spoken by you?
B. Does English spoken by you?
C. Is English being spoken by you?
D. Does English being spoken by you?

**14.** Had they seen me before?
A. Had myself been seen by them before?
B. Had me being seen by them before?
C. Had I been seen by them before?
D. Had I being seen by them before?

**15.** May I take this pen?
A. May this pen will be taken by me?
B. May this pen shall be taken by me?
C. May this pen should be taken by me?
D. May this pen be taken by me?

**16.** Can we send it by air?
A. Can this be sent by air?
B. Can it be sent by air?
C. Can it go by air?
D. Can it be send by air?

**17.** Who wrote this book?
A. By whom was this book written?
B. By whom is this book written?
C. By whom was this book being written?
D. By whom is this book being written?

**18.** What did you buy?
A. What is bought by you?
B. What is being bought by you?
C. What was bought by you?
D. What was being bought by you?

**19.** Whom do you want?
A. Who is wanted by you?
B. Who is being wanted by you?
C. You are wanted by whom?
D. You are being wanted by whom?

**20.** When will you raise this question?
A. When this question will be raised by you?
B. When will this question be raised by you?
C. When this question is being raised by you?
D. When is this question being raised by you?

**Directions (Qs. 21 to 35):** *In each of the following questions, a sentence is given in Active Voice. Below it are given four alternatives suggesting the Passive Voice form of the above sentence. Choose the correct alternative.*

**21.** Who did this?
- A. This was done by whom?
- B. By whom was this done?
- C. Who has done this?
- D. By whom this was done?

**22.** One should keep ones promises.
- A. Promises should be kept.
- B. Ones promises should be kept by one.
- C. Promises must be kept.
- D. Ones promises one should keep.

**23.** Give the order.
- A. Order given.
- B. Order be given.
- C. Let the order be given.
- D. Order may be given by you.

**24.** You will have to do it.
- A. It will be done by you.
- B. It will have to be done by you.
- C. It has to be done by you.
- D. It would have to be done by you.

**25.** Keep to the left.
- A. You are ordered to keep to the left.
- B. You ought to keep to the left.
- C. You are advised to keep to the left.
- D. You must keep to the left.

**26.** They will arrange a party.
- A. A party will have to be arranged by them.
- B. A party they will have to arrange.
- C. A party will be arranged by them.
- D. A party by them will be arranged.

**27.** Someone has picked my pocket.
- A. My pocket is picked.
- B. My pocket has picked.
- C. My pocket has been picked.
- D. My pocket was picked.

**28.** He kept me waiting.
- A. I kept waiting for him.
- B. I kept waiting by him.
- C. I was waiting for him.
- D. I was kept waiting by him.

**29.** Why do you tell a lie?
- A. Why is a lie told by you?
- B. Why is told a lie by you?
- C. Why is told by you a lie?
- D. Why has a lie been told by you?

**30.** I have written a letter.
- A. A letter is written by me.
- B. A letter has been written by me.
- C. A letter was written by me.
- D. A letter had been written by me.

**31.** They will have helped you.
- A. You will have helped by them.
- B. You will have been helped by them.
- C. You will be helped by them.
- D. You will be helped by them.

**32.** Open the door.
- A. Door may be opened.
- B. Let the door be open.
- C. Let the door be opened.
- D. Door be opened.

**33.** I am reading a book.
- A. A book is read by me.
- B. A book is being read by me.
- C. A book has been read by me.
- D. A book in been read by me.

**34.** Why did your brother write such a letter?
- A. Why your brother wrote such a letter?
- B. Why was by brother written such a letter?
- C. Why was such a letter written by your brother?
- D. Why was written such a letter by your brother?

**35.** Did you run a great risk?
- A. Was a great risk run by you?
- B. Was run a great risk by you?
- C. Was by you run a great risk?
- D. Had you run a great risk?

**Directions (Qs. 36 to 45):** *In each of the following questions, a sentence is given in Passive Voice. Below it are given four alternatives suggesting the Active Voice form of the above sentence. Choose the correct alternative.*

**36.** He was made king.
- A. He became king.
- B. They made him king.
- C. They had made him king.
- D. He has been made king.

**37.** Good news is expected by us.
- A. We are expecting good news.
- B. We have been expecting good news.
- C. We had expected good news.
- D. We expect good news.

**38.** The child must be looked after.
- A. The child you must look after.
- B. You must look after the child.
- C. You must look the child after.
- D. You may look after the child.

**39.** What is wanted by you?
- A. What you want?
- B. What did you want?
- C. What do you want?
- D. What you do want?

**40.** Your father is known to me.
- A. I am known to your father.
- B. I know your father.
- C. I have known your father.
- D. I knew your father.

**41.** She may be told the story by you.
- A. The story may be told by you to her.
- B. You may tell the story to her.
- C. You may tell her the story.
- D. You may tell to her the story.

**42.** Duty ought to be done.
- A. Let duty be done.
- B. One ought to do one's duty.
- C. One should do his duty.
- D. Do you duty.

**43.** Is English spoken by you?
- A. Did you speak English?
- B. Do you speak English?
- C. Have you spoken English?
- D. Do you know how to speak English?

**44.** Gold coins are contained in this box.
- A. This box contains gold coins.
- B. This box has contained gold coins.
- C. This box is containing gold coins.
- D. This box has gold coins.

**45.** Character is revealed by manners.
- A. Manners revealed character.
- B. Manners reveal character.
- C. Manners have revealed character.
- D. Manners do reveal character.

## ANSWERS

| 1 | 2 | 3 | 4 | 5 | 6 | 7 | 8 | 9 | 10 |
|---|---|---|---|---|---|---|---|---|---|
| D | C | B | D | C | A | C | B | D | A |
| **11** | **12** | **13** | **14** | **15** | **16** | **17** | **18** | **19** | **20** |
| C | B | A | C | D | B | A | C | A | B |
| **21** | **22** | **23** | **24** | **25** | **26** | **27** | **28** | **29** | **30** |
| B | A | C | B | C | C | C | D | A | B |
| **31** | **32** | **33** | **34** | **35** | **36** | **37** | **38** | **39** | **40** |
| B | C | B | C | A | B | D | B | C | B |
| **41** | **42** | **43** | **44** | **45** | | | | | |
| C | B | B | A | B | | | | | |

❑❑❑

# 10 Sentence Completion

*Filling the blanks is such an exercise that starts with the primary schools and continues at the highest level of competitive examinations. One must practise it regularly to score well.*

## Multiple Choice Questions

**Directions:** *Pick out the most effective word(s) from the given words to fill in the blanks and make the sentence meaningfully complete.*

**1.** One requires great ................. to teach and handle little children who are restless.

A. patience B. attitude
C. determination D. knowledge

**2.** The researchers will ................. some of the causes of increasing poverty in the state.

A. fund B. investigate
C. promote D. circulate

**3.** I usually perform ................. when nobody is watching me.

A. alone B. good
C. better D. hard

**4.** It was ................. to everyone that the minister had been drinking.

A. observed B. known
C. discovered D. realised

**5.** I would rather stay indoors ................. the rain stops.

A. so B. waiting
C. until D. usually

**6.** The process should be completed as far as possible within a week, ..... which the matter should be brought to notice of the officer concerned.

A. following B. failing
C. realizing D. referring

**7.** The officers are ..... to regular transfers.

A. free B. open
C. subject D. available

**8.** All letters received from Government should ..... be acknowledged.

A. suddenly
B. obviously
C. immediately
D. occasionally

**9.** Mumbai office ..... a meeting of senior officials to discuss the high incidence of frauds.

A. attended B. convened
C. reported D. registered

**10.** The note should be ..... to all the concerned departments for their consideration.

A. regulated B. requested
C. carried D. forwarded

**11.** Your present statement does not .............. what you said last week.

A. accord to B. accord in
C. accord with D. accord for

**12.** I had a vague ................ that the lady originally belonged to Scotland.

A. notion B. expression
C. imagination D. theory

**13.** The prisoner showed no .............. for his crimes.

A. hatred B. obstinacy
C. remorse D. anger

**14.** It is inconceivable that in many schools children are subjected to physical ............. in the name of discipline.

A. violation B. exercise
C. violence D. security

**15.** We have not yet fully realised the ................. consequences of the war.

A. happy B. pleasing
C. grim D. exciting

**16.** Happiness consists in being .............. what we have.

A. contented to B. contented with
C. contented for D. contented in

**17.** His rude behaviour is a ................. his organization.

A. disgrace for
B. disgrace on
C. disgrace upon
D. disgrace to

**18.** No child is ................... understanding. One has to wait and provide proper guidance.

A. dull to B. dull in
C. dull of D. dull for

**19.** I am fully .................. the problems facing the industry.

A. alive with B. alive to
C. alive for D. alive on

**20.** The Romans were ................ science.

A. bad in B. bad to
C. bad for D. bad at

**21.** Although I was ........... of his plans, I encouraged him, because there was no one else who was willing to help.

A. sceptical B. remorseful
C. fearful D. excited

**22.** You have no business to .......... pain on a weak and poor person.

A. inflict B. put
C. direct D. force

**23.** Her uncle died in a car accident. He was quite rich. She suddenly ......... all her uncle's money.

A. succeeded B. caught
C. gave D. inherited

**24.** There was a major accident. The plane crashed. The pilot .......... did not see the tower.

A. likely B. probably
C. scarcely D. hurriedly

**25.** The car we were travelling in ........... a mile from home.

A. broke off B. broke down
C. broke into D. broke up

**26.** What are you .......... in the kitchen cupboard?

A. looking in B. looking on
C. looking to D. looking for

**27.** I did not see the point of ......... waiting for them, so I went home.

A. hanging around B. hang on
C. hang together D. hanging up

**28.** He lost confidence and ......... of the deal at the last minute.

A. backed out B. backed on
C. backed down D. backed onto

**29.** To the dismay of all the students, the class monitor was ..... berated by the principal at a school assembly.

A. critically B. ignominiously
C. prudently D. fortuitously

**30.** All attempts to revive the fishing industry were ..... failure.

A. foredoomed to B. heading at
C. predicted for D. estimated to

**31.** There are ..... parked outside than yesterday.

A. fewer cars
B. few cars
C. less cars
D. a small number of cars

**32.** The minister had to ..... some awkward questions from reporters.
A. fend B. fend at
C. fend out D. fend off

**33.** The ..... of evidence was on the side of the plaintiff since all but one of the witnesses testified that his story was correct.
A. propensity B. force
C. preponderance D. brunt

**34.** Attention to detail is ..... of a fine craftsman.
A. hallmark B. stamp
C. seal of authority D. authenticity

**35.** Behaving in a ............ and serious way, even in a ............ situation, makes people respect you.
A. calm, difficult
B. steady, angry
C. flamboyant, tricky
D. cool astounding

**36.** Along with a sharp rise in ........., a recession would eventually result in more men, women, and children living in ........... .
A. crime, apathy
B. fatalities, poor
C. deaths, slums
D. unemployment, poverty

**37.** The government has .............. to provide financial aid to the ones ........... by severe floods in the city.
A. desired, troubled B. promised, havoc
C. failed, affected D. wanted, struck

**38.** An airplane with ............ passengers on board made an unscheduled ......... as the airport to which it was heading was covered with thick fog.
A. imitable, slip B. faulty, stop
C. variety, halt D. numerous, landing

**39.** Deemed universities ............ huge fees, but have not been successful in providing ............... education to our students.
A. collect, maintaining
B. pay, better
C. ask, good
D. charge, quality

**40.** If the banks desire to ......... profit, they should get rid of ......... measures.
A. lose, concentrate
B. increase, populist
C. earn, unhealthy
D. maximise, traditional

**41.** Leadership defines what the future should look like and ...... people with that vision.
A. aligns B. develops
C. trains D. encourages

**42.** We upset ourselves by responding in an ...... manner to someone else's actions.
A. unabashed B. irrational
C. arduous D. arguable

**43.** All the people involved in that issue feel a great ...... to his suggestion.
A. contradiction B. adherence
C. indifference D. repugnance

**44.** These elections will be remembered as much for its anti-incumbency mood as for its ...... mandate.
A. invincible B. rational
C. unprecedented D. deliberate

**45.** How do you expect us to stay in such a ...... building even if it can be hired on a nominal rent?
A. scruffy B. disperate
C. fragmented D. robust

**46.** ...... efforts from all concerned are required to raise the social and economic conditions of our countrymen.
A. Perpetual B. Dynamic
C. Massive D. Exploring

**47.** Many companies see technology as a ...... for a whole host of business problems.
A. consideration B. preference
C. linking D. panacea

**48.** Known as devout and serious person, she also has ...... sense of humour.
A. better B. plentiful
C. quick D. good

**49.** The matter would have become serious if ...... action had not been taken.
A. hasty B. fast
C. timely D. unusual

**50.** The ...... with which he is able to yield the paint brush is really remarkable.
A. ease B. practice
C. majesty D. sweep

**51.** You must ensure the correctness of the information before ................ .
A. drawing B. enabling
C. learning D. jumping

**52.** The rocket ................ the target and did not cause any casualty.
A. sensed B. reached
C. missed D. exploded

**53.** It is desirable to take ................ in any business if you want to make profit.
A. advice B. risk
C. loan D. recourse

**54.** They wasted all the money on purchase of some ................ items.
A. excellent B. important
C. significant D. trivial

**55.** When he found the wallet his face glowed but soon it faded as the wallet was ................ .
A. empty B. vacant
C. recovered D. stolen

**56.** He has served the country by ................ many significant positions.
A. appointing
B. creating
C. developing
D. holding

**57.** The frequent errors are a result of the student's ................ .
A. talent B. smartness
C. carelessness D. perception

**58.** The robbers eventually ................ in breaking into the house.
A. succeeded B. decided
C. caught D. trained

**59.** I finally ................ her to stay another day.
A. advised B. persuaded
C. suggested D. called

**60.** Most of the people who ................ the book exhibition were teachers.
A. witnessed B. presented
C. conducted D. attended

# ANSWERS

| 1 | 2 | 3 | 4 | 5 | 6 | 7 | 8 | 9 | 10 |
|---|---|---|---|---|---|---|---|---|---|
| A | B | C | A | C | B | C | C | B | D |
| **11** | **12** | **13** | **14** | **15** | **16** | **17** | **18** | **19** | **20** |
| C | A | C | C | C | B | D | B | B | D |
| **21** | **22** | **23** | **24** | **25** | **26** | **27** | **28** | **29** | **30** |
| B | C | C | B | C | C | D | A | B | A |
| **31** | **32** | **33** | **34** | **35** | **36** | **37** | **38** | **39** | **40** |
| A | D | D | A | A | D | C | D | C | B |
| **41** | **42** | **43** | **44** | **45** | **46** | **47** | **48** | **49** | **50** |
| A | A | D | C | A | A | D | D | C | A |
| **51** | **52** | **53** | **54** | **55** | **56** | **57** | **58** | **59** | **60** |
| A | C | B | D | A | D | C | A | B | D |

# 11 Sentence Improvement

*One may use the same words in many ways but the best way is only one that makes the perfect usage of the words and conveys the proper meaning of the expression. Try it yourself in the following questions.*

## Multiple Choice Questions

**Directions:** *In these questions, a part of the sentence is bold. Below are given alternatives to the bold part at A, B and C which may improve the sentence. Choose the correct alternative. In case no improvement is needed, your answer is 'D'.*

**1.** Discreet salience **is extremely important** to create that 'irresistible-yet-unattainable' image for brands that want to take India seriously

A. was extremely important
B. is mainly important
C. was important extremely
D. No Improvement

**2.** This, over a designer outfit that he wanted for a friend's party and **that his sensitive** parents refused him.

A. which his sensitive
B. which his insensitive
C. that his insensitive
D. No Improvement

**3.** Goa was full of non-Goa property hunters **rushing about buying up the place** like tomorrow was an expired lease.

A. rushing in buying up the place
B. rushed about buying up the place
C. rushing about to buy up the place
D. No Improvement

**4.** Property hunting is a **tired and hungry** making business.

A. is a tiresome and hungry
B. is a tiring and hungry
C. is a tiring and waste
D. No Improvement

**5.** Cultural differences aside, **till luxury need speaks** in a manner that befits.

A. luxury still needs to speak
B. luxury still need to speak
C. luxury till need to speak
D. No Improvement

**6.** Indian food—the culinary avatar of the subcontinent's social history presented on a platter—**is without doubt the best food** in the world.

A. is undoubtedly the greatest food
B. is without doubt greatest food
C. is best food without doubt
D. No Improvement

**7.** It must retain the language of poetry. **It needed to create** stories, and not statements.
A. It needed creating
B. It needs creating
C. It needs to create
D. No Improvement

**8.** This year, Asia-Pacific has become the first region **to reach aggregate profiting** in biotech.
A. to reach aggregated profitability
B. to reach aggregate profitability
C. to reach aggregate of profit
D. No Improvement

**9.** India is deviating to embrace the West. If Western luxury brands deviate a little, **albeit selectively**, they will find rich Indian arms open far and wide.
A. though selectively
B. however selectively
C. albeit selectedly
D. No Improvement

**10.** China and India continued to attract attention and deals, motivated by the desire to increase access to these **largest and growing** drug markets and by the need to lower the costs of drug development.
A. larger and growing
B. large and growing
C. larger and grown
D. No Improvement

**11.** Luxury brands are **still above of the** clover curve here, with their elite (small) audiences.
A. still ahead of the
B. still in the
C. still far of the
D. No Improvement

**12.** Agencies **hence needed to be** sure of returns before investing, say admen.
A. hence needs to be
B. so needs to be
C. hence need to be
D. No Improvement

**13.** India is still a nascent market and that's the spirit everyone's **looking at it**.
A. looking for it B. looking in it
C. looking with it D. No Improvement

**14.** Questioning the state's move to allow women to serve liquor but not dance in bars **of the ground that** dancing aroused physical lust.
A. on the grounds that
B. of the grounds that
C. over the grounds that
D. No Improvement

**15.** For England the positives from their crushing series lose come in the shape of James Anderson and Kevin Pietersen, **both of which** have made significant strides up the rankings.
A. both of which B. both of whom
C. both of who D. No Improvement

**16.** International campaigns can work well for luxury here, **but context cannot be** ignored.
A. so context cannot be
B. but context cannot
C. but context couldn't
D. No Improvement

**17.** For one, the Indian luxury context, **while evolved rapidly**, still has its own meaning, and its own implications.
A. while evolved rapid
B. which evolving rapidly
C. while evolving rapidly
D. No Improvement

**18.** But too much of availability can compromise a luxury brand or **made it lose** its lustre.
A. make her lose B. make him lose
C. make it lose D. No Improvement

**19.** Still, it's under-the-upper **layers themselves who** are aspiring for slivers of luxury.
A. layers themselves which
B. layer itself who
C. layers themself which
D. No Improvement

**20.** It is like saying Hindi movies, with skimpily dressed dancers, would **effect public** order.
A. effect your B. affect public
C. affected public D. No Improvement

**21.** The court held that a few women being involved in prostitution was no **justice to deny other** bar girls the right to livelihood.
A. justification to declare other
B. justification to deny other
C. justice to let other
D. No Improvement

**22.** All-rounder cricketer has also made some progress **over the** player rankings.
A. above the B. at the
C. up the D. No Improvement

**23.** Former minister on Sunday **joined hands** with a suspended Lok Sabha member to float a new political outfit.
A. folded hands
B. walked hand in hand
C. shaked hands
D. No Improvement

**24.** Pakistan's former ministers will meet in London on Monday **to ask** a strategy to return home from exile.
A. to chalk out
B. to negotiate
C. to create
D. No Improvement

**25.** It's a family potboiler, medical thriller and political drama **all in one**—except that it's all too real and all too grim.
A. all 3 in one
B. all coupled into one
C. all rolled into one
D. No Improvement

**26.** India's efforts to get international support for its civil nuclear energy programme got **a go ahead on** Sunday as Germany indicated it would not come in the way of the India-US nuclear deal.
A. a life in B. a boost on
C. a boost at D. No Improvement

**27.** Is it time for old bungalows to **bite the dust**?
A. go down B. get down
C. come down D. No Improvement

**28.** The bungalows was an outward manifestation of a certain **way in life**, and with that era gone.
A. way for life B. way of life
C. way at life D. No Improvement

**29.** The builder Mittals will reportedly **raise their money**-raking high-rise behind it.
A. highten their money
B. rise their money
C. raise there money
D. No Improvement

**30.** The impatient present has usually demolished **more of the** past before we wake up to the irretrievable loss.
A. much of B. much of their
C. much of the D. No Improvement

**31.** Preservation is a romantic notion; demolition **quiet** more practical reasons.
A. has many, B. had many,
C. have many, D. No Improvement

**32.** You must get back to your **charming self** and impress the audience with your social skills.
A. own self B. main self
C. own uniqueness D. No Improvement

**33.** Stay focused on your goals and don't **get disturbed by** non-materialistic possessions.
A. get involved by
B. get betrayed by
C. get distracted by
D. No Improvement

**34.** You may appear more optimistic than your detractors **may want it to be.**
A. want you to be
B. wish yourself to be
C. seek you be
D. No Improvement

**35.** There are a number of mineral springs in the Czech territory, which **has been used** for medicinal purposes since the early 15th century.
A. have been used B. had been used
C. has being used D. No Improvement

**36.** The picturesque mountains **offer**s excellent bungee jumping spots.

A. shows B. provides
C. offer D. No Improvement

**37.** Begin your **meal with** traditional faves like potato soup, beef soup with liver dumplings or dill soup made from sour milk.

A. meals with B. meal in
C. meals of D. No Improvement

**38.** You can also **go to the** National Museum building and the famous Prague State Opera.

A. went to B. visit the
C. saw D. No Improvement

**39.** If they close the Gulf for a **length of time** to shipping, then certainly we could look at $150, probably higher.

A. larger amount of time
B. larger duration of time
C. larger amount of hours
D. No Improvement

**40. More of them** are owned by the state and even the privately-owned ones are open to the public.

A. Most of which B. Most of them
C. Most of all D. No Improvement

**41.** Constructed in the ninth century by the Prince Booivoj, the castle has transformed **oneself** from a wooden fortress surrounded by earthen bulwarks to the imposing form it has today.

A. himself B. herself
C. itself D. No Improvement

**42.** Apart from frequent art exhibitions, **their are also** permanent collections devoted to archaeology, anthropology, mineralogy, natural history and numismatics.

A. there is also B. there are also
C. their are also D. No Improvement

**43.** You can visit the Czech Museum of Fine Arts, **at a** permanent exhibition on Czech Kubism.

A. with a
B. for a
C. in a
D. No Improvement

**44.** Tensions **above** Iran come at a time of strong demand for energy.

A. under B. inside
C. over D. No Improvement

**45.** Because its shores line the narrow Straits of Hormuz, Iran **could quickly hit** both military and commercial shipping.

A. will quickly hit
B. shall quickly hit
C. will be quick hitting
D. No Improvement

**46.** For most people who exercise **at the** morning, there is no getting around the question: Eat and run? Or run and eat later?

A. in the
B. in
C. at the time of
D. No Improvement

**47.** Are ad agencies even attempting to peer into the keyhole of this indulgence sanctum to garner consumer insights **ahead of** the curve?

A. above
B. over
C. within
D. No Improvement

**48.** Too many people rush into the world of credit and don't stop to think about how **their actions could affect their** credit score and ability to qualify for credit in the future.

A. their actions may affect their
B. their actions might affect their
C. their actions will affect their
D. No Improvement

**49.** According to the report, **number of deal with** vaccines were energized by concerns around avian flu, SARS, and biodefence products, while looming patent expirations led to more deals in generics.

A. number of deals in
B. number of deal in
C. number of deals with
D. No Improvement

**50.** This is how the Bombay High Court responded to the state government's purported **moral stand which** dance bars were causing grave harm to society.

A. moral stand in
B. moral stand at
C. moral stand that D. No Improvement

**51.** If you have a high credit limit, use **at least a** third of it.

A. atleast a
B. at last a
C. utmost a
D. No Improvement

**52.** Fitness experts will say that **first eating provides** fuel for a proper workout.

A. eating in the beginning provides
B. first eat provides
C. eating first provides
D. No Improvement

**53.** One study that examined the claim directly in 1995 found that a group of people did **burned much calories from fat on days** when they exercised on an empty stomach than on days when they had a small breakfast first.

A. burn more calories from fat on days
B. burn more calorie from fat on days
C. burnt more calories from fat on days
D. No Improvement

**54.** Carefree children spent their afternoons **to run about barefoot**, their clothes dusty, and telltale twigs of the neighbour's mango tree in their hair.

A. running barefoot in the sun
B. run about barefoot in the sun
C. running about barefoot in the sun
D. No Improvement

**55.** A year ago, a 13-year-old girl attempted suicide because her mother **refuses to pay his** mobile bills.

A. refuses to pay her
B. refused to pay her
C. refused to pay his
D. No Improvement

# ANSWERS

| 1 | 2 | 3 | 4 | 5 | 6 | 7 | 8 | 9 | 10 |
|---|---|---|---|---|---|---|---|---|---|
| D | C | D | B | A | D | C | C | D | B |
| **11** | **12** | **13** | **14** | **15** | **16** | **17** | **18** | **19** | **20** |
| C | C | D | A | C | D | C | C | C | C |
| **21** | **22** | **23** | **24** | **25** | **26** | **27** | **28** | **29** | **30** |
| B | C | C | A | C | B | D | B | D | C |
| **31** | **32** | **33** | **34** | **35** | **36** | **37** | **38** | **39** | **40** |
| A | D | C | A | D | C | A | B | D | B |
| **41** | **42** | **43** | **44** | **45** | **46** | **47** | **48** | **49** | **50** |
| C | B | A | C | D | A | D | C | A | C |
| **51** | **52** | **53** | **54** | **55** | | | | | |
| C | C | A | C | B | | | | | |

# 12 Reordering Words & Sentences

*Different words form a sentence and convey their meaning only when arranged in a proper order. A Paragraph is formed from sentences, it will convey its true meaning and purpose only when the sentences are arranged in a proper manner. Try and practise it in this exercise.*

## Multiple Choice Questions

**Directions (Qs. 1 to 20):** *In the following questions, some parts of the sentence have been jumbled up. You are required to rearrange these parts which are labelled P, Q, R and S to produce the correct sentence. Choose the option with proper sequence.*

**1.** We are doing
P : to the people
Q : to give relief
R : all we can
S : but more funds are needed
The correct sequence should be
A. P Q R S B. R Q P S
C. Q P R S D. S P Q R

**2.** The man
P : when he was
Q : in the office last evening
R : could not finish
S : all his work
The correct sequence should be
A. P Q R S B. Q R S P
C. R Q P S D. R S P Q

**3.** The people decided
P : they were going
Q : how much
R : to spend
S : on the construction of the school building
The correct sequence should be
A. Q P R S B. P Q R S
C. P R Q S D. S Q P R

**4.** The man said that
P : those workers
Q : would be given a raise
R : who did not go on
S : strike last month
The correct sequence should be
A. P Q R S B. P R S Q
C. Q P R S D. R S P Q

**5.** I think
P : the members
Q : are basically in agreement
R : of the group
S : on the following points
The correct sequence should be
A. R Q P S B. S Q R P
C. P R Q S D. P Q S R

**6.** While it was true that
P : I had
Q : to invest in industry
R : some lands and houses
S : I did not have ready cash

The correct sequence should be —

A. P Q R S B. P R S Q
C. S Q P R D. Q P R S

**7.** P : But for your help
Q : to finish this work
R : it would not have been possible
S : in time
The correct sequence should be
A. P R Q S B. S P Q R
C. R P Q S D. P Q R S

**8.** The boy
P : in the competition
Q : who was wearing spectacles
R : won many prizes
S : held in our college
The correct sequence should be
A. P Q R S B. R P S Q
C. Q R P S D. Q P S R

**9.** About 200 years ago,
P : in the south of India
Q : an old king
R : ruled over a kingdom
S : called Rajavarman
The correct sequence should be
A. Q S R P B. P Q R S
C. Q P S R D. Q S P R

**10.** P : his land
Q : a wooden plough
R : the Indian peasant still uses
S : to cultivate
The correct sequence should be
A. R Q P S B. Q P S R
C. S R Q P D. R Q S P

**11.** He was a man,
P : even if he had to starve
Q : who would not beg
R : borrow or steal
S : from anyone
The correct sequence should be
A. P Q R S B. P R Q S
C. Q R S P D. Q P R S

**12.** P : in the progress of
Q : universities play a crucial role
R : our civilization
S : in the present age
The correct sequence should be
A. S Q P R B. Q R S P
C. Q R P S D. S Q R P

**13.** P : far out into the sea
Q : for the next two weeks there were further explosions
R : which hurled
S : ashes and debris
The correct sequence should be
A. Q R P S B. R S P Q
C. Q R S P D. S R P Q

**14.** William Shakespeare,
P : in his lifetime
Q : the great English dramatist
R : wrote thirty-five plays
S : and several poems
The correct sequence should be
A. P Q R S B. R S P Q
C. Q S R P D. Q R S P

**15.** Whenever I am,
P : with an old friend of mine
Q : in New Delhi
R : to have dinner
S : I always try
The correct sequence should be
A. S Q P R B. Q S R P
C. R P S Q D. P R Q S

**16.** P : I don't know
Q : must have thought
R : what people sitting next to me
S : but I came away
The correct sequence should be
A. R S Q P B. R Q S P
C. P Q R S D. P R Q S

**17.** P : in estimating the size of the earth
Q : but they were hampered by the lack of instruments of precision
R : ancient astronomers
S : used methods which were theoretically valid
The correct sequence should be
A. R P Q S B. P R Q S
C. R S Q P D. R P S Q

**18.** P : It is a pity that
Q : by offering a handsome dowry
R : a number of parents think that
S : they will be able to ensure the happiness of their daughters

The correct sequence should be

A. S Q R P  B. P R S Q
C. P S R Q  D. P R Q S

**19.** The common man
P : in nurturing
Q : a more active role
R : communal harmony
S : should play

The correct sequence should be

A. P R S Q  B. S Q P R
C. S Q R P  D. P R Q S

**20.** The doctor
P : able to find out
Q : what has caused
R : the food poisoning
S : has not been

The correct sequence should be

A. S P R Q  B. P R Q S
C. P R S Q  D. S P Q R

**Directions (Qs. 21 to 40):** *A number of sentences are given below which when properly sequenced form a coherent paragraph. Each sentence is labelled as abcdef...... Choose the most logical order of sentences from among the given choices to construct a coherent paragraph:*

**21.** (a) Parts of northern region were pounded by heavy rains today,
(b) Vehicular traffic came to a near halt.
(c) As mid and high altitude areas of Himachal Pradesh were in grip of severe cold wave with snow lashing the tribal areas and mid ranges receiving showers.
(d) As the sky remained heavily overcast with dark clouds reducing the visibility considerably.
(e) A large number of tourists were forced to buy heavy woollens and stay indoors due to inclement weather.

A. ecabd  B. adecb
C. edabc  D. acbde

**22.** (a) The idea is that students should be able to find employment for themselves after the course.
(b) The Central Board of Secondary Education is planning a revamp of its vocational courses.
(c) For this it is necessary to tie up with the industry as well as mobilise schools for their support.
(d) While others will be made less academic and more in tune with the needs of the industry.
(e) A number of courses have been identified as 'deadwood' and will be done away with.

A. bedac  B. abcde
C. acebd  D. baced

**23.** (a) Clearly, age is not a deterrent in one's choice of learning.
(b) Perhaps, it was because of her childhood desire.
(c) When Rachna came to Delhi eight years back, she had not anticipated a career in the field of art.
(d) She has been successful in the various exhibitions that she has been part of in terms of business.
(e) She had got into expressing her thoughts with the help of a brush and colours only because her daughter refused to get initiated into it.
(f) She feels that her use of colour appeals to people.

A. aedcbf  B. cdefba
C. cebadf  D. acdebf

**24.** (a) The rehabilitation record has been dismal.
(b) It has been two years years since the earthquake rudely rattled the people of Gujarat.
(c) And since then, life has been a constant struggle.
(d) The quake set Gujarat's clock back by 10 years.
(e) Things changed forever.

A. bedca B. bcade
C. dbace D. edcba

**25.** (a) In fact, success in exams depended on rote learning from old notes.
(b) when he was studying civil engineering in a college in Gujarat.
(c) He was detained for lack of attendance.
(d) Lectures were soporific, classes rarely worth attending and 80 per cent attendance compulsory.
(e) The college became a trap he hated.
(f) His is a plight many engineers across India would identify with.
(g) He found the going tough.
A. abcdgef B. bgdacef
C. fabcdge D. abcdefg

**26.** (a) In a country that has close to 600 recognised engineering colleges, there are only seven IITs.
(b) Barring a few exeptions, the academic atmosphere in these is moribund.
(c) The very best students usually get there.
(d) many waste themselves in frustration.
(e) Most of those who get into engineering are good students.
(f) but about 1.25 lakh others and up in the remaining colleges.
A. aecfbd B. abecdf
C. abcdef D. acfbed

**27.** (a) Whatever the job market, common wisdom says that IIT graduates will find jobs where others have failed.
(b) The IIT brand name is a ticket to success.
(c) When recruiters go headhunting, the IITs are still top of their list.
(d) Its possessor is understood to have an excellent academic record and the will to succeed.
(e) In the job market, that counts.
A. bdeac B. abcde
C. abdce D. dbace

**28.** (a) It will pave the way .........
(b) signalling a new beginning in strategic ties......
(c) for a tangible Indian economic presence in Iran and Central Asia.
(d) Iran has offered India valuable road linkages to central Asia ......
(e) aimed at promoting peace and economic cooperation in the region.
A. dbeac B. debca
C. acebd D. abced

**29.** (a) A good college is essential for a successful career and admissions are based on marks.
(b) The marks-based system followed by all the boards in the country recognises only a small percentage of students as successful.
(c) The marks one scores in the crucial board exams dictate the path his life takes.
(d) Anyone scoring below a certain percentage is automatically branded a 'failure'.
(d) So if you cannot make it into the best college, your career is over even before it has started.
A. abcde B. bcdea
C. bdcae D. abdec

**30.** (a) The project has already started on an experimental basis in the west district.
(b) A website is soon going to be launched where application forms can be downloaded and submitted.
(c) Standing in a queue at a government office to submit application form will be a thing of the past.
(d) A unique code will be alloted while submitting the form which will help in finding the status of the application.
A. abcd B. dabc
C. cbda D. badc

**31.** (a) To curb bio-terrorism is a difficult task.
(b) To check these attacks and lessen their impact, we need an impartial team of sincere, strong and dedicated men.
(c) The media can play a strong role in stopping this unnecessary spread of panic.
(d) Since bio-terrorism is not visible or easily detectable, it can be used often.
(e) Men who honour the lives of their fellow countrymen before their own.

A. abcde B. dabce
C. adbec D. acbed

**32.** (a) He was dying.
(b) No one was ready to touch him as even shifting him from one place to another would lead to profuse bleeding.
(c) He was a five-day old infant, premature and bleeding profusely.
(d) Even if injected one small needle, blood would ooze out and continue to flow for an hour at a stretch.
(e) This small being had haematoma, a thick blood clot in his brain.
A. edbca B. cabde
C. eacdb D. cedba

**33.** (a) The day I don't treat a patient, I feel .......
(b) I have enough to eat, I crave for blessings now.
(c) But if a financially weak patient gives me only ₹ 50, I don't mind.
(d) Each month I do three to four operations free of cost.
(e) I have lost something in life.
(f) My consultation fee is ₹ 300.
A. fcdeab B. dfcbae
C. fcabde D. bdfcea

**34.** (a) When he was rushed to the nearby Primary Health Centre after his fall, the doctor referred him to a hospital.
(b) This worsened his injury.
(c) Had a little precaution been exercised after the accident, Tarun would have continued with his gymnastic classes.
(d) He was paralysed from waist downwards when he fell from the vaulting horse while doing gymnastics.
(e) However, the doctor forgot to tell Tarun's parents to take him on a stretcher as he had suffered spinal injuries.
(f) Tarun is wheelchair bound for two years.
A. fdeabc B. abcdef
C. fdcaeb D. fdbcae

**35.** (a) As the temperature rises, staying hydrated can become a greater challenge for people exercising both indoors and out.
(b) Several things can influence this process, including age, gender, physical conditioning. humidity and a lack of sufficient fluids.
(c) In hot weather, individuals can lose as much as two quarts of sweat per hour.
(d) As we age, we have a lower perceived level of thirst in response to fluid loss and early stages of dehydration.
(e) If not replenished, this can lead to dehydration, heat exhaustion and even heatstroke.
A. abcde B. dbcae
C. cbdea D. acebd

**36.** (a) The leopard was discovered in the servant quarters of a farmhouse.
(b) The injuries appeared to have been caused by the paws of the leopard, and were not teeth wounds.
(c) It took the wild life officials, Delhi Police and Delhi zoo vets eight hours to capture the leopard that had wandered into a factory in south Delhi.
(d) The leopard then jumped into the factory where the workers managed to lock it in a small generator room before calling in the police.
(e) Before its capture, the leopard attacked two women and a man in the farmhouse.
A. aebdc B. bdaec
C. eadbc D. adbec

**37.** (a) Police suspect a carpenter working at John's house as he has not reported for work since the day the boy went missing.
(b) John did not return home in the afternoon.
(c) John's mother had herself put the boy on the vehicle in the morning.
(d) John smiled at him and was last seen walking up to him.
(e) His parents called the school and were told John had not been to school at all and had been marked absent.
(f) He was about to enter the school when someone called out his name.

A. cfdbea B. debfca
C. bfdaec D. abcdef

**38.** (a) However, the mayhem over the last few months is deeply shocking.
(b) Yet I do not agree with the prophets of doom who see nothing but disaster ahead.
(c) When I came back to my motherland India after a stay in Switzerland, I felt I was trading a hotbed of intense religious and political violence for peace and quiet.
(d) I think our nation is searching for an identity.
(e) And a new vision of the future will emerge from this.
A. abcde B. cabde
C. cebad D. bedca

**39.** (a) An integrated and combined approach was required to reveal the mystery of the brain —its structure, composition and function.
(b) Since the early 80's, scientists were clear that the brain would be the final frontier to conquer.
(c) The initiative was flagged off and came to be known as the Human Brain Project.
(d) But that wasn't easy because understanding the brain involved completely integrating information from the level of the gene to the level of behaviour.
(e) To fulfill this requirement a group of American scientists from various disciplines decided to work together.
A. acbed B. bdaec
C. abdec D. badec

**40.** (a) A product is something that is made in a factory, a brand is something that is bought by a consumer.
(b) The trick therefore, lies in the brand positioning.
(c) For a consumer, the satisfaction of becoming associated with a name that is the 'best' and the 'leader' is far more important and at times makes him ignore the price factor.
(d) Brands come and go.
(e) Still there are those who manage to stay and develop an affinity with consumers.
A. aebcd B. debac
C. decab D. aecdb

# ANSWERS

| 1 | 2 | 3 | 4 | 5 | 6 | 7 | 8 | 9 | 10 |
|---|---|---|---|---|---|---|---|---|---|
| B | D | A | B | C | C | A | C | A | D |
| **11** | **12** | **13** | **14** | **15** | **16** | **17** | **18** | **19** | **20** |
| C | A | C | D | B | D | C | B | B | D |
| **21** | **22** | **23** | **24** | **25** | **26** | **27** | **28** | **29** | **30** |
| D | A | C | A | B | D | A | A | C | C |
| **31** | **32** | **33** | **34** | **35** | **36** | **37** | **38** | **39** | **40** |
| C | D | B | C | D | A | A | B | B | B |

# 13 Comprehension Passages

## PASSAGES

**Directions:** *Read the following passages and answer the questions given below each.*

### PASSAGE-1

In the Roman times, defected enemies were generally put to death as criminals for having offended the emperor of Rome. In the middle ages, however, the practice of ransoming of returning prisoners in exchange for money became common. Though some saw this custom as a step towards a most humane society, the primary reasons behind it were economic rather than humanitarian.

In those times, rulers had only a limited ability to raise taxes. They could neither force their subject to fight nor pay them to do so. The promise of material compensation in the form of goods and ransom was therefore the only way of inducing combatants to participate in a war. In the middle ages, the predominant incentive for the individual soldiers was the expectation of spoils. Although collecting ransom clearly brought financial gain, keeping a prisoner and arranging for his exchange had its cost. Consequently, procedures were devised to reduce transaction costs.

One such device was a rule asserting that the prisoner had to assess his own value. This compelled the prisoner to establish a value *without too much distortion;* indicating too low a value would increase, the captive's chances of being killed, while indicating too high a value would either ruin him financially or create a prohibitively expensive ransom that would also result in death.

**1.** It can be inferred from the passage that a medieval soldier

A. was less likely to kill captured members of opposing armies than was a soldier of the Roman Empire

B. was similar to a 20th century terrorist in that he operated on a basically independent level and was motivated solely by economic incentives

C. had few economic options and chose to fight because it was the only way to earn an adequate living

D. was motivated to spare prisoners' lives by humanitarian rather than economic ideals

**2.** Which of the following best describes the change in policy from executing prisoners in Roman times to ransoming prisoners in the middle ages?

A. The emperors of Rome demanded more respect than did medieval rulers and thus Roman subjects went to greater lengths to defend their nation

B. It was a reflection of the lesser degree of direct control medieval ruler had over subjects

C. It became a show of strength and honour warrior of the middles ages to be able to capture and return their enemies

D. Medieval soldiers were not as hum-anitarian as their ransoming practices might have indicated

3. The primary purpose of the passage is to
   A. discuss the economic basis of the medieval practice of exchanging prisoners for ransom
   B. examine the history of the treatment of prisoner of war
   C. emphasize the importance of a warrior's code of honour during the middle ages
   D. explore a way of reducing the cost of ransom

4. The author uses the phrase *"without too much distortion"* in order to
   A. indicate that prisoners would fairly assess their worth
   B. emphasize the important role medieval prisoners played in determining whether they should be ransomed
   C. explain how prisoners often paid more than an appropriate ransom in order to increase their chances for survival
   D. suggest that captors and captives often had understanding relationships

## PASSAGE-2

The world dismisses curiosity by calling it idle or mere idle curiosity—even though curious persons are seldom idle. Parents do their best to extinguish curiosity in their children because it makes life difficult to be faced everyday with a string of unanswerable questions about what makes fire hot or why grass grows. Children whose curiosity survives parental discipline are invited to join our university. With the university, they go on asking their questions and trying to find the answers. In the eyes of a scholar, that is what a university is for. Some of the questions which the scholars ask, seem to the world to be scarcely worth asking, let alone answering. They asked questions too minute specialised for you and me to understand without years of explanation. If the world inquires of one of them why he wants to know the answer to a particular question he may say especially if he is a scientist, that the answer will in some obscure way make possible a new machine or weapon or gadget. He talks that way because he knows that the world understands and respects utility.

But to you who are now part of the university, he will say that he wants to know the answer simply because he does not know it, the way the mountain climber wants to climb a mountain, simply because it is there. Similarly a historian asked by an outsider why he studies history may come out with the argument that he has learnt to repeat on such occasions, something about knowledge of the past making it possible to understand the present and mould the future. But if you really want to know why a historian studies the past, the answer is much simpler, something happened and he would like to know what. All this does not mean that the answers which scholars find to their questions have no consequences. They may have enormous consequences but these seldom form the reason for asking the questions or pursuing the answers. It is true that scholars can be put to work answering questions for the sake of the consequences as thousands are working, now, for example, in search of a cure for cancer. But this is not the primary function of the scholars. For the consequences are usually subordinate to the satisfaction of curiosity.

1. According to the passage, the children make life difficult for their parents
   A. by their ceaseless curiosity
   B. by unceasing bombardment of questions
   C. by asking irrelevant questions
   D. by posing profound questions

2. The common people consider some of the questions that the scholars ask unimportant
   A. as they are too lazy and idle
   B. as they are too modest
   C. as it's beyond their comprehension
   D. as it is considered a waste of time

3. A historian really studies the past
   A. to comprehend the present and to reconstruct the future
   B. to explain the present and plan the future
   C. to understand the present and make fortune
   D. to understand the present and mould the future

4. Children whose curiosity survives parental discipline means
   A. children retaining their curiosity in spite of being discouraged by their parents
   B. children pursuing their mental curiosity
   C. children's curiosity subdued due to parents' intervention
   D. children being disciplined by their parents

5. According to the passage, parents do their best to discourage curiosity in their children
   A. because they have no time
   B. because they have no patience to answer them
   C. because they feel that their children ask stupid questions continuously
   D. because they are unable to answer all their questions

## PASSAGE-3

The factor of geographical distribution is equally, possibly even more, significant that English is spoken as first or native language in at least four continents of the world, Russian in two, Chinese and the Indian languages in one. English is without question the closest approach to a world language today. It goes without saying that no two persons ever have an identical command of their common language. Certainly, they have not precisely the same vocabulary. There are at least minor differences in pronunciation, indeed the same individual will not pronounce his vowels and consonants in absolutely identical fashion everytime he utters them. Everyone possesses, in addition, certain individual traits of grammatical form and syntactical order, constituting that peculiar and personal quality of language which we term as style. All of this is implicit in the well-known phrase, 'Style is the man.' No men are identical, no two styles are the same. If this be true of but two persons, the potential of differences resident in a language spoken by more than 200 million truly staggers imagination.

1. The author argues that English is the closest approach to a world language because
   A. there are more native speakers of English than of any other language
   B. English has less number of mutually unintelligible dialects
   C. the geographical distribution of English covers a much greater area
   D. other languages are much too complex to be world languages

2. The fact that the same individual will not pronounce his vowels and consonants identically everytime shows that
   A. literary style varies from person to person
   B. mutual intelligibility is a myth
   C. vocabulary varies from individual to individual
   D. no two persons speak the same language exactly the same way

3. It is evident from the passage that style is
   A. a strange type of language
   B. a language where one does not have to be particular about correctness and grammar
   C. language used in a particular way by an individual
   D. a question of grammatical and syntactic correctness

4. According to some authorities
   A. more people speak Chinese dialect than English
   B. more people speak English as an auxiliary language than as a first language
   C. more people speak English in the UK than in England
   D. about one-fourth of the world's population speaks English

5. The overall implication of the passage is that
   A. to suppose that 230 million people speak English as a native language would certainly be an underestimate
   B. the 55 million inhabitants of the British Isles speak like the 30 million inhabitants of the dominions and colonies
   C. a little less than half the native English speakers in the world live in the US

D. about one-tenth of the total English-speaking world population lives in British dominions and colonies

## PASSAGE-4

What is the future which awaits our children? The underlying assumption of the question, that Indian children have a common future, is itself dubious. It can legitimately be asked whether a student who is well-fed, attending a boarding school in the salubrious climate of the hills and learning to use computers has any future in common with a malnourished child who goes to a school with no blackboards, if indeed he does go to school. The latter may have no worthwhile future at ali. And it might be worthwhile to analyse the significance of this marginalisation of more than 75 per cent of the children of this country.

The failure to provide an infrastructure for primary education in the villages of India more than 40 years after independence is in sharp contrast with the sophisticated institutions, for technical institutes of higher education are funded by the government, which essentially means that the money to support them comes from taxes. And, since indirect taxation forms a substantial part of the taxes collected by the government, the financial burden is borne by all the people. L.K. Jha put it graphically when he observed that 25 paise of every rupee spent on educating an IIT student comes from the pockets of men and women whose children may never enter a proper classroom.

**1.** The author is trying to highlight which of the following?

A. Faulty system of direct taxes
B. The greatness of L.K. Jha
C. Need of sophisticated education for rural poor
D. Need to have common future for Indian children

**2.** Which of the following pairs have been termed as 'sharp contrast' by the author?

(*i*) Infrastructure for technical education
(*ii*) Lack of infrastructure for rural primary schools
(*iii*) 25 paise of every rupee earned by Government is spent on education
(*iv*) The financial burden of higher technical education is borne by all people
(*v*) 75% of children have limited opportunities

A. (*ii*) and (*iv*) B. (*ii*) and (*iii*)
C. (*iii*) and (*iv*) D. (*i*) and (*ii*)

**3.** Which of the following statements is not true?

(*i*) The author welcomes Govt.'s initiative on primary education
(*ii*) 75% of the children have a bright future
(*iii*) 25% cost of educating a technocrat comes from poor people

A. Only (*i*) B. Only (*ii*)
C. Only (*iii*) D. Only (*i*) and (*ii*)

**4.** According to the author, who among the following does not have a hopeful and prosperous future?

(*i*) All students from technical institutes
(*ii*) All students financially supported by the Government

A. Only (*i*) B. Only (*ii*)
C. Both (*i*) and (*ii*) D. Neither (*i*) nor (*ii*)

**5.** What seems to be the likely answer of the author to the question posed by him in the first sentence of the passage?

(*i*) There is no common future for the Indian children
(*ii*) The future is worthwhile for majority of Indian children
(*iii*) The majority may never enter a proper classroom

A. Only (*i*) B. Only (*ii*)
C. Only (*iii*) D. Both (*i*) and (*ii*)

**6.** What seems to be the purpose of the author in writing this passage?

A. Setting goals for children of upper middle class
B. Questioning the legitimacy of public schools
C. Highlighting lack of infrastructural facilities for primary education
D. Focusing on inequality in educational opportunities

## PASSAGE-5

Cyber crime is the branded stigma defacing the culture and magnanimity of computer technology. It is upkeeping the flag with indomitable triumph against developing computer technology worldwide.

Modern age is striding with marching steps of technology revolution beating the past decade of ancestral belief with ultimate care. Computer invention has unfolded the mystery of quick access with the objective of minimum manpower and cutting the time consumption parameters.

As each coin has dual face of its portrait, likewise computer technology is sick of creeping virus. Synthetic man-made dilemma of site hackers activation is causing setback to the expanding anchor of revolutionary device with great loss of time, economy and data profile as suffered by consumers. A recent report from Internet security firm Websense estimates that 85.6 per cent of all the unwanted e-mails contained links to spam sites. The company's data suggests that the number of malicious sites grew 233 per cent in the last six months and saw 671 per cent growth in the number of malicious sites during the last year. In June alone, the total number of e-mails detected as containing viruses increased by 600 per cent compared to May.

Chat rooms, blogs and message-boards where the users post comments have been identified as the top targets of hackers and spammers due to the high traffic these attract. According to Websense, 95 per cent of user-generated comments to blogs, chat rooms and message-boards during the first half of the year were malicious.

It is advisable not to click on spurious links and stay away from keying in passwords at unknown sites as they are most likely to be spammed. Hackers can steal your passwords and log in to your account and access critical information like account numbers and contact details among other things.

1. The above passage is:
   A. an advisory for the computer users.
   B. an advisory for the Internet users.
   C. a warning against possible threat to the Internet users.
   D. related to chat rooms, blogs and message boards.
2. People who use chat rooms and blogs,
   A. are safe and have no threats from spam.
   B. are more prone to malicious e-mails.
   C. create virus and hack the accounts of others.
   D. are unsafe.
3. According to the writer, it is not safe to:
   A. log on to spurious links.
   B. access one's own account frequently.
   C. have essential information stored in a computer.
   D. include data-stealing code.
4. Hackers and spammers, according to the writer, are:
   A. a new threat to the Internet users and the economy.
   B. only pranksters and not serious threat to the system.
   C. trained, professional technocrats who are an asset.
   D. not expert professionals.
5. Which word in the passage is synonym of *weblog*?
   A. blog B. password
   C. site D. e-mail
6. Which agency has assessed the data record with spam sites?
   A. Microsoft
   B. Internet security from Google
   C. Websense
   D. Spammers
7. Which month dominates the e-mails detection data record?
   A. May B. June
   C. Last six months D. Last year

## PASSAGE-6

Progress in life depends a good deal on crossing one threshold after another. Some time ago, a man watched his little nephew try to write his name. It was hard work, very hard work. The little boy had arrived at an effort threshold. Today he writes his name with comparative ease. No new threshold confronts him. This is the way with all of us. As soon as we cross one threshold, as soon as we conquer one difficulty, a new difficulty appears, or should appear. Some people make the mistake of steering clear of thresholds. Anything that requires genuine thinking and use of energy, they avoid. They prefer to stay in a rut where thresholds are not met. Probably, they have been at their job a number of years. Things are easy for them. They make no effort to seek out new obstacles to overcome. Real progress stops under such circumstances.

Some middle-aged and elderly people greatly enrich their lives by continuing to cross thresholds. One man went into an entirely new business when he was past middle life and made success of it, De Morgan didn't start to write novels until he was past sixty. Psychologists have discovered that man can continue to learn throughout his life. And it is undoubtedly better to try and fail than not to try at all. There one can be placed in the category of the Swiss mountaineer of whom it was said, *"He died climbing"*. When a new difficulty arises to obstruct your path, do not complain. Accept the challenge. Determine to cross this threshold as you have crossed numerous other thresholds in your past. In the words of a poet, do not rest but strive *to pass from dream to grander dream.*

**1.** What obstructs real progress in life?
   A. Remaining at one and the same post
   B. Avoiding the thinking and energy
   C. Shunning every work
   D. Stopping education

**2.** What does progress in life depend upon?
   A. Good habits
   B. Hardwork
   C. Overcoming one difficulty after another
   D. Spirit of service and cooperation

**3.** What does *'He died climbing'* signify?
   A. He died when he was climbing the hill
   B. He died before getting at the top
   C. He strove hard till the last moment of life
   D. He climbed the hill and then died

**4.** What does *'to pass from dream to grander dream'* mean?
   A. Always having greater and greater aspiration in life
   B. Seeing one good dream and then greater aspiration in life
   C. Making plan after plan
   D. Seeing one dream after the other

**5.** What did the man entering a new business past middle life do of his business?
   A. He miserably failed in it
   B. He achieved partial success
   C. He dropped the business after some time
   D. He achieved good success in it

**6.** How can you accomplish the most difficult tasks?
   A. By mobilizing all possible resources
   B. By avoiding all obstacles
   C. By sticking to hardwork
   D. By doing it bit by bit and persisting in the effort

**7.** What does De Morgan's life teach?
   A. That it is futile to learn many things
   B. That one is never old in case he has vigour
   C. That it is never too late to learn
   D. That creative writing can be made even late in life

**8.** How do middle-aged and elderly people add brilliance to their lives?
   A. By overcoming difficulty one after another
   B. By getting sycophants to surround them
   C. By making fine speeches
   D. By acquiring resourcefulness

**9.** What should we do when a new difficulty obstructs our path?
   A. Run away from it
   B. Be bold and face it
   C. Manoeuvre to get it removed
   D. Enlist other people's help to get it over

**10.** When did De Morgan start to write novels?
   A. When he was sixty years old
   B. When he was below sixty
   C. When he studied psychology
   D. None of these

## PASSAGE-7

It is *heartening* to know that if one had not had any heart attack earlier and he stops smoking, his chances of having a heart attack *drop* to that of a non-smoker in about six months' time. Stopping of smoking is also the single most effective means of secondary prevention (recurrence of a heart attack) in heart patients.

Smoking leads to pain and stiffness in the legs while walking. No amount of drugs can help. The only remedy is to give up smoking. If women smoke during pregnancy, there is an increased risk of death of the baby in the womb or soon after birth. Even where the baby survives, there is likelihood of delayed physical and intellectual development of the baby till it reaches 11 years of age.

Still worse the fact about smoking is that passive smoking is equally dangerous. Passive smokers are those who do not smoke but being in the company of smokers have to inhale smoke exhaled by the smokers They are equally prone to heart diseases, lung cancer and bronchitis, for no fault of theirs. It is seen that the incidence of these diseases is greater among women whose husbands are *heavy* smokers As such, every non-smoker has a fundamental right to safeguard himself against the danger of passive smoking. "Your smoking is injurious to my health and I have a right to stop you from smoking" could be the slogan against passive smoking. It is a great threat to the health of the individual, the family and the society. In fact one has to choose between health and smoking including passive smoking. *One cannot have both.*

Another matter of *grave concern* about smoking is the long time interval between the start of smoking habit and the manifestation of deadly diseases like cancer, chronic bronchitis and heart attack. People are generally not aware of the link between smoking and the misery they have to undergo years later and younger people often fall victim to this menacing habit under the wrong impression that they are *immune* to its disastrous effects, not realising that they are *heading* towards catastrophe. The prolonged incubation period of many tobacco-related diseases has prevented recognition of the size of the threat and the *grim* picture of chronic and life-threatening diseases.

**1.** What is "passive smoking"?
- A. Giving up the habit of smoking abruptly
- B. Exhaling smoke by a non-smoker
- C. Unintended intake of smoke exhaled by smokers
- D. Smoking cigarettes which are harmless in nature

**2.** The effects of passive smoking are more and more prominently observed among
- A. the children
- B. the smokers
- C. the wives of smokers
- D. the non-smokers

**3.** Which of the following is a heartening thing, according to the author?
- A. People who have had a heart attack stop smoking
- B. It takes only six months for any person to quit smoking
- C. The smoker carries the risk of heart attack for six months
- D. None of these

**4.** Which of the following statements is/are false in the context of the passage?
- (*i*) Passive smokers are not free from risk of heart diseases
- (*ii*) Intake of certain medicines helps recover pain and stiffness in legs caused by smoking
- (*iii*) Younger people are immune to the disastrous effects if their regular smoking is under control

A. (*i*) and (*ii*) only  B. (*ii*) and (*iii*) only
C. (*ii*) only  D. (*iii*) only

**5.** Which of the following is not mentioned in the passage as a likely result of smoking by women during pregnancy?
- A. Death of baby before birth
- B. Death of baby after birth
- C. Survival of baby with some abnormality
- D. Abnormal delay in the childbirth

**6.** Which of the following is considered by the author as a matter of "grave concern"?
 A. Inordinate delay in appearance of symptoms of hazards of smoking
 B. Long time required for giving up the habit of smoking
 C. Manifestation of deadly diseases like cancer, bronchitis, etc.
 D. Lack of awareness of people regarding the hazards of smoking

**7.** The youth feel that they are immune to the hazardous effects of smoking because
 A. these effects of smoking are not visible within a short time span
 B. they do not realise that they are heading towards disaster
 C. they feel a great thrill in acquiring the habit of smoking
 D. the link between smoking and its disastrous effects cannot be established

**8.** Which factor prevents people from realising the extent of threat of smoking hazards?
 A. Their lack of awareness of civic responsibilities
 B. Their firm belief that they are not immune to these hazards
 C. The less disastrous effects of tobacco-related diseases
 D. None of these

**9.** The last sentence of the third para *"One cannot have both"* means
 A. active smoking and passive smoking
 B. smoking and risk of heart diseases
 C. threat to the individual and also to the family
 D. None of these

**Directions (Qs. 10 to 12):** *Choose the word which is most nearly the* ***SAME*** *in meaning as the word given in bold capitals as used in the passage.*

**10. HEADING**
 A. crowning  B. marching
 C. adorning  D. title

**11. HEAVY**
 A. excessive  B. bulky
 C. large  D. thick

**12. DROP**
 A. roll  B. escape
 C. remove  D. reduce

**Directions (Qs. 13 to 15):** *Choose the word which is most nearly the* ***OPPOSITE*** *in meaning of the word given in bold capitals as used in the passage.*

**13. GRIM**
 A. dim  B. dark
 C. presentable  D. pleasant

**14. IMMUNE**
 A. free  B. vulnerable
 C. powerful  D. weak

**15. HEARTENING**
 A. cheerful  B. miserable
 C. frightening  D. dangerous

## PASSAGE-8

The happy man is the man who lives objectively, who has free affections and wide interests, who secures his happiness through these interests and affections and through the fact that they, in turn, make him an object of interest and affection to many others. To be the recipient of affection is a potent cause of happiness, but the man who demands affection is not the man upon whom it is *bestowed.* The man who receives affection is, speaking broadly, the man who gives it. But it is useless to attempt to give it as a calculation, in the way in which one might lend money at interest, for a calculated affection is not genuine and is not felt to be so by the recipient.

What then can a man do who is unhappy because he is encased in self? So long as he continues to think about the causes of his unhappiness, he continues to be self-centred and therefore does not get outside the vicious circle, if he is to get outside it, it must be genuine interests, not by simulated interests adopted merely as a medicine. Although this difficulty is real, there is nevertheless much that he can do if he has rightly diagnosed his trouble. If, for example, his trouble is due to a sense of sin, conscious or unconscious, he can first persuade his conscious mind that he has no reason to feel sinful and then proceed, to plant his rational conviction in his unconscious mind, concerning himself meanwhile with some more or less neutral activity. If he succeeds in *dispelling* the sense of sin, it is possible that genuine objective interests will arise spontaneously. If his trouble is self-pity, he can deal with it in the same manner after first persuading himself that there is nothing extraordinarily unfortunate in his circumstances.

If fear is his trouble, let him practise exercises designed to give courage. Courage has been recognised from time immemorial as an important virtue, and a great part of training of boys and young men has been devoted to producing a type of character capable of fearlessness in battle. But moral courage and intellectual courage have been much less studied, they also, however, have their technique. Admit to yourself everyday at least one painful truth, you will find this quite useful. Teach yourself to feel that life still be worth living even if you were not, as of course you are, immeasurably superior to all your friends in virtue and in intelligence. Exercises of this sort prolonged through several years will at last enable you to admit facts *without flinching* and will, in so doing, free you from the empire of fear over a very large field.

**1.** Who according to the passage is the happy man?
A. who is encased in self
B. who has free affection and wide interests
C. who is free from worldly passions
D. who has externally centre passions

**2.** According to the passage, calculated affection
A. appears to be false and fabricated
B. makes other pen-on to love you
C. turns into permanent affection over a period of time
D. leads to self-pity

**3.** Which of the following virtues, according to the passage, has been recognised for long as an important virtue?
A. Patriotism B. Sacrifice
C. Courage D. Self-consciousness

**4.** Which of the following, according to the passage, has not been studied much?
A. Feeling of guilt and self-pity
B. The state of mind of an unhappy man
C. How to get absorbed in other interests
D. Moral and intellectual courage

**5.** If a man is suffering from a sense of sin
A. he should invite opinion of others
B. he should admit his sin at once
C. he should consciously realize that he has no reason to feel sinful
D. he should develop a fearless character

**6.** What happens to a man who demands affection?
A. His feelings are reciprocated by others
B. He tends to take a calculated risk
C. He becomes a victim of a viscious circle
D. None of these

**7.** What should a man do who is suffering from the feeling of self-pity?
A. He should control his passions and emotions
B. He should persuade himself that everything is alright in his circumstances
C. He should seek affection from others
D. He should develop a feeling of fearlessness

**8.** How to get out of the viscious circle mentioned in the passage?
A. By practicing skills of concentration
B. By inculcating the habits of self-absorption
C. Being true to others and one's internal circumstances
D. None of these

**9.** Which of the following statements is not *true* in the context of the passage?
A. Happy man has wide interests
B. Courage has been recognized as an important virtue
C. Unhappy man is encased in self

D. Issue of intellectual courage has been extensively studied

**10.** Which of the following words is ***SIMILAR*** in meaning of the word **'bestowed'** as used in the passage?

A. Conferred B. Accommodated
C. Trusted D. Withdrawn

**11.** Which of the following statements is *true* in the context of the passage?

A. All passions stem from unhappiness
B. The happy man lives in subjectively
C. Any virtue has a dark side also
D. One feels happy if one receives affection

**12.** Which of the following words is ***SIMILAR*** in meaning to the word **'flinching'** as used in the passage?

A. Wincing B. Convincing
C. Explaining D. Debating

**13.** What happens when you think about cause of your unhappiness?

A. You try to introspect and look critically at yourself
B. You realize that the life can be lived in different ways
C. You try to practice exercise designed to give courage
D. You remain a self-centred person

**14.** What according to the passage is the real cause of happiness?

A. Material rewards and incentives received
B. Critical analysis of the happy state of mind
C. Affection received from others
D. Calculated risks taken

**15.** Which of the following words is ***OPPOSITE*** in meaning of the word **'dispelling'** as used in the passage?

A. Giving B. Accumulating
C. Projecting D. Scattering

## PASSAGE-9

Education, particularly higher education, is the obvious but crucially important instrument for nation building. As Confucious has said:

"If you are thinking of one year, plant rice. If you are thinking of a decade, plant trees. If you are thinking of a century, educate the people."

When we set about the task of higher education, we should be absolutely clear in our perception of the goals of education in the specific context of our nation's development. No *doubt,* one of the important aims of education would be to create the required range and nature of trained manpower assessed to be needed by different sectors of national growth. The entire educational apparatus must be geared progressively to fulfill the requirements of different phases of our growth in every sector—primary, secondary and *tertiary*. The aim must be to ensure that our country does not experience either *paucity,* or a *surfeit* of trained manpower in any specific segment of our economy. The requirements of our country, as a free, democratic, secular, socialist, nation, *aspiring* for rapid development, *entail* a specific recipe for our educational institutions. Today's educational institutions must therefore be developed accordingly and must regulate themselves to give the country the precise nature and quantum of trained manpower as projected by the requirements of our planned economy.

**1.** The author has quoted thoughts of Confucious to stress

A. importance of planting trees for human beings
B. the worthless efforts in planting rice
C. the benefits of investing in education
D. the need for assessing manpower requirement

**2.** Which statement cannot be made on the basis of the passage?

A. Higher education should keep in view the requirements of national economy
B. Higher education has not been employed for nation building
C. All levels of education have a role to play in nation's growth
D. In our country we need to have a specially planned educational system

3. The writer believes that
   A. there are no problems related to higher education
   B. investment in education is of long-range
   C. higher education should be used to assess manpower needs
   D. aims of higher education in India are absolutely clear

4. The author's expectations from higher education, are essentially
   A. unrealistic  B. confusing
   C. critical  D. vague

5. The writer indicates that
   A. higher education did not play any role in national growth
   B. primary education did not play any role in national growth
   C. our nation experiences paucity of trained manpower in many sectors
   D. today's higher education has no precise goals to achieve

6. Author has used the word 'apparatus' to indicate the
   A. scientific nature of education
   B. complicated organization demanded by education
   C. readily visible benefits of education
   D. entire equipment of education to perform particular function

7. Which of the following has not been conveyed by the passage?
   A. Education at any level can contribute in nation building
   B. Manpower needs in many areas can be fulfilled through higher education
   C. Rapid development of our nation is possible through higher education
   D. Present higher education does not ensure surfeit of trained manpower

8. This passage is likely to be addressed to
   A. politicians only
   B. scientists only
   C. students only
   D. cannot be said

9. Choose a suitable title to the passage:
   A. Manpower Planning in India
   B. Importance of Higher Education
   C. Demands of Higher Education
   D. Role of Higher Education in India

**Directions (Qs.10 to 12):** *Choose the word which is most nearly the **SAME** in meaning as the word given in bold capitals as used in the passage.*

10. **DOUBT**
   A. suspicion  B. certain
   C. definite  D. sure

11. **TERTIARY**
   A. last  B. important
   C. third  D. terminal

12. **ASPIRING**
   A. inquiring  B. awaiting
   C. involving  D. striving

**Directions (Qs.13 to 15):** *Choose the word which is most **OPPOSITE** in meaning as the word given in bold capitals as used in the passage.*

13. **PAUCITY**
   A. moderate  B. enormity
   C. mediocrity  D. littleness

14. **SURFEIT**
   A. abundance  B. redundancy
   C. repletion  D. lack

15. **ENTAIL**
   A. entitled  B. ensure
   C. dismiss  D. retain

## PASSAGE-10

Books are a great treasurehouse of knowledge. They are the living examples of man's *march* on the path to higher and higher civilisation. The great men who died long ago, live in their books. We feel their very personality and existence when we read their books. We feel as if they were conversing with us.

Books not only store civilization but also carry it forward. All coming generations get the light of knowledge from the books written by their ancestors and try to improve upon that knowledge. Civilization cannot make much *headway* in a country where there are not many *great* books. We get through books the latest knowledge in the fields of arts, science, commerce, etc. This knowledge is helpful to us and *enables* us to achieve success in the field of our choice.

Books are never failing friends. They never *desert* us, not even when all fair-weather friends have deserted us. They dispel the dark clouds of gloom from our minds and increase our happiness if we are already happy. Through the ages, the scriptures and other great books have provided immeasurable *solace* to the wounded and strife-torn humanity.

There may be books prescribed for some course or profession, but then there are books for general study. The books of literature—poetry, drama, novel, short stories, etc., are generally highly thrilling and inspiring if they are written by a good author. There may be tragic, comical or humorous books. The question is that of an individual's choice.

To be a lover of books, though not to be bookworm, is a sign of good luck. A voracious reader gets much *more pleasure* from reading books than a miser gets in hoarding money. The knowledge embedded in books is valueless; so is pleasure obtained from reading them. A good book absorbs the whole spirit of man; the reader's pleasure is indescribable.

**1.** Which of the following, according to the passage, is not true about books?
A. They are source of inspiration
B. They are source of knowledge
C. They are source of happiness
D. They are means of livelihood

**2.** How do the books help in progress of civilization?
A. Based on the earlier books new knowledge is obtained
B. The books provide solution to many problems
C. The books inspire the scientists
D. Not mentioned in the passage

**3.** How do the books make people more happy?
A. They help the reader to overcome the shadows of uncertainty
B. They help bring in joy by amusing the reader through their content
C. They help the reader to understand the darker side of life
D. Not mentioned in the passage

**4.** Which of the following is the author's view about the knowledge and pleasure derived from books?
(*i*) We get more of knowledge and less of pleasure
(*ii*) We get more of pleasure and less of knowledge
(*iii*) We get knowledge and pleasure in equal measure
A. only (*i*) B. only (*ii*)
C. either (*i*) or (*ii*) D. only (*iii*)

**5.** The high quality of books produced by a country indicates:
A. it has a high rate of literacy
B. it has a progressive civilization
C. it is not an industrialised nation
D. it has learned ancestors

**6.** Why are the books, according to the passage, called never-failing friends?
A. Books do not betray individuals
B. Books are inanimate
C. Books always give companionship to the reader
D. Books are available in the market anytime unlike others

**7.** How do the books help in bringing peace in the minds of people?
A. Books provide information about the past civilization
B. Books help people learn to take correct steps with the help of the recorded information
C. Books act as a window to the minds of the great men
D. Not mentioned in the passage

**8.** Which of the following has been described as a sign of good luck?
A. Being a miser
B. Having lot of money
C. Advancing the culture
D. A passion for books

**Directions (Qs. 9 to 12):** *Choose the word which is most nearly the **SAME** in meaning as the word given in bold capitals as used in the passage.*

**9. SOLACE**
A. peace B. tranquillity
C. calmness D. console

**10. ENABLES**
A. helps B. succeeds
C. promotes D. stops

**11. HEADWAY**
A. higher B. forge
C. movement D. improve

**12. MARCH**
A. move B. progress
C. pass D. register

**Directions (Qs. 13 to 15):** *Choose the word which is most **OPPOSITE** in meaning of the word given in bold capitals as used in the passage.*

**13. GREAT**
A. small B. thin
C. short D. ordinary

**14. PLEASURE**
A. displeasure B. pain
C. happiness D. hardship

**15. DESERT**
A. waterhole B. bitter
C. accompany D. propel

# ANSWERS

**PASSAGE-1**

| 1 | 2 | 3 | 4 |
|---|---|---|---|
| A | B | A | A |

**PASSAGE-2**

| 1 | 2 | 3 | 4 | 5 |
|---|---|---|---|---|
| A | C | D | A | D |

**PASSAGE-3**

| 1 | 2 | 3 | 4 | 5 |
|---|---|---|---|---|
| A | D | C | D | A |

**PASSAGE-4**

| 1 | 2 | 3 | 4 | 5 | 6 |
|---|---|---|---|---|---|
| D | A | D | A | A | D |

**PASSAGE-5**

| 1 | 2 | 3 | 4 | 5 | 6 | 7 |
|---|---|---|---|---|---|---|
| A | D | A | A | A | C | B |

**PASSAGE-6**

| 1 | 2 | 3 | 4 | 5 |
|---|---|---|---|---|
| A | C | C | A | D |
| **6** | **7** | **8** | **9** | **10** |
| D | B | A | B | D |

**PASSAGE-7**

| 1 | 2 | 3 | 4 | 5 |
|---|---|---|---|---|
| C | C | D | B | D |
| **6** | **7** | **8** | **9** | **10** |
| A | A | D | D | B |
| **11** | **12** | **13** | **14** | **15** |
| A | D | D | B | C |

**PASSAGE-8**

| 1 | 2 | 3 | 4 | 5 |
|---|---|---|---|---|
| B | A | C | D | C |
| **6** | **7** | **8** | **9** | **10** |
| D | B | D | D | A |
| **11** | **12** | **13** | **14** | **15** |
| D | D | D | C | B |

**PASSAGE-9**

| 1 | 2 | 3 | 4 | 5 |
|---|---|---|---|---|
| D | D | C | D | D |
| **6** | **7** | **8** | **9** | **10** |
| D | A | D | B | A |
| **11** | **12** | **13** | **14** | **15** |
| C | D | B | D | C |

**PASSAGE-10**

| 1 | 2 | 3 | 4 | 5 |
|---|---|---|---|---|
| D | A | D | D | B |
| **6** | **7** | **8** | **9** | **10** |
| A | D | D | D | A |
| **11** | **12** | **13** | **14** | **15** |
| D | B | D | B | C |

❑❑❑

# 14 Cloze Test

*A cloze test is a procedure in which a person is asked to supply words that have been removed from a passage as a test of his ability to comprehend text. Practise it regularly to score well.*

## PASSAGES

**Directions:** *In each of the following passages some numbered blank spaces are given. For each numbered blank space four answer choices are given. Pick out the one which is the most appropriate for that blank space, keeping the trend of the passage in mind.*

### Passage-1

Mankind's most ....(1).... treasure of thoughts is carefully preserved in the golden casket of books. The ....(2).... of books is as vast as the universe, for there is no corner of it which they have left ....(3).... . There is no ....(4).... of books on any topic, be it as simple as the composition of sodium nitrate or as ....(5).... as the mechanism of a spacecraft rocketing towards Mars. The ....(6).... of books is not only most easily available but is enlightened, dependable and lifelong. In times of distress they make us stoically ....(7).... of the object that causes uneasiness and we learn to ....(8).... with the sting of adversity.

#### Questions

1. A. costly B. important C. valuable D. vast
2. A. area B. scope C. storage D. kingdom
3. A. unexplored B. unseen C. untouched D. unapproached
4. A. lack B. dearth C. shortage D. insufficiency
5. A. extricate B. intricate C. intrinsic D. internecine
6. A. company B. assistance C. friendship D. companionship
7. A. defiant B. defendant C. defensible D. delusive
8. A. adapt B. adopt C. exist D. co-exist

### Passage-2

Though the government has tried to ....(1).... Naxalism with all its might, much more needs to be done to totally root out the ....(2).... of Naxalism. The roots of Naxalism ....(3).... economic backwardness and social exploitation of the peasants and the weaker classes. Thus, the best way to ....(4).... Naxalism is to bring the naxals ....(5).... the mainstream. ....(6).... policies and schemes should be implemented effectively ....(7).... the Naxals economically stable. They should be ....(8).... to participate in democratic processes. The government has to ....(9).... the social upliftment of the Naxals. Use of force in ....(10).... Naxalism will yield little success.

## Questions

1. A. crush B. handle
   C. tackle D. suppress
2. A. menace B. whole
   C. gamut D. stems
3. A. lies in B. are in
   C. abound in D. exist in
4. A. crash B. crush
   C. break D. defy
5. A. in B. on
   C. into D. within
6. A. Current B. Latest
   C. Occurring D. Existing
7. A. so that B. so as to make
   C. such that D. to make
8. A. insisted B. brought
   C. encouraged D. forced
9. A. assure B. insure
   C. guarantee D. ensure
10. A. countering B. defying
    C. banishing D. desecrating

## Passage-3

We are living in very exciting ....(1).... . The ....(2).... change is dizzying and the impact this progress is having on our present and — more importantly — on our future is difficult to ....(3).... in its ...(4).... . This is the age of ....(5).... micro-processors, sophisticated software, new hardware technology and high bandwidth, high-speed networks. The PC gave us a new way to work, play and ....(6).... . In fact, it brought ....(7).... our desktops computing power, which until a few years ....(8).... had only been available to corporates. With the ....(9).... of the internet, the PC ....(10).... us the most convenient and flexible way to head on to the Net.

## Questions

1. A. periods B. days
   C. phase D. times
2. A. phase B. pace
   C. sphere D. drastic
3. A. guess B. forecast
   C. comprehend D. approximate
4. A. whole B. entirety
   C. fruition D. fullness
5. A. strong B. changing
   C. powerful D. sonorous
6. A. convey B. communicate
   C. entertain D. enjoy
7. A. onto B. to
   C. on D. at
8. A. back B. earlier
   C. behind D. before
9. A. addendum B. adherence
   C. afoot D. advent
10. A. allowed B. privileged
    C. brought D. offered

## Passage-4

What is required today in our country is ....(1).... of a new political culture based on full respect for human liberty, on pluralism and on a better social deal for all. The major ....(2).... facing us today is to carry out democratic transformation in all the ....(3)...., social, cultural, economic and political. The events of the 20th century ....(4).... one thing absolutely clear that human ....(5)...., everywhere, specially in countries whose political structures were ....(6).... to reflect the revolutionary aspirations of the people ....(7).... not only under stress and strain but are ....(8).... vast upheavals because of the ....(9).... of democracy. At the same time it has also to be understood that democracy cannot be ....(10).... into a static mould.

## Questions

1. A. growing B. developing
   C. creating D. creation
2. A. development B. crisis
   C. challenge D. drawback
3. A. corners B. context
   C. realm D. spheres
4. A. have made B. has made
   C. had made D. made

5. A. travails B. traverse
C. traps D. transverse

6. A. supposed B. meant
C. caused D. forced

7. A. were B. was
C. are D. have been

8. A. developing B. evolving
C. experiencing D. faced with

9. A. denial B. rebuff
C. rebuttal D. absence

10. A. shaped B. flex
C. frozen D. caused

## Passage-5

For centuries, women not only in India but all over the world ....(1).... treated as ....(2).... secondary position to men. ....(3).... human history men ....(4).... far greater power then women to name, classify, and order the worlds in which they both live. ....(5).... studies in various parts of the world point out to a wide ....(6).... in male and female roles ....(7).... cultures and demonstrate the possibility of change in these sex-determined roles. The 20th century in particular ....(8).... the cause of gender justice by internationalizing struggles for equality ....(9).... women and other oppressed people. Women's struggles against their ....(10).... were intertwined in ....(11).... degrees with ideologies and movements based on the values of freedom, self-determination, equality, democracy and justice.

### Questions

1. A. has been B. have been
C. had been D. were

2. A. occupying B. taking
C. possessing D. serving

3. A. All through B. Throughout
C. Since D. From

4. A. have B. had
C. have had D. enjoy

5. A. Sociological B. Anthropological
C. General D. Practical

6. A. concord B. repulsion
C. disagreement D. variation

7. A. among B. across
C. between D. of

8. A. developed B. evolved
C. promoted D. entertained

9. A. for B. to
C. among D. by

10. A. subsidiary B. subsequent
C. subservience D. subordination

11. A. various B. varying
C changing D. differing

## Passage-6

Visualisation is a strong ....(1).... to memory. Those persons who ......(2)..... a powerful memory cannot do so without taking the help of visualisation. Such persons have developed the skills to ....(3).... visualisation even in such ....(4).... tasks as remembering names and numbers. These persons have the names and numbers ....(5).... in their brain even after hearing those names and figures only once. On the other hand those who take the help of revising to memorise ....(6).... to forget it once they have ....(7).... the practice of revising ....(8).... the ones who have applied visualisation to memorise. Psychologists ....(9).... in visualisation a powerful tool for personality development. The more you visualise, the more you are ....(10).... your attitude and behaviour to the blue prints of your vision and ....(11).... more you are inching towards success.

### Questions

1. A. way B. path
C. aid D. symptom

2. A. command B. master
C. rule D. enjoy

3. A. use B. apply
C. put D. place

4. A. trivial B. difficult
C. mundane D. unscrupulous

5. A. impress B. imprinted
C. impinge D. store

6. A. bent B. incline
C. prone d. tend

7. A. dropped B. left
C. gave up D. given up

8. A. unlike B. opposite
C. contrary D. not like

9. A. found B. have found
C. sees D. finds

10. A. shaping B. moulding
C. making D. attuning

11. A. actually B. factually
C. subsequently D. consequently

## Passage-7

The development of an area depends on the resources ....(1).... in the area, the needs and ....(2).... of the people living there and the technological skill ....(3).... by them. Humans play an important and decisive role in the ....(4).... of development of an area. We choose the ....(5).... of resources which could be developed to our ....(6).... . The natural ....(7).... available in an area ....(8).... value as a resource only when people find a use for them. There are ....(9).... where large potential resources are available, but they ....(10).... developed for economic reasons. Lack of capital for investments, roads and railway lines, and other ....(11).... facilities may stand in the way of resource development.

### Questions

1. A. present B. prevalent
C. available D. exist

2. A. inspirations B. aspirations
C. ambitions D. curiosity

3. A. handled B. practised
C. availed D. possessed

4. A. system B. design
C. pattern D. style

5. A. class B. group
C. variety D. types

6. A. good B. advantage
C. approach D. favour

7. A. secrets B. phenomenon
C. products D. endowments

8. A. get B. acquire
C. possess D. takes

9. A. instances B. events
C. circumstances D. happenings

10. A. have not yet been
B. haven't been
C. are not yet
D. yet have not been

11. A. common B. general
C. infrastructural D. structural

## Passage-8

The Naxal problem in India is basically socio-economic in ....(1).... . The main reasons ....(2).... the Naxal movement in India are the ....(3).... of peasants and their weak social and economic position. ....(4).... of the peasants are landless labourers whose lands have been ....(5).... occupied by the landlords. Moreover, the landlords give ....(6).... wages to the peasants. Their ....(7).... suffering at the hands of the landlords thus encourage many peasants to take law ....(8).... their own hands. Due to their poor economic condition the peasants easily ....(9).... the trap of the naxal leaders who have their ....(10).... interests. Illiteracy, unemployment, police excesses, corruption and ....(11).... administration further ....(12).... this complex problem.

### Questions

1. A. form B. shape
C. behaviour D. nature

2. A. for B. of
C. in D. behind

3. A. complaisance B. exploitation
C. domination D. exculpation

4. A. Many B. Much
C. Most D. All

5. A. imperiously B. imperatively
C. forcefully D. forcibly

6. A. improper B. small
C. inadequate D. insufficient

7. A. long B. brutal
C. pathetic D. great

8. A. in B. into
C. on D. by

9. A. fall into B. fall in
C. fell in D. fell into

10. A. selfish B. vested
C. vicious D. vindictive

11. A. failed B. improper
C. inefficient D. bureaucratic

12. A. heighten B. deepen
C. add D. worsen

## Passage-9

No doubt various ....(1).... and Acts are there to eliminate the ....(2).... practice of child labour. But the ....(3).... is that, these are not being implemented in both letter and spirit, for which the ....(4).... of the problem remains as it was. Therefore a judicious, pragmatic, integrated and time-bound ....(5).... supplemented by ....(6).... follow-up action is essential to ....(7).... the problem that ....(8).... deep root in our Society. It is true that child labour can't be ....(9)... with a magic wand. If we ....(10).... time-bound goals and follow, of course, with the ....(11).... assistance of ILO and UNICEF, it is possible to eliminate the problem of child labour. With strong political will power and people's backing nothing is ....(12).... . Rather ....(13).... the bud we should let it blossom and spread its fragrance all around. ....(14).... lies the progress and prosperity of the society.

### Questions

1. A. means B. methods
C. source D. provisions

2. A. unjust B. inhuman
C. mal D. illegal

3. A. anxiety B. abrasion
C. tragedy D. conclusion

4. A. magnitude B. depth
C. gravity D. soaring

5. A. approach B. analysis
C. survey D. scheme

6. A. continuous B. thorough
C. throughout D. regular

7. A. outroot B. uproot
C. downroot D. grassroot

8. A. have B. has
C. had D. has taken

9. A. wipe out B. wipe off
C. wipe up D. wiped

10. A. keep B. put
C. put up D. set

11. A. ongoing B. continuing
C. unending D. frequent

12. A. insurmountable B. intangible
C. inscrutable D. incorrigible

13. A. killing B. hurting
C. destroying D. nipping

14. A. Here B. There
C. Therein D. Herein

## Passage-10

Every action we perform ....(1).... a result. And, naturally, we lay claim ....(2).... the results or fruits ....(3).... from that action in the ....(4).... that it is we who perform the action. This is .....(5).... ignorance because ....(6).... is it the Lord who ....(7).... the result of any action, it is by His will ....(8).... that even the action is accomplished. The will of the Lord ....(9).... whether we cooperate with His will or strive ....(10).... . If God wills that an action takes place, he arranges for the ....(11).... for it to happen. It is ....(12).... experience that sometimes despite our best efforts we ....(13).... achieve the results we desire, and at other times the seemingly most ....(14).... situations mysteriously get ....(15).... . ....(16).... way man chooses to act, both the act and the outcome of the cost are dependent ....(17).... on the will of the Lord.

### Questions

1. A. produce B. produces
C. causes D. undergoes

2. A. on B. at
C. to D. for

3. A. occurring B. obtaining
C. deriving D. falling

4. A. belief B. hope
C. fantasy D. folly

5. A. sheen B. keen
C. sheer D. sheathe

6. A. alone B. only that
C. not only D. for only

**7.** A. declares B. decides
C. ordains D. ornate

**8.** A. completely B. entirely
C. only D. alone

**9.** A. prevails always
B. prevails everywhere
C. is prevalent
D. always prevails

**10.** A. alone B. always
C. constantly D. independently

**11.** A. wherewithal B. whereabouts
C. whatsoever D. wherefore

**12.** A. usual B. general
C. universal D. common

**13.** A. does not B. may not
C. do not D. might not

**14.** A. intractable B. intangible
C. internecine D. intricate

**15.** A. subsided B. resolved
C. solved D. converted

**16.** A. Whatever B. All the
C. All those D. Whichever

**17.** A. mainly B. actually
C. entirely D. generally

# ANSWERS

### PASSAGE-1

| 1 | 2 | 3 | 4 | 5 | 6 |
|---|---|---|---|---|---|
| C | D | A | B | B | D |
| 7 | 8 | | | | |
| A | D | | | | |

### PASSAGE-2

| 1 | 2 | 3 | 4 | 5 | 6 |
|---|---|---|---|---|---|
| C | A | A | B | C | D |
| 7 | 8 | 9 | 10 | | |
| B | C | D | A | | |

### PASSAGE-3

| 1 | 2 | 3 | 4 | 5 | 6 |
|---|---|---|---|---|---|
| D | B | C | B | C | B |
| 7 | 8 | 9 | 10 | | |
| A | D | D | D | | |

### PASSAGE-4

| 1 | 2 | 3 | 4 | 5 | 6 |
|---|---|---|---|---|---|
| D | C | D | A | A | B |
| 7 | 8 | 9 | 10 | | |
| C | C | A | C | | |

### PASSAGE-5

| 1 | 2 | 3 | 4 | 5 | 6 |
|---|---|---|---|---|---|
| B | A | B | C | B | D |
| 7 | 8 | 9 | 10 | 11 | |
| B | C | D | D | B | |

### PASSAGE-6

| 1 | 2 | 3 | 4 | 5 | 6 |
|---|---|---|---|---|---|
| C | A | B | C | B | D |
| 7 | 8 | 9 | 10 | 11 | |
| A | A | B | D | D | |

### PASSAGE-7

| 1 | 2 | 3 | 4 | 5 | 6 |
|---|---|---|---|---|---|
| C | B | D | C | D | B |
| 7 | 8 | 9 | 10 | 11 | |
| D | B | A | A | C | |

### PASSAGE-8

| 1 | 2 | 3 | 4 | 5 | 6 |
|---|---|---|---|---|---|
| D | A | B | C | D | C |
| 7 | 8 | 9 | 10 | 11 | 12 |
| A | B | A | B | C | D |

### PASSAGE-9

| 1 | 2 | 3 | 4 | 5 | 6 |
|---|---|---|---|---|---|
| D | B | C | A | A | D |
| 7 | 8 | 9 | 10 | 11 | 12 |
| B | D | B | D | B | A |
| 13 | 14 | | | | |
| D | C | | | | |

### PASSAGE-10

| 1 | 2 | 3 | 4 | 5 | 6 |
|---|---|---|---|---|---|
| B | C | B | A | C | C |
| 7 | 8 | 9 | 10 | 11 | 12 |
| C | D | D | D | A | D |
| 13 | 14 | 15 | 16 | 17 | |
| C | A | B | D | C | |

# GENERAL INTELLIGENCE & REASONING

# 1. LETTER SERIES

In letter series, the letters follow a definite order. The given series of letters can be in natural order or in reverse order or combination of both. The letters may be skipped or repeated or consecutive. The given series may be single or may even comprise of two different series merged at alternate positions. While attempting questions on letter series one should note the pattern of alphabet series.

Alphabets in natural series are :

A B C D E F G H I J K L M N O P Q R S T U V W X Y Z

A ↓ 1st, E ↓ 5th, J ↓ 10th, O ↓ 15th, T ↓ 20th, Y ↓ 25th

Alphabets in reverse series are :

Z Y X W V U T S R Q P O N M L K J I H G F E D C B A

Z ↓ 1st, V ↓ 5th, Q ↓ 10th, L ↓ 15th, G ↓ 20th, B ↓ 25th

**Note :** On reaching Z, the series restarts from A and on reaching A, it restarts from Z.

## EXERCISE

**Directions :** *In each of the following series determine the order of the letters. Then from the given options select the one which will complete the given series.*

**1.** B Y C X D W E ?
(*a*) S (*b*) T
(*c*) U (*d*) V

**2.** B A F E J I P O ? U
(*a*) V (*b*) T
(*c*) S (*d*) Q

**3.** B A D C ? H G J I
(*a*) EF (*b*) FE
(*c*) FG (*d*) DF

**4.** ADG, XVT, BEH, WUS, ?
(*a*) VTR (*b*) CFI
(*c*) DFJ (*d*) STU

**5.** GMSY, IOUA, KQWC, ?
(*a*) MSYE (*b*) NSYE
(*c*) MTYE (*d*) MSYF

**6.** ADG, GJM, ?, SVY
(*a*) MPS (*b*) MQR
(*c*) MQS (*d*) SPM

**7.** XYZ, UVW, ?, OPQ
(*a*) RST (*b*) STU
(*c*) QRS (*d*) TUV

**8.** JOBS, KMEO, LKHK, ?, NGNC
(*a*) MJLH (*b*) LIKG
(*c*) MIKG (*d*) MNGM

**9.** AZ, GT, MN, ?, YB
(*a*) KF (*b*) TS
(*c*) RX (*d*) SH

**10.** BMY, DNW, FOU, ?
(*a*) HPT (*b*) HPS
(*c*) HQS (*d*) GPS

**11.** AZ, CX, EV, ?
(*a*) HU (*b*) GS
(*c*) GT (*d*) HT

**12.** DMP, FLN, HKL, JJJ, ?
(*a*) MIH (*b*) III
(*c*) LIH (*d*) MII

**13.** ECA, JHF, OMK, ?, YWU
(*a*) TRP (*b*) LNP
(*c*) QPN (*d*) RPT

**14.** ABP, CDQ, EFR, ?
(*a*) GHS (*b*) HGS
(*c*) GHR (*d*) GHT

**15.** BEH, KNQ, TWZ, ?
(*a*) IJL (*b*) BDF
(*c*) CFI (*d*) ADG

**16.** EJO, TYD, INS, XCH, ?
(*a*) MRW (*b*) NRV
(*c*) MRV (*d*) NRW

**17.** ABP, CDQ, EFR,?
(*a*) GHS (*b*) GIS
(*c*) GGS (*d*) GJS

**18.** NRA, PRC, RRE, TRG, ?
(*a*) USI (*b*) VRI
(*c*) WRJ (*d*) TRI

**19.** FJKP, ILMQ, LNOR, OPQS, ?
(*a*) RQTV (*b*) RQSS
(*c*) RRST (*d*) RTTU

**20.** DQCP, EPEN, FOGL, GNIJ, ?
(*a*) HNLG (*b*) HLJG
(*c*) HOMI (*d*) HMKH

**21.** DFST, FSTD, STDF, ?
(*a*) TSFD (*b*) FDTS
(*c*) TDFS (*d*) SFDT

**22.** IXT, MAV, QDX, ?
(*a*) WGX (*b*) VHY
(*c*) UGZ (*d*) YHZ

**23.** QYK, ?, ISG, EPE
(*a*) NWJ (*b*) MVI
(*c*) NVI (*d*) MVJ

**24.** JMC, CLT, KND, ?, LOE, GPX
(*a*) ENV (*b*) DMX
(*c*) EOU (*d*) DRX

**25.** ZDV, XGS, VJP, ?
(*a*) SNM (*b*) TMM
(*c*) TNR (*d*) SNT

## EXPLANATORY ANSWERS

**1. (*d*) :** There are two alternate series.

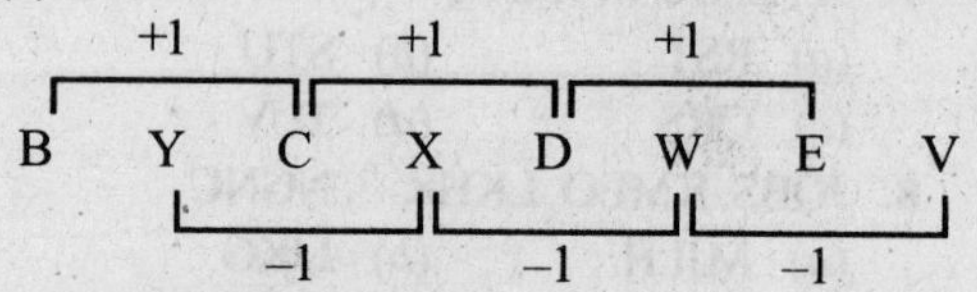


*Series I* : BCDE (natural order)
*Series II* : YXWV (reverse order)

**2. (*a*) :** Each vowel (AEIOU) is preceded by the letter that comes next to it in the natural alphabetical series.

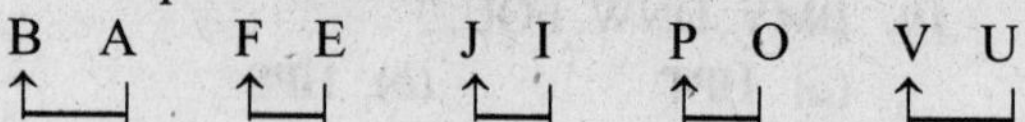


**3. (*b*) :** The letters in natural series are divided into sections of two letters each. The letters in each section are written backward.
BA DC FE HG JI

**4. (*b*) :** There are two alternate series.

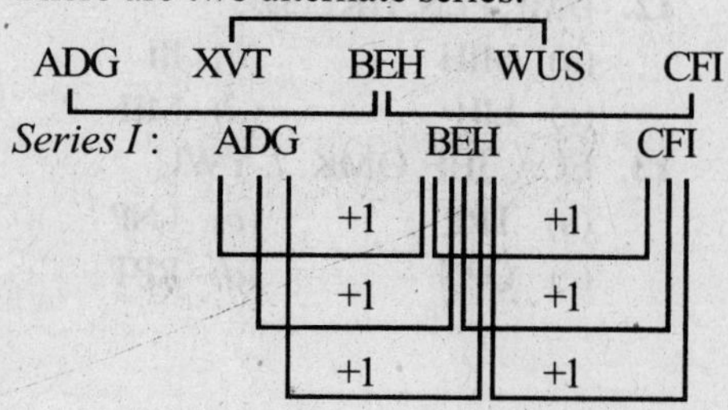


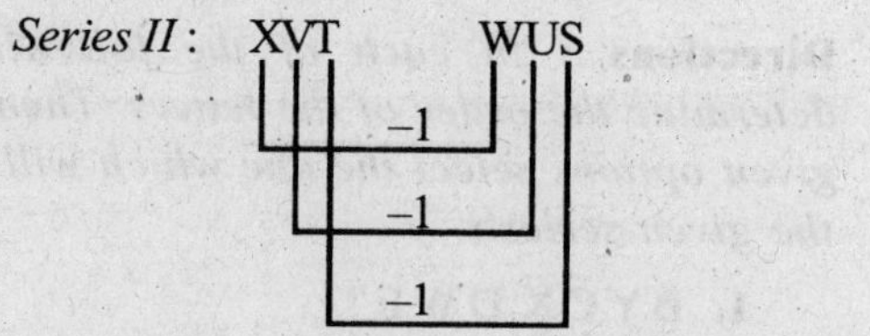


**5. (*a*) :** The series is formed by moving each letter two steps forward from one group to the next.

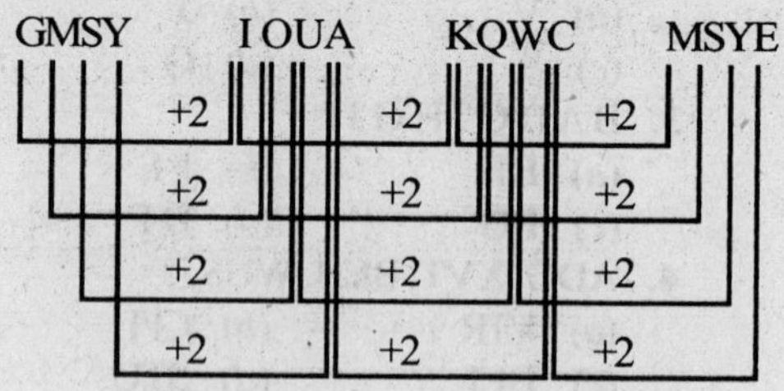


(The series restarts from A on reaching Z)

**6. (*a*) :** In each group of three letters the alphabet is in the succession of +3. The next group begins with the last alphabet of the previous group.

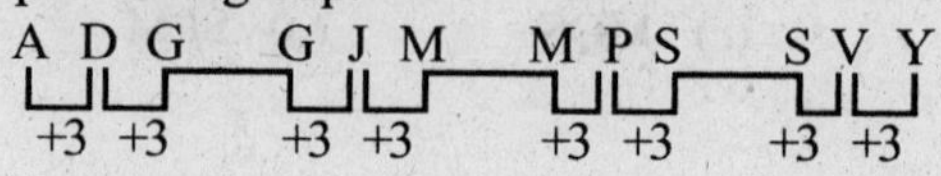

**7. (*a*) :** The alphabet from one group to the next are in recession of –3, *i.e.,*

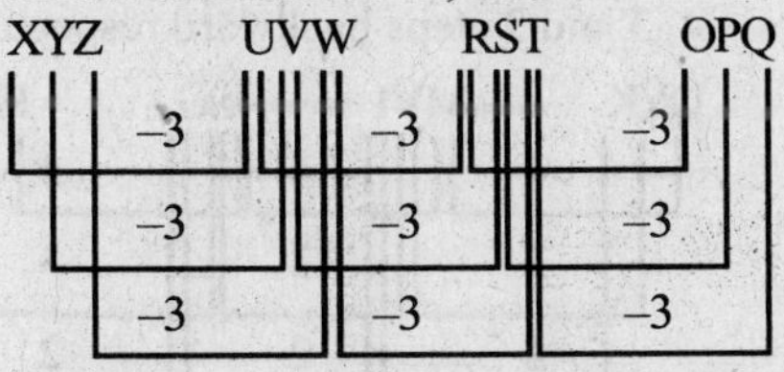


**8. (*c*) :** The alphabets in each group follow the pattern +1, –2, +3 and –4 respectively from one group to the next group.

**9. (*d*) :** The letters in one group correspond to the letters in the next group in the manner +6, –6 respectively, *i.e.,*

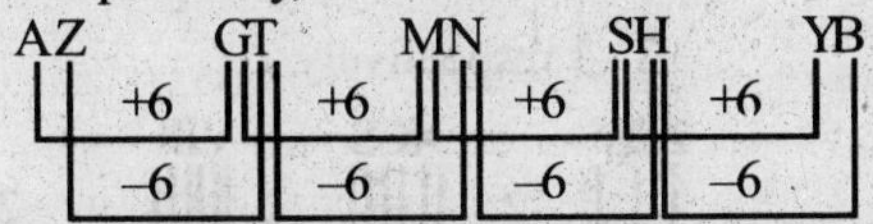


**10. (*b*) :** The letters in one group correspond to the letters in the next group in the manner +2, +1, -2 respectively, *i.e.,*

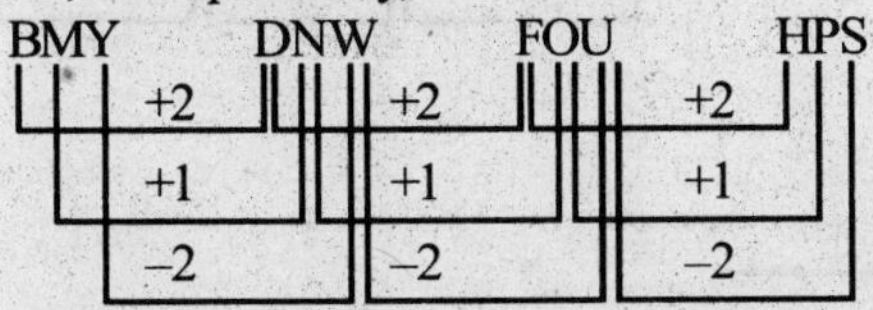


**11. (*c*) :** The letters in each group correspond to the letters in the next group in the manner +2, –2 respectively, *i.e.,*

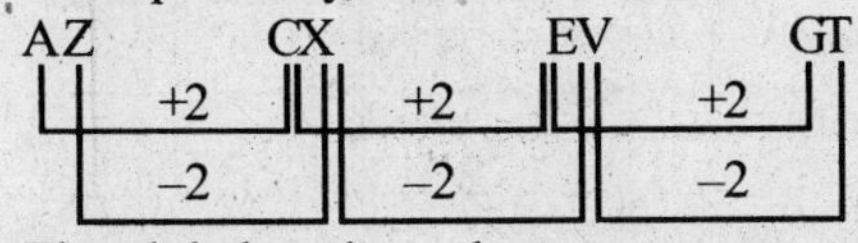


**12. (*c*) :** The alphabets in each group correspond to the alphabets in the next group in the manner +2, –1, –2 respectively, *i.e.,*

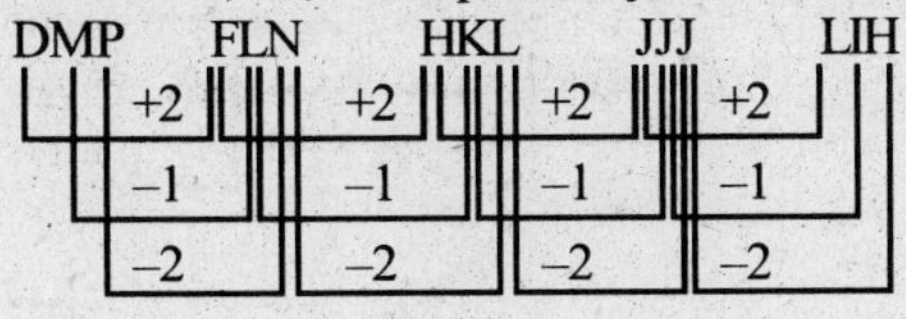


**13. (*a*) :** The alphabets in each group are moved five steps forward, *i.e.,*

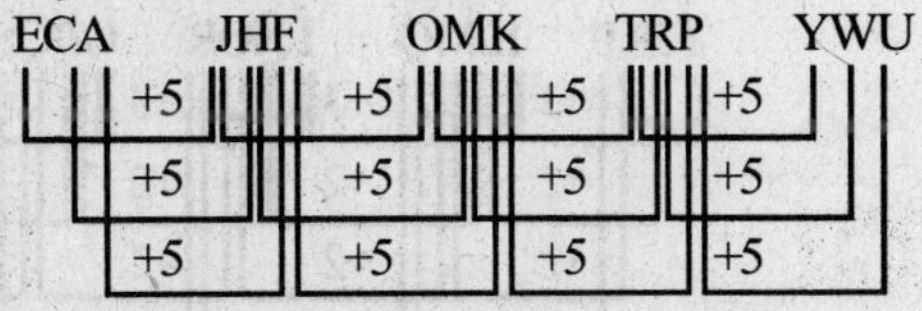


**14. (*a*) :** The letters in one group correspond to the letters in the next group in the manner +2, +2, +1 respectively, *i.e.,*

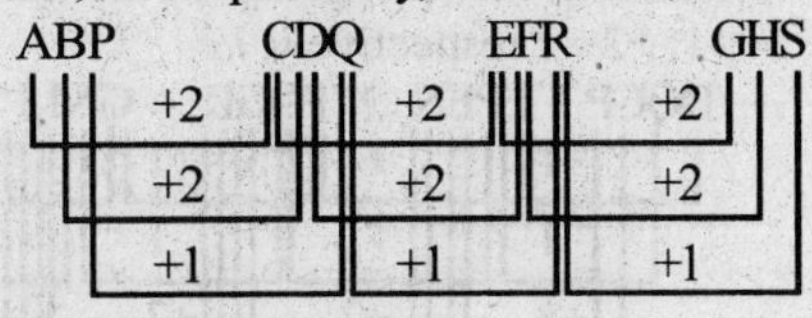


**15. (*c*) :** All the letters in each group are moved nine steps forward.

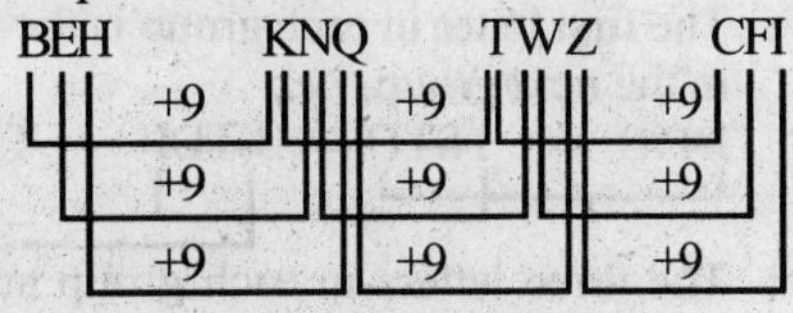


**16. (*a*) :** There are two alternate series :

*Series I* :

*Series II* :

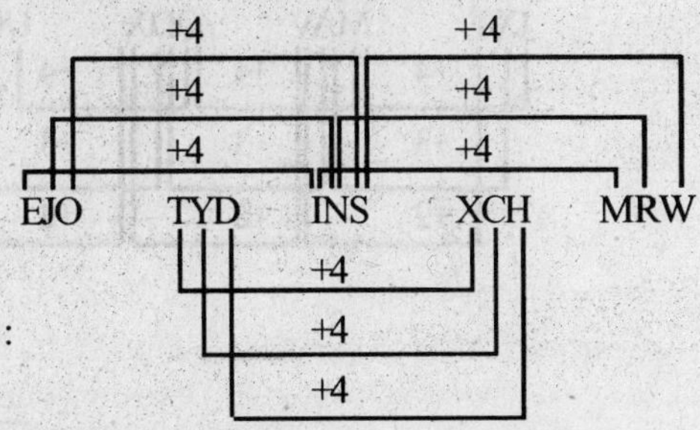


**17. (*a*) :** The letters in one group correspond to the letters in the next group in the manner +2, +2, +1 respectively, *i.e.,*

**18. (*b*) :** The first and third letters are moved two steps forwards while the middle letter remains unchanged, *i.e.,*

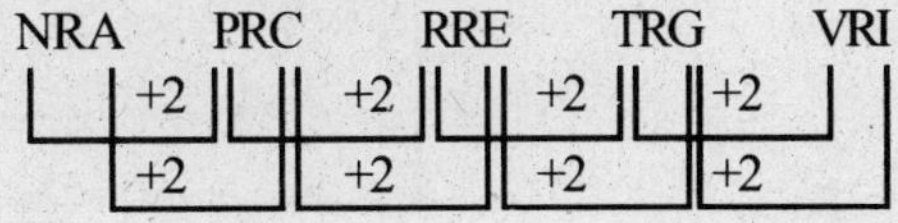

**19. (*c*) :** The four letters are moved 3, 2, 2, 1 steps forward respectively, *i.e.,*

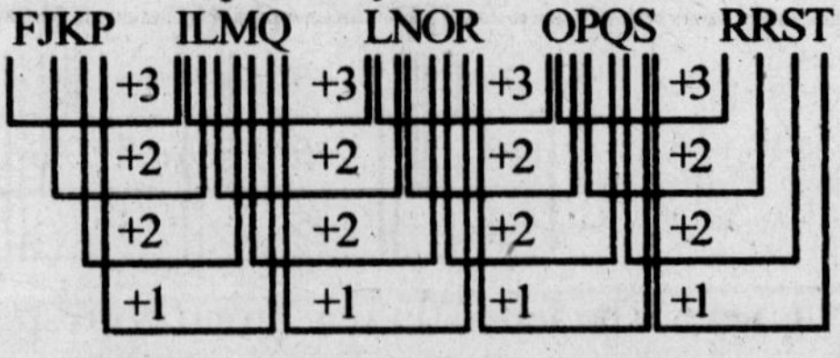


**20. (*d*) :** The letters in one group correspond to the letters in the next group in the manner, +1, –1, +2 –2 respectively, *i.e.,*

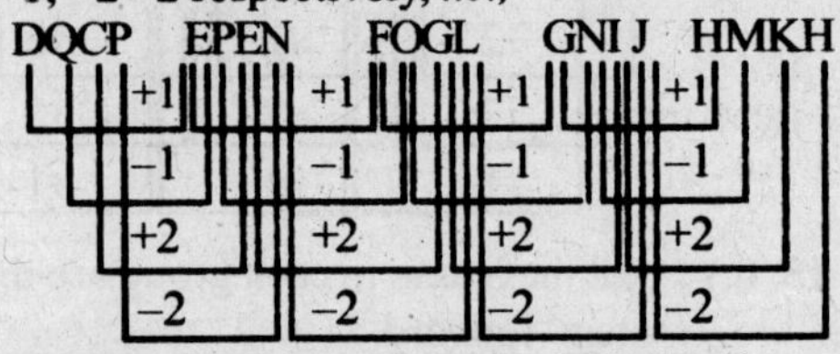


**21. (*c*) :** The first letter in each group is the last letter in the next group, *i.e.,*

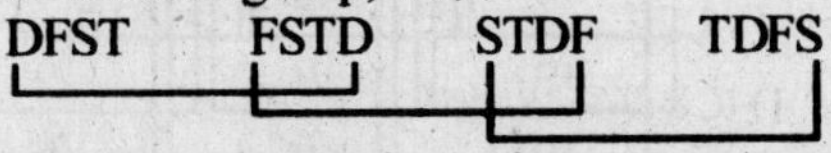


**22. (*c*) :** The three letters in each group are moved 4, 3 and 2 steps forward respectively, *i.e.,*

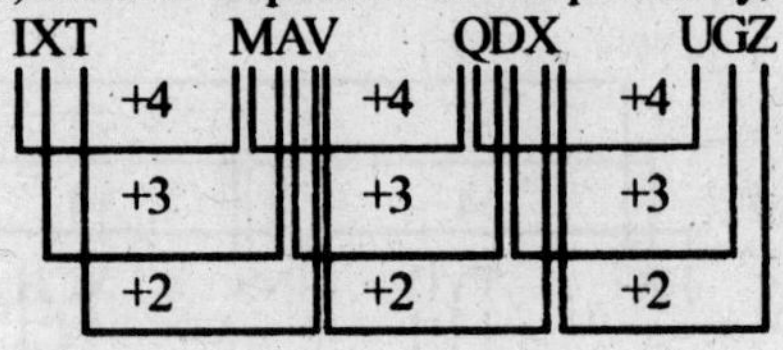


**23. (*b*) :** The three letters in each group are moved 4, 3 and 2 steps backward respectively, *i.e.,*

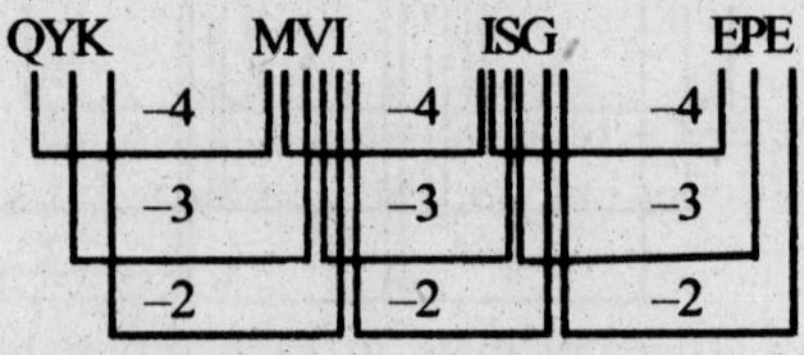


**24. (*a*) :** There are two alternate series :

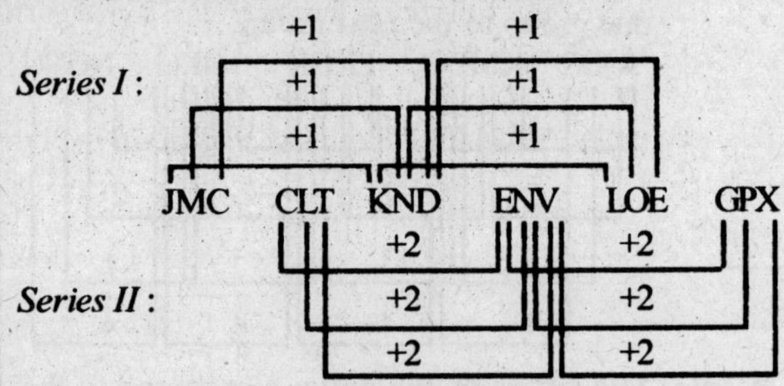


**25. (*b*) :** The letters in one group correspond to the letters in the next group in the manner –2, +3 –3 respectively, *i.e.,*

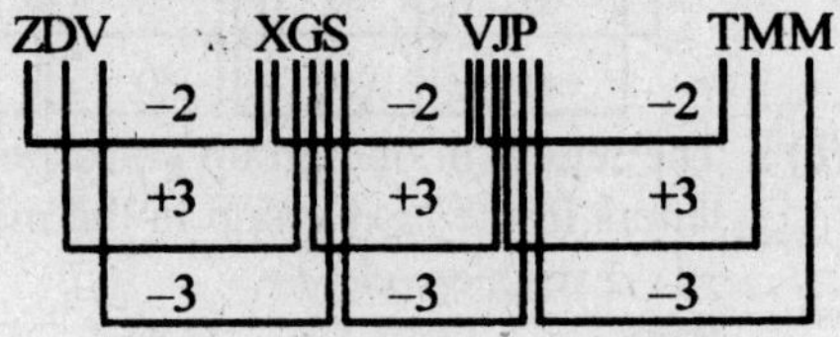

# 2. Wrong Letter Series

In this type of series, the candidates are not required to find the letter or group of letters which will complete the given series but, they have to identify the letter or number which is wrong or misfit in the given series.

## SOLVED EXAMPLE

**1.** Which of the following letters in the given series is wrong?

J M P T V Y

(*a*) J (*b*) P (*c*) T (*d*) Y

**Ans. (*c*) :** The letters in this series are moved three steps forward, *i.e.*,

J M P S V Y

+3 +3 +3 +3 +3

Letter 'T' should have been 'S'.

## EXERCISE

**Directions :** *Which letter(s) in each of the following series is wrong or is misfit in the series?*

**1.** A E H O U

(*a*) U (*b*) O
(*c*) H (*d*) E

**2.** C H M S W B

(*a*) C (*b*) S
(*c*) B (*d*) W

**3.** X S N I C Y

(*a*) Y (*b*) C
(*c*) S (*d*) I

**4.** Z A W B X C

(*a*) D (*b*) C
(*c*) X (*d*) W

**5.** M L O N Q P R

(*a*) R (*b*) O
(*c*) Q (*d*) L

**6.** D K R Y F L

(*a*) L (*b*) D
(*c*) R (*d*) Y

**7.** L N Q T W Z C F

(*a*) C (*b*) Q
(*c*) L (*d*) F

**8.** XW, DC, CB, NM, PQ

(*a*) NM (*b*) CB
(*c*) PQ (*d*) XW

**9.** B E I N S A I

(*a*) A (*b*) E
(*c*) S (*d*) I

**10.** Z T P K H F

(*a*) Z (*b*) P
(*c*) T (*d*) F

## EXPLANATORY ANSWERS

**1. (*c*) :** The series is made with vowels only. AEIOU. I should be in place of H.

**2. (*b*) :** The letters in the series are moved five steps forward.

C H M R W B

+5 +5 +5 +5 +5

R should be in place of S

(The series restarts from A on reaching Z)

**3. (*b*) :** The pattern in the series is –5, *i.e.*,

X S N I D Y

–5 –5 –5 –5 –5

D should be in place of C.

**4. (*d*) :** There are two alternate series

+1 +1

Z A Y B X C

−1 −1

*Series I* : ZYX (reverse series)
*Series II* : ABC (natural series)
Y should be in place of W.

**5. (*a*) :** Two consecutive letters are written backwards.

ML ON QP SR

S should be in place of R.

**6. (*a*) :** The pattern in this series in moving the letters seven steps forward.

D K R Y F M

+7 +7 +7 +7 +7

M should be in place of L.

**7. (*c*) :** The pattern in the series is +3

K N Q T W Z C F

+3 +3 +3 +3 +3 +3 +3

K should be in place of L.

**8. (*c*) :** The series is made with any two consecutive letters written backwards.

XW DC CB NM QP

← ← ← ← ←

Q should come before P in the series.

**9. (*c*) :** The difference between the letters is increased by one at each step.

B E I N T A I

+3 +4 +5 +6 +7 +8

T should be in place of S.

**10. (*b*) :** The difference between the letters is decreased by one at each step.

Z T O K H F

−6 −5 −4 −3 −2

O should be in place of P.

# 3. REPEAT SERIES

In this type of series, small letters of the alphabet are used to make a set of letters which are repeated. The candidate has to find the set of letters which will fit the blanks left in the given series in such a manner that one section of the series is further repeated in the same manner.

## SOLVED EXAMPLE

**1.** Which of the following groups of letters will complete the given series?
ba-b-aab-a-b
(*a*) baab (*b*) abba (*c*) abaa (*d*) babb

**Ans. (*b*) :** The series is baab, baab, baab. Here the section 'baab' is repeated in the series.

***Solving steps*** : The candidate has to look for clues to solve such series pattern. 'aab' in the Series indicates that 'b' in this series is preceded by two 'a' so, the first blank and the last blank will be filled by 'a'. Now the first set is formed, *i.e.,* 'baab' in the beginning. This set is repeated, so the second and third blanks will have 'b' filling them. Now, solve the exercise given below to know the different ways in which these series are formed.

## EXERCISE

**Directions :** *Which of the following groups of letters will complete the given series?*

**1.** ab---b-bbaa-
(*a*) babba (*b*) abaab
(*c*) abbab (*d*) baaab

**2.** aa-ab--aaa-a
(*a*) baaa (*b*) abab
(*c*) aaab (*d*) aabb

**3.** -baa-aab-a-a
(*a*) baab (*b*) abab
(*c*) aaba (*d*) aabb

**4.** -a cca-ccca-acccc-aaa
(*a*) ccaa (*b*) acca
(*c*) caac (*d*) caaa

**5.** c-bbb--abbbb-abbb-
(*a*) abccb (*b*) bacbb
(*c*) aabcb (*d*) abacb

**6.** ac-cab-baca-aba-acac
(*a*) bcbb (*b*) aacb
(*c*) babb (*d*) acbc

**7.** --aba--ba-ab
(*a*) abbab (*b*) bbaba
(*c*) baabb (*d*) abbba

**8.** --babbba-a--
(*a*) bbaba (*b*) babbb
(*c*) baaab (*d*) ababb

**9.** k-mk-lmkkl-kk-mk
(*a*) lklm (*b*) lkmk
(*c*) lkmm (*d*) lkml

**10.** abc-d-bc-d-b-dd
(*a*) decdb (*b*) dadac
(*c*) cdabe (*d*) bacde

**11.** b-abbc-bbca-bcabb-ab
(*a*) acba (*b*) acaa
(*c*) cacc (*d*) cabc

**12.** aca-ac--a-ac
(*a*) babc (*b*) aaac
(*c*) cacc (*d*) caca

**13.** ba-cb-b-bab-?
(*a*) acbb (*b*) bcaa
(*c*) cabb (*d*) bacc

**14.** ab-aa-caab-aab-a
(*a*) bcbc (*b*) bbca
(*c*) cbcc (*d*) caba

**15.** -bbcaa-bcaa-bc-a-bca
(*a*) bacab (*b*) abbab
(*c*) abcba (*d*) bcaab

**16.** a-bccb-ca-cca-baab-c
(*a*) accab (*b*) abcaa
(*c*) bacaa (*d*) ababc

**17.** b-dabbcd-b-c-ab
(*a*) cabd (*b*) bcad
(*c*) dcba (*d*) acbd

**18.** a-ba-caacb-bc-
(*a*) acbb (*b*) cbab
(*c*) cbaa (*d*) cbba

**19.** c-baa-aca-cacab-acac-bca
(*a*) acbaa (*b*) cbaac
(*c*) bccab (*d*) bbcaa

**20.** -bcc-ac-aabb-ab-cc
(*a*) bacab (*b*) abaca
(*c*) aabca (*d*) bcaca

**21.** ab-ccca-bccc-bbcc-
(*a*) abbc (*b*) bbac
(*c*) bbca (*d*) cabc

**22.** -cbc-a-bcaac-ca
(*a*) aaba (*b*) caab
(*c*) bcab (*d*) aacb

**23.** ab-ba--ba-
(*a*) abba (*b*) baab
(*c*) baba (*d*) abab

**24.** yx-yx-yxz-xzy-zyxz
(*a*) zzyx (*b*) xxzy
(*c*) yyzx (*d*) yzxz

**25.** xxxy-y-xxy-yxx-
(*a*) xyxy (*b*) yxyx
(*c*) yyxx (*d*) xxyy

## EXPLANATORY ANSWERS

**1. (*d*) :** The series is abbaab, abbaab.
**2. (*c*) :** The series is aaaaba, aaaaba.
**3. (*b*) :** The series is aba, aba, aba, aba.
**4. (*d*) :** The series is c,a,cc,aa, ccc, aaa, cccc, aaaa.
**5. (*a*) :** The series is cabbbb, cabbbb, cabbbb.
**6. (*b*) :** The series is acac, abab, acac, abab, acac.
**7. (*a*) :** The series is ab, ab, ab, ab, ab, ab.
**8. (*b*) :** The series is bababb, bababb.
**9. (*d*) :** The series is klmk, klmk, klmk, klmk.
**10. (*b*) :** The series is abcdd, abcdd, abcdd.
**11. (*d*) :** The series is bcab, bcab, bcab, bcab, bcab.
**12. (*c*) :** The series is ac, ac, ac, ac, ac, ac.
**13. (*d*) :** The series is babc, babc, babc.
**14. (*c*) :** The series is abca, abca, abca, abca.
**15. (*b*) :** The series is abbca, abbca, abbca, abbca.
**16. (*d*) :** The series is aabcc, bbcaa, ccabb, aabcc.
**17. (*a*) :** The series is bcdab, bcdab, bcdab.
**18. (*c*) :** The series is acbabca, acbabca.
**19. (*a*) :** The series is cabaac, acabca, cabaac, acabca.
**20. (*a*) :** The series is bbccaa, ccaabb, aabbcc.
**21. (*b*) :** The series is abbccc abbccc.
**22. (*d*) :** The series is acbca acbca acbca.
**23. (*d*) :** The series is ab ab ab ab ab.
**24. (*a*) :** The series is yxz yxz yxz yxz yxz yxz.
**25. (*b*) :** The series is xxx yyy xxx yyy xxx.

# 4. Number Series

In this type of series, the set of given numbers in a series are related to one another in a particular pattern or manner. The relationship between the numbers may be (i) consecutive odd/even numbers; (ii) consecutive prime numbers; (iii) squares/cubes of some numbers with/without variation of addition or subtraction of some number; (iv) sum/product/difference of preceding numbers; (v) addition/subtraction/multiplication/division by some number; and (vi) many more combinations of the relationships given above.

## EXERCISE

**Directions :** *In the following questions, select the number(s) from the given options for completing the given series.*

**1.** 7776, 1296, 216, 36, 6, ?
(*a*) 6 (*b*) 0
(*c*) 3 (*d*) 1

**2.** 29282, 2662, 242, 22, ?
(*a*) 1 (*b*) 2
(*c*) 0 (*d*) 11

**3.** 1, 2, 2, 4, 16, ?, 65536
(*a*) 276 (*b*) 64
(*c*) 256 (*d*) 198

**4.** 3, 5, 9, 15, 23, ?, 45
(*a*) 37 (*b*) 35
(*c*) 31 (*d*) 33

**5.** 7, 21, 35, 49, 63, ?
(*a*) 70 (*b*) 77
(*c*) 81 (*d*) 108

**6.** 10, 14, 23, 39, 64, ?, 149
(*a*) 78 (*b*) 128
(*c*) 103 (*d*) 100

**7.** 6, 24, 29, 116, 121, ?, 489
(*a*) 468 (*b*) 484
(*c*) 243 (*d*) 363

**8.** 5, 50, 45, 450, 445, ?, 4445
(*a*) 4450 (*b*) 4600
(*c*) 4550 (*d*) 4500

**9.** 6.25, 9, 12.25, 16, 20.25, 25, 30.25?
(*a*) 36 (*b*) 32
(*c*) 28.25 (*d*) 40.25

**10.** 243, 5, 81, 15, 27, 45, 9, ?
(*a*) 5 (*b*) 15
(*c*) 135 (*d*) 27

**11.** 2, 7, 14, 23, ?, 47
(*a*) 31 (*b*) 38
(*c*) 28 (*d*) 34

**12.** 0, 1, 8, 27, 64, ?
(*a*) 125 (*b*) 128
(*c*) 256 (*d*) 121

**13.** 37, 47, 58, ?, 79, 95
(*a*) 71 (*b*) 69
(*c*) 68 (*d*) 67

**14.** 4, –8, 14, –22, 32, ?
(*a*) –44 (*b*) 42
(*c*) –42 (*d*) 44

**15.** 6, 7, 9, 11, 15, 15, 24, 19, ?
(*a*) 32 (*b*) 34
(*c*) 36 (*d*) 37

**16.** 2, 6, 12, 20, 30, ?
(*a*) 42 (*b*) 36
(*c*) 41 (*d*) 40

**17.** 1, 4, 5, 11, 9, 18, ?, 25
(*a*) 12 (*b*) 13
(*c*) 19 (*d*) 23

**18.** 27, 45, 9, 15, 3, 5, ?
(*a*) 1 (*b*) 1/3
(*c*) 1/5 (*d*) 1/9

**19.** 3, 1/3, 14, 1/14, 25, 1/25, ?
(*a*) 1/36 (*b*) 34
(*c*) 35 (*d*) 36

**20.** 1/2, 3/4, 5/8, 7/16, ?
(*a*) 10/17 (*b*) 9/32
(*c*) 11/34 (*d*) 12/35

**21.** 4, 8, 7, 14, 12, 22, 19, ?, 28
(*a*) 12 (*b*) 24
(*c*) 28 (*d*) 32

**22.** 96, 90, 78, ?, 36, 6
(*a*) 60 (*b*) 72
(*c*) 48 (*d*) 54

**23.** 6, 3, 11, 8, 18, 15, 27, 24, ?, ?
(*a*) 36, 33 (*b*) 36, 35
(*c*) 38, 35 (*d*) 38, 34

**24.** 1, 6, 15, ?, 45, 66, 91
(*a*) 25 (*b*) 26
(*c*) 27 (*d*) 28

**25.** 1, 2, 5, 12, 27, 58, 121, ?
(*a*) 246
(*b*) 247
(*c*) 248
(*d*) 249

## EXPLANATORY ANSWERS

**1. (*d*) :** The numbers in this sequence are divided by 6 each time.

**2. (*b*) :** The numbers in the series are divided by 11 at each step.

**3. (*c*) :** The number in the series is product of all the numbers preceding it.

1 2 2 4 16 256 65536

(1×2)
(1×2×2)
(1×2×2×4)
(1×2×2×4×16)
(1×2×2×4×16×256)

**4. (*d*) :** The difference between consecutive numbers increases by 2 at each step.

3 5 9 15 23 33 45
+2 +4 +6 +8 +10 +12

**5. (*b*) :** The series is multiplication of 7 by odd numbers starting from 3.

7 21 35 49 63 77
×3
×5
×7
×9
×11

**6. (*d*) :** The number plus the square of numbers in natural order starting from 2 gives the next number in the series.

10 14 23 39 64 100 149
$+2^2$ $+3^2$ $+4^2$ $+5^2$ $+6^2$ $+7^2$

**7. (*b*) :** The sequence in the series is ×4, +5, which is repeated.

**8. (*a*) :** The sequence in the series is ×10, –5, which is repeated.

**9. (*a*) :** There are two alternate series :

+6 +8 +10
6.25 9 12.25 16 20.25 25 30.25 36
+7 +9 +11

*Series I* : 6.25, 12.25, 20.25, 30.25 (sequence is +6, +8, +10)
*Series II* : 9, 16, 25, 36 (sequence is +7, +9, +11)

**10. (*c*) :** There are two alternate series :

÷3 ÷3 ÷3
243 5 81 15 27 45 9 135
×3 ×3 ×3

*Series I* : 243, 81, 27, 9 (division by 3)
*Series II* : 5, 15, 45, 135 (multiplication by 3)

**11. (*d*) :** The difference between two consecutive numbers is increasing by 2 starting from 5.

2 7 14 23 34 47
+5 +7 +9 +11 +13

**12. (*a*) :** The numbers are cubes of numbers in natural order.

**13. (*a*) :** The sum of the digits of the number is added to the number to obtain the next number in the series.

37 47 58 71 79 95
+(3+7) +(4+7) +(5+8) +(7+1) +(7+9)

**14. *(a)* :** Alternate numbers are marked positive and negative, but the difference between their magnitude increases by 2 at each step.

4   −8   14   −22   32   −44

4   6   8   10   12

**15. *(c)* :** There are two alternate series :

+3   +6   +9   +12

6   7   9   11   15   15   24   19   36

+4   +4   +4

*Series I*: 6, 9, 15, 24, 36 (sequence is +3, +6, +9, +12)

*Series II* : 7, 11, 15, 19 (addition of 4 at each step)

**16. *(a)* :** The difference between the consecutive numbers in the series increases by 2 at each step.

2   6   12   20   30   42

+4   +6   +8   +10   +12

**17. *(b)* :** There are two alternate series :

+4   +4   +4

1   4   5   11   9   18   13   25

+7   +7   +7

*Series I* : 1, 5, 9, 13 (addition of 4)

*Series II* : 4, 11, 18, 25 (addition of 7)

**18. *(a)* :** There are two alternate series :

÷3   ÷3   ÷3

27   45   9   15   3   5   1

÷3   ÷3

*Series I* : 27, 9, 3, 1 (division by 3)

*Series II* : 45, 15, 5 (division by 3)

**19. *(d)* :** Two consecutive numbers form a pair. The difference between the numbers placed at odd places increases by 11 and the second number is the fraction part of the number.

$3 \quad \frac{1}{3} \quad 14 \quad \frac{1}{14} \quad 25 \quad \frac{1}{25} \quad 36$

+11   +11   +11

**20. *(b)* :** In this fraction series the numbers on the top are increased by 2 and at the bottom, multiplied by 2.

**21. *(d)* :** There are two alternate series :

+3   +5   +7   +9

4   8   7   14   12   22   19   32   28

+6   +8   +10

*Series I* : 4, 7, 12, 19, 28 (sequence is +3, +5, +7, +9)

*Series II* : 8, 14, 22, 32 (sequence is +6, +8, +10)

**22. *(a)* :** The series is formed by multiples of 6 in this manner :

$6 \times 16 = 96$

$6 \times 15 = 90 \quad (16-1) = 15$

$6 \times 13 = 78 \quad (15-2) = 13$

$6 \times 10 = 60 \quad (13-3) = 10$

$6 \times 6 = 36 \quad (10-4) = 6$

$6 \times 1 = 6 \quad (6-5) = 1$

**23. *(c)* :** There are two alternate series :

+5   +7   +9   +11

6   3   11   8   18   15   27   24   38   35

+5   +7   +9   +11

*Series I* : 6, 11, 18, 27, 38

*Series II* : 3, 8, 15, 24, 35

(Both series follow the pattern +5, +7, +9, +11)

**24. *(d)* :** The difference between the numbers in this series is increased by 4 at each step.

1   6   15   28   45   66   91

+5   +9   +13   +17   +21   +25

**25. *(c)* :** The sequence in this series is number into 2 plus the numbers in natural order starting from 0.

1   2   5   12   27   58   121   248

$(1\times2)+0 \quad (2\times2)+1 \quad (5\times2)+2 \quad (12\times2)+3 \quad (27\times2)+4 \quad (58\times2)+5 \quad (121\times2)+6$

# 5. WRONG NUMBER SERIES

In this type of series, the given series may be complete but what needs to be identified is the number in the given completed series which is disturbing the sequential pattern of that series and does not fit in with the relationship shared between the other numbers.

## EXERCISE

**Directions :** *In the given series find the number which is wrong.*

**1.** 5, 25, 120, 625, 3125, 15625
(*a*) 15625 (*b*) 625
(*c*) 120 (*d*) 5

**2.** 4, 8, 11, 22, 18, 36, 24, 50
(*a*) 8 (*b*) 22
(*c*) 36 (*d*) 24

**3.** 2, 4, 12, 24, 72, 142, 432
(*a*) 432 (*b*) 12
(*c*) 142 (*d*) 72

**4.** 2, 3, 4, 4, 6, 8, 9, 12, 16
(*a*) 3 (*b*) 9
(*c*) 6 (*d*) 12

**5.** 97, 91, 86, 83, 79, 77, 76, 76
(*a*) 86 (*b*) 76
(*c*) 91 (*d*) 83

**6.** 7, 11, 11, 9, 15, 7, 19, 5, 23, 1
(*a*) 5 (*b*) 7
(*c*) 1 (*d*) 9

**7.** 3, 7, 12, 28, 48, 118, 192, 448
(*a*) 12 (*b*) 118
(*c*) 28 (*d*) 7

**8.** 10, 100, 1100, 11000, 111000, 1210000
(*a*) 1210000 (*b*) 11000
(*c*) 100 (*d*) 111000

**9.** 24576, 6144, 1536, 386, 96, 24
(*a*) 386 (*b*) 6144
(*c*) 96 (*d*) 1536

**10.** 11, 13, 15, 17, 19, 23, 29, 31, 37
(*a*) 13 (*b*) 23
(*c*) 15 (*d*) 31

**11.** 36, 43, 49, 54, 60, 61, 63, 64
(*a*) 60 (*b*) 63
(*c*) 54 (*d*) 43

**12.** 3, 10, 41, 206, 1236, 8660
(*a*) 10 (*b*) 41
(*c*) 206 (*d*) 1236

**13.** 17, 25, 37, 50, 65, 82, 101
(*a*) 25 (*b*) 17
(*c*) 101 (*d*) 65

**14.** 12, 20, 38, 42, 56, 72
(*a*) 20 (*b*) 38
(*c*) 56 (*d*) 72

**15.** 5, 6, 11, 22, 42, 88, 176
(*a*) 5 (*b*) 42
(*c*) 176 (*d*) 11

**16.** 905, 180, 175, 35, 30, 6, 1
(*a*) 6 (*b*) 1
(*c*) 175 (*d*) 905

**17.** 5040, 840, 160, 42, 14, 7
(*a*) 7 (*b*) 160
(*c*) 14 (*d*) 840

**18.** 3, 32, 363, 3993, 43923
(*a*) 363 (*b*) 3
(*c*) 32 (*d*) 43923

**19.** 3, 18, 38, 78, 123, 178, 243
(*a*) 78 (*b*) 3
(*c*) 123 (*d*) 18

**20.** 0, 1, 2, 2, 4, 4, 6, 8, 8, 10
(*a*) 6 (*b*) 0
(*c*) 1 (*d*) 10

**21.** 5, 12, 16, 24, 27
(*a*) 12 (*b*) 16
(*c*) 24 (*d*) 27

**22.** 27, 36, 45, 60, 71, 99
(*a*) 27 (*b*) 45
(*c*) 60 (*d*) 71

**23.** 81, 64, 49, 35, 25, 16
(*a*) 64 (*b*) 35
(*c*) 25 (*d*) 16

**24.** 625, 125, 25, 5, 0
(*a*) 0 (*b*) 125
(*c*) 5 (*d*) 625

**25.** 25, 19, 17, 13, 11, 7
(*a*) 25 (*b*) 17
(*c*) 13 (*d*) 7

# EXPLANATORY ANSWERS

**1. (*c*) :** The numbers in the series are multiplied by 5 to get the next number.

∴ 125 should be in place of 120.

**2. (*d*) :** Two numbers form a pair. The first number increases by 7 for the next pair and the second number is the double of first number.

4 8 11 22 18 36 25 50
×2 ×2 ×2 ×2
+7 +7 +7

∴ 25 should be in place of 24.

**3. (*c*) :** There are two alternate series and in each series, the numbers are multiplied by 6 to get the next number.

×6 ×6 ×6
2 4 12 24 72 144 432
×6 ×6

∴ 144 should be in place of 142.

**4. (*b*) :** There are three alternate series and in each series, the numbers are multiplied by 2 to get the next number.

×2 ×2
2 3 4 4 6 8 8 12 16
×2 ×2
×2 ×2

*Series I* : 2, 4, 8
*Series II* : 3, 6, 12
*Series III* : 4, 8, 16

∴ 8 should be in place of 9.

**5. (*d*) :** The difference between the consecutive numbers in the series decreases by 1 at each step.

97 91 86 82 79 77 76 76
−6 −5 −4 −3 −2 −1 −0

∴ 82 should be in place of 83.

**6. (*c*) :** There are two alternate series :

+4 +4 +4 +4
7 11 11 9 15 7 19 5 21 3
−2 −2 −2 −2

*Series I* : 7, 11, 15, 19, 23 (addition of 4)
*Series II* : 11, 9, 7, 5, 3 (subtraction of 2)

∴ 3 should be in place of 1.

**7. (*b*) :** There are two alternate series and in each series, the numbers are multiplied by 4 to get the next number.

×4 ×4 ×4
3 7 12 28 48 112 192 448
×4 ×4 ×4

∴ 112 should be in place of 118.

**8. (*d*) :** The numbers in this series are multiplied by 10 and 11 alternately is, *i.e.,* × 10, × 11.

10 100 1100 11000 121000 1210000
× 10 × 11 × 10 × 11 × 10

∴ 121000 should be in place of 111000.

**9. (*a*) :** The numbers in this series are divided by 4 to get the next number.

24576 6144 1536 384 96 24
÷4 ÷4 ÷4 ÷4 ÷4

∴ 384 should be in place of 386.

**10. (*c*) :** The series comprises of prime numbers in increasing order. Only 15 is an exception.

**11. (a) :** The difference between two consecutive numbers is decreasing by 1 at each step.

36 43 49 54 58 61 63 64

+7 +6 +5 +4 +3 +2 +1

∴ 58 should be in place of 60.

**12. (d) :** The sequence followed in this series is :

$3 \times 3 + 1 = 10$
$10 \times 4 + 1 = 41$
$41 \times 5 + 1 = 206$
$206 \times 6 + 1 = 1237$; and
$1237 \times 7 + 1 = 8660$

∴ 1237 should be in place of 1236.

**13. (a) :** The numbers in the series are 1 plus the squares of numbers in natural order starting from 4.

17 26 37 50 65 82 101

↓ ↓ ↓ ↓ ↓ ↓ ↓

$4^2 + 1$ $5^2 + 1$ $6^2 + 1$ $7^2 + 1$ $8^2 + 1$ $9^2 + 1$ $10^2 + 1$

∴ 26 should be in place of 25.

**14. (b) :** The sequence followed in this series is :

$3 \times 4 = 12$
$4 \times 5 = 20$
$5 \times 6 = 30$
$6 \times 7 = 42$
$7 \times 8 = 56$
$8 \times 9 = 72$

∴ 30 should be in place of 38.

**15. (b) :** The numbers in the series are the sum of all the numbers preceding them.

5 6 11 22 44 88 176

(5 + 6)

(5 + 6 + 11)

(5 + 6 + 11 + 22)

(5 + 6 + 11 + 22 + 44)

(5 + 6 + 11 + 22 + 44 + 88)

∴ 44 should be in place of 42.

**16. (d) :** The sequence followed in the series is ÷ 5, – 5 which is repeated.

900 180 175 35 30 6 1

÷5 –5 ÷5 –5 ÷5 –5

∴ 900 should be in place of 905.

**17. (b) :** The numbers in the series are divided by numbers in reverse order starting from 6 to get the next number.

5040 840 168 42 14 7

÷6 ÷5 ÷4 ÷3 ÷2

∴ 168 should be in place of 160.

**18. (c) :** The numbers in this series are multiplied by 11 to get the next number.

3 33 363 3993 43923

×11 ×11 ×11 ×11

∴ 33 should be in place of 32.

**19. (b) :** 3 is the only prime number in the series.

**20. (d) :** There are two alternate series :

+2 +2 +2 +2

0 1 2 2 4 4 6 8 8 16

×2 ×2 ×2 ×2

*Series I* : 0, 2, 4, 6, 8, (addition of 2)

*Series II* : 1, 2, 4, 8, 16 (multiplication by 2)

∴ 16 should be in place of 10.

**21. (c) :** The sequence in the series is +7, +4 which is repeated, *i.e.*,

5 12 16 23 27

+7 +4 +7 +4

∴ 23 should be in place of 24.

**22. (d) :** All other numbers are divisible by 3.

**23. (b) :** The sequence is the square of the number in decreasing order starting from 9, *i.e.*,

$9^2 = 9 \times 9 = 81$
$8^2 = 8 \times 8 = 64$
$7^2 = 7 \times 7 = 49$
$6^2 = 6 \times 6 = 36$
$5^2 = 5 \times 5 = 25$
$4^2 = 4 \times 4 = 16$

∴ 36 should be in place of 35.

**24. (a) :** The number in the series are divided by 5 to get the next number

625 125 25 5 1

÷5 ÷5 ÷5 ÷5

∴ 1 should be in place of 0 digit.

**25. (a) :** Other numbers are prime numbers.

# 6. WORD ANALOGY

In Analogy Tests, the relationship between two given words is established and then applied to the other words. The type of relationship may vary, so while attempting such questions the first step is to identify the type of relationship, which can be any one of the following.

## EXERCISE

**Directions :** *In the questions given below one term is missing. Based on the relationship of the two given words find the missing term from the given options.*

**1.** HUNGER : FOOD : : THIRST : ?
(*a*) Water (*b*) Drink
(*c*) Tea (*d*) Coffee

**2.** HUNTER : GUN : : WRITER : ?
(*a*) Book (*b*) Pen
(*c*) Poem (*d*) Page

**3.** WOOL : SHEEP : : SILK : ?
(*a*) Saree (*b*) String
(*c*) Silkworm (*d*) Moth

**4.** FOOD : STOMACH : : FUEL : ?
(*a*) Engine (*b*) Automobile
(*c*) Rail (*d*) Aeroplane

**5.** WATER : SAND : : OCEAN : ?
(*a*) Island (*b*) River
(*c*) Desert (*d*) Waves

**6.** ADULT : BABY : : FLOWER : ?
(*a*) Seed (*b*) Bud
(*c*) Fruit (*d*) Butterfly

**7.** WRITER : READER : : PRODUCER : ?
(*a*) Creator (*b*) Contractor
(*c*) Creature (*d*) Consumer

**8.** ENTRANCE : EXIT : : LOYALTY : ?
(*a*) Treachery (*b*) Patriotism
(*c*) Fidelity (*d*) Reward

**9.** MOTHER : MATERNAL : : FATHER : ?
(*a*) Eternal (*b*) Detrimental
(*c*) Paternal (*d*) Formidable

**10.** PEARL : NECKLACE : : FLOWER : ?
(*a*) Plant (*b*) Garden
(*c*) Petal (*d*) Bouquet

**11.** ALPHABET : WORD : : WORD : ?
(*a*) Sound (*b*) Music
(*c*) Sentence (*d*) Dictionary

**12.** LIFE : DEATH : : HOPE : ?
(*a*) Cry (*b*) Pain
(*c*) Despair (*d*) Sad

**13.** GOOD : BAD : : VIRTUE : ?
(*a*) Blame (*b*) Sin
(*c*) Despair (*d*) Vice

**14.** BIRD : FLY : : SNAKE : ?
(*a*) Timid (*b*) Clatter
(*c*) Crawl (*d*) Hole

**15.** CAT : MOUSE : : BIRD : ?
(*a*) Cage (*b*) Trap
(*c*) Eagle (*d*) Worm

**16.** STATE : EXILE
(*a*) Police : Arrest
(*b*) Judge : Convict
(*c*) Constitution : Amendment
(*d*) Church : Excommunicate

**17.** CAPRICIOUSNESS : RELIABILITY
(*a*) Extemporaneous : Predictability
(*b*) Unreliable : Inhuman
(*c*) Tenacious : Practicality
(*d*) Arbitrary : Whimsical

**18.** LOATH : COERCION
(*a*) Detest : Caressing
(*b*) Irritate : Caressing
(*c*) Irate : Antagonism
(*d*) Reluctant : Persuasion

**19.** SCALES : FISH
(*a*) Lady : Dress (*b*) Tree : Leaves
(*c*) Bird : Feather (*d*) Skin : Man

**20.** TREE : SAPLING
(*a*) Hut : Mansion
(*b*) Giant : Dwarf
(*c*) Horse : Foal
(*d*) Ant : Elephant

**21.** CHALK : BLACKBOARD
(*a*) Door : Handle
(*b*) Table : Chair
(*c*) Ink : Paper
(*d*) Type : Paint

**22.** PRIMEVAL : MEDIEVAL
(*a*) Dinosaur : Dragon
(*b*) Gorilla : Soldier
(*c*) Evolution : Revelation
(*d*) Thorn : Rose

**23.** TRILOGY : NOVEL
(*a*) Rice : Husk
(*b*) Milk : Cream
(*c*) Fabric : Weaving
(*d*) Serial : Episode

**24.** PEDANT : ERUDITION
(*a*) Prude : Modesty
(*b*) Blunt : Politician
(*c*) Diplomats : Tactless
(*d*) Enemy : Friendly

**25.** FURY : IRE
(*a*) Convulsion : Spasm
(*b*) Amusement : Happiness
(*c*) Joke : Laugh
(*d*) Dispassion : Emotion

**26.** BaBy : TaTa : : LiLy : ?
(*a*) PooL (*b*) ROse
(*c*) HaNd (*d*) DoWN

**27.** BCDA : STUR : : KLMJ : ?
(*a*) VWXU (*b*) EFHG
(*c*) SRTU (*d*) QSRP

**28.** AEI : LPT : : CGK : ?
(*a*) OSV (*b*) RUY
(*c*) TXC (*d*) FJN

**29.** RUX : TRP : : BEH : ?
(*a*) SQN (*b*) QON
(*c*) QOM (*d*) QNL

**30.** CART : ART : : FOUR : ?
(*a*) RUN (*b*) TWO
(*c*) QUE (*d*) OUR

**31.** FIK : JGO : : DFR : ?
(*a*) BIO (*b*) HDV
(*c*) GCU (*d*) FLP

**32.** LJH : KKI : : CIA : ?
(*a*) BJB (*b*) DHB
(*c*) BJC (*d*) BBJ

**33.** ACE : HIL : : MOQ : ?
(*a*) SVW (*b*) TUX
(*c*) RTW (*d*) WUS

**34.** BCDE : WVUT : : QRST : ?
(*a*) EFHG (*b*) JIHG
(*c*) POML (*d*) GEDC

**35.** PNLJ : IGEC : : USQO : ?
(*a*) HJLN (*b*) LNJH
(*c*) NLJH (*d*) JHNL

**36.** DIMO : DMIO : : JUVR : ?
(*a*) JVRU (*b*) JRVU
(*c*) JVUR (*d*) JUVR

## EXPLANATORY ANSWERS

**1. (*a*) :** Hunger is satiated by food, thirst by water.

**2. (*b*) :** Weapon of a hunter is a gun, weapon of a writer is a pen.

**3. (*c*) :** Wool is obtained from sheep, silk is obtained from silkworm.

**4. (*a*) :** Food is consumed in stomach, fuel is consumed in engine.

**5. (*c*) :** The related words are near opposites.

**6. (*b*) :** The youngone of an adult is a baby and that of a flower is a bud.

**7. (*d*) :** A writer aims to please the readers by his writings, a producer aims to please the consumers by his products.

**8. (*a*) :** The related words are opposites.

**9. (*c*) :** Relations on the mother's side are maternal and on the father's side paternal.

**10.** ***(d)*** **:** Many pearls make a necklace, many flowers make a bouquet.

**11.** ***(c)*** **:** More than one alphabet make a word, more than one word make a sentence.

**12.** ***(c)*** **:** The related words are opposites.

**13.** ***(d)*** **:** The related words are opposites.

**14.** ***(c)*** **:** Birds fly, snakes crawl.

**15.** ***(d)*** **:** Cat chases the mouse, bird chases the worm.

**16.** ***(d)*** **:** Punishment of leaving the State is exile, punishment of leaving the Church is excommunication.

**17.** ***(c)*** **:** The related words are antonyms.

**18.** ***(d)*** **:** Loathing is the result of constant coersion, reluctance is the result of constant persuasion.

**19.** ***(d)*** **:** Covering of the fish is scales, covering of man is skin.

**20.** ***(c)*** **:** Young tree is a sapling, young horse is a foal.

**21.** ***(c)*** **:** Chalk is used to write on blackboard, ink is used to write on paper.

**22.** ***(a)*** **:** The related words represent almost the same time period and answer option represents almost the same sized creatures.

**23.** ***(d)*** **:** Trilogy is section of a novel, episode is a section of a serial.

**24.** ***(a)*** **:** The related words are synonyms.

**25.** ***(b)*** **:** Fury causes ire, amusement causes happiness.

**26.** ***(c)*** **:** In each group the alternate letters are capitals.

**27.** ***(a)*** **:** In each group the first three letters are consecutive and they follow the fourth letter.

ABCD : RSTU : : JKLM : UVWX

**28.** ***(d)*** **:** In each group the letters jump three letters between them, *i.e.,* they are moving to the fourth letter.

AEI : LPT :: CGK : FJN

+4 +4   +4 +4   +4 +4   +4 +4

**29.** ***(c)*** **:** The letters in first set are jumping two letters, *i.e.,* moving three steps forward and in the second they are jumping one letter, *i.e.* moving two steps backward.

RUX : TRP :: BEH : QOM

+3 +3   –2 –2   +3+3   –2 –2

**30.** ***(d)*** **:** The first set of letters drop the first letter to get the second set.

CART : ART :: FOUR : OUR

**31.** ***(b)*** **:** The three letters in first set are moved +4, –2, and +4 steps respectively.

FIK : JGO :: DFR : HDV

+4, –2, +4   +4, –2, +4

**32.** ***(a)*** **:** The letters in the first set are moved –1, +1 and +1 steps respectively.

LJH : KKI :: CIA : BJB

–1, +1, +1   –1, +1, +1

**33.** ***(b)*** **:** The three letters are moved +7, +6 and +7 steps forward respectively.

ACE : HIL :: MOQ : TUX

+7, +6, +7   +7, +6, +7

**34.** ***(b)*** **:** The consecutive letters in the first set are in natural order and in the second set, they are in reverse order.

BCDE → : WVUT ← :: QRST → : JIHG ←

**35.** ***(c)*** **:** The letters are moved seven steps backwards.

PNLJ : IGEC :: USQO : NLJH

–7, –7, –7, –7   –7, –7, –7, –7

**36.** ***(c)*** **:** Only the middle letters are reversed to obtain the second set of letters.

DIMO : DMIO :: JUVR : JVUR

# 7. NUMBER ANALOGY

In number analogy also, the relationship between the given numbers is detected and then applied to the second part to find the missing numbers. This relationship between the numbers can be based on any of the following patterns : *(i)* numbers can be odd/even/prime numbers; *(ii)* numbers can be multiples of one number; *(iii)* numbers can be squares/cubes of different numbers; *(iv)* some numbers can be added to/ subtracted from/multiplied to/divided into the first number to get the second number; *(v)* the second number can be the sum/product/difference of the digits of first number; and *(vi)* combinations of any mathematical calculations given above can apply to the relationship between the two given numbers.

## EXERCISE

**Directions :** *In the following questions, select the number from the given options which follows the same relationship as shared between the first two numbers.*

**1.** 1 : 11 : : 2 : ?
(*a*) 20 (*b*) 22
(*c*) 24 (*d*) 44

**2.** $\frac{1}{7} : \frac{1}{14} :: \frac{1}{9} : ?$
(*a*) $\frac{1}{88}$ (*b*) $\frac{1}{80}$
(*c*) $\frac{1}{81}$ (*d*) $\frac{1}{18}$

**3.** 0.16 : 0.0016 : : 1.02 : ?
(*a*) 10.20 (*b*) 0.102
(*c*) 0.0102 (*d*) 1.020

**4.** 663 : 884 : : 221 : ?
(*a*) 332 (*b*) 554
(*c*) 773 (*d*) 442

**5.** 16 : 0.16 : : ?
(*a*) 2 : 0.02 (*b*) 7 : 0.007
(*c*) 1.3 : 0.13 (*d*) 0.01 : 0.001

**6.** $3 : \frac{1}{3} :: ?$
(*a*) 6 : 12 (*b*) 5 : 2/15
(*c*) 8 : 1/8 (*d*) 9 : 27

**7.** 65 : 13 : : 180 : ?
(*a*) 93 (*b*) 36
(*c*) 133 (*d*) 102

**8.** 125 : 27 : : 343 : ?
(*a*) 729 (*b*) 64
(*c*) 216 (*d*) 512

**9.** 357 : 73 : : ?
(*a*) 429 : 94 (*b*) 201 : 21
(*c*) 138 : 38 (*d*) 93 : 39

**10.** 731 : 902 : : 655 : ?
(*a*) 646 (*b*) 800
(*c*) 793 (*d*) 556

**11.** 162 : 9 : : 310 : ?
(*a*) 33 (*b*) 27
(*c*) 16 (*d*) 4

**12.** 13 : 17 : : 15 : ?
(*a*) 19 (*b*) 11
(*c*) 21 (*d*) 16

**13.** 225 : 15 : : 256 : ?
(*a*) 26 (*b*) 16
(*c*) 20 (*d*) 28

**14.** 46 : 48 : : 54 : ?
(*a*) 59 (*b*) 40
(*c*) 67 (*d*) 62

**15.** 33 : 36 : : 21 : ?
(*a*) 9 (*b*) 18
(*c*) 25 (*d*) 32

**16.** 123 : 149 : : 201 : ?
(*a*) 202 (*b*) 404
(*c*) 401 (*d*) 227

**17.** 7 : 105 : : 5 : ?
(*a*) 97 (*b*) 83
(*c*) 75 (*d*) 61

**18.** 11 : 101 : : 73 : ?
(*a*) 153 (*b*) 330
(*c*) 543 (*d*) 703

**19.** 4 : 32 : : 8 : ?
(*a*) 34 (*b*) 68
(*c*) 92 (*d*) 128

**20.** 94 : 26 : : 62 : ?
(*a*) 16 (*b*) 22
(*c*) 39 (*d*) 48

## EXPLANATORY ANSWERS

**1. (*b*) :** The first number is repeated to obtain the second number.

**2. (*d*) :** The first fraction is multiplied by half to obtain the second fraction.

$\frac{1}{7} : \frac{1}{14} :: \frac{1}{9} : \frac{1}{18}$ ($\times \frac{1}{2}$, $\times \frac{1}{2}$)

**3. (*c*) :** The decimals are divided by 100.

0.16 : 0.0016 :: 1.02 : 0.0102 ($\div 100$, $\div 100$)

**4. (*d*) :** The digits at tens and hundreds place is same but the digit at the units place is half the other identical digits.

663 : 884 :: 221 : 442

**5. (*a*) :** Of the two related numbers, the second number is the result of first number divided by 100.

16 : 0.16 :: 2 : 0.02 ($\div 100$, $\div 100$)

**6. (*c*) :** Of the two related numbers, the second number is the part fraction of the first number, *i.e.* 3 is related to one-third $\left(\frac{1}{3}\right)$. Similarly, 8 will be related to one-eighth $\left(\frac{1}{8}\right)$.

**7. (*b*) :** The first number is divided by 5 to get the second number.

65 : 13 :: 180 : 36 ($\div 5$, $\div 5$)

**8. (*a*) :** The numbers are cubes of different odd numbers.

125 : 27 :: 343 : 729
$\downarrow$ $\downarrow$ $\downarrow$ $\downarrow$
$5^3$ $3^3$ $7^3$ $9^3$

**9. (*a*) :** The central digit of the first number is left out and the corner digits written in reverse order to get the second number.

357 : 73 :: 429 : 94

**10. (*a*) :** The sum of the digits of both the numbers is same.

$731 : 902 \rightarrow 7+3+1$
$= 9+0+2$ *i.e.* $11 = 11$
$655 : 646 \rightarrow 6+5+5$
$= 6+4+6$ *i.e.* $16 = 16$

**11. (*d*) :** The sum of the digits of the first number is the second number.

162 : 9 :: 310 : 4 ($1+6+2$, $3+1+0$)

**12. (*a*) :** First number plus 4 gives the second number.

13 : 17 :: 15 : 19 ($+4$, $+4$)

**13. (*b*) :** The root of first number is the second number.

225 : 15 :: 256 : 16 ($\sqrt{225}$, $\sqrt{256}$)

**14. (*b*) :** The product of the digits of first number is multiplied by 2 to get the second number.

46 : 48 :: 54 : 40 ($(4 \times 6)2$, $(5 \times 4)2$)

**15. *(a)*:** The square of the sum of the digits of the first number is the second number.

33 : 36 :: 21 : 9

$(3+3)^2$ $(2+1)^2$

**16. *(c)*:** Each digit of the first number are squared to get the digits of the second number.

123 : 149 :: 201 : 401

$1^2$, $2^2$, $3^2$ $2^2$, $0^2$, $1^2$

**17. *(c)*:** The first number is multiplied by 15 to get the second number.

7 : 105 :: 5 : 75

× 15 × 15

**18. *(d)*:** Zero is inserted in between the digits of the first number to get the second number.

11 : 101 :: 73 : 703

**19. *(d)*:** Double the first number multiplied by the number itself gives the second number.

4 : 32 :: 8 : 128

$(4 \times 2)\,4$ $(8 \times 2)\,8$

**20. *(a)*:** The sum of the digits of the first number multiplied by two gives the second number.

94 : 26 :: 62 : 16

$(9+4) \times 2$ $(6+2) \times 2$

# 8. ODD ONE OUT

In this type of classification, four words are given out of which three are almost same in matter or meaning and only one word is different from the common three. One has to find out the word which is different from the rest.

## EXERCISE

**Directions :** *In each of the following questions, three words are alike in some manner. Spot the odd one out.*

1. (*a*) Green (*b*) Red (*c*) Colour (*d*) Orange
2. (*a*) Stable (*b*) Hole (*c*) Canoe (*d*) Sty
3. (*a*) Nose (*b*) Eyes (*c*) Skin (*d*) Teeth
4. (*a*) Venus (*b*) Moon (*c*) Pluto (*d*) Mars
5. (*a*) Happy (*b*) Gloomy (*c*) Lively (*d*) Cheerful

**Directions :** *Three of the following four in each question are alike in a certain way and so form a group. Select the group of letters that does not belong to that group.*

6. (*a*) ACE (*b*) LOR (*c*) GIK (*d*) VXZ
7. (*a*) TSR (*b*) LKJ (*c*) PQO (*d*) HGF
8. (*a*) EF LM (*b*) KJ SR (*c*) XW HG (*d*) ED YX
9. (*a*) JOPK (*b*) BOPC (*c*) QOPR (*d*) TOPS
10. (*a*) DfH (*b*) MoQ (*c*) UwY (*d*) InO

**Directions :** *In each of the following questions, there are four options. Three numbers, in these options, are alike in certain manner. Only one number does not fit in. Choose the one which is different from the rest.*

11. (*a*) 1948 (*b*) 2401 (*c*) 966 (*d*) 1449
12. (*a*) 182 (*b*) 169 (*c*) 130 (*d*) 158
13. (*a*) 129 (*b*) 130 (*c*) 131 (*d*) 132
14. (*a*) 3215 (*b*) 9309 (*c*) 4721 (*d*) 2850
15. (*a*) 1776 (*b*) 2364 (*c*) 1976 (*d*) 3776

**Directions :** *In the following questions select the pair which is different from the other three.*

16. (*a*) Chair - Furniture
    (*b*) Shirt - Garment
    (*c*) Necklace - Jewellery
    (*d*) Bogie - Engine
17. (*a*) Crayon - Paper
    (*b*) Pencil - Lead
    (*c*) Pen - Ink
    (*d*) Brush - Paint
18. (*a*) War - Peace
    (*b*) Real - Natural
    (*c*) Premiere - First
    (*d*) Wrath - Anger
19. (*a*) Finger - Thimble
    (*b*) Head - Cap
    (*c*) Waist - Tiara
    (*d*) Foot - Shoe
20. (*a*) Day - Night
    (*b*) Clever - Foolish
    (*c*) Clear - Blurred
    (*d*) Arrive - Come

**Directions :** *In the following questions, which of the following pair of letters is different from the other three?*

**21.** (*a*) FGH - HIJ (*b*) PQR - RST (*c*) MNO - OPQ (*d*) CDE - DEF

**22.** (*a*) JuM - jUm (*b*) iLo - Ilo (*c*) PSa - psA (*d*) ZeX - zEx

**23.** (*a*) NQT - JMP (*b*) CFI - RUX (*c*) ADG - FGH (*d*) SVY - ORU

**24.** (*a*) DXD - XDX (*b*) KUK - UKU (*c*) FHF - EHE (*d*) RSR - SRS

**25.** (*a*) AYT - BZU (*b*) FNG - EMF (*c*) RWO - QVN (*d*) HJD - GIC

**Directions :** *Which of the following pair of numbers is different from the other three pairs?*

**26.** (*a*) 28, 4 (*b*) 63, 7 (*c*) 56, 8 (*d*) 35, 5

**27.** (*a*) 3, 11 (*b*) 8, 16 (*c*) 5, 13 (*d*) 14, 24

**28.** (*a*) 13, 156 (*b*) 12, 144 (*c*) 15, 180 (*d*) 16, 176

**29.** (*a*) 32, 13 (*b*) 46, 20 (*c*) 51, 24 (*d*) 72, 45

**30.** (*a*) 5, 25 (*b*) 9, 81 (*c*) 4, 64 (*d*) 6, 36

**31.** (*a*) 91, 10 (*b*) 57, 12 (*c*) 69, 15 (*d*) 72, 13

**32.** (*a*) 20, 10 (*b*) 45, 27 (*c*) 15, 12 (*d*) 30, 18

**33.** (*a*) 7, 3 (*b*) 13, 9 (*c*) 11, 7 (*d*) 17, 8

**34.** (*a*) 10, 20 (*b*) 40, 50 (*c*) 30, 40 (*d*) 50, 60

**35.** (*a*) 16, 26 (*b*) 3, 4 (*c*) 26, 24 (*d*) 27, 25

## EXPLANATORY ANSWERS

**1. (*c*) :** All others are types of colour.

**2. (*c*) :** Canoe is a boat. Others are resting places of birds/animals.

**3. (*d*) :** All others are sense organs.

**4. (*b*) :** All others are planets.

**5. (*b*) :** All others are expressions of joy.

**6. (*b*) :** The sequence in each group is +2. Only option (*b*) has sequence in +3, *i.e.*,

ABCDE (+2, +2)　　LMNOPQR (+3, +3)

GHIJK (+2, +2)　　VWXYZ (+2, +2)

**7. (*c*) :** The sequence of alphabet in each group is in reverse order. Only option (*c*) has sequence in disturbed order.

**8. (*a*) :** Two consecutive alphabet in each group are in reverse sequence (–1), *i.e.*,

KJ (–1) SR (–1); XW (–1) HG (–1); ED (–1) YX (–1)

Only in option (*a*) the sequence is in natural order (+1), *i.e.*,

EF (+1)　　LM (+1)

**9. (*d*) :** In each group, letters 'OP' are common. The two corner alphabet are in natural order (+1); *i.e.*,

JOPK (+1); BOPC (+1); QOPR (+1)

Only in option (*d*) they are in reverse order (–1); *i.e.*,

TOPS (–1)

**10. (*d*) :** In other groups, only the alphabet in the centre is of lower case. In this option letter 'L' on the left is also in lower case.

**11. (*a*) :** Other numbers are divisible by 7.

**12. (*d*) :** Other numbers are multiples of 13.

**13. (*c*) :** 131 is a prime number.

**14. (*b*) :** In other numbers, no digit is repeated.

**15. (*b*) :** In other numbers, the last two digits are same.

**16. (*d*) :** Bogie is a part of train which is a type of conveyance. Chair, Shirt and Necklace are types of furniture, garment and jewellery respectively.

**17. (a) :** The medium used for writing with pencil is lead, with pen it is ink and with brush, it is paint. With crayon it should be wax.

**18. (a) :** The pair of words are opposite. Other pairs are synonyms.

**19. (c) :** Tiara is worn on the head.

**20. (d) :** Other words are opposite to each other.

**21. (d) :** In all other groups, the letters are in natural series and the last letter of first part is the first letter of the second part.

**22. (b) :** In all other groups, only the vowel is in lower case in the first part and in second part the case is reversed.

**23. (c) :** In all other groups, the letters jump two letters in between them.

**24. (c) :** In all other groups, the single letter in first part is repeated in the second and vice versa.

**25. (a) :** In all other groups, the letters in the first part are one step forward than the corresponding letters in the second part.

**26. (b) :** In all other pairs 7 times the second number is the first number. In this option 9 times 7 is the first number.

**27. (d) :** In all other groups, the difference between the two numbers is 8.

**28. (d) :** In other groups 12 times, the first number is the second number. In this option 11 times the first number is the second number.

**29. (a) :** 13 is a prime number.

**30. (c) :** In all other pairs, the second number is a perfect square of the first.

**31. (d) :** In all other pairs, the second number is the sum of the digits of the first number.

**32. (a) :** In all other pairs, the numbers are divisible by 3.

**33. (d) :** In other groups, the difference between the numbers is 4.

**34. (a) :** In this option, the second number is double the first number. In other groups the difference between the two numbers is 10.

**35. (a) :** In other groups, the first digits of the two numbers are same (consider 3 and 4 as 03 and 04).

# 9. CODING AND DECODING

Coding is a secretive language which is used to change the representation of the actual term/word/value. This coded language can be framed by *(i)* moving the letters one or more steps forward or backward; *(ii)* substituting numbers for letters and vice–versa; *(iii)* writing the letters of the given word in reverse order in part or in whole; and *(iv)* replacing the letters in their natural series by the same positioned letters in their reverse series.

There is variety in ways of coding. Coding language is not only for words and numbers but also for hiding a group of words, statements or even sentences. This form of coding pattern may appear to be confusing but after solving only a few questions it is very easy to understand. Questions based on this coding pattern require no moving of steps or straining efforts of calculations, but only quick tallying or comparing ability. The codes can be letters or numbers.

## EXERCISE

**Directions :** *In the following questions select the right option which indicates the correct code for the word or letter given in the question.*

**1.** If MUSK is coded as 146816, then ZERO will be coded as :

(*a*) 113811 (*b*) 122912
(*c*) 15915 (*d*) 2651815

**2.** If BAD is coded as 7, HIS as 9, LOW will be coded as :

(*a*) 50 (*b*) 8
(*c*) 23 (*d*) 5

**3.** In a certain code LIBERATE is written as 56403170, TRIBAL will be written in the same code as :

(*a*) 734615 (*b*) 736415
(*c*) 136475 (*d*) 034615

**4.** In certain military code, SYSTEM is written as SYSMET, and NEARER as AENRER, what will be the code for FRACTION?

(*a*) CRAFNOIT (*b*) FRCAITNO
(*c*) CARFNOIT (*d*) FRACNOIT

**5.** If CRUDE is written as BSTED, then MOIST will be coded as :

(*a*) NNJRU (*b*) LNHRS
(*c*) NPJTU (*d*) LPHTS

**6.** In a certain code ALPACA is written as ACAPLA. How will ANIMAL be written in that code?

(*a*) LAMINA (*b*) ALAMIN
(*c*) LAMNIA (*d*) AAMLIN

**7.** In a certain code FINGER is written as DGLECP. What will be the code for KIDNEY?

(*a*) IGBLCW (*b*) IGCLBW
(*c*) IBCGLE (*d*) IGBKCV

**8.** In a certain code QUESTION is written as NXBVQLLQ. How will REPLY be coded?

(*a*) YHMOV (*b*) OBMVI
(*c*) VHSOB (*d*) OHMOV

**9.** If in a certain code SKEW is coded as PNCY, then what will JXQV will stand for?

(*a*) MUTS (*b*) MUST
(*c*) MTSU (*d*) STUM

**10.** In a certain code LONDON is written as MPOEPO. What will IVOHSZ mean in the same code?

(*a*) HUNGRY (*b*) HUNDRY
(*c*) GRUNHY (*d*) HONDUS

**11.** In a certain code language 8514 is a code for HEAD, 3945 for RIDE and 057 for BEG. What will be the code for GRADE?

(*a*) 71345 (*b*) 73415
(*c*) 74135 (*d*) 73145

**12.** If MOTHERLAND is coded as 9501623748, how will DREAM be coded?
(*a*) 82697 (*b*) 86297
(*c*) 82769 (*d*) 82679

**13.** If OATH is coded in a certain language as TEYL, then how will WORD be coded?
(*a*) BWRH (*b*) HRWB
(*c*) BSWH (*d*) CSXI

**14.** If FINANCE is coded as GKQESIL, then how will BANK be coded in the same manner?
(*a*) CBOL (*b*) CDRP
(*c*) CCQO (*d*) CCPN

**15.** PLANNING is coded in a certain language as UFFHSCSA. How will AUTHORITY be coded in the same language?
(*a*) FOYBTLNND
(*b*) FYOTBNNLT
(*c*) FBOYTLNTN
(*d*) FBOYTNLTN

**Directions :** *In the following questions study the coded patterns and then select the right option from the given alternatives.*

**16.** In a certain language, (a) 'go ju mi' stands for 'plenty of money'; (b) pao ju go nei vu' for 'money creates lots of problems'; (c) 'kol vu nei' for 'problems create tension'; and (d) 'sol tun ju haw' for 'still money is needed'. Which of the following words stand for 'money'?
(*a*) nei (*b*) ju
(*c*) haw (*d*) go

**17.** In a certain language, (a) 'FOR' stands for 'old is gold'; (b) 'ROT' stands for 'gold is pure'; (c) 'ROM' stands for 'gold is costly'. How will 'pure old gold is costly' be written?
(*a*) TFROM (*b*) FOTRM
(*c*) FTORM (*d*) TOMRF

**18.** In a certain code '415' means 'milk is hot'; '18' means 'hot soup'; and '895' means 'soup is tasty'. What number will indicate the word 'tasty'?
(*a*) 9 (*b*) 8
(*c*) 5 (*d*) 4

**19.** In a certain code '643' means 'she is beautiful', '593' means 'he is handsome', and '567' means 'handsome meets beautiful'. What number will indicate the word 'meets'?
(*a*) 5 (*b*) 3
(*c*) 7 (*d*) 6

**20.** In a certain code language, (a) 'dugo hui mul zo' stands for 'work is very hard'; (b) 'hui dugo ba ki' for 'Bingo is very smart'; (c) 'nano mul dugo' for 'cake is hard', and (d) 'mul ki qu' for 'smart and hard'. Which of the following words stand for 'Bingo'?
(*a*) jalu (*b*) dugo
(*c*) ki (*d*) ba

**Directions :** *Read the given coded information and choose the correct answer from the given options.*

**21.** If 'water' is called 'blue', 'blue' is called 'red', 'red' is called 'white', 'white' is called 'sky', 'sky' is called 'rain', 'rain' is called 'green', 'green' is called 'air' and 'air' is called 'table', which of the following is the colour of milk?
(*a*) white (*b*) rain
(*c*) sky (*d*) green

**22.** If 'light' is called 'dark', 'dark' is called 'green', 'green' is called 'blue', 'blue' is called 'red', 'red' is called 'white' and 'white' is called 'yellow', what is the colour of blood?
(*a*) red (*b*) dark
(*c*) white (*d*) yellow

**23.** If 'sky' is called 'sea', 'sea' is called 'water', 'water' is called 'air', 'air' is called 'cloud' and 'cloud' is called 'river', then what do we drink when thirsty?
(*a*) sky (*b*) air
(*c*) water (*d*) sea

**24.** If 'yellow' means 'red', 'white' means 'green', 'red' means 'orange', 'blue' means 'white' and 'green' means 'blue', then the colour of sky is :
(*a*) white (*b*) green
(*c*) blue (*d*) yellow

**25.** If 'land' is called 'sky', 'sky' is called 'air', 'air' is called 'water', 'water' is called 'sand' and 'sand' is called 'solid', where do fishes swim?
(*a*) air (*b*) sky
(*c*) water (*d*) sand

# EXPLANATORY ANSWERS

**1. *(b)*:** The coded number signifies the position of the alphabet in its reverse order of the alphabetical series (ZYXW...)

M U S K → MUSK
↓ ↓ ↓ ↓
14th 6th 8th 16th → 146816

Similarly,

Z E R O → ZERO
↓ ↓ ↓ ↓
1st 22nd 9th 12th → 122912

**2. *(d)*:** The coded number is the sum of number digits signifying the position of the alphabet in the natural order.

B A D
↓ ↓ ↓
2nd 1st 4th *i.e.,* 2 + 1 + 4 = 7

Similarly,

H I S
↓ ↓ ↓
8th 9th 19th *i.e.,* 8 + 9 + 19 = 36
further, 3 + 6 = 9

Also,

L O W
↓ ↓ ↓
12th 15th 23rd *i.e.,* 12 + 15 + 23 = 50
further, 5 + 0 = 0

**3. *(b)*:** The letters of the word TRIBAL are picked from LIBERATE. So will be the coded numbers.

L I B E R A T E → given word
5 6 4 0 3 1 7 0 → codes

Similarly,

T R I B A L → word to be coded
7 3 6 4 1 5 → answer codes

**4. *(c)*:** The word is divided into two equal parts and the letters of each part are written in reverse order.

SYS TEM SYS MET NEA RER AEN RER

Similarly,

FRAC TION CARF NOIT

**5. *(d)*:** The code is formed by moving the letters one step backwards and one step forward alternately.

CRUDE BSTED
−1
+1
−1
+1
−1

Similarly,

MOIST LPHTS
−1
+1
−1
+1
−1

**6. *(a)*:** The letters of the word are written backwards.

ALPACA ACAPLA

Similarly,

ANIMAL LAMINA

**7. *(a)*:** The word is coded by moving the letters two steps backwards.

FINGER DGLECP
−2
−2
−2
−2
−2
−2

Similarly,

KIDNEY IGBLCW
−2
−2
−2
−2
−2
−2

**8. *(d)* :** The letters of the word are coded by moving three steps backward and three steps forward alternately.

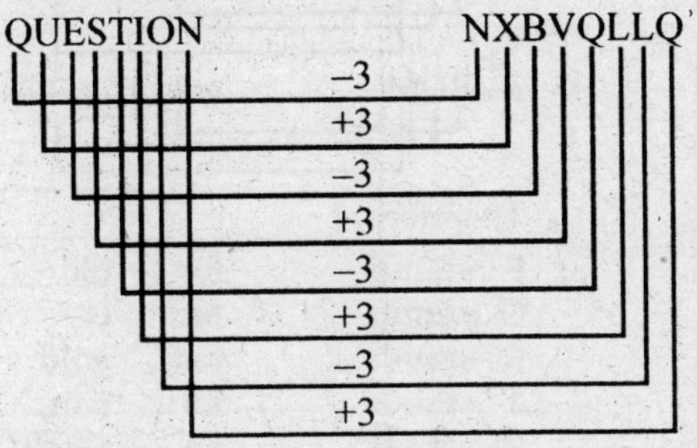


Similarly,

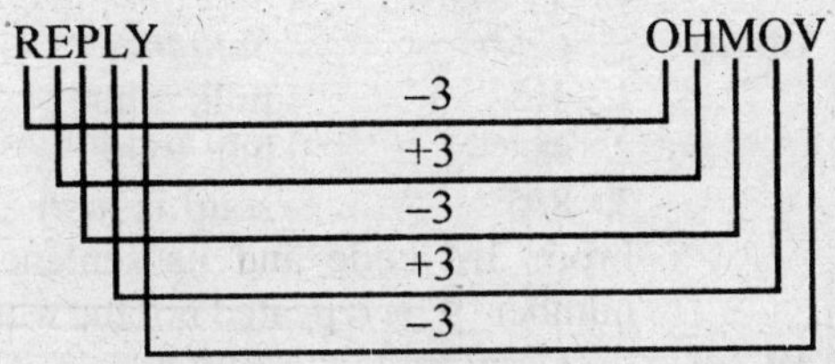


**9. *(b)* :** The letters are decoded by moving the letters +3, –3, +2 and –2 steps respectively.

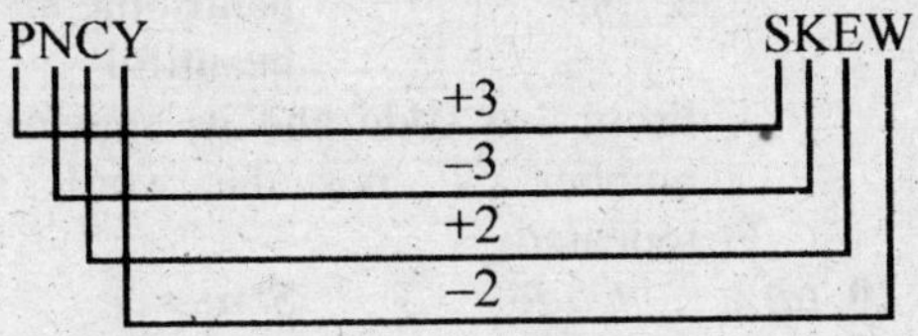


Similarly,

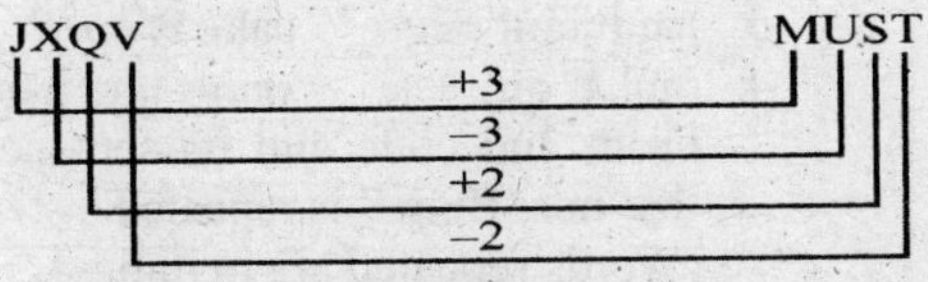


**10. *(a)* :** The letters of the coded word are moved one step backward.

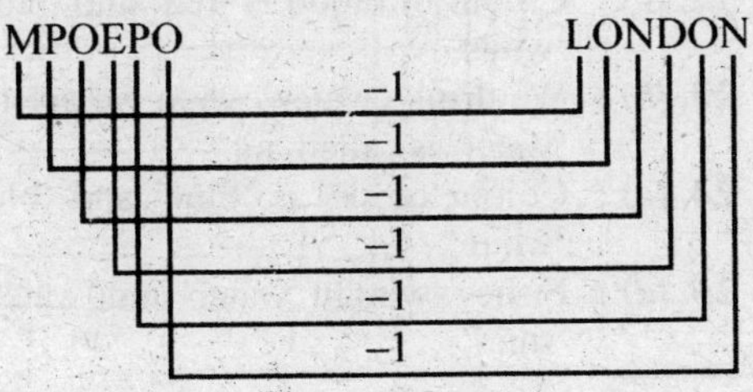


Similarly,

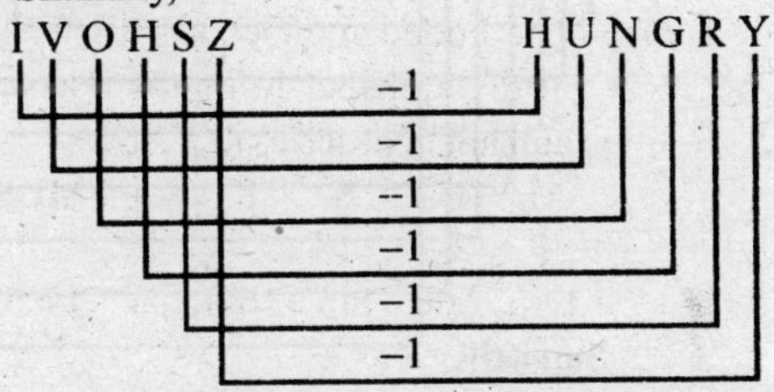


**11. *(d)* :** The word GRADE is framed by letters in the given words. So, in order to find the code for GRADE select the respective number codes.

H E A D R I D E B E G → letters
8 5 1 4 3 9 4 5 0 5 7 → codes

So,

G R A D E →letters
7 3 1 4 5 →answer codes

**12. *(d)* :** The letters of the word are coded by numbers. So to find the code for DREAM select the respective numbers.

M O T H E R L A N D → letters
9 5 0 1 6 2 3 7 4 8 → codes

So, D R E A M → letters
8 2 6 7 9 → answer codes

**13. *(c)* :** The letters are coded by moving five and four steps forward alternately.

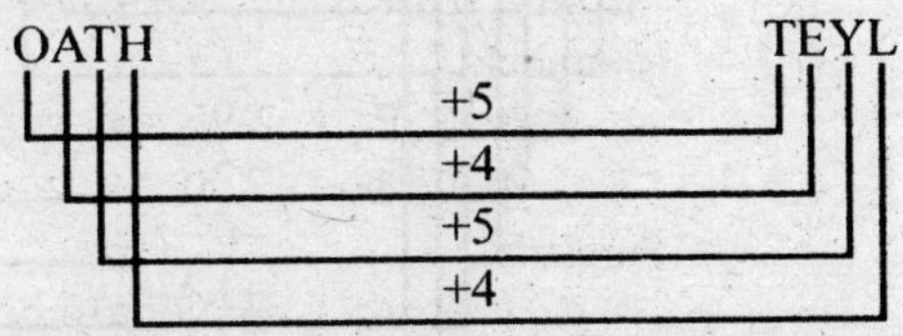


Similarly,

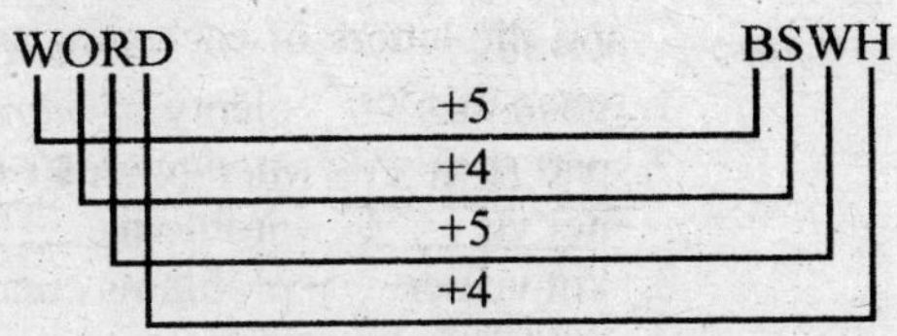


**14. *(c)* :** The letters of the word are coded by moving one step ahead and increasing the difference by one.

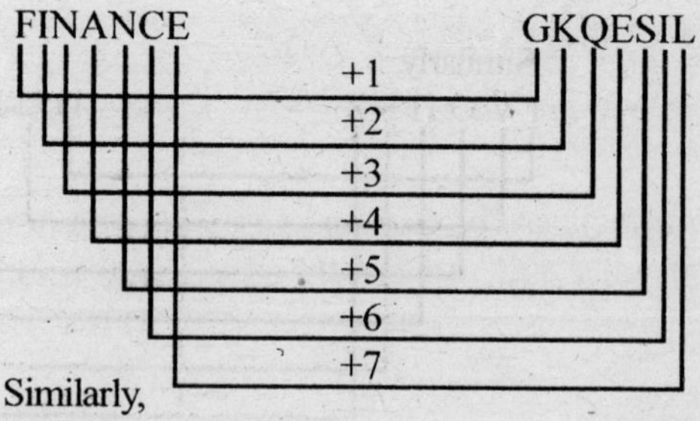


Similarly,

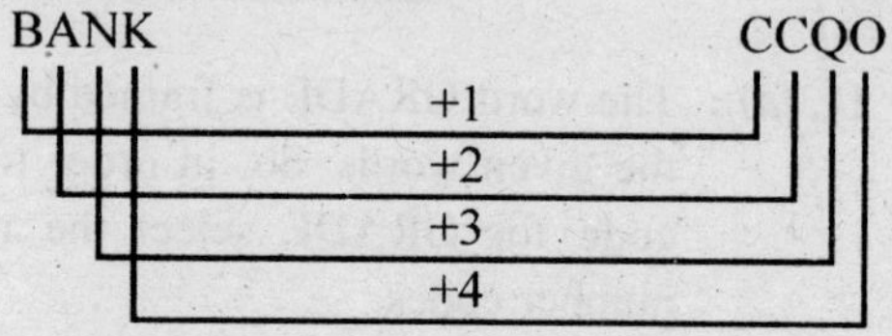


**15. *(a)* :** The letters of the word are coded by moving five steps forward and six steps backward alternately.

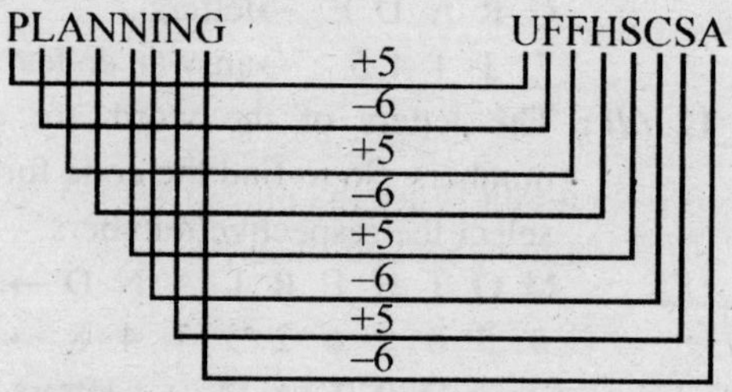


Similarly,

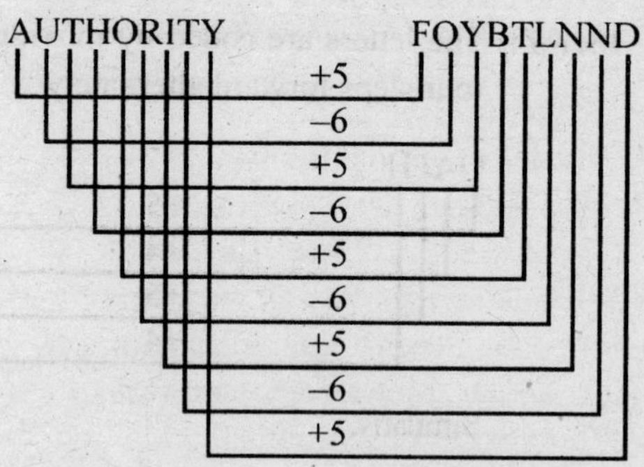


**16. *(b)* :**

| | *Code* | *Sentence* |
|---|---|---|
| 1. | go *ju* mi | plenty of *money* |
| 2. | pao *ju* go nei vu | *money* creates lots of problems |
| 3. | kol vu nei | problems create tension |
| 4. | sol tun *ju* haw | still *money* is needed |

In 1st, 2nd and 4th codes and their sentences the word 'ju' is repeated and so is 'money'.

**17. *(a)* :**

| | *Code* | *Sentence* |
|---|---|---|
| 1. | FOR | old is gold |
| 2. | ROT | gold is pure |
| 3. | ROM | gold is costly |

Therefore,

| | | | |
|---|---|---|---|
| F | stands | for | old |
| O | stands | for | is |
| R | stands | for | gold |
| T | stands | for | pure |
| M | stands | for | costly |

So, 'pure old gold is costly' will be written as 'TFROM'.

**18. *(a)* :**

| | *Code* | *Sentence* |
|---|---|---|
| 1. | 415 | milk is hot |
| 2. | 18 | hot soup |
| 3. | 895 | soup is *tasty* |

From 3rd code and its sentence neither number '9' is repeated nor the word 'tasty'.

**19. *(c)* :**

| | *Code* | *Sentence* |
|---|---|---|
| 1. | 643 | she is beautiful |
| 2. | 593 | he is handsome |
| 3. | 567 | handsome *meets* beautiful |

From 3rd code and its sentence, neither number '7' nor the word 'meets' is repeated.

**20. *(d)* :**

| | *Code* | *Sentence* |
|---|---|---|
| 1. | *dugo hui* mul zo | work *is very* hard |
| 2. | *hui dugo* **ba** *ki* | **Bingo** *is very smart* |
| 3. | nano mul *dugo* | cake is *hard* |
| 4. | mul *ki* qu | *smart* and hard |

From 2nd code and its sentence, neither 'ba' nor 'Bingo' is repeated.
(Words repeated are in italics)

**21. *(c)* :** Colour of milk is 'white' and 'white' is called 'sky'.

**22. *(c)* :** Colour of blood is 'red' and 'red' is called 'white'.

**23. *(b)* :** We drink 'water' when we are thirsty and 'water' is called 'air'.

**24. *(a)* :** Colour of sky is 'blue' and 'blue' means 'white'.

**25. *(d)* :** Fishes swim in 'water' and 'water' is called 'sand'.

# 10. STATEMENT ANALYSIS

In these type of questions, a few statements are given. Certain facts are broken up and mentioned in these statements. What is required is to analyse the statements, arrange and sort out the given facts and then answer the questions related to the given statements.

## EXERCISE

**1.** Among five friends, A is heavier than B; C is lighter than D; B is lighter than D but heavier than E. Who among them is the heaviest?

(*a*) B (*b*) C
(*c*) A (*d*) Can't say

**2.** Pune is bigger than Jhansi, Sitapur is bigger than Chittor. Raigarh is not as big as Jhansi, but is bigger than Sitapur. Chittor is not as big as Sitapur. Which is the smallest?

(*a*) Jhansi (*b*) Pune
(*c*) Chittor (*d*) Sitapur

**3.** Ajay works more than Ram. Alok works as much as Raju. Pankaj works less than Alok. Ram works more than Alok. Who works the most of all?

(*a*) Ajay (*b*) Ram
(*c*) Alok (*d*) Raju

**4.** Among five friends P, Q, R, S and T, who is the youngest? To arrive at the answer which of the following information given in the statements (A) and (B) is sufficient?

(A) R is younger than P and T.
(B) S is younger than Q.

(*a*) Only A alone is sufficient
(*b*) Either A or B is sufficient
(*c*) Both A and B together are needed
(*d*) Both A and B together are not sufficient

**5.** A is elder to B while C and D are elder to E who lies between A and B. If C be elder to B, which one of the following statements is necessarily true?

(*a*) E is elder to B
(*b*) A is elder to C
(*c*) C is elder to D
(*d*) D is elder to C

**6.** Suresh is as much older than Kamal as he is younger than Prabodh. Navin is as old as Kamal. Which of the following statements is wrong?

(*a*) Suresh is older than Navin
(*b*) Kamal is younger than Suresh
(*c*) Prabodh is not the oldest
(*d*) Navin is younger than Prabodh

**Directions (Qs. 7 to 9) :** *Ram, Sohan and Mohan play football, hockey and cricket. Ram, Ramesh and Mohan play hockey, cricket and basketball. Ram, Sohan, Rahim and Mohan play football and cricket. Now answer the following questions based on the above statements :*

**7.** Which game is played by all the boys?

(*a*) Football (*b*) Hockey
(*c*) Cricket (*d*) Basketball

**8.** Which two boys play all the games?

(*a*) Ram, Sohan (*b*) Ram, Ramesh
(*c*) Sohan, Mohan (*d*) Ram, Mohan

**9.** Who does not play football?

(*a*) Ramesh (*b*) Sohan
(*c*) Rahim (*d*) Mohan

**Directions (Qs. 10 to 12) :** *Read the following directions and answer the questions given below :*

There are five persons in a group. Out of these two are men. Only three persons know swimming, of which one is a man. There is a couple, of which the husband knows swimming. A is the younger sister of D and B is the husband of E. C is a swimming champion.

**10.** Who is the other man in the group?

(*a*) C (*b*) B

(*c*) A (*d*) D

**11.** The two women who know how to swim are:

(*a*) A and C (*b*) C and D

(*c*) D and E (*d*) A and E

**12.** The two persons who do not know how to swim are :

(*a*) B and D (*b*) D and E

(*c*) A and E (*d*) A and D

**Directions (Qs. 13 to 15) :** *Read the following statements and answer the questions given below :*

Rajat, Sushil and Nagesh play football, hockey and cricket. Rajat, Ramu and Nagesh play hockey, cricket and basketball. Rajat, Sushil, Mayank and Nagesh play football and cricket.

**13.** Which game is played by all the boys?

(*a*) Hockey (*b*) Basketball

(*c*) Football (*d*) Cricket

**14.** Who does not play football?

(*a*) Rajat (*b*) Nagesh

(*c*) Sushil (*d*) Ramu

**15.** Which of the following two boys play all the games?

(*a*) Nagesh, Rajat

(*b*) Mayank, Ramu

(*c*) Ramu, Nagesh

(*d*) Sushil, Mayank

**Directions (Qs. 16 to 20) :** *Read the following information and answer the questions given below:*

(*i*) P, Q, R, S, T and U are six members in a family in which there are two married couples.

(*ii*) T a teacher is married to the doctor who is mother of R and U.

(*iii*) Q the lawyer is married to P.

(*iv*) P has one son and one grandson.

(*v*) Of the two married ladies one is a housewife.

(*vi*) There is also one student and one male engineer in the family.

**16.** Who among the following is the housewife?

(*a*) Q (*b*) P

(*c*) S (*d*) T

**17.** Which of the following represents the group of females in the family?

(*a*) QTR (*b*) PSR

(*c*) PSU (*d*) Data inadequate

**18.** Which of the following is true about the granddaughter in the family?

(*a*) She is a student

(*b*) She is an engineer

(*c*) She is a lawyer

(*d*) Data Inadequate

**19.** How R is related to U?

(*a*) Brother

(*b*) Sister

(*c*) Brother or Sister

(*d*) Data inadequate

**20.** How is P related to R?

(*a*) Grandfather (*b*) Mother

(*c*) Sister (*d*) Grandmother

## EXPLANATORY ANSWERS

**1. (*d*) :** The five friends in descending order of weight are : A/D, B/C, E or A/D, B, C/E. Either A or D is the heaviest.

**2. (*c*) :** The order of cities in descending order of size is : Pune, Jhansi, Raigarh, Sitapur, Chittor.

**3. (*a*) :** On the basis of doing work, the descending order will be : Ajay, Ram, Alok/Raju, Pankaj.

**4. (*d*) :** Statements are not inter-related.

**5. (*a*) :** The order in descending seniority will be : A/C/D, E, B.

**6. (*c*) :** On the basis of age the descending order will be : Prabodh, Suresh, Kamal/Navin.

**Chart for Answers 7 to 9**

| *Boy* | *Games Played* |
|---|---|
| Ram | Football, Hocky, Cricket, Basketball |
| Sohan | Football, Hockey, Cricket |
| Mohan | Football, Hockey, Cricket, Basketball |
| Ramesh | Hockey, Cricket, Basketball |
| Rahim | Football, Cricket. |

**7.** ***(c)*** **8.** ***(d)*** **9.** ***(a)***

**For Answers 10 to 12 the information chart will be :**

A. Woman ((younger sister of D); knows swimming.

B. Man (husband of E); knows swimming

C. Woman; Swimming champion

D. Man (brother of A)

E. Woman (wife of B)

From the couple B & E, B (husband) knows swimming. C is a swimming champion. Three persons know how to swim of which only B is a man. So, the two women who know how to swim are C and A (the younger sister of D). There are two men in the group of five. One is B and the other will be D.

**10.** ***(d)*** **11.** ***(a)*** **12.** ***(b)***

**Chart for Answers 13 to 15**

| *Boy* | *Games Played* |
|---|---|
| Rajat | — Football, Hockey, Cricket, Basketball |
| Sushil | — Football, Hockey, Cricket, Basketball |
| Nagesh | — Football, Hockey, Cricket, Basketball |
| Ramu | — Hockey, Cricket, Basketball |
| Mayank | — Football, Cricket |

**13.** ***(d)*** **14.** ***(d)*** **15.** ***(a)***

**Chart for Answers 16 to 20**

P (female/housewife) — Q (male/lawyer) *Grandparents*

T (male/teacher) — S (female/doctor) *Parents*

R, U Children

(of R and U, one is a male engineer and one is a student)

**16.** ***(b)*** **:** One married lady S who is mother of R and U is a doctor. Q the lawyer is married to P. Of the two married ladies one is a house-wife. As Q is a lawyer the other married lady who is a housewife should be P.

**17.** ***(d)*** **:** Sex of R and U is not given.

**18.** ***(a)*** **:** P has one son T and one grandson either R or U one of whom is an engineer. So, the granddaughter is a student.

**19.** ***(c)*** **:** Sex of R and U is not given, but as both are children of S and one is a male engineer, the relationship between the two is of brother and sister.

**20.** ***(d)***

# 11. PLACE ARRANGEMENT

Place arrangement generally refers to the positioning of persons or objects in a manner indicated by set of information given. One has to understand the order of placement and then attempt questions following the given information.

## EXERCISE

**Directions :** *In the following questions, understand the arrangement pattern and then select the right answer from the given options :*

**1.** Five boys are sitting in a row. Raghu is not adjacent to Shyam or Amit. Ajay is not adjacent to Shyam. Raghu is adjacent to Mayank. If Mayank is at the middle in the row, then Ajay is adjacent to whom out of the following?

(*a*) Amit (*b*) Raghu
(*c*) Mayank (*d*) Shyam

**2.** Mini is to the right of Rajni but to the left of Ananta. Saya is to the right of Mini but to the left of Jaya. Who is on the extreme left if all the girls are facing North?

(*a*) Jaya (*b*) Mini
(*c*) Rajni (*d*) Saya

**3.** O, P, Q, R, S and T are standing on a bench according to their height. P is taller than O but shorter than S. Only S is taller than T. R is shorter than P but taller than Q. Who is the shortest?

(*a*) O (*b*) Q
(*c*) P (*d*) Cannot be said

**4.** Five personalities are living in a multistoried building. Mr. Effortless lives in a flat above Mr. Active, Mr. Charge lives in a flat below Mr. Diligent, Mr. Active lives in a flat above Mr. Diligent and Mr. Behaved lives in a flat below Mr. Charge. Who lives in the topmost flat?

(*a*) Mr. Charge (*b*) Mr. Diligent
(*c*) Mr. Effortless (*d*) Mr. Behaved

**5.** Six friends are sitting in a circle and playing cards. Kenny is to the left of Danny. Michael is in-between Bob and John. Roger is in between Kenny and Bob. Who is sitting to the right of Michael?

(*a*) Danny (*b*) John
(*c*) Kenny (*d*) Bob

**6.** Four girls A, B, C and D are sitting in a circle. B and C are facing each other. Which of the following is definitely true?

(*a*) A is to the left of C
(*b*) D is to the left of C
(*c*) A and D are facing each other
(*d*) A is not between B and C

**7.** Brijesh, Jayesh, Amar and Praveer are playing a game of cards. Amar is to the right of Jayesh who is to the right of Brijesh. Who is to the right of Amar?

(*a*) Brijesh
(*b*) Praveer
(*c*) Brijesh or Praveer
(*d*) Jayesh

**8.** In a pile of 10 books there are 3 of History, 3 of Hindi, 2 of Maths, and 2 of English. Taking from above there is an English book between a History and Maths book, a History book between a Maths and an English book, a Hindi book between an English and a Maths book, a Maths book between two Hindi books, and two Hindi books between a Maths and a History book. Book of which subject is at the sixth position from the top?

(*a*) English (*b*) Hindi
(*c*) History (*d*) Maths

**9.** Five persons A, B, C, D and E are sitting in a row facing you such that D is on the left of C and B is on the right of E. A is on the right of C and B is on the left of D. If E occupies a corner position, then who is sitting in the centre?

(*a*) A (*b*) B
(*c*) C (*d*) D

**10.** Six friends A, B, C, D, E and F are standing in a circle. B is between F and C; A is between E and D; F is to the left of D. Who is between A and F?

(*a*) C (*b*) B
(*c*) D (*d*) E

## EXPLANATORY ANSWERS

**1. (*b*) :** The order of sitting is :
Amit, Shyam, Mayank, Ajay, Raghu
*or*
Ajay, Raghu, Mayank, Amit, Shyam

**2. (*c*) :** The order in which the girls are positioned is :
Rajni, Mini, Ananta, Saya, Jaya
*or*
Saya, Jaya, Ananta
*or*
Saya, Ananta, Jaya

**3. (*d*) :** In descending order of height, the standing positions are :

| S | | S |
|---|---|---|
| T | | T |
| P | *or* | P |
| R | | R |
| O | | Q |
| Q | | O |

Either O or Q is the shortest. The informa-tion given is not enough to clarify the answer.

**4. (*c*) :** The personalities living in flats in multi-storied building are in order given below :
Mr. Effortless
Mr. Active
Mr. Diligent
Mr. Charge
Mr. Behaved

**5. (*d*) :** The order in which the friends are sitting is :

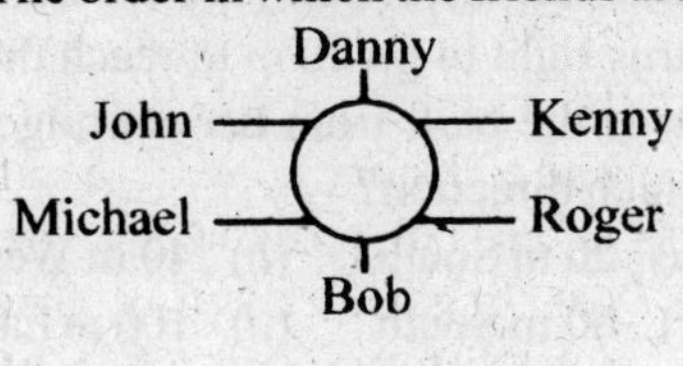


**6. (*c*) :** The sitting positions are :

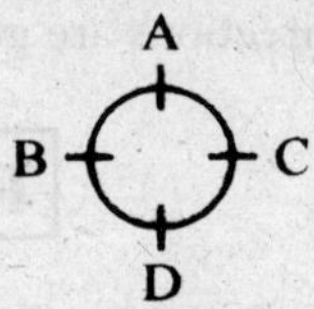


*or*

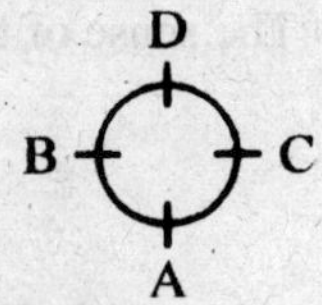


**7. (*b*) :** The order from left to right is :
Brijesh, Jayesh, Amar, Praveer

**8. (*b*) :** The pile of books is in the order :
1st — History
English
Maths
History
English
6th — Hindi
Maths
Hindi
Hindi
10th — History

**9. (*d*) :** Sitting order while facing us is :
A, C, D, B, E

**10. (*c*) :** The pattern of standing is :

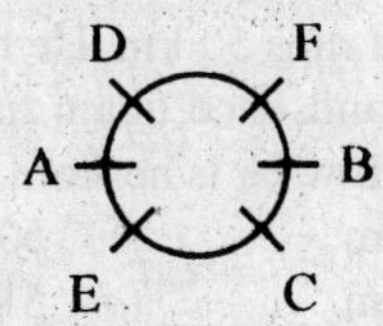

# 12. Direction Sense

In these type of tests, the directions in questions needs to be perceived. Such questions are based on the direction chart.

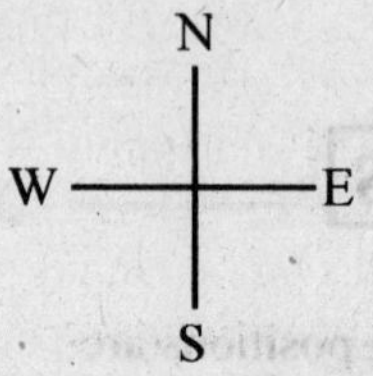


N = North S = South E = East W = West

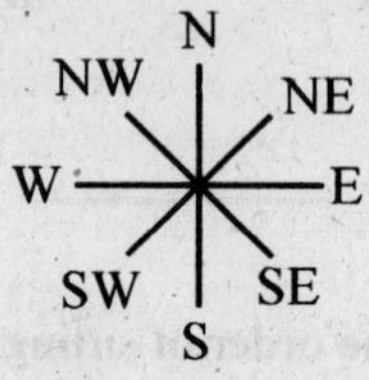


The sense of the different directions are guided by the left and right turns or angular turns.

## EXERCISE

**Directions :** *In the following questions, select the right answer from the given options to depict the correct direction/distance.*

**1.** Kittu walks towards East and then towards South. After walking some distance he turns towards West and then turns to his left. In which direction is he walking now?

(*a*) North (*b*) South
(*c*) East (*d*) West

**2.** A person is driving towards West. What sequence of directions should he follow so that he is driving towards South?

(*a*) left, right, right
(*b*) right, right, left
(*c*) left, left, left
(*d*) right, right, right

**3.** Richa drives 8 km to the South, turns left and drives 5 km. Again, she turns left and drives 8 km. How far is she from her starting point?

(*a*) 3 km (*b*) 5 km
(*c*) 8 km (*d*) 13 km

**4.** Dingi runs 40 km towards North then turns right and runs 50 km. He turns right and runs 30 km, and once again turns right and runs 50 km. How far is he from his starting point?

(*a*) 90 km (*b*) 50 km
(*c*) 10 km (*d*) 5 km

**5.** If North is called North-West, North-West is called West, West is called South-West and so on. What will South-East be called?

(*a*) East (*b*) West
(*c*) North-East (*d*) South-East

**6.** A man travels 100 km towards South. From there he turns right and travels 100 km and again turns right to travel 50 km. Which direction is he in from his starting point?

(*a*) North (*b*) North-East
(*c*) East (*d*) South-West

**7.** A train runs 120 km in West direction, 30 km in South direction and then 80 km in east direction before reaching the station. In which direction is the station from the train's starting point?

(*a*) South-West (*b*) North-West
(*c*) South-East (*d*) South

**8.** Facing the West direction, Priya jogs for 20 m, turns left and goes further 40 m. She turns left again and jogs for 20 m. Then she turns right to go 20 m to reach the park. How far is the park from her starting point and in which direction?

(*a*) 20 m South (*b*) 40 m West
(*c*) 60 m South (*d*) 100 m East

**9.** If all the directions are rotated, *i.e.,* if North is changed to West and East to North and so on, then what will come in place of North-West?

(*a*) South-West (*b*) North-East
(*c*) East-North (*d*) East-West

**10.** A and B start together from one point. They walk 10 km towards North. A turns left and covers 5 km whereas B turns right and covers 3 km. A turns left again and covers 15 km whereas B turns right and covers his 15 km. How far is A from B?

(*a*) 18 km (*b*) 10 km
(*c*) 5 km (*d*) 8 km

**11.** Tarun is walking towards East. What direction he should not follow if he should walk towards North?

(*a*) right, right, left, right, right
(*b*) right, right, left, left, left
(*c*) right, right, right
(*d*) right, left, right, left

**12.** Sony and Moni start walking from a point. Sony walks in West direction and Moni in South direction. After covering 20 km, Soni turns left and walks 15 km. Moni walks 10 km, turns left and walks 5 km. Soni, then turns left again and walks 25 km, whereas Moni turns right and walks 5 km. How far are Sony and Moni from each other?

(*a*) 5 km
(*b*) They are back at the starting point
(*c*) They are at same place at the finishing point
(*d*) Data is insufficient

**13.** I was walking in South-East direction. After a while I turned 90º to the right and walked ahead. Later I turned 45º to the right. In which direction am I walking now?

(*a*) North (*b*) North-East
(*c*) South-West (*d*) East

**14.** Two friends Jack and Bunny start a race, and together they run for 50 mts. Jack turns right and runs 60 mts while Bunny turns left and runs 40 mts. Then Jack turns left and runs 50 mts while Bunny turns right and runs 50 mts. How far are the two friends now from each other?

(*a*) 60 mts. (*b*) 100 mts
(*c*) 20 mts (*d*) 150 mts

**15.** A policeman left his police post and proceeded south 4 km, after hearing a loud sound from point A. On reaching the place he heard another sound and proceeded 4 km to his left to the point B, only to find that the sound was coming from left of B. From B he proceeded left to reach that place 4 km away. In which direction he has to go to reach his police post?

(*a*) North (*b*) South
(*c*) East (*d*) West

## EXPLANATORY ANSWERS

**1. (*b*) :**

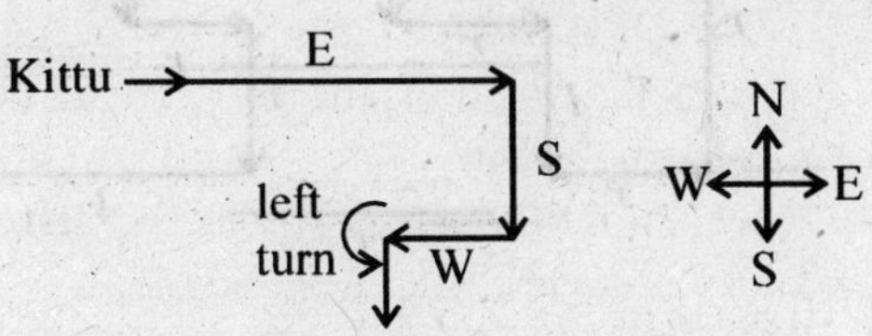


**2. (*d*) :**

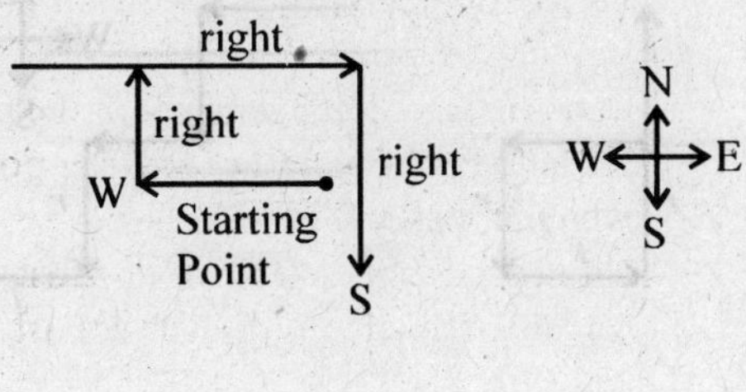


**3. (*b*) :**

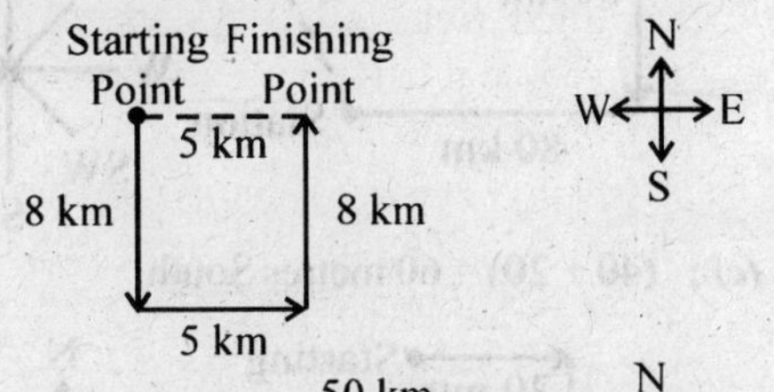


**4. (*c*) :**

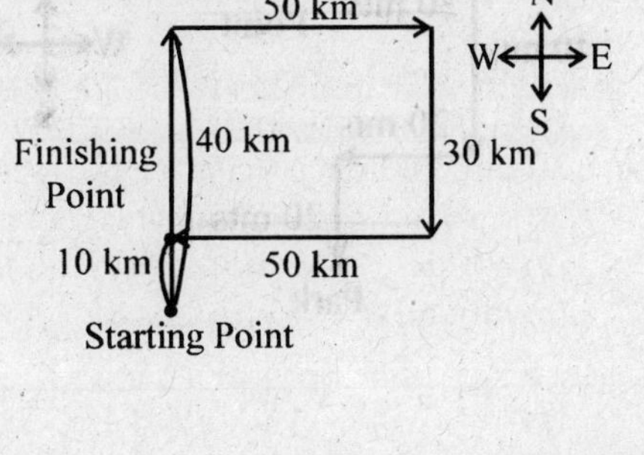

**5.** ***(a)*** **:** **Original Directions**

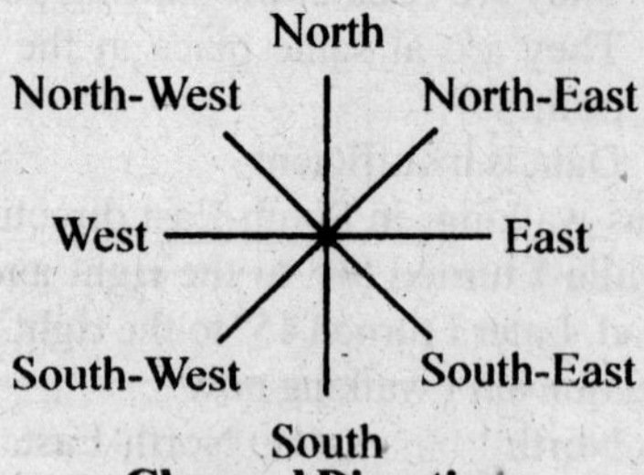


**Changed Directions**

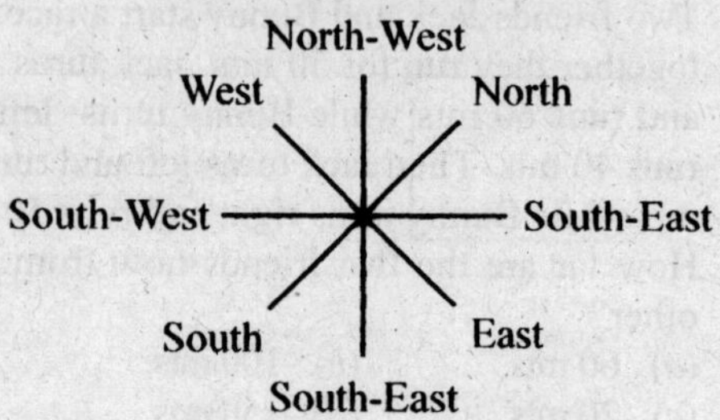


**6.** ***(d)*** **:**

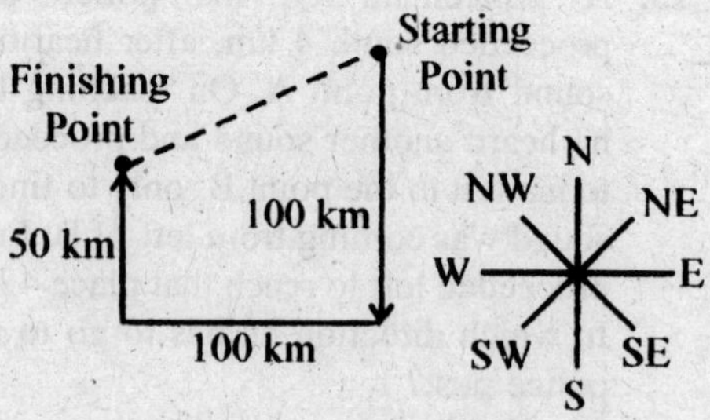


**7.** ***(a)*** **:**

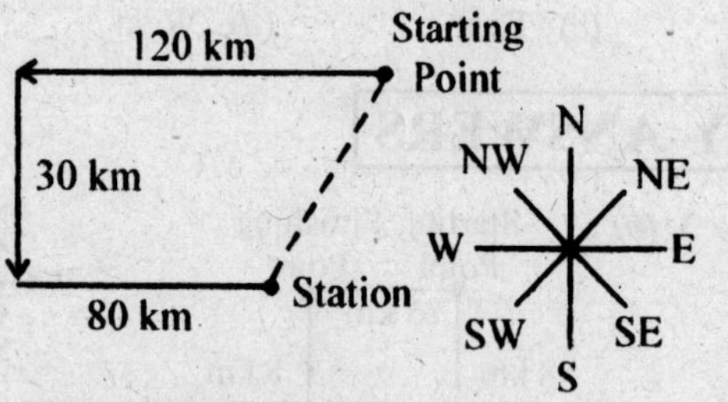


**8.** ***(c)*** **:** (40 + 20) = 60 metres South

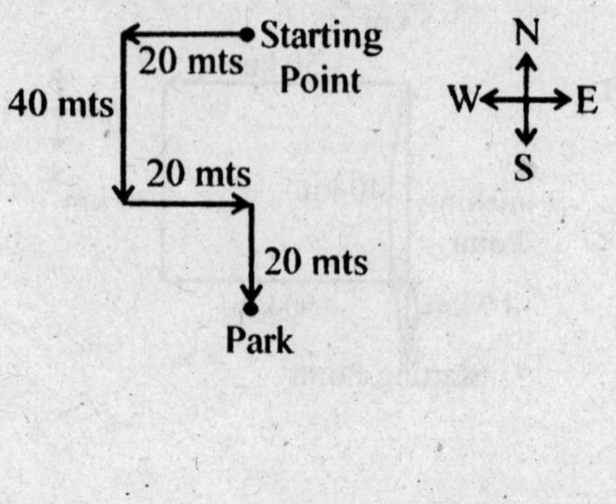


**9.** ***(a)*** **:** **Original Directions**

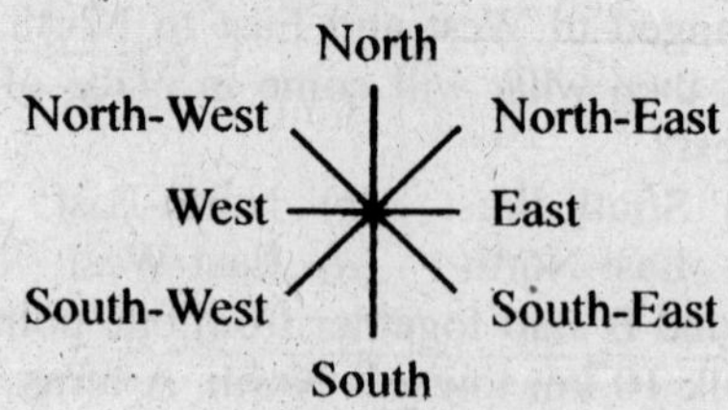


**Changed Directions**

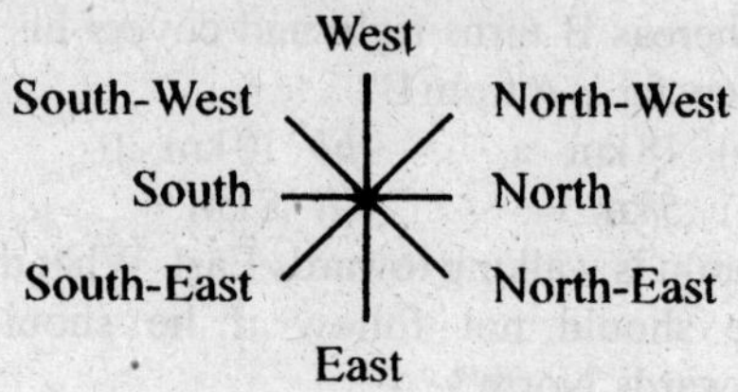


**10.** ***(d)*** **:**

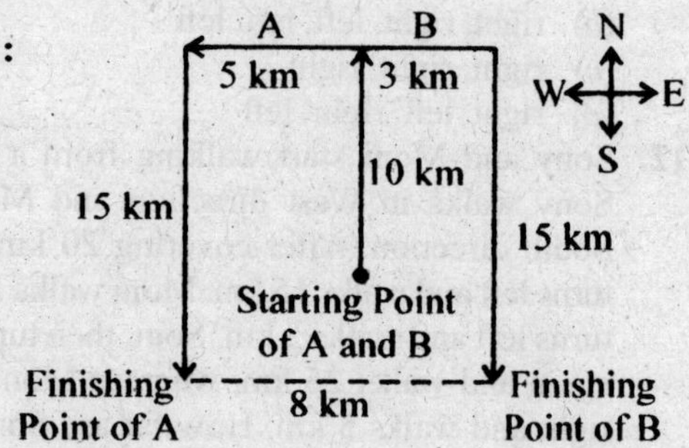


**11.** ***(d)*** **:**

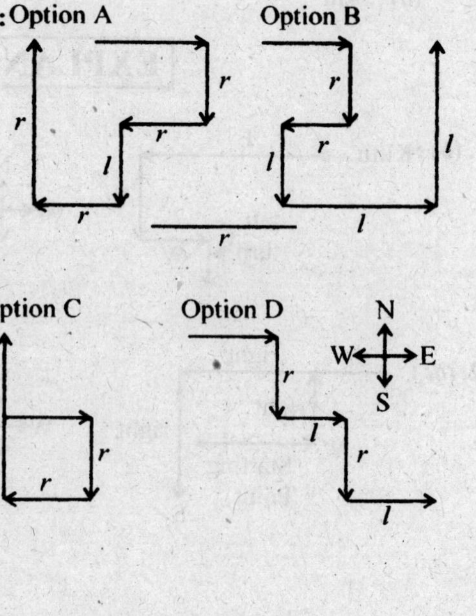

**12. *(c)* :**

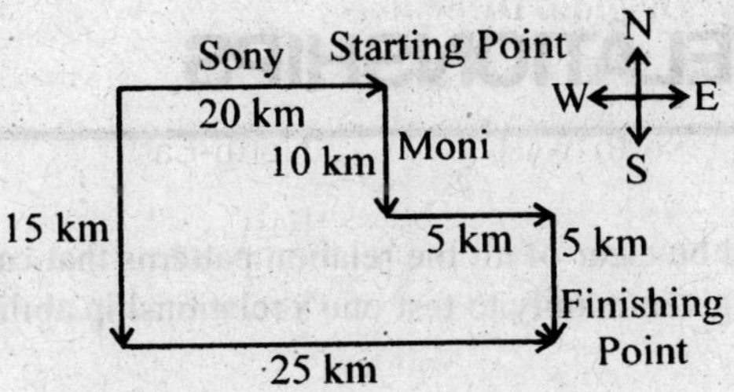


**13. *(a)* :** The direction of the movement is :

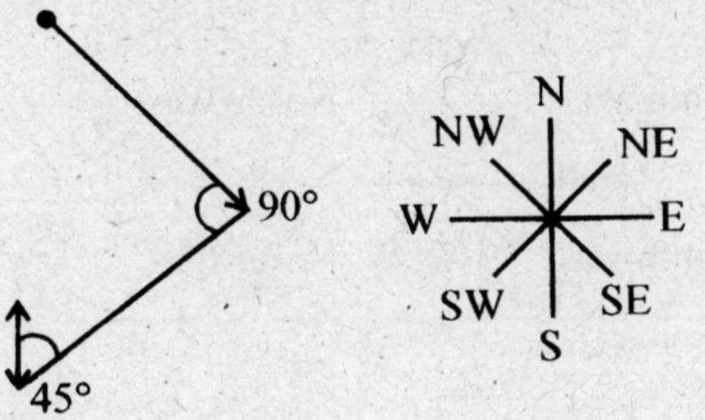


**14. *(b)* :** The track of both the friends is :

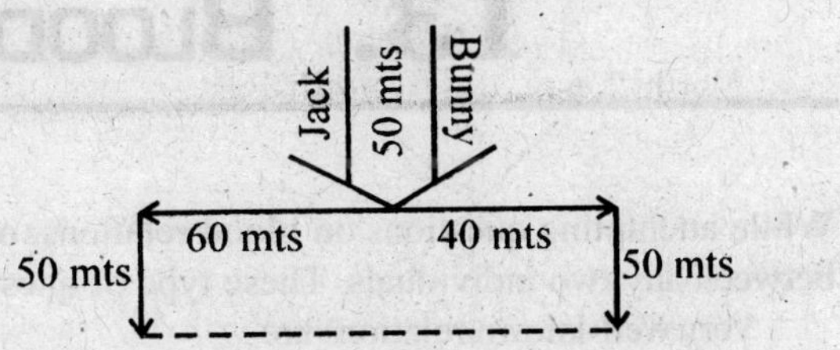


The two friends are 60 + 40 = 100 mts apart

**15. *(d)* :**

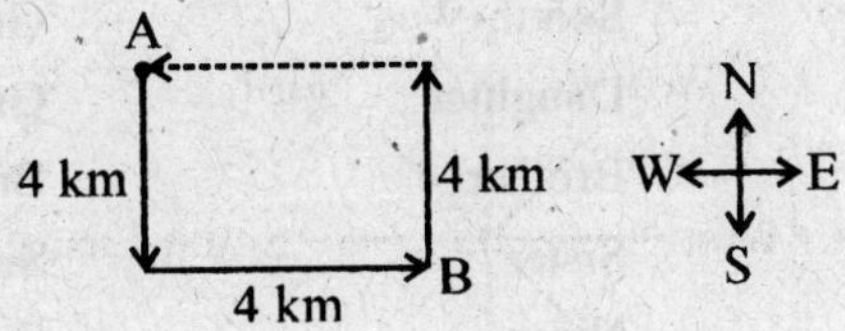

# 13. Blood Relationships

While attempting questions on blood relations, one should be clear of all the relation patterns that can exist between any two individuals. These type of questions are given mainly to test one's relationship ability.

Very well-known relations are :

| | |
|---|---|
| Mother | Grandmother |
| Father | Grandfather |
| Son | Grandson |
| Daughter | Granddaughter |
| Brother | Brother-in-law |
| Sister | Sister-in-law |
| Niece | Father-in-law |
| Nephew | Mother-in-law |
| Uncle | Son-in-law |
| Aunt | Daughter-in-law |
| Husband | Cousin |
| Wife | |

The patterns of some relationships which help in solving questions in these tests are :

| | | |
|---|---|---|
| Father's *or* Mother's Father | — | Grandfather (Paternal *or* Maternal) |
| Father's *or* Mother's Mother | — | Grandmother (Paternal *or* Maternal) |
| Father's *or* Mother's Son | — | Brother |
| Father's *or* Mother's Daughter | — | Sister |
| Father's Brother | — | Paternal Uncle |
| Father's Sister | — | Paternal Aunt |
| Mother's Brother | — | Maternal Uncle |
| Mother's Sister | — | Maternal Aunt |
| Uncle *or* Aunt's Son *or* Daughter | — | Cousin |
| Son's Wife | — | Daughter-in-law |
| Daughter's Husband | — | Son-in-law |
| Husband's *or* Wife's Brother | — | Brother-in-law |
| Husband's *or* Wife's Sister | — | Sister-in-law |
| Brother's Wife | — | Sister-in-law |
| Sister's Husband | — | Brother-in-law |
| Brother's Son | — | Nephew |
| Brother's Daughter | — | Niece |

# EXERCISE

**Directions :** *In each of the following questions keenly study the relationship mentioned between the persons, and then from the given options select the right relationship as the answer.*

**1.** A lady said, "The person standing there is my grandfather's only son's daughter". How is the lady related to the standing person?

(*a*) Sister
(*b*) Mother
(*c*) Aunt
(*d*) Cousin

**2.** Ajay is the brother of Vijay. Mili is the sister of Ajay. Sanjay is the brother of Rahul and Mehul is the daughter of Vijay. Who is Sanjay's Uncle?

(*a*) Rahul
(*b*) Ajay
(*c*) Mehul
(*d*) Data inadequate

**3.** A man introduced the boy coming with him as "He is son of the father of my wife's daughter". What relation did the boy bear to the man?

(*a*) Son-in-law
(*b*) Son
(*c*) Brother
(*d*) Father

**4.** If Amit's father is Billoo's father's only son and Billoo has neither a brother nor a daughter, what is the relationship between Amit and Billoo?

(*a*) Uncle — Nephew
(*b*) Father — Daughter
(*c*) Father — Son
(*d*) Cousins

**5.** Pointing to a woman in the photograph a man said, "She is the daughter of my grandmother's only son. How is the woman related to the man?

(*a*) Mother (*b*) Daughter
(*c*) Sister-in-law (*d*) Sister

**6.** Pointing to a photograph, a woman said, "She is the only daughter of my mother's father." How is the woman related to the person in the photograph?

(*a*) Mother
(*b*) Grandmother
(*c*) Daughter
(*d*) Cannot be determined

**7.** Ram is the brother of Shyam and Mahesh is the father of Ram. Jagat is the brother of Priya and Priya is daughter of Shyam. Who is the uncle of Jagat ?

(*a*) Shyam
(*b*) Mahesh
(*c*) Ram
(*d*) Data insufficient

**8.** Introducing a man, a woman said, "His wife is the only daughter of my father". How is the man related to the woman?

(*a*) Husband
(*b*) Father
(*c*) Father-in-law
(*d*) Brother

**9.** If Maya is the only daughter of Richa's grandmother's brother, how is Maya's daughter related to Richa?

(*a*) Niece
(*b*) Cousin
(*c*) Aunt
(*d*) Mother

**10.** Pointing to a woman, a man said, "Her husband's mother is the wife of my father's only son". How is the man related to the woman?

(*a*) Son
(*b*) Brother-in-law
(*c*) Uncle
(*d*) Father-in-law

## EXPLANATORY ANSWERS

**1. (*a*) :**

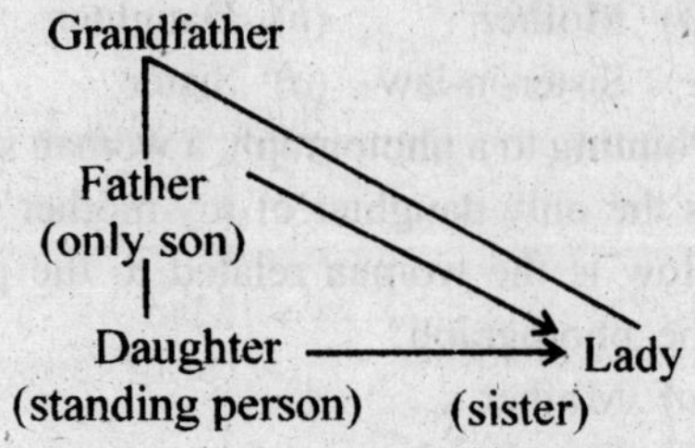


Lady's grandfather's son is lady's father and father's daughter will only be lady's sister.

**2. (*d*) :** 1. Mili ➤ Ajay ➤ Vijay ↓ Mehul
(sister) (brother) (daughter)

2. Sanjay ➤ Rahul
(brother)

There are two sets of relationship. Information given is incomplete and no relation can be established between the two sets.

**3. (*b*) :** The relationship chart based on problem is :

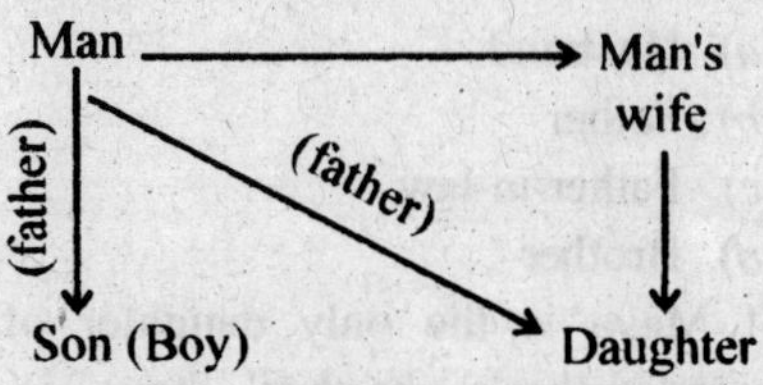


'Father of the man's wife's daughter' is the man himself and the boy in question is the man's son.

**4. (*c*) :** The relationship chart based on problem is :

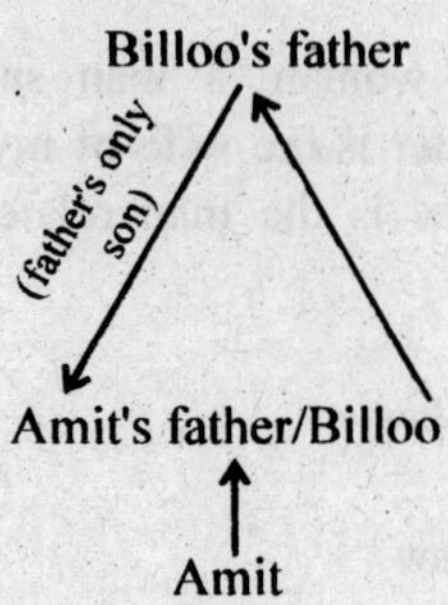


Amit's father is Billoo's father's only son means Billoo is the only son in question also, he is the father of Amit. It must be noted that Billoo has no brother which means he is single and also, when he has no daughter, Amit is his only son.

**5. (*d*) :**

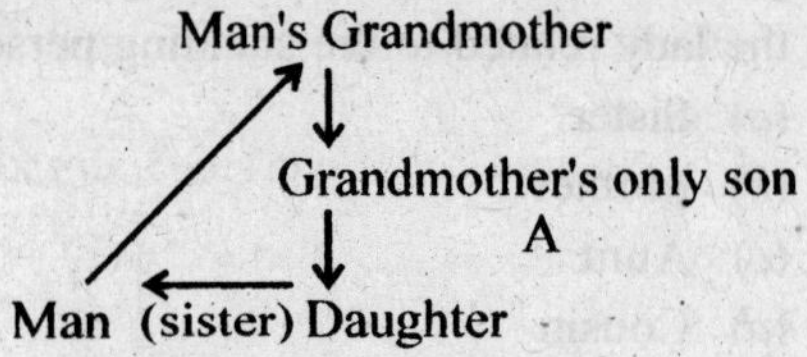


'My grandmother's only son' is the father of the man, and 'daughter of my grandmother's only son' is the sister of the man.

**6. (*c*) :** Woman's mother's father

↕

Person in photograph
(woman's mother/only daughter)

↑ (daughter)
Woman

'Only daughter of my mother's father' is the person in the photograph and she is also the mother of the woman. So, the woman is the daughter of the person in the photograph.

**7. (*c*) :**

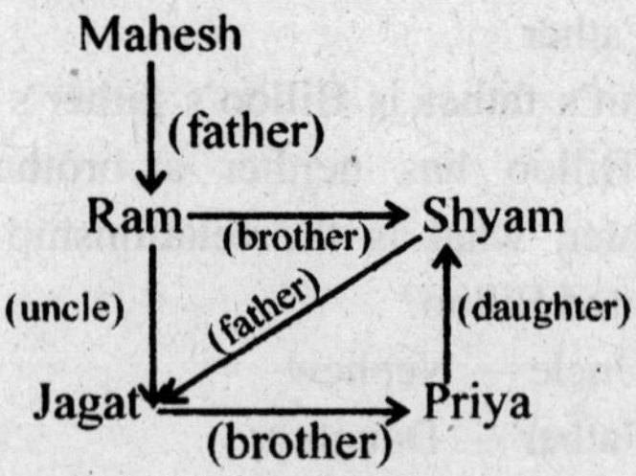


Jagat is brother of Priya and Priya is daughter of Shyam. So Shyam is also the father of Jagat. Ram is the brother of Shyam. So, Jagat's father's brother Ram is the uncle of Jagat.

**8. (*a*) :**

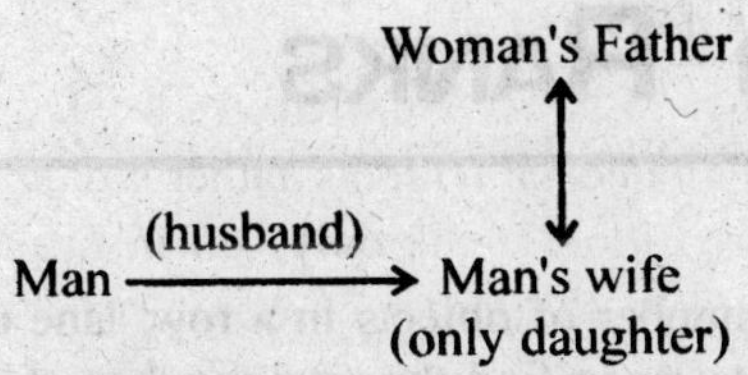


'Only daughter of my father' is the woman herself and the man is her husband.

**9. (*b*) :**

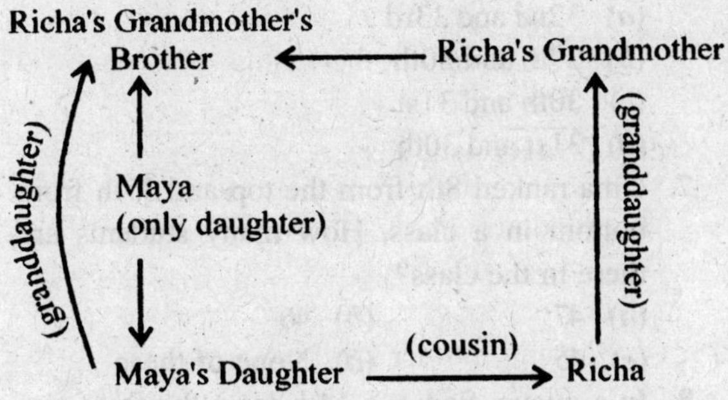


Both Maya's Daughter and Richa are granddaughters of a brother and a sister respectively. So Maya's daughter is the cousin of Richa.

**10. (*d*) :**

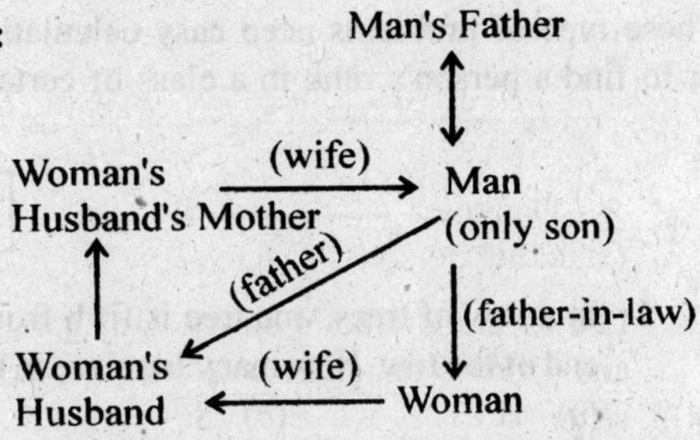


'My father's only son' is the man himself. 'Her husband's mother' is the wife of the man and so the man is the father of the woman's husband. As the woman is the wife of man's son, the man is the father-in-law of the woman.

# 14. Rows and Ranks

These type of problems need easy calculations to find out the number of objects in a row, lane or queue or to find a person's rank in a class of certain number of students; or to find the total number of students.

## EXERCISE

**1.** In a row of trees, one tree is fifth from either end of the row. How many trees are in the row?

(*a*) 11 (*b*) 8
(*c*) 10 (*d*) 9

**2.** Jaya ranks 5th in a class of 53. What is her rank from the bottom in the class?

(*a*) 49th (*b*) 48th
(*c*) 47th (*d*) 50th

**3.** Mohan ranks twenty-first in a class of sixty-five students. What will be his (Mohan's) rank if the lowest candidate is assigned rank 1?

(*a*) 44th (*b*) 45th
(*c*) 46th (*d*) Data inadequate

**4.** If Rahul finds that he is 12th from the right in a line of boys and 4th from the left, how many boys should be added to the line such that there are 28 boys in the line?

(*a*) 12 (*b*) 14
(*c*) 20 (*d*) 13

**5.** In a row of boys, Rajan is tenth from the right and Suraj is tenth from the left. When Rajan and Suraj interchange their positions, Suraj will be twenty-seventh from the left. Which of the following will be Rajan's position from the right?

(*a*) Tenth
(*b*) Twenty-sixth
(*c*) Twenty-ninth
(*d*) None of these

**6.** Mahesh and Suresh are ranked 11th and 12th respectively from the top in a class of 41 students. What will be their respective ranks from the bottom?

(*a*) 32nd and 33rd
(*b*) 29th and 30th
(*c*) 30th and 31st
(*d*) 31st and 30th

**7.** Uma ranked 8th from the top and 37th from bottom in a class. How many students are there in the class?

(*a*) 47 (*b*) 46
(*c*) 45 (*d*) None of these

**8.** In a queue, Sadiq is 14th from the front and Joseph is 17th from the end, while Jane is in between Sadiq and Joseph. If Sadiq be ahead of Joseph and there be 48 persons in the queue, how many persons are there between Sadiq and Jane?

(*a*) 5 (*b*) 6
(*c*) 7 (*d*) 8

**9.** Rohan ranked eleventh from the top and twenty-seventh from the bottom among the students who passed the annual examination in a class. If the number of students who failed in the examination was 12, how many students appeared for the examination?

(*a*) 48
(*b*) 49
(*c*) 50
(*d*) Cannot be determined

**10.** Some boys are sitting in a row. P is sitting fourteenth from the left and Q is seventh from the right. If there are four boys between P and Q, how many boys are there in the row?

(*a*) 19 (*b*) 21
(*c*) 25 (*d*) 23

# EXPLANATORY ANSWERS

**1. (*d*):**

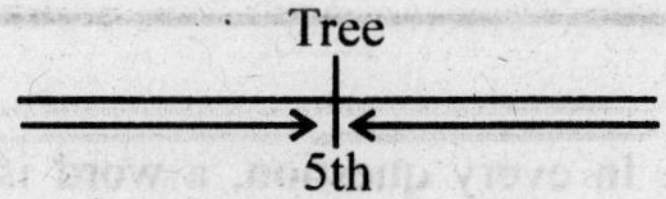


Total number of trees in the row are :
$(5+5)-1=9$.

**2. (*a*) :**

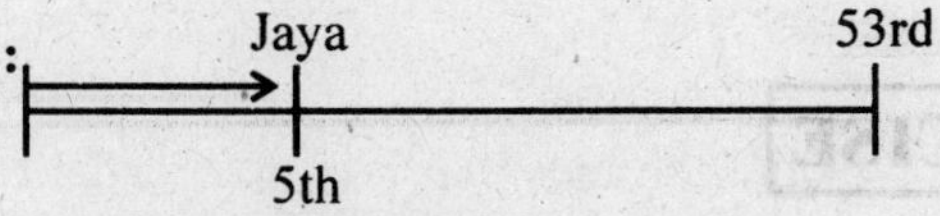


Jaya's rank from the bottom is :
$(53-5)+1=49$th.

**3. (*b*) :**

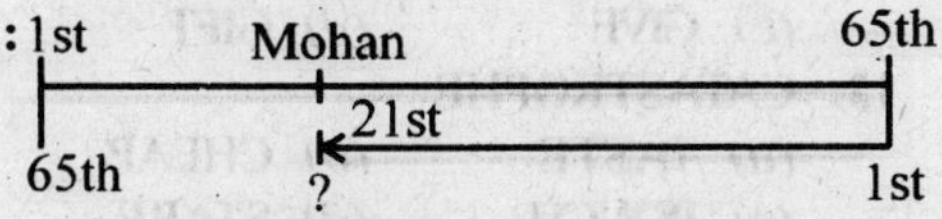


*Note :* Mohan's rank from the last or the question asked means the same.

Mohan's rank is $(65-21)+1=45$th.

**4. (*d*) :**

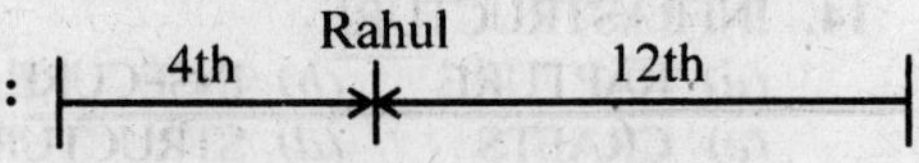


The number of boys in the line are :
$(4+12)-1=15$
To make a line of 28 boys, $(28-15)$ *i.e.* 13 more boys are needed.

**5. (*d*) :**

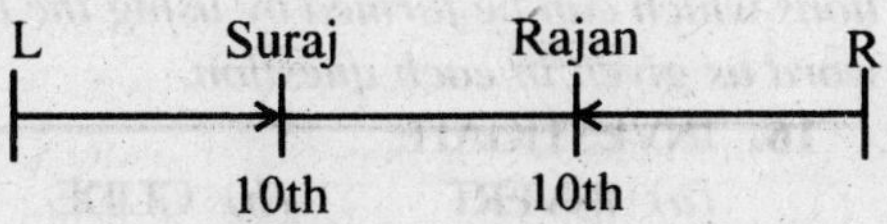


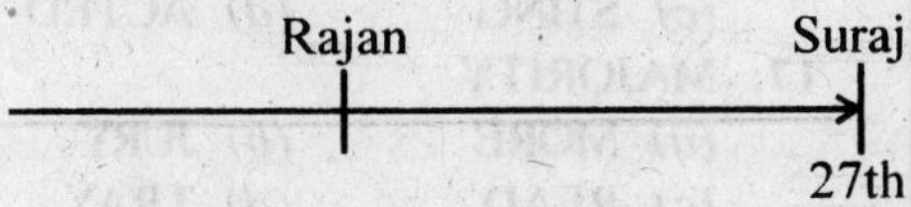


As the position of boys is equal from both ends, Rajan will also be 27th from the right after changing positions.

**6. (*d*) :**

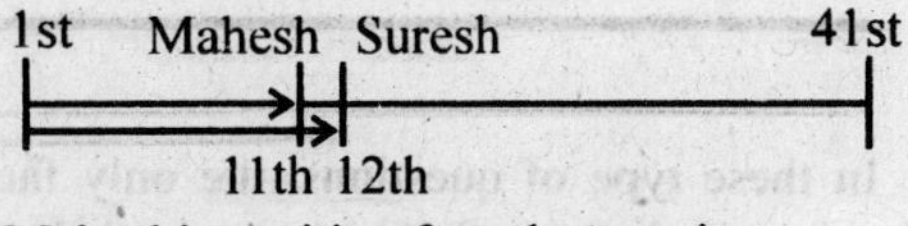


Mahesh's position from bottom is :
$(41-11)+1=31$st
Suresh's position from bottom is :
$(41-12)+1=30$th.

**7. (*d*) :**

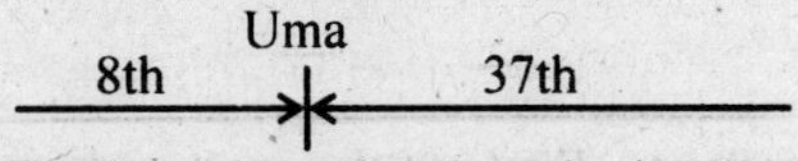


Total number of students in the class are :
$(8+37)-1=44$.

**8. (*d*) :**

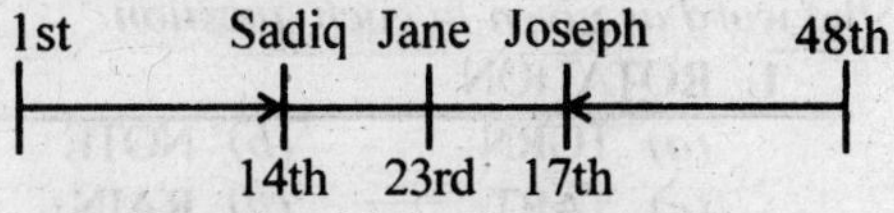


Sadiq's position from front : 14th
Joseph's position from last :
17th or $48-17+1=32$nd from front.
Middle postion between Sadiq & Joseph

$$=\frac{(32-14)}{2}+14=23\text{ rd.}$$

Hence, Jane position is 23rd from front
Person between Sadiq & Jane
$=23-14-1=8$.

**9. (*b*) :**

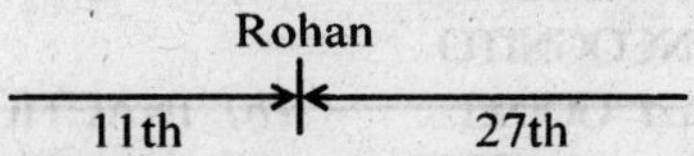


Number of students who passed the examination $(11+27)-1=37$
Those who failed = 12
Total number of students who appeared in the examination $=37+12=49$.

**10. (*c*) :**

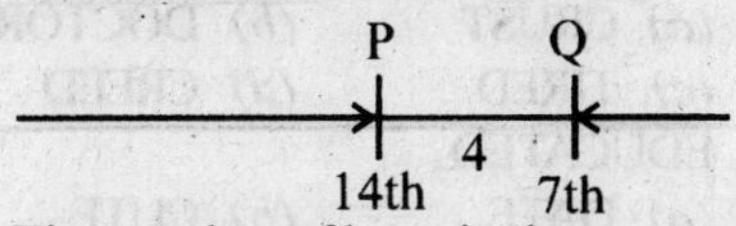


The number of boys in the row are :
$(14+4+7)=25$.

# 15. Permutations and Combinations

In these type of questions, the only factor essential is alertness. In every question, a word is given. By using the letters of this given word the options are formed. The candidates are required to find from the given options the word *(i)* which cannot be formed by using the letters of the given word or *(ii)* which can be formed by using the letters of the given word.

## EXERCISE

**Directions :** *Find out the one word among the options which cannot be formed by using the letters of the word as given in each question.*

**1.** ROTATION
(a) TORN (b) NOTE
(c) TART (d) RAIN

**2.** PHILOSOPHY
(a) SOIL (b) SHIP
(c) SOLO (d) SPIN

**3.** SLAVATION
(a) SNORT (b) LATVIA
(c) SALIVA (d) AVAIL

**4.** ACADEMY
(a) DEMY (b) MACE
(c) DIRE (d) MADE

**5.** INCOGNITO
(a) GOING (b) INACTION
(c) IGNITION (d) TONGO

**6.** JUDICIARY
(a) INJURY (b) CADDY
(c) DICY (d) ACRID

**7.** DOCTRINE
(a) CRUST (b) DOCTOR
(c) TIRED (d) CREED

**8.** EDUCATED
(a) DATE (b) CUTE
(c) EAST (d) DUCT

**9.** INSUFFICIENT
(a) ENTICE (b) SCENT
(c) SUFFICE (d) THENCE

**10.** DECEMBER
(a) REDEEM (b) DECREE
(c) BRACED (d) MEMBER

**11.** FUGITIVE
(a) EXIT (b) FIVE
(c) GIVE (d) GIFT

**12.** CATASTROPHE
(a) TASTE (b) CHEAP
(c) POUCH (d) STARE

**13.** TORRENTIAL
(a) TRAIL (b) MENTAL
(c) LEARN (d) RETAIL

**14.** INFRASTRUCTURE
(a) RAPTURE (b) INSECURE
(c) CRAFTS (d) STRUCTURE

**15.** RECOMMEND
(a) MEND (b) ROME
(c) CANE (d) OMEN

**Directions :** *Find out the one word among the options which can be formed by using the letters of the word as given in each question.*

**16.** INVESTIGATE
(a) INVERT (b) GLIDE
(c) STING (d) ACTED

**17.** MAJORITY
(a) MORE (b) JURY
(c) READ (d) TRAY

**18.** WATERMELON
(a) MAKER (b) WRITE
(c) TOWER (d) NOVEL

**19.** PREDICTION
(a) DESIRE (b) CREDIT
(c) ACTION (d) PICKED

**20.** BARGAIN
(a) GRAIN (b) BARGE
(c) ANGRY (d) TRING

**21.** THERMOSTAT
(*a*) MOTHER (*b*) STAMEN
(*c*) THRUST (*d*) HOIST

**22.** LEARNED
(*a*) DREAM (*b*) CLEAR
(*c*) ELDER (*d*) DRAPE

**23.** ADVENTURE
(*a*) AWARE (*b*) EVENT
(*c*) TRUCE (*d*) DRIED

**24.** THANKSGIVING
(*a*) AVENGE (*b*) HAUNTS
(*c*) GRAINS (*d*) SAVING

**25.** NOCTURNAL
(*a*) CRUST (*b*) TRAIL
(*c*) CORAL (*d*) OCEAN

## ANSWERS

| 1 | 2 | 3 | 4 | 5 | 6 | 7 | 8 | 9 | 10 |
|---|---|---|---|---|---|---|---|---|---|
| (*b*) | (*d*) | (*a*) | (*c*) | (*b*) | (*a*) | (*a*) | (*c*) | (*d*) | (*c*) |
| **11** | **12** | **13** | **14** | **15** | **16** | **17** | **18** | **19** | **20** |
| (*a*) | (*c*) | (*b*) | (*a*) | (*c*) | (*c*) | (*d*) | (*c*) | (*b*) | (*a*) |
| **21** | **22** | **23** | **24** | **25** | | | | | |
| (*a*) | (*c*) | (*b*) | (*d*) | (*c*) | | | | | |

# 16. Symbol Substitution

Questions in these category are easy to attempt. Candidates must be quick in substituting symbols and calculations. The common pattern of questions asked are given below.

## EXERCISE

**1.** If "+" means "–"; "–" means "×"; "×"means "÷" and "÷" means "+", then
$15 \times 5 \div 10 + 5 - 3 = ?$
(a) 9.5 (b) 0
(c) –2 (d) 24

**2.** If "+" means "×"; "–" means "÷"; "÷"means "+" and "×" means "–", then what will be the value of $20 \div 40 - 4 \times 5 + 6 = ?$
(a) 60 (b) 1.67
(c) 150 (d) 0

**3.** If × stands for addition, < for subtraction, + stands for division, > for multiplication, – stands for equal to, ÷ for greater than, and = stands for less than, state which of the following is true?
(a) $5 \times 3 < 7 \div 8 + 4 \times 1$
(b) $3 \times 4 > 2 - 9 + 3 < 3$
(c) $5 > 2 + 2 = 10 < 4 \times 8$
(d) $3 \times 2 < 4 \div 16 > 2 + 4$

**4.** If $\rightarrow$ stands for subract, $\leftarrow$ stands for add, •$\uparrow\uparrow$ stands for multiply, $\downarrow\downarrow$ stands for divide, $\leftrightarrow$ for greater than, $\longleftrightarrow$ stands for equal to, then which of the following alternatives is true?
(a) $4 \leftarrow 6 \uparrow\uparrow 2 \longleftrightarrow 3 \rightarrow 12 \leftarrow 12$
(b) $10 \downarrow\downarrow 5 \uparrow\uparrow 5 \longleftrightarrow 9 \rightarrow 3 \leftarrow 4$
(c) $15 \uparrow\uparrow 2 \rightarrow 5 \longleftrightarrow 12 \downarrow\downarrow 4 \leftarrow 3$
(d) $13 \downarrow\downarrow 13 \leftarrow 1 \leftrightarrow 20 \rightarrow 5 \uparrow\uparrow 2$

**5.** If Δ denotes =; + denotes >, – denotes <, □ denotes ≠, × denotes > and ÷ denotes < then a + b – c denotes
(a) b Δ c □ a
(b) b □ a ÷ c
(c) a ÷ b × c
(d) b – a + c

**6.** If '✱' denotes '×', 'Δ' denotes '÷', '□' denotes '–', '●' denotes '+', 'α' denotes '=' and 'β' denotes ≠, then which of the following euations is correct?
(a) 2 □ 10 ✱ 4 Δ 5 α 5 ● 12 Δ 6
(b) 27 Δ 9 ● 6 β 3 ✱ 6 □ 9
(c) 4 Δ 2 ✱ 0 α 7 Δ 1 ✱ 0
(d) 5 ● 6 Δ 3 □ 2 α 8 Δ 4 ✱ 3

**7.** If $\downarrow$ stands for '÷', $\uparrow$ stands for '×', $\rightarrow$ stands for '+' and $\leftarrow$ stands for '–', then
$25 \downarrow 5 \rightarrow 3 \uparrow 6 \leftarrow 8 = ?$
(a) 9 (b) 12
(c) 16 (d) 15

**8.** If the + and × signs of the following equations are interchanged, which will be the correct equation?
(a) $7 \times 5 + 3 = 20$
(b) $4 + 9 \times 1 = 42$
(c) $6 \times 5 + 8 = 46$
(d) $2 + 11 \times 4 = 28$

**9.** If '+' stands for multiplication, '×' stands for addition, '÷' stands for subtraction and '–' stands for division, then what will be the result of the following equation?
$7 \times 4 \div 10 \times 2 + 5 = ?$
(a) 7 (b) 0
(c) 11 (d) 15

**10.** If 'A' means '÷', 'B' means '+', 'C' means '×' and 'D' means '–', then
12 C 4 A 24 D 10 B 1 = ?
(a) $11\frac{1}{3}$ (b) 23
(c) –7 (d) $16\frac{4}{5}$

# EXPLANATORY ANSWERS

**1. *(c)* :** $15 \div 5 + 10 - 5 \times 3$
$3 + 10 - 15 = -2$

**2. *(d)* :** $20 + 40 \div 4 - 5 \times 6$
$20 + 10 - 30 = 0$

**3. *(c)* :** *(a)* $5 + 3 - 7 > 8 \div 4 + 1$
$1 > 3$
*(b)* $3 + 4 \times 2 = 9 \div 3 - 3$
$11 = 0$
*(c)* $5 \times 2 \div 2 < 10 - 4 + 8$
$5 < 14$
*(d)* $3 + 2 - 4 > 16 \times 2 \div 4$
$1 > 8$

**4. *(b)* :** *(a)* $4 + 6 \times 2 = 3 - 12 + 12$
$16 = 3$
*(b)* $10 \div 5 \times 5 = 9 - 3 + 4$
$10 = 10$
*(c)* $15 \times 2 - 5 = 12 \div 4 + 3$
$25 = 6$
*(d)* $13 \div 13 + 1 > 20 - 5 \times 2$
$2 > 10$

**5. *(d)* :** What is given is $a > b < c$
The equations are :
*(a)* $b = c \neq a$ which is wrong
*(b)* $b \neq a < c$ which is wrong
*(c)* $a < b > c$ which is wrong
*(d)* $b < a > c$ which is correct
Therefore, *(d)* is the answer.

**6. *(c)* :** The solved equations will be :
*(a)* $2 - 10 \times 4 \div 5 = 5 + 12 \div 6$
$2 - 8 = 5 + 2$
$-6 = 7$ which is wrong
*(b)* $27 \div 9 + 6 \neq 3 \times 6 - 9$
$3 + 6 \neq 18 - 9$
$9 \neq 9$ which is wrong
*(c)* $4 \div 2 \times 0 = 7 \div 1 \times 0$
$2 \times 0 = 7 \times 0$
$0 = 0$ which is correct
*(d)* $5 + 6 \div 3 - 2 = 8 \div 4 \times 3$
$5 = 6$ which is wrong

**7. *(d)* :** $25 \div 5 + 3 \times 6 - 8$
$5 + 18 - 8 = 15$

**8. *(c)* :** After interchanging the signs the equations are :
*(a)* $7 + 5 \times 3 = 22$ which is wrong
*(b)* $4 \times 9 + 1 = 37$ which is wrong
*(c)* $6 + 5 \times 8 = 46$ which is correct
*(d)* $2 \times 11 + 4 = 26$ which is wrong

**9. *(c)* :** $7 + 4 - 10 + 2 \times 5$
$7 + 4 - 10 + 10 = 11$

**10. *(c)* :** $12 \times 4 \div 24 - 10 + 1$
$2 - 10 + 1 = -7$

# 17. Missing Numbers

Playing with numbers and mathematical skills are needed to attempt these type of tests. The candidates have to work out the right combination of arithmetical symbols to arrive at the answer options which will take the place of the interrogation sign in the given questions.

## EXERCISE

**Directions:** *In each question given below which one number can be placed at the sign of interrogation?*

1. 

(a) 693 (b) 939
(c) 981 (d) 993

2. 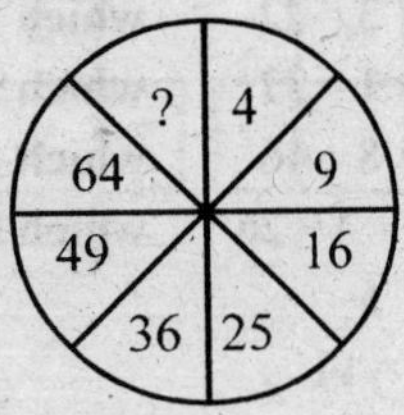


(a) 68 (b) 100
(c) 72 (d) 81

3. 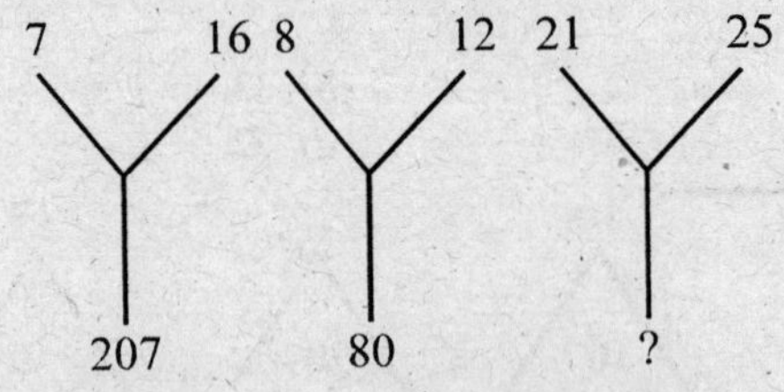


(a) 425 (b) 184
(c) 241 (d) 210

4. 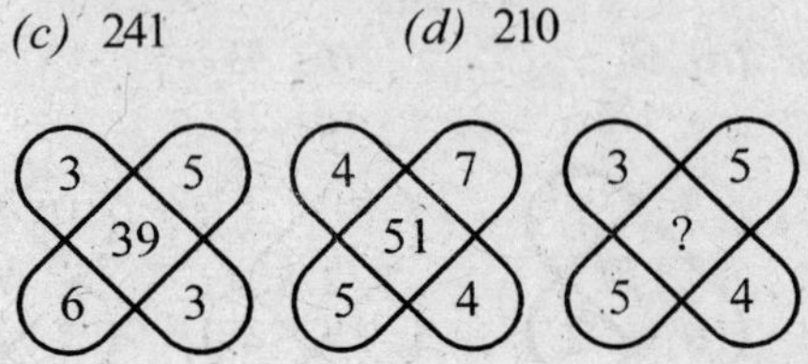


(a) 35 (b) 37
(c) 45 (d) 48

5. 

(a) 4 (b) 8
(c) 20 (d) 14

6.

| | | |
|---|---|---|
| 14 | 9 | 4 |
| 12 | 7 | 2 |
| 10 | 5 | 0 |
| 16 | 11 | ? |

(a) 9 (b) 6
(c) 3 (d) 7

7. 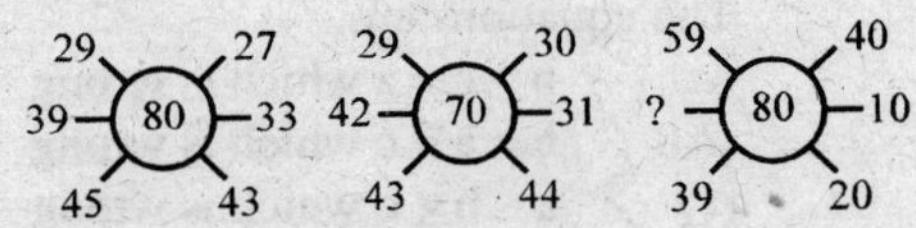


(a) 69 (b) 49
(c) 50 (d) 60

8. 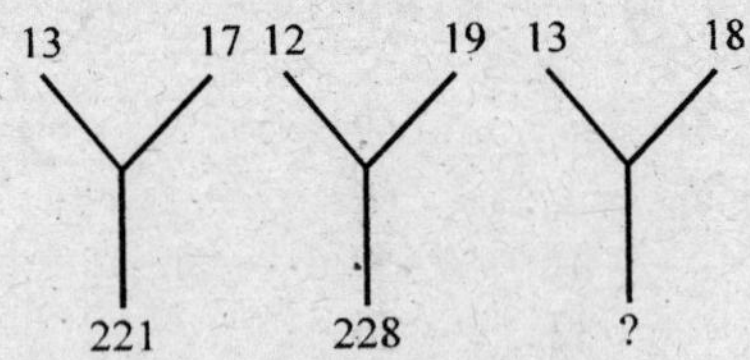


(a) 31 (b) 229
(c) 234 (d) 312

9. 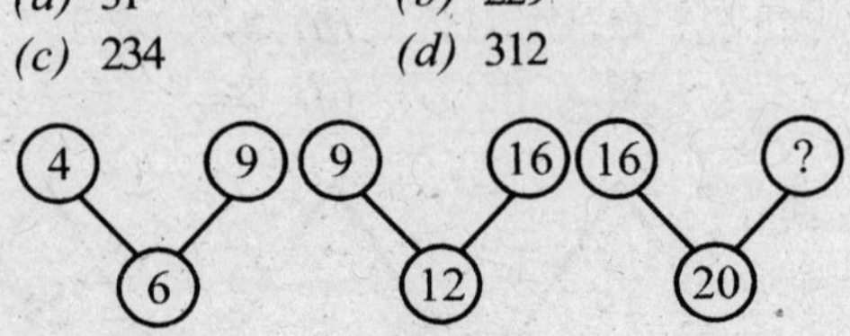


(a) 21 (b) 25
(c) 50 (d) 60

**10.**

| 51 | (11) | 61 |
|---|---|---|
| 64 | (30) | 32 |
| 35 | (?) | 43 |

*(a)* 25 *(b)* 27
*(c)* 32 *(d)* 37

**11.**

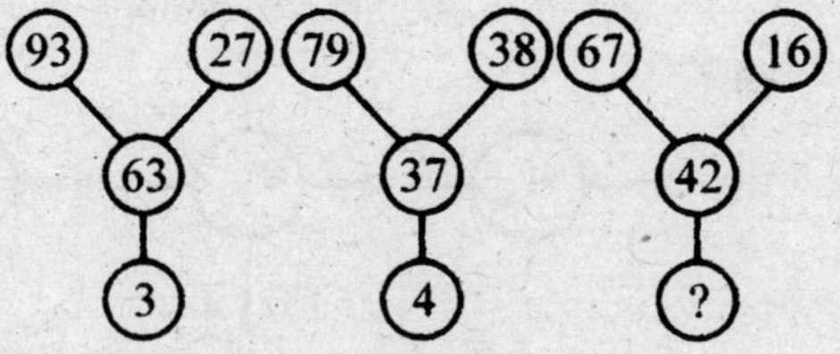


*(a)* 5 *(b)* 6
*(c)* 8 *(d)* 9

**12.**

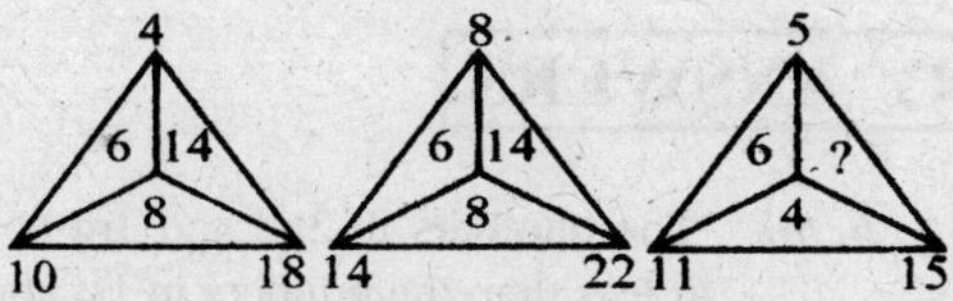


*(a)* 8 *(b)* 14
*(c)* 10 *(d)* 6

**13.**

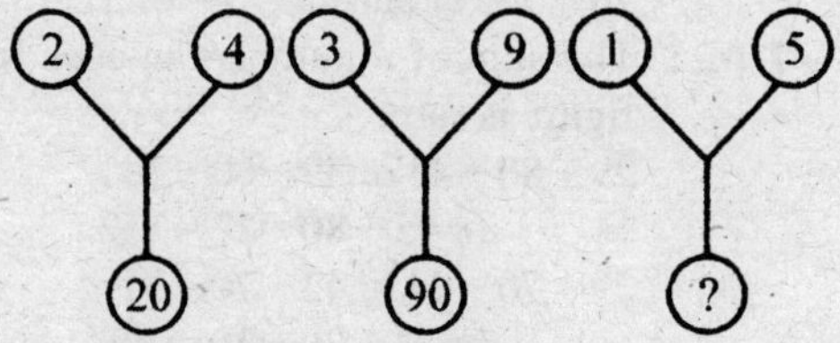


*(a)* 20 *(b)* 25
*(c)* 26 *(d)* 75

**14.**

| 27 | 22 | 50 |
|---|---|---|
| 13 | 12 | 26 |
| 9 | 2 | ? |

*(a)* 12 *(b)* 39
*(c)* 18 *(d)* 24

**15.**

*(a)* 25 *(b)* 47
*(c)* 37 *(d)* 41

**16.**

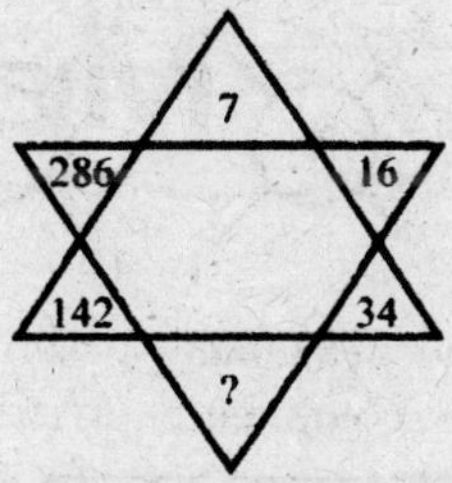


*(a)* 70 *(b)* 68
*(c)* 56 *(d)* 92

**17.**

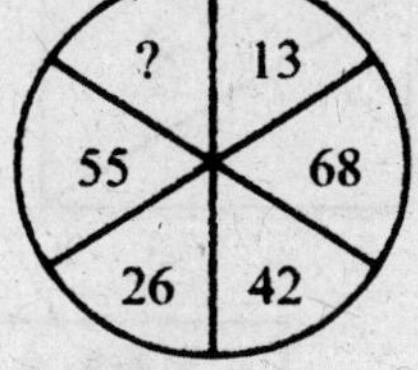


*(a)* 41 *(b)* 37
*(c)* 29 *(d)* 25

**18.**

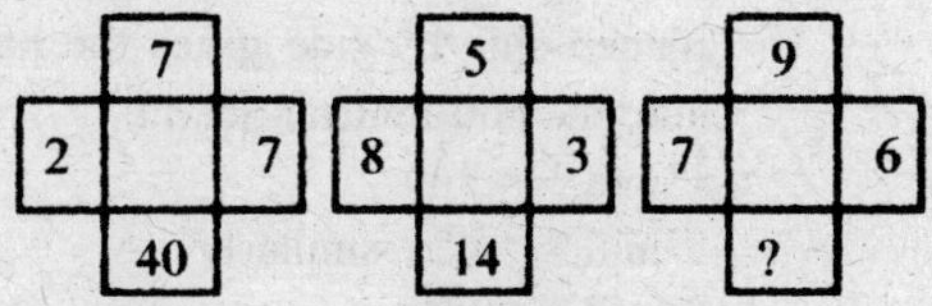


*(a)* 72 *(b)* 68
*(c)* 82 *(d)* 96

**19.**

| 42 | (21) | 22 |
|---|---|---|
| 78 | (?) | 84 |
| 162 | (18) | 99 |

*(a)* 12 *(b)* 13
*(c)* 60 *(d)* 72

**20.**

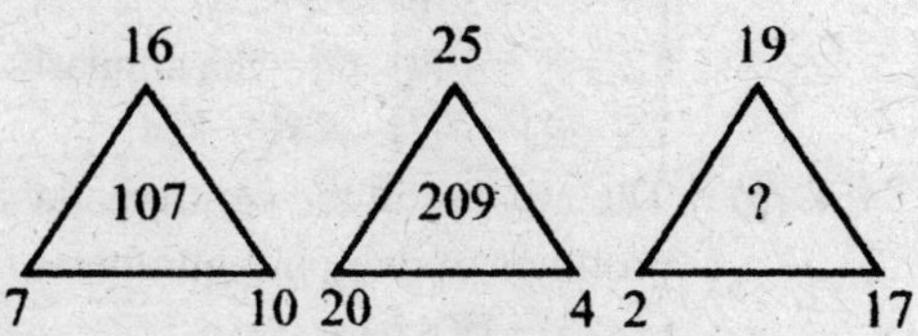


*(a)* 68 *(b)* 93
*(c)* 175 *(d)* 217

**21.**

*(a)* 960 *(b)* 628
*(c)* 830 *(d)* 492

**22.**

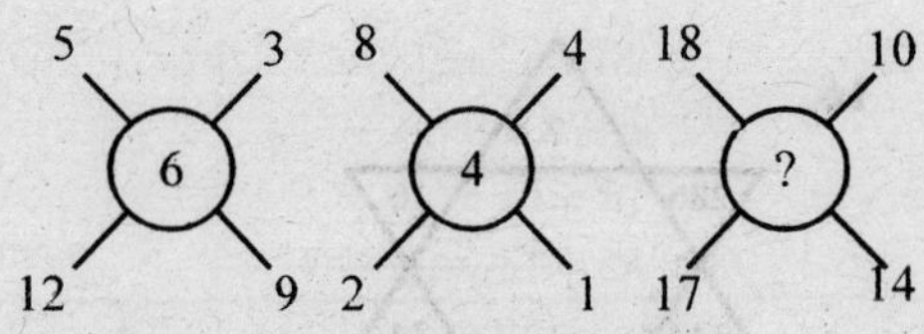


(a) 18 (b) 10
(c) 36 (d) 24

**23.**

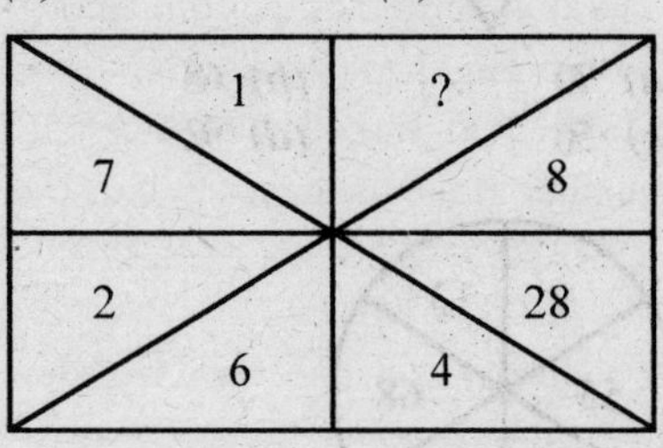


(a) 24 (b) 10
(c) 32 (d) 12

**24.**

| | |
|---|---|
| 6 (40) | 4 |
| 3 (12) | 3 |
| 7 (?) | 2 |

(a) 51 (b) 36
(c) 22 (d) 4

**25.**

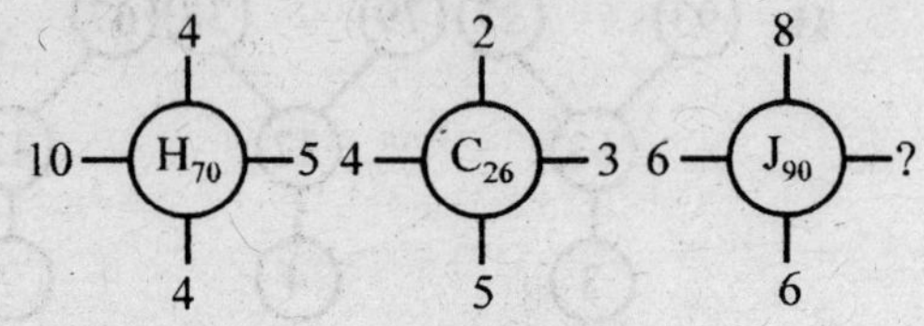


(a) 5 (b) 4
(c) 2 (d) 1

## EXPLANATORY ANSWERS

**1. (c) :** The squares of two numbers on the top placed side by side gives the number inside the bottom triangle, *i.e.,*
$6^2$ and $3^2 = 369$
$2^2$ and $5^2 = 425$, similarly
$3^2$ and $9^2 = 981$.

**2. (d) :** Starting from number 4 the numbers are the squares of numbers in natural order *i.e.,* $2^2 = 4, 3^2 = 9, 4^2 = 16 \ldots\ldots 9^2 = 81$.

**3. (b) :** The number at the bottom is the difference of the squares of two numbers at the top, *i.e.,*
$16^2 - 7^2 = 256 - 49 = 207$
$12^2 - 8^2 = 144 - 64 = 80$, similarly
$25^2 - 21^2 = 625 - 441 = 184$.

**4. (b) :** The number in the centre is the sum of the products of diagonal numbers, *i.e.,*
$(3 \times 3) + (5 \times 6) = 39$
$(4 \times 4) + (7 \times 5) = 51$, similarly
$(3 \times 4) + (5 \times 5) = 37$.

**5. (d) :** Sum of two numbers on the top divided by 2 gives the third number, *i.e.,*
$(7 + 5) \div 2 = 6$
$(5 + 21) \div 2 = 13$, similarly
$(24 + 4) \div 2 = 14$.

**6. (b) :** The numbers in 2nd and 3rd columns are 5 less than the nunbers in 1st and 2nd columns respectively, *i.e.,*
$14 - 5 = 9$ and $9 - 5 = 4$
$12 - 5 = 7$ and $7 - 5 = 2, \ldots$ similarly
$16 - 5 = 11$ and $11 - 5 = 6$.

**7. (a) :** The sum of 3 numbers in each line in one figure is same, *i.e.,*
$29 + 80 + 43$ or $39 + 80 + 33$
or $45 + 80 + 27 = 152$
$29 + 70 + 44$ or $42 + 70 + 31$
or $43 + 70 + 30 = 143$,
similarly $59 + 80 + 20$ or $39 + 80 + 40 = 159$.
The missing number is :
$159 - (80 + 10) = 69$.

**8. (c) :** The number at the bottom is the product of two numbers at the top, *i.e.,*
$13 \times 17 = 221$
$12 \times 19 = 228$, similarly
$13 \times 18 = 234$.

**9. (b) :** Square of number at the bottom is equal to the product of two numbers at the top, *i.e.,*
$6^2 = 4 \times 9$, *i.e.,* 36
$12^2 = 9 \times 16$, *i.e.,* 144, similarly
$20^2 = 16 \times ?$, *i.e.,* 400. The missing number is $400 \div 16 = 25$.

**10. *(b)* :** The sum of the products of the digits of numbers in 1st and 3rd columns is the number in the 2nd column, *i.e.,*
$(5 \times 1) + (6 \times 1) = 11$
$(6 \times 4) + (3 \times 2) = 30$, similarly
$(3 \times 5) + (4 \times 3) = 27$.

**11. *(d)* :** The sum of numbers on right and centre subtracted from the number on the left gives the number at the bottom, *i.e.,*
$93 - (27 + 63) = 3$
$79 - (38 + 37) = 4$, similarly
$67 - (16 + 42) = 9$.

**12. *(c)* :** The number inside each triangle is the difference of the numbers at its base *i.e.*
$10 - 4 = 6$, $18 - 4 = 14$ and $18 - 10 = 8$
$14 - 8 = 6$, $22 - 8 = 14$ and $22 - 14 = 8$, similarly
$11 - 5 = 6$, $15 - 5 = 10$ and $15 - 11 = 4$.

**13. *(c)* :** The sum of squares of two numbers at the top gives the third number below, *i.e.,*
$2^2 + 4^2 = 20$
$3^2 + 9^2 = 90$, similarly
$1^2 + 5^2 = 26$.

**14. *(a)* :** The sum of numbers in 1st and 2nd column plus 1 is the number in the 3rd column, *i.e.,*
$27 + 22 + 1 = 50$
$13 + 12 + 1 = 26$, similarly
$9 + 2 + 1 = 12$.

**15. *(d)* :** The product of numbers on either side of the triangle plus the number at the base is the number inside the triangle, *i.e.,*
$(5 \times 3) + 4 = 19$
$(6 \times 4) + 5 = 29$, similarly
$(7 \times 5) + 6 = 41$.

**16. *(a)* :** Clockwise starting from number 7, the next number is obtained by doubling the number and adding 2, *i.e.,*
$(7 \times 2) + 2 = 16$
$(16 \times 2) + 2 = 34 \ldots$, similarly
$(34 \times 2) + 2 = 70$
$(70 \times 2) + 2 = 142$
$(142 \times 2) + 2 = 286$.

**17. *(c)* :** The difference between the numbers in opposite sectors is 13, *i.e.,*
$26 - 13 = 13$
$68 - 55 = 13$, similarly
The missing number is $42 - 13 = 29$
($42 + 13 = 55$ is not given as option).

**18. *(b)* :** The number at the bottom is obtained by subtracting the sum of two numbers in the centre grid line from the square of the number at the top, *i.e.,*
$7^2 - (2 + 7) = 40$
$5^2 - (8 + 3) = 14$, similarly
$9^2 - (7 + 6) = 68$.

**19. *(b)* :** The number inside the brackets is obtained by multiplying the number on the left by 2 and then dividing the product by the sum of digits of number on the right, *i.e.,*
$(42 \times 2) \div (2 + 2) = 21$
$(162 \times 2) \div (9 + 9) = 18$, similarly
$(78 \times 2) \div (8 + 4) = 13$.

**20. *(a)* :** Subtracting the sum of squares of two numbers at the base from the square of number at the apex gives the number inside the triangle, *i.e.,*
$16^2 - (7^2 + 10^2) = 107$
$25^2 - (20^2 + 4^2) = 209$, similarly
$19^2 - (2^2 + 17^2) = 68$.

**21. *(c)* :** The number in the centre is the product of all the 4 numbers minus 10, *i.e.,*
$(3 \times 5 \times 2 \times 6) - 10 = 170$
$(8 \times 1 \times 4 \times 9) - 10 = 278$, similarly
$(10 \times 6 \times 7 \times 2) - 10 = 830$.

**22. *(d)* :** The number inside the circle is the product of difference of two numbers above and difference of two numbers below, *i.e.,*
$(5 - 3)(12 - 9) = 6$
$(8 - 4)(2 - 1) = 4$, similarly
$(18 - 10)(17 - 14) = 24$.

**23. *(a)* :** Starting from number 1 anticlockwise the number in the diagonally opposite section is its multiplication by 4, *i.e.,*
$1 \times 4 = 4$, $7 \times 4 = 28$, $2 \times 4 = 8$, similarly
$6 \times 4 = 24$.

**24. *(a)* :** Square of the number on the left plus the number on the right is the number within brackets, *i.e.*,

$6^2+4=40$

$3^2+3=12$, similarly

$7^2+2=51$.

**25. *(b)* :** Letter H is 8th in order of alphabetical series. Taking the sum of numbers placed vertically outside the circle + 8; multiplying it by the number on the right; then subtracting from the product the number on the left, gives the number inside the circle, *i.e.*,

Step I $\rightarrow$ $4+8+4 = 16$

Step II $\rightarrow$ $16\times5 = 80$

Step III $\rightarrow$ $80-10 = 70$

Letter C is 3rd in order, so

Step I $\rightarrow$ $2+3+5 = 10$

Step II $\rightarrow$ $10\times3 = 30$

Step III $\rightarrow$ $30-4 = 26$

Similarly, J is 10th in order, so

Step I $\rightarrow$ $8+10+6 = 24$

Step II $\rightarrow$ $24\times?$

Step III $\rightarrow$ $(24\times?)-6=90$

Simplifying the above equation :

$24\times? = 90+6$, *i.e.*, 96

$? = 96\div24=4$.

# 18. Alphabet Problems

Alphabet problems are fun to attempt. They are based on alphabetical series in natural as well as reverse order.

**Natural Order**

A B C D E F G H I J K L M N O P Q R S T U V W X Y Z

**Reverse Order**

Z Y X W V U T S R Q P O N M L K J I H G F E D C B A

**Note :** The series starts from A on reaching Z and from Z on reaching A. Of these A E I O U are vowels and the rest are consonants.

## EXERCISE

**1.** Which letter should be ninth letter to the left of ninth letter from the right if the first half of the alphabet is reversed?

*(a)* I *(b)* D

*(c)* F *(d)* E

**2.** Starting from the fifth letter from the left, if twelve letters are written in reverse order, then which letter will be the seventh to the left of the fourteenth letter from the right?

*(a)* N *(b)* H

*(c)* L *(d)* O

**3.** What letter will come in the centre of sixth letter from the right and thirteenth letter from the left?

*(a)* Q *(b)* R

*(c)* P *(d)* S

**4.** If in the word "DISTURBANCE", the first letter is interchanged with the last letter, the second letter is interchanged with the tenth letter and so on, which letter would come after the letter "T" in the newly formed word?

*(a)* I *(b)* U

*(c)* N *(d)* S

**5.** If it is possible to make a meaningful word with the third, the fifth, the seventh and the tenth letters of the word PROJECTION. If no such word can be made, give 'O' as the answer. If more than one such word can be made, give 'M' as the answer.

*(a)* T *(b)* N

*(c)* O *(d)* M

**6.** A meaningful word is made if we take the first, fourth, fifth, seventh, tenth, eleventh and the twelfth letters of the word "FELICITATIONS". Which of the following will be the fifth letter of that word from the right end of that word?

*(a)* T *(b)* C

*(c)* N *(d)* I

**7.** On rearranging the jumbled spelling of the word SKARTINS, a language is obtained. What is the fifth letter from the right of the rearranged word?

*(a)* N *(b)* K

*(c)* R *(d)* S

**8.** If the 1st, 3rd, 5th, 7th, 10th and 13th letters of the word "ENTERTAINMENT" are used to make a meaningful word, then what two letters will come in the centre?

*(a)* AM *(b)* TT

*(c)* RE *(d)* NA

**9.** On rearranging the jumbled spelling of the word GRUBY a sport is obtained. What is the letter in the centre?

*(a)* R *(b)* B

*(c)* G *(d)* U

**10.** If the letters 'ERVSECI' can be rearranged to form a meaningful word what will be the fifth letter from the right?

(*a*) R (*b*) V

(*c*) E (*d*) None of these

**11.** From the word HASTEN how many independent meaningful English words can be made without changing the order of the letters and using each letter only once?

(*a*) 1 (*b*) 2

(*c*) 3 (*d*) 4

## EXPLANATORY ANSWERS

**1. (*d*) :** MLKJIGHFEDCBANOPQRSTUVWXYZ

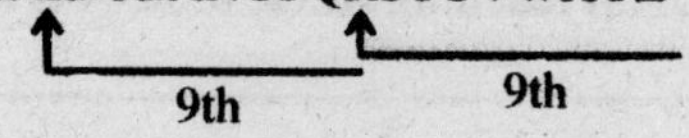


**2. (*d*) :** ABCDPONMLKJIHGFEQRSTUVWXYZ

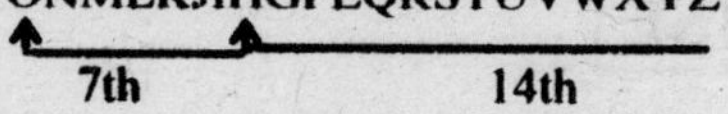


**3. (*a*) :**

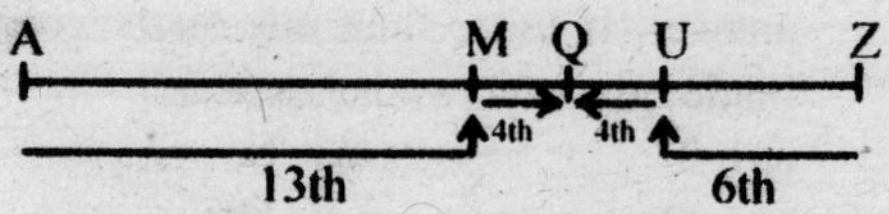


13th letter from left is 'M' and 6th letter from right is 'U'. The letter in the centre of 'M' and 'U' is 'Q'.

**4. (*d*) :** ECNABRUTSID

**5. (*d*) :** PROJECTION

The 3rd, 5th, 7th and 10th letters are OETN.

The words formed are TONE and NOTE.

**6. (*b*) :** FELICITATIONS

The 1st, 4th, 5th, 7th, 10th, 11th and 12th lettes are FICTION.

The word is FICTION and 5th letter from right is 'C'.

**7. (*d*) :** The word is SANSKRIT and 5th letter from right is 'S'.

**8. (*b*) :** ENTERTAINMENT

The 1st, 3rd, 5th 7th, 10th and 13th letters are ETRAMT.

The word formed is MATTER.

**9. (*c*) :** The sport is RUGBY. The letter in the centre is 'G'.

**10. (*a*) :** The word is SERVICE and fifth letter from right is 'R'.

**11. (*b*) :** The words formed are : HAS, TEN.

# 19. Logical Diagram

In these type of questions, a set of five different figures is given as options. Each figure represents a logical pattern of certain groups of related words wherein each word represents a class. One has to identify the most appropriate logical figure for the set of words given. Some of the relationships represented by these diagrams are given below. Understand the relationship patterns and then attempt the exercise following the explanation.

## EXERCISE

**Directions :** *From the five logical Diagrams, select one which best illustrates the relationship among three given classes in the questions 1 to 10.*

*(a)*

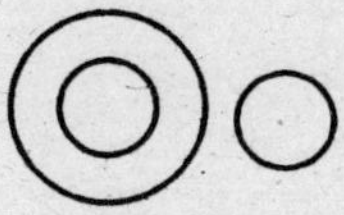

*(b)*

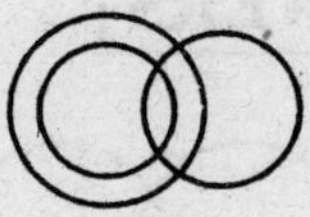

*(c)*

*(d)*

*(e)*

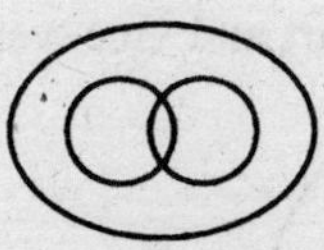

**1.** Birds, fruits, mangoes
**2.** Criminals, lawyers, bandits
**3.** Swimmers, bachelors, men
**4.** Smart, engineers, women
**5.** Vegetables, potatoes, brinjals
**6.** Grapes, sweet, fruit
**7.** Doctors, architects, humans
**8.** Scholars, people, Indians
**9.** Children, naughty, studious
**10.** Pens, pencils, stationery

**Directions :** *From the five logical diagrams select one which best illustrates the relationship among three given classes in questions 11 to 20.*

*(a)*

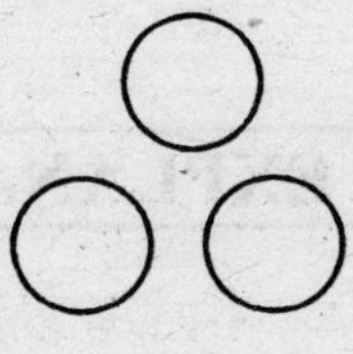

*(b)*

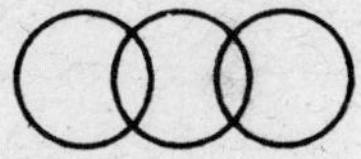

*(c)*

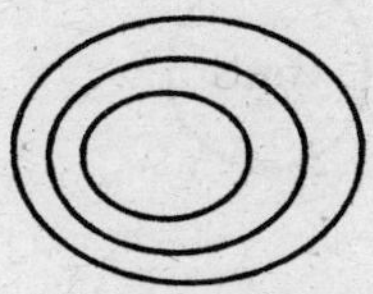

*(d)*

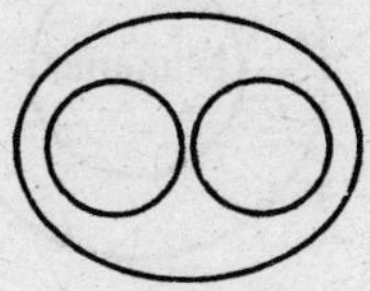

*(e)*

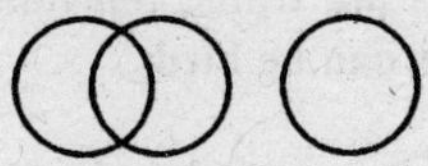

**11.** Ink, crayons, red
**12.** Canines, dogs, pups
**13.** Table, chair, stool
**14.** Ripe, mangoes, basket
**15.** Scholars, studious, illiterates
**16.** Cars, ships, means of conveyance
**17.** Age, number, thirteen
**18.** Country, state, continent
**19.** Father, parent, mother
**20.** Iron, metal, mercury

**Directions :** *From the five logical diagrams select one which best illustrates the relationship among three given classes in the questions 21 to 30.*

*(a)*

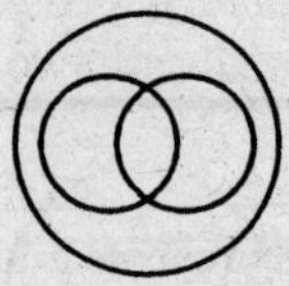

*(b)*

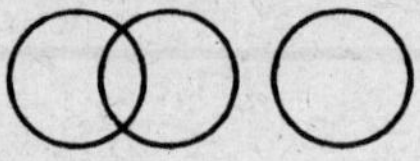

*(c)*

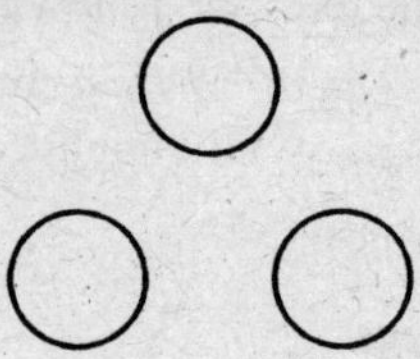

*(d)*

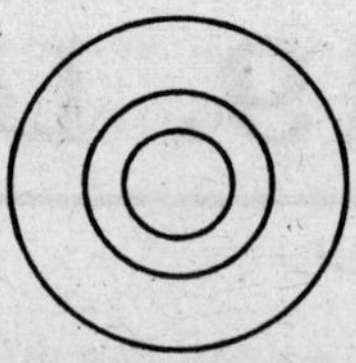

*(e)*

**21.** Lizards, Reptiles, Crocodiles
**22.** Whales, Tortoise, Fishes
**23.** Birds, Crows, Parrots
**24.** Sisters, Women, Mothers
**25.** Plants, Scientists, Men
**26.** Novels, Album, English
**27.** Sentences, Words, Paragraph
**28.** Beef, Mutton, Flesh
**29.** Principal, Student, Parent
**30.** Lily, Rose, Flower.

## EXPLANATORY ANSWERS

**1.** ***(a)*** :

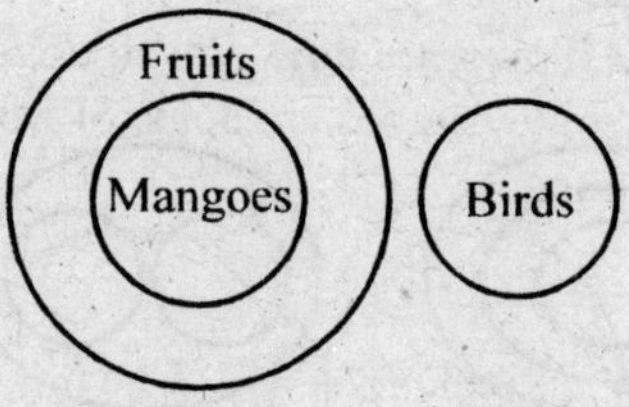


All mangoes are fruits, but neither fruits, nor mangoes can be birds.

**2.** ***(a)*** :

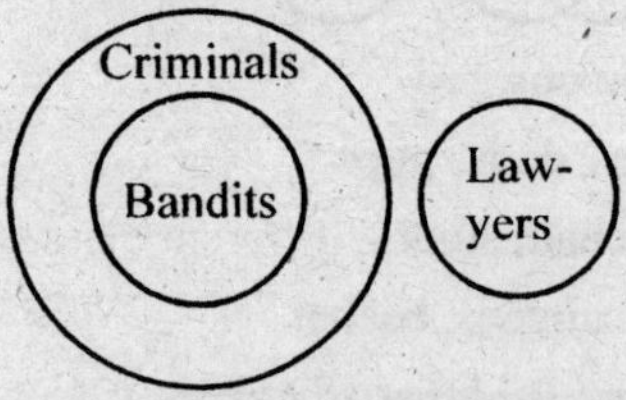


All bandits are criminal, but neither criminals nor bandits can be lawyers.

**3.** ***(b)*** :

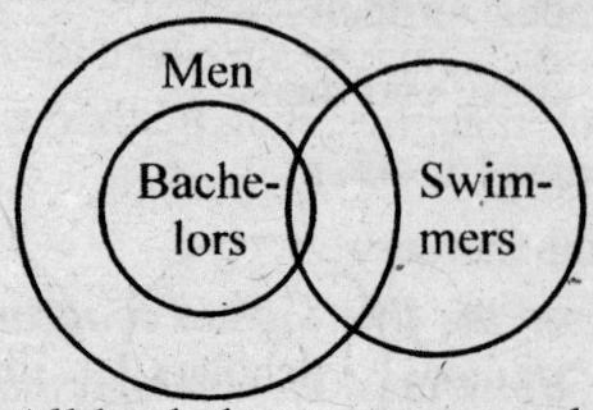


All bachelors are men and some men and bachelors can be swimmers.

**4.** ***(c)*** :

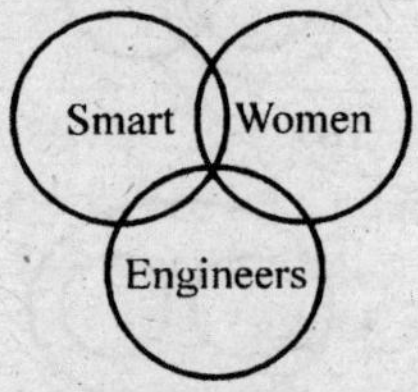


Some women can be smart and some women can be engineers and vice–versa. Some engineers can be women and some engineers can be smart and vice–versa.

**5.** ***(d)*** :

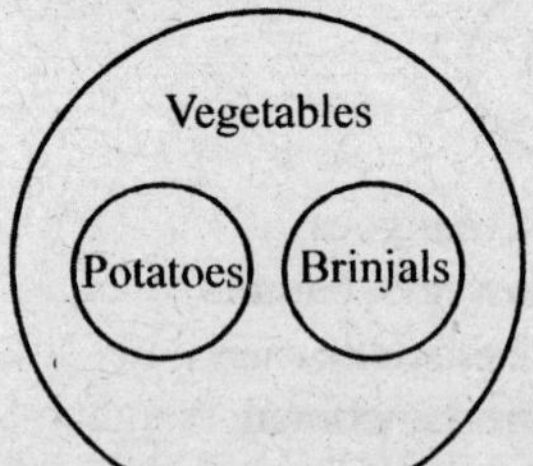


Potatoes and brinjals are vegetables but they have nothing in common. Some vegetables are potatoes and some are brinjals.

**6.** ***(b)*** :

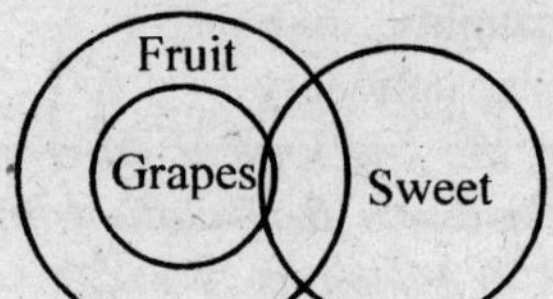

Some grapes are sweet and all grapes are fruit. But not all that is sweet is fruit.

**7. *(d)* :**

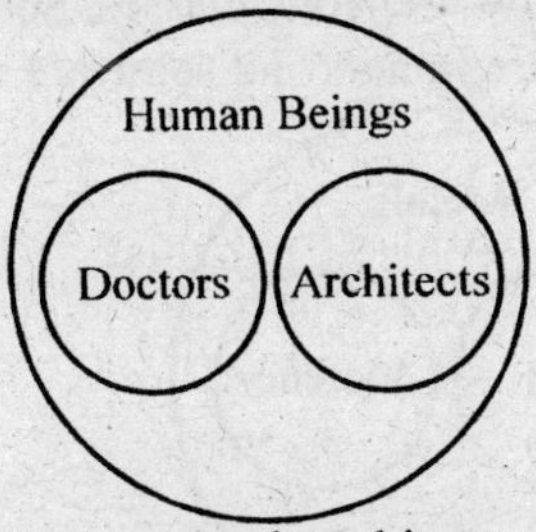


Doctors and architects are two separate classes, but all doctors and architects are humans and some humans are either doctors or architects.

**8. *(e)* :**

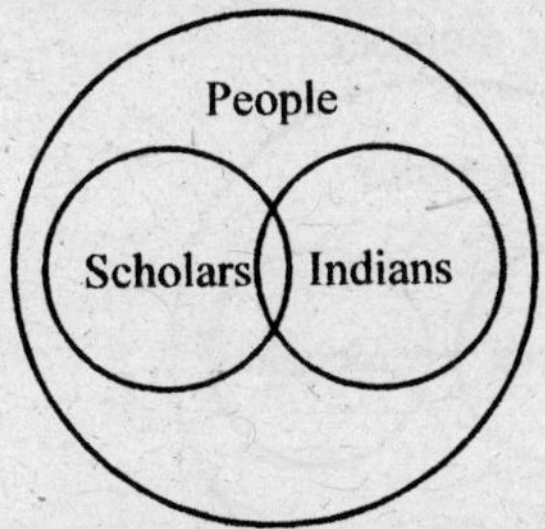


Some Indians can be scholars and some scholars can be Indians. All scholars and Indians are people.

**9. *(c)* :**

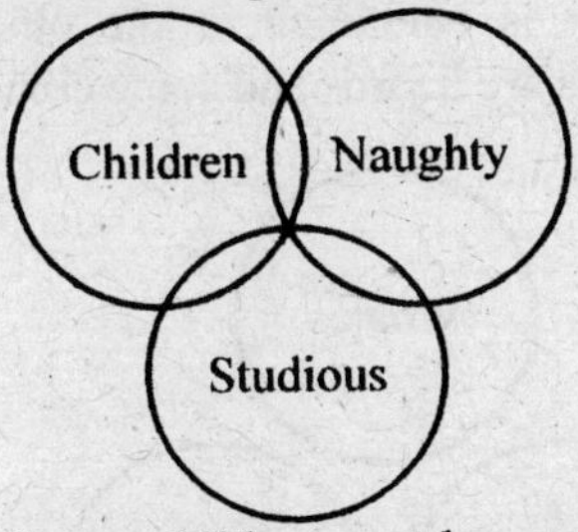


Some children can be naughty and some can be studious, some studious can be children and some naughty. Some naughty can be studious and some children.

**10. *(d)* :**

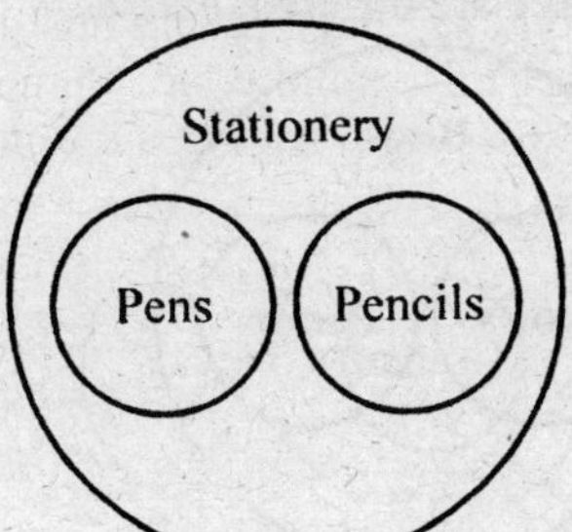


Pens and pencils both are items of stationery and some stationery is pens and pencils, but pens and pencils are two separate classes.

**11. *(b)* :**

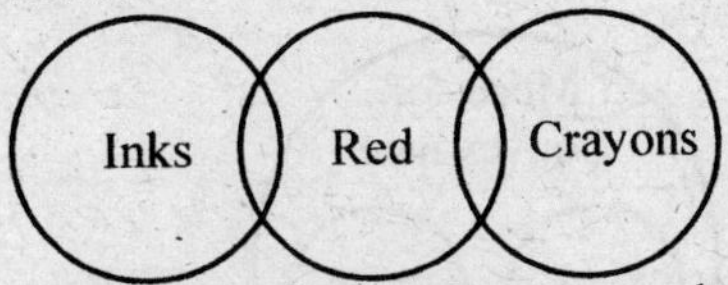


Some ink and some crayons can be red and some red units can be inks and crayons, but ink and crayon have nothing in common.

**12. *(c)* :**

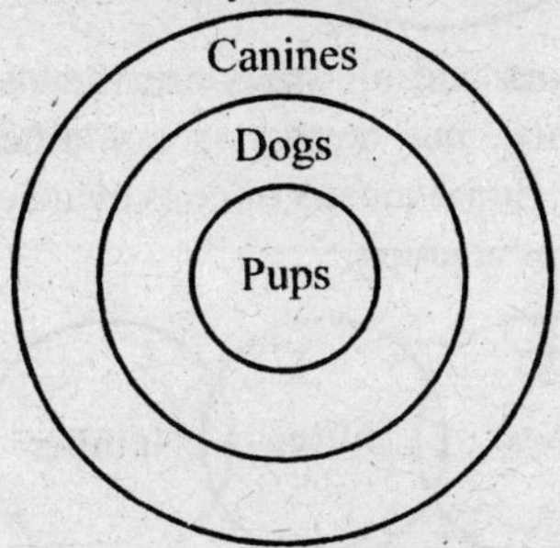


All pups are dogs and all dogs are canines. Some canines are dogs, of which some are pups.

**13. *(a)* :**

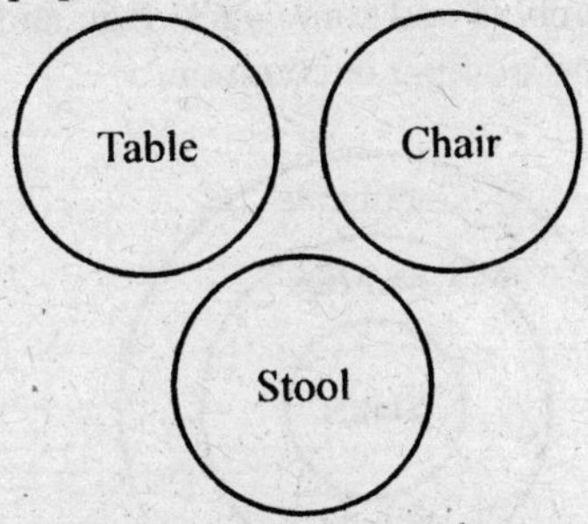


All three are different classes.

**14. *(e)* :**

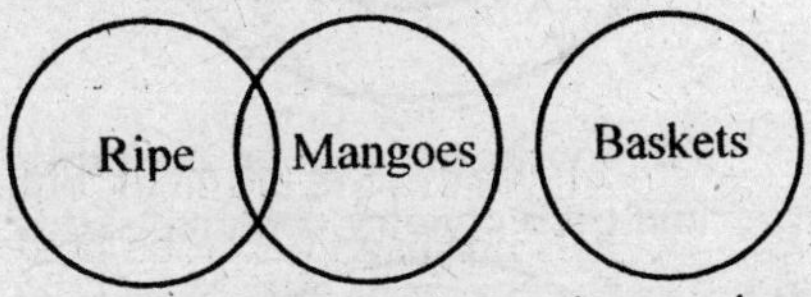


Some mangoes are ripe and some ripe units are mangoes, but neither ripe units nor mangoes can be baskets.

**15. *(e)* :**

Some studious can be scholars and some scholars can be studious, but neither studious nor scholars can be illiterates.

**16.** ***(d)*** **:**

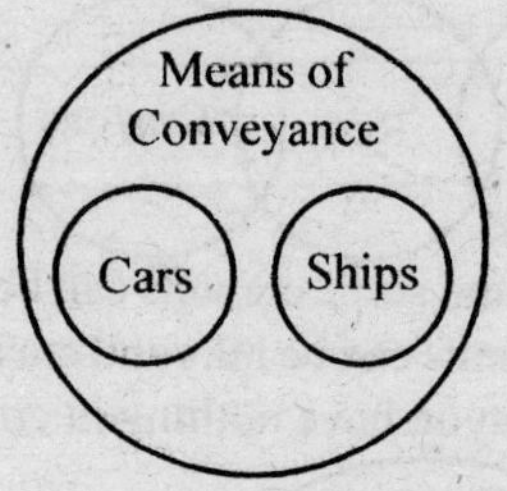


All cars and all ships are means of conveyance, but neither is contained in the other. Some means of conveyance are cars and some ships.

**17.** ***(b)*** **:**

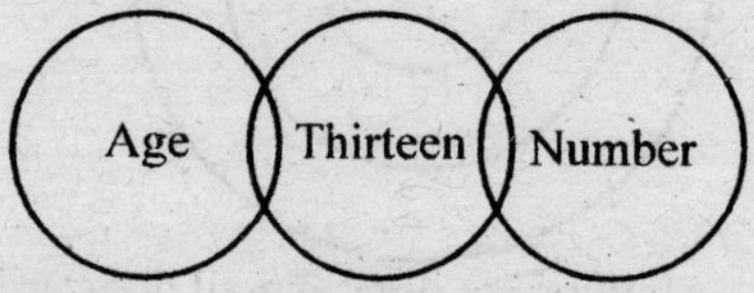


Some are aged thirteen and some numbers are thirteen. Some thirteen units are numbers and some ages. Age and number have nothing in common.

**18.** ***(c)*** **:**

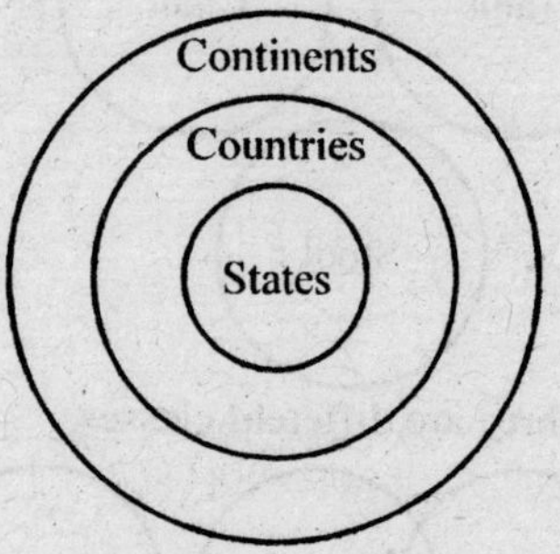


All continents contain countries within it and each country contains states within it.

**19.** ***(d)*** **:**

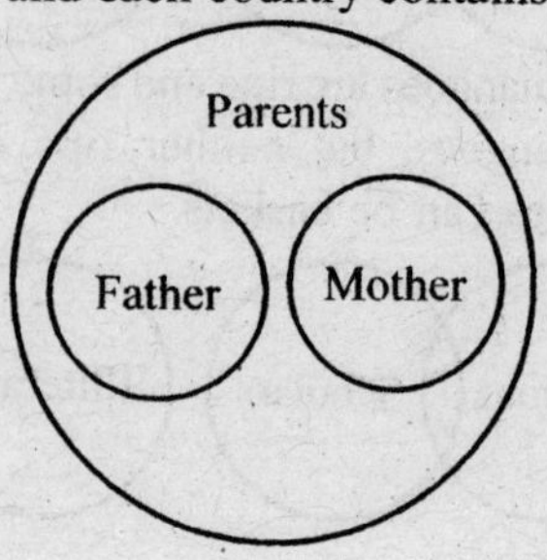


All fathers and mothers are parents, but they are two separate classes. Some of the parents are fathers and some are mothers.

**20.** ***(d)*** **:**

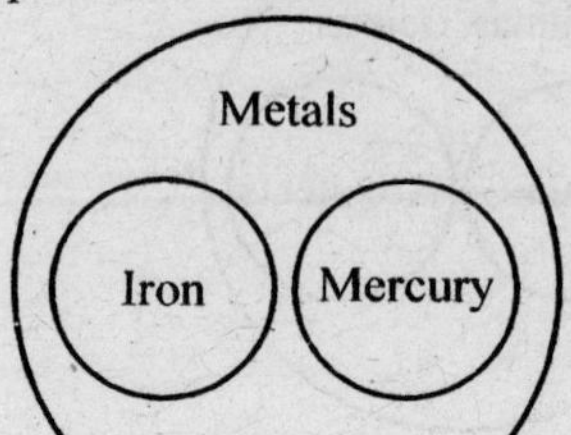


Iron and mercury are metals, but they have nothing in common. Some metals are iron and some mercury.

**21.** ***(d)*** **:**

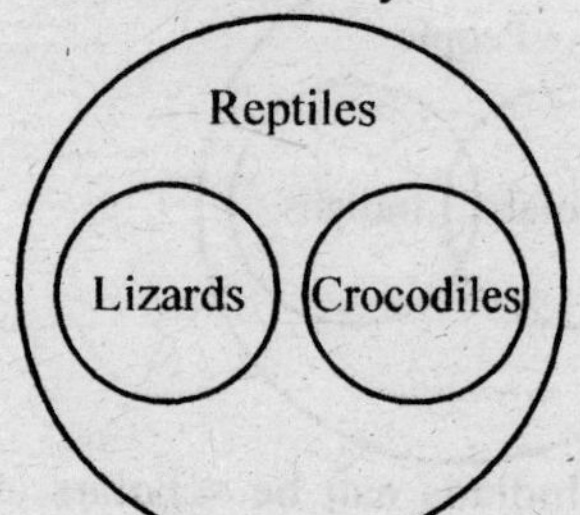


All lizards and crocodiles are reptiles, but neither is contained in the other. Some reptiles are lizards and some crocodiles.

**22.** ***(c)*** **:**

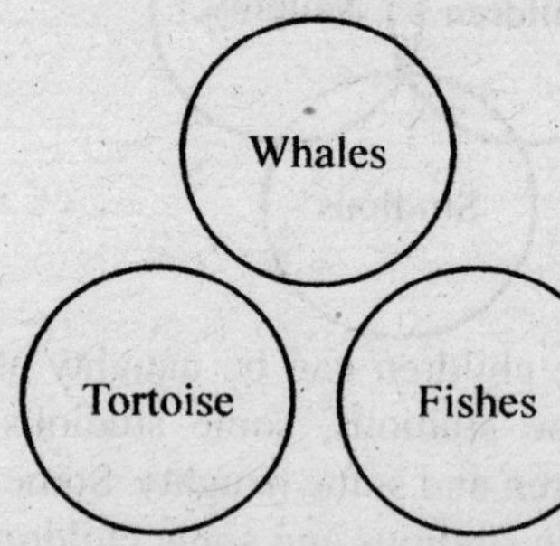


All three are different classes.

**23.** ***(d)*** **:**

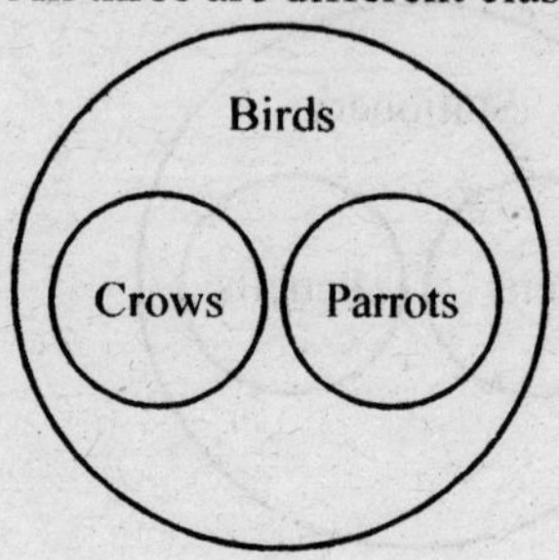

All crows and parrots are birds but neither is contained in the other. Some birds are crows and some parrots.

**24.** ***(a)*** **:**

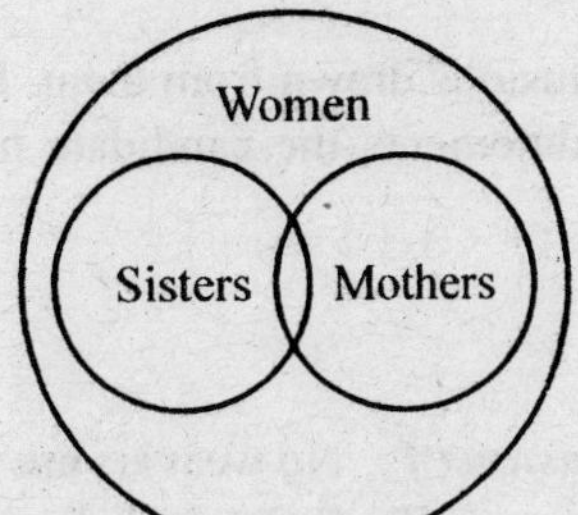


Some sisters can be mothers and some mothers can be sisters. All sisters and mothers are women.

**25.** ***(b)*** **:**

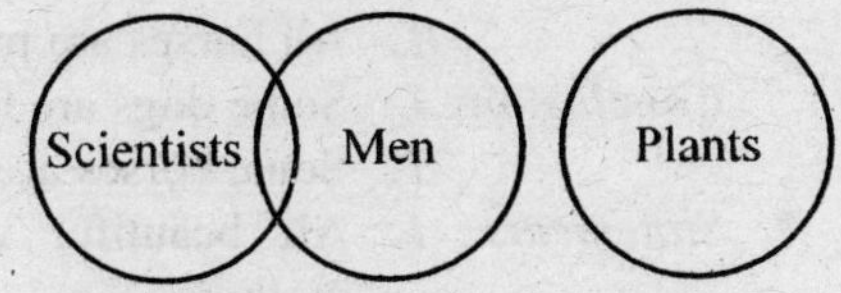


Some scientists can be men and some men can be scientists, but neither scientists nor men can be plants.

**26.** ***(b)*** **:**

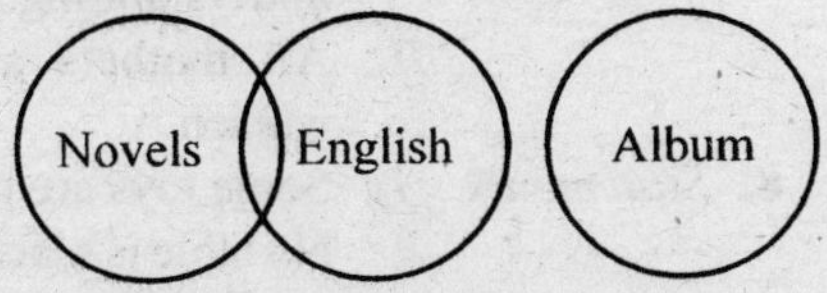


Some novels can be in English and some written material in English can be novels, but neither novels nor English can be album.

**27.** ***(e)*** **:**

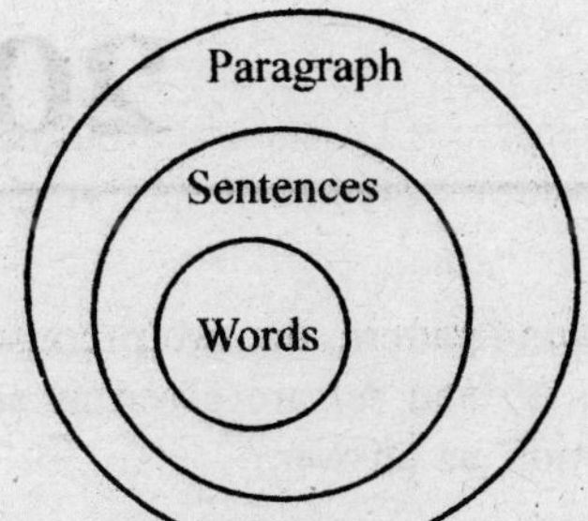


All paragraphs contain sentences within it and all sentences contain words within it.

**28.** ***(d)*** **:**

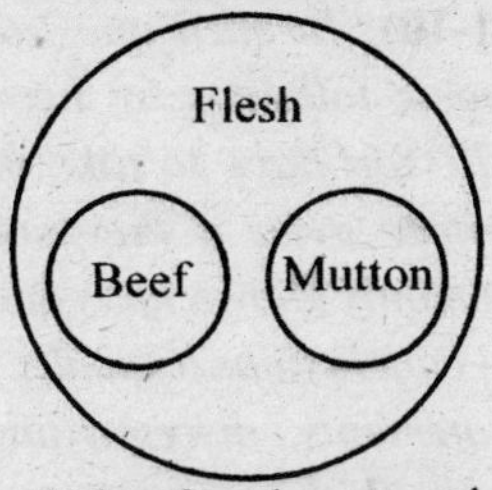


All beef and mutton is flesh of some animals. Some flesh is beef and some mutton.

**29.** ***(b)*** **:**

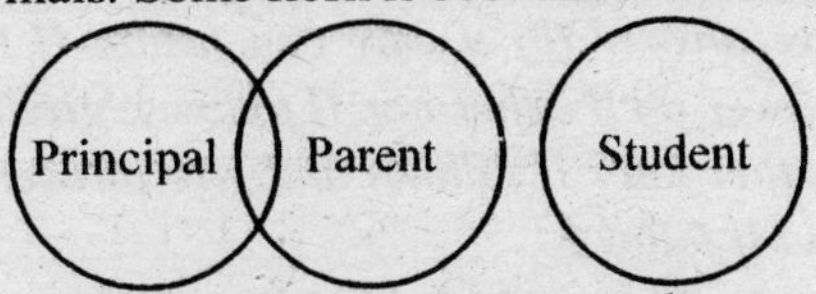


A Principal can be a parent and parent can be a principal. A student is a different class.

**30.** ***(d)*** **:**

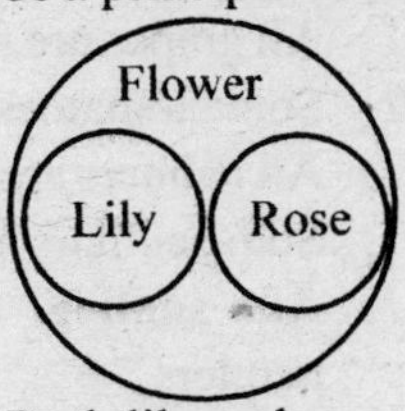


Both lily and rose are flowers. But neither is contained in the other.

# 20. SYLLOGISM

In this reasoning pattern, the two premises are followed by two conclusions drawn from them. Five options *(a)*, *(b)*, *(c)*, *(d)* and *(e)* are given as answers. Based on the two statements the candidate has to select the right option as answer.

## EXERCISE

**Directions (Qs. 1-10):** *In each question below are given two statements followed by two conclusions numbered I and II. You have to take the two given statements to be true even if they seem to be at variance from commonly known facts and then decide which of the given conclusions logically follows from the two given statements, disregarding commonly known facts. Read both the statements and—*

*Give answer (a) if only conclusion I follows; give answer (b) if only conclusion II follows; give answer (c) if either I or II follows; give answer (d) if neither I nor II follows and give answer (e) if both I and II follows.*

**1.** *Statements* *I:* All tomatoes are red.
*II:* All grapes are tomatoes.
*Conclusions* *I:* All grapes are red.
*II:* Some tomatoes are grapes.

**2.** *Statements* *I:* All painters are smilling.
*II:* Some authors are painters.
*Conclusions* *I:* All smiling authors are painters.
*II:* Some authors are smiling.

**3.** *Statements* *I:* All peons in this office are efficient.
*II:* Ramu is not efficient.
*Conclusions* *I:* Ramu is not peon in this office.
*II:* Ramu should be more efficient.

**4.** *Statements* *I:* All weavers are hard working.
*II:* No hard working men are foolish.
*Conclusions* *I:* No weavers are foolish.
*II:* Some foolish are weavers.

**5.** *Statements* *I:* All fishes are cars.
*II:* All cars are vegetables.
*Conclusions* *I:* Some vegetables are cars.
*II:* Some vegetables are fishes.

**6.** *Statements* *I:* Some dogs are pups.
*II:* All horses are pups.
*Conclusions* *I:* Some dogs are horses.
*II:* Some horses are dogs.

**7.** *Statements* *I:* All beautiful women are mothers.
*II:* All mothers are understanding.
*Conclusions* *I:* All beautiful women are understanding.
*II:* All mothers are beautiful women.

**8.** *Statements* *I:* Some toys are tables.
*II:* No table is black.
*Conclusions* *I:* Some toys are black.
*II:* Some toys are not black.

**9.** *Statements* *I:* All rivers are mountains.
*II:* Some rivers are deserts.
*Conclusions* *I:* Some mountains are deserts.
*II:* Some deserts are not mountains.

**10.** *Statements* *I:* All men are horses.
*II:* All horses are elephants.
*Conclusions* *I:* All men are elephants.
*II:* All elephants are men.

**Directions (Qs. 11-15):** *In the following questions, select the set of conclusion which logically follows from the given statements.*

**11.** *Statements* *I :* All foxes are plates.
*II :* All plates are trees.
*Conclusions* *I :* All foxes are trees.
*II :* All trees are foxes.
*III :* Some trees are foxes.
*IV :* Some trees are plates.
*(a)* All conclusions are correct.
*(b)* Only conclusions I, III, and IV follow.
*(c)* Only conclusions II, III, and IV follow.
*(d)* Only conclusions I and IV follow.
*(e)* None of the above.

**12.** *Statements* *I :* Some cubes are squares.
*II :* All squares are circles.
*Conclusions* *I :* All cubes are circles.
*II :* Some circles are cubes.
*III :* Some circles are squares.
*IV :* All squares are cubes.
*(a)* Only conclusion I follows.
*(b)* Only conclusion I, II and III follow.
*(c)* All conclusions are correct.
*(d)* Only conclusions II and III follow.
*(e)* None of the above.

**13.** *Statements* *I :* All cups are goats.
*II :* All goats are tins.
*Conclusions* *I :* All goats are cups.
*II :* All tins are goats.
*III :* No cups are tins.
*IV :* No tins are cups.
*(a)* Only conclusions III and IV follow.
*(b)* Only conclusios I and II follow.
*(c)* Only conclusions I, II and III follow.
*(d)* All conclusions are correct.
*(e)* None of the above.

**14.** *Statements* *I :* All bombs are bags.
*II :* Some bags are jets.
*Conclusions* *I :* All bombs are jets.
*II :* All jets are bombs.
*III :* Some jets are bombs.
*IV :* Some bombs are jets.
*(a)* Only conclusion III follows.
*(b)* Only conclusions I and II follow.
*(c)* All conclusions are correct.
*(d)* Only conclusions III and IV follow.
*(e)* None of these.

**15.** *Statements* *I :* Some thorns are jackets.
*II :* Some jackets are boats.
*Conclusions* *I :* No thorns are boats.
*II :* All jackets are boats.
*III :* Some boats are thorns.
*IV :* No jackets are thorns.
*(a)* Either conclusion I or IV follows.
*(b)* Either conclusion I or II follows.
*(c)* Either conclusion I or III follows.
*(d)* No conclusion is correct.
*(e)* All conclusions are correct.

## EXPLANATORY ANSWERS

**1. *(e)* :** When all tomatoes are red and all grapes are tomatoes, then all grapes are also red. When all grapes are tomatoes, then some tomatoes must be grapes. Therefore, both conclusions I and II are correct.

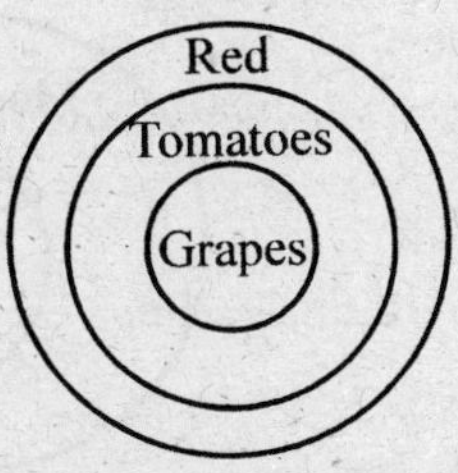


**2. *(b)* :** When all painters are smiling and some authors are painters, then some authors are smiling. Therefore, only conclusion II is correct.

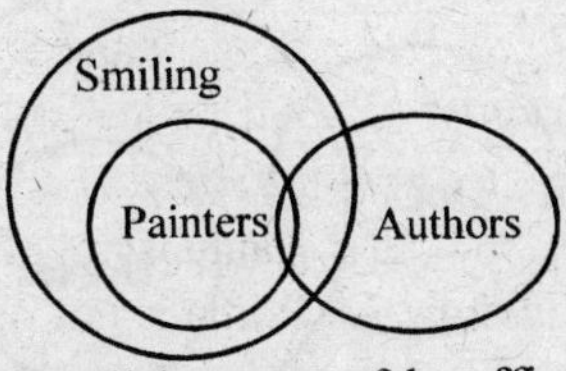


**3. *(a)* :** When all the peons of the office are efficient, then Ramu cannot be a peon in this office. Therefore, only conclusion I is correct.

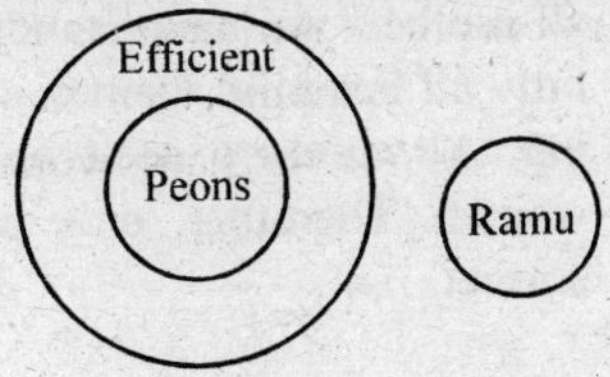

**4. *(a)* :** When all weavers are hardworking and no hardworking men are foolish, then no weavers are foolish. Therefore, only conclusion I is correct.

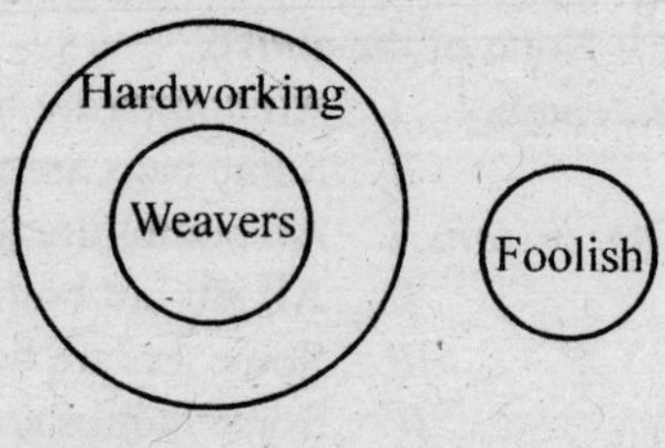


**5. *(e)* :** When all fishes are cars and all cars are vegetables, then all fishes will naturally be vegetables. This means that some vegetables are fishes. And when all cars are vegetables, then some vegetables will be cars naturally. Therefore, both the conclusions I and II are correct.

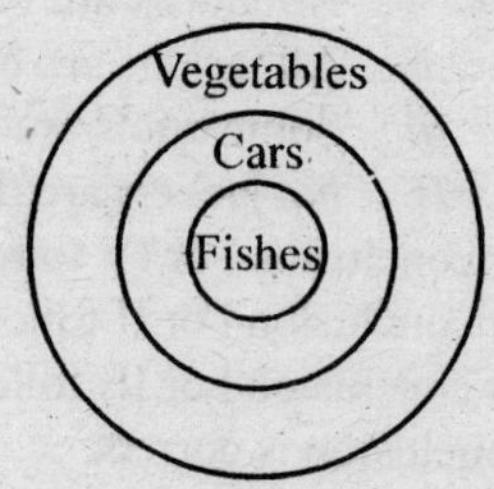


**6. *(d)* :** No relationship can be established between the two statements. Therefore, neither conclusion I nor conclusion II is correct.

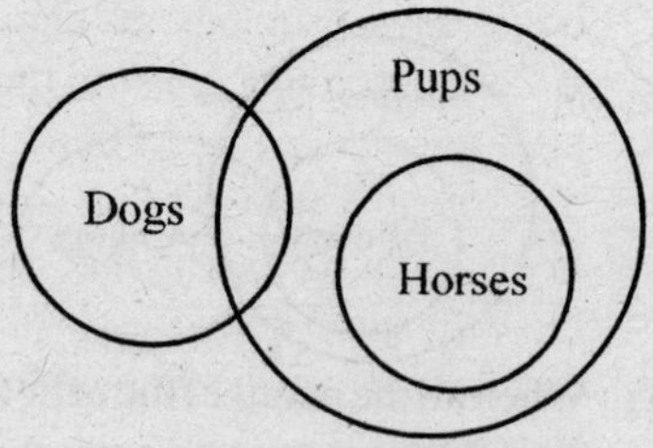


**7. *(a)* :** When all beautiful women are mothers and all mothers are understanding, then naturally all beautiful women are understanding. All mothers need not be beautiful women. Therefore, only conclusion I is correct.

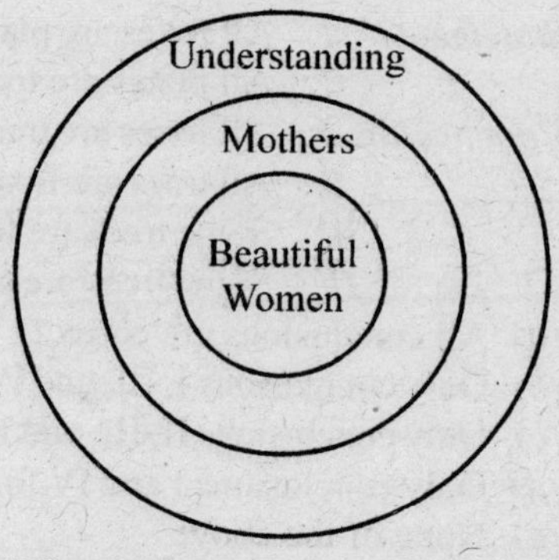


**8. *(c)* :** When some toys are tables and no table is black, then it is indicated that some toys can be black, as all toys are not tables. On the other hand, some toys may not be black. Therefore, there is a possibility that some toys may or may not be black. As such, either conclusion I or conclusion II can be correct.

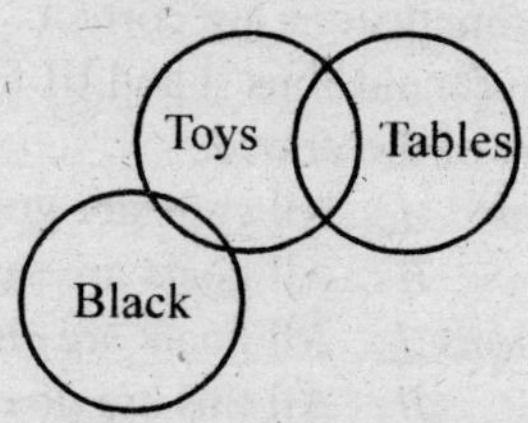


**9. *(e)* :** When all rivers are mountains and some rivers are deserts, then some deserts cannot be mountains and also, some mountains need not be deserts. Therefore, both conclusion I and conclusion II are correct.

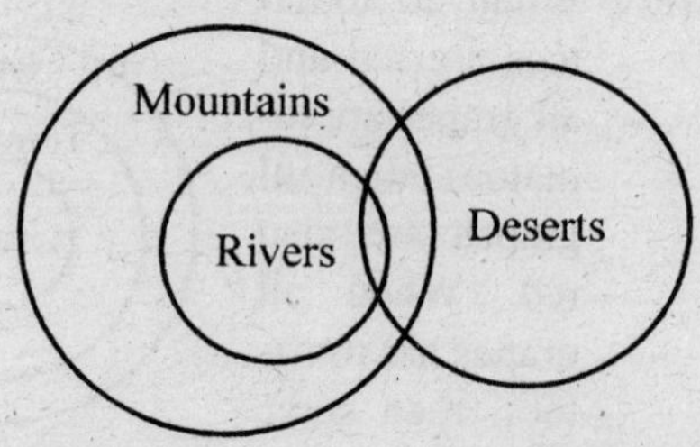


**10. *(a)* :** When all men are horses and all horses are elephants then, naturally all men are elephants, but all elephants need not be men. Therefore, only conclusion I is correct.

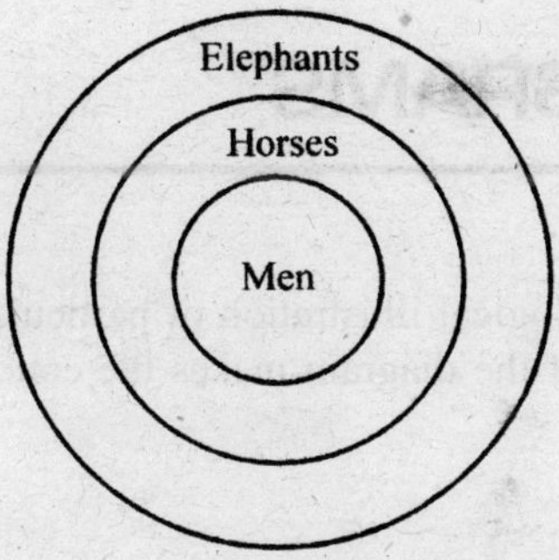


**11. *(b)* :**

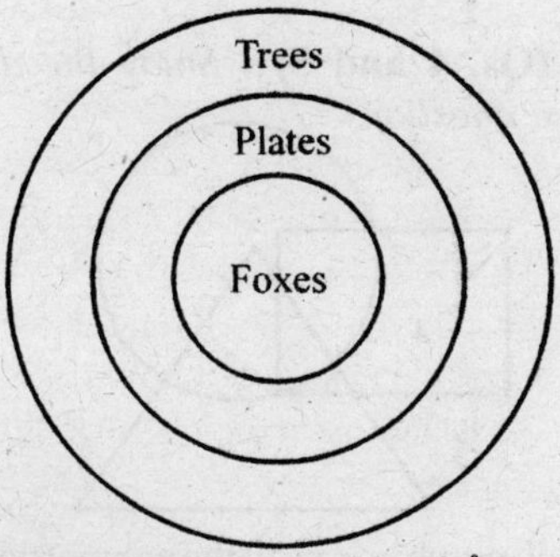


When all foxes are plates and all plates are trees, then naturally all foxes will be trees and some trees will then have to be foxes. And when all plates are trees then some trees will have to be plates. Therefore, only conclusions I, III and IV are correct.

**12. *(d)* :** When it is given that some cubes are squares and all squares are circles, then some cubes will naturally be circles, though all cubes cannot be circles. When some cubes are circles, then some circles will have to be cubes. And when all squares are circles, then some circles will have to be squares. As per given statement II, all squares are circles. Therefore all squares cannot be cubes. As such only conclusions II and III are correct.

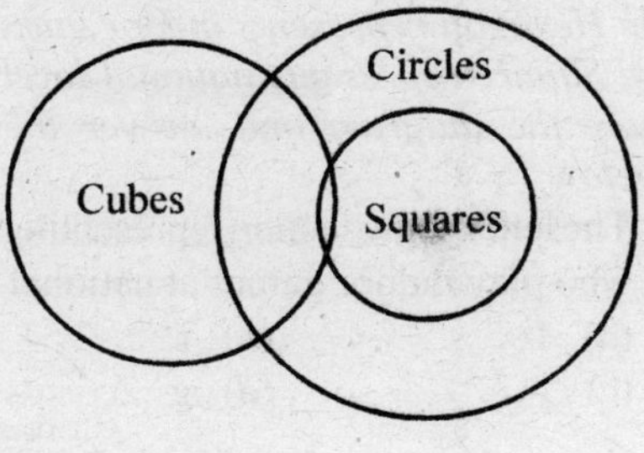


**13. *(e)* :** When all cups are goats, then only some goats can be cups. When all goats are tins, then only some tins can be goats. When all cups are goats and all goats are tins, then naturally all cups are tins and some tins must be cups. Therefore, all the conclusions are incorrect.

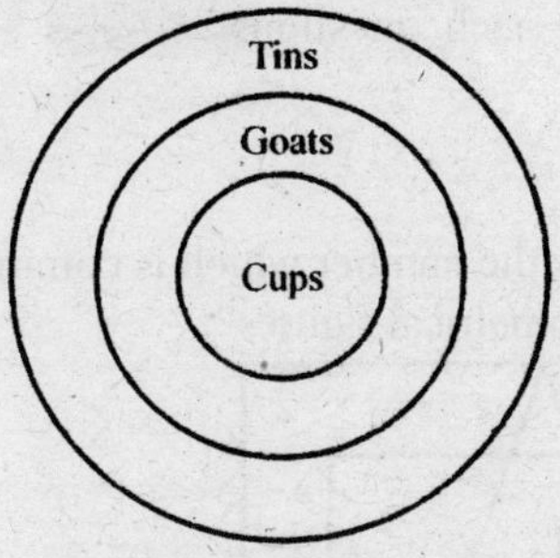


**14. *(e)* :** When all bombs are bags and some bags are jets then all bombs cannot be jets. 'Some bags' indicate that there is no chance of some bombs being jets, or some jets being bombs. Further all jets cannot be bombs. Therefore, all conclusions are incorrect.

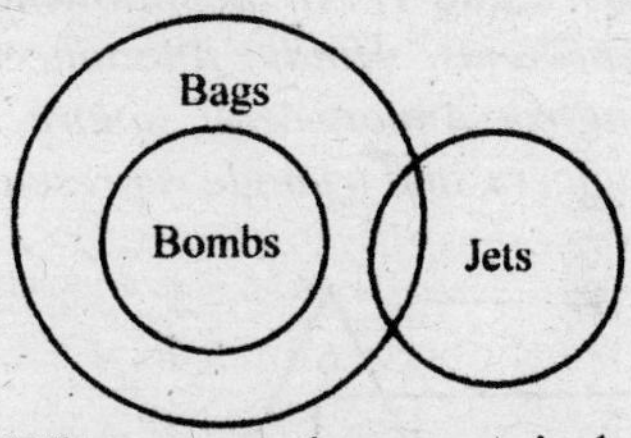


**15. *(d)* :** When some thorns are jackets and some jackets are boats, then some thorns may be boats but some boats cannot be thorns. As per Statement I, some thorns are jackets, some jackets need to be thorns. When Statement II conveys that some jackets are boats, then it is clear that all jackets cannot be boats. Therefore, no particular given conclusion can be drawn from the given statements.

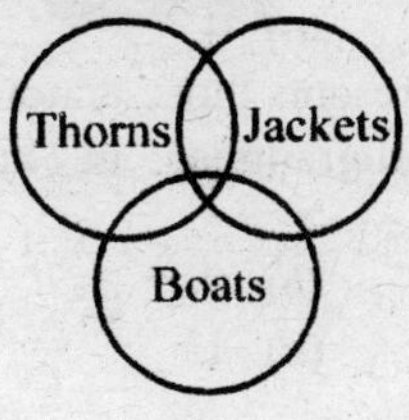

# 21. Venn Diagrams

In these type of questions, diagrammatic representation presents a logical illustration of particular class or statements based on which the questions are asked. A clear view of the diagram makes the concepts clear for attempting such questions.

## EXERCISE

1. What is the number which is common to only two geometrical figures?

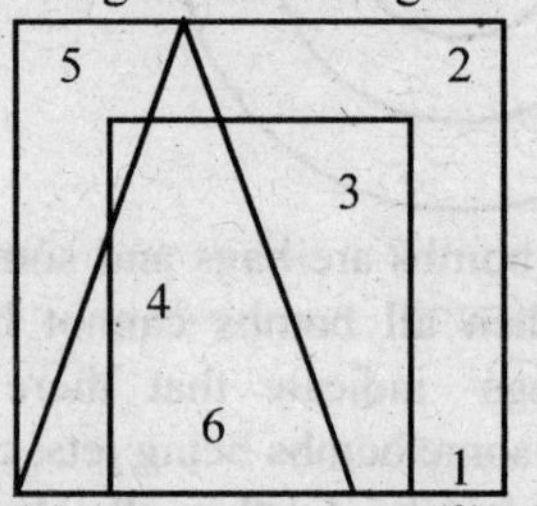


(*a*) 4 (*b*) 3
(*c*) 5 (*d*) 2

**Directions (Qs. 2 and 3) :** *In the following diagram, rectangle represents Hindi Announcers, circle represents English Announcers, square represents French Announcers, and triangle represents German Announcers.*

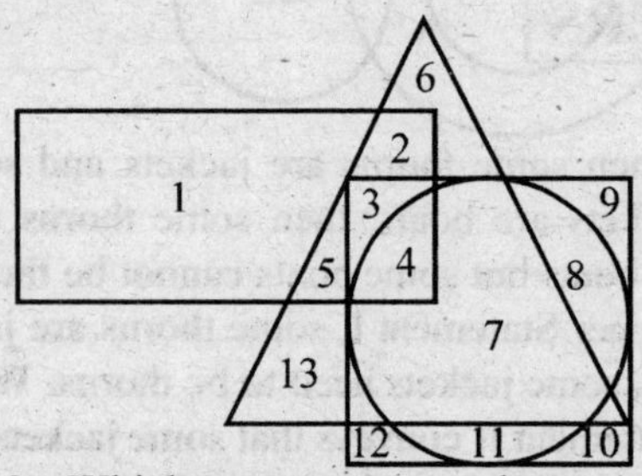


2. Which area represents those announcers who can present programmes in Hindi, French and German only?
(*a*) 1 (*b*) 2
(*c*) 3 (*d*) 4

3 Which area represents those announcers who can present programmes in French and English only?
(*a*) 7 (*b*) 9
(*c*) 11 (*d*) 13

**Directions (Qs. 4 and 5) :** *Study the diagram to answer these questions.*

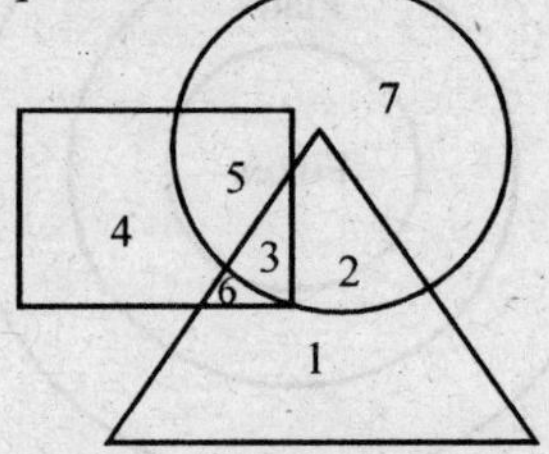


4. Which number is in all the geometrical figures?
(*a*) 5 (*b*) 6
(*c*) 2 (*d*) 3

5. Number 6 is in :
(*a*) Rectangle and triangle
(*b*) Circle and traingle
(*c*) Rectangle and circle
(*d*) Rectangle only

**Directions ( Qs. 6 to 9) :** *In the following diagram*

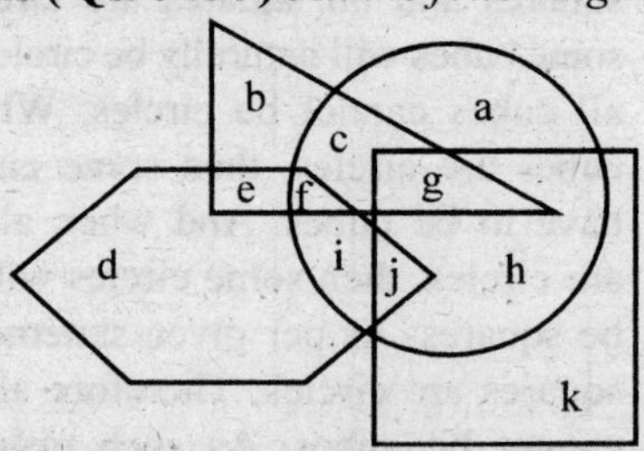


*The Circle represents players*
*The Triangle represents outdoor games*
*The Hexagon represents indoor games and*
*The Square represents national level players*
*Study the diagram and answer the questions given below :*

6. The letter in the section representing the players who play indoor games at national level is :
(*a*) f (*b*) i
(*c*) j (*d*) g

**7.** The letter representing the section of outdoor as well as indoor game players who do not play at the national level is :

(*a*) c (*b*) f
(*c*) e (*d*) i

**8.** The section representing national level players who do not play either outdoor or indoor games but still come under the category of players is :

(*a*) k (*b*) g
(*c*) c (*d*) h

**9.** Persons who play outdoor games but do not come under the category of players are represented in the section marked :

(*a*) b (*b*) c
(*c*) a (*d*) d

**Directions (Qs. 10 to 13) :** *Study the diagram given below.*

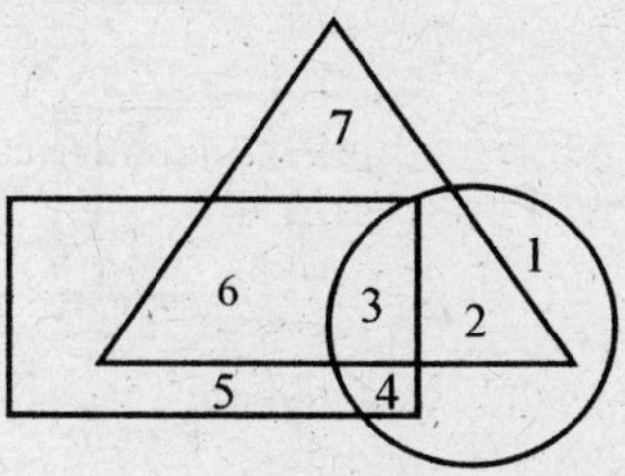


A college provides three different activities, students union represented by triangle, literary society represented by rectangle and social service league represented by circle.

**10.** Those who take part in both literary society and social service league but not in students union are represented by :

(*a*) 3 & 4 (*b*) 5 & 6
(*c*) 5 & 1 (*d*) 4

**11.** Those who take part in students union but not in social service league are represented by :

(*a*) 2 & 7 (*b*) 6 & 7
(*c*) 6 (*d*) 7

**12.** Those students who are members of literary society only and not of any other activity are represented by :

(*a*) 2 (*b*) 5
(*c*) 3 & 4 (*d*) 3

**13.** Those students who are members of all three groups are represented by :

(*a*) 2 (*b*) 3
(*c*) 4 (*d*) 6

## EXPLANATORY ANSWERS

**1.** ***(b)*** **:**

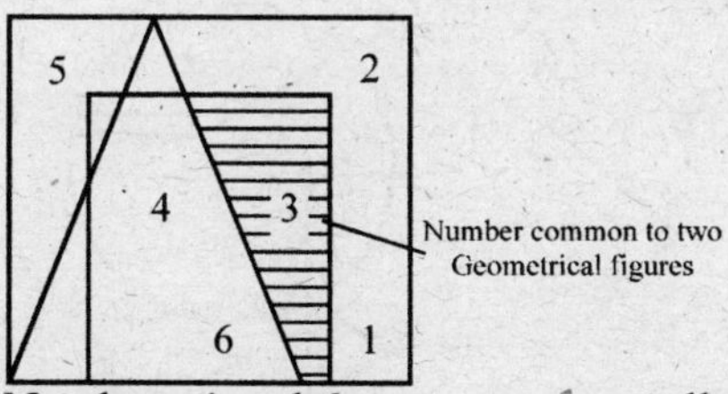


*Note :* Numbers 4 and 6 are common to all three geometrical figures.

**2.** ***(c)*****,** **3.** ***(c)*** **:**

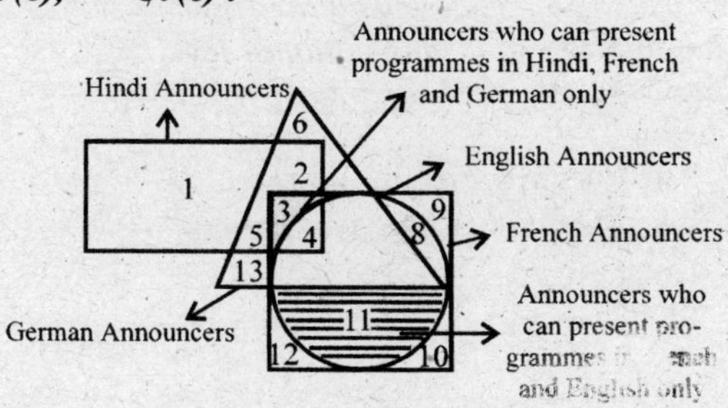


**4.** ***(d)*****,** **5.** ***(a)*** **:**

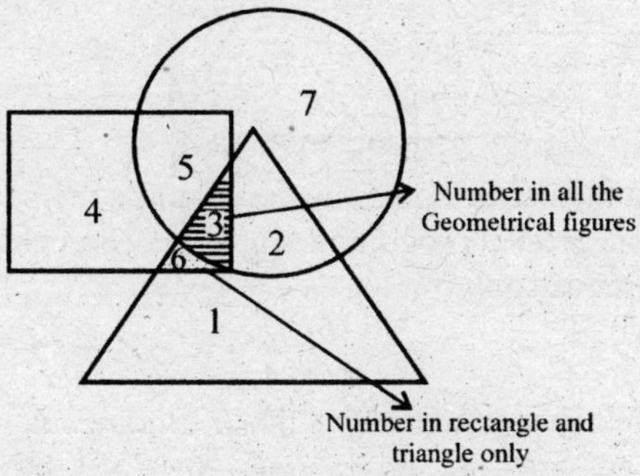


**6.** ***(c)*****,**

**7.** ***(b)*****,**

**8.** ***(d)*****,**

**9.** ***(a)*** **:**

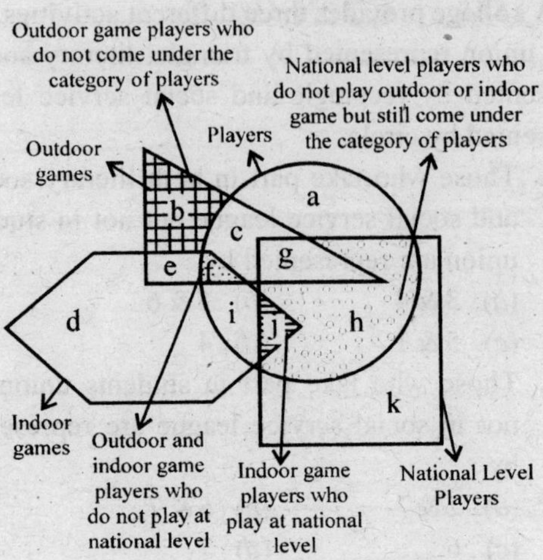


**10.** ***(d)***, **11.** ***(b)***, **12.** ***(b)***, **13.** ***(b)*** **:**

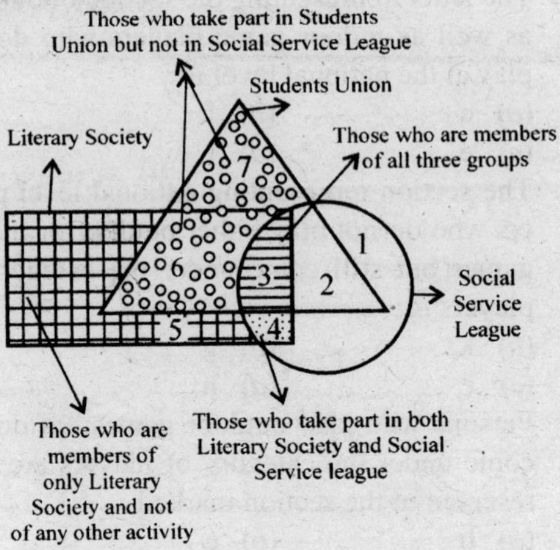

# 22. NON-VERBAL SERIES

## EXERCISE

**Directions (Q. 1–10) :** *In each of the following questions which one of the five answer figures given below should come after the problem figures if the sequence are continued?*

**Problem Figures** **Answer Figures**

1.  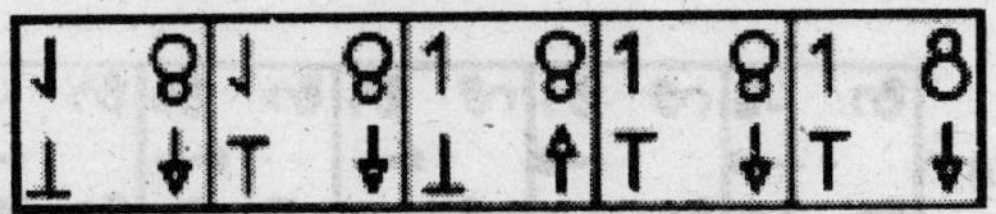

*(a)* *(b)* *(c)* *(d)* *(e)*

2. 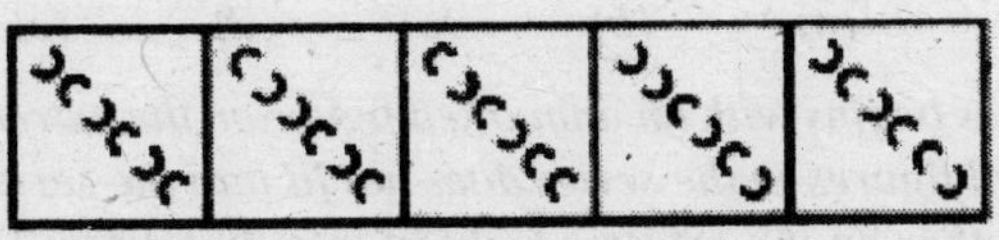 

*(a)* *(b)* *(c)* *(d)* *(e)*

3. 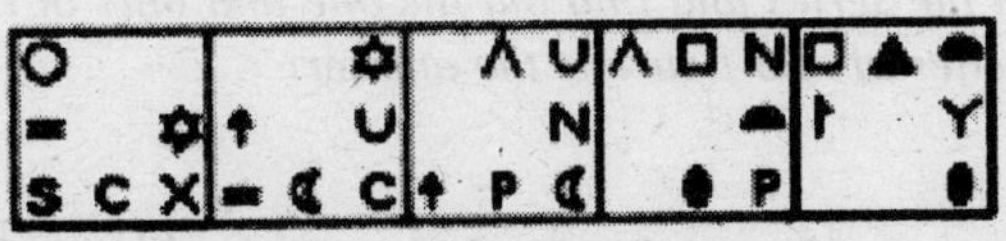 

*(a)* *(b)* *(c)* *(d)* *(e)*

4.  

*(a)* *(b)* *(c)* *(d)* *(e)*

5.  

*(a)* *(b)* *(c)* *(d)* *(e)*

6.  

*(a)* *(b)* *(c)* *(d)* *(e)*

7.  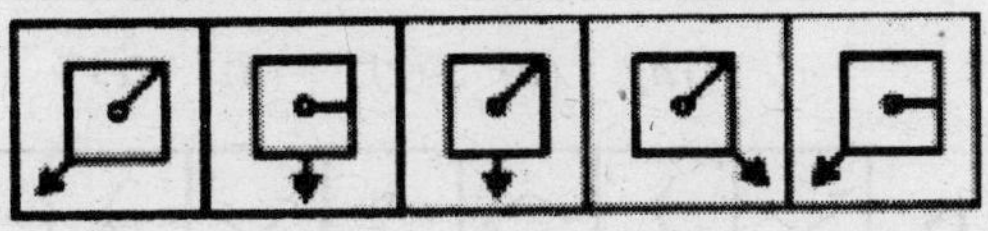

*(a)* *(b)* *(c)* *(d)* *(e)*

**Problem Figures** **Answer Figures**

8. 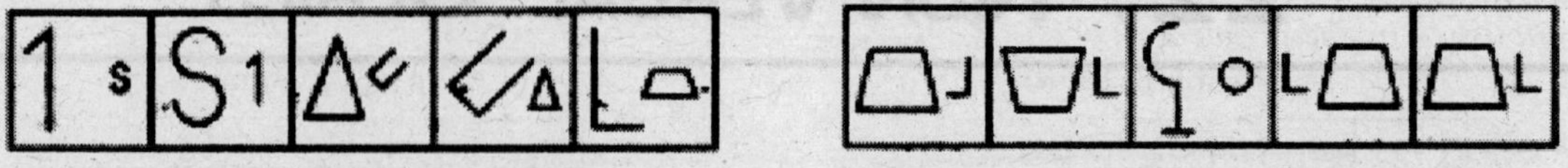

(a) (b) (c) (d) (e)

9. 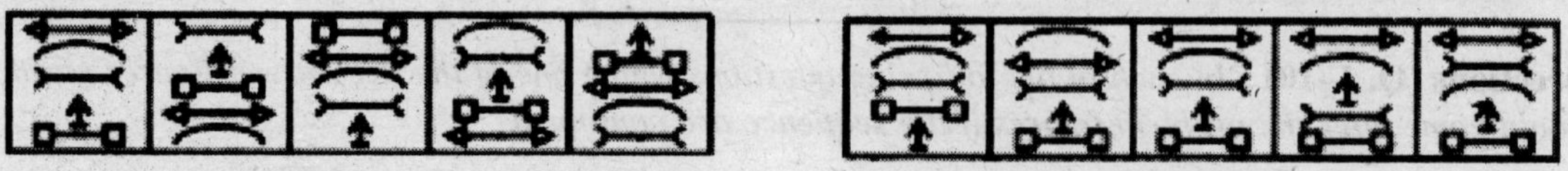

(a) (b) (c) (d) (e)

10. 

(a) (b) (c) (d) (e)

**Directions (Q. 11-20) :** *In each of these questions, a series begins with an unmarked figure on the extreme left in the row of figures. One and only one of the five lettered figures in the series does not fit into the series. The two unmarked figures, one on the extreme left and the other on the extreme right fit into the series. Take as many aspects into account as possible of the figures in the series and find out the one and only of the five marked figures which does not fit into the series. The letter of that figure is the answer.*

11. 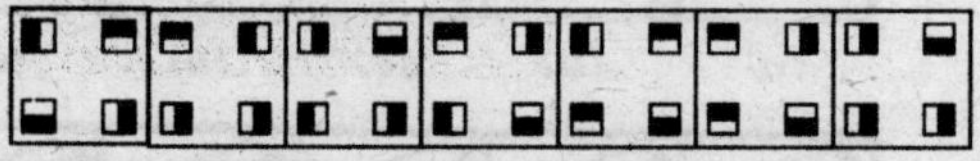

(a) (b) (c) (d) (e)

12. 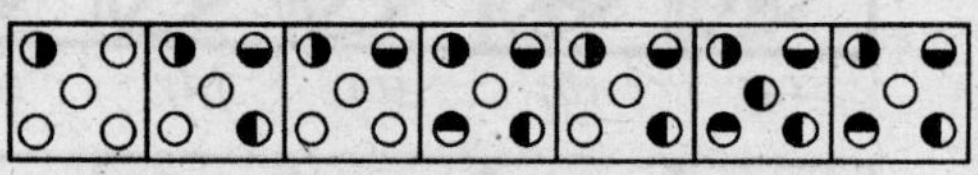

(a) (b) (c) (d) (e)

13. 

(a) (b) (c) (d) (e)

14. 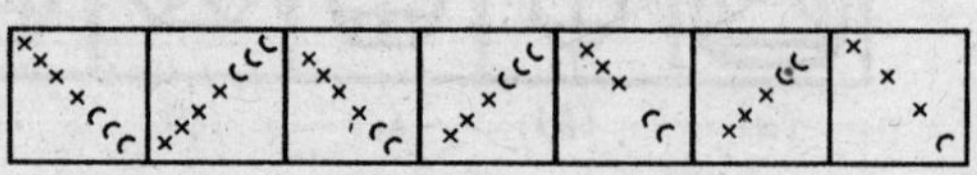

(a) (b) (c) (d) (e)

15. 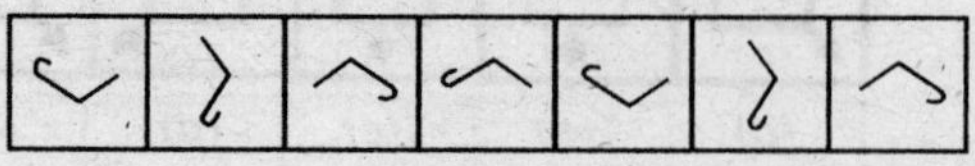

(a) (b) (c) (d) (e)

16. 

(a) (b) (c) (d) (e)

17. 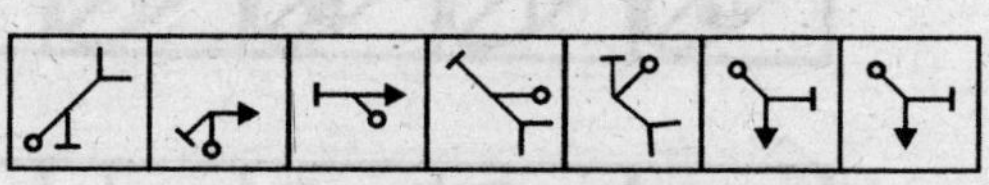

(a) (b) (c) (d) (e)

18. 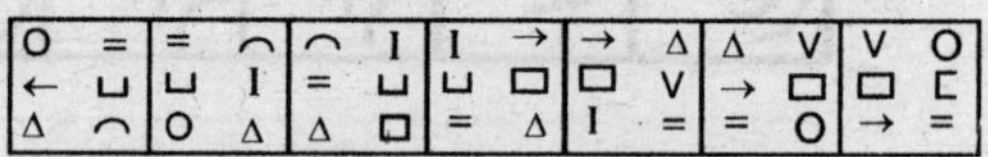

(a) (b) (c) (d) (e)

19. 

(a) (b) (c) (d) (e)

20. 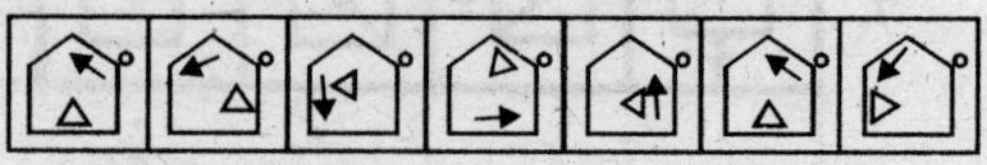

(a) (b) (c) (d) (e)

**Directions (Q. 21–30) :** *Each of the following questions consist of problem figures followed by answer figures. Select a figure from amongst the answer figures which will continue the same series or pattern as established by the problem figures.*

**Problem Figures** | **Answer Figures**

21. 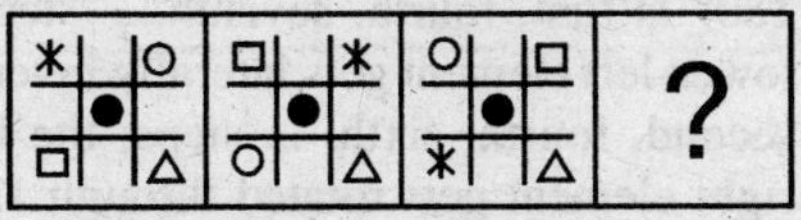 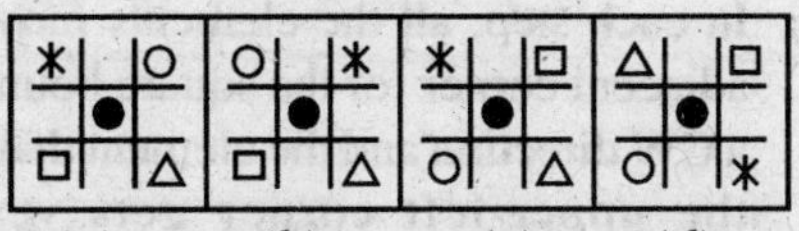

(a) (b) (c) (d)

22. 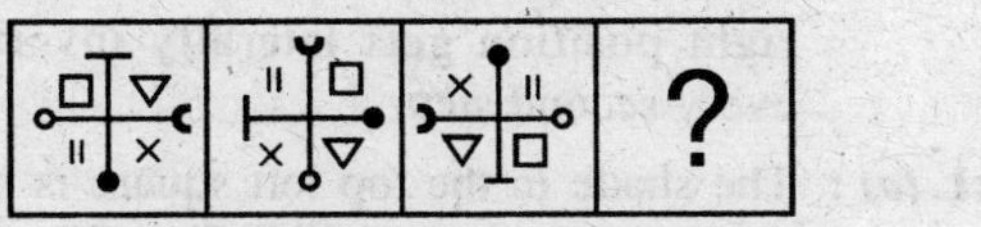 

(a) (b) (c) (d) (e)

23. 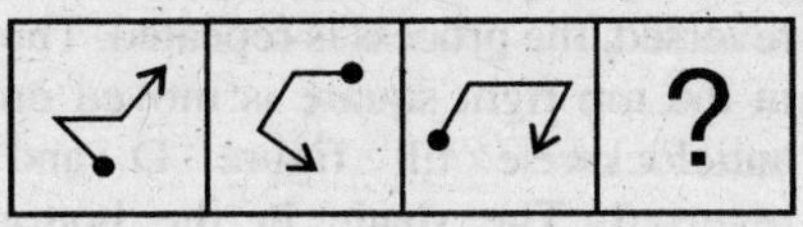 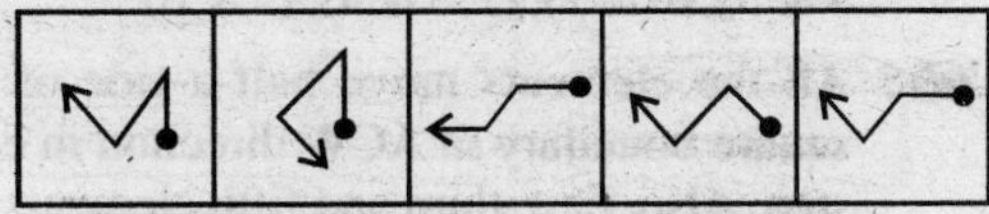

(a) (b) (c) (d) (e)

24. 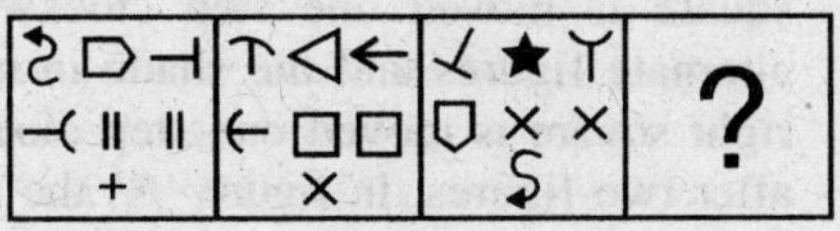 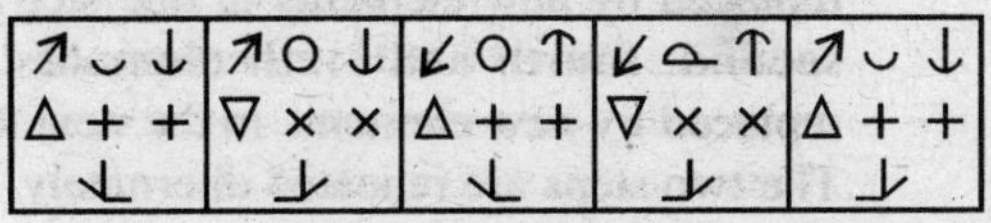

(a) (b) (c) (d) (e)

25. 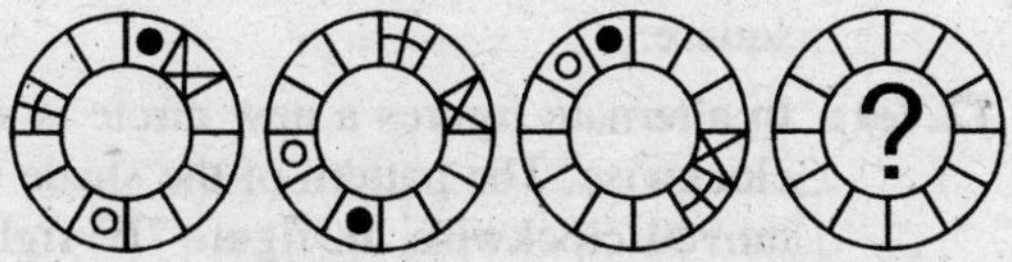 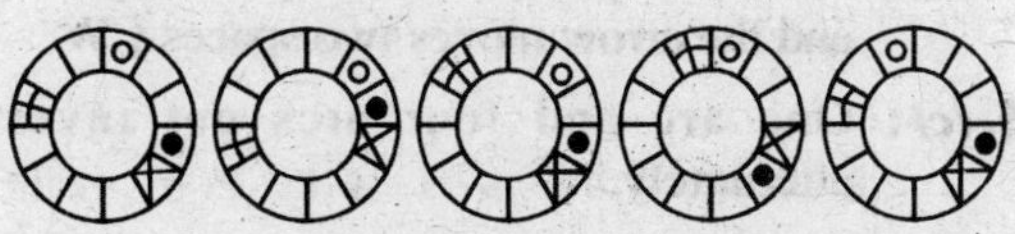

(a) (b) (c) (d) (e)

26. 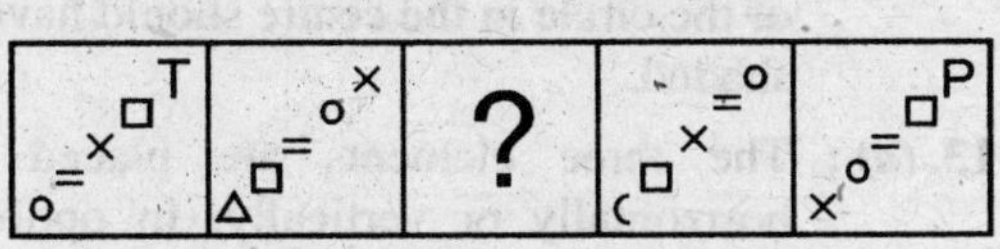 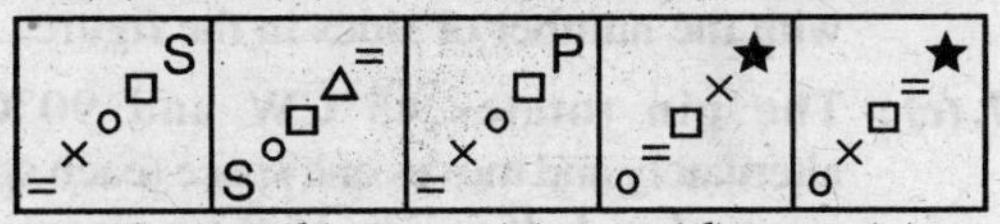

(a) (b) (c) (d) (e)

27. 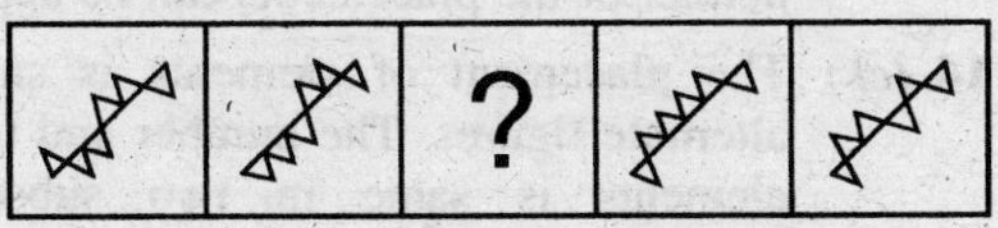 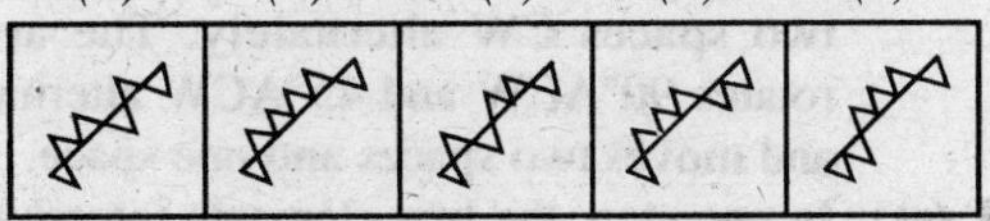

(a) (b) (c) (d) (e)

28. 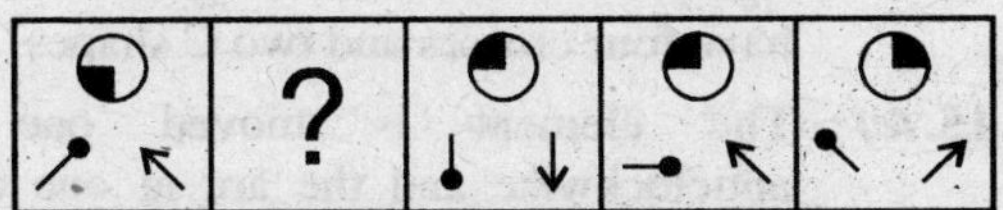 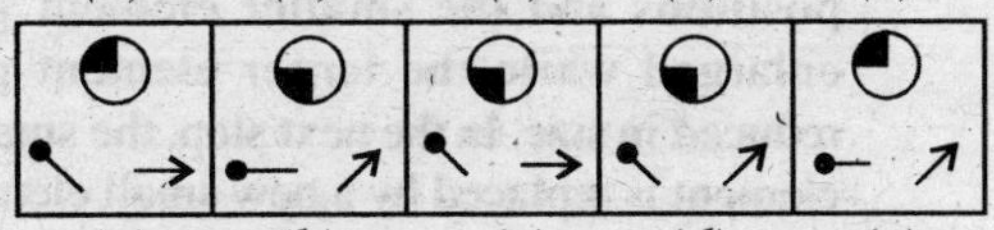

(a) (b) (c) (d) (e)

29. 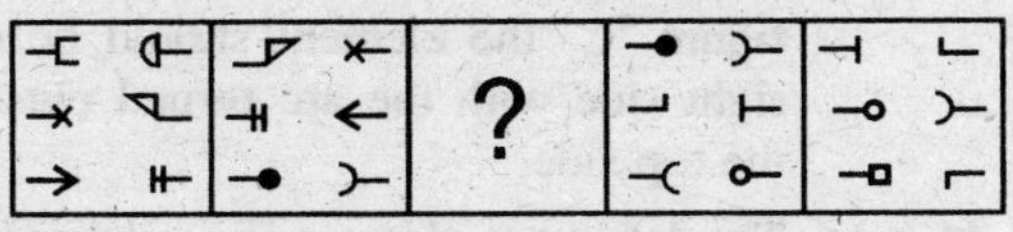 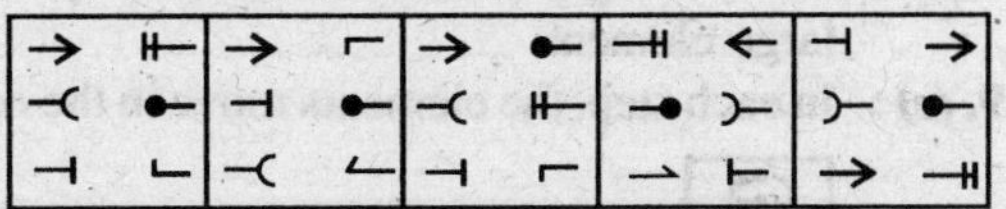

(a) (b) (c) (d) (e)

30. 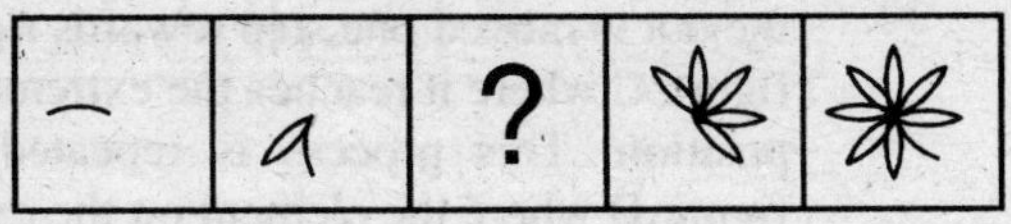 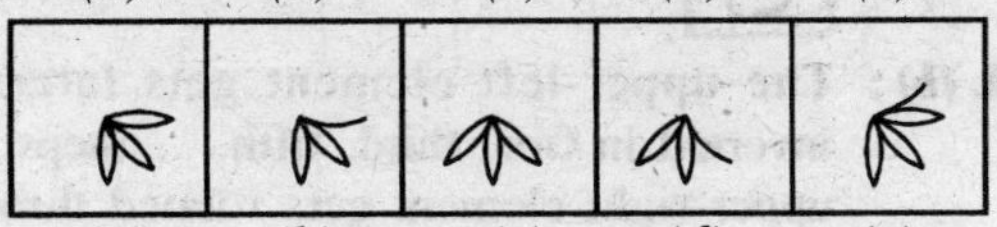

(a) (b) (c) (d) (e)

# EXPLANATORY ANSWERS

**1. *(d)* :** In each step, all the elements move to the adjacent corner (of the square boundary) in a CW direction and the element that reaches the upper-left corner gets vertically inverted.

**2. *(c)* :** We can label the arcs as shown . The arcs get inverted in the sequence (1 & 2), (3, 4 & 5), (6 & 1), (2, 3 & 4), (5 & 6), ............

**3. *(d)* :** All the elements move half-a-side of the square boundary in ACW direction in each step. Also, first, third and fifth elements are replaced by new elements in one step and second, fourth and sixth elements are replaced by new elements in the next step. The two steps are repeated alternately.

**4. *(a)* :** In each step, the dot moves one space CW and the arrow moves two spaces CW.

**5. *(c)* :** One arc and four arcs get inverted alternately.

**6. *(e)* :** The number of parts increases by one along with the number of sides in the figure.

**7. *(c)* :** The pin rotates 45°CW and 90°CW alternately and moves one space (each space is equal to half-a-side of the square) and two spaces CW alternately. The arrow rotates 90°ACW and 45°ACW alternately and moves two spaces and one space.

**8. *(e)* :** In one step, the two elements interchange positions and the smaller element gets enlarged while the larger element gets reduced in size. In the next step, the smaller element is replaced by a new small element and the larger element is replaced by a new large element.

**9. *(c)* :** In each step, the elements move in the order

.

**10. *(b)* :** The upper-left element gets laterally inverted in first, third, fifth. .... steps; the upper-right element gets rotated through 180° is first, fourth, seventh,.... steps; the lower-left element gets laterally inverted in second, fourth, sixth, ... steps; the lower-right element gets rotated through 180° in third, sixth,... steps and the pin at the middle-right position gets laterally inverted in every second step.

**11. *(a)* :** The shade in the top left square is moved one step clockwise till figure B and then reversed, the process is repeated. The shade in the top right square is moved one step anticlockwise till figure D and then reversed. The shade in the bottom left square is moved one step clockwise in alternate figures and the shade in bottom right square is moved one step clockwise after two figures. In figure 'A' the rule is isolated by the shade in the bottom left square.

**12. *(e)* :** In alternate figures a new circle is shaded clockwise. The pattern of the shade is also moved clockwise. In figure 'E' right half of the circle in the centre should have been shaded.

**13. *(a)* :** The three elements are placed either horizontally or vertically. In option 'A' neither of the placements can be applied.

**14. *(c)* :** The placement of elements is same in alternate figures. The number and type of elements is same in two subsequent figures. In this manner, figure 'C' should have four crosses and two C shapes.

**15. *(c)* :** The element is moved one step anticlockwise and the arc at one end is turned outside and inside alternately. In figure 'C' the element should be on the right side with the arc turned outside on the top side.

**16. *(e)* :** The left most element, line segment with the dot is moved one step towards right till figure C where it reaches the extreme right position. This process is repeated from figure D where the element on the extreme left, line segment with a circle, is moved. In figure 'E' the placement of the elements does not follow the rule of the series.

**17.** ***(e)*** **:** The 'T' line is rotated 45° clockwise and the line with the circle 45° anticlockwise. The 'Y' shape and the arrow are repeated twice after two figures. In option E, the 'T' shape and the line with the circle are rotated by 90°.

**18.** ***(e)*** **:** First the elements in the four corners are moved one step anticlockwise, next the four elements from the top are moved one step anticlockwise and then the four elements from the bottom are moved one step anticlockwise. Of the remaining two elements, the one on the left is made new each time and then their places are interchanged. This process is repeated from figure D. In option 'E' open square should have been in place of circle to continue the series.

**19.** ***(a)*** **:** At each step the outermost figure is removed and a new figure is placed right in the centre of other two figures. In option 'A' the triangle is turned upside down, which violates the rule of the series.

**20.** ***(a)*** **:** The arrow is moved one step anticlockwise and the triangle one step clockwise. In figure 'A' the triangle should have been on the left side of the figure.

**21.** ***(a)*** **:** The places of star, circle and square are moved one step clockwise at each step.

**22.** ***(e)*** **:** The elements in the four quadrants are moved one step clockwise and the elements at the ends of the cross are moved one step anticlockwise in this series.

**23.** ***(a)*** **:** In alternate figures, the line with the dot is turned 90° clockwise and the arrow 180° clockwise.

**24.** ***(e)*** **:** In alternate figures, the element in the top left position is horizontally inverted and moved one and half steps anticlockwise, the top middle element is turned 90° clockwise and moved one step anticlockwise, the top right element is turned 135° clockwise and moved one step anticlockwise, the element at the bottom is replaced by a new element and moved to the top middle position, and the two identical elements are replaced by two new identical elements.

**25.** ***(a)*** **:** The cross and the circle move one and two steps clockwise respectively (at each step), the plus moves 3, 4 and 5 steps clockwise, and the dot 6, 5 and 4 steps clockwise.

**26.** ***(a)*** **:** At first step, the fifth or the bottom most element is moved to the second place from top, the second element moved to the fourth place, the fourth element is moved to the third place, the third element is moved to the first or the topmost place and the element on the top, which is made new, is moved to the last or the fifth place. At second step i.e., from second problem figure to third problem figure the above process is reversed. The bottom most element is the first and the top most element is the last or fifth. Hereafter, the process is repeated from the beginning. Option 'A' is the right answer.

**27.** ***(c)*** **:** Starting from the bottom, one triangle is moved to the opposite side at each step in upward order. Option 'C' fits into the question marked space.

**28.** ***(c)*** **:** The shade inside the circle is rotated clockwise in alternate figures; the line segment with a dot is rotated 135° clockwise in alternate figures and the arrow is rotated 135° anticlockwise in alternate figures. By this process answer figure 'C' completes the series.

**29.** ***(a)*** **:** At each step the elements are moved diagonally upward and then laterally inverted, and the top two elements are made new and placed at the bottom line. By this process, option figure 'A' completes the series.

**30.** ***(a)*** **:** The number of arcs making the petals of the flower are increased by one, one and half, two, two and half respectively at each step. Also, the flower is turned 45° anticlockwise. By this process, option 'A' is the right answer.

# 23. Non-Verbal Analogy

## EXERCISE

### TYPE-I

**Directions (Q. 1-15):** *The second figure in the first unit of the Problem Figures bears a certain relationship to the first figure. Similarly, one of the figures in the Answer Figures bears the same relationship to the first figures in the second unit of the Problem Figures. Locate the figure which would fit the questions marks.*

**Problem Figures** | **Answer Figures**

**1.**

1 2 3 4

(a) (b) (c) (d) (e)

**2.**

1 2 3 4

(a) (b) (c) (d) (e)

**3.**
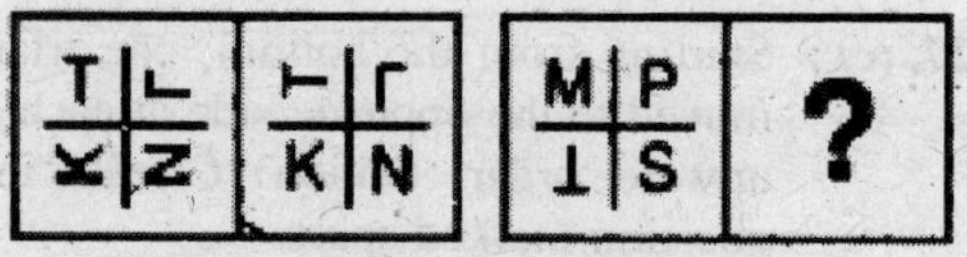
1 2 3 4
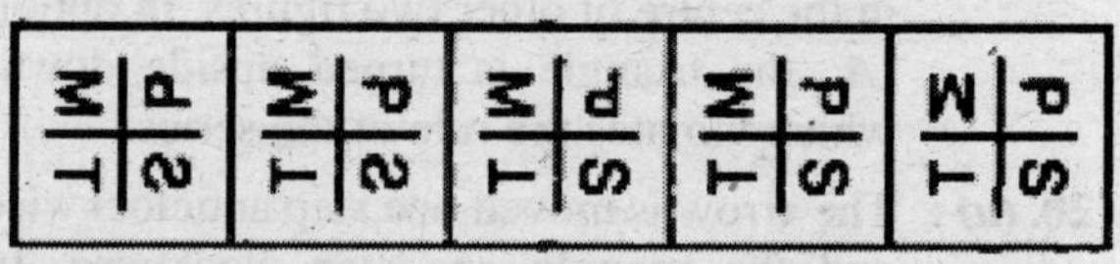
(a) (b) (c) (d) (e)

**4.**

1 2 3 4

(a) (b) (c) (d) (e)

**5.**
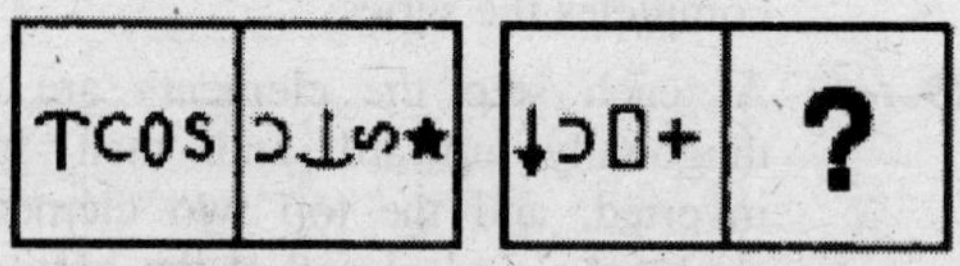
1 2 3 4
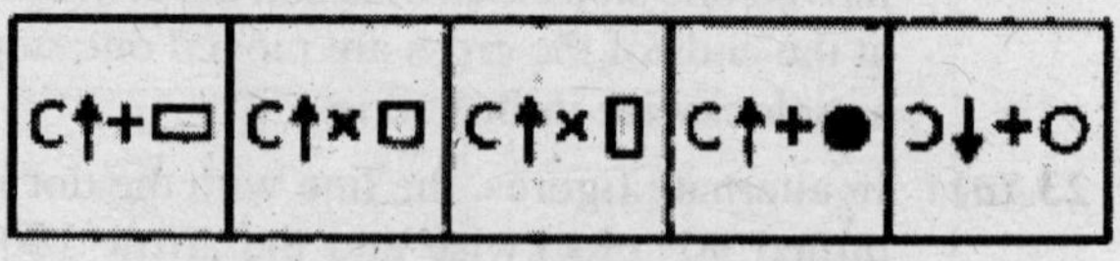
(a) (b) (c) (d) (e)

**6.**

1 2 3 4

(a) (b) (c) (d) (e)

**Problem Figures** **Answer Figures**

7. 
1 2 3 4

(a) (b) (c) (d) (e)

8. 
1 2 3 4

(a) (b) (c) (d) (e)

9. 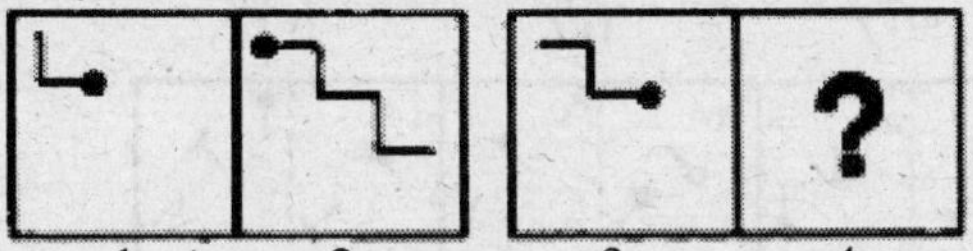
1 2 3 4
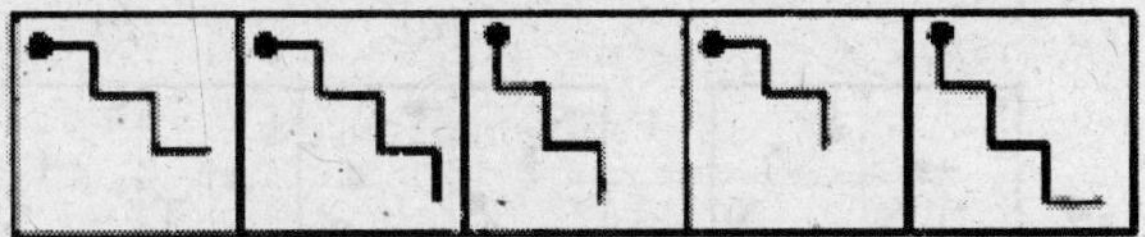
(a) (b) (c) (d) (e)

10. 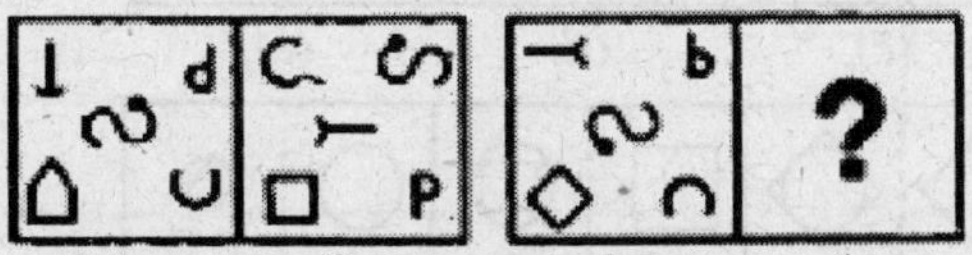
1 2 3 4

(a) (b) (c) (d) (e)

11. 
1 2 3 4

(a) (b) (c) (d) (e)

12. 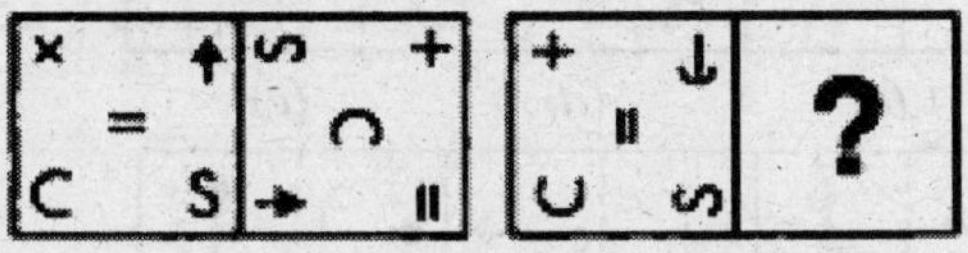
1 2 3 4
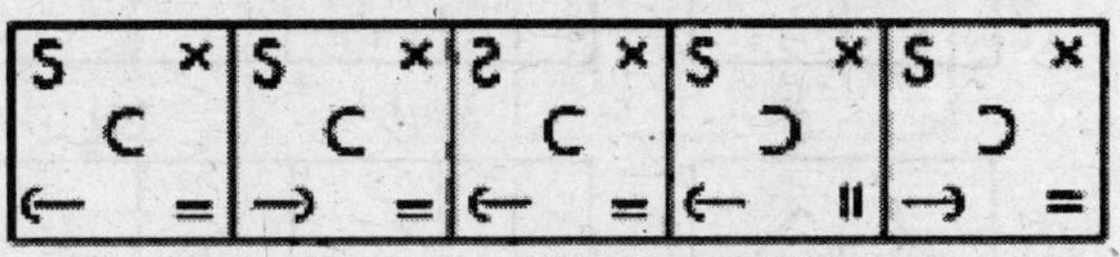
(a) (b) (c) (d) (e)

13. 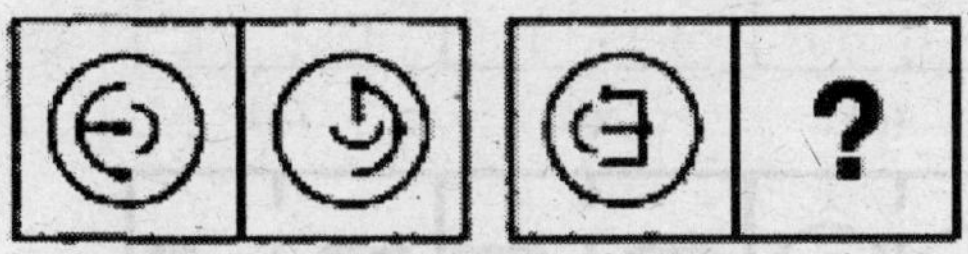
1 2 3 4

(a) (b) (c) (d) (e)

14. 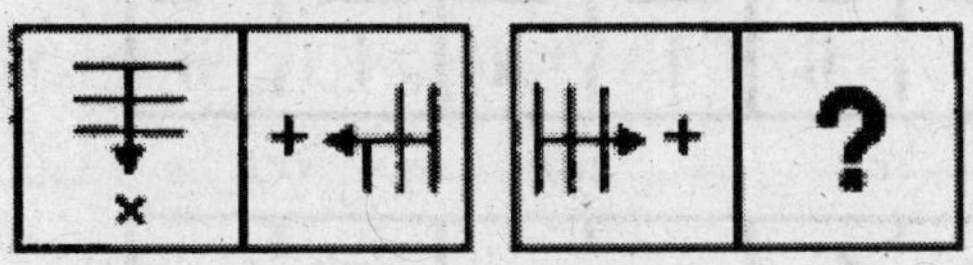
1 2 3 4

(a) (b) (c) (d) (e)

15. 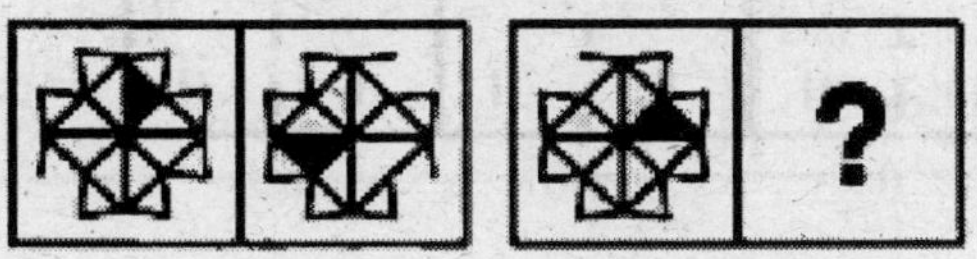
1 2 3 4

(a) (b) (c) (d) (e)

# TYPE-II

**Directions (Q. 16–30):** *In each of the following questions, a related pair of figures is followed by five numbered pairs of figures. Select the pair that has a relationship* ***similar*** *to that in the unnumbered pair.*

**Problem Figure** **Answer Figures**

16. 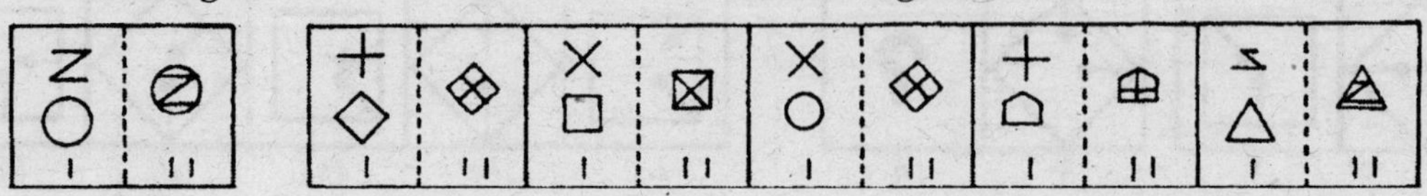

(a) (b) (c) (d) (e)

17. 

(a) (b) (c) (d) (e)

18. 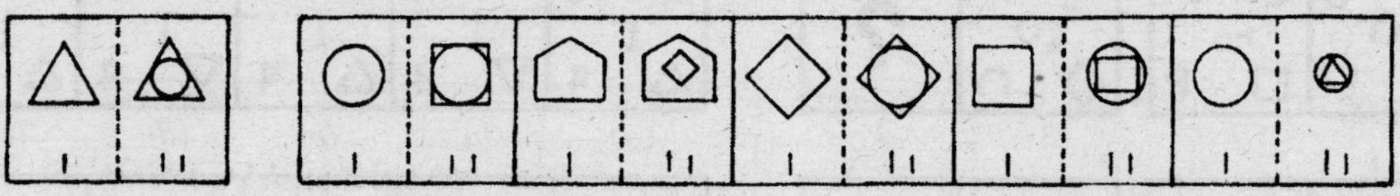

(a) (b) (c) (d) (e)

19. 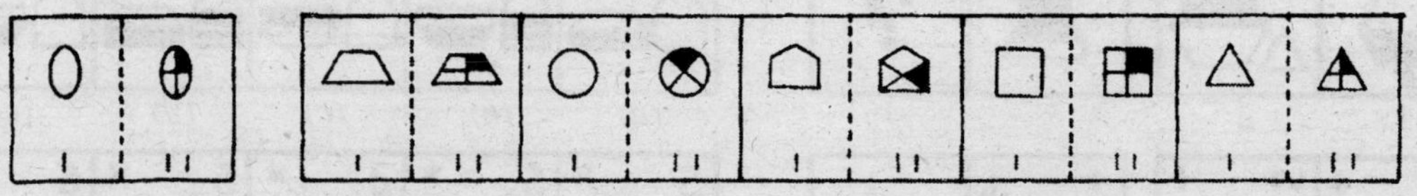

(a) (b) (c) (d) (e)

20. 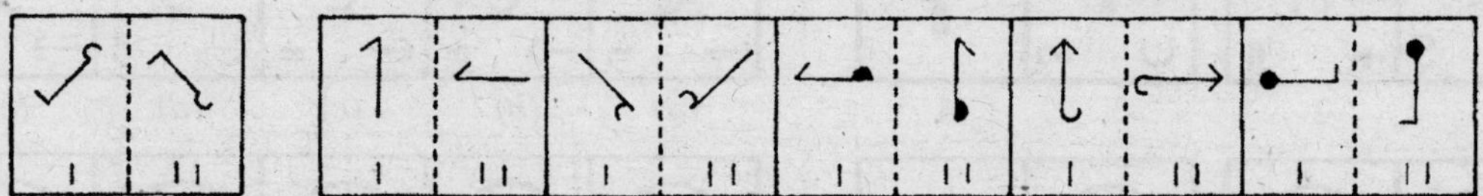

(a) (b) (c) (d) (e)

21. 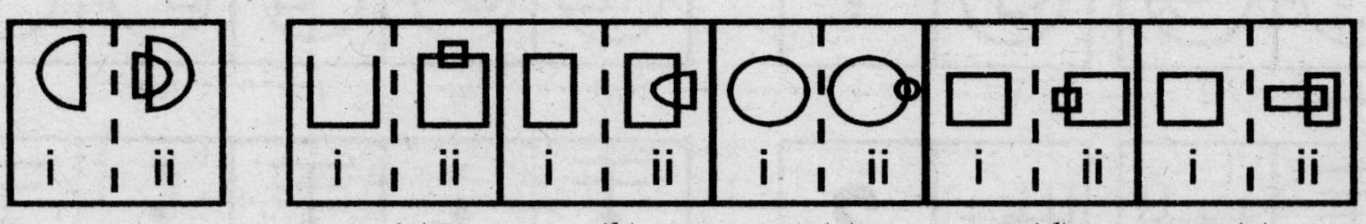

(a) (b) (c) (d) (e)

22. 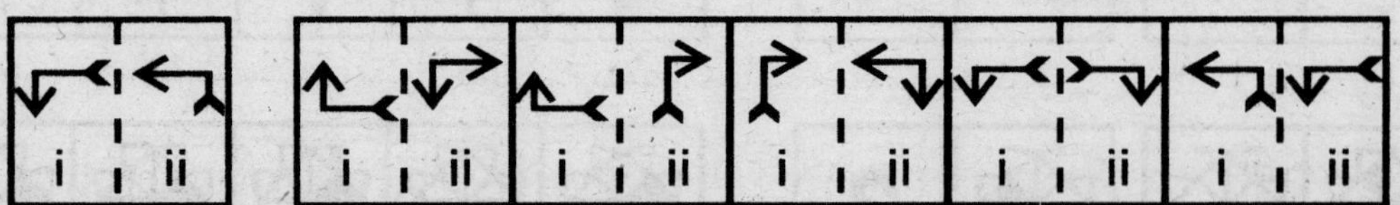

(a) (b) (c) (d) (e)

**Problem Figure** **Answer Figures**

23.

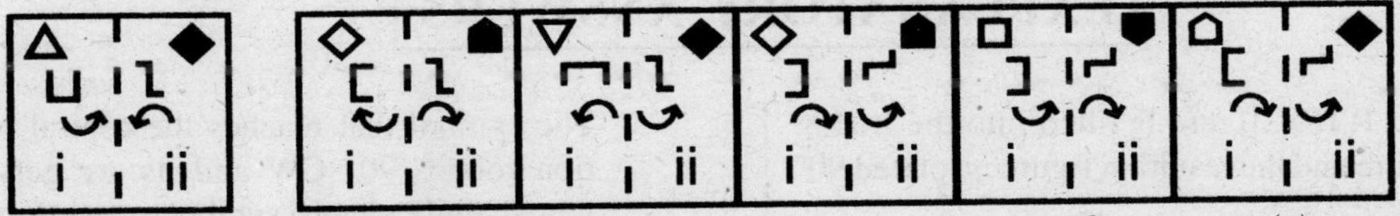


(a) (b) (c) (d) (e)

24.

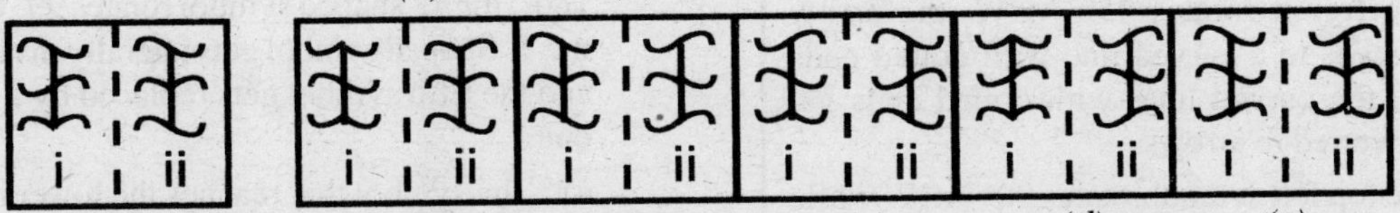


(a) (b) (c) (d) (e)

25.

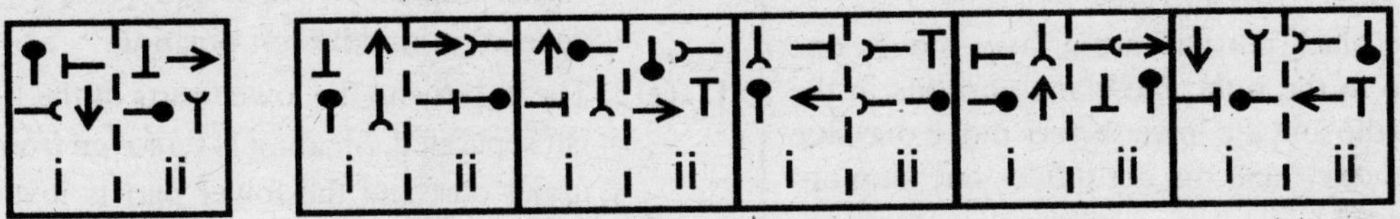


(a) (b) (c) (d) (e)

26.

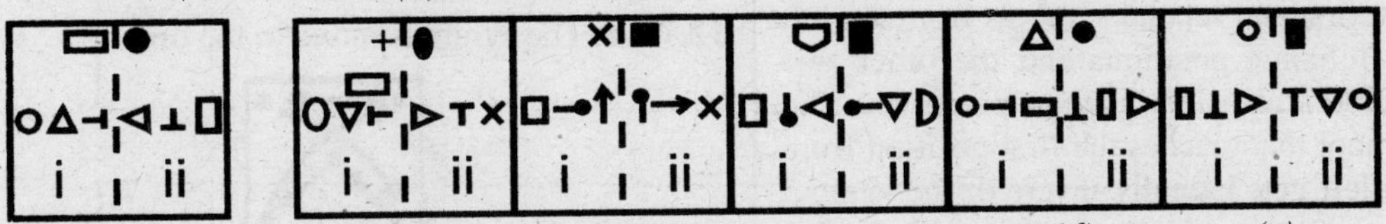


(a) (b) (c) (d) (e)

27.

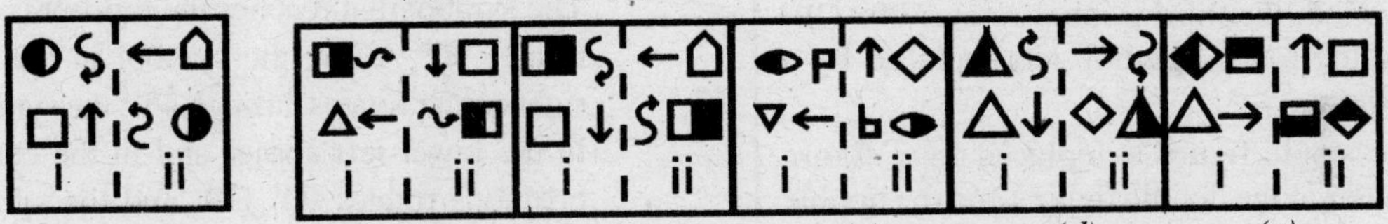


(a) (b) (c) (d) (e)

28.

(a) (b) (c) (d) (e)

29.

(a) (b) (c) (d) (e)

30.

(a) (b) (c) (d) (e)

# EXPLANATORY ANSWERS

**1. (b) :** The R.H.S. figure is fitted into the L.H.S. figure and the resulting figure is rotated 90° CW.

**2. (b) :** The figure rotates 45° ACW, the arrow changes to a curved line with dotted ends and the curved lines with dotted ends get converted to arrows.

**3. (d) :** The top left symbol rotates 90° ACW while all other symbols rotate 90° CW.

**4. (e) :** The black portion in top layer moves one step to the right; the black portions in the middle and the lower layers move one step to the left and the dot moves one step upwards.

**5. (d) :** The first and second symbols from the left interchange positions and the other two symbols also interchange positions. The symbol that reaches the first position from the left gets laterally inverted; the symbol that reaches the second position gets inverted, the third symbol rotates 90° CW and the fourth symbol gets replaced by a new one.

**6. (d) :** The single figure is replaced by a figure similar to the double figures and the double figures are replaced by figures similar to the single figure.

**7. (e) :** The figure rotates 135° ACW; a 'T' appears diagonally opposite to the black leaf and a 'Y' appears diagonally opposite to the white leaf.

**8. (c) :** The square rotates through 45°. The arrow moves 90° ACW and the pin moves 45° ACW.

**9. (b) :** The figure rotates through 180° and three lines forming a zig-zag, get attached to its lower end.

**10. (d) :** The symbols move in the order

The symbol that reaches the central position rotates 90° CW and its arc gets inverted; the 'P' shaped symbol rotates through 180°; the 'C' shaped symbol rotates 90° CW; the 'S' Shaped symbol gets laterally inverted and the fifth symbol gets replaced by a new one.

45°, the symbol that reaches the lower right corner rotates 90° ACW and a new symbol appears in middle-left position.

**11. (e) :** The upper and the lower parts of the figure get separated. Shading is removed from the upper part and the lower part is inverted. The two parts are then placed side by side.

**12. (a) :** The symbols move in the order

The symbol that reaches the top-left corner rotates 90° ACW; the symbol in the top-right corner rotates through 45°; the symbols in the lower-left corner and in the central positions rotates 90° CW and the symbol that reaches the lower-right corner rotates through 90°.

**13. (e) :** The figure gets laterally inverted. The dot on the larger arc, the pin and the small arc rotate 90° ACW. Also, the pin gets inverted.

**14. (c) :** The figure rotates 90° CW. One half of one of the lines on the arrow is lost. The figure in front of the arrowhead rotates through 45°.

**15. (d) :** The missing line segment in the first figure is replaced in second. Then moving ACW, the third line segment is removed along the two next consecutive sides of the square. Shaded portion in the first figure moves three steps ACW. Similarly, the third figure gives figure (D).

**16. *(b)* :** The uppermost design enters into innerside side of the lower design from Ist figure to the IInd figure.

**17. *(a)* :** In element I to II upper left design comes at lower right rotating 135° C.W. Middle design goes to upper left and rotates 90° CW. While lower right design goes to middle and it also rotates 90° C.W. The same changes occur in option A.

**18. *(e)* :** In element I to II and ellipse is put in the triangle. Similarly in option E a triangle is put in the ellipse.

**19. *(d)* :** From first figure to IInd figure, design is divided into four equal parts and right side of the upper portion becomes shaded.

**20. *(e)* :** From Ist figure to IInd figure, design is reversed after moving 90° anticlockwise direction.

**21. *(d)* :** The figure in the first part is laterally inverted and a similar but smaller design is placed on its left side in the second part.

**22. *(e)* :** The element in first part is moved by 90° and the places of short and long line segments are interchanged.

**23. *(c)* :** The number of sides making the top left figure is increased by one and a new figure is made, shaded and moved to the top right position. The element in the centre is turned 90° anticlockwise and the small line on the other side is turned by 180°. The element in the bottom right is turned upside down and moved to the bottom left position.

**24. *(a)* :** The direction of both arcs on the top, are on the middle right and arc on the bottom left in first part are turned to the other side in the second part.

**25. *(b)* :** From part one to part two, the element in the top left is turned 90° clockwise and the other three 90° anticlockwise, also the elements are moved one step anticlockwise.

**26. *(b)* :** From part one to part two, the top right element is turned by 90° and moved down, the lower right and middle elements are turned 90° clockwise and 90° anticlockwise respectively and moved to the left and the lower left element is shaded and moved up.

**27. *(a)* :** All the four elements exchange place diagonally and in doing so the top left element is laterally inverted, the top right element is horizontally inverted, the bottom right element is turned 90° anticlockwise and the number of lines making the element in bottom left is increased by one.

**28. *(e)* :** The innermost figure is removed and the new innermost figure also encloses the other two figures. The innermost and smallest figure is then shaded.

**29. *(b)* :** The design in the first part is horizontally inverted in the second.

**30. *(b)* :** All the elements in the first part are turned upside down and then 1st, 2nd, 3rd and 4th positioned elements become 3rd, 4th, 1st and 2nd elements in the second part.

# 24. ODD MAN OUT

In this type of reasoning a statement is followed by inferences drawn from it. From these inferences only one definitely follows which is the hidden proposition of the sentence and it is the right answer to the question.

## EXERCISE

**Directions (Q. 1–10) :** *In each question below five figures are given. Four are similar in a certain way and so form a group. The question is— which one of the figures* **does not** *belong to that group?*

1. 

(a) (b) (c) (d) (e)

2. 

(a) (b) (c) (d) (e)

3. 

(a) (b) (c) (d) (e)

4. 

(a) (b) (c) (d) (e)

5. 

(a) (b) (c) (d) (e)

6. 

(a) (b) (c) (d) (e)

7. 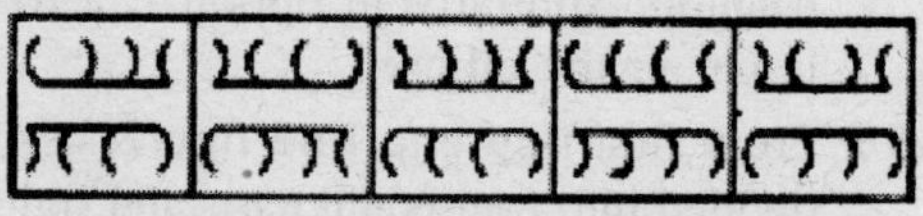

(a) (b) (c) (d) (e)

8. 

(a) (b) (c) (d) (e)

9. 

(a) (b) (c) (d) (e)

10. 

(a) (b) (c) (d) (e)

**Directions (Q. 11–20) :** *In each of the following questions, in four out of the five figures, element I is related to element II in the same particular way. Find out the figure in which the element I is* **not** *so related to element II.*

11. 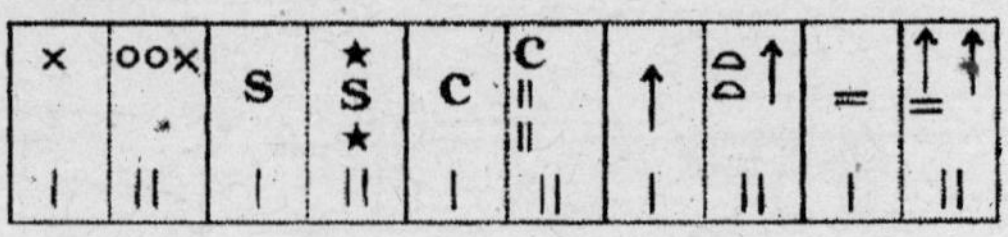

(a) (b) (c) (d) (e)

12. 

(a) (b) (c) (d) (e)

**13.** 

(a) (b) (c) (d) (e)

**14.** 

(a) (b) (c) (d) (e)

**15.** 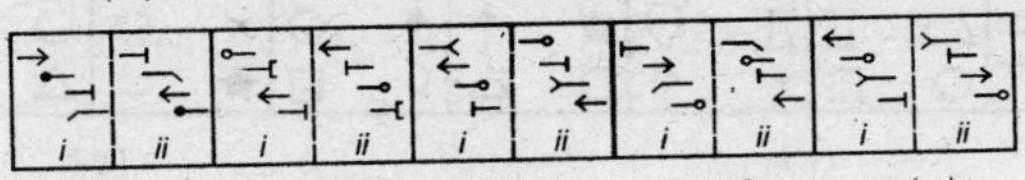

(a) (b) (c) (d) (e)

**16.** 

(a) (b) (c) (d) (e)

**17.** 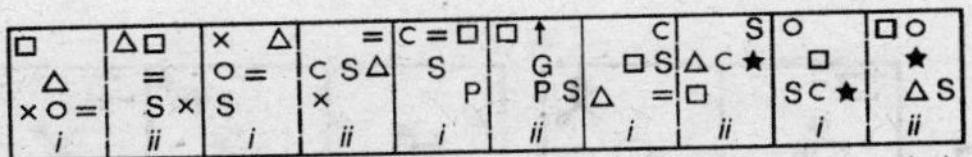

(a) (b) (c) (d) (e)

**18.** 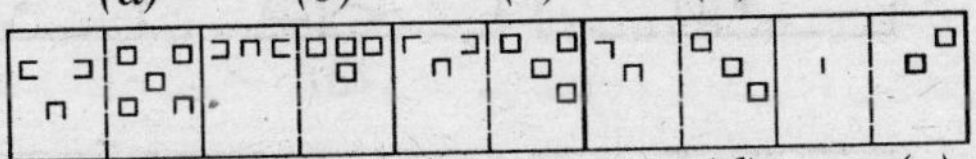

(a) (b) (c) (d) (e)

**19.** 

(a) (b) (c) (d) (e)

**20.** 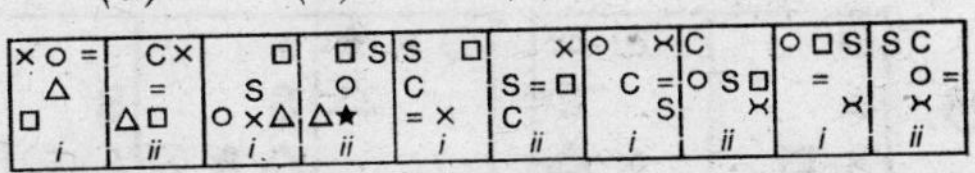

(a) (b) (c) (d) (e)

**Directions (Q. 21–30) :** *In each of the following questions, a related pair of figures (unnumbered) is followed by five numbered pairs of figures. Out of these five, four have relationship similar to that in the unnumbered pair. Only one pair of figures does not have similar relationship. Select that pair of figures which does not have a similar relationship to that in the unnumbered pair. Number of that pair is your answer.*

**21.** 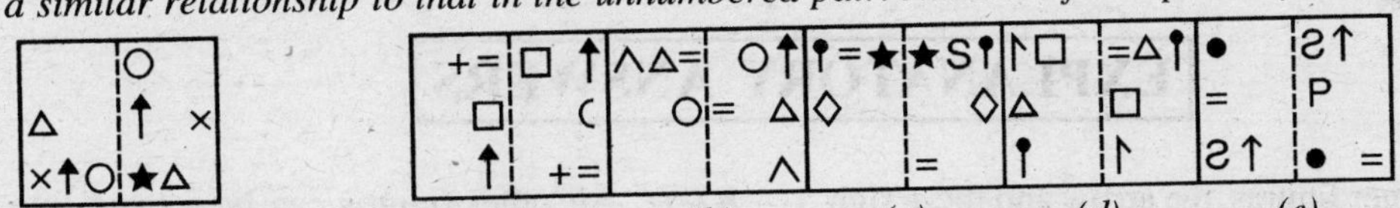

(a) (b) (c) (d) (e)

**22.** 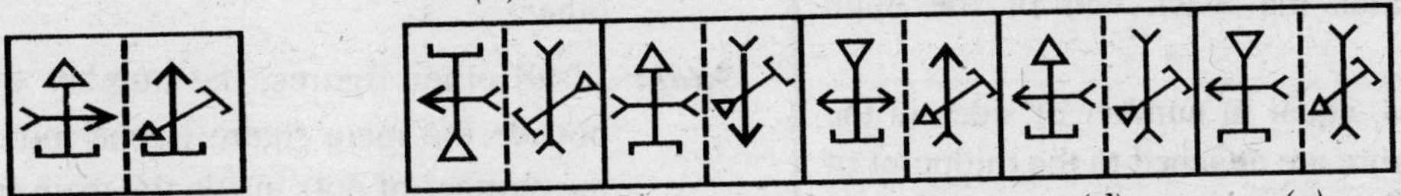

(a) (b) (c) (d) (e)

**23.** 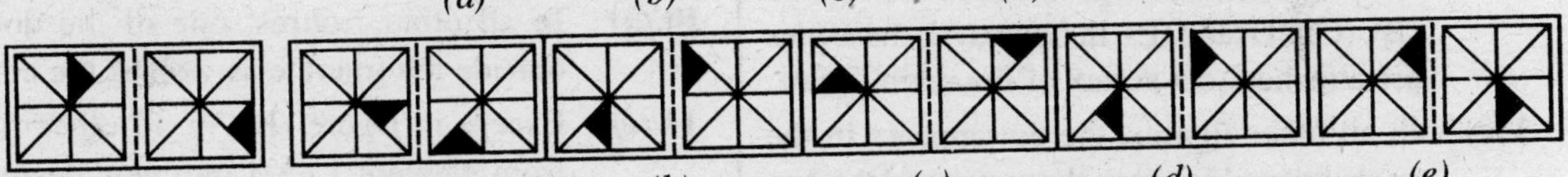

(a) (b) (c) (d) (e)

**24.** 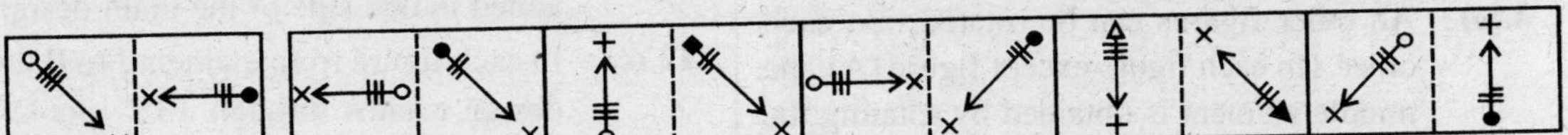

(a) (b) (c) (d) (e)

**25.** 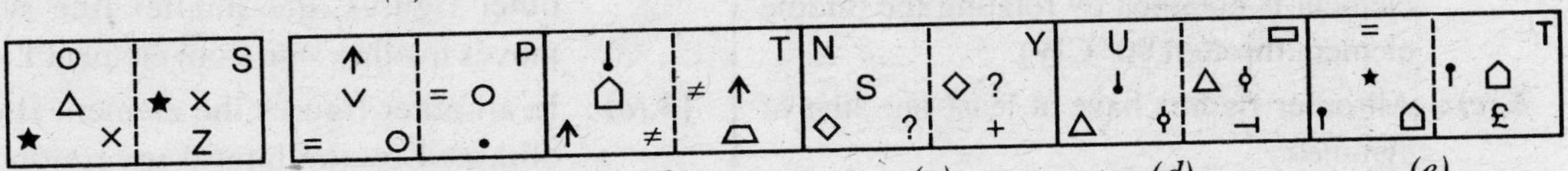

(a) (b) (c) (d) (e)

**26.** 

(a) (b) (c) (d) (e)

27.

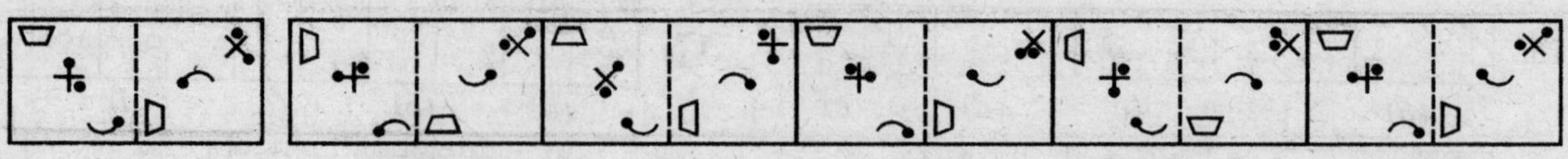

(a) (b) (c) (d) (e)

28.

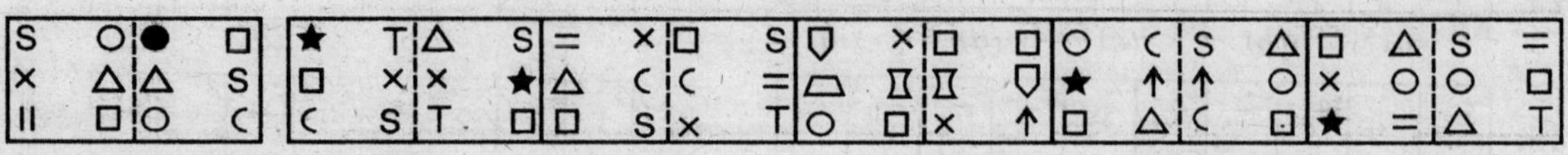

(a) (b) (c) (d) (e)

29.

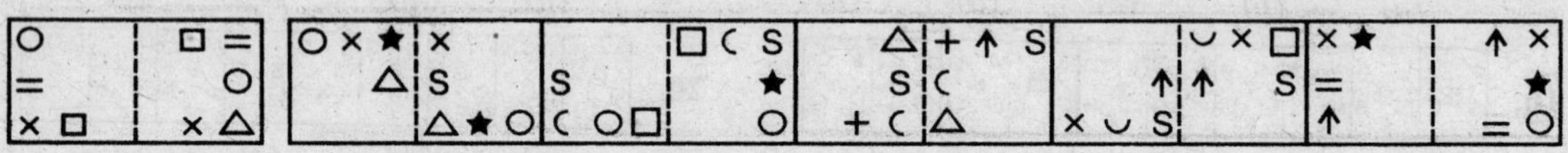

(a) (b) (c) (d) (e)

30.

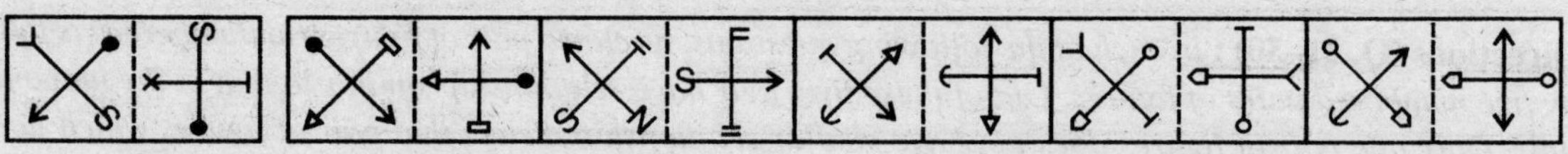

(a) (b) (c) (d) (e)

# EXPLANATORY ANSWERS

**1. *(d)* :** In all other figures, the arrow and the + sign lie towards the black end of the main figure.

**2.*(a)* :** The pins, equal in number of sides in the main figure are attached to the midpoint of a side of the main figure in case of figures (B), (C), (D) and (E). In figure (A), these pins are attached to a vertex of the main figure.

**3.*(c)* :** In all other figures, the dot appears in the angle formed between the arrow and the pin.

**4.*(a)* :** All other figures can be rotated into each other. (In each figure except figure (A), the middle element is obtained by rotating the outer element through 90° CW and the inner element is obtained by rotating the middle element through 90° CW).

**5.*(c)* :** All other figures have at least one line of symmetry.

**6.*(c)* :** All other figures can be rotated into each other.

**7.*(e)* :** In each one of the other four figures, four arcs are curved towards the left and four other arcs are curved towards the right.

**8.*(c)* :** All other figures can be rotated into each other.

**9.*(d)* :** In all other figures, the number of dots outside the main figure is one more than the number of dots inside the main figure.

**10.*(a)* :** In all other figures, one of the dots lies outside the triangle as well as the circle.

**11.*(e)* :** Except in figure (B), in all other figures, from element I to II two new designs are added in one side of the main design.

**12.*(c)* :** In each figure from element I to II the main design rotates through 135° clockwise or anticlockwise. Except in figure (C), in all other figures, the smaller line segment moves to other side from element I to II.

**13.*(a)* :** In all other figures the element II can be obtained by the lateral inversion of the element I. In figure (A), the lower design has not been inverted.

**14.*(b)* :** In figure (B), the small segment is on the same side as that of the half shaded circle in both the elements.

**15.(*d*) :** The first design is inverted and moved to third place, the second design is moved to the fourth place, third design to the first place and fourth design is inverted and moved to the second place. Option (D) violates this.

**16.(*b*) :** In all other options the top-left element is moved to the centre with 90° clockwise rotation. Here, it is rotated anticlockwise.

**17.(*d*) :** All the designs are shifted in a set pattern one behind the other. The fourth design in all others is changed and placed in the last. Here, the fifth and last designs are changed.

**18.(*a*) :** In all other pair of figures, all incomplete squares in the first elements are completed and an extra square is added in the second element.

**19.(*a*) :** From element I to element II, the 'S' shape is turned 90° clockwise and moved down, the double arrow shape '⇒' is turned 90° clockwise and moved to the right, the two parallel lines one turned by 90°; one parallel line is added and all three lines are moved up, the line with a dot is turned 90° clockwise and moved to the centre and the 'C' shape in the centre is turned by 180° and moved to top left position. Here, the double arrow is turned anticlockwise.

**20.(*c*) :** Starting from one unit, all units are moved in a set pattern, the places of last two units moved are interchanged and the last unit is then made new. Here, no changes are made in the last two units.

**21.(*d*) :** From element I to element II clockwise the first unit is moved 2 steps forward, the second unit 1 step forward, the third unit 2½ steps forward and the fourth unit 3 steps forward. In option 'D' the third unit violates the rule.

**22.(*e*) :** From element I to element II, the horizontal bar is turned 135° anticlockwise and the unit at the lower end is turned by 180°. The vertical bar is turned 90° anticlockwise and the unit at the lower end is turned by 180°. In option 'E' one more unit at the top is turned by 180°.

**23.(*e*) :** In element II, the shade is moved two sections clockwise and shifted from the centre to the base. In option 'E' it is not so.

**24.(*a*) :** In element II, the arrow is turned 135° clockwise. In option 'A' it is turned anticlockwise.

**25.(*b*) :** From element I to element II, the bottom right unit and bottom left unit are moved to the centre and middle left position respectively. The other two units are removed and two new elements are placed in the top right and bottom centre position respectively. In option 'B' the placement of bottom right and left elements is not right.

**26.(*c*) :** In element II, the shades are shifted one petal clockwise. In option 'C' one of the shades is not moved.

**27.(*b*) :** From element I to element II, the unit on the top left is turned 90° anticlockwise and moved to the bottom right corner position, the unit in the centre is turned 135° anticlockwise and moved to the top right position, and the unit in the bottom right is turned by 180° and moved to the centre. In option 'B', the middle unit is turned 135° clockwise.

**28.(*a*) :** From element I to element II, a new unit is placed in the top left position, the top left unit is moved to the middle right position, the middle right unit is moved to the left position, the middle left unit is replaced by a new unit and placed in bottom right position, the bottom right unit is moved to the top right position, and the top right unit is moved diagonally to replace the bottom left unit. In option 'A', the middle left unit is not changed when moved to the bottom right position.

**29.(*e*) :** From element I to element II starting anticlockwise, the first and second units are moved 1½ steps clockwise respectively, the third unit ½ step anticlockwise, the fourth unit 2 steps clockwise, and a new unit is placed ahead of the first unit. Option 'E' violates the rules.

**30.(*e*) :** In element II, the cross is turned 135° clockwise and then the positions of left and top units on the cross are interchanged. In option 'E' it is not so.

# YOUR SPACE

# ARITHMETICAL AND NUMERICAL ABILITY

# NUMBER SYSTEM

1. There are four numbers A, B, C and D. Average of the first three i.e., A, B and C is 15 and that of B, C and D is 16. If the last number, i.e., D is 19, then the first number is—

   A. 15 B. 16
   C. 17 D. 18

2. Of the three numbers, the first is twice the second and thrice the third. If the average of three is 22, the three numbers are—

   A. 12, 18, 36 B. 18, 12, 36
   C. 36, 12, 18 D. 36, 18, 12

3. If a person is standing on the sixth number in the queue from both the ends, the total persons in the queue are—

   A. 9 B. 11
   C. 12 D. 13

4. A number '*x*' when multiplied by 5 and added to three times its own gives 64; the number is—

   A. 8 B. 12
   C. 14 D. 18

5. A number which when multiplied by 11 is as much above 180 as it was originally below it. The number is—

   A. 25 B. 30
   C. 40 D. 45

6. The sum of a number and its reciprocal is thrice the difference of the number and its reciprocal. Find the number.

   A. $\sqrt{2}$ B. $\sqrt{3}$
   C. $\sqrt{5}$ D. $\sqrt{7}$

7. A boy was asked to find $\frac{7}{9}$ of a fraction. He made a mistake of dividing the fraction by $\frac{7}{9}$ and so got an answer which exceeded the correct answer by $\frac{8}{21}$. Find the correct answer.

   A. $\frac{2}{3}$ B. $\frac{5}{7}$
   C. $\frac{7}{12}$ D. $\frac{7}{15}$

8. There are 408 boys and 312 girls in a school, which are to be divided into equal sections of either boys or girls alone. Find the maximum number of boys or girls that can be placed in a section. Also find the total number of sections thus formed.

   A. 10, 20 B. 24, 30
   C. 24, 40 D. 30, 30

9. The sum of all possible two-digit number formed from three different one-digit natural numbers, when divided by the sum of the original three numbers is equal to—

   A. 11 B. 18
   C. 22 D. 36

10. There are four prime numbers written in ascending order. The product of the first three is 385 and that of the last three is 1001. The last number is—

    A. 19 B. 17
    C. 13 D. 11

11. If the number 357 ★ 25 ★ is divisible by both 3 and 5, then the missing digits in the unit's place and thousandth place respectively are—

    A. 0, 4 B. 5, 4
    C. 5, 6 D. 0, 6

12. The difference between two numbers is 1365. When the larger number is divided by the smaller one, the quotient is 6 and the remainder is 15. The smaller number is:

A. 360 B. 295
C. 270 D. 240

**13.** When a number is divided by 31, the remainder is 29. When the same number is divided by 16, what will be the remainder?
A. 15 B. 13
C. 11 D. Data inadequate

**14.** In dividing a number by 585, a student applied the method of short division. He divided the number successively by 5, 9 and 13 (factor of 585) and got the remainders 4, 8 and 12. If he had divided the number by 585, the remainder would have been:
A. 584 B. 292
C. 144 D. 24

**15.** When a number divided by 6 leaves a remainder 3. When the square of the same number is divided by 6, the remainder is:
A. 3 B. 2
C. 1 D. zero

## ANSWERS

| 1 | 2 | 3 | 4 | 5 | 6 | 7 | 8 | 9 | 10 |
|---|---|---|---|---|---|---|---|---|---|
| B | D | B | A | B | A | C | B | C | C |
| **11** | **12** | **13** | **14** | **15** | | | | | |
| C | C | D | A | A | | | | | |

## SOME SELECTED EXPLANATORY ANSWERS

**1.** $\frac{A+B+C}{3} = 15,$

or, $A + B + C = 15 \times 3 = 45$ ... *(i)*

$\frac{B+C+D}{3} = 16,$

or $B + C + D = 48$ ... *(ii)*

$D = 19$

$\therefore\ B + C + 19 = 48$

or, $B + C = 48 - 19 = 29$

But, $A + B + C = 45$

Putting the value of $B + C = 29$ in the above equation *(i)*, we get $A + 29 = 45$

$\therefore\ A = 45 - 29 = 16.$

**2.** Let the third number $= x$

$\therefore$ First number $= 3x$

Second number $= \frac{3x}{2}$

$\therefore\ \frac{1}{3}\left[x+3x+\frac{3x}{2}\right] = 22 \Rightarrow \frac{11}{2}x = 66$

$\Rightarrow x = \frac{66\times 2}{11} = 12 =$ Third number,

$12 \times 3 = 36 =$ First number,

$\frac{12\times 3}{2} = 18 =$ Second number.

**3.** If the person is standing at sixth number in the queue from both sides, that means there are five persons ahead and five persons behind him. Hence, total number of persons in the queue is $5 + 1 + 5 = 11$.

**4.** $5 \times x + 3x = 64 \quad \Rightarrow 8x = 64$

$\therefore\quad x = \frac{64}{8} = 8.$

**5.** Let the number is $x$

$\therefore\quad 180 - x = 11x - 180$

$\Rightarrow\quad 180 + 180 = 11x + x$

$\Rightarrow\quad 360 = 12x,$

$\Rightarrow\quad x = \frac{360}{12} = 30.$

**6.** Let the no. $= x$ then its reciprocal $= \frac{1}{x}$

By the question, $\left(x+\frac{1}{x}\right) = 3\left(x-\frac{1}{x}\right)$

$$\Rightarrow \quad \frac{x^2+1}{x} = \frac{3(x^2-1)}{x}$$

$$\Rightarrow \quad x^2 + 1 = 3x^2 - 3$$

$$\Rightarrow \quad 3x^2 - x^2 = 3 + 1$$

$$\therefore \quad x = \sqrt{2}.$$

**7.** Let the required fraction = $x$

then, by the question $x \div \frac{7}{9} - x \times \frac{7}{9} = \frac{8}{21}$

$$\Rightarrow \quad x \times \frac{9}{7} - \frac{7x}{9} = \frac{8}{21}$$

$$\Rightarrow \quad \frac{32x}{63} = \frac{8}{21}$$

$$\Rightarrow \quad x = \frac{8}{21} \times \frac{63}{32} = \frac{3}{4}$$

Hence, the correct answer = $\frac{3}{4} \times \frac{7}{9} = \frac{7}{12}$.

**8.**

```
312) 408(1
     312
     ---
      96) 312 (3
          288
          ---
           24) 96 (4
               96
               --
               ×
```

$\therefore$ Maximum number of girls or boys that can be placed in a section = 24 and total number of such section = $\frac{408}{24} + \frac{312}{24}$

$= 17 + 13 = 30$

**9.** Let three different one digit natural numbers be $x$, $y$ and $z$.

Then, sum of all possible two digits numbers

$= (10x + y) + (10y + x) + (10x + z)$
$+ (10z + x) + (10y + z) + (10z + y)$

$= 22x + 22y + 22z = 22(x + y + z)$

Hence, required number = 22.

**10.** Let four prime numbers be $a$, $b$, $c$ and $d$ respectively.

Now, $\frac{abc}{bcd} = \frac{385}{1001} \Rightarrow \frac{c}{d} = \frac{5}{13}$

Hence, $a = 5$ and $d = 13$

**11.** 357 ★ 25 ★

For divisible by 5, the last digit must be either 0 or 5.

If last digit is 0, then other required digit will be 2 or 5 or 8

Hence, the numbers are (0, 2) or (0, 5) or (0, 8)

If last digit is 5, then other required digit will be 0 or 3 or 6 or 9

Hence, the numbers are (5, 0) or (5, 3) or (5, 6) or (5, 9)

So, correct option is (c).

**12.** Here, $(x + 1365) = 6x + 15$

$\Rightarrow 5x = 1350$

$\therefore x = \frac{1350}{5} = 270$

Hence, the smaller number = 270.

**13.** The number = $31x + 29$.

Here, given data is inadequate.

**14.**

| | |
|---|---|
| 5 | $a$ |
| 9 | $b - 4$ |
| 13 | $c - 8$ |
| | $1 - 12$ |

Now, $c = 13 \times 1 + 12 = 25$

$b = 9c + 8 = 9 \times 25 + 8 = 233$

$a = 5b + 4 = 5 \times 233 + 4$

$= 1165 + 4 = 1169$

$1169 = 585 \times 1 + 584$

Hence, required remainder = 584.

**15.** The number = $6x + 3$

Now, $(6x + 3)^2 = 36x^2 + 36x + 9$

$= (36x^2 + 36x + 6) + 3$

$= 6(6x^2 + 6x + 1) + 3$

Hence, required remainder = 3.

# LCM AND HCF

**1.** The L.C.M. and H.C.F. of two numbers are 4284 and 32 respectively. If one of the numbers is 204, the other is

A. 672 B. 576
C. 676 D. 572

**2.** Two numbers are in the ratio of 8 : 15. If their H.C.F. is 4, the numbers are

A. 32 and 60 B. 16 and 30
C. 80 and 150 D. 64 and 120

**3.** The greatest number that will divide 366, 513 and 324 leaving the same remainder in each case is

A. 21 B. 18
C. 27 D. 42

**4.** The L.C.M. of two numbers is 45 times their H.C.F. If the sum of the L.C.M. and the H.C.F. of these two numbers is 1150 and one of the numbers is 125, then the other number is

A. 256 B. 225
C. 250 D. 255

**5.** The H.C.F. and the L.C.M. of two numbers are 50 and 250 respectively. On dividing one of these numbers by 2, 50 is obtained as quotient. The numbrs are

A. 100, 125 B. 80, 100
C. 125, 100 D. 200, 250

**6.** Three bells ring respectively at an interval of 15 seconds, 20 seconds and 24 seconds. If they ring continuously for 12 minutes then how many times, during this period, will they ring together?

A. 2 times B. 6 times
C. 5 times D. 3 times

**7.** If the sum of two numbers is 55 and the H.C.F. and L.C.M. of these numbers are 5 and 120 respectively. Find the sum of their reciprocals.

A. $\frac{120}{11}$ B. $\frac{11}{120}$
C. $\frac{601}{55}$ D. $\frac{55}{601}$

**8.** The LCM of two numbers is 48. The numbers are in the ratio of 2 : 3. The sum of the numbers is

A. 64 B. 40
C. 32 D. 28

**9.** Find the greatest number that will divide 43, 91 and 183 so as to leave the same remainder in each case.

A. 13 B. 9
C. 7 D. 4

**10.** The greatest possible length which can be used to measure exactly the length 7m, 3m 85cm, 12m 95 cm is

A. 42 cm B. 35 cm
C. 25 cm D. 15 cm

**11.** A, B and C start at the same time in the same direction to run around a circular park. A completes a round in 252 seconds, B in 308 seconds and C in 198 seconds, all starting at the same point. After what time will they meet again at the starting point?

A. 46 minutes 12 seconds
B. 45 minutes
C. 42 minutes 36 seconds
D. 26 minutes 18 seconds

**12.** Which of the following has most numbers of divisors?

A. 182 B. 176
C. 101 D. 99

**13.** Which is of the following is a co-primes?

A. (23, 92) B. (21, 35)
C. (18, 25) D. (16, 62)

**14.** Let N be the greatest number that will divide 1305, 4665 and 6905, leaving the same remainder in each case. Then find the sum of the digits in N.

A. 8 B. 6
C. 5 D. 4

**15.** The greatest number which one dividing 1657 and 2037 leaves remainder 6 and 5 respectively, is:

A. 305 B. 235
C. 127 D. 123

## ANSWERS

| 1 | 2 | 3 | 4 | 5 | 6 | 7 | 8 | 9 | 10 |
|---|---|---|---|---|---|---|---|---|---|
| A | A | A | B | A | B | B | B | D | B |
| **11** | **12** | **13** | **14** | **15** | | | | | |
| A | B | C | D | C | | | | | |

## SOME SELECTED EXPLANATORY ANSWERS

**1.** 1st number × 2nd number = LCM × HCF

$\therefore$ 204 × 2nd number = 4284 × 32

$\therefore$ 2nd number $= \dfrac{4284 \times 32}{204} = 672$

$\therefore$ 2nd number = 672

**2.** Let the numbers be $8x$ and $15x$

$8x = 2 \times 2 \times 2 \times x$

$15x = 3 \times 5 \times x$

$\therefore$ LCM of $8x$ and $15x = 2 \times 2 \times 2 \times x \times 3 \times 5$
$= 120x$

Now, 1st number × 2nd number = HCF × LCM

$\Rightarrow \quad 8x \times 15x = 4 \times 120x$

$\Rightarrow \quad 120x^2 = 4 \times 120x$

$\Rightarrow \quad x = 4$

$\therefore$ Numbers are 8 × 4 = 32 and 15 × 4 = 60

**3.** Difference between 366 and 513 = 513 − 366
= 147

and difference between 513 and 324
= 513 − 324 = 189

$\therefore$ HCF of 147 and 189

```
147) 189 (1
     147
     ----
      42) 147 (3
          126
          ---
           21) 42 (2
               42
               --
                ×
```

$\therefore$ The required largest number is 21.

**4.** LCM of the two numbers = 45 × HCF

and LCM + HCF = 1150

$\Rightarrow$ 45 × HCF + HCF = 1150

$\Rightarrow$ HCF(45 + 1) = 1150

$\Rightarrow$ HCF $= \dfrac{1150}{46} = 25$

$\therefore$ LCM = 45 × 25 = 1125

$\because$ 1st number × 2nd number = LCM × HCF

$\therefore$ 125 × 2nd number = 1125 × 25

$\therefore$ 2nd number $= \dfrac{1125 \times 25}{125} = 225.$

**5.** According to the condition of the problem, 50 is obtained on dividing one of the numbers by 2

$\therefore$ One of the numbers = 50 × 2 = 100

Now, 1st number × 2nd number = LCM × HCF

$\therefore$ 100 × 2nd number = 250 × 50

$\therefore$ 2nd number $= \dfrac{250 \times 50}{100} = 125$

Hence, numbers are 100 and 125.

**6.** LCM of 15, 20 and 24

```
5 | 15, 20, 24
--+-----------
4 |  3,  4, 24
--+-----------
3 |  3,  1,  6
--+-----------
  |  1,  1,  2
```

LCM = 5 × 4 × 3 × 2 = 120

$\because$ 12 minutes = 12 × 60 = 720 seconds
$\therefore$ Number of times the bells will ring together during 12 minutes

$$= \frac{720}{120} = 6 \text{ times.}$$

**7.** Let the number be $x$ and $y$.
Then, $x + y = 55$;
$xy$ = HCF × LCM = 5 × 120
$\therefore$ Sum of their reciprocals

$$= \frac{1}{x} + \frac{1}{y} = \frac{x+y}{xy} = \frac{55}{5 \times 120} = \frac{11}{120}.$$

**8.** Let the two numbers be $2x$ and $3x$;
their LCM = $6x$
Now, $6x = 48$ $\therefore$ $x = 8$
Hence, the numbers are 2 × 8, 3 × 8 = 16, 24
Their sum = 16 + 24 = 40.

**9.**

```
2240) 3360 (1          1120) 5600 (5
      2240                   5600
      1120 ) 2240 (2           ×
             2240
               ×
```

Hence, N = HCF of 3360, 2240 and 5600 = 1120
Sum of digits in N = 1 + 1 + 2 + 0 = 4.

**10.** 7m = 700 cm;
3m 85 = 385 cm;
12m 95cm = 1295 cm

```
385) 700 (1
     385
     315) 385 (1
          315
           70) 315 (4
               280
                35 ) 70 (2
                     70
                      ×

35) 1295 (37
    105
     245
     245
      ×
```

Hence, required length = HCF of 700 cm, 385 cm, 1295 cm = 35 cm.

**11.**

| | |
|---|---|
| 2 | 252, 308, 198 |
| 2 | 126, 154, 99 |
| 3 | 63, 77, 99 |
| 3 | 21, 77, 33 |
| 7 | 7, 77, 11 |
| 11 | 1, 11, 11 |
| | 1, 1, 1 |

Hence, LCM = 2 × 2 × 3 × 3 × 7 × 11 = 2772
Hence, A, B, C will meet again at the starting point after 2772 sec. = 46 min 12 sec.

**12.**

| ***Numbers*** | ***Their divisors*** |
|---|---|
| 182 | → 1, 2, 7, 13, 14, 26, 91 and 182 |
| 176 | → 1, 2, 4, 8, 16, 22, 44, 88 and 176 |
| 101 | → 1 and 101 |
| 99 | → 1, 3, 9, 11, 33 and 99 |

Therefore, 176 has the most number of divisors.

**13.** HCF of 23 and 92 = 23
HCF of 21 and 35 = 7
HCF of 18 and 25 = 1
HCF of 16 and 62 = 2
Hence, 18 and 25 are co-prime numbers.

**14.** N = HCF of (4665 – 1305), (6905 – 4665) and (6905 – 1305)
= HCF of 3360, 2240 and 5600 = 112
Sum of digit of 1 + 1 + 2 = 4.

**15.** Required number = HCF of (1657 – 6) and (2037 – 5) = HCF of 1651 and 2032 = 127.

```
1651) 2032 (1
      1651
       381) 1651 (4
            1524
             127) 381 (3
                  381
                   ×
```

# AVERAGE

1. One-third of a certain journey was covered at the rate of 25 km per hour, one-fourth at the rate of 30 km per hour and the rest at the 50 km per hour. What is the average speed per hour for whole journey?

   A. $33\frac{1}{3}$ kmph  B. $44\frac{1}{4}$ kmph
   C. $22\frac{1}{2}$ kmph  D. 33 kmph

2. A batsman has a certain average of runs for 16 innings. In the 17th innings, he makes a score of 85 runs thereby increasing his average by 3. What is the average after the 17th inning?

   A. 33 runs  B. 34 runs
   C. 37 runs  D. 36 runs

3. The average of 6 observations is 12. A new seventh observation is included and the new average is decreased by 1. The seventh observation is

   A. 1  B. 3
   C. 5  D. 6

4. The average age of 30 students in a class is 12 years. The average age of a group of 5 of the students is 10 years and that of another group of 5 of them is 14 years. The average age of the remaining students is

   A. 8 years  B. 10 years
   C. 12 years  D. 14 years

5. Out of the three given numbers, the first number is twice the second and thrice the third. If the average of three numbers is 121, what is the difference between the first and third number?

   A. 144  B. 77
   C. 99  D. 132

6. If the average marks of three batches of 55, 60 and 45 students is 50, 55 and 60, then average marks of all the students is:

   A. 55  B. 54
   C. 54.68  D. 55.68

7. The average of 8 numbers is 20. The average of first two numbers is $15\frac{1}{2}$ and that of the next three is $21\frac{1}{3}$. If the sixth number is less than the seventh and eighth numbers by 4 and 7 respectively, then the eighth number is:

   A. 27  B. 25
   C. 22  D. 18

8. A pupil's marks were wrongly entered as 83 instead of 63. Due to that the average marks for the class got increased by half. What is the number of pupils in the class?

   A. 73  B. 40
   C. 40  D. 10

9. A cricketer whose bowling average is 12.4 runs per wicket takes 5 wickets for 26 runs and thereby decreases his average by 0.4. The number of wickets taken by him till the last match was:

   A. 85  B. 80
   C. 72  D. 64

10. The average weight of a class of 24 students is 35 kg. If the weight of the teacher is included, the average rises by 400 g. What is the weight of the teacher?

    A. 55 kg  B. 53 kg
    C. 50 kg  D. 45 kg

**11.** Nine men went to a hotel. Eight of them spent Rs. 3 for each over their meals and the ninth spent Rs. 2 more than the average expenditure of all the nine. What is the total money spent by them?

A. Rs. 29.25  B. Rs. 29.50
C. Rs. 29  D. Rs. 30

**12.** The average age of 24 students in a class is 10. If the teacher's age is included, the average increases by one. The age of the teacher is

A. 25  B. 30
C. 35  D. 40

**13.** The average of 5 consecutive even numbers A, B, C, D and E is 34. What is the product of B and D?

A. 1152  B. 1368
C. 1224  D. 1088

**14.** The average of 50 numbers is 30. If two numbers, 35 and 40 are discarded, then the average of the remaining numbers is nearly:

A. 29.68  B. 29.27
C. 28.78  D. 28.32

**15.** The average monthly salary of 20 employees of an organisation is Rs. 1500. If the manager's salary is added, then the average salary increases by Rs. 100. Find the manager's monthly salary?

A. Rs. 4800  B. Rs. 3600
C. Rs. 2400  D. Rs. 2000

## ANSWERS

| 1 | 2 | 3 | 4 | 5 | 6 | 7 | 8 | 9 | 10 |
|---|---|---|---|---|---|---|---|---|---|
| A | C | C | C | D | C | B | B | A | D |
| **11** | **12** | **13** | **14** | **15** | | | | | |
| A | C | A | A | B | | | | | |

## SOME SELECTED EXPLANATORY ANSWERS

**1.** Let the total distance covered during journey = 60 km

$\frac{1}{3}$ of the distance covered during journey

$$= 60 \times \frac{1}{3} = 20 \text{ km}$$

$\frac{1}{4}$ of the distance covered during journey

$$= \frac{1}{4} \times 60 = 15 \text{ km}$$

$\therefore$ The distance covered during the rest of journey = 60 – (20 + 15) = 25 km

Time taken to cover 20 km at 25 km/h

$$= \frac{20}{25} \text{ hours} = \frac{4}{5} \text{ hour}$$

Time taken to cover 15 km at 30 km/h

$$= \frac{15}{30} \text{ hours} = \frac{1}{2} \text{ hour}$$

Time taken to cover 25 km at 50 km/h

$$= \frac{25}{50} \text{ hours} = \frac{1}{2} \text{ hour}$$

$$\text{Total time taken} = \frac{4}{5} + \frac{1}{2} + \frac{1}{2}$$

$$= \frac{9}{5} \text{ hours}$$

$$\text{Hence average speed per hour} = 60 \div \frac{9}{5}$$

$$= \frac{60 \times 5}{9} = \frac{100}{3} \text{ km/h}$$

$$= 33\frac{1}{3} \text{ km/h}$$

**2.** Average increase in the score of 17 innings = 3 runs

Total increase in the score of 17 innings = 3 × 17 = 51 runs

$\therefore$ His average of 16 innings = 85 – 51 = 34 runs

Hence, average after the 17th innings
$= 34 + 3 = 37$ runs

**3.** Seventh observation $= (7 \times 11 - 6 \times 12) = 5$

**4.** Let, the required average age be $x$
Then, $5 \times 10 + 5 \times 14 + 20 \times x = 30 \times 12$
$\Rightarrow \quad 20x = 360 - 120$
$\Rightarrow \quad 20x = 240$
$\Rightarrow \quad x = 12$

**5.** Let the three numbers be $x$, $\frac{x}{2}$ and $\frac{x}{3}$ respectively,

Now, $\frac{1}{3}\left(x + \frac{x}{2} + \frac{x}{3}\right) = 121$

$\Rightarrow \frac{11x}{6} = 121 \times 3$

$\therefore x = \frac{121 \times 3 \times 6}{11} = 198$

Hence, required difference $= x - \frac{x}{3} = \frac{2x}{3}$

$= \frac{2}{3} \times 198 = 132$

**6.** Required average Marks

$= \frac{55 \times 50 + 60 \times 55 + 45 \times 60}{55 + 60 + 45} = \frac{8750}{160} = 54.68$

**7.** Let the sixth, seventh and eighth numbers are $x$, $x + 4$ and $x + 7$.
Sum of last three numbers

$= 8 \times 20 - (2 \times \frac{31}{2} + 3 \times \frac{64}{3})$

$\Rightarrow x + x + 4 + x + 7 = 160 - 95$
$\Rightarrow 3x + 11 = 65$
$\Rightarrow 3x = 54 \qquad \therefore x = 18$
New eighth number $= x + 7 = 18 + 7 = 25$

**8.** Let the total number of pupils in the class be $x$; then,

$\frac{83 - 63}{x} = \frac{1}{2} \quad \Rightarrow \frac{20}{x} = \frac{1}{2} \qquad \therefore x = 40$

**9.** Let the number of wickets taken by him be $x$ till the last match.

Then, $\frac{x \times 12.4 + 26}{x + 5} = 12$

$\Rightarrow 12.4x + 26 = 12x + 60$

$\Rightarrow 0.4x = 34 \quad \therefore \quad x = \frac{340}{4} = 85$

**10.** Let the weight of the teacher be $x$ kgs, then

$\frac{24 \times 35 + x}{25} = 35.4$

$\Rightarrow 840 + x = 885 \quad \therefore \quad x = 45$ kgs

**12.** Age of the teacher $= (25 \times 11 - 24 \times 10)$ years
$= 35$ years

**13.** Let 5 consecutive even numbers A, B, C, D and E be $x$, $x + 2$, $x + 4$, $x + 6$ and $x + 8$ respectively.

Now, $\frac{x + x + 2 + x + 4 + x + 6 + x + 8}{5} = 34$

$\Rightarrow 5x + 20 = 170$
$\Rightarrow 5x = 150 \qquad \therefore x = 30$
Then, $B = x + 2 = 30 + 2 = 32$;
$D = x + 6 = 30 + 6 = 36$
Hence, their product $= 32 \times 36 = 1152$

**14.** The average of remaining 48 numbers

$= \frac{50 \times 30 - (35 + 40)}{48} = \frac{1500 - 75}{48}$

$= \frac{1425}{48} = 29.68$

**15.** Let manager's salary be Rs. $x$, then

$\frac{20 \times 1500 + x}{21} = 1600$

$\Rightarrow 30,000 + x = 33600$
$\therefore \quad x =$ Rs. 3600

# PROBLEMS BASED ON AGES

**1.** The ratio of ages of A and B is 3 : 11. After 3 years the ratio becomes 1 : 3. What are the ages of A and B?

A. 9 years, 33 years  B. 10 years, 40 years
C. 9 years, 27 years  D. None of these

**2.** Two years ago, the ratio of Ram's and Mohan's age was 3 : 2 and at present 7 : 5. What are their present ages?

A. 14 years, 10 years  B. 15 years, 10 years
C. 13 years, 9 years  D. None of these

**3.** The ages of Samir and Saurabh are in the ratio of 8 : 15 respectively. After 9 years the ratio of their ages will be 11 : 18. What is the difference between their ages in years?

A. 20 years  B. 21 years
C. 22 years  D. 24 years

**4.** The present age of father is 34 years more than that of his son. 12 years ago, father's age was 18 times the age of his son. The present age of son in years is:

A. 12  B. 14
C. 16  D. 18

**5.** A mother is 25 years older than her daughter. Five years ago, the age of the mother was 6 times the age of the daughter. What is the present age of mother?

A. 25 years  B. 29 years
C. 32 years  D. 35 years

**6.** The difference between the present ages of P and Q is 4 years. The ratio of their ages after 5 years will be 9 : 8. The present age of P is:

A. 24 years  B. 30 years
C. 32 years  D. None of these

**7.** Ten years ago, the age of Divya was half of the age of Namrata. If the ratio of present ages of both is 3 : 4, the sum of their present ages is:

A. 35 years  B. 30 years
C. 25 years  D. 18 years

**8.** The ratio between the present ages of A and B is 5 : 3 respectively. The ratio between A's age 4 years ago and B's age 4 years hence is 1 : 1. The ratio between A's age 4 years hence and B's age 4 years ago is:

A. 4 : 1  B. 3 : 1
C. 2 : 1  D. 1 : 3

**9.** Ram got married 8 years ago. His present age is $\frac{6}{5}$ times his age at the time of marriage. Ram's sister was 10 years younger to him at the time of his marriage. What is the present age of Ram's sister?

A. 40 years  B. 38 years
C. 36 years  D. 32 years

**10.** A father said to his son, "I was as old as you are at present at the time of your birth." If the father's age is 38 years now. Five years ago the age of son was:

A. 38 years  B. 33 years
C. 19 years  D. 14 years

## ANSWERS

| 1 | 2 | 3 | 4 | 5 | 6 | 7 | 8 | 9 | 10 |
|---|---|---|---|---|---|---|---|---|---|
| A | A | B | B | D | D | A | B | B | D |

# SOME SELECTED EXPLANATORY ANSWERS

1. Let the ages of A and B be $3x$ and $11x$ years; then

$$\frac{3x+3}{11x+3}=\frac{1}{3} \Rightarrow 9x + 9 = 11x + 3$$

$\Rightarrow 2x = 6 \quad \therefore x = 3$

Hence, their present age, $3x = 3 \times 3 = 9$ years; $11x = 11 \times 3 = 33$ years

2. Let the present ages of Ram and Mohan are $7x$ and $5x$ years; then

$$\frac{7x-2}{5x-2}=\frac{3}{2} \Rightarrow 14x - 4 = 15x - 6$$

$\therefore x = 2$

Hence, their present ages : $7 \times 2 = 14$ years and $5 \times 2 = 10$ years

3. Let the present ages of Samir and Saurabh are $8x$ and $15x$ years respectively; then

$$\frac{8x+9}{15x+9}=\frac{11}{18} \Rightarrow 144x + 162 = 165x + 99$$

$\Rightarrow 21x = 63 \quad \therefore x = 3$

Hence, difference of their ages $= 15x - 8x = 7x = 7 \times 3 = 21$ years

4. Let the present ages of father and his son be $x + 34$ and $x$ years respectively; then

$18(x - 12) = x + 34 - 12$

$\Rightarrow 18x - 216 = x + 22$

$\Rightarrow 17x = 238 \quad \therefore x = 14$

Hence, present age of his son = 14 years

5. Let the present ages of mother and her daughter are $(x + 25)$ and $x$ years respectively; then

$6(x - 5) = x + 25 - 5$

$\Rightarrow 6x - 30 = x + 20$

$\Rightarrow 5x = 50 \quad \therefore x = 10$

Hence, the age of the mother $= 10 + 25 = 35$ years

6. Let the present ages of P and Q be $(x + 4)$ and $x$ years;

then, $\frac{x+4+5}{x+5}=\frac{9}{8} \Rightarrow 8x + 72 = 9x + 45 \quad \therefore x = 27$

Hence, present age of P = 27 + 4 = 31 years

7. Let the present ages of Divya and Namrata are $3x$ and $4x$ years respectively; then

$$\frac{3x-10}{4x-10}=\frac{1}{2}$$

$\Rightarrow 6x - 20 = 4x - 10$

$\Rightarrow 2x = 10 \quad \therefore x = 5$

Hence, sum of their ages $= 3x + 4x = 7x = 7 \times 5 = 35$ years

8. Let the present ages of A and B are $5x$ and $3x$ years respectively; then,

$$\frac{5x-4}{3x+4}=1 \Rightarrow 5x - 4 = 3x + 4$$

$\Rightarrow 2x = 8 \quad \therefore x = 4$

Hence, their present ages are 20 years and 12 years.

So, required ratio $= (20 + 4) : (12 - 4) = 24 : 8 = 3 : 1$

9. Let the present age of Ram be $x$ years; then

$$\frac{x}{x-8}=\frac{6}{5} \Rightarrow 5x = 6x - 48$$

$\therefore x = 48$

Hence, present age of Ram's sister $= 48 - 10 = 38$ years.

10. Let the age of father was $x$ years at the time of his son's birth, then present age of father and his son will be $2x$ and $x$ years,

Now, $2x = 38 \quad \therefore x = 19$ years

Hence, 5 years ago the age of son was $19 - 5 = 14$ years

# CHAIN RULE

**1.** A fort has provision for 50 days. After 15 days a reinforcement of 150 men arrives and the provision now lasts 25 days. How many men were there in the fort?

A. 300 B. 225
C. 275 D. 200

**2.** In a fort there is provisions for 40 days for 275 persons. If after 16 days 125 persons leave the fort for how many more days the provisions will last?

A. 35 days B. 44 days
C. 45 days D. 53 days

**3.** 60 men could complete a work in 250 days. They worked together for 200 days. After that the work had to be stopped for 10 days due to bad weather. How many more men should be engaged to complete the work in time?

A. 20 B. 18
C. 15 D. 10

**4.** A contractor undertook to complete a project in 90 days and employed 60 men on it. After 60 days, he found that $\frac{3}{4}$ of the work has already been completed. How many men can he discharge so that the project may completed exactly on time?

A. 15 B. 20
C. 30 D. 40

**5.** A flagstaff 17.5 m high casts a shadow of length 40.25 m. The height of the building, which casts a shadow of length 28.75m under similar condition will be:

A. 21.25 m B. 17.5 m
C. 12.5 m D. 10 m

**6.** If 5 men or 9 women can do a piece of work in 19 days, then 3 men and 6 women will do the same work in how many days?

A. 21 B. 18
C. 15 D. 12

**7.** A certain number of men can finish a piece of work in 100 days. If there were 10 men less, it will take 10 days more for the work to be finished. How many men were there originally?

A. 110 B. 100
C. 82 D. 75

**8.** Some persons can do a piece of work in 12 days. Two times the number of such persons will do half of that work in:

A. 12 days B. 3 days
C. 6 days D. 4 days

**9.** 2 men and 7 boys can do a piece of work in 14 days; 3 men and 8 boys can do the same in 11 days. Then 8 men and 6 boys can do three times of this work in

A. 30 days B. 4 days
C. 21 days D. 18 days

**10.** If 3 men or 6 boys, working 7 hours a day can do a piece of work in 10 days; how many days will it take to complete a piece of work twice as large with 6 men and 2 boys working together for 8 hours a day?

A. 9 B. $8\frac{1}{2}$
C. $7\frac{1}{2}$ D. $6\frac{1}{2}$

**11.** If 15 men can do a certain amount of work in 20 days working 8 hours a day, in how many days will 10 men do three times the work working 6 hours a day?

A. 120 days B. 70 days
C. 100 days D. None of these

**12.** 40 men consume 60 kgs of rice in 15 days, then in how many days will 30 men consume 12 kgs of rice?

A. 9 days B. $6\frac{1}{4}$ days
C. 4 days D. $3\frac{1}{4}$ days

**13.** 56 men can complete a piece of work in 24 days. In how many days can 42 men complete the same piece of work?

A. 48 B. 32
C. 20 D. 16

**14.** Running at the same constant rate, 6 identical machines can produce a total of 270 bottles per minute. At this rate, how many bottles could 10 such machines produce in 4 minutes?

A. 1400 B. 1600
C. 1800 D. 2000

**15.** 400 persons, working 9 hours a day complete $\frac{1}{4}th$ of the work in 10 days. The number of additional persons, working 8 hours a day, required to complete the remaining work in 20 days, is:

A. 275 B. 250
C. 675 D. 200

## ANSWERS

| 1 | 2 | 3 | 4 | 5 | 6 | 7 | 8 | 9 | 10 |
|---|---|---|---|---|---|---|---|---|---|
| B | B | C | B | C | C | A | B | C | C |
| **11** | **12** | **13** | **14** | **15** | | | | | |
| A | C | B | C | C | | | | | |

## SOME SELECTED EXPLANATORY ANSWERS

**1.** Days: 35 ↑ 25; Men: $x$ ↓ $x + 150$

$$\Rightarrow \frac{x+150}{x} = \frac{35}{25} \quad \Rightarrow 1 + \frac{150}{x} = \frac{35}{25}$$

$$\Rightarrow \frac{150}{x} = \frac{10}{25}$$

$$\therefore x = \frac{25}{10} \times 150 = 375$$

Required number of men = 375 – 150 = 225

**2.** Persons: 275 ↑ 150; Days: 24 ↓ $x$

$$\Rightarrow \frac{x}{24} = \frac{275}{150} \quad \therefore x = \frac{275}{150} \times 24 = 44 \text{ days}$$

**3.** Days: 50 ↑ 40; Men: 60 ↓ $x$

$$\Rightarrow \frac{x}{60} = \frac{50}{40} \quad \therefore x = \frac{50}{40} \times 60 = 75 \text{ men}$$

Hence, number of additional men = 75 – 60 = 15

**4.** Work: $\frac{3}{4}$ ↓ $\frac{1}{4}$; Days: 60 ↑ 30; Men: 60 ↓ $x$

$$\Rightarrow \frac{x}{60} = \frac{60}{30} \times \frac{1/4}{3/4}$$

$$\therefore x = \frac{60}{30} \times \frac{1}{3} \times 60 = 40 \text{ days}$$

Hence, number of men to be discharged = 60 – 40 = 20

**5.** Shadow (m) — Object (m)

40.25 ↓ 17.5 ↓

28.75 ↓ $x$ ↓

$$\Rightarrow \frac{x}{17.5} = \frac{28.75}{40.25}$$

$$\therefore\ x = \frac{28.75 \times 17.5}{40.25} = 12.5 \text{ m}$$

**6.** 5 men ≡ 9 women

$$\therefore\ 3 \text{ men} = \frac{9}{5} \times 3 = \frac{27}{5} \text{ women}$$

$$\text{Hence, 3 men and 6 women} = \frac{27}{5} + 6 = \frac{57}{5} \text{ women}$$

Women ↑: 9, $\frac{57}{5}$ — Days ↓: 19, $x$

$$\Rightarrow \frac{x}{19} = \frac{9 \times 5}{57}$$

$$\therefore\ x = \frac{9 \times 5}{57} \times 19 = 15 \text{ days}$$

**7.** Days ↑: 100, 110 — Men ↓: $x$, $x - 10$

$$\Rightarrow \frac{x-10}{x} = \frac{100}{110} \quad \Rightarrow \quad 110x - 1100 = 100x$$

$\Rightarrow 10x = 1100 \qquad \therefore\ x = 110$

Hence, initially the number of men = 110

**8.** Work ↓: 1, $\frac{1}{2}$ — Persons ↑: $x$, $2x$ — Days ↓: 12, $a$

$$\Rightarrow \frac{a}{12} = \frac{x}{2x} \times \frac{1}{2} \qquad \therefore\ a = \frac{1}{4} \times 12 = 3 \text{ days}$$

**9.** Here, $14 \times 2$ men + $14 \times 7$ boys ≡ $11 \times 3$ men + $11 \times 8$ boys

⇒ 28 men + 98 boys ≡ 33 men + 88 boys

⇒ 5 men = 10 boys ∴ 1 man = 2 boys

Then, 2 men and 7 boys ≡ 4 boys + 7 boys = 11 boys

& also, 8 men and 6 boys ≡ 16 boys + 6 boys = 22 boys

Work ↓: 1, 3 — Boys ↑: 11, 22 — Days ↓: 14, $x$

$$\Rightarrow \frac{x}{14} = \frac{11}{22} \times \frac{3}{1}$$

$$\therefore\ x = \frac{1}{2} \times 3 \times 14 = 21 \text{ days}$$

**12.** Men ↑: 40, 30 — Rice (kgs) ↓: 60, 12 — Days ↓: 15, $x$

$$\Rightarrow \frac{x}{15} = \frac{12}{60} \times \frac{40}{30}$$

$$\therefore\ x = \frac{12}{60} \times \frac{40}{30} \times 15 = 4 \text{ days}$$

**14.** Machines ↓: 6, 10 — Time (minutes) ↓: 1, 4 — Bottles ↓: 270, $x$

$$\Rightarrow \frac{x}{270} = \frac{4}{1} \times \frac{10}{6}$$

$$\therefore\ x = \frac{4 \times 10}{6} \times 270 = 1800 \text{ bottles}$$

**15.** Work ↓: $\frac{1}{4}$, $\frac{3}{4}$ — Hours ↑: 9, 8 — Days ↑: 10, 20 — Persons ↓: 400, $x$

$$\Rightarrow \frac{x}{400} = \frac{10}{20} \times \frac{9}{8} \times \frac{3/4}{1/4}$$

$$\therefore\ x = \frac{1}{2} \times \frac{9}{8} \times 3 \times 400 = 675$$

Hence, number of additional persons = 675 − 400 = 275

# TIME AND DISTANCE

**1.** Starting from a point at a speed of 4 km/hr a man reaches at a cerain place and returns back to the point from where he had started journey on bicycle at the speed of 16 km/hr. His average speed during the entire journey will be :

A. 6.4 km/h B. 8.4 km/h
C. 5.4 km/h D. 10 km/h

**2.** A motorist covers a certain distance at a average speed of 48 km/h in 45 minutes. What speed in km/h he must maintain to cover the same distance in 30 minutes?

A. 66 km/h B. 79 km/h
C. 80 km/h D. 72 km/h

**3.** A policeman saw a thief at a distance of 200 m. The policeman and the thief started running at the same time. If the policeman runs at a speed of $4\frac{1}{6}$ m per second and the thief at a speed of $3\frac{1}{3}$ m per second, after what time the policeman will catch the thief?

A. 12 min B. 10 min
C. 9 min D. 4 min

**4.** A monkey wants to climb up a glazed pole. He climbs 12 metres in 1 minute and then he slips back 3 metres in the next minute. If the pole is 63 metre high, how long does he take to climb at the top of the pole?

A. $11\frac{1}{4}$ min B. $12\frac{1}{2}$ min
C. $12\frac{3}{4}$ min D. $14\frac{3}{4}$ min

**5.** The distance between two stations A and B is 300 km. A train leaves the station A with a speed of 40 km/hr. At the same time another train departs from the station B with a speed of 50 km/hr. How much time will these two trains take to cross each other?

A. 3 hrs 40 min B. 3 hrs 20 min
C. 2 hrs 20 min D. 3 hrs 45 min

**6.** Nilesh goes to school from his village at the speed of 4 km/hr and returns from school to village at the speed of 2 km/hr. If he takes 6 hours in all, then what is the distance between the village and the school?

A. 8 km B. 6 km
C. 5 km D. 4 km

**7.** By increasing the speed of the bus by 10 km/hr the time of journey for 72 km is reduced by 36 minutes. What was the original speed of the bus?

A. 30 km/hr B. 35 km/hr
C. 40 km/hr D. 45 km/hr

**8.** A train covers a distance in 50 minutes, if it runs at a speed of 48 km/hr on an average. The speed at which the train must run to reduce the time of journey to 40 minutes will be:

A. 70 km/hr B. 60 km/hr
C. 55 km/hr D. 50 km/hr

**9.** A certain distance is covered by a vehicle at a certain speed. If half of this distance is covered by another vehicle in double the time, the ratio of the speeds of the two vehicles is:

A. 4 : 1 B. 1 : 4
C. 2 : 1 D. 1 : 2

**10.** A is faster than B. A and B each walk 24 km. The sum of their speeds is 7 km/hr and sum of times taken by them is 14 hours. What is the speed of A?

A. 7 km/hr B. 5 km/hr
C. 4 km/hr D. 3 km/hr

# ANSWERS

| 1 | 2 | 3 | 4 | 5 | 6 | 7 | 8 | 9 | 10 |
|---|---|---|---|---|---|---|---|---|---|
| A | D | D | C | B | A | A | B | A | C |

# SOME SELECTED EXPLANATORY ANSWERS

**1.** Average speed during the entire journey

$= \frac{2xy}{x+y} = \frac{2\times4\times16}{4+16} = \frac{8\times16}{20} = 6.4$ km/hr.

**2.** Let required speed be $x$ km/hr; then

$x \times \frac{1}{2} = 48 \times \frac{3}{4}$ $\therefore$ $x = 48 \times \frac{3}{4} \times 2$

$= 72$ km/hr

**3.** Suppose the policeman will catch the thief after $t$ seconds

then, $\left(\frac{25}{6} - \frac{10}{3}\right)t = 200 \Rightarrow \frac{5}{6}t = 200$

$\therefore t = \frac{200\times6}{5} = 240$ sec $= 4$ min.

**4.** The monkey climbs 12 metres in 1 minute and then he slips back 3 metres in the next minute

$\therefore$ The monkey climbs in the first 2 minutes $= 12 - 3 = 9$ metres

$\therefore$ In the first 12 minutes the monkey climbs $= 9 \times 6 = 54$ metres

Remaining height of the pole to be covered by the monkey $= 63 - 54 = 9$ metre

$\therefore$ The monkey will climb the height of 9 metres in the 13th minute

$\because$ The monkey climbs 12 metres in 1 minute

$\therefore$ The monkey will climb 9 metres in $\frac{1}{12} \times 9$

$= \frac{3}{4}$ minute

$\therefore$ Time spent in climbing at the top of the pole $= \left(12 + \frac{3}{4}\right)$ minutes $= 12\frac{3}{4}$ minutes

**5.** The two trains are moving in the opposite directions

$\therefore$ Relative speed $= 40 + 50 = 90$ km/hr.

$\therefore$ Time taken to cross each other $= \frac{300}{90} = 3\frac{1}{3}$ hours or, 3 hours 20 minutes.

**6.** Let $x$ km be the distance between village and the school; then

$\frac{x}{4} + \frac{x}{2} = 6 \quad \Rightarrow \frac{3x}{4} = 6$

$\therefore \quad x = \frac{6\times4}{3} = 8$ km

**8.** Let $x$ km/hr be the required speed of the train; then

$x \times \frac{40}{60} = 48 \times \frac{50}{60}$

$\therefore \quad x = \frac{48\times50}{40} = 60$ km/hr

**9.** Let $x$ km/hr and $t$ hr be the certain speed and certain time.

Then, ratio of their speeds $= \frac{x}{t} : \frac{x}{2\times2t} = 1 : \frac{1}{4}$

$= 4 : 1$

**10.** Let speeds of A and B are $x_1$ and $x_2$ km/hr and times taken by them are $t_1$ and $t_2$ hrs, then

$x_1 + x_2 = 7$ km/hr ...(i)

$t_1 + t_2 = 14$ hrs ...(ii)

Now, $\frac{24}{x_1} + \frac{24}{x_2} = 14 \Rightarrow \frac{24(x_1 + x_2)}{x_1x_2} = 14$

$\therefore \quad x_1x_2 = \frac{24\times7}{14} = 12$

Then, $x_1 - x_2 = \sqrt{(x_1 + x_2)^2 - 4x_1x_2}$

$= \sqrt{(7)^2 - 4\times12} = 1$ ...(iii)

Solving *(i)* and *(iii)* we get $x_1 = 4$ km/hr

# TIME AND WORK

**1.** A and B working together complete a work in 35 days. If A takes 60 days to complete it, how long would B alone take to complete it?

A. 64 days B. 72 days
C. 81 days D. 84 days

**2.** A few children working together can do a piece of work in 18 days. If the number of children employed on the work is made double, how long would they take to complete half of the work?

A. $4\frac{1}{2}$ days B. $2\frac{1}{3}$ days
C. $8\frac{3}{4}$ days D. $6\frac{1}{2}$ days

**3.** 10 men or 18 boys can do a piece of work in 15 days. In how many days would 25 men and 15 boys complete the same work working together?

A. $5\frac{1}{2}$ days B. $4\frac{1}{2}$ days
C. $6\frac{2}{3}$ days D. $2\frac{1}{3}$ days

**4.** A cistern is filled by a tap in $3\frac{1}{2}$ hours. Due to a leak in the bottom of the cistern, it takes half an hour longer to fill the cistern. If the cistern is full, how long will it take the leak to empty it?

A. 28 hours B. 29 hours
C. $31\frac{1}{3}$ hours D. 38 hours

**5.** A is twice as good a workman as B and thrice as good a workman as C. If C alone can do a piece of work in 24 days, how long would the three persons take to finish the work working together?

A. $3\frac{3}{11}$ days B. $4\frac{4}{7}$ days
C. $4\frac{4}{11}$ days D. $3\frac{4}{11}$ days

**6.** If 3 men and 5 women can do a piece of work in 8 days and 2 men and 7 boys can do the same work in 12 days. Find the number of boys, the work done by whom can equate the work done by 10 women.

A. 19 boys B. 21 boys
C. 23 boys D. 15 boys

**7.** 8 men alone can complete a piece of work in 12 days. 4 women alone can complete the same piece of work in 48 days and 10 children alone can complete the piece of work in 24 days. In how many days can 10 men, 4 women and 10 children together complete the piece of work?

A. 6 B. 8
C. 10 D. 15

**8.** A works twice as fast as B. If B can complete a piece of work independently in 12 days. Find in how many days A and B together can complete the work?

A. 8 days B. 6 days
C. 4 days D. 18 days

**9.** A contractor undertook to complete a project in 90 days and employed 60 men on it. After 60 days, he found that $\frac{3}{4}$ of the work has already been completed. How many men can he discharge so that the project may be completed exactly on time?

A. 15 B. 20
C. 30 D. 40

**10.** A can do a piece of work in 25 days and B can do it in 20 days. They work together for 5 days and then A goes away. In how many days will B finish the remaining work?

A. 33 days B. 20 days
C. 11 days D. 10 days

## ANSWERS

| 1 | 2 | 3 | 4 | 5 | 6 | 7 | 8 | 9 | 10 |
|---|---|---|---|---|---|---|---|---|---|
| D | A | B | A | C | B | A | C | B | C |

## SOME SELECTED EXPLANATORY ANSWERS

**1.** (A + B)'s 1 day's work $= \frac{1}{35}$

and also, A's 1 day's work $= \frac{1}{60}$

Hence, B's 1 day's work $= \frac{1}{35} - \frac{1}{60} = \frac{5}{420} = \frac{1}{84}$

So, B will do the whole work in 84 days.

**3.** 10 men $\equiv$ 18 boys

25 men $\equiv \frac{18}{10} \times 25 = 45$ boys

Hence, 25 men + 15 boys = 45 + 15 = 60 boys

Now, 18 boys can do a piece of work in 15 days.

Hence, 60 boys will do a piece of work in

$\frac{15 \times 18}{60} = \frac{9}{2}$ days $= 4\frac{1}{2}$ days.

**4.** In 1 hour $\frac{2}{7}$ cistern is filled by the tap.

Hence, in $\frac{1}{2}$ hour $\frac{2}{14} = \frac{1}{7}$ cistern is filled by the tap.

So, $\frac{1}{7}$ cistern is emptied by the leakage in 4 hours.

So, 1 cistern will be emptied by the leakage in 28 hours.

**6.** Here, (3 men + 5 women) × 8

$\equiv$ (2 men + 7 boys) × 12

$\Rightarrow$ 40 women $\equiv$ 84 boys

$\therefore$ 10 women $\equiv \frac{84}{40} \times 10 = 21$ boys

Hence, work done by 10 women

= work done of 21 boys.

**7.** B's 1 day's work $= \frac{1}{4} - \frac{1}{12} = \frac{2}{12} = \frac{1}{6}$

Hence, B alone will complete the work in 6 days.

**8.** Ratio of efficiency of A and B = 2 : 1

Then, ratio of their time taking = 1 : 2

Hence, if B can complete the work in 12 days, then A in 6 days.

Now, (A + B)'s 1 day's work $= \frac{1}{6} + \frac{1}{12} = \frac{3}{12} = \frac{1}{4}$

So, A and B together can complete the work in 4 days.

**9.** After 60 days remaining work $= 1 - \frac{3}{4} = \frac{1}{4}$

In 60 days $\frac{3}{4}$ work has been done by 60 men

In 30 days $\frac{1}{4}$ work will be done by

$60 \times \frac{4}{3} \times \frac{1}{4} \times \frac{60}{30} = 40$ men.

Hence, required number of men = 60 – 40 = 20 (which are to be discharged).

# BOATS AND STREAMS

1. A boat goes 6 km upstream and back to the starting point in 2 hours. If the current of the stream runs at the rate of 4 km/hr, find the speed of the boat in still water.
A. 6 km/hr B. 8 km/hr
C. 10 km/hr D. 12 km/hr

2. A boat covers 24 km upstream and 36 km downstream in 6 hours, while it covers 36 km upstream and 24 km downstream in 6½ horus. Find the speed of the current.
A. 2 km/hr B. 4 km/hr
C. 6 km/hr D. 8 km/hr

3. A man can row 5 km/hr in still water and the speed of the stream is 1.5 km/hr. He takes an hour when he travels upstream to a place and back again to the starting point. How far is the place from the starting point?
A. 2.275 km B. 3.5 km
C. 1.5 km D. None of these

4. The speed of a boat in still water is 6 km/hr and the speed of the stream is 1.5 km/hr. A man rows to a place at a distance of 22.5 km and comes back to the starting point. Find the total time taken by him.
A. 8 hours B. 10 hours
C. 12 hours D. 4 hours

5. A boat covers 20 km downstream and 6 km upstream in 3 hours, while it covers 30 km downstream and 12 km upstream in 5 hours. What is the speed of boat in still water?
A. 6 km/hr B. 8 km/hr
C. 10 km/hr D. 12 km/hr.

6. Samir can travel 12 miles downstream in a certain river in 6 hours less than it takes him to travel the same distance upstream. But when he could double his rowing rate for his 24-mile round trip, the downstream 12 miles would then take only one hour less than the upstream 12 miles. Find the speed of the current in miles/hour.
A. $2\frac{2}{3}$ B. $2\frac{1}{3}$
C. $1\frac{2}{3}$ D. $1\frac{1}{3}$

7. A boat takes 6 hours to travel from place M to N downstream and back from N to M upstream. If the speed of the boat in still water is 4 km/hr; what is the distance between two places?
A. 6 kms B. 8 kms
C. 12 kms D. Data inadequate

8. A man can row upstream at 8 km/hr and downstream at 13 km/hr. The speed of the stream is:
A. 2.5 km/hr B. 4.2 km/hr
C. 5 km/hr D. 10.5 km/hr

9. A man's speed with the current is 15 km/hr and the speed of the current is 2.5 km/hr. The man's speed against the current is:
A. 12.5 km/hr B. 10 km/hr
C. 9 km/hr D. 8.5 km/hr

10. A motorboat, whose speed is 15 km/hr in still water goes 30 km downstream and comes back in a total of 4 hours 30 minutes. What is the speed of the stream (in km/hr)?
A. 10 B. 6
C. 5 D. 4

## ANSWERS

| 1 | 2 | 3 | 4 | 5 | 6 | 7 | 8 | 9 | 10 |
|---|---|---|---|---|---|---|---|---|---|
| B | A | A | A | B | B | D | A | B | C |

## SOME SELECTED EXPLANATORY ANSWERS

**1.** Let the speed of a boat in still water = $x$ km/hr; then

$$\frac{6}{x-4}+\frac{6}{x+4}=2 \quad\Rightarrow\quad \frac{2x}{x^2-16}=\frac{1}{3}$$

$\Rightarrow x^2 - 6x - 16 = 0$

$\Rightarrow (x - 8)(x + 2) = 0$

Hence, the speed of the boat = 8 km/hr.

**2.** Let $x$ km/hr and $y$ km/hr be the speeds of the boat in still water and the speed of the current respectively, then

$$\frac{24}{x-y}+\frac{36}{x+y}=6 \Rightarrow \frac{4}{x-y}+\frac{6}{x+y}=1 \quad \text{...(i)}$$

And, $$\frac{36}{x-y}+\frac{24}{x+y}=\frac{13}{2} \quad \text{...(ii)}$$

Solving these two equations, we get

$x + y = 12;\ x - y = 8$

Hence, $y = \frac{1}{2}(12-8) = 2$ km/hr.

**3.** Let required distance be $x$ km, then

$$\frac{x}{5-1.5}+\frac{x}{5+1.5}=1 \Rightarrow \frac{x\times 2}{7}+\frac{x\times 2}{13}=1$$

$\Rightarrow 40x = 91 \qquad \therefore x = 91/40 = 2.275$ km

**4.** Required time period $= \frac{22.5}{6+1.5}+\frac{22.5}{6-1.5}$

$$= \frac{45}{15}+\frac{45}{9} = 8 \text{ hours.}$$

**5.** Let $x$ km/hr and $y$ km/hr be the speed of boat in still water and speed of current respectively; then

$$\frac{20}{x+y}+\frac{6}{x-y}=3 \quad \text{...(i)}$$

and also, $$\frac{30}{x+y}+\frac{12}{x-y}=5$$

$$\Rightarrow \frac{15}{x+y}+\frac{6}{x-y}=\frac{5}{2} \quad \text{...(ii)}$$

Solving equations *(i)* & *(ii)*, we get $x + y = 10$ and $x - y = 6$

Since, $x = \frac{1}{2}(10 + 6) = 8$ km/hr.

**6.** Let $x$ km/hr and $y$ km/hr be the speed of rowing in still water and speed of the current respectively; then

$$\frac{12}{x-y}-\frac{12}{x+y}=6 \quad\Rightarrow\quad \frac{24y}{x^2-y^2}=6$$

$$\Rightarrow x^2 = y^2 + 4y \quad \text{...(i)}$$

Again, $$\frac{12}{2x-y}-\frac{12}{2x+y}=1$$

$$\Rightarrow \frac{24y}{4x^2-y^2}=1 \quad\Rightarrow\quad x^2=\frac{y^2+24y}{4} \quad \text{...(ii)}$$

From equations (i) and (ii), we get

$$y^2 + 4y = \frac{y^2+24y}{4} \Rightarrow 3y^2 = 8y$$

$$\therefore\ y = \frac{8}{3} = 2\frac{1}{3} \text{ miles/hr.}$$

**8.** The speed of the stream $= \frac{1}{2}(13 - 8) = \frac{5}{2}$

$= 2.5$ km/hr.

**9.** The man's speed in still water

$= 15 - 2.5 = 12.5$ km/hr

Hence, the men's speed against the current

$= 12.5 - 2.5 = 10$ km/hr

**10.** Let speed of the stream be $x$ km/hr, then

$$\frac{30}{15+x}+\frac{30}{15-x}=4\frac{1}{2} \quad\Rightarrow\quad \frac{30\times 30}{225-x^2}=\frac{9}{2}$$

$$\Rightarrow \frac{200}{225-x^2}=1 \quad\Rightarrow\quad x^2 = 225 - 200$$

$\Rightarrow x^2 = 25 \qquad \therefore\ x = 5$ km/hr.

# ALLIGATION OR MIXTURE

1. A shopkeeper buys 26 kgs of milk @ Rs. 16 per kg. He also buys from another source an inferior quality of milk @ Rs. 10 per kg. How much quantity of the latter should he buy to mix it with the former so that he can sell the mixture @ Rs. 14 per kg without making any loss?

A. 13 kgs B. 12 kgs
C. 14 kgs D. 16 kgs

2. Two vessels A and B contain mixture of milk and water in the ratio 4 : 1 and 9 : 11 respectively. They are mixed in the ratio of 3 : 2. Find the ratio of milk : water in the resulting mixture.

A. 34 : 16 B. 33 : 17
C. 16 : 34 D. 17 : 33

3. A shopkeeper has 50 kgs of rice. He sells a part of it at 20% profit and the rest at 40% profit. If he gains 25% on the whole, find the quantity of each part.

A. 12.5 kgs and 37.5 kgs
B. 37.5 kgs and 12.5 kgs
C. 23.5 kgs and 21.5 kgs
D. 21.5 kgs and 23.5 kgs

4. A man bought a certain quantity of sugar for Rs. 8000. He sells one-fourth of it at 20% loss. At what per cent profit should he sell the remainder stock so as to make an overall profit of 20%?

A. 20% B. 30%
C. 35% D. 40%

5. Rs. 675 was divided among 75 boys and girls. Each boy gets Rs. 20 whereas a girl gets Rs. 5. Find the number of boys and girls.

A. 20, 55 B. 15, 60
C. 25, 50 D. 30, 45

6. A vessel contains mixture of liquids A and B in the ratio 3 : 2. When 20 litres of the mixture is taken out and replaced by 20 litres of liquid B, the ratio changes to 1 : 4. How many litres of liquid A was there initially present in the vessel?

A. 12 litres B. 18 litres
C. 24 litres D. 22 litres

7. A container is full of milk. One-third of milk is taken out of it and replaced by same quantity of water. Then again one-third of the mixture is taken out of it and replaced by the same quantity of water. The process is repeated 4 times. If 16 litres of milk is left in the container at the end of 4th operation, find the capacity of the container.

A. 76 litres B. 81 litres
C. 82 litres D. 85 litres

8. The cost of type-I rice is Rs. 15 per kg and type-II is Rs. 20 per kg. If both type I and type II are mixed in the ratio of 2 : 3, then find the price per kg of the mixed variety.

A. Rs. 19.50 B. Rs. 19
C. Rs. 18.50 D. Rs. 18

9. In what ratio must a grocer mix two varieties of tea worth Rs. 60 a kg and Rs. 65 a kg so that by selling the mixture at Rs. 68.20 a kg he may gain 10%?

A. 4 : 5 B. 3 : 5
C. 3 : 4 D. 3 : 2

**10.** A vessel contains 80 litres of milk. 16 litres of milk was taken out of the vessel and replaced by water. Then 16 litres of mixture was withdrawn and again replaced by water. The operation was repeated for third time. How much milk is now left in the vessel?

A. 96.40 litres B. 50.36 litres
C. 40.96 litres D. 32.76 litres

## ANSWERS

| 1 | 2 | 3 | 4 | 5 | 6 | 7 | 8 | 9 | 10 |
|---|---|---|---|---|---|---|---|---|---|
| A | B | B | B | A | B | B | D | D | C |

## SOME SELECTED EXPLANATORY ANSWERS

**1.** 16  10

14

4  2

$$\text{or } 2:1 \quad \frac{\text{Quantity of milk @ Rs.10 per kg}}{\text{Quantity of milk @ Rs. 16 per kg}} = \frac{1}{2}$$

$$\text{So, quantity of milk @ Rs. 10 per kg.} = \frac{26}{2} = 13 \text{ kgs.}$$

**2.** Fraction is

| | *Milk* | *Water* |
|---|---|---|
| A : | $\frac{4}{5}$ | $\frac{1}{5}$ |
| B : | $\frac{9}{20}$ | $\frac{11}{20}$ |

$$(3A + 2B) = \text{A and B} : \left(\frac{12}{5}+\frac{9}{10}\right) \left(\frac{3}{5}+\frac{11}{10}\right)$$

$$\frac{33}{10} \qquad \frac{17}{10}$$

So, Ratio of milk : water in the resulting mixture = 33 : 17.

**3.** 20%  40%

25%

15  5

or 3 : 1

$$\text{Quantity sold at 20\% profit} = \frac{3}{3+1} \times 50 = 37.5 \text{ kgs.}$$

$$\text{Quantity sold at 40\% profit} = (50 - 37.5) = 12.5 \text{ kgs.}$$

**4.** Let the remainder stock be sold at $x$% profit.

– 10  + $x$

+20

($x$–20)  30

$$\frac{x-20}{30} = \frac{1/4}{3/4}$$

$$\text{or} \quad x - 20 = 30 \times \frac{1}{3}$$

$$\text{or} \quad x = 20 + 10$$

$$x = 30\% \text{ profit.}$$

**5.** Average money per head (boy or girl)

$$= \text{Rs. } \frac{675}{75} = \text{Rs. } 9$$

(Boys) Rs. 20  (Girls) Rs. 5

(Average) Rs. 9

4  11

Number of boys $= \frac{4}{4+11} \times 75 = 20$

Number of girls $= \frac{11}{4+11} \times 75 = 55.$

**6.** % of liquid B initially present in the vessel

$$= \frac{2}{3+2} \times 100 = 40\%$$

% of liquid B finally present in the vessel

$$= \frac{4}{1+4} \times 100 = 80\%$$

The second solution is liquid B which is being mixed and it has 100% liquid B.
80% of liquid B present in the resultant mixture may be taken as average percentage. So, using rule of alligation on liquid B per cent, we can write,

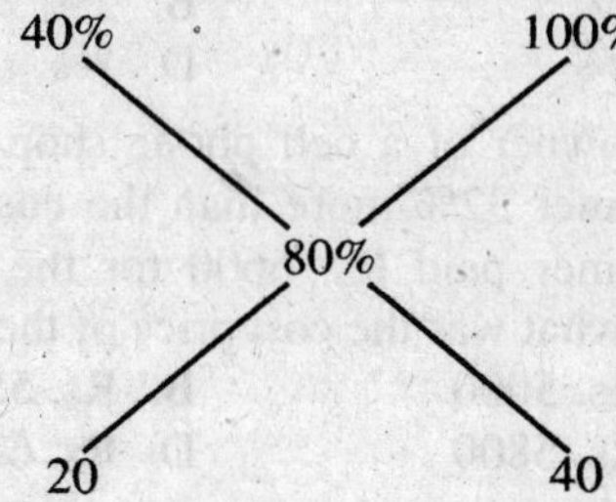


or 1 : 2
The ratio of liquid left in the vessel to liquid B being mixed = 1 : 2
Since the quantity of liquid B being mixed is 20 litres, the quantity of liquid left in the vessel is 10 litres.
Therefore, the total quantity of liquid initially present in the vessel

$$= 10 + 20 = 30 \text{ litres}$$

Quantity of liquid A $= \frac{3}{2+3} \times 30$

$= 18$ litres.

**7.** Let capacity of the container be $x$ litre; then

$$x(1 - 1/3)^4 = 16 \Rightarrow x\left(\frac{2}{3}\right)^4 = 16$$

$$\Rightarrow x \times \frac{16}{81} = 16 \quad \therefore x = 81 \text{ litres}$$

**8.** Let the price per kg of mixed variety be Rs. $x$; then

By the rule of alligation,

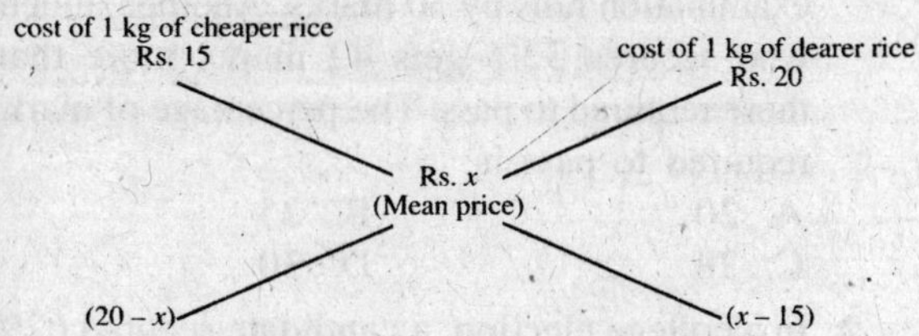


Now, $\frac{20-x}{x-15} = \frac{2}{3} \Rightarrow 60 - 3x = 2x - 30$

$\Rightarrow 5x = 90 \quad \therefore x = \text{Rs. } 18$

**9.** S.P. of 1 kg mixture = Rs. 68.20,
Gain % = 10%

Hence, C.P. of 1 kg mixture $= \frac{100}{110} \times \text{Rs. } 68.20$

$= \text{Rs. } 62$

By the rule of alligation

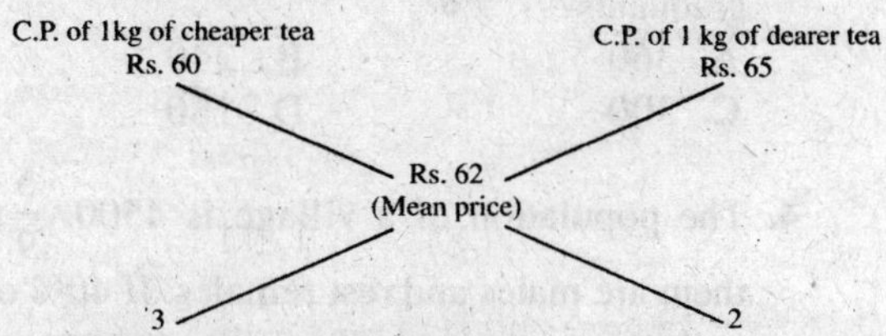


Hence, required ratio = 3 : 2

**10.** Amount of milk left $= 80\left(1 - \frac{16}{80}\right)^3$

$$= 80\left(\frac{4}{5}\right)^3$$

$$80 \times \frac{64}{125} = 40.96 \text{ litres.}$$

# PERCENTAGE

**1.** A student who secures 20% marks in an examination fails by 30 marks. Another student who secures 32% gets 42 marks more than those required to pass. The percentage of marks required to pass is:

A. 20 B. 25
C. 28 D. 30

**2.** In a college election, a candidate secured 62% of the votes and is elected by a majority of 144 votes. The total number of votes polled is:

A. 600 B. 800
C. 925 D. 1200

**3.** In an organisation, 40% of the employees are matriculates, 50% of the remaining are graduates and the remaining 180 are postgraduates. How many employees are graduates?

A. 360 B. 240
C. 300 D. 180

**4.** The population of a village is 4500. $\frac{5}{9}$th of them are males and rest females. If 40% of the males are married, then the percentage of married female is :

A. 35 B. 40
C. 50 D. 60

**5.** A's income is 10% more than B's. How much per cent is B's income is less than A's?

A. 10% B. 7%
C. $9\frac{1}{11}\%$ D. $6\frac{1}{2}\%$

**6.** If the price of a television set is increased by 25%, then by what percentage should the new price be reduced to bring the price back to original level?

A. 15% B. 20%
C. 25% D. 30%

**7.** In an election one of the two candidates gets 40% votes and loses by 100 votes. Total number of votes is :

A. 500 B. 400
C. 600 D. 1000

**8.** The gross income of a person is Rs. 20000. 10% of his income is exempted from income tax and his net income is Rs. 19100. The rate of income tax is :

A. 3% B. 2%
C. 4% D. 5%

**9.** The owner of a cell phone shop charges his customer 32% more than the cost price. If a customer paid Rs. 6600 for the cell phone, then what was the cost price of the cell phone?

A. Rs. 5000 B. Rs. 5500
C. Rs. 5800 D. Rs. 6100

**10.** If the cost of pins reduced by Rs. 4 per dozen, 12 more pins can be purchased for Rs. 48. The cost of pins per dozen after reduction is:

A. Rs. 8 B. Rs. 12
C. Rs. 16 D. Rs. 20

**11.** In an examination 80% of the students passed in Mathematics and 70% passed in English, while 10% students failed in both the subjects. If 360 students passed in both the subjects, find the total number of students who appeared in the examination.

A. 400 B. 600
C. 630 D. 640

**12.** Electric tax is increased by 20% and its consumption is decreased by 20%. The change in the expenditure is:

A. 4% decrease B. 4% increase
C. 5% decrease D. 5% increase

**13.** The selling price of certain commodity was reduced by 25%. As a result of it, the sales increased by 30%. What was the effect of it on cash collected by daily sales?

A. 2.5% decrease    B. 2.5% increase
C. 5% decrease    D. 5% increase

**14.** The wheat sold by a grocer contained 10% low quality wheat. What quantity of good quality wheat should be added to 150 kgs of wheat so that the percentage of low quality wheat becomes 5%?

A. 50 kgs    B. 85 kgs
C. 135 kgs    D. 150 kgs

**15.** Nilam spends 15% of her monthly income on household expenses. She spends 17% of the monthly income in travelling and 6% on medical expenses and saves the rest Rs. 15,500. What is her monthly income?

A. Rs. 20,000
B. Rs. 25,000
C. Rs. 30,000
D. Rs. 35,000

## ANSWERS

| 1 | 2 | 3 | 4 | 5 | 6 | 7 | 8 | 9 | 10 |
|---|---|---|---|---|---|---|---|---|---|
| B | A | D | C | C | B | A | D | A | B |
| **11** | **12** | **13** | **14** | **15** | | | | | |
| B | A | A | D | B | | | | | |

## SOME SELECTED EXPLANATORY ANSWERS

**1.** $20\% \text{ of } x + 30 = 32\% \text{ of } x - 42$

$\Rightarrow 12\% \text{ of } x = 72$

$$\Rightarrow x = \frac{72 \times 100}{12} = 600$$

Pass Mark $= 20\% \text{ of } 600 + 30 = 150$

$$\text{Pass percentage} = \left(\frac{150}{600} \times 100\right)\% = 25\%$$

**2.** $(62\% \text{ of } x - 38\% \text{ of } x) = 144$

$$\Rightarrow 24\% \text{ of } x = 144 \quad \Rightarrow x = \frac{144 \times 100}{24} = 600$$

**3.** $$\text{Matriculates} = \frac{40}{100}x = \frac{2x}{5}$$

$$\text{Remaining} = \left(x - \frac{2x}{5}\right) = \frac{3x}{5}$$

$$\text{Graduates} = \frac{50}{100} \times \frac{3x}{5} = \frac{3x}{10}$$

$$\text{Remaining} = \frac{3x}{5} - \frac{3x}{10} = \frac{3x}{10}$$

$$\text{Now, } \frac{3x}{10} = 180$$

$$\therefore x = \frac{10 \times 180}{3} = 600$$

$$\therefore \text{Graduates} = \frac{3 \times 600}{10} = 180.$$

**4.** $$\text{Males} = \left(\frac{5}{9} \times 4500\right) = 2500$$

Females $= 2000$

$$\therefore \quad \text{Married males} = \frac{40}{100} \times 2500 = 1000$$

and married females $= 1000$

$\therefore$ Percentage of married females

$$= \left(\frac{1000}{2000} \times 100\right)\% = 50\%.$$

**5.** $$\text{Required percentage} = \left[\frac{10}{(100+10)} \times 100\right]\%$$

$$= 9\frac{1}{11}\%.$$

**6.** $$\text{Required reduction} = \frac{25}{100+25} \times 100 = 20\%.$$

**7.** Out of 100, difference in votes = (60 – 40) = 20

20% of $x$ = 100

$$\therefore x = \frac{100 \times 100}{20} = 500.$$

**8.** Gross income = Rs. 20000

Income exempted from income tax = 10% of gross income

∴ Income on which income tax is chargeable = (100 – 10%) = 90% of gross income

$$= 20000 \times \frac{90}{100} = \text{Rs. } 18000$$

∴ Total income tax paid on

= Rs. 20000 – Rs. 19100

= Rs. 900

$$\therefore \text{Rate per cent of income tax} = \frac{900}{18000} \times 100 = 5\%$$

**9.** Let cost price of the cell phone be Rs. $x$; then

$$x + \frac{32}{100} \times x = 6600 \quad \Rightarrow \frac{132x}{100} = 6600$$

$$\therefore x = \frac{100 \times 6600}{132} = \text{Rs. } 5000.$$

**10.** Let reduced price by Rs. $x$ per dozen, then

$$\frac{48}{x} - \frac{48}{x+4} = 1 \quad \Rightarrow \frac{48 \times 4}{x^2 + 4x} = 1$$

$$\Rightarrow \quad x^2 + 4x - 192 = 0$$

$$\Rightarrow (x + 16)(x - 12) = 0$$

$$\therefore \quad x = \text{Rs. } 12.$$

**11.** Here, percentage of students failed in Mathematics and English be 30% and 20% respectively.

Percentage of students failed either one or both subjects = 30 + 20 – 10 = 40%

Hence, percentage of pass students = 100 – 40 = 60%

Now, 60% = 360

$$\therefore 100\% = \frac{360}{60} \times 100 = 600.$$

**12.** Let initially electric tax is Rs. 100 and consumption = 100 units

Decrease in consumption

= 100 × 100 – 120 × 80 = Rs. 400

$$\text{Hence, decrease percentage} = \frac{400 \times 100}{100 \times 100} = 4\%.$$

**13.** Let the selling price of a commodity be Rs. 100 and number of sales = 100 units

Decrease in daily cash = 100 × 100 – 75 × 130 = Rs. 250

Hence, decrease percentage

$$= \frac{250 \times 100}{100 \times 100} = 2.5\%.$$

**14.** Let $x$ kg of good wheat be added; then

$$\frac{10}{100} \times 150 = \frac{5}{100}(150 + x)$$

$$\Rightarrow 150 + x = 300 \quad \therefore x = 150 \text{ kg}.$$

**15.** Let her monthly income be Rs. $x$; then

$$x - \left(\frac{15}{100} \times x + \frac{17}{100} \times x + \frac{6}{100} \times x\right) = 15{,}500$$

$$\Rightarrow x - \frac{38x}{100} = 15500 \quad \Rightarrow \frac{62x}{100} = 15500$$

$$\therefore x = \frac{15500 \times 100}{62} = \text{Rs. } 25000.$$

# PROFIT AND LOSS

**1.** Ashok bought 25 kg of rice at the rate of Rs. 6 per kg and 35 kg of rice at the rate of Rs. 7 per kg. He mixed the two and sold the mixture at the rate of Rs. 6.75 per kg. What was his gain or loss in the transaction?

A. Rs. 16 gain B. Rs. 16 loss
C. Rs. 10 gain D. None of these

**2.** Profit after selling a commodity for Rs. 425 is same as loss after selling it for Rs. 355. The cost of the commodity is :

A. Rs. 285 B. Rs. 390
C. Rs. 295 D. Rs. 400

**3.** Ram bought 4 dozen apples at Rs. 12 per dozen and 2 dozen at Rs. 16 per dozen. He sold all of them to earn 20%. At what price per dozen did he sell the apples?

A. Rs. 14.40 B. Rs. 16.00
C. Rs. 16.80 D. Rs. 16.20

**4.** At what price must Kantilal sell a mixture of 80 kg sugar at Rs. 6.75 per kg with 120 kg at Rs. 8 per kg to gain 20%?

A. Rs. 7.50 per kg B. Rs. 8.20 per kg
C. Rs. 8.35 per kg D. Rs. 9 per kg

**5.** A person bought an article and sold it at a loss of 10%. If he had bought it for 20% less and sold it for Rs. 55 more, he would have had a profit of 40%. The C.P. of the article is :

A. Rs. 200 B. Rs. 225
C. Rs. 250 D. None of these

**6.** A dealer sold a machine to a shopkeeper at 20% profit. The shopkeeper sold the machine to a customer so as to get 25% profit for himself. The difference between the selling price of the dealer and that of the shopkeeper was found to be Rs. 129. What is the initial price of the machine?

A. Rs. 410 B. Rs. 420
C. Rs. 430 D. Rs. 440

**7.** A man bought a horse and cart. If he sold the horse at 10% loss and the cart at 20% gain he would not loss anything. If he sold the horse at 5% loss and the cart at 5% gain he would lose Rs. 10 in the bargain. What did he pay for each?

A. Rs. 400, Rs. 200 B. Rs. 300, Rs. 300
C. Rs. 250, Rs. 350 D. Rs. 350, Rs. 250

**8.** The marked price of a radio is 20% more than its cost price. If a discount of 10% is given on the marked price, the gain percentage is:

A. 8 B. 10
C. 12 D. 15

**9.** A dishonest dealer sells his goods at the cost price and still earns a profit of 60% by underweight. What weight does he use for a kg?

A. 625 gms B. 750 gms
C. 800 gms D. 850 gms

**10.** A man sells two horses for Rs. 990 each. On one he gains 10% and the other he loses 10%. What is his total percentage of gain or loss in the transaction?

A. 1% gain B. 1% loss
C. 2% gain D. 2% loss

## ANSWERS

| 1 | 2 | 3 | 4 | 5 | 6 | 7 | 8 | 9 | 10 |
|---|---|---|---|---|---|---|---|---|---|
| C | B | B | D | C | C | A | A | A | B |

# SOME SELECTED EXPLANATORY ANSWERS

**1.** C.P. of 60 kg mixture = Rs. $(25 \times 6 + 35 \times 7)$ = Rs. 395

S.P. of 60 kg mixtire = Rs. $(60 \times 6.75)$ = Rs. 405

$\therefore$ Gain = Rs. $(405 - 395)$ = Rs. 10

**2.** Let C.P. = Rs. $x$

Then, $425 - x = x - 355 \Rightarrow 2x = 780$

$\therefore$ $x =$ Rs. 390

**3.** C.P. of 6 dozen apples = Rs. $(12 \times 4 + 16 \times 2)$ = Rs. 80

$\therefore$ S.P. = Rs. $\left(\frac{120}{100} \times 80\right)$ = Rs. 96

$\therefore$ S.P. per dozen = Rs. $\left(\frac{96}{6}\right)$ = Rs. 16

**4.** C.P. of 1 kg sugar = $\frac{80 \times 6.75 + 120 \times 8}{200}$ = Rs. 7.50

$\therefore$ S.P. of 1 kg = Rs. $\left(\frac{120}{100} \times 7.50\right)$ = Rs. 9 per kg

**5.** Let C.P. = Rs. $x$,

then S.P. = $\frac{90}{100} \times x$ = Rs. $\frac{9x}{10}$

Now, when C.P. = Rs. $\frac{80x}{100}$ = Rs. $\frac{4x}{5}$;

then S.P. = $\frac{140}{100} \times \frac{4x}{5}$ = Rs. $\frac{28x}{25}$

But, $\frac{28x}{25} - \frac{9x}{10} = 55 \Rightarrow \frac{11x}{50} = 55$

$\therefore$ $x =$ Rs. 250

**6.** Let the initial price = Rs. $x$; then C.P. for dealer

$= \frac{120}{100} \times x =$ Rs. $\frac{6x}{5}$

Again, C.P. for shopkeeper = $\frac{125}{100} \times \frac{6x}{5}$ = Rs. $\frac{3x}{2}$

Now, $\frac{3x}{2} - \frac{6x}{5} = 129 \Rightarrow \frac{3x}{10} = 129$

$\therefore x = \frac{10 \times 129}{3}$ = Rs. 430

**7.** Here, 10% C.P. of horse = 20% C.P. of cart;
Hence, C.P. of horse = $2 \times$ C.P. of cart;
Let C.P. of cart and horse be Rs. $x$ and Rs. $2x$ respectively; then,

$\frac{5}{100} \times 2x - \frac{5}{100} \times x = 10 \Rightarrow \frac{1}{20}x = 10$

$\therefore x = 200$

Hence, C.P. of a cart = Rs. 200 and C.P. of a horse = $2 \times 200$ = Rs. 400

**8.** Let C.P. be Rs. 100; then marked price = Rs. 120

Since, S.P. = $\frac{90}{100} \times 120$ = Rs. 108

$\therefore$ Profit = $108 - 100$ = Rs. 8, Hence, gain = 8%.

**9.** Required weight = $\frac{100}{160} \times 1000$ = 625 gms.

**10.** Here, loss % = $\left(\frac{10}{10}\right)^2$ = 1%.

# SIMPLE INTEREST

1. A lent a sum of Rs. 1250 to B at a certain rate of interest for 3 years and a sum of Rs. 1500 to C at the same rate of interest for 2 years. If he was paid total Rs. 258.75 as interest in both cases, find the rate of interest at which money was lent by him.

   A. $4\frac{1}{6}\%$   B. $6\frac{1}{4}\%$
   C. $2\frac{1}{7}\%$   D. $3\frac{5}{6}\%$

2. A invested Rs. 5000 at a certain rate of simple interest and Rs. 4000 for the same period at 1% higher rate of interest. If the interest in both cases is same, the former rate of interest is :

   A. 3%   B. 4%
   C. 6%   D. 5%

3. If a certain sum of money at simple interest amounts to Rs. 1900 in 3 years and to Rs. 2050 in 5 years, the rate per cent per annum is :

   A. 4½%   B. 3½%
   C. 2½%   D. 5¼%

4. A certain sum of money lent out on simple interest amounts to Rs. 1760 in 2 years and to Rs. 2000 in 5 years. Find the sum.

   A. Rs. 1650   B. Rs. 1500
   C. Rs. 1580   D. Rs. 1600

5. Out of the sum of Rs. 1550, a part was lent out at 5% p.a. simple interest and the remaining at 8% p.a. simple interest. If the total interest in both cases after 3 years is Rs. 300, the sum of money lent out at 8% p.a. simple interest was:

   A. Rs. 760   B. Rs. 775
   C. Rs. 750   D. Rs. 780

6. If simple interest on a certain sum of money for 4 years at 5% p.a. is same as the simple interest on Rs. 840 for 10 years at the rate of 4% p.a., the sum of money is:

   A. Rs. 1780   B. Rs. 1660
   C. Rs. 1680   D. Rs. 1620

7. What equal instalment of annual payment will discharge a debt which is due as Rs. 848 at the end of 4 years at 4% per annum simple interest?

   A. Rs. 200   B. Rs. 212
   C. Rs. 225   D. Rs. 250

8. Madhavi lent Rs. 5000 to Kamla for 5 years and Rs. 3000 to Vimla for 4 years. Find the rate of interest, if Madhavi gets an interest of Rs. 600 in the end.

   A. 1.62%   B. 2.5%
   C. 3%   D. 4%

9. A sum of money doubles itself in 7 years at simple interest. In how many years it will become four fold?

   A. 10 years   B. 14 years
   C. 21 years   D. 35 years

10. An amount doubles itself at the end of 8 years with a certain rate of simple interest. What will be the total simple interest on Rs. 8000 at that rate at the end of 4 years?

    A. Rs. 2000   B. Rs. 4000
    C. Rs. 6000   D. None of these

## ANSWERS

| 1 | 2 | 3 | 4 | 5 | 6 | 7 | 8 | 9 | 10 |
|---|---|---|---|---|---|---|---|---|---|
| D | B | A | D | C | C | A | A | C | B |

# SOME SELECTED EXPLANATORY ANSWERS

**1.** $\frac{1250 \times R \times 3}{100} + \frac{1500 \times R \times 2}{100} = 258.75$

$\Rightarrow 6750\ R = 25875$

$\therefore \quad R = \frac{25875}{6750} = \frac{23}{6} = 3\frac{5}{6}\%$

**2.** Here, $\frac{5000 \times R \times T}{100} = \frac{4000 \times (R+1) \times T}{100}$

$\Rightarrow 5R = 4R + 4 \quad \therefore \; R = 4\%$

**3.** Simple interest for 2 years

= Rs. 2050 − Rs. 1900 = Rs. 150

$\therefore$ Simple interest for 1 year = Rs. $\frac{150}{2}$

= Rs. 75

Since simple interest for 3 years = Rs. 75 × 3

= Rs. 225

$\therefore$ Principal = Rs. 1900 − Rs. 225

= Rs. 1675

Hence, Rate = $\frac{75 \times 100}{1675 \times 1} = 4\frac{1}{2}\%$

**4.** Interest for 3 years = Rs. 2000 − Rs. 1760

= Rs. 240

$\therefore$ Interest for 1 year = Rs. $\frac{240}{3}$ = Rs. 80

And interest for 2 years = Rs. 80 × 2 = Rs. 160

$\therefore$ Principal = Rs. 1760 − Rs. 160 = Rs. 1600

**5.** Let Rs. $x$ and Rs $(1550 - x)$ were lent out at 8% and 5% respectively; then

$\frac{x \times 8 \times 3}{100} + \frac{(1550 - x) \times 5 \times 3}{100} = 300$

$\Rightarrow 24x + 23250 - 15x = 30000$

$\Rightarrow 9x = 6750 \quad \therefore \; x = \frac{6750}{9}$ = Rs. 750

**6.** Here, $\frac{P \times 5 \times 4}{100} = \frac{840 \times 4 \times 10}{100} \Rightarrow 5P = 8400$

$\therefore P = \frac{8400}{5}$ = Rs. 1680

**7.** Let equal instalment be Rs. $x$; then

$x + \frac{x \times 4 \times 3}{100} + x + \frac{x \times 4 \times 2}{100} + x + \frac{x \times 4 \times 1}{100} + x = 848$

$\Rightarrow 4x + \frac{24x}{100} = 848 \quad \Rightarrow \frac{106x}{25} = 848$

$\therefore x = \frac{848 \times 25}{106}$ = Rs. 200

**8.** $\frac{5000 \times R \times 5}{100} + \frac{3000 \times R \times 4}{100} = 600$

$\Rightarrow \quad 250\ R + 120\ R = 600$

$\Rightarrow \quad 370R = 600$

$\therefore \quad R = \frac{600}{370} = 1.62\%$

**9.** Let principal be Rs. $x$; then amount = Rs. $2x$, Hence, I = $2x - x$ = Rs. $x$.

$R = \frac{x \times 100}{x \times 7} = \frac{100}{7}\%$ p.a.

Now, amount = Rs. $4x$; then I = $4x - x$

= Rs. $3x$

Hence, $T = \frac{3x \times 100}{x \times \frac{100}{7}} = \frac{3 \times 100 \times 7}{100} = 21$ years

**10.** Let principal = Rs. $x$; then amount = Rs. $2x$; I = $2x - x$ = Rs. $x$

$R = \frac{x \times 100}{x \times 8} = \frac{25}{2}\%$

Again, $I = \frac{8000 \times 25 \times 4}{100 \times 2}$ = Rs. 4000

# COMPOUND INTEREST

**1.** The compound interest on a certain sum of money invested for 3 years at 5% per annum is Rs. 1891.50. What will be the simple interest on the same sum at the same rate for 2 years?

A. Rs. 1700 B. Rs. 1200
C. Rs. 1500 D. Rs. 2100

**2.** A sum of money lent out at a certain rate of simple interest amounts to Rs. 6600 in 2 years and to Rs. 6900 in 3 years. What will be the compound interest on the same sum of money if lent out at the same rate for 2 years?

A. Rs. 605 B. Rs. 715
C. Rs. 615 D. Rs. 595

**3.** A man deposits Rs. 1200 in a bank on the 1st day of each year. If the bank pays 5% per annum compound interest on deposited sum of money, what will be the amount to his credit on the 10th day of the second year?

A. Rs. 2560 B. Rs. 2460
C. Rs. 2370 D. Rs. 2860

**4.** If the difference between compound and simple interest on a certain sum of money for 3 years at 5% per annum is Rs. 244. the sum is :

A. Rs. 40000 B. Rs. 25000
C. Rs. 30000 D. Rs. 32000

**5.** A man purchased a sewing machine for Rs. 5000. If due to sustained use value of this sewing machine depreciates by 6% annually, find its value after 3 years.

A. Rs. 3775.67 B. Rs. 4152.92
C. Rs. 4250.25 D. Rs. 4356.25

**6.** Find the sum on which the difference between compound and simple interest for 3 years at 10% per annum will be Rs. 868.

A. Rs. 29500 B. Rs. 27625
C. Rs. 28500 D. Rs. 28000

**7.** Samir invested Rs. 15000 at the rate of interest 10% p.a. for 1 year. If the interest compounded six months. What amount will Samir get at the end of the year?

A. Rs. 16,500 B. Rs. 16525.50
C. Rs. 16537.50 D. Rs. 18,150

**8.** The compound interest on a certain sum for 2 years at 10% per annum is Rs. 525. The simple interest on the same sum for double the time at half the rate per cent per annum is:

A. Rs. 800 B. Rs. 600
C. Rs. 500 D. Rs. 400

**9.** The least number of complete years in which a sum of money put at 20% compound interest will be more than doubled is:

A. 6 B. 5
C. 4 D. 3

**10.** On a sum of money, the simple interest for 2 years is Rs. 660, while the compound interest is Rs. 696.30, the rate of interest being the same in both cases. Find the rate of interest.

A. Rs. 12% B. 11%
C. 10% D. 9%

## ANSWERS

| 1 | 2 | 3 | 4 | 5 | 6 | 7 | 8 | 9 | 10 |
|---|---|---|---|---|---|---|---|---|---|
| B | C | B | D | B | D | C | C | C | B |

# SOME SELECTED EXPLANATORY ANSWERS

**1.** Here, $1891.50 = P\left[\left(1+\frac{5}{100}\right)^3 - 1\right]$

$\Rightarrow 1891.50 = P\left[\left(\frac{21}{20}\right)^3 - 1\right]$

$\Rightarrow 1891.50 = P\left(\frac{1261}{8000}\right)$

$\therefore P = \frac{1891.50 \times 8000}{1261} = \text{Rs. } 12000$

Now, $\text{S.I.} = \frac{12000 \times 5 \times 2}{100} = \text{Rs. } 1200$

**2.** Here, 1 year's S.I. = Rs. 6900 – Rs. 6600 = Rs. 300

$\therefore$ 2 year's S.I. = 300 × 2 = Rs. 600

$\therefore$ Principal = Rs. 6600 – Rs. 600 = Rs. 6000

Hence, $\text{Rate} = \frac{600 \times 100}{6000 \times 2} = 5\%$

$\therefore \text{C.I.} = 6000\left[\left(1+\frac{5}{100}\right)^2 - 1\right]$

$= 6000\left[\left(\frac{21}{20}\right)^2 - 1\right] = \frac{6000 \times 41}{400} = \text{Rs. } 615$

**3.** Required amount $= 1200\left(1+\frac{5}{100}\right) + 1200$

$= 1200 \times \frac{21}{20} + 1200 = 1260 + 1200 = \text{Rs. } 2460$

**4.** Here, $P\left[\left(1+\frac{5}{100}\right)^3 - 1\right] - \frac{P \times 5 \times 3}{100} = 244$

$\Rightarrow P \times \frac{1261}{8000} - \frac{3P}{20} = 244 \Rightarrow P \times \frac{61}{8000} = 244$

$\therefore P = \frac{244 \times 8000}{61} = \text{Rs. } 32000$

**5.** Here, value of the machine after 3 years

$= 5000\left(1-\frac{6}{100}\right)^3 = 5000 \times \frac{47}{50} \times \frac{47}{50} \times \frac{47}{50}$

= Rs. 4152.92.

**6.** Here, $P\left[\left(1+\frac{10}{100}\right)^3 - 1\right] - \frac{P \times 10 \times 3}{100} = 868$

$\Rightarrow P \times \frac{331}{1000} - \frac{3P}{10} = 868$

$\Rightarrow P \times \frac{31}{1000} = 868 \therefore P = \frac{868 \times 1000}{31}$

= Rs. 28000

**7.** $A = 15000\left(1+\frac{5}{100}\right)^2 = 15000 \times \frac{441}{400}$

= Rs. 16537.50

**8.** Here, $P\left[\left(1+\frac{10}{100}\right)^2 - 1\right] = 525$

$\Rightarrow P\left[\frac{121}{100} - 1\right] = 525 \Rightarrow P \times \frac{21}{100} = 525$

$\therefore P = \frac{525 \times 100}{21} = \text{Rs. } 2500$

Hence, required $\text{S.I.} = \frac{2500 \times 5 \times 4}{100} = \text{Rs. } 500$

**9.** Here, $P\left(1+\frac{20}{100}\right)^n > 2P \Rightarrow \left(\frac{6}{5}\right)^n > 2$

Hence, if $n = 4$ then, $\left(\frac{6}{5}\right)^4 = \frac{1296}{625} > 2$

So, $n = 4$ years

**10.** Here, S.I. for 1 year = Rs. 330

Since, simple interest of Rs. 330 for 1 year = 696.30 – 660 = Rs. 36.30

Hence, required rate $= \frac{36.30 \times 100}{330 \times 1} = \frac{3630}{330}$

= 11%

# AREA AND PERIMETER

**1.** If side of a square is reduced by 50%, its area will be reduced by

A. 50% B. 75%
C. 80% D. 60%

**2.** If each side of a square is doubled, its area will become

A. double
B. four times
C. three times
D. eight times

**3.** Three sides of a triangle are in the ratio of 17 : 15 : 8. If the perimeter of this triangle is 40 m, find its area

A. 50 sq. m. B. 49 sq. m.
C. 60 sq. m. D. 69 sq. m.

**4.** If the length of a rectangle is increased by 20% and width is decreased by 15%, then its area

A. decreases by 4% B. increases by 2%
C. decreases by 2% D. increases by 3%

**5.** If the length of a rectangle is increased by 20%, then by how much per cent its breadth must be decreased so as to keep its area unaltered?

A. 25% B. $8\frac{1}{3}\%$
C. $16\frac{2}{3}\%$ D. 20%

**6.** The ratio of length and breadth of a rectangular plot is 71 : 61 respectively. The area of the plot is 17324 $m^2$. What is perimeter of the plot?

A. 264 m B. 284 m
C. 528 m D. 614 m.

**7.** If the length and breadth of a rectangular field are increased, the area increases by 50%. If the increase in length was 20%, by what ' ntage was the breadth increased?

A. 20% B. 25%
C. 30% D. 40%

**8.** The length and breadth of a varandah is 40 m and 15 m respectively. How many stone slabs of size 6 decimetre × 5 decimetre each are needed in flooring it:

A. 1000 B. 2000
C. 3000 D. 4000

**9.** The circumference of a circular plot is 396 m. What is the area of the circular plot?

A. 9,446 $m^2$ B. 9,856 $m^2$
C. 12,474 $m^2$ D. 18,634 $m^2$

**10.** If the sides of an equilateral triangle are increased by 20%, 30% and 50% respectively to form a new triangle, the increase in the perimeter of the equilateral triangle is:

A. 25% B. $33\frac{1}{3}\%$
C. 50% D. 100%

## ANSWERS

| 1 | 2 | 3 | 4 | 5 | 6 | 7 | 8 | 9 | 10 |
|---|---|---|---|---|---|---|---|---|---|
| B | B | C | B | C | C | B | B | C | B |

# SOME SELECTED EXPLANATORY ANSWERS

**1.** Area of the square = $x^2$ sq. m.

Side of the new square = $x - 50\%$ of $x = \frac{x}{2}$ m

$\therefore$ Area of the new square = $\left(\frac{x}{2}\right)^2 = \frac{x^2}{4}$ sq. m.

$\therefore$ Reduction in area of the square = $x^2 - \frac{x^2}{4}$

$= \frac{3x^2}{4}$ sq. m.

$\therefore$ Percentage reduction = $\frac{3x^2/4}{x^2} \times 100 = 75\%$

**2.** Area of the square = $x^2$ sq. m
Now, area of the new square = $(2x)^2 = 4x^2$ sq. m
Hence, it is clear that if side of a square is doubled, its area becomes four times.

**3.** Suppose sides of the triangle are $17x$ m, $15x$ m and $8x$ metres

$\therefore$ Perimeter $= 17x + 15x + 8x = 40x$

Now, $40x = 40$

$\Rightarrow x = 1$ m

Therefore, the sides are $17 \times 1 = 17$ m, $15 \times 1 = 15$ m and $8 \times 1 = 8$ m

$\because (17)^2 = (15)^2 + (8)^2$,

*i.e.*, it is a right angled triangle

$\therefore$ Area of the right angled triangle

$= \frac{1}{2} \times 8 \times 15 = 60$ sq. m.

**4.** Area of the rectangle = $xy$ sq. metre

Area of the new rectangle = $\frac{120}{100} x \times \frac{85}{100} y$

$= 1.020\, xy$ sq. metre

$\therefore$ Increase in the area = $1.02\, xy - xy$

$= .02\, xy$ sq. m.

$\therefore$ Percentage increase = $\frac{.02xy}{xy} \times 100 = 2\%$

**5.** Area of the rectangle = $xy$
On reducing the breadth by A% and increasing the length by 20%

Length of the new rectangle = $\frac{120x}{100} x = 1.2x$

Breadth of the new rectangle = $y -$ A% of $y$

$= y\left(1 - \frac{A}{100}\right)$

$\therefore$ Area of the new rectangle = $1.2x \times y\left(1 - \frac{A}{100}\right)$

Now, $xy = 1.2\, xy\left(1 - \frac{A}{100}\right) \Rightarrow 1 = 1.2 \frac{(100 - A)}{100}$

$\Rightarrow 1.2\, A = 120 - 100$

$\therefore A = \frac{20}{1.2} = 16\frac{2}{3}\%$

**6.** Let length and breadth of a rectangle be $71x$ and $61x$ m; then

$71x \times 61x = 17324 \Rightarrow x^2 = \frac{17324}{71 \times 61} = 4$

$\therefore x = 2$

Hence, length = $71 \times 2 = 142$ m; breadth $= 61 \times 2 = 122$ m

Since, perimeter $= 2(142 + 122) = 2 \times 264 = 528$ m

**7.** Here, $20 + x + \frac{20 \times x}{100} = 50 \Rightarrow x + \frac{x}{5} = 30$

$\Rightarrow \frac{6x}{5} = 30 \qquad \therefore x = \frac{5 \times 30}{6} = 25$

Hence, breadth was increased by 25%

**8.** Required number of stone slabs = $\frac{40 \times 15}{\frac{6}{10} \times \frac{5}{10}}$

$= \frac{40 \times 15 \times 100}{6 \times 5} = 2000$

**9.** Radius of circular plot = $\frac{396 \times 7}{2 \times 22} = 63$ m

Area of the circular plot = $\frac{22}{7} \times 63 \times 63$

$= 12{,}474\ m^2$

# VOLUME AND SURFACE AREA

**1.** If a solid sphere of 3 cm radius is melted and recast into a right circular cone whose base radius is same as that of the sphere, the height of the cone will be

A. 8 cm B. 12 cm
C. 6 cm D. 5 cm

**2.** Diameter of a roller is 2.4 m and it is 1.68 m long. If it takes 1000 complete revolutions once over to level a field, the area of the field is

A. 12672 sq. m B. 12671 sq. m
C. 12762 sq. m D. 11768 sq. m

**3.** If each edge of a cube is increased by 10%, then by how much per cent will the surface area of this cube be increased?

A. 21% B. 18%
C. 15% D. 20%

**4.** Height and base radius of a solid cylinder are 14 m and 4 m respectively. It is melted and recast into a solid cone of the same base radius as that of the cylinder, what will be the height of the cone?

A. 21 m B. 42 m
C. 48 m D. 54 m

**5.** A room is in the form of a cube of side 10 m. How many bales of cotton can be kept in it if each bale covers 5 cu m space?

A. 100 B. 175
C. 200 D. 225

**6.** Three cubes having side 2 cm, 3 cm and 4 cm respectively are melted together to form a new cube. The side of the new cube will be

A. 3.526 cm B. 4.628 cm
C. 4.626 cm D. 4.528 cm

**7.** If base diameter of a cylinder is increased by 50%, then by how much per cent its height must be decreased so as to keep its volume unaltered?

A. 45.56% B. 55.56%
C. 50.16% D. 62.33%

**8.** The surface area of a cube is 600 sq. m. Its diagonal is

A. $10\sqrt{3}$ cm B. $5\sqrt{3}$ cm
C. $4\sqrt{2}$ cm D. $10\sqrt{2}$ cm

**9.** The base diameter of a conical tomb is 28 m and its slant height is 50 m. Find the cost of white washing its curved surface at the rate of 80 paise per sq. m?

A. Rs. 1860 B. Rs. 1760
C. Rs. 1950 D. Rs. 1875

**10.** The volume of a cuboid is 1120 cu cm and its height is 5 cm while the length and the breadth of the cuboid are in the ratio 8 : 7. The length of this cylinder exceeds the breadth by

A. 4 cm B. 2 cm
C. 7 cm D. 5 cm

## ANSWERS

| 1 | 2 | 3 | 4 | 5 | 6 | 7 | 8 | 9 | 10 |
|---|---|---|---|---|---|---|---|---|---|
| B | A | A | B | C | C | B | A | B | B |

## SOME SELECTED EXPLANATORY ANSWERS

**1.** Volume of the cone = Volume of the sphere

$\therefore \quad \frac{1}{3}\pi(3)^2 \times h = \frac{4}{3}\pi \times 3^3 \Rightarrow h = 12$ cm

Hence, height of the cone = 12 cm.

**2.** Surface area of the roller = $2\pi rh$

$= 2 \times \frac{22}{7} \times 1.2 \times 1.68 = 12.672$ sq. m

In one complete revolution, the roller covers 12.672 sq. m.

$\therefore$ It will cover in 1000 revolutions

$= 12.672 \times 1000 = 12672$ sq. m

Hence, area of the field = 12672 sq. m.

**3.** Percentage increase in the surface area of the cube $= \left(x + y + \frac{xy}{100}\right)\%$

$= \left(10 + 10 + \frac{10 \times 10}{100}\right)\% = 21\%.$

**4.** Here,

volume of the cone = Volume of the cylinder

$\Rightarrow \quad \frac{1}{3}\pi r^2 \times \text{height} = \pi r^2 \times 14$

$\therefore \quad$ Height $= 14 \times 3 = 42$ m

Thus, height of the cone = 42 m.

**5.** Volume of the cubical room $= (10)^3$

$= 1000$ cu m

Number of cotton bales which can be placed in the room

$= \frac{\text{Volume of the room}}{\text{Volume of each cotton bale}} = \frac{1000}{5} = 200.$

**6.** Volume of the new cube $= 2^3 + 3^3 + 4^3$

$= 8 + 27 + 64 = 99$cu cm

$\therefore$ Side of the new cube $= \sqrt[3]{99} = 4.626$ cm.

**7.** Change in the volume of the cylinder

$= \left(x + y + (-z) + \frac{xy + y(-z) + (-zx)}{100} + \frac{xy(-z)}{100^2}\right)\%$

Since volume of the cylinder remains unchanged.

$\therefore \quad$ Change = 0%

Now, $\left(50 + 50 + (-z) + \frac{50 \times 50 - 50z - 50z}{100} + \frac{50 \times 50 \times (-z)}{100^2}\right) = 0$

$\therefore \quad 100 - z + 25 - z - .25z = 0$

$\Rightarrow 2.25z = 125 \Rightarrow z = \frac{125}{2.25} = 55.56$

$\therefore$ Height of the cylinder should be decreased by 55.56%.

**8.** Here, $\quad 6 \times (\text{side})^2 = 600$

$\Rightarrow \quad \text{side}^2 = 100$

$\Rightarrow \quad \text{side} = \sqrt{100} = 10$ cm

$\therefore$ Diagonal of the cube $= \sqrt{3} \times \text{side}$

$= \sqrt{3} \times 10$

$= 10\sqrt{3}$ cm.

**9.** Area of the curved surface of the cone

$= \frac{22}{7} \times \frac{28}{2} \times 50 = 2200$ sq. m.

$\therefore$ Cost of white washing at 80 paise per sq. m

$= 2200 \times \frac{80}{100} = $ Rs. 1760.

**10.** Suppose the length and the breadth of the cuboid are $8x$ cm and $7x$ cm

$\therefore$ Here, $\quad 8x \times 7x \times 5 = 1120$

$\Rightarrow x^2 = \frac{1120}{280} = 4 = (2)^2 \Rightarrow x = 2$

$\therefore$ Length of the cuboid $= 8 \times 2 = 16$ cm

Breadth of the cuboid $= 7 \times 2 = 14$ cm

Hence, it is clear that length of the cuboid exceeds the breadth by 2 cm.

# AREA AND PERIMETER

1. The length of a plot is four times its breadth. A playground measuring 1200 square metres occupies a third of the total area of the plot. What is the length of the plot, in metres?
   A. 20 B. 30
   C. 60 D. None of these
2. The width of a rectangular hall is $\frac{3}{4}$ of its length. If the area of the hall is 300 $m^2$, then the difference between its length and width is:
   A. 3 m B. 4 m
   C. 5 m D. 15 m
3. The length and breadth of a rectangular piece of land are in ratio of 5 : 3. The owner spent ₹ 3000 for surrounding it from all the sides at ₹ 7.50 per metre. The difference between its length and breadth is:
   A. 50 m
   B. 100 m
   C. 150 m
   D. 200 m
4. A room 8 m × 6 m is to be carpeted by a carpet 2 m wide. The length of carpet required is:
   A. 12 m B. 36 m
   C. 24 m D. 48 m
5. The length of a rectangle is increased by 60%. By what per cent would the width have to be decreased to maintain the same area?
   A. $37\frac{1}{2}$% B. 60%
   C. 75% D. 120%
6. A man walked 20 m to cross a rectangular field diagonally. If the length of the field is 16 m, the breadth of the rectangle is:
   A. 4 m
   B. 16 m
   C. 12 m
   D. Cannot be determined
7. If the ratio of the areas of two squares is 9 : 1, the ratio of their perimeters is:
   A. 9 : 1 B. 3 : 1
   C. 3 : 4 D. 1 : 3
8. The perimeter of both, a square and a rectangle are each equal to 48 m and the difference between their areas is 4 $m^2$. The breadth of the rectangle is:
   A. 10 m B. 12 m
   C. 14 m D. None of these
9. Area of a square with side $x$ is equal to the area of a triangle with base $x$. The altitude of the triangle is:
   A. $\frac{x}{2}$ B. $x$
   C. $2x$ D. $4x$
10. If only the length of the rectangular plot is reduced to $\frac{2}{3}$rd of its original length, the ratio of original area to reduced area is:
    A. 2 : 3 B. 3 : 2
    C. 1 : 2 D. None of these
11. If the radius of a circle be reduced by 50%, its area is reduced by:
    A. 25% B. 50%
    C. 75% D. 100%
12. The perimeter of a rhombus is 52 m while its longer diagonal is 24 m. Its other diagonal is:
    A. 5 m B. 10 m
    C. 20 m D. 28 m
13. The circumference of a circle is 352 m, then its area in $m^2$ is:
    A. 9856 B. 8956
    C. 6589 D. 5986

## ANSWERS

| 1 | 2 | 3 | 4 | 5 | 6 | 7 | 8 | 9 | 10 |
|---|---|---|---|---|---|---|---|---|---|
| D | C | A | C | A | C | B | A | C | B |
| **11** | **12** | **13** | | | | | | | |
| C | B | A | | | | | | | |

## SOME SELECTED EXPLANATORY ANSWERS

**1.** Area of the plot $= 3 \times 1200 = 3600$ m$^2$
Let breadth be $x$ m. Then length $= 4x$ m
According to the question,
$4x \times x = 3600 \Rightarrow x^2 = 900 \Rightarrow x = 30$
Hence, length of the plot $= 4 \times 30 = 120$ m.

**2.** Let length be $x$ m, then breadth $= \frac{3x}{4}$ m

Area of the hall $= x \times \frac{3x}{4} = \frac{3x^2}{4}$

According to the question,

$\frac{3x^2}{4} = 300 \Rightarrow x^2 = 400 \Rightarrow x = 20$

Length $= 20$ m and breadth $= \frac{3}{4} \times 20 = 15$ m

Difference $= 20 - 15 = 5$ m

**3.** Let length $= 5x$ m and breadth $= 3x$ m
Perimeter of rectangle $= 2(5x + 3x) = 16x$ m

But perimeter $= \frac{\text{Total cost}}{\text{Rate}} = \frac{3000}{7.50} = 400$ m

Now, $16x = 400 \Rightarrow x = 25$
length $= 5x = 5 \times 25 = 125$ m
breadth $= 3x = 25 \times 3 = 75$ m
Difference $= 125 - 75 = 50$ m

**4.** Length of the carpet $= \frac{8 \times 6}{2} = 24$ m.

**7.** Let the areas of the squares be $(9x^2)$ m$^2$ and $(x^2)$ m$^2$
Then, their sides are $3x$ m and $x$ m respectively

Ratio of their perimeters $= \frac{12x}{4x} = 3 : 1$

**9.** According to the question,

$$x^2 = \frac{1}{2} \times x \times h$$

$$\Rightarrow \quad h = \frac{2x^2}{x} = 2x$$

**10.** Let length $= x$ and breadth $= y$

New length $= \frac{2}{3}x$

$$\therefore \frac{\text{Original area}}{\text{Reduced area}} = \frac{xy}{\frac{2}{3}xy} = \frac{3}{2} = 3 : 2$$

**11.** Original area $= \pi r^2$, New area $= \pi\left(\frac{r}{2}\right)^2 = \frac{\pi r^2}{4}$

Reduction in area $= \pi r^2 - \frac{\pi r^2}{4} = \frac{3\pi r^2}{4}$

Reduction per cent $= \frac{3\pi r^2}{4} \times \frac{1}{\pi r^2} \times 100 = 75\%$

**12.** Side of rhombus $= \frac{52}{4} = 13$ m

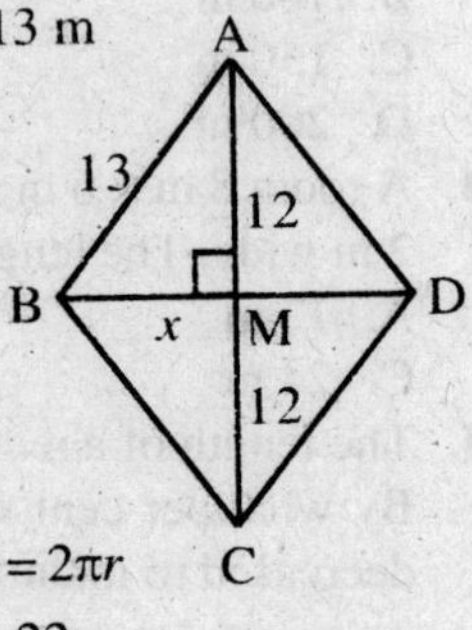


In $\Delta$ABM,
$x^2 = (13)^2 - (12)^2$
$x^2 = 169 - 144$
$x^2 = 25$
$\Rightarrow \quad x = 5$ m
$\therefore$ Another diagonal
$= 2 \times 5 = 10$ m

**13.** Circumference of a circle $= 2\pi r$

$$\Rightarrow \quad 352 = 2 \times \frac{22}{7} \times r$$

$$\Rightarrow \quad r = \frac{352 \times 7}{44} = 56 \text{ m}$$

Area of circle $= \pi r^2 = \frac{22}{7} \times 56 \times 56$

$= 9856$ m$^2$

# FINANCIAL AND COMMERCIAL ACCOUNTS

# UNIT-I

# ADVANCED ACCOUNTING

## INTRODUCTION: COMPANY ACCOUNTS

Sole proprietorship is the most common type of business when the size of business is small. Partnership became popular as the size increased. As firms became very big requiring more amount of capital and involving more risks, it lead to the formation of Companies. A company is an association of persons who contribute money or money's worth to a common stock (capital), for carrying on business for the purposes of profit. The capital is divided into shares, which are held by the members (shareholders) in any proportion and are transferable. It is a legal person, and in law exists like an individual, but with no physical existence.Section 3(1)(i) of the Companies Act, 1956, defines a company as "a company formed and registered under this Act or an existing company". An existing company means a company formed and registered under any of the previous Companies Act.

## CHARACTERISTICS

A company has the following essential characteristics:

**1. Voluntary Association**

It is a voluntary association of persons. No law can compel persons to form a company. It is their own creation and voluntary act.

**2. Limited Liability**

The liability of shareholders is limited to the amount he has agreed to pay to the company, either by purchasing shares or by giving a guarantee.

**3. Separate Legal Entity**

Company can hold, buy and sell properties. It can open bank account in its name and can enter into contracts. It can sue and be sued.

**4. Common Seal**

Being an artificial person, it cannot sign the documents and can act only through natural persons, called Directors. Every company must, therefore have a common seal with its name engraved on it. The common seal of the company is regarded as the official signature of the company. Any documents prepared by the directors belongs to the company only when it contains the common seal.

**5. Perpetual Succession**

It is independent of members and its existence is not affected by the coming in and going out of its members. Its continuity is not affected by the changes in the membership.

**6. Ownership and Management are separated**

As the number of shareholders are large in number, it becomes difficult for them to carry on the day-to-day affairs of the business so the ownership and management are separated. The management of the company is in the hands of the Board of Directors.

**7.Transferability of shares**

Shares are freely transferable without restriction.

**8.Compulsory Registration**

All companies must be registered under the Companies Act, 1956.

**9. Maintenance of Books**

A company is required by law to keep a prescribed set of account books and it has to observe the regulations carefully.

**10. Periodic Audit**

Audit of company's accounts is compulsory by a practicing chartered accountant, who is appointed by the shareholders on the recommendation of Board of Directors, at the Annual General Meeting.

## KINDS OF COMPANIES

Companies may be classified into various kinds on the following basis :

### I. Classification on the Basis of Incorporation

**1. Statutory companies :** These are the companies which are created by a special Act of the Legislature *e.g.*, the Reserve Bank of India, the State Bank of India, the Life Insurance Corporation, the Industrial Finance Corporation, the Unit Trust of India. These are mostly concerned with public utilities, *e.g.*, railways, tramways, gas and electricity companies and enterprises of national importance. The provisions of the Companies Act, 1956 apply to them, if they are not inconsistent with the provisions of the special Acts under which they are formed.

**2. Registered companies :** These are the companies which are formed and registered under the Companies Act, 1956, or were registered under any of the earlier Companies Acts. These are by far the most commonly found companies.

### II. Classification on the Basis of Liability

On the basis of liability companies may be classified into :

1. Companies with limited liability. These may be—
   (*a*) companies limited by shares, or
   (*b*) companies limited by guarantee, or
2. Companies with unlimited liability [Sec. 12(2)].

**1. Companies with limited liability**

**(*a*)** *Companies limited by shares* : Where the liability of the members of a company is limited to the amount unpaid on the shares, such a company is known as a company limited by shares. The liability can be enforced during the existence of the company as also during the winding up of the company. If the shares are fully paid, the liability of the members holding such shares is nil.

**(*b*)** *Companies limited by guarantee* : Where the liability of the members of a company is limited to a fixed amount which the members undertake to contribute to the assets of the company in the event of its being wound up, the company is called a company limited by guarantee.

**2. Companies with unlimited liability**

Sec. 12 specifically provides that any 7 or more persons (2 or more in case of a private company) may form an incorporated company, with or without limited liability. A company without limited liability is known as an unlimited company.

### III. Classification on the Basis of Number of Members

From the point of view of the general public and on the basis of number of members, a company may be—

1. a private company, or
2. a public company.

**1. Private company**

A private company is normally what the Americans call a 'close corporation'. According to Sec. 3(1) *(iii)*, a 'private company' means a company which has a minimum paid-up capital of Rs. 1,00,000 or such higher paid-up capital as may be prescribed, and by its Articles—

(*a*) restricts the right to transfer its shares, if any. This restriction is meant to preserve the private character of the company.

(*b*) limits the number of its members to 50 not including its employee-members (present or past).

(*c*) prohibits any invitation to the public to subscribe for any shares in, or debentures of, the company.

(*d*) prohibits any invitation or acceptance of deposits from persons other than its members, directors or their relatives.

**2. Public company :** A public company means a company which—

(*a*) has a minimum paid-up capital of Rs. 5 lakh or such high paid-up capital, as may be prescribed:

(*b*) is a private company which is a subsidiary of a company which is not a private company.

Every public company, existing on the commencement of the Companies (Amendment) Act, 2000, with a paid-up of less than Rs. 5, 00,000 shall, within a period of two years from such commencement, enhance its paid-up capital to Rs. 5,00,000.

**IV. Classification on the Basis of Control**

On the basis of control, companies may be classified into :

1. Holding companies, and
2. Subsidiary companies (Sec. 4).

**1. Holding company [Sec. 4(4)]**

A company is known as the holding company of another company if it has control over that other company. According to Sec. 4(4), a company is "deemed to be the holding company of another if, but only if, that other is its subsidiary". Now the question is : What is a subsidiary company?

**2. Subsidiary company [Sec. 4(1)]**

A company is known as a subsidiary of another company when control is exercised by the latter (called holding company) over the former called a subsidiary company. According to Sec. 4(1), a company (say, company 5) is deemed to be a subsidiary of another company (say, Company H) in the following cases :

**(a)** *Company controlling composition of Board of directors* : Where a company (Company H) controls the composition of Board of directors of another company (Company S), the latter (Company S) becomes the subsidiary of the former (Company H). For this purpose the composition of Company S's Board of directors is deemed to be controlled by Company H if Company H can appoint or remove all or a majority of directors of Company S.

**(b)** *Holding of majority of shares* : Where a company (Company H) holds more than half in nominal value of equity share capital of another company (Company S), the latter (Company S) becomes the subsidiary of the former (Company H). The words '*nominal value of equity capital*' in Sec. 4 means the face value of the equity capital which has been subscribed for.

**(c)** *Subsidiary of another subsidiary* : Where a company (Company S) is subsidiary of another company (say Company $H_1$) which is itself subsidiary of the controlling company (Company H), the former (Company S) becomes the subsidiary of the controlling company (Company H).

**V. Classification on the Basis of Ownership**

On the basis of ownership, a company may be a—

1. Government company, or
2. Non-Government company.

The latter is controlled and operated by private capital.

**Government company**

A Government company means any company in which not less than 51 per cent of the paid-up share capital is held by

*(a)* the Central Government, or

*(b)* any State Government or Governments, or

*(c)* partly by the Central Government and partly by one or more State Governments. For example, State Trading Corporation of India Ltd. and Minerals and Metals Trading Corporation fo India Ltd. are Government companies. The subsideary of a Government company is also a Government company (Sec. 617).

**Foreign Company**

It means any company incorporated outside India which has an established place of business in India [Sec. 591(1)]. Where, for example, representatives of a foreign company frequently come and stay in a hotel in India for purchasing raw material, machinery, cotton etc., the foreign company has a place of business in India.

Where a minimum of 50 per cent of the paid-up share capital (whether equity or preference or partly equity and partly preference) of a foreign company is held by one or more citizens of India or/and by one or more bodies corporate incorporated in India, whether singly or jointly, such company shall comply with such provisions as may be prescribed as if it were an Indian company [Sec. 591 (2)].

### One-Man Company

This is a company (usually private) in which one man holds practically the whole of the share capital of the company, and in order to meet the statutory requirement of minimum number of members, some dummy members who are mostly his relations or friends, hold just 1 or 2 shares each. The dummy members are usually nominees of the principal shareholder who is the virtual owner of the business and who carries it on with limited liability.

## INCORPORATION OF COMPANY

### Mode of forming incorporated company (Sec. 12)

Any 7 or more persons (2 or more in case of a private company) associated for any lawful purpose may form an incorporated company, with or without limited liability. They shall *subscribe their names* to a Memorandum of Association and also comply with other formalities in respect of registration. A company so formed may be:

1. a company limited by shares, or
2. a company limited by guarantee, or
3. an unlimited company.

Companies limited by shares are the most popular and in the rest of this Chapter, we shall be chiefly concerned with them.

### Documents to be filed with the Registrar

Before a company is registered, it is desirable to ascertain from the Registrar of Companies (for the State in which the registered office of the company is to be situate) if the proposed name of the company is approved. Then the following documents duly stamped together with the necessary fees are to be filed with the Registrar :

1. *The Memorandum of Association* duly signed by the subscribers.
2. The *Articles of Association*, if any, signed by the subscribers to the Memorandum of Association. A public company limited by shares need not have its own Articles of Association. It may instead adopt Table A in Schedule I to the Act.
3. The *agreement*, if any, which the company proposes to enter into with any individual for appointment as its managing or whole-time director or manager [Sec. 33(1)].
4. A *list of the directors* who have agreed to become the first directors of the company (this applies to a public company limited by shares) and their written consent to act as directors and take up qualification shares (Sec. 266).
5. A *declaration* stating that all the requirements of the Companies Act and other formalities relating to registration have been complied with. Such declaration shall be signed by any of the following persons : *viz.*
   *(a)* an Advocate of the Supreme Court or of a High Court; or
   *(b)* an attorney or a pleader entitled to appear before a High Court; or
   *(c)* a secretary or a chartered a accountant in whole-time practice in India, who is engaged in the formation of the company; or
   *(d)* a person named in the Articles as a director, manager or secretary of the company [Sec. 33(2)].

Then within 30 days of the date of incorporation of the company, a notice of the situation of the registered office of the company shall be given to the Registrar who shall record the same (Sec. 146).

### Certificate of Incorporation

When the requisite documents are filed with the Registrar, the Registrar shall satisfy himself that the statutory requirements regarding registration have been duly complied with. In exercising this duty, the Registrar is not required to carry out any investigation. If the Registrar is satisfied as to the compliance of statutory requirements, he retains and registers the Memorandum, the Articles and other documents filed with him and issues a 'certificate of incorporation'. *i.e.,* of the formation of the company [Sec. 33(3)].

By issuing certificate of incorporation the Registrar certifies under his hand that the company is incorporated and in the case of a limited company, that the company is limited (Sec. 34).

## MEMBERS OF A COMPANY

### Members and Shareholders

The 'members' or 'shareholders' of a company are the persons who collectively constitute the company as a corporate entity. The terms 'member' and 'shareholder' and 'holder of a share' are used interchangeably. They are synonymous in the case of a company limited by shares, a company limited by guarantee and having a share capital and an unlimited company whose capital is held in definite shares. But in the case of an unlimited company or a company limited by guarantee, a member may not be a shareholder, for such a company may not have a share capital.

### Who can become a member ?

Any person who is competent to contract (Sec. 11 of the Indian Contract Act, 1872) may become a member of a company. This is subject to the provisions of the Memorandum and the articles of the company. The Articles may provide that certain persons cannot become members of the company.

*Minor*: A minor is not competent to become the member of a company because an agreement with a minor is absolutely void [*Mohiri Bibi* Vs. *Dharamodas Ghose*, (1903) I.L.R. 30 Cal, 539].

### How to become a Member ?

A person may become a member of a company in the following ways:

**1. Membership by subscription :** The subscribers to the Memorandum of Association of a company are deemed to have agreed to become its members. When the company is registered, their names are entered as members in the register of members [Sec. 41 (1)]. Neither application nor allotment of shares is necessary.

**2. Membership by application and registration:** Apart from the subsribers of memorandum, every other person, who *agrees in writing* to become a member and whose name is *entered in the register of members,* is a member of the company [Sec. 41(2)]. A written application for allotment of shares is, therefore, necessary before a person can be entered as a member in the register of members.

Registration of the name of a person as member of a company may result from any one of the following ways:

*(a) By application and allotment* : An application for shares is an offer to take shares; allotment is acceptance of that offer by the company which creates a binding contract between the applicant and the company. The application may be absolute or conditional. If it is absolute, an allotment and its notice is a sufficient acceptance. If it is conditional, the allotment must be according to the terms of the application, otherwise there will be no contract.

*(b) By transfer* : A person may purchase shares in the open market. He becomes a member when the transfer of shares is effected and his name is entered in the register of members.

*(c) By succession* : A deceased member continues to be member of the company so long as his name appears in the register of members. His legal representative who acquires a legal right to shares is entitled to have his name entered in the register of members. The company also has the power to register any person as a shareholder to whom the right to any shares (also debentures) in the company has been transmitted by operation of law (Sec. 108), and in such a case an instrument of transfer is not necessary.

*(d) Agreement to be in writing* : An agreement for becoming a member has to be in *writing*. As such a person cannot be deemed to have become a member by means of acquiescence or estoppel simply because his name is entered in the register of members.

**3. Membership by beneficial wornership :** Every person holding equity share capital of a company and whose name is entered as *beneficial owner* in the records of the depository shall be deemed to be a member of the concerned company [Sec. 41(3)].

**4. Membership by qualification shares :** Before a person can be appointed a director of a public company, he must take, or sign an undertaking to take and pay for, the qualification shares, if any. He thus becomes a member and is in the same position as a subscriber to the Memorandum of the company is (Sec. 266).

## MAINTENANCE OF BOOKS OF ACCOUNT

Section 209 of the Companies Act states that books of account shall be maintained at the company's registered office unless the Board of Directors decide to keep them at another place in India. It is a duty of the company to inform the Registrar of Companies within seven days of the decision in case the Board of Directors decides to maintain books at the place other than the registered office.Where the company has a branch office, whether in or outside India the proper books of accounts relating to the transactions effected at the branch office are kept at that office and proper summarised returns made up to date at intervals of not more than three months are prepared and sent within reasonable time to head office.

Every company is required to keep proper books of account showing (i) all monies received and spent and the details thereof, (ii) sales and purchases of goods, and (iii) assets and liabilities. A company engaged in production, processing, manufacturing or mining activities has also to maintain, if required by the Central Government, cost accounting records *i.e.*,particulars relating to utilisation of material, labour and other items of costs.

Proper books of accounts shall not be deemed to be kept if there are not kept such books as are necessary to give a *true and fair view* of the state of affairs of the company or branch office, as the case may be, and to explain its transactions. Also if such books are not kept on *accrual basis* and according to system of double entry book keeping, proper books of accounts shall not be deemed to have been kept.

## STATUTORY BOOKS

The following statutory books are required to be maintained by a company under different sections of the Companies Act :

- Register of Investments of the company not held in its own name (Section 49).
- Register of Mortgages and Charges (Section 143).
- Register of Members and Index (Sections 150 & 151).
- Register of Debenture-holders and Index (Section 152).
- Foreign Register of Members and of Debenture-holders and their duplicates (Sections 157 and 158).
- Minute Books (Section 193).
- Register of Contracts, Companies, and firms in which directors are interested (Section 301).
- Register of directors, managing director, manager and secretary (Section 303).
- Register of Directors. share-holding (Section 307).
- Register of investments in securities of any other body corporate, loans made, guarantees given or securities provided to any body corporate.

In addition, a company usually maintains a number of statistical books to keep a record of its transactions which have resulted either in the payment of money to it or constitute the basis on which certain payments have been made by it. Registers and documents relating to the issue of shares are :

(i) Share Application and Allotment Book ;

(ii) Share Call Book ; and

(iii) Certificate Book.

In respect of shares, the company, in addition to maintain Register of Members, which it has to maintain statutorily, it also maintains (*a*) Share Transfer Book ; and (*b*) Dividend Register.

## FINAL ACCOUNTS

Under Section 210 of the Companies Act, at the annual general meeting of a company, the Board of Directors of the company shall lay before the company:

(a) a balance sheet as at the end of the period;

(b) a profit & loss account for that period.

In case of a company not carrying on business for profit, an income and expenditure account shall be laid before the company at its annual general meeting instead of profit and loss account.Every balance-sheet of the company shall give a true and fair view of the state of affairs of the company as at the end of the financial year and shall subject to the provisions of the section be in the Form set out in Part I of Schedule VI, or as near thereto as circumstances admit. Any insurance or banking company or any company engaged in generation or supply of electricity or any other class of company for which a Form of balance sheet has been prescribed under the Act governing such class of company need not follow such form (Section 211). Every Profit and Loss Account of a company shall also give a true and fair view of profit or loss of the company for the financial year and shall comply with the requirements of Part II of Schedule VI. Every insurance or banking company or any company engaged in the generation of electricity or any other class of company for which a Form of Profit and Loss Account has been specified under the Act governing such class of company need not follow the Form given in the Schedule VI to this Act.

While preparing the final accounts of a company the following should be kept in mind :

* Requirements of Schedule VI;

* Other statutory requirements;

* Accounting Standards issued by the Institute of Chartered Accountants of India on different accounting matters (AS-1 to AS-32);

* Statements and Guidance Notes issued by the Institute of Chartered Accountants of India;

Recently, the Companies (Amendment) Act, 1999 which shall be deemed to have come into force on 31st day of October, 1998, has made the compliance of accounting standards mandatory by adding Sub-sections 3A, 3B and 3C in Section 211.These are :

**(*3A*) :** Every profit and loss account and balance sheet of the company shall comply with the accounting standards.

**(*3B*) :** Where the profit and loss account and the balance sheet of the company do not comply with the accounting standards, such companies shall disclose in its profit and loss account and balance sheet, the following, namely :

(a) the deviation from the accounting standards;

(b) the reasons for such deviation; and

(c) the financial effect, if any, arising due to such deviation.

**(*3C*) :** For the purposes of this section, the expression .accounting standards. means the standards of accounting recommended by the Institute of Chartered Accountants of India constituted under the Chartered Accountants Act, 1949, as may be prescribed by the Central Government in consultation with the National Advisory Committee on Accounting Standards established under Sub-section (*1*) of Section 210A :Provided that the standard of accounting specified by the Institute of Chartered Accountants of India shall be deemed to be the Accounting Standards until the Accounting Standards are prescribed by the Central Government under this sub-section..

The balance sheet can be prepared either in Horizontal Form or in Vertical Form. However, there is no specified Form of Profit and Loss Account. Schedule VI - Part II gives only

**(i)** As regards Loans and Advances, [the amount due from other companies under the same management within the meaning of sub-section (1B) of section 370 should also be given with the names of the companies] the maximum amount due from every one of these at any time during the year must be shown.

**(j)** Particulars of any redeemed debentures which the company has power to issue should be given.

**(k)** Where any of the company's debentures are held by a nominee or a trustee for the company, the nominal amount of the debentures and the amount at which they are stated in the books of the company shall be stated.

**(l)** A statement of investments [whether shown under Investment or under Current Assets, as stock-in-trade] separately classifying trade investments and other investments should be annexed to the balance sheet, showing the names of the bodies corporate (indicating separately the names of the bodies corporate under the same management) in whose shares or debentures, investments have been made (including all investments, whether existing or not, made subsequent to the date as at which the previous balance sheet was made out) and the nature and extent of the investment so made in each such body corporate;

provided that in the case of an investment company,that is to say, a company whose principal business is the acquisition of shares, stock, debentures or other securities, it shall be sufficient if the statement shows only the investments existing on the date as at which the balance sheet has been made out. In regard to the investments in the capital of partnership firms, the names of the firms (with the names of all their partners, total capital and the shares of each partner), shall be given in the statement.

**(m)** If, in the opinion of the Board, any of the current assets, loans and advances have not a value on realisation in the ordinary course of business at least equal to the amount at which they are stated, the fact that the Board is of that opinion shall be stated.

**(n)** Except in the case of the first balance sheet laid before the company after the commencement of the Act, the corresponding amounts for the immediately preceding financial year for all items shown in the balance sheet shall be also given in the balance sheet. The requirement in this behalf shall, in the case of companies preparing quarterly or half-yearly accounts, etc., relate to the balance sheet for the corresponding date in the previous year.

**(o)** The amounts to be shown under Sundry Debtors shall include the amounts due in respect of goods sold or services rendered or in respect of other contractual obligations but shall not include the amounts which are in the nature of loans or advances.

**(p)** Current accounts with directors, and manager, whether they are in credit, or debit, shall be shown separately.

**Sources of Finance**

The company raises its finance through internal and external sources.

*Internal Sources*

It includes:

a) Share capital

b) Undistributed profits of the companies.

*External Sources*

It includes:

a) Issue of Debentures

b) Accepting Deposits from the public

c) Loans from Commercial Banks

d) Loans from Financial Institutions - such as, Industrial Finance Corporation, State Finance Corporation, Industrial Development Bank of India, Industrial Credit and Investment Corporation of India etc.

**Share capital of a company**

Part I Schedule VI of the Companies Act 1956 deals with this aspect. Every business is expected to have a capital. Generally 'capital' means a particular amount of money used in the business for the purpose of earning revenue. In the context of the Company Law, the capital may be:

**Nominal or Authorised Capital**

This is the maximum amount of capital which a company is authorised to raise and is stated in the Memorandum of Association. It can also be called as **'Registered Capital'**.***For example :*** A Ltd has been incorporated with an Authorised Capital of Rs.10,00,000 divided into 1,00,000 shares of Rs.10 each.

**Issued Capital**

This represents part of the authorised capital, which is issued to public for subscription, say 60,000 shares of Rs.10 each.The difference between the authorised capital and the issued capital represents **unissued capital**. This can be offered to the public at a later date.

**Subscribed capital**

This refers to that part of the issued capital which has been subscribed by the public, say 50,000 shares of Rs.10/- each.

**Unsubscribed Capital**

The difference between the issued capital and subscribed capital represents unsubscribed capital, say 10,000 shares of Rs.10/- each in the above example.

**Called-up Capital**

This refers to that part of the subscribed capital which has been called up by the company for payment. ***For example:*** If 50,000 shares of Rs.10/- each have been subscribed by the public of which Rs.5/-

per share has been called up, then the subscribed capital of the company is Rs 5,00,000, of which the called up capital is Rs.2,50,000 ( Rs.5 x 50,000).

**Uncalled capital**

The difference between subscribed and called up capital is called **uncalled capital**. Taking the previous example, uncalled capital would be Rs.2,50,000 (Rs.5 x 50000).***For example:*** If 50,000 shares of Rs.10/- each have been subscribed by the public of which Rs.5/- per share has been called up, then the subscribed capital of the company is Rs 5,00,000, of which the called up capital is Rs.2,50,000 ( Rs.5 x 50,000).

**Uncalled capital**

The difference between subscribed and called up capital is called **uncalled capital**. Taking the previous example, uncalled capital would be Rs.2,50,000 (Rs.5 x 50000).

**Paid up capital**

This refers to that part of the called-up capital, which has been actually paid up by the shareholders. Some of the shareholders might have defaulted in paying a part of the called-up money. Such amount defaulted is known as **calls-in-arrears**.In other words the difference between called-up capital and paid up capital is known as calls-in-arrears.***For example***, one shareholder holding 500 shares failed to pay the call @ Rs.2 per share, then paid up capital is Rs.2,49,000, and calls-in-arrears is Rs.1000.

**Reserve Capital**

A company can reserve part of its uncalled capital to be called up only at the time of winding up. A special resolution has to be passed for that purpose. This is called Reserve Capital. It is not disclosed in the companies balance sheet.

**Shares**

The capital of the company is divided into units of small denomination. These units are called **shares**. Sec. 2(46) of the Companies Act explains the meaning of share as a share in the share capital of a company. Holders of shares are called **shareholders**.***For example :*** If the authorised capital Rs.10,00,000 is divided into 1,00,000 units of Rs.10 each, then each unit of Rs.10 is called a share of Rs.10 each. Thus, in the above case, the company is said to have 1,00,000 shares of Rs.10 each.Shares must be numbered so that they may be identified. They are transferable in the manner provided by the Articles of Association.

**Types of Shares**

According to the Companies (Amendment) Act, 2000, the share capital of a company limited by share, shall be of two kinds only namely:

I. Preference Shares and

II. Equity Shares

**I. Preference Shares**

The Companies Act, 1956, Sec. 85 deals with preference shares.Preference shares are those which satisfy the following two conditions.

1. The right to receive dividend at a specified rate before any dividend is paid.
2. Right to return of capital in case of winding up before the capital of equity share holders is returned.

**From the point of view of dividend payment**

**Cumulative Preference Shares:** Holders of these shares have the right to receive arrears of dividend out of the subsequent years' profit.

**Non cumulative Preference Shares:** In this case, arrears of dividend are not paid.

From the point of view of redemption

**Redeemable Preference Shares:** These shares are redeemed or repaid in accordance with the terms of issue after a specified period.In India, companies can now issue only this category of preference shares.

**Irredeemable Preference Shares:** These are shares, which cannot be refunded before winding-up (Now all preference shares must be redeemable)

From the point of view of participating in profits

**Participating Preference Shares:** The holders of this class of preference shares have the right to share profits remaining after the payment of dividend to the equity shareholders. They also enjoy the right to participate in the surplus remaining after the repayment of capital of equity shareholders in case of winding-up of the company.

**Non Participating Shares:** It is as good as ordinary preference shares, which carry only fixed rate of dividend.

**From the point of view of convertibility**

**Convertible Preference Shares:** These are shares, which can be converted into an equity shares.

**Non-Convertible Preference Shares:** Shares which cannot be converted into equity shares, is called a non-convertible preference share. Unless the Articles or terms of issue provide preference shares are deemed to be non-convertible.

**II. Equity Shares**

Shares which are not preference shares are called **Equity Shares**.In other words, equity shares are those which are entitled to dividend and repayment of capital after the preference share holders are paid. The rate of dividend is decided by the Board of Directors. Normally,equity shareholders control the affairs of the business.

**Issue of Shares**

The shares of the company can be issued in two ways;

1) for consideration other than cash and

2) for cash

For consideration other than cash:

Some times the company agrees to pay the vendors from whom it has bought assets like land and building, etc., fully paid up shares of the company instead of giving cash for the same.

**Issue of Shares for cash**

The procedure of issuing shares for cash is given below:

**1. Issue of Prospectus**

When shares are issued to public for cash it should satisfy the provisions of the Companies Act and the Securities Exchange Board of India (SEBI) guidelines. Every public issue must be accompanied by an issue of prospectus. The terms and conditions of the issue of shares are stated in the prospectus. On reading the prospectus, the public will have to apply for the shares in the prescribed form.

**2. Receipt of application money**

Whenever a public company issues shares, advertisements appear in the leading newspapers about the issue. Those who are interested in purchasing the shares may get an application form along with a copy of the prospectus. If he is satisfied with the information available in the prospectus, he remits the application money along with the filled-in application form to any one of the banks (branches) mentioned in the application. The applicant is required to remit at least 5% of the nominal value of the share with the application as application money (Sec 69(3)). However, as per the SEBI guidelines, the minimum application should be 25% of its issue price. The accounting entry passed to record the same is

Bank (Cash) A/c Dr. [Total amount received on application ]

To Share Application A/c

(Amount received on application on ——— shares @ Rs —— per share)

The banker will send the application money to the company along with a list of applicants. The public issue must be kept open for at least three working days and not more than ten working days. The issue price of shares may be received in one instalment or in different instalments.

**Journal Entries:** There are two types of journal entries connected with issue of shares. They are called **cash entries** and **transfer entries**. Cash entries involve the receipt of various instalments of the share. Transfer entries relate to transfer of these amounts to share capital. In case of share application, cash entry is made first followed by transfer entry. But in case of allotment and calls the transfer entry is passed first, then on receiving cash, cash entry is passed. This is because immediately allotment or call is made, money becomes due and therefore share capital is credited without waiting for the receipt of cash.

**3. Allotment of Shares**

While application is an offer to buy shares, allotment of shares by the company constitutes an acceptance of such offer. If the company does not receive the minimum subscription (is the least amount of shares which should be subscribed for by the public before the Directors can proceed to allotment) of 90% of the issued amount, the company has to refund the entire subscription. Once the shares are allotted, the applicants now get the status of shareholders or members of the company.

**Transfer of Application money**

On the date of allotment the company considers the application money on those shares which are allotted as a part of the share capital.Therefore the application money has to be transferred to share capital account. The accounting entry passed to record the same is:

Share Application A/c Dr [No. of shares allotted x Application money per share]

To Share Capital A/c

(Application money on —— shares transferred to Share capital)

**Amount Due on Allotment**

As soon as shares are allotted, the shareholders are liable to pay the allotment money, which is due. The accounting entry passed to record the same is:

Share Allotment A/c Dr [No. of shares allotted x Allotment amount per share]

To Share Capital A/c

(Amount due on the allotment of — shares @ Rs.— per share)

**Receipt of Allotment money**

On receipt of allotment money, the following entry is made:

Bank A/c Dr

To Share Allotment A/c

(Allotment money received)

**4. Call on Shares**

If the shares are not fully called up after allotment the Directors have the right to call the remaining amount. Call is an instalment due on shares. A call letter will be generally issued to every shareholder. The maximum number of calls that a company can make is three. There should be at least one month gap between two calls unless otherwise provided by the Articles of Association of the company.

**Terms of Issue:**

Shares of a company may be issued in any of the following three ways;

(*a*) Issue of shares at par

(*b*) Issue of shares at premium and

(*c*) Issue of shares at discount

The accounting treatment of issue of shares in case of each of the above is different. We shall now discuss these three situations in detail.

**(*a*) Issue of shares at par**

If the issue price is equal to the face value, it is said to be issued at par. For example when shares of Rs 10 each (face value) are issued at Rs 10 only.

**Under-subscription**

Due to poor response, all the shares offered may not be taken by the public. This is under-subscription. However the shares cannot be allotted if the minimum subscription is not received. Under-subscription does not require any special treatment. Journal entries are made on the basis of shares applied for.

**Over-subscription**

When the applications received are more than that has been issued to the public, it is called as over-subscription. A company cannot allot more shares than that were offered to public through the prospectus.When there is over subscription the allotment must follow SEBI guidelines to ensure proportional (Pro-rata) allotment.When there is over - subscription the directors have three alternatives to deal with the situation.

1. Some applicants may not be allotted any shares – **rejection of shares**.
2. Some applicants may be allotted less number of shares than they applied for – **prorata allotment.**
3. Some applicants may be allotted full number of shares they applied for – **full allotment.**

**Calls- in- Arrears**

Sometimes shareholders may fail to pay the amount due on calls.The total amount not received on the calls by the company are called as **Calls-in-Arrears**. This amount is shown as a deduction from the called up capital to arrive the paid up share capital in the Balance Sheet.

**Calls-in-Advance**

When an applicant sends more money than what is called by the company, the excess money is called **Calls-in-Advance**.According to Section 92 calls-in-advance can be accepted only when a company is so authorised by its Articles.

**(b) Issue of shares at premium**

When a company issues its shares at a price more than the face value, it is said to be issued at premium. Premium is the excess money collected over and above the face value of the share. When share of Rs.10 (face value) are issued at Rs.12, it is said to be issued at a premium of Rs.2.When shares are issued at premium, the amount of premium shall be credited to a separate account called as **'Securities Premium Account'** 1. It is not a part of the share capital. It is shown separately in the Balance sheet under the heading **'Reserves and Surplus'**. Under Sec. 78 the amount to the credit of the securities premium account may be used for the following purposes:

1. issue of fully paid bonus shares
2. writing off the preliminary expenses
3. writing off expenses like commission paid or discount allowed on shares / debentures and
4. for the premium payable on redemption of preference shares / debentures.

The amount of premium can be collected with the application money or with the allotment money. **But normally it is collected with the allotment money only.**

**(*c*) Issue of Shares at Discount**

When a company issues its shares at a price less than the face value, it is said to be issued at discount. Discount is the difference between the face value and the issue price. For example a share of Rs.10 (face value) is issued at Rs 9, it is said that shares are issued at discount of Re.1.A company can issue shares at a discount only when the following conditions are satisfied (Sec. 79).

(*a*) Issue of shares at discount is authorised by an ordinary resolution passed by the company in its general body meeting and sanctioned by Company Law Board.

(*b*) The shares must belong to a class already issued.

(*c*) The maximum amount of discount can not exceed 10%, however, if the Company Law Board is convinced the shares can be issued at a higher discount rate.

(*d*) The company has to be in existence at least for one year.Whenever shares are issued at a discount the amount of discount is brought into account with the instalment due on allotment.

The shares will appear at the full face value on the liability side of the Balance Sheet. The amount of discount on issue of shares being loss of capital nature shown on the asset side and written off against the Profit and Loss account over a period of time. The amount of discount not yet written off will appear in the asset side of the Balance Sheet under the heading **'Miscellaneous Expenditure'**.

**Forfeiture of Shares**

Sometimes a shareholder may fail to pay any of the instalments i.e allotment or call money. In such a situation after giving due notice and following the procedures laid down in the Articles of Association, the Directors of the company can forfeit the shares that were already issued.Forfeiture of shares means to cancel the allotment to the defaulting shareholder. Once the shares are forfeited, these shares will not form part of the share capital and the shareholders will not be the members of the company.

**Forfeiture of shares – issued at Par**

The effect of forfeiture is to cancel the allotment given to the shareholder. So, all entries passed earlier must be reversed now.It should be noted that share capital is debited with the amount called up till the stage of forfeiture and not the nominal value of shares.The balance in the share forfeited account is shown as an addition to the total paid-up capital of the company under the heading 'Share Capital' on the liability side of the Balance Sheet.

**Forfeiture of shares – issued at Premium**

**1. When premium is received :** When shares originally issued at premium, on which premium amount has been received are forfeited, then the premium once collected cannot be cancelled (Sec.78).

**2. When premium is not received:** When shares originally issued at a premium on which the premium amount has not yet been received are forfeited, Securities Premium account has to be debited now.

**Forfeiture of shares – issued at Discount**

When shares originally issued at discount are forfeited then discount on shares account should be cancelled. This can be done by crediting discount on shares account.

**Reissue of forfeited shares**

The Directors of a company have the right to reissue the shares that were forfeited by them already as and when they find it suitable and convenient. In this connection the following points need to be noted.

**Reissue Price:** Forfeited shares can be reissued at any price the company prefers. But the reissue price plus amount already collected from the defaulting member should not be less than the amount credited as paid up on reissue of shares.

***When shares are fully paid:*** If a share of Rs.10 (face value) on which Rs.3 has been already been collected is now forfeited then the minimum reissue price should be Rs.7 (Rs.10 – Rs.3).

***When shares are partly paid:*** In the above example if the company has called only Rs.8 then the minimum reissue price should be Rs.5 (Rs.8 – Rs.3).

**Forfeited shares account:** The discount on reissue (paid-up value – reissue price) of forfeited shares is debited to 'Forfeited shares account'.

**Capital Reserve:** The balance if any in the forfeited share account is a capital profit and will be transferred to 'Capital reserve account'.

**Reissue of shares issued at Premium:** When shares previously issued at a premium on which premium has been already received fully, share premium need not be recorded again on reissue of shares.

**Reissue of shares issued at Discount:** When shares previously issued at discount are reissued after forfeiture the discount should be brought into account.

**Partial Reissue :** When all forfeited shares are not reissued then only profit made on such reissued shares is transferred to capital reserve. The amount relating to that part of shares that are not reissued will remain in the shares forfeited account which will be transferred to the liability side of the Balance Sheet.

**DEBENTURES**

The most common method of supplementing the capital available to a company is to issue debentures which may either be simple or naked carrying no charge on assets, or mortgage debentures carrying either a fixed or a floating charge on some or all of the assets of the company. A debenture is a bond issued by a company under its seal, acknowledging a debt and containing provisions as regards repayment of the principal and interest. If a charge has been created on any or the entire asset of the company, the nature of the charge and the assets charged are described therein. Since the charge is not valid unless registered with the Registrar, his certificate registering the charge is printed on the bond. It is also customary to create a trusteeship in favour of one or more persons in the case of mortgage debentures. The trustees of debenture holders have all powers of a mortgage of a property and can act in whatever way they think necessary to safeguard the interest of debenture holders.

Debentures are usually redeemable, but a company may also issue irredeemable debentures. Redeemable debentures may be redeemed after a fixed number of years or any time after a certain number of years has elapsed since their issue, on giving a specified notice, or by annual drawing. A company may also purchase its debentures, as and when convenient in the open market and when debentures are quoted at a discount on the Stock Exchange, it may be profitable for the company to purchase and cancel them or, when it is desired, to keep the debentures alive with a view of issuing them again at a later date. Usually, according to the conditions of the issue, the company is required to create a sinking fund described as Debenture Redemption Reserve Fund, by appropriating annually a certain percentage of, or a fixed sum out of, its profit to its credit and investing the amount thereof either in the purchase of securities which are readily saleable or taking out a policy that shall mature at the time the debentures will fall due for payment. Such an arrangement would ensure that the company will have sufficient liquid funds for the redemption of debentures at the time they shall fall due for payment.

Usually, the balance to the credit of Debenture Redemption Fund, after adjusting therein the amount of appreciation and depreciation of investments on their sale, is either more or less as compared to the amount of debentures which are proposed to be redeemed. If it is in excess, the amount is transferred to the Capital Reserve, on the assumption that it is a capital profit received on the appreciation in the value of investments or settlement of liability for a lesser amount that what was usually payable. On the other hand, if it is short, the deficit is made up by the transfer from Profit and Loss Account. The balance in the account, equal to the amount of debentures redeemed is subsequently transferred to General Reserve.

Debentures sometimes are redeemable at a premium. In such a case, the appropriation to the Redemption Reserve Fund should be sufficient to pay both the amount of debentures and the premium on redemption. If no sinking fund is created a provision for the premium payable for the same should be made out of profit over the period of debentures.When the company decides to establish the sinking fund at the end of the first year, the amount indicated by the sinking funds tables is credited to the sinking fund account and debited to profit and loss account in the appropriation section. That shows the intention of the company to set aside regular sums of money to build up a fund for redeeming debentures. Immediately, the company should also purchase outside investments. The entry for the purpose naturally will be to debit sinking fund investments and credit bank. It is sometimes thought that since Government securities or individual debentures are available in multiples of Rs. 100 the investments should be made to the nearest of Rs. 100. This may be true in the case of a new issue otherwise, if securities are purchased from the market, it is possible generally to invest any sum of money that may be desired.In the subsequent years, when interest is received on investments, the bank account will be debited and interest on sinking fund investments account will be credited. The balance in the latter account will be transferred to the sinking fund account; the annual installment will be debited to the profit and loss appropriation account and credited to the sinking fund account.The investments every year will be of an amount equal to the annual installment plus the interest which may have been received in the year concerned. Thus, the sinking fund will go on accumulating each year. [ Note : Infact, a notional entry of transfer of interest (and also profit or loss on realisation of sinking fund investments) to the profit and loss account and then again to sinking fund will meet strict requirement of law and AS 13 as well.]

From the accounting point of view, the purchase of debentures involves two problems first, adjustment of the premium or discount, if any paid on their purchase and second, adjustment of interest payable on them. Where a sinking fund is kept the amount of premium or discount is adjusted therein on cancellation so that at the date of redemption, the balance of the Debenture Investments Account, is equal to the Debenture Account. But, if there is none, Debenture Investments are treated like other investments.

As regards interest, where there is a sinking fund, the interest on debentures held as an investment made out of the fund is credited to the sinking fund in exactly the same way as the debentures are outside investments. But where there is no sinking fund, since the adjustment of interest on debentures held as investments would merely involve crediting and debiting the Profit and Loss Account by the same amount, often it is not made. However, on their purchase or cancellation an amount equal to the nominal value of debentures is transferred to General Reserve from the Profit & Loss Account on the consideration that to such an extent the profits will not be available for distribution.

If the debentures are purchased within the interest period, the price would be inclusive of interest provided these are purchased cum interest; but if purchased 'ex Interest' the interest to the date of purchase would be payable to the seller in addition. In order to adjust the effect thereof the amount of interest accrued till the date of purchase, if paid, is debited to the Interest Account against which the interest for the whole period will be credited. Thus, in result, a balance in the Account would be left, equal to the interest for the period the debentures were held by the company.

**Some Important Facts**

***(i)*** Profit or loss on redemption of debenture arises only on sale or cancellation; if debentures are purchased but not cancelled the total amount paid (minus the interest to the date of purchase) should be debited to Own Debentures Account and shown as investment in the Balance Sheet. On cancellation, the account will be credited and Debenture Account debited: the difference between the nominal value of the debentures cancelled and the amount standing to the debit on Own Debentures Account will be profit or loss on redemption of debentures.

***(ii)*** If debentures are straightway cancelled on purchase, the profit or loss on redemption of debentures will be ascertained by comparing (*a*) the nominal value of debentures cancelled, and (*b*) the price paid less interest to the date of purchase (if the transaction is cum-interest).

***(iii)*** In case the transaction is ex-interest, the interest to the date of transaction will be paid in addition to the settled price and hence profit on redemption will be nominal value minus the settled price.

**BUY BACK OF SECURITIES**

The Companies (Amendment) Act, 1999 has introduced Section 77A in the Companies Act,1956, permitting companies to buyback their own shares and other securities. A company may now, purchase its own shares or other specified securities out of -

*(i)* its free reserves; or

*(ii)* the securities premium account; or

*(iii)* the proceeds of any shares or other specified securities.

**PROVISIONS OF SECTION 77B OF COMPANIES ACT**

*As per Section 77B :*

(1) No company shall directly or indirectly purchase its own shares or other specified securities.

(*a*) through any subsidiary company including its own subsidiary companies; or

(*b*) through any investment company or group of investment companies; or

(*c*) if a default, by the company, in repayment of deposit or interest payable thereon, redemption of debentures or preference shares or payment of dividend to any shareholder or repayment of any term loan or interest payable thereon to any financial institutions or bank, is subsisting.

(2) No company shall directly or indirectly purchase its own shares or other specified securities in case such company has not complied with provisions of Sections 159, 207 and 211.

**CASH FLOW STATEMENTS**

Accounting Standard 3, Cash Flow Statements, was issued in March, 2004. This revised Accounting Standard super seeded the Accounting Standard (AS 3) on changes in Financial Position, issued in June 1981.Cash flow statement provides information about the changes in cash and cash equivalents of an enterprise. Cash flow statement is based on cash concept of profit. Cash flow statement seems to be useful because it identifies cash generated from trading operations, the operating cash surplus which can be applied for investment in fixed assets. In fact a portion of cash from operations is used to pay dividend and tax and the other portion is ploughed back. What can be ploughed back is directly identifiable from cash flow statement. In projected form, this statement is a very useful tool of planning.Cash flow statements are prepared to explain the cash movements between two points of time.

**Sources of Cash:**

1. Issue of shares and debentures and raising long-term loan.

2. Sale of investments and other fixed assets.
3. Cash from operations.
4. Decrease in Cash.

**Applications of Cash:**

1. Redemption of preference shares and debentures and repayment of long-term loan.
2. Purchase of investments and other fixed assets.
3. Payment of tax.
4. Payment of dividend.
5. Increase in cash.

Increase in cash or decrease in cash is put in the applications and the sources respectively just to balance the cash flow statement. At this juncture students may note that in cash flow statement changes in all balance sheet items are to be taken into consideration separately for explaining movement of cash.

## ELEMENTS OF CASH FUND

As per AS 3, issued by the Council of the ICAI, Cash Funds include:

(i) Cash in hand,

(ii) Demand deposits with banks, and

(iii) Cash equivalents.

Cash equivalents which are considered as part of funds for calculation of cash flows are defined as .short term highly liquid investments that are readily convertible into known amounts of cash and which are subject to an insignificant risk of changes in value.. Basic objective of acquisition of cash equivalents is to deploy, for a short period, idle cash required to meet short-term cash-commitments. Securities with short maturity period of, say, three months or less from the date of acquisition qualify as a cash equivalent. Examples are: acquisition of preference shares, shortly before their specified redemption date, bank deposits with short maturity period, etc. Thus, cash flow statement deals with flow of cash funds but does not consider the movements among cash, bank balance payable on demand and investment of excess cash in cash equivalents. Examples are cash withdrawn from current account, cash deposited in bank for 60 days, etc.

## CLASSIFICATION OF CASH FLOW ACTIVITIES

Transactions, which increase cash, are classified as cash inflow and transactions which decrease cash are classified as cash outflow. Thus, cash flow statement provides explanation for changes in cash position of the business entity. Accounting Standard issued by the Institute of Chartered Accountants of India require that the cash flow statement should report cash flows during the period classified by operating, investing and financing activities:

**Operating Activities:** These are the principal revenue producing activities of the enterprise. Net impact of operating activities on flow of cash is reported as .Cash flows from operating activities or cash from operation. The amount of cash flows from operating activities is a key indicator of the extent to which the operations of the enterprises have generated sufficient cash flows to maintain the operating capability of the enterprise, pay dividends, repay loans, and make new investments without recourse to external sources of financing. It provides useful information about internal financing. Information about the specific components of historical operating cash flows is useful, in conjunction with other information, in forecasting future operating cash flows.

**Investing activities:** These are the acquisition and disposal of long-term assets and other investments not included in cash equivalents. The separate disclosure of cash flows arising from investing activities is important because the cash flows represent the extent to which the expenditures have been made for resources intended to generate future incomes and cash flows.

**Financing activities:** These are the activities that result in changes in the size and composition of the owner's capital (including preference share capital) and borrowings of the enterprise. The separate disclosure of cash flows arising from financing activities is important because it is useful in predicting claims on future cash flows by providers of funds (both capital and borrowings) to the enterprise.

# OBJECTIVE TYPE QUESTIONS

**1.** In setting the accounts of a firm after its dissolution the assets of the firm shall be applied first in paying
(a) Each partner proportionately what is due to him on account of loans advanced by him
(b) Each partner proportionately what is due to him on account of capital
(c) Each partner proportionately what is due to him on account of past profits
(d) The debts of the firm to third parties

**2.** Capital employed in a business is Rs. 1,50,000, profits are Rs. 50,000 and the normal rate of profit is 20%. The amount of goodwill as per capitalisation method would be
(a) Rs. 1,00,000 (b) Rs. 1,50,000
(c) Rs. 2,00,000 (d) Rs. 3,00,000

**3.** 'A' and 'B' are sharing profits and losses in the ratio of 4 : 1 'C' is admitted as a new partner for 1/3rd share of profits for which he pays Rs. 30,000 as goodwill. If 'A' and 'B' agree to share future profits equally, then the amount of goodwill to be credited to 'A' would be
(a) Rs. 30,000 (b) Rs. 90,000
(c) Rs. 48,000 (d) Rs. 42,000

**4. Assertion (A) :** Share premium amount can be refunded in cash to equity share holders

**Reason (R) :** Share premium is usually collected when the market price of the shares is higher than the face value of the share

*In the context of the above two statements, which one of the following is correct?*
(a) Both A and R are true, but R is the correct explanation of A
(b) Both A and R are true, but R is NOT correct explanation of A
(c) A is true, but R is false
(d) A is false, but R is true

**5.** Match List I with List II and select the correct answer from the codes given bolow the lists :

| List I (Item) | List II (Nature of Item) |
|---|---|
| I. Cash | A. Share holder's equity |
| II. Profits | B. Fixed assets |
| III. Discount on issue of shares | C. Current assets |
| IV. Plant and machinery | D. Fictitious assets |
| | E. Intangible assets |

***Codes :***
(a) I-B, II-E, III-A, IV-C
(b) I-C, II-A, III-D, IV-B
(c) I-C, II-D, III-D, IV-E
(d) I-A, II-C, III-D, IV-B

**6.** When a goodwill account is raised at the time of admission of a new partner, credit is given to old partners in their
(a) New profit sharing ratio
(b) Old profit sharing ratio
(c) Ratio of sacrifice
(d) Capital ratio

**7.** A and B were equal partners in a firm on 1.1.1982, they admitted C on the following conditions: C should bring Rs. 10,000 as capital, and Rs. 5,000 as goodwill. In future A, B and C would share profits and losses in the ratio of 2: 1:2. A and B will share the goodwill in the ratio of
(a) 1 : 1 (b) 3 : 1
(c) 1 : 3 (d) 2 : 1

**8.** On 31st December 1982, the assets and liabilities of a firm were Rs. 40,000 and Rs. 30,000 respectively

The firm was dissolved and a sum of 60 paise in a rupee was paid to the creditors. What was the loss on realisation?
(a) Rs. 10,000 (b) Rs. 12,000
(c) Rs. 18,000 (d) Rs. 22,000

**9.** When an incoming partner purchases his share from one of the existing partners

(a) The total assets of the firm do not change.
(b) The assets of the firm will be augmented to the extent of the payment received from the new partner.
(c) The assets of the firm will be augmented to the extent of the payment received from the new partner and existing partner with draws the share surrendered.
(d) The changes in the total assets of the firm will depend upon the structure of the assets.

**10.** While preparing the final accounts from incomplete records, the capital is to be taken as equal to the
(a) Value of fixed assets.
(b) Total assets.
(c) Difference between the current assets and current liabilities.
(d) Net assets.

**11.** Profit on reissue of forfeited shares is transferred to
(a) Profit and loss A/c
(b) Capital reserve A/c
(c) Share capital A/c
(d) General reserve A/c

**12.** Consider the following items which appear under "Reserves and Surplus" of balance sheet of a company
I. Profit and loss Account
II. Capital Redemption Reserve
III. Share Premium
IV. Capital Reserve
*The correct sequence of these items is*
(a) IV, II, III, I (b) IV, III, II, I
(c) I, II, III, IV (d) II, IV, III, I

**13.** The term current assets does not include
(a) Stock (b) Cash
(c) Advance payment (d) Furniture

**14.** Bonus share are issued by the companies because
(a) Surplus cash is available.
(b) There are heavy accumulated general reserves.
(c) There is heavy competition from similar companies.
(d) They have high gross profit ratio.

**15.** Profit can be fraudulently inflated by
(a) Suppression of sales returns.
(b) Treating capital expenditure as revenue.
(c) Overestimation of liabilities.
(d) Omission of prepaid expenses.

**16.** The trial balance of a manufacturing concern at the close of its financial year showed the following revenue balances

| | Rs. |
|---|---|
| Raw materials and stores consumed | 2,00,000 |
| Salaries and wages | 50,000 |
| Other manufacturing expenses | 1,00,000 |
| Sales | 3,00,000 |

The closing stock at selling rates amounted to Rs. 80,000. The management wants to change the basis of valuation of closing stock from selling rates to cost or market price, whichever is lower. Besides the figures given above, no other data are available
*The closing stock value is*
(a) Rs. 83,674.30 (b) Rs. 75,933.50
(c) Rs. 73,684.22 (d) Rs. 64,385.40

**17.** What is the correct sequence in which the capital of a company is raised?
(a) Issued, Nominal, Subscribed, Called-up.
(b) Issued, Nominal, Calledup, Subscribed.
(c) Nominal, Issued, Called-up, Subscribed.
(d) Nominal, Issued, Subscribed, Called-up.

**18.** Secret reserves may result by
(a) Creating general reserve.
(b) Providing excessive depreciation.
(c) Over valuation of stocks.
(d) Under valuation of liabilities.

**19.** Which of the following is not a capital reserve?
(a) Profits prior to incorporation.
(b) Dividend equalisation reserve.
(c) Profit on sale of fixed assets.
(d) All of these.

**20.** Which of the following is created by debiting the Profit and Loss Account?
(a) Provision
(b) Sinking fund for redemption of debentures
(c) Dividend equalisation fund
(d) All of these.

**21.** Any reserve which is not apparent on the face of the balance sheet is known as
(a) Secret reserve. (b) Hidden reserve.
(c) Inner reserve. (d) Any of these.

**22.** A provision is a
(a) General reserve. (b) Specific reserve.
(c) Capital reserve. (d) None of these.

**23.** If a company issues 1000 equity shares of Rs. 10 each will be legally all right if it asks an application.
(a) Rs. 2.50 (b) Rs. 3.50
(c) Rs. 4.50 (d) Rs. 5.00

**24.** If a share of Rs. 10 issued at a premium of Re.1, on which Rs. 9 (including premium) have been called and Rs. 7 (including premium) paid is forfeited the capital account should be debited by
(a) Rs. 8 (b) Rs. 9
(c) Rs. 7 (d) Rs. 6

**25.** A partnership firm is compulsorily dissolved when its business becomes illegal is described in which section of Partnership Act.
(a) Section 42 (b) Section 43
(c) Section 41 (d) Section 44

**26.** If vendors are issued fully paid shares of Rs. 1,00,000 in consideration of Net Assets of Rs. 1,20,000, the balance of Rs. 20,000 will be credited to
(a) Goodwill Account.
(b) Capital Reserve Account.
(c) Profit and Loss Account.
(d) Vendor's Account.
(e) None of these.

**27.** Partner's salaries to be debited to
(a) Profit and loss Account.
(b) Trading Account.
(c) Profit and Loss Appropriation Account.
(d) None of these.

**28.** In the absence of any partnership deed, interest on partner's loan will be allowed at the rate of
(a) 5% (b) 6%
(c) 9% (d) 12%

**29.** If A and B who are sharing profit in the ratio of 3:1. They admit C to one profits, the profit sharing ratio shall be
(a) A: 9/16; B: 3/16; C: 4/16
(b) A: 10/16; B: 2/16; C: 4/16
(c) A: 8/16; B: 4/16; C: 4/16
(d) A: 7/16; B: 5/16; C: 4/16

**30.** On the admission of a new partner the decrease in the value of Assets is debited to
(a) Revaluation Account.
(b) Old partner's capital Account.
(c) New partner's capital Account.
(d) Assets Account.

**31.** X, Y and Z are partners in the ratio of 1/2: 2/5: 1/10, what will be the new ratio of the remaining partners if X retires?
(a) 2 : 1 (b) 4 : 1
(c) 5 : 1 (d) 3 : 1

**32.** Goodwill of a firm of A and B is valued at Rs. 30,000. It is appearing in the books at Rs. 12,000 C is admitted for 1/4 share. What amount he is supposed to bring for goodwill?
(a) Rs. 3,000 (b) Rs. 4,500
(c) Rs. 7,500 (d) Rs. 10,500

**33.** A and B are partners in the ratio of 2:1. They admit C for 1/4 share who contributes for Rs. 3,000 for his share of goodwill. The total value of good will of the firm is
(a) Rs. 3,000 (b) Rs. 9,000
(c) Rs. 12,000 (d) Rs. 15,000

**34.** When a firm is dissolved, profit or loss on realisation is shared by the partners
(a) Equal
(b) In the ratio of their capital balances.
(c) In the profit sharing ratio.
(d) In the ratio laid down in Garner V. Murray.

**35.** C and D are equal partners. Their capital balances on dissolution of the firm are C–Rs. 25000 and D–Rs. 15,000
Total cash available is Rs. 30,000
How should this cash be distributed between C and D?
(a) Rs. 15,000 each.
(b) Rs. 20,000 to C and Rs. 10,000 to D.
(c) Rs. 18,750 to C and 11,250 to D.
(d) According to decision in Garner V. Murray.

**36.** At the time of dissolution, an unrecorded asset taken by Mr. X, a partner should be debited to
(a) Mr. X's capital A/c.
(b) Realisation A/c.
(c) Assets A/c.
(d) None of these.

**37.** The term fixed assets include
(a) Bank balance.
(b) Stock of finished goods.
(c) Goodwill.
(b) Loose tools.

**38.** Secret reserves serve the purpose of
(a) Enabling the directors to tide over unfavourable times.
(b) Meeting exceptional losses.
(c) Increasing the working capital.
(d) None of these.

**39.** In *Garner V. Murray* the deficiency of the insolvent partners is borne by other partner in the
(a) Profit sharing ratio.
(b) Ratio of their capitals.
(c) Equal share by each.
(d) None of these.

**40.** The remuneration payable to a whole-time director of the company should not exceed
(a) 5% of the net profits.
(b) 6% of the net profits.
(c) 7% of the net profits.
(d) 10% of the net profits.

**41.** In what order the following items are shown on the liability side of the balance sheet?
I. Share capital
II. Debentures
III. Sundry creditors
IV. Proposed dividends
***Codes:***
(a) I, II, III, IV (b) I, III, II, IV
(c) II, III, IV, I (d) I, IV, II, III

**42.** If on a share of Rs. 100 and called -up capital Rs.90 while the company received Rs.80, the capital account should be credited with
(a) Rs. 100 (b) Rs. 90
(c) Rs. 80 (d) Rs. 70

**43.** Unclaimed dividend is shown in the balance sheet under the heading as
(a) Current liabilities.
(b) Unsecured loans.
(c) Reserves and surplus.
(d) None of these.

**44.** Contingent liability is shown due to
(a) Convention of full disclosure.
(b) Convention of conservatism.
(c) Convention of materiality.
(d) Dual aspect concept.

**45.** Assets of a business are Rs. 21,315 and liabilities Rs. 4,120. What is the amount of owner's equity?
(a) Rs. 21,315 (b) Rs. 17,195
(c) Rs. 25,435 (d) Rs. 4,120

**46.** Which of the following transactions will increase an asset and also decrease an asset?
(a) Stores purchased on account.
(b) Stores purchased on cash.
(c) Payment of a promissory note with cash.
(d) Declaration of a dividend.

**47.** Which of the following transactions results in decrease in owner's equity and increase in liabilities?
(a) Declaration of a dividend, payable in cash next month
(b) Shares forfeited, on which call money is not paid
(c) Reduction in the par value of shares, from Rs. 10 to Rs. 5
(d) Reduction in the paid-up value of shares, from Rs. 5 to Rs. 3

**48.** "A three year permium paid on a fire insurance policy" should be classified as
(a) Accrued asset (b) Accrued liability
(c) Unearned revenue (d) Prepaid expense

**49.** "Wages outstanding" is appearing in the trial balance of a company while preparing Income statement and balance sheet, wages outstanding should appear in
(a) The balance sheet only.
(b) Income statement only.
(c) Both income statement as well as balance sheet.
(d) Either income statement or balance sheet.

**50.** The income statement reports the
(a) Net effect of income generating activities.
(b) Net effect of profit generating activities.
(c) The financial position of business.
(d) The overall effect on funds.

**51.** An example of an intangible asset is
(a) Goodwill.
(b) Debit balance of Profit and Loss A/c.
(c) Preliminary expenses.
(d) Deferred revenue expenditure.

**52.** How the following liabilities are to be shown on the liability side of the balance sheet in the order of permanence
I. Current liabilities and provisions
II. Secured loans
III. Share capital
IV. Unsecured loans
V. Reserves and surplus
***Codes:***
(a) III, V, II, IV, I (b) III, II, I, IV, V
(c) I, IV, II, V, III (d) V, IV, III, II, I

**53.** How should the following items shown in the balance sheet in the liquidity order?
I. Cash at bank
II. Cash in hand
III. Plant and machinery
IV. Sundry debtors
V. Goodwill
***Codes:***
(a) I, II, IV, V, III (b) I, II, III, IV, V
(c) II, I, III, IV, V (d) II, I, IV, III, V

**54.** On an equity share of Rs. 100, the minimum amount of application money under the laws should be
(a) Rs. 2 (b) Rs. 5
(c) Rs. 10 (d) Rs. 50

**55.** Rights shares mean the shares which are
(a) Issued to the directors of the company.
(b) First offered to the debenture-holders
(c) First offered to the existing shareholders.
(d) Issued by a newly formed company

**56.** For which of the following purposes, share premium can be used?
(a) In writing off the discount on debentures of the company.
(b) In writting off the preliminary expenses of the company.
(c) Issuing bonus shares.
(d) In providing for the premium payable on the redemption of preference shares.

**57.** Issue of shares at a discount of 10% or less must be
(a) Authorised by the central government
(b) Authorised by the court.
(c) Authorised by the resolution passed by the company general meeting
(d) Authorised by the resolution passed by the company in general meeting and sanctioned by company Law Board.

**58.** In case the shares have been issued at a premium and the amount of premium has been received, then at the time of forfeiture of such shares.
(a) Share premium account should be debited.
(b) Share premium account should be credited.
(c) Share premium account should be neither debited nor credited.
(d) It should be written off.

**59.** X Ltd. forfeited 30 shares of Rs. 10 each fully called-up for non- payment of allotment money of Rs. 3 per share and call money of Rs. 4 per share. These share are re-issued for Rs. 8 per share fully paid. What is the amount to be trans- ferred to capital reserve account?
(a) Rs. 300 (b) Rs. 60
(c) Rs. 30 (d) Rs. 90

**60.** X Ltd. forfeited 20 shares of Rs. 10 each, Rs. 8 called-up, on which John had paid application and allotment money of Rs. 5 per share of these, 15 shares were re-issued to parker as fully paid-up for Rs. 6 per share. What is the balance in the share forfeiture account after the relevant amount has been transferred to capital Reserve Amount.
(a) Nil (b) Rs. 5
(c) Rs. 25 (d) Rs. 100

**61.** A Ltd. issued a prospectus inviting applications for 2,000 shares. Applications were received for 3,000 shares and pro rata allotment was made on the application for 2, 400 shares. If white had been alloted 40 shares, how many shares he must have applied for?
(a) 40 (b) 44
(c) 48 (d) 52

**62.** X Ltd. forfeited 20 shares of Rs. 10 each and on which Rs. 4 per share were paid, what minimum price company must charge if the forfeited shares are re-issued as Rs. 8 per share paid-up?
(a) Rs. 2 per share. (b) Rs. 4 per share.
(c) Rs. 8 per share. (d) Rs. 10 per share.

**63.** Which of the following may be utilised by a limited company for the redemption of redeemable perference shares?
(a) General Reserve.
(b) Dividend Equilisation Fund.
(c) Profit and loss account balance.
(d) All of these.

**64.** If preference share are redeemed at premium, then such premium may be provided out of the
(a) Share premium account.
(b) Proceeds of a fresh issue of shares.
(c) Share forfeiture account.
(d) Capital redemption reserve account.

**65.** "Capital Redemption Reserve Account" is created
(a) voluntarily to accumulated funds to redeem preference shares in future.
(b) to meet legal requirements regarding redemption of preference shares.
(c) out of share premium account to redeem preference shares.
(d) out of share forfeiture account to redeem preference shares.

**66.** Redeemable preference shares of Rs. 2,00,000 are redeemed at par for which purpose fresh equity capital of Rs. 80, 000 is issued at par. What amount should be transferred to capital Redemption Reserve Account?
(a) Nil (b) Rs. 80,000
(c) Rs. 1,20,000 (d) Rs. 2,00,000

**67.** Redeemable preference shares of Rs. 2,00,000 are redeemed at par for which purpose fresh equity capital of Rs. 80,000 is issued at a discount of 10%. What amount should be transferred to capital Redemption Reserve Account?
(a) Rs. 1,20,000 (b) Rs. 1,28,000
(c) Rs. 2,00,000 (d) Rs. 72,000

**68.** X Ltd. purchased land and building worth Rs. 28,80,000 and in lieu issued debentures of Rs. 100 each at a discount of 4%. What is the number of debentures issued?
(a) 28,800 (b) 30,000
(c) 32,000 (d) 32,000

**69.** When shares are forfeited, capital account is debited by
(a) Nominal value of shares.
(b) Paid-up amount on shares.
(c) Called-up amount on shares.
(d) Forfeited amount.

**70.** When all the debentures are redeemed, the balance left in the 'Debenture Sinking Fund account's is transferred to
(a) General Reserve.
(b) Sinking Fund Investment A/c.
(c) Debentures A/c.
(d) Capital Redemption Reserve.

**71.** The Balance sheet of a company
(a) Must be prepared in the form set by law
(b) May be prepared in any form
(c) Should be prepared in any form so as to give a true and fair picture of the state of affairs of the company.
(d) Items should be shown in order of performance.

**72.** Share forfeited Account is shown on the liability side of the balance sheet.
(a) Under the heading "Reserves and Surplus".
(b) By adding to the paid-up capital.
(c) Under the heading "current liabilities and provisions".
(d) Under the heading "Miscellaneous".

**73.** The profit or loss disclosed by the accounts of a company is
(a) Transferred to share capital account.
(b) Shown in the column of "Current liabilities and provisions".
(c) Shown in the column of 'Reserves and surplus' under a separate account.
(d) Transferred to General Reserve.

**74.** Unclaimed dividends is shown on the liability side of the balance sheet under the heading.
(a) Reserve and Surplus
(b) Provisions
(c) Current Liabilities
(d) Miscellaneous items

**75.** The remuneration payable to a whole time director of the company should not exceed
(a) 5% of the net profits.
(b) 6% of the net profits.
(c) 7% of the net profits.
(d) 10% of the net profits.

**76.** Which of the following is not required to be made under statutes?
(a) Profit & Loss
(b) Funds Flow Statement.
(c) Balance Sheet
(d) None of these.

**77.** 6% Debentures A/c Rs. 3,00,000; Debenture Interest Rs. 6,000
*What amount should be shown in P and L A/c ?*
(a) Rs. 6,000 (b) Rs. 12,000
(c) Rs. 18,000 (d) None of these

**78.** ' Non-convertible' debentures refers to
(a) Owners' capital. (b) Loan capital.
(c) Short-trem debts. (d) All of these.

**79.** The authorised capital of a company is Rs. 5 lakhs, issued capital Rs. 3 lakhs and subscribed capital Rs. 2 lakhs. It has received Rs.5 per Share on application and allotment and Rs.2 per share on first-call except on 2,500 shares. Share capital is credited with.
(a) Rs. 3,00,000 (b) Rs. 2,00,000
(c) Rs. 1,40,000 (d) Rs. 1,35,000

**80.** Which of the following is not a current liability?
(a) Unclaimed dividends
(b) Minority interest
(c) Bills payable
(d) Bank overdraft

**81.** A company has a share capital of Rs. 1,00,000 and general reserve of Rs. 1,20,000. It proposes to issue shares out of general reserve in such a way that after issue of shares the remaining balance in General Reserve should be equal to 25% of the total capital (new). Find the remaining reserve from the following:
(a) Rs. 25,000 (b) Rs. 30,000
(c) Rs. 44,000 (d) Rs. 70,000

**82.** 30 shares of a company on which application money of Rs. 3 per share has been duly paid are forfeited for non-payment of allotment money of Rs. 3 each and first and find call of Rs. 4 each. These shares are then re-issued at Rs. 8 per share fully paid. How much money should be transferred to Capital Reserve?
(a) Rs. 30 (b) Rs. 60
(c) Rs. 90 (d) Rs. 120

**83.** Which of the following is current liability?
(a) Outstanding wages
(b) Debentures
(c) Long-term loans
(d) Share capital

**84.** Account books for how many proceeding years should be preserved in good condition?
(a) 5 (b) 8
(c) 10 (d) 13

**85.** Provision for discount on debtors shall be made on
(a) Book debts before incurring bad debt and before providing for bad debt.
(b) Book debts after incurring bad debt and after providing for bad debt.
(c) Book debts before incurring bad debt but after providing for bad debt.
(d) Book debts after incurring bad debt but before providing for bad debt.

**86.** Closing stock appearing in trial balance will be taken to
(a) Trading Account only.
(b) Balance Sheet only.
(c) Trading Account and Balance Sheet.
(d) Profit and Loss Account only.

**87.** In a trial balance, debtors appear at Rs. 45,00. Provision for doubtful debts at 5% is to be made after considering the following adjustments.
I. An amount of Rs. 1,000 is included in debtor who is bankrupt and his estate is expected to realise 50 (fifty) paise in the rupee.
II. Debtors include an account of Rs. 2, 000 for goods supplied to proprietor.
III. Bill receivable include a dishonoured bill for Rs. 1,000.
IV. Goods sold in 'Sale of Return' basis not approval by the customer for Rs.5,000 recorded as sale.
V. Debtor includes as amount of Rs. 500 from a customer whose financial position is doubtful.
The total provision to be made for doubtful debts is
(a) Rs. 1,900 (b) Rs. 2,250
(c) Rs. 2,425 (d) None of these.

**88.** In the event of dissolution of a firm, the partners' personal assets are first applied for payment of

(a) the personal liabilities.
(b) the firm's liabilities.
(c) both the personal and firm's liabilities.
(d) the preferential and tax liabilities.

**89.** 'A' and 'B' are partners in a business sharing profits in the ratio of 5:3. They admit 'C' as a partner with 1/4 share in the profits. Which he acquires 3/4 from 'A' and 1/4 from 'B'. He pays Rs. 4, 000 as his share of goodwill. 'A' and 'B' will be credited by
(a) Rs. 2,500 and Rs. 1,500 respectively
(b) Rs. 200 each
(c) Rs. 1,000 and Rs. 300 respectively
(d) Rs. 3,000 and Rs. 1,000 respectively

**90.** 'A' and 'B' who are partners, share profits in the ratio of 7:3. 'C' is admitted as a new partner. 'A' surrenders 1/7 of his share and 'B' surrenders 1/3 of his share in favour of 'C'. The new profit sharing ratio will be
(a) 6:2:2 (b) 4:1:1
(c) 3:2:2 (d) None of these.

**91.** 'A' and 'B' are two partners of a firm having capitals of Rs. 15,000 and Rs. 5, 000 respectively, sharing profit and loss in the ratio of 2:1. On dissolution of the firm the assets realised is:

1st instalment Rs. 3,000
2nd instalment Rs. 5,000

*Under Proportionate capital Method, the loss to 'B' will be*
(a) Rs. 100 (c) Rs. 2,100
(c) Rs. 3,000 (d) Rs. 4,000

**92.** A, B, C, D are partners sharing profits and losses in the ratio 3:3:2:1. The partnership is dissolved and D becomes insolvent. C brings only his share of loss and shows his inability to contribute anything towards D's deficiency. According to Garner vs. Murray ruling, D's deficiency in the total will be shared by
(a) A and B in their capital ratio.
(b) A, B and C in their profit sharing ratio.
(c) A, B and C in their capital ratio.
(d) A, B and C equally.

**93.** According to companies Act, a "reserve capital" is created
(a) For a specific purpose at anytime during its working life.
(b) For issue to the existing shareholders as rights issue of shares.
(c) As the uncalled portion of share capital of a limited company to be called only in the event of winding up.
(d) For conversion of FCDS into equity shares.

**94.** Match List I with List II and select the correct answer using the codes given below the Lists:

| List I (Items of balance sheets of company) | List II (Headings of balancesheet) |
|---|---|
| I. Profit prior to Incorporation | A. Provisions |
| II. Proposed dividend | B. Miscellaneous expenditure. |
| III. Interest paid out of capital | C. Current liabilities |
| IV. Unclaimed dividend | D. Reserves and surplus |

*Codes :*
(a) I-D, II-A, III-C, IV-B
(b) I-D, II-A, III-B, IV-C
(c) I-A, II-D, III-B, IV-C
(d) I-A, II-D, III-C, IV-B

**95.** Amount set a part to meet probable losses on account of bad debts is a
(a) Liability
(b) Reserve
(c) Provision
(d) Contingent liability

**96.** *Consider the following statements.*
Redeemable preference shares can be redeemed out of
I. sale proceeds of the new issue of shares.
II. sale proceeds of the new issue of debentures.
III. profits available for dividends.
IV. sales proceeds of the assets of the company.
*Of these statements:*
(a) I and III are correct.
(b) I alone is correct.
(c) II, III, and IV are correct.
(d) I, II, III and IV are correct.

**97.** Match List I with List II and select he correct answer using the codes given below the Lists:

| List I | List II |
|---|---|
| I. Balance of Debenture Redemption Fund Account | A. Realisation Account |
| II. Balance of Sinking Fund Account for replacement of an asset. | B. Funds-flow Statement. |
| III. On dissolution of a firm, the provisions made for doubtful debts appearing in Balance Sheet. | C. General Reserve |
| IV. Financial Consequences of business operations | D. Asset Account |

*Codes:*

(a) I-A, II-B, III-C, IV-D
(b) I-C, II-D, III-A, IV-B
(c) I-A, II-B, III-D, IV-C
(d) I-C, II-D, III-B, IV-A

**98.** A company issue 10,000 shares of Rs. 10 each at a discount of 10% payable as follows:

| | |
|---|---|
| on application | Rs. 2.50 |
| on allotment | Rs. 3.00 |
| on first and final call | Rs. 3.50 |

*A holder of 100 shares did not pay the final call and his shares were forfeited. Share capital A/c will be debited by*

(a) Rs. 650 (b) Rs. 1,000
(c) Rs. 850 (d) Rs. 900

**99.** Owner's equity stands for

(a) Fixed Assets minus Fixed Liabilities.
(b) Fixed Assets minus Current Liabilities.
(c) Current Assets minus Fixed Liabilities.
(d) Total Assets minus Total Liabilities.

**100.** Which one of the following is an intangible asset?

(a) Furniture
(b) Patent right
(c) Investment in shares
(d) Losse tools.

**101.** Match List I (Names of accounts) with List II (Matters with which the accounts are concerned) and select the correct answer using the codes given below the lists:

| List I | List II |
|---|---|
| I. Patners' current account | A. Dissolution of partnership |
| II. Goodwill account | B. Revaluation of assets on the admission of a partner. |
| III. Partners' drawings accounts | C. Fixed capitals of Partners. |
| IV. Profit and Loss adjustment account | D. Goods taken by partners for private consumption. |

*Codes:*

(a) I-A, II-C, III-B, IV-D
(b) I-A, II-C, III-D, IV-B
(c) I-C, II-A, III-D, IV-B
(d) I-C, II-A, III-B, IV-D

**102.** Whenever debentures are cancelled, any profit on cancellation is transferred to

(a) Profit and loss account.
(b) Sinking fund account.
(c) Capital redemption reserve account.
(d) Capital reserve account.

**103.** Match List I (Transaction) with List II (Entry to be made) and select the correct answer by using the codes given below the lists:

| List I | List II |
|---|---|
| I. Loss on realisation | A. Debits partner's capital account |
| II. Profit on realisation | B. Credit realisation A/c |
| III. Assets sold | C. Credit partner's capital A/c |
| IV. Creditors paid | D. Debit realisation A/c |

*Codes:*

(a) I-A, II-C, III-B, IV-D
(b) I-C, II-A, III-B, IV-D
(c) I-C, II-A, III-D, IV-B
(d) I-A, II-C, III-D, IV-B

**104.** Which of the following statements are appropriate in respect of partnership accounts?

I. In the absence of any provision in the partnership agreement to the contrary, partners can charge interest at 6% per annum on loans given by them to the partnership firm.

II. An ordinary partnership firm can have not more than 50 partnership.
III. A banking partnership firm can have not more than 10 partnership.
IV. In the absence of any provision in the partnership agreement to the contrary, profits and losses are shared by the partners in the ratio of their capitals.

*Select the correct answer using the codes given below:*

***Codes:***

(a) I and II (b) I and III
(c) II, III and IV (d) I, III, and IV

**105.** A and B are equal partners in a firm. They admitted C as one-sixth partner who brought in Rs. 60,000 as good will. The new profit sharing ratio is 3:2:1. If good will of Rs. 60,000 is to be paid to the old partners as per profit sacrificing ratio, B will receive

(a) Rs. 30,000 (b) Rs. 60,000
(c) Rs. 45,000 (d) None of these.

**106.** R admitted as a new partner for one-fourth share of future profits, fails to bring in cash of Rs.5,000 towards good will, but the existing (old) partners S and T sharing profits in the ratio of 3:2, raise the goodwill account at its full value. Therefore the partners will be credited for goodwill as

| | S (Rs.) | T (Rs.) | R (Rs.) |
|---|---|---|---|
| (a) | 3,000 | 2,000 | Nil |
| (b) | 9,000 | 6,000 | 5,000 |
| (c) | 12,000 | 8,000 | Nil |
| (d) | 2,250 | 1,500 | 1,250 |

**107.** What is the correct sequence of the following action required for the preparation of Final Accounts?

I. Preparation of Trial Accounts
II. Balancing of Accounts
III. Preparation of Annual Financial statement
IV. Making Adjusting Entries

*Select the correct answer using the codes given below:*

(a) IV, II, I, III (b) II, IV, III, I
(c) II, I, IV, III (d) IV, II, III, I

**108.** A business entity has an opening balance of Rs. 4,000 as provision for bad and debts. Total sales amounts to Rs. 6,00,000 and out of which Rs. 1,00,000 worth of sales is for cash. A provision of 1% is to be made on outstanding debtors. The amount to be debited to profit and loss account for current year's provision on debtors will be

(a) Rs. 6,000 (b) Rs. 5,000
(c) Rs. 1,000 (d) None of these

**109.** Having reissued all forfeited shares, the credit balance remaining in forfeited shares account is transferred to

(a) General reserve. (b) Reserve capital.
(c) Capital reserve. (d) None of the these.

**110.** Rights issue refers to the share issued to

(a) Employees.
(b) Public.
(c) Existing directors.
(d) None of these.

**111.** That portion of the share capital which can be called up only on the winding up of the company is the

(a) Authorised capital
(b) Issued capital
(c) Subscribed capital
(d) Reserve capital

**112.** If vendors are issued fully paid shares of Rs. 80,000 in consideration of net assets of Rs. 60,000, then the balance of Rs. 20,000 will be

(a) Debited to profit and loss account.
(b) Debited to goodwill account.
(c) Credited to capital reserve account.
(d) Credited to share premium account.

**113.** Which of the following method (s) is/are followed for the purpose of 'piecemeal distribution' in the case of dissolution of a partnership firm?

I. Proportionate Capital Method.
II. Maximum Possible Loss Method.
III. Reconstruction and Distribution Method.

*Select the correct answer using the codes given below:*

(a) III alone (b) I and III
(c) III and II (d) I and II

**114.** Consider the following parties:

I. Secured creditors
II. Unsecured creditors
III. Partners who granted loans
IV. Partners who contributed capitals in excess as compared to the profit sharing ratio.

*The correct sequence in which payment are to be made to these parties in the event of the dissolution of a partnership firm is*

(a) II, I, III, IV (b) I, II, IV, III
(c) I, II, III, IV (d) II, I, IV, III

**115.** Match List I (Provision of partnership Act with List II (Matters with which the provision are related) and select the correct answer using the codes given below the lists:

| List I | List II |
|---|---|
| I. Interest must be allowed @ 6% p.a. | A. Drawing of Partners |
| II. No interest shall be allowed. | B. Net loss of the firm for an accounting year. |
| III. No interest shall be charged | C. Capitals contributed by the partners. |
| IV. Must be shared equally by all the partners unless otherwise agreed | D. Loan given by a partner to the firm. |

***Codes :***

(a) I-A, II-C, III-B, IV-D
(b) I-D, II-C, III-B, IV-A
(c) I-C, II-B, III-D, IV-A
(d) I-D, II-C, III-A, IV-B

**116.** The minimum share application money is

(a) Rs. 5 per share.
(b) 5% of the nominal value of shares.
(c) 10% of the nominal value of shares.
(d) 20% of the nominal value of shares.

**117.** Balance sheet prepared after the new partnership agreement, assets and liabilities are recorded at

(a) Original Value (b) Revalued Figure
(c) At realisable Value (d) At current cost

**118.** After the redemption of debentures, the balance of debenture sinking fund is transferred to

(a) Debenture Account.
(b) General Reserve.
(c) Profit and Loss Account.
(d) Capital Reserve.

**119.** Debentures can be redeemed by

(a) purchase of own debentures in the open market.
(b) converting them into a new class of debentures.
(c) converting them into shares.
(d) any of the methods mentioned in (a), (b) and (c) above.

**120.** A company wishes to redeem its preference shares amounting to Rs. 1,00,000 at a premium of 5% and for this purpose issues 5, 000 equity shares of Rs. 10 each at a premium of 5%. The company also has a balance of Rs.1,00,000 as General Reserves and Rs.50,000 in profit and loss account. The amount to be transferred to Capital Redemption Reserve Account for the purpose of redemption is

(a) Rs. 47,500 (b) Rs. 50,000
(c) Rs. 52,500 (d) Rs. 1,05,000

**121.** The Balance sheet of a limited company as on 31.12. 1992 is as under:

| | Rs. | Rs. |
|---|---|---|
| Share capital : | | 1,16,000 |
| 5,000 equity shares of Rs. 10 each | 50,000 | |
| 2,000 equity shares of Rs. 10 each, Rs. 8 per share paid up | 16,000 | |
| General Reserve | 50,000 | |
| | 1,16,000 | 1,16,000 |

*The company decided to capitalise the necessary part of the General Reserve by issuing*

I. a bonus share per share on the partly paid up shares in order to make them fully paid and

II. fully paid bonus shares at premium of 5% per share amongst the existing share holders to be distributed in the ratio of one share for every five shares held

*The amount to be transferred from the General Reserve Account*

(a) Rs. 14,700 (b) Rs. 15,000
(c) Rs. 18,000 (d) Rs. 21,000

**122.** The main objective of providing depreciation is to

(a) Create secret reserves.
(b) Reduce the book value of assets.
(c) Value the assets property.
(d) Allocate cost of the assets.

**123.** Match List I (Items) with List II (Head in Balance sheet) and select the correct answer using the codes given below the lists:

| List I | List II |
|---|---|
| I. Loss on issue of debentures | A. Reserves and surplus |
| II. Unclaimed dividend | B. Miscellaneous Expenditure |
| III. Prepaid rent | C. Current Liabilities |
| IV. Profit prior to incorporation | D. Current Assets. |

***Codes :***

(a) I-C, II-B, III-A, IV-D
(b) I-C, II-B, III-D, IV-A
(c) I-B, II-C, III-D, IV-A
(d) I-B, II-C, III-A, IV-D

**124.** Interim payments to partners of a dissolved partnership firm are made according to the

(a) Assumption that remaining unrealised assets would be able to realise their book value.
(b) Balances of capital of the partners.
(c) Existing profit sharing ratios of the partners.
(d) Assumption that the realisable value of the remaining assets is zero.

**125.** A, B and C are partners is a business sharing profits at the ratio of 2:2:1. C dies on 31.3.94. The profits for the financial year 93-94 (April-March) is Rs. 64,000. The share of the deceased partner in the profits for the year will be rupees.

(a) Rs. 12,800 (b) Rs. 9,600
(c) Rs. 6,400 (d) Rs. 3,200

**126.** Match List I (Items) with List II (Headings) and select the correct answer using the codes given below the lists:

| List I | List II |
|---|---|
| I. Interim Dividend | A. Miscellaneous expenses |
| II. Share premium | B. Current Liabilitites |
| III. Unclaimed Dividend | C. Reserves and surplus |
| IV. Discount on Issue of shares | D. Profit and loss appr-opriation account |

***Codes :***

(a) I-C, II-D, III-A, IV-B
(b) I-D, II-C, III-A, IV-B
(c) I-C, II-D, III-B, IV-A
(d) I-D, II-C, III-B, IV-A

**127.** Consider the following Balance sheet as on 1.1.94

| Liabilities | Rs. | Assets | Rs. |
|---|---|---|---|
| Salaries out standings | 300 | Cash | 350 |
| XXXX | 12,350 | Furniture Books and Buildings | 1,000<br>11,000 |
| | | Subscriptions outstanding | 300 |
| | 12,650 | | 12,650 |

*In the above balance sheet, the missing narration XXXX is*

(a) Capital. (b) Capital Fund.
(c) Profit for the year. (d) Reserve Fund.

**128.** Which one of the following statements is correct?

(a) Share premium received on issue of shares can be utilised for writing off the preliminary expenses of the company.
(b) Capital Redemption Reserve is available only for issuing fully paid bonus share.
(c) Discount on issue of shares is shown as a reduction from capital Account in the Balance sheet.
(d) At the time of Rights issue, the existing share holders gain because the shares are generally issued at a price lower than the market price.

**129.** The Directors of a Limited company resolved to forfeit 1, 000 equity shares of Rs. 10 each, Rs.7.50 paid up, for non-payment of the final call money of Rs. 2, 50 per share. 700 of these shares were reissued at Rs. 7 per share. The amount to be transferred to the capital Reserve Account would be

(a) Rs. 2,500 (b) Rs. 3,150
(c) Rs. 3,500 (d) Rs. 3,750

**130.** The nominal and book value of sinking Fund Investments. Account are respectively Rs. 1,00,000 and Rs. 96, 000. The company has sold investments of the nominal value of Rs. 20,000 at a price that was sufficient to redeem the debentures of Rs. 20,000 at Rs. 102. The profit on sale of investment is
(a) Rs. 800 (b) Rs. 1,000
(c) Rs. 1,200 (d) None of these.

**131.** A company's Balance Sheet interatia contains Rs. 1,60,000 fully paid 10% redeemable preference shares, Rs. 1,000 as share premium and Rs. 1,31,000 as Revenue Reserves. It resolves to immediately redeem the above mentioned shares at 5% premium by maximum utilisation of earnings from fresh issue. If the issue is made at 20% premium, the MINIMUM amount of fresh equity issue proceeds will be
(a) Rs. 28,800 (b) Rs. 32,000
(c) Rs. 36,000 (d) Rs. 37,000

**132.** The following accounting entries are required in connection with the allotment of shares of a company.
I. Adjustment entry in respect of the discount allowed if any, on the issue of shares.
II. Transfer entry for the application money received on shares alloted
III. Adjustment entry for the excess application money, if any, being adjusted against the allotment money due

*The correct sequence of these entires is*
(a) I, II, II (b) II, I, III
(c) II, III, I (d) III, II, I

**133.** When shares are forfeited, called up amount on shares is debited to
(a) Forfeiture Account.
(b) Capital Reserve Account.
(c) General Reserve Account.
(d) Capital Account.

**134.** The value of which one of the following assets increases in the initial years of its life, remains constant there after and finally begins to decline?
(a) Live stock (b) Patents
(c) Good will (d) Machinery

**135.** Which of the following pairs is/are correctly matched?

| | List I | List II |
|---|---|---|
| I. | Sinking Fund | Replacement of wasting assets |
| II. | Secret Reserve | Over valuation of liabilities |
| III. | General Reserve | Provision for drop in value of assets |

*Select the correct answer using the codes given below:*
(a) I, II, and III (b) I and III
(c) II alone (d) I alone

**136.** An estimate of the assets and liabilities of a firm as on a given date is called
(a) Balance Sheet.
(b) Statement of affairs.
(c) Statement of capital.
(d) Income statement.

**137.** Which of the following is a compulsory to revalue at the time of admission of a new partner:
(a) Stock (b) Fixed Assets
(c) Investments (d) Good will

**138.** A limited company issued equity share of each. It has called up Rs. 75 on each share but recived Rs. 60 per share. The share capital account will be credited.
(a) Rs. 60 per share
(b) Rs. 75 per share
(c) Rs. 100 per share
(d) None of these

**139.** Redeemable preference shares can be redeemed
(a) Only if they are fully paid.
(b) Even if they are partly paid.
(c) If they are paid not less than 50% of the nominal value of shares.
(d) Only if they are issued at a premium.

**140.** Advance received from customers is
(a) An item of current liability.
(b) An item of non-current asset.
(c) An item of contingent liability.
(d) An item of non-cash cost.

**141.** Final Accounts of a manufacturing company generally include the following types of documents:

I. Balance sheet
II. Manufacturing Account
III. Profit and Loss Account
IV. Trading Account
V. Profit and Loss Application Account

*The correct sequence in which these documents are prepared*

(a) I, IV, III, II, V (b) II, IV, III, V, I
(c) I, II, IV, III, V (d) II, IV, V, III, I

**142.** A and B are partners sharing profits and losses in the ratio of 2:5. They admit C on the on condition that he will bring goodwill in cash which is distributed between A and B. C's share in future profits or losses is to be one fourth. The new profit sharing ratio of A, B and C will be

(a) 6:15:7 (b) 15:6:7
(c) 7:6:15 (d) 6:7:15

**143.** Where all the debentures are redeemed, the balance left in the Debenture Sinking Fund Accounting is transferable to

(a) Debenture Account.
(b) Sinking Fund Investment Account
(c) Capital Redemption Reserve.
(d) General Reserve.

**144.** The balance in share forfeiture account after the reissue of all forfeited shares, should be

(a) Added to paid-up capital
(b) Transferred to goodwill account
(c) Transferred to Capital Reserve Account
(d) Shown as share Forfieiture Account

**145.** A company issued Rs. 2,00,000, 4% bonds repayable on equal instalments over 10 years. What is the amount required in the initial year, to pay interest and to redeem the bonds (Ignore tax and D.C.F.)

(a) Rs. 56,000 (b) Rs. 28,000
(c) Rs. 20,000 (d) Rs. 8,000

**146.** Match List I with List II and select the correct answer using the codes given below the lists:

| List I | List II |
|---|---|
| I. Deferred shares | A. Repayment obligation |
| II. Preference shares | B. Redembles stock dividend |
| III. Bonus shares | C. No dividend obligation |
| IV. Equity shares | D. Not being used |

***Codes :***

(a) I-D, II-C, III-A, IV-B
(b) I-D, II-B, III-C, IV-A
(c) I-C, II-B, III-A, IV-D
(d) I-D, II-A, III-B, IV-C

**147.** Which one of the following statement is false?

(a) The process of issue of bonus shares is also known as capitalisation of reserves.
(b) Fully paid bonus shares are issued only out of capital reserves.
(c) Only revenue reserves should be used when bonus is declared in order to make partly paid shares into fully paid shares.
(d) Bonus shares are shares issued without payment.

**148.** The Balancesheet of a company showed the following balances at the end of the year under the head 'Reserves and Surplus':
*General reserve Rs. 5,00,000, share premium accounts Rs. 50,000 : Premium on issue of Debentures account Rs. 20,000 : Dividends equalisation fund Rs. 40,000. Surplus on revaluation of assets Rs. 30,000; Profit and loss account (credit) Rs. 60,000. Maximum amount available for distribution as dividend to the share holders of the company will be*

(a) Rs. 60,000 (b) Rs. 1,00,000
(c) Rs. 6,00,000 (d) Rs. 6,70,000

**149.** A, B and C are partners with profit sharing ratio 4:3:2. B retires and Goodwill Rs. 10,800 shown in books of account. If A and B share profits of B in 5:3, then find the value of goodwill shared between A and C

(a) Rs. 18,50 and Rs. 1,950
(b) Rs. 1,650 and Rs. 1,750
(c) Rs. 2,000 and Rs. 1,600
(d) Rs. 1,950 and Rs. 1,650

**150. Assertion (A):** The amounts realised on sale of shares at a premium is credited to share premium account but not to profit and loss account.

**Reason (R)** : The amount of share premium is excluded from the distribution to shareholders as it is not current year's profits

*In the context of the above two statement, which one of the following is correct?*

(a) Both A and R are ture, and R is the correct explanation of A.
(b) Both A and R are true, but R is not a correct explation of A
(c) A is true, but R is false
(d) A is false, but R is true.

**151.** While preparing 'Annual financial statements' 'Credit Balance' shown by the Bank Pass Book should be treated as

(a) A liability
(b) An income
(c) An excess of payments over receipts.
(d) An asset.

**152.** The joint life policy account received on the death of a partner is credited to the

(a) Joint life policy reserve account.
(b) Capital accounts of all the partners in their profit sharing ratio.
(c) General ratio.
(d) Profit and loss account

**153.** Consider the following activities connected with the accounting information system:

I. Preparation of the table of accounting.
II. Communication of accounting information
III. Preparation of accounting information report.
IV. Collection of accounting data.

*The correct sequence of these activities is*

(a) IV, I, III, II (b) I, IV, III, II
(c) IV, III, I, II (d) I, II, IV, III

**154.** A cooperative store having a turnover of Rs. 10 lakh and profit of Rs. 50, 000 purchased locks costing Rs. 300 for use in the shop. The accountant charged it in the P & L A/C of current year, but the auditor raised an objection saying that it should be capitalised. On which one of the following conventions could the accountant be defended?

(a) Disclosure (b) Materiality
(c) Conservatism (d) Consistency.

**155.** Consider the following statements:

*Notes forming part of accounts of companies invariably display significant Accounting Policies*

I. as per the requirement of SEBI guidelines for disclosure and investor protection.
II. because it is a mandatory requirement under the Companies Act, 1956.
III. as required by As-I-disclosure of accounting policies, which is mendatory.
IV. as it is required under the listing agreement with the stock exchanges.

*Which of the above statements are correct?*

(a) I, II, and III (b) II, and III
(c) II, III and IV (d) I and IV

**156.** Match List I with List II and select the correct answer using the codes given below the Lists:

| List I | List II |
|---|---|
| I. Showing joint life policy at surrender value | A. Concept of consistency |
| II. Team spirit and dedication of cost employees are not recorded in the books of accounts | B. Concept of cost |
| III. Methods of depreciation and inventory valuation should not be changed frequently | C. Concept of conserva-tism |
| IV. Fixed assets are recorded at 'cost less depreciation' | D. Concept of money meas-urement |

***Codes :***

(a) I-C, II-D, III-A, IV-B
(b) I-C, II-D, III-B, IV-A
(c) I- D, II-C, III-A, IV-B
(d) I- D, II-C, III-B, IV-A

**157.** If depreciation is calculated on the basis of the formula, $\frac{n(n+1)}{2}$, then which one of the following methods is adopted?
(a) Diminishing value method
(b) Annuity method
(c) Sum of years Digits Method
(d) Sinking Fund Method.

**158.** Consider the following methods of inventory valuation:
I. Simple Average
II. First-in-first-out
III. Last-in-first-out
IV. Weighted Average
*Which of these methods do not match current cost with current revenues?*
(a) I and III (b) I, II and III
(c) I, II, and IV (d) II, III and IV

**159.** Consider the following fundamental assumptions:
I. Prudence II. Going concern
III. Accrual IV. Consistency
As per Accounting standard-1, which of these assumptions are taken into consideration while preparing financial statements?
(a) I and IV (b) II and III
(c) I, II, III and IV (d) II, III, and IV

**160.** Which one of the following statements is correct?
(a) Preliminary expenses are revenue expenses.
(b) Cost of issuing shares and debentures and raising loans, such as legal expenses and underwriting commission are capital expenditure.
(c) Interest on loan is a capital expenditure.
(d) Cost of machinery purchased is a revenue expenditure.

**161.** The ending balance of owner's equity is Rs. 21,000. During the years the owner contributed Rs. 6,000 and withdrew Rs. 4,000. If the firm had Rs. 8,000 net income for the year, what was the owner's equity at the beginning?
(a) Rs. 23,000 (b) Rs. 21,000
(c) Rs. 19,000 (d) Rs. 11,000

**162.** The ending balance of the accounts receivable amount was Rs. 12,000. Services billed to customers for the period were Rs. 21,500 and collection on account from customers was Rs. 23,600. The beginning balance of account receivable was
(a) Rs. 33,500 (b) Rs. 14,100
(c) Rs. 9,800 (d) Rs. 33,300

**163.** Which one of the following is a capital expenditure?
(a) Compensation paid for breach of a contract of supply of goods.
(b) Interest on borrowings during the period of construction of works.
(c) Loss of stock by fire.
(d) Loss due to embezzlement by the Manager.

**164.** A company issued 14% debentures of Rs. 10,00,000 at a discount of 10%. The discount allowed will be treated in the account books as
(a) Capital expenditure.
(b) Revenue expenditure.
(c) Deferred revenue expenditure.
(d) Capital loss.

**165.** A building standing in the books at Rs. 30,000 was sold for Rs. 45,000. The gain on the sale of building was transferred to profit and loss account thus taking the net profit to Rs. 1,70,000. The fund from operation will be
(a) Rs. 2,15,000 (b) Rs. 1,17,000
(c) Rs. 1,55,000 (d) Rs. 2,00,000

**166.** Match List I with List II and select the correct answer using the codes given below the Lists:

| List I | List II |
|---|---|
| I. Lease hold property | A. Depreciation Fund Method |
| II. Mines, quarries, etc. | B. Annuity Method |
| III. The interest lost on the acquisition of an asset. | C. Fixed Instalment Method |
| IV. To provide for replacement of asset at the end of its useful life. | D. Depletion Method. |

*Codes:*
(a) I-B, II-A, III-D, IV-C
(b) I-C, II-D, III-A, IV-B
(c) I-C, II-D, III-B, IV-A
(d) I-D, II-C, III-A, IV-B

**167.** Following are the extracts from the Trial Balance of a firm:

| Particulars | Rs. Dr. | Rs. Cr. |
|---|---|---|
| Sundry debtors | 50,000 | – |
| Provision for doubtful debts | – | 5,000 |
| Bad debts | 3,000 | – |

*Additional Information:*

I. Additional bad debts Rs.3,000.

II. Keep the provision for bad debts @ 10% on debtors.

The net amount of bad debts that will appear in the Profit and Loss Account will be

(a) Rs. 8,000 (b) Rs. 7,500
(c) Rs. 5,700 (d) Rs. 4,500

**168.** A and B sharing profits in the ratio of 3:2 and having capitals of Rs. 30,000 and Rs. 15,000 respectively decided to dissolve the firm. After paying off all liabilities, they realised from various assets is Rs. 15,000. This amount will be distributed between A and B as

(a) Rs. 9,000 and Rs.6,000 respectively
(b) Rs. 10,000 and Rs.5,000 respectively
(c) Rs. 7,500 and Rs.7,500 respectively
(d) Rs. 12,000 and Rs.3,000 respectively

**169.** A, B and C are partners sharing profits in the ratio of 6:3:1. They dicided to dissolve the firm when their capitals were Rs. 8,000, Rs. 3,000 and Rs. (–1) 1,000 respectively other liabilities and assets were-Bank over draft Rs. 3,500; A's advance to the firm Rs. 500; sundry creditors Rs. 2,500; plant and machinery Rs. 7,500; stock-in trade Rs. 2,500; Sundry debtors Rs. 6,000 and Cash Rs. 500. Plant and machinery realised at 20% less, stock-in trade at 25% less and sundry debtors at 30% less than their respective book value. Expenses of dissolution amounted to Rs. 250. C become inslovent and his private estate yielded Rs. 100 only. What is the loss on realisation?

(a) Rs. 4,125 (b) Rs. 4,150
(c) Rs. 4,175 (d) Rs. 4,225

**170.** A, B and C are the partners in a business firm sharing their profits in the ratio of 4:3:2. A new partner D enters the firm. The new profit. Sharing ratio fo A, B, C and D is 5:4:2:1.D contributes a good will of Rs. 36,000. This good-will is to be allocated among A, B and C. Which one of the following will be the correct allocation?

| | A Rs. | B Rs. | C Rs. |
|---|---|---|---|
| (a) | 16,000 | 12,000 | 8,000 |
| (b) | 12,000 | 8,000 | 16,000 |
| (c) | 12,000 | Nil | 24,000 |
| (d) | 24,000 | Nil | 12,000 |

**171.** A, B and C are equal partners in a firm with capital of Rs. 16,800, Rs. 12,600 and Rs. 6,000 respectively with bills payable Rs. 3,300; cerditors Rs. 6,000; cash Rs. 600; debtors Rs. 10,800; stocks Rs. 11,400; furniture Rs. 2,400 and building Rs. 19, 500. E is admitted to the firm and brings Rs. 9,000 as goodwill and Rs. 15,000 as capital. Half the goodwill is withdrawn by old partners, and stock and furniture is depreciated by 10%. A provision of 5% on debtors is created and value of building is taken at Rs. 27,000. The profit on revaluation will be

(a) Rs. 5,500 (b) Rs. 5,580
(c) Rs. 5,400 (d) Rs. 5,680

**172.** A and B are partners in a firm sharing profits in the ratio of 3:2. They admit C as a new partner for 1/3 share in the profits of the firm. The new profit-sharing ratio of A, B and C is

(a) 3:2:1 (b) 3:2:2
(c) 3:2:3 (d) 6:4:5

**173.** Under the net worth method, the basis of ascertaining profit is the

(a) Difference between the liabilities on two dates.
(b) Difference between the gross assets on two dates.
(c) Difference between the capital on two dates.
(d) Increase in net worth before adjusting for drawings and additions to capital.

**174.** A non-performing asset with a financial institution denotes an asset on which

(a) Regular dividend is not being received.
(b) Interest is on default for two quarters or more.
(c) Repayment of capital appears difficult.
(d) There is no earning of profit

**175.** A company forfeited 100 shares of Rs. 10 each owing to the default in the payment of share call money of Rs. 5 each. These shares were issued at Rs. 9 each, payable at Rs. 2 on application Rs. 2 on allotment and the balance of Rs. 5 on call. The shares were then reissued to another share holder at a price of Rs. 6 per share

*The amount to be debited to forfrited shares account on account of discount on reissue of shares would be*

(a) Rs. 100 (b) Rs. 300
(c) Rs. 400 (d) Rs. 500

**176.** The issue of bonus shares must be in accordance with the guidelines issued by the
(a) Company Law Board
(b) Controller of Capital Issues
(c) Securities and Exchange Board of India
(d) Registrar of Companies

**177.** Consider the following statements:
I. Obsolescence of some of the stock
II. Slow-moving inventory
III. Frequent stock-outs
IV. Fast- moving inventory

*Which of the above statement (s) is/are correct?*

(a) I and II (b) IV alone
(c) II alone (d) II and III

**178.** Consider the following ratios:
I. Acid test ratio.
II. Capital turnover ratio.
III. Bad debts to sales ratio.
IV. Inventory turnover ratio.

*Which of these ratios are more appropriate for testing the liquidity of a concern?*

(a) I and III (b) I and IV
(c) II and IV (d) II and III

**179.** Consider the given data:
I. Proprietory ratio = 0.75
II. Current ratio = 2:1
III. Proprietory fund = Rs. 60,000
IV. Fixed assets = Rs. 50.000

*The working capital will be computed as*

(a) Rs. 10,000 (b) Rs. 15,000
(c) Rs. 20,000 (d) Rs. 25,000

**180.** Consider the following Balance sheet of ABC Company Limited as on March 31, 1999:

| Liabilities | Rs. | Assets | | Rs. |
|---|---|---|---|---|
| Equity shares capital | 20,00,000 | Fixed assets | 60,00,000 | |
| Preference share capital | 10,00,000 | Less depre- ciation | 20,00,000 | 40,00,000 |
| General reserve | 5,00,000 | | | |
| 10% debentures | 11,00,000 | Debtors | | 10,00,000 |
| Creditors | 7,00,000 | Stock | | 6,00,000 |
| Out standing expenses | 3,00,000 | Cash | | 1,00,000 |
| Profit & Loss A/c | 1,05,000 | Format- ion Exp- enses | | 5,000 |
| | 57,05,000 | | | 57,05,000 |

*The current ratio of ABC company is*

(a) 2.00 (b) 1.90
(c) 1.85 (d) 1.70

**181.** Match List I with List II and select the correct answer using the codes given below the Lists:

| List I | List II |
|---|---|
| I. Current assets ÷ Current liabilities | A. Performance of equity capital |
| II. Fixed assets ÷ Long-term funds | B. Short-term solvency |
| III. Debt Equity | C. Capital structure |
| IV. Earnings after interest and taxes ÷ Number of shares issued | D. Over all perfor- mance |

***Codes:***

(a) I-B, II-E, III-C, IV-D
(b) I-A, II-B, III-C, IV-D
(c) I-B, II-E, III-D, IV-C
(d) I-A, II-B, III-D, IV-C

**Directions (182-183):** *These questions are based on the following Balance sheet of M/s. A Ltd. as on 31st Dec., 1998:*

| Liabilities | Rs. (in lakhs) | Assets | Rs. (in lakhs) |
|---|---|---|---|
| Owned funds | 25.00 | Fixed assets | 27.00 |
| Long term bebt | 1.50 | Current assets | 6.10 |
| Current liabilities | 5.00 | Other assets | 0.40 |
| Unclaimed dividends | 0.20 | | |
| Provisions | 1.80 | | |
| | 33.50 | | 33.50 |

*Study the Balance sheet carefully and attempt the following questions:*

**182.** 'Owned funds' would be
(a) Rs. 25 lakh (b) Rs. 8.50 lakh
(c) Rs. 25. 20 lakh (d) Rs. 27 lakh

**183.** The 'margin of safety'. *i.e.*, the cushion of protection for creditors is
(a) 4.06:1 (b) Rs. 4.60 lakh.
(c) 0.20:1 (d) Rs. 22 lakh.

**184.** If the management of A Limited want to evaluate the general efficiency, which one of the following additional information is required?
(a) Sales and earnings after income-tax and interest.
(b) Break-up of owned funds into share capital, reserves and surpluses, etc.
(c) Earnings before income-tax and interest.
(d) Operating expenses and sales.

**185.** Financial indicators of four companies are as follows:

| Com-pany | Current ratio | Debt equity ratio | Rate of return on investment | Fixed assets turnover |
|---|---|---|---|---|
| A | 2.0:1 | 2.5:1 | 10% | 5 |
| B | 2.5:1 | 3.0:1 | 25% | 4 |
| C | 1.5:1 | 4.0:1 | 20% | 3 |
| D | 1.0:1 | 3.5:1 | 15% | 2 |

*In general, which of the above companies would fall in the highest risk class?*
(a) A and B (b) B and C
(c) C and D (d) A and D

**186.** Consider the particulars given below:
Sales = Rs. 60,000
Variable cost = Rs. 25,000
Fixed cost = Rs. 30,000

*Based on these data, the operating leverage shall be*
(a) 5 (b) 7
(c) 8 (d) 9

**187.** Consider the following statements:
*Redeemable preference shares of a company can be redeemed out of*
I. Profits of the company which would otherwise be available for dividend.
II. Company's share premium account.
III. Fresh issue of shares made for the purpose of redemption.
*Which of the above shatements are correct?*
(a) I and II (b) I and III
(c) II and III (d) I, II and III

**188.** The main purpose of depreciation accounting is to
(a) Charge the cost of asset.
(b) Allocate the cost of the asset over its estimated useful life.
(c) Provide of replacement of the asset on the expiry of its useful life.
(d) Value the assets on the closing date of the year.

**189.** Which one of the following pairs is not correctly matched?
(a) Increase in working capital ____ Application of fund
(b) Increase in current liability ____ Source of fund.
(c) Issue of shares ____ Source of fund.
(d) Issue of bonus shares ____ Source of fund.

**190.** Consider the following statements:
I. Operational loss is a source of funds.
II. Decrease in working capital is a source of funds.
III. Additions to fixed assets are an application of funds.
IV. Fresh introduction of capital is an application of funds.
*Which of the above statements are applicable while preparing the funds flow statements?*
(a) I and II (b) I and III
(c) II and III (d) I, III and IV

**191.** A company's reported current profit is Rs. 70,000 after incorporating the following: Loss on sale of investments Rs. 10,000; Premium on redemption of debentures Rs. 1,500; Depreciation on machinery and plant Rs. 20,000; Goodwill and preliminary expenses written off Rs. 30,000; Gain from sale of non current assets Rs. 40,000. The net inflow of funds from the operation would be

(a) Rs. 91,500 (b) Rs. 80,000
(c) Rs. 70,000 (d) Rs. 59,500

**192.** For the purpose of analysing changes in financial position, enterprises prepare
(a) Balance sheet and Profit and Loss A/c.
(b) Cash flow statement and funds flow statement.
(c) Statement of cash from operations and Balance sheet.
(d) Statement of changes in working capital and statement of cash from operations.

**193.** Materiality in accounting is decided
(a) By the size of an item.
(b) By the knowledge as to whether an individual item is having a significant influence on financial statement.
(c) Solely by the discretion of the accountant.
(d) By the physical volume of the transaction.

**194.** Match List I (Event) with List II(Result) and select the correct answer using the codes given below the Lists:

| List I | List II |
|---|---|
| I. Collusion between two or more persons | A. Payments of dividends othrwise not possible |
| II. Falsification of accounts to increase apparent profits. | B. Error of principle committed. |
| III. Operation of an effective system of internal check | C. Trial balance may agree. |
| IV. Purchase of raw materials is debited to Loose tools and concealed. | D. Frauds perpetrated and account |
| | E. Possiblility of errors and frauds is considerably reduced |

*Codes:*
(a) I-C, II-D, III-E, IV-B
(b) I-D, II-A, III-E, IV-B
(c) I-D, II-A, III-B, IV-E
(d) I-B, II-D, III-A, IV-C

**195.** Accounting is the process of matching
(a) Benefits and costs
(b) Revenues and costs
(c) Cash inflows and outflows.
(d) Potential and real performance.

**196.** A had started business with Rs. 20,000 in the beginning of the year. During the year he borrowed Rs. 10,000 from B. He further Introduced Rs. 20,000 in the business. He also gave Rs. 5,000 as loan to his son. Goods given away as charity by him was Rs.2,000. Profits earned by him was Rs. 25,000. He also withdrew Rs. 3,000 from the business His capital at the end of the year would be

(a) Rs. 50,000 (b) Rs. 40,000
(c) Rs. 62,000 (d) Rs. 48,000

**197.** Match List I with List II and select the correct answer using the codes given below the list

| List I | List II |
|---|---|
| I. A long term debt instrument on which interest is accumulated and paid on maturity | A. Mutual fund |
| II. A debt instrument on which rebate is available under the Income Tax Act | B. Deep Discount Bond |
| III. Pooling together the money of different investors and investing it in diversified securities | C. Infrastructure Bond |
| IV. Buying the right but not the obligation to sell a security for a specific price | D. Put option |

*Codes:*
(a) I-D, II-A, III-B, IV-C
(b) I-B, II-C, III-A, IV-D
(c) I-C, II-A, III-B, IV-D
(d) I-C, II-A, III-D, IV-B

**198.** To guard against the dangers of excess payment arising out of double insurance or over-insurance made by the insured, insurance companies provide in their agreement.
(a) Average clause.
(b) Subrogation clause.
(c) Risk clause.
(d) Indemnity clause.

**199.** A person insured his property worth Rs. 10,000 against fire for Rs. 8,000. His actual loss by fire is Rs. 5,000 and there is an average clause in the policy. His claim will be
(a) Rs. 10,000 (b) Rs. 8,000
(c) Rs. 5,000 (d) Rs. 4,000

**200.** In the Balance sheet, under the sub-heading 'current liabilities and provisions', disclosure of the name (s) of small-scale industries/under takings is required if the company owes a sum
(a) Exceeding Rs. 1 lakh as outstanding for more than 6 months.
(b) Not exceeding Rs. 1 lakh as outstanding for more than 6 months.
(c) Exceeding Rs. 1 lakh as outstanding for more than 30 days.
(d) Exceeding Rs. 50,000 as outstanding for more than 2 months.

**Directions** - *These questions (Q.201-216)consist of two statements, one labelled the Assertion (A) and the other labelled the Reason (R). You are to examine these two statements carefully and decide if the Assertion A and the Reason R are individually true and if so, whether the Reason is a correct explanation of the Assertion. Select your answers to these items using the codes.*

**201. Assertion (A) :** Management accounting provides management with information for decision making

**Reason (R) :** Management accounting is a branch of cost accounting.

***Codes:***
(a) Both A and R, are true, and R is the correct explanation of A.
(b) Both A and R are true, but R is not a correct explanation of A.
(c) A is true but R is false.
(d) A is false but R is true.

**202. Assertion (A) :** Under diminishing balance method of depreciation, the charge for depreciation keeps on diminishing year after year in all subsequent years.

**Reason (R) :** Under diminishing balance method, the rate per cent at which depreciation is written off goes on diminishing form year to year.

***Codes:***
(a) Both A and R are true, and R is the correct. explanation of A.
(b) Both A and R are , true but R is not a correct explanation of A.
(c) A is ture but R is false.
(d) A is false but R is true.

**203. Assertion (A) :** No item of capital expendit-ure finds its place in the Trading and profit & Loss Account or some other form of revenue accounts.

**Reason (R) :** Capital expenditure consists of expenditure, the benefit of which is not fully consumed in one accounting period but is spread over several periods.

***Codes:***
(a) Both A and R, are true, and R is the correct explanation of A.
(b) Both A and R, are true, but R is not a correct explanation of A.
(c) A is true, but R is false.
(d) A is false, but R is true.

**204. Assertion (A):** Now-a-days many companies prepare their Balance sheet in a vertical form rather than in the traditional horizontal form.

**Reason (R) :** Part IV of schedule IV to the companies Act, 1956 permits both the forms.

*Codes:*

(a) Both A and R are true, and R is the correct explanation of A.

(b) Both A and R are true, but R is not a correct explanation of A

(c) A is true, but R is false

(d) A is false, but R is true.

**205. Assertion (A) :** When pro-rata allotment of shares is made, the surplus application money is transferred to share allotment A/c.

**Reason (R) :** The company is not required to pay any interest on such surplus application money.

*Codes:*

(a) Both A and R are true, and R is the correct explanation of A.

(b) Both A and R are true, but R is not a correct explanation of A.

(c) A is true, but R is false.

(d) A is false, but R is true.

**206. Assertion (A) :** One single primary ratio, that measures the financial out come of all recorded business activities, is ROI.

**Reason (R) :** In practice, however, variations are also found in the ratio because capital and return are subject to different interpretations by firms.

*Codes:*

(a) Both A and R, are true, and R is the correct explanation of A.

(b) Both A and R, are true,but R is not a correct explanation of A.

(c) A is true, but R is false.

(d) A is false, but R is true.

**207. Assertion (A) :** ROI is the index to study management efficiency.

**Reason (R) :** Earning power in relation to total investment is measured by ROI.

*Codes:*

(a) Both A and R, are true, and R is the correct explanation of A.

(b) Both A and R, are true, but R is not a correct explanation of A.

(c) A is true, but R is false.

(d) A is false, but R is true.

**208. Assertion (A) :** For a company, every debt is not a loan, but every loan is a debt.

**Reason (R) :** In the case of deposit of money with the company, it is the depositor who is the prime mover, where as in the case of loan it is the company who is the prime mover.

*Codes:*

(a) Both A and R, are true, and R is the correct explanation of A.

(b) Both A and R, are true,but R is not a correct explanation of A.

(c) A is true, but R is false.

(d) A is false, but R is true.

**209. Assertion (A) :** A company is accountable to the society since it makes use of community owned assets and other infrastructural facilities and concessions provided by the state from the tax payers' money.

**Reason (R) :** The best way of social responsibility reporting is to prepare a Value-Added Statement (VAS) which shows the income earned by share holders.

*Codes:*

(a) Both A and R, are true, and R is the correct explanation of A.

(b) Both A and R, are true, but R is not a correct explanation of A.

(c) A is true, but R is false.

(d) A is false, but R is true.

**210. Assertion (A) :** The matching concept requires that costs be recognised as expenses in the period in which revenue is realised.

**Reason (R)** : There may not be a match between expenditure and expenses over a short period.

*Codes:*

(a) Both A and R, are true, and R is the correct explanation of A.
(b) Both A and R, are true, but R is not a correct explanation of A.
(c) A is true, but R is false.
(d) A is false, but R is true.

**211. Assertion (A) :** According to International Accounting Standards Committee, fixed production expenses should be included in inventory valuation on the basis of normal capacity. According to the Institute of chartered Accountants of India, it is for the management to decide the Question.

**Reason (R)** : The Question to be decided is whether the fixed product- ion expenses be excluded from inventory valuation and charged wholly to the revenue of that year or whether these expenses be included on the basis of normal level of production.The former method, is called 'marginal costing' and the latter 'absorption costing?

*Codes:*

(a) Both A and R, are true, and R is the correct explanation of A.
(b) Both A and R, are true,but R is not a correct explanation of A.
(c) A is true, but R is false.
(d) A is false, but R is true.

**212. Assertion (A) :** The fixed assets in the balance sheet of a limited company are required to be shown at cost less depreciation.

**Reason (R)** : The balance sheet and profit and loss account are to disclose a true and fair view.

*Codes:*

(a) Both A and R, are true, and R is the correct explanation of A.
(b) Both A and R, are true, but R is not a correct explanation of A.
(c) A is true, but R is false.
(d) A is false, but R is true.

**213. Assertion (A) :** Share premium amount can be refunded in cash to equity share holders.

**Reason (R)** : Share premium is usually collected when the market price of the shares is higher than the face value of the share.

*Codes:*

(a) Both A and R, are true, and R is the correct explanation of A.
(b) Both A and R, are true,but R is not a correct explanation of A.
(c) A is true, but R is false.
(d) A is false, but R is true.

**214. Assertion (A) :** Conventionally, a newly-started company should adopt a low geared capital structure where the share of equity capital and reserves is higher than the share of fixed interest bearing securities.

**Reason (R)** : During initial years, the profit is low and the company tries to strengthen its financial position.

*Codes:*

(a) Both A and R, are true, and R is the correct explanation of A.
(b) Both A and R, are true,but R is not a correct explanation of A.
(c) A is true, but R is false.
(d) A is false, but R is true.

**215. Assertion (A) :** A new firm can be profittable and yet not be able to pay its debts as they become due.

**Reason (R)** : New firms often have the problem of having increased investments in inventory and fixed assets at an amount which exceeds cash generated from operations.

*Codes:*

(a) Both A and R, are true, and R is the correct explanation of A.
(b) Both A and R, are true, but R is not a correct explanation of A.
(c) A is true, but R is false.
(d) A is false, but R is true.

**216.** Which one of the following routines best describes the chronology of steps taken in the selling process?
(a) Receipt of order, invoicing, processing order, shipment of goods.
(b) Invoicing, processing order, shipment of goods, accounting for sale.
(c) Receipt of order, processing order, accounting for sale, shipment of goods
(d) Processing order, invoicing, shipment of goods, accounting for sale.

**217.** When prices show a rising trend, which one of the following methods of inventory valuation will result in lower income and lower valuation of inventory?
(a) F I F O
(b) L I F O
(c) Simple average method.
(d) Weighted average method.

**218.** Under which one of the following methods of depreciation is the amount of the assets never reduced to zero?
(a) Staright line method
(b) Diminishing balance method
(c) Sum of years digit method
(d) Annuity method

**219.** Consider the following statements :
*Secret reserves serve the purpose of*
I. enabling the directors to tide over unfavourable items
II. meeting exceptional losses
III. increasing the working capital
*of these statement*
(a) I and II are correct
(b) II and III are corect
(c) I and III are correct
(d) I, II and III are correct

**220.** ABC analysis is a
(a) system of profit and loss appropriation
(b) technique of financial planning
(c) technique of inventory control
(d) technique of profit determination

**221.** A sum of Rs. 50,000 was spent by a factory in over – hauling its existing plant and machinery and it enhanced its working life by five years.
*The aforesaid expenditure is*
(a) Capital expenditure
(b) Partly capital and partly revenue expenditure.
(c) Revenue loss.
(d) Deferred revenue expenditure.

**222.** Match List I (Items of Expenditure and receipt) with List II (Nature of Expenditure and Receipt) and select the correct answer using the codes given bolow the lists:

| List I | List II |
|---|---|
| I. Replacement cost of an old asset | A. Revenue expenditure |
| II. Special repairing charges of an asset | B. Capital receipt |
| III. Huge advertisement expenses | C. Defered revenue expenditure |
| IV. Sale value of an old motorcar | D. Capital expenditure |

*Codes:*
(a) I-D, II-A, III-C, IV-B
(b) I-D, II-A, III-B, IV-C
(c) I-A, II-D, III-C, IV-B
(d) I-A, II-D, III-B, IV-C

**223.** Which one of the following is not a capital expenditure
(a) Legal expenses incurred in raising a debenture loan
(b) Compensation paid to a dismissed employee
(c) Brokerage paid to the broker at the time of purchase
(d) Expenses for pulling down on old structure

**224.** Out standing wages is an item of
(a) Current asset
(b) Curent liability
(c) Non-current asset
(d) Non-current liability

**225.** A and B partners sharing profits and losses in the ratio of 3 : 1. They have agreed to admit C into the partnership firm C is given 1/4 th share of future profits which he acquires in the ratio 2: 1 from A and B. The new profit sharing ratio would be :

(a) 4:3:1 (b) 7:2:3
(c) 3:1:7 (d) 7:3:2

**226.** A, B, C were partners sharing profits in the proportion of 1/2, 1/3 and 1/6 respectively. On 31st March, 1997 their capital stood as follows:

A = Rs. 4,00,000
B = Rs. 3,00.000
C = Rs. 2,50,000

A sum of Rs. 1,20,000 also appeared as reserve fund in their balance sheet on this date. B retires on this date when the goodwill of the firm was valued at Rs. 1,80,000.

Profit and loss adjustment account prepared on that date without taking good will and reserve fund into consideration showed a net profit of Rs. 28500. The net amount payable to B will be:

(a) Rs. 3,82,500 (b) Rs. 4,09,500
(c) Rs. 3,63,800 (d) Rs. 4,04,000

**227.** X and Y are partners sharing profits in the ratio of 1:1. They admit Z for 1/5 th share who contributed Rs. 25,000 for his share of goodwill. The total value of the goodwill of the firm will be

(a) Rs. 25,000 (b) Rs. 50,000
(c) Rs. 1,00,000 (d) Rs. 1,25,000

**228.** On the death of a partner, the amount of joint life policy should be credited to the capital accounts of

(a) all partners including the deceased partner in their profit-sharing ratio.
(b) remaining partners in the new profit sharing ratio.
(c) remaining partners equally.
(d) all partners including the deceased partners in their capital ratio.

**229.** In the absence of any contract to the contrary, capital profit or arising on dissolution of a partnership firm is credited to the partners' capital account in

(a) Equal proportion.
(b) Capital ratio.
(c) Profit-sharing ratio.
(d) Proportion to assets realised.

**230.** Writing off the expired cost of an intangible asset is called

(a) Amortisation (b) Capitalisation
(c) Depletion (d) Depreciation.

**231.** The debt equity ratio of a company is 8:1. It was decided to issue bonus shares in the ratio of 1:2. The debt equity ratio after the issue of bonus shares would be

(a) 8:1 (b) 4:1
(c) 1:8 (d) 1:4

**232.** Profit prior to incorporation is an example of

(a) Revenue reserve (b) Secret reserve
(c) Capital reserve (d) General reserve

**233.** To provide funds to pay to the retiring partner or to the representatives of a deceased partner, generally partners:

(a) Create a Sinking Fund
(b) Create Joint Life Policy
(c) Create Reserve Fund
(d) Create a Separate Bank A/C

**234.** The ratios which measure the relative contribution of financing by owners and financing provided by out siders are called

(a) Liquidity ratios.
(b) Leverage ratios.
(c) Activity ratios.
(d) Profitability ratios.

**235.** Right's shares are the shares that are offered to the

(a) Directors of the company.
(b) Debenture holders.
(c) Existing share holders.
(d) Creditors of the company.

**236.** Unpaid calls are shown in the balance sheet of a company.

(a) By adding it to the share capital.
(b) By deducting it from the called-up share capital.
(c) Under the head, 'current assets'.
(d) Under the head, 'current liabilities.

**237.** Pro-rata allotment of shares means allotment of shares

(a) Equally amongst the applicants.
(b) At the discretion of the directors.
(c) To all the applicants in proportion to the shares applied for.
(d) To only a few selected applicants.

**238.** Match List I with List II and select the correct answer using the codes given below the Lists :

| List I | List II |
|---|---|
| I. Acid test ratio. | A. Liquidity ratio. |
| II. Gearing ratio. | B. Profitability ratio. |
| III. Working capital turnover ratio. | C. Leverage ratio. |
| IV. Return on capital employed. | D. Long-term solvency ratio. |
| | E. Activity ratio. |

*Codes:*
(a) I-A, II-C, III-E, IV-B
(b) I-B, II-E, III-A, IV-C
(c) I-A, II-E, III-D, IV-B
(d) I-E, II-C, III-D, IV-A

**239.** Which of the following transaction(s) will improve the Current Ratio?
I. Bills receivable dishonoured.
II. Cash collected from customers.
III. Issue of new shares.
IV. Payment of preliminary expenses by way of equity shares.
*Select the correct answer using the codes given below:*
*Codes:*
(a) I, II and III (b) IV alone
(c) III alone (d) II and IV

**240.** In the case of a particular depreciation method, the periodic depreciation is smaller than the asset's actual annual depreciation cost. The annual net incidence on profit and loss account remains constant due to incroporation of only fixed depreciation. The periodic depreciation is not recorded through the asset account. The depreciation method used in this case is.
(a) Sinking fund method.
(b) Diminishing balance method.
(c) Annuity method.
(d) Sum-of-years digits method.

**241.** X Ltd. forfeited 30 shares of Rs. 10 each fully called up for non-payment of allotment money of Rs. 3 per share and call money of Rs. 4 per share. These shares are re-issued for Rs. 8 per share fully paid. What is the amount to be transferred to capital Reserve Account?
(a) Rs. 300 (b) Rs. 60
(c) Rs. 30 (d) Rs. 90

**242.** Credit sales of a company during the year are Rs. 1,20,000. Debtors Rs. 20,000 and Bills Receivable Rs. 10,000. The average collection period is
(a) 3 Months (b) 4 Months
(c) 5 Months (d) 6 Months

**243.** Collection of sundry debtors would
(a) Increase current ratio.
(b) Decrease current ratio.
(c) Have no effect on current ratio.
(d) Increase debtors turnover.

**244.** Which one of the following statements is not correct?
*A high gross profit margin ratio is the result of*
(a) higher sales price,cost of goods sold remaining constant
(b) lower cost of goods sold, sales price remaining constant
(c) an increase in the proportionate volume of higher margin items
(d) increase in the sales return, cost of goods sold remaining the same

**245.** A company with a paid -up capital of 5000 equity shares of Rs. 10 each has a turnover of four times with a margin of 8% on sales. The ROI of the company will be
(a) 28% (b) 32%
(c) 35% (d) 42%

**246.** The best definition of 'Capital employed' in calculating the rate of return on investment is
(a) Current assets + gross fixed assets
(b) Current assets + net fixed assets
(c) Working capital + gross fixed assets
(d) Working capital + net fixed assets

**247.** While calculating the net present value under discounted cash flow method of return on investment analysis, the calculations involved are :
I. Cash outflow
II. Discounted net cash flow
III. Cash inflow
IV. Net present value
*The correct sequence of these calculations is*
(a) IV, I, III, II (b) I, III, II, IV
(c) I, II, III, IV (d) III, I, IV, II

**248.** Patents and copyrights fall under sthe catetgory of
(a) Current assets (b) Liquid assets
(c) Intangible assets (d) Nominal assets

**249.** Match List I (Balance sheet items) with is List II (classification) and select the correct answer using the codes given below the Lists:

| List I | List II |
|---|---|
| I. Discount on debenture | A. Current liability |
| II. Forfeited shares | B. Non-current asset account |
| III. Incometax payable | C. Current asset |
| IV. Debtors' acceptance | D. Non-current liability. |

***Codes :***
(a) I-B, II-D, III-A, IV-C
(b) I-D, II-B, III-C, IV-A
(c) I-B, II-D, III-C, IV-A
(d) I-D, II-B, III-A, IV-C

**250.** Ajoy Ltd. makes a net profit of Rs. 1,00,000, after providing for depreciation on assets amounting to Rs. 20.000 and writing off preliminary expenses amounting to Rs. 10,000 and gain of Rs. 5,000 on sale of a piece of machinery. Funds from operation of Ajoy Ltd. would be
(a) Rs. 1,00,000 (b) Rs. 1,20,000
(c) Rs. 1,25,000 (d) Rs. 1,35,000

**251.** Which one of the following statements is correct?
(a) A decrease in current liabilities causes and increase in the working capital.
(b) An increase in current liabilities causes a decrease in the working capital
(c) A decrease in the current assets causes an increase in the working capital.
(d) An increase in the current assets causes a decrease in the working capital.

**252.** Match List I with List II and select the correct answer using the codes given below the Lists:

| List I | List II |
|---|---|
| I. Net loss from operations | A. Source of funds. |
| II. Changes in working capital | B. Drain on working capital |
| III. Depreciation | C. Flow of funds. |
| IV. Issue of fully paid bonus shares. | D. Neither source nor application of funds. |

***Codes :***
(a) I-C, II-B, III-A, IV-D
(b) I-B, II-C, III-D, IV-A
(c) I-B, II-C, III-A, IV-D
(d) I-C, II-B, III-D, IV-A

**253.** Which of the following are the means of marketing new issues of securities?
I. By listing of securities.
II. Through jobbers and brokers.
III. By private placing of securities
IV. Through privileged subscripitions.
*Select the correct answer using the codes given below*
***Codes:***
(a) I and II (b) I, II and III
(b) III and IV (c) I, II, III and IV

**254.** On death of a partner, his executor is paid the share of profits of the dying partner for the relevant period. This payment is recorded in which account?
(a) Profit and Loss Adjustment A/C
(b) Profit and Loss Appropriation A/C
(c) Profit and Loss Suspense A/C
(d) Profit and Loss Reserve A/C

**255.** Match List I with List II and select the correct answer using the codes given below the Lists:

| List I | List II |
|---|---|
| I. LUT | A. D G F T |
| II. EPZ | B. exports promotion |
| III. E P C G Scheme | C. 100% exports |
| IV. Value Addition | D. 100% E O U |

***Codes :***
(a) I-A, II-C, III-B, IV-D
(b) I-C, II-B, III-A, IV-D
(c) I-A, II-D, III-C, IV-B
(d) I-B, II-D, III-A, IV-C

**256.** A second hand machinery was purchased for Rs. 1,00,000 five years ago and was overhauled by carrying out some current repairs at a cost of Rs. 10,000. It has also an accumulated depreciation of Rs. 50,000. It has been disposed

of in the beginning of the six the year for Rs. 60,000. Profit/ Loss on such disposal shall be.
(a) Profit of Rs. 10,000
(b) Loss of Rs. 50,000
(c) Loss of Rs. 40,000
(d) No profit, no loss.

**257.** Match List I with List II and select the correct answer using the codes given below the lists:

| List I | List II |
|---|---|
| I. Income measurement | A. Accrues to owner's equity |
| II. Expense recognition | B. Revenue recognition |
| III. Basis for realisation accounting | C. Matching revenues and expenses |
| IV. Recognised revenue | D. Accounting period |

*Codes :*
(a) I-C, II-D, III-B, IV-A
(b) I-C, II-D, III-A, IV-B
(c) I-B, II-C, III-D, IV-A
(d) I-B, II-C, III-A, IV-D

**258.** Charging a period for the proportionate cost of an intangible asset is termed as
(a) Depreciation (b) Diminution
(c) Amortisation (d) Expiration

**259.** Obsolescence means decline in the value due to
(a) Fall in the market price.
(b) Physical wear and tear.
(c) Innovations and inventions.
(d) Efflux of time.

**260.** Concept of conservatism refers to taking into account
(a) All profit.
(b) Only cash profit.
(c) Only profit realised.
(d) Profit realised and all possible losses.

**261.** Which one of the following accounting standards is not mandatory in India?
(a) Fixed assets accounting and revenue recognition.
(b) Inventory and depreciation accounting.
(c) Non-monetary assets and fixed assets.
(d) Monetary assets and depreciation accounting.

**262.** If the total charge of depreciation and maintenance is considered, the method which would provide a uniform charge is
(a) Annuity method.
(b) Straight line method.
(c) Diminishing balance method.
(d) Insurance policy method.

**263.** Which of the following expenditures are to be treated as revenue expenditure?
I. Interest paid on money borrowed during construction period.
II. Cost of patent Rights.
III. Loss of uninsured stock due to fire.
IV. Retirement gratuity paid to an employee.
*Select the correct answer using the codes given below:*
*Codes:*
(a) I, II, and III (b) II, III, and IV
(c) III, and IV (d) I and II

**264.** Payment of compensation to a worker, who has been discharged from service, is a
(a) Capital expenditure
(b) Revenue expenditure
(c) Deferred revenue expenditure
(d) Non-business expenditure

**265.** Expenditure incurred on research is an example of
(a) Capital expenditure
(b) Revenue expenditure
(c) Deferred revenue expenditure
(d) Partly capital expenditure and partly revenue expenditure

**266.** Rs. 19,500 debited to building repairs on 31st Dec. 1993 included Rs. 9,500 as the cost of building a small room for the watchman. A bill of Rs. 800 for colour wash of the whole building during the year was not received till 1993 Dec. The amount to be debited to profit and loss account would be
(a) Rs. 20,300 (b) Rs. 19,500
(c) Rs. 10,800 (d) Rs. 9,500

267. The term loan of Rs. 5,00,000 was received from IFCI. It was used as under

I. Rs. 2,00,000 was advanced to suppliers for capital work-in-progress and

II. Rs. 3,00,000 was used for financing the working capital

*The interest payable would be treated*

(a) On both I and II as capital expenditure

(b) On I as capital expenditure and on II as revenue expenditure

(c) On I as deferred expenditure and on II as revenue expenditure

(d) On I as deferred revenue expenditure and on II as capital expenditure

268. A, B and C are partners sharing profit and losses in the ratio 9:4:3. They took joint life policy of Rs. 25,000 for A, Rs. 20,000 for B and Rs. 51,000 for C. What is the share of C is JLP amount ?

(a) Rs. 18,000 (b) Rs. 25,000
(c) Rs. 51,000 (d) Rs. 20,000

269. Which of the following statement is false

(a) Interest on calls -in-advance is paid from the date of receipt of the advance to the date of relevant call.

(b) Interest on calls-in-advance is paid from the date of receipt of advance to the date of appropriation to the relevant call.

(c) Interest on calls-in-advance is paid at the rate of 6% P.A..

(d) Payment of interest on calls-in-advance is at the discretion of the company.

270. T Ltd. proposed to issue 6,000 equity shares of Rs. 100 each at a premium of 40%. The minimum amount of application money to be collected per share is

(a) Rs. 5.00 (b) Rs. 6.00
(c) Rs. 7.00 (d) Rs. 8.40

271. The directors of B Ltd. made the final call of Rs. 30 per share on January 15,2004 indicating the last date of payment of call money to be January 31,2004. Mr. C holding 7,500 shares paid the call money on March 15,2004.
If the company adopts Table A of the Companies Act the amount of interest on calls-in-Arrears by Mr. C. Will be

(a) Rs. 937.50 (b) Rs. 1,406.25
(c) Rs. 1,125.00 (d) Rs. 1,687.50

272. Dividends are usually paid as a percentage of

(a) Authorized share Capital
(b) Net Profit
(c) Paid-up Capital
(d) Called-up capital

273. E Ltd. had alloted 10,000 shares to the applicants of 14,000 shares on pro rata basis. The amount payable on application is Rs 2. F applied for 420 shares. The number of shares alloted and the amount carried forward for adjustment against allotment money due from F is

(a) 60 shares; Rs. 120
(b) 340 shares; Rs. 160
(c) 320 shares; Rs. 200
(d) 300 shares; Rs. 240

274. A Company forfeited 2,000 shares of Rs. 10 each (which were issued at par) held by Mr. John for non-payment of allotment money of Rs. 4 per share. The called-up value per share was Rs. 9 on forfeiture, the amount debited to share capital is

(a) Rs. 10,000 (b) Rs. 8,000
(c) Rs. 2,000 (d) Rs. 18,000

275. If forfeited shares ( which were originally issued at discount) are reissued at a premium, the amount of such premium will be credited to

(a) Share Forfeiture A/C
(b) Share Premium A/C
(c) Capital Reserve A/C
(d) Discount on issue of shares A/C

276. The maximum amount beyond which a company is not allowed to raise funds, by issue of share is its

(a) Issued Capital (b) Reserve Capital
(c) Nominal Capital (d) Subscribed capital

277. Declared dividend should be classified in the Balance Sheet as a

(a) Provision
(b) Current liability
(c) Reserve
(d) Current Asset

**278.** As per schedule VI of the Companies Act, 1956, under which of the following heads is 'Premium on issue of preference shares' shown in the balance sheet of a company.
(a) Miscellaneous Expenditure
(b) Debentures
(c) Reserves and Surplus
(d) Current Liabilities Provisions

**279.** When sale is Rs. 4,80,000, gross loss is 25% on cost, purchase is Rs. 3,50,000 and closing stock is Rs. 60,000, the stock in the beginning would be
(a) Rs. 70,000 (b) Rs. 94,000
(c) Rs. 1,34,000 (d) Rs. 3,50,000

**280.** Which one of the following is NOT a current liability?
(a) Acceptances
(b) Loan instalment payable in the current year.
(c) Temporary bank overdraft.
(d) Arrears of preference dividend.

**281.** It is given that the cost of the stock is Rs. 100. However, its current market price is Rs. 95 (buying) and Rs. 90 (selling). If the market price is interpreted in the sense of replacement cost, the stock should be valued at
(a) Rs. 95 (b) Rs. 100
(c) Rs. 90 (d) Rs. 93

**282.** When ever debentures are cancelled ,any profit on cancellation is transferred to
(a) Profit and loss account.
(b) Sinking fund account.
(c) Capital redemption reserve account.
(d) Capital reserve account.

**283.** Given that

| | | |
|---|---|---|
| Closing stock | Rs. | 30,000 |
| Opening stock | Rs. | 20,000 |
| Sales | Rs. | 1,00,000 |
| Administrative and selling Expenses | Rs. | 20,000 |
| Purchases | Rs. | 70,000 |

*The operating ratio is*
(a) 50% (b) 65%
(c) 75% (d) 80%

**284.** A company issue 10,000 shares of Rs. 10 each at a discount of 10% payable as follows:
On application Rs. 2.50
On allotment Rs. 30.00
On first and final call Rs. 3.50
A holder of 100 shares did not pay the finalcall and his shares were forfeited. Share Capital A/c will be debited by
(a) Rs. 650
(b) Rs. 850
(c) Rs. 1,000
(d) Rs. 900

**285.** Consider the following statements:
Redeemable preference shares can be redeemed out of
I. Sale proceeds of the new issue of shares.
II. Sale proceeds of the new issue of debentures.
III. Profits available for dividends.
IV. Sales proceeds of the assets of the company.
*Of these statements:*
(a) I and III are correct.
(b) I alone is correct.
(c) II, III, and IV are correct.
(d) I, II, III, and IV are correct.

**286.** Match List I with List II and select the correct answer using the codes given below the Lists:

| List I | List II |
|---|---|
| I. Balance of Debenture Redemption fund account. | A. Realisation account. |
| II. Balance of sinking fund account for replacement of an asset | B. Funds flow Statement |
| III. On dissolution of a firm, the provisions made for doubtful debts appearing in Balance sheet | C. General Reserve |
| IV. Financial consequences of business operations | D. Asset Account. |

*Codes :*
(a) I-A, II-B, III-C, IV-D
(b) I-C, II-D, III-A, IV-B
(c) I-A, II-B, III-D, IV-C
(d) I-C, II-D, III-B, IV-A

**287.** Consider the following Income statement creditside :

| | |
|---|---|
| By Gross Income .................... | 1,00,000 |
| By profit on sale of investment | 5,000 |
| | 1,05,000 |
| Debit side : | |
| To salaries.............................. | 8,000 |
| Add out standing..................... | 2,000 |
| | 10,000 |
| To stationery.......................... | 2,000 |
| To rent.................................... | 3,000 |
| To provision for depreciation.. | 10,000 |
| To bad debts............................ | 2,000 |
| To loss on sale of machinery.... | 3,000 |
| To provision for taxation ......... | 10,000 |
| To net income ......................... | 65,000 |
| | 1,05,000 |

*Which one of the following will be the correct 'fund from operation'?*

(a) Rs. 73,000 (b) Rs. 75,000
(c) Rs. 83,000 (d) Rs. 92,000

**288.** Match List I with List II and select the correct answer using the codes given below the Lists:

| List I | List II |
|---|---|
| I. EAIT No. of equity shares | A. Liquidity |
| II. Outstanding Debt equity | B. Solvency |
| III. FA Long -term funds | C. Capital structure |
| IV. CA CL | D. Over all performance. |

*Codes :*

(a) I-D, II-C, III-B, IV-A
(b) I-D, II-C, III-A, IV-B
(c) I-B, II-C, III-A, IV-D
(d) I-B, II-C, III-D, IV-A

**289.** If the stock turnover ratio is 4 times and the collection period is 30 days, the operating cycle would be

(a) 30 days (b) 60 days
(c) 90 days (d) 120 days

**290.** Given:

| | |
|---|---|
| Fixed Assets ..................... | Rs.10,00,000 |
| Current Assets ................ | Rs. 6,00,000 |
| Total net profit .............. | Rs. 2,60,000 |
| Current Liabilities........... | Rs. 3,00,000 |

*Which one of the following will be correct ROI?*

(a) 26% (b) 25%
(c) 20% (d) 16.5%

**291.** Non-registration of a partnership does not affect

(a) The right of a partner to sue the firm.
(b) The right of the firm to sue third parties.
(c) The right of the third party to proceed against the firm or its partner.
(d) Any of these.

**292.** Steps to be taken in a selling systems includes:

I. Receipt of order
II. Processing order
III. Shipment of merchandise
IV. Accounting for sale

*The correct chronological sequence of these steps is*

***Codes:***

(a) I, IV, III, II (b) I, IV, II, III
(c) I, II, IV, III (d) I, II, III, IV

**Directions-** *The following questions (Q. 293-296)consist of two statements, one labelled the Assertion A and the other labelled Reason R. You are to examine these two statements carefully and decide if the Assertion A and the Reason R are individually true and if so, whether the Reason is a correct explanation of the Assertion. Select your answer to these question using the codes.*

**293. Assertion (A):** Amount realised on the disposal sale of a discarded machine of the factory should be treated as revenue receipt.

**Reason (R)** : Sale proceeds are usually of revenue in nature

***Codes:***

(a) Both A and R are true, and R is the correct explanation of A.
(b) Both A and R are true, but R is not the correct explanation of A.
(c) A is true, but R is false.
(d) A is false, but R is true.

**294. Assertion (A) :** An accounting is principle that the relatively small item and values should be ignored from accounts.

**Reason (R)** : The cost of the effort in the allocation of small items over along period does not justify the benefit derived from this operation and the cost of such items is treated as expense for the period in which they are incurred.

*Codes:*
(a) Both A and R are true, and R is the correct explanation of A.
(b) Both A and R are true, but R is not the correct explanation of A.
(c) A is true, but R is false.
(d) A is false, but R is true.

**295. Assertion (A) :** Financial leverage is beneficial only when the rate of earning is higher than the cost of debt.

**Reason (R)** : Debt-equity ratio indicates the short-term financial soundness of a business concern.

*Codes:*
(a) Both A and R are true, and R is the correct explanation of A.
(b) Both A and R are true, but R is not the correct explanation of A.
(c) A is true, but R is false.
(d) A is false, but R is true.

**296. Assertion (A) :** Break-even chart merely depicts the relationship between sales and expenses in such a way as to show at what volume revenues exactly cover expenses.

**Reason (R)** : The break-even chart shows that at any lesser volume of sale, the company would suffer a loss, and at a greater volume of sale it would enjoy a profit.

*Codes:*
(a) Both A and R are true, and R is the correct explanation of A.
(b) Both A and R are true, but R is not the correct explanation of A.
(c) A is true, but R is false.
(d) A is false, but R is true.

**297.** Share premium received by issuing shares can be used for
(a) Payment of dividend.
(b) Issue of bonus shares.
(c) Remuneration to management.
(d) Any business purpose.

**298.** Which of the following signifies the difference between par value and an issue price below par?
(a) Securities Premium
(b) Discount on issue of shares
(c) Calls-in arrear
(d) Calls in advance

**299.** Financial disintermediation results in larger
(a) Access to financial institutions.
(b) Participation of foreign financial institutions
(c) Fee-based income.
(d) Securities-related income.

**300.** Match List I with List II and select the correct answer using the codes given below the Lists:

| List I (Type of Manual Fund) | List II (Features) |
|---|---|
| I. Open-ended fund | A. Maximises short term to investors. |
| II. Income fund | B. Can sell ultimaited number of units |
| III. Close-ended fund | C. The units are not redeemable at their NAV |
| IV. Growth fund | D. Maximises long-term return to investors. |

*Codes :*
(a) I-C, II-D, III-B, IV-A
(b) I-C, II-D, III-A, IV-B
(c) I-B, II-A, III-D, IV-C
(d) I-B, II-A, III-C, IV-D

**301.** Match List I with List II and select the correct answer using the codes given below the Lists:

| List I | List II |
|---|---|
| I. Screen trading | A. Capital Market reforms |
| II. G.V. Rama Krishna Committed Report | B. Industrial Sickness |

III. BIFR — C. Disinvestment of PSU shares

IV. SEBI — D. Stock Exchange.

***Codes :***

(a) I-C, II-D, III-A, IV-B
(b) I-D, II-C, III-B, IV-A
(c) I-D, II-C, III-A, IV-B
(d) I-C, II-D, III-B, IV-A

**302.** In the last-in first out (LIFO) method, the closing stock is valued at

(a) A price which is paid for the last consignment.
(b) A price which is paid for the earlier consignments.
(c) An average price of all the consignments.
(d) None of these.

**303.** If the operating expenses exceed gross profit, the excess is referred to as

(a) Operating income.
(b) Operating loss.
(c) Non-operating expenses.
(d) Non-operating income.

**304.** On using reducing balance method on an asset of Rs. 20,000 at the rate of 10% per annum, depreciation of 3rd year will be

(a) Rs. 6,000 (b) Rs. 1,800
(c) Rs. 1,620 (d) Rs. 2,000

**305.** Accounting is

(a) The art of recording,classifying and summarising in a significant manner and in terms of money, transactions and events which are, in part at best financial in character, and interpreting there of.
(b) A systematic and regular record of events affecting a firm with a view to obtaining a clear financial picture.
(c) Preparation of various financial statements over a period of time of a firm to measure its performance in monetary terms.
(d) Nothing but book-keeping.

**306.** Aush started business on 1st April, 1995 with a capital of Rs. 25,000 and a loan of Rs. 12,500. Total assets and liabilities at the end of 31st March,1996 amounted to Rs. 75,000 and Rs. 12,500 respectively. He invested a further capital of Rs. 12, 500 during the year and with drew Rs. 7,500 during the relevant financial period. His closing capital and profits would be respectively.

(a) Rs. 62, 500 and Rs. 32,500
(b) Rs. 50,000 and Rs. 40,000
(c) Rs. 70,000 and Rs. 47,500
(d) Rs. 55,000 and Rs. 42,500

**307.** A person started business with a cash of Rs.22,000 and stock of Rs.3,000 on 1st January, 1996. During the year he made a profit of Rs. 6,000. His creditors were paid Rs. 4,500 for the office furniture supplied. He took goods worth Rs. 3,500 for his daughter's wedding on 30th June, 1996. The gross assets of his business on 31st December, 1996 was

(a) Rs. 27,500 (c) Rs. 26,500
(b) Rs. 23,500 (c) Rs. 20,500

**308.** In stock valuation, application of the principle 'at cost price or market price which ever is lower' will result in the valuation of stock sometimes at cost price and at other times at market price. *This is an application of the principle of*

(a) Consistency (b) Materiaity
(c) Conservatism (d) Disclosure

**309.** Match List I with List II and select the correct answer using the codes given below the Lists:

| List I | List II |
|---|---|
| I. Heavy amount of premium on redemption of preference shares. | A. Capital expenditure |
| II. Excess of sale proceeds of fixed assets over their original cost. | B. Deferred revenue expenditure |
| III. Cost of installation of an old machine | C. Capital gain |
| IV. Freight paid on purchase of raw material | D. Revenue expenditure |

***Codes :***

(a) I-B, II-C, III-D, IV-A
(b) I-C, II-B, III-D, IV-A
(c) I-B, II-C, III-A, IV-D
(d) I-C, II-B, III-A, IV-D

**310.** Amount spent on an advertisement compaign, the benefit of which is likely to last for three years is a
(a) Capital expenditure.
(b) Revenue expenditure.
(c) Deferred revenue expenditure.
(d) Contingent expenditure.

**311.** Match List I with List II and select the correct answer using the codes given belwo the lists:

| List I | List II |
|---|---|
| I. Preliminary expense | A. Capital expenditure. |
| II. Travelling expenses of the salesman | B. Revenue expenditure. |
| III. Profit on sale of a part of the business building | C. Capital gain |
| IV. Nazrana paid on the purchase of land for business | D. Deferred revenue expenditure |

***Codes:***
(a) I-D, II-B, III-C, IV-A
(b) I-D, II-B, III-A, IV-C
(c) I-B, II-D, III-C, IV-A
(d) I-B, II-D, III-A, IV-C

**312.** Revenue is generally recoginsed as being earned at that point of time when
(a) Sale is effected.
(b) Cash is received.
(c) Production is completed.
(d) Debts are collected.

**313.** Which one of the following will be treated as revenue expenditure?
(a) Cost incurred for a new exit as required under the local bodies' buy laws.
(b) Interest paid on loan during the construction of works.
(c) Cost of pulling down on old building as also the payment made to the architect for the plan of a new building.
(d) A dealer in sewing machines purchases sewing machines and spends some money on the repair of ten machines damaged while in transit.

**314.** Which one of the following is capital expenditure?
(a) Cost of advertisement.
(b) Purchase of a delivery van.
(c) Purchase of raw material.
(d) Purchase of machine oil.

**315.** Which one of the following depreciation methods is most suitable for a coal mine?
(a) Diminishing balance method.
(b) Depletion method.
(c) Fixed instalment method.
(d) Sum of years'digits method.

**316.** In the case of a sole proprietorship, Assets in Balance sheet items are conveniently shown in
(a) Order of fixity.
(b) Order of liquidity.
(c) Alphabetical order.
(d) Order of dates of acquisition.

**317.** A business concorn provides the following details:

| | |
|---|---|
| Cost of goods sold | Rs. 1,50,000 |
| Sales | Rs. 2,00,000 |
| Opening stock | Rs. 60,000 |
| Closing stock | Rs. 40,000 |
| Debtors | Rs. 45,000 |
| Creditors | Rs. 50,000 |

*The concerns' purchases would amount to (in Rs.)*
(a) 1,30,000 (b) 2,20,000
(c) 2,60,000 (d) 2,90,000

**318.** The following figures (all in Rs.) relate to non trading concern:

| | |
|---|---|
| 1st January,1995 stock of medicines | 5,000 |
| 1st January, 1995 Outstanding creditors for medicines | 3,000 |
| Amount paid for medicines during the years | 15,000 |
| Value of medicines spoiled during the year | 400 |
| Stock of medicines on 31st December, 1995 | 3,500 |

*The amount to be debited to Income and Expenditure account would be*
(a) Rs. 15,000 (b) Rs. 18,500
(c) Rs. 18,000 (d) Rs. 13,500

**319.** Which one of the following statement is correct?

(a) Depreciation is not the process of valuation of asset it is a process of allocation of cost of asset to the period of its economic life.

(b) If the cost of machinery is more than the book value, then depreciation need not be provided.

(c) When the plant machinery and maintained in good condition, through repairs and renewals, depreciation need not be provi- ded.

(d) In the absence of any legal provisions, if the auditor finds that provision made for depreciation is inadequate, then he is not required to refer to it in his report.

**320.** Which of the following items should be entered in the Receipts and Payments account of a club?

I. Sale of old newspapers.

II. Loss on sale of some asset.

III. Payments for investment.

*Select the correct answer using the codes given below:*

***Codes:***

(a) I, II and III (b) I and III

(c) I and II (d) II and III

**321.** A cultural club discloses that subscriptions received during a particular accounting period as per Receipts and payments account amount to Rs. 57,360. Subscription out standing (opening and closing ) was Rs. 4,800 and Rs. 6,000 respectively. Subscription received in advance (opening balance and closing balance) amounted to Rs. 3,600 and Rs. 2,160 respecti-vely. The amount to be posted to Income and Expenditure account would be

(a) Rs. 57,360 (b) Rs. 54,000

(c) Rs. 60,000 (d) Rs. 63,360

**Directions:** *The following questions (Q. 322-328) consist of two statements, one labelled the Assertion A and the other labelled Reason R. You are to examine these two statements carefully and decide if the Assertion A and the Reason R are individually true and if so, whether the Reason is a correct explanation of the Assertion. Select your answer to these questions using the codes.*

**322. Assertion (A) :** In accounting, a distinction is made between the business and the owner.

**Reason (R) :** Accounting concepts are based on adjectivity and not on subjectivity.

***Codes:***

(a) Both A and R are true, and R is the correct explanation of A.

(b) Both A and R are true, but R is not the correct explanation of A.

(c) A is true, but R is false.

(d) A is false, but R is true.

**323. Assertion (A) :** Materiality concept refers to the state of ignoring relatively small items and values from accounts.

**Reason (R) :** The effort involved in allocat-ing the cost of a small item over long period should be justified in terms of the benefit derived from this operation. Therefore cost of such items may be treated as expenses for the period in which they are acquired.

***Codes:***

(a) Both A and R are true, and R is the corret explanation of A.

(b) Both A and R are true, but R is not the correct explanation of A.

(c) A is true, but R is false.

(d) A is false, but R is true.

**324. Assertion (A) :** A minor can be admitted to the benefits of partnership with the consent of all the partners.

**Reason (R) :** This liability is confined only to the extent of his share in the profits and property of the firm.

***Codes:***

(a) Both A and R are true, and R is the corret explanation of A.

(b) Both A and R are true, but R is not the correct explanation of A.

(c) A is true, but R is false.

(d) A is false, but R is true.

**325. Assertion (A) :** The investors in the capital market have been showing a decisive shift in favour of fixed income instruments.

**Reason (R)** : The debt instruments have active secondary market.

***Codes:***

(a) Both A and R are true, and R is the corret explanation of A.

(b) Both A and R are true, but R is not the correct explanation of A.

(c) A is true, but R is false.

(d) A is false, but R is true.

**326. Assertion (A) :** The floating policy protects the policy holder against errors and omissions.

**Reason (R)** : Goods are insured even if the policy holder fails to report that goods have already been forwarded from the place of shipment.

***Codes:***

(a) Both A and R are true, and R is the correct explanation of A.

(b) Both A and R are true, but R is not the correct explanation of A.

(c) A is true, but R is false.

(d) A is false, but R is true.

**327. Assetion (A) :** Once incorporated, the name of a public limited company can not be changed.

**Reason (R)** : The name of a public limited company must be distinct and should not mislead or resemble that of only other company.

***Codes:***

(a) Both A and R are true, and R is the correct explanation of A.

(b) Both A and R are true, but R is not the correct explanation of A.

(c) A is true, but R is false.

(d) A is false, but R is true.

**328. Assertion (A) :** A transferee of shares cannot sue the promoters of a company for misinformation in the prospectus.

**Reason (R)** : The information provided by the company promoters in the prospectus is addressed only to the original allottees.

***Codes:***

(a) Both A and R are true, and R is the correct explanation of A.

(b) Both A and R are true, but R is not the correct explanation of A.

(c) A is true, but R is false.

(d) A is false, but R is true.

**329.** Owner's equity stands for

(a) Fixed Assets minus Fixed Liabilities.

(b) Fixed Assets minus Current Liabilities.

(c) Current Assets minus Fixed Liabilities.

(d) Total Assets minus Total Liabilities.

**330.** Which one of the following is an intangible asset?

(a) Furniture.

(b) Patent Right.

(c) Investment in shares.

(d) Losse tolls.

**331.** Match List I (Name of accounts) with List II (Matters with which the accounts are concerned) and select the correct answer using the codes given below the lists:

| List I | List II |
|---|---|
| I. Partners' current accounts | A. Dissolution of partnership |
| II. Goodwill account | B. Revaluation of assets on the admission of a partner |
| III. Partners' drawings accounts | C. Fixed capitals of partners. |
| IV. Profit and loss adjustment account | D. Goods taken by partners for private consumption. |

***Codes:***

(a) I-A, II-C, III-B, IV-D

(b) I-A, II-C, III-D, IV-B

(c) I-C, II-A, III-D, IV-B

(d) I-C, II-A, III-B, IV-D

**332.** Match List I (Transaction) with List II (Entry to be made) and select the correct answer by using the codes given below the lists:

| List I | List II |
|---|---|
| I. Loss on realisation | A. Debits partner's capital A/c |
| II. Profit on realisation | B. Credit realisation A/c |
| III. Assets sold | C. Credit partner's capital A/c |
| IV. Creditors paid | D. Debit realisation A/c |

*Codes:*
(a) I-A, II-C, III-B, IV-D
(b) I-C, II-A, III-B, IV-D
(c) I-C, II-A, III-D, IV-B
(d) I-A, II-C, III-D, IV-B

**333.** Which of the following statements are appropriate in respect of partrnership accounts?

I. In the absence of any provision in the partnership agreement to the country, partners can charge interest at 6% per annum on loans given by them to the partnership firm.

II. An ordinary partnership firm can have not more than 50 partner.

III. A banking partnership firm can have not more than 10 partnership.

IV. In the absence of any provision in the partnership agreement to the contrary, profits and losses are shared by the partners in the ratio of their capitals.

*Select the correct answer using the codes given below :*

***Codes:***
(a) I, and II (c) I, II and IV
(b) I and III (d) I, III and IV

**334.** G Ltd. acquired assets worth Rs. 7,50,000 from H Ltd. by issue of shares of Rs. 100 at a premium of 25%. The number of shares to be issued by G Ltd. to settle the purchase consideration is
(a) 6,000 shares (b) 7,500 shares
(c) 9,375 shares (d) 5,625 shares

**335.** B Ltd. a listed company, proposed to issue 1,00,000 equity shares of Rs. 10 each at par by way of private placement. The maximum amount of brokerage that can be paid by company is
(a) Rs. 5,000 (b) Rs. 10,000
(c) Rs. 50,000 (d) Rs. 25,000

**336.** The excess price received over the par value of Shares, should be credited to
(a) Calls in advance account
(b) Share capital account
(c) Reserve capital account
(d) Securities premium account

**337.** On approval from the central Government, the rate of discount on the issue of shares can be — per cent of the nominal value of shares
(a) 10 (b) 20
(c) 15 (d) 5

**338.** The Share Premium Account should be shown under
(a) Share Capital
(b) Current Liabilities
(c) Current Assets
(d) Reserves and Surplus

**339.** That portion of the share capital which can be called up only on the winding-up of the company is the
(a) Authorised capital
(c) Issued capital
(b) Subsrcibed capital
(c) Reserve capital

**340.** If vendors are issued fully paid shares of Rs. 80,000 in consideration of net assets of Rs. 60,000 then the balance of Rs.20,000 will be
(a) Debited to profit and loss account.
(b) Debited to good will account.
(c) Credited to capital reserve account.
(d) Credited to share premium account.

**341.** Match List I with List II and select the correct answer using the codes given below the lists:

| List I (Item) | List II (Type of asset) |
|---|---|
| I. Brand equity | A. Tangible |
| II. Plant and machinery | B. Current |
| III. Advances to suppliers | C. Intangible |
| IV. Deferred revenue expenditure | D. Fictitious |

*Codes :*

(a) I-C, II-A, III-D, IV-B
(b) I-C, II-A, III-B, IV-D
(c) I-A, II-C, III-B, IV-D
(d) I-A, II-C, III-D, IV-B

**342.** Consider the following items:
I. Debentures.
II. Prepaid rent.
III. Accrued interest.
IV. Bank overdraft.
*Current liabilities would include*
(a) II, III and IV (b) I, II and III
(c) III and IV (d) I, II, III and IV

**343.** Match List I with List II and select the correct answer using the codes given below the lists:

| List I | List II |
|---|---|
| I. G.P. Ratio | A. Convention of conservatism |
| II. Cash budget | B. Profitability. |
| III. E.O.Q. | C. Inventory management |
| IV. Provision for bad debts | D. Management of liquid assets. |

*Codes :*
(a) I-B, II-D, III-A, IV-C
(b) I-D, II-B, III-C, IV-A
(c) I-D, II-B, III-A, IV-C
(d) I-B, II-D, III-C, IV-A

**344.** Given that the current ratio is 2:1, if the net working capital is Rs. 60,600, then the amount of current liabilities would be
(a) Rs. 30,300 (b) Rs. 60.600
(c) Rs. 1,21,200 (d) Rs. 90,900

**345.** Project Engineering Ltd. has an adverse current ratio. Which one of the following would improve this ratio?
(a) Sale of fixed assets for cash.
(b) Collection of some of the current accounts receivables.
(c) Use of cash to pay off some long-term debts
(d) Collection from sundry debtors.

**346.** XYZ Ltd. incurs a net loss of Rs. 5,000 during an accounting year. Depreciation for the relevant year amounts Rs. 1,000, preliminary expenses written off during the accounting year is Rs. 3,000 and a loss of Rs.4,000 is due to sale of plant and machinery. Based on this data, funds from operations would amount to
(a) Rs. 3,000 (c) Rs. 2,000
(b) Rs. 5,000 (c) Rs. 4,000

**347.** One of the consequences of non-registration of a partnership firm is that
(a) A partner cannot sue the other partner to enforce a right arising from a contract.
(b) The partner of such a firm cannot sue third parties.
(c) Third parties cannot sue the firm for claims exceeding Rs.100
(d) The official Assignee or Receiver will have no power on the property of the dissolved firm.

**348.** Consider the following rights:
I. Right to take part in the business.
II. Right to share profits.
III. Right to interest on advances in excess of capital.
IV. Right to expel a non-cooperative partner
*Codes:*
(a) I and II (b) II and IV
(c) I, I and III (d) I, III and IV

**349.** Match List I with List II and select the correct answer using the codes given below the lists:

| List I (Type of combi-nations) | List II (Illustrations) |
|---|---|
| I. Association | A. Cartel |
| II. Federation | B. Chamber of commerce and industry. |
| III. Partial consolidation | C. Holding company. |
| IV. Complete consolidation | D. Amalgamation. |

*Codes :*
(a) I-B, II-A, III-C, IV-D
(b) I-A, II-B, III-C, IV-D
(c) I-B, II-A, III-D, IV-C
(d) I-A, II-B, III-D, IV-C

**350.** Which one of the fòllowing is an example of a company incorproated by a special Act of parliament?
(a) Life Insurance Corporation of India
(b) Indian Oil Corporation.
(c) State Trading Corporation of India.
(d) Bharat Heavy Electricals Limited.

**351.** Match List I (Activity) with List II (Associated organisation) and select the correct answer by using the codes given below the lists:

| | List I | | List II |
|---|---|---|---|
| I. | Mutual fund | A. | Stock exchange |
| II. | Public issue of capital | B. | Assets management company |
| III. | Forward trading | C. | Merchant banking |
| IV. | Option pricing | D. | Forex market. |

***Codes :***
(a) I-C, II-B, III-D, IV-A
(b) I-C, II-B, III-A, IV-D
(c) I-B, II-C, III-A, IV-D
(d) I-B, II-C, III-D, IV-A

**352.** In the context of foreign trade, the CIF cost may be obtained by
(a) Adding freight and marine insurance premium to the FOB price.
(b) Deducting freight and marine insurance premium to the FOB price.
(c) Adding customs duties, freight and marine insurance premium to the cost.
(d) Deducting customs duties, freight and marine insurance premium from the price.

**353.** Paid-up value is payable on a life insurance policy
(a) On the maturity of the policy.
(b) When the policy lapses.
(c) When the policy is surrendered.
(d) On maturity or death which ever is earlier.

**354.** An important aspect of control is that the
(a) Manager motivates his subordinates to give better performance.
(b) Manager sets as effective management information system.
(c) Plans are checked before implementation against predetermined measures of performance.
(d) Performance is checked against predetermined standards.

**355.** Consider the following steps:
(a) Analysis of variances.
(b) Initiating corrective action.
(c) Measurement of actual performance.
(d) Establishment of standards.
*What is the sequence of steps?*
(a) I, II, III, IV (b) II, III, I, IV
(c) III, I, II, IV (d) IV, III, I, II

**356.** Rights issue refers to the shares issued to
(a) Employees
(b) Public
(c) Existing directors
(c) None of these.

**357.** Social obligation of accounting refers to
(a) The completion of journal entires.
(b) The preparation of final accounts.
(c) Cost recording.
(d) Servicing the needs of various stake-holders.

**358.** An asset is purchased for Rs. 50,000 on which depreciation is to be provided annually according to the straight line method. The useful life of the asset is 10 years and the residual value is Rs. 10,000. The rate of depreciation is
(a) 20% (c) 18%
(b) 10% (c) 8%

**359.** Bonus shares can be issued by a company
(a) Out of the Reserves created by revaluation of fixed assets.
(b) Out of share premium not collected in cash
(c) Without any provision for it in the Articles of Association of the company.
(d) Out of free Reserves built of genuine profits.

**360.** During a period of declining prices, which one of the following inventory pricing methods will result in lower cost of goods sold?
(a) F I F O.
(b) L I F O.
(c) Simple average method.
(d) Inflated price method.

# ANSWERS

| 1 | 2 | 3 | 4 | 5 | 6 | 7 | 8 | 9 | 10 |
|---|---|---|---|---|---|---|---|---|---|
| (d) | (a) | (d) | (d) | (b) | (b) | (c) | (d) | (c) | (d) |
| **11** | **12** | **13** | **14** | **15** | **16** | **17** | **18** | **19** | **20** |
| (b) | (a) | (d) | (b) | (a) | (c) | (d) | (b) | (b) | (d) |
| **21** | **22** | **23** | **24** | **25** | **26** | **27** | **28** | **29** | **30** |
| (a) | (b) | (a) | (a) | (c) | (b) | (c) | (b) | (a) | (a) |
| **31** | **32** | **33** | **34** | **35** | **36** | **37** | **38** | **39** | **40** |
| (b) | (b) | (c) | (c) | (b) | (a) | (c) | (a) | (b) | (a) |
| **41** | **42** | **43** | **44** | **45** | **46** | **47** | **48** | **49** | **50** |
| (a) | (b) | (a) | (a) | (b) | (b) | (a) | (d) | (c) | (b) |
| **51** | **52** | **53** | **54** | **55** | **56** | **57** | **58** | **59** | **60** |
| (a) | (a) | (d) | (b) | (c) | (c) | (d) | (c) | (c) | (c) |
| **61** | **62** | **63** | **64** | **65** | **66** | **67** | **68** | **69** | **70** |
| (c) | (b) | (d) | (a) | (b) | (c) | (b) | (b) | (c) | (a) |
| **71** | **72** | **73** | **74** | **75** | **76** | **77** | **78** | **79** | **80** |
| (a) | (b) | (c) | (c) | (a) | (b) | (a) | (b) | (c) | (b) |
| **81** | **82** | **83** | **84** | **85** | **86** | **87** | **88** | **89** | **90** |
| (c) | (a) | (a) | (b) | (b) | (c) | (a) | (a) | (d) | (a) |
| **91** | **92** | **93** | **94** | **95** | **96** | **97** | **98** | **99** | **100** |
| (d) | (c) | (c) | (b) | (c) | (a) | (c) | (c) | (d) | (b) |
| **101** | **102** | **103** | **104** | **105** | **106** | **107** | **108** | **109** | **110** |
| (c) | (d) | (a) | (b) | (b) | (c) | (c) | (c) | (c) | (d) |
| **111** | **112** | **113** | **114** | **115** | **116** | **117** | **118** | **119** | **120** |
| (d) | (b) | (d) | (c) | (d) | (b) | (b) | (b) | (d) | (b) |
| **121** | **122** | **123** | **124** | **125** | **126** | **127** | **128** | **129** | **130** |
| (c) | (d) | (c) | (d) | (a) | (d) | (a) | (a) | (b) | (c) |
| **131** | **132** | **133** | **134** | **135** | **136** | **137** | **138** | **139** | **140** |
| (c) | (b) | (d) | (a) | (d) | (b) | (d) | (b) | (a) | (a) |
| **141** | **142** | **143** | **144** | **145** | **146** | **147** | **148** | **149** | **150** |
| (b) | (a) | (d) | (c) | (b) | (d) | (c) | (c) | (c) | (d) |
| **151** | **152** | **153** | **154** | **155** | **156** | **157** | **158** | **159** | **160** |
| (d) | (b) | (a) | (b) | (b) | (a) | (c) | (c) | (d) | (b) |
| **161** | **162** | **163** | **164** | **165** | **166** | **167** | **168** | **169** | **170** |
| (d) | (b) | (b) | (c) | (c) | (c) | (c) | (d) | (c) | (c) |
| **171** | **172** | **173** | **174** | **175** | **176** | **177** | **178** | **179** | **180** |
| (b) | (d) | (d) | (d) | (b) | (c) | (c) | (a) | (b) | (d) |
| **181** | **182** | **183** | **184** | **185** | **186** | **187** | **188** | **189** | **190** |
| (a) | (a) | (d) | (d) | (c) | (b) | (b) | (b) | (d) | (c) |
| **191** | **192** | **193** | **194** | **195** | **196** | **197** | **198** | **199** | **200** |
| (a) | (b) | (b) | (b) | (b) | (c) | (b) | (d) | (d) | (c) |

| 201 | 202 | 203 | 204 | 205 | 206 | 207 | 208 | 209 | 210 |
|---|---|---|---|---|---|---|---|---|---|
| (c) | (c) | (a) | (a) | (c) | (b) | (a) | (a) | (c) | (c) |
| **211** | **212** | **213** | **214** | **215** | **216** | **217** | **218** | **219** | **220** |
| (c) | (a) | (c) | (a) | (a) | (d) | (b) | (b) | (a) | (c) |
| **221** | **222** | **223** | **224** | **225** | **226** | **227** | **228** | **229** | **230** |
| (a) | (a) | (d) | (b) | (b) | (b) | (d) | (a) | (a) | (a) |
| **231** | **232** | **233** | **234** | **235** | **236** | **237** | **238** | **239** | **240** |
| (a) | (c) | (b) | (b) | (c) | (b) | (c) | (a) | (c) | (a) |
| **241** | **242** | **243** | **244** | **245** | **246** | **247** | **248** | **249** | **250** |
| (c) | (a) | (c) | (d) | (b) | (d) | (b) | (c) | (a) | (c) |
| **251** | **252** | **253** | **254** | **255** | **256** | **257** | **258** | **259** | **260** |
| (a) | (c) | (d) | (c) | (c) | (c) | (a) | (c) | (c) | (d) |
| **261** | **262** | **263** | **264** | **265** | **266** | **267** | **268** | **269** | **270** |
| (c) | (b) | (c) | (b) | (c) | (c) | (b) | (c) | (d) | (a) |
| **271** | **272** | **273** | **274** | **275** | **276** | **277** | **278** | **279** | **280** |
| (b) | (c) | (d) | (d) | (b) | (c) | (b) | (c) | (d) | (d) |
| **281** | **282** | **283** | **284** | **285** | **286** | **287** | **288** | **289** | **290** |
| (a) | (d) | (d) | (c) | (a) | (c) | (c) | (a) | (d) | (c) |
| **291** | **292** | **293** | **294** | **295** | **296** | **297** | **298** | **299** | **300** |
| (c) | (d) | (b) | (a) | (c) | (a) | (b) | (b) | (c) | (d) |
| **301** | **302** | **303** | **304** | **305** | **306** | **307** | **308** | **309** | **310** |
| (b) | (b) | (b) | (c) | (a) | (a) | (a) | (c) | (c) | (c) |
| **311** | **312** | **313** | **314** | **315** | **316** | **317** | **318** | **319** | **320** |
| (a) | (a) | (a) | (b) | (b) | (b) | (a) | (d) | (a) | (b) |
| **321** | **322** | **323** | **324** | **325** | **326** | **327** | **328** | **329** | **330** |
| (c) | (b) | (a) | (b) | (c) | (d) | (d) | (a) | (d) | (b) |
| **331** | **332** | **333** | **334** | **335** | **336** | **337** | **338** | **339** | **340** |
| (c) | (a) | (b) | (a) | (a) | (d) | (b) | (d) | (d) | (b) |
| **341** | **342** | **343** | **344** | **345** | **346** | **347** | **348** | **349** | **350** |
| (b) | (c) | (d) | (b) | (a) | (a) | (b) | (c) | (b) | (a) |
| **351** | **352** | **353** | **354** | **355** | **356** | **357** | **358** | **359** | **360** |
| (d) | (c) | (d) | (d) | (d) | (c) | (d) | (d) | (d) | (c) |

# UNIT-II

# AUDITING

## MEANING OF AUDITING

The word "AUDIT" has been derived from the Latin word "audire" which means to hear. In olden times whenever the owners of a business organisation suspected fraud, they appointed certain persons to check the accounts. Such persons asked the accountant to appear before them and heard whatever he had to explain in connection with the accounts.

Auditing is primarily concerned with verification of accounting and financial records in order to determine their accuracy, authenticity and reliability.

Let us discuss some of the important definitions of the word "auditing" given by eminent authorities.

## F.R.M. DE PAULA

According to him, "auditing is" the examination of a Balance Sheet and Profit and Loss Account prepared by others, together with the books, accounts and vouchers relating there to in such a manner that the auditor may be able to satisfy himself and honestly report that, in his opinion, such Balance Sheet is properly drawn up so as to exihibit a true and correct view of the state of affairs of the particular concern, according to the information and explanation given to him and as shown by the books."

## SPICER AND PEGLER

They have defined "Audit as such an examination of the books, accounts and vouchers of a business, as will enable the auditor to satisfy himself that the Balance Sheet is properly drawn up, so as to give a true and fair view of the state of the affairs of the business, and whether the profit and loss Account gives a true and fair view of the profit and loss for the financial period, according to the best of his information and the explanation given to him, and as shown by the books, and if hot, in what respect he is not satisfied."

## LAWRENCE R. DICKSEE

According to him, "An audit is an examination of accounting records undertaken with a view to estabilishing whether they correctly and completely reflect the transactions to which they relate. In some instances it may be necessary to ascertain whether the transactions themselves are supported by authority."

**The Institute of Chartered Accountants of India** has defined auditing as "a systematic and independent examination of data, statements, records, operations and performances (financial or other wise) of an enterprise for a state purpose. In any auditing situation the auditor perceives and recognises the propositions before him for examination, collects evidence, evaluates the same and on this basis formulates his judgement which is communicated through his reports."

## MONTGOMERY

"Auditing is a systematic examination of the books and records of a business or other organisation, in order to ascertain or verify and to report upon the facts regarding its financial operations and the result there of."

## JOSEPH LANCASTER

"The process of checking, vouching, and verification by which the auditor seeks to establish the accuracy or other wise of a Balance Sheet is known as audit and may be conveniently defined as an investigation into books of account and the documents and vouchers from which the auditor has to make a report on the Balance Sheet or other statements of figures prepared from the books, to the persons for whom he has been appointed to report."

From the analysis of the above difinitions we may summarise the salient features of an audit as follows :

**1.** *It is a systematic and independent examination* of the books of account to ascertain whether the Balance Sheet show a true and fair view of the financial position and the Profit and Loss Account gives a true and fair view of the Profit and Loss for the financial period.

**2.** *It is done by independent qualified persons.* Audit will be useful only when it is conducted by an independent and qualified person. Needless to say that audit is undertaken to exercise a check upon persons who handle receipts and payments of money belonging to others.

**3.** *It is based on Documentary evidence* such as books of accounts, vauchers including information and explanation given to the auditor during the course of his audit.

**4.** *The object of an audit is to ascertain truth and fairness* of the financial statements. The auditor has to ensure that the financial statements have been prepared from the relevant books of account according to the generally accepted standard practices. They exhibit a true and fair view of both the financial position and the profit and loss position relating to the period and review.

## OBJECTS OF AUDITING

Objects of auditing is to ascertain whether the financial statements, *i.e.,* Balance Sheet and Profit and Loss Account show a true and fair view of the company's affairs at the end of its financial year and its working results during that financial year.

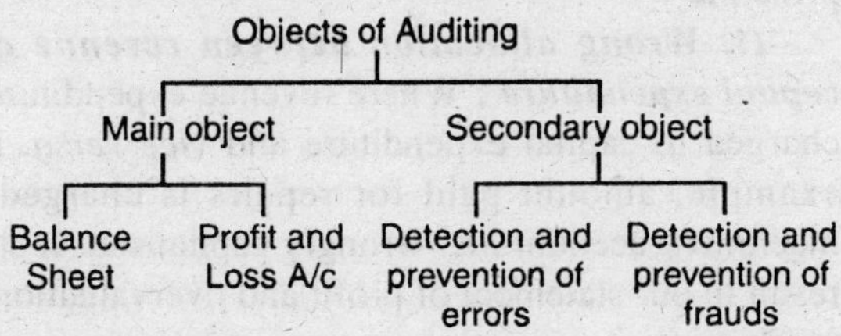


**Main Object**

(*i*) *Balance Sheet* exhibit a true and fairview of financial position at the end of the year.

(*ii*) *Profit and Loss A/C* exhibit a true and fair view of profit and loss during the year.

The main object of auditing is to ascertain whether the financial statements show a true and fair view of the financial position and its working results.

**Secondary Objects**

The auditor in order to ascertain whether the financial statements show a true and fair view of the financial position and working result must eusure that there are no errors and frauds which render them untrue and unfair.

(*i*) **Detection and provention of errors :** An error means an innocent mistake made by a person while recording a transaction in the books of account or other record.

**Types of errors :**

1. Errors of omission
2. Errors of commission
3. Errors of principle
4. Compensating errors
5. Errors of Duplication

**1. Errors of Omission.** An error of omission as its name suggests, means to omit to write or record something. When a transaction is omitted, i.e., not recorded partially or wholly, there is an error of omission. For example, a transaction of sale may not be recorded. In case a transaction is not recorded in a book of original entry, it will not affect the trial balance. For example if a sale of Rs. 100 is not recorded in the sales book, it will also not be posted to the customer's account. Thus, it will not affect the trial balance. However, in certain cases an error may be obvious (apparent) from the balance of an account. If the rent paid for the last 2 months is not recorded, the rent account will show payment of Rs. 1000 in place of the usual Rs. 1,200.

**2. Errors of Commission :** Errors of commission as its name suggests means mistake committed recording something. Where a transaction is incorrectly recorded in the books, it is called an error of commission. These errors often arise due to negligence or inadvertance on the part of the person recording or posting the transaction in the books of account. Such errors include wrong totalling, balancing or carry forward of totals.

The following are some examples of errors of commission :

(*i*) ***Recording a transaction wrongly wholly or partially*** : Where a transaction is wrongly recorded in the books of original entry or posted in the ledger.

**Types of Errors**

| Errors of Omission | Errors of Commission | Errors of Principle | Compensating Errors | Errors of duplication |
|---|---|---|---|---|
| (*i*) Not recording a transation. (*a*) Wholly or (*b*) partly | (*i*) Recording a transaction wrongly<br>(*ii*) Posting a transaction wrongly<br>(*iii*) Errors made in totalling and balancing<br>(*iv*) Errors made in carrying forward any balance or total | (*i*) Wrong allocation between capital and revenues expenditure<br>(*ii*) Debiting expenditure to personal account<br>(*iii*) Valuing assets and liabilities against fundamental principles of accountancy | | |

For example, a sale of Rs. 560 recorded as Rs. 650 in the Sales Book. Needless to say such an error will not affect the trial balance.

*(ii)* ***Posting a transaction wrongly :*** Where a transaction is correctly entered in the books of original entry but while posting in the ledger, a wrong amount may be entered or it may be posted to a wrong account. For example,a sale of Rs. 260 may be debited to the customer's account as Rs. 620. It means debiting the customers's account by Rs. 360 more than actual. Thus, the error will be detected as the trial balance will be out by (show a difference of) Rs. 360 *i.e.*, credit side will be short by Rs. 360.

Again, a transaction may be posted in a wrong account. For example, goods may be sold to Ram but may be debited to Sham. Such an error will not affect the trial balance and as such will be rather difficult to detect.

*(iii)* ***Errors made in totalling and balancing :*** These errors are due to wrong castings (Totalling) and balancing of accounts. These errors will affect the trail balance. The error would be reflected in the total of the trial balance on the same side.

*(iv)* ***Errors made in carrying forward any balance or total trial balance :*** Such errors happen when balance or totals of various accounts are carried forward or posted to the trial balance *i.e.*, the balances or totals carried forward may be more or less than the actual figures. For example, balance of Rs. 2,600 may be carried forward as Rs. 2,060. Such an error will cause difference in trial balance. Again, the balance in an account may be carried forward correctly but to the wrong side *i.e.*, debit balance may be written as credit balance and *vice versa*. Such an error will put the trial balance out by double the amount. For example,a debit balance of Rs. 200 posted wrongly on the credit side will make the debit side of the trial balance short by Rs. 400 and *vice versa*.

**3. Errors of Principle :** An error of principle arises, when a mistake of accepted accounting principles is made. For example, where revenue expenditure is charged to capital expenditure or *vice versa*. Sometimes such errors are made intentionally *i.e.*, knowingly with a view to overstate or understate profits.

The following are some examples of errors of principle :

*(i)* ***Wrong allocation between revenue and capital expenditure :*** Where revenue expenditure is charged to capital expenditure and *vice versa*. For example, amount paid for repairs is charged to machinery account *i.e.*, wrongly capitalised. It shall result in our statement of profit and overvaluation of machinery.

*(ii)* ***Debiting expenditure to personal account*** **:** This may happen when rent paid to the landlord is debited to the personal account of the landlord. This will result in overstatement of profit and overvaluation of debtors in the balance sheet. Needless to say rent paid is an expenditure and landlord is not a debtor as he has rendered service by providing his building premises for the business.

***(iii) Valuing assets and liabilities against fundamental principles of accountancy*** **:** Such errors arise where assets are not valued in accordance with the accepted accounting principles. This may result in overstatment or understatement of profits. The errors of principle do not affect the trial balance. As such it may be difficult, if not impossible, to detect such errors. Therefore, these errors can be detected only if the auditor makes a thorough and careful examination of the transactions.

Some more examples of errors of principle are :

(*i*) inadequate or excess provision for depreciation;

(*ii*) no provision at all for depreciation;

(*iii*) under or over valuation of assets, particularly of stock in trade;

(*iv*) no provision, inadequate provision or excess provision for outstanding expenses;

(*v*) inadequate or excess provision for bad and doubtful debts;

(*vi*) wrong adjustment or no adjustment of prepaid expenses;

(*vii*) superfluous adjustment for deferred revenue expenditure, *e.g.*, treating normal advertisement expenditure as deferred advertisement expenditure.

**4. Compensating Erros :** These errors are not a new type of errors. An error which wholly or partially compensates or balances another error is called a compensating error. For example, a sale of Rs. 500 may be recorded as a sale of Rs. 900 and a purchase of Rs. 800 may be recorded as of Rs. 400. Thus, recorded excess sale of Rs. 400 may be compensated by recording short purchase of Rs. 400. This mistake will not be disclosed by the trial balance as the trial balance will agree. Therefore, agreement of trial balance is no guarantee that there is no error. There may be compensating errors inspite of the agreement of the trial balance.

Compensating errors may or may not affect the profit. If both the compensating errors are made in revenue accounts, it will affect the profit. However, if the compensating errors are in revenue account and in asset or liability account, these will over or understate the profit.

**5. Errors of Duplication :** Again, these errors are also not of a new type. An error of duplication happens when a transaction is recorded twice in the books. Such an item shall also be posted twice. Such errors may occur due to mistakes made by the book-keeper or because of confusion caued by duplicate invoices or vouchers. Such errors cannot be detected with the help of the trial balance. Hence careful and thorough examination only by the auditor shall reveal such errors.

**Detection of Errors**

According to Batliboi detection of errors is the primary duty of the auditor. His clients would naturally expect him (auditor) to place before them accurate statement of accounts indicating a true and correct (now fair) view of their business.

Strictly speaking, it is no part of auditor's duty to detect errors. Whenever he is called upon to do so, he would be acting in the capacity of an accountant rather than that of an auditor. Nevertheless he has to detect errors in order to state whether or not in his opinion the accounts show a true and fair view of the company's affairs at the end of the financial year and its profit and loss for the financial year.

There are no hard and fast rules which the auditor may follow. It would depend upon the facts and circumstances of each and every case. He should take the following steps to locate the errors :

1. He should find out whether his client is maintaining books on self-balancing system.
2. In case his client is following the self-balancing system, it would be easier for him to locate the mistake.
3. In case his client is not following the self-balancing system he should thoroughly check the trial balance.
4. He should check and re-check the totals of the trial balance.
5. He should compare the items of trial balance of the current year with those of the previous year to check if any item has not been left out.
6. He should compare the items with the ledger accounts to see that no balances have been left out.

7. He should check the opening balances of the ledger account brought forward from the previous year.
8. He should check and re-check the totals of the various ledger accounts.
9. The lists of debtors and creditors should be properly compared with the trial balance and their totals checked thoroughly.
10. Ascertain from the nature of accounts, which always have debit or credit balance, whether or not those have been posted on the correct side. For example, rent paid should be posted on the debit side of the trial balance.
11. Difference involving a round figure *e.g.*, 100, 1000, etc should be traced to totallings.
12. Difference divisible by 2 should be traced to posting to the wrong side. For example, a difference of Rs. 100 in the trial balance may be due to posting on wrong side *i.e.*, debit in place of credit or *vice versa*.
13. Difference divisible by 9 may indicate exchange of digits. For example, writing 45 in place of 54 or 98 instead of 89.
14. Check the journal to ensure that the total of debit side equals that of credit side.
15. Special care should be taken to check over-writing of figures and fraudulent striking off figures, if any.
16. Difference of odd amount, *e.g.*, Rs. 298.17 may indicate that certain items might have not been posted correctly.
17. If the errors still remain undetected, he should carry out a thorough checking of the books of account and the trial balance.

## DETECTION AND PREVENTION OF FRAUD

Fraud is an error or mistake made wilfully or knowingly with a view to defraud others *i.e.*, to deceive or cheat people.

Broadly speaking fraud can be classified into :

1. Misappropriation or embezzlement of cash
2. Misappropriation of goods
3. Manipulation of accounts
4. Window-dressing.

### 1. Misappropriation or embezzlement of cash

Misappropriation or embezzlement of cash means wrongful conversion or fraudulent application of cash. It virtually takes the form of actual theft of cash.

Misappropriation or embezzlement of cash may be made in any of the following manner :

(*i*) non-recording or under-recording of cash sales, or
(*ii*) omitting to record cash received, or
(*iii*) recording less amount of cash than received, or
(*iv*) recording fictitious payment of cash, or
(*v*) recording more amount on the payment side of the cash book than paid, or
(*vi*) teeming and lading.

It will be difficult for the auditor to detect fraud unless there is a good internal control and internal check system in operation in the organisation.

The system of receiving and paying cash in a big business house should be such that the work of one clerk is automatically checked by another clerk.

In the absence of such a system he should advise his client to adopt a reliable system of internal checks and internal control. He will do well to disown his liability in case there is no internal check or internal control system.

To detect fraud of the first three types mentioned above, he should compare the cash book with the rough cash book, salesmen's summary, counterfoils of receipt books. To detect fraud of the least two types, he should compare the cash book with the invoices, vouchers, wage sheets and salary book.

If feasible, he should advise his client to use carbon type of counterfoils rather than duplicate type of counterfoil with perforation between the customer's copy and the record copy. Again, he should advise his clent to obtain payee's signature on the counterfoil of the receipt in order to check entry of less cash than actually received. The payer shall not sign on the counterfoil if lesser amount than paid is entered in the receipt book.

**"Teeming and Lading" or Lapping :** It is another method of misappropriation of cash. According to Meigs, "Lapping" may be defined as the "concealment of a shortage (of cash) by delaying the recording of cash receipts." Under this method of cash misappropriation, no entry is made by the cashier when the cash is received by him say, from a debtor X. He misappropriates the cash. When cash is received from another debtor. Y the amount is recorded in the cash book in the name of X. When amount is received from Y, it is credited in the name of Z and so on. Later, say, at the end of the month, the cashier returns the money and credits it in the name of the person whose account he has not credited so far *i.e.*, Z.

In this manner he misuses the money without authority and without paying any interest. The auditor has to check such type of frauds. He should check the cash book with counterfoils or carbon copies of the cash receipt book. With the consent of his client the auditor should obtain confirmation of their balances from the debtors directly.

**2. Misappropriation of goods**

Misappropriation of goods may be done in the following manner :

(*i*) **Actual theft of goods :** Which are costly and handy *i.e.*, not bulky. Such goods may be concealed and carried easily without the possibility of being detected.

(*ii*) **Inflating sales :** Misappropriation of goods may be done by recording sales of larger quantities than actual and misappropriating the balance.

(*iii*) **Deflating Purchases :** Similarly, goods may be misappropriate by recording purchases of smaller quantities than actual and misappropriating the balance.

(*iv*) Issuing fictitious credit not for goods returned in collision with the customers.

Misappropriation of goods can be checked by proper internal check and control system, in purchases, purchases returns, sales and sales returns. In addition regular and periodical stock taking and security check up of the workers leaving the factory through metal detectors and and X-ray machines. Monthly comparison of gross profit ratio to sales will also help in reducing misappropriation of goods.

**3. Fraudulent manipulation of accounts**

This type of fraud is committed by falsification of accounts without defalcation of cash or goods. It is done by making fictitious entries in respect of sales, purchases, assets and liabilities. It is difficult to detect such frauds because these are committed by high officials like directors, managers etc. who are trusted servants of the company and as such there is no suspicion. It may be committed with the object of —

**1. Showing more profits then actual —**

(*i*) in order to get more commission on profit if commission is based on profit;

(*ii*) to win confidence of the shareholders, to show that higher profits are due to their hard works or efforts;

(*iii*) to sell their shares at higher prices as increased profit will higher dividends;

(*iv*) to show better financial position in order to get financial assistance; and

(*v*) to get more subscription of shares or public deposits.

**2. Showing less profits than actual in order —**

(*i*) to evade taxes;

(*ii*) to mislead competitors;

(*iii*) to indulge in insider trading of shares by purchasing them at lower prices and later on selling them at higher prices.

**3. Falsification of accounts** may be done —

(*i*) by under or over valuation of assets particularly stock in trade;

**Types of Frauds**

- Misappropriation or embezzlement of cash
  Teeming and Lading or Lapping
- Misappropriation or theft of goods
- Fraudulent manipulation of accounts
  (*i*) Showing more profit than actual.
  (*ii*) Showing less profits than actual.
- Window dressing

(*ii*) by not providing depreciation at all or providing inadequate or excess duplication;

(*iii*) by showing bogus sales or purchases or sales return or purchases returns;

(*iv*) by creating secret reserve or by utilising secret reserve when the organisation is running into losses without disclosing the fact to the shareholders;

(*v*) by treating revenue expenditure as capital expenditure and *vice versa;* and

(*vi*) by showing income of next year in the current year or by suppressing accrued income by not showing it in the current year.

**4. Window dressing**

Infact it is also one of the ways of falsification or manipulation of accounts. Window dressing implies showing a more prosperous position than what actually it is. It is done by arranging the balance sheet in such a way that it shows a state of affairs far better than what actually it is. For example, an overdraft may be cleared on the eve of the date of the balance sheet by arranging a short term loan from its subsidiary with the object of showing á better working capital position. Similarly loans given to directors and other managerial personnel may be shown to have been received at the end of the year.

**Auditor's position as regards fraud and errors**

An auditor is required to express his opinion on the truth and fairness of the financial position and profit and loss made by an organisation as disclosed by its financial statements. He is under an obligation to ensure that the opinion expressed by him on the financial statements is true and fair free from errors and frauds. If he has exercised reasonable care and diligence he cannot be held guilty for errors or frauds discovered later on.

An auditor is an expert in his won field. As such he is expected to possess specialised skills and professional diligence to do his job. In Foments Ltd. vs. Selsdon Ltd. it was held "that an auditor is not to be merely written off as adder, upper and subtractor. His vital task is to take care to see that errors are not made by their errors of computation, or omission,or commission,or downright untruths. To perform this task properly, he must come to it with an inquiring mind, not suspicious of dishonesty but nevertheless suspecting that someone may have made a mistake somewhere and that a check must be made to ensure that there is none." He must discharge his duties with utmost care. He is expected to apply reasonable skill and diligence as is expected of a professional of his stature. The degree of skill and care will depend upon facts and circumstances of each and every case. He is not required to do anything more.

In Kingston Cotton Mills' case the learned judge held that the auditor is only a watch dog and not a blood hound. As such he is not bound to be a detective,or as was said, to approach his work with suspicion or with a foregone conclusion that there is something wrong, "Auditors must not be made liable for not tracing out ingenious and carefully laid schemes of fraud when there is nothing to arouse their suspicion and when those frauds are perpetrated by tried servants of the company and are undected for years by the directors."

However, the judgement in Kingston Cotton Mills' case does not absolve them of their responsibility of reasonable care and diligence. In case there is suspicion, the auditor must probe to the botton.

In international Laboratories Ltd. vs. Dewar, it was held that "while the auditor may be only a watch dog, he will not have performed the function of his office if, after one howl, he retreats under the barn or if he confines his protest to a fellow watch dog."

"Is not the watch dog bound to bark and chase too, if necessary? If when sniffing sound, you hit upon a trail of something wrong, surely you must follow it up and there is just as much obligation on the auditor, who is bound to keep his eyes open and his nose too. It may be that by vigilantly following this trail up to the end, he may root up something from which fraud is exposed."

In view of the above judicial observations, position of an auditor in connection with detection of errors and frauds can be summarised as follows :

1. He must exercise reasonable care and skill to detect errors and frauds.
2. If he has taken reasonable care he is not liable for any errors or frauds discovered later on.

3. In case there is suspicion, he should probe the matter to the bottom to discover errors and frauds. He must enlarge the extent of his investigation and modify his checking strategies and procedures to meet the situation.

## TYPES OF AUDIT

An audit may be classified on number of bases :

(*i*) On the basis of Legislative control

(*ii*) On the basis of relationship between the management and the auditor.

(*iii*) On the basis of period of audit covered

(*iv*) On the basis of object

(*v*) On the basis of coverage of audit

### I. On the basis of Legislative Control

An audit may be classified as follows :

**1. Statutory Audit :** As its name indicates statutory audit is that audit which has been made compulsory by the statute *i.e.*, Law. For example, audit has been made compulsory by the Co. Act for companies to protect and safeguard the interests of the shareholders of the co. Statutory audit is conducted with the object to check the accuracy of accounts of a company.

Statutory Audit has been prescribed for the following :

(*a*) Companies registred under the companies Act.

(*b*) Goverment companies.

(*c*) Corporations established by Parliament or state legislatures.

(*d*) Banking companies governed by the Banking Regulation Act, 1949.

(*e*) Electricity supply companies governed by the Electricity Supply Act 1948.

(*f*) Co-operative Societies registered under various co-oprative Societies Acts.

(*g*) Societies registered under the Societies Registered Act, 1860.

(*h*) Public and other charitable trust registered under the Trusts Act, 1882.

**2. Non-Statutory Audit :** It means an Audit which is not compulsory. As such it means an audit undertaken voluntarily. A partnership firm or a sole propritory firm may also get its accounts audited. An Internal Audit is also in the nature of no-statutory Audit.

(*i*) ***Internal Audit*** **:** It is also necessary for the directors to eusure that the policies framed by them are properly executed by the employees of the company. "Internal Auditing is the continuous and systematic process of examining and reporting on the administrative systems and accounting methods of a company or a group of companies. It is carried out by the employees of the company."

Objects of Internal audit are :

(*a*) To confirm that the policies of management are being properly executed and to draw attention to those areas where policies appear to be inadequate.

(*b*) To verify that the information used by the management to control the undertaking is both adequate and accurate.

**3. Government Audit :** Under the constitution of India, the comptroller and Auditor General of India has been empowered to conduct Government audit. Audit of Government departments, Government companies and various statutory corporations is conducted under his direct control.

### II. On the basis of relationship between the management and the auditor

On this basis there are two types of audit :

(*i*) External Audit

(*ii*) Internal Audit

(*i*) **External Audit :** It implies an audit conducted by the external auditor or independent person.

(*ii*) **Internal Audit :** Internal Auditing is the continuous and systemative process of examining and reporting on the administrative systems and accounting methods of a company or a group of companies. It is carried out by the employees of the company."

### III. On the basis of period of audit covered

**1. Continuous Audit :** Continuous Audit, as its name suggests, is an audit which is continously done through the year. The auditor regulary visits the client's office to audit the accounts after a certain interval say, a fortnightly or monthly depending upon the volume of work.

According to spicer and Pegler "a continuous audit is one where the auditor's staff is occupied continuously on the accounts the whole year round, or where the auditors attends at intervals, fixed or otherwise during the currency of the financial year and performs an interim audit, such audits are adopted where the work involved is considerable and have many points in their favour although they are subject to certain disadvantages."

**2. Final or Completed or Periodical or Annual Audit :** According to spicer and Pegler, "a final or completed audit is commonly understood to be an audit which is not commenced until after the end of the financial period, and is then carried on until completed."

In simple words final audit is an audit which is done after the financial period is over and the accounts are ready. It is continued in a session until the complete audit work is over.

Infact the term audit, in the absence of anything to the contrary, implies a final or completed audit. It is also called periodical audit as it is done after the close of the financial period.

Final Audit is also called annual audit as it is usually done every year *i.e.,* annually.

**3. Interim Audit :** An audit conducted in between two annual audits is called interim audit. In case a company wants to declare an interim dividend it becomes necessary to get interim audit of the accounts done upto the date at which the company wants to declare interim dividend. For example, a company may decide to declare the interim dividend after the close of the half year.

Interim audits involves a complete audit of accounts for a part of the year *i.e.,* from the date of the last balance sheet to the date of the interim accounting period.

**4. Occasional Audit :** As its name indicates occasional audit means an audit which is done on a particular occasion or on the happening of some event and not regularly.

For example, the occasion may be admission or retirement of a partner or the event may be that a partner is suspecting fraud. Infact it is done is such cases where audit is optional. For example, in case of a sole proprietory or partnership concern occasional audit may be got done where fraud is suspected by the proprietor or any partner. An occasional audit is the audit is hardly done in case of companies or other statutory bodies as annual audit is compulsory for such organisations.

An occasional audit may be in the form of special audit or an investigation.

**IV. On the basis of object**

An audit may be classified on the basis of objects. Those are given here bleow :

1. **Financial Audit**
2. **Cost Audit**
3. **Management Audit**
4. **Operational Audit**
5. **Performance Audit**
6. **Propriety Audit**
7. **Cash Audit**

**1. Financial Audit :** Infact most of the audits discussed so far such as statutory audits, final audit, continuous audit, internal audit etc. are all financial audits.

**2. Cost Audit :** According to R.W. Dobson, "Cost audit is the verification of the cost accounts and of the adherence to the cost accounting paln."

**3. Management Audit :** According to Taylor and Parry, "Management and auditing is a method to evaluate the efficiency of management at all levels through out the organisation, or more specifically, it comprises the investigation of a bussiness by an independent body from the highest executive level downwards in order to ascertain whether sound management prevails throughout, and to report as to its efficiency or otherwise with recommendations to ensure its effectiveness where such is not the case."

Thus, the main object of management audit is to achieve the most efficient administration of the enterprise.

**4. Operational Audit :** It has been defined as "a systematic independent appraisal activity within an organisation for a review of the entire departmental operation as a service to management. The overall objective of operational auditing is to assist all level of management in the effective discharge of their responsibilities by furnishing them with objective analysis apparaisals, recommendations and pertain comments concerning the activities reviewed."

**5. Performance Audit :** The term "performance audit" implies review of performance of various internal control and internal cheek systems.

The object of performance audit is to improve the efficiency and the efficacy of the management.

**6. Propriety Audit :** Propriety audit is an examination of actions and decisions to find out whether they are in public interest and meet the standards of proper conduct. In propriety audit, the auditor does not verifies the evidence supporting a particular transactions, he tries to ascertain that it is proper and in accordance with the established principles or customs approved by the authorities. The propriety audit is concerned with examining that there is no leakage of revenue or wastage of funds by mistake or fraud. It is concerned with ascrtaining appropriateness or justness from legal, financial or economic point of view.

**7. Cash Audit :** Cash audit is the detailed examination of cash transactions with the help of cash book and relevenat evidence.

### V. On the basis of coverage of audit

**1. Partial Audit :** When the auditor examines only a part of the record or books for the whole year or all the books and record for a part of the year, it is called partial audit.

**2. Detailed Audit :** In detailed audit all the books and transactions are thoroughly checked.

**3. Balance Sheet Audit :** Balance sheet audit as its name indicates is the verification of the values of various assets and liabilities appearing in the balance sheet. These include share capital, reserves and provisions and the amount of profit earned etc. on the liability side. On the asset side items included are land and buildings, plant and machinery and the amount of loss incurred etc. Since the item profit and loss also appear in the balance sheet, the auditor will have to review the items appearing in the profits & loss Account.

## AUDIT PROCESS

An auditor has to prepare his audit report. To give his report he has to examine sufficient evidence to certify the truth and fairness of the financial statements examined by him. This he can do with the help of audit process *i.e.,* tests and audit techniques.

There are two types of audit process :

### I. Compliance Processes

These processes are designed to ensure that internal controls, on which the auditor has to rely, are in operation. He has to check :

(*i*) Whether the controls exist

(*ii*) Whether these are working off

(*iii*) If so, whether these operated throughout the period under audit.

### II. Substantive Process

These processes are designed to ensure the completeness, accuracy and validity of the data produced by the accounting system. Substantive processes are of two types :

(*i*) test of details of transactions such as checking of casts, sub-casts, carry-for ward and their calculation etc.

(*ii*) analysis of significant ratios and trends including an enquiry into abnormal fluctuations and items.

It should be noted that the nature, timing and extent of substantive processes to be applied are determined by the results of compliance tests. For example, if the internal check system for cash sales in operation is found satisfactory *i.e.,* efficient and effective by an auditor, he may apply only test checks in vouching cash sales. If no error or fraud is detected by test checks, he may assume that the rest of the cash sales are alright *i.e.,* there is no error of fraud in cash sales in the absence of any suspicion.

On the other hand if the internal check system is not satisfactory or there is no internal check system at all, he should probe the matter to the bottom *i.e.,* thoroughly.

An auditor collects evidence with the help of audit techniques. In fact both the audit processes-compliance and substantive, discussed above are performed with the help of audit techniques.

Audit techniques are the tools and methods of processes applied by the auditor to collect audit evidence. These vary from situation to situation depending upon facts and circumstance of a case. As such an auditor may change the techniques if the finds that it is not suitable in a particular case. The important audit techniques are as follows :

1. Vouching
2. Physical Examination (verification)
3. Observation
4. Confirmation
5. Test checking
6. Inquiry

7. Scanning
8. Analysis of financial statement
9. Reconciliation
10. Flow charting
11. Electronic data processing records

**1. Vouching**

Vouching is the most important technique of auditing. It is because of this it is remarked that vouching is the "essence of auditing."

Vouching means examination and evaluation of documentary evidence. According to De Paula, Vouching. "does not mean merely the inspection of receipts with the cash book, but includes the examination of receipts with the transactions of a business together with documentary and other evidence of sufficient validity to satisfy an auditor that such transactions are in order, have been properly authorized and are correctly recorded in the books of account."

**2. Physical Examination (Verification)**

Tangible assets of a business shown in the balançe sheet physically examined *i.e.*, verified. Such verification involves identifications, counting or quantitative measurement and valuation of the asset concerned.

**3. Observation**

In fact it is also a part of physical Examination. It means observing any process or act being performed by others. For example, an auditor may observe the process of stock taking being done by the client of the staff when the accounts are being audited.

**4. Confirmation**

Confirmation implies independent verification of a fact or figure from a third party. For example, confirming client's bank balance from the bank or confirming the debtor's balance from the debtors directly. In confirmation emphasis is laid an 'independence' so that the truth may be revealed.

**5. Test Checking**

It involves testing a samples from the bulk *i.e.*, a small number of representative items are selected at random from the lot. On the basis of the result of the sample a conclusion is drawn about the whole lot (information). It should be noted that to get proper result the sample should be :

(*i*) representative, and
(*ii*) large enough to represent the characteristics of the lot.

**6. Inquiry**

Where it is necessary to examine any matter in detail, inquiry techniques is used to collect and analyse the information. Under this method searching questions are asked to obtain necessary information and explanation. It is usual to use a pre-designed questionaire for the purpose of conducting inquiry.

**7. Scanning**

It implies a close scrutiny of transactions where the transaction appear to be useful must be done by the experienced and skilled auditor as it is necessary to ask searching questions to extract necessary information and explanation and to correlate the collected information to draw meanigful condusions.

**8. Analysis of financial statement**

To draw conclusion an auditor may examine and analyse accounting figures. For instance consistency of the accounts can be checked by calculating accounting ratios. Similarly consistency of profitability can be checked with the help of profitability ratio.

**9. Reconciliation**

It means scarching the reason for variance *i.e.*, difference in two figures. For example, bank balance of the client can be verified by preparing a bank reconciliation statement.

**10. Flow charting**

Flow chart involves graphical presentation of various operations, controls and stages of a system with the help of a flow chart an auditor can analyse a system to judge its efficiency and effectiveness.

**11. Electronic data processing records**

With the growing use of computers in the field of basic accounting records it has become necessary for an auditor to audit computerised accounts. Some of these techniques have also computised. The auditor has to safeguard not only aganist technical errors and errors due to the fault of the operator but also frauds perpetuated by the computer operator intentionally to commit fraud.

# OBJECTIVE TYPE QUESTIONS

**1.** Vouching implies
(a) Inspection of reciepts
(b) Examination of vouchers to check authenticity of records.
(c) Surprise checking of accounting records.
(d) Examining the various assets.

**2.** Payment for goods purchased should be vouched with the help of
(a) Creditors' statement.
(b) Correspondence with the suppliers.
(c) Cash Memos.
(d) Ledger Accounts.

**3.** The most reliable voucher is one which originates
(a) In the concern.
(b) Out side the concern.
(c) Out side the concern and sent directly to the auditor.
(d) In the concern and sent directly to the auditor.

**4.** Purchases Returns should be vouched with the help of
(a) Bought Notes
(b) Credit Notes
(c) Goods Inwards Book
(d) Cash Book

**5.** Verification refers to
(a) Examination of journal and ledger
(b) Examination of vouchers related to assets.
(c) Examining the physical existence and valuation of assests.
(d) Calculation of value of assets.

**6.** Which of the following statements is correct?
(a) Valuation is a part of verification.
(b) Verification is a part of valuation.
(c) Valuation has nothing to do with verification.
(d) Auditor is a valuer.

**7.** Stock should be valued at
(a) Cost.
(b) Market price.
(c) Cost or market price whichever is lower.
(d) Cost less depreciation.

**8.** Valuation mean
(a) Calculation value of assets.
(b) Checking the value of assets.
(c) Checking the physical existence of assets.
(d) Examining the authenticity of assets.

**9.** "Auditor is not a valuer" was stated in
(a) King ston Cotton Mills case.
(b) London and General Bank case.
(c) Les V. Neuchated Co. Ltd. case
(d) London Oil Storage Co. case.

**10.** First auditor of a company is appointed by the
(a) Share holders
(b) Central Government.
(c) Company Law Board.
(d) Board of Directors.

**11.** The following cannot be appointed as an auditor of the company.
(a) A chartered Accountant
(b) A firm of C.A.
(c) A Body corporated.
(d) None of these.

**12.** The first auditor of company will hold office.
(a) For a period of one year.
(b) Till holding of statutory meeting.
(c) Till the conclusion of first annual general meeting.
(d) Till a new auditor is appointed.

**13.** An auditor in a casued vacancy is appointed by the
(a) Board of Directors.
(b) Sharehoders.
(c) Central Government
(d) Company Law Board

**14.** If an auditor, not appointed at annual general meeting, is appointed by the
(a) The Central Government.
(b) Board of Directors.
(c) Shareholders
(d) Company Law Board.

**15.** A special Auditor is appointed by the
(a) Shareholders.
(b) Board of Directors
(c) Central Government.
(d) Comptoroller and Auditor General.

**16.** A Government auditor may be appointed by the
(a) Central Government on the advice of comptroller and Auditor General.
(b) Shareholders.
(c) Board of Directors.
(d) Comptorller and Auditor General.

**17.** A company auditor can be removed before expiry of his term by.
(a) Shareholders with prior-permission of Central Government.
(b) Board of Directors.
(c) Central Government.
(d) State Government.

**18.** A company auditor, in general, has to submit this report to
(a) Shareholders
(b) Central Government
(c) Comptroller and Auditor General
(d) Board of Directors.

**19.** A special auditor has to submit his report to the
(a) Shareholders.
(b) Central Government.
(c) Comptroller and Auditor General.
(d) Board of Directors

**20.** An auditor of Government company has to submit his report to
(a) Shareholders
(b) Central Government
(c) Comptroller and Auditor General
(d) Ministry concerned.

**21.** Auditor, in general, is an
(a) Employee of the company.
(b) Agent of the company.
(c) Agent of the shareholders.
(d) None of these.

**22.** Auditor should see that the return of allotment has been sent to Registrar within
(a) 1 month (b) 2 months
(c) 3 months (d) 40 days

**23.** Application money should not be withdrawn, unless
(a) Allotment is made.
(b) Cash book has been prepared.
(c) Certificate to commence business obtained.
(d) Certificate of incorporation obtained.

**24.** Divisible profit should not include.
(a) Interest on capital (b) Capital
(c) Depreciation (d) None of these.

**25.** Dividend can be paid out of
(a) Capital profits. (b) Capital receipts.
(c) Revenue receipts (d) None of these.

**26.** Capital profits imply profits earned.
(a) Through business transactions.
(b) From capital.
(c) From sale of fixed assets.
(d) From sale of current assets.

**27.** A company auditor should see that the dividend should be paid.
(a) After charging depreciation.
(b) Without charging depreciation.
(c) Out of capital
(d) None of these.

**28.** In his report, the auditor gives his
(a) Judgement
(b) Opinion
(c) Guarantee to correctness of accounts.
(d) True state of affairs.

**29.** In his report, the company auditor states
(a) Correct state of affairs.
(b) True state of affairs.
(c) True and fair state of affairs.
(d) Fair state of affairs.

**30.** The company has earned profits on sale of its machinery and wants to pay dividend out of it. As auditor, you should
(a) Allow it.
(b) Not allow it.
(c) Allow it with certain conditions.
(d) None of these.

**31.** In the general meeting of company, shareholders want dividend @10% where as directors recommended @7 ½%. As an auditor would you.
(a) Allow it. (b) Not allow 10%
(c) Allow only 7 ½% (d) None of these.

**32.** Auditor finds that there is a change in the method of valuation of stock, whether he should

(a) Allow it.
(b) Disallow it.
(c) Allow it with a note to this effect.
(d) Ignore it.

**33.** In the annual general meeting of a company, the auditor is questioned as why he has signed the balance sheet when assets would not realise the value shown in it. Which of the following arguments given by auditor is correct?
(a) Market value of assets has nothing to do with assets.
(b) Market value of assets cannot be as certained.
(c) Assets are shown treating it as a going concern.
(d) None of these.

**34.** The auditor did not care to check adequacy of provision for Bad and Doubtful Debts. Whether he can be held.
(a) Liable for it.
(b) Not liable for it.
(c) Liable criminally for it.
(d) None of these.

**35.** The auditor resorted to test checking and, with the result, he could not disclose certain frauds. Whether he can be held.
(a) Liable for it.
(b) Not liable for it.
(c) Liable criminally for it.
(d) None of these.

**36.** During the course of an audit, an auditor finds that no vouchers are available for certain payments. Whether he should.
(a) Seek proper explanation for it.
(b) Demand vouchers for it.
(c) Ignore it.
(d) Accept cartificate for it.

**37.** During a company audit, the management argues with the auditor, that machinery has been very well maintained and is as good as new. Hence there is no need for charging depreciation on it. Whether the auditor should
(a) Accept it (b) ignore it
(c) Reject it (d) None of these

**38.** Civil liability of an auditor implies liability for
(a) Misappropriation of cash.
(b) Misappropriation of goods.
(c) Fraud.
(d) Misfeasance.

**39.** Auditor is liable for
(a) Not verifying petty cash.
(b) Not determining stock.
(c) Not checking accounts property.
(d) All of these.

**40.** If an auditor allows publication of annual reports knowing them to be materially false to deceive shareholders, he incurs
(a) Contractual liability.
(b) Civil liability.
(c) Criminal liability.
(d) None of these.

**41.** An auditor can be held liable under C.A. Act, 1949 for
(a) Negligence.
(b) Criminal offence.
(c) Professional misconduct.
(d) Breach of contract.

**42.** If a company auditor has misapplied money of a company, he may be held liable for
(a) Negligence.
(b) Misfeasance.
(c) Criminal liability.
(d) Contractual liability.

**43.** If an auditor is found guilty of falsification of company books, he will incur
(a) Criminal liability.
(b) Civil liability.
(c) Contractual liability.
(d) None of these.

**44.** For misstatement in a company prospectus, the auditor incurs
(a) Civil liability
(b) Criminal liability
(c) Contractual liability
(d) None of these

**45.** A chartered Accountant sent circular letters soliciting work can he be held liable
(a) For misfeasance.
(b) For negligence.
(c) Criminally
(d) For professional misconduct.

**46.** The main object of audit of accounts of a partnership firm is to
(a) Meet the statutory requirements.
(b) Increase the profits.
(c) Increase the goodwill.
(d) Detect errors and frauds.

**47.** Auditing begins where......ends
(a) Selling.
(b) Accounting.
(c) Inventory valuation.
(d) Business.

**48.** Auditing is compulsory in the case of
(a) Sole tradership.
(b) Partnership.
(c) Joint stock companies.
(d) All of these.

**49.** Auditing can be defined as
(a) Preparation of books of accounts.
(b) Examination of books of accounts.
(c) Rendering expert advice to management regarding accounting matters.
(d) Checking that accounts are correct.

**50.** The existence of a good system of internal check reduces to a great extent
(a) The work of the auditor.
(b) The liability of the auditor.
(c) Neither work nor liability of the auditor.
(d) Both work and liability of an auditor.

**51.** Government audit means
(a) Auditing of the accounts of Government departments.
(b) Auditing of companies by persons appointed by the Government.
(c) Audit under the provisions of law.
(d) Audit of Government company.

**52.** Cost audit means
(a) Auditing the cost of goods produced.
(b) Audit of cost accounts.
(c) Audit by a cost accountant.
(d) Audit by A.C.A. of accounts.

**53.** Interim audit is conducted between two.....audits.
(a) Continuous (b) Costs
(c) Final audits (d) All of these.

**54.** When at an annual general meeting of a company no auditors are appointed or re-appointed. In that case
(a) The central government appoints a person to fill the vacancy.
(b) The Board of Directors appoint a person to fill the vacancy.
(c) The Managing Director appoints a person to fill the vacancy.
(d) The extra ordinary general meeting is called to appoint auditors.

**55.** It is a right of the company auditor to have access
(a) To the books of account of the company.
(b) To the books of accounts and vouchers of the company.
(c) To all the statutory, statistical, costing and account books and vouchers of the company.
(d) None of these.

**56.** Where the provision of the companies Act are violated, the auditor must report the same to the.
(a) Central Government.
(b) Board of directors.
(c) Managing Director.
(d) Shareholders.

**57.** A voucher is a
(a) Document in support of an entry made in the books of accounts.
(b) Invoice received from suppliers.
(c) Receipt issued to a customer for cash recieved.
(d) All of these.

**58.** Except in special cases, the retiring auditor is automatically
(a) Re-appointed (b) Dismissed
(c) Disqualified (d) Suspended

**59.** The company shall intimate to the auditor appointed stating that he has been appointed as auditor of the company within
(a) 30 days (b) 20 days
(c) 10 days (d) 7 days

**60.** Audit programme implies planning of audit work by
(a) The managing director.
(b) The accounting staff.
(c) The audit staff.
(d) The auditor.

**61.** Audit note book contains
(a) Various dates for reference
(b) Details of work done.
(c) Notes regarding item requiring clarification, explanations etc.
(d) All of these.

**62.** The liability of an auditor can be
(a) Civil.
(b) Criminal.
(c) Civil and / or criminal.
(d) All of these.

**63.** Balance sheet audit is an audit in which
(a) Balance sheets of a number of years are audited.
(b) Audit is done at the end of the financial year.
(c) Verification of assets and liabilities is done.
(d) None of these.

**64.** The duties of auditor of a partnership firm are regulated by
(a) Partnership Act.
(b) Partnership deed.
(c) Agreement between partnership and auditor.
(d) Institute of chartered Accountants.

**65.** Under or over valuation of assets and liabilities are due to
(a) Clerical errors.
(b) Errors of principles.
(c) Fraudulent manipulation of accounts.
(d) None of these.

**66.** Civil liability of a company auditor is for
(a) Wilfully making a false statement.
(b) Negligence.
(c) Mis-statement in porspectus.
(d) All of these.

**67.** The difference between internal audit and statutory audit is that
(a) Internal auditor should be a qualified chartered accountant whereas statutory auditor need not hold such a qualifiaction.
(b) Internal auditor has to submit his report to the shareholders while a statutory auditor has to submit his report to the management.
(c) Appointment of internal auditor is optional while the appointment of statutory auditor is obligatory.
(d) None of these

**68.** Internal audit is helpful in
(a) Prevention of errors and frauds.
(b) Detection of errors and frauds.
(c) Auditing items in depth.
(d) Final audit.

**69.** Audit is depth refers to
(a) Audit of each and every item.
(b) Intensive audit of a few items.
(c) Audit of a few items selected at random.
(d) Detailed audit of each and every item.

**70.** Test checking implies
(a) Checking only few items in detail.
(b) Checking each and every item.
(c) Checking a representative sample of items.
(d) None of these.

**71.** Auditor are appointed by
(a) Board of Directors.
(b) Shareholders in the annual general meeting.
(c) Managing Director.
(d) Central Government.

**72.** In the case of a partnership the auditor is appointed.
(a) Under the partnership Act.
(b) By the partners them selves.
(c) Under the chartered Accountants Act.
(d) None of these.

**73.** Auditing is compulsory in the case of
(a) Joint stock companies.
(b) Sole tradership
(c) Partnership
(d) All of these.

**74.** Which of the following persons areeligible for appointment as auditor of a company
(a) A person who owes Rs. 1900 to company.
(b) A person who is a chartered accountant.
(c) A chartered accountant but of unsound mind.
(d) A person who is a chartered accountant but is a secretary of the company.

**75.** The duties of auditor of a partnership firm is regulated by the
(a) Deed of partnership
(b) Partnership Act.
(c) Agreement between the partners and the auditor.
(d) None of these.

**76.** Balance sheet audit is useful when
(a) The concern is a big one.
(b) The concern is a small one.
(c) The internal check is weak.
(d) The concern is a bank.

**77.** Continuous audit is useful for
(a) Medium sized concerns.
(b) Big concerns.
(c) Small concerns.
(d) None of these.

**78.** The principal object of audit is
(a) To exhibit a true and fair view of the state of Affairs of the undertaking.
(b) Detection of errors.
(c) Detection and prevention of frauds.
(d) Checking accuracy of accounts.

**79.** While doing the audit, the auditor found a balance Rs. 6,000 in good will A/C and ascertained that the amount has not been written off for a long period. The auditor can
(a) Advise the concern to write off the goodwill.
(b) Insist the concern to write off goodwill in the same year.
(c) Recommend the concern to write off goodwill over a period of 5 year.
(d) Allow good will to appear forever.

**80.** Management Audit means
(a) Systematic appraisal of management's objectives and procedures.
(b) Audit of management accounting.
(c) Audit on behalf of management.
(d) Criticism of policies.

**81.** Internal audit is helpful in
(a) Making record ready for official audit.
(b) Prevention of errors and frauds.
(c) Detection of errors and frauds.
(d) Auditing for self-satisfaction.

**82.** Audit in depth refers to
(a) Audit of each and every item of the account.
(b) Intensive audit of a few items.
(c) Audit of a few selected items.
(d) Detailed audit of each and every item.

**83.** The objective of Auditing is
(a) Expression of opinion as to truthfulness and fairness of financial statements
(b) Detection and prevention of frauds and errors
(c) Both (a) and (b)
(d) None of these

**84.** Internal audit is
(a) Statutory Audit
(b) Annual Audit
(c) Internal control
(d) Yearly audit by some people.

**85.** An audtior is like a
(a) Mad dog (b) Watch dog
(c) Foolish dog (d) Watchman.

**86.** The company shall inform to the auditor appointed stating that he has been appointed as auditor of the company within
(a) 10 days (b) 8 days
(c) 7 days (d) 30 days

**87.** The audtior shall inform the Registrar of Companies in writing about his acceptance of appointment within
(a) 20 days (b) 30 days
(c) 40 days (d) 45 days

**88.** A voucher is a document
(a) Insupport of an entry made in the books of accounts.
(b) Receipt received from the person who delivered goods to the company.
(c) Invoice received from suppliers.
(d) All of these.

**89.** A vacancy caused by the resignation of an auditor is filled only
(a) By the general meeting of the shareholders.
(b) By the Board of Directors.
(c) Company Law Board.
(d) By the Managing Director of the company.

**90.** Audit of the Modern corporation is codnucted in order to
(a) Control over losses.
(b) Increase in porfits.
(c) To meet the statutory requirement of the law.
(d) Satisfy the shareholders and members.

**91.** Audit at the end of the years is known as
(a) Periodical audit (b) Standard audit
(c) Statutory audit (d) Efficient audit

**92.** Government audit means
(a) Auditing of the accounts of government departments.
(b) Auditing by the government appointed auditor.
(c) Auditing under the provision of law.
(d) None of these.

**93.** Remuneration of an auditor is fixed by
(a) Article of Association of the company.
(b) Memorandum of Association of the company.
(c) Managing Director of the company.
(d) The appointing authority.

**94.** The liabilities of an auditor can be
(a) Civil (b) Criminal
(c) Civil and criminal (d) None of these.

**95.** Civil liability of a company auditor is for
(a) Wilfully making a false statement.
(b) Negligence.
(c) Misstatement in the report.
(d) All of these.

**96.** Balance sheet audit is an audit in which
(a) B/S of various year is audited
(b) Verification of assets and liabilities is done.
(c) Auditing is done at the end of the financial year.
(d) None of these.

**97.** An employee connot be an auditor of the company because
(a) He may give bias and subjective views.
(b) A person connot audit his own accounts.
(c) It is prohibited by company law.
(d) He cannot find his own mistakes.

**98.** Test checking means
(a) Checking each and every item.
(b) Checking a few items in detail.
(c) Checking a representative sample of item.
(d) Intensive audit of a few items.

**99.** The auditor should inform the Registrar of Companies about the acceptance of appointment within
(a) 7 days (b) 18 days
(c) 20 days (d) 30 days.

**100.** Internal audit is helpful in
(a) Audit in depth.
(b) Internal check.
(c) Prevention of errors and frauds.
(d) Statutory audit.

**101.** Audit of sole tradership is
(a) Unnecessary (b) Advisable
(c) Compulsory (d) Optional

**102.** Which of the following is the most detailed audit.
(a) Statutory audit
(b) Balance sheet audit
(c) Continuous audit
(d) Interim audit.

**103.** Which among these are clerical errors
(a) Errors of Principle
(b) Errors of Duplication
(c) Errors of Omission
(d) Comepensating Errors

**104.** An auditor of a company gives
(a) Critical review of accounts.
(b) His expert opinion about the accounts.
(c) Collaborative evidence that accounts are properly drawn up.
(d) Actual position about the accounts of the firm.

**105.** Consider the following statements:

**Assertion (A)** : A body corporate cannot be the auditor of a company.

**Reason (R)** : It is prohibited under company law.

(a) Both A and R are true, and R is the correct explanation of A.
(b) Both A and R are true, but R is not the correct explanation of A.
(c) A is true, but R is false.
(d) A is false, but R is true.

**106.** Internal check serves the purpose of
(a) Detection of errors.
(b) Prevention of errors.
(c) Detection and prevention of errors.
(d) All of these.

**107.** Auditors of a company are ordinarily appointed by
(a) Managing Director
(b) Chairman of the Board of Directors.
(c) Shareholders in the Annual General Meeting.
(d) General Manager of the company.

**108.** Internal check is a part of the whole system of
(a) Internal control (b) Internal audit
(c) Final audit (d) Interim audit

**109.** The main object of auditing is to
(a) Detect errors.
(b) Prevent errors.
(c) Detect and prevent errors.
(d) None of these.

**110.** Auditing Means
(a) Detection and prevention of frauds.
(b) Detection and prevention of errors.
(c) Detection and prevention of errors and frauds.
(d) Controlling of accounts.

**111.** Civil liabilitiy of a company auditor is for
(a) Wilfully making a false statement
(b) Mis-statement .
(c) Negligence.
(d) Not being over cautious.

**112.** Audit report along with annual accounts is given by
(a) Statutory Auditor.
(b) Internal Auditor.
(c) Government Auditor.
(d) Secretarial Auditor.

**113.** Consider the following statements:
*Management audit may*
I. Cover performance audit.
II. Protect the interests of the shareholders.
III. Cover properietory audit
IV. Refer to audit of work done by the management accountant.
*Of these statements.*
(a) I and II are correct.
(b) III and IV are correct.
(c) I and III are correct.
(d) II and IV are correct.

**114.** Management audit is ordered by the
(a) Workers of a company.
(b) Government.
(c) Board of Directors
(d) Securities Exchange Board of India.

**115.** When an auditor detects material weaknesses in the internal checks and control system of the company under audit, It should report his finding as per.
(a) ICAI orders
(b) SEVI orders
(c) MAOCARO orders
(d) ICWAI orders

**116.** The remuneration of an auditor of a partnership firm is fixed by
(a) The partnership Act
(b) The companies Act
(c) The Government
(d) None of these

**117.** If the shareholders fail to appoint or reappoint auditors of a limited company in an Annual General Meeting, the Vacancy will be filled by the
(a) Securities Exchange Board of India.
(b) Comptroller and Auditor General of India.
(c) Central Government.
(d) A Registrar of company.

**118.** Match List I with List II and select the correct answer using the codes given below the lists:

| | **List I** (Appointment of Auditor) | | **List II** (Appointing Authority) |
|---|---|---|---|
| I. | First auditor of a non-Government limited company. | A. | Shareholders of the company. |
| II. | Reappointment of a retiring auditor of a non-Government limited company. | B. | Board of Directors of the Company. |
| III. | Auditor of a Government Company. | C. | Central Government on the advice of the comptroller and Auditor General of India. |
| IV. | Auditor of a non Government limited Company. When shareholders fail to appoint or reappoint an auditor. | D. | Central Government. |

***Codes:***
(a) I-A, II-B, III-D, IV-C
(b) I-B, II-A, III-C, IV-D
(c) I-A, II-B, III-C, IV-D
(d) I-B, II-A, III-D, IV-C

**119.** As far as a company is concerned, which one of the following pairs is NOT correctly matched?
(a) Internal audit ____ Obligatory
(b) Statutory audit ____ Mandatory
(c) Continuous audit ____ Optional
(d) Management audit ____ Voluntary.

**120.** Where the auditor places a high degree of reliance on an internal control procedure, the acceptable risk of over reliance would be
(a) Low (b) High
(c) Moderate (d) Nil

**121.** A file which contains rules governing the organisation under audit is known as
(a) Current file (b) Permanent file
(c) Routine file (d) Procedence file

**122.** Special audit can be ordered by
(a) Preference shareholders.
(b) The Central Government.
(c) SEBI
(d) Debenture holders.

**123.** Management audit is conducted by
(a) The statutory auditors
(b) Government auditors
(c) Cost auditors
(d) None of these.

**124.** System of internal check is said to exist in an organisation when
(a) An employee is specifically deputed to check the work of another employee.
(b) The departmental head checks the work of his subordinate.
(c) Some outside experts check the work of employees.
(d) Another employee of the same department check.

**125.** Internal Auditor is appointed by the
(a) Shareholders of the company.
(b) Statutory auditor.
(c) Institute of Internal Auditors of India.
(d) Board of Directors of the company.

**126.** Which one of the following is true of the position of an auditor regarding the system of internal check in the organisation?
(a) He should acquaint himself with the system of internal check.
(b) He should monitor and supervise the system of internal check.
(c) He himself should lay down the system of internal check.
(d) He has nothing to do with the system of internal check.

**127.** The auditor has a right to ask for information and explanation from the
(a) Past auditors of the company.
(b) Directors of the company.
(c) Officers of the company.
(d) Intrernal auditors of the company.

**128.** In the case of audit of statutory report, an auditor is expected to give his report on the
(a) Number of shares allotted, amount received in cash and summarised Receipts and payments account.
(b) Authorised capital, subscribed capital and paid up capital.
(c) Profit and loss account, Balance sheet and directors' report.
(d) Directors' qualification shares, calls in arrears and calls in advance.

**129.** Working papers which contain a record of the audit work are the property of the
(a) Company.
(b) Auditor.
(c) Registrar of Companies.
(d) Government of India.

**130.** Sampling is used in the case of
(a) Collection of debts by the accountant.
(b) Test checks by the auditor.
(c) Supervision by the works manager.
(d) Checking pass-book entries by the accountant.

**131.** A continuous audit is not suitable where the
(a) Transactions are few but complicated.
(b) There is no urgency to finalise the accounts on a particular date.
(c) Internal audit work is being carried on in a satisfactory manner.
(d) System of internal check in operation is not satisfactory.

**132.** Management audit is
(a) An independent appraisal of the total management process.
(b) A statutory requirement.
(c) An investigation into the conduct of director.
(d) An idependent appraisal of competitiveness of business.

**133.** The first auditors of a company are appointed by the
(a) Registrar of Companies.
(b) Shareholders of the company.
(c) Promoters of the company.
(d) Board of Directors of the company.

**Directions : (Q 134-138)** *The following questions consist of two statements, one labelled the Assertion A and the other labelled Reason R. You are to examine these two statements carefully and decide if the Assertion A and the Reason R are individually true and if so, whether the Reason is a correct explanation of the Assertion. Select your answer to these questions using the codes given below and mark your answer sheet accordingly.*

***Codes:***
(a) Both A and R are true, and R is the correct explanation of A.
(b) Both A and R are true, but R is not the correct explanation of A.
(c) A is true, but R is false.
(d) A is false, but R is true.

**134. Assertion (A) :** Now-a-days, it is obligatory on the part of companies to disclose in their Annual Report, work done for the benefit of the society.
**Reason (R) :** Annual Reports are used by members of the society in one capacity or another.

**135. Assertion (A) :** The auditor should examine the "objects" clause of the Memorandum of Association.
**Reason (R) :** This would ensure that the company is carrying on business as specified in the Memorandum of Association.

**136. Assertion (A) :** The auditor of a proprietory firm need not be bound by professional propriety.
**Reason (R) :** Proprietory auditor is responsible only to the person (s) who appoint (s) him.

**137. Assertion (A) :** The main purpose of auditing is to verify that the accounts have been prepared according to the principles of accounting and to see whether the financial statement so prepared reflect a true and fair view of the state of affairs of a business.
**Reason (R) :** Auditing starts after the completion of recording of transactions in the books of account.

**138. Assertion (A) :** The auditor should visit the particular concern at intervals and check the book of accounts.
**Reason (R) :** Some precaution is required to be taken by the auditor to avoid weaknesses of continuous audit.

**139.** When the auditor examines and tests the client's accounting and other control systems to see whether or not they constitute a reliable base for the preparation of acccounts, then it is known as.
(a) Balance sheet audit.
(b) System audit.
(c) Continuous audit.
(d) Internal audit.

**140.** Audit Note book is a
(a) Personal note book of an auditor
(b) Record of work performed by an auditor .
(c) Record of important points and enquiries which an auditor has to refer to his clients.
(d) Records of mistakes and errors detected during the course of audit of account books.

**141.** Which one of the following statements regarding the internal check system is correct?
(a) Have an accurate record of all the business transactions.
(b) Known the accounting method follow in the business.
(c) Plan for future audit works.
(d) As certain the profit earning capacity of the business.

**142.** By observing, testing and assessing , an auditor examines the system of
(a) Internal audit.
(b) Internal control.
(c) Continuous audit.
(d) Statutory audit.

**143.** An auditor of a partnership firm is appointed as per
(a) Statute.
(b) Government order.
(c) Agreement.
(d) Convention.

**144.** A company auditor may be removed in the meeting of the
(a) Board of Director when the Managing Director is also present
(b) Board of Directors.
(c) Majority shareholders
(d) General Body of shareholders.

**145.** According to sec 224 of the companies Act, 1956, a company auditor may be appointed by any of the three appointing authorities. The correct sequence of the order in which they can exercise their power to appoint a company auditor in the life of a company other than a government company is
(a) Board of Directors, Central Government' shareholders.
(b) Central Government, shareholders, Board of Directors.
(c) Shareholders, Board of Directors, Central Government.
(d) Board of Directors, shareholders, Central Government.

**146.** The liability of auditor can be
(a) Only civil.
(b) Only criminal.
(c) Either civil or criminal
(d) Civil and criminal.

**147.** Consider the following activites:
I. Valuation.
II. Verification.
III. Vouching.
*The correct sequence of the activities are*
(a) III, I, II (b) III, II, I
(c) II, III, I (d) I, II, III

**148.** Consider the following statements:
*Continuous audit is useful because*
I. More detailed checking is possible.
II. Audit can be completed quite quickly.
III. Figures in the accounts cannot be altered as the auditor visits several times during the year.
IV. Internal check can be done a way with
*Of these statements:*
(a) I and II are correct.
(b) II and IV are correct.
(c) II, III and IV are correct.
(d) I, III, and IV are correct.

**149.** Match List I (Nature of audit) with List II (Related types of audit) and select the correct answer by using the codes given below the lists:

| List I | List II |
|---|---|
| I. Audit work is carried on almost simultaneously with the reacording of transactions. | A. Balance sheet Audit. |
| II. Auditor Start his work when the final acounts have been prepared. | B. Continuous Audit |
| III. Audit conducted in between two annual audits. | C. Interim Audit. |
| IV. Some of the books and records of the whole period or specific period are audited. | D. Cost Audit. |
| | E. Partial Audit. |

***Codes:***
(a) I-D, II-A, III-B, IV-C
(b) I-B, II-A, III-E, IV-C
(c) I-B, II-A, III-C, IV-E
(d) I-A, II-B, III-C, IV-D

**150.** Which one of the following would be a sufficient ground for an auditor to submit a qualified report even though the management had given a note to the accounts?

I. Securities belonging to the client are lodged with a depository.

II. Fixed assets have been mortgaged.

III. Bank balance as show by the pass book is different from that indicated by the pass book.

IV. Closing stock is valued at cost plus loy.

*Select the correct answer using the codes given below.*

(a) III, I, II (b) III, II, I

(c) II, III, I (d) I, II, III

**151.** Consider the following documents:

I. Audit Note book.

II. Audit Programme.

III. Audit Report.

IV. Audit Files.

*The correct sequence in which an auditor prepares these documents is*

(a) I, II, III, IV (b) II, I, III, IV

(c) II, I, IV, III (d) I, II, IV, III

**152.** Which of the following pairs are correctly matched?

(a) Test check...............Random checking

(b) Internal check................A system of automatic checking

(c) Internal control.................includes internal check and internal audit.

(d) Investigation................General examiantion of all accounting records.

**153.** The scope of external audit in the case of a partnership firm is decided by the

(a) Companies Act.

(b) Partnership Act.

(c) Letter of appointment of the auditor.

(d) Income Tax Act.

**154.** A chartered Accountant who has purchased on credit goods worth Rs. 2, 000 from a company 'Z' Ltd., is

(a) Not disqualified from being appointed an auditor of Z Ltd.

(b) Disqualified from being appointed an auditor of any company of the group.

(c) Disqualified from being appointed an auditor of Z Ltd.

(d) Disqualified from being appointed an auditor of any company having dealings with Z Ltd.

**155.** The auditor of a company are NOT supposed to issue qualified report when

(a) Goodwill worth Rs. 1,00,000 built up by the company is not shown in the Balance sheet.

(b) Goodwill is shown in the Balancesheet of the company although it has been totally lost.

(c) Balance sheet and profit and Loss Account show a true and correct view of the company's affairs and are drawn in conformity with the law.

(d) Proper Books of Accounts as required by law have been kept by the company but the auditor has been refused access to some of these books.

**156.** 'Surprise checks' are part of

(a) An auditor's working papers.

(b) An audit programme.

(c) An auditor's report.

(d) An accounting standard.

**157.** Physical verification of fixed assets is the primary responsibility of the

(a) Auditor (b) Management

(c) Government (d) Shareholders

**158.** Auditing standards differ from auditing procedures in that the procedures relate to

(a) Measures of performance.

(b) Audit principles.

(c) Acts to be performed.

(d) Audit judgements.

**159.** Consider the following situations:

I. The business of the company is being conducted fraudulently.

II. The persons connected with the formation of the company have been quility or fraud.

III. The company so desires it by way of a special Resolution.

*The Central Government need not necessarily appoint Inspectors to investigate the affairs of the company in respect of situations listed at*

(a) I, II and III (b) I and II

(c) I and III (d) II and III.

**160.** What is the correct sequence of the following assignments?

I. Internal control.
II. Test check.
III. Internal check.
IV. Statutory audit.

*Select the correct answer using the codes given below:*

***Codes:***

(a) I, II, III, IV (b) III, I, IV, II
(c) III, I, II, IV (d) IV, III, II, I

**161.** Statutory auditor of a company is the case of a casual vacancy may be appointed by the

(a) Board of Directors.
(b) Managing Director.
(c) Extra Ordinary General Meeting.
(d) Government concerned.

**162.** Which of the following are included in the 'Statutory Books' for the purpose of company audit?

I. Register of charges.
II. Minutes Books for the Board Meetings.
III. Articles of Association.
IV. Minutes Book for the share holder's meeting
V. Register of members.
IV. Memorandum of Association.

*Select the correct answer using the codes given below:*

***Codes:***

(a) I, II, IV and V
(b) III, II, IV and VI
(c) I, III, V and VI
(d) II, III, V and VI

**163.** Consider the following statements:
A statutory auditor of a pubic limited company claims that he has the following legal right in relation to his duties.

I. Right to refuse to make a report.
II. Right of access to books of accounts and registers.
III. Right to seek explanation from directors and officers.
IV. Right to make statement in the general meeting.

*Of these statements:*

(a) I, II and III are correct.
(b) I, II and IV are correct.
(c) I, III and IV are correct.
(d) II, III and IV are correct.

**164.** Which one of the following practices is permissible under the code of ethics to be followed by an auditor?

(a) An auditor who gives an expert opinion on a client company may be an under writer of the same.
(b) Understatement of the facts only for tax planning purposes.
(c) Prescribing a fee contingent upon the tax liabilities/savings effected.
(d) Engaging in a business conjointly with the client.

**165.** The auditor is generally expected to carry out the following in a particular seriatim.

I. Verification of Assets and liabilities.
II. Vouching of transactions.
III. Checking of Valuation of Assets and liabilities.

***Codes:***

(a) I, II and III (b) II, I and III
(c) II, III and I (d) III, II and I

**166.** Match List I with List II and select the correct answer using the codes given below the lists:

| List I | List II |
|---|---|
| I. Duties of auditors | A. Access to books of the company. |
| II. Rights of auditors | B. Penalty for non-compliance with sections 227 to 229. |
| III. Liabilities of auditors | C. Company in generals meeting. |
| IV. Removal of auditors | D. To make a report. |

***Codes:***

(a) I-D, II-A, III-B, IV-C
(b) I-A, II-C, III-A, IV-D
(c) I-A, II-D, III-C, IV-B
(d) I-C, II-B, III-C, IV-A

**167.** For granting subsidy to the sick units, the audit required would be
(a) Financial Audit
(b) Internal Audit
(c) Management Audit
(d) Statutory Audit

**168.** When a company engages a chartered Accountant as its internal auditor, the external auditor.
(a) Need not check as covered by internal audit.
(b) Should ignore the existence of internal audit.
(c) Should incorporat the internal auditor's report with his own.
(d) Should examine the system and efficiency of internal audit and devise a suitable audit programme.

**169.** Companies Act restricts the maximum number of companies, with paid up capital of Rs. 25 lakhs or more each, to which one can be appointed as an auditor to
(a) 5 (b) 10
(c) 15 (d) 20

**170.** When at an Annual General Meeting of a company no auditor is appointed or re-appointed. In that case
(a) The Central Government appoints a person to fill the vacancy.
(b) The Board of Directors appoints a person to fill the vacancy.
(c) The Managing Director of the company appoints a person to fill the vacancy.
(d) None of these can appoint a person to fill that vacancy.

**171.** Which among these is a fraud
(a) Employee fraud
(b) Management fraud
(c) Both (a) and (b)
(d) None of these

**172.** Cost audit under Section 233 (b) of the companies Act is
(a) Voluntary (b) Compulsory
(c) Advisable (d) None of these

**173.** Duties of a company auditor are defined by
(a) Memorandum of Association.
(b) Articles of Association.
(c) Companies Act, 1956.
(d) Agreement between company and the auditor.

**174.** A person is disqualified from being appointed as a director of a company if
(a) He has applied to be adjudged insolvent.
(b) He is of unsound mind.
(c) He is an undischarged inslovent.
(d) All of these.

**175.** A chartered Accountant is not disqualified to be an auditor of a company if he is
(a) An employee of the company.
(b) The managing director of that company.
(c) Indebted to the company for Rs. 1,000.
(d) A shareholder in that company.

**176.** 'Audit in depth' means
(a) Audit of each and every item.
(b) Intensive audit of each and every.
(c) Intensive audit of a few items.
(d) Audit of a few selected items.

**177.** A company auditor can be removed by
(a) Board of Directors.
(b) Managing Director.
(c) Any Director
(d) General meeting.

**178.** A vacancy caused by resignation of an auditor is filled by
(a) Board of Directors.
(b) Managing Director
(c) General meeting
(d) Central Government.

**179.** Audit of company accounts is
(a) Compulsory
(b) Advisable
(c) Unnecessary
(d) Depends upon Directors

**180.** Auditing is luxury for a
(a) Joint stock company
(b) Partnership firm
(c) Small shop company
(d) Government company

**181.** Limitations of audit is
(a) That is does not reveal complete picture.
(b) That is does not guarantee accuracy of accounts.
(c) That auditor may be biased.
(d) All of these.

**182.** Auditing is compulsory for
(a) Small-scale business enterprises.
(b) All partnership firms.
(c) All joint stock companies.
(d) All proprietory concerns.

**183.** Government may order for special Audit under
(a) Section 227 (b) Section 233 (A)
(c) Section 233 (B) (d) Section 224

**184.** Special audit is necessary for
(a) Manufacturing concern.
(b) Processing concern.
(c) Inefficient concern.
(d) Trading concern.

**185.** Interim audit refers to
(a) Examination of accounts continuously.
(b) Examination of accounts intermittently.
(c) Audit work to find out and check interim profits of a company.
(d) Carrying an audit for bonus purposes at the end of the year.

**186.** Internal auditor of a company must be a
(a) Chartered accountant.
(b) Cost accountant.
(c) Chartered or cost accountant
(d) Need not possess any porfessional qualification.

**187.** Final audit implies
(a) Audit of acounts at the end of the year.
(b) Finally checking of accounts to reveal frauds.
(c) Audit for submitting report immediately at the end of the year.
(d) Audit of banking companies.

**188.** Alteration of a figures after audit is a limitation of
(a) Final audit. (b) Continuous.
(c) Interim audit. (d) None of these.

**189.** Joint audit implies
(a) Audit of two concerns together.
(b) Audit of joint stock companies.
(c) Audit of joint sector companies.
(d) Audit of two firms by C.A.

**190.** Management audit means
(a) Audit under taken on behalf of the management.
(b) Evaluating peroformance of various management process and functions.
(c) Audit under taken on behalf of Government to publish management.
(d) Compulsory audit of company management.

**191.** Systems audit implies.
(a) Systematic examination of accounts.
(b) Audit under taken to improve auditing systems.
(c) Enquiring accounting and control systems.
(d) Checking the performance of management.

**192.** Internal audit is
(a) Compulsory for a company with paid-up capital of Rs. 25 lakh and above.
(b) Voluntary for a company.
(c) Not necessary for a company.
(d) Necessary for a company.

**193.** The scope of work of internal audit is decided by the
(a) Shareholders. (b) Management.
(c) Government. (d) Law.

**194.** The scope of work of statutory audit for a company is decided by the
(a) Shareholders (b) Management
(c) Government (d) Law

**195.** Internal auditor can be removed by the
(a) Government
(b) Shareholders
(c) Management
(d) Company Law Board.

**196.** Management of audit profession is in the hands of
(a) Government.
(b) Comptroller and Auditor General.
(c) Institute of chartered accountants of India.
(d) Institute of cost and work accountants of India.

**197.** Institute of chartered Accountants of India was established on
(a) April 1, 1956 (b) April 1, 1949
(c) July 1, 1956 (d) July 1, 1949

**198.** The object of internal check is to
(a) Control wastages of resources.
(b) Prevent errors and frauds.
(c) Verify the cash receipts and payments.
(d) Facilitate quick decision by the management

**199.** Internal check is a part of
(a) Internal audit
(b) Internal accounting
(c) External audit
(d) Internal control.

**200.** Internal check is carried on by
(a) Special staff (b) Internal auditor
(c) Accountant (d) None of these.

**201.** Internal check involves
(a) Reduction of work of cashier.
(b) Division of responsibilities of members of staff.
(c) Verification of inventory.
(d) Collusion among the members of staff.

**202.** Internal check is essential for
(a) Petty traders
(b) Cash transactions in a large concern.
(c) A concern using automatic equipments.
(d) None of these.

**203.** Misappropriation of goods may be checked by
(a) Proper super vision over stock.
(b) Checking of employees.
(c) Punishment of employees.
(d) None of these.

**204.** Window Dressing implies
(a) Curtailment of expenses.
(b) Checking wastages.
(c) Under-valuation of assets.
(d) Over-valuation of assets.

**205.** Falsification of accounts is undertaken by
(a) Auditors
(b) Clerks.
(c) Accountants.
(d) Responsible officials.

**206.** Valuation of assets on wrong basis is
(a) Technical error.
(b) Clerical error.
(c) Error of principle.
(d) Compensation error.

**207.** In which section has the limitations of Auditing been mentioned:
(a) AAs-4 (b) AAs-5
(c) AAs-6 (d) AAs-7

**208.** Test checking should not be applied to
(a) Sales book
(b) Purchase book
(c) Bank re-concilialion statement
(d) Bills book

**209.** In vouching, an auditor verifies
(a) The authority of transactions only.
(b) The authenticity of transactions only.
(c) Both the authority and authenticity of transactions only.
(d) The arithmetical accuracy of the transactions only.

**210.** Consider the following statements regarding Information Memorandum :
I. A company inviting subscription by an information memorandum shall be bound to file a prospectus prior to the opening of the subscription lists and the offer as a red-herring pospectus, at least 10 days before the opening of the offer.
II. The information memorandum and red-herring prospectus shall carry same obligations as are applicable in the case of a prospectus.
III. Any variation between the information memorandum and the red-herring prospectus shall be high lighted as variations by the issuing company.

*Which of the statements given above is /are correct?*
(a) I only (b) I, II and III
(c) II and III (d) III only

**211.** Which one of the following statement related to auditing is not correct?
(a) Chances of frauds are maximum in the case of cash sales.
(b) While routine checking is carried out, vouching may be considered unnecessary.
(c) While vouching the cash receipts, the auditor should study the system of internal check in operation.
(d) Vouching is the essence of auditing.

**212.** Under which one of the following circumstances, the Central Government is empowered to direct special audit of the companies?
(a) Where any director has misapporpriated the company's fund.
(b) Where a shareholder has complained to the Government about the non payment of dividend.

(c) Where the company has continuously defaulted in the payment of interest to the debenture holders.
(d) Where the conduct of management is in the manner which is injurious to trade, industry or business to which it pertains.

**213.** Consider the following statements
I. Audit, programme is the management's plan of action.
II. The primary basis of preparing an audit programme is the system of internal control.
III. The idea implied in the preparation of an audit programme is to ensure to the auditor a complete grip over his staff.
*Which of the statements given above is /are correct?*
(a) III only (b) I, II and III
(c) I and II (d) II and III

**214.** Which of the following are included in auditor's working papers?
I. Audit manuals.
II. Audit programme.
III. Audit procedures.
IV. Audit note-book.
*Select the correct answer using the codes given below:*
(a) I and II (b) III and IV
(c) I, II and III (d) II and IV

**215.** The tool used by auditor to monitor and control the progress of audit work is
(a) Engagement diary.
(b) Audit programme.
(c) Audit working papers.
(d) Audit notes.

**216.** Which of the following is called 'Backbone of auditing'?
(a) Routine checking
(b) Vouching
(c) Internal checks
(d) Internal control

**217.** While auditing the financial statements of non-corporate enterprises, the auditor's duties and scope of work would be governed by
(a) The statute passed by the parliament.
(b) The companies Act, 1956 and the client concerned jointly.
(c) The agreement with his client.
(d) The provisions of the Income Tax Act, 1961.

**218.** Consider the following statements:
I. First auditors of a company are appointed by the Board of Directors within one month of the incorporation.
II. Subsequent auditors of a company are appointed every year by the shareholders in the Annual General Meeting.
III. A body corporate can be appointed as auditor of a company.
IV. Section 226 of the companies Act, 1956 prescribes the qualifications and disqualifications for appointment of the auditors of companies.
*Which of the statements given above are correct?*
(a) I, II and III (b) I and III
(c) I, II and IV (d) II and III

**219.** Consider the following statements:
I. The auditor should verify that the Directors do not enter into contracts for which they are not authorised to do so by the Articles of Associations, the Board and the statute.
II. The auditor should ensure that the qualification shares are held by the Directors as laid down by the Articles of Association.
III. The auditor should refer to the Minutes of the Meeting of Board of Directors if remuneration has been paid on the bill of their attendance at the Board's Meetings.
*Which of the statements given above is /are correct?*
(a) I only (b) II and III
(c) II only (d) I, II and III

**220.** The auditor must ensure that the amount of premium on the issue of shares is not utilised for
(a) Issue of bonus shares.
(b) Writing off commission paid on the issue of shares.
(c) Providing of premium payable on redemption of preference shares.
(d) Transfer to capital redemption reserve.

**221.** Under which of the following circumstances can an auditor give a qualfied report?

I. When the accounts have not been prepared in accordance with the provisions of the companies Act.
II. When books of accounts have not been kept.
III. When the financial statements are in agreement with books of accounts and returns.
IV. When the accounts of the company do not show a true and fair view of the company as at the end of the financial year.

*Select the correct answer using the codes given below:*

(a) I, II and IV (b) I, II and III
(c) II, III and IV (d) I, III and IV

**222.** The system of internal check ensures that
(a) Work is distributed among the employees according to their merit and qualifications.
(b) Work is completed as per the prescribed time schedule.
(c) Work performed by one employee is automatically checked by another employee.
(d) Work preformed by an employee is checked by internal audit staff.

**223.** Which of the following is not disqualified for appointment as auditor of a company?
(a) A firm having chartered accountants as its partners.
(b) An officer or employee of the company.
(c) A person who is a partner or who is in the employment of an officer or employee of the company.
(d) A person who is indebted to the company for an amount exceeding Rs. 1000 or a guarantor for more than Rs. 1000

**224.** The auditor is generally expected to carry out following in a particular sequence:
I. Verification of asssets and liabilities.
II. Vouching the transactions.
III. Checking the valuation of assets and liabilities.

*Select the correct sequence using the codes given below:*

(a) II, III, I (b) I, II, III
(c) II, I, III (d) III, I, II

**225.** Any casual vacancy in the office of a statutory auditor caused by the resignation of the auditors shall be filled by the company
(a) At the Board Meeting
(b) At the Annual General Meeting
(c) By means of a circular resolution.
(d) At the statutory Meeting.

**226.** In verification of assets, the duty of the auditor is
(a) To ensure that assets have actually been acquired.
(b) To ensure that they are clearly stated in the balance sheet.
(c) To satisfy himself that they are properly valued.
(d) To satisfy himself with regard to the existence, ownership and value of the assets.

**227.** Match List I (Type of Audit) with List II (Feature) and select the correct answer using the codes given below the lists:

| **List I** (Type of Audit) | **List II** (Feature) |
|---|---|
| I. Continuous audit | A. Continuous review of the operations and records of the business by special staff. |
| II. Internal audit | B. Audit which is not statutory. |
| III. Occasiaonal audit | C. Audit convenient and useful specially is the case of small concerns. |
| IV. Periodical audit | D. Audit work carried on almost simultaneously with the recording of transactions. |

***Codes:***

(a) I-B, II-A, III-D, IV-C
(b) I-D, II-C, III-B, IV-A
(c) I-B, II-C, III-D, IV-A
(d) I-D, II-A, III-B, IV-C

**228.** An audit in which the auditor examines the financial statements of an enterprise to express an opinion as to whether or not they reflect a true and fair view of its state of affairs and working results is known as

(a) Management audit.
(b) Cost audit.
(c) Financial audit.
(d) Periodical audit.

**229.** Which of the following are statutory audits?

I. financial audit of insurance companies.
II. financial audit of partnership firms.
III. financial audit of proprietorship firms.
IV. financial audit of manufacturing companies,

*Select the correct answer using codes given below.*

(a) I and IV (b) I and II
(c) I and III (d) III and IV

**230.** Continuous audit is used

(a) Where volume of the transactions is not very large.
(b) Where it is desired to present the accounts just after the close of the financial year and where the statement of accounts is to be presented to the management after every month or quarter.
(c) Where satisfactory system of internal check is not in operation.
(d) Where interim audit is not in operation.

**231.** Auditing is compulsory in case of

(a) Joint-stock company.
(b) Charitable Trust.
(c) Cooperative society.
(d) All of these.

**Directions : (Q 232-235)** *The questions consist of two statements, one labelled as 'Assertion (A)' and the other labelled as 'Reason (R). You are to examine these two statements carefully and select the answers to these items using the codes given below:*

***Codes:***

(a) Both A and R are true, and R is the correct explanation of A.
(b) Both A and R are true, but R is not a correct explanation of A.
(c) A is true, but R is false.
(d) A is false, but R is true.

**232. Assertion (A) :** Vouching refers to examination by the auditor of documentory evidence supp- orting and substantiating a transaction recorded in books.

**Reason (R) :** Verification refers to confirming the actual existence, possession, ownership basis of valuation and freedom from encumbrance.

**233. Assertion (A) :** Management Audit should be conducted by a team of experts.

**Reason (R) :** Management Audit is a critical examination of policy and practices of management from the highest level to down ward in order to as certain that sound management prevails in the business concern.

**234. Assertion (A) :** If it is found that some errors and /or frauds are remaining undetected due to the fact that a statutory auditor depended upon test checking, then the said auditor will be held responsible for negligence in the performance of his duties.

**Reason (R) :** A statutory auditor cannot, in anyway, avoid or reduce the responsibility laid on him by the statutes.

**235. Assertion (A) :** An auditor of a large business concern has to adopt test checking based on scientific statistical sampling technique instead of checking the whole of transacation of a particular class.

**Reason (R) :** Test checking based on scientific statistical sampling technique, reduces the volume of unnecessarily cumber some audit work involved in detailed checking of all transactions.

**236.** Financial audit in Joint-stock company in India
(a) Necessary.
(b) Voluntary.
(c) Statutory.
(d) Voluntary for companies which operate in certain activities only.

**237.** Select the pairs which are correctly match
I. Statutory Audit: Review of various operations of a company.
II. Management Audit: Verification of top level policy and its implications.
III. Operational Audit: Examining the production planning and control operations.
IV. Internal Audit: According to the company objectives.
*Select the correct answer using the codes given below:*
(a) I and II (b) I and III
(c) II and III (d) I and IV

**238.** Internal Auditor is appointed by the
(a) Board of Directors of the company.
(b) Shareholders of the company.
(c) Institute of chartered Accountants of India.
(d) Company secretary.

**239.** Consider the following statements:
An 'Internal Audit' is not a part of
I. Continuous statutory Audit.
II. Internal check system.
III. Internal control system.
*Which of these statements are correct:*
(a) I, II and III (b) I and II
(c) II and III (d) I and III

**240.** Consider the following statements:
The Auditor is generally expected to carry out. the following in a particular seriatim:
I. Verification of assets and liabilities.
II. Vouching of transactions.
III. Checking of valuation of assets and liabilities
*The correct chronological sequence of these acts is*
(a) I-III-II (b) III-II-I
(c) II-I-III (d) III-I-II

**241.** Consider the following functions:
I. Checking of valuation and physical verification of assets.
II. Routine checking and vouching.
III. Scrutiny of internal check system.
*The correct sequence of these functions to be performed by an Auditor during the course of auditing is*
(a) II-I-III (b) III-I-II
(c) III-II-I (d) I-II-III

**242.** Four important acts performed by an Auditor in connection with an audit work as
I. Verification of assets and checking valuation of the same.
II. Checking of Annual Accounts and Balance sheet.
III. Preparation of an audit programme.
IV. Test checking of financial transactions.
*The correct sequence in which these acts are performed by the Auditor is*
(a) II-I-III-IV (b) II-III-IV-I
(c) III-I-IV-II (d) III-IV-I-II

**243.** Which of following may be included in 'Audit working papers'?
I. Audit note book.
II. Audit Programmes.
III. Schedules of sundry debtors and sundry creditors.
IV. Audit Manuals.
*Select the correct answer using the codes given below :*
***Codes :***
(a) I and IV (b) I and II
(c) II, III and IV (d) I, II and III

**244.** Consider the following statements :
An 'Internal Control System' may include
I. Interim audit
II. Internal audit
III. Financial controls
*Which of these statements are correct?*
(a) I, II and III (b) I and II
(c) II and III (d) I and III

**245.** Which one of the following pairs is NOT correctly matched?
(a) Suppression of invoices........window dressing.
(b) Over charging depreciation.........reserves secret.
(c) Omission of cash receipts.....under statement of sales.
(d) Omission of credit sale..........under statement of debtors.

**246.** The main purpose of auditing is to
(a) Detect accounting offences and to punish the offender.
(b) Prepare and authernticate the accounts.
(c) Prepare the accounts and authenticate their true and fair view.
(d) Certify the financial position of the business.

**247.** Statements on Standard Auditing Practices (SAPs) are important while discharging the auditing function by a member of the ICAI in case of a company, because SAPs are
(a) Prescribed by the ICAI.
(b) Contained in the companies Act, 1956.
(c) Approved by the Department of company Affairs.
(d) Approved by the central Government in consultation with comptroller and Auditor-General.

**248.** The selection of items, to be included in the audit on a subjective basis without consideration of sample size or method of section, is
(a) Probability sampling.
(b) Systematic sampling.
(c) Random sampling.
(d) Judgement sampling.

**249.** Internal audit report is submitted to
(a) Government.
(b) Shareholders.
(c) Creditors.
(d) Board of Directors.

**250.** The scope of audit in a partnership firm is governed by
(a) Partnership act.
(b) Partnership deed.
(c) Agreement between partnership firm and auditor.
(d) Number of partners of the firm.

**251.** If an auditor does something wrong fully in the performance of his duties resulting in financial loss to the company, he will be held guilty of
(a) Civil negligence.
(b) Mis feasance.
(c) Criminal negligence.
(d) Financial irregularity.

**252.** What are the aspects to be considered while qualifying the audit report on the accounts of a company?
I. An item requiring specific disclosure under the companies Act is not so disclosed
II. where the auditor has not been able to form an opinion due to his inability to obtain sufficient, appropriate evidence, information and explanation.
III. An auditor realises that items in a financial statement are misstated to such an extent that the financial statement does not give a true and fair view.

*Select the correct answer using the codes given below:*

***Codes:***
(a) I only (b) I and II
(c) II and III (d) I, II and III

**253.** Match List I with List II and select the correct answer using the codes given below the lists:

| | List I | | List II |
|---|---|---|---|
| I. | Reduction of share capital | A. | Sec. 100 |
| II. | Reissue of redeemed debentures | B. | Sec. 228 |
| III. | Branch audit | C. | Sec. 121 |
| IV. | Presentation of annual Accounts | D. | Sec. 210 |

***Codes:***
(a) I-D, II-B, III-C, IV-A
(b) I-A, II-C, III-B, IV-D
(c) I-D, II-C, III-B, IV-A
(d) I-A, II-B, III-C, IV-D

**254.** Match List I with List II and select the correct answer using the codes given below the lists:

| List I | List II |
|---|---|
| I. Statutory report | A. Sec. 200 |
| II. Prohibition of tax-free or remuneration | B. Sec. 165 |
| III. Under writing commission | C. Sec. 78 |
| IV. Issue of shares at premium | D. Sec. 76 |

*Codes:*

(a) I-D, II-A, III-B, IV-C
(b) I-B, II-C, III-D, IV-A
(c) I-D, II-C, III-B, IV-A
(d) I-B, II-A, III-D, IV-C

**255.** The first Standard Auditing practice (SAP-1) is related to

(a) Objectives and scope of the audit of financial statements
(b) Basic principles governing an audit.
(c) Documentation.
(d) Detecting fraud and error.

**256.** Which of the following relating to Audit programme is NOT correct?

(a) The auditor cannot defend himself on the basis of audit programme if there is a charge of negligence against him.
(b) It is useful basis for planning the programme for the subsequent year.
(c) It helps in the final review before the report is signed.
(d) It simplifies the allocation of work amongst the audit staff.

**257.** The scope of 'management audit' is determined by the

(a) Shareholders.
(b) Board of directors.
(c) Comptroller and Auditor-General (C&AG).
(d) Comptrollers and Auditor-General in consultation with the Central Government.

**258.** What is an audit conducted between two annual audits called

(a) Annual Audit
(b) Interim Audit
(c) Spice Audit
(d) Pleger Audit

**259.** Test checking reduces

(a) The work of an auditor.
(b) The liability of an auditor.
(c) Both work and liability of an auditor.
(d) The remuneration of an auditor.

**260.** While establishing the statistical sampling plan, the degree of precision required is determined by

(a) Keenness of the management.
(b) Suitability of accounting systems and procedures.
(c) Allowable margine of error the auditors are willing to accept.
(d) Random number table used for the purpose.

**261.** Every auditor appointed under section 224 (1) of the companies Act, 1956 shall inform in writing as to whether he has accepted or refused to accept the appointment. Such an intimation shall be given by him to the

(a) Company within 30 days of receipt from the company of the intimation of his appointment.
(b) Company Law Board within 30 days of receipt from the company of the intimation of his appointment.
(c) Company within 7 days of receipt from the company of the intimation of his appointment.
(d) Registrar with in 30 days of receipt from the company of the intimation of his appointment.

**262.** Audit committee shall act in accordance with the terms of reference to be specified by

(a) Statutory Auditors.
(b) SEBI
(c) Board of Directors.
(d) Central Government.

**263.** X is proposed to be appointed as the auditor of ABC Co. Ltd. at the ensuing AGM in place of the retiring auditor Y. This requires

(a) A special resolution and approval of the company Law Board.
(b) A special notice.

(c) An ordinary resolution and approval of the Company Law Board.
(d) A special resolution and approval of Central Government.

**264.** In the case of an audiw.tor appointed under section 619 of the companies Act, 1956 by the comptroller and Auditor-General of India, the remuneration shall be fixed by the
(a) Company in general meeting.
(b) Comptroller and Auditor-General of India.
(c) Comptroller and Auditor-General of India in consultation with the Central Govenment.
(d) Company Law Board.

**Directions -** *In the given context (Q. 265-271) of the statement mark the answer according to the following codes:*

***Codes:***
(a) Both A and R are true, and R is the correct explanation of A.
(b) Both A and R are true, but R is NOT a correct explanation of A.
(c) A is true but R is false.
(d) A is false but R is true.

**265. Assertion (A) :** It is the duty of the auditor to see that costing records as required udner Section 209 (1) (d) of the companies Act, 1956, have been maintained by certain class of companies.

**Reason (R) :** More maintenance of cost records does not make manufacturing companies cost-effective.

**266. Assertion (A) :** Analytical Review is not the part of company statutory Audit.

**Reason (R) :** Analytical Review goes beyond true and fair prsentation of the financial position.

**267. Assertion (A) :** Management audit is a statutory audit.

**Reason (R) :** Management audit is performed through innovative ideas.

**268. Assertion (A) :** The auditors Report is very singificant, it should be read very carefully, particularly any qualificatory notes that it may contain. The manufact- uring and other companies (Auditors Report) orders, 1975, as amended in Sept. 1998, required the auditors to include a statement of certain matters in their report on the accounts, of the company.

**Reason (R) :** The auditor should make a specific observation and in case the report is qualified, then reason for such qualification should also be mentioned. In case the auditor is not able to give any answer against any particular point, he should also explain the reasons there of.

**269. Assertion (A) :** Audit requires application of porfessional judgement in a tremendously wide variety of situation and circumstances. An auditor broadly expresses his judgement of the fairness with which those statements present the state of affairs of a particular organisation. Thus even the audited accounts may be incorrect, sometimes.

**Reason (R) :** The very object of auditing is to find out the truth and fairness of the financial position of the concern and also to prevent and detect errors and frands. Auditor will be liable for any incorrect information in the audited accounts.

**270. Assertion (A) :** An auditor of a company gives a critical review of accounts.

**Reason (R)** : He gives collaborative evidence that accounts are properly drawn up.

**271. Assertion (A)** : Internal Audit does not comprise a means by which the management of a business concern maintains Internal control.

**Reason (R)** : Internal Audit is a continuous critical examination of accounts of a businees concern by its employees.

**272.** When audit is carried out during the accounting period with some interval, it is called
(a) Periodic audit
(b) Partial audit
(c) Continuous audit
(d) Interim audit

**273.** Analytical review by an auditor mainly includes
(a) Examining vouchers and other documents.
(b) Physical verification of assets.
(c) Examining day books with ledgers.
(d) Study of ratios and trends.

**274.** Consider the following statements:
*The important techniques of auditing are*
I. Test check and sampling.
II. Flow charting of interrelated operations in the accounting system of an organisation.
III. Using Internal Control Questionnaire.
IV. Collecting information on price fluctuations from market -research organisations.
*Which of the above statements are correct?*
(a) I, II and III (b) I, II and IV
(c) I, III and IV (d) I, III and IV

**275.** Match List I with List II and select the correct answer using the codes given below the lists:

| List I | List II |
|---|---|
| I. Auditor is a watch dog but not a blood hound | A. Union bank of Allahabad case. |
| II. An auditor should and sign the balance sheet with open eyes. He should not depend on the officials of the company | B. Hedley Byrne and Co. Ltd. Vs Hille 4 partners case. |
| III. Capital pofit cannot be divided as dividend unless all the assets have been revalued and the profit has been acatually realised. | C. Kingston Cotton Mills case. |
| IV. An action for negligence can be the auditor in tort by a person with whom he is not in a contractual relationship but to whom he owes duty. | D. Fostar Vs The Trinidad Lake brought against Ashalte Co. case. |

*Codes:*
(a) I-A, II-C, III-B, IV-D
(b) I-C, II-A, III-B, IV-D
(c) I-A, II-C, III-D, IV-B
(d) I-C, II-A, III-D, IV-B

**276.** Consider the following documents
I. Audit Report.
II. Audit final Accounts.
III. Audit Note Book
IV. List of Lost Vouchers
V. Audit programme
*Which of the above doucment are Auditor working papers?*
(a) I, II and III (b) I, III and IV
(c) I, III, IV and V (d) II, III, IV and V

**277.** Which of the following is not correct about the management auditor?
(a) He appraises and reviews the past performance and future plans of the company.
(b) He evaluates the performance of management and finds out whether they are efficient or not.
(c) He works simultaneously with the statutory auditor verifying the financial state of affairs of the company.
(d) He examines both financial and non financial records of the organisation.

**278.** Which one of the following pairs is not correctly matched?
(a) Internal check........ staff of the concern.
(b) Internal Audit........ chartered Accountant
(c) Cost Audit............ cost Account or chartered Accountant.

(d) Propriety Audit...... Comptroller and Auditor General of India.

**279.** Consider the following statements:

I. Audit working papers enable the auditor to know the weaknesses of the internal check system.

II. Audit programme assures adherence to the principles of auditing and accounting.

III. Manipulation of accounts are done by under valuation of assets.

IV. Internal check maximises the possibilities of erros and frauds.

*Which of the above statements are correct?*

(a) I, II and III (b) II, III and IV
(c) I, II and IV (d) I, II, III and IV

**280.** Consider the following duties of auditor:

I. He should see that the provision sec.78 have been complied with

II. He should see that sum available has been utilized in the mannner as laid down by the Articles.

III. He should examine the prospectus, the Articles and the minutes of the directors meeting to see whether the issue of shares at a premium is duly authorised or not.

*The correct sequence of these duties in case of audit of issue of shares at a premium is*

(a) I, II, III (b) II, I, III
(c) III, I, II (d) III, II, I

**281.** The accounts of a company shall be audited by the company auditor, or by a person qualified to be appointed as auditor, if the company has to

(a) Wind up
(b) Amalgamate.
(c) Finalise branch office accounts.
(d) Declare interim dividend.

**282.** Consider the following actions taken by an auditor

I. Carrying on vouching.
II. Preparing the audit report;
III. Checking the valuation of assets
IV. Decision to qualify the report.

*The correct sequence of the actions is*

(a) I, III, IV, II (b) IV, I, III, II
(c) III, IV, II, I (d) I, II, IV, III

**283.** It is necessary that an auditor should prepare an 'Audit programme': maintain an 'Audit note book': use an 'Internal control Questionnarie' and a 'Flow chart of Accouting system': adopt 'special Ticks' for each class of transaction checked and divide work as well as responsibility among the members of his staff for an efficient conduct of audit work. All these refer to.

(a) General principles of internal auditing.
(b) General principles of internal checking
(c) Basic principles of auditing.
(d) General techniques of auditing.

**284.** Which one of the following is the main object of auditing?

(a) Ascertaining whether all cash receipts and payments of an organisation have been correctly recorded and accounted for.
(b) Preventing errors and frauds connected with financial transactions of an organisation.
(c) Verifying books of accounts and annual financial statements of an organisation so as to give a report on the view presented by the said accounts and statements.
(d) Recording properly all financial transactions in various books of accounts and preparing annual financial statements indicating the results of such transacations.

**285.** Management audit refers to

(a) Audit on behalf of the management.
(b) Audit of management accounting system in operation.
(c) Systematic appraisal of management's objectives and procedures.
(d) Audit of managerially initiated financial transactions.

**286.** In evaluating internal control, the first step is to prepare an internal control questionnaire or a flow chart of the system.

*The subsequent steps should be to*

I. Determine the extent of audit work necessary to form an opinion.

II. Gather enough evidence to determine as to whether the internal control system is functioning as described.

III. Write a letter to the management describing the weakness in the internal control system.

IV. From a final judgement on the effectiveness of the internal control system.

*The correct sequence of these steps would be*

(a) I, II, III, IV (b) II, IV, I, III
(c) II, I, III, IV (d) II, IV, III, I

**287.** When an auditor tests sales transactions, one step is tracing a sample of sales invoices to debits in the accounts receivable ledger. Based upon this step, he will form an opinion as to whether
(a) Each sales invoice represents a valid sale.
(b) All sales have been recorded.
(c) All debits in accounts receivable ledger are supported by sales invoices.
(d) Recorded sales invoices are properly posted to customer accounts.

**288.** The comprehensive meaning of an efficient stock market is that it is a market which
(a) Allocates resources efficiently.
(b) Reflects the effective use of information in the price of the shares traded there in .
(c) Signals the changes in the listed company's performance.
(d) Safe guards the investor's money.

**289.** Global Depository Receipts (GDRs) are issued by successful corporations with a view to attracting.
(a) Overseas loan funds.
(b) Remittances from NRTs.
(c) Foreign equity capital.
(d) Foreign direct investment.

**290.** If an auditor, after his appointment, becomes disqualified as specified in Section 226 (3) and (4) of the companies Act, 1956.
(a) The appointed authority will ask him to Vacate his office.
(b) The company Law Board will ask him to tender his resignation.
(c) He will be deemed to have vacated his office.
(d) The institute of Chartered Accountants of India will terminate him from office.

**291.** The cost auditor in a company shall be appointed by
(a) The Board of Directors.
(b) The Board of Directors with the previous approval of the Central Government.
(c) The members of the company with the previous approval of the Central Government.
(d) The C & AG.

**292.** For appointing an auditor other than a retiring auditor
(a) Special resolution is required.
(b) Ordinary resolution and approved of C & AG are required
(c) Unanimous resolution and approval of the central Government are required.
(d) Special notice is required.

**293.** Secretarial Audit is
(a) Compulsory in companies having paid-up share capital of less-than Rs. 50 lakhs.
(b) Compulsory where the statutory audit reveals inadequacy of internal check in secretarial department.
(c) Optional and would help the Board of Directors and the Registrar of Companies in regard to compliance aspects, mainly under the companies Act, 1956.
(d) Compulsory in such companies as may be notified by the central Government.

**Directions (294-295):** *The following questions consists of two statements, one labelled the Assertion (A) and the other labelled the Reason (R). You are to examine these two statements carefully and decide if the Assertion A and the Reason R are individually true and if so, whether the Reason is a correct explanation of the Assertion. Select your answers to these items using the codes.*

**294. Assertion (A)** : Detection of errors is not of considerable importance to an auditor.

**Reason (R)** : Some mistakes which appear to be in the first instance merely clerical errors are ultimately found to be fraudulent manipulation of accounts, but vast majority of mistakes are merely clerical errors committed due to either carelessness or ignorance on the part of clerical staff.

**Codes:**
(a) Both A and R, are true, and R is the correct explanation of A.
(b) Both A and R, are true,but R is not a correct explanation of A.
(c) A is true, but R is false.
(d) A is false, but R is true.

**295. Assertion (A) :** Detection of frauds committed by the manipulation of accounts is a very difficult task for an auditor.

**Reason (R) :** Frauds of the type 'Manipulation of Accounts' are committed without any misappropriation of cash or goods.

**Codes:**
(a) Both A and R, are true, and R is the correct explanation of A.
(b) Both A and R, are true,but R is not a correct explanation of A.
(c) A is true, but R is false.
(d) A is false, but R is true.

**296.** Special audit of the accounts of a company is directed by
(a) Shareholders of the company.
(b) Comptroller and Auditor-General of India.
(c) Company Law Board.
(d) Central Government.

**297.** Match List I (Items) with List II (Section of companies Act, 1956) and select the correct answer using the codes given below the lists:

| List I | List II |
|---|---|
| I. Appointment of Auditors by central Govt. | A. Sec. 226 (1) |
| II. Qualification of Auditors | B. Sec. 224 (5) |
| III. Appointment of Auditors by Board of Directors. | C. Sec. 224 (8) |
| IV. Remuneration of Auditors | D. Sec. 224 (3) |

**Codes :**
(a) I-D, II-A, III-C, IV-B
(b) I-A, II-D, III-B, IV-C
(c) I-D, II-A, III-B, IV-C
(d) I-A, II-D, III-C, IV-B

**Directions (298-299): -** *The following questions consists of two statements, one labelled the Assertion (A) and the other labelled the Reason (R). You are to examine these two statements carefully and decide if the Assertion (A) and the Reason (R) are individually true and if so, whether the Reason is a correct explanation of the Assertion. Select your answers to these questions using the codes.*

**298. Assertion (A) :** Audit procedure and audit techniques are two different aspects of auditing but are complementary to each other.

**Reason (R) :** Audit procedure is concerned with determining the existence of documentary evidence and audit techniques are concerned with examination of those evidences.

**Codes:**
(a) Both A and R, are true, and R is the correct explanation of A.
(b) Both A and R, are true,but R is not a correct explanation of A.
(c) A is true, but R is false.
(d) A is false, but R is true.

**299. Assertion (A) :** The auditor of a partnership firm is appointed under a contract with the firm but not under any statute.

**Reason (R) :** The firm can also appoint him to act as an accountant for preparation of accounts.

**Codes:**
(a) Both A and R, are true, and R is the correct explanation of A.
(b) Both A and R, are true, but R is not a correct explanation of A.
(c) A is true, but R is false.
(d) A is false, but R is true.

**300.** An arrangement in which the accounting work of each individual is checked by other members is known as
(a) Internal audit (b) External audit
(c) Internal check (d) Test checking

**301.** The most important objective of internal audit is
(a) Early detection of error and fraud.
(b) Facilitating final audit.
(c) Early finalisation of annual accounts.
(d) Ensuring systematic accounting.

**302.** Consider the following documents.
I. Audit Note Book
II. Audit Programme
III. Audit Report.
IV. Audit Files.
*The correct sequence, in which an auditor prepares these documents is.*
(a) II, I, IV, III (b) I, II, III, IV
(c) II, I, III, IV (d) I, II, IV, III

**303.** Test-checking reduces the
(a) Powers of an auditor.
(b) Expenses of audit.
(c) Work of an auditor.
(d) Liability of an auditor.

**304.** Which one of the following is the first industrial organisation to have conducted social audit of its performance?
(a) Associated Cement Companies.
(b) Reliance Indus tries Limited.
(c) Bharat Heavy Electricals Limited.
(d) Tata Iron & Steel company.

**305.** The main purpose of an independent audit is to.
(a) Check and correct frauds and errors.
(b) Help in detecting frauds and errors.
(c) Determine if the financial statements fairly represent the actual financial position and the working results of the organisation.
(d) Help in formulating future plans.

**306.** Match List I (Types of audit) with List II (Purposes) and select the correct answer using the codes given below the lists:

| List I | List II |
|---|---|
| I. Continuous audit | A. To ensure efficient conduct of the business and prevent wastage. |
| II. Periodical audit. | B. Detailed examination of the books of accounts at regular intervals |
| III. Interim audit | C. Audit taken up at the close of the financial period. |
| IV. Internal audit | D. Audit conducted between the end of two financial periods. |

***Codes :***
(a) I-A, II-C, III-D, IV-B
(b) I-B, II-C, III-D, IV-A
(c) I-C, II-B, III-A, IV-D
(d) I-C, II-A, III-B, IV-D

**307.** Management audit refers to
(a) Examination of books and audit of accounts done by the management.
(b) The periodic assessment of company's activities by the statutory auditor.
(c) Periodic assessment of company's managerial planning, organising, actuating and controlling compared to form of successful operation.
(d) Auditor's assessment of the financial statement of the entity.

**308.** Vouching may be termed as
(a) Identification of the documentary evidence supporting the transaction.
(b) Verification of the documentary supporting the transaction.
(c) Authentication of the document supporting the transaction.
(d) Verification of the accuracy and authenticity of the transaction.

**309.** Interim audit refers to an audit conducted
(a) In two different accounting years.
(b) In-between two statutory annual audits with in the some accounting period.
(c) In-between two statutory audit and an internal audit in the same accounting period.
(d) In-between one statutory audit, one management audit and one internal audit.

**310.** Audit techniques are concerned with the
(a) Examination of those evidences which have been traced by audit procedures.
(b) Application of generally accepted accounting principles to particular phases of a financial statement.

(c) Accuracy and validity of management authorisation to the account section employees.

(d) Method of conducting a business affair and reporting in annual report.

**311.** What is the correct sequence of the following aspects in auditing?

I. Special audit. II. Internal audit.
III. Internal check. IV. Annual audit.

*Select the correct answer using the codes given below*

*Codes:*

(a) I, III, II, IV (b) III, IV, I, II
(c) III, II, IV, I (d) I, II, III, IV

**312.** Match List I with List II and select the correct answer using the codes given below the lists:

| List I | List II |
|---|---|
| I. Compensating errors | A. Not recording a business transaction. |
| II. Errors of ommission | B. Charging a Revenue item to capital. |
| III. Errors of principle | C. Writing a debit item on the credit side and a credit item on the debit side of equal amount. |
| IV. Errors of commission | D. Posting a correct amount to a wrong Account. |

*Codes :*

(a) I-C, II-A, III-D, IV-B
(b) I-B, II-A, III-D, IV-C
(c) I-C, II-A, III-B, IV-D
(d) I-B, II-A, III-C, IV-D

**Directions (313-314):** - *The following questions consist of two statements, one labelled the Assertion A and the other labelled the Reason R. You are to examine these two statements carefully and decide if the Assertion A and the Reason R are individually true and if so, whether the Reason is a correct explanation of the Assertion. Select your answers to these questions using the codes.*

**313. Assertion (A) :** Audit is conducted to find out the financial position of a concern.

**Reason (R) :** The objects of audit are the detection and prevention of errors and frauds.

*Codes:*

(a) Both A and R, are true, and R is the correct explanation of A.
(b) Both A and R, are true, but R is not a correct explanation of A.
(c) A is true, but R is false.
(d) A is false, but R is true.

**314. Assertion (A) :** Internal audit must be carried out by a qualified chartered Accountant.

**Reason (R) :** It is a management tool.

*Codes:*

(a) Both A and R, are true, and R is the correct explanation of A.
(b) Both A and R, are true,but R is not a correct explanation of A.
(c) A is true, but R is false.
(d) A is false, but R is true.

**315.** According to AAs-1, Basic Principles Governing an Audit, issued by the ICAI, principles which government auditor's professional obligations are

(a) Integrity, objectivity and Independence
(b) Confidentiality
(c) Work performed by others
(d) All of these

**316.** The basic postulates of financial auditing theory includes

(a) Accounting system and internal control
(b) Audit conclusion and report
(c) Financial statement and data are verifiable
(d) Audit evidence

**317.** The qualities of an auditor includes

(a) Independence
(b) Integrity
(c) Ability for expression and communication
(d) All of the above

**318.** In which year was the CAG's duties been specified by the Controller and auditor Generals (Duties, Powers and Condition of Service) Act

(a) 1971 (b) 1972
(c) 1973 (d) 1974

**319.** Which among the following must be kept into consideration while modifying or disigning an audit programme
(a) Internal control system
(b) Nature of client's activities
(c) Clear cut instructions
(d) Both (a) and (b)

**320.** Which among the following are advantages of Audit Notebook
(a) Important matters relating to audit work may be easily remembered
(b) Technical details about business
(c) Total of important ledger accounts
(d) Bound Register

**321.** What is the connecting link between the client's accounting records and the auditors report
(a) Audit Notebook
(b) Audit working papers
(c) Audit Report
(d) Audit Design

**322.** The guidance as the relationship between the external and internal auditor is given by
(a) AAs-6 (b) AAs-7
(c) AAs-8 (d) AAs-9

**323.** Which among the following is not an audit report
(a) Standard unqualified report
(b) Adverse report
(c) Disclaimer of opinion report
(d) Disclosure report

**324.** When did Income-tax Act come in force?
(a) 1960 (b) 1961
(c) 1962 (d) 1963

**325.** In which section of Companies Act, 1956, to power to summon persons suspected of having property of a company etc been classified
(a) Section 477 (b) Section 539
(c) Section 545 (d) Section 240

**326.** The verification of the correctness of cost accounts and of adherence to cost acounting plan is known as
(a) Financial Accounting
(b) Financial Audit
(c) Management Audit
(d) Cost Audit

**327.** The Management Auditor can be appointed by
(a) Share holders
(b) Board of Directors
(c) Debenture holders
(d) Both (a) & (b)

**328.** The process of collecting and evaluating evidence to determine whether a computer system safeguards assets, maintain data integrity, achieves organisational goals effectively and consumes resources efficiently is known as
(a) EDP Auditing
(b) Financial Auditing
(c) Cost Auditing
(d) Management Auditing

**329.** System development and documentation control is a type of
(a) General control
(b) Application control
(c) both (a) & (b)
(d) None of the above

**330.** An entity's internal control system encompasses much more than entiti's record-keeping procedures. It consists of the following components:
(a) Accounting control
(b) Control environment
(c) Control Procedures
(d) All of the above

**331.** Which system controls the cash payment of small amounts through petty cash
(a) Imprest system (b) Payroll system
(c) Hiring system (d) Payment system

**332.** Which section of the Companies Act, 1956 deals about prosecution of deliquent officers and members of the company
(a) Section 545 (b) Section 539
(c) Section 538 (d) Section 544

**333.** In which Auditing and Assurance standards the auditor's duties related to internal control in CIS environment has been described

(a) AAs-28 (b) AAs-29
(c) AAs-30 (d) AAs-31

**334.** The compliance procedures are audit tests designed to obtain a reasonable assurance as to reliability of internal control system. They seek to test

(a) existence (b) effectiveness
(c) continuity (d) All of the Above

**335.** Audit procedures can be classified into

(a) Compliance procedure
(b) Substantive procedure
(c) Both (a) & (b)
(d) None of these

**336.** Auditing and assurance standards 5, issued by the Institute of Chartered Accountants of India deals with the basic principles relating to

(a) Audit Evidence
(b) Management Evidence
(c) Non-Compliance
(d) Statutory Evidence

**337.** Section 229 A of the Companies Directors Act, 1956 has put an obligation on board of direction that any recommendation made by the Audit committee, in respect of financial management and statutony audit report, shall be

(a) Binding (b) Not binding
(c) Evaluating (d) None of these

**338.** An internal check system with regards to purchase returns should operate at following points

(a) Authorising returns
(b) Preparing advice note for returns
(C) Preparing outward return notes
(D) All of the above

## ANSWERS

| 1 | 2 | 3 | 4 | 5 | 6 | 7 | 8 | 9 | 10 |
|---|---|---|---|---|---|---|---|---|---|
| (b) | (d) | (c) | (b) | (c) | (a) | (c) | (a) | (a) | (d) |
| **11** | **12** | **13** | **14** | **15** | **16** | **17** | **18** | **19** | **20** |
| (c) | (c) | (a) | (a) | (c) | (a) | (a) | (a) | (b) | (c) |
| **21** | **22** | **23** | **24** | **25** | **26** | **27** | **28** | **29** | **30** |
| (d) | (a) | (c) | (c) | (a) | (c) | (a) | (b) | (c) | (c) |
| **31** | **32** | **33** | **34** | **35** | **36** | **37** | **38** | **39** | **40** |
| (d) | (c) | (c) | (a) | (a) | (d) | (c) | (d) | (d) | (c) |
| **41** | **42** | **43** | **44** | **45** | **46** | **47** | **48** | **49** | **50** |
| (c) | (c) | (a) | (b) | (d) | (d) | (b) | (c) | (b) | (a) |
| **51** | **52** | **53** | **54** | **55** | **56** | **57** | **58** | **59** | **60** |
| (a) | (b) | (c) | (a) | (c) | (d) | (d) | (a) | (d) | (c) |
| **61** | **62** | **63** | **64** | **65** | **66** | **67** | **68** | **69** | **70** |
| (d) | (c) | (b) | (c) | (c) | (b) | (c) | (a) | (b) | (c) |
| **71** | **72** | **73** | **74** | **75** | **76** | **77** | **78** | **79** | **80** |
| (b) | (b) | (a) | (b) | (c) | (c) | (b) | (a) | (a) | (a) |
| **81** | **82** | **83** | **84** | **85** | **86** | **87** | **88** | **89** | **90** |
| (b) | (b) | (c) | (c) | (b) | (c) | (b) | (d) | (a) | (c) |
| **91** | **92** | **93** | **94** | **95** | **96** | **97** | **98** | **99** | **100** |
| (a) | (a) | (d) | (c) | (b) | (c) | (c) | (c) | (d) | (c) |
| **101** | **102** | **103** | **104** | **105** | **106** | **107** | **108** | **109** | **110** |
| (b) | (c) | (c) | (b) | (a) | (c) | (c) | (a) | (c) | (c) |

| 111 | 112 | 113 | 114 | 115 | 116 | 117 | 118 | 119 | 120 |
|---|---|---|---|---|---|---|---|---|---|
| (c) | (a) | (a) | (c) | (c) | (d) | (c) | (b) | (a) | (b) |
| **121** | **122** | **123** | **124** | **125** | **126** | **127** | **128** | **129** | **130** |
| (b) | (b) | (d) | (d) | (d) | (b) | (c) | (a) | (b) | (b) |
| **131** | **132** | **133** | **134** | **135** | **136** | **137** | **138** | **139** | **140** |
| (c) | (a) | (d) | (c) | (a) | (c) | (a) | (a) | (d) | (c) |
| **141** | **142** | **143** | **144** | **145** | **146** | **147** | **148** | **149** | **150** |
| (b) | (b) | (c) | (d) | (d) | (d) | (a) | (a) | (c) | (d) |
| **151** | **152** | **153** | **154** | **155** | **156** | **157** | **158** | **159** | **160** |
| (c) | (d) | (c) | (c) | (d) | (b) | (a) | (c) | (d) | (c) |
| **161** | **162** | **163** | **164** | **165** | **166** | **167** | **168** | **169** | **170** |
| (a) | (a) | (d) | (a) | (c) | (a) | (a) | (d) | (b) | (a) |
| **171** | **172** | **173** | **174** | **175** | **176** | **177** | **178** | **179** | **180** |
| (c) | (c) | (c) | (d) | (d) | (c) | (d) | (c) | (a) | (c) |
| **181** | **182** | **183** | **184** | **185** | **186** | **187** | **188** | **189** | **190** |
| (d) | (c) | (b) | (c) | (c) | (d) | (a) | (b) | (d) | (b) |
| **191** | **192** | **193** | **194** | **195** | **196** | **197** | **198** | **199** | **200** |
| (b) | (a) | (b) | (d) | (c) | (c) | (b) | (b) | (d) | (d) |
| **201** | **202** | **203** | **204** | **205** | **206** | **207** | **208** | **209** | **210** |
| (b) | (b) | (a) | (d) | (d) | (a) | (a) | (c) | (c) | (c) |
| **211** | **212** | **213** | **214** | **215** | **216** | **217** | **218** | **219** | **220** |
| (b) | (d) | (a) | (d) | (b) | (b) | (c) | (c) | (d) | (d) |
| **221** | **222** | **223** | **224** | **225** | **226** | **227** | **228** | **229** | **230** |
| (a) | (c) | (a) | (c) | (b) | (d) | (d) | (c) | (a) | (b) |
| **231** | **232** | **233** | **234** | **235** | **236** | **237** | **238** | **239** | **240** |
| (d) | (b) | (a) | (a) | (a) | (c) | (c) | (a) | (b) | (c) |
| **241** | **242** | **243** | **244** | **245** | **246** | **247** | **248** | **249** | **250** |
| (c) | (d) | (d) | (c) | (c) | (c) | (a) | (d) | (d) | (c) |
| **251** | **252** | **253** | **254** | **255** | **256** | **257** | **258** | **259** | **260** |
| (c) | (d) | (b) | (d) | (b) | (a) | (b) | (b) | (a) | (c) |
| **261** | **262** | **263** | **264** | **265** | **266** | **267** | **268** | **269** | **270** |
| (d) | (c) | (d) | (a) | (b) | (a) | (d) | (a) | (a) | (a) |
| **271** | **272** | **273** | **274** | **275** | **276** | **277** | **278** | **279** | **280** |
| (d) | (d) | (d) | (a) | (d) | (d) | (b) | (b) | (a) | (c) |
| **281** | **282** | **283** | **284** | **285** | **286** | **287** | **288** | **289** | **290** |
| (d) | (a) | (d) | (c) | (c) | (d) | (d) | (a) | (c) | (c) |
| **291** | **292** | **293** | **294** | **295** | **296** | **297** | **298** | **299** | **300** |
| (b) | (d) | (c) | (d) | (b) | (d) | (c) | (a) | (b) | (c) |
| **301** | **302** | **303** | **304** | **305** | **306** | **307** | **308** | **309** | **310** |
| (a) | (a) | (c) | (a) | (c) | (b) | (c) | (d) | (b) | (a) |
| **311** | **312** | **313** | **314** | **315** | **316** | **317** | **318** | **319** | **320** |
| (c) | (c) | (c) | (d) | (d) | (c) | (d) | (a) | (d) | (a) |
| **321** | **322** | **323** | **324** | **325** | **326** | **327** | **328** | **329** | **330** |
| (b) | (b) | (d) | (b) | (a) | (d) | (d) | (a) | (a) | (d) |
| **331** | **332** | **333** | **334** | **335** | **336** | **337** | **338** | | |
| (a) | (a) | (b) | (d) | (c) | (a) | (a) | (d) | | |

# UNIT-III

# FINANCIAL MANAGEMENT—AN OVER VIEW

## MEANING OF FINANCIAL MANAGEMENT

Financial management is that managerial activity which is concerned with the planning and controlling of the firm's financial resources. It is an integrated decision making process concerned with acquiring, financing and managing assets to accomplish the overall goal of a business organisation. It can also be stated as the process of planning decisions in order to maximise the shareholder's wealth. Financial managers have a major role in cash management, acquisition of funds and in all aspects of raising and allocating capital. As far as business organisations are concerned, the objective of financial management is to maximize the value of business.

Financial management comprises the forecasting, planning, organising, directing, coordinating and controlling of all activities relating to acquisition and application of the financial resources of an undertaking in keeping with its financial objective. This definition of financial management by Raymond Chambers aptly sums up the vital role played by it in any organisation. Another very elaborate definition given by Phillippatus is .Financial Management is concerned with the managerial decisions that result in the acquisition and financing of short term and long term credits for the firm. As such it deals with the situations that require selection of specific assets (or combination of assets), the selection of specific problem of size and growth of an enterprise. The analysis of these decisions is based on the expected inflows and outflows of funds and their effect on managerial objectives. One more definition of financial management is that .Financial management deals with procurement of funds and their effective utilisation in the business.Financial management can also be stated as .The management of all the processes associated with the efficient acquisition and deployment of both short and long term financial resources.

There are, thus, two basic aspects of financial management viz., procurement of funds and an effective use of these funds to achieve business objectives.

## PROCUREMENT OF FUNDS

Since funds can be obtained from different sources therefore their procurement is always considered as a complex problem by business concerns. Funds procured from different sources have different characteristics in terms of risk, cost and control. The funds raised by the issue of equity shares are the best from the risk point of view for the firm, since there is no question of repayment of equity capital except when the firm is under liquidation. From the cost point of view, however, equity capital is usually the most expensive source of funds. This is because the dividend expectations of shareholders are normally higher than prevalent interest rate and also because dividends are an appropriation of profit,not allowed as an expense under the Income Tax Act. Also the issue of new shares to public may dilute the control of the existing shareholders.

Debentures as a source of funds are comparatively cheaper than the shares because of their tax advantage. The interest the company pays on a debenture is free of tax, unlike a dividend payment which is made from the taxed profits. However, even when times are hard, interest on debenture loans must be paid whereas dividends need not be. However, debentures entail a high degree of risk since they have to be repaid as per the terms of agreement; also, the interest payment has to be made whether or not the company makes profits.

There are thus risk, cost and control considerations which a finance manager must consider while procuring funds. The cost of funds should be at the minimum level for that a proper balancing of risk and control factors must be carried out. Funds can also be procured from banks and financial institutions; they generally provide funds subject to certain restrictive covenants. These covenants restrict the freedom of the borrower to raise loans from other sources.

The reform process is also moving in the direction of a closer monitoring of 'end use'of resources mobilised through capital markets. Such restrictions are essential for the safety of funds provided by institutions and investors. Besides above there are several other financial instruments used today for raising long term, medium term and short term funds e.g., commercial paper, deep discount bonds etc. The finance manager has to balance the availability of funds and the restrictive provisions tied with such funds resulting in lack of flexibility.

In the globalised competitive scenario it is not enough to depend on the available ways of raising finance but resource mobilisation has to be undertaken through innovative ways or financial products which may meet the needs of investors. Multiple option convertible bonds can be sighted as an example. Funds can be raised indigenously as well as from abroad.Foreign Direct Investment (FDI) and Foreign Institutional Investors (FII) are two major routes for raising funds from foreign sources besides ADR.s (American depository receipts) and GDR.s (Global depository receipts). Obviously, the mechanism of procurement of funds has to be modified in the light of the requirements of foreign investors. Procurement of funds inter alia includes identification of sources of finance, determination of finance mix, raising of funds and division of profits between dividends and retention of profits i.e. internal fund generation.

## EFFECTIVE UTILISATION OF FUNDS

The finance manager is also responsible for effective utilisation of funds. He has to point out situations where the funds are being kept idle or where proper use of funds is not being made.All the funds are procured at a certain cost and after entailing a certain amount of risk. If these funds are not utilised in the manner so that they generate an income higher than the cost of procuring them, there is no point in running the business. This is also an important consideration in dividend decision. Hence, it is crucial to employ the funds properly and profitably. The funds are to be invested in the manner so that the company can produce at its optimum level without endangering its financial solvency. Thus, financial implications of each decision to invest in fixed assets are to be properly analysed. For this, the finance manager would be required to possess sound knowledge of techniques of capital budgeting. He must also keep in view the need of adequate working capital and ensure that while the firms enjoy an optimum level of working capital they do not keep too much funds blocked in inventories, book debts and cash, etc.

## EVOLUTION OF FINANCIAL MANAGEMENT

Financial management evolved gradually over the past 50 years. The evolution of financial management is divided into three phases. Financial Management evolved as a separate field of study at the beginning of the century. The three stages of its evolution are:

**The Traditional Phase:** During this phase, financial management was considered necessary only during occasional events such as takeovers, mergers, expansion, liquidation, etc. Also,when taking financial decisions in the organisation, the needs of outsiders (investment bankers, people who lend money to the business and other such people) to the business was kept in mind.

**The Transitional Phase:** During this phase, the day-to-day problems that financial managers faced were given importance. The general problems related to funds analysis, planning and control were given more attention in this phase.

**The Modern Phase:** Modern phase is still going on. The scope of financial management has greatly increased now. It is important to carry out financial analysis for a company. This analysis helps in decision making. During this phase, many theories have been developed regarding efficient markets, capital budgeting, option pricing, valuation models and also in several other important fields in financial management.

## IMPORTANCE OF FINANCIAL MANAGEMENT

Financial management is all about managing expenditure within a limited budget. It is about allocating money to the necessary items first. If after that, you have some money left, it must be used to pay off the debts. If there is still some money left you can use it as you like.Financial management means management of all matters related to an organisation's finances. This principle is the same whether it is an organisation, a family, or even a country's economy. We must balance expenditure and income. Let us understand this better by taking an example of a company, Cotton Textiles Limited. The company earns money by selling textiles. Let us assume that it earns Rs. 10 lakhs every month. This is known as revenue. A company has many expenses. Some of the major expenses of the company can be listed as wages to workers, raw materials for making the textile, electricity and water bills and purchase and repair of machines that are used to manufacture the textile.All these expenses are paid out of the revenues. If the revenues are more than the expenses,then the company will make profits. But, if the expenses are more than revenues, then it will face losses. If it continues like that, eventually, it will lose all its assets. In other words it will lose its property and all that it owns. In that case, even the workers may be asked to leave the company. To avoid this situation, the company has to manage the cash inflows (cash coming into the company) and outflows (various expenses that the company has to meet).

## SCOPE OF FINANCIAL MANAGEMENT

As an integral part of the overall management, financial management is mainly concerned with acquisition and use of funds by an organization. Based on financial management guru Ezra Solomon's concept of financial management, following aspects are taken up in detail under the study of financial management:

(a) Determination of size of the enterprise and determination of rate of growth.

(b) Determining the composition of assets of the enterprise.

(c) Determining the mix of enterprise's financing i.e. consideration of level of debt to equity etc.

(d) Analyse planning and control of financial affairs of the enterprise.

The scope of financial management has undergone changes over the years. Until the middle of this century, its scope was limited to procurement of funds under major events in the life of the enterprise such as promotion, expansion, merger, etc. In the modern times, the financial management includes besides procurement of funds, the three different kinds of decisions as well namely, investment, financing and dividend.

## OBJECTIVES OF FINANCIAL MANAGEMENT

Efficient financial management requires the existence of some objectives or goals because judgment as to whether or not a financial decision is efficient must be made in the light of some objective. Although various objectives are possible but we assume two objectives of financial management for elaborate discussion. These are:

## PROFIT MAXIMISATION

It has traditionally been argued that the objective of a company is to earn profit, hence the objective of financial management is also profit maximisation. This implies that the finance manager has to make his decisions in a manner so that the profits of the concern are maximised. Each alternative, therefore, is to be seen as to whether or not it gives maximum profit.However, profit maximisation cannot be the sole objective of a company. It is at best a limited objective. If profit is given undue importance, a number of problems can arise. Some of these have been discussed below:

**(i)** The term profit is vague. It does not clarify what exactly it means. It conveys a different meaning to different people. For example, profit may be in short term or long term period; it may be total profit or rate of profit etc.

**(ii)** Profit maximisation has to be attempted with a realisation of risks involved. There is a direct relationship between risk and profit. Many risky propositions yield high profit. Higher the risk,higher is the possibility of profits. If profit maximisation is the only goal, then risk factor is altogether ignored. This implies that finance manager will accept highly risky proposals also, if they give high profits. In practice, however, risk is very important consideration and has to be balanced with the profit objective.

**(iii)** Profit maximisation as an objective does not take into account the time pattern of returns. Proposal A may give a higher amount of profits as compared to proposal B, yet if the returns begin to flow say 10 years later, proposal B may be preferred which may have lower overall profit but the returns flow is more early and quick.

**(iv)** Profit maximisation as an objective is too narrow. It fails to take into account the social considerations as also the obligations to various interests of workers, consumers, society, as well as ethical trade practices. If these factors are ignored, a company cannot survive for long. Profit maximisation at the cost of social and moral obligations is a short sighted policy.

## WEALTH / VALUE MAXIMISATION

People buy the shares as an investment. It means that they expect these shares to give them some returns. It is the duty of the finance manager to see that the shareholders get good returns on the shares. Hence, the value of the share should increase in the share market. The share value is affected by many things. If a company is able to make good sales and build a good name for itself, in the industry, the company's share value goes up. If the company makes a risky investment, people may lose confidence in the company and the share value will come down. So, this means that the finance manager has the power to influence decisions regarding finances of the company. The decisions should be such that the share value does not decrease. Thus, wealth or value maximisation is the most important goal of financial management.

How do we measure the value/wealth of a firm? According to Van Horne, Value of a firm is represented by the market price of the company's common stock. The market price of a firm's stock represents the focal judgment of all market participants as to what the value of the particular firm is. It takes into account present and prospective future earnings per share, the timing and risk of these earnings, the dividend policy of the firm and many other factors that bear upon the market price of the stock. The market price serves as a performance index or report card of the firm's progress. It indicates how well management is doing on behalf of stockholders.Of course, there are other goals too like:

- Achieving a higher growth rate
- Attaining a larger market share
- Gaining leadership in the market in terms of products and technology
- Promoting employee welfare
- Increasing customer satisfaction

Many companies have several other goals for the welfare of the society, like improving community life, supporting education and research, solving societal problems, etc. But wealth maximisation means that the company is using its resources in a good manner. If the share value is to stay high, the company has to reduce its costs and use the resources properly. If the company follows the goal of wealth maximisation, it means that the company will promote only those policies that will lead to an efficient allocation of resources.To achieve wealth maximization, the finance manager has to take careful decision in respect of:

1. **Investment decisions**: These decisions determine how scarce resources in terms of funds available are committed to projects which can range from acquiring a piece of plant to the acquisition of another company. Funds procured from different sources have to be invested in various kinds of assets. Long term funds are used in a project for various fixed assets and also for current assets. The investment of funds in a project has to be made after careful assessment of the

various projects through capital budgeting. A part of long term funds is also to be kept for financing the working capital requirements. Asset management policies are to be laid down regarding various items of current assets. The inventory policy would be determined by the production manager and the finance manager keeping in view the requirement of production and the future price estimates of raw materials and the availability of funds.

2. **Financing decisions:** These decisions relate to acquiring the optimum finance to meet financial objectives and seeing that fixed and working capital are effectively managed. The financial manager needs to possess a good knowledge of the sources of available funds and their respective costs, and needs to ensure that the company has a sound capital structure, i.e. a proper balance between equity capital and debt. Such managers also need to have a very clear understanding as to the difference between profit and cash flow, bearing in mind that profit is of little avail unless the organisation is adequately supported by cash to pay for assets and sustain the working capital cycle.

Financing decisions also call for a good knowledge of evaluation of risk, e.g. excessive debt carried high risk for an organisation's equity because of the priority rights of the lenders. A major area for risk-related decisions is in overseas trading, where an organisation is vulnerable to currency fluctuations, and the manager must be well aware of the various protective procedures such as hedging (it is a strategy designed to minimise, reduce or cancel out the risk in another investment) available to him. For example, someone who has a shop, takes care of the risk of the goods being destroyed by fire by hedging it via a fire insurance contract.

3. **Dividend decisions:** These decisions relate to the determination as to how much and how frequently cash can be paid out of the profits of an organisation as income for its owners/shareholders. The owner of any profit-making organization looks for reward for his investment in two ways, the growth of the capital invested and the cash paid out as income; for a sole trader this income would be termed as drawings and for a limited liability company the term is *dividends*.The dividend decisions thus has two elements , the amount to be paid out and the amount to be retained to support the growth of the organisation, the latter being also a financing decision; the level and regular growth of dividends represent a significant factor in determining a profit-making company's market value, i.e. the value placed on its shares by the stock market.

All three types of decisions are interrelated, the first two pertaining to any kind of organization while the third relates only to profit-making organisations, thus it can be seen that financial management is of vital importance at every level of business activity, from a sole trader to the largest multinational corporation. It is instructive to think this point through by taking the case of the sole trader; thus he has to invest capital in a shop, fittings and equipment and in the purchase of stock and sustaining debtors (working capital), he has to have sources of capital to finance his investment such as his own capital and bank borrowings, and he has to make dividend decisions to determine how much can be reasonably withdrawn from the business to ensure that it will remain sufficiently liquid and, if desired, capable of growth.

## FINANCIAL MANAGEMENT AND ACCOUNTING

The relationship between financial management and accounting are closely related to the extent that accounting is an important input in financial decision making. In other words, accounting is a necessary input into the financial management function. Financial accounting generates information relating to operations of the organisation. The outcome of accounting is the financial statements such as balance sheet, income statement, and the statement of changes in financial position. The information contained in these statements and reports helps the financial managers in gauging the past performance and future directions of the organisation. Though financial management and accounting are closely related, still they differ in the treatment of funds and also with regards to decision making.

**Treatment of Funds:** In accounting, the measurement of funds is based on the accrual principle i.e. revenue is recognised at the point of sale and not when collected and expenses are recognised when they are incurred rather than when actually paid. The accrual based accounting data do not reflect fully the financial conditions of the organisation. An organization which has earned profit (sales less expenses) may said to be profitable in the accounting sense but it may not be able to meet its current obligations due to shortage of liquidity as a result of say, uncollectible receivables. Such an organisation will not survive regardless of its levels of profits. Whereas, the treatment of funds, in financial management is based on cash flows. The revenues are recognised only when cash is actually received (i.e. cash inflow) and expenses are recognised on actual payment (i.e. cash outflow). This is so because the finance manager is concerned with maintaining solvency of the organisation by providing the cash flows necessary to satisfy its obligations and acquiring and financing the assets needed to achieve the goals of the organisation. Thus, cash flow based returns help financial managers to avoid insolvency and achieve desired financial goals.

**Decision making:** The purpose of accounting is to collect and present financial data on the past, present and future operations of the organisation. The financial manager uses these data for financial decision making. It is not that the financial managers cannot collect data or accountants cannot make decisions. But the chief focus of an accountant is to collect data and present the data while the financial manager's primary responsibility relates to financial planning, controlling and decision making. Thus, in a way it can be stated that financial management begins where accounting ends.

## FINANCIAL MANAGEMENT AND OTHER RELATED DISCIPLINES

For its day to day decision making process, financial management also draws on other related disciplines such as marketing, production and quantitative methods apart from accounting. For instance, financial managers should consider the impact of new product development and promotion plans made in marketing area since their plans will require capital outlays and have an impact on the projected cash flows. Likewise, changes in the production process may require capital expenditures which the financial managers must evaluate and finance. Finally, the tools and techniques of analysis developed in the quantitative methods discipline are helpful in analyzing complex financial management problems.

# OBJECTIVE TYPE QUESTIONS

**1.** Which one of the following does not constitute the purpose of setting up SEBI?
(a) To protect the interests of the investors in securities
(b) To promote the development of the securities markets
(c) To regulate the global securities markets
(d) To deal with matters connected with Fraudulent and unfair trade practices relating to securities markets

**2.** Match **List-I** (Activity) with **List-II** (Associated organisation) and select the correct answer by using the codes given below the lists :

| **List-I** | **List-II** |
|---|---|
| A. Mutual Fund | 1. Stock exchange |
| B. Public issue of capital | 2. Assets management company |
| C. Forward trading | 3. Merchant banking |
| D. Option pricing | 4. Forex market |

**Codes:**

| | A | B | C | D |
|---|---|---|---|---|
| (a) | 3 | 2 | 4 | 1 |
| (b) | 3 | 2 | 1 | 4 |
| (c) | 2 | 3 | 1 | 4 |
| (d) | 2 | 3 | 4 | 1 |

**3.** EXIM bank can be described as a—
(a) non-banking financial company
(b) commercial bank
(c) non-banking non-financial company
(d) schedule bank

**4.** Integration of various units of similar character producing similar products or engaged in the same sphere of business activity under a single form of management and control is called—

(a) vertical combination
(b) horizontal combination
(c) circular or mixed combination
(d) lateral or allied combination

**5.** Paid-up value is payable on a life insurance policy—
(a) on the maturity of the policy
(b) when the policy lapses
(c) when the policy is surrendered
(d) on maturity or death which ever is earlier

**6. Assertion (A):** The investors in the capital market have been showing a decisive shift in favour of fixed income instruments.

**Reason (R):** The debt instruments have active secondary market
(a) Both A and R are true and R is the correct explanation of A
(b) Both A and R are true but R is not a correct explanation of A
(c) A is true but R is false
(d) A is false but R is true

**7. Assertion (A):** The floating policy protects the policy holder against errors and omissions.

**Reason (R):** Goods are insured even if the policy holder fails to reports that goods have already been forwarded from the place of shipment.
(a) Both A and R are true and R is the correct explanation of A
(b) Both A and R are true but R is not a correct explanation of A
(c) A is true but R is false
(d) A is false but R is true

**8.** It is compulsory for a share broker to register with the—
(a) Concerned Stock Exchange
(b) Securities and Exchange Board of India
(c) Department of Company Affairs
(d) Concerned Stock Exchange in concurrence with the securities and Exchange Board of India

**9.** Who among the following is not a speculator in stock Exchange?
(a) Broker (b) Bull
(c) Bear (d) Stag

**10.** The gilt-edged market refers to the market for
(a) Industrial Securities
(b) Govt. and semi-govt. securities
(c) Shares and debentures
(d) Public limited company securities

**11.** "*Causa promixa*" implies that the loss must arise from—
(a) the nearest place
(b) an ascertainable source
(c) the cause insured against
(d) unforeseen sources

**12.** Which one of the following statements is true?
(a) Supplier's credit and buyer's credit are one and the same thing
(b) EXIM bank generally deals with export transactions above Rs.5 crore
(c) The main focus of EXIM bank is one Export and Import credits for short-term
(d) ECGC provides no protection against hazards of nature

**13.** Life insurance is a contact on the life of a man in which the insurer promises to pay a sum of money. For the consideration of a definite premium, to the insured person on his death or an attaining a particular age, which one of the following assumptions is implicit in the above definition?
(a) It is a contract of indemnity
(b) It is a contract of guarantee
(c) It is a contract of compensation
(d) It is a contract of return on investment

**14.** Trading on equity takes place—
(a) when capital other than that of equity shareholders is also employed
(b) only when equity capital is employed
(c) only when debenture funds are employed
(d) when profits are ploughed back

**15.** Letter of credit is now becoming an increasingly popular method of financing—
(a) fixed capital needs
(b) working capital needs
(c) redemption of debentures
(d) distribution of dividend

**16.** Which of the following are the methods of market new issues of securities?

I. Listing of securities
II. Jobbers and brokers
III. Private placement of securities
IV. Privileged subscriptions

Select the correct answer using the codes given below :

**Codes :**

(a) I and II (b) II and III
(c) III and IV (d) I, II, III and IV

**17.** Which one of the following statements is correct?

(a) EXIM Bank promotes Indian exports through a wide variety and range of lending programmes
(b) EXIM Bank does not extend non-funded facility to Indian exports
(c) Overseas Investment Finance facility is not a part of the function of EXIM Bank
(d) EXIM Bank was established to provide assistance in raising capital in international markets

**18.** In which of the following types of insurance should insurable interest be present only at the time when policy is taken?

(a) Fire insurance
(b) Life insurance
(c) Marine insurance
(d) Life and Marine insurance

**19.** Capital gearing ratio denotes the relationship between—

(a) assets and capital
(b) loans and capital
(c) equity shareholders funds and long term borrowed funds
(d) debentures and share capital

**20.** Consider the following functions of a stock exchange—

I. Providing a ready market for securities
II. Helping capital formation
III. Regulating the capital structure of a company
IV. Regulating the public deposits with companies of these statements :

(a) I, II, III and IV are correct
(b) I, II and III are correct
(c) I and II are correct
(d) None of these

**21.** Both 'security' and 'investment' elements are available—

(a) only in Life Insurance
(b) in both Life and Fire Insurance
(c) in both Marine and Fire Insurance
(d) in Life, Marine and Fire Insurance

**22.** Match List-I with List-II and select the correct answer using the codes given below the lists:

| | List-I | List-II |
|---|---|---|
| I. | Bull | 1. Buys the shares for sale but finds it difficult to meet his commitment |
| II. | Bear | 2. Buys the shares to sell them in future expecting a price rise |
| III. | Lane duck | 3. Neither buys nor sells but merely applies for shares to sell at a premium |
| IV. | Stag | 4. Agrees to sell on a fixed date expecting a fall in the price |
| | | 5. Buys and sells shares on the same date |
| | | 6. Agrees to sell on a fixed date but finds it difficult to meet his commitment |
| | | 7. A genuine investor |

**Codes:**

| | A | B | C | D |
|---|---|---|---|---|
| (a) | 4 | 2 | 1 | 7 |
| (b) | 4 | 2 | 3 | 5 |
| (c) | 2 | 4 | 5 | 1 |
| (d) | 2 | 4 | 6 | 3 |

**23.** Which one of the following pairs is not correctly matched?

| | | |
|---|---|---|
| A. | Value of any security | 1. The real value of any security is determined by the prior rights to the return of income. |
| B. | Debenture | 2. It possesses maximum safety and normally offers regular and fixed income |

| | | | |
|---|---|---|---|
| C. | Preference Share | 3. | It offers reasonable safety as well as regular and fixed income by way of dividend |
| D. | Equity Shares | 4. | It invites speculative tendency. There is risk of loss in such a share |

Select the correct answer using the codes given below :

**Codes:**

| | A | B | C | D |
|---|---|---|---|---|
| (a) | 1 | 2 | 3 | 4 |
| (b) | 2 | 1 | 3 | 4 |
| (c) | 1 | 2 | 4 | 3 |
| (d) | 2 | 1 | 4 | 3 |

**24.** In stock exchange operations, when the speculator buys the right to sell a certain number of shares on an agreed date at a specified time it is known as—

(a) no option (b) put option
(c) call option (d) double option

**25.** The Jurisdiction of the MRTP Commission with respect to monopolistic trade practices is not exercisable upon/under—

(a) a reference made to it by the Central Government
(b) an application made to it by the Director General
(c) ts own knowledge or information
(d) any of the above mentioned circumstances

**26.** Consider the following statements:
The EXIM Bank plays an active role in boosting exports by

I. Civil Construction Contract abroad
II. Providing long-term finance for export of capital goods
III. Providing short-term finance for import of capital goods
IV. Providing short-term finance for export of quality goods

Of these statements :

(a) I and II are correct
(b) I and IV are correct
(c) II and III are correct
(d) III and IV are correct

**27.** In option dealings, speculation means—

(a) buying in one market at cheaper price and selling the same in another at a higher price
(b) agreeing to illegitimate trading in securities outside the reorganised stock exchange
(c) acquiring a right to buy or sell a certain quantity of security at a stated price within a prescribed time
(d) postponing the payment to and delivery of securities if market conditions turn adverse

**28. Assertion (A):** The liability of share holders in a private limited company is limited to the amount unpaid on shares

**Reason (R):** The number of share holders of a private limited company is limited to fifty

(a) Both A and R are true and R is the correct explanation of A
(b) Both A and R are true but R is not a correct explanation of A
(c) A is true but R is false
(d) A is false but R is true

**29. Assertion (A):** High capital gearing leads to greater speculation

**Reason (R):** Proportion of equity share capital in relation to the total capital comprising the other securities is small leading to capitalisation being highly geared

(a) Both A and R are true and R is the correct explanation of A
(b) Both A and R are true but R is not a correct explanation of A
(c) A is true but R is false
(d) A is false but R is true

**30. Assertion (A):** Special rules and procedures are followed in the import and export trade

**Reason (R):** The need for import and export trade is explained by the principles of 'Comparative Cost Theory'.

(a) Both A and R are true and R is the correct explanation of A
(b) Both A and R are true but R is not a correct explanation of A
(c) A is true but R is false
(d) A is false but R is true

**31.** Partnership is a form of business organisation in which business debts can be recovered from—
(a) the managing partners
(b) all the managers and partners
(c) the firm and the managers
(d) the firm and all the partners

**32.** Of the following organisations, the easiest to wind up is the—
(a) Public Limited Company
(b) Multinational Corporation
(c) Private Limited Company
(d) Partnership Firm

**33.** The main objective of Stock Exchange is to—
(a) provide facilities for speculation
(b) safeguard the interest of investors
(c) help in the capital formation in the country
(d) provide a ready market for securities

**34.** The maximum number of partners in a firm for a general business is—
(a) 7 (b) 10
(c) 50 (d) 20

**35.** The agreement of partnership—
(a) must be oral
(b) must be in writing
(c) can be either oral or in writing
(d) must be in writing on a stamp paper

**36.** The minimum number of members requires for registration of a co-operative society is—
(a) two (b) seven
(c) ten (d) twenty

**37.** Co-operative and public companies are similar in respect of—
(a) the liability of members
(b) the minimum number of members required for registration
(c) the maximum number of members
(d) method of distribution of profit
(e) none of these

**38.** The term 'Capitalisation' is used in relation to—
(a) Sole-proprietorship
(b) Partnership
(c) Joint Stock Companies
(d) Co-operative Societies

**39.** Watered Capital means—
(a) Over-Capitalisation
(b) Under-Capitalisation
(c) Excessive capital
(d) Part of the capital not represented by assets

**40.** Over-Capitalisation may be remedied by—
(a) increasing the number of equity shares
(b) increasing the par value of shares
(c) issuing additional preference shares
(d) redemption of debentures

**41.** Under-Capitalisation can be remedied by
(a) Issue of bonus shares
(b) Redemption of preference shares
(c) Redemption of debentures
(d) Reduction of interest of debentures

**42.** The first Stock Exchange was set up in India in
(a) 1887 (b) 1905
(c) 1908 (d) 1923

**43.** Capital gearing means
(a) proper capitalisation
(b) watered capital
(c) fixation of a proper ratio between two or more types of securities
(d) trading on equity

**44.** A company is said to be low geared when the proportion of
(a) equity capital to the total capital is small
(b) preference capital to the total capital is small
(c) debentures capital to the total capital is small
(d) both preference and debenture capital to the total capital is small

**45.** Working capital can be used for the purchase of
(a) machinery
(b) goodwill
(c) land and building
(d) raw material
(e) all of these

**46.** Which of the following sources is not used for medium term financing?
(a) issue of equity shares
(b) issue of preference shares

(c) issue of debentures
(d) term loans from banks

**47.** Working capital is represented by
(a) current liabilities
(b) current assets minus current liabilities
(c) total assets minus current liabilities
(d) cash-in-hand plus stock-in-trade

**48.** Participating preference shares are those which participate
(a) in the voting
(b) in the general meeting of the company
(c) in the management of the company
(d) in the profits over and above their fixed dividend

**49.** In which of the following, rate of interest/dividend is not fixed?
(a) Equity capital (b) Debentures
(c) Preference capital (d) Public deposits

**50.** To which of the following types of companies, debentures suit as a source of finance?
(a) Companies with fluctuating earnings
(b) Companies with stable earnings
(c) Companies which cannot earn a rate of profit higher than the rate of interest payable on debentures
(d) All of these

**51.** First debentures are those
(a) which are issued before share capital
(b) which are repayable before other debentures
(c) which are secured by a floating charges
(d) which are secured by a fixed charge

**52.** The first stock exchange was set up in India in
(a) Kolkata (b) Mumbai
(c) Delhi (d) Chennai

**53.** Under writers are persons who
(a) purchase the shares and debentures of a company
(b) work as agents of the company for the sale of shares and debentures
(c) manage the issue of shares and debentures
(d) undertake to buy those shares and debentures not subscribed for by the public

**54.** Which of the following institutions undertake underwriting of shares and debentures of companies?
(a) Unit Trust of India
(b) Industrial Development Bank of India
(c) State Finance Corporations
(d) All of these

**55.** Which of the following sources of finance do not pose a burden on the finances of the company?
(a) Public deposits
(b) Debentures
(c) Loans from financial institutions
(d) Retained earnings

**56.** Which of the following is not a component of the new issue market?
(a) Stock exchange
(b) Unit Trust of India
(c) Financial Institution like IFC, IDBI
(d) LIC

**57.** When an existing company offers its shares for sale to the existing shareholders, it is known as
(a) Private placing (b) Bonus issue
(c) Rights issue (d) Offer for sale

**58.** Which of the speculators expects the price of securities to rise in the near future?
(a) Bull (b) Bear
(c) Stag (d) Lane duck

**59.** Which of the following speculative activities is based on disparity in quote prices in different markets?
(a) Option dealings
(b) Arbitrage
(c) Margin trading
(d) Blank Transfers

**60.** Contango charge is paid by a
(a) bull speculator to bear speculator
(b) bear speculator to bull speculator
(c) lane duck to bull speculator
(d) bull to lane duck speculator

**61.** Listing of securities in a stock exchange for the purpose of trading indicates that
(a) at the time of listing, the company is financially sound

(b) at the time of listing, the company is legally organised
(c) the stock exchange guarantees about the financial soundness of the company
(d) all of these

**62.** An existing company raising additional capital
(a) must offer the new shares to the existing share holders
(b) need not offer the new shares to the existing share holders
(c) issues share to debenture-holders
(d) issues shares to preference shareholders

**63.** Stock exchange deals with the
(a) second-hand Securities
(b) issue of equity shares
(c) issue of preference shares
(d) issue of debentures

**64.** FICCI was formed in the year
(a) 1920 (b) 1925
(c) 1926 (d) 1951

**65.** MRTP Act came into force in
(a) 1969 (b) 1970
(c) 1971 (d) 1980

**66.** If income is more than expenditure, a company will be able to show profits.
(a) True (b) False

**67.** Management of all matters related to an organisation.s finances is called:
(a) Cash inflows and outflows
(b) Allocation of resources
(c) Financial management
(d) Finance

**68.** Allocation of resources means paying all expenses on time to avoid interest expenditure.
(a) True (b) False

**69.** Which of the following is not an element of financial management?
(a) Allocation of resources
(b) Financial Planning
(c) Financial Decision-making
(d) Financial control

**70.** Financial management is concerned with the actual cash flows of the organisation, while financial accounting is concerned with recording the flow of cash.
(a) True (b) False

**71.** The most important goal of financial management is:
(a) Profit maximisation
(b) Matching income and expenditure
(c) Using business assets effectively
(d) Wealth maximisation

**72.** In the traditional phase, the importance of financial management was limited to major events such as mergers and takeovers.
(a) True (b) False

**73.** To achieve wealth maximization, the finance manager has to take careful decision in respect of:
(a) Investment (b) Financing
(c) Dividend (d) All the above

**74.** Early in the history of finance, an important issue was:
(a) Liquidity (b) Technology
(c) Capital structure (d) Financing options

**75.** Which of the following are microeconomic variables that help define and explain the discipline of finance?
(a) Risk and return (b) Capital structure
(c) Inflation (d) All of the above

**76.** According to Companies (Amendment) Act 2000, a company limited by share can issue _______ kinds of shares.
(a) 1 (b) 2
(c) 3 (d) None of these

**77.** The public issue must be kept open for atleast
(a) 3days (b) 5 days
(c) 7 days (d) None of these

**78.** Minimum amount to be collected by a company as application money according to SEBI is _____% of the issue price.
(a) 10% (b) 25%
(c) 50% (d) None of these

**79.** When more number of applications are received than that are offered to the public, it is called ____________.
(a) Over subscription (b) Under subscription
(c) Full subscription (d) None of these

**80.** The maximum calls that a company can makeis
(a) one (b) two
(c) three (d) None of these

**81.** Calls-in-arrears is shown in the Balance Sheet as
(a) deduction from called up capital

(b) addition to paid up capital
(c) addition to issued capital
(d) none of these

**82.** Capital Reserve is shown on the ________ side of Balance Sheet.
(a) Asset (b) Liability
(c) Both (d) None of these

**83.** A company can issue shares
(a) at par only
(b) at par and at premium
(c) at par, at premium & at discount
(d) none of these

**84.** When the company issue shares at a price more than the face value it is called as an issue at ________.
(a) Par (b) Premium
(c) Discount (d) None of these

**85.** Normally companies can issue shares at ________% of discount
(a) 5 (b) 10
(c) 20 (d) None of these

**86.** When shares are forfeited the share capital of the company will ________.
(a) remain same (b) reduce
(c) increase (d) none of these

**87.** Securities premium will appear in the ________ side of the Balance Sheet.
(a) Asset (b) Liability
(c) Assets & Liabilities (d) none of these

**88.** The balance of forfeited share account is________ in the Balance Sheet.
(a) added to paid up capital
(b) added to authorised capital
(c) deducted from paid up capital
(d) none of these

## ANSWERS

| 1 | 2 | 3 | 4 | 5 | 6 | 7 | 8 | 9 | 10 |
|---|---|---|---|---|---|---|---|---|---|
| (c) | (d) | (a) | (b) | (d) | (c) | (d) | (d) | (a) | (b) |
| **11** | **12** | **13** | **14** | **15** | **16** | **17** | **18** | **19** | **20** |
| (c) | (c) | (b) | (a) | (b) | (c) | (a) | (b) | (c) | (c) |
| **21** | **22** | **23** | **24** | **25** | **26** | **27** | **28** | **29** | **30** |
| (a) | (d) | (a) | (c) | (d) | (c) | (c) | (b) | (d) | (b) |
| **31** | **32** | **33** | **34** | **35** | **36** | **37** | **38** | **39** | **40** |
| (d) | (d) | (b) | (d) | (c) | (c) | (a) | (c) | (d) | (d) |
| **41** | **42** | **43** | **44** | **45** | **46** | **47** | **48** | **49** | **50** |
| (a) | (a) | (d) | (d) | (d) | (a) | (b) | (d) | (a) | (b) |
| **51** | **52** | **53** | **54** | **55** | **56** | **57** | **58** | **59** | **60** |
| (b) | (b) | (d) | (d) | (d) | (a) | (c) | (a) | (b) | (a) |
| **61** | **62** | **63** | **64** | **65** | **66** | **67** | **68** | **69** | **70** |
| (b) | (a) | (a) | (c) | (b) | (a) | (c) | (b) | (d) | (a) |
| **71** | **72** | **73** | **74** | **75** | **76** | **77** | **78** | **79** | **80** |
| (d) | (a) | (d) | (a) | (d) | (b) | (a) | (b) | (a) | (c) |
| **81** | **82** | **83** | **84** | **85** | **86** | **87** | **88** | | |
| (a) | (b) | (c) | (b) | (b) | (b) | (b) | (a) | | |

# UNIT-IV

# FINANCIAL STATEMENTS

**Definition of Accounting**

Accounting is defined as "the art of recording, classifying, and summarising in terms of money transactions and events of a financial character and interpreting the results thereof".

**Objectives of Accounting**

The objectives of the term 'accounting' can be stated as follows:

(*a*) To maintain records of a business
(*b*) Calculation of profit or loss
(*c*) Depiction of financial position, and
(*d*) To make information available to various groups and users.

**Functions of Accounting**

Accounting embraces the following functions:

1. Keeping systematic records
2. Protecting properties of the business
3. Communicating the results
4. Meeting legal requirements

**CONCEPTS OF ACCOUNTANCY**

Accounting is the language of business. The financial transactions are recorded and reported by means of financial statements to a number of interested parties. In the absence of systematic approach, accountants may use their own language and whatever they will be writing, will not be understood necessarily in the same sense by others concerned. Thus, the uniformity in understanding of accounting records is possible only when some standard language is used. With a view to make the accounting language a standard language, certain accounting principles or concepts have been developed.

Accounting principles or rules or concepts are general guidelines for sound accounting practices. Their usefulness depend on general acceptability rather than individual acceptability. These are known as 'generally accepted accounting principles' having been formalised on the basis of usage, reason, and experience. As stated by the AICPA (American Institute of Certified Public Accountants) :

"Generally accepted accounting principles incorporate the consensus at any time as to which economic resources and obligations should be recorded as assets and liabilities, which changes in them should be recorded, when these changes should be recorded, how the recorded assets and liabilities and changes in them should be measured, what information should be disclosed and how should it be disclosed, and which financial statements should be prepared." Thus, generally accepted accounting principles (GAAP) comprises a set of rules, concepts and guidelines used in preparing financial accounting reports.

Following is a list of accounting concepts agreed to by accountants:

1. Business entity concept
2. Dual aspect concept
3. Going concern concept
4. Accounting period concept
5. Money measurement concept
6. Cost concept
7. Periodic matching of cost and revenue concept
8. Verifiable objective evidence concept
9. Realisation concept
10. Accrual concept
11. Disclosure concept
12. Materiality concept
13. Consistency concept
14. Conservatism concept

**1. Business Entity Concept**

According to this concept, 'business is treated as a unit or entity apart from its owner, creditor, managers and others'. This concept is applicable to all forms of business organisations.

**2. Dual Aspect Concept**

According to this principle of accounting, every transaction has a dual aspect, i.e., two fold effect. Every receiver is also a giver and every giver is also a receiver.

Receiving and giving aspects are the two aspects of every business transaction. This principle is called double entry system of book-keeping. As per dual aspect, total assets and total liabilities must be equal. This equality is called 'Balance sheet equation or accounting equation. It can be stated as:

Liabilities = Assets

or

Capital + Liabilities (outside) = Assets

or

Capital = Assets – Liabilities.

**3. Going Concern Concept**

According to Kohler's Dictionary for Accountants, a going concern is defined as "any enterprise which is expected to continue operating indefinitely in the future".

This concept assumes that a business entity will continue to operate in definitely. Indefinitely existence means that the business enterprise will not be wound up within the foreseable future and therefore would be able to meet its contractual obligations and use its resources according to the plans and predetermined goals. This concept forms the basis for depreciation.

**4. Accounting Period Concepts**

Life of business is indefinitely, so, the measurement of income is not possible for a very, very long period. At frequent intervals properietor has to know "how things are going". Therefore, accountants choose some shorter and convenient time for the measurement of income. Normally, twelve month period is adopted for this purpose. The time interval is called "Accounting period."

**5. Money Measurement Concept**

The money measurement concept underlines the fact that is terms of money. A fact or a happening which cannot be expressed in terms of money is not recorded in the account book. As general health condition of the chairman of the company quality of products introduced by the enterprise etc. cannot be expressed in terms of money and thus are not recorded in the books.

As per this concept a transaction is recorded at its money value on the date of occurrence and the subsequent changes in the money value are ignored. Here, correct fact cannot be recorded in the book.

**6. Cost Concept**

The idea of cost assumption in that:

(*i*) asset is recorded at the price paid to acquire it-that is, at cost;

(*ii*) this cost is the basis for all subsequent accounting for the asset.

The cost concept implies that if nothing has been paid for acquiring something, it not be shown is the accounting books as an asset.

**7. Periodic Matching of cost and Revenue concept**

To compare profit or loss of an accounting period., it is necessary to match all expenses incurred in an accounting period with the revenue earned during that year.

Net income = Revenues – Expenses

**8. Verifiable Objective Evidence Concept**

This concept means that all accounting transactions should be evidenced and supported by business documents. These supporting documents (invoices, vouchers etc) provide the basis for making accounting entries and for later verification by auditors.

**9. Realisation Concept**

Kohler defines realisation concept as follows:

(*i*) A concept which gives accounting recognition to an exchange transaction, such as sale of goods or services only, when an inflow or outflow of cash equivalent results.

(*ii*) The realisation principle holds that revenue should be recognised with accompanying gains or losses at the point of sale in an arm's length transaction if the earning process is virtually complete.

**10. Accrual Concept**

Accrual means the recognition of events and conditions as they occur, rather than in the period of their incurrence, receipts or payments. Also the partial recognition of an item of revenue or expense and its related asset or liability: the result of the lack of coincidence of the accounting period and the contractual or benefit period.

**11. Disclosure Concept**

The disclosure principle implies that accounts must be prepared honestly, and all material information must be disclosed therein.

**12. Materiality Concept**

American Accounting Association (AAA) defines the term materiality as "An item should be regarded as material if there is reason to believe that knowledge if it would influence the decision of informed investor". It should be noted that an item material for one concern may be immaterial for another.

**13. Consistency Concept**

The principle of consistency plays its role when alternative accounting method is equally accepted.

**14. Conservatism Concept**

This is the policy of' Playing safe. It takes into consideration all prospective losses but leaves all prospective profit. Kohler defines 'Conservatism' as "a guidelines which chooses between acceptable accounting alternatives for recording events or transactions so that the least faveurable immediate effect on assets, income and owner's equity is reported." Following are the examples of this concept:

(*a*) Making the provision for doubtful debts and discount on debtors in anticipation of actual bad debts and discount.

(*b*) Valuing the stock-in-trade at market price or cost price whichever is less.

## INCOME MEASUREMENT

The main purpose of accounting is to measure the income of a business because the business is started with the sole aim of organizing the various factors of production for the purpose of increasing its wealths.

**Definition of Income :** Income can be defined as the amount of change (favourable) in wealth which results from business activities.

The AAA Committee has defined the term 'Income' as "the realised net income of an enterprise measures its effectiveness as an operating unit and is the change in its net assets arising out of:

(*a*) the excess or deficiency of revenue compared with related expired cost, and

(*b*) Other gains or losses to the enterprise from sales, exchanges or other conventions of assets ..." The measurement of income is influenced by many concepts: Conservatism, consistancy, the entity business, the periodicity, the cost basis, and the realisation principles.

**Conservatism**

The approach of conservatism in the measurment of income, although shifts the income from one period to another, has been defended on the argument that the risk of understatement of income under the concept of conservatism cannot be equated with the danger of its over statement. The later approach to measurement of income may prove more disastrous for the business. The measurement of stock at cost or market price whichever is lower, the principle of amortization of intangible assets not recognizing the appreciation in the value of assets, are the examples of concepts of conservatism as applied to the measurement of income. But the concept of conservatism does not and must not lead towards bais for understatement of income by providing excessive depreciation, excessive reserves etc.

**Consistency**

To facilitate the comparison of performance of one year with that of another, it is essential that basis of measurement of income should remain the same from year to year. Therefore, the measurement of income in any particular year depends upon the basis followed in the previous year (s).

**The Entity**

The entity concept maintains that business should be regarded as an institution separate and distinct from its legal owners. Thus any measurement of income is to be done from the business point of view and not from the proprietor's point of view. The interest on the capital of partners, though income to individual partners, is considered as an expense of measuring income of a business.

**The Accounting Period**

It should be appreciated that income of an enterprise can precisely be determied only at the termination of entity's life. But inderterminable life-span of the entity makes the period so long and uncertain that no business can wait that long for finding out the fruit of hard work put in carrying the business. Moreover, if unfortunately, at that time it is found that results are unfavourable, it will be too late to correct the decision. It is thus essential for correct decision that interim progress of the business must be calculated. The satisfactory period for measuring income is either the calender year or a natural business year.

**The Accrual Concept**

With the choosing of calender year or natural business year as a period for reporting income, the continuous process of business does not come to standstill simply because the accounting period has ended. The flow of entity transactions does not confirm exactly to the prescribed time interval. Instead, there will be quantities unsold, goods-in-transit, accounts and bills to be collected, contract for services in the various stages of completion. This period convention has given rise to the accrual basis of accounting. This entails the necessity of recognising the revenue with the preiod in which it was realised and the application of costs to the period benefiting from services. For example, revenue from sales will be considered in the year in which shipment takes place regardless of when the payment is received. Rent, insurance, interest, salary etc., paid in advance will be prorated between successive years according to the specific period covered by the payments.

**The Going Concern**

Since the termination of business at the end of accounting period is a fiction and since life span of the business is indefinite, the determination of profits by means of assets appraisal is not considered proper. Any valuation of accounting income on the basis of appraisal of its assets on market value is much influenced by excessive emphasis on the liquidation rather than continuity.

## EXPIRED COST AND INCOME MEASUREMENT

It has already been stated in the definition of income given by AAA that it is "... the excess or deficiency of revenue compared with related expired cost...". Thus any attempt to measure accounting income will be futile unless the correct measurement of the expired cost is available.

The costs which helps income determination may be direct cost or indirect cost, may be fixed cost or variable cost. The cost may be inclusive of purchase discount. Costs may be historical or standard. In order to have a more precise idea about the cost and its influence on the determination of income, it is studied under the following majorheads :

***(a)* Cost of property and its expiration**

Property is constructed or acquired to provide a source of revenue and so long as it helps in providing revenue, each revenue increment derived from its usage should bear its proportionate share of the total actual cost of the property. As to what part of the cost of asset should go to determine income would much depend upon the determination of cost of asset itself.

The determination of the cost of asset, is a dificult process. The allocation of various overheads makes the cost of asset an intelligent expression of estimates if not an arbitrary one. Determination of life expectancy and scrap value of the asset pose a serious problem. The calculation of cost expiration for measuring income cannot be very accurate.

***(b)* Inventory Costs**

Inventory costs include costs of those *(i)* which are held for resale, *(ii)* are in the process of production for sale, and *(iii)* are those which are currently consumed in the production of goods.

Determination of income depends much upon the determination of cost inventory as an expired cost. The calculation of inventory cost depends upon the direct cost, indirect cost efficiency on allocating costs between joint costs, by product costs, and so-on.

***(c)* Intangible Costs**

The calculation of expiration costs of intangible assets like patent rights leasehold rights, goodwill, development expenses, advertisement, etc. is also in the way of determining correct income. But these intangible assets pose a serious problem because their useful life is absolutely unknown.

***(d)* Imputed Cost**

In determining accounting income, besides taking same explicit or actual costs, some implicit or imputed costs like interest on capital, salary of a partner or proprietor, rent of the building owned by the proprietor are considered. The imputed costs are carved to facilitate comparison and management decision.

## THE REALISATION PRINCIPLE AND INCOME MEASUREMENT

The definition of accounting concept of income by AAA lays emphasis on the realisation aspect of income. It aims at comparing the realised revenue with the corresponding expired cost. Thus in order to calculate proper amount of income it is essential and imperative to have a proper recognition of revenue.

The recognition of revenue leads to the problem of determination of precise point of time in income producing cycle when its realisation can be considered to be worthwhile and acceptable to standards. This leads to the consideration of following point :

- *(a)* The sale as a basis of revenue recognition.
- *(b)* The asset as a basis of revenue recognition, i.e., cash vs. mercantile system.
- *(c)* Completed production as the basis of revenue recognition
- *(d)* Recognition of revenue prior to productive completion, and
- *(e)* Appreciation as the basis of revenue recognition.

***(a)* The sale as a basis of revenue recognition**

The sale completes the transaction and receives the primary objective of manufacturing or purchasing goods, it provides a satisfactory measure of recognition of revenue. The sale also denotes the expiration of all proportionate costs and permits their comparison with revenue for measuring income. It eliminates all future speculation as to whether they will be selling or not and also to their prices at which they will be selling. From legal point of view also, sale point recognition is justified.

**(b) Asset received as a basis of revenue recognition**

The advocates of this principle want to postpone the recognition of revenue till its actual relisation in cash.

**Cash vs. Accrual or Mercantile Basis of Accounting :** According to cash basis, the actual receipts and payment in cash is the real basis of recording transaction in the accounting period. The revenue will be considered in a particular accounting period only when it is realised in cash. Similarly, an expense will be considered only when it is paid in actual cash in the accounting period.

**(c) Completed production as the basis of revenue recognition**

Where there are compelling reasons for the maintenance of large inventory for any purpose whatsoever, the revenue is recognised even before the sale takes place. The main purpose of holding the inventory in such business houses is to push up the sale price. The retention of goods in such industries serves the purpose of getting the revenues. The production basis of revenue recognition has its utility in agriculture, extractive industries (oil, gold, silver, other metals), etc.

**(d) Recognition of Revenue prior to productive completion**

In long-term contracts, the basis of recognition of revenue is discarded in as much as this will result in the postponement of income for a very long period. When all of a sudden heavy amount of revenue will be recognised. This type of procedure will bring frustration to shareholders during the period it is not recognised and also will attract high rate of income tax when it is recognised.

**(e) Appreciation as the basis of revenue recognition**

The value of an asset sometimes appreciates due to change in general price. Any increment in the value of asset due to above mentioned reasons, is treated as fictitious increment. It does not add to the source of revenue. It is more an expression of original cost into the currency as per the changed index number.

## CONCLUSION

The calculation of income is an important affair in as much as its correct calculation determines the divident policy, acts as an important tool for measuring the effective use of money and managerial proficiency. It determines the future policy of the concern. But its determination is a difficult process as it is affected by:

(a) Various concepts and conventions

(b) Correct calculation of expired cost and

(c) Correct recognition of revenue

The concepts and conventions affecting the calculation of income are numerous, the calculation of expired cost is a difficult process and recognition of revenue is affected by various considerations. The job of measuring income is not an easy one.

## FINAL ACCOUNTS

### Meaning

Final accounts are prepared on the last date of the accounting period. Final account has two parts :

(i) *Trading and profit and loss account*

Trading account shows the results of trading i.e., buying and selling of goods during a trading period.

All items of expenses and losses and all revenues and gains occuring during the accounting period are reported in profit and loss account.

(ii) *Balance Sheet*

Balance sheet is prepared to know the exact financial position of the business on the last date of the accounting period.

These two satements trading and profit and loss account and balance sheet are known as Final Accounts. They are also called Financial Statements. Both these statements are prepared from the balances appearing in the trial balance extracted from ledger accounts as on the last date of the accounting period. After the preparation of trading and profit and loss account, balances remaining in the trial balance represent either assets or liabilities existing on the last day of the accounting period. These assets and liabilities are arranged in a proper way and the resultant statement is called a balance sheet or position statement.

## PREPARATION OF FINAL ACCOUNTS

Final accounts are prepared from the balances appearing in the trial balance at the end of an accounting period.

In order to decide the place where the particular balance should be taken, following rules may be noted:

**(i) For the debit side of the trial balance**

Balance appearing on the debit side of the trial balance may either be a loss or expense or an asset. If the debit balance of the account represents such an item that it is likely to benefit in the future, then it is an asset and is taken to the asset side of the balance sheet. Building, machinary, tools, bills receivable, debtors balances are examples of assets. If the balance of the account is such that the benefit out of it has already expired then it is an expense, and is likely to the debit side of trading account or profit and loss account as the case may be. Cost of goods sold, wages, cartage, freight, commission, rent, salary, insurance, stationery, postage and carriage are examples of expenses.

**(ii) For the credit side of trial balance**

Balance appearing on the credit side of the trial balance may either be a gain or a revenue or a liability. If the credit balance of the account is payable then it is a liability and is taken to the balance sheet. Examples are : Capital, loan, creditors, outstanding expenses. If the balance is not payable then it is a gain or revenue and is taken to the profit and loss account. Examples are : sale of goods or services, income from interest, rent, dividend.

### Trading Account

The aim of the trading account to find out gross profit or gross loss. Gross profit or gross loss is the difference between the 'cost of goods' and 'sales'.

The total amount of sales can be known from the sales account in the ledger.

Gross Profit = Sales – Cost of goods sold

**Trading Account**
for the year ending ...

| *Dr.* *Particulars* | *Amount (Rs.)* | *Particular* | *Cr. Amount (Rs.)* |
|---|---|---|---|
| To stock in the begining | | By Sales | |
| To purchases | | | |
| Less : return outwards | | Less : Return inwards | |
| To direct expenses[1]. | | By stock at the end. | |
| To gross profit[2]. | | | |

1. This heading is replaced by actual items of direct expenses, e.g., wages and salaries, freight, carriage in, cartage, etc.

2. Gross profit is the balancing figure. In case debit side exceeds the credit side, the difference is part on the credit side and it is termed as gross loss.

**Advantages of trading account**

1. It depicts the gross income or profit from the buying and selling of goods.
2. A comparison is possible of the purchases, sales, opening, and closing stocks and direct expenses of one period with similar items of previous periods to help detect the various causes of changes in them and to find out strong or weak spots of the trading activity.
3. Gross profit ratio or the ratio of gross profit to the net sales can be ascertained to find out how for the anticipated or planned results have been achieved.
4. Effective control over stocks can be ensure by comparing stock figures with those of previous periods reasons for wide fluctuations in stocks can be investigated.
5. Theft or leakage of goods can also be detected.

**Profit and Loss Account**

All the remaining expenses and loses are shown on the debit side and incomes and gains on the credit side of this account. The difference of the sides is either net profit or net loss which is taken to the capital account of the proprietor. Net profit is added to the capital and net loss is deducted from the capital. General form of the profit and loss account is as follows :

**Profit and Loss Account**

for the year ending 31st December 20...

Dr. Cr.

| *Particulars* | *Amount (Rs.)* | *Particulars* | *Amount (Rs.)* |
|---|---|---|---|
| To gross loss | | By gross profit | |
| To office salaries and wages | | By cash discounts received. | |
| To office rent, rates and taxes | | By bad debts recovered | |
| To office lighting and insurance | | By income from investments | |
| To printing and stationery | | By commission received | |
| To postage, telegrams | | By interest on deposits | |
| To legal expenses | | By interest on renewal of bills of exchange | |
| To Trade expenses | | By gain on sale of fixed assets | |
| To Audit fees | | By apprenticeship premium | |
| To car upkeep expenses | | By Interest on-drawings | |
| To Telephone expenses | | By Net loss (transferred to capital accounts). | |
| To General expenses | | | |
| To cash discounts allowed | | | |
| To interest on capital | | | |
| To interest on loans | | | |
| To discounts or rebate on bills of exchange | | | |
| To bad debts | | | |
| To selling and distribution expeneses. | | | |
| To packing of finished goods | | | |
| To store charges | | | |
| To carriage, freight, cartage outwards | | | |
| To cost of samples, catalogue expenses. | | | |
| To salesmen's salaries, expenses and commission | | | |
| To advertising expenses. | | | |
| To depreciation on fixed assets | | | |
| To loss on sale of fixed assets | | | |
| To Net profit (transferred to capital account). | | | |

**Manufacturing Account**

A manufacturing account is prepared in a manufacturing business, in addition to trading account. Thus, a firm engaged in manufacturing business prepares manufacturing account, trading account and profit and loss account. In case a manufacturing firm is engaged in manufacturing more than one product then it prepares a separate manufacturing account for each type of product. Manufacturing account may serve to indicate the results of the manufacturing department.

A manufacturing account is intended to disclose the factory cost of production. It consists of following:

**Cost of Materials Consumed**

This is also referred to as direct materials. It is the cost of such materials that actually become part of the cost unit. It is calculated as under :

| | Rs. |
|---|---|
| Opening stock of raw materials | ... |
| Add : purchases of raw materials | ... |
| Less : Closing stock of raw materials | ... |
| Cost of materials consumed. | |

**Direct Labour Cost**

Wages paid to employees for the time they are engaged in working on the direct materials.

**Direct Expenses**

Expenses incurred specifically on behalf of the cost unit. A manufacturing business is set up for manufacturing something may that be pens, ball pens, pencils, bricks, electrical appliances, etc. These things, that the enterprise is set up to provide, are termed "cost units".

**Prime Cost**

It is also referred to as "direct cost". It is the aggregate of direct materials, direct wages and direct expenses.

**Factory Overheads**

In addition to the above direct materials cost, direct labour cost and direct expenses there are many other costs which are incurred. Examples are : costs incurred in factory, costs incurred in the office and costs incurred in the selling and distribution department. All indirect costs incurred in the factory are termed as factory overheads. Factory overheads are also termed as production overheads. Examples of factory overheads are : factory rent, factory insurance, depreciation of plant, plant repair, factory fuel, factory stationery, factory telephone bill, factory supervisor remuneration, storekeeper's salary, works manager's salary, etc.

**Gross works cost of production**

The total of prime cost and factory overheads is sometimes termed as gross works cost of production or gross works cost of manufacture. This cost does not take into consideration the cost of work-in-progress both in the begining and at the end.

**Net works cost of production**

If the cost of work-in-progress in the beginning is added to the gross works cost of production and from the sum of the two the cost of work-in-progress at the end is subtracted then the balance left is termed as net works cost of production.

**Pro forma of a Manufacturing Account**

... (Name of the Firm)

Manufacturing Account for the year ending ...

Dr. Cr.

| *Particulars* | *Amount (Rs.)* | *Particular* | *Amount (Rs.)* |
|---|---|---|---|
| To Direct materials used : Rs.<br>Opening stock of Raw materisls ...<br>Add : purchases ...<br>Less : returns ...<br>Add: carriage inwards ...<br>Less : closing stock...<br>To Direct labour or wages<br>To Direct expenses<br>To Factory overheads:<br>Factory rent<br>Factory insurance<br>Factory supervisor's Remuneration<br>Plant repairs<br>Plant depreciation<br>Lighting & heating<br>Motive power<br>Indirect wages | | By net works cost of production (transferred to trading accounts | ... |

| *Particulars* | *Amount (Rs.)* | *Particular* | *Amount (Rs.)* |
|---|---|---|---|
| Depreciation on facotry<br>Building<br>Gross works cost of production<br>Add : work-in-progress (openings)<br>Less : work-in-progress (closing)<br>Net works cost | | | |

## BALANCE SHEET

It is a statement prepared with an aim to know the exact financial position of the business on the last date of the financial year. All nominal accounts, e.g., salaries, wages, carriage, commission, rent, etc., in the trial balance are transferred to trading and profit and loss account. Now accounts left out are the real accounts and personal accounts of customors are grouped under the heading sundry debtors and likewise all the balance of the suppliers are grouped under one heading sundry creditors. These balances of real and personal accounts are grouped as assets and liabilities and are arranged in a proper way and the resultant statement is called a balance sheet or position statement. Assets are shown on the right-hand side and liabilities on the left hand side.

## MARSHALLING OF BALANCE SHEET

The arrangement of the items in balance sheet in a proper way is known as marshalling of balance sheet. This marshalling is of two types :

*(i)* Liquidity order and

*(ii)* Permanence order

Following is an example of the balance sheet of a sole trader's business in the order of liquidity, i.e., ease of conversion of the assets into cash. The more liquid asset is shown first and then less liquid one, and soon. Similarly, on the liabilities side, current liabilities in order of payment are shown first, then fixed or long-term and, lastly, the capital of the proprietor.

**Balance Sheet**
as on March 31, 20...

| *Liabilities* | *Rs.* | *Assets* | *Rs.* |
|---|---|---|---|
| **Current Liabilities** | | **Current Assets** | |
| Creditors | | Cash in hand | |
| Bills payable | | Cash at bank | |
| Bank overdraft | | Stock-in-trade | |
| Outstanding expenses | | Debtors | |
| Income received in advance | | Bills receivable | |
| | | Prepaid expenses | |
| **Fixed Liabilities** | | **Investments** | |
| Loan | | **Fixed Assets** | |
| Mortagage | | Furniture & Fixtures | |
| Capital | | Plant & Machinery | |
| | | Building | |
| | | Land | |
| | | Goodwill | |

The assets of a business can also be shown in the balance sheet in the order of performance, i.e., in order of the desire to keep them in use.

For examples, goodwill, patents & trade marks, furniture & fitting, plant & machinery, unexpired expenses, stock-in-trade, sundry debtors, investments, bills receivable, cash at bank, cash in hand.

Sole proprietors, partnership firm, and banks usually follow the order of liquidity but join stock companies are required under the Companies Act, to follow the order of permanence in showing their assets in the balance sheet.

### Features of Balance Sheet

1. Balance sheet is a statement of financial position.
2. It is prepared after the preparation of trading and profit and loss account, i.e., after trans ferring all nominal accounts to them. Those remaining are classified into assets and liabilities and are taken to balance sheet.
3. Assets represent debit balances in the ledger while liabilities represent credit balances.
4. Liabilities are shown on the left-hand side of the balance sheet while assets on the right-hand side.
5. The words 'To' or 'By' are not used into the items. Similarly 'Dr.' or 'Cr.' are not used. Instead, the words liabilities and assets are used.
6. Assets and liabilities are presented either in order of liquidity or permanence.
7. Balance sheet indicates the financial position of the business on a particular date.

It is usually headed as :

Balance Sheet as at ...

### Presentation of Final Accounts in Vertical Form

So, for the final or financial statements – Trading, profit and loss account and balance sheet – have been presented in a 'T' form. This is also called the account form, horizontal form or traditional form. This form of presentation, which is quite simple and easy to understand, is known as 'vertical form' or presentation which is also called Report Form. Columnar Form or Running Form. Many firms and companies use this vertical form to present their final accounts or financial statements.

It is a system of presentation of information in trading, profit and loss account and Balance Sheet in which items relating to income or gains and expenses or losses and assets and liabilities are placed one after another, instead of side by side, in such a manner that significant information relating to cost of goods sold, gross profit, net profit, current assets, current liabilities, fixed assets, proprietor's funds etc. are revealed to the readers at a glance.

Following are the proforma of trading and profit and loss account and Balance Sheet in vertical form.

... (Name of the firm)

**Trading and profit and loss Account**

for the year ended ...

| *Items* | | *Rs.* | *Rs.* |
|---|---|---|---|
| | Rs. | | |
| Sales | ... | | |
| Less : Return | ... | | |
| Net: Sales | | ... | |
| Less : Cost of goods sold | | | |
| Opening stock | | ... | |
| Add : Purchases less return | | ... | |
| Add : Direct expenses e.g., carriage inwards | | | |
| Cartage, wages, etc. | | ... | |
| Less : Closing stock | | | |
| Gross Profit | | | |
| Add : Interest, Rent, Commission, Profit on sale of assets etc. | | ... | |

| *Items* | *Rs.* | *Rs.* |
|---|---|---|
| Less : Indirect expenses, e.g., General Administration, selling expenses | ... | |
| Less on sale of assets | ... | |
| Net profit | | ... |

... (Name of the firm)

Balance Sheet

as on ...

| *Items* | *Rs.* | *Rs.* |
|---|---|---|
| **Fixed Assets :** | | |
| Goodwill | | ... |
| Land & Building less depreciation | | ... |
| Plant & Machinery less depreciation | | ... |
| Furniture less depreciation | | ... |
| Office equipments less depreciation | | ... |
| Motor vehicles less depreciation | | ... |
| **Current Assets :** | | |
| Stores and spare parts | | ... |
| Stock-in-trade (Closing stock) | | ... |
| Investment-short term | | ... |
| Sundry debtor less provision for bad debts | | ... |
| Unexpired payments | | ... |
| Bills Receivable | | ... |
| Accred Income | | ... |
| Cash in bank | | ... |
| Cash in hand | | ... |
| **Less Current Liabilities :** | | |
| Sundry creditors | ... | |
| Bills Payable | ... | |
| Outstanding liabilities for expenses | ... | ... |
| **Net Working Capital** | | |
| Financial by | | |
| Capital : | | |
| Balance | | |
| Add : Net profit | ... | |
| Less : Drawings | ... | |
| Loans | ... | |

**Limitations of final Accounts**

The nature of figures reported and the way in which they are reported tend to give the impression of that financial statements are precise, exact and final. But this is not the case. These statements have the following limitations:

*(i)* The profit reported by the profit and loss account and financial position disclosed by the balance sheet cannot be exact in that these are interim reports. Exact position can be known only when the business is liquidated or sold.

*(ii)* Many items are influenced by the personal judgement and since the "soundness of the judgement necessarily depends on the competence and integrity of those who make them" the quality of statements, in its turn, gets affected by the quality of the team which organises the whole show.

*(iii)* The balance sheet is affected by various concepts, e.g., fixed assets by going concern concept, debtors and stock in trade by conservatism. Because of this, balance sheet does not show the financial position of the concern as is claimed by it.

*(iv)* The net income as disclosed by the profit and loss account is not absolute but relative in that this statement is the outcome of:

*(a)* Conventions and concepts

*(b)* Correct calculation of expired costs

*(c)* Correct recognition of revenue

The concept and conventions affecting the calculation of income are many: the calculation of expired cost is a difficult process, and recognition of revenue is affected by various considerations.

*(v)* Financial statements do not record and reveal any fact which cannot be expressed in terms of money. General health conditions of the chairman of the company, working conditions in which a worker has to work, growth of a team of loyal workers, sales policy pursued by the Co., quality of product introduced by the Co. etc., are not exhibited in financial statements because they cannot be expressed in terms of money.

## ACCOUNTING STANDARDS

Accounting Standards (ASs) are written policy documents issued by expert accounting body or by government or other regulatory body covering the aspects of recognition, measurement, presentation and disclosure of accounting transactions in the financial statements. The ostensible purpose of the standard setting bodies is to promote the dissemination of timely and useful financial information to investors and certain other parties having an interest in thecompany's economic performance. Accounting Standards reduce the accounting alternatives in the preparation of financial statements within the bounds of rationality, thereby ensuring comparability of financial statements of different enterprises. Accounting Standards deal with the issues of

(i) recognition of events and transactions in the financial statements,

(ii) measurement of these transactions and events,

(iii) presentation of these transactions and events in the financial statements in a manner that is meaningful and understandable to the reader, and

(iv) the disclosure requirements which should be there to enable the public at large and the stakeholders and the potential investors in particular, to get an insight into what these financial statements are trying to reflect and thereby facilitating them to take prudent and informed business decisions.

Accounting Standards standardize diverse accounting policies with a view to eliminate, to the maximum possible extent,

(i) the non-comparability of financial statements and thereby improving the reliability of financial statements, and

(ii) to provide a set of standard accounting policies, valuation norms and disclosure requirements.

## HOW MANY ACCOUNTING STANDARDS?

The council of the Institute of Chartered Accountants of India has, so far, issued thirty two Accounting Standards. However, AS 8 on 'Accounting for Research and Development' has been withdrawn consequent to the issuance of AS 26 on 'Intangible Assets'. Thus effectively,there are 31 Accounting Standards at present. The 'Accounting Standards' issued by the Accounting Standards Board establish standards which have to be complied by the business entities so that the financial statements are prepared in accordance with generally accepted accounting principles.

## LIST OF ACCOUNTING STANDARDS

Following is the list of Accounting Standards :

| AS No. | AS Title |
|---|---|
| 1 | Disclosure of Accounting Policies |
| 2 | Valuation of Inventories (Revised) |
| 3 | Cash Flow Statement (Revised) |
| 4 | Contingencies and Events Occurring after the Balance Sheet Date |
| 5 | Net Profit or Loss for the Period, Prior Period Items and Changes in Accounting Policies (Revised) |
| 6 | Depreciation Accounting (Revised) |
| 7 | Construction Contracts (Revised) |

| | |
|---|---|
| 8 | Research & Development Now included in AS . 26 |
| 9 | Revenue Recognition |
| 10 | Accounting for Fixed Assets |
| 11 | The Effects of Changes in ForeignExchange Rates (Revised) |
| 12 | Accounting for Government Grants |
| 13 | Accounting for Investments |
| 14 | Accounting for Amalgamations |
| 15 | Employee Benefits |
| 16 | Borrowing Costs |
| 17 | Segment Reporting |
| 18 | Related Party Disclosures |
| 19 | Leases |
| 20 | Earning Per Shares |
| 21 | Consolidated Financial Statement |
| 22 | Accounting for Taxes on Income |
| 23 | Accounting for Investment in Associates in Consolidated Financial Statement |
| 24 | Discontinuing Operations |
| 25 | Interim Financial Statement |
| 26 | Intangible Assets |
| 27 | Financial Reporting of Interests in Joint Ventures |
| 28 | Impairment of Assets |
| 29 | Provisions, Contingent Liabilities and Contingent Assets |
| 30 | Financial Instruments: Recognition and Measurement |
| 31 | Financial Instruments: Presentation |
| 32 | Financial Instruments: Disclosures |

## ADJUSTMENTS

Some important and common items, which need to be adjusted at the time of preparing the final accounts are discussed below.

1. Closing stock
2. Outstanding expenses
3. Prepaid Expenses
4. Accrued incomes
5. Incomes received in advance
6. Interest on capital
7. Interest on drawings
8. Interest on loan
9. Interest on investment
10. Depreciation
11. Bad Debts
12. Provision for bad and doubtful debts
13. Provision for discount on debtors
14. Provision for discount on creditors.

### Closing Stock

The unsold goods in stock at the end of the accounting period is called as closing stock. This is to be valued at cost or market price whichever is lower.Value of closing stock will appear

i) on the credit side of trading account and

ii) on the assets side of balance sheet.

### Outstanding Expenses

Expenses which have been incurred but not yet paid during the accounting period for which the final accounts are being prepared are called as outstanding expenses. Outstanding expenses will be shown

i) on the debit side of Profit and Loss account by way of additions to the particular expenses and

ii) on the liabilities side of the Balance Sheet.

### Prepaid Expenses

Expenses which have been paid in advance are called as prepaid (unexpired) expenses.Prepaid expenses will be shown

i) on the debit side of the Profit and Loss account by way of deduction from the particular expenses and

ii) on the assets side of the Balance Sheet.

### Accrued Incomes or Outstanding Incomes

Income which has been earned but not received during the accounting period is called as accrued income.

**Accrued income will be shown**

i) on the credit side of Profit and Loss account by way of addition to particular income and

ii) on the assets side of the Balance Sheet

**Incomes Received in Advance**

Income received during a particular accounting period for the work to be done in future period is called as income received in advance. Incomes received in advance will be shown

i) on the credit side of the Profit and Loss account by way of deducting from the particular income and

ii) on the liabilities side of the Balance sheet.

**Interest on Capital**

In order to see whether the business is really earning profit or not,it is desirable to charge interest on capital at a certain rate.Interest on capital will be shown

i) on the debit side of Profit and Loss account and

ii) on the liabilities side of the Balance Sheet by way of addition to the capital.

**Interest on Drawings**

Amount withdrawn by the owner for his personal use is called as drawings. When interest on capital is allowed, then interest on drawings is charged from the owner. Interest on drawings is an income for thebusiness and will reduce the capital of the owner.Interest on drawings will be shown

i) on the credit side of Profit and Loss account and

ii) on the liabilities side of the Balance Sheet by way of addition to the drawings which are ultimately deducted from the capital.

**Interest on Loan (Outstanding)**

Borrowings from banks, financial institutions and outsiders for business are called loans. Amount payable towards interest on loan is an expense for the business.Interest on loan outstanding will be shown

i) on the debit side of the Profit and Loss account by way of addition to the appropriate interest account and

ii) on the liability side of the Balance sheet by way of addition to the particular loan account.

**Interest on Investment**

Interest receivable on investments is an income for the business.Accrued interest on investments (outstanding interest receivable) will be shown

i) On the credit side of the Profit and Loss account by way of addition to the appropriate interest account and

ii) On the assets side of the balance sheet by way of addition to the investments account.

**Depreciation**

Depreciation is the reduction in the value of fixed assets due to its use or obsolescence. Generally depreciation is charged at some percentage on the value of fixed asset. Depreciation will be shown

i) on the debit side of Profit and Loss account and

ii) on the assets side of the Balance Sheet by way of deduction from the value of concerned asset.

**Bad Debts**

Debts which cannot be recovered are called **bad debts**. It is a loss for the business.Bad debts will be shown

i) on the debit side of Profit and Loss account and

ii) on the assets side of the Balance Sheet by way of deduction from sundry debtors.

**Provision for Bad and Doubtful Debts**

Every business suffers a percentage of bad debts over and above the debts definitely known as irrecoverable and written off as Bad (Bad debts written off). If Sundry debtors figure is to be shown correctly in the Balance sheet provision for bad and doubtful debts must be adjusted.This Provision for bad and doubtful debts is generally provided at a certain percentage on Debtors, based on past experience.While preparing final accounts, the bad debts written off given in adjustment is first deducted from the Sundry debtors then on the balance amount (Sundry debtors – Bad debt written off) provision for bad and doubtful debts calculated.Provision for bad and doubtful debts will be shown

i) on the debit side of Profit and Loss Account and

ii) on the assets side of the Balance sheet by way of deduction from Sundry debtors (after Bad debts written off if any).

**Provision for Discount on Debtors**

To motivate the debtors to make prompt payments, cash discount may be allowed to them. After providing provision for bad and doubtful debts, the remaining debtors are called as **good debtors.** They may pay their dues in time and avail themselves of the cash discount permissable. So a provision for discount on good debtors at a certain percentage may have to be created.Provision for discount on debtors will be shown

i) on the debit side of Profit and Loss account and

ii) on the asset side of the Balance sheet by way of deduction from Sundry debtors (after deducting bad debts written off and provision for bad and doubtful debts).

**Provision for Discount on Creditors**

Similar to cash discount allowed to debtors, the firm may have a chance to receive the cash discount from the creditors for prompt payment. Provision for discount on Creditors is calculated at a certain percentage on Sundry Creditors.Provision for discount on creditors will be shown

i) on the credit side of Profit and Loss account and

ii) on the liabilities side of the Balance sheet by way of deduction from Sundry creditors.

## FINANCIAL STATEMENT ANALYSIS

Financial statements are final result of accounting work done during the accounting period. Financial statements normally include Trading, Profit and Loss Account and Balance Sheet. The users of accounting information may not be able to get direct reply to certain questions from the above statements. However, by expressing the items in the financial statements, in relation to each other we can get meaningful information.

Analysis of financial statement has been defined as "a process of evaluating the relationship between the component parts of the financial statements to obtain a better understanding of a firm's position and performance".

Financial statement analysis is an important part of the overall financial assessment. The different users look at the business concern from their respective view point and are interested in knowing about its profitability and financial condition. A detailed cause and effect study of the profitability and financial condition is the overall objective of financial statement analysis.

**Significance of Financial Statement Analysis**

1. Judging the earning capacity or profitability of a business concern.

2. Analysing the short term and long term solvency of the business concern.

3. Helps in making comparative studies between various firms.

4. Assists in preparing budgets.

**Limitations of Financial Statement Analysis**

Analysis of financial statements helps to ascertain the strength and weakness of the business concern, but at the same time it suffers from the following limitations.

1. It analyses what has happened till date and does not reflect the future.

2. It ignores price level changes.

3. Financial analysis takes into consideration only monetary matters, qualitative aspects are ignored.

4. The conclusions of the analysis is based on the correctness of the financial statements.

5. Analysis is a means to an end and not the end itself.

6. As there is variation in accounting practices followed by different firms a valid comparison of their financial analysis is not possible.

**Ratio Analysis**

Ratio is an expression of one number in relation to another. Ratio analysis is the process of determining and interpreting the numerical relationship between figures of financial statements. A ratio is a mathematical relationship between two items expressed in a quantitative form. An absolute figure does not convey much meaning. Generally, with the help of other related information the significance of the absolute figure could be understood better.

**Expression of Ratios**

*Ratios are expressed in three ways:*

**1. Time:** In this type of expression one number is divided by another number and the quotient is taken as number of times. For example,expressing the attendance of 40 students present in a class of 80 students would be:

$$\frac{40}{80} = 0.5 \text{ times}$$

**2. Percentage:** It is expressed in Percentage. When the above example is expressed as percentage, it would be as under

$$\frac{40}{80} \times 100 = 50\%$$

**3. Pure:** It is expressed as a proportion. In the above example, this would be as under

$$\frac{40}{80} = \frac{1}{2} = 0.5$$

This may also be expressed as 0.5:1.The study of relationships between various items or groups of items in financial statements is known as 'Financial Ratio Analysis'.

**Objectives**

The objectives of using ratios are to test the profitability, financial position (liquidity and solvency) and the operating efficiency of a concern.

**Advantages of Ratio Analysis**

Ratio analysis is an important technique in financial analysis. It is a means for judging the financial soundness of the concern. The advantages of accounting ratios are as follows:

1. It is an useful device for analysing the financial statements.

2. It simplifies, summarizes the accounting figures to make it understandable.

3. It helps in financial forecasting.

4. It facilitates interfirm and intrafirm comparisons.

Ratio analysis is useful in finding the strength and weakness of a business concern. After identifying the weakness, the ratios are also helpful in determining the causes of the weakness.

## CLASSIFICATION OF RATIOS

### I. Liquidity Ratios

Liquidity Ratios measure the firms' ability to pay off current dues i.e., repayable within a year. Liquidity ratios are otherwise called as Short Term Solvency Ratios. The important liquidity ratios are

1. Current Ratio
2. Liquid Ratio
3. Absolute Liquid Ratio

**1. Current Ratio**

This ratio is used to assess the firm's ability to meet its current liabilities. The relationship of current assets to current liabilities is known as current ratio. The ratio is calculated as:

$$\text{Current Ratio} = \frac{\text{Current Assets}}{\text{Current Liabilities}}$$

Current Assets are those assets, which are easily convertible into cash within one year. This includes cash in hand, cash at bank, sundry debtors, bills receivable, short term investment or marketable securities, stock and prepaid expenses.Current Liabilities are those liabilities which are payable within one year. This includes bank overdraft, sundry creditors, bills payable and outstanding expenses.

**2. Liquid Ratio**

This ratio is used to assess the firm's short term liquidity. The relationship of liquid assets to current liabilities is known as liquid ratio. It is otherwise called as Quick ratio or Acid Test ratio. The ratio is calculated as:

$$\text{Liquid Ratio} = \frac{\text{Liquid Assets}}{\text{Current Liabilities}}$$

Liquid assets means current assets less stock and prepaid expenses.

**3. Absolute Liquid Ratio**

It is a modified form of liquid ratio. The relationship of absolute liquid assets to liquid liabilities is known as absolute liquid ratio. This ratio is also called as 'Super Quick Ratio'. The ratio is calculated as:

$$\text{Absolute Liquid Ratio} = \frac{\text{Absolute Liquid Assets}}{\text{Liquid Liabilities}}$$

Absolute liquid assets means cash, bank and short term investments. Liquid liabilities means current liabilities less bank overdraft.

**II. Solvency Ratios**

Solvency refers to the firms ability to meet its long term indebtedness. Solvency ratio studies the firms ability to meet its long term obligations. The following are the important solvency ratios:

1. Debt-Equity Ratio
2. Proprietory Ratio

**1. Debt Equity Ratio**

This ratio helps to ascertain the soundness of the long term financial position of the concern. It indicates the proportion between total long term debt and shareholders funds. This also indicates the extent to which the firm depends upon outsiders for its existence. The ratio is calculated as:

$$\text{Debt-Equity Ratio} = \frac{\text{Total long term Debt}}{\text{Shareholders funds}}$$

Total long term debt includes Debentures, long term loans from banks and financial institutions. Shareholders funds includes Equity share capital, Preference share capital, Reserves and surplus.

**2. Proprietory Ratio**

This ratio shows the relationship between proprietors or shareholders funds and total tangible assets. The ratio is calculated as:

Proprietory Ratio

$$= \frac{\text{Share holders funds (Proprietors funds)}}{\text{Total tangible assets}}$$

Tangible assets will include all assets except goodwill, preliminary expenses etc.

**III. Profitability Ratios**

Efficiency of a business is measured by profitability. Profitability ratio measures the profit earning capacity of the business concern. The important profitability ratios are discussed below:

1. Gross Profit Ratio
2. Net Profit Ratio
3. Operating Profit Ratio
4. Operating Ratio

**1. Gross Profit Ratio**

This ratio indicates the efficiency of trading activities. The relationship of Gross profit to Sales is known as gross profit ratio.The ratio is calculated as:

$$\text{Gross Profit Ratio} = \frac{\text{Gross Profit}}{\text{Sales}} \times 100$$

Gross profit is taken from the Trading Account of a business concern. Otherwise Gross profit can be calculated by deducting cost of goods sold from sales. Sales means Net sales.

Gross Profit = Sales — Cost of goods sold

Cost of goods sold = Opening Stock + Purchases– – Closing Stock

(or)

Sales — Gross Profit

**2. Net Profit Ratio**

This ratio determines the overall efficiency of the business. The relationship of Net profit to Sales is known as **net profit ratio**. The ratio is calculated as:

$$\text{Net Profit Ratio} = \frac{\text{Net Profit}}{\text{Sales}} \times 100$$

Net profit is taken from the Profit and Loss account of the business concern or the gross profit of the concern less administration expenses,selling and distribution expenses and financial expenses.

**3. Operating Profit Ratio**

This ratio is an indicator of the operational efficiency of the management. It establishes the relationship between Operating profit and Sales. The ratio is calculated as:

$$\text{Operating Profit Ratio} = \frac{\text{Operating Profit}}{\text{Sales}} \times 100$$

Where operating profit is Net profit + Non-operating expenses — Non-operating income. Where, Non-operating expenses are interest on loan and loss on sale of assets. Non-operating income are dividend, interest received and profit on sale of asset.

Operating profit = Gross profit — Operating expenses.

Operating expenses include administration, selling and distribution expenses. Financial expenses like interest on loan are excluded for this purpose.

### 4. Operating Ratio

This ratio determines the operating efficiency of the business concern. Operating ratio measures the amount of expenditure incurred in production, sales and distribution of output. The relationship between Operating cost to Sales is known as Operating Ratio. The ratio is calculated as:

$$\text{Operating Ratio} = \frac{\text{Cost of goods sold + Operating expenses}}{\text{Sales}} \times 100$$

## IV. Activity Ratios

Activity ratios indicate the performance of the business. The performance of a business is judged with its sales (turnover) or cost of goods sold. These ratios are thus referred to as **turnover ratios**. A few important activity ratios are discussed below:

1. Capital turnover ratio
2. Fixed assets turnover ratio
3. Stock turnover ratio
4. Debtors turnover ratio
5. Creditors turnover ratio

### 1. Capital Turnover Ratio

This shows the number of times the capital has been rotated in the process of carrying on business. Efficient utilisation of capital would lead to higher profitability. The relationship between Sales and Capital employed is known as Capital Turnover Ratio. The ratio is calculated as:

$$\text{Capital Turnover Ratio} = \frac{\text{Sales}}{\text{Capital Employed}} \times 100$$

Where Sales means Sales less sales returns and Capital employed refers to total long term funds of the business concern i.e., Equity share capital, Preference share capital, Reserves and surplus and Long term borrowed funds.

### 2. Fixed Assets Turnover Ratio:

This shows how best the fixed assets are being utilised in the business concern. The relationship between Sales and Fixed assets is known as Fixed assets turnover ratio. The ratio is calculated as:

$$\text{Fixed assets turnover Ratio} = \frac{\text{Sales}}{\text{Fixed assets}}$$

Fixed assets means Fixed assets less depreciation.

### 3. Stock Turnover Ratio

This ratio is otherwise called as inventory turnover ratio. It indicates whether stock has been efficiently used or not. It establishes a relationship between the cost of goods sold during a particular period and the average amount of stock in the concern. The ratio is calculated as:

$$\text{Stock turnover ratio} = \frac{\text{Cost of goods sold}}{\text{Average stock}}$$

$$\text{Average stock} = \frac{\text{Opening stock + closing stock}}{2}$$

If information to calculate average stock is not given then closing stock may be taken as average stock.

### 4. Debtors Turnover Ratio

This establishes the relationship between credit sales and average accounts receivable. Debtors turnover ratio indicates the efficiency of the business concern towards the collection of amount due from debtors. The ratio is calculated as:

Debtors turnover Ratio

$$= \frac{\text{Credit Sales}}{\text{Average Accounts Receivable}}$$

Accounts receivable includes sundry debtors and bills receivable.

Average accounts receivable

$$= \frac{\text{Opening (debtors + bills receivable)} + \text{Closing (debtors + bills receivable)}}{2}$$

In case credit sales is not given, total sales can be taken as credit sales.

**5. Creditors Turnover Ratio**

This establishes the relationship between credit purchases and average accounts payable. Creditors turnover ratio indicates the period in which the payments are made to creditors. The ratio is calculated as:

Creditors turnover ratio

$$= \frac{\text{Credit Purchases}}{\text{Average Accounts payable}}$$

Accounts payable include sundry creditors and bills payable.

Average accounts payable

$$= \frac{\text{Opening (creditors + bills payable)} + \text{Closing (creditors + bills payable)}}{2}$$

In case credit purchases is not given total purchases can be taken as credit purchases.

## COST-VOLUME-PROFIT ANALYSIS (BREAK-EVEN ANALYSIS)

As the name suggests, cost volume profit (CVP) analysis is the analysis of three variables cost, volume and profit. Such an analysis explores the relationship between costs, revenue, activity levels and the resulting profit. It aims at measuring variations in cost and volume. CVP analysis is based on the following assumptions:

**1.** Changes in the levels of revenues and costs arise only because of changes in the number of product (or service) units produced and sold for example, the number of television sets produced and sold by Sony Corporation or the number of packages delivered by Overnight Express. The number of output units is the only revenue driver and the only cost driver. Just as a cost driver is any factor that affects costs, a revenue driver is a variable, such as volume, that causally affects revenues.

**2.** Total costs can be separated into two components; a fixed component that does not vary with output level and a variable component that changes with respect to output level. Furthermore, variable costs include both direct variable costs and indirect variable costs of a product. Similarly, fixed costs include both direct fixed costs and indirect fixed costs of a product.

**3.** When represented graphically, the behaviours of total revenues and total costs are linear (meaning they can be represented as a straight line) in relation to output level within a relevant range (and time period).

**4.** Selling price, variable cost per unit, and total fixed costs (within a relevant range and time period) are known and constant.

**5.** The analysis either covers a single product or assumes that the proportion of different products when multiple products are sold will remain constant as the level of total units sold changes.

**6.** All revenues and costs can be added, subtracted, and compared without taking into account the time value of money.

### Breakeven Point

The word contribution has been given its name because of the fact that it literally contributes towards the recovery of fixed costs and the making of profits. The contribution grows along with the sales revenue till the time it just covers the fixed cost. This point where neither profits nor losses have been made is known as a break-even point. This implies that in order to break even the amount of contribution generated should be exactly equal to the fixed costs incurred. Hence, if we know how much contribution is generated from each unit sold we shall have sufficient information for computing the number of units to be sold in order to break even. Mathematically, Break even point in units = Fixed costs / Contribution per unit.

**Limitations of Breakeven Analysis**

The limitations of the practical applicability of breakeven analysis and breakeven charts stem mostly from the assumptions underlying CVP which have been mentioned above. Assumptions like costs behaving in a linear fashion or sales revenue remain constant at different sales levels or the stocks shall remain constant period after period are unrealistic. Similarly, the assumption that the only factor which influences costs is the 'activity level achieved' Is erroneous because other factors like inflation also have a bearing on costs.

## LEVERAGE

Leverage refers to the ability of a firm in employing long term funds having a fixed cost, to enhance returns to the owners. In other words, leverage is the amount of debt that a firm uses to finance its assets.The use of various financial instruments or borrowed capital, to increase the potential return of an investment. A firm with a lot of debt in its capital structure is said to be highly levered. A firm with no debt is said to be unlevered. Leverage can occur in either the *operating or financing* portions of the income statement. The effect of leverage is to *magnify* the effects of changes in sales volume on earnings. Leverage serves to increase both expected return and risk to the firm's stockholders. Leverage helps both the investor and the firm to invest or operate. However, it comes with greater risk.

If an investor uses leverage to make an investment and the investment moves against the investor, his or her loss is much greater than it would have been if the investment had not been leveraged - leverage magnifies both gains and losses. In the business world, a company can use leverage to try to generate shareholder wealth, but if it fails to do so, the interest expense and credit risk of default destroys shareholder value.

## TYPES OF LEVERAGE

The term Leverage in general refers to a relationship between two interrelated variables. In financial analysis it represents the influence of one financial variable over some other related financial variable. These financial variables may be costs, output, sales revenue, Earnings Before Interest and Tax (EBIT), Earning per share (EPS) etc.

There are three commonly used measures of leverage in financial analysis. These are:

(i) Operating Leverage

(ii) Financial Leverage

(iii) Combined Leverage

## OPERATING LEVERAGE

Operating leverage (OL) maybe defined as the employment of an asset with a fixed cost in the hope that sufficient revenue will be generated to cover all the fixed and variable costs. The use of assets for which a company pays a fixed cost is called operating leverage. With fixed costs the percentage change in profits accompanying a change in volume is greater than the percentage change in volume. The higher the turnover of operating assets, the greater will be the revenue in relation to the fixed charge on those assets.Operating leverage is a function of three factors:

(i) Rupee amount of fixed cost,

(ii) Variable contribution margin, and

(iii) Volume of sales.

Operating leverage is the ratio of net operating income before fixed charges to net operating income after fixed charges. Degree of operating leverage is equal to the percentage increase in the net operating income to the percentage increase in the output.

$$OL = N(P-V) / N(P-V)-F$$

Where,

OL = Operating leverage

N = Number of units sold

P = Selling price per unit

V = Variable cost per unit

F = Fixed cost

Operating leverage is directly proportional to business risk. More operating leverage leads to more business risk, for then a small sales decline causes a big profit.

## FINANCIAL LEVERAGE

Financial leverage (FL) maybe defined as .the use of funds with a fixed cost in order to increase earnings per share.. In other words, it is the use of company funds on which it pays a limited return. Financial leverage involves the use of funds obtained at a fixed cost in the hope of increasing the return to common stockholders. Degree of financial leverage is the ratio of the percentage increase in earning per share (EPS) to the percentage increase in earnings before interest and taxes (EBIT).

## DEGREE OF COMBINED LEVERAGE

Combined leverage maybe defined as the potential use of fixed costs, both operating and financial, which magnifies the effect of sales volume change on the earning per share of the firm.Degree of combined leverage (DCL) is the ratio of percentage change in earning per share to the percentage change in sales. It indicates the effect the sales changes will have on EPS.

Degree of combined leverage = Degree of operating leverage × Degree of financial leverage

# OBJECTIVE TYPE QUESTIONS

**1.** Profits can be frauduletly inflated by
(a) Suppression of sales returns
(b) Treating capital expenditure as revenue
(c) Overestimation of liabilities
(d) Omission of prepaid expenses

**2.** A credit sale of goods to shivendra should be debited to
(a) Sales Account
(b) Goods Account
(c) Shivendra Account
(d) Purchase Account

**3.** Which of the following assets does not depreciate?
(a) Machinery and equipment
(b) Patents
(c) Land
(d) Furniture

**4.** Valuing the stock in trade at market price or cost price which is less is an example of the convention of
(a) consistency (b) disclosure
(c) knowing the value (d) none of these

**5.** Double entry principle means
(a) Having debit for every credit and similarly credit for each debit.
(b) Writing all the entries twice in the book.
(c) Maintaining the double account for all busness transactions.
(d) Writing two times the same entry.

**6.** A sale of goods to Vaibhav Deep for cash should be debited to
(a) Vaibhav's A/C (b) Cash A/C
(c) Sale of goods A/C (d) None of these

**7.** A withdrawal of cash from business by the proprietor of the firm should be credited to
(a) Capital Account
(b) Cash Account
(c) Drawing Account
(d) Proprietor's Account

**8.** The preparation of a trial balance helps in
(a) Locating errors of principle
(b) Locating errors of ommission
(c) Locating clerical errors
(d) Locating compensatory errors

**9.** A cheque received and deposited in the bank on the same day is recorded in the
(a) Cash column of the cash book
(b) Bank column of the cash book
(c) Credited in the cash book
(d) Debited in the cash book

**10.** Petty cash may be used to pay
(a) the expenses relating to postages and conveyance
(b) salaries and wages to the final staff
(c) for the purchase of furniture and fittings
(d) none of these

**11.** A reserve is charge against
(a) Trading account
(b) Profit and loss account
(c) Profit and loss appropriation account
(d) None of these

**12.** The payment side of cash book is under cost by Rs 200 when over draft as per pass book is the starting point
(a) Rs. 200 will be deducted
(b) Rs. 200 will be added
(c) No effect will be in the pass book
(d) None of these.

**13.** An amount of Rs. 300 is debited twice in the pass book when overdraft as per the cash book is the starting point
(a) Rs. 600 will be added
(b) Rs. 500 will be deducted
(c) No effect will be in the cash book
(d) None of these

**14.** Expenditure incurred by a publisher for acquiring copy rights is a
(a) Capital expenditure
(b) Revenue expenditure
(c) Deferred revenue expenditure
(d) None of these.

**15.** Immediately after purchasing a new truck Rs. 1,000 is paid to have the name of the company and other advertising material painted on the truck this Rs.1,000 is a
(a) Capitalexpenditure
(b) Deferred revenue expenditure
(c) Revenue expenditure
(d) None of these

**16.** A return Inwards book is kept to record
(a) return of goods sold
(b) returns of anything purchased
(c) returns of goods purchased
(d) returns of anything sold

**17.** Bill Receivable Book is a part of the
(a) Ledger
(b) Balancesheet
(c) Journal
(d) Profit and Loss Account

**18.** A sales of Rs. 2000 wrongly entered in the purchase book
(a) decreases the gross profit by Rs. 2000
(b) increases the gross profit by Rs. 2000
(c) increases the gross profit by Rs. 4000
(d) none of these.

**19.** Which of the following are current assets?
(a) Bank loan for three years
(b) Account receivable
(c) Long-term investments
(d) Debentures sinking fund investments

**20.** Insurance unexpires accounts is a
(a) Real account
(b) Personal account
(c) Nominal account
(d) None of these.

**21.** Goodwill account is a
(a) Nominal Account (b) Real Account
(c) Personal Account (d) None of these.

**22.** Bank overdraft account is a
(a) Personal Account (b) Real Account
(c) Nominal Account (d) All of these.

**23.** Contingent liability is shocon due to
(a) Convention of full disclosure.
(b) Convention of conservatism.
(c) Convention of materiality.
(d) Dual aspect concept.

**24.** Which item is shown on the debit side of a trial balance?
(a) Rent outstanding
(b) Prepaid Expenses
(c) Purchases
(d) Excess of income over expenses by the firm

**25.** Purchase for office furniture on account is recorded in
(a) General Journal (b) Cash book
(c) Purchase book (d) Sales book

**26.** Sales on account is recorded in
(a) Cash book (b) Journal
(c) Sales book (d) General Journal

**27.** The credit balance in the bank account is
(a) Capital (b) a liability
(c) an asset (d) an expense

**28.** Cash sales are recorded in
(a) Sales book (b) Cash book
(c) Journal (d) Purchase book

**29.** Error of commission do not permit
(a) The trial balance to agree
(b) Correct the total of balance sheet
(c) Correct totalling of trial balance
(d) None of these

**30.** An item of Rs.72 has been debited to a personal account as Rs. 27, is an error of
(a) Commission (b) Omission
(c) Principle (d) None of these

**31.** Sales to shyam of Rs. 500 not recorded in the books would affect
(a) Shyam's account (b) Sales account
(c) Sales account (d) Cash account

**32.** Which of the following accounts is increased by credit entries?
(a) Bank Overdraft
(b) Purchases Account
(c) Goodwill Account
(d) Sales Returns Account

**33.** Profit and loss account of business shows the
(a) Net profit earned
(b) Gross profit earned
(c) Balance of all accounts
(d) Capital employed in business

**34.** If a receipt of Rs. 200 from Rajesh out debtor has not been recorded in the books the profit would show
(a) an increase of Rs. 200
(b) a decrease of Rs. 200
(c) neither an increase nor a decrease
(d) none of these

**35.** Closing stock is valued at
(a) Market price
(b) Cost price
(c) Cost price or market price whichever is lower
(d) Cost price or market price whichever is higher

**36.** Unearned income account is
(a) an asset (b) a liability
(c) an expernse (d) an income

**37.** Depreciation is provided on
(a) Current Assets (b) Liquid Assets
(c) Fictitious Assets (d) Fixed Assets

**38.** A bill of exchange is drawn by a
(a) Creditor (b) Debtor
(c) Shareholder (d) Debentureholder

**39.** Bills receivable account is
(a) an expense Account
(b) an asset Account
(c) a liability Account
(d) a revenue Account

**40.** When goods are purchased for the joint venture out of joint bank A/C the amount is debited to
(a) Joint bank A/C
(b) Joint venture A/C
(c) Purchases account
(d) None of these

**41.** Bills receivable endorsed are debited to
(a) Debtor's Account
(b) Creditor's Account
(c) Bills payable Account
(d) Bills receivable Account

**42.** Subscription received during the year were Rs. 800 for the current year. Rs.100 for the previous year and Rs. 100 for the next year. In the receipts and payments account the receipts from subscriptions would appear at
(a) Rs. 700 (b) Rs. 800
(c) Rs. 900 (d) Rs. 1000

**43.** Any donation received for a specific purpose is a
(a) Liability (b) Assets
(c) Revenue receipts (d) Capital receipts

**44.** The convention of conservatism will have the effect of
(a) Over statement of assets
(b) Under statement of assets
(c) Under statement of liabilities
(d) Under statement of provision for bad and doubtful debts

**45.** An accountant is mainly concerned with
(a) Audit work
(b) Preparation of budget for his employees
(c) Management Constancy Services
(d) Filling tax returns

**46.** Expenses incurred on research and development is an example of
(a) Capital expenditure
(b) Revenue expenditure
(c) Deferred revenue expenditure
(d) None of these

**47.** Amount spent on increasing the seating capacity in a cinema hall is
(a) Capital expenditure
(b) Revenue expenditure
(c) Deferred revenue expenditure
(d) None of these

**48.** Which of the following is not capital expenditure?
(a) Cost of issuing shares and debentures
(b) Wages paid for construction of building
(c) Repairs on a second-hand machinery newly purchased
(d) Purchase of new spark plug at a cost of Rs. 8.50 for a two-year old car

**49.** Window dressing is prohibited due to
(a) Convention of conservatism
(b) Convention of disclosure
(c) Convention of materiality
(d) Accrual concept

**50.** Quantitative transactions are not recorded in accounts due to
(a) dual concept
(b) accrual concept
(c) money measurement concept
(d) none of these

**51.** Concept of Realisation implies
(a) When cash is received from debtors
(b) When goods are delivered to customer
(c) When order is received
(d) None of these

**52.** Which of the following are not current liabilities?
(a) Bank overdraft
(b) Redeemable debentures
(c) Provision for doubtful debts
(d) Accounts payable

**53.** Provision for doubtful debts account is a
(a) Personal account
(b) Real account
(c) Nominal account
(d) None of these

**54.** LIFO inventory method was used in year I, FIFO in year II and weighted average in year III. Which accounting principle is violated?
(a) Cost principle
(b) Consistency
(c) Materiality
(d) No principle of accounting is violated

**55.** Land was reported at its selling price which is substantially higher than its cost. The increase in value was included in the income statement, which accounting principle is violated ?
(a) Cost principle
(b) Going concern concept
(c) Entity concept
(d) Conservatism

**56.** The cost of three small files (of Rs. 4 each) was charged to expenses when purchased even though they had a useful life of several years. This was done according to the
(a) Cost principle
(b) Conservatism principle
(c) Full disclosure
(d) Materiality

**57.** The amount spent on unsuccessful patent rights is a
(a) Capital expenditure
(b) Deferred revenue expenditure (if the amount is large)
(c) Revenue expenditure (even though the amount is large)
(d) None of these

**58.** Double entry system of bookkeeping refers to a system where
(a) the number of accounts with a debit balance must agree with the number of accounts with the credit balance
(b) each transaction is recorded twice, once in journal and then in legder
(c) equal debit and credit entries are made for each transaction
(d) each transaction is recorded in two set of account books

**59.** An entry of Rs. 500 was wrongly posted to wages account instead of machinery account, as wages are to be capitalised. It is an error of
(a) Commission (b) Omission
(c) Principle (d) Clerical error

**60.** Which of the following statements best explains the relationship between journal and ledger?
(a) First recording in journal and then posting to ledger completes the double entry of the transaction.

(b) The journal is the book of original entry where as the ledger is the book of second entry.
(c) The journal is the book for analytical record and ledger is the book for chronological record.
(d) The process of recording, in the journal is called journalising, the process of recording in the ledger is called posting.

**61.** In order to determine the amount of sales, to which of the following records one should refer?
(a) Sales book
(b) Sales account
(c) Journal
(d) Total debtors account

**62.** Which of the following errors is revealed by trial balance?
(a) Wrong amount entered in the book of original entry
(b) Wrong amount entered in a ledger account
(c) Complete omission of an entry from the book of original entry
(d) All of these

**63.** Which of the following errors are revealed by trial balance?
(a) Omission of an amount from the trial balance
(b) Posting of the wrong amount
(c) Wrong totalling of the book of original entry
(d) None of these

**64.** Which of the following errors will cause the trial balance to be out of balance?
(a) The total of the purchase book is Rs. 1000 short
(b) Goods received back from mahesh, Rs. 250 have not been entered in the Returns inward book
(c) Office furniture purchased from Ravi and Co. Rs. 950 has been entered in the purchase book
(d) A purchase of Rs. 251 from Gopal and Co. has been entered in the purchase book as Rs. 215.

**65.** Which of the following errors will not cause the trial balance to be out of order?
(a) Rs. 590 received from P. Das has been debited to (b) Rs. 10 Das
(b) A purchase of Rs. 258 from Lekhi has been debited to his account as Rs. 285
(c) The total of the discount columm of the cash book (cr.) is Rs. 20 short
(d) An invoice for Rs. 460 is entered in the sales book as Rs. 640

**66.** Which of the following errors will not cause the trial balance to be out of balance?
(a) Rs. 310 for goods sold, was posted to the credit of charges
(b) Purchases returns book for December 1978 was overcast by Rs. 220
(c) Sales book carried forward Rs. 2400 instead of Rs. 2004
(d) All of these

**67.** An invoice of Rs. 560 is entered in the sales book as Rs. 650. The total of the debit side of the trial balance is Rs. 21,440. Assuming no other error what is the total of the credit side of the trial balance?
(a) Rs. 21,240 (b) Rs. 21,350
(c) Rs. 21,330 (d) None of these

**68.** Which of the following books should be used to record purchase of a type writer on account?
(a) Cash books (b) Purchase book
(c) Sales book (d) Journal

**69.** Which of the following books should be used to record purchase of merchandise an account?
(a) Cash book (b) Purchase book
(c) Sales book (d) Journal

**70.** Agreement of the trial balance may not indicate that
(a) no error remains undetected
(b) double entry has been completed
(c) arithmetic accuracy is reasonably proved
(d) all ledger accounts have been correctly posted

**71.** Use of subsidary books can be made by
(a) Only large business concerns
(b) Only small business concerns
(c) Only medium size business concerns
(d) All of these

**72.** Petty cash system is designed
(a) to meet the needs of small businesses
(b) to cover small and miscellaneous income
(c) to cover the small expenditure to be paid in cash
(d) to cover both small incomes and expenditures

**73.** The term "Imprest system" is used in relation to
(a) Purchase book (b) Sales book
(c) Cash book (d) Petty cash book

**74.** Trial balance is a proof that
(a) every transaction is recorded twice
(b) no error remains in the books of accounts
(c) books are authentically and correctly written
(d) none of these

**75.** Which of the following is an error of commission?
(a) A sale of Rs. 560 ommitted to be recorded
(b) A purchase of Rs. 840 was wrongly posted
(c) Treating charges as addition to asset
(d) Sales book over cost by Rs. 600 and purchase book was under cost by the same amount

**76.** Which of the following errors is disclosed by trial balance?
(a) Error of principle
(b) Wrong amount posted in ledger account
(c) Non-recording of a transaction in the book of original entry
(d) None of these

**77.** 'Bank over draft' should be classified as
(a) Current asset (b) Current liability
(c) Intengible asset (d) Intangible asset

**78.** Assets appearing in the book but having no value are known as
(a) Wasting assets (b) Intangible assets
(c) Current assets (d) Fictitious assets

**79.** Which of the following is an accounting equation
(a) Capital – Assets – Liabilities
(b) Capital – Assets – Liabilities
(c) Assets – Liabilities – Capital
(d) Liabilities – Assets – Capital

**80.** Which of the following is an equation?
(a) Assets = Equities
(b) Assets = Liabilities – Capital
(c) Assets = Liabilities – Equities
(d) Assets = Equities + Liabilities

**81.** The capital in a business on Jan. 1 and Jan. 31 is Rs. 17,000 and Rs. 17,200 respectively. Investment by owner and withdrawal by owner during Jan amount to Rs. 1,000 and Rs.700 respectively. What is the net income for January?
(a) Rs. 100 (Loss) (b) Rs. 300
(c) Rs. 200 (d) Rs. 500

**82.** Which of the following transactions will result in decrease in assets and decrease in liabilities?
(a) Payment of a promissory note with cash
(b) Materials returned to supplier on account
(c) Redemption of debentures
(d) All of these

**83.** Cost of goods sold – Rs. 13,300, Gross Profit – Rs. 3,200, Netprofit – Rs. 700, what is the amount of sales?
(a) Rs. 14,000 (b) Rs. 10,100
(c) Rs. 16,500 (d) Rs. 17,200

**84.** Select the correct amount of purchases, given the following information :

| | |
|---|---|
| Cost of goods sold | – Rs. 1,20,000; |
| Carriage in wards | – Rs. 1,890; |
| Opening stock | – Rs. 43,640; |
| Closing stock | – Rs. 38,500; |
| Purchase returns | – Rs. 2,150; |
| Sales | – Rs. 2,82,650 |

(a) Rs. 1,15,120 (b) Rs. 62,650
(c) Rs. 1,10,420 (d) None of these

**85.** Depreciation is appearing in the trial balance of a company. While making final accounts, it should be shown in
(a) the profit and loss account
(b) the balance sheet as a deduction from the asset concerned
(c) the profit and loss account and balance sheet
(d) the profit and loss account or balance sheet

**86.** From the following find out the correct equation
I. A represents opening stock
II. B represents purchases
III. C represents closing stock
IV. D represents cost of goods sold
(a) A - C = D - B (b) A + B = D - C
(c) D - A = B + C (d) None of these

**87.** While assertaining profit in single entry system the amount of additional capital introduced is

(a) added to the capital in the beginning
(b) deducted from the capital in the beginning
(c) added to the capital at the end
(d) deducted from the capital at the end

**88.** When capital at the end is Rs. 21,500 drawings Rs. 4,300 and capital in the begining Rs.19,400, what is the amount of profit or loss?
(a) Rs. 2,200 (profit) (b) Rs. 2,200 (loss)
(c) Rs. 6,400 (profit) (d) Rs. 6,400 (loss)

**89.** Generally, under single entry system
(a) only personal accounts are maintained
(b) only personal, cash and bank accounts are maintained
(c) all accounts are maintained
(d) no account is maintained

**90.** Opening debtors Rs.12,000,closing debtors Rs.15,000 cash received from debtors Rs. 25,000 what is the amount for sales?
(a) Rs. 22,000 (b) Rs. 28,000
(c) Rs. 2,000 (d) None of these

**91.** If the rate of gross profit on sales is 25% and the cost of goods sold is Rs. 75,000, then the amount of total sales will be
(a) Rs. 1,00,000
(b) Rs. 93,750
(c) Rs. 92,150
(d) Cannot be known

**92.** Total debtors account will be affected by
(a) Cash sales (b) Credit sales
(c) B/R closing balance (d) All of these

**93.** If the cost of goods sold is Rs. 1,20,000 and the rate of gross loss is 1/4 on sales,the amount of sales is
(a) Rs. 1,20,000 (b) Rs. 90,000
(c) Rs. 80,000 (d) Rs. 96,000

**94.** Cost of goods sold is Rs.1,00,000 rate of gross profit on sales is 20%. What is the amount of sales?
(a) Rs. 1,20,000 (b) Rs. 80,000
(c) Rs. 1,25,000 (d) None of these

**95.** The single entry system is defective because
I. only one account is maintained
II. the trial balance cannot be prepared
III. the net profit cannot be accurately calculated
IV. the possibility of fraud and misappropriation is great

*Select the correct answer from the following:*
(a) I, III and IV (b) I and II
(c) II, III and IV (d) I only

**96.** Assets in the beginning of the year Rs. 10,000, Assets at the end of the year Rs. 18,000 Drawing during the year Rs. 2,000. Therefore the profit is
(a) Rs. 6,000 (b) Rs. 8,000
(c) Rs. 10,000 (d) None of these

**97.** Depreciation, as the term is used in accounting, means
(a) physical deterioration of a fixed asset
(b) decline in the market value of an asset
(c) allocation of the cost of fixed asset over its useful life
(d) making a provision for the replacement of the fixed asset

**98.** The term depletion is used in relation to
(a) Fixed assets (b) Wasting assets
(c) Current assets (d) Intangible assets

**99.** Under the annuity method the amount of total depreciation is determined by
(a) deducting the scrap value from the cost of the asset
(b) deducting the amount of interest from the cost of the asset
(c) adding the cost of the assets and interest there on
(d) adding the cost of the assets and expected cost of maintenance

**100.** Which method of depreciation is suggested for coal mines?
(a) Dimishing balance
(b) Fixed instalment method
(c) Sum of years' digits method
(d) Depletion method

**101.** In which of the following methods, the asset account appears at its original cost through out its life?
(a) Annuity method
(b) Depreciation fund method
(c) Sum of years, digits method
(d) Machine hour rate method

**102.** The amount of depreciation provided in the sinking fund method when compared to annuity method is
(a) higher (b) lower
(c) equal (d) unpredictable

**103.** The cost of a machine having a span of life of 5 years is Rs. 1,00,000. It has a scrap value of Rs.10,000. The amount of depreciation under the sum of years, digit method will be
(a) Rs. 16,000 (b) Rs. 18,000
(c) Rs. 25,000 (d) Rs. 30,000

**104.** Stock as on January 5 – Rs. 27,000; purchases between Dec.31st and Jan. 5 – Rs. 700; cost of sales between Dec. 31st and Jan. 5 – Rs. 1,500 what was the stock on Dec.31
(a) Rs. 27,800 (b) Rs. 26,200
(c) Rs. 26,300 (d) Rs. 28,500

**105.** Which method of inventory valuation is most widely used in accounting ?
(a) Cost price
(b) Market price
(c) Cost or market price whichever is greater
(d) Cost or market price whichever is lower

**106.** A company may resort to "window dressing" by manipulating the data such as
I. inventory valuation
II. omission of liability for goods purchased
III. treating a short-term liability long-term debt
(d) recording in advance cash receipts applicable to next accounting period
(a) I, III and IV (b) II and IV
(c) I, II and III (d) I, II, III and IV

**107.** Match List I with List II and select the correct answer using the codes given below the list:

| List I | List II |
|---|---|
| I. Compensating errors | A. Not recording a business transaction |
| II. Errors of omission | B. Charging a Revenue item to capital |
| III. Errors of principle | C. Writing a debit item on the credit side and a credit item on the debit side of equal amount |
| IV. Errors of commission | D. Posting a correct amount to a wrong account |

*Codes:*
(a) I-C, II-A, III-D, IV-B
(b) I- B, II-A, III-D, IV-C
(c) I- C, II-A, III-B, IV-D
(d) I- B, II-A, III-C, IV-D

**Directions Q. 108-109 :** *These questions consist of two statements, Assertion (A) and Reason (R). You have to examine these two statements and select your answers to these items using the codes given below:-*

*Codes:*
(a) Both A and R are true, and R is the correct explanation of A
(b) Both A and R are true, but R is not a correct explanation of A
(c) A is true, but R is false
(d) A is false, but R is true

**108.** **Assertion (A)** : Amount realised on the disposal (sale of a discarded) machine of the factory should be treated as revenue receipt

**Reason (R)** : Sale proceeds are usually of revenue in nature

**109.** **Assertion (A)** : An accounting principle is that the relatively small item and values should be ignored from accounts

**Reason (R)** : The cost of the effort in the allocation of small items over a long period does not justify the benefit derived from this operation and the cost of such items is treated as expense for the period in which they are incurred

**110.** A second hand machinery was purchased for Rs.1,00,000 five years ago and was overhauled by carrying out some current repairs at a cost of Rs. 10,000. It has also an accumulated depreciation of Rs. 50,000. It has been disposed of in the beginning of the sixth year for Rs.60,000. Profit/loss on such disposal shall be

(a) Profit of Rs. 10,000
(b) Loss of Rs. 50,000
(c) Loss of Rs. 40,000
(d) No profit, no loss

**111.** Match List I with List II and select the correct answer using the codes given below the lists:

| List I | List II |
|---|---|
| I. Income measurement | A. Accrues to owner's equity |
| II. Expense recognition | B. Revenue recognition |
| III. Basis for realisation in accounting | C. Matching revenues |
| IV. Recognised revenue | D. Accounting period |

***Codes:***
(a) I-C, II-D, III-B, IV-A
(b) I-C, II-D, III-A, IV-B
(c) I-B, II-C, III-D, IV-A
(d) I-B, II-C, III-A, IV-D

**112.** Charging a period for the proportionate cost of an Intangible asset is termed as
(a) depreciation (b) diminution
(c) amortisation (d) expiration

**113.** Obsolescence means decline in the value due to
(a) Fall in the market price
(b) Physical wear and tear
(c) Innovations and inventions
(d) Efflux of time

**114.** Concept of conservatism refers to taking into account
(a) all profit
(b) only cash profit
(c) only profit realised
(d) profit realised and all possible losses

**115.** Which one of the following accounting standards is not mandatory in india?
(a) Fixed assets accounting and revenue recognition
(b) Inventory and depreciation accounting
(c) Non-monetary assets and fixed assets
(d) Monetary assets and depreciation accounting

**116.** If the total charge of depreciation and maintenance is considered,the method which would provide a unifrom charge is
(a) annuity method
(b) straight line method
(c) diminishing balance method
(d) insurance policy method

**117.** Which of the following expenditures are to be treated as revenue expenditure?
I. Interest paid on money borrowed during construction period
II. Cost of patent rights
III. Loss of uninsured stock due to fire
IV. Retirement gratuity paid to an employee

*Select the correct answer using the codes given below*

***Codes:***
(a) I, II and III (b) II, III, and IV
(c) III and IV (d) I and II

**118.** Payment of compensation to a worker, who has been discharged from service, is a
(a) Capital expenditure
(b) Revenue expenditure
(c) Deferred – revenue expenditure
(d) Non-business expenditure

**119.** Book-keeping is often confused with
(a) Algebra (b) Statistics
(c) Cashier (d) Accounting

**120.** If the operating expenses exceed gross profit, the excess is referred to as
(a) Operating income
(b) Operating loss
(c) Non-operating expenses
(d) Non-operating income

**121.** On using reducing balance method on an asset of Rs.20,000 at the rate of 10% per annum, depreciation of 3rd year will be
(a) Rs. 6,000 (b) Rs. 1,800
(c) Rs. 1,620 (d) Rs. 2,000

**122.** Rs.19,500 debited to building repairs on 31st Dec.1993 included Rs. 9,500 as the cost of building a small room for the watch man. A bill of Rs. 800 for colour wash of the whole building during the year was not received till 1993

Dec.The amount to be debited to profit and loss account would be

(a) Rs. 20,300 (b) Rs. 19,500
(c) Rs. 10,800 (d) Rs. 9,500

**123.** The term loan of Rs. 5,00,000 was received from IFCI. It was used as under

I. Rs. 2,00,000 was advanced to suppliers for capital-work-in-progress and
II. Rs. 3,00,000 was used for financing the working capital

*The interest payable would be treated*

(a) on both I and II as capital expenditure
(b) on I as capital expenditure and on II as revenue expenditure
(c) on I as deferred expenditure and on II as revenue expenditure
(d) on I as deferred revenue expenditure and on II as capital expenditure

**124.** Accounting is

(a) the art of recording, classifying and summarising in a significant manner and in terms of money, transactions and events which are, in part at best financial in character, and interpreting there of
(b) a systematic and regular record of events affecting a firm with a view to obtaining a clear financial picture
(c) preparation of various financial statements over a period of time of a firm to measure its performance in monetary terms
(d) nothing but book-keeping

**125.** Ayush started business on 1st April,1995 with a capital of Rs. 25,000 and a loan of Rs. 12,500. Total assets and liabilities at the end of 31st March, 1996 amounted to Rs .75,000 and Rs. 12,500 respectively. He invested a further capital of Rs. 12,500 during the year and withdrew Rs. 7,500 during the relevant financial, period. His closing capital and profits would be respectively

(a) Rs. 62,500 and Rs. 32,500
(b) Rs. 50,000 and Rs. 40,000
(c) Rs. 70,000 and Rs. 47,500
(d) Rs. 55,000 and Rs. 42,500

**126.** A person started business with a cash of Rs. 22,000 and stock of Rs. 3,000 on 1st January, 1996. During the year he made a profit of Rs. 6,000. His creditors were paid Rs. 4,500 for the office furniture supplied. He took goods worth Rs. 3,500 for his daugher's wedding on 30th June, 1996. The gross assets of his business on 31st December, 1996 was

(a) Rs. 27,500 (b) Rs. 26,500
(c) Rs. 23,500 (d) Rs. 20,500

**127.** In stock valuation, appilcation of the principle 'at cost price or market price whichever is lower' will result in the valuation of stock sometimes at cost price and at other times at market price. This is an application of the principle of

(a) Consistency (b) Materiality
(c) Conservatism (d) Disclosure

**128.** Match List I with List II and select the correct answer using the codes given below the lists:

| List I | List II |
|---|---|
| I. Heavy amount of premium on redemption of preference shares | A. Capital expenditure |
| II. Excess of sale proceeds fixed assets over their original cost | B. Deferred revenue expenditure |
| III. Cost of installation of an old machine | C. Capital gain |
| IV. Freight paid on purchase of raw material | D. Revenue of expenditure |

***Codes:***

(a) I-B, II-C, III-D, IV-A
(b) I-C, II-B, III-D, IV-A
(c) I-B, II-C, III-A, IV-D
(d) I-C, II-B, III-A, IV-D

**129.** Amount spent on an advertisement campaign, the benefit of which is likely to last for three years is a

(a) Capital expenditure
(b) Revenue expenditure
(c) Deferred revenue expenditure
(d) Contingent expenditure

**130.** Match List I with List II and select the correct answer using the codes given below the lists:

| List I | List II |
|---|---|
| I. Preliminary expense | A. Capital expenditure |
| II. Travelling expenses of the salesman | B. Revenue expenditure |
| III. Profit on sale of a part of the business building | C. Capital gain |
| IV. Nazrana paid on the purchase of land for business | D. Deferred revenue |

***Codes:***

(a) I-D, II-B, III-C, IV-A
(b) I-D, II-B, III-A, IV-C
(c) I-B, II-D, III-C, IV-A
(d) I-B, II-D, III-A, IV-C

**131.** Revenue is generally recognised as being earned at that point of time when
(a) Sale is effected
(b) Cash is received
(c) Production is completed
(d) Debts are collected

**132.** Which one of the following will be treated as revenue expenditure?
(a) Cost incurred for a new exit as required under the local bodies, by laws
(b) Interest paid on loan during the construction of works
(c) Cost of pulling down on old building as also the payment made to the architect for the plan of a new building
(d) A dealer in purchases sewing machines and spends some money on the repair of the machines damaged while goods in transit

**133.** Which one of the following is capital expenditure?
(a) Cost of advertisement
(b) Purchase of a delivery van
(c) Purchase of raw material
(d) Purchase of machine oil

**134.** Which one of the following depreciation methods is most suitable for a coal mine?
(a) Diminishing balance method
(b) Depletion method
(c) Fixed instalment method
(d) Sum of year's digits method

**135.** In the case of a sole proprietorship, Assets in Balancesheet items are conveniently shown in
(a) Order of fixity
(b) Order of liquidity
(c) Alphabetical order
(d) Order of dates of acquisition

**136.** A business concern provides the following details

| | |
|---|---|
| Cost of goods sold | ............Rs.1,50,000 |
| Sales | ............Rs.2,00,000 |
| Opening stock | ..............Rs. 60,000 |
| Closing stock | ..............Rs. 40,000 |
| Debtors | ...............Rs.45,000 |
| Creditors | ...............Rs.50,000 |

*The concerns, purchses would amount to(in Rs.)*
(a) 1,30,000 (b) 2,20,000
(c) 2,60,000 (d) 2,90,000

**137.** The following figures (all in Rs.) relate to non trading concern:

| | |
|---|---|
| 1st January , 1995 stock of medicines | 5,000 |
| 1st January ,1995 outstanding creditors for medicines | 3,000 |
| Amount paid for medicines during the years | 15,000 |
| Value of medicines spoiled during the year stock of medicines | 400 |
| On 31st December,1995 | 3,500 |

*The amount to be debited to income and expenditure account would be*
(a) Rs.15,000 (b) Rs.18,500
(c) Rs.18,000 (d) Rs.13,500

**138.** Which one of the following statements is correct?
(a) Depreciation is not the process of valuation of asset–it is a process of allocation of cost of asset to the period of its economic life
(b) If the cost of machinery is more than the book value, then depreciation need not be provided
(c) When the plant and machinery and maintained in good condition, through repairs and renewals, depreciation need not be provided

(d) In the absence of any legal provisions, if the auditor finds that provision made for depreciation is inadequate, then he is not repuired to refer to it in his report

**139.** Which of the following items should be entered in the receipts and payments account of a club?

I. Sale of old newspapers
II. Loss on sale of some asset
III. Payments for investment

*Select the correct answer using the codes given below*

***Codes:***

(a) I, II and III (b) I and III
(c) I and II (d) II and III

**140.** A cultural club discloses that subscriptions received during a particular accounting period as per receipts and payments account amount to Rs. 57,360. Subscription outstanding (opening and closing) was Rs. 4,800 and Rs. 6,000 respectively. Subscription received in advance (opening balance and closing balance) amounted to Rs. 3,600 and Rs. 2,160 respectively. The amount to be posted to income and expenditure account would be

(a) Rs. 57,360 (b) Rs. 54,000
(c) Rs. 60,000 (d) Rs. 63,360

**Directions Q.141-144 :** *These questions consist of two statements, Assertion (A) and Reason (R). You have to examine these two statements and select your answers to these items using the codes given below:-*

***Codes:***

(a) Both A and R are true, and R is the correct explanation of A
(b) Both A and R are true,but R is NOT a correct explanation of A
(c) A is true,but R is false
(d) A is false, but R is true

**141. Assertion (A) :** In accounting, a distinction is made between the business and the owner

**Reason (R) :** Accounting concepts are based on adjectivity and not on subjectivity

**142. Assertion (A) :** Materiality concept refers to the state of ignoring relatively small items and values from accounts

**Reason (R) :** The effort involved in allocating the cost of a small item over a long period should be justified in terms of the benefit derived from this operation. Therefore cost of such items may be treated as expenses for the period in which they are acquired

**143. Assertion (A) :** The balance sheet fails to reveal the worth of a business

**Reason (R) :** Assets are merel unamortised costs

**144. Assertion (A) :** The cost of demolishing an old building preparatory to the construction of a new building in that place is to be treated as capital expenditure

**Reason (R) :** Such cost is not incidental to the construction of the new building

**145.** The fundamental accounting equation, Assets = Equities + liabilities is the formal expression of

(a) dual aspect concept
(b) matching concept
(c) going – concern concept
(d) money measurement concept

**146.** A business is considered to be having and indefinite life according to

(a) accounting period concept
(b) cost concept
(c) going concern concept
(d) dual aspect concept

**147.** Which of the following pairs are correctly matched

I. Business entity – Accounting standard
II. Stock valuation – Consistency
III. Capital – Drawings
IV. Going concern – Assumption

*Select the correct answer using the codes given below*

***Codes:***

(a) I, III and IV (b) I, II and III

(c) I, II and IV (d) I, III and IV

**148.** Money measurement concept of accounting theory is based on the assumption that the value of money will

(a) remain constant (b) fluctuate

(c) decrease (d) go up

**149.** Match List I (Items of expenditure and receipt) with List II (Nature of expenditure and receipt) and select the correct answer using the codes given below the lists :

| List I | List II |
|---|---|
| I. Premium paid for a lease hold property | A. Revenue experditure |
| II. Insurance premium paid for risks against accidental losses of properties (fixed assets) | B. Capital receipt |
| III. Amount realised from the sale of securities (investment) \purchased earlier | C. Deferred revenue expenditure |
| IV. Huge sales promotion expenses | D. Capital expenditure |

***Codes:***

(a) I-D, II-B, III-A, IV-C

(b) I-C, II-B, III-A, IV-D

(c) I-D, II-A, III-B, IV-C

(d) I-C, II-A, III-B, IV-D

**150.** Match List I (Items of expenditure and receipt) with List II (Nature of expenditure and receipt) and select the correct answer using the codes given below the lists:

| List I | List II |
|---|---|
| I. Compensation paid to retrenched workers of the factory for the loss of service | A. Capital expenditure |
| II. Legal expenses incurred in connection with the purchase of a plot of land | B. Capital receipt |
| III. Compensation received from the government for the compulsory removal of a business premises to another place | C. Revenue expenditure |
| IV. Sale proceeds of merchandise (goods) | D. Revenue receipt |

***Codes:***

(a) I-A, II-C, III-D, IV-B

(b) I-A, II-C, III-B, IV-D

(c) I-C, II-A, III-D, IV-B

(d) I-C, II-A, III-B, IV-D

**151.** The cash price of a machine is Rs. 1,20,000 and its hire purchase price is Rs. 1,50,000 to be paid in five equal yearly instalments. If a company purchases the machine on hire purchase basis, the amount of capital expenditure will be

(a) Rs.1,20,000 (b) Rs.1,35,000

(c) Rs.1,50,000 (d) Rs.1,60,000

**152.** Which one of the following is a capital expenditure

(a) Compensation paid to directors on termination of their services

(b) Expenditure incurred in connection with the renewal of a Trade Mark

(c) Gratuities paid to employees on their retirement

(d) Royalty paid in instalments for the purchase of rights to manufacture and sell patient medicines

**153.** The following information pertains to a cultural club :

Stock of tinned provisions : Rs. 25,000 (as on 1.4.94 )

Purchased during the year: Rs. 1,50,000

Stock of tinned provisions : Rs. 50,000 (as on 31.3.95 )

Sale of tinned provisions : Rs. 1,50,000 during the year

*The amounts to be debited and credited respectively to the Income and Expenditure account would be*

(a) Rs. 1,75,000 and Rs. 1,50,000
(b) Rs. 1,25,000 and Rs. 1,75,000
(c) Rs. 1,25,000 and Rs. 1,50,000
(d) Rs. 1,75,000 and Rs. 1,25,000

**154.** A cricket club has 50 members and each member pays Rs. 200 as monthly subscription 5 members paid advance subscription for the financial year 1994–95 and 10 members failed to pay subscription for the year 1993–94. The amount to be credited as subscription to income and expenditure account would be

(a) Rs. 12,000 (b) Rs. 10,000
(c) Rs. 9,600 (d) Rs. 8,000

**155.** The following information is provided by a cultural club :

| | |
|---|---|
| Stock of sports goods | : Rs.20,000 |
| Purchase of sports goods during the accounting period | : Rs. 80,000 |
| Sports goods sold as scrap | : Rs. 500 |
| Closing balance | : Rs.30,000 |

*The amount to be charged to Income and Expenditure Accounts as sports goods consumed will be*

(a) Rs. 69,500 (b) Rs. 70,000
(c) Rs. 70,500 (d) Rs. 80,000

**156.** A trader maintains his books of accounts on Single Entry basis. His books of accounts show that his total purchases during the year were Rs. 90,000 of which he returned goods worth Rs. 10,000. His credit sales were Rs. 50,000 and cash sales were Rs. 80,000 of the total sales goods returned were Rs. 30,000. Closing stock is Rs. 12,000. He sells his goods at cost plus $33\frac{1}{3}$ %. His opening stock is.

(a) Rs. 12,000 (b) Rs. 10,000
(c) Rs. 8,000 (d) Rs. 7,000

**157.** A firm which keeps its books of accounts on single entry system has opening balance and closing balance of Bills Receivable as Rs. 9,000 and Rs.11,000 respectively. Bills collected during the financial period amount to Rs. 20,000. Bills receivable received during the financial period amount to

(a) Rs. 22,000 (b) Rs. 18,000
(c) Rs. 12,000 (d) Rs. 11,000

**158.** Which preparing accounts from incomplete records,the amount of credit sales is determined by

(a) preparing total creditors account
(b) preparing total debtors account
(c) ascertaining the balance in trading account other than closing stock
(d) ascretaining the balance in debtors account and cash book

**159.** An asset is purchased for Rs. 50,000 on which depreciation is to be provided annually according to the straight line method. The useful life to the asset is 10 years and the residual value is Rs. 10,000. The rate of depreciation is

(a) 20 % (b) 18 %
(c) 10 % (d) 8 %

**160.** An asset is never reduced to zero in the

(a) fixed instalment method
(b) reducing balance method
(c) annuity method
(d) sum of years method

**161.** The main objective of providing depreciation is to

(a) create secret reserves
(b) reduce the book value of assets
(c) value the assets properly
(d) allocate cost of the assets

**162.** Match List I (financial statements and accounts) with List II (special matters associated with statements and accounts) and select the correct answer using the codes given below the lists :

| List I | List II |
|---|---|
| I. Receipts and payments | A. Revenue account |
| II. Income and expenditure account | B. Cash |
| III. Dividend equalisation reserve | C. Liability |
| IV. Club subscription received in advance account | D. Balancesheet |
| | E. General reserve |

*Codes:*
(a) I-B, II-A, III-D, IV-C
(b) I-C, II-B, III-D, IV-E
(c) I-B, II-A, III-E, IV-C
(d) I-A, II-B, III-D, IV-E

**163.** Profit under single entry system of Book Keeping means
(a) the difference between opening and closing cash balances and reduced by fresh capital introduced
(b) the difference between opening net assets and closing net assets as increased by drawings and reduced by new capital introduced
(c) profit shown by Trading and Profit and Loss Account and Balance sheet
(d) the amount of closing cash balance as reduced by expenses

**164.** Given that

| | |
|---|---|
| Opening capital | : Rs. 5,000 |
| Closing capital | : Rs. 6,000 |
| Drawings | : Rs. 1,000 |
| New capital invested | : Rs. 500 |

the profit for the year will be
(a) Rs. 2,000 (b) Rs. 1,500
(c) Rs. 1,000 (d) Rs. 500

**165.** Which of the following are prepared by the organisations keeping only incomplete accounting records?
I. Cash book
II. Customer's Accounts
III. Expenses Accounts
IV. Day Books
*Choose the correct answer using the codes given below :*
*Codes:*
(a) I, II and III (b) I, II and IV
(c) I, III and IV (d) II, III and IV

**166.** Depreciation Accounting is a process of
(a) allocation of cost
(b) valuation of assets
(c) provision for replacement of assets
(d) estimation of net profit

**167.** Given that the value of furniture on 1.1.93 is Rs. 8,000, furniture purchased during the year is Rs. 4,000, sale of furniture no loss no profit basis is Rs. 2,000, and the furniture is valued at Rs. 7,000 on 31.12.93, the depreciation for the year 1993 will be
(a) Rs. 1,000 (b) Rs. 3,000
(c) Rs. 5,000 (d) Rs. 7,000

**168.** Which of the following are applicable to sinking fund method of depreciation?
I. Periodic depreciation is smaller than the assets, actual annual depreciable cost
II. Amount of interest constantly declines due to assets, reducing balances
III. Annual net incidence on profit and loss account remains constant due to incorporation of only fixed depreciation
IV. Periodic depreciation is recorded through the assets account
*Select the correect answer using the codes given below:*
*Codes:*
(a) II and IV (b) I and III
(c) I, II and III (d) II, III and IV

**169.** Match List I with List II and select the correct answer using the codes given below the lists :

| List I | List II |
|---|---|
| I. Amortisation | A. Diminition in the life of the assets due to excessive use |
| II. Depreciation | B. Exhaustion of natural resource |
| III. Depletion | C. Expiration of tangible assets |
| IV. Obsolescence | D. Expiration of intangible assets |
| | E. Economic deterioration due toimproved inventions |

*Codes:*
(a) I-A, II-B, III-C, IV-D
(b) I-A, II-B, III-D, IV-E
(c) I-E, II-B, III-C, IV-D
(d) I-D, II-C, III-B, IV-E

**170.** Match List I with List II and select the correct answer using the codes given below the lists :

| List I (Accounting concept) | List II (Principle involved) |
|---|---|
| I. Consistency | A. Losses are anticipated and accounted for in advance but profits are not accounted for until realised |
| II. Comparability | B. All the relevant financial informations should be summarised and presented in the accounting statements |
| III. Conservatism | C. Accounting procedures in an entity should be followed uniformly from period to period |
| IV. Disclosure | D. Accounting statement of different periods of an entity and those of different entities of a period should be based on the same accounting principles and procedures. |
| | E. Personal Judgement of accountants should not influence accounting measurements. |

*Codes:*
(a) I-D, II-C, III-E, IV-B
(b) I-C, II-D, III-A, IV-B
(c) I-D, II-C, III-A, IV-E
(d) I-C, II-D, III-B, IV-E

**171.** Which one of the following should be considered a revenue expenditure?
(a) Rs. 1,000 paid for the erection of a new plant
(b) Cost of Rs. 10,000 incurred in increasing the sitting accommodation of a hotel
(c) Damages paid on account of breach of a contract to supply certain goods
(d) Repairs to machinery purchased second hand

**172.** The written down value of a plant is 6,000 (the original value being Rs.10,000). It is sold for Rs. 12,000 during the current financial year. Which one of the following is true in this regard?
(a) Capital profit = Rs. 6,000
(b) Revenue profit = Rs. 6,000
(c) Capital profit = Rs. 2,000 and
(d) Revenue profit = Rs. 4,000
(e) Capital profit = Rs. 12,000

**173.** Match List I (Item of expenditure/receipt) with List II (Nature of expenditure/receipt)and select the correct answer using the codes given below the lists :

| List I | List II |
|---|---|
| I. Carriage charges on a new machine purchased for factory | A. Revenue receipt |
| II. Legal expenses incurred in defending a case of violation of a provision of Factories Act | B. Revenue expenditure |
| III. Grant-in-aid received from the Goverment for the construction of a building | C. Deferred revenue expenditure |
| IV. Amount received for a part of the office building sublet | D. Capital expenditure |
| | E. Capital receipt |

*Codes:*

(a) I-B, II-C, III-A, IV-E
(b) I-D, II-B, III-E, IV-A
(c) I-C, II-D, III-A, IV-E
(d) I-D, II-C, III-A, IV-E

**174.** While preparing the annual financial statements, the balance of rent account should be treated as the balance of a

(a) Personal Account
(b) Nominal Account
(c) Real Account
(d) Deferred Expenditure Account

**175.** What is the correct sequence of the preparation of the following accounts and statement of a non–profit organisation?

I. Income and expenditure account
II. Receipts and payment account
III. Balance sheet

*Select the correct answer from the codes given balow:*

*Codes:*

(a) I, II, III (b) I, III, II
(c) II, I, III (d) II, III, I

**176.** Profit as per accounts from incomplete records may constructed as equivalent of

(a) Excess of assets over liabilities at the close of the period
(b) Excess of capital at the end over the capital at the beginning
(c) Excess of assets over liabilities at the commencement of the period
(d) Excess of capital at the begining over the capital at the end

**177.** According to records of a firm which not keep its accounts on double entry systems, all sales were made on credit so as to realise a profit of $33\frac{1}{3}$ per cent on sales proceeds. The stock of unsold goods at the beginning and at the end of the trading period were valued at Rs. 21,000 and 18,000 respectively. Goods worth Rs. 1,39,500 were purchased for resale during the period

*The proprietor withdraw goods worth Rs. 1,500 during accounting period for personal use. What were the total sales during the period?*

(a) Rs. 1,80,000 (b) Rs. 2,11,500
(c) Rs. 2,25,000 (d) Rs. 2,31,500

**178.** Consider the following statement, while preparing annual financial statements,the balance of bills receivable account can be treated as

I. an accrued income
II. an item of assets
III. a "personal account" balance

*Of these statement*

(a) II and III are correct
(b) I and III are correct
(c) I and II are correct
(d) None of these

**179.** On January 1,1992 there was a balance of Rs. 4,000 in the plant and machinery account. An addition of Rs. 2,000 was made on July 1,1992. Accounts were closed for the year on December 31,1992. If depreciation was charged at 10% per annum, the balance in the plant and machinery account on the closing date would be

(a) Rs. 5,300 (b) Rs. 5,400
(c) Rs. 5,500 (d) Rs. 5,600

**180.** A machinery having a residual value of Rs. 5,000 was purchased on 1.1.1998 for Rs. 1,00,000 and was depreciated @ 9.5% on a straight line method. On 1.1.1998, it was estimated that its useful life has been reduced to eight years. Under the changed circum stances, the annual depreciation charges for the year 1991 and onwards will be

(a) Rs. 11,875 (b) Rs. 13,300
(c) Rs. 9,500 (d) Rs. 12,500

**181.** In which one of the following methods of charge depreciation shall be balance never be reduced to zero ?

(a) Fixed instalment method
(b) Depreciation fund method
(c) Diminishing balance method
(d) Depletion unit method

**182.** "Holding gains in relation to stocks should not be used for payment of dividend." Which one of the following accounting principles is involved in this?

(a) Consistency (b) Cost
(c) Materiality (d) Realisation

**183.** X started business with a capital of Rs. 20,000 and purchased goods worth Rs. 2,000 on credit. These transactions may be expressed in the from of 'Accounting equation' such as
(a) Rs. 22,000 = Rs. 20,000 + Rs. 2,000
(b) Rs. 20,000 = Rs. 22,000 – Rs. 2,000
(c) Rs. 22,000 = Rs. 22,000 + 0
(d) Rs. 22,000 = 0 + Rs. 22,000

**184.** Long-term liabilities are
(a) Fixed assets minus current assets
(b) Fixed assets minus current liabilities
(c) Current assets plus current liabilities
(d) Total liabilities minus current liabilities

**185.** A business entity has assets of Rs. 26,000 and liabilities of Rs. 6,000. Owner's equity in this case is
(a) Rs. 32,000 (b) Rs. 26,000
(c) Rs. 20,000 (d) Rs. 6,000

**186.** Accounting records transactions in terms of
(a) Commodity units
(b) Monetary units
(c) Production units
(d) None of these

**187.** Market price or actual cost, whichever is less, is the generally accepted accouting principle for valuation of
(a) Stock-in-trade (b) Fixed assets
(c) Current assets (d) All of these

**188.** Match List I with List II and select the correct answer using the codes given below the lists :

| **List I** (Types of accounts) | **List II** (Principles) |
|---|---|
| I. Real Accounts | A. Debit the receiver credit the giver |
| II. Nominal Accounts | B. Debit what comes in credit what goes out |
| III. Personal Accounts | C. Debit all expenses credit all gains |

*Codes:*
(a) I-C, II-B, III-A (b) I-A, II-C, III-B
(c) I-B, II-C, III-A (d) I-A, II-B, III-C

**189.** Renewal fee for patents is a
(a) Capital expenditure
(b) Revenue expenditure
(c) Deferred reveue expenditure
(d) Development expenditure

**190.** A manufacturing company spent the following amounts on the import and installation of machine
(a) Rs. 50,000 : Price of the machine
(b) Rs. 5,000 : Freight
(c) Rs. 1,050 : Insurance premium
(d) Rs. 6,000 : Replacement of a part damaged intransit, not covered under the insurance policy

*Based on the above data, capital expenditure would be*
(a) Rs. 50,000 (b) Rs. 56,050
(c) Rs. 62,050 (d) Rs. 51,050

**191.** If trial a balance does not tally inspite of through scruting and the diffrence is substantial, then which one of the following courses would be accountant adopt?
(a) Defer preparation of financial statements
(b) Open suspense A/C
(c) Write off the difference to profit and loss A/C
(d) Ignore the difference and prepare financial statements

**192.** Given, subscription received in 1990
For the year 1989 – Rs. 500
For the year 1990 – Rs. 7,000
For the year 1991 – Rs. 400
1990 – subscription outstanding on 31st December, 1990 : Rs. 250
*The amount of subscription to be posted to income and expenditure account of 1990 is*
(a) Rs. 7,000 (b) Rs. 7,250
(c) Rs. 7,900 (d) Rs. 8,150

**193. Assertion (A) :** The matching concept requires that costs should be recognised as expenses in the period in which revenue is realised

**Reason (R) :** There may not be a matching between expenditure and expense over a short period

*In the context given above, which one of the following is correct ?*

(a) Both A and R are true, and R is the correct explanation of A
(b) Both A and R are true, but R is not a correct explanation of A
(c) A is true, but R is false
(d) A is False,but R is true

**194.** In financial statements, adequate disclosure is ensured by companies as per the requirements of

I. management policies
II. materiality concept
III. disclosure concept
IV. relevant provision of the companies Act
V. internal control

*Of these a statements:*

(a) I and III are correct
(b) I, II and III are correct
(c) II, III and V are correct
(d) II, III and IV are correct

**195.** The proprietor of a business is treated as a creditor for capital introduced by him according to

(a) money measurement concept
(b) cost concept
(c) business entity concept
(d) dual aspect concept

**196.** Which one of the following statements is correct?

(a) Capital of a firm is reduced by borrowing
(b) When there is no change in proprietor's capital it is an indication of loss in business
(c) Nominal accounts refer to false transactions
(d) Real accounts relate to assets of a business

**197.** Trade discount allowed on sales is

(a) debited to customer's account
(b) credited to customer's account
(c) debited to profit and loss account
(d) None of these

**198.** Accounting principles represent

(a) a consensus at a particular time to the recording of accounting transactions
(b) inviolable laws fixed by the legal boards
(c) laws fixed by accounting experts
(d) laws fixed by the respective governments

**199.** How does an over costing of purchase day book affect the cost of sales and profit?

(a) Cost of sales is decreased while profit is increased
(b) Cost of sales is increased while profit is decreased
(c) Both cost of sales and profit are increased
(d) Cost of sales is increased, gross profit is decreased,but net profit remains unaffected

**200.** Consistency with reference to application of accounting principles refers to the fact that

(a) Companies in the same industry use identical accounting procedures and methods, and are consistent
(b) Income and assets have not been over stated
(c) Accounting methods and procedures used have been consistently applied from year to year
(d) All methods and procedures have been utilised

**201.** What is the correct sequence of the following in the preparation of periodical financial statements?

I. preparation of Balancesheet
II. preparation of Funds flow statement
III. preparation of Trial balance
IV. preparation of Profit/Loss statement

*Select the correct answer from the codes given below and mark your answer sheet accordingly*

***Codes:***

(a) IV, II, I, III (b) III, IV, I, II
(c) II, IV, III, I (d) I, III, II, IV

**202.** Depreciation is

(a) A source of fund
(b) A use of fund
(c) Neither a source nor a use of fund
(d) Partly a source and partly an application of fund

**203.** The following are the figures relating to a trader

Opening stock – Rs. 10,000
Closing stock – Rs. 11,000
Purchse – Rs. 70,000

*The goods are sold at a profit of 30% on cost. The amount of sales will be*

(a) Rs. 1,04,000 (b) Rs. 91,000
(c) Rs. 89,700 (d) Rs. 21,000

**204.** Subscriptions amounting to Rs. 7,500 appear on the credit side of income and expenditure account after adjusting subscriptions out standing Rs. 600 and subscriptions received in advance Rs. 450. The amount of subscriptions to be shown in the receipts and payments account for the same year will be

(a) Rs. 6,450 (b) Rs. 7,350
(c) Rs. 7,650 (d) Rs. 8,550

**205.** Which of the following item/items will be included in income and expenditure account?

I. Accrued expenses
II. Credit purchases
III. Prepaid expenses
IV. Opening cash balance

*Select the correct answer from the codes given below and mark your answer sheet accordingly*

***Codes :***

(a) I (b) I and II
(c) II and III (d) III and IV

**206.** If

| | | |
|---|---|---|
| Capital at the end | = | Rs. 7,000 |
| Capital introduced | = | Rs. 5,000 |
| Drawings | = | Rs. 8,000 |
| Loss | = | Rs.10,000 |

*Then capital in the beginning is equal to*

(a) Rs. 12,000 (b) Rs. 16,000
(c) Rs. 20,000 (d) Rs. 30,000

**207.** Company accounting conforms more to dual aspect concept than to incomplete recording system because

I. companies Act insists upon the adoption of double entry systems of book keeping
II. balance sheet could not be preprared under sec. 211of company's Act according to the incomplete recording system
III. to show true and fair view of the affairs of the company
IV. to ensure adequate disclosure

*Select the correct answer from the codes given below and mark your answer sheet accordingly:*

***Codes :***

(a) I and II (b) II and III
(c) II, III and IV (d) I, II and III

**208.** The purpose of depreciation is to

(a) reduce fixed assets to market value each year
(b) save income tax and wealth tax
(c) reduce fixed assets to nil as soon as possible assets top expense over their working lives
(d) allocate the cost of fixed

**209.** The amount of depreciation under straight line method vis-a-vis written down value method, when the rate of depreciation is same,would be

(a) equal in all years
(b) equal in the first year but higher is subsequent years
(c) equal in the first year but lower in subsequent years
(d) lower in the first year but equal in subsequent years

**210.** If on January 1,1983 a plant is purchased for Rs. 1,20,000, its estimated life is ten years and its salvage value is Rs. 10,000 under which one of the following method would the 1983 depreciation be the largest?

(a) Straight line method
(b) Double-declining balance method
(c) Sum of the year's digits method
(d) 15% on original cost

**211.** Accumulated depreciation account is shown in the final accounts

(a) on the liability side of the balance sheet
(b) on the debit side of the profit and loss account
(c) by deducting from the related asset account in the balance sheet
(d) on the credit side of the profit and loss account

**212.** A particular firm provided the following data for an accounting year

Current ratio.......................... 2.5 :1
Liquid ratio........................... 1.5 :1
Net working capital............... Rs. 6,00,000

*Current assets and current liabilities of the firm are, respectively,*

(a) Rs. 9,00,000 and Rs. 3,00,000
(b) Rs. 10,00,000 and Rs. 4,00,000
(c) Rs. 8,50,000 and Rs. 2,50,000
(d) Rs. 7,50,000 and Rs. 1,50,000

**213.** When shares are forfeited, the share capital account is debited by
(a) Paid-up amount
(b) Called-up amount
(c) Nominal value of the shares
(d) Market value of the shares

**214.** When one of the following reflects the over all efficiency with which capital is used?
(a) Return on shareholders funds
(b) Investment turnover ratio
(c) Earning per share
(d) Operating ratio

**215.** A company pays dividend out of
(a) Profits of the company for year for which dividends are to be paid
(b) Undistributed profit of the previous financial years
(c) Money provided by the central and state governments for the payment of dividends in pursuance of their guaranters
(d) All of these

**216.** A limited company has to redeem redeemable preference shares of the value of Rs. 1,00,000 for which the company has issuerd 3000 equity shares of Rs.10 each at a premium of 10 %. The amount to be transferred to capital redemption reserve account will be
(a) Rs. 1,00,000 (b) Rs. 97,000
(c) Rs. 70,000 (d) Rs. 67,000

**217.** To test the liquidity of a concern, which of the following ratios are useful?
I. Acid test ratio
II. Capital turnover ratio
III. Bad debts to sales ratio
IV. Inventory turnover ratio
*Select the correct answer using the codes given below:*
(a) I and III (b) I and IV
(c) II and IV (d) II and III

**218.** The following figures are taken from a balance sheet :

| | (Rs.) |
|---|---|
| Equity share capital................ | 1,10,000 |
| 6% preference share capital... | 30,000 |
| General reserve.................... | 50,000 |
| Reserve for contingencies...... | 20,000 |
| 6% mortgage debentures...... | 50,000 |
| Sundry creditors................. | 20,000 |
| Preliminary expenses............ | 5,000 |
| Prepaid expenses................. | 4,000 |

*In this case, the debt equity ratio is*
(a) 1 : 2 (b) 2 : 1
(c) 24 : 1 (d) None of these

**219.** Who among the following is a bear operator
(a) A stock broker who sells shares now and buys the same shares later
(b) An investor who expects the price of a security or that of the whole securities market to rise
(c) An investor who sells securities anticipation of being able to repurchase them later at a lower price
(d) A broker who indulges in rigging of share prices

**220.** Match List I with List II and select the correct answer using the codes given below the lists:

| List I | List II |
|---|---|
| I. Financial leverage | A. Efficiency |
| II. Quick ratio | B. Profitability |
| III. Stock turnover | C. Liquidity |
| IV. Margin on sales | D. Risk |

*Codes:*
(a) I-D, II-C, III-A, IV-B
(b) I-A, II-B, III-D, IV-C
(c) I-D, II-B, III-A, IV-C
(d) I-A, II-C, III-D, IV-B

**221.** In a partnership business if there is no specific agreement among partners, profit is distributed in the
(a) ratio of capital contributions
(b) ratio of time spent in the business
(c) ratio to be decided by the court
(d) equal ratio

**222.** Consider the following statements
I. In case of the marine insurance, the insurable interest must exist at the time the loss occurs
II. In case of fire insurance, insurable interest must exist both at the time of the contract and at the time of loss

*Which of the statements given above is/are correct ?*

(a) I only (b) II only
(c) Both I and II (d) Neither I nor II

**223.** Consider the following statements :

I. Workmen's compensation and third party insurance are examples of guarantee insurance

II. Re-insurance is more common under fire and marine insurance

*Which of the statements given above is/are correct ?*

(a) I only (b) II only
(c) Both I and II (d) Neither I nor II

**224.** The dividend pershare in a company is Rs. 2, earning per share is Rs. 5, and the market value is Rs. 25. What will be its yield?

(a) 20 per cent (b) 12.5 per cent
(c) 8 per cent (d) 25 per cent

**225.** When an incoming partner purchases his share from any one of the existing partners,then

(a) total assets of the firm do not change
(b) total assets of the firm will be augmented to the extent of payment received from the new partner
(c) total assets of the firm will be reduced to the extent of payment received from the new partner
(d) change in total assets of the firm will depend upon the new profit sharing ratio of the partners

**226.** If the good will raised at the time of retirement of a partner is to be written off, then the capital accounts of the remaining partners are debited in

(a) New profit sharing ratio
(b) Capital ratio
(c) Old profit sharing ratio
(d) Sacrificing ratio

**227.** Match List I with List II and select the correct answer using the codes given below the Lists :

| List I | List II |
|---|---|
| I. Partner's current accounts | A. Dissolution of partnership |
| II. Goodwill account | B. Admission of a partner |
| III. Partner's drawings account | C. Fixed capital of partners |
| IV. Realisation account | D. Goods taken by a partner for self-consumption |

***Codes:***

(a) I-A, II-D, III-B, IV-C
(b) I-C, II-B, III-D, IV-A
(c) I-A, II-B, III-D, IV-C
(d) I-C, II-D, III-B, IV-A

**228.** Which one of the following securities cannot be issued by a public limited company in India?

(a) Participating preference shares
(b) Redeemable preference shares
(c) Deferred shares
(d) Debentures

**229.** Match List I with List II and select the correct answer using the codes given below the lists :

| List I | List II |
|---|---|
| I. Receipts and payments account | A. Revenue |
| II. Income and expenditure account | B. Cash |
| III. Dividend equalization reserve | C. Liability |
| IV. Subscription received in advance account | D. General reserve |

***Codes:***

(a) I-B, II-A, III-D, IV-C
(b) I-C, II-D, III-A, IV-B
(c) I-B, II-D, III-A, IV-C
(d) I-C, II-A, III-D, IV-B

**230.** Which one of the following is not a valid observation with reference to the declaration or payment of dividend for any financial year?

(a) Depreciation for the current financial year must be provided
(b) Arrears of depreciation must be provided
(c) Losses incurred in previous year (s) must be set off
(d) 10% of the profit must be transferred to the reserves in all cases

*Codes:*
(a) I-B, II-A, III-D, IV-B
(b) I-C, II-D, III-A, IV-B
(c) I-B, II-D, III-A, IV-C
(d) I-C, II-A, III-D, IV-B

**231.** Which of the following amounts shall be credited to Investor Education and protection Fund, if they remain unpaid/unclaimed for seven years from the date they become due?
(a) Matured debentures of a company
(b) Tax arrears
(c) Proceeds of sale of property
(d) Provision for doubtful debts

**232.** Match List I with List II and select the correct answer using the codes given below the lists :

| | List I | | List II |
|---|---|---|---|
| I. | Uncertain liability | A. | Amortisation |
| II. | Expiry of tangible asset | B. | Long term liability |
| III. | Basis for all valuations in the balancesheet | C. | Research and development |
| IV. | Accounting standard-As-8 | D. | Estimated obligation |
| | | E. | Conservatism convention |

*Codes:*
(a) I-E, II-A, III-B, IV-C
(b) I-D, II-C, III-E, IV-A
(c) I-E, II-C, III-D, IV-A
(d) I-D, II-A, III-E, IV-C

**233.** Consistency with reference to application of accounting principles refer to the fact that
(a) Companies in the same industry use identical accounting procedures and methods
(b) Income and assets have not been over stated
(c) Accounting methods and procedures used have been consistently applied from year to year
(d) All the methods and procedures have been utilised

**234.** A company purchased the following assets and paid through 1,00,000 fully paid equity shares of Rs. 10 at a premium of Rs. 2 :
Building________ Rs.5,00,000
Machinery________ Rs.4,00,000
Stock in trade ________ Rs.1,00,000
*In the context of funds flow statement,this transaction will result in*
(a) Funds in flow of Rs. ________10,00,000
(b) Funds in flow of Rs. ________12,00,000
(c) Funds in flow of Rs. ________ 1,00,000
(d) Funds in flow of Rs. ________ 9,00,000

**235.** Call option is
(a) a contract to buy a certain number of shares at a stated price within a specified period of time
(b) a contract to sell a certain number of shares at a stated price within a specified period of time
(c) the option of the issuing company to demand the shareholders to pay for the partly paid shares
(d) the option available to the convertible debenture holders to demand equity shares in conversion of debentures.

**Directions : (Q. 236-238)** *The questions consist of two statements, one labelled as (Assertion (A) and the other labelled as 'Reason (R)'. You are to examine these two statements carefully and select the answers to these items using the codes.*

**236. Assertion (A)** : Holding company is a partial consolidation
**Reason (R)** : If company C is the subsidiary of B, and B is a subsidiary of A, then C will be deemed to be a subsidiary of A through the medium of B

*Codes :*
(a) Both A and R are true, and R is the correct explanation of A
(b) Both A and R are true, but R is not a correct explanation of A
(c) A is true,but R is false
(d) A is false, but R is true

**237. Assertion (A) :** While preparing trading and profit and loss A/C and balancesheet, the adjustments given out side the trial balance are to be shown in final accounts at two places, if treated directly

**Reason (R)** : Adjustment are to be made to comply with the matching principle

*Codes:*

(a) Both A and R are true, and R is the correct explanation of A
(b) Both A and R are true, but R is not a correct explanation of A
(c) A is true, but R is false
(d) A is false, but R is true

**238. Assertion (A) :** Current ratio shows the ability of the firm to meet its short term obligations

**Reason (R)** : Current ratio is also used in inventory valuation

*Codes:*

(a) Both A and R are true, and R is the correct explanation of A
(b) Both A and R are true, but R is not a correct explanation of A
(c) A is true, but R is false
(d) A is false, but R is true

**239.** Making the provision for bad and doubtful debts in anticipation of actual bad debts is on basis of

(a) Convention of disclosure
(b) Convention of consistency
(c) Convention of conservatism
(d) Conventions of disclosures and consistency

**240.** Following data appear in the books of XY & Co.as on 31- 03 - 03

Capital account...................Rs. 13,00,000
Drawings account...............Rs. 12,000
Land & building account.... Rs. 10,00,000
Goodwill account...............Rs. 3,50,000
Suspense account (Dr)........ Rs. 50,000
Loss by theft account......... Rs. 20,000
Business loss......................Rs.50,000
Loan given to AB & Co..... Rs. 60,000

*What will be the amount of sundry creditors?*

(a) Rs. 2,30,000 (b) Rs. 1,72,000
(c) Rs. 3,42,000 (d) Rs. 2,42,000

**241.** Under the accrual concept, which one of the following will not be shown as an asset/liability in the balancesheet of an entity?

(a) Interest due but not paid
(b) Interest due but not received
(c) Interest due and paid
(d) Interest paid but not due

**242.** A Company purchased 8% bonds at a cost of Rs.12,00,000 (face value Rs.10,00,000) on January 1,2003. Half yearly interest is payable on this investment on June 30 and December 31st each year. The company closes its accounts on 31-3-2003. The amount of accured interest shown in profit and loss account for the year ended is

(a) Rs. 40,000 (b) Rs. 60,000
(c) Rs. 20,000 (d) Rs. 80,000

**243.** Goods worth Rs. 24,000 were returned by X. The accountant, however, credited the sales returns account by Rs. 42,000. Inorder to rectify this error, what should be done?

(a) Debit the sales return account by Rs. 42,000
(b) Credit the sales return account by Rs. 24,000
(c) Debit the sales return account by Rs. 66,000
(b) Debit the sales return account by Rs. 18,000

**244.** A machine with a written down value of Rs. 10,000 has been sold for Rs. 13,000. The amount realized is a

(a) Capital receipt and profit involved should be transferred to capital reserve
(b) Revenue receipt
(c) Capital receipt and profit involved should be transferred to General Reserve
(d) Capital receipt and profit involved should be transferred to profit and loss A/C

**245.** Rs.10,000 spent on the replacement of worn-out parts of an electronic machinery is treated as

(a) Capital expenditure
(b) Revenue expenditure
(c) Deferred revenue expenditure
(d) Capital loss

**246.** Preliminary expenses are an example of

(a) Revenue expenditure
(b) Capital expenditure
(c) Deferred revenue expenditure
(d) All of these

**247.** Which of the following is/are capitalised along with the purchase price a fixed asset?
I. Import duty
II. Delivery and handling cost
III. Cash discount
IV. Cost of installation
*Select the correct answer using the codes given below:*
(a) III only (b) II and III
(c) I, II and IV (d) I, II, III and IV

**248.** Match List I (Items) with List II (Standards) and select the correct answer using the codes given below the lists:

| List I (Items) | List II (Standards) |
|---|---|
| I. Accounting for fixed assets | A. AS-9 assets |
| II. Revenue recognition | B. AS-10 |
| III. Depreciation accounting | C. AS-3 |
| IV. Cash flow statement | D. AS-6 |

*Codes:*
(a) I-B, II-C, III-D, IV-A
(b) I-D, II-A, III-B, IV-C
(c) I-B, II-A, III-D, IV-C
(d) I-D, II-C, III-B, IV-A

**249.** Accounting standard-AS-2 provides that inventories should be valued at
(a) lower of historical cost and net realisable value
(b) lower of historical cost and market value
(c) only estimated selling price
(d) All of these

*ABC company purchased cassettes during three months as follows:*

| Months (2003) | Quantity | Amount (Rs.) |
|---|---|---|
| January | 200 | 20,000 |
| February | 1000 | 60,000 |
| March | 800 | 96,000 |

*The company sold 1600 cassettes at Rs. 100 each. What will be the value of closing stock if the cost flow assumption of weighted average method is followed?*
(a) Rs. 23,500 (b) Rs. 35,200
(c) Rs. 37,500 (d) Rs. 36,200

**250.** While making an adjustment entry in respect of interest on capital, credit is made to
(a) Capital account
(b) Interest on capital account
(c) Profit & loss account
(d) Interest account

**251.** Given the following data extracted from the book of Abdul traders :

| | (Rs.) |
|---|---|
| Opening stock.................... | 30,000 |
| Closing stock.................... | 40,000 |
| Purchases.......................... | 1,25,000 |
| Carriage inwards................ | 2,000 |
| Carriage outwards.............. | 3,000 |
| Return outwards................. | 5,000 |
| Sales.................................. | 1,50,000 |

*The cost of goods sold will be*
(a) Rs. 1,30,000 (b) Rs. 1,12,000
(c) Rs. 1,20,000 (d) Rs. 1,15,000

**252.** Consider the following statements :
A credit purchase during the accounting year which was not recorded in the books of account but included in the closing stock is to be
I. added to the credit purchases account
II. added to the creditors account
III. subtracted from the closing stock
IV. added to the opening stock
*Which of the statements given above is/are correct?*
(a) III only (b) I and II
(c) II and III (d) II, III and IV

**253.** Match List I (Items) with List II (Headings) and select the correct answer using the codes given below the lists:

| List I (Items) | List II (Headings) |
|---|---|
| I. Provision for income tax | A. Miscellaneous expenses not written off |
| II. Share premium | B. Current liabilities |
| III. Unclaimed dividend | C. Reserves and surplus |
| IV. Discount issue of shares | D. Profit and loss account |

*Codes:*
(a) I-D, II-C, III-B, IV-A
(b) I-B, II-C, III-D, IV-A
(c) I-D, II-A, III-B, IV-C
(d) I-B, II-A, III-D, IV-C

**254.** Match List I (Items of balance sheet) with List II (Head in the balance sheet) and select the correct answer using the codes given below the lists:

| List I (Items of balancesheet) | List II (Head in the balancesheet) |
|---|---|
| I. Govt. securities | A. Current liabilities |
| II. Stock in trade | B. Provisions |
| III. Unclaimed dividend | C. Liquid assets |
| IV. Proposed dividend | D. Current assets |

*Codes:*
(a) I-C, II-A, III-D, IV-B
(b) I-B, II-D, III-A, IV-C
(c) I-C, II-D, III-A, IV-B
(d) I-B, II-A, III-D, IV-C

**255.** Secret reserves are created by means of
(a) transfer to general reserve
(b) providing excessive depreciation
(c) over valuation of inventories
(d) under valuation of liabilities

**256.** Match List I with List II and select the correct answer using the codes given below the lists:

| List I | List II |
|---|---|
| I. Inventory of material | A. Shareholders' equity |
| II. Retained earnings | B. Fixed asset |
| III. Listing fees of shares in a stock exchange | C. Current asset |
| IV. Plant and machinery | D. Fictitious asset |
| | E. Intangible asset |

*Codes:*
(a) I-C, II-D, III-E, IV-B
(b) I-B, II-A, III-D, IV-C
(c) I-C, II-A, III-D, IV-B
(d) I-B, II-D, III-E, IV-C

**257.** In case of a cultural club subscriptions received during a particular accounting period as per receipt and payment account amount to Rs. 57,360 subscription outstanding (opening and closing) were Rs. 4,800 and Rs. 6,000 respectively. Subscriptions received in advance (opening and closing) were Rs. 3,600 and Rs. 2,160 respectively
*The amount to be credited to income and expenditure account would be*
(a) Rs. 57,360 (b) Rs. 54,000
(c) Rs. 60,000 (d) Rs. 63,360

**258.** Receipts and payments account records transactions of
(a) Revenue receipts and payments only
(b) Capital receipts and payments only
(c) All receipts and payments relating to the current year only
(d) All receipts and payments relating to the current year succeeding year as well as preceding year

**259.** X and Y are sharing profits in the ratio of 2: 1. They admit Z into the firm with 1/4 shares in profits for which he brings Rs. 12,000. as his share of capital. The partners decide to have their capitals according to the new profits sharing ratio. As a result, the adjusted capital of Y will be
(a) Rs. 10,000 (b) Rs. 12,000
(c) Rs. 16,000 (d) Rs. 24,000

**260.** Which of the following will not be the source for buying back of shares by a company?
(a) Company's free reserves
(b) Company's securities premium account
(c) Proceeds of any shares or other specified securities as per section 77 A (1) (iii)
(d) Company's borrowings from financial institutions

**261.** Match List I (Different type of shares/events) with List II (Transaction by the company) and select the correct answer using the codes given below the lists:

| List I (Different type of ) shares events) | List II (Transaction by the company) |
|---|---|
| I. Sweet equity shares | A. A company gives its shares to the shareholders in the form of extra dividend |

II. Bonus shares — B. Shares issued by the company at a discount

III. Rights shares — C. A company provides an opportunity to the existing shareholders to purchase subsequent issue of share on priority basis

IV. Buy-back of shares — D. Acompany exercises its call option to buy shares from the shareholders

***Codes:***

(a) I-C, II-A, III-B, IV-D
(b) I-B, II-D, III-C, IV-A
(c) I-C, II-D, III-B, IV-A
(d) I-B, II-A, III-C, IV-D

**262.** If net profits are Rs. 30,000 and expenses not resulting in the application of fund are Rs. 10,000, then the funds from operation will be

(a) Rs. 30,000 (b) Rs. 40,000
(c) Rs. 10,000 (d) Rs. 20,000

**263.** Cost of goods purchased for resale is an example of

(a) Capital expenditure
(b) Revenue expenditure
(c) Deferred revenue expenditure
(d) None of these

**264.** Which of the following is/are included in income and expenditure account?

I. Accrued expenses
II. Credit purchases
III. Prepaid expenses
IV. Opening cash balance

*Select the correct answer using the codes given below*

***Codes:***

(a) I only (b) I and II
(c) II and III (d) III and IV

**265.** Within how much period a copy of the profit and loss account and balance sheet of company are to be filed with the Registrar?

(a) 14 days of Annual meeting of the company
(b) 21 days of Annual meeting of the company
(c) 30 days of Annual meeting of the company
(d) 45 days of Annual meeting of the company

**266.** Following particular are given for a firm

Closing stock.................... Rs. 45,000
Other current assets........... Rs. 1,05,000
Current liabilities.............. Rs. 70,000
Sales................................ Rs. 3,20,000

*The working capital turnover ratio is*

(a) 5: 1 (b) 4: 1
(c) 3: 1 (d) 2: 1

**267.** Match List I with List II and select the correct answer using the codes given below the lists

| List I | List II |
|---|---|
| I. VED Analysis | A. Sources and uses of fund |
| II. Ratio Analysis | B. Inventory control |
| III. Fund-flow Analysis | C. Analysis and interpretation of financial statements |
| IV. Income and Expenditure Analysis | D. Non-profit organisation |

***Codes:***

(a) I-A, II-D, III-B, IV-C
(b) I-B, II-C, III-A, IV-D
(c) I-A, II-C, III-B, IV-D
(d) I-B, II-D, III-A, IV-C

**268.** Match List I with List II and select the correct answer using the codes given below the lists:

| List I | List II |
|---|---|
| I. Partners and firm | A. Agent and principle relationship |
| II. Sole proprietor ship | B. Prospectus |
| III. Public limited company | C. Personal |
| IV. Nominal partnership | D. Firm image |

***Codes:***

(a) I-A, II-C, III-B, IV-D
(b) I-D, II-B, III-C, IV-A
(c) I-A, II-B, III-C, IV-D
(d) I-D, II-C, III-B, IV-A

**269.** Following particulars are given for a firm

Quick ratio .............. 1.5
Current Assets.......... Rs. 1,50,000
Current liabilities...... Rs. 60,000

*The value of stock is*
(a) Rs. 60,000 (b) Rs. 70,000
(c) Rs. 80,000 (d) Rs. 90,000

**270.** The cost of a machine is Rs.70,000. It has 10 year life at the end of which it is expected to realise Rs. 5,000. The depreciation for first four years on a straight line basis is
(a) Rs. 28,000 (b) Rs. 26,000
(c) Rs. 22,000 (d) Rs. 20,000

**271.** A partner's capital at the end of a year was Rs. 3,00,000. His share of profit for the year was Rs. 60,000 and he had drawn Rs. 20,000 from the firm during the year
*Then his capital at the beginning of the year was*
(a) Rs. 3,00,000 (b) Rs. 3,20,000
(c) Rs. 3,80,000 (d) Rs. 2,60,000

**272.** Under writers are persons who
(a) Purchase the shares and debentures of a company
(b) Workas agents of the company for the sale of shares a nd debentures.
(c) Undertake to buy those shares and debenteres not subscribed for by the public.
(d) Publicise the share-issueon behalf of the company

**273.** A company takes a loan of Rs. 70 lakhs on which it has to pay interest @ 15% p.a company's return on invesment is 25% before tax and the tax payable on net earning is 60%. What gain accrues to the shareholders because of this loan?
(a) Rs. 2,40,000 (b) Rs. 2,43,000
(c) Rs. 2,77,000 (d) Rs. 2,80,000

**274.** Equity shares represent owner's capital. Therefore, an equity shareholder
(a) has preferential claim over income and wealth of the company
(b) has residual claim over income and wealth of the company
(c) has no right over income and wealth of the company
(d) is personally liable for all the liabilities of the company even beyond his paid-up capital

**275.** In case of retirement of a partner, the partner's loan account would be shown
(a) in his capital account
(b) in his wife's loan account
(c) in his loan account
(d) in the total amount due to him

**276.** As per Garner V Murray Rule, the loss resulting from a partner's insolvency is borne by other partners in
(a) equal ratio
(b) their capital ratio
(c) their profit sharing ratio
(d) 3 : 1 ratio

**277.** The movement of securities from one stock exchange to another with the object of reaping a profit from the disparity in share prices is called
(a) Averaging
(b) Arbitraging
(c) Back wardation
(d) Forward trading

**278.** Consider the following statements:
I. Transfer and transmission of shares are the same thing
II. 'Stag' is a speculative person who applies for shares in a new issue expected to be over-subscribed to make profit by selling such shares at a premium
III. Stock is a bundle of fully paid shares put together for convenience
*Which of the above statements is/are correct ?*
(a) I and II (b) II and III
(c) III only (d) II only

**279.** Consider the following statements :
Issue of bonus shares can be made out of the
I. General reserve Account
II. Realised capital profits Account
III. Revaluation Reserve Account
IV. Profit and loss Account (Cr)
*Which of these statement are correct?*
(a) I and IV (b) II and III
(c) I, II and IV (d) II, III and IV

**280.** Which one of the following transactions can change the current ratio?
(a) Purchase of goods for cash
(b) Payment to outstanding trade creditors

(c) Acceptance on a Bill of Exchange written by a trade creditor
(d) Dishonour of a Bill of Exchange

**281.** Which one of the following pairs is not correctly matched?
(a) Company.........Authorised capital
(b) Shares............Face value
(c) Bonus shares....Market value
(d) Preference shares...Fixed dividend

**Directions :** *The following questions (282-287) consist of two statements,one labelled as the Assertion (A) and the other as Reason (R) You are to examine these two statements carefully and decide if the Assertion (A) and the Reason (R) are indivisually true and if so, whether the Reason is a Correct explanation of the Assertion (A) select your answers of these question using the codes given below and mark your Answer sheet accordingly*

***Codes :***
(a) Both A and R are individually true, and R is the correct explanation of A
(b) Both A and R are individually true, but R is not the correct explanation of A
(c) A is true, but R is false
(d) A is false, but R is true

**282. Assertion (A) :** Revenue expenditure is written off in the year in which it occurs
**Reason (R) :** The benefit of revenue expenditure is consumed in the year in which it arises

**283. Assertion (A) :** Cash flow statement and fund flow statement disclose same information
**Reason (R) :** Both are prepared out of the same data

**284. Assertion (A) :** Liquid ratio reveals strenght of liquidity of a business unit
**Reason (R) :** Liquid ratio analyses liquid assets and liquid liabilities of a business unit inorder to assest the extent of liquidity

**285. Assertion (A) :** Profit and loss Account,and balancesheet are finacial statement showing financial position of a business unit
**Reason (R) :** Profit and loss Account, and Balancesheet are prepared at the end of the financial year

**286. Assertion (A) :** The interest on debentures canbe capitalised up to the complete construction of the fixed assets
**Reason (R) :** The construction of fixed assets could only be completed by the use of these funds

**287. Assertion (A) :** Capital expenditure is incurred for the purpose of acquiring fixed assets
**Reason (R) :** Capital expenditure item is shown in the asset side of the balancesheet

**288.** Z is admitted in a firm of a 1/4 share in the profits for which he brings Rs. 30,000 for goodwill. It will be taken away by the old partner's X and Y in
(a) Old profit–sharing ratio
(b) New profit–sharing ratio
(c) Sacrificing ratio
(d) Capital ratio

**289.** Forty thousand 10% redeemable preference shares of Rs. 10 each are redeemed at a premium of Rs. 10 each by the issue of 20000 equity shares of Rs. 10 each at a premium of Rs. 10 each. The amount transferred to capital Redemption Reserve Account would be
(a) Rs. 1,80,000 (b) Rs. 2,00,000
(c) Rs. 2,20,000 (d) Rs. 2,40,000

**290.** In a draft balance sheet, the stock at valuation Rs. 1,00,000 was shown on assets side while finalising the balancesheet, an item which was valued at Rs. 37,400 had realisable of Rs. 26,000 only. In the profit and loss account, the stock would be shown at

(a) Rs. 62,600 (b) Rs. 88,600
(c) Rs. 1,00,000 (d) Rs. 1,26,000

**291.** Consider the following statements :
Capital expenditure is incurred for the purpose of
I. obtaining along term benefit for the business
II. increasing earning capacity of the business
III. purchasing of marketable securities
IV. acquiring of an asset in the business
*Which of these statements are correct ?*
(a) I and IV (b) I, II and IV
(c) II and III (d) III and IV

**292.** Which one among the following shall result in 'capital loss' to a firm?
(a) Pilferage of certain items
(b) Loss of goods in transit
(c) Loss due to delay in delivery by port authorities
(d) Confiscation of goods by custom authorities on account of false declaration

**293.** Which one of the following is the correct sequence regarding preparation of final accounts?
(a) Ledger-Trial Balance-Journal-Profit and Loss Account-Balance sheet
(b) Journal-Ledger-Trial Balance-Profit and Loss Account-Balance sheet
(c) Trial Balance-Ledger-Journal-Balance-sheet-Profit and Loss Account
(d) Journal-Trial Balance-Ledger-Profit and Loss Account-Balance sheet

**294.** A, B and C are equal partners. After distributing the loss on realisation of assets and paying all liabilities, their capital accounts show the following balances:
(a) Rs. 10,000 (Cr)
(b) Rs. 4,000 (Cr)
(c) Rs. 14,000 (Dr)
*What is the amount of cash with the firm ?*
(a) Rs. 18,000 (b) Rs. 4,000
(c) Rs. 14,000 (d) Rs. 10,000

**295.** An investor while trading in a stock in the share market lays greatest emphasis upon
(a) earning before interest and tax
(b) rate of return on equity
(c) earning price ratio
(d) dividend price ratio

**296.** Which one of the following statement is true of bonus shares
(a) Bonus shares are issued to the promoters only
(b) Bonus shares are issued only to the existing shareholders
(c) Bonus shares are the shares issued to the employees of the company as an incentive
(d) Bonus shares are issued at parvalue

**297.** Profit from re-issue of forfeited shares should be transferred to
(a) Profit and loss Account
(b) General Reserve
(c) Share premium Account
(d) Capital Account

**298.** Which one of the following pairs is correctly matched ?
(a) Adjusted profit and loss Account : Fund from operations
(b) Proposed dividend:current liability
(c) Investment : current assets
(d) Depreciation : Inflow of fund

**299.** Consider the following
I. Preparation of balancesheet
II. Preparation of funds flow statement
III. Preparation of trial balance
IV. Preparation of profit and loss Account
*The correct chronological sequence of the above in the preparation of periodical financial statement is*
(a) IV - II - III - I (b) III - IV - I - II
(c) II - IV - III - I (d) I - III - II - IV

**300.** The current assets to the current liabilities ratio is said to be satisfactory if it is
(a) 1 : 2 (b) 2 : 1
(c) 1 : 1 (d) 1.5 : 1

**301.** The balance left in the capital accounts on dissolution of a firm is transferred to
(a) Realisation Account
(b) Profit and loss Account
(c) Bank Account
(d) None of these

**302.** Consider the following statements :
The purposes of charging depreciation to the profit and loss Account are
I. to provide for replacement of assets
II. to ascertain true profit
III. to present real financial position
IV. to arrive at the scrap value of the asset
*Which of these statement are correct ?*
(a) I and IV (b) I and II
(c) I, II and III (d) II, III and IV

**303.** What is the kind of expenditure incurred on heavy advertising whose benefit is to continue for years to come?
(a) Revenue Expenditure
(b) Capital Expenditure
(c) Deferred Revenue Expenditure
(d) Prepaid Expenditure

**304.** Match List I (Concepts of Accounting) with List II (Suitability of the Accounting concepts) and select the correct answer using the codes given below the lists:

| List I (Concepts of Accounting) | List II (Suitability of the Accounting concepts) |
|---|---|
| I. Money measurement concept | A. Application to all forms of business organisations |
| II. Business entity concept | B. Basic accounting |
| III. Cost concept | C. Original purchase price of assets |
| IV. Dual aspect concept | D. Application to those transactions / events which are of financial nature in accounting |

*Codes:*
(a) I-D, II-B, III-C, IV-A
(b) I-C, II-A, III-D, IV-B
(c) I-D, II-A, III-C, IV-B
(d) I-C, II-B, III-D, IV-A

**305.** For a firm
Opening stock.............. Rs. 32,000
Closing stock................ Rs. 34,000
Sales............................ Rs. 4,40,000
Gross profit ratio ......... 25% on sales
*The stock turnover ratio of the firm is*
(a) 8.0 (b) 8.5
(c) 9.0 (d) 10.0

**306.** Consider the following statements :
An unregistered partnership firm suffers from the following disabilities :
I. A partner of such firm cannot file a suit for the dissolution of the firm
II. The firm cannot file a suit against any third party for realisation of its dues
III. A partner cannot file a suit against any other partner to enforce any right arising out of partnership deal
*Which of the above statements are correct*
(a) I, II and III (b) I and III
(c) I and II (d) II and III

**307.** The distinctive characteristic of "perpetual succession' of a joint stock company refers to
(a) un interrupted business inspite of continuous losses
(b) immunity from government direction for the closure of the company
(c) immunity from resolution passed in the annual general body meeting for closure of the company
(d) uninterrupted existence not affected by the death or insolvency of members of the company

**308.** Who is a 'bull'?
(a) A stock broker who deals or specializes in a few shares
(b) An investor who sells securities in anticipation of being able to rebuy them later at a lower price
(c) An investor who buys securities in anticipation of being able to sell them later at a highter price
(d) An investor who expects the price of a security or of the market as a whole to fall.

**309.** Commercial paper is a
(a) long-term corporate security meant for small investors
(b) medium-term corporate security meant for institutional investors
(c) treasury paper meant for corporate investors
(d) short-term corporate security meant for large scale investors

**310.** A cartel is a combination firms
(a) Which are functioning in a particular industry
(b) Whose combined assets are worth more than 90% of total assets of the industry
(c) Who control major chunk of the market
(d) Whose combined profits are enormous

**311.** The take over of a company in which most of the purchase price is paid with borrowed money is referred to as
(a) hostile takeover
(b) illegal takeover
(c) lever aged buy-out
(d) management buy-out

**312.** One of the major difficulties in improving the industrial efficiency in enterprises is
(a) low investment
(b) low productivity
(c) ineffective marketing
(d) poor inventory control

**313.** Exim bank of india provides financial assistance to exporters and importers in India
(a) in foreign currency only
(b) both in Indian currency and foreign currencies
(c) as Zero-interest loans
(d) as subsidies

**314.** The national-insurer in India is
(a) General Insurance Corporation of India
(b) United India Insurance Company Ltd.
(c) Insurance Regulatory and Development Authority
(d) Oriental Fire and General Insurance Company Ltd.

**315.** In life insurance,the risk insured is
(a) certain to occur and also the timing of its occurrence is known
(b) certain to occur,but its timing of occurrence is not known
(c) not certain to occur and also the timming of its occurrence is not known
(d) not likely to occur

**316.** Which one of the following risks is not insured by the export credit and guarantee corporation?
(a) The risks of non-payment by the foreign buyer
(b) The risk that the importer may return to goods on the ground of lower quality
(c) The political risk that the import licence may be revoked
(d) The risk of war, revolution, etc. in the buyer's country

**317.** Financial year of a company shall not exceed
(a) Calendar year
(b) 15 months
(c) 18 months with special permission of Registrar of Companies
(d) 15 months with special permission of Registrar of Companies

**Directions :** *The following questions (Q. 318-323) consists of two statements one labelled the Assertion (A) and other labelled the Reason (R). You are to examine these two statements carefully and decide if the Assertion (A) and the Reason (R) are individually true and if so,whether the Reason is a correct explanation of the Assertion. Select your answers to these items using the codes given below*

***Codes:***
(a) Both A and R are true and R is the correct explanation of A
(b) Both A and R are true but R is NOT a correct explanation of A
(c) A is true but R is false
(d) A is false but R is true

**318. Assertion (A) :** There is no error, when the totals of the debit side and the credit side of the trial balance are equal

**Reason (R) :** Trial Balance is a two columm statement showing names and balances of all the accounts in the order in which they appear in the ledger

**319. Assertion (A) :** Companies are required to use Written Down Value (WDV) method and the rates specified to schedule XIV to the companies Act

**Reason(R)** : A change from WDV method of providing depreciation to Straight Line Method (SLM) should made if it is considered that the change would result in a more appropriate preparation or presentation of the financial statements of the company.

**320. Assertion (A)** : Entrance fees in case of non profit concerns can be treated as revenue receipt or capital receipt

**Reason (R)** : Some accountants consider entrance fees to be recurring in nature, where as others consider it to be non recurring

**321. Assertion (A)** : Performance ratios show where we are

**Reason (R)** : Balancesheet ratios show how we stand

**322. Assertion (A)** : One single primary ratio that measures the final outcome of all recorded business activities is ROI

**Reason (R)** : In practice, however variations are also found in the ratio because capital and return are subject to different interpretations by firms

**323. Assertion (A)** : According to Accounting standard 3(revised) of the Institute of Chartered Accountants of India a cash flow from investing activites and cash flows from financing activities

**Reason (R)** : According to Accounting standard 3 (revised) of the Institute of Chartered Accountants of India a cash flow statement should be devided into three heads cash flows from operating activities, cash flows from investing activities and cash flows from financing activities.

**324.** Accounting is generally understood as
I. Summarisation of business transactions
II. Language of the business
III. Source of business information
IV. Means of communication
*Select the correct answer using the codes given below:*
(a) I only (b) I and II
(c) II and III (d) I, II, III and IV

**325.** Which one of the following types of information, a creditors would be interested to gather while reading Annual Reports of an enterprise?
(a) Profitability (b) Liquidity
(c) Continuity (d) Solvency

**326.** Consider the following statements:
I. Closing stock is valued on the principle of cost price or market price which ever is lower
II. The manufactured goods in a year are transferred from the manufacturing account to trading account at selling price
III. The going concern concept assumes that a business will continue its operations indefinitely
IV. Revenue is not increased by taking loans at though assets and liabilities are increased
*Which of the above statements are correct?*
(a) I, III and IV (b) I and II
(c) II and III (d) II, III and IV

**327.** In case of disclosure of accounting policies, the following fundamental accounting assumptions may NOT be required to be stated if they are followed in the preparation of final accounts of a company :
I. Materiality and accounting period
II. Going concern and consistency
III. Accrual basis of accounting
IV. Conservatism and accounting period
*Select the correct answer using the codes given below :*
(a) II and III (b) I and IV
(c) I, II and III (d) I, II, III and IV

**328.** Match List I (Accounting Standards (AS) issued by the Institute of Chartered Accountants of India with List II (Standard on) select the correct answer using the codes given below the lists:

| List I | List II |
|---|---|
| I. AS-1 | A. Valuation of Inventories |
| II. AS-2 | B. Disclosure of Accounting Policies |
| III. AS-3 | C. Depreciation Accounting |
| IV. AS-6 | D. Cash flow Statement |

*Codes:*
(a) I-B, II-C, III-D, IV-A
(b) I-D, II-A, III-B, IV-C
(c) I-D, II-C, III-B, IV-A
(d) I-B, II-A, III-D, IV-C

**329.** Which one of the following pairs is NOT correctly matched ?
(a) Accounting equation........Assets liabilities capital
(b) Accounting year.......1st April to 31st March
(c) Accrual concept.......Recognising revenue on receipt of cash
(d) Cost concept ........ Recognising transactions at historical cost

**330.** Included in production overhead of hardware division of Rs. 3,00,000 is Rs. 50,000, being the cost of prototype computers manufactured by the compnay itself. These are not to be sold but to be kept for demonstrating alive the medical imaging software programme.
*The cost of prototype computers of Rs. 50,000 should be treated as*
(a) Fixed assets
(b) Deferred revenue expenditure
(c) Production over head cost of hardware division
(d) Advertising cost

**331.** The loss on the sale of old furniture is debited to
(a) Profit and loss Account
(b) Furniture Account
(c) Trading Account
(d) Depreciation Account

**332.** If the purchases made during the year were Rs. 60,000 the balance of stock in trade at the beginning and at the end of the year were Rs. 12,000 and Rs. 9,000 respectively and the gross profit on sale was 1/5th then which one of the following represents the figure of gross profit for the year?
(a) Rs. 15,750 (b) Rs. 14,000
(c) Rs. 12,500 (d) Rs. 17,250

**333.** Given :

| | | |
|---|---|---|
| Opening stock.................... | Rs. | 5,000 |
| Closing stock..................... | Rs. | 7,000 |
| Purchases.......................... | Rs. | 10,000 |
| Manufacturing expenses..... | Rs. | 20,000 |
| Loss of materials due .......... to fire | Rs. | 1,000 |

*The cost of production would be*
(a) Rs. 28,000 (b) Rs. 29,000
(c) Rs. 27,000 (d) Rs. 30,000

**334.** A and B are sharing profits in the ratio of 2:1. They admit C into the firm with 1/4th share in profits for which he brings Rs. 12,000 as his share of capital. Therefore, the adjusted capital of B will be
(a) Rs. 48,000 (b) Rs. 12,000
(c) Rs. 16,000 (d) Rs. 24,000

**335.** While making an adjusting entry in respect of interest on capital,we credit
(a) Capital Account
(b) Profit and loss Account
(c) Interest on capital Account
(d) Drawing Account

**336.** A and B are partners sharing profits and losses in proportion 2:1. They admit new partner C whom they give 1/5th share in profits. The new profit sharing ratio will be
(a) 8 : 4 : 3 (b) 3 : 2 : 1
(c) 2 : 1 : 1 (d) 4 : 2 : 1

**337.** Match List I with List II and select the correct answer using the codes given below the lists :

| List I | List II |
|---|---|
| I. Revaluation account | A. Retirement of a partner |

| | |
|---|---|
| II. Realisation account | B. Maximum loss method |
| III. Piecemeal distribution | C. Admission of a partner |
| IV. Gaining ratio | D. Dissolution of partnership firm |

***Codes:***
(a) I-B, II-A, III-C, IV-D
(b) I-C, II-D, III-B, IV-A
(c) I-B, II-D, III-C, IV-A
(d) I-C, II-A, III-B, IV-D

**338.** Dividend can be paid generally out of
(a) Share premium account
(b) Capital redemption reserve account
(c) Currrent year's profits
(d) All of these

**339.** The following four assets normally appear in the balance sheet
I. Advance salary
II. Copy right
III. Preliminary expenses
IV. Loose tools
*The correct order in which these are to appear in the balance sheet if drawn in order of permanency will be*
(a) IV, II, I, III (b) III, II, IV, I
(c) I, II, III, IV (d) II, IV, I, III

**340.** What is the correct sequence of the following items of current assets in the balance sheet of a company, as per the companies Act,1956?
I. Cash balance in hand
II. Interest accrued on investments
III. Stores and spare parts
IV. Loose tools
V. Sundry debtors
VI. Stock-in-trade
VII. Work-in-progress
*Select the correct answer using the codes given below :*
(a) II, V, IV, VI, VII, III, I
(b) I, II, IV, III, V, VII, VI
(c) VII, VI, IV, I, II, V, III
(d) II, III, IV, VI, VII, V, I

**341.** Under the head 'provisions' in the balance sheet of a limited company the following provisions made for, are to be disclosed:
I. Proposed dividend
II. PF schemes
III. Pension and other staff-benefit schemes
IV. Taxation
*The correct chronological order of their disclosure is*
(a) IV, II, I, III (b) III, II, I, IV
(c) IV, I, II, III (d) III, I, II, IV

**342.** Under the head 'Current liabilities' the following are disclosed
I. Unclaimed dividend
II. Sundry creditors
III. Unexpired discounts
IV. Bills payable
*The correct chronological order of their disclosure is*
(a) IV, III, II, I (b) I, III, II, IV
(c) IV, II, III, I (d) I, II, III, IV

**343.** A company can forfeit shares if the
(a) Shareholder fails to pay the amount of the call during the stipulated time
(b) Shareholder pays calls in advance
(c) Shareholder does not pay the application money
(d) Shares have been issued at par

**344.** The balances appearing in the books of a company at the end of the financial year were:
Capital redemption reserve account Rs. 50,000; share premium account Rs.10,000; General reserve account Rs. 5,000; revaluation reserve Rs. 2,000; profit and loss account (debit) Rs. 10,000
*Maximum amount available for distribution as Bonus Shares' will be*
(a) Rs. 50,000 (b) Rs. 55,000
(c) Rs. 45,000 (d) Rs. 57,000

**345.** A company forfeited 30 equity shares of Rs. 10 each fully called up, for non-payment of allotment money of Rs. 3 and call money of Rs. 4 per share. If these shares are reissued at Rs. 8 per share fully paid, the amount transferable to capital reserve will be
(a) Rs. 300 (b) Rs. 60
(c) Rs. 90 (d) Rs. 30

**346.** Match List I with List II and select the correct answer using the codes given below the lists:

| List I | List II |
|---|---|
| I. Nominal share capital | A. Capitalisation of reserve |
| II. Right shares | B. Fixed dividend |
| III. Bonus shares | C. Maximum amount of share capital of a company |
| IV. Preference shares | D. First offered to the existing share holders |

*Codes:*

(a) I-C, II-D, III-A, IV-B
(b) I-B, II-A, III-D, IV-C
(c) I-B, II-D, III-A, IV-C
(d) I-C, II-A, III-D, IV-B

**347.** The current ratio is 3: 2 and the amount of current liabilities is Rs. 40,000. What is the amount of current assets?

(a) Rs. 60,000 (b) Rs. 70,000
(c) Rs. 80,000 (d) Rs. 1,00,000

**348.** Which one of the following ratios is likely to be affected the most on account of price level charges?

(a) Current ratio
(b) Inventory turnover ratio
(c) Debtors turnover ratio
(d) Fixed assets turnover ratio

**349.** Consider the following satements
The current ratio would reduce by
I. Collection of book debts
II. Payment to trade creditors
III. Purchase of machinery for cash
IV. Cash deposited into bank
*Which of the above statements are correct ?*

(a) I and III (b) only III
(c) II and IV (d) I, III, and IV

**350.** The return on capital employed shows the combined effect of

(a) net profit ratio and inventory turnover ratio
(b) operating ratio and net profit ratio
(c) net profit ratio and capital turnover ratio
(d) gross profit ratio and capital turn over ratio

**351.** Which among the following is the socielaigation of accounting?

(a) To ascertain profit correctly
(b) To maintain the records of the assets and liabilities of organisation
(c) To establish effective orgainisational control
(d) To be helpful in correct tax assessment

**352.** With regard to the rate of return on investment (ROI),which one of the following statements is NOT valid?

(a) It is an overall indicator of the profitability of an enterprise
(b) It is a triangular relationship in the sense that ROI = Profit margin X Asset turn over
(c) It is a superior measure compared to the cash flow generated per share
(d) It was first developed by du Pont,USA

**353.** Alfa Company Limited acquired the business of M/s Bharat Traders. The valuation of the items acquired was buildings Rs. 1,20,000; machinery Rs. 80,000 and stock-in-trade Rs. 30,000. The company issued in lieu of the above items 800, 10% debentures of Rs. 100 each at par and 15000 quaity shares of Rs. 10 each *How much was the flow of funds in the above transaction ?*

(a) Rs. 2,30,000 (b) Rs. 1,00,000
(c) Rs. 50,000 (d) Rs. 30,000

**Directions:** *The following questions (Q. 354-358) consists of two statements, one labelled the Assertion (A) and the other labelled the Reason (R) You are to examine these two statements carefully and decide if the Assertion (A) and the Reason (R) are individually true and if so, whether the Reason is a correct explanation of the Assertion. Select your answers to those items using the codes given below :*

*Codes:*

(a) Both A and R are true and R is the correct explanation of A
(b) Both A and R, are true, but R is not the correct explanation of A
(c) A is true, but R is false
(d) A is false, but R is true

**354. Assertion (A) :** The interest on borrowed funds canbe capitalised up to the completion of fixed assets

**Reason (R) :** The completion of fixed assets has been possible only because of these funds

**355. Assertion (A) :** A claim lodges with Railways in March 1998 for loss of goods of Rs. 2,00,000 had been passed by payment in March 2001 for Rs. 1,50,000. No entry was passed in 1998

**Reason (R) :** The collectability of the claim was not certain in 1998

**356. Assertion (A) :** ROI measures the final out come of all recorded business activities. It is the ratio that measures the performance of the firm that generates returns.

**Reason (R) :** However, interpretation regarding the amount of capital invested and size of returns generated by a firm differ from one interpreter to another and one organisation to another. In other words, practices are not uniform and as such the acceptability of the concept is being questind

**357. Assertion (A) :** The dissolution of partnership may or may not include the dissolution of the firm, but the dissolution of the firm includes dissolution of partnership.

**Reason (R) :** When the dissolution of partnership takes place, all businesses come to a close, but on the dissolution of the firm, the business may be carried on by a reconstituted firm.

**358. Assertion (A) :** Among efficiency conscious enterprises, integrated office is becoming popular

**Reason (R) :** Greater flexibility, better work flow and lower operating cost are benefits of open office

**359.** Which one of the following is an ingredient of the entity convention of accounting?

(a) The owner of a unit and the unit itself is one and the same.

(b) The owner and the unit are treated separately.

(c) No separate accounts for the unit is required.

(d) The unit is a private affair of the owner, hence no accounting is required.

**360.** Which one of the following accounting equations is correct?

(a) Assets = Owner's Equity

(b) Assets = Liabilities + Owner's Equity

(c) Assets = Liabilities – Owner's Equity

(c) Assets + Liabilities = Owner's Equity

**361.** Which one of the following accounting conventions stipulates that contingent assets appear as a foot note in the balancesheet?

(a) Materiality (b) Consistency

(c) Disclosure (d) Conservatism

**362.** Which one of the following is not related to the convention of conservatism?

(a) Making provision for doubtful debts and discount on debtors in anticipation of actual bad debts and discount

(b) Valuation of stock at market price or cost price whichever is higher

(c) Charging of small capital items as Revenue

(d) Adopting written-down value method of depreciation as against straight–line method

**363.** Match List I (Standards issued by ICAI) with List II (Objects/areas covered) and select the correct answer using the codes given below the lists:

| List I | List II |
|---|---|
| I. AS-1 | (A) Valuation of Inventories |
| II. AS-2 | (B) Cash flow Statement |

III. AS-3 (C) Revenue Recognition
IV. AS-9 (D). Disclosure of Accounting Policies

*Codes:*

(a) I-D, II-A, III-B, IV-C
(b) I-D, II-A, III-C, IV-B
(c) I-A, II-D, III-C, IV-B
(d) I-A, II-D, III-B, IV-C

**364.** On March 31, 2001, the closing stock of X Ltd. was Rs. 3,45,000 was destroyed by fire. The company closes its account on March 31. If the balance sheet of the company on March 31, 2001 was finalised on April 25, 2001, then the balance sheet will show the closing stock at

(a) Rs. 3,45,000 with no mention of fire
(b) Rs. 1,20,000 with no mention of fire
(c) Rs. 3,45,000 showing loss by fire in foot note
(d) Rs. 1,20,000 showing loss by fire in foot note

**365.** Consider the following

The investment port folio of a business man as on 31-12-2000 stood as follows :

I. 8% Debentures of X Co. Ltd. (Rs. 6,000). Interest payable on March 31 and Sept. 30
II. 7% Debentures of Y Co. Ltd. (Rs. 4,000). Interest payable on June 30 and Dec. 31
III. 10% Debentures of Z Co. Ltd. (Rs. 9,000). Interest payable on June 1 and Dec. 1

*Amount of interest accrued on the closing data will be*

(a) Rs. 335 (b) Rs. 1,025
(c) Rs. 195 (d) Rs. 830

**366.** Which one of the following is correct with respect to going concern convention

(a) The enterprise is not going to terminate its operations in the period a head
(b) The enterprise may go out of business in the next accounting period
(c) The enterprise may not divest or diversify its operational spheres
(d) The enterprise may not revalue its assets during the current accounting period?

**367.** Consider the following statements:-

Continuous evaluation of the relevance of generally accepted accounting principles is required, because

I. They are the everlasting operating realiries
II. The environment, in which business operates, under goes constant change
III. The business enterprises can develop financial statements of value to the end-users
IV. Realities of social,economic and legal frame work have to be considered by professional accountants

*Which of the above statements are correct ?*

(a) I, II and III (b) I, II and IV
(c) III and IV (d) I and IV

**368.** Which one of the following will lead to under statement of net profit?

(a) Amortisation of fictitous Assets
(b) Treating capital expenditure as revenue expenditure
(c) Treating revenue expenditure as capital expenditure
(d) Creation of general reserve

**369.** Which one of the following items is considered revenue expenditure ?

(a) Expenditure by way of maintenance that has increased productivity
(b) Repair of a gear box in a car that has enhanced its operational life
(c) Complete over haul of a machines pending around 20% of its value
(d) Changing a small component of a machine to maintain its operating efficiency

**370.** After the construction of their new factory building M/s XYZ Co. shifted to it. During this process Rs. 20,000 were spend on pulling down the old structure and Rs.2,000 weres spent on shifting the stocks to new building. This expenditures are to be classified as

(a) Capital expenditure
(b) Revenue expenditure
(c) Capital and revenue expenditure respectively
(d) Deferred revenue expenditure

**371.** Match List I with List II select the correct answer :

| List I | List II |
|---|---|
| I. Reducing capital | A. Contribution margin |
| II. Sales > variable cost | B. Reorganisation |
| III. Sales > Break even sales | C. Absorption |
| IV. Take–over of firm | D. Margin of safety |

*Codes:*
(a) I-B, II-A, III-C, IV-D
(b) I-A, II-B, III-C, IV-D
(c) I-A, II-B, III-D, IV-C
(d) I-B, II-A, III-D, IV-C

**372.** Preparation of Trial Balance helps, mainly, in
(a) summarising business transactions
(b) verifying that 'generally accepted accounting principles' have been observed
(c) finalising the 'sources and uses of funds' statement
(d) locating errors if any in books of accounts

**373.** Match List I with List II select the correct answer:

| List I | List II |
|---|---|
| I. Goodwill | A. Current liability |
| II. Over-draft | B. Fixed assets |
| III. Preliminary expenses | C. Reserves and surpluses |
| IV. Premium on issue of shares | D. Fictitious assets |

*Codes:*
(a) I-B, II-A, III-D, IV-C
(b) I-A, II-B, III-D, IV-C
(c) I-A, II-B, III-C, IV-D
(d) I-B, II-A, III-C, IV-D

**374.** If opening stock = Rs. 2,45,000, purchases = Rs. 15,00,000, sales = Rs. 17,40,000 and rate of gross profit = 20% on cost of goods sold, the closing stock would be at
(a) Rs. 3,53,000 (b) Rs. 2,95,000
(c) Rs. 2,45,000 (d) Rs. 1,95,000

**375.** Match List I (Items) with List II (Recorded in) and select the correct answer :

| List I | List II |
|---|---|
| I. Wrapping material | A. Trading account |
| II. Wages and salaries | B. Profit and loss account |
| III. Prepaid expenses | C. Balance sheet |
| IV. Opening stock | |

*Codes:*
(a) I-B, II-A, III-A, IV-C
(b) I-B, II-A, III-C, IV-A
(c) I-C, II-B, III-B, IV-A
(d) I-C, II-B, III-A, IV-C

**376.** The basis adopted for piecemeal distribution of cash among the partners should be such that amounts finally left unpaid are in the ratio in which
(a) Capital stands on the data of dissolution
(b) Profit and losses are shared
(c) Capital balance stood at the beginning of partnership
(d) Private assets appear on the date of dissolution

**377.** The capital of a firm is Rs. 80,000. The reasonable return in the industry is 7.5 per cent. If the profit earned by the firm during past five years was Rs. 8,000; Rs. 9,000; Rs. 7,000; Rs. 8,500 and Rs. 10,000; then the super profit of the firm will be
(a) Rs. 2,000 (b) Rs. 2,500
(c) Rs. 3,000 (d) Rs. 3,500

**378.** Consider the following :
A football club has received the following subscriptions during the year ending March 31, 2001:

| | 31-3-2000 | 31-3-2001 |
|---|---|---|
| Out standing Subscription | 19,500 | 25,500 |
| Subscription | 12,800 | 9,500 |

Subscription received during the year 2000-01: Rs. 2,45,000. The subscription income of the club for the year 2000-01 was
(a) Rs. 2,63,800 (b) Rs. 2,80,000
(c) Rs. 2,47,700 (d) Rs. 2,84,000

**379.** 'A' and 'B' are partners in a firm sharing profits and losses in the ratio of 2:3 'C' a new partner is admitted for 1/4 th share. 'A' and 'B' old partners share C's profit into their profit sharing ratio.

The new profit sharing ratio of 'A', 'B' and 'C' would be.

(a) 1 : 1 : 1 (b) 2 : 3 : 4
(c) 1 : 2 : 2 (d) 6 : 9 : 5

**380.** Consider the following statements with respect to the sinking-fund method of depreciation :

I. Depreciation is smaller than the assets' annual depreciable cost
II. Amount of interest constantly declines due to assets' reducing balance
III. Amount net incidence on profit and loss account remains constant due to changing fixed depreciation
IV. Periodic depreciation is recorded through the asset account

*Which of the above statements are correct*

(a) II and III (b) I and III
(c) I, II and IV (d) II, III and IV

**381.** The following information about share capital is required to be disclosed in the balance sheet of a Ltd. company.

I. Issues, subscribed and paid-up capital
II. Add forfeited shares
III. Less calls in arrear from directors
IV. Less calls in arrear from others

*The chronological order of their disclosure under the head'share capital, in the balance sheet would be*

(a) I, II, III ,IV (b) I, III, IV, II
(c) I, IV, III, II (d) I, II, IV, III

**382.** Match List I (Fund) with List II (Purpose of fund) and select the correct answer :

| List I | List II |
|---|---|
| I. Sinking fund | A. Maintaining stable rate of dividend |
| II. Capital redemption reserve fund | B. Periodical of debentures redemption |
| III. Dividend equalisation fund | C. Strengthening financial position |
| IV. General reserve fund | D. Redeeming preference shares |

*Codes:*

(a) I-C, II-B, III-A, IV-C
(b) I-B, II-D, III-C, IV-A
(c) I-D, II-B, III-C, IV-A
(d) I-B, II-D, III-A, IV-C

**383.** Provisions are amounts set a side out of profits and other surpluses for

(a) meeting a liability, the amount of which can be determined with exact figure
(b) any known liability of which the amount cannot be determined with substantial accuracy
(c) meeting an eventuality arising out of revaluation of assets in ordinary course of business
(d) meeting a liability arising out of arbitration

**384.** A trader does not keep a complete set of books and gives the following information :

He started business with Rs. 10,000 on June 1, 2000.

He drew at the rate of Rs. 500 per month for the last six months. He also introduced further capital of Rs. 2,000 in the business during the year.

His total assets on Dec. 31, 2000 were Rs. 23,700 and his creditors were Rs. 3,000 on the same date. Outstanding expenses on Dec. 31, 2000, were Rs. 500. His net profit during the year would be

(a) Rs. 11,200 (b) Rs. 11,500
(c) Rs. 13,000 (d) Rs. 14,200

**385.** X who holds 100 shares of Rs. 10 each, fails to pay a final call of 2 Rs. The directors forfeited all the shares and subsequently reissued 50 shares of Rs. 6 each as fully paid. The amount to be transferred to Capital Reserve A/C would be

(a) Rs. 200 (b) Rs. 300
(c) Rs. 400 (d) Rs. 800

**386.** A Ltd. company issues 3000,15% debentures of Rs. 100 each at a discount of 7.5% repayable at a premium of 5% at the end of 5 years. The loss on issue of debentures will be

(a) Rs. 22,500 (b) Rs. 30,000
(c) Rs. 37,500 (d) Rs. 45,000

**387.** Match List I with List II and select the correct answer

| List I | List II |
|---|---|
| I. Technique of cash management | A. Fund flow Analysis |
| II. Technique of working capital management | B. Economic order quantity |
| III. Technique of inventory management | C. Common size balancesheets |
| IV. Technique of Analysis of financial statement | D. Cash flow Analysis |

*Codes:*

(a) I-A, II-D, III-B, IV-C
(b) I-A, II-D, III-C, IV-B
(c) I-D, II-A, III-C, IV-B
(d) I-D, II-A, III-B, IV-C

**388.** Match List I (Transactions) with List II (Impact on current ratio) and select the correct answer using the codes given below the lists:

| List I | List II |
|---|---|
| I. Goods sold at profit | A. Improvement |
| II. Creditors paid | B. Deterioration |
| III. Debts realised | C. No change |
| IV. Materials purchased on credit | |

*Codes:*

(a) I-A, II-C, III-B, IV-B
(b) I-B, II-C, III-A, IV-C
(c) I-A, II-A, III-C, IV-B
(d) I-B, II-A, III-C, IV-C

**389.** The following information had been made available from the profit and loss account for the year ending on March 31, 200 :

| | |
|---|---|
| Gross profit........................ | Rs. 2,00,000 |
| Gross profit margin........... | 20% |
| Stock velocity.................... | 4 |

*If, in current year, the sales are expected to increase by 50 %, then the average inventory required would be*

(a) Rs. 2,00,000 (b) Rs. 2,50,000
(c) Rs. 3,00,000 (d) Rs. 3,50,000

**390.** X Ltd. has current ratio of 2 :1 and quick ratio of 1.5:1. If its current liabilities are Rs. 80,000, then the value of stock would be

(a) Rs. 1,60,000 (b) Rs. 1,20,000
(c) Rs. 40,000 (d) Rs. 80,000

**391.** If earning per share of a company is Rs.5 and the price earning ratio of other similar companies is 4,then the market value of the share of the company would be

(a) Rs. 0.80 (b) Rs. 1.25
(c) Rs. 9 (d) Rs. 20

**392.** If the cost of goods sold is Rs. 1,00,000 the value of opening stock is Rs. 20,000 and the value of closing stock is Rs. 80,000. Then the stock turnover ratio would be

(a) 5 times (b) 4 times
(c) 2 times (d) 1 time

**393.** Match List I with List II and select the correct answer using the codes given below the lists:

| List I | List II |
|---|---|
| I. Current ratio | A. Sufficiency of EBIT to cover interest charges |
| II. Debt equity ratio | B. Short term solvency |
| III. Net profit margin ratio | C. Exposure to financial risk |
| IV. Interest coverage ratio | D. Earnings left for share holders |

*Codes:*

(a) I-B, II-C, III-A, IV-D
(b) I-C, II-B, III-A, IV-D
(c) I-C, II-B, III-D, IV-A
(d) I-B, II-C, III-D, IV-A

**394.** Match List I with List II and select the correct answer :

| List I | List II |
|---|---|
| I. Leverage ratio | A. Short-term solvency |
| II. Liquid ratio | B. Earning capacity |
| III. Turn-over ratio | C. Relationship of debt and Equity |
| IV. Profitability ratio | D. Efficiency of Assets management |

*Codes:*

(a) I-B, II-A, III-D, IV-C
(b) I-C, II-B, III-A, IV-D
(c) I-D, II-C, III-A, IV-B
(d) I-C, II-A, III-D, IV-B

**395.** PEPs is calculated as

(a) $\frac{\text{EBIT Equity shares}}{\text{Equity Shares}}$

(b) $\frac{\text{EBIT - Preference Dividend}}{\text{Equity Shares}}$

(c) $\frac{\text{EAT}}{\text{Equity Shares}}$

(d) $\frac{\text{EAT-Preference Dividend}}{\text{Equity Shares,}}$

**396.** Consider the following information provided by XY Ltd. :

Net profit before depreciation and taxes .................................... Rs. 44,000
Depreciation for the year ............ Rs. 8,000
Goodwill written off during the year............................................ Rs. 10,000
Rate of tax.................................... Rs. 50%

*The cash flow of XY Ltd. form perations will be*

(a) Rs. 36,000 (b) Rs. 28,000
(c) Rs. 26,000 (d) Rs. 13,000

**397.** If profit made during the year Rs.10,000; increase and decrease in the current assets is Rs. 5,000 and Rs. 4,000 respectively, then the cash from operation equals

(a) Rs. 9,000 (b) Rs. 10,000
(c) Rs. 11,000 (d) Rs. 19,000

**398.** Match List I with List II select and the correct answer :

| List I | List II |
|---|---|
| I. Interest on capital in construction works | A. Performance and propriety |
| II. Management Audit | B. Capital expenditure |
| III. Financial Audit | C. Authorisation of expenditure |
| IV. Valuation in balance sheet | D. Critical review by management |
| | E. Entity concept |

*Codes:*

(a) I-B, II-D, III-E, IV-C
(b) I-D, II-A, III-B, IV-E
(c) I-B, II-A, III-C, IV-E
(d) I-D, II-B, III-C, IV-A

**399.** Consider the following with regard to furniture and fixtures:

I. Valuation with reference to bills and invoices
II. Authorisation of expenditure and its capitalisation
III. Adequate provison of depreciation
IV. Whether furniture is mortgaged or free from any mortgage

*The correct sequence to be adopted by the auditor during the course of analytical review, vouching and examination of documents, would be*

*Codes:*

(a) I, II, III, IV (b) II, III, I, IV
(c) III, IV, II, I (d) IV, I, II, III

**400.** Match List I with List II and select the correct answer using the codes given below the lists:

| List I | List II |
|---|---|
| I. Public limited company | A. One man one vote |
| II. Partnership firm | B. Can make public issue |
| III. Cooperative society | C. Restricted membership |
| IV. Private limited company | D. Unlimited liability |
| | E. Direct supervision |

*Codes:*

(a) I-E, II-D, III-B, IV-C
(b) I-B, II-D, III-A, IV-C
(c) I-E, II-C, III-B, IV-A
(d) I-B, II-C, III-A, IV-D

**401.** Consider the following rights

I. The right of a partner to sue for dissolution the firm or for accounts there of
II. The power of the receiver to realise the properties of an insolvent partner
III. The right of the firm to sue any partner
IV. The right of a partner to file a suit against the firm for enforcing his rights

*Which of the above rights are NOT affected due to non registration of a partnership firm?*

(a) I and II (b) II and III

(c) I, II and III (d) II, III and IV

**402.** Which one of the following firms is considered to be illegal to do trading business?

(a) A firm with XI partners

(b) A firm with XVIII partners

(c) A firm with XX partners

(d) A firm with XXII partners

**403.** The fund available with a company after paying all claims including tax and dividend is called

(a) net profit

(b) net operating profit

(c) capital profit

(d) retained earnings

**404.** The Net Asset Value (NAV) of a unit of mutual fund scheme is compared as

Market value of the fund's investments + Receivables + Accrued income–liablities-

(a) -Accrued expenses/No. of units outstanding

(b) Market value of the fund's investment/No. of units outstanding

(c) Assets of the fund liabilities of the fund No. of units outstanding

(d) Face value of the unit + Dividend per unit

**405.** Who among the following does NOT have insurable interest in fire insurance?

(a) A shop owner in the property of his customers

(b) A creditor in the property mortgaged with him

(c) A trustee in the property of the trust

(d) An insurance company in the property insured

**406.** In marine insurance,warranty means a guarantee

(a) against the loss of the ship in the voyage

(b) for the safety of the captain of the ship

(c) for payment of shipping freight

(d) to comply with condition mentioned in the policy

**407.** In a consequential loss policy which one of the following losses in indemnified ?

(a) Loss of corporate image

(b) Loss of net profits due to fire

(c) Loss due to theft during fire

(d) Loss due to damage around the venue of fire

**408.** All solvency ratios are expressed in terms of

(a) Proportion (b) Times

(c) Percentage (d) None of these

**409.** All activity ratios are expressed in terms of

(a) Proportion (b) Times

(c) Percentage (d) None of these

**410.** All profitability ratios are expressed in terms of

(*a*) Proportion (*b*) Times

(*c*) Percentage (*d*) None of these

**411.** Liquid liabilities means

(a) Current liabilities

(b) Current liabilities – Bank overdraft

(c) Current liabilities + Bank overdraft

(d) None of these

**412.** Shareholders funds includes

(a) Equity share capital, Preference share capital, Reserves &Surplus

(b) Loans from banks and financial institutions

(c) Equity share capital, Preference share capital, Reserves &Surplus and Loans from banks and financial institutions

(d) None of these

**413.** Which of the following option is correct

(a) Tangible Assets = Land + Building + Furniture

(b) Tangible Assets = Land + Building + Goodwill

(c) Tabgible Assets = Land + Furniture + Goodwill + Copy right

(d) None of these

**414.** Gross profit ratio establishes the relationship between

(a) Gross profit & Total sales

(b) Gross profit & Credit sales

(c) Gross profit & Cash sales

(d) None of these

**415.** Opening stock is equal to Rs.10,000, Purchase Rs.2,00,000 and closing stock is Rs.5,000. Cost of goods sold is equal to

(a) Rs. 2,15,000 (b) Rs. 2,10,000

(c) Rs. 2,05,000 (d) None of these

**416.** Operating ratio is equal to
(a) 100 – Operating profit ratio
(b) 100 + Operating profit ratio
(c) Operating profit ratio
(d) None of these

**417.** Total sales is Rs,3,40,000 and the gross profit made is Rs.1,40,000. The cost of goods sold will be ________
(a) Rs.2,00,000 (b) Rs. 4,80,000
(c) Rs. 3,40,000 (d) None of these

**418.** Total sales of a business concern is Rs.8,75,000. If cash sales is Rs.3,75,000, then credit sales will be
(a) Rs.12,50,000 (b) Rs.5,00,000
(c) 12,00,000 (d) None of these

**419.** Cost of goods sold is Rs.4,00,000 and average stock is Rs.80,000.Stock turnover ratio will be
(a) 5 times (b) 4 times
(c) 7 times (d) None of these

**420.** Current assets of a business concern is Rs.60,000 and current liabilities are Rs.30,000.Current ratio will be
(a) 1 : 2 (b) 1 : 1
(c) 2 : 1 (d) None of these

**421.** Equity share capital is Rs.2,00,000, Reserves & surplus is Rs.30,000. Debenture Rs.40,000 and the shareholders funds will be
(a) Rs.2,00,000 (b) Rs. 2,30,000
(c) Rs. 1,90,000 (d) None of these

**422.** Accounting Standards cover the aspect of
(a) Recognition of events and transactions in the financial transactions
(b) Measurement of events and transactions in the financial transactions
(c) Presentation and disclosure of events and transactions in the financial transactions
(d) All of the above

**423.** Which of the following statement is not true?
(a) Standards reduce to reasonable extent confusing variations in the accounting treatments
(b) Standards may call for disclosures beyond that required by law
(c) The application of accounting standards facilitate comparison of financial statements of companies though there legal systems, traditions and accounting policies adopted are different
(d) Accounting standards cannot override the statute

**424.** Which of the following accounting standard has been withdrawn by ICAI?
(a) AS 2 on Valuation of Inventories
(b) AS 8 on Accounting for Research and Development
(c) AS 13 on Accounting for Investments
(d) AS 10 on Accounting for Fixed Assets

**425.** A firm's cost of capital is the:
(a) Cost of borrowing money
(b) Cost of issuing stock
(c) Cost of bonds
(d) Overall cost of financing to the firm

**426.** The cost of debt financing is generally ________ the cost of preferred or common equity financing.
(a) Less than
(b) More than
(c) Equal to
(d) Not enough information to tell

**427.** The cost of issuing new stock is called:
(a) The cost of equity
(b) Flotation costs
(c) Marginal cost of capital
(d) None of the above

**428.** The cost of each component of a firm's capital structure multiplied by its weight in the capital structure is called the:
(a) Marginal cost of capital
(b) The cost of debt
(c) Weighted average cost of capital
(d) None of the above

**429.** When establishing their optimal capital structure, firms should strive to:
(a) Minimize the weighted average cost of capital
(b) Minimize the amount of debt financing used
(c) Maximize the marginal cost of capital
(d) None of the above

**430.** The ________ is the percentage change in operating income that results from a percentage change in sales.

(a) Degree of financial leverage
(b) Breakeven point
(c) Degree of operating leverage
(d) Degree of combined leverage

**431.** If interest expenses for a firm rise, we know that firm has taken on more ________.
(a) Financial leverage
(b) Operating leverage
(c) Fixed assets
(d) None of the above.

**432.** The ________________ is the percentage change in earnings per share that results from a percentage change in operating income.
(a) Degree of combined leverage
(b) Degree of financial leverage
(c) Breakeven point
(d) Degree of operating leverage

**433.** Combined leverage is the percentage change in relationship between sales and ____________.
(a) Operating income
(b) Operating leverage
(c) Earnings per share
(d) Breakeven point

**434.** A highly leveraged firm is __________ risky than its peers.
(a) Less (b) More
(c) The same (*d*) None of the above

**435.** An advantage of debt financing is:
(a) Interest payments are tax deductible
(b) The use of debt, up to a point, lowers the firm's cost of capital
(c) Does not dilute owner's earnings
(d) All of the above

**436.** The cost of equity capital is all of the following EXCEPT:
(a) The minimum rate that a firm should earn on the equity-financed part of an investment
(b) A return on the equity-financed portion of an investment that, at worst, leaves the market price of the tock unchanged
(c) By far the most difficult component cost to estimate
(d) Generally lower than the before-tax cost of debt.

**437.** In calculating the costs of the individual components of a firm.s financing, the corporate tax rate is important to which of the following component cost formulae?
(a) Common stock
(b) Debt
(c) Preferred stock
(d) None of the above

**438.** Market values are often used in computing the weighted average cost of capital because
(a) This is the simplest way to do the calculation
(b) This is consistent with the goal of maximizing shareholder value
(c) This is required in India by the SEBI
(d) This is a very common mistake

439. An EBIT-EPS indifference analysis chart is used for________
(a) Evaluating the effects of business risk on EPS
(b) Examining EPS results for alternative financing plans at varying EBIT levels
(c) Determining the impact of a change in sales on EBIT
(d) Showing the changes in EPS quality over time.

**440.** A company makes and sells a single product. If the fixed cost incurred in making and selling the product increase:
(a) The breakeven point will increase
(b) The breakeven point will decrease
(c) The breakeven point will remain the same
(d) Neither a nor b nor c

**441.** ABC Ltd manufactures a single product which it sells for Rs. 20 per unit. Fixed costs are Rs. 60,000 per annum. The contribution to sales ratio is 40 percent. ABC Ltd breakeven point in units is
(a) 7,500 (b) 8,000
(c) 7,000 (d) 7,400

**442.** ABC Ltd sells a single product for Rs. 9 per unit. The variable cost is Rs. 6 per unit and the fixed cost total Rs. 54,000 per month. In a period when the actual sales were Rs.1,80,000, ABC Ltd. Margin of Safety , in units was
(a) 16,000 (b) 18,000
(c) 2,000 (d) 17,000

**443.** Variable costs are budgeted to be 60% of the sales value whereas the fixed costs are estimated as 10% of the sales value. If the company increases its selling price by 10% and fixed cost per unit, variable cost per unit and the sales volume remain the same, the effect of the contribution will be
(a) An increase by 3%
(b) An increase by 10%
(c) A increase by 25%
(d) A increase by 30%

**444.** ABC Ltd plans to produce and sell 4,000 units of product C each month, at a selling price of Rs. 18 per unit. The unit cost comprises of Rs. 8 variable cost and Rs. 4 fixed cost. Calculate the monthly margin of safety, as a percentage of planned sales
(a) 60% (b) 70%
(c) 65% (d) 75%

**445.** Product X generates a contribution to sales ratio of 30%. Fixed costs directly attributable to X amount to Rs. 75,000 per month. Calculate the sales revenue required to achieve a monthly profit of Rs. 15,000
(a) Rs. 2,00,000 (b) Rs. 2,76,000
(c) Rs. 3,00,000 (d) Rs. 2,50,000

**446.** Which of the statements about the profit . volume graph are true?
(a) The profit lines passes through the origin
(b) Other things being equal, the angle of the profit line becomes steeper when the selling price increases
(c) Contribution cannot be read directly from the chart
(d) Fixed costs are shown as line parallel to the horizontal axis

**447.** When comparing the profits reported under marginal and absorption costing during a period when the level of stocks increased
(a) Absorption costing profits will be higher and closing stock valuations lower than those under marginal costing
(b) Absorption profits will be higher and closing stock valuations higher than those under marginal costing
(c) Marginal costing profits will be higher and closing stock valuations lower than those under absorption costing
(d) Marginal costing profits will be lower and closing stock valuations higher than those under absorption costing

**448.** A company made 17,500 units at a total cost of Rs. 16 each. Three quarters of the cost were variable and one quarter fixed. 15,000 units were sold at Rs. 25 each. There were no opening stocks. By how much will profit calculated under absorption costing differ from the profit if marginal costing principles were used?
(a) Absorption costing profit will be Rs. 22,500 less
(b) Absorption costing profit would be Rs. 10,000 greater
(c) Absorption costing profit would be Rs. 1,35,000 greater
(d) Costing profit would be Rs. 10,000 less

**449.** A Rs. 1,30,000 absorption costing profit was made in a particular period which had an opening and closing stock of 15,000 and 20,000 units respectively. If the fixed overhead absorption rate is Rs. 8 per unit, the marginal costing profit would be
(a) Rs. 90,000
(b) Rs. 1,30,000
(c) Rs. 1,70,000
(d) Impossible to calculate

## ANSWERS

| 1 | 2 | 3 | 4 | 5 | 6 | 7 | 8 | 9 | 10 |
|---|---|---|---|---|---|---|---|---|---|
| (a) | (c) | (c) | (d) | (a) | (b) | (b) | (c) | (b) | (a) |
| **11** | **12** | **13** | **14** | **15** | **16** | **17** | **18** | **19** | **20** |
| (c) | (b) | (b) | (a) | (c) | (a) | (c) | (d) | (b) | (b) |

| 21 | 22 | 23 | 24 | 25 | 26 | 27 | 28 | 29 | 30 |
|---|---|---|---|---|---|---|---|---|---|
| (b) | (b) | (a) | (b) | (a) | (c) | (b) | (b) | (a) | (a) |
| **31** | **32** | **33** | **34** | **35** | **36** | **37** | **38** | **39** | **40** |
| (c) | (a) | (a) | (c) | (c) | (b) | (d) | (a) | (b) | (b) |
| **41** | **42** | **43** | **44** | **45** | **46** | **47** | **48** | **49** | **50** |
| (b) | (d) | (d) | (b) | (a) | (c) | (a) | (d) | (b) | (c) |
| **51** | **52** | **53** | **54** | **55** | **56** | **57** | **58** | **59** | **60** |
| (b) | (b) | (b) | (b) | (b) | (d) | (c) | (c) | (c) | (d) |
| **61** | **62** | **63** | **64** | **65** | **66** | **67** | **68** | **69** | **70** |
| (b) | (b) | (c) | (a) | (d) | (d) | (b) | (d) | (b) | (d) |
| **71** | **72** | **73** | **74** | **75** | **76** | **77** | **78** | **79** | **80** |
| (d) | (c) | (d) | (a) | (b) | (b) | (b) | (d) | (b) | (d) |
| **81** | **82** | **83** | **84** | **85** | **86** | **87** | **88** | **89** | **90** |
| (a) | (d) | (c) | (d) | (a) | (a) | (d) | (c) | (b) | (b) |
| **91** | **92** | **93** | **94** | **95** | **96** | **97** | **98** | **99** | **100** |
| (a) | (b) | (c) | (c) | (c) | (c) | (c) | (b) | (c) | (d) |
| **101** | **102** | **103** | **104** | **105** | **106** | **107** | **108** | **109** | **110** |
| (b) | (b) | (d) | (b) | (d) | (c) | (c) | (b) | (a) | (d) |
| **111** | **112** | **113** | **114** | **115** | **116** | **117** | **118** | **119** | **120** |
| (a) | (c) | (c) | (d) | (c) | (b) | (c) | (b) | (d) | (b) |
| **121** | **122** | **123** | **124** | **125** | **126** | **127** | **128** | **129** | **130** |
| (c) | (c) | (b) | (a) | (a) | (a) | (c) | (c) | (c) | (a) |
| **131** | **132** | **133** | **134** | **135** | **136** | **137** | **138** | **139** | **140** |
| (a) | (a) | (b) | (b) | (b) | (a) | (d) | (a) | (b) | (c) |
| **141** | **142** | **143** | **144** | **145** | **146** | **147** | **148** | **149** | **150** |
| (b) | (a) | (d) | (c) | (a) | (c) | (d) | (a) | (c) | (d) |
| **151** | **152** | **153** | **154** | **155** | **156** | **157** | **158** | **159** | **160** |
| (a) | (a) | (c) | (b) | (a) | (d) | (a) | (b) | (d) | (b) |
| **161** | **162** | **163** | **164** | **165** | **166** | **167** | **168** | **169** | **170** |
| (d) | (a) | (b) | (b) | (b) | (a) | (b) | (b) | (d) | (b) |
| **171** | **172** | **173** | **174** | **175** | **176** | **177** | **178** | **179** | **180** |
| (c) | (a) | (b) | (a) | (c) | (b) | (b) | (a) | (c) | (a) |
| **181** | **182** | **183** | **184** | **185** | **186** | **187** | **188** | **189** | **190** |
| (c) | (d) | (a) | (d) | (c) | (b) | (a) | (c) | (b) | (c) |
| **191** | **192** | **193** | **194** | **195** | **196** | **197** | **198** | **199** | **200** |
| (b) | (b) | (b) | (d) | (c) | (d) | (c) | (a) | (b) | (c) |
| **201** | **202** | **203** | **204** | **205** | **206** | **207** | **208** | **209** | **210** |
| (b) | (a) | (c) | (b) | (b) | (c) | (d) | (d) | (b) | (c) |

| | | | | | | | | | |
|---|---|---|---|---|---|---|---|---|---|
| **211** | **212** | **213** | **214** | **215** | **216** | **217** | **218** | **219** | **220** |
| (a) | (b) | (b) | (a) | (d) | (c) | (b) | (d) | (c) | (a) |
| **221** | **222** | **223** | **224** | **225** | **226** | **227** | **228** | **229** | **230** |
| (d) | (c) | (c) | (a) | (a) | (c) | (b) | (c) | (a) | (d) |
| **231** | **232** | **233** | **234** | **235** | **236** | **237** | **238** | **239** | **240** |
| (a) | (d) | (c) | (c) | (a) | (d) | (c) | (c) | (c) | (d) |
| **241** | **242** | **243** | **244** | **245** | **246** | **247** | **248** | **249** | **250** |
| (c) | (c) | (c) | (a) | (b) | (c) | (c) | (c) | (a) | (a) |
| **251** | **252** | **253** | **254** | **255** | **256** | **257** | **258** | **259** | **260** |
| (b) | (b) | (a) | (c) | (b) | (c) | (c) | (d) | (b) | (b) |
| **261** | **262** | **263** | **264** | **265** | **266** | **267** | **268** | **269** | **270** |
| (d) | (b) | (b) | (a) | (c) | (b) | (b) | (a) | (a) | (b) |
| **271** | **272** | **273** | **274** | **275** | **276** | **277** | **278** | **279** | **280** |
| (d) | (c) | (d) | (b) | (d) | (b) | (b) | (c) | (a) | (b) |
| **281** | **282** | **283** | **284** | **285** | **286** | **287** | **288** | **289** | **290** |
| (c) | (a) | (c) | (a) | (a) | (a) | (a) | (c) | (c) | (b) |
| **291** | **292** | **293** | **294** | **295** | **296** | **297** | **298** | **299** | **300** |
| (b) | (d) | (b) | (d) | (c) | (b) | (d) | (a) | (b) | (b) |
| **301** | **302** | **303** | **304** | **305** | **306** | **307** | **308** | **309** | **310** |
| (c) | (c) | (c) | (c) | (d) | (d) | (d) | (d) | (c) | (a) |
| **311** | **312** | **313** | **314** | **315** | **316** | **317** | **318** | **319** | **320** |
| (c) | (b) | (b) | (a) | (c) | (b) | (c) | (d) | (b) | (a) |
| **321** | **322** | **323** | **324** | **325** | **326** | **327** | **328** | **329** | **330** |
| (d) | (d) | (a) | (a) | (a) | (a) | (b) | (d) | (d) | (a) |
| **331** | **332** | **333** | **334** | **335** | **336** | **337** | **338** | **339** | **340** |
| (a) | (a) | (a) | (b) | (a) | (a) | (b) | (c) | (d) | (d) |
| **341** | **342** | **343** | **344** | **345** | **346** | **347** | **348** | **349** | **350** |
| (c) | (c) | (a) | (b) | (d) | (a) | (a) | (b) | (b) | (d) |
| **351** | **352** | **353** | **354** | **355** | **356** | **357** | **358** | **359** | **360** |
| (d) | (b) | (d) | (c) | (d) | (b) | (c) | (b) | (b) | (b) |
| **361** | **362** | **363** | **364** | **365** | **366** | **367** | **368** | **369** | **370** |
| (d) | (b) | (a) | (c) | (c) | (a) | (b) | (b) | (d) | (a) |
| **371** | **372** | **373** | **374** | **375** | **376** | **377** | **378** | **379** | **380** |
| (d) | (d) | (a) | (b) | (b) | (b) | (b) | (d) | (d) | (b) |
| **381** | **382** | **383** | **384** | **385** | **386** | **387** | **388** | **389** | **390** |
| (b) | (d) | (b) | (a) | (a) | (c) | (d) | (c) | (c) | (a) |
| **391** | **392** | **393** | **394** | **395** | **396** | **397** | **398** | **399** | **400** |
| (b) | (c) | (d) | (d) | (d) | (b) | (a) | (a) | (b) | (b) |

| 401 | 402 | 403 | 404 | 405 | 406 | 407 | 408 | 409 | 410 |
|---|---|---|---|---|---|---|---|---|---|
| (a) | (d) | (d) | (c) | (a) | (a) | (b) | (a) | (b) | (c) |
| **411** | **412** | **413** | **414** | **415** | **416** | **417** | **418** | **419** | **420** |
| (b) | (a) | (a) | (a) | (c) | (a) | (a) | (b) | (a) | (c) |
| **421** | **422** | **423** | **424** | **425** | **426** | **427** | **428** | **429** | **430** |
| (b) | (d) | (c) | (b) | (d) | (a) | (b) | (c) | (a) | (c) |
| **431** | **432** | **433** | **434** | **435** | **436** | **437** | **438** | **439** | **440** |
| (a) | (b) | (c) | (b) | (d) | (d) | (b) | (b) | (b) | (a) |
| **441** | **442** | **443** | **444** | **445** | **446** | **447** | **448** | **449** | |
| (a) | (c) | (c) | (a) | (c) | (d) | (b) | (a) | (b) | |

UNIT-V

# FINANCIAL MANAGEMENT IN PUBLIC SECTOR ENTERPRISES

## CAPITAL BUDGETING

The capital budgeting decisions are decisions as to whether or not money should be invested in long term projects. It includes analysis of various proposals regarding capital expenditure to evaluate their impact on the financial situation of the company and to choose the best out of the various alternatives. The function of finance in this area is to enable the management to take a proper capital budgeting decision.

### Importance of Capital Budgeting

Capital budgeting decisions are the most crucial and critical decisions for a business to take. This is the fact due to the various seasons.

1. Capital budgeting decisions have long term implications on the operations of the business. A wrong decision may affect the long term survival of the company. The investment in fixed assets which is more than required may increase the operating costs of the company. The inadequate investment in fixed assets may make it difficult for the company to compete may affect its market share.
2. Capital budgeting decisions involve large amount of the funds. As such, it is necessary to take the decision very very carefully and to make the arrangement of the funds for the procurement of these assets.
3. The capital budgeting decisions are irreversible due to the fact that it is difficult to find the market for such capital goods. The only alternative is to scrap these assets which involves huge losses.
4. Capital budgeting decisions are difficult to make because it involves the assessment of future events which are difficult to ascertain. The investments are required to be made immediately but the returns are expected over a number of years.

### The Process of Capital Budgeting

The process of capital budgeting involves generally the following steps.

1. **Project Generation :** The generation of the proposals may fall under any of the following categories :
   (a) Additions to the present product line.
   (b) Expand the capacity of the existing product line.
   (c) Proposals to reduce costs of the existing product life without affecting the scale of operations.

   The generation of the projects may take place at the levels of top management or at the level of workers also. For example, proposal to replace an old machine or to improve the production techniques may originate at the worker's level also.
2. **Project Evaluation :** As in case of any types of decision makings, the capital budgeting decisions also have two faces. Firstly, estimation of the benefits and costs measured in terms of cash flows and secondly, selection of an certain project to judge the desirability of the projects. It is necessary that the evaluation of the project is done by impartial group and experts in the field. Care must be

taken to choose the criteria to judge the desirability of the projects and it should be consistent with the company's basic objective to maximize the wealth.

2. **Project Selection :** There is no fixed and laid down procedure to select the final criteria among the various available alternatives. Generally, the selection of the final project is done by the top management though it may be scrutinized at various levels. In many cases, top management may delegate the authority to approve certain projects to lower management also.

4. **Project Execution :** After the final selection of the project is made, the funds are appropriated and the execution of the project is carried on. However, there has to be a proper system to check that the execution of the project is being made as per the predecided plans and schedules.

**Evaluation of the Projects**

As discussed earlier, the process of evaluation of the projects necessarily involves the cost benefit analysis. This cost benefit analysis will generally be made in financial terms, though in some cases non-financial considerations may also come into play. For example, sometimes a project may be undertaken to get established in the market or to satisfy certain legal requirements or for some social welfare benefits or just for some emotional reasons. However, financial cost benefit analysis will be the basic evaluation criteria.

There are many techniques and tools to evaluate the various investment proposal. But before going into the details of these various techniques, one most important aspect of the evaluation has to be studied and that is 'how to compute the cash flows?'

**How to compute the Cash Flows ?**

As the estimation of cash flows–both outflows as well as inflows–is the crux for evaluating the projects, this estimation should be made as carefully as possible. The following stages should be considered for this purpose.

1. Following items constitute the cash outflow :
   (i) Cost of new equipment.
   (ii) Cost for demolition of old equipment (Similarly, if there is some scrap value receivable from the disposal of the old equipment, the outflow on account of the new equipment should be suitably adjusted).
   (iii) Cost of preparing site and installation charges incurred with respect to the new equipment.

   Following factors should also be taken into consideration :

   (a) If the cost of the new equipment is not to be incurred in one single installment, but is to be paid over a period of years, it will involve the cash outflow not only in the first year but in the subsequent years also. Similarly, if the cost of the equipment/ project is met by raising the term borrowing, the cash outflow will come into consideration as and when the installment of terms borrowings and interest on the same are paid.

   (b) If the new equipment/project brings certain scrap value after the usual life is over, the amount realised as scrap value will institute the cash inflow, but in relation to the year in which the amount is actually received.

   (c) In some cases, implementation of the project may involve investment in the form of additional working capital due to increased inventory, increased debtors etc. This additional investment in working capital constitutes cash outflow. Similarly, after the useful life of the project is over, this investment in the working capital is released and hence should be considered as inflow but only with respect to the year in which it is so released. Further, if the company resorts to some outside source of funds for financing working capital requirements, the cash outflow on account of investment in working capital will be the amount invested by the company itself. The amount received from the outside source of working capital finance constitute the cash outflow.

(d) If a new asset is intended to be purchased in order to replace an existing asset, the sale proceeds of the old asset should be considered as the cash inflow and the cash outflow required to purchase new asset should be adjusted accordingly.

2. Following factors should be considered while computing cash inflows :

(i) Computation of cash inflows highly depends upon correct estimation of production and sales. On the basis of additional production units which can be sold and the price at which they can be sold, the gross revenue from the project can be worked out. However, while doing so, the possibility of reduction in selling price, introduction of a cheaper product by competitors, etc. should also be considered.

(ii) Second state in deciding the cash inflows is to estimate the costs attached to the project. These costs may be in the form of fixed costs or variable costs or depreciation.

(iii) The difference between the gross revenue and the costs give the result of net value which should be adjusted for taxation factor for computation of cash inflows as it involves the actual payment of cash. However, the amount of depreciation, if it is already included in the cost to consider the taxation factor should be added back while computing the cash inflows as depreciation does not involve the cash outflow. In simple words, the cash inflows should be computed in the following stages :

Sales Revenue
Less : Costs (including depreciation)
Net Revenue
Less : Tax Liability
Revenue after Taxes
Add : Depreciation
Net cash inflow.

(iv) Care should be taken not to include the cost of interests and dividends while considering the costs attached to the project. This is due to the fact that for evaluating the proposals if cost of capital is considered as the discounting factor (as discussed in details later), the amounts of interest and dividend are already given due consideration while computing the cost of capital.

(v) Sometimes the cash inflows may be considered in terms of net savings in cost rather than in terms of excess of sales over the additional cost. Thus, for computing the cash inflows these savings in costs will be the starting point which will have to be adjusted further for taxation and depreciation factor. The cash inflows will be computed as below :

Saving in costs
(Other than Depreciation)
Less : Depreciation
Net Savings in costs
Less : Tax liability
Savings after Tax
Add : Depreciation
Net cash inflows.

**Time Value of Money**

It has already been discussed that the evaluation of capital expenditure proposals involves the comparison between cash outflows and cash inflows. The peculiarity of evaluation of capital expenditure proposals is that it involves the decisions to be taken today whereas the flow of funds, either outflow or inflow, may be spread over a number of years. It goes without saying that for a meaningful comparison between the cash outflows and cash inflows, both the variables should be on comparable basis. As such, the question which arises is that ''is the value of flows arising in future the same in terms of today ?'' For example, if the proposals involves the cash inflows of Rs. 10,000 after one year, is the value of this cash inflow really Rs. 10,000 as on today when the capital expenditure proposal is to be evaluated ? The ideal reply to this question is 'no'. The value of Rs. 10,000 received after one year is less than Rs. 10,000 if received today. The reasons for this can be stated as below :

1. There is always an element of uncertainty attached with the future cash flows.
2. The purchasing power of cash inflows received after the year may be less than that of equivalent sum is received today.
3. There may be investment opportunities available if the amount is received today which cannot be exploited if the equivalent sum is received after one year.

In the capital budgeting decision, if there has to be meaningful comparison between the cash outflows and cash inflows which may arise in future at different points of time whereas the evaluation is required to be done as on today, both the future cash outflows and cash inflows are required to be expressed in terms of today.

There are two techniques available for this :

(a) Compounding.

(b) Discounting.

**(a) Compounding**

In this technique, the interest is compounded & becomes a part of initial principal at the and of compounding period.

The compounding of interest can be calculated with the help of following equation :

$A = P(1+i)^n$ where

A = Amount at the end of the period.

P = Amount of principal at the beginning of the period.

i = Rate of interest.

n = Number of years.

**(b) Discounting**

This technique involves the process which is exactly opposite to that involved in the technique of compounding. This technique tries to find out the present value of Re 1 if received or spent after *n* years, provided that the interest rate of *i* can be earned on investment. The present value is calculated with the help of following equation.

$$P = \frac{A}{(1+i)^n} \text{ where,}$$

P = Present value of sum received or spent.

A = Sum received or spent in future.

i = Rate of interest.

n = Number of years.

**Present Value Tables**

To simplify the computation of present value, use can be made of Table A given in the Appendix which gives the present value of rupee one for the various interest rates (*i*) and years (*n*). For computing the present value of a future lump sum, the said sum can be multiplied by choosing the interest factor/discounting factor/present value factor for the relevant combination of *i* and *n*.

**Present Value of Series of Cash Flows**

In capital budgeting decisions, the cash flows, either cash outflow or cash inflow, may occur at various points of time. For finding out the present value of this series of cash flows, it is necessary to find out the present value of each future cashflow and then aggregate them.

**Relevance in Capital Budgeting Decisions**

As discussed earlier, to make the value of cash outflows and cash inflows comparable, it is necessary to reduce future cash outflows on cash inflows to their present value of discounting them by proper discounting factor or interest factor or present value factor. Usually, weighted average cost of capital is considered as the discounting factor in capital budgeting decisions.

**Techniques for Evaluation of Capital Expenditure Proposals**

Various techniques are available for evaluation of capital expenditure proposals. They can be broadly categorised under two heads.

(a) Techniques not considering time value of money.

(b) Techniques considering time value of money.

**(a) Techniques not considering time value of money :**

## 1. Pay Back Period

Pay back period indicates the period within which the cost of the project will be completely recovered. In other words, it indicates the product within which the total cash inflows equal to the total cash outflows. Thus,

$$\text{Pay back period} = \frac{\text{Cash outlay}}{\text{Annual cash inflow}}$$

**Acceptance Rule**

Pay back period method can be used as an accept or reject criteria or as a method of ranking the project. If the pay back period computed for a project is more than maximum pay back period estimated by the management it would be rejected or vice versa. As a ranking method, the projects having shortest pay back period will be ranked highest.

**Advantages**

1. If is quite simple to calculate and easy to understand. It makes it quite clear that there are no profits on a project unless pay back period is over.
2. It costs less.
3. It may be a suitable technique where risk of obsolescence is high. In such cases, projects with shorten pay back period may be preferred as the changes in technology may make other projects obsolete before their costs are recovered.

**Disadvantages**

1. It does not consider the returns from a project after its pay back period is over. Thus, one project A may have a pay back period of 5 years while another project B may have a pay back period of 3 years, thus making project B most preferable. But it is quite possible the project A may generate good cash inflows after 5 years till the end of 10 years, while project B may stop generating cash inflows after 3 years only. In such cases, project A may prove to be more advantageous.
2. It may not be a suitable method to evaluate the projects if they involve uneven cash inflows.
3. It ignores time value of money.
4. To decide the acceptable pay back period is a difficult task. There is no rational basis for deciding the maximum pay back period. It is a subjective decision.

## 2. Accounting Rate of Return

Accounting rate of return (ARR) computes the average annual yield on the net investment in the project. ARR is computed by dividing the average profits after depreciation and taxes by net investments in the project. Thus ARR can be computed as :

$$\frac{\text{Total profit}}{\text{Net investment in project} \times \text{No. of years of profits}} \times 100$$

**(b) Techniques considering time value of money :**

## 1. Discounted Pay Back Period

This is an improvement over the pay back period method in the sense that it considers time value of money. Thus, discounted pay back period indicates that period within which the discounted cash inflows equal to the discounted cash outflows involved in a project.

## 2. Net Present Value

Net present value (NPV) is a method of calculating present value of cash inflows and cash outflows in an investment project, by using cost of capital as the discounting rate, and finding out net present value by subtracting present value of cash outflows from present value of cash inflows. Thus,

$$\text{NPV} = \begin{Bmatrix} \Sigma \text{ Discounted} \\ \text{cash inflows} \end{Bmatrix} \text{ Less } \begin{Bmatrix} \Sigma \text{ Discounted} \\ \text{cash outflows} \end{Bmatrix}$$

## 5. Internal Rate of Return

Internal rate of return (IRR) is that rate at which the discounted cash inflows match with discounted cash outflows. The indication given by IRR is that this is the maximum rate at which the company will be able to pay towards the interest on amounts borrowed for investing in the projects, without losing anything. Thus, IRR may be called as the "break even rate" of borrowing for the company.

In simple words, IRR indicates that discounting rate at which NPV is zero. If by applying 10% as the discounting rate, the resultant NPV is positive, while by applying 12% discount rate the resultant NPV is negative, it means that IRR, i.e. the discounting rate at which NPV is zero, falls between 10% and 12%. Thus, by applying the trial and error method, one can find out the discounting rate at which NPV is zero. The process to compute IRR will be to select any discounting rate and compute NPV. If NPV is negative, a lower discounting rate should be tried and the process should be repeated till the NPV becomes zero. Following illustration explains the process to calculate IRR.

**Limitations of Capital Budgeting**

The basic limitation of the capital budgeting process lies in this fact that it involves various estimations. These estimations are specifically in respect of :

(a) Cash outflow.
(b) Revenues/Savings and costs attached with projects.
(c) Life of the projects.

Whereas the cash outflows can be estimated with a reasonable accuracy, the cash inflows and life of the projects can't be estimated accurately. Further, the changes in fiscal and taxation policies of the Government also have the impact on determination of cash inflows. If the techniques use the discounted flows to evaluate the projects, the cost of capital is used as discounting rate. Difficulties in deciding the cost of capital, prove to be the limitation of capital budgeting process.

**Evaluation Criteria in certain typical situations**

(a) In certain cases, the capital expenditure may not involve any specific inflow of funds, but only outflow of funds. For example, if a machine manufactures such products which themselves cannot be marketed, there may not be any specific inflow of funds associated with such machines. Under such situations, if the company is required to make the choice between two machines, the company should choose that machine which involves less amount of present value of outflow of funds.

**Planning, Organization and Control of Capital Expenditure**

It has already been discussed that the various proposals for incurring capital expenditue may be generated either at top managment level or even at lower management level though latter is the rare possibility. The various proposals generated are evaluated with the help of various techniques as discussed above. The ultimate selection for proposals depends upon the evaluation made by these techniques, however the factors like urgency or availability of funds may also play important role.

The ultimate power to reject or accept various capital expenditure proposals rests with the top management which may be in the form of Board of Directors of Executive Committee or Management Committee. In some cases, the power may rest with the Chairman or Managing Director. The proposals involving the outlay to a certain extent may fall within the powers of chief executive also and the proposals involving the outlay beyond that extent will have to be referred to top managment as described above. If the actual implementation of the selected proposals involved the arrangement of funds from the financial institutions or require certain Government approvals, it is the responsibility of middle management to arrange for the same.

If it is intended to exercise proper control on the capital budgeting process, an organization may be required to take the following steps :

1. **Planning :** The capital expenditure has to be planned properly taking into consideration the present and future needs of the business. It should be planned in such a way as to ensure the balanced development of all the section of the organization individually as well as of the organisation as a whole. Usually the plans in respect of capital expenditure are prepared in the form of capital expenditure budget. Care should be taken to select the period for which capital expenditure budget should be prepared. Too long a period may not be useful.
2. **Evaluation :** Utmost care should be taken while evaluating the capital expenditure proposals. As the capital expenditure proposals involve long term and irreversible decisions, a wrong decision may disturb the entire financial structure of the organisation. The evaluation of various proposals should be done as rationally as possible. Proper weightage should be given to the elements of risk and uncertaintly.
3. **Control over progress :** Usually, the implementation of capital/expenditure proposals are spread over more than one year. As such proper control is required to be exercised over issue of work orders/purchase orders, acquisition of material, labour force and other assets, supply of funds etc.

4. **Periodic and post-completion audit :** These are required to be conducted in order to confirm whether the proposal has been implemented as per the original plan or not. If some faults are pointed out regarding planning process, they may be corrected while considering future projects. If some faults are pointed out during mid-term review of the projects, corrective actions may be taken during the remaining period of implementation.
5. **Forms and procedures :** In order to ensure proper control over capital expenditure, certain forms and procedures may be prescribed. Care should be taken that the said forms are used and procedures are followed at each and every stage of implementation of the capital expenditure proposals.

## WORKING CAPITAL MANAGEMENT

Working Capital Management is considered to be a very important function of finance, as a very large amount of funds is blocked in current assets. Net working capital means current assets less current liabilities. Unless otherwise specified, working capital means net working capital. As such, working capital management refers to proper management of current assets and current liabilities.

The term current assets refers to those assets held by a business which can be converted in the form of cash or used during the course of normal operations within a short span of time say one year, without any deduction in value. Current assets change the shape very frequently. The current assets ensure smooth and fluent business operations and considered to be life blood of the business. In case of a manufacturing organization, current assets may be found in the form of stocks, receivables, cash and bank balances and sundry loans & advances.

The term current liabilities refers to those liabilities which are to be paid off during the course of business, within a short span of time say one year. They are expected to be paid out of current assets or the earnings of the business. Current liabilities consists of sundry creditors, bills payable, bank overdraft or cash credit, outstanding expenses etc.

### Principles of Working Capital Management

The basic objective of working capital management is to avoid over investment or under investment in current assets, as both the extremes involve the adverse consequences. Over investment in current assets may lead to the reduced profitability due to cost of funds blocked, extra storing space required, extra efforts for follow up and recovery required, possibility of malpractice etc. The objective of working capital management is to ensure optimum investment in current assets. In other words, working capital management intends to ensure that the investment in current assets is reduced to the minimum possible extent. However, the normal operations of the organisations are affected adversely, reducing the investment in current assets is fruitless.

### Why the need for working capital arises ?

Generally, it will not be possible for any organisation to operate without the working capital. Let us assume that a manufacturing organisation commences its business with a certain amount of cash. This cash will be invested to buy the raw material. The purchased raw material will be processed with the help of various infrastructural facilities like labour, machinery etc. to convert the same in the form of finished products. These finished products will be sold in the market on credit basis whereby the receivables get created. And when receivables make the payment to the organisation, cash is generated again. As such, there is a cycle in which cash available to the organisation is converted back in the form of cash. This cycle is referred to as working capital cycle.

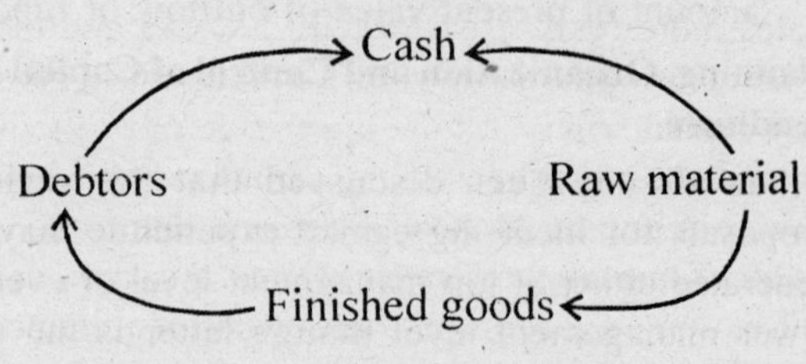


In between each of these stages, there is some time gap involved. The entire requirement of working capital arises due to this time gap. As this time gap is unavoidable, requirement of working capital is unavoidable. The finance professional is interested in reducing this time gap to the minimum possible in order to merge the working capital properly.

**Factors affecting Working Capital requirement**

**(a) Nature of business**

Some businesses are such that due to their very nature, their requirement of fixed capital is more rather than working capital. These businesses may sell services and not the commodities and that too on cash basis. As such, no funds are blocked in piling the inventories and no funds are blocked in receivables; e.g., public utility services like railways, electricity boards, infrastructure oriented projects etc. Their requirement of working capital is less. Whereas if the organisation is a trading organisation, the requirement of working capital will be on the higher side, as huge amount of funds get blocked in mainly two types of current assets, stock and receivables.

**(b) Size of the organisation**

In small scale organizations, requirement of working capital is quite high due to high amount of overheads, high buying costs and high selling costs. As such, medium sized organisations have an edge over the small scale organizations. However, if the business grows beyond a certain limit, the requirement of working capital may be adversely affected by the increasing size.

**(c) Phase of trade cycles**

During the inflationary conditions, the working capital requirement will be on the higher side as the company may like to buy more raw material, may increase the production to take the advantage of favourable market conditions and due to increased sales more funds are blocked in stocks and receivables. During the depression, the requirement of working capital will be on the lower side due to reduced operations but more working capital may be required due to piling up of inventories and due to nonpayment of dues by customers in time. As such, in both the extreme situations of trade cycles, requirement of working capital may be high.

**(d) Trading terms**

The terms on which the organisation makes the purchases and sales affect the requirement of working capital in a big way. If the purchases are required to be made on cash basis and sales are to be made on credit basis to cope with competitions existing in the market, it will result into high requirement of working capital. Whereas, if the purchases can be made on credit basis and sales can be made of cash basis, it will reduce the requirement of working capital as a part of working capital requirement can be financed out of credit offered by the suppliers.

**(e) Length of production cycle**

The term production cycle refers to the time duration from the stage raw materials is acquired till the stage finished product is manufactured. The principle will be "longer the duration of production cycle, higher the requirement of working capital." In some businesses like machine tools industry, the time gap between the acquisition of raw material till the completion of production is quite high. As such more amount is blocked in raw materials or work in progress or finished goods and even in receivables. Requirement of working capital is always very high in this case. Whereas in case of the industries like paper industry or sugar industry, the production cycle is very short. As such, the requirement of working capital, at least for stocks, may be very less.

**(f) Profitability**

High profitability reduces the strain on working capital as the profit to the extent they are earned in cash can be used for financing the requirement of working capital. However, the profit which reduces the strain on working capital is the post-tax profit (*i.e.* the profit earned after paying of the tax liability) and post-dividend profit (*i.e.* the profit remaining in the business after paying the dividend on the shares).

Financing of Working Capital Requirement

Before we go ahead with the discussions on the various methods available for financing the working capital requirement, the term working capital needs to be viewed from one more angle.

(a) Fixed or permanent working capital.

(b) Variable or temporary working capital.

Fixed working capital is the minimum working capital required to be maintained in the business on permanent or uninterrupted basis. The requirement for this type of working capital is unaffected due to the changes in the level of activity.

Variable working capital is the working capital required over and above the fixed or permanent working capital and changes with the fluctuations in the level of activity as a result of changes in production and sales.

The relationship between fixed and variable working capital can be shown with the help of following diagram.

The basic principle of finance states that the permanent requirements of working capital should be financed out of long term or permanent sources *viz.* own generation of funds, cash profits, shares or debentures etc.

For financing temporary requirement of working capital, the organisation can go for various sources which can be discussed as below :

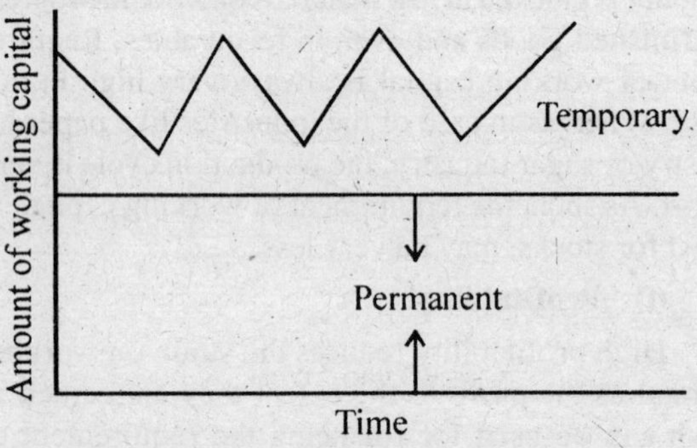


(a) Spontaneous sources
(b) Inter-corporate deposits
(c) Commercial papers
(d) Banks

**Spontaneous Sources**

Spontaneous sources for financing the working capital requirement arise during the course of normal business operations. During the course of business operations, the company may be able to buy certain goods or services for which the payment is to be made after a certain time gap. As such, the company is able to buy goods or services without making payment for the same. These spontaneous sources are unsecured in nature and vary with the level of sales. These spontaneous sources do not have any explicit cost attached to the same. They are generally known as "Current Liabilities." Following forms of current liabilities may be used as spontaneous sources for financing the working capital requirement :

**(a) Trade Credit**

If the company buys the raw material from the suppliers on credit basis, it gets the raw materials for utilization immediately with the facility to make the payment at a delayed of time. By accepting the delayed payment, the suppliers of raw material finance the requirement of working capital. For using this source, certain factors may play an important role :

1. Trends in the industry.
2. Liquidity position of the company.
3. Earnings of the company over a period of time.
4. Record of payment by the company to the suppliers over a period of time.
5. Relationship of the company with the suppliers.

**(b) Outstanding Expenses**

All the services enjoyed by the company are not required to be paid for immediately. They are paid for after a certain time gap. As such, the company is able to get the benefits of these services without paying for the same immediately, thus getting the finance for working capital purposes. These are called "outstanding expenses". This may apply to salaries, wages, telephone expenses, electricity expenses, water charges etc.

**Inter-Corporate Deposits (ICD)**

Inter-Corporate Deposits indicates the amount of funds borrowed by one company from another company. Usually both the companies being under the same management but not necessarily so. Point to be noted here is that ICDs are not considered to be deposits as per the provisions of section - 58A of the Companies Act, 1956 and as such the regulations applicable to the public deposits do not apply to ICDs.

Inter-Corporate Deposits as a source for financing the working capital requirement has the following characteristics features :

(a) ICDs are for a very short period of time, viz. three months or six months.

(b) ICDs is an unsecured source for raising the funds required for working capital purposes.

(c) ICDs as a source is not regulated by any law. As such, the rate of interest, period of ICD etc. can be decided by the company on its own.

(d) ICDs is a relationship based borrowing made by the company.

**Commercial Papers**

In the recent past, commercial papers (CPs) have become one of the best methods for financing the working capital requirements of the companies.

The companies trying to raise the funds by issuing the CP are regulated by guidelines for issue of commercial papers (CP), 2000 issued by Reserve Bank of India on October 10, 2000. These guidelines apply to the companies trying to raise the bonds by issuing the CPs. As per these guidelines, a company means a company as defined in sector 45-1 (aa) of Reserve Bank of India Act, 1934.

Section 45-(aa) of Reserve Bank Act, 1934 defines a company as the company as defined in section 3 of the Companies Act. 1956.

**What is a CP?**

Commercial paper is an unsecured promissory note issued at a discount. The rate of discount is required to be decided by the issue and is not regulated; e.g., A CP of Rs. 100 may be issued at Rs. 98, indicating that the investor has to pay Rs. 98 while at the time of maturity, he will get Rs. 100. It means that difference between Rs. 98 and Rs. 100 i.e. Rs. 2 is in the form of interest on investment made by the investor.

**Who can issue the CP?**

A company will be eligible to issue the CP provided :

(a) The tangible net worth of the company as per latest audited balance sheet is not less than Rs. 4 crores.

**Note :** Tangible net worth means share capital plus free reserves duly reduced by intangible assets like accumulated losses, deferred revenue expenditure etc. Free Reserves include share premium and debenture redemption reserve but do not include revaluation reserve.

(b) Company has been sanctioned working capital limits by banks.

(c) Borrowed amount of the company is classified as a standard asset by the bank.

Before the company issues the CPs it is required to obtain satisfactory credit rating from an approved credit rating agency. Presently, following credit rating agencies have been approved by RBI for this purpose :

(a) Credit Rating Information Services of India Ltd. (CRISIL)

(b) Investment Information and Credit Rating Agency of India Ltd. (ICRA)

(c) Credit Analysis and Research Ltd. (CARE)

(d) FITCH Rating India (P) Ltd.

The minimum credit rating required is P-2 of CRISIL. If the rating is given by any other agency, equivalent minimum rating will be required. The rating so obtained by the company should be current and should not have fallen due for review.

**Who can invest in CP?**

Following persons can invest in the CP :

(a) Individuals

(b) Banks

(c) Corporate bodies incorporated in India

(d) Unincorporated bodies

(e) Non-resident Indians

(f) Foreign institutional investors

**Nature of a CP**

(a) A CP can be issued for the maturity period of 15 days to one year.

(b) A CP has the denomination of Rs. 5 lakhs and every single investor should invest minimum Rs. 5 lakhs in the CP.

(c) Every issue of CP, including the renewal, will be considered to be the fresh issue.

(d) The amount of CP shall be within the overall limit sanctioned by the Board of Directors. It can be issued as a "stand alone" product. Banks will be free to adjust the working capital limits after considering the CPs issued by the company.

It will not be out of place to mention here that CP is not treated as a deposit as per the provisions of section 5B-A of the Companies Act, 1956.

**Procedure for issuing the CPs**

Every company issuing the CP should appoint a scheduled bank as the issuing the paying agent (IPA). IPA will satisfy itself that the company has obtained satisfactory credit rating. It shall also verify the documents submitted by the issuing company and issue a certificate that the documents are in order. IPA should also certify that it has a valid agreement with the issuing company.

The issuing company shall arrange to place the CPs on private placement basis with the investors. The issuing company shall disclose to the potential investor its financial position. After the deal is confirmed, the issuing company shall issue physical certificates to the investor. Investors shall be given a copy of IPA certificate to the effect that the issuing company has a valid agreement with the IPA and documents are in order.

Every issue of CP should be reported to RBI through the IPA within three days from the date of completion of the issue.

**Advantages of Commercial Papers**

(a) As CPs are required to be rated, good rating reduces the cost of capital for the company.

(b) CP is one of the best possible ways available to the company to take the advantage of short term interest fluctuations in the market.

(d) As CPs are unsecured, no change is required to be created on the assets of the issuing company.

**Disadvantages of Commercial Papers**

(a) CP is a source for short term financing available only to a few selected blue chip and profitable companies.

(b) By issuing CP, the credit available from the banks may get reduced.

(c) Issue of CP is very closely regulated by the RBI guidelines.

**Banks**

In the Indian circumstances, bank play a very major role in the financing the working capital requirement of the organisations. We will consider the bank as a source for financing the working capital requirement of the organisations under the following heads :

(a) What should be the amount of assistance ?

(b) What should be the form in which working capital assistance is extended ?

(c) What security should be obtained for working capital assistance ?

(d) What are the various applicable regulations to be considered by the banks while extending the working capital assistance ?

**Amount of Assistance**

To obtain the bank credit for financing the working capital requirements, the company is required to estimate the working capital requirement properly. To estimate the requirement of working capital requirement properly, the company will be required to estimate its level of current assets and current liabilities properly, as working capital is the difference between current assets and current liabilities. For this, the techniques like ratio analysis, trend analysis etc. can be used by the company. More accurate the estimation of the level of current assets and current liabilities, more accurate will be estimation of the requirement of working capital. Then, the company will have to approach the bank along with the necessary supporting data on the basis of the estimates submitted by the company, the bank may decide the amount of assistance that can be extended. While extending the working capital assistance, the bank may describe the margin money requirement. The margin money stipulation is made by the banks in order to ensure the borrowing company's own state in the business and also to provide the cushion against the possible reduction in the value of security offered to the bank. The percentage of margin money stipulation may depend upon the credit standing of the borrowing company, fluctuations in the price of the security and the directives of RBI from time to time. The general principle applicable will be, "more diecy the nature of security, higher will be the margin money stipulations."

## FORM OF ASSISTANCE

After deciding the amount of overall assistance to be extended the company, the bank can disburse the amount in any of the following forms :

(a) Non-fund based lending

(b) Fund based lending

### Non-fund based Lending

In case of Non-fund based lending, the lending bank does not commit any physical outflow of funds. As such, the funds position of the lending bank remains intact. The non-fund based lending can be made by the banks in two forms.

**(a) Bank Guarantees**

The mechanism of bank guarantee is described below :

Suppose company A is the selling company and company B is the purchasing company. Company A does not know company B and as such is concerned whether company B will make the payment or not. In such circumstances, D who is the Bank of company B, opens the Bank Guarantee in favour of company A in which it undertakes to make the payment to company A, if company B fails to honour its commitment to make the payment in future. As such, interests of company A are protected as it is assured to get the payment, either from company B or from its bank D. As such, Bank Guarantee is the mode which will be found typically in the seller's market. As far as Bank D is concerned, while issuing the guarantee in favour of company A, it does not commit any outflow of funds. As such, it is a non-fund based lending for banks. If on due date, Bank D is required to make the payment to company A due to failure on account of company B to make the payment, this non-fund based lending becomes the fund based lending for Bank D which can be recovered by bank D from company B. For issuing the Bank Guarantee, bank D charges the Bank Guarantee commission from company B which gets decided on the basis of two factors viz. what is the amount of Bank Guarantee and what is the period of validity of Bank Guarantee. In case of this conventional form of Bank Guarantee, both company A as well as company B gets benefited. Company A is benefited as it is assured to get the payment. Company B is benefited, as it is able to make the credit purchases from company A without knowing company A. As such, Bank Guarantee transactions will be applicable in case of credit transactions.

In some cases, interest of purchasing company are also to be protected. Suppose that company A which manufactures capital goods takes some advance from the purchasing company B. If company A fails to fulfil its part of the contract to supply the capital goods to company B, there needs to be some protection available to company B. In such circumstances bank C which is the banker of company A opens a Bank Guarantee in favour of company B in which it undertakes that if company A fails to fulfil its parts of the contract, it will reimburse any losses incurred by company B due to this non-fulfilment of contractual obligations. Such Bank Guarantee is technically referred to as Performance Bank Guarantee and is ideally found in the buyer's market.

**(b) Letter of Credit**

The non-fund based lending in the form of Letter of Credit (LC) is very regularly found in the international trade, the exporter and importer are unknown to each other. Under these circumstances, exporter is worried about getting the payment from importer and the importer is worried as to whether he will get the goods or not. In this case, the importer implies to his bank in his country to open a letter of credit in favour of the exporter whereby the importer's bank undertakes to pay the exporter or accept the bills or drafts drawn by the exporter on the exporter fulfilling the terms and conditions specified in the letter of credit. Thus there are essentially three parties in the case of a letter of credit :

(a) The importer.

(b) The issuer who is the bank of importer.

(c) The exporter who is the beneficiary in case of Letter of Credit.

In practical circumstances, there may be some other parties involved in case of letter of credit.

(a) **Advising bank :** This banks is in the exporter's country, which notifies the exporter about opening of Letter of Credit.

**(b) Confirming bank :** If the exporter is not satisfied about the security offered by the importer he may insist that the letter of credit be confirmed by any other bank, other than the issuing bank. In this case, both the banks are liable to honour the bills of exchanges.

The letter of credit may be of different varieties:

**(a) Revocable or Irrevocable :** In case of revocable letter of credit, the issuing bank can cancel or change in the obligation to make the payment or honour the bills or drafts drawn upon it. In case of irrevocable letter of credit, the issuing bank agrees not to cancel or modify the terms of letter of credit.

**(b) Confirmed or unconfirmed :** If the exporter is not satisfied with the security offered by the importer, he insits upon the contamination of a bank, other than the issuing bank which guarantees the payment and/or acceptance of the drafts or bills drawn by the exporter. In case of unconfirmed letter of credit, there is no such confirmation.

The combination of irrevocable and confirmed letter of credit can be considered to be a guaranteed payment on the part of exporter.

The mechanism of letter of credit proves to be beneficial both for the exporter as well as the importer.

**Advantages to the Exporter**

(a) Exporter is assured to get the payment for the goods exported by him, if he satisfies all the terms and conditions specified in the letter of credit. This eliminates the risk of dealing with an unknown importer in a different country.

(b) If the exporter has fulfilled all the terms and conditions of the letter of credit, he can approach its local bank and get the advance pending the export proceeds receivable from the importer.

**Advantages to the Importer**

(a) The issuing bank specifies various terms and conditions in the letter of credit which are required to be fulfilled by the exporter, compliance of which is carefully examined by the issuing bank. As such, the importer is assured to get the proper supply of the goods.

(b) As the letter of credit assures the payment to the exporter, the importer can bargain for better trading terms with the exporter.

It should be noted here that the mechanism of letter of credit could be equally applicable in case of domestic trade also.

**Fund based Lending**

In case of fund based lending, the lending bank commits the physical outflow of funds. As such the funds position of the lending bank does get affected. The fund based lending can be made by the banks the following forms :

1. **Loan :** In this case, the entire amount of assistance is disbursed at one time only, either in cash or by transfer to the company's account. It is a single advance. The loan may be repaid in installments, the interest will be charged on outstanding balance.

2. **Ourdraft :** In this case, the company is allowed to withdraw in excess of the balance standing in its bank account. However a fixed limit is stipulated by the bank beyond which the company will not be able to overdraw the account. Granting of the assistance in the form of overdraft presupposes the opening of a formal current account. Legally, overdraft is a demand assistance given by the bank *i.e.*, bank can ask for the repayment at any point of time. Overdraft is given by the bank for a very short period of time, at the end of which the company is supposed to repay the same. Interest is payable on the actual amount drawn and is calculated on daily product basis.

3. **Cash credit :** In practice, the operations in cash credit facility are similar to those of overdraft facility except the fact that the company need not have a normal current account. Here also a fixed limit is stipulated beyond which the company is not able to withdraw the amount. Legally, cash credit also is a demand facility, but in practice, it is on continuous basis. Here also, the interest is payable on actual amount drawn and is calculated on daily product basis.

4. **Bills purchased / discounted :** This form of assistance is comparatively of recent origin. This facility enables the company to get the immediate pay-

ment against the credit bills/invoices raised by the company. The bank holds the bills as a security till the payment is made by the customer. The entire amount of bill is not paid to the company. The company gets only the present worth of the amount of the bill, the difference between the face value of the bill and the amount of assistance being in the form of discount charges. However, on maturity, bank collects the full amount of bill from the customer. While granting this facility to the company, The bank inevitably satisfies itself about the credit worthiness of the customer and the genuineness of the bill. A fixed limit is stipulated in case of the company beyond which the bills are not purchased or discounted by bank.

**5. Working capital term loans :** To meet the working capital needs for the company, banks may grant the working capital term loans for a period of 3 to 7 years, payable in yearly or half yearly instalments.

**6. Packing credit :** This type of assistance may be considered by the bank to take care of specific needs of the company when it receives some export order. Packing credit is a facility given by the bank to enable the company to buy / manufacture the goods to be exported. If the company holds a confirmed export order placed by the overseas buyer or on irrecoverable letter of credit in its favour, it can approach the bank for packing credit facility. Basically, packing credit facility may take two forms :

(i) Pre-shipment packing credit : To take care of needs of the company before the goods are shipped to the overseas buyer.

(ii) Post-shipment packing credit : To take care of needs of the company from the shipment of goods to the overseas buyer till the date of collection of from boom him.

Necessarily, both these facilities are short-term facilities. The company may be required to repay the same within a predecided span or out or the export proceeds of the goods exported.

**(c) Security for Assistance**

The bank may provide the assistance in any of the modes as stated above. But normally no assistance will be available unless the company offers some security in any of the following booms.

**1. Hypothecation :** Under this mode of a security, bank extends the assistance to the company against the security of movable property, usually inventories. Under this mode of security neither the property not the possession of the goods hypothecated is to transferred to the bank. But the bank has the right to sell the goods hypothecated to realise the outstanding amount of assistance granted by it to the company.

**2. Pledge :** Under this mode of security, bank extends the assistance to the company against the security of movable property. But unlike in case of hypothecation, possession of the goods is with the bank and the goods pledged are in the custody of the bank. As such, it is the duty of the bank to take care of the goods in its custody. In case of default on the part of company to repay the amount of assistance, the bank has the right to sell the goods to realise the outstanding amount of assistance.

**3. Lien :** Under this mode of security, the bank has a right to retain the goods belonging to the company until the debt due to the bank is paid. Lien can be of two types:-

**(i) Particular Lien :** It is valid till the claims pertaining to specific goods are fully paid.

**(ii) General Lien :** It is valid till all the dues payable to the bank are paid.

Normally, banks enjoy general Lien.

**4. Mortgage :** This mode of security pertains to immovable properties like land and buildings. It indicates transfer of legal interest in a specific immovable property as security for the payment of dent. Under this mode, the possession of the property remains with the borrower while the bank gets full legal title there to subject to borrower's right to repay the debt. The party who transfers the interest (*i.e.* the company) is called mortgagor and the party in whose favour the interest is so transferred (*i.e.* the bank) is called mortgage.

## CONTROL OVER WORKING CAPITAL

It can be seen from the preceding discussions that the commercial banks play a very significant role in financing working capital needs. These working capital needs used to be met mainly in the form of cash credit facilities and these advances used to be totally security oriented rather than end use oriented. As such, the units which were able to provide securities to the banks were able to get main chunk of the finances provided by the bankes whereas others experienced shortage of inputs, lower capacity utilisation, high cost of production and ultimately threat of closure. Reserve bank of India has attempted to identify major weakness in the system of financing of working capital needs by banks in order to control the same properly. These attempts were mainly in the form of appointment of following committees :

(a) Dahejia Committee
(b) Tandon Committee
(c) Choore Committee
(d) Marathe Committee
(e) Nayak Committee and Vaz Committee.

## OBJECTIVE TYPE QUESTIONS

**1.** Registered companies are the companies which are incorporated
(a) By a royal character.
(b) By a special Act of Parliament.
(c) Under the companies Act, 1956.
(d) By a special Act of Legislative Assembly.

**2.** A company limited by guarantee and having as share capital .
(a) Can be only public company.
(b) Can be only a private company.
(c) May be both a public company or a private company.
(d) None of these.

**3.** Under the companies Act, 1956, a private company
(a) Must have at least 7 members.
(b) Cannot have more than 20 members.
(c) Must prohibit invitation to the public to subscribe for its shares.
(d) Must issue a prospectus or a statement in lieu of prospectus.

**4.** A private company can commence business.
(a) Immediately after its incorporation.
(b) After it is able to raise minimum subscription.
(c) After it gets certificate to commence business.
(d) After it gets permission from the registered of companies to commence business.

**5.** If a private company becomes a public company by altering its articles by a special resolution, it must file a copy the resolution altering the articles with the registrar within.
(a) 15 days of the passing of the resolution.
(b) 21days of the passing of the resolution.
(c) 30 days of the passing of the resolution.
(d) 3 months of the passing of the resolution.

**6.** A public company can be converted into a private company by passing
(a) A special resolution to after the aricles to include the restrictions on private companies.
(b) An ordinary resolution.
(c) A special resolution to alter the articles and obtaining the approval of the company of the Central Government.
(d) By passing a special resolution and obtaining the approval of the company law Board.

**7.** A company is deemed to be a subsidiary of another company.
(a) When the latter controls the composition of the board of directors of the former.
(b) When the former controls the composition of the Board of the Directors of the latter.
(c) When the former holds more than half in nominal value of equity share capital of the latter.
(d) None of these.

**8.** A Government company is one in which
(a) The entire share capital is held by the Central Government or by one or more States Governments.
(b) Not less than 51 per cent of the share capital is held by the Central Government or one or more State Governments.
(c) More than 40 per cent of the share capital is held by the Central Government or one or more State Government.

(d) 50 per cent of the share capital is held by the Central Government and 50 per cent by one or more State Government.

**9.** An illegal association under the company Act is
(a) An unlawfull association of persons
(b) A partnership formed for carrying out illegal activities
(c) A partnership with more than 20 members
(d) A partnership dissolved by a court of law

**10.** The secretary of a company may be
(a) Any individual, firm or body corporate
(b) Only an individual
(c) Only a body corporate
(d) Only a firm

**11.** A secretary is appointed by the articles. His appointment must be confirmed by
(a) The shareholders in the statutory meeting
(b) The shareholders in the first annual general meeting
(c) The board of director by a resolution passed in the first meeting of the Board after his appointment
(d) The Central Government

**12.** The particular of the appointment of a secretary must be filed with the Registrar of companies within
(a) 15 days of his appointment.
(b) 21 days of his appointment.
(c) 30 days of his appointment.
(d) 3 months of his appointment.

**13.** When a company is registered and a certificate of incorporation is issued by the Registrar
(a) It acquires a perpetual succession.
(b) Its property becomes the property of the shareholders.
(c) Any liability of the company is the liability of the individual shareholders.
(d) Pre–incorporation contracts becomes binding on the company.

**14.** For pre–incorporation contracts entered into by the promoters on bahalf of a company.
(a) The company becomes liable when it acquires certificate of incorporation.
(b) The promoters are personally liable.
(c) Both the company and the promoters are liable.
(d) None of these.

**15.** The certificate of incorporation can be disputed on the following grounds:
(a) Where all the signatories are minors.
(b) Where signatures to the memorandum are forged.
(c) Where the memorandum is signed by only 1 person for all the7 subscribers.
(d) None of these.

**16.** The minimum number of persons required to form public company is
(a) 2 (b) 7
(c) 2 (d) 50

**17.** The purpose of a memorandum of a company is to
(a) Inform the Registrar that the company is under incorporation.
(b) Inform the shareholders as to what the object of the company are.
(c) Invite the public to subscribe for the shares of the company.
(d) None of these.

**18.** A company may change its name by passing
(a) A special resolution.
(b) An ordinary equal resolution.
(c) A special as well as an ordinary resolution as the case may be.
(d) An unanimous resolution of the Board of Directors.

**19.** In case of change of registered office of a company from the place to another in the same town, a notice is to be given to the registered or within
(a) 21 days of the change.
(b) 30 days of the change.
(c) 1 month of the change.
(d) 3 months of the change.

**20.** Where the registered office of a company is changed from one state to another, a certified copy of the order of the company law Board confirming the alteration must be filed by the company with
(a) The Registrar of the state in which the company was originally located.

(b) The Registrar of the state in which the registered office is shifted.
(c) The Registrar of both the states.
(d) The Central Government.

21. After a special resolution for the alteration of the objects of a company has been passed, the alteration must be confirmed by
(a) The company law board
(b) The court
(c) The Central Government
(d) The creditiors of the company

22. An act is said to be ultravires a company when it is beyond the power, third party .
(a) Can hold the company liable
(b) Can hold the directors liable for breach of implied authority
(c) Cannot hold the directors liable
(d) None of these

23. The altered memorandum must be filed with the Registrar within
(a) 1 month of the company Law Board order
(b) 2 months of the company Law Board order
(c) 3 months of the company Law Board order
(d) 4 months of the company Law Board order

24. If a public company limited by a share does not have its own articles, it may adopt
(a) Table A in schedule I to the Act
(b) Table B in schedule I to the Act
(c) Table C in schedule I to the Act
(d) Table D in schedule I to the Act

25. A copy of every special resolution altering the articles be filed with the Registrar within
(a) 15 days of its passing
(b) 21 days of its passing
(c) 30 days of its passing
(d) 3 months of its passing

26. If the Articles of a company conflict with the memorandum
(a) The articles shall prevail
(b) The memorandum shall prevail
(c) The director will resolve the conflict
(d) The court will resolve the conflict

27. The memorandum and articles of a company are open to inspection by only
(a) The members of the company
(b) The members and creditors of the company
(c) All of these
(d) The Company Law Board

28. Doctrine of constructive notice means
(a) Notice of altreration of objects clause to the Registrar
(b) Notice of change of name to members
(c) Notice to outsides dealing with the company as to contents of memorandum and articles
(d) Notice to public as to issue of prospectus

29. The object or purpose of a company are included in the
(a) Articles of Association
(b) Memorandum of Association
(c) Annual return
(d) Statutory report

30. Table A given in schedule I to the companies Act, 1956 gives the model
(a) Memorandum of Association
(b) Articles of Association
(c) Share Transfer Form
(d) Prospectus

31. A prospectus is a document.
(a) Filed by a company with the Registrar before its incorporation
(b) Issued by a company inviting deposits from the public
(c) Which governs the relationship of a company with the creditors dealing with the company
(d) None of these

32. When a copy of a prospectus has been delivered to the Registrar for registration, the prospectus must be issued to the public within.
(a) 30 days of its delivery to the Registrar for registration
(b) 50 days of its delivery to the Registrar for registration
(c) 90 days of its delivery to the Registrar for registration
(d) 120 days of its delivery to the Registrar for registration

33. A person who has been induced to buy shares in a company on the faith of a fraudulent prospectus has remedies against
(a) The company only
(b) The directors only

(c) The promoters only
(d) The company and its directors, promoters and experts

**34.** A shareholders purchased in the open market shares of a company whose prospectus contained some mis-statements. He
(a) Can resend the contract only but cannot claim damages.
(b) Can claim damages only but cannot resend the contract.
(c) Has no remedy against the company.
(d) Has remedy against the directors responsible for the issue of the prospectus

**35.** Share capital of a company means
(a) Equity share capital
(b) Preference share capital
(c) Equity and preference share capital
(d) Equity and preference share capital and debentures

**36.** The share capital of a company can be reduced by
(a) An ordinary resolution after a special notice
(b) A special resolution after a special notice
(c) A special resolution with the sanction of the court
(d) By the unanimous resolution of the Board of Directors and the approval of the central Government

**37.** The special resolution for reducing capital of a company as confirmed by the court takes effect.
(a) From the day it was passed
(b) From the day it was confirmed by the court
(c) On its registration by the Registrar
(d) On its publication in some local news paper

**38.** A company which alters its share capital must give notice of alteration to the Registrar within
(a) 15 days of doing so
(b) 21 days of doing so
(c) 30 days of doing so
(d) 45 days fo doing so

**39.** Rights shares mean shares which are
(a) Issued by a newly formed company
(b) Legally issued to the public
(c) Offered to existing share holders
(d) Issued to the Central Government on conversion of debentures into shares.

**40.** The terms "members" and "share holders" are used interchangeably in the case of
(a) A company limited by shares
(b) A company limited by guarantee
(c) A companylimited by guarantee and having a share capital
(d) An unlimited company

**41.** At any one time a company may close its register of members for a period not exceeding
(a) 10 days (b) 15 days
(c) 21 days (d) 30 days

**42.** Equity shareholders of a company are
(a) Creditors of the company
(b) Owners of the company
(c) Customers of the company
(d) None of these

**43.** Preference shareholders of a company are
(a) Creditors of the company
(b) Owners of the company
(c) Customers of the company
(d) None of these

**44.** An allotment is completed only when
(a) It is communicated to the subscriber
(b) The subscriber pays the allotment money
(c) The subscriber acknowledges the receipt of allotment letter
(d) The resolution for allotment has been passed by the Board of Directors

**45.** A company may convert all or any of its fully paid up shares into stock
(a) By passing an ordinary resolution
(b) By passing a special resolution
(c) With the permission of the Company Law Board
(d) With the permission of the Central Government

**46.** Before a company can issue shares at a discount, it must have been working for at least
(a) 6 months from the date it was entitled to commence business
(b) 1 year from the date it was entitled to commence business
(c) 2 years from the date it was entitled to commence business
(d) 5 years from the date it was entitled to commence business

47. Public limited companies cannot issue
   (a) Equity shares
   (b) Preference shares
   (c) Debentures shares
   (d) Deffered shares

48. Subject to the permission allowed, the maximum allowable discount on equity shares is
   (a) 5 per cernt (b) 10 per cent
   (c) 15 per cent (d) 20 per cent

49. The rate of discount on equity shares
   (a) Should not exceed 10 per cent
   (b) Can exceed 10 per cent if a special resolution is passed to that effect
   (c) Can exceed 10 per cent if the Company Law Board permits
   (d) Cannot exceed 10 per cent in any case

50. A company must deliver share certificates within
   (a) 15 days of the transfer of shares
   (b) 2 months of the transfer of shares
   (c) 3 months of the transfer of shares
   (d) 6 months of the transfer of shares

51. A bearer of a share warrant of a company is
   (a) A member of the company
   (b) Not a member of the company unless the Articles otherwise provide
   (c) A member subject to certain conditions
   (d) None of these

52. Which of the following are not conditions for the issue of share warrants by a company?
   (a) The shares must be fully paid up
   (b) The articles must authories the issue of share warrants
   (c) The prior approval of the Central Government must be obtained
   (d) The company must have been working for at least 2 years prior to the issue of share warrants

53. If a call of larger amount is made on some share holders than the other of the same class, the call is
   (a) Valid
   (b) Voidable
   (c) Void
   (d) Valid only for the smaller amount of the call

54. The power to make calls can be exercised by the
   (a) Board of directors of the company
   (b) Shareholders of the company in general meeting
   (c) The secretary on his own
   (d) The class of shares on whome the call is to be made

55. If a company refuse to register a transfer of shares it must notify its refusal to the transfer within
   (a) 15 days of its refusal
   (b) 1 month of its refusal
   (c) 2 months of its refusal
   (d) 3 months of its refusal

56. In the case of a public company the transferor or transferee may appeal against any refusal of the company to register the the transfer to
   (a) The court
   (b) The Company Law Board
   (c) The general body of shareholders
   (d) The Board of Directors

57. An instrument of transfer of shares must be presented to the prescribed authorities for
   (a) verification of the instrument
   (b) as certaining the bonafides of the transferor
   (c) as certaining the bonafides of the transferee
   (d) endorsement of the date of presentation

58. A transferee becomes a member of a company when
   (a) The instrument of transfer is presented to the prescribed authority
   (b) The instrument of transfer is presented to the company
   (c) The instrument of transferd is registered by the company
   (d) The company acknowledge receipt the instrument of transfer

59. Certification of transfer means
   (a) Completion of act of transfer of shares
   (b) Indorsement on the instrument of transfer by an officer of company that the share certificate relating to the shares to be transferred has been lodged with the company
   (c) Filling in the prescribed from the transfer of shares
   (d) Presenting the instrument of transfer to the company

**60.** Transmission of share takes place
(a) By operation of law
(b) By act of the holder of shares
(c) When the transferee applies to the company for transfer
(d) In case of loss of share certificate

**61.** The shareholders of a company in a general meeting can
(a) Insists on payment of dividend at a certain rate
(b) Increase the rate of dividend recommended by the Board of Director but cannot decrease it
(c) Descrease the rate of dividend recommended by the Board of Directors but cannot decrease it
(d) Remove the director for recommended a low rate of dividend

**62.** After the dividend has been declared by a company it should be paid, or the warrant in respect there of should be posted, within
(a) 21 days of the declaration of dividend
(b) 30 days of the declaration of dividend
(c) 42 days of the declaration of dividend
(d) 90 days of the declaration of dividend

**63.** Dividend declared by a company
(a) May be paid in cash
(b) May be paid in cash or in kind
(c) Must be paid in cash only
(d) May be paid in any form

**64.** The statutory meeting of a public company must be held
(a) Within 1 year of its incorporation
(b) Within 6 months of its incorporation
(c) Within 6 months of its commencement of business
(d) Within a period of not less than 1 month and not more than 6 months from the date at which the company is entitled to commence business

**65.** A statutory meeting is required to be held by
(a) All companies
(b) Only private companies
(c) Only public companies
(d) Only Government companies.

**66.** The first annual general meeting of a company must be held within
(a) 1 year of its incorporation
(b) 15 months of its incorporation
(c) 18 months of its incorporation
(d) 2 years of its incorporation

**67.** The notice for a general meeting of a company must be given atleast.
(a) 7 days before the meeting
(b) 14 days before the meeting
(c) 21 days before the meeting
(d) 30 days before the meeting

**68.** The requisition for an extra ordinary meeting of a compnay limited by shares must come from
(a) 50 members
(b) 100 members
(c) The holders of not less than 1/5th of the paid-up capital.
(d) The holders of not less than 1/10th of the paid-up capital.

**69.** The proper authority for convening a general meeting of a company is the
(a) Board of Directors
(b) Managing Director
(c) Chairman of the Board of Directors
(d) Shareholders

**70.** Unless the article otherwise provide, the quorum for the general meeting of a public company is
(a) 1/3rd of the members personally present
(b) 2 members personally present
(c) 5 members personally present
(d) 7 members personally present

**71.** Proxy is appointed by a shareholder to
(a) Vote at meeting of the shareholders
(b) Speak at a meeting of the shareholders
(c) Speak and vote at a meeting of the share holders
(d) Attend the meeting without the right to vote or to speak

**72.** An ordinary resolution is one which is passed in a general meeting by
(a) A simple majority of votes including the casting vote of the chairman
(b) 3/4 ths majority of votes
(c) 2/3 rds majority of votes
(d) A simple majority of the total members of the company

**73.** A special resolution is one to pass which the votes cast in favour must be
(a) Twice the votes cast against it
(b) 3 times the votes cast against it
(c) 3/4 ths of the totel votes cast
(d) More than the vote cast against it

**74.** A special resolution must be filed with the Registrar for registration within
(a) 14 days of its passing
(b) 21 days of its passing
(c) 30 days of its passing
(d) 45 days of its passing

**75.** A private company must have at least
(a) 1 Director (b) 2 Directors
(c) 3 Directors (d) 5 Directors

**76.** The minimum number of directors in a public company is.
(a) 2 (b) 3
(c) 5 (d) 7

**77.** Unless the articles provide for the retirement of all directors at every annual general meeting , at least of total number of director are liable to retire by rotation
(a) Two thirds (b) One third
(c) One half (d) One fourth

**78.** A person cannot hold office as a director simultaneously in more than
(a) 5 companies (b) 10 companies
(c) 20 companies (d) 50 companies

**79.** The office of a director becomes vacant if he, fails to obtain his qualification shares, if any within
(a) 30 days of his appointment
(b) 1 month of his appointment
(c) 2 months of his appointment
(d) 3 months of his appointment

**80.** The over all maximum managerial remuneration of a public limited company must not exceed.
(a) 5 per cent of its net profit
(b) 10 per cent of its net profit
(c) 11 per cent of its net profit
(d) 15 per cent of his net profit

**81.** The quorum for a Board meeting is
(a) One half of the total strength of the Board or 2 directors which ever is less
(b) One third of its strength
(c) One half of its strength
(d) One third of its strength or 2 directors which ever is higher

**82.** A meeting of the Board of Directors must be held at least once in every.
(a) 4 months and at least 3 such meetings much be held in every year
(b) 3 months
(c) 2 months
(d) 3 months and at least 4 such meetings must be held in every year

**83.** After accepting his appointment as an auditor of a company, the auditor shall inform the Registrar that he has accepted the appointment within on the receipt from the company of the intimation of his appointment.
(a) 7 days (b) 14 days
(c) 21 days (d) 30 days

**84.** An auditor is to make a report on the accounts examined by him to the
(a) Share holders
(b) Directors
(c) Managing Director
(d) Secretary

**85.** Which are of the following is NOT an advantage of the incorporation of a company?
(a) Perpetual succession
(b) Limited liability of members
(c) Capital contributions forming part of the joint stock of the company
(d) Freedom to do any business

**86.** Match List I with List II and select the correct answer using the codes given below the lists:

| List I (Organisation) | List II (Associated with) |
|---|---|
| I. Joint stock company | A. Memorandum of association |
| II. Co- operative society | B. Special act |
| III. Statutory corporation | C. Mutual contract |
| IV. Partnership | D. Bye – laws |

***Codes:***
(a) I-A, II-D, III-B, IV-C
(b) I-A, II-B, III-D, IV-C
(c) I-A, II-C, III-D, IV-B
(d) I-A, II-B, III-C, IV-D

**87.** Economic oligarchy, fraudulent practices bureaucratic management and difficulty information are the limitation o f a
(a) Sole properties concern
(b) Partnership firm
(c) Joint stock company
(d) Co-operative society

**88.** According to the latest guidelines a company cannot issue
(a) Both equity and preference shares simultaneously
(b) Non-convertible debentures
(c) Irredeemable peference shares
(d) Partially convertible debentures

**89.** To enable a company to pay dividends, a special authority is
(a) Not needed either in the memorandum or in the articles
(b) Needed either in the memorandum or in the articles
(c) Needed only in the memorandum
(d) Needed only in the articles

**90.** A company can invest money another company only if it is so authorised by its
(a) Memorandum of Association
(b) Articles of Association
(c) Auditors
(d) Company Secretary

**91.** Which one of the following is NOT feature of a private company as per Indian Companies Act
(a) Limitation on the number of its members
(b) Restriction on the right to transfer its shares
(c) Ban on floating of debentures
(d) Prohibition of any invitation to the public

**92.** According to the companies Act, which one of the following companies can commence allotment of shares even before the minimum subscription is subscribed or paid?
(a) Chartered company
(b) Private company
(c) Government company
(d) Public limited company

**93.** Which one of the following types of companies deals with only its shareholders for their benefit?
(a) Private limited company
(b) Chit fund company
(c) Nidhi company
(d) Banking company

**94.** Those companies which can register themselves without the word "limited" under licence granted by the Central Government
(a) Private companies
(b) Charitable companies
(c) Public companies
(d) None of these

**95.** Which one of the following reports is to be placed before the parliament by a Government company?
(a) Director's report (b) Annual report
(c) Income report (d) Statutory report

**96.** Share premium recieved by issuing shares can be used for
(a) Payment of dividend
(b) Issue of bonus shares
(c) Remuneration to management
(d) Any business purpose

**97.** Which of the following statement is false
(a) A company can issue convertible debentures
(b) Debentures cannot be secured
(c) A company can issue redeemable debentures
(d) Debentures have no right to participate in profits over and above their fixed interest.

**98.** Which one of the following documents is known as doctrine of constructive notice?
(a) The prospectus of the company
(b) The certificate of commencement of business
(c) The memorandum and the article of association
(d) List of working directors

**99.** Under the companies act, which one of the following power can be exercised by the Board of Director?
(a) Power to sell any of the Company's undertakings
(b) Power to make call
(c) Power to borrow money in excess of the paid up capital
(d) Power to reappoint on auditor

**100.** The statutory meeting of the company must be held within six months

(a) From filing of statement in lieu of prospectus
(b) Of obtaining the certificate of commencement of business
(c) Of obtaining the certificate of incorporation
(d) From the date when the first board of directors meetings was held

**101.** A public limited company can offer pre-emptive rights only to the
(a) Director of the company
(b) Existing equity shareholders
(c) Debentures holders
(d) Short term creditors of the company

**102.** Under the law, the inspector who does the inspection of the company's account has to submit his report to the
(a) Company's Board of Directors
(b) Secretary to the company
(c) Central Government
(d) Shareholders of the company

**103.** If a company adopt table 'A', the company is required to pay interest on calls in advance at the rate of
(a) 8% (b) 7%
(c) 6% (d) 5%

**104.** Which one of the following types of registered companies will be the most appropriate for the promotion of science, culture, religion etc.?
(a) Company limited by share
(b) Company limited by guarantee
(c) Unlimited company
(d) Government company

**105.** A joint stock company's letter head must, by law have the address of the
(a) Managing director
(b) Factory
(c) Registered office
(d) Head office

## ANSWERS

| 1 | 2 | 3 | 4 | 5 | 6 | 7 | 8 | 9 | 10 |
|---|---|---|---|---|---|---|---|---|---|
| (c) | (c) | (c) | (a) | (c) | (c) | (a) | (b) | (c) | (b) |
| 11 | 12 | 13 | 14 | 15 | 16 | 17 | 18 | 19 | 20 |
| (c) | (c) | (a) | (b) | (d) | (b) | (b) | (a) | (b) | (c) |
| 21 | 22 | 23 | 24 | 25 | 26 | 27 | 28 | 29 | 30 |
| (a) | (b) | (c) | (a) | (c) | (b) | (c) | (c) | (b) | (b) |
| 31 | 32 | 33 | 34 | 35 | 36 | 37 | 38 | 39 | 40 |
| (b) | (c) | (d) | (c) | (c) | (c) | (c) | (c) | (c) | (a) |
| 41 | 42 | 43 | 44 | 45 | 46 | 47 | 48 | 49 | 50 |
| (d) | (b) | (d) | (d) | (a) | (b) | (d) | (b) | (c) | (c) |
| 51 | 52 | 53 | 54 | 55 | 56 | 57 | 58 | 59 | 60 |
| (d) | (d) | (c) | (a) | (c) | (b) | (d) | (c) | (b) | (a) |
| 61 | 62 | 63 | 64 | 65 | 66 | 67 | 68 | 69 | 70 |
| (c) | (c) | (c) | (d) | (c) | (c) | (c) | (d) | (a) | (c) |
| 71 | 72 | 73 | 74 | 75 | 76 | 77 | 78 | 79 | 80 |
| (a) | (a) | (c) | (c) | (b) | (b) | (a) | (c) | (c) | (c) |
| 81 | 82 | 83 | 84 | 85 | 86 | 87 | 88 | 89 | 90 |
| (d) | (d) | (a) | (a) | (d) | (a) | (c) | (c) | (a) | (b) |
| 91 | 92 | 93 | 94 | 95 | 96 | 97 | 98 | 99 | 100 |
| (c) | (b) | (c) | (b) | (b) | (b) | (b) | (c) | (b) | (b) |
| 101 | 102 | 103 | 104 | 105 | | | | | |
| (b) | (c) | (c) | (b) | (c) | | | | | |

# UNIT-VI

# BARE ACTS

## THE COMPANIES ACT, 1956

The Companies Act, 1956, has been in force for the last 53 years. The Act confers a variety of powers on the Central Government and the Company Law Board to monitor, regulate and control the affairs of the companies.

## THE PAYMENT OF BONUS ACT, 1965

This is an Act intended to provide for the payment of bonus to persons employed in certain establishments and for matters connected therewith. It came into force from September 25,1965. It extends to the whole of India. Unless it is provided otherwise in the Act, it shall apply to : (*a*) every factory and (*b*) every other establishment in which 20 or more persons are employed on any day during an accounting year. But the appropriate Government may apply the provisions of the Act with effect from such accounting year as may be notified in the Gazette to any establishment or class of establishments [including an establishment as defined by Section 2(*m*) (*ii*) of the Factories Act], employing persons between 10 and 19 in number [Proviso to Section 1(3)].An establishment in which 20 or more persons are employed on any day during an accounting year, must continue to be governed by this Act, in spite of the fact that the number of persons employed therein falls below 20.

## THE PAYMENT OF GRATUITY ACT, 1972

Gratuity is a word derived from a Latin word 'Gratuitas.' which simply means a 'Gift'. In the industrial sector, it can be treated as a gift from the employer to his employee for the services rendered to his establishment by him for the development and prosperity of the same.Gratuity is a benefit, which an employee gets at the time of retirement or when he leaves the establishment. Gratuity is a amount ( as a lump sum payment) which is paid by an employer to his employee for his past services when the employment is terminated. When the employment comes to an end due to the retirement or superannuation of the workers, it becomes a good help to the workers, it becomes a good help to the effected employee to meet the new situation which often comes due to reduction in regular earnings or even total

stoppage of earnings. In case of death of the worker, it provides financial assistance to the members of his family for their survival, if they have got no other means for their survival.Thus, this gratuity scheme serves as an instrument of social security as well as a reward to a person who sacrifices his whole life in the betterment, development and prosperity of an establishment, and in other way for the Nation.

## ACT 39 OF 1972

The payment of Gratuity Bill passed by both of the houses of parliament was signed by the President of India on 21st August 1972 and came into force on 16th September, 1972 as THE PAYMENT OF GRATUITY ACT, 1972 (39 of 1972). This Act was amended time to time as per requirement, the years 1984, 1987, 1994 and 1998.

## INDUSTRIAL DISPUTES ACT 1947

The Industrial Disputes act 1947 provides for the investigation and settlement of industrial disputes in an industrial establishment relating to lockouts, layoffs, retrenchment etc. It provides the machinery for the reconciliation and adjudication of disputes or differences between the employees and the employers. Industrial undertaking includes an undertaking carrying any business, trade, manufacture etc. The

Act lays down the conditions that shall be complied before the termination/retrenchment or layoff of a workman who has been in continuous service for not less than one year under an employer. The workman shall be given one month's notice in writing, indicating the reasons for retrenchment and the period of the notice that has expired or the workman has been paid, in lieu of such notice, wages for the period of the notice. The workman shall also be paid compensation equivalent to 15 days' average pay for each completed year of continuous service. A notice shall also be served on the appropriate government.

## INDIAN CONTRACT ACT, 1872

### DEFINITION OF CONTRACT

A contract is an agreement made between two or more parties which the law will enforce. According to sec. 2(*h*), a contract is an agreement enforceable by law. An agreement comes into existence by the process of offer by one party and its unqualified acceptance by the other party.

The parties who enter into an agreement must agree upon the subject matter in the same sense and at the same time, *i.e.*, there must be consensus and idem. An agreement may be a social agreement or a legal agreement. A social agreement is that which does not give rise to legal consequences. In case of its breach the parties cannot go to the law court to enforce a right. A legal agreement is that which gives rise to legal consequences and remedies in the law court in case of its breach.

### ESSENTIAL OF CONTRACT

1. There must be an agree. This involves two parties, one party making the offer and the other party accepting it.
2. The parties must intend to create legal relationship.
3. The parties must be capable of entering into an agreement as regards age and understanding.
4. The agreement must be supported by consideration on both sides.
5. The consent of the parties must be free and genuine.
6. The object of the agreement must be lawful.
7. The terms of the agreement must be certain and capable of performance.
8. The agreement must not have been expressly declared as void.

### CLASSIFICATION OF CONTRACTS

Void agreement—an agreement not enforceable by law (Sec. 2(*g*)].

Void contract—a contract which ceases to be enforceable by law [Sec. 2(*f*)]

Voidable contract—a contract which is enforceable by law at the option of one party thereto, but not at the option of the other [Sec. 2(*i*)]

Illegal Agreement—an agreement which involves the transgression of some rule of basic public policy and is criminal in nature or immoral. It is not only void as between the immediate parties but it also taints the collateral transactions with illegality.

Implied Contract—a contract which is inferred from the circumstances of the case or from the conduct of the parties.

Express Contract—a contract is which the terms are stated in words (written or spoken) by the parties.

Quasi-Contract—an obligation created by law, regardless of agreement.

Executed Contract—a contract which is wholly performed by both the parties.

Executory Contract—a contract in which the promises of both the parties have yet to be performed.

Partly executory, partly executed—a contract in which one party has performed his obligation, but the other party has yet to perform his obligation.

Unilateral Contract—a contract in which only one party has yet to perform his obligation.

Bilateral Contract—a contract in which both the parties have yet to perform their obligations.

### CAPACITY TO CONTRACT

Every person is competent to contract who is of the age of majority according to the law to which he is subject, and who is of sound mind, and is not disqualified from contracting by any law to which he is subject (Sec. 11).

### 1. Minor

A minor is a person who has not completed eighteen years of age. But where a guardian has been appointed to a minor under the Guardians and Wards Act or where a minor is under the guardianship of the Court of Wards, he attains majority at the age of twenty one. The position as regards his agreements is as follows:

**1.** His agreement is altogether void and inoperative. **2.** He can be a promisee or a beneficiary in a contract. **3.** His estate is liable for the necessary goods supplied or necessary services rendered to him or to anyone whom he is legally bound to support or for money lent to him to buy necessaries. **4.** He may enter into contracts of apprenticeship, service, education and instruction provided these are beneficial to him. **5.** He can be an agent. **6.** He cannot be a partner. But he can be admitted to the benefits of an already existing partnership with the consent of the other partners. **7.** If he has received any benefit under a void agreement, he cannot be asked to compensate or pay for it. **8.** The court never orders specific performance of his agreements. **9.** He can always plead minority and is not estopped from doing so even when he enters into an agreement by falsely misrepresenting his age. **10.** He cannot be adjudged insolvent.

### 2. Persons of unsound mind

*Lunatics.* A lunatic can enter into a contract when he is of sound mind.

*Idiots.* An agreement of an idiot like that of a minor is altogether void.

*Drunken or intoxicated persons.* Their position is similar to that of lunatics.

These persons, like a minor, are liable for necessaries supplied to them or their minor dependants.

### 3. Other persons

*Alien enemies.* During the war an Indian citizen cannot enter into a contract with an alien enemy. Contracts made before the war are either suspended or dissolved.

*Foreign sovereigns and accredited representatives of a foreign state.* They can enter into contracts and enforce these contracts in our Courts. But they cannot be sued in our Courts without the prior sanction of the Central Government.

*Corporations.* The contractual capacity of a statutory corporation is limited by the Statute governing it. As regards a company registered under the Companies Act, 1956, its contractual capacity is regulated by its Memorandum of Association and the Companies Act, 1956.

*Insolvents.* When a debtor is adjudged insolvent he is deprived of his power to leal in his property divisible among his creditors.

*Convicts.* A convict when undergoing imprisonment is incapable of entering into a contract.

## FREE CONSENT

All agreements are contract if they are made by the free consent of the parties. Two or more persons are said to consent when they agree upon the same thing in the same sense [Sec. 13] consent is said to be free when it is not caused by; *(i)* coercion or *(ii)* undue influence, or *(iii)* fraud, or *(iv)* misrepresentation, or *(v)* mistake subject to the provisions of sec. 20, 21 and 22.

### Effect of agreement without free consent

When consent to an agreement is caused by coercion, fraud, misrepresentation, or undue influence, the agreement is a contract voidable at the option of the party whose consent was so caused (Secs. 19 and 19-A).

### Coercion

"Coercion" is the committing or threatening to commit any act forbidden by the Indian Penal Code, 1860 or the unlawful detaining, or threatening to detain, any property, to the prejudice of any person whatever, with the intention of causing any person to enter into an agreement (Sec. 15).

A threat to commit suicide amounts to coercion.

### Undue Influence

A contract is said to be induced by "undue influence" where the relations subsisting between the parties are such that one of the parties is in a position to dominate the will of the other, and uses that position to obtain an unfair advantage over the other. A person is deemed to be in a position to dominate the will of another where he—*(a)* holds real or apparent authority over the other, or *(b)* stands in a fiduciary relation to the other; or *(c)* makes a contract with a person whose mental capacity is temporarily or permanently affected by reason of age, illness or mental or bodily distress. Where a person who is in a position to dominate the will of another, enters into a contract with him, and the transaction appears to be *unconscionable*, the burden of proving that such contract was not induced by undue influence lies upon the person in a position to dominate the will of the other (Sec. 16).

*Relationships which raise presumption of undue influence :* **1.** parent and child, **2.** trustee and beneficiary, **3.** religious guru and disciple. **4.** guardian and ward, **5.** solicitor and client, **6.** doctor and patient, and **7.** fiance and fiancee.

*No presumption of undue influence in the following cases :* **1.** husband and wife, **2.** landlord and tenant, **3.** creditor and debtor.

**Misrepresentation and Fraud**

"Misrepresentation" is a mis-statement of a material fact made innocently with an honest belief as to its truth or non-disclosure of a material fact, without any intent to deceive the other party.

"Fraud" exists when it is shown that a false representation has been made, **1.** knowingly, or **2.** without belief in its truth, or **3.** recklessly, not caring whether it is true or false, and **4.** the maker intends the other party to act upon it. It also exists when there is a concealment of a material fact.

**Mistake**

Mistake is erroneous belief about something. It may be a **1.** mistake of law, or **2.** mistake of fact.

**1.** *Mistake of law* : It may be a **1.** mistake of law of the country, or **2.** mistake of law of a foreign country. The general rule as regards mistake of law of the country is that ignorance of law is no excuse. Mistake of law of a foreign country is regarded as a mistake of fact.

**2.** *Mistake of fact,* it may be a—**1.** *Bilateral mistake.* Where *both* the parties to an agreement are under a mistake as to a matter of fact essential to the agreement, the agreement is void (Sec. 20).

Mistake of fact (bilateral mistake) may relate to :

*(a) Subject-matter* : Mistake of fact regarding subject-matter may relate to existence of the subject-matter; *(ii)* price of the subject-matter; *(iii)* quantity of the subject-matter; *(iv)* identity of the subject-matter; *(v)* quality of the subject-matter, or *(vi)* title to the subject-matter.

*(b) Possibility of performance* : Mistake of fact may also relate to *(i)* physical, or *(ii)* legal, impossibility of performance.

In both these cases, the agreement is void.

**2.** *Unilateral mistake* : Where only *one* of the parties is under a mistake as to a matter of fact, the contract is not voidable (Sec. 22). There are however two exceptions to this rule.

*(i) Identity of the person contracted with* : If A intends to enter into a contract with B, C cannot give himself any right in respect of the contract by accepting the offer. In such a case the contract is void.

*(ii) Nature of contract* : Where a person is made to enter into a contract through the inducement of another but through no fault of his own, there is a mistake as to the nature of the contract, and the contract is void.

**Legality of Object**

An agreement is a contract if it is made for a lawful consideration and with a lawful object (Sec. 10).

Every agreement of which the object or consideration is unlawful is void. The consideration or object of an agreement is unlawful if—it is forbidden by law; or it is fraudulent; or involves or implies injury to the person or property of another; or the Court regards it as immoral, or opposed to public policy (Sec. 23).

**Effects of illegality**

No action is allowed on an illegal agreement. This rule is based on the following two maxims : **1.** No action arises from a base cause. **2.** Where there is equal guilt, the defendant is in a better position.

The effects of illegality are summed up as follows: **1.** The collateral transactions to an illegal agreement also become tainted with illegality. **2.** No action can be taken for the *(a)* recovery of money paid or property transferred under an illegal agreement, and *(b)* breach of an illegal agreement.

**Agreements Opposed to Public Policy**

An agreement is said to be opposed to public policy when it is injurious to the welfare of the society or it tends to be harmful to the public interest. The following agreements are, or have been held to be, opposed to public policy:

**1.** Agreements of trading with enemy. **2.** Agreement to commit a crime. **3.** Agreements interfering with administration of justic. These include *(a)* agreements for stifling prosecution and *(b)* agreements which interfere with the course of justice. **4.** Agreements in restraint of legal proceedings. These include *(a)* agreements to oust the jurisdiction of Courts, and *(b)* agreements to vary periods of limitation. **5.** Agreements for the sale of public offices. **6.** Agreements tending to create interest opposed to duty. **7.** Agreements in restraint of parental rights. **8.** Agreements restricting personal liberty. **9.** Agreements in restraint of marriage. **10.** Marriage brokerage agreements. **11.** Agreements interfering with marital duties. **12.** Agreements in fraud of creditors or revenue authorities. **13.** Agreements in restraint of trade. An agreement in restraint of trade is one which restrains a person from freely exercising his trade, business or profession. Every agreement, by which anyone is restrained from exercising a lawful profession, trade or business of any kind is, to that extent, void (Sec. 27). Exceptions are made.

In case of agreements for sale of goodwill and partners' agreements provided the restraint is reasonable.

**Void Agreements**

A void agreement is one which is not enforceable by law (Sec. 2(*g*)].

The following agreements have been expressly declared to be void :

**1.** Agreements made by incompetent persons (Sec. 11). **2.** Agreements made under a mutual mistake of fact (Sec. 20). **3.** Agreements the consideration or object of which is unlawful (Sec. 23). **4.** Agreements the consideration or object of which unlawful in part (Sec. 24). **5.** Agreements made without consideration (Sec. 25). **6.** Agreements in restraint of marriage (Sec. 26). **7.** Agreements in restraint of trade (Sec. 27). **8.** Agreements in restraint of legal proceedings (Sec. 28). **9.** Agreements the meaning of which is uncertain (Sec. 29). **10.** Agreements by way of wager (Sec. 30). **11.** Agreements contingent on impossible events (Sec. 36). **12.** Agreements to do impossible acts (Sec. 56).

**Wagering agreements**

A wagering agreement is an agreement to pay money or money's worth on the happening or non-happening of a specified uncertain event. Wagering agreements are void in India. In the States of Maharashtra and Gujarat, however, they have been declared to be illegal. The collateral transactions to such wagering agreements in the States of Maharashtra and Gujarat also become illegal. In the rest of India collateral transactions are valid.

**Uncertain agreements**

Agreements the meaning of which is not certain, or capable of being made certain, are void.

**Restitution**

It means return of the benefit received from the plaintiff under a void contract. The principle of restitution is that the defendant who has been unjustly enriched at the expense of the plaintiff is required to make restitution to the plaintiff.

**Contingent Contract**

A contingent contract is a contract to do or not to do something. If some event, collateral to such contract, does or does not happen.

**Characteristics of contingent contract**

1. Its performance depends upon the happen-ing or non-happening in future of some event.
2. The event must be uncertain.
3. The uncertain future event must be collateral to the contract.

**Rules regarding contingent contracts**

1. If a contingent contract is to be performed if an uncertain future event happens, it cannot be enforced until the event has happened. If it is to be performed if a particular event does not happen, its performance can be enforced if the event becomes impossible.
2. If a contingent contract depends for its performance on doing of an act by the promisor, the contract becomes void where the promisor makes the performance impossible.
3. If a contingent contract contemplates doing of a thing if a specified event happens within a fixed time, it becomes void if the event does not happen within that time.
4. If a contingent contract contemplates to do anything if an impossible event happens, it is void.

**Assignment of contract**

Assignment of a contract means transfer of contractual rights and liabilities under the contract to a third party. It may take place by—

**1.** *Act of the parties* : This is subject to the following rules:

1. Contracts involving personal skill or ability or other personal qualifications cannot be assigned.
2. A promisor cannot assign his liabilities or obligations under a contract.
3. The rights and benefits under a contract may be assigned if the obligation under the contract is not of a personal nature.
4. An actionable claim can always be assigned but the assignment to be complete and effectual must be effected by an instrument in writing. Notice of such assignment must also be given to the debtor.

**2.** *Operation of law* : This takes place in case of death or insolvency of a party to the contract.

**Discharge of Contract**

A contract is said to be discharged when the obligations created by it come to an end. The various modes of discharge of a contract are as follows :

**1. Discharge by performance**

Discharge of a contract by performance takes place when the parties to the contract fulfil their obligations arising under the contract within the time and in the manner prescribed. The performance may be *(i)* actual performance, or *(ii)* attempted performance.

**2. Discharge by agreement or consent**

A contract rests on the agreement of the parties. As it is agreement which binds them, so by their agreement or consent they may be discharged.

The discharge by consent may be express or implied. Discharge by implied consent takes place by—*(a) Novation, i.e.,* when a new contract is substituted for an existing one, either between the same parties or between one of the parties and a third party. *(b) Alternation, i.e.,* when one or more of the terms of the contract is/are altered by the mutual consent of the parties to the contract. *(c) Rescission, i.e.,* when all or some of the terms of the contract are cancelled. *(d) Remission, i.e.,* acceptance of a lesser fulfillment of the promise made. *(e) Waiver* which means intentional relinquishment or giving up of a right by a party entitled thereto under a contract. *(f) Merger, i.e.,* when an inferior right accruing to a party under a contract merges into a superior right accruing to the same party under a new contract.

**3. Discharge by impossibility**

Impossibility of performance may be—

**Initial impossibility :** An agreement to do an act impossible in itself is void.

**Supervening impossibility :** Impossibility which arises subsequent to the formation of a contract (which could be performed at the time when the contract was entered into) is called subsequent or supervening impossibility. The cases covered by supervening impossibility include; *(a)* Destruction of subject-matter of contract; *(b)* Non-existence or non-occurrence of a particular state of things; *(c)* Death or incapacity for personal service; *(d)* Change of law or stepping in of a person with statutory authority; *(e)* Outbreak of war. The contract is descharged in these cases.

The following cases are not covered by supervening impossibility; *(a)* Difficulty of performance;

*(b)* Commercial impossibility; *(c)* Failure of a third person on whose work the promisor relied; *(d)* Strikes, lock-outs and civil disturbances; *(e)* Failure of one of the objects. The contract is not discharged in these cases.

**4. Discharge by lapse of time**

If a contract is not performed within the period of limitation and if no action is taken by the promisee in a Law Court, the contract is discharged.

**5. Discharge by operation of law**

This includes discharge by *(a)* death, *(b)* merger, *(c)* inolvency, *(d)* unauthorised alternation of the terms of a written agreement, and *(e)* rights and liabilities becoming vested in the same person.

**6. Discharge by breach of contract**

If a party breaks his obligation which the contract imposes, there takes place breach of contract. Breach of contract may be **1.** actual breach, or **2.** anticipatory breach.

1. *Actual breach of contract* may occur *(a)* at the time when the performance is due, or *(b)* during the performance of the contract.
2. *Anticipatory breach of contract occurs* when a party repudiates his liability or obligation under the contract before the time for performance arrives.

**Quasi Contract**

In certain cases the law imposes an obligation and allows an action to be brought on it as if it arose out of an agreement, though none was present in fact. Such cases, strictly speaking, are not contracts, but the law recognises them as "certain relations resembling those created by contracts". In English Law, such relations are called quasi-contracts.

Quasi-contracts rest on the ground of equity that a person shall not be allowed to enrich himself unjustly at the expense of another.

Secs. 68 to 72 deal with the following quasi-contracts :

1. Claim for necessaries supplied to a person incapable of contracting or on his account (Sec. 68).
2. Reimbursement of a person paying money due by another in payment of which he is interested (Sec. 69).
3. Obligation of a person enjoying benefit of a non-gratuitous act (Sec. 70).
4. Responsibility of finder of goods (Sec. 71)
5. Liability of person to whom money is paid or thing delivered by mistake or under coercion (Sec. 72).

Quantum meruit

This means "as much as is earned".

Indemnity and Gurantee

Contract of Indemnity

A contract by which one party promises to save the other from loss caused to him by the conduct of the promisor himself, or by the conduct of any other person, is called a 'contract of indemnity' (Sec. 124). The person who promises to make good the loss is called the *indemnified* (promisor) and the person whose loss is to be made good is called the *indemnified* (promisee) or *indemnity-holder.*

A contract of indemnity is a species of the general contract. It must as such have all the essential elements of a valid contract. It may be *express* or *implied.*

**Contract of Guarantee**

A 'contract of guarantee' is a contract to perform the promise, or discharge the liability, of a third person in case of his default. The person who gives the guarantee is called the '*surety*', the person in respect of whose default the guarantee is given is called the '*principal debtor*', and the person to whom the guarantee is given is called the '*creditor*'. A guarantee may be either oral or written (See. 126).

A contract of guarantee must have all the essential elements of a valid contract. But the principal debtor may be a person suffering from incapacity to contract and it is not necessary that the contract must necessarily result in some benefit to the surely himself.

**Kinds of guarantee :** A guarantee may be given **1.** for the payment of a debt, or **2.** for the payment of the price of the goods sold on credit, or **3.** for the good conduct or honesty of a person employed in a particular office, in which case the guarantee is called a 'fidelity guarantee'. A guarantee may also be a *specific* or *simple* guarantee (which extends to a *single transaction*) or a *continuing* guarantee which extends to a *series of transactions* (Sec. 129).

## BAILMENT AND PLEDGE

### Bailment

A 'bailment' is the *delivery of goods* by one person to another for some *purpose,* upon a contract, that they shall, when the purpose is accomplished, be *returned* or otherwise *disposed* of according to the directions of the person delivering them. The person delivering the goods is called the '*bailor*' and the person to whom they are delivered is called the 'bailee' (Sec. 148).

**Requisites of bailment : 1.** Contract. **2.** Delivery of possession of goods for some purpose. **3.** Return of goods when the purpose is accomplished.

### Pledge

The *bailment* of goods *as security for payment of a debt or performance of a promise is called 'pledge'*. The bailor is, in this case, called the '*pawnor*' or '*pledger*' and the bailee is called the '*pawnee*' or '*pledge*' (Sec. 172).

### Contract of Agency

An 'agent' is a person employed *to do any act for another* or to represent another in dealings with third persons. The person for whom such act is done, or who is so represented, is called the '*principal*'(Sec. 182).

### Rules of agency

*(a)* Whatever a person competent to contract may do himself, he may do through an agent. *(b)* He, who does through another, does by himself.

The acts of an agent, therefore, are the acts of the principal. This is of course subject to certain conditions.

# SALE OF GOODS ACT, 1930

## SALE OF GOODS

### Contract of sale

A contract of sale of goods is a contract whereby the seller *transfers* or *agrees to transfer* the property in goods to the buyer for a price (Sec. 4).

### Sale and agreement to sell

Where under a contract of sale the property in the goods is transferred from the seller to the buyer, the contract is called a sale, but where the transfer of the property in the goods is to take place at a future time or subject to some condition therafter to be fulfilled the contract is called an agreement to sell. An agreement to sell becomes a sale when the time elapses or the conditions are fulfilled subject to which the property in the goods is to be transferred.

### Contract of sale how made

A contract of sale is made by an offer to buy or sell goods for a price and the acceptance of such offer. It may provide for the immediate delivery of the goods or immediate payment of the price or both, or for the delivery or payment by instalments or that the delivery or payment or both shall be postponed. It may be made in writing or by word of mouth or partly in writing and partly by word of mouth, or may be implied from the conduct of the parties (Sec. 5).

### Subject-matter of sale

'Good' form the subject of a contract of sale. They mean *every kind of movable property* other than actionable claims and money, and include stock and shares, growing crops, grass and things attached to or forming part of the land which are agreed to be severed before sale or under the contract of sale [Sec. 2(7)] Goods may be : **1.** *Existing goods, i.e.,* goods which are owned and possessed by the seller at the time of sale. These goods may be specific ascertained or unascertained. **2.** *Future goods, i.e.,* goods which the seller does not possess at the time of the contract and which will be acquired, manufactured or produced by him at some future date. **3.** *Contingent goods i.e.,* goods the acquisition of which by the seller depends upon a contingency which may or may not happen.

**Price :** The price in a contract of sale must be expressed in money. It **1.** may be fixed by the contract itself, or **2.** may be left to be fixed in an agreed manner, or **3.** may be determined from the course of dealing between the parties. Where the price is not determined in accordance with these provisions, the buyer must pay the seller a reasonable price (Sec. 9).

## CONDITIONS AND WARRANTIES

A stipulation in a contract of sale with reference to goods which are the subject thereof may be a *condition* or a *warranty* [Sec. 12(1)]. A condition is a stipulation *essential to the main purpose* of the contract. Its breach gives a right to the buyer to treat the contract as repudiated [Sec. 12(2)]. A warranty is a stipulation *collateral* to the main purpose of the contract. Its breach gives rise to a claim for damages but not a right to reject the goods and treat the contract as repudiated [Sec. 12(3)].

## EXPRESS AND IMPLIED CONDITIONS AND WARRANTIES

In a contract of sale, conditions and warranties may be *express* or *implied*. Express conditions and warranties are those which are agreed upon between the parties at the time of the contract. Implied conditions and warranties are those which are implied by law unless the parties stipulated to the contrary.

### Implied conditions

**1.** *Condition as to title :* In a contract of sale there is an implied condition on the part of the seller that *(a)* in the case of a sale, he has a right to sell the goods, and *(b)* in the case of an agreement to sell, he will have a right to sell the goods at the time when the property is to pass [Sec. 14(1)].

**2.** *Sale by description* : Where there is a contract for the sale of goods by description, there is an implied condition that the goods shall correspond with the description. If the sale is by sample as well as by description, the goods shall correspond both with the sample and the description (Sec. 15).

**3.** *Condition as to quality or fitness* : The condition as to quality or fitness is implied where *(a)* the goods sold are such as the seller deals in the ordinary course of his business; *(b)* the buyer relies on the seller's skill or judgment as to the fitness of the goods for any particular purpose; and *(c)* the buyer expressly or impliedly makes known to the seller that he wants the goods for that particular purpose [Sec. 16(1)].

**4.** *Condition as to merchantability* : Where goods are bought by description from a seller who deals in goods of that description (whether he is the manufacturer or producer or not), there is an implied condition that the goods shall be of merchantable quality [Sec. 16(2)].

**5.** *Condition implied by custom* : An implied condition as to quality or fitness for a particular purpose may be annexed by the usage of trade [Sec. 16(3)].

**6.** *Sale by sample* : In the case of a contract for sale by sample there is an implied condition *(a)* that the bulk shall correspond with the sample in quality; *(b)* that the buyer shall have a reasonable opportunity of comparing the bulk with the sample; and *(c)* that the goods shall be free from any defect, rendering them unmerchantable, which would not be apparent on a reasonable examination of the sample (Sec. 17).

**7.** *Condition as to wholesomeness* : In case of eatables and provisions, there is an implied condition that the goods shall be wholesome and fit for human consumption.

### Implied warranties

In a contract of sale, unless there is a contrary intention, there is an implied warranty that **1.** the buyer shall have and enjoy *quiet possession* of the goods [Sec. 14(*b*)], and **2.** the goods are free from any change or encumbrance in favour of any third party [Sec. 14(*c*)].

*Caveat emptor* : This means "let the buyer beware". The doctrine of *caveat emptor* does not apply—**1.** In case of implied conditions and warranties; **2.** When the buyer intimates the purpose to the seller and depends upon his skill or judgment; **3.** When there is a usage of trade; **4.** When there is a fraud by the seller.

## AUCTION SALE

A sale by auction is a public sale where different intending buyers try to outbid each other. The goods are ultimately sold to the highest bidder. The law on auction sales is contained is Sec. 64 of the Sale of Goods Act.

# PARTNERSHIP ACT, 1932

## DEFINITION NATURE OF PARTNERSHIP

Partnership is the relation between persons who have agreed to share the profits of a business carried on by all or any of them acting for all (Sec. 4).

**Characteristics of partnership**

**1.** Association of two or more persons. **2.** Agreement. **3.** Business. **4.** Sharing of profits of the business. **5.** Mutual agency.

**Partners, firm and firm name**

Persons who have entered into partnership with one another are called individually *partners* and collectively a *firm.* The name under which their business is carried on is called the *firm name.* The partners may carry on business under any name and style. But the name should not resemble the name of any existing firm and it should not show or imply the parronage of the Government.

Law of partnership is an extension of the law of agency.

**Partnership and firm**

Partnership is merely an abstract legal relationship between partners. A firm is a collective name for all the partners. Partnership is an abstract thing; a firm is a concrete thing.

**Formation of partnership**

Partnership is a special type of contract. As such all the essential elements of a valid contract must be present. But a minor may be admitted to the benefits of partnership with the consent of all the partners for the time being, and no consideration is required to create partnership.

**Duration of partnership**

A partnership may be for a *fixed period of time.* Where no provision is made by the partners for the duration of the partnership, it is *partnership-at-will.* When a person becomes a partner with another person or persons in a particular adventure or undertaking, it is *a particular partnership.*

**Test of Partnership**

In order to determine the existence of partnership between a group of persons, one has look to the agreement between them. If there is no agreement, we shall have to refer to Sec. 6. In determining whether a group of persons is or is not a firm, or whether a person is or not a partner in a firm, regard shall be had to the *real relation* between the parties as shown by all relevant facts taken together. The sharing of profits or of gross returns arising from property by persons holding a joint or common interest in that property does not of itself make such persons partners. Again the receipt by a person of a share of the profits of a business does not of itself make him a partner with the persons carrying on the business. The business. The test of partnership is *mutual agency* and not necessarily the sharing of profits or the contribution of capital or the holding of a particular property jointly.

**REGISTRATION OF FIRMS**

The Partnership Act does not provide for the compulsory registration of firms. But by creating certain disabilities from which an unregistered firm suffers, the law has made the registration of firms compulsory.

**Effects of non-registration**

**1.** A partner of an unregistered firm cannot file a suit against the firm or any partner thereof for the purpose of enforcing a right arising from a contract or a right conferred by the Partnership Act, **2.** No suit can be filed on behalf of an unregistered firm against any third party for the purpose of enforcing a right arising from a contract. **3.** An unregistered firm cannot claim a set-off exceeding Rs. 100.

*Procedure for registration* : The registration of a firm may be effected any time by filing an application in the form of a statement giving the necessary details with the Registrar of Firms of the area. The application for registration should be accompanied by the prescribed registration fee. When the Registrar is satisfied that the provisions as laid down in the Act have been duly complied with, he records an entry of the statement in the Register of Firms, and files the statement. He then issues a certificate of registration.

**RELATION OF PARTNER**

**Relation of Partners to one another**

The relations of the partners to one another are usually governed by the agreement among them. Where there is no specific agreement, their relations to one another are governed by Secs. 9 to 17 of the Partnership Act.

**Relations of Partners to third parties**

Every partner is the agent of the firm for the purposes of the business of the firm (Sec. 18).

*Authority of a partner* : The authority of a partner means the right of a partner to bind the firm by his acts. This authority of a partner to bind the firm may be an *express* authority or *implied* authority. Where, there is no partnership agreement or where the agreement is silent. Sec. 19 (1) provides that the act of a partner, which is done to carry on, in the usual way, business of the kind carried on by the firm, binds the firm. This authority of a partner is called his *implied authority*.

*No implied authority* : In the absence of any usage or custom of trade to the contrary, the implied authority of a partner *does not empower* him to—

*(a)* submit a dispute relating to the business of the firm to arbitration;

*(b)* open a baking account on behalf of the firm in his own name;

*(c)* compromise or relinquish any claim or portion of claim by the firm;

*(d)* withdraw a suit or proceeding filed on behalf of the firm;

*(e)* admit any liability in a suit or proceeding against the firm;

*(f)* acquire immovable property on behalf of the firm;

*(g)* transfer immovable property belonging to the firm;

*(h)* enter into partnership on behalf of the firm [Sec. 19(2)].

A partner can do any of the above things if—

1. he has specific or express authority of the partners; or
2. the usage or custom of trade permits him.

**Types of partners**

1. *Actual partner, i.e.*, one who becomes a partner by an agreement and is actively engaged in the conduct of the business of partnership.
2. *Sleeping partner, i.e.*, one who does not take an active part in the conduct of the business of the firm. He is, however, liable for the debts of the firm.
3. *Nominal partner, i.e.*, one who lends his name to the firm, without having any real interest in it. He is, however, liable to outsiders for the debts of the firm.
4. *Partner in profits only. i.e.*, one who gets a share in profits only and is not to contribute towards losses. He is, however, liable to outsiders for the debts of the firm.
5. *Partner by estoppel or holding out.* Anyone who by words spoken or written or by conduct prepresents himself, or knowingly permits himself to be represented to be a partner in a firm, is liable as a partner in that firm to anyone who has on the faith of any such representation given credit to the firm, whether the person representing himself or represented to be a partner does or does not know that the representation has reached the person so giving credit.
6. *Minor partner.* With the consent of all the partners for the time being, a minor may be admitted to the benefits of partnership. A minor partner has a right to such share of the property and of the profits of the firm as may have been agreed upon. He has also a right to have access to and to inspect and, copy any of the accounts, but not the books, of the firm. His liability is, however, confined only the extent of his share in the profits and property of the firm. He may, at any time within six months of his attaining majority, give public notice that he has elected to *(a)* become, or *(b)* not to become a partner in the firm. If he fails to give a public notice, he is deemed to have become a partner in the firm on the expiry of the said six months.

**RECONSTITUTION OF A FIRM**

**1.** *Introduction of a new partner* (Sec. 31) : Subject to contract between the partners, on person can be introduced as a partner into a firm without the consent of all the existing partners. An incoming partner is not liable for any act of the firm done prior to his admission.

**2.** *Retirement of a partner* (Sec. 32) : A partner may retire from a firm with the consent of all the other partners. Where the partnership is at will, a partner may retire by giving notice in writing to all the other partners of his intention to retire.

**3.** *Explusion of partner* (Sec. 38) : A majority of partners can expel a partner only if such power is conferred by contract between the partners, and the power is exercised *bonafide* by the majority of partners.

**4.** *Insolvency of a partner* (Sec. 34) : Where a partner in a firm is adjudicated insolvent, he ceases to be a partner on the date on which the order of adjudication is made, whether or not the firm is thereby dissolved.

**5.** *Death of a partner* [Sec. 42*(c)*] : Subject to contract between the partners, a firm is dissolved by the death fo a partner.

**Dissolution of firm**

The *dissolution of partnership* between all the partners of a firm is called the *dissolution of the firm* (Sec. 39). Dissolution of firm means complete breakdown of the relation of partnership between all the partners. If this breakdown of partnership relation is between a few and not all the partners, this amounts to dissolution of partnership which simply involves only a change in the relation of the partners.

Dissolution of a firm may be voluntary or without the order of Court, or it may take place by the order of Court.

**Dissolution without the order of court**

This takes place in the following ways :

**1.** *Dissolution by agreement* (Sec. 40). A firm may be dissolved *(i)* with the consent of all the partners, or *(ii)* in accordance with a contract between the partners.

**2.** *Compulsory dissolution* (Sec. 41). A firm is compulsorily dissolved *(a)* when all the partners or all the partners but one are adjudicated insolvent. *(b)* on the happening of any event which makes it unlawful for the business of the firm to be carried on, or for the partners to carry it on in partnership.

**3.** *Dissolution on the happening of certain contingencies* (Sec. 42). Subject to contract between the partners, a firm is dissolved *(a)* it constituted for a fixed term, by the expiry of that term; *(b)* if constituted to carry out one or more adventures or undertakings, by the completion thereof; *(c)* by the death of a partner; and *(d)* by the adjudication of a partner as an insolvent.

**4.** *Dissolution by notice of partnership-at-will* (Sec. 43). Where a partnership is at will, the firm may be dissolved by any partner by giving a notice in writing to all the other partners of his intention to dissolve the firm.

**Dissolution by the Court (Sec. 44)**

At the suit of a partner, the Court may dissolve a firm on any of the folloiwng grounds, viz., *(a)* Insanity of a partner, *(b)* Permanent incapacity of a partner, *(c)* Misconduct of a partner, *(d)* Persistent breach of agreement by a partner, *(e)* Transfer of interest by a partner, *(f)* Business working at a loss, *(g)* Any other ground which the Court deems just and equitable.

**Rights and Liabilities of Partners on Dissolution**

**Rights :** On the dissolution of a firm, a partner has the right to **1.** have the business of the firm would up and the debts of the firm settled out of the property of the firm; **2.** share in the profits of the firm earned after dissolution; **3.** have the premium returned on premature dissolution; **4.** restrain the use of firm name or property by any partner for his own benefit.

In case the partnership is rescinded on the ground of fraud or misrepresentation, the partner has the right of *(a)* lien on the surplus assets, *(b)* subrogation, and *(c)* indemnification.

**Liabilities :** If a public notice is not given of the dissolution of a firm the partners continue to be liable to third parties for any act done by any of them after dissolution. After the dissolution of the firm, the partners continue to be liable for acts done to wind up the affairs of the firm and to complete transactions begun but unfinished at the time of the dissolution.

## CONSUMER PROTECTION — HISTORY, CONCEPT, OBJECT AND OTHER RELATED ASPECTS OF LEGISLATION

The history of the consumer protection legislation at the International level can be traced back to a movement that took place in 1983 when the guidelines for the protection of consumer were submitted to the Economic and Social Council (UNESCO) by the Secretary General of the United Nations in consultation with governments. Thereafter, a resolution was passed by the UN assembly on 9th April 1985 for providing guidelines to the governments to make the law for better protection of the interest of the consumers. Such law being the essence of the time aimed at providing a cheaper and speedier justice to the consumer.

At the national level the growing industrialization demanded better laws for protecting the rights of the consumer. The advertisement in television, newspaper and magazine showing their impact on the minds of the consumer also brought with themselves the chances of misleading consumers by hiding the defect, imperfections or short comings in the quality, quantity and the purity of the goods. In cases of services rendered there increased chances of deficiencies in service which affected the consumer adversely. The earlier statutes like the Code of Civil Procedure, 1908, Indian Contract Act, 1872, Sale of Goods Act, 1930, Indian Penal Code, 1860, Standards of Weights and Measures Act, 1976 and the Motor Vehicle Act, 1988 could not achieve the object of protecting the rights of the consumer in a proper manner although the Monopolistic and Restrictive Trade Practices Act, 1969 and the Prevention of Food Adulteration Act, 1954 worked well in the direction. Yet a special statute for the purpose became the essence of the time, so on 5th December, 1986 the Consumer Protection Bill, 1986 as introduced in Lok Sabha.

Interpreting the preamble in the Consumer Protection Act, 1986 the Supreme Court in the case of J. J. Merchant (Dr.) v. Srinath Chaturvedi (2002) 6 SCC 635 held that the object of the Act lies is providing speedy, inexpensive and simple redressal to consumer disputes and for that purpose a quasi-judicial machinery has been set up at district, state and central level. The relief of specific nature has to be provided by these quasi-judicial bodies and they are empowered to award compensation to the consumers in appropriate cases. Furthermore, the power to penalise has also been conferred to them in cases of non-compliance of the orders given by these bodies.

## MEANING OF CONSUMER

"Consumer" means any person who-

(*i*) buys any goods for a consideration which has been paid or promised or partly paid and partly promised or under any system of deferred payment and includes any user of such goods other than the person who buys such goods for consideration paid or promised or partly paid or partly promised, or under any system of deferred payment, when such use is made with the approval of such person, but does not include a person who obtains such goods for resale or for any commercial purpose; or

(*ii*) hires or avails of any services for a consideration which has been paid or promised or partly paid and partly promised, or under any system of deferred payment and includes any beneficiary of such services other than the person who hires or avails of the services for consideration paid or promised, or partly paid and partly promised, or under any system of deferred payment, when such services are availed of with the approval of the first mentioned person but does not include a personal who avails of such services for any commercial purpose;

Here "commercial purpose" does not include use by a person of goods bought and used by him and services availed by him exclusively for the purposes of earning his livelihood by means of self-employment;

And the term "Person" includes

(*i*) a firm whether registered or not;
(*ii*) a Hindu undivided family;
(*iii*) a co-operative society;
(*iv*) every other association of person whether registered under the Societies Registration Act, 1860 (21 of 1860) or not;

After the changes made in the Consumer Protection Act, 1986 by the Consumer Protection (Amendment) Act, 2002 (Act 62 of 2002) it is to be noted that the services availed by the user exclusively for the purposes of earning his livelihood by means of self-employment has also been excluded from the interpretation to the term "Commercial Purpose". So, now the term "consumer" includes the user of goods bought and used by him and services availed by him for the purposes of earning his livelihood by means of self-employment. It becomes necessary to understand the meaning of the term "Service" within the ambit of the Consumer Protection Act, 1986. "Service" means service of any description which is made available to potential users and includes, but not limited to the provision of facilities in connection with banking, financing insurance, transport, processing, supply of electrical or other energy, board or lodging or both, housing construction, entertainment, amusement or purviewing of news or other information but does not include the rendering of any service free of charge or under a contract of personal service.

## DEFINITION OF "GOODS"

**Section 2 (1)(*i*)** of the Consumer Protection Act, 1986 defines "goods" as "goods defined in the Sale of Goods Act, 1930". So, "Goods" means every kind of movable property other than actionable claims and money; and includes stock and shares, growing crops, grass, and things attached to or forming part of the land which are agreed to be severed.

In *R.D. Goyal* v. *Reliance Industries Ltd.* (2003) 1 SCC 81 it was held that the definition of goods is in pari-materia with the provisions of the Sale of Goods Act, 1932.

## CONSUMER - WHO IS NOT

In *Laxmiben Laxmichand Shah* v. *Sakerben Kanji Chandan,* (2001) 9 SCC 604, the Supreme Court upheld the view of the National Commission wherein the claim for compensation by the tenant against his landlord was not accepted. The term of lease in this case did not contain any provision for cleaning, repairing and maintenance of the building by landlord and as such it was observed that the tenant was not a consumer. The omission to render such services on the part of landlord did not entitle the tenant to claim compensation for the same.

Complaint by the holder of power of attorney is not maintainable under the Act (Punjab National Bank v. Ramakant Yadav, (1997) 1 CPJ 44 (Bihar)).

Education does not lie within the ambit of the Consumer Protection Act, 1986 (N. Taneja v. Consumer District Forum AIR 1992 Cal 95).

Subscriber to a law reporter does not come within the meaning of "Consumer" (Delhi Law Times Office v. Jadish Prasad (1996) 2 CPJ 78 (Bihar)).

The Supreme Court in *Savami Roadlines* v. *Sundaram Textiles Ltd.* AIR 2001 SC 2630 held that the consumer complaint made by the insurance company is not tenable for the reason that the insurance company is not a consumer. In this case on the non-delivery of goods by carrier, the value of goods was paid to the consignor by insurer and he obtained from him a letter of subrogation in which the main terms were similar to those involved in Oberoi forwarding case (2000) 2 SCC 407. It was held that the alleged letter of subrogation was an assignment and as such the complaint filed by the insurer against the carrier, although impleading the consignor also, was not tenable. But, the insurer could seek remedy before a Civil Court. A significant question that remains unanswered in this case is that in case of mere subrogation whether the insurer, who had compensated the consignor for loss of goods by the carrier, could maintain a complaint against the carrier.

In the case of *Vinitha Ashok* v. *Lakshmi Hospital,* (2001) 8 SCC 731 the Apex Court held that the doctor would come within the purview of negligence regardless of his diagnosis and treatment being approved by a body of professional opinion, in case such opinion is not established to be reasonable or responsible. Professional opinion needs to match with the logical analysis so as to be described as reasonable and responsible. In this case the appellant had a cervical pregnancy, a rare and complicated condition discovered during D & C procedure for MTP and hysterectomy (removal of uterus) operation was performed by the respondent which resulted in excessive bleeding. On facts of the case it was held that the respondents had followed procedure commonly used through out the state of Kerala and could not be said to have acted negligently. Furthermore, the fact that certain experts had stopped use of D & C method would not be of much importance. The Supreme Court upheld the view of the National Commission wherein the claim of the appellant for compensation was dismissed.

Telephone services come under the purview of Consumer Protection Act (Mahaveer Electricals v. District Engineer, Telecommunication, (1991) 2 CPJ 296 (Andh. Pra.)).

Where suit was instituted in the Civil Court after the payment of "court fees" it was held that it did not mean the "hiring" or "availing of " service of the Court after the payment of consideration. As such the complaint was not tenable before consumer forum on the basis of deficiencies in the set up of the Civil Judicial Administration.

A claim for compensation against the advocate who had rendered service free of charge and without compensation was not tenable (G. Swaminathan v. E. Kumar (1991) 1 MWN (CP) 71 (T.N)).

Where person registered himself for release of L.P.G. connection with the distributer it was held that the person was "consumer" irrespective of the fact that at the time of registration he pays nothing and the payment is deferred till the time of release of gas connection (Dharam Chand v. Mandeep Gas Service, (1993) 2 CPJ 985 (Punj.)).

Nominee of a life insurance policy is a "Consumer" (Jagdish Prasad Dagar v. Senior Divisional Manager, LIC, (1992) 2 CPJ 493 (NC)).

Where a person was using electricity for a Commercial Purpose he was held to be "Consumer" within the meaning of the Act (Sub-Divisional Officer, HSEB v. Sita Ram (1992) 2 CPJ 819 (Haryana)).

The "Commercial Purchase" as envisaged in clause 2(*d*) of the Consumer Protection Act, 1986 has been illustrated by the Court in a number of cases. For instance, where the vehicle was purchased for running it as a taxi it was held to be a purchase for commercial purpose (Pushpa Meena v. Shah Enterprises (Rajsthan) Ltd. (1992) 1 CPJ 271(Raj)).

Where goods were purchased for resale it was held to be purchased for commercial purpose (Zohia Starlinger Ltd. v. Lenith Computers Ltd. (1991) 1 CPJ 145 (NC)).

Similarly, where the VCR was purchased for running video parlour, it was a purchase for commercial purpose (Assistant Manager, BPL India v. SR Tushar, (1991) CPJ 155).

The grant of state carriage permit was held to be commercial purchase (*Re.* State Transport Authority, (1992) 2 CPJ 677 (Cal HC)).

The purchase of photocopier machine was held to be a purchase for commercial purpose (*Re.* State Transport Authority, (1992) 2 CPJ 677 (Cal HC)).

In *Kalpavruksha Charitable Trust* v. *Toshniwal Bros.* (*Bombay*) (*P*) *Ltd*, (2000) 1 SCC 512 where a charitable trust ran a diagnostic center where the patients used to take advantage of scanning, etc. and were usually required to pay for the same. Only 10% of the patient users were given free service. It was held by the Supreme Court that the purpose of purchase of machines by the Diagnostic Center was purchased for "Commercial purpose".

**CONSUMER DISPUTE**

"Consumer dispute' means a dispute where the person against whom a complaint has been made, denies or disputes the allegations contained in the complaint.

**DEFICIENCY IN SERVICE**

"Service" means service of any description which is made available to potential users and includes, but not limited to, the provision of facilities in connection with banking, financing, insurance, transport, processing, supply of electrical or other energy, board or lodging or both, housing construction, entertainment, amusement or the purveying of news or other information, but does not include the rendering of any service free of charge or under a contract of personal service.

On the other hand "deficiency" means any fault, imperfection, shortcoming or inadequacy in quality, nature and manner of performance which is required to be maintained by or under any law for the time being in force or has been undertaken to be performed by a person in pursuance of a contract or otherwise in relation to any service.

In *Swastic Industries* v. *Maharashtra State Electricity Board* AIR 1997 SC 1101 the Supreme Court observed that where the supplementary demand for escaped energy charges was made by the State Electricity Board, it was not a deficiency in service as per Section 2(*1*)(*g*) of Consumer Protection Act, 1986.

In *Viswalakshmi Sasidharan* v. *Branch Manager, Syndicate Bank*, (1997) 1 CPR 107, where the bank could not disburse the total amount of loan contracted with the petitioner it was held by the Supreme Court that it amounts to deficiency in service. Furthermore, it was observed that the admission of the petitioner to the effect that they might not be able to repay the loan later on was not sufficient for the commission to decline from taking up the case.

The Supreme Court in *Ravneet Singh Bagga* v. *KLM Royal Dutch Airlines* (2000) 1 SCC 66 upheld the orders of National Commission and observed that verification of the visa by the concerned airlines second time enroute on certain suspicious grounds was a bonafide act, and the bonafide action of the respondent staff can't tantamount to deficiency in service and therefore the appellant was not entitled to any relief under this Act.

## UNFAIR TRADE PRACTICES

"Unfair Trade Practice" has been defined in *Section 2(1)(r)* of the Consumer Protection Act, 1986 as:

"Unfair trade practice" means a trade practice which, for the purpose of promoting the sale, use or supply of any goods or for the provision of any service, adopts any unfair method or unfair or deceptive practice including any of the following practices namely:

(1) the practice of making any statement, whether orally or in writing or by visible representation which,

- (*i*) falsely represents that the goods are of a particular standard, quality, quantity, grade, composition,, style or model;
- (*ii*) falsely represents that the services are of a particular standard , quality or grade;
- (*iii*) falsely represents any re-built, second-hand, renovated, reconditioned or old goods as new goods;
- (*iv*) represents that the goods or services have sponsorship, approval, performance, characteristics, accessories, uses or benefits which such goods or services do not have;
- (*v*) represents that the seller or the supplier has a sponsorship or approval or affiliation which such seller or supplier does not have;
- (*vi*) makes a false or misleading representation concerning the need for, or the usefulness of, any goods or services;
- (*vii*) gives to the public any warranty or guarantee of the performance, efficacy or length of life of a product or of any goods that is not based on an adequate or proper test thereof:

  provided that where a defense is raised to the effect that such warranty or guarantee is based on adequate or proper test, the burden of proof of such defence shall lie on the person raising such defence;
- (*viii*) makes to the public a representation in a form that purports to be:
  - (*a*) a warranty or guarantee of a product or of any goods or services; or
  - (*b*) a promise to replace, maintain or repair an article or any part thereof or to repeat or continue a service until it has achieved a specified result, if such purported warranty or guarantee or promise is materially misleading or if there is no reasonable prospect that such warranty, guarantee or promise will be carried out;
- (*ix*) materially misleads the public concerning the price at which a product or like products or goods or services, have been or are, ordinarily sold or provided, and, for this purpose, a representation as to price shall be deemed to refer to the price at which the product or goods or services has or have been sold by sellers or provided by suppliers generally in the relevant market unless it is clearly specified to be the price at which the product as been sold or services have been provided by the person by whom or on whose behalf the representation is made;

(*x*) gives false or misleading fact disparaging the goods, service or trade of another person.

*Explanation*: For the purpose of clause (1), a statement that is:

(*a*) expressed on an article offered or displayed for sale or on its wrapper or container; or

(*b*) expressed on anything attached to, inserted in, or accompanying, an article offered or displayed for sale or on anything on which the article is mounted for display or sale; or

(*c*) contained in or on anything that is sold, sent, delivered, transmitted or in any other manner whatsoever made available to a member of the public, shall be deemed to be a statement made to the public by, and only by, the person who had caused the statement to be so expressed, made or contained;

(2) permits the publication of any advertisement whether in any newspaper or other wise, for the sale or supply at a bargain price, of goods or services that are not intended to be offered for sale or supply at the bargain price, or for a period that is, and in quantities that are, reasonable, having regard to the nature of the market in which the business is carried on, the nature and size of business, and the nature of the advertisement.

***Explanation***—For the purpose of clause (2), "bargaining price" means:

(*a*) a price that is stated in any advertisement to be a bargain price, by reference to an ordinary price or otherwise, or

(*b*) a price that a person who reads, hears or sees the advertisement, would reasonable understand to be bargain price having regard to the prices at which the production advertised or like products are ordinarily sold;

(3) permits-

(*i*) the offering of gifts, prizes or other items with the intention of not providing them as offered or creating impression that something is being given or offered free of charge when it is fully or partly covered by the amount charged in the transactions as a whole;

(*ii*) the conduct of any contest, lottery, game of chance or skill, for the purpose of promoting, directly or indirectly, the sale, use or supply of any product or any business interest;

(3A) withholding from the participants of any scheme offering gifts, prizes or other items free of charge, on its closure the information about final results of the scheme.

***Explanation***—For the purposes of this subclause, the participants of a scheme shall be deemed to have been informed of the final results of the scheme where such results of the scheme where such results are within a reasonable time published, prominently in the same newspapers in which the scheme was originally advertised;

(4) permits the sale or supply of goods intended to be used, or are of a kind likely to be used, by consumers, knowing or having reason to believe that the goods do not comply with the standards prescribed by competent authority relating to performance, composition, contents, design, constructions, finishing or packaging as are necessary to prevent or reduce the risk of injury to the person using the goods;

(5) permits the hoarding or destruction of goods, refuses to sell the goods or to make them available for sale or to provide any service, if such hoarding or destruction or refusal raises or refusal raises or tends to raise or is intended to raise, the cost of those or other similar goods or services.

(6) manufacture of spurious goods or offering such goods for sale or adopting deceptive practices in the provision of services.

In Colgate Palmolive Ltd. v. Hindustan Lever Ltd., 1986-2002 consumer 6101 (NS) the Supreme Court held that for holding a trade practice to be unfair trade practice, it must be found that it causes loss or injury to the consumer.

## RESTRICTIVE TRADE PRACTICE

"Restrictive Trade Practice" has been defined in *Section 2(1)(nnn)* of the Consumer Protection Act, 1986 as:

"restrictive trade practice" means a trade practice which tends to bring about manipulation of price or its conditions of delivery or to affect flow of supplies in the market relating to goods or services in such a manner as to impose on the consumers unjustified costs or restrictions and shall include-

(*a*) delay beyond the period agreed to by a trader in supply of such goods or in providing the services which has led or is likely to lead to rise in the price;

(*b*) any trade practice which requires a consumer to buy, hire or avail of any goods or, as case may be, services as condition precedent to buying, hiring or availing of other goods or services;

"Trader" in relation to any goods means a person who sells or distributes any goods for sale and includes the manufacturer thereof and where such goods are sold or distributed in package form includes, the packer thereof.

## "MANUFACTURER" MEANING OF

"Manufacturer" means a person who-

(*i*) makes or manufactures any goods or parts thereof; or

(*ii*) does not make or manufacture any goods but assembles parts thereof made or manufactured by others; or

(*iii*) puts or causes to be put his own mark on any goods made or manufactured by any other manufacturer;

Where a manufacturer dispatches any goods or part thereof to any branch office maintained by him, such branch office shall not be deemed to be the manufacturer even though the parts so dispatched to it are assembled at such branch office and are sold or distributed from such branch office.

# OBJECTIVE TYPE QUESTIONS

**1.** The minimum number of members in a private company and public company are
(*a*) Three and Seven respectively
(*b*) Two and seven respectively
(*c*) Two and nine respectively
(*d*) None of the above

**2.** A public Company can commence business after receiving
(*a*) Certificate of incorporation
(*b*) Certificate to commence business
(*c*) Both (a) and (b)
(*d*) None of the above

**3.** As per Companies (Amendment) Act, 2000, a private company and public company must have paid up capital of
(*a*) Rs. One lakh and two lakhs respectively
(*b*) Rs. One lakh and five lakhs respectively
(*c*) Rs. Two lakhs and six lakhs respectively
(*d*) None of the above.

**4.** Contacts, which entered into, by agents or trustees on behalf of a prospective company before it has come into existence are called
(*a*) Provisional contracts
(*b*) Preliminary or pre-incorporation contracts
(*c*) Both (a) and (b)
(*d*) None of the above

**5.** A private company can be converted into a public company under
(*a*) Conversion by default
(*b*) Conversion by operation law
(*c*) Conversion by choice
(*d*) Any of the above

**6.** A company limited by shares
(*a*) Has unlimited liability
(*b*) Exists only in contemplation of law
(*c*) Has a perpetual succession
(*d*) Comes to an end on the death of all the members

7. An Act is said to be ultra virus a company when it is beyond the powers.
(a) Of the company
(b) Of the directors
(c) Of the directors but not the company
(d) Conferred on the company by the Articles

8. The charter of a company is its
(a) Articles of Association
(b) Prospectus
(c) Statement in lieu of Prospectus
(d) Memorandum of Association.

9. Which of the following is benefit from incorporation of a company?
(a) Loss of privacy
(b) Possibilities of frauds
(c) Greater public accountability
(d) Independent legal entity

10. Which one of the following is not the content of the memorandum of association?
(a) Name clause
(b) The registered office clause
(c) The objects clause
(d) The Board of Directors clause.

11. The limit of salary of a worker entitled to get bonus is
(a) 5000/- per month
(b) 3,500/- per month
(c) 2,500/- per month
(d) None of the above

12. As per Section 38 of the Payment of Bonus Act, 1965 the power to make/frame rules is vested with
(a) Cabinet Secretary
(b) Ministry of Finance
(c) Ministry of Labour
(d) Central Government

13. Who is entitled to entitled to bonus under the Payment of Bonus Act, 1965?
(a) A part time employee who is engaged on a regular basis
(b) A probationer employee
(c) A dismissed employee reinstated with back wages
(d) All of the above

14. Ordinarily, the Payment of Bonus Act, 1965 cannot apply on an establishment employing less than 20 persons.
(a) True (b) False

15. Once the Bonus Act is applicable on an establishment, the Act will continue to apply even if the number of employees comes below the required minimum.
(a) True. (b) False.

16. Completed year of service means
(a) Service for one year
(b) Continuous service
(c) Continuous service for one year
(d) Number of years of service

17. Superannuation means
(a) The attainment of age of 58 years
(b) The attainment of age of 60 years
(c) Attainment of age as fixed in the contract or condition of services
(d) Such age certified medically to be fit

18. Gratuity shall be paid to an employee after he has surrendered continuous service for
(a) Not less than three years
(b) Not less than five years
(c) Not less than seven years
(d) None of the above

19. For calculation of gratuity under the payment of Gratuity Act, 1972 the number of days in a month is to be taken as
(a) Actual number of days on employment
(b) 26 days
(c) 15 days
(d) 30 days

20. The Payment of Gratuity come into force on
(a) 23rd Oct., 1971 (b) 16th Sept., 1972
(c) 16th Sept., 1971 (d) 23rd Oct., 1972

21. Gratuity is a benefit, which an employee gets at the time of only retirement.
(a) True (b) False

22. Forfeiture of Gratuity is possible under certain circumstances.
(a) True (b) False

**23.** On which of the following states the Indian Partnership Act, 1932 does not applies?
(*a*) The State of Sikkim
(*b*) The North-Eastern States of India
(*c*) The State of Jammu and Kashmir
(*d*) All the above

**24.** On which of the following date section 69 of the Indian Partnership Act, 1932 came into force?
(*a*) 1st October, 1933
(*b*) 1st April, 1938
(*c*) 11 November 1933
(*d*) 1st October, 1936

**25.** The date on which the Indian Partnership Act, 1932 came into force is:
(*a*) 1st October, 1932
(*b*) 4th October, 1932
(*c*) 1st May, 1934
(*d*) 1st April,1832

**26.** Under Indian Partnership Act 1932, act of a firm means.
(*a*) Only such acts which give rise to a right enforceable by or against the firm
(*b*) All acts which do not give any right enforceable by the firm
(*c*) All acts of the partners
(*d*) None of these

**27.** In which of the following Act, Partnership law was containted?
(*a*) The Transfer of Property Act, 1908
(*b*) The Sale of Goods Act, 1930
(*c*) The Indian Contract Act, 1872
(*d*) All the above

**28.** In which of the following Act, the partnership related provisions were contained before Indian Partnership Act,1932?
(*a*) Indian Contract Act, 1872
(*b*) C.P.C
(*c*) Companies Act, 1913
(*d*) All the above

**29.** Which of the following is included in 'business' under section 2(b) of the Indian Partnership Act, 1932.
(*a*) Every trade, occupation and profession
(*b*) Every occupation
(*c*) Every trade and occupation
(*d*) None of these

**30.** Under which of the following section of the Indian Partnership Act 1932, the term 'business' has been defined?
(*a*) Section 2(b) (*b*) Section 2(c)
(*c*) Seftion 2(e) (*d*) Section 2(a)

**31.** The question that an act of a partner is of an act of firm or not; it is a question of :
(*a*) Fact
(*b*) Law
(*c*) Fact and Law both
(*d*) None of these

**32.** The act of a firm is an act of :
(*a*) Any one partner (*b*) Any one agent
(*c*) All the partners (*d*) All the above

**33.** Partnership is a :
(*a*) creation of the choice and voluntarily agreement between the concerned parties
(*b*) compulsory legal relation
(*c*) (*a*) and (*b*) both
(*d*) None of these

**34.** Which of the following section of the Indian Partnership Act 1932 defines the term "partnership" :
(*a*) Section 4 (*b*) Section 2
(*c*) Section 3 (*d*) Section 7

**35.** Which of the following statement is correct?
(*a*) A Partnership can be a general partnership
(*b*) A Partnership can be a particular partnership
(*c*) (*a*) or (*b*) any one
(*d*) None of these

**36.** Which statement is correct?
(*a*) A partnership firm is a distinct legal entity from its partners
(*b*) A partnership firm is not a distinct legal entity from its partners
(*c*) A partnership firm is a juristic person
(*d*) All the above

**37.** For which of the following section 7 of the Indian Partnership Act provides:
(*a*) General partnership
(*b*) Partnership at will
(*c*) Partnership in a particular adventure
(*d*) All the above

**38.** Which of the following is provided under section 8 of the Indian Partnership Act, 1932:
(*a*) A general partnership
(*b*) A particular partnership
(*c*) (*a*) and (*b*) both
(*d*) None of these

**39.** Which of the fowllowing section prescribes that the reation of partnership arises not from status :
(*a*) Section 5 (*b*) Section 2
(*c*) Section 8 (*d*) Section 9

**40.** By which of the following a partnership cannot be constituted?
(*a*) Two U.H.F. (*b*) Two individuals
(*c*) (*a*) and (*b*) both (*d*) None of these

**41.** With, which of the following a joint Hindu family is entitled to enter into an agreement of partnership :
(*a*) All individuals
(*b*) Another U.H.F.
(*c*) All partnership firms
(*d*) None of these

**42.** The nature of a Mutual agency is :
(*a*) A legal incidence of partnership
(*b*) A test to determine the existence of a partnership
(*c*) (*a*) and (*b*) both
(*d*) None of these

**43.** With which of the following a partnership firm is entitled to enter into a partnership?
(*a*) An individual (*b*) Another firm
(*c*) H.U.F. (*d*) None of these

**44.** A valid partnership is, between :
(*a*) Individual members of one firm and the individual members of another firm
(*b*) Two partnership firms and an individual
(*c*) One Partnership firm and an individual
(*d*) All the above

**45.** To constitute a partnership under the Indian Partnership Act, 1932. Which of the following in itself is not sufficient?
(*a*) Receipt by a person of a payment varying with the profits earned by a business
(*b*) Sharing of profits by persons having a joint or common interest
(*c*) Receipt by a person of a share of the profits
(*d*) All the above

**46.** Which of the following section of the Indian Partnership Act, 1932 describes the mode of determining the existence of partnership?
(*a*) Section 3 (*b*) Section 8
(*c*) Section 6 (*d*) Section 11

**47.** The state on which this act does not applies, is:
(*a*) Sikkim
(*b*) Nagaland
(*c*) Jammu and Kashmir
(*d*) All the above

**48.** A valid partnership, under this Act, is:
(*a*) Partnership between two UHFs
(*b*) Partnership between the *Karta* of a UHF in his representative capacity and an individual co-parcener of the same family
(*c*) (*a*) and (*b*) both
(*d*) None of these

**49.** To, which of the following, section 5 of the Indian Partnership Act, 1932 does not applies?
(*a*) Burmese Buddhist husband and wife carrying on the business
(*b*) Any Muslim Trading Family
(*c*) Any Trading Company
(*d*) All the above

**50.** From which of the following date the disoldution of firm by notice becomes effective under section 43 of the Indian Partnership Act 1932?
(*a*) mentioned in the noitce as the date of dissolution
(*b*) on which the notice is sent
(*c*) on which the notice is received
(*d*) None of these

**51.** With which of the following the concept of partnership commensurate?
(*a*) Joint owners of property
(*b*) Principal and agent
(*c*) Co-owners of property
(*d*) None of these

**52.** The Indian Partnership Act, came into force on:
(*a*)1 August, 1934 (*b*) 1 October, 1932
(*c*) 7 July, 1933 (*d*) None of these

**53.** For creating a partnership under section 4 of the Indian Partnership Act,1932 which of the following is not essential?
(*a*) Sharing of losses (*b*) An agreement
(*c*) Profit sharing (*d*) All the above

**54.** For which of the following a partnership is provided and recognised in the Indian Partnership Act, 1932 ?
(*a*) For a specified and fixed venture
(*b*) For a specified and fixed period
(*c*) (*a*) and (*b*) both
(d) None of these

**55.** Incase a partnership for unfixed, period under the Indian Partnership Act, 1932 such partnership is :
(*a*) Partnership at will
(*b*) Illegal partnership
(*c*) General partnership
(*d*) None of these

**56.** Partnership at will is subject to:
(*a*) Two exceptions (*b*) Four exceptions
(*c*) Six exceptions (*d*) One exceptions

**57.** If after the expiration of fix period, for which a partnership firm was constituted the firm continues to carry on business,without any new agreement in such condition:
(*a*) The partnership becomes partnership at will
(*b*) The partnership stands extended till the new agreement is made
(*c*) The partnership dissolves
(*d*) None of these

**58.** Which of the following statement is correct?
(*a*) In a partnership at will a partner of a firm can dissolve the firm at any time by giving a notice of his intention to his co-partners
(*b*) In a partnership at will a partner of a firm can retire from the firm at any time by giving a notice of his intention to his co-partners
(*c*) (*a*) and (*b*) both
(*d*) None of these

**59.** Indian Partnership Act came into existence in :
(*a*) 1832 (*b*) 1932
(*c*) 1950 (*d*) None of these

**60.** Which of the following is correct regarding constituting a partnership under section 4 of the Indian Partnership Act,1932?
(*a*) It is immaterial as to whether the business is of temporary or permanent nature
(*b*) The business has to be of permanent nature
(*c*) The business can be of temporary nature
(*d*) None of these

**61.** In which of the following section of Indian Partnership Act,1932. General duties of partners have been provided?
(*a*) Section 15 (*b*) Section 18
(*c*) Section 9 (*d*) None of these

**62.** Which of the following statement is correct?
(*a*) Section 12 of the Indian Partnership Act, 1932 is a mixed statement of rights and duties of partners in reference to the conduct of the business
(*b*) Section 12 of the Indian Partnership Act, 1932 is a statement of rights of the partners in reference to the conduct of business
(*c*) Section 12 of the Indian Partnership Act, 1932 is a statement of duties of the partners in the conduct of the business
(*d*) None of these

**63.** Under section 11 of the Indian Partnership Act,1932 an agreement in restraint of trade in a partnership is :

(*a*) Against public policy
(*b*) void
(*c*) valid
(*d*) illegal

**64.** Partnership at will is described under section :
(*a*) 2 (*b*) 5
(*c*) 7 (*d*) 9

**65.** The rights and duties of partners *inter se* can be regulated under section :
(*a*) section 11 (*b*) section 15
(*c*) section 16 (*d*) section 17

**66.** Section 7 of the Indian Partnership Act, 1932 describes about :
(*a*) Partnership at will
(*b*) Right of partners
(*c*) Minor related provision
(*d*) None of these

**67.** Which of the following is a duty of every partner under section 10 of the Indian Partnership Act?
(*a*) To render true accounts
(*b*) Not to carry on any business other than that of the firm
(*c*) To indemnify the firm for any loss caused to it by his fraud in the conduct of the business of the firm
(*d*) All the above

**68.** To which of the following the rule of unanimity of the Indian Partnership Act, 1932 has a reference :
(*a*) Every type matters
(*b*) Fundamental matters
(*c*) Ordinary matters
(*d*) None of these

**69.** In which of the following matters section 12 (c) of the Indian Partnership Act, 1932 is applicable:
(*a*) Ordinary matters
(*b*) Fundamental matters
(*c*) All matters
(*d*) None of these

**71.** Which of the following is provided under section 12 (c) of the Indian Partnership Act, 1932?
(*a*) Rule of unaimity
(*b*) Rule of majority
(*c*) (a) and (b) both
(*d*) None of these

**71.** It is a question of........ that whether a partnership exists or not
(*a*) Fact and law both
(*b*) Fact
(*c*) Law
(*d*) (*b*) or (*c*)

**72.** Section 24 of the Indian Partnership Act, 1932 describes :
(*a*) Notice to a partner is a notice to the firm
(*b*) Notice to a partner is not a notice to the firm
(*c*) A partner can retire without any notice to other partners
(*d*) None of these

**73.** Which of the following is the minimum number of persons required for a partnership?
(*a*) 6 (*b*) 8
(*c*) 2 (*d*) 15

**74.** Duties of the partners are described under which of the following section of Indian Partnership Act 1932?
(*a*) 16 (*b*) 14
(*c*) 11 (*d*) 10

**75.** Incase an illegal partnership, such partnership can :
(*a*) Be sued (*b*) Sue and be sued
(*c*) Sue (*d*) Not be sued

**76.** Which of the following remedy is available to the members of an illegal partnership?
(*a*) For the partnership dealings and transaction only with the permission of the court againt other partners
(*b*) For the partnership dealings and transactions, against each partner
(*c*) Have no remedy against each other for the partnership dealings and transactions
(*d*) None of these

**77.** The account books of the firm can be examined by a partner:

(*a*) Twice a year
(*b*) As many number of times without any restriction
(*c*) Once a month
(*d*) Twice a month

**78.** During which of the following period a partner can access all the books of accounts:
(*a*) After the dissolution of the firm
(*b*) The subsistence of the partnership
(*c*) The proceedings for the dissolution of the firm
(*d*) All the above

**79.** The account books etc. of the firm can be examined by a partner:
(*a*) Through any representative
(*b*) Himself
(*c*) Through his advocate
(*d*) All the above

**80.** Which of the following statement is correct?
(*a*) Section 13 of the Indian Partnership Act, is a mixed statement of rights, duties and liabilities of the partners.
(*b*) Section 13 of the Indian Partnership Act, 1932 is a mixed statement of rights and duties of the partners
(*c*) Section 13 of the Indian Partnership Act, 1932 is a mixed statement of duties and liabilities of the partners
(*d*) Scetion 13 of the Indian Partnership Act, 1932 is a mixed statement of rights and liabilities of the partners

**81.** The rate of interest prescribed under section 13, is:
(*a*) Nine per cent (*b*) Twelve per cent
(*c*) Six per cent (*d*) None of these

**82.** The conduct of the business is described under section :
(*a*) 13 (*b*) 16
(*c*) 12 (*d*) 18

**83.** Which of the following is provided by section 13(a) of the Indian Partnership Act, 1932:
(*a*) Payment of remuneration to a partner only when there is an agreement to that effect between the partners
(*b*) Payment of remuneration to a partner as a matter of right
(*c*) (*a*) and (*b*) both
(*d*) None of these

**84.** To which of the following all the partners are entitled under section 13 (b) of the Indian Partnership Act, 1932?
(*a*) Share the profits and losses equally in the absence of any agreement to the contrary between them
(*b*) Share the profits and losses in the ratio of their capital contributions
(*c*) Share the profits and losses equally as in agreement to the contrary
(*d*) All the above

**85.** Which of the following statement is correct, by virtue of section 13 of the Indian Partnership Act, 1932?
(*a*) Partner is not entitled to interest on the advance made over and above the share of capital
(*b*) Partner is not entitled to interest on the capital subscribed by him
(*c*) (a) and (b) both
(*d*) None of these

**86.** If a partner contributes in the partnership business then his status is of :
(*a*) A partner of the firm
(*b*) An employee of the firm
(*c*) A creditor of the firm
(*d*) None of these

**87.** Incase dissolution of the partnership the interest on capital :
(*a*) As well as on advances keeps running upto the date of payment.
(*b*) Ceases run whereas interest of advances keeping runing upto the date of payment
(*c*) And the interest on advances cease to run
(*d*) None of these

**88.** If a partner overdraws from the firm, in such case :
(*a*) Interest is chargeable 18% p.a.
(*b*) Interest is chargeable 9% p.a.

(*c*) No Interest is chargeable
(*d*) None of these

**89.** In which of the following condition the right to indemnity is lost under this Act?
(*a*) The death of the partner
(*b*) The retirement of the partner
(*c*) The dissolution of the partnership
(*d*) None of these

**90.** Which of the following is provided under section 13 (f) of the Indian Partnership Act, 1932?
(*a*) Indemnity in favour of the firm against a partner
(*b*) Indemnity in favour of the parties against the firm
(*c*) Indemnity in favour of the partner against the firm
(*d*) None of these

**91.** By which of the following an action for indemnity against a partner can be brought?
(*a*) An individual partner
(*b*) The firm only
(*c*) (*a*) and (*b*) both
(*d*) None of these

**92.** Which of the following section of the Indian Partnership Act describes regarding what constitutes the property of the firm :
(*a*) Section 14 (*b*) Section 19
(*c*) Section 18 (*d*) Section 15

**93.** Section 14 of the Indian Partnership Act, 1932 is :
(*a*) Inclusive (*b*) Conclusive
(*c*) Voidable (*d*) None of these

**94.** Section 2 of the Indian Partnership Act defines the term :
(*a*) Partnership (*b*) Partner
(*c*) Property of firm (*d*) All the above

**95.** Which of the following section of the Indian Partnership Act 1932 describes about dissolution of a firm by court?
(*a*) 44 (*b*) 46
(*c*) 49 (*d*) 50

**96.** For the purpose of this act the term property includes all the property of the firm :
(*a*) Property purchase with money of the firm
(b) Acquired by the firm
(*c*) For the purposes or in the course of business of the firm
(*d*) None of these

**97.** The property purchased by a partner out of the partnership funds is :
(*a*) A question of fact
(*b*) An estate of the partner
(*c*) A joint estate
(*d*) None of these

**98.** The Act, on which the Sale of Goods Act, is based, is:
(*a*) The English Sale of Goods Act, 1893
(*b*) The Indian Contract Act, 1872
(*c*) (*a*) and (*b*) both
(*d*) None of these

**99.** On which State of India, the Sale of Goods Act, 1930 does not applies?
(*a*) Arunachal Pradesh
(*b*) Sikkim
(*c*) Jammu and Kashmir
(*d*) All the above

**100.** In its operation the Sale of Goods Act, is:
(*a*) retrospective (*b*) prospective
(*c*) (*a*) and (*b*) both (*d*) None of these

**101.** Under the Sale of Goods Act, the term 'delivery' means:
(*a*) voluntary transfer of possession form one person to another
(*b*) forcefully transfer of possession from one person to another
(*c*) transfer of possession in any manner such as gratuitous, involuntary or voluntary.
(*d*) None of these

**102.** The definition of the documents of title of goods described in this Act is:
(*a*) descriptive
(*b*) exhaustive
(*c*) can not be determined
(*d*) None of these

**103.** Which of the following sections of the Sale of Goods Act defines the term 'goods'?
(*a*) section 2(4) (*b*) section 9
(*c*) section 6 (*d*) section 2(7)

**104.** Which section of the Sale of Goods Act describes 'Future' Goods?
(*a*) sec. 2(6) (*b*) sec. 2(4)
(*c*) sec. 2(3) (*d*) sec. 2(1)

**105.** Which of the following is included in Goods under section 2(7)?
(*a*) money (*b*) actionable claim
(*c*) all claims (*d*) None of these

**106.** Under the Sale of Goods Act, the term 'property' means:
(*a*) a special property
(*b*) immovable property
(*c*) immovable and movable properties both
(*d*) the general property in goods and not merely a special property.

**107.** The term 'Goods' under the Sale of Goods Act, means:
(*a*) every kind of immovable property
(*b*) every kind of movable and immovable property.
(*c*) Actionable claims and money only than actionable claims and money.
(*d*) every kind of movable property other than actionable claims and money.

**108.** The term, Feature goods, under section 2 of the Sale of Goods Act, means:
(*a*) goods to be manufactured or produced or acquired by the seller after the making of contract of sale.
(*b*) goods not to be manufactured or produced or acquired by the seller after the making of contract of sale.
(*c*) goods to be manufactured or produced or acquired by the seller before the making of contract of sale.
(*d*) None of these

**109.** For the purpose of operation the Sale of Goods Act, 1930 is:
(*a*) retrospective (*b*) prospective
(*c*) (*a*) and (*b*) both (*d*) None of these

**110.** Under the Sale of Goods Act the term 'Seller' means:
(*a*) salesman
(*b*) a person who sells
(*c*) a person who sells or agrees to sell goods.
(*d*) None of theses

**111.** 'Document of title to goods' under section 2(4) of the Sale of Goods Act, includes:
(*a*) wharfinger's certificate only
(*b*) dock warrant only
(*c*) bill of lading only
(*d*) All the above

**112.** Under the Sale of Goods Act, 1930 the delivery can be:
(*a*) symbolic only (*b*) actual only
(*c*) constructive only (*d*) All the above

**113.** The term 'goods' under section 2(7) of this Act does not includes:
(*a*) growing crops
(*b*) stock and share
(*c*) things attached to or forming part of the land
(*d*) actionable claims and money

**114.** On which of the following Acts the Sale of Goods Act 1930 is based?
(*a*) the Indian Contract Act, 1872
(*b*) the transfer of property Act, 1893
(*c*) the English Sales of Goods Act, 1893
(*d*) All the above

**115.** The term 'buyer' under section 2(2) of the Sale of Goods Act, 1930 means:
(*a*) a person who buys
(*b*) a person who agrees to buy.
(*c*) (*a*) and (*b*) both
(*d*) None of these

**116.** Which of the following sections of the Sale of Goods Act 1930 defines the term delivery:
(*a*) sec. 2(6) (*b*) sec. 2(3)
(*c*) sec. 2(5) (*d*) None of these

**117.** Under which of the following sections the insolvent has been defined?
(*a*) sec. 2(5) (*b*) sec. 2(6)
(*c*) sec. 2(7) (*d*) sec. 2(8)

**118.** Which of the following is included in document of title to goods?
(*a*) railway receipt
(*b*) warrant or order for the delivery of goods
(*c*) bill of lading
(*d*) All the above

**119.** The nature of a bill of lading is as a :
(*a*) banders cheque
(*b*) promissory note
(*c*) (*a*) and (*b*) both
(*d*) None of these

**120.** Which of the following sections of the Sale of Goods Act 1930 describes the documents of title to goods?
(*a*) section 2(1) (*b*) section 2(2)
(*c*) section 2(3) (*d*) section 2(4)

**121.** Which of the following documents is not a document of title to goods?
(*a*) wharfinger's certificate
(*b*) warehouse keeper's certificate
(*c*) railway receipt
(*d*) None of these

**122.** In which section of the Sale of Goods Act, 1930 the provision related to the application of provisions of the Indian Contract Act 1872 is provided?
(*a*) section 4 (*b*) section 6
(*c*) section 7 (*d*) section 3

**123.** Section 3 of the Sale of Goods Act 1930 provides the provision related to:
(*a*) sale and agreement to sell
(*b*) existing or future goods
(*c*) (*a*) and (*b*) both
(*d*) application of provisions of the Indian Contract Act, 1872.

**124.** According to section 4 of the Sale of Goods Act 1930, A contract of sell of goods is a contract whereby:
(*a*) the seller transfers the property
(*b*) the seller agrees to transfer the property
(*c*) the seller transfers or agrees to transfer the property
(*d*) None of these

**125.** According to section 4(2) of the Sale of Goods Act 1930; a contract of the sale may be:
(*a*) absolute only
(*b*) conditional only
(*c*) absolute or conditional
(*d*) None of these

**126.** Which of the following sections of the Sale of Goods Act 1930, the term property defines?
(*a*) section 2(11) (*b*) section 2(10)
(*c*) section 2(1) (*d*) section 2(3)

**127.** Under section 2(5) of the Sale of Goods Act 1930, the term fault means:
(*a*) fault in goods
(*b*) wrorngful act or default
(*c*) wrongful act
(*d*) None of these

**128.** The term insolvent is defined under section:
(*a*) 2(6) (*b*) 2(4)
(*c*) 2(8) (*d*) 2(9)

**129.** 'Mercantile agent' is defined under section:
(*a*) 2(6) (*b*) 2(7)
(*c*) 2(8) (*d*) 2(9)

**130.** Under section 2(9) of the Sale of Goods Act 1930 mercantile agent means the person
(*a*) who sells the goods
(*b*) who buys the goods
(*c*) who sells the goods or consings goods for the purpose of, sale or buys goods, or raise money on the security of goods.
(*d*) None of these

**131.** Which of the following sections of the Sale of Goods Act 1930 defines the term piece?
(*a*) section 2(8) (*b*) section 2(4)
(*c*) section 2(10) (*d*) None of these

**132.** Which of the following is not a feature of a mercantile agent described in section 2(9) of the Sale of Goods Act 1930?
(*a*) having authority to sell goods
(*b*) having authority to consign goods
(*c*) having authority to buy goods
(*d*) None of these

**133.** Which of the following is the meaning of the term piece used in the Sale of Goods Act 1930?
(*a*) consideration in any form
(*b*) consideration in foreign currency only
(*c*) money consideration
(*d*) money consideration and consideration in goods both.

**134.** Under section 2(12) of the Sale of Goods Act 1930 the terms quality of Goods includes:
(*a*) a only stale of Goods
(*b*) only condition of Goods
(*c*) state or condition of Goods
(*d*) None of these

**135.** Which of the following terms is defined under section 2(12) of the Sale of Goods Act 1930?
(*a*) feature goods (*b*) price
(*c*) quality of goods (*d*) seller

**136.** The term property used in Section 2(11) of the Sale of Goods Act 1930 means:
(*a*) a special property only
(*b*) all types of property
(*c*) the general property in goods and not merely a special property
(*d*) None of these

**137.** Under which of the following sections of the Sale of Goods Act 1930 the term property has been defined?
(*a*) section 2(5) (*b*) section 4
(*c*) section 11 (*d*) section 2(11)

**138.** Under section 4 of the Sale of Goods Act, 1930 the contract in which the transfer of the property in the goods is to take place at a feature time or subject to same conditions thereafter to be fulfilled, is called:
(*a*) a sale
(*b*) an agreement to sell
(*c*) a sale and an agreement to sell both
(*d*) None of these

**139.** Which of the following is the meaning of the term specific goods used in section 2(14) of the Sale of Goods Act, 1930?
(*a*) goods identified and agreed upon at the time a contract of a sale is made
(*b*) any type of goods
(*c*) goods available in market at the time of a contract of a sale is made
(*d*) None of these

**140.** Section 2(14) of the Sale of Goods Act, 1930 defines the term:
(*a*) price (*b*) seller
(*c*) goods (*d*) specific goods

**141.** In case at the time of making a contract to sell the goods are not specific or ascertained in such condition the contract can be:
(*a*) null and void (*b*) illegal
(*c*) agreement to sell (*d*) None of these

**142.** In the Sale of Goods Act, 1930 the provision regarding sale and agreement to sell is provided under section:
(*a*) 4 (*b*) 5
(*c*) 3 (*d*) 2

**143.** Under section 4 of the Sale of Goods Act 1930 the conditions for the purpose of conditional contract of Sale of Goods may be:
(*a*) promissory only
(*b*) either contingent or promissory
(*c*) contingent only
(*d*) None of these

**144.** Section 5 of the Sâle of Goods Act, 1930 provides the provisions related to:
(*a*) subject matter of contract
(*b*) conditions and warranties
(*c*) the piece
(*d*) formalities of the contract

**145.** Which of the following Acts, deals with Quasi contract?
(*a*) the English Sale of Goods Act 1893
(*b*) the Indian contract Act 1873
(*c*) the Sale of Goods Act 1930
(*d*) All the above

**146.** In which of the following the property in goods transferred in future?
(*a*) contract of sale
(*b*) contingent contract of sale
(*c*) (*a*) and (*b*) both
(*d*) agreement to sell

**147.** Which of the following is necessary for the formation of a contract under the Sale of Goods Act 1930?
(*a*) offer and acceptance of offer
(*b*) delivery of goods
(*c*) cash payment
(*d*) None of these

**148.** A contract of sale under the Sale of Goods Act 1930 is made by:
(*a*) price
(*b*) delivery of the goods
(*c*) an offer to buy or sell goods for a price and the acceptance of such offer.
(*d*) None of these

**149.** Subject matter of the contract is described in the Sale of Goods Act, 1930 under section:
(*a*) 4 (*b*) 3
(*c*) 6 (*d*) None of these

**150.** In which of the following conditions section 7 of the Sale of Goods Act, 1930 is applicable?
(*a*) in case Goods perishing before making of contract
(*b*) in case Goods perishing after making of contract
(*c*) *(a)* and *(b)* both
(*d*) None of these

**151.** In which of the following conditions a contract for sale of specific goods is void under section 7 of the Sale of Goods Act, 1930?
(*a*) in case perishing the goods to the knowledge of the seller
(*b*) in case perusing the goods to the knowledge of the buyer.
(*c*) In case perishing the goods without knowledge of the seller
(*d*) None of these

**152.** A contract, under section 7 of the Sale of Goods Act, 1930:
(*a*) void
(*b*) voidable at the instance of the seller
(*c*) illegal
(*d*) None of these

**153.** Which of the following is beyond the application of Section 7 of the Sale of Goods Act, 1930?
(*a*) c. i. f. contract (*b*) f.o.b. contract
(*c*) (a) and (b) both (*d*) None of these

**154.** In case of application, Section 8 of the Sale of Goods Act, 1930, is :
(*a*) confined to contract of sale
(*b*) confined to agreement to sell
(*c*) *(a)* and *(b)* both
(*d*) None of these

**155.** Which of the following cases are dealt under section 8 of the Sales of Goods Act, 1930?
(*a*) goods perishing before sale but after agreement to sell
(*b*) goods perishing after sale
(*c*) *(a)* and *(b)* both
(*d*) None of these

**156.** On which of the following section 8 of the Sale of Goods Act, 1930 does not applies?
(*a*) specific goods
(*b*) unascertained goods
(*c*) generic goods
(*d*) None of these

**157.** Which of the following type effect depicts on contract under section 8 of the Sale of Goods Act, 1930?
(*a*) avoided from the date of perishing goods
(*b*) avoided from the date of knowledge of perishing goods
(*c*) void
(*d*) All the above

**158.** In which of the following condition a contract for Sale of Goods can be avoided under section 8 of the Sale of Goods Act 1930? If the goods have perished/ damaged due to the:
(*a*) fault of either the buyer or the seller
(*b*) fault neither of the buyer /nor the seller
(*c*) fault of the seller
(*d*) fault of the buyer

**159.** In case goods having been perished /damaged subsequent to the formation of the contract when such contract can be avoided under section 8 of the Sale of Goods Act, 1930?

(a) after the property in goods has passed to the buyer
(b) before the property in goods has passed to the buyer
(c) (a) and (b) both
(d) None of above

**160.** Which of the following is provided under section 9 of the Sale of Goods Act, 1930?
(a) ascertainment of price
(b) conditions and warranties
(c) agreement to sell
(d) All the above

**161.** Under which type of agreement for a contract, the buyer has a right to return the goods at any time?
(a) hiring (b) agency
(c) bailment (d) sale

**162.** Which of the following to created by a sale of Goods under the Sale of Goods Act, 1930?
(a) *a jus in personam* (b) *a jus in rem*
(c) *either (a) or (b)* (d) None of these

**163.** In respect of Goods, regarding the agreement of sell, which of the following statement is not correct?
(a) it is not executory contract which creates *jus in rem*
(b) it is an executed contract which creates a *jus in rem*
(c) *(a)* and *(b)* both
(d) None of these

**164.** Which of the following is described by the distinction between sell and agreement to sell?
(a) nature the subject matter of the contract
(b) nature of property
(c) rights and liabilities of the parties to contract
(d) All of above

**165.** Section 5 of this Act describes:
(a) contract of sale how made
(b) sale and agreement to sell
(c) exhausting or future goods
(d) None of these

**166.** Which of the following type is the condition if a condition provides for the defeasance of a certain ion right on the happening of a specified event under a contract?
(a) condition subsequent
(b) condition concurrent
(c) condition precedent
(d) None of these

**167.** Which of the following can be the subject matter under section 6 of the Sale of Goods Act, 1930?
(a) either existing or future goods
(b) the existing goods only
(c) the future goods only
(d) None of these

**168.** Which of the following statement is true?
(a) a contract for Sale of Goods to be delivered at a future date shall not be invalid if the seller has not got the goods in present possession nor has contracted for the purchase of the same nor has any expectation of getting them.
(b) a contract for sale of Goods to be delivered at a future date shall be invalid if the seller has not the goods in present possession
(c) a contract for sale of Goods to be delivered at a future date shall be invalid if the seller has not contracted for the purchase of those goods
(d) None of these

**169.** In which of the following manner a contract of present sale of future goods is treated under section 6(3) of the Sale of Goods Act, 1930?
(a) agreement to sell
(b) contract of sale
(c) (a) and (b) both
(d) None of these

**170.** If transfer of title or registration is not created, in such condition, which of the following treatment the purchaser have?
(a) cannot claim damages for breach of conditions and warranties

(*b*) can claim damages for breach of conditions or warranties
(*c*) either (*a*) or (*b*)
(*d*) None of these

**171.** Effect of part delivery is described under section on of this Act.
(*a*) 15 (*b*) 18
(*c*) 34 (*d*) 35

**172.** Which of the following is true?
(*a*) a wagering contract is not unenforceable
(*b*) a wagering contract is not forbidden by law
(*c*) a wagering contract is not void
(*d*) None of these

**173.** Consumer Protection Act came into existence in:
(*a*) 1946 (*b*) 1886
(*c*) 1986 (*d*) 1966

**174.** Which of the followings is not correct?
(*a*) Consumer means any person who buy any goods for a consideration
(*b*) Consumer means any person who hires or avails of any services for a consideration
(*c*) (*a*) and (*b*) both
(*d*) None of these

**175.** Which of the following is not included in the term 'person' under consumer protection Act 1986?
(*a*) a Hindu undivided family
(*b*) a co-operative society
(*c*) a firm
(*d*) None of these

**176.** Under the consumer protection Act 1986, 'Goods' means:
(*a*) every kind of movable property only
(*b*) every kind of immovable property only
(*c*) every kinds of movable property other than
(*d*) None of these

**177.** The Consumer Protection Act 1986 was amended in:
(*a*) 1987 (*b*) 2000
(*c*) 2002 (*d*) 1996

**178.** Incase goods are purchase for resale, these goods under the Consumer Protection Act 1986, are:
(*a*) for business
(*b*) for commercial purpose
(*c*) for sale
(*d*) None of these

**179.** Consumer dispute, under the Consumer Protection Act 1986, means:
(*a*) A dispute between two consumers
(*b*) A dispute between a shopkeeper and a consumer
(*c*) A dispute, where the person against whom a complaint has been made, denies or disputes the allegations contained in the complaint
(*d*) None of these

**180.** Under the Consumer Protection Act 1986 'deficiency' means:
(*a*) any fault in goods only
(*b*) any imperfection only
(*c*) any fault, imperfection, shortcoming or inadequacy in quality, nature and manner of performance
(*d*) None of these

**181.** Unfair Trade Practice, under section 2(1)(r) of the Consumer Protection Act 1986 means:
(*a*) Trade practice without paying Trade Tax
(*b*) Trade Practice without registration of firm
(*c*) Trade practice which for the purpose of promoting the sale, use or supply of any goods or for the provision of any service, adopts any unfair methods or unfair or deceptive practice
(*d*) None of these

**182.** The maximum limits of the Central Consumer Protection Act 1986, is:
(*a*) 75 (*b*) 11
(*c*) 150 (*d*) 45

**183.** The term of the Central Consumer Protection council under the Consumer Protection Act 1986 is:
(*a*) 2 years (*b*) 5 years
(*c*) 4 years (*d*) 3 years

**184.** Which of the followings is not an object of the State Consumer Protection Councils?
(*a*) to promote and protect the right to be informed about the quality, quantity, potency, purity etc
(*b*) to promote and protect the right to be heard and to be assured that Consumer's interests will receive due consideration
(*c*) (*a*) and (*b*) both
(*d*) None of these

**185.** The District Consumer Dispute Redressal forum is:
(*a*) Judicial forum
(*b*) Quasi-Judicial forum
(*c*) Arbitrary forum
(*d*) None of theses

**186.** The District Consumer Dispute Redressal forum consists of:
(*a*) A president, two vice-presidents and two other members
(*b*) A president and two other members
(*c*) A chairman and three other members
(*d*) None of these

**187.** Generally the District forum under the Consumer Protection Act 1986 has the jurisdiction to entertain complaints where the value of the goods or services and the compensation does not exceed rupees:
(*a*) 5 lakhs (*b*) 10 lakhs
(*c*) 20 lakhs (*d*) 50 lakhs

**188.** Any person aggrieved by an order made by the state commission in exercise of its powers may prefer an appeal against such order to the:
(*a*) High Court
(*b*) Supreme Court
(*c*) National Commission
(*d*) None of these

**189.** Against the order of National Commission, a person can appeal to:
(*a*) Supreme Court
(*b*) High Court
(*c*) there is no provision of appeal against the order of National Commission
(*d*) None of these

**190.** Every member of the National Commission shall hold office for a term of:
(*a*) Five years or upto the age of seventy years.
(*b*) Four years or up to the age of 65 years
(*c*) Three years or upto the age of 65 years
(*d*) Two years or upto the age of 65 years

**191.** The limitation period to file a complaint, as provided in the Cosumer Protection Act 1986 is:
(*a*) one year from the date on which the cause of action has arisen.
(*b*) two years from the date on which the cause of action has arisen
(*c*) five years from the date on which the cause of action has arisen.
(*d*) no limitation period is provided.

**192.** The principal of Res-judicata is:
(*a*) not applicable in consumer cases
(*b*) applicable in consumer cases
(*c*) applicable only in some consumer cases
(*d*) None of these

**193.** The person who does not make or manufacture any goods but assembles parts thereof made or manufactured by others, under the Consumer Protection Act 1986, is a:
(*a*) Consumer
(*b*) Manufactuer
(*c*) Trader
(*d*) None of these

**194.** Which of the followings is not an object of the central council under the Consumer Protection Act 1986?
(*a*) to promote and protect the right to consumer education
(*b*) to promote and protect the right to seek redressal against unfair trade practices
(*c*) (*a*) and (*b*) both
(*d*) None of these

**195.** The Consumer Protection Act 1986 provides regarding establishment of the district consumer protection councils in:
(*a*) 5 districts in a State
(*b*) Every district in a State
(*c*) Atleast 10 district in a state
(*d*) None of these

**196.** Under Section 2 (1) (*b*) of the Consumer Protection Act 1986, 'Complainant' means:
(*a*) a consumer
(*b*) the central government or state government who makes a complainant
(*c*) any voluntary consumer association registered under any law for the time being inforce
(*d*) All the above

**197.** Under the Consumer Protection Act-1986, appropriate laboratory means:
(*a*) laboratory organisation recognised by the Central Government
(*b*) laboratory or organisation recognised by the State Government
(*c*) laboratory or organisation established by or under any law for the time being inforce
(*d*) All the above

## ANSWERS

| **1** | **2** | **3** | **4** | **5** | **6** | **7** | **8** | **9** | **10** |
|---|---|---|---|---|---|---|---|---|---|
| (*b*) | (*c*) | (*b*) | (*b*) | (*d*) | (*c*) | (*a*) | (*d*) | (*d*) | (*d*) |
| **11** | **12** | **13** | **14** | **15** | **16** | **17** | **18** | **19** | **20** |
| (*b*) | (*d*) | (*d*) | (*a*) | (*a*) | (*c*) | (*c*) | (*b*) | (*b*) | (*b*) |
| **21** | **22** | **23** | **24** | **25** | **26** | **27** | **28** | **29** | **30** |
| (*b*) | (*a*) | (*c*) | (*a*) | (*a*) | (*a*) | (*c*) | (*a*) | (*a*) | (*a*) |
| **31** | **32** | **33** | **34** | **35** | **36** | **37** | **38** | **39** | **40** |
| (*c*) | (*c*) | (*a*) | (*a*) | (*c*) | (*b*) | (*b*) | (*b*) | (*a*) | (*a*) |
| **41** | **42** | **43** | **44** | **45** | **46** | **47** | **48** | **49** | **50** |
| (*d*) | (*c*) | (*d*) | (*a*) | (*d*) | (*c*) | (*c*) | (*b*) | (*d*) | (*a*) |
| **51** | **52** | **53** | **54** | **55** | **56** | **57** | **58** | **59** | **60** |
| (*b*) | (*b*) | (*a*) | (*c*) | (*a*) | (*a*) | (*a*) | (*c*) | (*b*) | (*a*) |
| **61** | **62** | **63** | **64** | **65** | **66** | **67** | **68** | **69** | **70** |
| (*c*) | (*a*) | (*c*) | (*c*) | (*a*) | (*c*) | (*c*) | (*b*) | (*b*) | (*c*) |
| **71** | **72** | **73** | **74** | **75** | **76** | **77** | **78** | **79** | **80** |
| (*d*) | (*a*) | (*c*) | (*a*) | (*a*) | (*c*) | (*b*) | (*d*) | (*d*) | (*a*) |
| **81** | **82** | **83** | **84** | **85** | **86** | **87** | **88** | **89** | **90** |
| (*c*) | (*c*) | (*a*) | (*a*) | (*a*) | (*a*) | (*b*) | (*c*) | (*a*) | (*a*) |
| **91** | **92** | **93** | **94** | **95** | **96** | **97** | **98** | **99** | **100** |
| (*b*) | (*a*) | (*a*) | (*a*) | (*a*) | (*c*) | (*a*) | (*a*) | (*c*) | (*b*) |
| **101** | **102** | **103** | **104** | **105** | **106** | **107** | **108** | **109** | **110** |
| (*a*) | (*a*) | (*d*) | (*a*) | (*d*) | (*d*) | (*d*) | (*a*) | (*b*) | (*c*) |
| **111** | **112** | **113** | **114** | **115** | **116** | **117** | **118** | **119** | **120** |
| (*d*) | (*d*) | (*d*) | (*c*) | (*c*) | (*d*) | (*d*) | (*d*) | (*d*) | (*d*) |
| **121** | **122** | **123** | **124** | **125** | **126** | **127** | **128** | **129** | **130** |
| (*d*) | (*d*) | (*d*) | (*c*) | (*c*) | (*a*) | (*b*) | (*c*) | (*d*) | (*c*) |

| 131 | 132 | 133 | 134 | 135 | 136 | 137 | 138 | 139 | 140 |
|---|---|---|---|---|---|---|---|---|---|
| (*c*) | (*d*) | (*c*) | (*c*) | (*c*) | (*c*) | (*d*) | (*b*) | (*a*) | (*d*) |
| **141** | **142** | **143** | **144** | **145** | **146** | **147** | **148** | **149** | **150** |
| (*c*) | (*a*) | (*b*) | (*d*) | (*b*) | (*d*) | (*a*) | (*c*) | (*c*) | (*a*) |
| **151** | **152** | **153** | **154** | **155** | **156** | **157** | **158** | **159** | **160** |
| (*c*) | (*a*) | (*a*) | (*b*) | (*a*) | (*c*) | (*a*) | (*b*) | (*b*) | (*a*) |
| **161** | **162** | **163** | **164** | **165** | **166** | **167** | **168** | **169** | **170** |
| (*a*) | (*b*) | (*b*) | (*c*) | (*a*) | (*a*) | (*a*) | (*a*) | (*a*) | (*a*) |
| **171** | **172** | **173** | **174** | **175** | **176** | **177** | **178** | **179** | **180** |
| (*c*) | (*b*) | (*c*) | (*d*) | (*d*) | (*c*) | (*c*) | (*b*) | (*c*) | (*c*) |
| **181** | **182** | **183** | **184** | **185** | **186** | **187** | **188** | **189** | **190** |
| (*c*) | (*c*) | (*d*) | (*d*) | (*b*) | (*b*) | (*c*) | (*c*) | (*a*) | (*a*) |
| **191** | **192** | **193** | **194** | **195** | **196** | **197** | | | |
| (*b*) | (*b*) | (*b*) | (*d*) | (*b*) | (*d*) | (*d*) | | | |

# GENERAL AWARENESS

# 1. Our India

## INDIA : AT A GLANCE

| | | |
|---|---|---|
| Population (2011) | : | 1,21,08,54,977 |
| Capital | : | New Delhi |
| Area | : | 32,87,263 sq km |
| Geographic Location | : | Between 8°4' and 37°6' north latitudes |
| | : | Between 68°7' and 97°25' east longitudes |
| Coastline Length | : | 7,516.6 km including the coastline of Lakshadweep, Andaman & Nicobar Islands. |
| Major Languages | : | 22 |
| National Anthem | : | Jana Gana Mana |
| National Currency | : | Rupee (₹) |
| National Animal | : | Tiger |
| National Aquatic Animal | : | Dolphin |
| National Bird | : | Peacock |
| National River | : | Ganga |
| Characteristics of Indian | : | Socialist, Secular, Democratic, Republic |
| Legislature | : | Bicameral Legislature at the Centre |
| | | Uni/Bicameral Legislatures in States |
| Executive | : | President, Vice-President and Council of Ministers at the Centre |
| | | Governor and Council of Ministers in States |
| Judiciary | : | Independent from Executive with Supreme Court at the apex of the hierarchy |
| Total Road Length | : | 63.32 Lakh kms (December, 2022) |

## India: States & Union Territories

| States/Union Territories | Capital | Area in (Sq. Km.) | Language |
|---|---|---|---|
| Andhra Pradesh | Amravati | 1,60,229 | Telugu |
| Arunachal Pradesh | Itanagar | 83,743 | Nyishi, Miji, Wancho etc. |
| Assam | Dispur | 78,438 | Assamese |
| Bihar | Patna | 94,163 | Hindi, Maithili |
| Chhattisgarh | Raipur | 136,034 | Hindi |
| Goa | Panji | 3,702 | Marathi and Konkani |
| Gujarat | Gandhinagar | 1,96,024 | Gujarati |
| Haryana | Chandigarh | 44,212 | Hindi |
| Himachal Pradesh | Shimla | 55,673 | Hindi and Pahari |
| Jharkhand | Ranchi | 79,714 | Hindi, Santhali |
| Karnataka | Bengaluru | 1,91,791 | Kannada |
| Kerala | Thiruvananthapuram | 38,863 | Malayalam |
| Madhya Pradesh | Bhopal | 308,000 | Hindi |
| Maharashtra | Mumbai | 307,713 | Marathi |
| Manipur | Imphal | 22,327 | Manipuri |
| Meghalaya | Shillong | 22,429 | Khasi, Garo and English |
| Mizoram | Aizawl | 21,081 | Mizo and English |
| Nagaland | Kohima | 16,579 | Sema, English |
| Odisha | Bhubaneswar | 155,707 | Odia |
| Punjab | Chandigarh | 50,362 | Punjabi |
| Rajasthan | Jaipur | 3,42,239 | Hindi and Rajasthani |
| Sikkim | Gangtok | 7,096 | Bhutia, Nepali, Lepcha and Limbu |
| Tamil Nadu | Chennai | 1,30,058 | Tamil |
| Telangana | Hyderabad | 1,14,840 | Telugu |
| Tripura | Agartala | 10,491 | Bengali, Kakborak |
| Uttar Pradesh | Lucknow | 2,40,928 | Hindi and Urdu |
| Uttarakhand | Dehradun | 53,484 | Hindi |
| West Bengal | Kolkata | 88,752 | Bengali |
| Jammu & Kashmir | Srinagar (Summer) Jammu (Winter) | 2,22,236* | Kashmiri, Urdu, Dogri |
| Andaman & Nicobar Island | Port Blair | 8,249 | Bengali, Hindi, Nicobarese, Tamil, Telugu, and Malayalam |
| Chandigarh | Chandigarh | 114 | Hindi, Punjabi |
| Dadra & Nagar Haveli and Daman and Diu | Daman | 603 | Gujarati and Hindi |
| Delhi | Delhi | 1483 | Hindi, Punjabi and Urdu |
| Lakshadweep | Kavaratti | 32 | Malayalam |
| Puducherry | Puducherry | 492 | Tamil, Telugu, Malayalam, English and French |
| Ladakh | Leh | — | Ladakhi |

** Including areas of Ladakh and illegally occupied by China and Pakistan.*

# POPULATION

**Second Largest Nation :** In terms of the size of population, India is the second largest country in the world, next only to China. China tops the list with 1341.0 million people. India's population constitutes nearly 17.5 per cent of the total world population while her geographical area is only 2.42 per cent of the world area. With such a huge population to support on so small an area, the country finds herself in great difficulty in making any significant dent on its poverty and economic backwardness. India's national income, which is barely 2 per cent of the total global income, clearly shows the tremendous strain of population on her economy.

## 2011 Census Highlights

| | | |
|---|---|---|
| Population of India–Total Indian population is 17.7% of total world population | : | 1,21,08,54,977 (Male: 62,32,70,258; Female: 58,75,84,719) |
| Decadal Growth (2001-2011) | : | 17.7 per cent (Males: 17.1 per cent; Females: 18.3 per cent) |
| Hightest Decadal Growth (State-wise) | : | Meghalaya (27.9 per cent) |
| Lowest Decadal Growth (State-wise) | : | Nagaland (–0.6 per cent) |
| Most populous State | : | Uttar Pradesh |
| Density of population | : | 382 persons per sq. km. |
| Most densly populated State | : | Bihar : 1106 per sq. km |
| Sex Ratio | : | 943 females per 1000 males |
| Total Literacy Rate | : | 73% (Males – 80.9%), (Females – 64.6%) |
| Highest Literacy (State-wise) | : | Kerala (94%) |
| Lowest Literacy (State-wise) | : | Bihar (61.8%) |

## OTHER DETAILS

**(a) Population of India**

| | | | |
|---|---|---|---|
| 1951 | 36,10,88,090 | 1961 | 43,92,34,771 |
| 1971 | 54,81,59,652 | 1981 | 68,33,29,097 |
| 1991 | 84,64,21,039 | 2001 | 102,87,37,436 |
| 2011 | 1,21,08,54,977 | | |

**(b) Density of Population (Persons per square kilometre)**

| | | | |
|---|---|---|---|
| 1951 | 113 | 1961 | 138 |
| 1971 | 177 | 1981 | 216 |
| 1991 | 267 | 2001 | 324 |
| 2011 | 382 | | |

**(c) Annual Compound Rate of Growth**

| | | | |
|---|---|---|---|
| 1941-1951 | 1.25 per cent | 1951-1961 | 1.96 per cent |
| 1961-1971 | 2.22 per cent | 1971-1981 | 2.20 per cent |
| 1981-1991 | 2.14 per cent | 1991-2001 | 1.95 per cent |
| 2001-2011 | 1.64 per cent | | |

### *India's Population At A Glance : 2011 (Final Data)*

| S.I. No. | State/UTs | Population | Sex Ratio | Density | Literacy Rate | (%) Decadel Growth Rate (2001-2011) |
|---|---|---|---|---|---|---|
| 1. | Jammu & Kashmir | 1,25,41,302 | 889 | 124 | 67.2 | 23.6 |
| 2. | Himachal Pradesh | 68,64,602 | 972 | 123 | 82.8 | 12.9 |
| 3. | Punjab | 2,77,43,338 | 895 | 551 | 75.8 | 13.9 |
| 4. | Chandigarh | 10,55,450 | 818 | 9258 | 86.0 | 17.2 |
| 5. | Uttarakhand | 1,00,86,292 | 963 | 189 | 78.8 | 18.8 |
| 6. | Haryana | 2,53,51,462 | 879 | 573 | 75.6 | 19.9 |
| 7. | Delhi | 1,67,87,941 | 868 | 11320 | 86.2 | 21.2 |
| 8. | Rajasthan | 6,85,48,437 | 928 | 200 | 66.1 | 21.3 |
| 9. | Uttar Pradesh | 19,98,12,341 | 912 | 829 | 66.7 | 20.2 |
| 10. | Bihar | 10,40,99,452 | 918 | 1106 | 61.8 | 25.4 |
| 11. | Sikkim | 6,10,577 | 890 | 86 | 81.4 | 12.9 |
| 12. | Arunachal Pradesh | 13,83,727 | 938 | 17 | 65.4 | 26.0 |
| 13. | Nagaland | 19,78,502 | 931 | 119 | 79.6 | –0.6 |
| 14. | Manipur | 28,55,794 | 985 | 128 | 79.2 | 24.50 |
| 15. | Mizoram | 10,97,206 | 976 | 52 | 91.3 | 23.5 |
| 16. | Tripura | 36,73,917 | 960 | 350 | 87.2 | 14.8 |
| 17. | Meghalaya | 29,66,889 | 989 | 132 | 74.4 | 27.9 |
| 18. | Assam | 3,12,05,576 | 958 | 398 | 72.2 | 17.1 |
| 19. | West Bengal | 9,12,76,115 | 950 | 1028 | 76.3 | 13.8 |
| 20. | Jharkhand | 3,29,88,134 | 949 | 414 | 66.4 | 22.4 |
| 21. | Odisha | 4,19,74,218 | 979 | 270 | 72.9 | 14.0 |
| 22. | Chhattisgarh | 2,55,45,198 | 991 | 189 | 70.3 | 22.6 |
| 23. | Madhya Pradesh | 7,26,26,809 | 931 | 236 | 69.3 | 20.3 |
| 24. | Gujarat | 6,04,39,692 | 919 | 308 | 78.0 | 19.3 |
| 25. | Daman & Diu | 2,43,247 | 618 | 2191 | 87.1 | 53.8 |
| 26. | Dadra & Nagar Haveli | 3,43,709 | 774 | 700 | 76.2 | 55.9 |
| 27. | Maharashtra | 11,23,74,333 | 929 | 365 | 82.3 | 16.0 |
| 28. | Andhra Pradesh | 4,93,86,799 | 993 | 308 | 67.0 | 11.0 |
| 29. | Karnataka | 6,10,95,297 | 973 | 319 | 75.4 | 15.6 |
| 30. | Goa | 14,58,545 | 973 | 394 | 88.7 | 8.2 |
| 31. | Lakshadweep | 64,473 | 947 | 2149 | 91.8 | 6.3 |
| 32. | Kerala | 3,34,06,061 | 1084 | 860 | 94.0 | 4.9 |
| 33. | Tamil Nadu | 7,21,47,030 | 996 | 555 | 80.1 | 15.6 |
| 34. | Puducherry | 12,47,953 | 1037 | 2546 | 85.8 | 28.1 |
| 35. | Andaman & Nicobar Island | 3,80,581 | 876 | 46 | 86.6 | 6.9 |
| 36. | Telangana | 3,51,93,978 | 988 | 307 | 66.4 | 13.58 |
| | **India** | **1,21,08,54,977** | **943** | **382** | **73.0** | **17.7** |

* * * * *

# 2. National Symbols

**State Emblem:** State Emblem of India is an adaptation from the Sarnath Lion Capital of Ashoka. It was adopted by the Government of India on January 26, 1950. In the adapted form, only three lions are visible, the fourth being hidden from the view. The wheel (Dharma Chakra) appears in relief in the centre of the abacus with a bull on the right and a horse on the left. The bell-shaped lotus has been omitted. The words "Satyameva Jayate" meaning "Truth alone triumphs" are inscribed below the Emblem in Devanagari script.

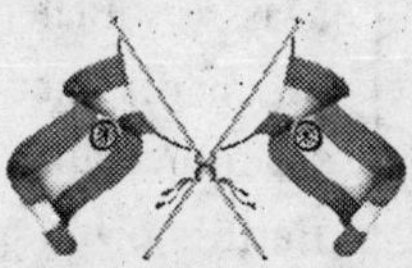

**National Flag:** The National Flag of India is a horizontal tricolour of deep saffron (Kesari), white and dark green in equal proportion. In the centre of the white band there is a wheel in navy blue colour. It has 24 spokes. The ratio of the length and the breadth of the flag is 3 : 2. Its design was adopted by the Constituent Assembly of India on July 22, 1947.

**National Anthem:** Rabindranath Tagore's song 'Jana-gana-mana' was adopted by the Constituent Assembly as the National Anthem of India on January 24, 1950.

*Jana-gan-mana-adhinayaka jaya he,*
*Bharata-bhagya-vidhata*
*Punjab-Sindh-Gujarat-Maratha-Dravida-*
*Utkala-Banga*
*Vindhya-Himachala-Yamuna-Ganga Uchhala-*
*jaladhi-taranga.*
*Tava subha name jage, Tava subha asisa mange,*
*Gahe tava jaya gatha,*
*Jana-gana-mangala-dayak, jaya he Bharata*
*bhagya vidhata,*
*Jaya he, jaya he, jaya he, Jaya jaya jaya,*
*jaya he.*

**National Song:** Bankim Chandra Chatterji's 'Vande Mataram' which was a source of inspiration to the people in their struggle for freedom, has been adopted as National Song. It has an equal status with the National Anthem.

*Vande Mataram*
*Sujalam, suphalam, malayaja-shitalam,*
*Shasya shyamalam, Mataram*
*Shubhrajyotsna,pulkita yaminim,*
*Phulla kusumita drumadalashobhinim,*
*Subhasinim sumadhura—bhashinim,*
*Sukhadam, Varadam, Mataram.*

**National Bird and Animal of India:** Peacock and Tiger; **National Aquatic Animal:** Dolphin; **National Flower:** Lotus; **National Calendar:** It was adopted on March 22, 1957. It has 365 days in the year and the first month of the year is Chaitra.

## Months of the National Calendar

(1) Chaitra, (2) Vaishakha, (3) Jaishtha, (4) Ashadha, (5) Shravan, (6) Bhadra, (7) Ashvina, (8) Kartika, (9) Marga-Shirsha, (10) Pausha, (11) Magha, (12) Phalguna.

* * * * *

# 3. THE UNIVERSE

## The Solar System: Some Facts

**Number of Planets:** 8—Mercury, Venus, Earth, Mars, Jupiter, Saturn, Uranus and Neptune.

**Largest most**

| | |
|---|---|
| Massive planet | Jupiter |
| Brightest planet | Venus |
| Brightest star | Sirius |
| Fastest orbiting planet | Mercury |
| Longest (Synodic) day | Mercury |
| Planet with largest moon | Jupiter |
| Greatest average density | Earth |
| Tallest mountain | Mars |
| Strongest magnetic fields | Jupiter |
| Most circular orbit | Venus |
| Shortest (synodic) day | Jupiter |
| Hottest planet | Venus |
| No moons | Mercury, Venus |
| Planet with moon with most eccentric orbit | Neptune |
| Lowest average density | Saturn |
| Greatest amount of liquid on the surface | Earth |

## The Earth: Facts and Data

**Composition of the Earth:** Aluminium (0.4%), Sulphur (2.7%), Silicon (13%), Oxygen (28%), Calcium (1.2%), Nickel (2.7%), Magnesium (17%), Iron (35%)

| | | |
|---|---|---|
| Surface area | : | 510100500 sq km |
| Land Surface (29.1%) | : | 148950800 sq km |
| Ocean Surface (70.9%) | : | 361149700 sq km |
| Type of water | : | 97% salt, 3% fresh |
| Total area of water | : | 382672000 sq km |
| Equatorial diameter | : | 12753 km |
| Equatorial Circumference | : | 40066 km |
| Polar Circumference | : | 39992 km |
| Polar diameter | : | 12710 km |
| Equatorial radius | : | 6376 km |
| Polar radius | : | 6335 km |
| Mass (estimated weight) | : | $594 \times 10^{19}$ metric tons |
| Mean distance from the Sun | : | 149407000 km |
| Earth's orbit speed (around sun) | : | 107320 kmph |
| Period of Revolution (round the sun) | : | 365 days 5 hrs 48 min. 45.51 seconds |
| Time of Rotation (on its axis) | : | 23 hrs 56 min. 4.09 seconds |
| Inclination of the axis (to the plane of the eclipitc) | : | 23°27' |

## Solar Statistics

| | | |
|---|---|---|
| Distance from the Earth | : | 149.8 million km |
| Absolute Visual Magnitude | : | 4.75 |
| Diameter Core | : | 13,84,000 km |
| Temperature | : | 15000000 K |
| Photosphere Temperature | : | 5770 K |

| | | |
|---|---|---|
| Rotation as seen from the Earth (at the equator) | : | 25.38 days |
| Rotation as seen from the Earth (near the poles) | : | 33 days |
| Chemical Composition | : | Hydrogen 71%<br>Helium 26.5%<br>Other elements 2.5% |
| Age | : | About 4.5 billion years |
| Expected lifetime of a normal star | : | About 10 billion years |

## Oceans of the World

| | |
|---|---|
| Pacific | 16,62,41,000 sq km |
| Atlantic | 8,65,57,000 sq km |
| Indian | 7,34,27,000 sq km |
| Arctic | 94,85,000 sq km |

## Longest Rivers

| *Name* | *Country/ Continent* | *Length in Kilometres* |
|---|---|---|
| Nile | Africa | 6650 |
| Amazon | S. America | 6437 |
| Mississippi-Missouri | USA | 6020 |
| Yangtze-Kiang | China | 5494 |
| Ob-Irtysh | Russia | 5410 |
| Lena | Russia | 4400 |
| Hwang Ho | China | 4344 |
| Niger | Africa | 4180 |
| St. Lawrence | Canada (USA) | 4023 |
| Murray-Darling | Australia | 3780 |
| Volga | Russia | 3690 |
| Indus | Asia | 2900 |
| Danube | Europe | 2850 |
| Orinoco | S. America | 2575 |

## Major Riverside Cities

| *City* | *River* | *Country* |
|---|---|---|
| Alexandria | Nile | Egypt |
| Amsterdam | Amsel | The Netherland |
| Ankara | Kizil | Turkiye |
| Baghdad | Tigris | Iraq |
| Bangkok | Menam | Thailand |
| Belgrade | Danube | Serbia |
| Berlin | Spree | Germany |
| Budapest | Danube | Hungary |
| Cairo | Nile | Egypt |
| Chittagong | Karnaphuli | Bangladesh |
| Karachi | Indus | Pakistan |
| Khartoum | Blue & White Nile | Sudan |
| Lahore | Ravi | Pakistan |
| Lisbon | Tagus | Portugal |
| Liverpool | Mersey | England |
| London | Thames | England |
| Moscow New | Moskva | Russia |
| Orleans | Mississipi | USA |
| New York | Hudson | USA |
| Paris | Seine | France |
| Yangon | Irawadi | Myanmar |
| Rome | Tiber | Italy |

## Major Gulfs of the World

| *Names* | *Areas (Sq. Km.)* |
|---|---|
| Gulf of Mexico | 15,44,000 |
| Gulf of Hudson | 12,33,000 |
| Arabian Gulf | 2,38,000 |
| Gulf of St. Lawrence | 2,37,000 |
| Gulf of California | 1,62,000 |
| English Channel | 89,900 |

## Major Mountain Ranges of the World

| *Range* | *Location* | *Length (km)* |
|---|---|---|
| Andes | South America | 7,200 |
| Himalayas-Karakoram-Hindukush | South Central Asia | 5,000 |
| Rockies | North America | 4,800 |

| Range | Location | Length (km) |
|---|---|---|
| Great Dividing Range | East Australia | 3,600 |
| Atlas | North West Africa | 1,930 |
| Western Ghats | Western India | 1,610 |
| Caucasus | Europe | 1,200 |
| Alaska | USA | 1,130 |
| Alps | Europe | 1,050 |

## Largest Deserts of the World

**Subtropical**

| | |
|---|---|
| Sahara, North Africa | 94,00,000 sq. km. |
| Kalahari, Southern Africa | 9,00,000 sq. km. |
| Thar, India/Pakistan | 2,00,000 sq. km. |
| Great Sandy, Australia | 4,00,000 sq. km. |

**Cool Coastal**

| | |
|---|---|
| Atacama, Chile S.A. | 1,40,000 sq. km |

**Cool Winter**

| | |
|---|---|
| Gobi, China | 13,00,000 sq. km. |
| Colorado, Western USA (also called the painted desert) | 3,37,000 sq. km. |

## Atmosphere

### Composition of Gases in Atmosphere

| | |
|---|---|
| Nitrogen | 78.03% |
| Oxygen | 20.99% |
| Argon | 0.93% |
| Carbon dioxide | 0.03% |
| Hydrogen | 0.01% |
| Neon | 0.0018% |
| Helium | 0.0005% |
| Crypton | 0.0001% |
| Xenon | 0.000,005% |
| Ozone | 0.000,0001% |

## World Important Local Winds

**Chinoon:** A warm day wind frequently experienced on the eastern side of the Rocky Mountains.

**Fohn:** A warm dry wind descending a mountain, as on the north side of the Alps.

**Haboob:** A sand storm or a dust storm in north and north-east Sudan near Khartoum.

**Bagrrio:** It is the tropical cyclone of the Philippine Island.

**Loo:** A hot wind which blows in summer season in Indian sub-continent.

**Papasago:** A cold northerly wind sometimes felt on the Mexico plateau.

**Bora:** It is the name given to the cold dry wind experienced particularly in winter along the eastern coast of the Atlantic Ocean and in northern Italy.

**Black Toller:** A hot dust wind which blows in the vast plain of North America.

## Principal Mountain Peaks of the World

| Mountains | Height in Metres | Range | Date of First Ascent |
|---|---|---|---|
| 1. Mount Everest | 8,848 | Himalayas | May 29, 1953 |
| 2. K-2 (Godwin Austen) | 8,611 | Karakoram | July 31, 1954 |
| 3. Kanchenjunga | 8,597 | Himalayas | May 25, 1955 |
| 4. Lhotse | 8,511 | Himalayas | May 18, 1956 |
| 5. Makalu I | 8,481 | Himalayas | May 15, 1955 |
| 6. Dhaulagiri I | 8,167 | Himalayas | May 13, 1960 |
| 7. Mansalu I | 8,156 | Himalayas | May 9, 1956 |
| 8. Chollyo | 8,153 | Himalayas | Oct. 19, 1954 |
| 9. Nanga Parbat | 8,124 | Himalayas | July 3, 1953 |
| 10. Annapurna I | 8,091 | Himalayas | June 3, 1950 |

| Mountains | Height in Metres | Range | Date of First Ascent |
|---|---|---|---|
| 11. Gasherbrum I | 8,068 | Karakoram | July 5, 1958 |
| 12. Broad Peak I | 8,047 | Karakoram | June 9, 1957 |
| 13. Gasherbrum II | 8,034 | Karakoram | July 7, 1956 |
| 14. Shisha Pangma (Gosainthan) | 8,014 | Himalayas | May 2, 1964 |
| 15. Gasherbrum III | 7,952 | Karakoram | Aug. 11, 1975 |

## Types of World Agriculture

**Viticulture**: The cultivation of the vine for production of grapes and wine.
**Pisciculture:** The breeding, rearing and transplantation of fish by artificial means.
**Sericulture:** The raising of silk worms for the production of raw silk.
**Horticulture:** To grow flower front, vegetables on small plots.

**Apiculture:** Bee keeping on a commercial scale for the sale of honey.
**Floriculture:** The cultivation of flowers or flowering plants.
**Mariculture:** Sea farming, or the cultivation of marine plants and animals for commercial purposes.
**Olericulture:** The cultivation of vegetables and kitchen herbs.

## Famous Straits of the World

| Strait | Between | Country |
|---|---|---|
| Malacca Strait | Andaman Sea and South China Sea | Indonesia |
| Palk Strait | Mannar and Bay of Bengal | India-Sri Lanka |
| Magellan Strait | Pacific and South Atlantic Ocean | Chile |
| Dover Strait | English Channel and North Sea | England-France |
| Berring Strait | Berring Sea and Chukasi Sea | Alaska-Russia |
| Sugaroo Strait | Japan Sea and Pacific Ocean | Japan |
| Sunda Strait | Java and Indian Ocean | Indonesia |
| Gibralter Strait | Mediterranean Sea and Atlantic Ocean | Spain |
| Harmuj Strait | Persia and Bay of Oman | Oman-Iran |
| Hudson Strait | Bay of Hudson and Atlantic Ocean | Canada |

## World's Famous Official Documents

**White Paper:** India; **Orange Book:** Netherlands; **Yellow Book:** France; **Green Book:** Italy and Iran; **White Book:** Portugal, China and Germany; **Grey Book:** Japan and Belgium.

## Famous Newspapers of the World

| Newspaper | Place of Publishing | Language |
|---|---|---|
| Daily News | New York (America) | English |
| Guardian | London (Britain) | English |
| Pravada | Moscow (Russia) | Russian |
| Al-Ahram | Cairo (Egypt) | Arabic |
| Merdeca | Jakarta (Indonesia) | Indonesian |
| Times | London (Britain) | English |
| People's Daily | Beijing (China) | Chinese |
| New Statesman | Britain | English |
| Daily Mirror | Britain | English |
| Hindu, Hindustan Times, Times of India, Tribune, Statesman, Indian Express, Economic Times | India | English |
| Hindustan, Nav Bharat Times, Rashtriya Sahara, Dainik Jagaran, Punjab Kesari | India | Hindi |

## Important Boundary Lines

| Boundary Line | Countries |
|---|---|
| Hindenberg Line | Germany-Poland |
| Maginot Line | France and Germany |
| Mannerhein Line | Russia-Finland |
| Mc Mahon Line | India and China |
| Order Niesse Line | Germany-Poland |
| Radcliff Line | India-Pakistan |
| Seigfrid Line | Germany-France |
| Durand Line | Pakistan and Afghani-stan |
| 17th Parallel | The line which defined the boundary between North Vietnam and South Vietnam before the two were united. |
| 38th Parallel | North Korea and South Korea |
| 49th Parallel | U.S.A. and Canada |

## Areawise 10 Big and Small Countries

### 10 Big Countries

| S. No. | Country | Area (sq. km) |
|---|---|---|
| 1. | Russia (Europe-Asia) | 17,098,242 |
| 2. | Canada (N. America) | 99,84,670 |
| 3. | China (Asia) | 95,96,961 |
| 4. | U.S.A. (N. America) | 93,72,614 |
| 5. | Brazil (S. America) | 85,14,877 |
| 6. | Australia (S. Pacific) | 77,41,220 |
| 7. | India (Asia) | 32,87,263 |
| 8. | Argentina (S. America) | 27,80,400 |
| 9. | Kazakhstan (Europe-Asia) | 27,24,900 |
| 10. | Algeria (Africa) | 23,81,741 |

### 10 Small Countries

| S. No. | Country | Area (Sq. km) |
|---|---|---|
| 1. | Vatican City (Europe) | 0.44 |
| 2. | Monaco (Europe) | 1.95 |
| 3. | Nauru (Southern Pacific) | 21.10 |
| 4. | Tuvalu | 26.00 |
| 5. | San Marino (Europe) | 61.00 |
| 6. | Liechtenstein (Europe) | 160.00 |
| 7. | Marshall Island (Central Pacific) | 181.00 |
| 8. | St. Kitts and Nevis (Eastern Caribbean) | 261.00 |
| 9. | Maldives | 298.00 |
| 10. | Malta | 316.00 |

## Populationwise 10 Big and Small Countries

### 10 Big Countries

| S. No. | Country | Population (2021) (In Million) |
|---|---|---|
| 1. | China (Asia) | 1,397.898 |
| 2. | India (Asia) | 1,339 |
| 3. | U.S.A. (North America) | 334.998 |
| 4. | Indonesia (Asia) | 275.122 |
| 5. | Pakistan (Asia) | 238.181 |
| 6. | Nigeria (Africa) | 219.464 |
| 7. | Brazil (South America) | 213.445 |
| 8. | Bangladesh (Asia) | 164.099 |
| 9. | Russia (Europe-Asia) | 142.321 |
| 10. | Japan (Asia) | 124.687 |

### 10 Small Countries

| S. No. | Country | Population (2021) |
|---|---|---|
| 1. | Vatican City (Europe) | 1000 |
| 2. | Tuvalu (Southern Pacific) | 11,448 |
| 3. | Palau (Western Pacific) | 21,613 |
| 4. | San Marino (Europe) | 34,467 |
| 5. | Monaco (Europe) | 31,223 |
| 6. | Liechstein (Europe) | 39,425 |
| 7. | St. Kitts and Nevis (Eastern Caribbean) | 54,149 |
| 8. | Marshall Island (Central Pacific) | 78,831 |
| 9. | Seychelles | 96,387 |
| 10. | St. Vincent and The Grenadines | 1,01,145 |

## Signals/Signs and Meaning

| Signal/Sign | Meaning |
|---|---|
| Red Triangle | Family Planning |
| Red Cross | Medical Help |
| Red Light | Danger, 'Stop' for the movement of vehicles |
| Green Light | Go |
| Olive Branch | Peace |
| White Pigeon or Dove | Peace |
| Black Strip on Arm | (i) Opposition (ii) Sorrow |
| Black Flag | Opposition |
| Red Flag | (i) Danger (ii) Revolution |
| White Flag | Treaty or Surrender |
| Yellow Flag | Vehicles with patients of contagious diseases |
| Two Bones across with a Skull | Danger of electricity |
| Half mast flown Flag | National mourning |
| Lotus | Sign of civilization and culture |
| Wheel (Chakra) | Sign of Progress |
| A blind folded woman with scale in hand | Sign of Justice |
| Reversed flown | National calamity flag· |

## National Emblems of Important Countries

| Country | National Emblem |
|---|---|
| America | Golden Rod |
| Australia | Kangaroo |
| Ireland | Shamrock |
| Italy | White Lily |
| Israel | Candelabrum |
| Iran | Rose |
| Canada | White Lily |
| Great Britain | Rose |
| Chile | Candor and Huemul |
| Germany | Corn Flower |
| Japan | Chrysanthemum |
| Zimbabwe | Zimbabwe Bird |
| Denmark | Beach |
| Turkiye | Crescent and Star |
| The Netherlands | Lion |
| New Zealand | Kiwi, Fern Southern Cross |
| Norway | Lion |
| Nepal | Kukri |
| Pakistan | Crescent |
| Poland | Eagle |
| France | Lily |
| Belgium | Lion |
| Bangladesh | Water Lily |
| Mongolia | The Soyombo |
| Russia | Double headed eagle |
| Lebanon | Cedar Tree |
| Sudan | Secretary Bird |
| Syria | Eagle |
| India | Lioned Capital |

## The Continents of the World

| Name | Area (In sq. km.) | Population (2021) (In million) | Per cent of the World's Population |
|---|---|---|---|
| Asia (including the Middle East) | 44,579,000 | 4,584 | 59.1 |
| Africa | 30,065,000 | 1,375 | 17.4 |
| North America | 24,256,000 | 373 | 4.78 |
| South America | 17,819,000 | 651 | 8.4 |
| Antarctica | 13,209,000 | — | — |
| Europe | 99,38,000 | 747 | 9.8 |
| Australia (plus Oceania) | 76,87,000 | 41.66 | 0.5 |

## International Date Line

It roughly corresponds to 180°E or W meridian of longitude which falls on the opposite side of the Greenwich meridian and the date changes by one day (i.e. 24 hours), as this line is crossed. On crossing this line from east to west a day is added, and a day is subtracted on crossing it from west to east.

* * * * *

# 4. United Nations

- **Origin:** UN Charter was signed by 50 members on June 26, 1945. It officially came into existence on October 24, 1945.
- **UN Charter:** The Charter is the Constitution of the UNO and contains its aims and objectives and rules and regulations for its functioning.
- **Aims and Objectives:** They are security, welfare and human rights.
- **Headquarters:** New York.
- **Flag:** The flag is light blue in colour, and emblazoned in white, in its centre is the UN symbol—a polar map of world embraced by twin olive branches open at the top.
- **Official Languages:** The official languages of the UN are: English, French, Chinese, Russian, Arabic and Spanish. However, working languages are English & French only.
- **Main Organs of the UN:** There are six main organs:

  1. General Assembly
  2. Security Council
  3. Economic and Social Council
  4. Trusteeship Council
  5. International Court of Justice, and
  6. Secretariat.

  1. **General Assembly:** It consists of representative of all members of the UN. Each member country has only one vote. It meets once a year and passes UN Budget.
  2. **Security Council:** It is the Executive body of the UN and is mainly responsible for maintaining international peace and security. It has 15 members, 5 of which (USA, UK, France, Russia and China) are permanent members. The 10 non-permanent members are elected by General Assembly for two-year term and are not eligible for immediate re-election.
  3. **Economic and Social Council:** It has 54 members elected by General Assembly.
  4. **Trusteeship Council:** It looks after interest of the people in areas not yet independent and leads them towards self-government.
  5. **International Court of Justice:** It has 15 judges, no two of whom may be nationals of the same state. They are elected by General Assembly and Security Council for a term of 9 years. The Court elects its President and Vice-President for a 3-year term.
  6. **Secretariat:** It is the Secretariat of the UN and is headed by the Secretary General.

## Years Observed by United Nations

1967: International Tourism Year
1968: Human Rights Year
1970: International Education Year
1972: International Book Year
1973: Copernicus Year
1974: World Population Year
1975: International Women's Year
1979: International Year of the Child
1981: International Year of Disabled
1983: World Communication Year
1985: International Youth Year
1986: International Year of Peace
1987: International Year of Shelter for the Homeless

1990: International Literacy Year
1992: International Space Year
1993: International Year for World's Indigenous People
1994: International Year of Family
1995: International Year of Tolerance
1996: International Year for Eradication of Poverty
1998: Human Rights Year
1999: Year of Older Persons
2000: Year of the Culture of Peace
2001: International Year of Volunteer
2002: International Year of Eco-tourism
2003: International Year of Fresh Water
2004: International Rice Year
2005: International Year of Sports and Physical Education
2006: International Year of Deserts and Desertification
2008: International Year of Potato
2009: International Year of Astronomy
2010: International Year of Bio-diversity
2011: International Year of Forest
2012: International Year of Cooperatives
2013: International Year of Water Cooperation
2014: International Year of Family Farming
2015: International Year of Soils
2016: International Year of Pulses
2017: International Year of Sustainable Tourism for Development
2019: International Year of Indigenous Languages.
2020: International Year of Plant Health
2021: International Year of Peace and Trust
2022: International Year of Artisanal Fisheries and Aquaculture
2023: International Year of Millets
2024: International Year of Camelids

- **Present Membership:** At present 193 countries are members of the UN. South Sudan is the latest entrant to this world organisation.

## Famous International Organisations, Headquarters and Year of Establishment

| *International Organisations* | *Headquarters* | *Year of Establishment* |
|---|---|---|
| United Nations (U.N.) | New York | 1945 |
| International Monetary Fund (I.M.F.) | Washington D.C. | 1945 |
| World Health Organisation (W.H.O.) | Geneva | 1948 |
| Food & Agricultural Organisation (FAO) | Rome | 1945 |
| International Labour Organisation (ILO) | Geneva | 1919 |
| UNESCO | Paris | 1946 |
| International Court of Justice | The Hague | 1945 |
| Universal Postal Union (UPU) | Berne | 1874 |
| International Civil Aviation Organisation (ICAO) | Montreal | 1947 |
| UNIDO | Vienna | 1966 |
| International Atomic Energy Agency (IAEA) | Vienna | 1957 |
| International Finance Corporation (IFC) | Washington | 1956 |
| United Nations Development Programme (UNDP) | New York | 1965 |
| UNICEF | New York | 1946 |
| International Maritime Organisation (IMO) | London | 1948 |
| World Meteorological Organisation (WMO) | Geneva | 1950 |
| International Telecommunication Union (ITU) | Geneva | 1865 |
| Arab League | Cairo | 1945 |
| Commonwealth of Nations | London | 1931 |
| World Trade Organisation (WTO) | Geneva | 1995 |

| *International Organisations* | *Headquarters* | *Year of Establishment* |
|---|---|---|
| International Development Association (IDA) | Washington D.C. | 1960 |
| International Bank for Reconstruction and Development (IBRD) | Washington D.C. | 1944 |
| World Intellectual Property Organisation (WIPO) | Geneva | 1967 |
| Organisation of Islamic Conference (OIC) | Jeddah (Saudi Arabia) | 1969 |
| Red Cross | Geneva | 1863 |
| Interpol | Lyons | 1923 |
| Asian Development Bank (ADB) | Manila | 1966 |
| North Atlantic Treaty Organisation (NATO) | Brussels | 1949 |
| Association of South East Asian Nations (ASEAN) | Jakarta | 1967 |
| South Asian Association for Regional Cooperation (SAARC) | Kathmandu | 1985 |
| Asia-Pacific Economic Cooperation (APEC) | Singapore | 1989 |
| Organisation for Economic Cooperation and Development (OECD) | Paris | 1961 |
| Organisation of Petroleum Exporting Countries (OPEC) | Vienna | 1960 |
| Common Wealth of Independent States (CIS) | Minsk | 1991 |
| International Olympic Committee (IOC) | Lausanne | 1894 |
| European Union (EU) | Brussels | Changed form of EEC Established in 1958 |
| Amnesty International (AI) | London | 1961 |
| Shanghai Cooperation Organisation (SCO) | Beijing | 2002 |
| BRICS Bank | Shanghai | 2014 |

* * * * *

# 5. Indian Constitution & Polity

Indian Constitution is a comprehensive document and it is the lengthiest written Constitution in the World.

**The Preamble of the Constitution:** "We the people of India, having solemnly resolved to Constitute India into a Sovereign, Socialist, Secular Democratic Republic and to secure to all its citizen."

**Justice:** Social, economic and political.

**Liberty:** Of thought, expression, belief, faith and worship.

**Equality:** Of status and of opportunity, and to promote among them all.

**Fraternity:** Assuring the dignity of the individual and the unity and integrity of the nation. In our Constituent Assembly this twenty-sixth day of November, 1949, do hereby adopt, enact and give to ourselves this Constitution.

## SCHEDULES TO THE CONSTITUTION

The Constitution of India originally contained only eight schedules. Presently there are 12 schedules in the constitution.

***First Schedule:*** It consists the list of the States and Union territories. ***Second Schedule:*** This Schedule is related to salary and allowances of the President, Governors, Speaker, Supreme Court and High Court Judges etc. ***Third Schedule:*** Contains forms of oath and affirmation. ***Fourth Schedule:*** Contains allocation of seats to each State and Union territory in the Council of States. ***Fifth Schedule:*** Provides for administration and control of scheduled areas and scheduled tribes. ***Sixth Schedule:*** Provides for administration of Tribal Areas in Assam, Meghalaya and Mizoram. ***Seventh Schedule:*** Distribution of powers and functions between the centre and state governments under three lists. ***Eighth Schedule:*** The languages recognised by Parliament. ***Ninth Schedule:*** It contains laws passed by the Union or States which cannot be taken to courts. ***Tenth Schedule:*** Provisions as to disqualification on the ground of political defection. ***Eleventh Schedule:*** Provisions regarding powers, authority etc. of Panchayati Raj institutions. ***Twelfth Schedule:*** Provisions regarding powers, authority etc. of Municipalities etc.

### Foreign Sources of Indian Constitution

| *Foreign Sources* | *Subject* |
|---|---|
| Britain | Parliamentary system, collective responsibilities of Cabinet |
| America | Fundamental right, Citizenship, Independent Judiciary, Judicial review |
| Canada | Division of powers |
| Ireland | Directive principles |
| Germany | Emergency provisions |
| Russia | Fundamental duties |
| Australia | Concurrent list |

## THE SUPREME COURT

The Supreme Court of India consists of the Chief Justice and other Judges whose number is prescribed by the Parliament from time to time. In 1950 there was a Chief Justice and there were 7 Judges. But the number of Judges continued increasing as per the need. The Supreme Court, at present, consists of the Chief Justice and 33 Judges.

The Chief Justice and other Judges of the Supreme Court are appointed by the President of India. For appointing the Chief Justice of India, the other Judges of the Supreme or High Courts may be consulted. Usually, the senior-most Judge in the Supreme Court is appointed as the Chief Justice. For the appointment of other Judges of the Supreme Court, the Chief Justice has to be consulted. Usually, the Chief Justice himself consults a collegium of the four senior-most Judges, and all of them need to agree for any candidate to be recommended for the appointment of a judge.

A person can be appointed as a Judge of the Supreme Court only if he/she:

I. is a citizen of India;

II. must have been at least a Judge of a High Court or of two or more such Courts in succession for at least five years; or

III. must have been an advocate of a High Court or of two or more such Courts in succession for at least ten years; or

IV. is, in the opinion of the President, a distinguished jurist.

Judges of the Supreme Court hold office till they attain the age of 65 years. But they may be removed from office by an order of the President, passed after an address by each House of Parliament supported by a special majority on the ground of proved misbehaviour or incapacity.

## The Jurisdiction and Powers of the Supreme Court

The Supreme Court of India is a powerful judiciary. The Constitution of India has defined its jurisdiction and powers in detail, it has Original. Appellate and Advisory Jurisdictions Besides these jurisdictions, it has a few other important functions.

(*i*) **Original Jurisdiction:** The Supreme Court alone has the authority to hear directly certain cases. These are:

(*a*) Disputes between the Union government and one or more State governments,

(*b*) Disputes between two or more States,

(*c*) Disputes between the Government of India and one or more States on the one side and one or more States on the other side.

(*ii*) **Appellate Jurisdiction:** The power of a superior or higher court to hear and decide appeals against the judgment of the lower court is called appellate jurisdiction. The Supreme Court is a court of appeal for constitutional, civil and criminal cases. It can hear appeals against the judgments of the High Courts. It also has the power to review its own judgment. It may in its own discretion grant special lease to appeal against any judgment or order delivered or passed by any court or tribunal within the territory of India.

Moreover, an Appeal may come to the Supreme Court in any criminal case, if the High Court certifies that the case is fit for appeal to the Supreme Court. The special appellate power has become a handy weapon in the hands of the Court to review the decisions pertaining to elections and Labour and Industrial Tribunals.

(*iii*) **Advisory Jurisdiction:** The Supreme Court has a special advisory jurisdiction in matters which may specifically be referred to it by the President of India. If at any time, it appears to the President that a question of law or fact has arisen or is likely to arise, which is of such public importance that it is urgent to obtain the opinion of the Supreme Court on it, he/she may refer it to the Supreme Court. The Supreme Court may, after such hearing as it thinks fit, report to the President its opinion thereon. The report or the opinion of the Supreme Court is of course, not binding on the President. Similarly, there is no compulsion for the Court to give its advice.

(*iv*) **Judicial Review:** The Supreme Court of India has the power to examine the validity of laws or executive orders. The Supreme Court has the powers to interpret the Constitution, and through this it has assumed the power of judicial review.

(*v*) **Guardian of the Constitution:** As the interpreter of the Constitution, the Supreme Court has the power to protect and defend the Constitution. If the Court finds that any law or executive order is against the Constitution, the same can be declared unconstitutional or invalid. Similarly the Supreme Court also acts as the custodian and protector of Fundamental Rights.

## PARLIAMENT

Parliament is the national legislature of the Indian Union. It consists of two Houses known as the Council of States or the Rajya Sabha and the House of People or Lok Sabha. The President is an integal part of Parliament.

**Rajya Sabha:** The Rajya Sabha is the Upper House of the Parliament and it is constituted of representatives from the States or the Constituent units of the Indian Union. It is a permanent body, one third of its members retiring after every two years. Its maximum strength is 250. Out of these, twelve members are nominated by the President from well-known personalities in the realm of Science, Art, Literature and Social Service. Rest of 238 representatives of the States and Union Territories are elected.

**Lok Sabha:** The Lok Sabha whose life is five years, is the Lower House of Parliament and comprises of members directly elected by the people. The House of the people (Lok Sabha) at present consists of 543 members directly elected from the states and from Union Territories. By the 104th amendment of the Constitution the reservation for two members of Anglo Indian Community nominated by President have been abolished. The House of the People shall continue for five years (unless sooner dissolved) from the date of its meeting and no longer and the expiry of the said period of 5 years shall operate as dissolution of the House.

### DIFFERENCE BETWEEN LOK SABHA AND RAJYA SABHA

- Members of Lok Sabha are directly elected by the eligible voters. Members of Rajya Sabha are elected by the elected members of State Legislative Assemblies in accordance with the system of proportional representation by means of single transferable vote.
- The normal life of every Lok Sabha is 5 years only while Rajya Sabha is a permanent body.
- Lok Sabha is the House to which the Council of Ministers is responsible under the Constitution. Money Bills can only be introduced in Lok Sabha. Also it is Lok Sabha, which grants the money for running the administration of the country.
- Rajya Sabha has special powers to declare that it is necessary and expedient in the national interest that Parliament may make laws with respect to a matter in the State List or to create by law one or more all-India services common to the Union and the States.

**Parliamentary Committees:** There are several Parliamentary Committees to assist the Parliament in its deliberations. These are appointed or elected by the respective Houses of Lok Sabha and Rajya Sabha on a motion made or are nominated by their presiding officers, i.e., the Speaker of Lok Sabha and the Chairman of Rajya Sabha respectively. Broadly, Parliamentary Committees are of two kinds–standing committees and ad-hoc committees. Among the Standing Committees, three are financial Committees:

(*i*) Public Account Committee;
(*ii*) Estimate Committee;
(*iii*) Public undertaking Committee.

Ad-hoc Committees are appointed as the need arises and cease to exist when the work is over.

**Speaker of Lok Sabha:** Speaker is elected by the Lok Sabha from among its members. The Speaker will have the final power to maintain order within the House of the People and to interpret its rules of procedure. Speaker decides whether a bill is a money bill or a non-money bill.

- There shall be a Speaker to preside over the house of the people. Speaker and Deputy-Speaker will be chosen among the members as soon as after the first sitting.
- They normally hold the office during the life of the house and may terminate earlier by the following ways:

(*a*) By ceasing to be a member of house

(*b*) By resignation addressed to Deputy-Speaker or vice-versa

(*c*) By removal from office by a resolution passed by a majority of all the then members of the House.

- He has the power to maintain order within the house, interpret its Rules of procedures, adjourn or suspend the House.
- The speaker shall preside over the joint sitting of the two houses of the parliament and when a money bill is transmitted from Lok Sabha to Rajya Sabha, the speaker shall endorse on the bill his certificate that it is a money bill.
- The deputy-speaker presides when the speaker is vacant or absent.
- The Speaker exercises a casting vote in case of tie.

## Indian States and Union Territories: Allocation of Seats

| S. No. | State/UTs | Seats of Lok Sabha | Seats of Rajya Sabha | Legislative Assembly | Legislative Council |
|---|---|---|---|---|---|
| 1. | Andhra Pradesh | 25 | 11 | 175 | 58 |
| 2. | Arunachal Pradesh | 2 | 1 | 60 | |
| 3. | Assam | 14 | 7 | 126 | |
| 4. | Bihar | 40 | 16 | 243 | 75 |
| 5. | Chhattisgarh | 11 | 5 | 90 | |
| 6. | Goa | 2 | 1 | 40 | |
| 7. | Gujarat | 26 | 11 | 182 | |
| 8. | Haryana | 10 | 5 | 90 | |
| 9. | Himachal Pradesh | 4 | 3 | 68 | |
| 10. | Jharkhand | 14 | 6 | 81 | |
| 11. | Karnataka | 28 | 12 | 224 | 75 |
| 12. | Kerala | 20 | 9 | 140 | |
| 13. | Madhya Pradesh | 29 | 11 | 230 | |
| 14. | Maharashtra | 48 | 19 | 288 | 78 |
| 15. | Manipur | 2 | 1 | 60 | |
| 16. | Meghalaya | 2 | 1 | 60 | |
| 17. | Mizoram | 1 | 1 | 40 | |
| 18. | Nagaland | 1 | 1 | 60 | |
| 19. | Odisha | 21 | 10 | 147 | |
| 20. | Punjab | 13 | 7 | 117 | |
| 21. | Rajasthan | 25 | 10 | 200 | |
| 22. | Sikkim | 1 | 1 | 32 | |
| 23. | Tamil Nadu | 39 | 18 | 234 | |
| 24. | Telangana | 17 | 7 | 119 | 40 |
| 25. | Tripura | 2 | 1 | 60 | |
| 26. | Uttar Pradesh | 80 | 31 | 403 | 100 |
| 27. | Uttarakhand | 5 | 3 | 70 | |
| 28. | West Bengal | 42 | 16 | 294 | |

| S. No. | State/UTs | Seats of Lok Sabha | Seats of Rajya Sabha | Legislative Assembly | Legislative Council |
|---|---|---|---|---|---|
| 29. | Jammu & Kashmir | 5 | 4 | — | — |
| 30. | Andaman & Nicobar Islands | 1 | — | — | — |
| 31. | Chandigarh | 1 | — | — | — |
| 32. | Dadra & Nagar Haveli and Daman & Diu | 2 | — | — | — |
| 33. | Delhi | 7 | 3 | 70 | — |
| 34. | Lakshadweep | 1 | — | — | — |
| 35. | Puduchery | 1 | 1 | 30 | — |
| 36. | Ladakh | 1 | — | — | — |

## Table of Precedence

1. President
2. Vice-President
3. Prime Minister
4. Governors of States within their respective states
5. Former Presidents

5A. Deputy Prime Minister

6. Chief Justice of India, Speaker of Lok Sabha
7. Cabinet Ministers of the Union, Chief Ministers of States within their respective States, Deputy Chairman NITI Aayog.

   Leaders of opposition in Rajya Sabha and Lok Sabha

7A. Holders of the Bharat Ratna Decoration

8. Ambassadors Extraordinary and Plenipotentiary and High Commissioners of Commonwealth Countries accredited to India

   Chief Ministers of States outside their respective States
9. Judges of the Supreme Court
10. Deputy Chairman Rajya Sabha, Deputy Chief Minister of States

    Deputy Speaker Lok Sabha, Members of the NITI Aayog, Minister of State of the Union and Other Minister in the Ministry of Defence.

## PRESIDENT

The President is the Constitutional head of the Republic of India. He is more or less the titular head of the executive. Really speaking, he is the constitutional head but not the real executive. The real power is vested in the hands of the Council of Ministers.

**Qualifications:**

(*i*) Indian citizen,

(*ii*) age not less than 35 years,

(*iii*) should have qualification for election to Lok Sabha,

(*iv*) should not hold any office of profit,

(*v*) should not be a Member of Parliament or State Legislature.

### Impeachment

- Impeachment is a quasi-judicial procedure in the parliament to remove the president from office due to the violation of the constitution. Either house may prefer this charge of violation of constitution before the other house. A house cannot prefer the charge unless
  - 14 days notice in writing signed by not less than ¼ of the total members of that house
  - the resolution should be passed by not less than 2/3 of the total membership of that house.
- The house may investigate or cause it to investigate and the president has the right to appear and to be represented before such investigation. As a result of such investigation, a resolution is passed by not less than 2/3 of the total membership of the house before which the charge has been preferred, such resolution shall has the effect of removing the president from the date on which the resolution is passed.

- A vacancy in the office of president may arise
  - On the expiry of his term
  - By death, resignation, impeachment or otherwise, *i.e.*, by setting aside of his election as president.
- If the vacancy is caused to the delay in the election of the president, the outgoing president must continue to hold the office and for all other occasions the vice-president shall act as the president. If the vice-president is not available, the chief justice will act as the president.

### Powers of President

- Art. 53 says that the Executive Power of the Union shall be vested in the President. The executive power consists of—
  - Administrative Power
  - Diplomatic Power
  - Military Power
  - Legislative Power
  - Pardoning Power

## VICE-PRESIDENT

The Vice-President acts as the ex-officio Chairman of the Council of States (Rajya Sabha). He is elected by an electoral college consisting of the members of both Houses of Parliament in accordance with the system of proportional representation by means of the single transferable vote. He must be a citizen of India, not less than 35 years of age, and should be eligible for election as a member of the Council of States. Disputes in connection with election of president or a vice-president are to be a dealt with in accordance with Article-71. Such disputes shall be decided by the Supreme Court.

## COUNCIL OF MINISTERS

- India adopted the British pattern of parliamentary form of government with the President as the formal head of executive acting on the advice of ministers responsible to the popular house of the legislature.
- The constitution prescribes that there shall be a council of ministers with the Prime minister at the head to assist and advice the president. (Art. 74)
- The Prime Minister is selected by the President, the other ministers are appointed by the President on the advice of the Prime Minister (Art. 75) and the allocation of portfolios amongst them is also made by him
- Ministers may be chosen from the members of either House and a minister has the right to speak in and take part in the proceedings of the other house though he has no right to vote in the House of which he is not a member.
- There is no bar to the appointment of a person from the outside the legislature as Minister. But he cannot continue as minister for more than 6 months unless he secures a seat in either house of the parliament.
- Art. 75(3) of the constitution says that the council of ministers shall be collectively responsible to the house of the people. So the ministry has to resign if it loses the confidence of the Lok Sabha.

### CATEGORIES OF COUNCIL OF MINISTERS

- There are three categories of council of ministers. Cabinet Ministers, Ministers of State and Deputy Ministers.
- The cabinet meetings can be attended by all cabinet ministers, Minister of state and deputy minister attend only if invited.
- The constitution provides for the collective responsibility of the council of ministers to the house of people only. The ministry as body has to resign as soon as it loses the confidence of the Lok Sabha.

## PRIME MINISTER

The Constitution lays down that there shall be a Council of Ministers headed by the Prime Minister to aid and advise the President in the exercise of his functions. The Prime Minister is the head of the Cabinet. Other Ministers are appointed by the President on his advice. He is the leader of the majority party in the Lok Sabha.

## FUNDAMENTAL RIGHTS

Following fundamental rights are enjoyed by every Indian citizen, irrespective of caste, colour, creed and sex:

**1. Right to Equality:** No special privileges, no distinction on grounds of religion, caste, creed and sex.

**2. Right to Freedom:** The right to freedom of expression and speech, the right to choose one's own profession, the right to reside in any part of the Indian Union.

**3. Right to Freedom to Religion:** Except when it is in the interest of public order, morality, health or other conditions, everybody has the right to profess, practice and propagate his religion freely.

**4. Cultural and Educational Rights:** The Constitution provides that every community can run its own institutions to preserve its own culture and language.

**5. Right against Exploitation:** Traffic in human beings and forced labour and the employment of children under 14 years in factories or mines, are punishable offences.

**6. Rights to Constitutional Remedies:** When a citizen finds that any of his fundamental rights has been encroached upon, he can move the Supreme Court, which has been empowered to safeguard the fundamental rights of a citizen (Article 32).

## Jurisdiction and Seat of High Courts

| *Name* | *Year* | *Territorial Jurisdiction* | *Seat* |
|---|---|---|---|
| Allahabad | 1866 | Uttar Pradesh | Prayagraj (Bench at Lucknow) |
| Andhra Pradesh | 2019 | Andhra Pradesh | Amaravati |
| Bombay | 1862 | Maharashtra, Goa, Dadar and Nagar Haveli and Daman and Diu | Mumbai (Benches at Nagpur, Panaji and Aurangabad) |
| Calcutta | 1862 | West Bengal and Andaman & Nicobar | Kolkata (Circuit Benches at Port Blair and Jalpaiguri) |
| Chhattisgarh | 2000 | Chhattisgarh | Bilaspur |
| Delhi | 1966 | Delhi | Delhi |
| Guwahati | 1948 | Assam, Nagaland, Mizoram and Arunachal Pradesh | Guwahati (Benches at Kohima, Aizawl and Itanagar) |
| Gujarat | 1960 | Gujarat | Ahmedabad |
| Himachal Pradesh | 1971 | Himachal Pradesh | Shimla |
| Jammu & Kashmir and Ladakh | 1928 | Jammu & Kashmir, Ladakh | Srinagar and Jammu |
| Jharkhand | 2000 | Jharkhand | Ranchi |
| Karnataka | 1884 | Karnataka | Bengaluru (Circuit Benches at Dharwar and Gulbarga) |
| Kerala | 1958 | Kerala & Lakshadweep | Ernakulam |
| Madhya Pradesh | 1956 | Madhya Pradesh | Jabalpur (Benches at Gwalior and Indore) |
| Madras | 1862 | Tamil Nadu & Puducherry | Chennai (Bench at Madurai) |
| Orissa | 1948 | Odisha | Cuttack |
| Patna | 1916 | Bihar | Patna |
| Punjab and Haryana | 1966 | Punjab, Haryana and Chandigarh | Chandigarh |
| Rajasthan | 1949 | Rajasthan | Jodhpur (Bench at Jaipur) |
| Sikkim | 1975 | Sikkim | Gangtok |

| Name | Year | Territorial Jurisdiction | Seat |
|---|---|---|---|
| Uttarakhand | 2000 | Uttarakhand | Nainital |
| Tripura | 2013 | Tripura | Agartala |
| Meghalaya | 2013 | Meghalaya | Shillong |
| Manipur | 2013 | Manipur | Imphal |
| Telangana | 2019 | Telangana | Hyderabad |

## FUNDAMENTAL DUTIES

The fundamental duties for the Indian citizens have been incorporated in the Constitution through the Constitution (42nd) Amendment Act, 1976. These duties are: (*i*) to abide by the Constitution and respect its ideals and institutions, the National Flag and the National Anthem; (*ii*) to cherish and follow the noble deeds which inspired our national struggle for freedom; (*iii*) to uphold and protect the sovereignty, unity and integrity of India; (*iv*) to defend the country and render national service when called upon to do so; (*v*) to promote harmony and the spirit of common brotherhood amongst all the people transcending religious, regional or sectional diversities and to renounce practices derogatory to the dignity of women; (*vi*) to value and preserve the rich heritage of our composite culture; (*vii*) to protect and improve natural environment including forests, lakes, rivers and wildlife, and to have compassion for living creatures; (*viii*) to develop the scientific temper, humanism and the spirit of inquiry and reform; (*ix*) to safeguard public property and to abjure violence; (*x*) to strive towards excellence in all spheres of individual and collective activity so that the nation constantly rises to higher levels of endeavour and achievement. (*xi*) who is parent or guardian to provide opportunities for education to his child or, as the case may be, ward between age of six and fourteen years.

## DIRECTIVE PRINCIPLES OF STATE POLICY

The Directive Principles of State Policy are contained in Article 36 to 51 in Part IV of the constitutions. Directive principles are not enforceable through courts. Main aim of Directive principles is to provide social and economic base of a genuine democracy.

**Some Important Directive Principles:**

- Provisions for adequate means of livelihood for all citizens (Art. 39).
- Right to work (Art. 41).
- Right to human condition of work and maternity relief (Art. 42).
- Right to a living wage and condition of work ensuring decent standard of life of worker (Art. 43).
- Common Civil Code (Art. 44).
- Prohibit consumption of liquor (Art. 47).
- Prevent slaughter of useful cattle (Art. 48).
- Organise Panchayati Raj (Art. 40).
- Separate the judiciary from the executive (Art. 50).
- Protect and maintain places of historic monuments (Art. 49).
- International peace (Art. 51).

**Voting Age:** The voting age in the election to the Lok Sabha and State Legislative Assemblies has been reduced from 21 to 18 years by the Constitution (61st) Amendment Act, 1989.

## GOVERNOR

The Governor is appointed by the President and holds office during the pleasure of the President. Apart from the power to appoint the council of ministers, if the governor finds that the government of state cannot be carried on in accordance with the provisions of the constitution (Art. 356), he may send his report to the President who may assume to himself the functions of the government of the state. (This is popularly known as 'President's Rule').

## THE ATTORNEY GENERAL OF INDIA

The Attorney General of India is the first law officer of the Government of India. Though he is not a member of cabinet he has the right to speak in the House of Parliament, but he has no right to vote. The Attorney General of India shall be appointed by the President and shall hold office during his pleasure.

His duty shall be to give advice on such legal matter from time to time as may be referred to him by the President.

## COMPTROLLER & AUDITOR GENERAL OF INDIA (CAG)

The Comptroller and Auditor General of India is guardian of the public purse and it is his duty to see that not a *paisa* is spent out of consolidated fund of India or of a state without the authority of the appropriate legislature. He is appointed by President of India.

**Status**

- Appointed by the President.
- A person with long administrative experience & knowledge of accounts is appointed.
- Holds office for 6 yrs or till 65 yrs of age.
- The President can remove him only on the recommendation of the 2 houses of Parliament (as in case of judge of Supreme Court).

## UNION PUBLIC SERVICE COMMISSION (U.P.S.C.)

This Commission is responsible for (i) recruitment to all civil services and posts, under the Union Government by written examinations, interviews and promotions, and (ii) advising the Government on all matters relating to methods of recruitment, principles to be followed in making promotions and transfers. Its Chairman is appointed by the President.

## INTER-STATE COUNCILS

Article 263 provides for inter-state councils. The power of the President to set up Inter-State Councils not only for advising upon disputes but also for investigating and discussing subjects in which some or all of the states, or the Union and one or more of the states have common interest.

## STAFF SELECTION COMMISSION

The Union Government has constituted the Staff Selection Commission for recruitment to non-technical Group C and some of Group B posts in the central departments and in subordinate offices. The administrative Reforms Commission had recommended the setting up of such a Commission.

## ELECTION COMMISSIONER

- The Constitution provides for an independent election commission to ensure free and fair election to the Parliament, the State legislature and the offices of President and Vice-President.
- Consists of Chief Election Commissioner +2 Election Commissioners. They all enjoy equal powers.
- The Chief Election Commissioner is appointed by the President and the other Election Commissioners are appointed by the President after consultation with the Chief Election Commissioner. Article 324 also provides for the appointment of Regional Commissioners at the time of General Elections after consultation with the Election Commissioner.
- Election Commissioners are appointed for a term of 5 years.
- They are not eligible for re-appointment. Also, they cannot hold any office of profit after their retirement.
- The term of 5 years can by cut short by resignation or removal by President on recommendation of the Parliament (Same as that of Judge of the Supreme Court).

* * * * *

# 6. Planning In India

The need for planning was felt in India even before independence. A National Planning Committee was set up by the Indian National Congress as early as 1938. The Planning Commission was set up in 1950. It was an advisory body engaged in the task of meaningful national planning. The main objectives of India's Economic Planning are as follows : (*i*) securing an increase in National Income; (*ii*) achieving a planned rate of investment within a given period to bring the actual investment as a proportion of national income to a higher level; (*iii*) reducing inequality in the distribution of income and wealth; (*iv*) providing additional employment; (*v*) adopting measures to increase agricultural production, manufacturing capacity for producers and a favourable balance of payments.

### Five Year Plans in India

| Plans | Period | Investment (₹ Crore) | Objectives |
|---|---|---|---|
| First Plan | April 1, 1951–March 31, 1956 | 1,960 | Priority to agriculture, electricity and irrigation. |
| Second Plan | April 1, 1956–March 31, 1961 | 4,672 | Development of basic and heavy industries. |
| Third Plan | April 1, 1961–March 31, 1966 | 8,577 | Long term development of India's economy. |
| Annual Plan | April 1, 1966–March 31, 1967 | 2,137 | |
| Annual Plan | April 1, 1967–March 31, 1968 | 2,205 | |
| Annual Plan | April 1, 1968–March 31, 1969 | 2,283 | |
| Fourth Plan | April 1, 1969–March 31, 1974 | 15,779 | Enlarge the income of rural population and supply of goods of mass consumption. |
| Fifth Plan | April 1, 1974–March 31, 1979 | 39,426 | Attain increased self reliance and employment avenues. |
| Annual Plan | April 1, 1979–March 31, 1980 | 12,176 | |
| Sixth Plan | April 1, 1980–March 31, 1985 | 1,09,292 | Removal of unemployment |
| Seventh Plan | April 1, 1985–March 31, 1990 | 2,18,730 | Food work and productivity were the basic priorities. |
| Eighth Plan | April, 1992–March 31, 1997 | 4,95,670 | Raising employment |
| Ninth Plan | April 1, 1997–March 31, 2002 | 9,41,041 | Agriculture and rural development |
| Tenth Plan | April 1, 2002–March 31, 2007 | 14,91,610 | Growth rate 7.8 percent per annum. |
| Eleventh Plan | April 1, 2007–March 31, 2012 | 36,44,718 | Literacy, Employment, Rural development & Transport development. |
| Twelfth Plan | April 1, 2012–March 31, 2017 | 43,30,000 | Long term development of India's economy. |

## 15-YEAR VISION PLAN

With the end of the Twelfth Plan in March 2017 the era of five year plans came to an end. NITI Aayog has come forward with a draft 15-year vision plan to catapult the country's economy to more than three times as compared to the present day. The new plan is set to replace the centralised five-year plans the country has been following for decades. The new plan is accompanied by shorter sub-plans—a seven-year strategy for 2017-24, and a three-year 'Action Agenda' from 2017-18 to 2019-20. No less than 300 specific action points covering a wide range of sectors have been drawn up as part of the 15-year vision. The 15-year vision document has a seven-year strategy document for 2017-24 as the 'National Development Agenda'. Separately, a three-year 'Action Agenda' from 2017-18 to 2019-20 is also under works to assess funding requirements. The three-year agenda is further divided into seven parts, with a number of specific action points for each part to boost economic growth. India's urban population is expected to increase by 22 crores by 2031. The plan is likely to lay emphasis on urban development, taking a note from China's elaborate long-term development agenda.

## NITI AAYOG

The planning commission which has a legacy of 65 years has replaced by NITI Aayog. The utility and significance of the Planning Commission had been questioned for long. The replacement seems to be more relevant and responsive to the present economic needs and scenario in the country.

### *Evolution of NITI Aayog*

The NITI Aayog was formed on January 1, 2015. In Sanskrit, the word "NITI" means morality, behaviour, guidance, etc. But, in the present context, it means policy and the NITI stand for National Institution for Transforming India. It is country's premier policy-making institution which is expected to bolster the economic growth of the country. It aims to construct a strong state that will help to create a dynamic and strong nation. This helps India to emerge as a major economy in the world. The NITI Aayog's creation has two hubs called "Team India Hub" and Knowledge and innovation Hub.

1. The Team India: It leads the participation of Indian states with the central government.
2. The Knowledge and innovation hub: it builds institution's think tank capabilities.

NITI Aayog is additionally creating itself as a State of the Art Resource Center, with the essential resources, knowledge, and skills that will empower it to act with speed, advance research and innovation, bestow crucial policy vision to the government and manage unforeseen issues. The reason for setting up the NITI Aayog is that the people had expectations for growth and development in the administration through their participation. This required institutional changes in administration and active strategy shifts that could seed and foster substantial scale change. The institution has completed four year of its life.

### *Members of NITI Aayog*

The NITI Aayog comprises the following:

1. Prime Minister of India as the Chairperson
2. Governing Council comprising the Chief Ministers of all the States and Union territories with Legislatures and lieutenant governors of other Union territories.
3. Regional Councils will be formed to address specific issues and contingencies impacting more than one state or a region. These will be formed for a specified tenure.
4. Experts, specialists and practitioners with relevant domain knowledge as special invitees nominated by the Prime Minister
5. Full-time organizational framework (in addition to Prime Minister as the Chair-person) comprising
   (*i*) *Vice-Chairperson*
   (*ii*) *Members:* Three (3) Full-time
   (*iii*) *Part-time members:* Maximum of two from leading universities research organi-zations and other relevant institutions in an ex-officio capacity. Part-time members will be on a rotational basis.
   (*iv*) *Ex Officio members:* Maximum of four members of the Union Council of Ministers to be nominated by the Prime Minister.

(v) *Chief Executive Officer:* To be appointed by the Prime Minister for a fixed tenure, in the rank of Secretary to the Government of India.

## FINANCE COMMISSION

Article 280 of the Constitution provides for the appointment of a finance commission every five year. President appoints chairman and members of this commission. Finance commission are to recommend to President the basis for the distribution of the net proceeds of taxes between the centre and the states and the principles which should govern the grants-in-aid to be given to the states out of the consolidated funds of India.

## GOODS AND SERVICES TAX

At the stroke of midnight of June 30, 2017 as the world slept, India woke up to one of the biggest tax reforms since Independence. The New GST tax regime is expected to transform India into one single market. President shared the dais with the Prime Minister Narendra Modi, Speaker, Vice-President and Finance Minister for the launch of the GST. Also present were the country's corporate honchos. The new tax regime replaces 17 different Central and State taxes and 23 cesses, including service tax, value added tax, entry tax, excise duty among others. The GST is expected to remove the cascading effect of tax-on-tax and make it easier to do business in the country. After GST, goods will have uniform prices across the country. There are 4 tax slabs for goods and services—5%, 12%, 18% and 28%.

## NATIONAL DEVELOPMENT COUNCIL

The National Development Council, set-up in 1952, consists of representatives of the Central Government as well as the State governments. It is the supreme body insofar as planning is concerned and it determines policies, issues guidelines, reviews working of the plan and finally approves the plan. The Council consists of the Prime Minister (Chairman), all Union Cabinet Ministers, Chief Ministers of all States and Union Territories and the Vice Chairman and members of the NITI Aayog. For matters relating to Plans and planning, the Union Minister of Planning is responsible to the Parliament.

## RESERVE BANK OF INDIA

- It is the Central Bank of the country.
- It was established on April 1, 1935 with a capital of ₹ 5 crore. This capital of ₹ 5 crore was divided into 5 lakh equity shares of ₹ 100 each. In the beginning, the ownership of almost all the share capital was with the non-government shareholders.
- It was nationalized on Jan 1, 1949 as govt. acquired the private shareholdings.
- **Governors:** Ist Governor - Sir Smith (1935-37)
  Ist Indian Governor - C.D. Deshmukh (1948-49)

### Other Financial Institutions

- **Industrial Credit & Investment Corporation of India Bank (ICICI Bank) :** Established in 1955 as a public limited company to encourage and assist industrial units of the nation. It has been converted into a bank with effect from May 3, 2002.
- **Small Industries Development Bank of India (SIDBI) :** Established in 1990; promotes small scale sector.
- **National Bank of Agriculture & Rural Development (NABARD) :** Established on Nov 5, 1982; gives credit facilities to farmers.
- **Export-Import Bank of India (EXIM) :** Set-up on Jan 1, 1982; grants deferred credit to Indian exporters in order to operate in the International market.
- **Industrial Development Bank of India (IDBI) :** Established in 1964; to provide financial assistance to industrial enterprises.
- **Industrial Reconstruction Bank of India (IRBI) :** Set-up in 1971 with the objective of reviving and revitalizing sick industrial units in public and private sectors.

* * * * *

# 7. GENERAL SCIENCE

## INVENTIONS AND DISCOVERIES

### Important Inventions

| *Name of Invention* | *Inventor* | *Nationality* | *Year* |
|---|---|---|---|
| Aeroplane | Orville & Wilbur Wright | U.S.A. | 1903 |
| Ball-Point Pen | John J. Loud | U.S.A. | 1888 |
| Barometer | Evangelista Torricelli | Italy | 1644 |
| Bicycle | Kirkpatrick Macmillan | Britain | 1839-40 |
| Bifocal Lens | Benjamin Franklin | U.S.A. | 1780 |
| Car (Petrol) | Karl Benz | Germany | 1888 |
| Celluloid | Alexander Parkes | Britain | 1861 |
| Cinema | Nicolas & Jean Lumiere | France | 1895 |
| Clock (mechanical) | I-Hsing & Liang Ling-Tsan | China | 725 |
| Diesel Engine | Rudolf Diesel | Germany | 1895 |
| Dynamo | Hypolite Pixii | France | 1832 |
| Electric Lamp | Thomas Alva Edison | U.S.A. | 1879 |
| Electric Motor (DC) | Zenobe Gramme | Belgium | 1873 |
| Electric Motor (AC) | Nikola Tesla | U.S.A. | 1888 |
| Electro-magnet | William Sturgeon | Britain | 1824 |
| Electronic Computer | Dr. Alan M. Turing | Britain | 1943 |
| Film (moving outlines) | Louis Prince | France | 1885 |
| Film (musical sound) | Dr. Le de Forest | U.S.A. | 1923 |
| Fountain Pen | Lewis E. Waterman | U.S.A. | 1884 |
| Gramophone | Thomas Alva Edison | U.S.A. | 1878 |
| Helicopter | Etienne Oehmichen | France | 1924 |
| Jet Engine | Sir Frank Whittle | Britain | 1937 |
| Laser | Charles H. Townes | U.S.A. | 1960 |
| Lift (Mechanical) | Elisha G. Otis | U.S.A. | 1852 |
| Locomotive | Richard Trevithick | Britain | 1804 |
| Machine Gun | James Puckle | Britain | 1718 |
| Microphone | Alexander Graham Bell | U.S.A. | 1876 |
| Microscope | Z. Janssen | Netherlands | 1590 |
| Motor Cycle | G. Daimler | Germany | 1885 |
| Photography (on film) | John Carbutt | U.S.A. | 1888 |
| Printing Press | Johann Gutenberg | Germany | c.1455 |
| Razor (safety) | King C. Gillette | U.S.A. | 1895 |
| Refrigerator | James Harrison & Alexander Catlin | U.S.A. | 1850 |

| Name of Invention | Inventor | Nationality | Year |
|---|---|---|---|
| Safety Pin | Walter Hunt | U.S.A. | 1849 |
| Sewing machine | Barthelemy Thimmonnier | France | 1829 |
| Ship (steam) | J.C. Perier | France | 1775 |
| Ship (turbine) | Hon. Sir C. Parsons | Britain | 1894 |
| Skyscraper | W. Le Baron Jenny | U.S.A. | 1882 |
| Slide Rule | William Oughtred | Britain | 1621 |
| Steam Engine (condenser) | James Watt | Britain | 1765 |
| Steel Production | Henry Bessemer | Britain | 1855 |
| Steel (stainless) | Harry Brearley | Britain | 1913 |
| Submarine | David Bushnell | U.S.A. | 1776 |
| Tank | Sir Ernest Swinton | Britain | 1914 |
| Telegraph | M. Lammond | France | 1787 |
| Telegraph Code | Samuel F.B. Morse | U.S.A. | 1837 |
| Telephone (perfected) | Alexander Graham Bell | U.S.A. | 1876 |
| Television (mechanical) | John Logie Baird | Britain | 1926 |
| Television (electronic) | P.T. Farnsworth | U.S.A. | 1927 |
| Thermometer | Galileo Galilei | Italy | 1593 |
| Transformer | Michael Faraday | Britain | 1831 |
| Transistor | Bardeen, Shockley & Brattain | U.S.A. | 1948 |
| Washing Machine (elec.) | Hurley Machine Co. | U.S.A. | 1907 |
| Zip-Fastener | W.L. Judson | U.S.A. | 1891 |

## Important Discoveries

| Discovery | Discoverer | Nationality | Year |
|---|---|---|---|
| Aluminium | Hans Christian Oerstedt | Denmark | 1827 |
| Atomic number | Henry Moseley | England | 1913 |
| Atomic structure of matter | John Dalton | England | 1803 |
| Chlorine | C.W. Scheele | Sweden | 1774 |
| Electromagnetic induction | Michael Faraday | England | 1831 |
| Electromagnetic waves | Heinrich Hertz | Germany | 1886 |
| Electromagnetism | Hans Christian Oersted | Denmark | 1920 |
| Electron | Sir Joseph Thomson | England | 1897 |
| General theory of relativity | Albert Einstein | Switzerland | 1915 |
| Hydrogen | Henry Cavendish | England | 1766 |
| Law of electric conduction | Georg Ohm | Germany | 1827 |
| Law of electromagnetism | Andre Ampere | France | 1826 |
| Law of falling bodies | Galileo | Italy | 1590 |
| Laws of gravitation & motion | Isaac Newton | England | 1687 |
| Laws of planetary motion | Johannes Kepler | Germany | 1609-19 |
| Magnesium | Sir Humphry Davy | England | 1808 |
| Neptune (Planet) | Johann Galle | Germany | 1846 |
| Neutron | James Chadwick | England | 1932 |
| Nickel | Axel Cronstedt | Sweden | 1751 |
| Nitrogen | Daniel Rutherford | England | 1772 |

| Discovery | Discoverer | Nationality | Year |
|---|---|---|---|
| Oxygen | Joseph Priestly C.W. Scheele | England Sweden | 1772 |
| Ozone | Christian Schonbein | Germany | 1839 |
| Pluto (Planet) | Clyde Tombaugh | U.S.A | 1930 |
| Plutonium | G.T. Seaborg | U.S.A | 1940 |
| Proton | Ernest Rutherford | England | 1919 |
| Quantum Theory | Max Planck | Germany | 1900 |
| Radioactivity | Antoine Bacquerel | France | 1896 |
| Radium | Pierre & Marie Curie | France | 1898 |
| Silicon | Jons Berzelius | Sweden | 1824 |
| Special theory of relativity | Albert Einstein | Switzerland | 1905 |
| Sun as centre of solar system | Copernicus | Poland | 1543 |
| Uranium | Martin Klaproth | Germany | 1789 |
| Uranus (Planet) | William Herschel | England | 1781 |
| X-rays | Wilhelm Roentgen | Germany | 1895 |

## Geographical Explorations/Discoveries

| Place | Explorer/Discoverer | Nationality | Year |
|---|---|---|---|
| America | Christopher Columbus | Italy | 1492 |
| Hawaii Islands (Sandwich Islands) | Captain James Cook | England | 1778 |
| Newfoundland | John Cabot | England | 1497 |
| New Zealand | Abel Janszoon Tasman | Holland | 1642 |
| North Pole | Robert Peary | USA | 1909 |
| Sea Route to India (via Cape of Good Hope) | Vasco da Gama | Portugal | 1498 |
| South Pole | Roald Amundsen | Norway | 1911 |

## Scientific Instruments

| Name of Instrument | Used for |
|---|---|
| Altimeter | measuring altitude |
| Ammeter | measuring strength of an electric current |
| Anemometer | measuring the velocity of wind |
| Audiometer | measuring level of hearing |
| Barometer | measuring atmospheric pressure |
| Callipers | measuring the internal and external diameters of tubes |
| Calorimeter | measuring quantity of heat |
| Compass | finding out direction |
| Dynamo | converting mechanical energy into electrical energy |
| Eudiometer | measuring volume changes during chemical reactions between gases |
| Galvanometer | detecting and determining the strength of small electric currents |
| Hydrometer | measuring specific gravity of a liquid |
| Hygrometer | measuring the humidity in the atmosphere |
| Lactometer | measuring the purity of milk |
| Manometer | measuring the gaseous pressure |
| Micrometer | measuring minute distances, angles, etc. |

| Name of Instrument | Used for |
|---|---|
| Microscope | seeing magnified view of very small objects |
| Periscope | with the help of this instrument an observer in a submarine can see what is going on the surface of the sea |
| Photometer | measuring intensity of light from distant stars |
| Pyrometer | measuring high temperatures |
| Radar | detecting and finding the presence and location of moving objects like aircraft, missile, etc. |
| Radiometer | measuring the emission of radiant energy |
| Rain Gauge | measuring the amount of rainfall |
| Seismograph | measuring and recording the intensity and origin of earthquake shocks |
| Sextant | measuring altitude and angular distances between two objects or heavenly bodies |
| Spectrometer | measuring the refractive indices |
| Spherometer | measuring the curvature of spherical objects/surface |
| Sphygmomanometer | measuring blood pressure |
| Stethoscope | ascertaining the condition of heart and lungs by listening to their function |
| Stroboscope | viewing objects that are moving rapidly with a periodic motion as if they were at rest |
| Tachometer | measuring the rate of revolution or angular speed of a revolving shaft |
| Telescope | viewing magnified images of distant objects |
| Theodolite | measuring the horizontal and vertical angles |
| Thermocouple | measuring the temperature inside furnaces and jet engines |
| Thermometer | measuring human body temperature |
| Thermostat | regulating constant temperature |
| Ultrasonoscope | measuring utrasonic sounds |
| Viscometer | measuring the viscosity of a fluid |
| Voltmeter | measuring potential difference between two points. |

## Diseases and the Parts of Body they Affect

| Disease | Part of body affected |
|---|---|
| AIDS | Immune system of body |
| Arthritis | Inflammation of joints |
| Asthma | Lungs |
| Cataract | Eyes |
| Conjunctivitis | Eyes |
| Diabetes | Pancreas |
| Diphtheria | Throat |
| Glaucoma | Eyes |
| Eczema | Skin |
| Goitre | Front of the neck (due to enlargement of thyroid gland) |
| Gout | Joints of bone |

| Disease | Part of body affected |
|---|---|
| Jaundice | Liver |
| Meningitis | Brain or spinal cord |
| Pleurisy | Pleura (inflammation of) |
| Polio | motor neurons |
| Pneumonia | Lungs |
| Pyorrhoea | Sockets of teeth |
| Tuberculosis | Lungs |
| Typhoid | Intestine |
| Malaria | Spleen |
| Leukaemia | Blood |
| Rickets | Bones |

* * * * *

# 8. Space Research

## First in Space

| | |
|---|---|
| First creator of rules regarding space research | — Isaac Newton |
| First artificial satellite launched in space | — Sputnik-1 (1957) |
| First living being sent in space | — Louika (a dog) |
| Firstever manned spacecraft | — Vostok-I |
| First man in space | — Yuri Gagarin, U.S.S.R. (1961) |
| First woman in space | — Valentina Tereshkova, U.S.S.R. (June 1963) |
| First man who moved in space out of the spacecraft | — Alexi Livonov, U.S.S.R. (June 1965) |
| First person to land on moon | — Neil Armstrong, America (21st July, 1969) |
| First fourwheeled carriage without human being on moon | — Leunokhev-I, U.S.S.R. (1970) |
| First space lab in orbit | — Skylab (America, 1973) |
| First space shuttle | — Columbia (America, 1981) |
| First Indian (man) in space | — Sq. led. Rakesh Sharma (13th April, 1984) |
| First Indian (Woman) in space | — Kalpana Chawla (19th Nov., 1997) |
| First American woman in space | — Sailyride (1983) |
| First spacecraft on Mars | — Pathfinder (6 July, 1997) |
| First woman who lead spacecraft | — Allin Collis (America) |
| First spacecraft without man | — Shenzoo, China (20th Nov. 1999) |
| First country in the world to succeed in an inter-planetary mission on mars in the maiden attempt | — India (MOM Spacecraft) |

## Indian Space Programme : At a Glance

| Satellite | Date | Type | Launch Vehicle | Result |
|---|---|---|---|---|
| Aryabhatta | 19-04-75 | Scientific | Cosmos | successful |
| Bhaskara I | 07-06-79 | Geosurvey | Cosmos | successful |
| Rohini | 10-08-79 | Geosurvey | S.L.V.3 | unsuccessful |
| Rohini D-1 | 18-07-80 | Geosurvey | S.L.V.3 | successful |
| Rohini | 31-05-81 | Scientific | S.L.V.3 | successful |
| Apple | 19-06-81 | Communication | Ariane | successful |
| Bhaskara II | 20-11-81 | Geosurvey | Cosonos | successful |
| INSAT-1A | 10-04-82 | Multipurpose | Delta | unsuccessful |
| Rohini | 17-04-83 | Scientific | S.L.V.3 | successful |
| INSAT-1B | 30-08-83 | Multipurpose | Space Shuttle | successful |
| SROSS I | 24-03-87 | Technical | ASLV-D1 | unsuccessful |
| IRS-1A | 17-03-88 | Remote sensing | Vostok | successful |
| SROSS II | 17-07-88 | Technical | ASLV-D2 | unsuccessful |
| INSAT-1C | 21-07-88 | Multipurpose | Ariane-4 | unsuccessful |

| Satellite | Date | Type | Launch Vehicle | Result |
|---|---|---|---|---|
| INSAT-1D | 12-06-90 | Multipurpose | Delta | successful |
| IRS-1B | 29-08-91 | Remote sensing | Vostok | successful |
| SROSS-4 | 04-05-94 | Scientific | ASLV-D3 | successful |
| IRS-1C | 28-12-95 | Remote sensing | PSLV-D3 | successful |
| INSAT-3B | 22-03-2000 | Multipurpose | Ariane | successful |
| G-SAT-1 | 18-04-2001 | Multipurpose | GSLV-D | successful |
| INSAT-3C | 24-01-2002 | Communication | Ariane-4 | successful |
| MAT SAT | 12-09-2002 | Meteorology | PSLVC-4 | successful |
| INSAT-3E | 28-09-2003 | Communication | Ariane-5 | successful |
| Cartosat-1 & HAMSAT | 05-05-2005 | Maping and Communication | PSLV-C6 | successful |
| INSAT-4a | 22-12-2005 | Communication | Ariane-5 | successful |
| CARTOSAT-2 | 10-01-2007 | Communication | PSLV-C7 | successful |
| INSAT-4CR | 02-09-2007 | Communication | GSLV-Fo4 | successful |
| Cartosat-2A | 28-04-2008 | Communication | PSLV-C9 | successful |
| Chandrayaan-I | 22-10-2008 | Maping and Scientific | PSLV-C11 | successful |
| RISAT-2 & ANUSAT | 20-04-2009 | Maping and Communication | PSLV-C12 | successful |
| Oceansat-2 | 24-09-2009 | Remote Sensing | PSLV-C14 | successful |
| CARTOSAT-2B | 12-07-2010 | Communication | PSLV-C15 | successful |
| RESOURCESAT-2 | 20-04-2011 | Remote Sensing | PSLV-C16 | successful |
| Megha-Tropiques | 12-10-2011 | Maping and Scientific | PSLV-C18 | successful |
| RISAT-1 | 26-04-2012 | Remote Sensing | PSLV-C19 | successful |
| Spot-6 | 09-09-2012 | Remote Sensing | PSLV-C21 | successful |
| Saral | 25-02-2013 | Scientific | PSLV-C20 | successful |
| GSAT-7 | 30-08-2013 | Defence | Ariane-5 | successful |
| MOM | 5-11-2013 | Mapping | PSLV-C25 | successful |
| GSAT-14 | 05-01-2014 | Communication | GSLV-D5 | successful |
| Spot-7 | 30-06-2014 | Remote Sensing | PSLV-C23 | successful |
| GSAT-16 | 07-12-2014 | Communication | Ariane-5 | successful |
| Astrosat | 28-09-2015 | Mapping and Scientific | PSLV-C30 | successful |
| GSAT-15 | 11-11-2015 | Communication | Ariane-5 | successful |
| TELEOS-1 & others | 16-12-2015 | Mapping and Scientific | PSLV-C29 | successful |
| IRNSS-1E | 20-01-2016 | Mapping and Scientific | PSLV-C31 | successful |
| IRNSS-1F | 10-03-2016 | Mapping and Scientific | PSLV-C32 | successful |
| IRNSS-1G | 28-04-2016 | Mapping and Scientific | PSLV-C33 | successful |
| INSAT-3DR | 08-09-2016 | Meteorology | GSLV-F05 | successful |
| SCATSAT-1 & others | 26-09-2016 | Multipurpose | PSLV-C35 | successful |
| RESOURCESAT-2A | 07-12-2016 | Remote Sensing | PSLV-C36 | successful |
| CARTOSAT-2 & 103 others | 15-02-2017 | Multipurpose | PSLV-C37 | successful |
| GSAT-19 | 05-06-2017 | Communication | GSLV MK-III-D1 | successful |
| CARTOSAT-2E | 23-06-2017 | Earth observation Satellite | PSLV-C38 | successful |
| GSAT-17 | 29-06-2017 | Earth observation Satellite | Ariane-5 ECA | successful |
| INS-1C | 10-01-2018 | Technology Applications | PSLV-C40 | successful |
| CARTOSAT-2F & 30 others | 12-01-2018 | Earth observation Satellite | PSLV-C40 | successful |
| GSAT-6A | 29-03-2018 | Communications | GSLV-F08 | successful |
| GSAT-7A | 19-12-2018 | Military Satellite | GSLV-MKII-F11 | successful |
| GSAT-31 | 06-02-2019 | Communication | Ariane-5 VCA | successful |
| Chandrayaan-II | 22-07-2019 | Mapping and Scientific | GSLV-MK-III | successful |
| RISAT 2BR1 & 9 others | 11-12-2019 | Mapping and Scientific | PSLV-C48 | successful |
| GSAT-30 | 17-01-2020 | Communication | Ariane-5 | successful |
| EOS-01 | 07-11-2020 | Earth observation | PSLV-C49 | successful |
| CMS-01 | 17-12-2020 | Communication | PSLV-XLC50 | successful |
| EOS-04 and INS-2TD | 14-02-2022 | Earth observation | PSLV-C52 | successful |
| DS-EO and others | 30-06-2022 | Earth observation | PSLV-C53 | successful |
| 36 Satellites of one web | 23-10-2022 | Earth observation | GSLV-Mark-3 | successful |
| EOS-07 | 10-02-2023 | Earth observation | SSLV-02 | successful |
| TeLEOS-2 and LUMILITE-4 | 22-04-2023 | Earth observation | PSLV-C55 | successful |
| Chandrayaan-3 | 14-07-2023 | Mapping and Scientific | LVM-3 M4 | successful |
| Aditya-L1 | 02-09-2023 | Solar observation | PSLV-C57 | successful |
| XPoSAT | 01-01-2024 | Earth Observation | PSLV-C58 | successful |

* * * * *

# 9. Indian History

## Famous Sites of Indus Valley Civilization

| Name of Site | Year of Excavation | River/ Sea coast | Discoverer |
|---|---|---|---|
| Harappa (Montgomery–Pakistan) | 1921 | Ravi River | Dayaram Sahney |
| Mohanjodaro (Larkana–Pakistan) | 1922 | Indus River | Rakhal Das Banerjee |
| Chanhudaro (Sindh–Pakistan) | 1931 | Indus River | N.G. Mazumdar |
| Alamgir pur (Meerut – U.P.) | 1952-55 | Hindan River | Yagyadatta Sharma |
| Ropar (Punjab) | 1953 | Sutlej River | Yagyadatta Sharma |
| Rangpur (Kathiabar–Gujarat) | 1953 | Bhabar River | Madho Swaroop Vatsa, Rang Nath Rao |
| Kotdigi (Sindh–Pakistan) | 1953 | Indus River | Fazal Ahmed Khan |
| Lothal (Ahmedabad–Gujarat) | 1954 | Bhogwa River | Rang Nath Rao |
| Kalibanga (Ganganagar–Rajasthan) | 1961 | Ghaggar | Brajwasi Lal |
| Surkotara (Kutch–Gujarat) | 1967 | Ghaggar River | Ravindra Singh Vishta |
| Banawali (Hissar–Haryana) | 1973 | Ghaggar River | Ravindra Singh Vishta |
| Balakote | 1979 | Arabian Sea | George F. Dales |
| Dhaulavira (Gujarat) | 1963-68 | — | J.P. Joshi |
| | 1990-91 | — | Dr. R.S. Vishta |

## Wellknown Quotations

| | |
|---|---|
| *"Swarajya is My Birthright"* | — Bal Gangadhar Tilak |
| *"Give me blood, I shall give you freedom"* | — Netajee Subhash Chandra Bose |
| *"Inqalab Zindabad"* | — Bhagat Singh |
| *"Saare Jahan Se Achcha, Hindustan Hamara"* | — Dr. Mohammed Iqbal |
| *"Dilli Chalo"* | — Subhash Chandra Bose |
| *"Sarfaroshi ki tamanna, Ab Hamare Dil Mein Hai."* | — Ram Prasad Bismil |
| *"I am socialist by nature".* | — Jawahar Lal Nehru |
| *"Go to Vedas"* | — Swami Dayanand |
| *"Aaram Haram Hai"* | — Jawahar Lal Nehru |
| *"Jai Jawan, Jai Kisan"* | — Lal Bahadur Shastri |
| *"Jai Jawan, Jai Kisan, Jai Vigyan"* | — Atal Bihari Vajpayee |
| *"Speak less, work more"* | — Sanjay Gandhi |
| *"Vijayee Vishwa Tiranga Pyara"* | — Shyam Lal Gupta |

| | |
|---|---|
| *"Quit India"* | — Mahatma Gandhi |
| *"Hindi, Hindu, Hindustan"* | — Bhartendu Harishchandra |
| *"Purna Swarajya"* | — Jawahar Lal Nehru |
| *"Every lathi blow inflicted on my body will prove a nail in British coffin"* | — Lala Lajpat Rai |
| *"Jai Hind"* | — Subhash Chandra Bose |
| *"Do or die"* | — Mahatma Gandhi |
| *"Who lives if India dies"* | — Jawahar Lal Nehru |
| *"Vande Mataram"* | — Bankim Chandra Chatterjee |
| *"Jana Gana Mana Adhinayaka Jai Hai"* | —Rabindranath Tagore |
| *"Hate sin, not the sinner."* | — Mahatma Gandhi |
| *"Service of the people is the service of God"* | — Swami Vivekananda |
| *"Truth and non-violence are my God."* | — Mahatma Gandhi |

## Battles and Wars In India

| War | Year | Result |
|---|---|---|
| *Battle of Kalinga* | (261 B.C.) | Ashoka defeated the king of Kalinga |
| *Second battle of Tarain* | (1192 A.D.) | Muhammad Gori defeated Prithviraj Chauhan |
| *First battle of Panipat* | (1526 A.D.) | Babar defeated Ibrahim Lodi |
| *Battle of Khanwa* | (1527 A.D.) | Babar defeated Rana Sanga |
| *Battle of Chausa* | (1539 A.D.) | Shershah Suri defeated Humayun and became ruler of Delhi |
| *Second Battle of Panipat* | (1556 A.D.) | Akbar defeated Hemu |
| *Battle of Talikota* | (1565 A.D.) | Allied forces of Bijapur, Bidar, Golkunda and Ahamadnagar defeated the King of Vijay Nagar |
| *Battle of Haldighati* | (1576 A.D.) | Some historian say that this battle was indecisive but some say that Rana Pratap was defeated by Akbar |
| *Battle of Palasey* | (1757 A.D.) | British forces defeated Nawab of Bengal Sirajudoulla |
| *Battle of Wandiwash* | (1760 A.D.) | British forces defeated the French |
| *Third battle of Panipat* | (1761 A.D.) | Maratha were defeated by Ahmad Shah Abadali |
| *Battle of Buxar* | (1764 A.D.) | British forces defeated the combined forces of Mir Quasim, Shah Alam Mughal empire and Awadh's Nawab |
| *Third Anglo-Maratha War* | (1792 A.D.) | Maratha were conclusively defeated |
| *Fourth Anglo-Mysore War* | (1799 A.D.) | Tipu Sultan died fighting the British forces |
| *Second Anglo-Sikh War* | (1848 A.D.) | British forces annexed Punjab from Sikh rulers |
| *Indo-China War* | (1962 A.D.) | China attacked India unilaterally and annexed some area |
| *Indo-Pak War* | (1965 A.D.) | Pakistan attacked India but had to suffer severe set-backs |
| *Indo-Pak War* | (1971 A.D.) | Pak declare war against India. |

* * * * *

# 10. World Geography

**Earth:** The earth constitutes land, water and air. Land is made up of rocks and soil. It is distributed in continents and islands. The water found in oceans, seas, lakes, etc. occupies about 2/3 of the earth's surface. The earth is surrounded by a cover of air, called atmosphere, which extends up to several hundred kilometres above its surface.

**Shape:** In ancient times people believed that the earth was flat in shape. Greek philosopher Pythagoras (6th century BC) was the first person to declare that the earth was round. After careful measurement, the scientists have found that the earth is slightly oblate (flattened at poles) and not exactly round.

**Motions:** The earth has two motions: *(i) Rotation:* Earth makes a complete round on its axis once each 24 hours (more exactly 23 hours, 56 minutes and 4.09 seconds). It causes days and night on the earth. *(ii) Revolution:* The earth makes a complete round of the Sun in one year. This revolution of earth produces alternate seasons.

***Some Facts:*** **(1)** Equal Day and Night — March 21 and September 23. **(2)** Longest Day — June 21. **(3)** Shortest Day — December 22. **(4)** The sunlight takes eight minutes in travelling from the Sun to the Earth. **(5)** Average speed of the earth in orbit ---- 66,600 miles (107,220 km) per hour. **(6)** Earth's equatorial diameter is about 7926 miles (12,756 km). **(7)** Water (oceans, seas, lakes and rivers) occupies nearly 75 per cent of the surface of the earth. **(8)** Earth's average distance from the Moon — 2,38,857 miles (3,84,400 km). **(9)** Earth's average distance from the Sun — 93 million miles (149.4 million km).

**Greenwich Time:** It is the local time of the Greenwich observatory in London on $0^{o}$ meridian. Greenwich time is international standard time.

**International Date Line:** Half way round the earth from the Greenwich is International Date Line on $180^{o}$ longitude. It runs down mid-Pacific. It is one day earlier on the east of this line than it is on the west of the line. When it is Monday east of the line, it is Tuesday west of the line.

**Zones:** On the basis of temperature and distribution of solar heat on the surface of the earth, the earth has been divided into five zones: (1) Torrid Zone, (2) North Temperate Zone, (3) South Temperate Zone, (4) Arctic Zone, and (5) Antarctic Zone.

**Continents:** Large land masses forming large geographical divisions are called continents. There are seven continents: (1) Asia (30.0%), (2) Africa (20.3%), (3) North America (16.3%), (4) South America (12.0%), (5) Antarctica (8.9%), (6) Europe (6.7%) and (7) Australia (5.2%).

**Highest Mountain Peaks:** (1) Everest (Asia-8848 metres), (2) Aconcagua (South America-6960 metres), (3) Mckinley (North America-6194 metres), (4) Kilimanjaro (Africa-5895 metres), (5) Elbrus (Europe-5642 metres), (6) Vinson Massif (Antarctica-5140 metres), (7) Kosciusko (Australia-2228 metres).

**Largest Oceans:** (1) Pacific Ocean (The largest, covers almost 1/3 of the earth's total area, and the deepest about 6.8 miles at Mariana Trench in western Pacific); (2) Atlantic Ocean, and (3) Indian Ocean. Other seas and gulfs are — the Mediterranean Sea, South China Sea, Bering Sea, Caribbean Sea, East China Sea, Sea of Japan, North Sea, Baltic Sea, Hudson Bay and Gulf of Mexico.

**Longest Rivers:** (1) Nile (6650 km-Africa), (2) Amazon (6570 km-South America), (3) Mississippi-Missouri (5970 km-North America), (4) Yangtze Kiang (5470 km-Asia), (5) Ob Irtysh (5150 km-Europe), (6) Congo (4666 km-Africa).

**Great Deserts:** (1) Sahara (94 lakh sq km-North Africa), (2) Libyan (11.65 lakh sq km-North Africa), (3) Australian (16 lakh sq km-Australia), (4) Gobi (13 lakh sq km-Mongolia), (5) Great Victoria (6,47,000 sq km-Australia), (6) Syrian (5,20,000 sq km Arabia), (7) Arabian (23,30,000 sq km Arabia).

**Largest Islands:** (1) Greenland (21,75,600 sq km) (2) New Guinea (7,77,000 sq km), (3) Borneo (7,25,545 sq km), (4) Malagasy (5,90,000 sq km), (5) Baffin Island (4,76,070 sq km).

**Highest Waterfalls:** (1) Angel (807 m-Venezuela), (2) Mongefossen (774 m-Norway), (3) Kukenaam (610 m-Venezuela), (4) Ribbon (491 m-USA), (5) King George VI (487 m-Guyana), (6) Upper Yosemite (435 m-USA).

## Major Producers of Crops, Minerals and Industrial goods

| | | | |
|---|---|---|---|
| **Coal** | China, USA, India, Australia, Indonesia, Russia | **Manganese** | South Africa, China, Australia |
| **Cocoa** | Cote d'Ivaire, Ghana, Indonesia, Nigeria | **Petroleum** | Russia, Saudi Arabia, USA, Iraq |
| **Coffee** | Brazil, Vietnam, Columbia, Indonesia | **Rice** | China, India, Indonesia, Bangladesh |
| **Copper** | Chile, Peru, China, USA | **Rubber** | Thailand, Indonesia, Malaysia, Vietnam, India |
| **Cotton** | China, India, USA, Pakistan, Brazil | **Silk** | China, India, Uzbekistan, Thailand |
| **Gold** | China, Australia, Russia, USA, Canada | **Silver** | Mexico, Peru, China, Chili |
| **Grapes** | China, Italy, USA, France, Spain | **Steel** | China, Japan, India, USA |
| **Iron ore** | Australia, Brazil, China, India | **Tea** | China, India, Kenya, Sri Lanka |
| **Jute** | India, Bangladesh, China | **Wheat** | China, India, USA, France, Russia |
| | | **Diamond** | Russia, Australia, Congo, Botswana |
| | | **Tobacco** | China, Brazil, India, USA, Indonesia |

## The Highest, Biggest and Longest in the World

| | | |
|---|---|---|
| **Airport** | *Largest* | King Fahd International Airport, Dammon (Saudi Arabia) |
| **Animal** | *Tallest* | Giraffe (Average height 6.09 m) |
| | *Largest & Heaviest* | Blue Whale (190 tonnes) |
| | *Longest recorded* | Boot lace Worm (55 m) |
| | *Fastest* | Cheetah (Approximately 100 km/hr) |
| **Bay** | *With maximum area* | Bay of Bengal (India: 217 million hc) |
| **Building** | *Tallest* | Burj Khalifa in Dubai (818 meter) |
| **Canal** | *Big ship (longest)* | Suez Canal (160 km) Busiest Kiel Canal (North Sea) |
| **Church** | *Largest* | Basilica of St. Peter (Vatican City Rome–Area 23000 sq. m. |
| **Continent** | *biggest* | Asia (31,845,872 $km^2$) |
| | *Smallest* | Australia Mainland (Area 76,17,930 $km^2$) |

| | | |
|---|---|---|
| **Country** | *Largest in Population* | China (over 140 crore) |
| | *Largest in Area* | Russia (17,098,242 sq. km) |
| | *With largest electorate* | India (over 90 crores) |
| | *Smallest independent* | State of Vatican City (0.44 $km^2$) |
| **Delta** | *Largest* | Sundarban's Ganga-Brahmaputra delta (1,05,000 sq. km) |
| **Epic** | *Longest* | Mahabharata |
| **Film** | *Most Oscars* | Ben Hur (11 Oscars—1959); Titanic (11 Oscars—1998); The Lord of Rings : The Return of the King (11 Oscars—2003). |
| **Island** | *Biggest* | Greenland (now known as Kalaatdlit Nunaat–2,175,600 sq km) |
| **Lake** | *Largest* | Caspian Sea (Azerbaijan, Russia, Iran border: 37.18 lakh $km^2$) |
| | *Deepest* | Baikal (Siberia) |
| | *Largest (fresh water)* | Superior Lake (USA—Canada border: 82,350 $km^2$) |
| **Mountain** | *Highest peak* | Mt. Everest (8848 m; Nepal) |
| | *Highest range* | Himalayas, Asia (upto 4200 m) |
| | *Greatest mountain range* | Himalaya-Karakoram (96 out of 109 peaks over 7315 m are here) |
| **Ocean** | *Largest and Deepest* | The Pacific (Area: 166,240,000 $km^2$; Depth: 10,924 m) |
| **Planet** | *Biggest* | Jupiter (equatorial diameter 142984 km) |
| | *Brightest, hottest and nearest to Earth* | Venus |
| | *Nearest to Sun* | Mercury |
| **Plateau** | *Highest* | Tibetan Plateau (Central Asia: 4900 m) |
| **Platform** | *Longest (rail)* | Shree Siddharoodha Swamiji Railway Station Hubballi, Karnataka (India) |
| **Religion** | *Oldest* | Hinduism |
| **Religion** | *Largest* | Christianity |
| **Rivers** | *Longest* | (i) Nile (6650 km) (ii) Amazon (6437 km) |
| **Sea** | *Largest* | South China Sea (2,974,600 sq. km) |
| | *Largest (inland)* | Mediterranean |
| **Star** | *Brightest* | Sirius A (also called Dog Star) |
| **Swimming course** | *Longest recognised* | English Channel |
| **Tunnel** | *Longest (railway)* | Gotthard Base Rail Tunnel (Switzerland; 57.1 km) |
| | *Largest (road)* | Laerdal, Norway (24.51 km) |
| **Wall** | *Longest* | Great Wall of China (main length 3460 km; branches length 2860 km) |
| **Waterfall** | *Highest* | Salto-Angel (in Venezuela on a branch of river Carrao, 807 m.) |

## Capital & Currencies

| Country | Capital | Currency |
|---|---|---|
| ✶ Afghanistan | Kabul | Afghani |
| ✶ Albania | Tirana | Lek |
| ✶ Algeria | Algiers | Dinar |
| ✶ Angola | Luanda | New Kwanza |
| ✶ Argentina | Buenos Aires | Peso |
| ✶ Armenia | Yeravan | Dram |
| ✶ Australia | Canberra | Dollar |
| ✶ Austria | Vienna | Euro |
| ✶ Azerbaijan | Baku | Manat |
| ✶ Bahrain | Manama | Dinar |
| ✶ Bangladesh | Dhaka | Taka |
| ✶ Barbados | Bridgetown | Dollar |
| ✶ Belarus | Minsk | Ruble |
| ✶ Belgium | Brussels | Euro |
| ✶ Benin | Porto Novo | Franc |
| ✶ Bhutan | Thimphu | Ngultrum[1] |
| ✶ Bolivia | La paz | Dollar |
| ✶ Botswana | Gaborone | Pula |
| ✶ Brazil | Brasilia | Real |
| ✶ Bosnia Herzegovina | Sarajevo | Dinar |
| ✶ Bulgaria | Sofia | Lev |
| ✶ Cambodia | Phnom-Penh | Riel |
| ✶ Canada | Ottawa | Dollar |
| ✶ Chile | Santiago | Peso |
| ✶ China | Beijing | Yuan |
| ✶ Colombia | Bogota | Peso |
| ✶ Congo | Brazzaville | Franc |
| ✶ Croatia | Zagreb | Kuna |
| ✶ Cuba | Havana | Peso |
| ✶ Cyprus | Nicosia | Euro |
| ✶ Czech Republic | Prague | Koruna |
| ✶ Denmark | Copenhagen | Krone |
| ✶ Ecuador | Quito | Sucre |
| ✶ Egypt | Cairo | Pound |
| ✶ Estonia | Tallinn | Euro |
| ✶ Ethiopia | Addis Ababa | Birr |
| ✶ Fiji | Suva | Dollar |
| ✶ Finland | Helsinki | Euro |
| ✶ France | Paris | Euro |
| ✶ Georgia | Tbilisi | Lari |
| ✶ Germany | Berlin | Euro |
| ✶ Ghana | Accra | Cedi |
| ✶ Greece | Athens | Euro |
| ✶ Guatemala | Guatemala City | Quetzal |

| Country | Capital | Currency |
|---|---|---|
| ✶ Guyana | George Town | Dollar |
| ✶ Hungary | Budapest | Forint |
| ✶ Iceland | Reykjavik | Krona |
| ✶ India | New Delhi | Rupee |
| ✶ Indonesia | Jakarta | Rupiah |
| ✶ Iran | Teheran | Rial |
| ✶ Iraq | Baghdad | Dinar |
| ✶ Ireland | Dublin | Euro |
| ✶ Israel | Jerusalem | Shekel |
| ✶ Italy | Rome | Euro |
| ✶ Jamaica | Kingston | Dollar |
| ✶ Japan | Tokyo | Yen |
| ✶ Jordan | Amman | Dinar |
| ✶ Kazakhstan | Akmola | Tenge |
| ✶ Kenya | Nairobi | Shilling |
| ✶ Korea (S) | Seoul | Won |
| ✶ Korea (N) | Pyongyang | Won |
| ✶ Kyrgyzstan | Bishkek | Som |
| ✶ Kuwait | Kuwait City | Dinar |
| ✶ Laos | Vientiane | Kip |
| ✶ Latvia | Riga | Euro |
| ✶ Lebanon | Beirut | Pound |
| ✶ Liberia | Monrovia | Dollar |
| ✶ Libya | Tripoli | Dinar |
| ✶ Lithuania | Vilnius | Litas |
| ✶ Luxembourg | Luxembourg | Euro |
| ✶ Macedonia | Skopje | Dinar |
| ✶ Malawi | Lilongwe | Kwacha |
| ✶ Malaysia | Kuala Lumpur | Ringgit |
| ✶ Maldives | Male | Rufiyaa |
| ✶ Mali | Bamako | Franc |
| ✶ Mauritius | Port Louis | Rupee |
| ✶ Mexico | Mexico City | Peso |
| ✶ Moldavia | Chisinau | Leu |
| ✶ Mongolia | Ulan Bator | Tugrik |
| ✶ Morocco | Rabat | Dirham |
| ✶ Mozambique | Maputo | Metical |
| ✶ Myanmar | Nay Pyi Taw | Kyat |
| ✶ Namibia | Winohoek | Dollar |
| ✶ Nepal | Kathmandu | Rupee |
| ✶ Netherlands | Amsterdam | Euro |
| ✶ New Zealand | Wellington | Dollar |
| ✶ Nigeria | Abuja | Naira |
| ✶ Norway | Oslo | Krone |
| ✶ Oman | Muscat | Rial |
| ✶ Pakistan | Islamabad | Rupee |

| Country | Capital | Currency |
|---|---|---|
| ✶ Panama | Panama City | Balboa |
| ✶ Peru | Lima | New Sole |
| ✶ Philippines | Manila | Peso |
| ✶ Poland | Warsaw | Zloty |
| ✶ Portugal | Lisbon | Euro |
| ✶ Qatar | Doha | Riyal |
| ✶ Romania | Bucharest | Leu |
| ✶ Russia | Moscow | Ruble |
| ✶ Saudi Arabia | Riyadh | Rial |
| ✶ Senegal | Dakar | Franc |
| ✶ Slovakia | Bratislava | Euro |
| ✶ Spain | Madrid | Euro |
| ✶ Sri Lanka | Colombo | Rupee |
| ✶ Sudan | Khartoum | Dinar |
| ✶ Suriname | Paramaribo | Guilder |
| ✶ Sweden | Stockholm | Krona |
| ✶ Switzerland | Berne | Swiss Francs |
| ✶ Syria | Damascus | Pound |
| ✶ South Africa | Capetown (Legislative) Pretoria *(Administrative)* | Rand |
| ✶ Tadzhikistan | Dushanbe | Ruble |
| ✶ Taiwan | Taipei | Dollar |
| ✶ Tanzania | Dodoma | Shilling |
| ✶ Thailand | Bangkok | Baht |
| ✶ Tunisia | Tunis | Dinar |
| ✶ Turkiye | Ankara | Lira |
| ✶ Turkmania | Ashikabad | Manat |
| ✶ Uganda | Kampala | Shilling |
| ✶ Ukraine | Kiev | Hyrvnia |
| ✶ United Arab Emirates | Abu Dhabi | Dirham |
| ✶ U.K. | London | Pound Sterling |
| ✶ U.S.A. | Washington | Dollar |
| ✶ Uruguay | Montevideo | Peso |
| ✶ Uzbekistan | Tashkent | Som |
| ✶ Venezuela | Caracas | Bolivar |
| ✶ Vietnam | Hanoi | Dong |
| ✶ Yemen | Sana'a | Rial |
| ✶ Zimbabwe | Harare | Dollar |
| ✶ Congo (Zaire) | Kinshasa | Zaire |
| ✶ Zambia | Lusaka | Kwacha |

## First in the World

| | |
|---|---|
| First Chinese visitor to India | Fahien |
| First foreign invader of India | Alexander, the Great (Greek) |
| First person to climb Mt. Everest | Tenzing Norgay (India) and Edmund Hillary (New Zealand) (1953) |
| First atom bomb dropped at | Hiroshima (Japan) |
| First man in the space | Yuri Gagarin (former USSR) |
| First woman in the space | Valentina Tereshkova (former USSR) |
| First person to walk in the space | Alexei Leonov (former USSR) |
| First person to land on the moon | Neil Armstrong (USA) |
| First and the only woman to have climbed Mt. Everest twice | Santosh Yadav (Indian; May 12, 1992; May 10, 1993) |
| First person on Mt. Everest without oxygen | Phu Dorjee (Indian; May 9, 1984) |
| First person to climb Mt. Everest twice | Nawang Gombu |
| First President of the USA | George Washington |
| First woman Prime Minister | Sirimavo Bandaranaike (Sri Lanka) |
| First person to swim across English Channel | Mathew Webb |
| First woman to swim across English Channel | Gertrude Caroline Ederle |
| First woman to climb Mt. Everest | Junko Tabei (Japan) |
| First woman to climb Mt. Everest alone and without oxygen supplies | Alison Hargreaves (Britain: May 13, 1995) |

| | |
|---|---|
| First Aeroplane to fly around the world without refuelling | Voyager (Dec. 1986) |
| First test-tube Baby | Louise Brown (UK; 1978) |
| First all-talking Film | Jaz Singer (1927) |
| First Secretary-General of the UN | Trygve Lie (Norway: 1946-53) |
| First woman President of the UN General Assembly | Vijayalakshmi Pandit (India: 1953) |
| First woman to reach North Pole | Ann Bancroft (1986) |
| First person to reach North Pole | Robert Peary |
| First person to reach South Pole | Amundsen (1911) |
| First woman to command Spacecraft in space | Ellin Collins |

## Popular Names

| *Popular Name* | *Real Name* |
|---|---|
| Badshah Khan | Abdul Ghaffar Khan |
| Bapu, Father of Nation | M.K. Gandhi |
| Bard of Avon | William Shakespeare |
| Chachaji *or* Panditji | Jawaharlal Nehru |
| Desert Fox | Gen. Rommel (Germany) |
| Desh Bandhu | C.R. Das |
| Father of English Poetry | Geoffrey Chaucer |
| Fuhrer | Adolf Hitler |
| Grand Old Man of India | Dadabhai Naoroji |
| Grand Old Man of Britain | W.E. Gladstone |
| Gurudev | Rabindra Nath Tagore |
| Guruji | M.S. Golwalkar |
| Grand Commoner | Pitt, the younger |
| Iron Man of India | Sardar Patel |
| Lady with the Lamp | Florence Nightingale |
| Lal, Bal, Pal | Lala Lajpat Rai, Bal Gangadhar Tilak, Bipin Chandra Pal |
| Li-Kwan | Pearl Buck |
| Little Corporal *or* Man of Destiny | Napoleon Bonaparte |
| Lokmanya | Bal Gangadhar Tilak |
| Lok Nayak | Jayaprakash Narain |
| Mahamana | Pt. Madan Mohan Malaviya |
| Maid of Orleans | Joan of Arc |
| Maiden Queen | Queen Elizabeth I |
| Man of Blood and Iron | Prince Bismark |
| Netaji | Subhash Chandra Bose |
| Nightingale of India | Sarojini Naidu |
| Priyadarshini | Indira Gandhi |
| Punjab Kesari | Lala Lajpat Rai |
| Wizard of the North | Walter Scott |

## Geographical Surnames

| *Geographical Surname* | *Real Name* |
|---|---|
| Bengal's Sorrow | Damodar River |
| Blue Mountains | Nilgiri Hills |
| China's Sorrow | Hwang-Ho |
| City of Palaces | Kolkata |
| City of Skyscrapers *or* Empire City | New York |
| City of Dreaming Spires | Oxford |
| Cockpit of Europe | Belgium |
| Dark Continent | Africa |
| Emerald Isle | Ireland |
| Eternal City | Rome |
| Gateway of India | Mumbai |
| Gate of Tears | Strait of Bab-el-mandab |
| Gift of the Nile | Egypt |
| Granite City | Aberdeen (Scotland) |
| Hermit Kingdom | Korea |
| Holy Land | Jerusalem |
| Island of Pearls | Bahrain (Persian Gulf) |
| Island of Cloves | Zanzibar |
| Key to the Mediterranean | Gibraltar |
| Land of Five Rivers | Punjab |
| Land of Golden Pagoda | Myanmar (Burma) |
| Land of Kangaroo | Australia |
| Land of Maple Leaf/Lillies | Canada |
| Land of Midnight Sun | Norway |
| Land of Morning Calm | Korea |
| Land of the Rising Sun | Japan |
| Land of Thousand Lakes | Finland |
| Land of Thunderbolt | Bhutan |
| Land of the White Elephants | Thailand |
| Manchester of the Orient | Osaka (Japan) |
| Pearl of the Antilles *or* Sugar Bowl of the World | Cuba |
| Pink City | Jaipur |
| Playground of Europe | Switzerland |
| Queen of the Adriatic | Venice (Italy) |
| Roof of the World | Pamirs |
| Sick Man of Europe | Turkiye |
| Venice of the North | Stockholm (Sweden) |
| Windy City | Chicago |
| Whiteman's Grave | Guinea Coast of Africa |
| World's Loneliest Island | Tristan de Cunha |

## Countries'/Cities' Names—Old and New

| Old Name | New Name | Old Name | New Name |
|---|---|---|---|
| Abyssinia | Ethiopia | Leningrad | St. Petersburg |
| Basutoland | Lesotho | Leopoldville | Kinshasa |
| Bechuanaland | Botswana | Mesopotamia | Iraq |
| British Honduras | Belize | North Rhodesia | Zambia |
| Burma | Myanmar | Nyasaland | Malawi |
| Ceylon | Sri Lanka | Peking | Beijing |
| Zaire | Congo | Persia | Iran |
| Constantinople | Istanbul | Rangoon | Yangon |
| Dahomey | Benin | Salisbury | Harare |
| Dutch East Indies | Indonesia | Siam | Thailand |
| East Pakistan | Bangladesh | South West Africa | Namibia |
| Formosa | Taiwan | Southern Rhodesia | Zimbabwe |
| Gold Coast | Ghana | Turkey | Turkiye |

## IMPORTANT RESIDENCES

• **Buckingham Palace (London):** King/Queen of Britain • **10, Downing Street (London):** Prime Minister, Britain • **Elysee Palace (Paris):** President, France • **Rashtrapati Bhawan (New Delhi):** President, India • **White House (Washington):** President, USA • **Vatican (Rome):** Pope

## Important towns situated on the River Banks

| Town | River | Town | River |
|---|---|---|---|
| Agra | Yamuna | Leh | Indus |
| Ahmedabad | Sabarmati | London | Thames |
| Ayodhya | Saryu | Lucknow | Gomati |
| Baghdad | Tigris | Nasik | Godavari |
| Berlin | Spree | New York | Hudson |
| Cairo | Nile | Paris | Seine |
| Kolkata | Hooghly | Patna | Ganga |
| Cuttack | Mahanadi | Prayagraj | Confluence of the Ganga and the Yamuna |
| Delhi | Yamuna | | |
| Dibrugarh | Brahmaputra | Rome | Tiber |
| Dublin | Liffey | Srinagar | Jhelum |
| Hardwar | Ganga | Surat | Tapti |
| Hyderabad | Musi | Sydney | Murray-Darling |
| Jabalpur | Narbada | Varanasi | Ganga |
| Kanpur | Ganga | Vienna | Danube |
| Karachi | Indus | Washington | Potamac |
| Lahore | Ravi | Yangon | Irawadi |

## Books and Authors

### FOREIGN

| Book | Author |
|---|---|
| Aesop's Fables | Aesop |
| Adventure of Robinson Crusoe | Daniel Defoe |
| Adventures of Sherlok Holmes | Arthur Conan Doyle |
| Alice in Wonderland | Lewis Carrol |
| Apple Cart | G.B. Shaw |
| Arabian Nights | Sir Richard Burton |
| As You Like It | William Shakespeare |
| A Tale of Two Cities | Charles Dickens |
| A Tale of Two Gardens | Octavio Paz |
| A Thousand Suns | Dominique Lapierre |
| August Coup | Mikhail S. Gorbachev |
| Ben Hur | Lewis Wallace |
| Candida | G.B. Shaw |
| Das Kapital | Karl Marx |
| David Copperfield | Charles Dickens |
| Divine Comedy | A. Dante |
| Doctor's Dilemma | G.B. Shaw |
| Famished Road | Ben Okri |
| Freedom From Fear | Aung San Suu Kyi |
| Gulistan Bostan | Sheikh Saadi |
| Gulliver's Travels | Jonathan Swift |
| Hamlet | William Shakespeare |
| Iliad | Homer |
| Inferno | A. Dante |
| In Memoriam | Lord Tennyson |
| Ivanhoe | Walter Scott |
| Julius Caesar | William Shakespeare |
| Lady Chatterley's Lover | D.H. Lawrence |
| Lajja | Taslima Nasreen |
| Les Miserable | Victor Hugo |
| Leviathan | Thomas Hobbes |
| Lolita | V. Nobokov |
| Lycidas | John Milton |
| Mein Kampf | Adolf Hitler |
| Merchant of Venice | William Shakespeare |
| Midnight's Children | Salman Rushdie |
| Moor's Last Sigh | Salman Rushdie |
| Mother | Maxim Gorky |
| Mother India | Katherine Mayo |
| Nana | Emile Zola |
| Ninteen Eighty Four | George Orwell |
| Odyssey | Homer |
| Origin of Species | Charles Darwin |
| Othello | William Shakespeare |
| Paradise Lost | John Milton |
| Paradise Regained | John Milton |
| Path to Power | Margaret Thatcher |
| Pickwick Papers | Charles Dickens |
| Pride and Prejudice | Jane Austen |
| Razor's Edge | Somerset Maugham |
| Republic | Plato |
| Romeo and Juliet | William Shakespeare |
| Round the World in Eighty Days | Jules Verne |
| Rubaiyat-i-Omar Khayyam | Edward Fitzgerald (Translator) |
| Shape of Things to Come | H.G. Wells |
| The Satanic Verses | Salman Rushdie |
| The Social Contract | Rousseau |
| The Tempest | William Shakespeare |
| Time Machine | H.G. Wells |
| Tom Sawyer | Mark Twain |
| Treasure Island | R.L. Stevenson |
| Twelfth Night | William Shakespeare |
| Uncle Tom's Cabin | H.B. Stowe |
| Unto This Last | John Ruskin |
| Utopia | Thomas More |
| Universe Around Us | James Jeans |
| Vicar of Wakefield | Oliver Goldsmith |
| War and Peace | Leo Tolstoy |
| Wealth of Nations | Adam Smith |
| Wonder That was India | A.L. Basham |
| Wuthering Heights | Emily Bronte |

### INDIAN

| Book | Author |
|---|---|
| Abhigyan Shakuntalam | Kalidas |
| Ain-i-Akbari | Abul Fazal |
| Anand Math | Bankim Chandra Chatterjee |

| Book | Author |
|---|---|
| Arthashastra | Kautilya |
| A Suitable Boy | Vikram Seth |
| Bhagwat Gita | Ved Vyas |
| Chidambara | Sumitranandan Pant |
| Devdas | Sarat Chandra Chatterjee |
| Diwan-i-Ghalib | Mirza Ghalib |
| Discovery of India | Jawaharlal Nehru |
| Essays on Gita | Aurobindo Ghosh |
| Eternal India | Indira Gandhi |
| Faces of Everest | Major H.P.S. Ahluwalia |
| Ganadevata | Tarashankar Bandopadhyaya |
| Geet Govind | Jaya Dev |
| Geetanjali | R.N. Tagore |
| Glimpses of World History | Jawaharlal Nehru |
| Godaan | Prem Chand |
| Gul-e-Nagma | Firaq Gorakhpuri |
| Gunahon ka Devta | Dharmveer Bharti |
| Harsh Charita | Bana Bhatta |
| Hindu View of Life | S. Radhakrishnan |
| Idols | Sunil Gavaskar |
| India Divided | Dr. Rajendra Prasad |
| The Judgement | Kuldip Nayyar |
| Juhi ki Kali | Surya Kant Tripathi 'Nirala' |
| Justice of Peace ke Aansu | Janardan Prasad Singh |
| Chand ka Munh Terha Hai | Muktibodh |
| Kapalkundala | Bankim Chandra Chatterjee |
| Kadambari | Bana Bhatta |
| Kagaz Te Kanwas | Amrita Pritam |
| Kamayani | Jai Shankar Prasad |
| Kitni Nawon | S.H. Vatsyayan |
| Kumar Sambhav | Kalidas |
| Mahabharata | Ved Vyas |
| Malgudi Days | R.K. Narayan |
| Manvini Bhavai | Pannalal Patel |
| Mati Matal | Gopi Nath Mohanty |
| Meghdoot | Kalidas |
| Meri Ekyavan Kavitain | Atal Bihari Vajpayee |
| Meri Sansadiya Yatra | Atal Bihari Vajpayee |
| Mritunjaya | B.K. Bhattacharya |
| Mudrarakshasa | Vishakhadatta |
| My Experiments with Truth | M.K. Gandhi |
| My Own Boswell | M. Hidayatullah |
| My Presidential Years | R. Venkataraman |
| Nisheeth | Uma Shankar Joshi |
| 'No, Sir' | P.G. Mavlankar |
| One Day Wonders | Sunil Gavaskar |
| Panchtantra | Vishnu Sharma |
| Passage to England | Nirad C. Chaudhuri |
| Prison Diary | Jaya Prakash Narayan |
| Raghuvansha | Kalidas |
| Rajtarangini | Kalhana |
| Ramayana | Balmiki |
| Ramcharit Manas | Tulsidas |
| Rukh Te Rishi | Harbhajan Singh |
| Satyarth Prakash | Swami Dayanand |
| Sur Sagar | Surdas |
| The Guide | R.K. Narayan |
| The Insider | P.V. Narasimharao |
| The Post Office — *Dak Ghar* | Rabindra Nath Tagore |
| The God of Small Things | Arundhati Roy |
| Urvashi | Ram Dhari Singh 'Dinkar' |
| Yama | Mahadevi Verma |
| My Country : My Life (Autobiography) | L.K. Advani |
| The Test of My Life | Yuvraj Singh |
| Twenty Years in a Decade | Shah Rukh Khan |

## IMPORTANT BOOKS WRITTEN IN JAIL

| Book | Author |
|---|---|
| My Experiments with Truth | Mahatma Gandhi |
| Glimpses of World History Discovery of India | Jawaharlal Nehru |
| Gita Rahasya | Lokmanya Bal Gangadhar Tilak |
| Pilgrim's Progress | John Bunyan |
| Bible (in German language) | Martin Luther |
| Les Miserables | Victor Hugo |
| Long Walk to Freedom | Nelson Mandela |

* * * * *

# 11. FIRST IN INDIA

## First in India

| | |
|---|---|
| Nobel Prize for Literature (1913) | Rabindra Nath Tagore |
| Nobel Prize for Physics (1929) | C.V. Raman |
| Nobel Prize for Peace (1979) | Mother Teresa |
| Nobel Prize for Economics (1998) | Amartya Sen |
| Special Oscar award winner (1992) | Satyajit Ray |
| Governor-General of free India (Last also) | C. Rajagopalachari |
| Woman Governor of the State | Smt. Sarojini Naidu |
| Indian Chief of the Army Staff* | General K.M. Cariappa |
| Woman Chief Minister of a State | Smt. Sucheta Kripalani |
| Woman President of United Nations General Assembly (1954) | Smt. Vijaylakshmi Pandit |
| President of International Court of Justice | Dr. Nagendra Singh |
| Woman to swim across the English Channel | Ms. Aarti Saha |
| Miss Universe | Miss Sushmita Sen |
| Miss World | Reita Faria |
| Indian to swim across the English Channel | Mihir Sen |
| Field Marshal | S.H.F.J. Manekshaw |
| Indian recipient of Victoria Cross | Khudadad Khan |
| Indian to conquer Mt. Everest | Sherpa Tenzing, May 29, 1953 |
| Indian male cosmonaut (1984) | Rakesh Sharma |
| Indian female cosmonaut | Kalpana Chawla (19 Nov., 1997) |
| Woman to climb Mt. Everest | Miss Bachendri Pal, May 23, 1984 |
| Woman to get Olympic Medal | Karnam Malleswari |
| Indian to address the UN General Assembly in Hindi | Atal Bihari Vajpayee |
| Newspaper | Bengal Gazette, Jan 27, 1780 |
| Postage Stamp issued | In 1852 |
| Telegraph line laid | In 1851, Kolkata; Diamond Harbour |
| Railways run | April 16, 1853; Bombay-Thana |
| Electric Train run | 1925: Bombay-Kurla |
| Atomic Power Station | Tarapore (Maharashtra) |
| Passenger-cum-cargo ship made in India | Harshavardhan |
| Satellite | Aryabhatta (1975) |
| Rocket | Rohini (1967) |
| Atomic Reactor | Apsara (1956) |
| Climb Everest without oxygen | Phu Dorjee (1987) |
| First film (movie) | Raja Harishchandra (1913) |
| First film (talkie) | Alam Ara (1931) |
| Metro Railway | Kolkata Metro Railway |

| | |
|---|---|
| Test-tube baby, scientifically documented | Born on August 6, 1986 at K.E.M. Hospital, Mumbai |
| TV Centre | At Delhi |
| Indian to get an Oscar | Bhanu Athaiya |
| Woman pilot in IAF | Ms Harita Kaur Deol |
| Cellular Phone | Kolkata, August 1, 1995 |
| Women president of Indian National Congress | Smt. Annie Besant |
| President of Indian National Congress | W.C. Banerjee (1885) |
| Indian who passed in I.C.S. Examination | Satendra Nath Tagore |
| Woman chief justice of High Court | Lila Saith (Himachal Pradesh) |
| Woman Foreign Secretary | Chokila Iyyar |

## First Important Officials of India

| | |
|---|---|
| The Governor-General of free India | Lord Mountbatten |
| President | Dr. Rajendra Prasad |
| President (Female) | Pratibha Patil |
| Vice-President | Dr. S. Radhakrishnan |
| Prime Minister | Jawahar Lal Nehru |
| Prime Minister (Female) | Indira Gandhi |
| Deputy Prime Minister | Sardar Vallabhbhai Patel |
| Chief Justice | Harilal J. Kania |
| First Female Judge in Supreme Court | Smt. Meera Sahib Fatima Bibi |
| Speaker, Lok Sabha | Ganesh Vasudeo Mawlankar |
| Woman Speaker of Lok Sabha | Meira Kumar |
| Chief Election Commissioner | Sukumar Sen |
| Commander-in-Chief | General Sir Roy Bucher |
| Chief of Army Staff | General Maharaj Rajendra Sinhji |
| Chief of Air Staff | Air Marshal Sir Thomas Elmhirst |
| Chief of Naval Staff | Vice Admiral Ramdas Katari |
| Chief of Defence Staff (CDS) | General Bipin Rawat |
| Female Minister | Raj Kumari Amrit Kaur (Health Minister) |
| Female Governor | Sarojini Naidu (U.P.) |
| Female Chief Minister | Sucheta Kripalani (U.P. 1963) |
| Finance Commissioner | K.C. Niyogi |
| Leader of Opposition in Lok Sabha (Recognised) | Y.V. Chavan (Congress) |
| Leader of Opposition in Rajya Sabha (Recognised) | Kamalapati Tripathi (Congress) |

## Highest, Biggest, Largest & Longest in India

| | |
|---|---|
| Award for Gallantry, Highest | Param Vir Chakra |
| Award, highest civilian | Bharat Ratna |
| Bank with largest number of branches | State Bank of India |
| River bridge, Longest | Bhupen Hazarika bridge Assam Lohit (Brahamputra) River |
| Cantilever Span Bridge, Largest | Howrah Bridge (Kolkata) |
| Cattle Fair, Largest | Sonepur Fair (Bihar) |
| City, Most Populous | Mumbai |
| Corridor, Longest | Ramanathaswamy Corridor, Tamil Nadu (1,220 mt.) |
| Desert, Largest | Thar (Rajasthan) |
| Dam, Longest | Hirakud Dam (Odisha) |

| | |
|---|---|
| Dam, Highest | Tehri Dam on Bhagirathi river in Uttarakhand (855 ft.) |
| Delta, Largest | Sunderban (12,872 Sq. km.) |
| Gateway, Highest | Buland Darwaja at Fatehpur Sikri (54 m.) |
| Lake, Largest (Fresh Water) | Wular Lake (Kashmir) |
| Literacy, Highest | Kerala |
| Museum, Largest | Indian Museum (Kolkata) |
| Mosque, Biggest | Jama Masjid (Delhi) |
| Peak, Highest | K-2 (8,611 mt.) |
| Railway Platform, Longest | Shree Siddharoodha Swamiji Railway Station Hubballi, Karnataka (1507 m) |
| Railway Bridge, Largest | Vembanad Bridge, Kerala (4.6 km) |
| River, Longest | The Ganga river (2,525 km.) |
| Rainfall, Highest (annual mean) | Mowsynram near Cherrapunji (Meghalaya) |
| Road, Longest | Grand Trunk Road |
| Road-Rail Longest Bridge | Bogibeel bridge, Assam (4.94 km) |
| Rock-cut Temple, Largest | Kailash Temples, Ellora (Maharashtra) |
| State, maximum forest cover | Madhya Pradesh |
| State, Largest (area) | Rajasthan (3,42,239 sq. km.) |
| State, Most Populous | Uttar Pradesh (19,98,12,341) |
| State with Maximum density of population | Bihar (1106 persons per sq. km.) |
| Tunnel, Longest (Road) | Dr. Shyama Prasad Mukherjee Tunnel (J & K—9.28 kms) |
| Tunnel, Longest (Railway) | Pir Panjal Tunnel (Qazigund to Banihal) (11.2 kms) (J&K) |
| Waterfall, Highest | Kunchikal Waterfall, Karnataka (455 m.) |
| Zoo, Largest | Zoological Gardens, Kolkata |
| Man-made Lake, Largest | Govind Sagar (Bhakra) |

## Indian Banks

- **Reserve Bank of India:** It was established in 1935 and nationalised in 1949. It is the Central Bank of the country and issues all currency notes except one rupee note. It acts as a banker to the Government and exercises control over other commercial banks in the country. Headquarters of Reserve Bank of India is in Mumbai.
- **The State Bank of India:** Largest commercial bank, alongwith its seven other associate banks was nationalised in 1955. On 1st April, 2017, the State Bank of India, which was India's largest bank, merged with five of its associate banks (State Bank of Bikaner & Jaipur, State Bank of Hyderabad, State Bank of Mysore, State Bank of Patiala and State Bank of Travancore), and with the Bharatiya Mahila Bank.
- **Nationalisation of Banks:** The Government of India on July 19, 1969, took over 14 biggest commercial banks incorporated in the country. On April 15, 1980, six more banks were nationalised. In March 1994, the Parliament passed the Banking Regulation (Amendment) Bill, 1994 which inter alia provided for establishment of private sector banks. Till June 2023 there were 12 public sector banks including SBI in India.

## Insurance

- **Life Insurance Corporation of India:** The Life Insurance Corporation of India was founded in September 1, 1956 when the Parliament of India passed the Life Insurance of India Act that nationalised the private insurance industry in India.
- **General Insurance Corporation of India:** The entire general insurance business in India was nationalized by the Government of India (GOI) through the General Insurance Business (Nationalization) Act (GIBNA) of 1972. 55 Indian insurance companies and 52 other general insurance operations of other companies were nationalized.

* * * * *

# 12. CULTURAL ACTIVITIES

## AKADEMIES

There are three akademies for promotion of creative art.

1. **Lalit Kala Akademi, New Delhi:** Established in 1954, the Lalit Kala Akademi strives for the popularisation of Indian art within the country and in various countries of the world through exhibitions, publications, workshops and camps. Every three year it organises the Triennale India, an international exhibition. It publishes research papers on Indian arts. Besides organising seminars, it honours eminent artists. The Akademi has set up regional centres called Rashtriya Lalit Kala Kendras at Lucknow, Kolkata, Chennai and Bhubaneswar and a small office at Mumbai.
2. **Sangeet Natak Akademi, New Delhi:** The Sangeet Natak Akademi, set-up in 1953, aims at the promotion and development of dance, drama and music. It holds seminars and festivals, presents awards to the eminent artists and extends financial assistance to traditional teachers and scholarships to students. It also operates a scheme of exchange of troupes.
3. **Sahitya Akademi, New Delhi:** The Sahitya Akademi, established in 1954, has the main functions of development of Indian letters, setting up high literary standards, translation of literary works of one Indian language into other Indian languages, publication of books on history of literature and criticism, bibliographies and reference books. The Akademy has regional offices at Mumbai, Kolkata, Bengaluru and Chennai.
4. **National School of Drama:** It is one of the top theatre training institutes in the world and only one of its kind in India. It was set up in 1959 under Sangeet Natak Akademi but was later made autonomous organisation in 1975.

## SCULPTURE

Archaeological Survey of India, set up in 1861, is responsible for preservation and maintenance of sculptures and historical monuments and manages a number of archaeological museums.

National Archives of India, established in 1891, it is the official custodian of all non-current records of permanent value of the Government of India and its predecessor bodies.

## MUSEUMS

They are repositories of the cultural heritage and conserve and preserve historical technical and other materials against decay and transmit them to posterity as records of history.

## MUSIC

**Main Schools of Classical Music:** There are two main schools of classical music, namely, the Hindustani and the Carnatic. The Hindustani school of classical music is in vogue in north-western India, eastern India and northern parts of the South India.

**Musical Instruments:** They are: Tabla, Mridangam, Pakhawaj, Chandai, Dholak, Veena, Sitar, Sarod, Gootuvadhyam, Sarangi, Flute, Nadaswaram, Shehnai, Shringi and Turahi.

## DANCE

India has a very rich tradition of tribal, folk and classical dances.

## Classical Dance

| Dance | State | Famous Artists |
|---|---|---|
| Bharat Natyam | Tamil Nadu | Yamini Krishnamurthy, Rukmini Devi Arundale, Swapna Sundari, Sonal Mansingh, Vaijanti Mala, Mrinalini Sarabhai, Chandralekha, Indrani, Ram Gopal, Bal Saraswati |
| Kathakali | Kerala | Gopinath, K.K. Nayar, Kunju-Kurup, T.K. Chandu |
| Kuchipudi | Andhra Pradesh | Sapna Sundari, Raja Reddy, Shobha Nayar, Radha Reddy, Vedantam Satyanarayan, Vimpanti Chinna Satyam. |
| Kathak | North India | Birju Maharaj, Gopi Krishna, Shambhu Maharaj, Sitara Devi, Vishnu Sharma, Durga Lal, Shobhana Narayan |
| Odissi | Odisha | Kelucharan Mahapatra, Indrani Rehman, Madhavi Mudgal, Protima Bedi, Samyukta Panigrahi, Sonal Mansingh, Debudas |
| Manipuri | Manipur | Uday Shankar, Bipin Singh, Suryamukhi, Darohra Jhaveri |

## Famous Folk-Dance

| State | Folk Dance |
|---|---|
| Andhra Pradesh | Dandari, Banjara |
| Asom | Bihu, Keli Gopal, Sataria |
| Bihar | Chhau, Magahi, Durga dance |
| W. Bengal | Kirtan, Kalatri, Asweabadh, Brita, Kalidance |
| Chhattisgarh | Saila, Karama, Bhagoria |
| Gujarat | Garba, Rasalila, Tippani, Dandia, |
| Haryana | Damyal, Lahoor |
| Himachal Pradesh | Dussehra dance, Hikat, Notio |
| Jammu & Kashmir | Dumhal |
| Jharkhand | Jhau, Ghumakudia, Jadur, Sarhul, Soharai, Karama, Vaima, Loojhari, Jat-Jatin, Vidayat |
| Karnataka | Yakshagan, Dolu Kunitha |
| Kerala | Mohini Attam, Padayuni |
| Madhya Pradesh | Lota Nritya, Jawara |
| Maharashtra | Tamasha, Dahi Handi, Gof, Deepak Dindi |
| Manipur | Dhol Cholam |
| Meghalaya | Nongakarem |
| Nagaland | Bamboo dance |
| Odisha | Chhau, Maya Shabari, Dalachai |
| Punjab | Gidda, Bhangra, Panihari |
| Rajasthan | Thumar, Kathaputali, Tera Tali |
| Tamil Nadu | Terukalathu, Kabalatam, Kargam, Pulivesham |
| Tripura | Hazagiri |
| Uttar Pradesh | Rasalila, Nautanki, Thali, Dhurang, Jhumela, Huraka, Bol. |
| Uttarakhand | Kajari, Karan |
| Goa | Dhode Modini |

## Musical Instruments and Artists

| Musical Instrument | Artists | Musical Instrument | Artists |
|---|---|---|---|
| Flute | Hari Prasad Chaurasia, Panna Lal Ghosh, T.R. Mahalingam, N. Ramani, Vijaya Raghava Rao | Sitar | Pandit Ravishankar, Vilayat Khan |
| | | Santur | Shiv Kumar Sharma |
| | | Rudraveena | Zia Mohiuddin Dagar |
| | | Pakhawaj | Govind Rao, Anokhe Lal, Kanthi Maharaj |
| Tabla | Allah Rakha, Gudai Maharaj, Latif Khan, Zakir Hussain | Mridanga | Palghat R. Raghu, U.S. Burman |
| Violin | Lalgudi Jayaraman, L. Subramaniam, M.S. Gopal Krishnan, S. Subrahmaniam, V.G. Jog, N. Rajan | Harmonium | Purushottam Walawakar, M. Dhaulpuri |
| | | Guitar | Pt. Vishnu Mohan Bhatt, Brij Bhushan Kalra |
| Shehnai | Bismilla Khan, Imrat Khan Ali Akbar | Ghatam | T.H. Vinayakaram |
| Sarod | Khan, Amjad Ali Khan, Alauddin Khan, Saren Rani, Brij Narayan | Janjira | V. Nagarajan |
| | | Symphony | Jubin Mehta |

## Major Park & Wild Life Sanctuaries in India

India is rich in flora and fauna. However, due to increasing population and industrial and commercial activities, there has been acute pressure on forests. The Government has taken several steps to check the sharp fall in the number of these species. Among the measures are declaration of certain habitats as national parks and sanctuaries. 106 national parks and 573 sanctuaries have been established till July 2023, important ones being given below:

**Assam:** Kaziranga National Park (know for one-horn Rhinoceroses); Manas Sanctuary.

**Jharkhand:** Hazaribagh National Park; Betla Tiger Reserve Palamau.

**Gujarat:** Valvadar National Park, Bhavnagar; Marine National Park, Gir Forests.

**Himachal Pradesh:** Rohla National Park; Motichur Sanctuary.

**Jammu & Kashmir:** Dachigam Sanctuary.

**Karnataka:** Bandipur National Park; Bannargheta National Park, Bangalore; Nagorhole National Park, Coorg; Ranganthitto Bird Sanctuary.

**Kerala:** Eravikulam Rajmallay National Park, Idduki; Periyar Game Sanctuary.

**Madhya Pradesh:** Kanha National Park; Bandhavgarh National Park, Shahdol; Shivpuri National Park.

**Maharashtra:** Taloba National Park, Chandrapur; Panch National Park, Nagpur; Borivali National Park, Mumbai; Nawagaon National Park, Bandara; Melghat National Park.

**Manipur:** Keibul Lamjao National Park.

**Odisha:** Simlipal, Tiger Sanctuary.

**Rajasthan:** Sariska Sanctuary; Ghana Bird Sanctuary, Ranthambhor Sanctuary.

**Sikkim:** Khangchandzenda National Park, Gangtok.

**Tamil Nadu:** Vedanthangal Bird Sanctuary; Guindy National Park, Chennai; Mudumalai Sanctuary; Kalakad-Munden Thurai Reserve.

**Uttar Pradesh:** Chandraprabha Sanctuary; Dudhwa National Park, Lakhimpur.

**West Bengal:** Jaldapara Sanctuary; Sunderbans.

**Uttarakhand:** Corbett National Park; Nainital.

* * * * *

# 13. AWARDS

## NATIONAL AWARDS

1. **Bharat Ratna:** This is India's highest civilian award. It is given for exceptional work on art, literature, science and recognition of public service of the highest order. Government servants are not eligible for it. The table shows the recipients of the award:

**Bharat Ratna Award Winners:**

| | | |
|---|---|---|
| **1.** | Dr. S. Radhakrishnan | 1954 |
| **2.** | C. Rajagopalachari | 1954 |
| **3.** | Dr. C.V. Raman | 1954 |
| **4.** | Dr. Bhagwan Das | 1955 |
| **5.** | Dr. M. Visvesvaraya | 1955 |
| **6.** | Jawahar Lal Nehru | 1955 |
| **7.** | Govind Ballabh Pant | 1957 |
| **8.** | Dr. D.K. Karve | 1958 |
| **9.** | Dr. Bidhan Chandra Roy | 1961 |
| **10.** | Purushottam Das Tandon | 1961 |
| **11.** | Dr. Rajendra Prasad | 1962 |
| **12.** | Dr. Zakir Hussain | 1963 |
| **13.** | Dr. Pandurang Vaman Kane | 1963 |
| **14.** | Lal Bahadur Shastri* | 1966 |
| **15.** | Indira Gandhi | 1971 |
| **16.** | V.V. Giri | 1975 |
| **17.** | K. Kamraj* | 1976 |
| **18.** | Mother Teresa | 1980 |
| **19.** | Acharya Vinoba Bhave* | 1983 |
| **20.** | Khan Abdul Ghaffar Khan | 1987 |
| **21.** | M.G. Ramachandran* | 1988 |
| **22.** | Dr. B.R. Ambedkar* | 1990 |
| **23.** | Dr. Nelson R. Mandela | 1990 |
| **24.** | Rajiv Gandhi* | 1991 |
| **25.** | Sardar Vallabhbhai Patel* | 1991 |
| **26.** | Morarji R. Desai | 1991 |
| **27.** | Maulana Abul Kalam Azad* | 1992 |
| **28.** | Jehangir Ratanji Dadabhai Tata | 1992 |
| **29.** | Satyajit Roy* | 1992 |
| **30.** | Shri Gulzari Lal Nanda* | 1997 |
| **31.** | Mrs. Aruna Asaf Ali* | 1997 |
| **32.** | Dr. A.P.J. Abdul Kalam | 1998 |
| **33.** | M.S. Subbalakshmi | 1998 |
| **34.** | C. Subramaniam | 1998 |
| **35.** | Jaya Prakash Narayan* | 1999 |
| **36.** | Prof. Amartya Sen | 1999 |
| **37.** | Pt. Ravi Shankar | 1999 |
| **38.** | Gopinath Bardoloi* | 1999 |
| **39.** | Lata Mangeshkar | 2001 |
| **40.** | Bismillah Khan | 2001 |
| **41.** | Bhimsen Joshi | 2009 |
| **42.** | C.N.R. Rao | 2014 |
| **43.** | Sachin Tendulakar | 2014 |
| **44.** | Pt. Madan Mohan Malaviya* | 2015 |
| **45.** | Atal Bihari Vajpayee | 2015 |
| **46.** | Nanaji Deshmukh* | 2019 |
| **47.** | Bhupen Hazarika* | 2019 |
| **48.** | Pranab Mukherjee | 2019 |
| **49.** | Karpoori Thakur* | 2024 |
| **50.** | L.K. Advani | 2024 |
| **51.** | Charan Singh* | 2024 |
| **52.** | P.V. Narasimha Rao* | 2024 |
| **53.** | M.S. Swaminathan* | 2024 |

* Posthumous

2. **Padma Vibhushan:** This award is given for exceptional and distinguished service in any field, including service rendered by Govt. servants.
3. **Padma Bhushan:** This award is given for distinguished service of a high order in any field, including service rendered by Govt. servants.
4. **Padma Shri:** This award is given for distinguished service in any field, including service rendered by Government servants.

## GALLANTRY AWARDS

1. **Param Vir Chakra:** The highest award for bravery or some daring and pre-eminent act of valour or self-sacrifice in the presence of the enemy, whether on land, at sea or in the air.
2. **Mahavir Chakra:** It is the second highest decoration and is awarded for acts of conspicuous gallantry in the presence of the enemy, whether on land, at sea or in the air.

3. **Vir Chakra:** It is the third in order of awards given for acts of gallantry in the presence of enemy, whether on land, at sea or in the air.
4. **Ashok Chakra:** This medal is awarded for the most conspicuous bravery or some daring or pre-eminent act of valour or self-sacrifice on land, at sea or in the air but not in the presence of enemy.
5. **Vishishta Sewa Medal:** It is awarded to personnel of all the three Services in class I, II and III in recognition of distinguished service of the "most exceptional" and "exceptional" and a "high" order respectively. Prefixes *Parma* and *Ati* are added before first two categories of medals respectively.
6. **Jeewan Raksha Padak:** Awarded for meritorious acts or a series of acts of a human nature displayed in saving life from drowning, fire and rescue operations in mines etc.

## Dada Saheb Phalke Award Winners:

| | |
|---|---|
| Mrs Devika Rani Roerich | 1969 |
| B.N. Sirkar | 1970 |
| Prithvi Raj Kapoor | 1971 |
| Pankaj Mallick | 1972 |
| Mrs Ruby Myers | 1973 |
| B.N. Reddy | 1974 |
| Dhiren Ganguly | 1975 |
| Mrs Kanan Devi | 1976 |
| Nitin Bose | 1977 |
| R.C. Boral | 1978 |
| Sohrab Modi | 1979 |
| P. Jai Raj | 1980 |
| Naushad Ali | 1981 |
| L.V. Prasad | 1982 |
| Mrs. Durga Khote | 1983 |
| Satyajit Roy | 1984 |
| V. Shantaram | 1985 |
| B. Nagi Reddy | 1986 |
| Raj Kapoor | 1987 |
| Ashok Kumar | 1988 |
| Lata Mangeshkar | 1989 |
| A. Nageshwar Rao | 1990 |
| Bhalji Pendharkar | 1991 |
| Bhupen Hazarika | 1992 |
| Majrooh Sultanpuri | 1993 |
| Dilip Kumar | 1994 |
| Dr Raj Kumar (Kannada actor) | 1995 |
| Sivaji Ganesan (Tamil Actor) | 1996 |
| Pradeepji (Poet, lyricist) | 1997 |
| B.R. Chopra | 1998 |
| Hrishikesh Mukherjee | 1999 |
| Asha Bhonsle (Playback singer) | 2000 |
| Yash Chopra | 2001 |
| Devanand | 2002 |
| Mrinal Sen | 2003 |
| Ador Gopala Krishnan | 2004 |
| Shyam Benegal | 2005 |
| Tapan Sinha | 2006 |
| Manna Dey | 2007 |
| V.K. Murthy | 2008 |
| D. Ramanaidu | 2009 |
| K. Balachander | 2010 |
| Soumitra Chatterjee | 2011 |
| Pran | 2012 |
| Gulzar | 2013 |
| Shashi Kapoor | 2014 |
| Manoj Kumar | 2015 |
| K. Viswanath | 2016 |
| Vinod Khanna | 2017 |
| Amitabh Bachchan | 2018 |
| Rajinikanth | 2019 |
| Asha Parekh | 2020 |
| Waheeda Rehman | 2021 |

## Highest Honours of Some Countries

| *Country* | *Highest Honour* |
|---|---|
| India | Bharat Ratna |
| Pakistan | Nishan-e-Pakistan |
| Kuwait | Mubarak-Al-kabir Medal |
| Saudi Arabia | Shah Abdul Aziz Medal |
| Argentina | The Order of Sona Martin |
| Nicaragua | Augusto-Caesar Sandino Order |
| Vietnam | The order of the Golden Star |
| Hungary | The Order of Banner |
| Britain | Member of British Empire, Victoria Cross |
| Japan | Order of Moulovenice Sun |
| Denmark | Order of Diana Brog |
| France | Legend of Honour |
| America | Presidential Medal of Freedom |
| Germany | Pore Lee Merit Iron Cross |
| The Netherlands | Netherlands Lion |

* * * * *

# COMPUTERS

## Introduction

The term computer is derived from the Latin word compute, which means to calculate. A computer is an electronic machine, devised for performing calculations and controlling operations that can be expressed either in logical or numerical terms. In simple terms, a computer is an electronic device that performs diverse operations with the help of instructions to process the information in order to achieve the desired results. A Computer application extends to cover huge area including education, industries, government, medicine, scientific research etc.

A computer is one of the most influential forces available in modern times. Due to its memory, high speed and perfection, its application can be extended to almost infinite levels. Millions of complex calculations can be done in mere fraction of time. Difficult decisions can be made with accuracy for comparatively little cost. Computers are widely seen as instruments for future progress and as tools to achieve substantiality by way of improved access to information by means of video conferencing and e-mail. Indeed computers have left such on impression on modern civilization that we call this era as the information age.

## Computer System

A computer system is a combination of various components. It performs the system functions such as input, processing, output, storage and control. A computer system consists of the following components: 1. Hardware; 2. Software

### Hardware

The physical components of the computer, such as electrical, electronics and mechanical unit are known as the hardware of the computer. That is, the input units, output units and CPU are called hardware. Thus hardware is the equipment involved in the function of a computer. It consists of the components that can be physically handled.

### Software

The computer performs operations like addition, subtraction, multiplication and division only when the user instructs it to do so. The user issues instructions and the CPU acts in accordance with the instructions. The sets of instructions, which control the sequence of operations, are known as programs, and collectively programs are called software. The software can be broadly classified into two types. They are: (a) System Software (b) Application Software.

### Difference between Hardware & Software

***Hardware***

1. It is the physical unit of the computer
2. Hardware understands only machine language, lower level language or binary
3. It works with binary code, the presence or absence of Pulses as 1's or 0's.

***Software***

1. It is a collection of programs to bring the hardware system into operation
2. It is written by a well versed programmer and generally in higher level language which is readable by human being.
3. It is represented by the Higher Level Languages such as BASIC, COBOL, *etc.,*

### System Software

System software consists of several Programs, which are directly responsible for controlling, integrating and managing the individual hardware components of a computer system. They provide basic functionality like file management, visual display and keyboard input which are used by application software. Some examples of system software are operating system, device drivers, language translators, system utilities.

### Application Software

A computer program used to perform a specific task, rather than just managing a computer system. Some examples of application software are word processing, spread sheets, database management systems.

## Two Types of Computer Systems

**Analog Computers :** The analog computers operate by measuring instead of counting. The analog computer works on the supply of continuous electrical signals. The display is also continuous. Its output is in the form of graphs.

**Digital Computers :** These computers work with quantities represented as digits. They operate on discrete quantities. In digital computer, both numeric and non-numeric information are represented as strings of digits. These computers use binary codes, 0's and 1's, to represent the information. The information is given to the computer in the form of discrete electrical signals.

## Input/Output Devices

**Input Devices :** An input device is any machine that feeds data into a computer. For example, a keyboard is an input device. Input devices other than the keyboard are sometimes called alternate devices. Trackballs, mouse and light pens are all alternate input devices.

**Output Devices :** Output is anything that comes out of a computer. Output can be meaningful information or gibberish, and it can appear in a variety of forms - as binary numbers, as characters, as pictures, and as printed pages. Output devices include display screens, loudspeakers, printers, plotters, etc.

## Computer Memory

There are two kinds of computer memory: primary and secondary. Primary memory is accessible directly by the processing unit. RAM is an example of primary memory. As soon as the computer is switched off the contents of the primary memory is lost. You can store and retrieve data much faster with primary memory compared to secondary memory. Secondary memory such as floppy disks, magnetic disk, etc., is located outside the computer. Primary memory is more expensive than secondary memory. Because of this the size of primary memory is less than that of secondary memory.

### Types of Primary Memory

- Random Access Memory (RAM)
- Read Only Memory (ROM)
- Programmable Read Only Memory (PROM)
- Erasable Programmable Read Only Memory (EPROM)

### Cache Memory

To decrease the mismatch in operating speed, a small memory chip is attached between CPU and Main memory whose access time is very close to the processing speed of CPU. It is called CACHE memory. CACHE memories are accessed much faster than conventional RAM. It is used to store programs or data currently being executed or temporary data frequently used by the CPU.

### Types of Secondary Memory

- Magnetic Tape
- Magnetic Disk
- Floppy Disk
- Optical Disk–1. Compact Disk/ Read Only Memory (CD-ROM), 2. Erasable Optical Disk.

The memory is measured by the following units:

(*a*) **BIT (Binary digit):** It is the smallest possible unit of information. It can be either 0 or 1.

(*b*) **NIBBLE:** Four bits form one nibble.

(*c*) **BYTE:** It is a unit of information consisting of fixed number of bits. It is a combination of 8 bits.

(*d*) **CHARACTER:** It is represented by one byte. It can be a letter, digit, punctuation mark or special characters.

(*e*) **WORD:** The combination of 2 bytes or 4 bytes or 8 bytes is a word.

The data measurement is as follows:

8 bits - 1 byte

1024 bytes - 1 Kilo Byte (KB)

1024 KB - 1 Mega Byte (MB)

1024 MB - 1 Giga Byte (GB)

1024 GB - 1 Tera Byte (TB)

**Word keyboard shortcuts**

| *Action* | *Key Stroke* |
|---|---|
| Open a file | Ctrl + O |
| New file | Ctrl + N |
| Close a file | Ctrl + W |
| Save As | F12 |
| Save | Ctrl+S or Shift+F12 |
| Print Preview | Ctrl + F2 |
| Print | Ctrl + P |
| Show/Hide paragraph symbols | Ctrl + * |
| Spelling and grammar | F7 |
| Help | F1 |
| Find | Ctrl + F |
| Replace | Ctrl + H |
| Go To | Ctrl + G |
| Select all - entire document | Ctrl + A |
| Select from cursor to beginning of line | Shift + Home |
| Select from cursor to end of line | Shift + End |
| Go to beginning of line | Home |
| Go to end of line | End |
| Go to beginning of document | Ctrl + Home |
| Go to end of document | Ctrl + End |
| Cut | Ctrl + X |
| Copy | Ctrl + C |
| Paste | Ctrl + V |
| Undo | Ctrl + Z |
| Redo | Ctrl + Y |
| Format painter | Ctrl + Shift + C |
| Left alignment | Ctrl + L |
| Center alignment | Ctrl + E |
| Right alignment | Ctrl + R |
| Justified | Ctrl + J |
| Delete previous word | Ctrl + Backspace |
| Apply bulleted list | Ctrl + Shift + L |
| Indent | Ctrl + M |
| Page break | Ctrl + Enter |
| Font face | Ctrl + Shift + F |
| Font size | Ctrl + Shift + P |
| Bold | Ctrl + B |
| Italics | Ctrl + I |
| Underline | Ctrl + U |
| Double underline | Ctrl + Shift + D |
| Word underline | Ctrl + Shift + A |
| Change case | Shift + F3 |
| Subscript | Ctrl + = |
| Superscript | Ctrl + Shift + = |
| Make web hyperlink | Ctrl + K |
| Go to next cell | Tab |
| Go to previous cell | Shift + Tab |
| Go to beginning of column | Alt + PageUp |
| Highlight to beginning of column | Alt + Shift + PageUp |
| Go to end of column | Alt + PageDown |
| Highlight to end of column | Alt + Shift + PageDown |
| Go to beginning of row | Alt + Home |
| Highlight to beginning of row | Alt + Shift + Home |
| Go to end of row | Alt + End |
| Highlight to end of row | Alt + Shift + End |
| Column break | Ctrl + Shift + Enter |
| Copyright © | Alt + Ctrl + C |
| Date field | Alt + Shift + D |
| Go to footnotes | Alt + Ctrl + F |
| Show/Hide ¶ | Ctrl + Shift + 8 |
| Theasaurus | Shift + F7 |

**Operating System**

It is the first layer of software loaded into computer memory when it starts up. As the first software layer, all other software that gets loaded after it depends on it for various common core services. In simple words, the operating system organizes and controls the hardware. Examples of operating systems are Windows XP, UNIX, and Linux.

## Programming Languages

Computers are machines. Unfortunately they cannot understand natural languages, such as Hindi, English, Tamil, etc. that human beings speak and understand. Therefore, to give instructions to computers, different languages have been developed. These languages are called computer languages. It is a general purpose language that is designed to combine business and scientific processing features and that can easily learned by novice programmers, yet contains advanced features for experienced programmers.

Computer languages are classified into three categories: 1. Low Level Language; 2. Machine language; 3. High level languages.

### Compiler

A compiler is a kind of translator that translates a program into another program, known as target language. Usually, the term compiler is used for language translator of high-level language into machine language. The compiler replaces single high-level statement with a series of machine language instruction.

### Interpreter

Unlike compilers, an interpreter translates a statement in a program and executes the statement immediately, before translating the next source language statement. Similar to compilers, every interpreted language such as BASIC and LISP has its own interpreters.

## Computer Networks

A **computer network**, often simply referred to as a **network**, is a collection of computers and devices connected by communications channels that facilitates communications among users and allows users to share resources with other users.

### Categories of Network

(*i*) **LAN :** LAN stands for Local Area Network. These networks evolved around the PC revolution. LANs enabled multiple users in a relatively small geographical area to exchange files and messages, as well as access shared resources such as file servers.

(*ii*) **WAN :** WAN stands for Wide Area Network. The interconnection of various LAN's through telephone network, which unites geographically distributed users, is achieved through WAN. In short when we log on to the internet, we become a part of a WAN.

(*iii*) **MAN :** MAN stands for Metropolitan Area Network. It is usually the interconnection between various LAN's in a particular geographical area like a metropolitan city like Bombay.

## Internet

Internet is a communication network which bridges all the small computer networks worldwide as a whole. Internet is based upon Internet technology, in particular World Wide Web (WWW), to build Information System within organization or enterprise to accomplish standardization and automation. Fundamentally, it means network computing environments which let the users share the information through the Internet and Web browsers.

### Characteristics of Intranet

The following are the important characteristics of the Intranet.

(*a*) It is an extended internet-private business networks located outside of the corporate firewall.

(*b*) It can be referred to an intranet that is partially accessible to authorized outsiders.

(*c*) It is a network that uses the internet to link businesses with others that share the common goals.

### E-MAIL

E-mail is an electronic message sent from one computer to another. We can send or receive personal and business-related messages with attachments, such as pictures or formatted documents. We can even send songs and computer programs.

* * * * *

# 14. SPORTS

## Important Cups & Trophies

### International

| | | | |
|---|---|---|---|
| • *American Cup* | : Yacht Racing | • *Walker Cup* | : Golf |
| • *Ashes* | : Cricket | • *Westchester Cup* | : Polo |
| • *Benson and Hedges* | : Cricket | • *Wightman Cup* | : Lawn Tennis |
| • *Canada Cup* | : Golf | • *World Cup* | : Cricket |
| • *Colombo Cup* | : Football | • *World Cup* | : Hockey |
| • *Corbitton Cup* | : Table Tennis (Women) | • *Reliance Cup* | : Cricket |
| • *Davis Cup* | : Lawn Tennis | • *Rothman's Trophy* | : Cricket |
| • *Derby* | : Horse Race | • *William's Cup* | : Basketball |
| • *Grand National* | : Horse Streple Chase Race | • *European Champions Cup* | : Football |
| • *Jules Rimet Trophy* | : World Soccer Cup | • *Eisenhower Cup* | : Golf |
| • *King's Cup* | : Air Races | • *Essande Champions Cup* | : Hockey |
| • *Merdeka Cup* | : Football | • *Rene Frank Trophy* | : Hockey |
| • *Ryder Cup* | : Golf | • *Grand Prix* | : Table Tennis |
| • *Swaythling Cup* | : Table Tennis (Men) | • *Edgbaston Cup* | : Lawn Tennis |
| • *Thomas Cup* | : Badminton | • *Grand Prix* | : Lawn Tennis |
| • *Uber Cup* | : Badminton (Women) | • *World Cup* | : Weightlifting |
| • *U. Thant Cup* | : Tennis | | |

### National

| | | | |
|---|---|---|---|
| • *Agarwal Cup* | : Badminton | • *C.K. Naidu Trophy* | : Cricket |
| • *Agha Khan Cup* | : Hockey | • *Chakola Gold Trophy* | : Football |
| • *All India Women's Guru Nanak Championship* | : Hockey | • *Divan Cup* | : Badminton |
| | | • *Deodhar Trophy* | : Cricket |
| | | • *Duleep Trophy* | : Cricket |
| • *Bandodkar Trophy* | : Football | • *D.C.M. Cup* | : Football |
| • *Bangalore Blues Challenge Cup* | : Basketball | • *Durand Cup* | : Football |
| | | • *Dhyan Chand Trophy* | : Hockey |
| • *Barna-Bellack Cup* | : Table Tennis | • *Dr. B.C. Roy Trophy* | : Football (Junior) |
| • *Beighton Cup* | : Hockey | • *Ezra Cup* | : Polo |
| • *Bombay Gold Cup* | : Hockey | • *F.A. Cup* | : Football |
| • *Burdwan Trophy* | : Weightlifting | • *G.D. Birla Trophy* | : Cricket |
| • *Charminar Trophy* | : Atheletics | • *Ghulam Ahmed Trophy* | : Cricket |
| • *Chadha Cup* | : Badminton | • *Gurmeet Trophy* | : Hockey |

- *Guru Nanak Cup* : Hockey
- *Gyanvati Devi Trophy* : Hockey
- *Holkar Trophy* : Bridge
- *Irani Trophy* : Cricket
- *I.F.A. Shield* : Football
- *Indira Gold Cup* : Hockey
- *Jawaharlal Challenge* : Air Racing
- *Jaswant Singh Trophy* : Best Services Sportsman
- *Kuppuswamy Naidu Trophy* : Hockey
- *Lady Rattan Tata Trophy* : Hockey
- *MCC Trophy* : Hockey
- *Moinuddaula Gold Cup* : Cricket
- *Murugappa Gold Cup* : Hockey
- *Modi Gold Cup* : Hockey
- *Narang Cup* : Badminton
- *Nehru Trophy* : Hockey
- *Nixan Gold Cup* : Football
- *Obaidullah Gold Cup* : Hockey
- *Prithi Singh Cup* : Polo
- *Rani Jhansi Trophy* : Cricket
- *Ranji Trophy* : Cricket
- *Rangaswami Cup* : Hockey
- *Ranjit Singh Gold Cup* : Hockey
- *Rajendra Prasad Cup* : Tennis
- *Ramanujan Trophy* : Table Tennis
- *Rene Frank Trophy* : Hockey
- *Radha Mohan Cup* : Polo
- *Raghbir Singh Memorial* : Football
- *Rohinton Baria Trophy* : Cricket
- *Rovers Cup* : Football
- *Sanjay Gold Cup* : Football
- *Santosh Trophy* : Football
- *Sir Ashutosh Mukherjee* : Football
- *Subroto Cup* : Football
- *Scindia Gold Cup* : Hockey
- *Sahni Trophy* : Hockey
- *Sheesh Mahal Trophy* : Cricket
- *Todd Memorial Trophy* : Football
- *Tommy Eman Gold Cup* : Hockey
- *Vittal Trophy* : Football
- *Vizzy Trophy* : Cricket
- *Vijay Merchant Trophy* : Cricket
- *Wellington Trophy* : Rowing
- *Wills Trophy* : Cricket

## Sports Measurements

- *Badminton Courts:* 44 ft. by 20 ft. (doubles) 44 ft. by 17 ft. (singles)
- *Boxing Ring:* 12 ft. by 28 ft. Sq.
- *Cricket Pitch:* 22 yards (distance)
- *Derby Course:* 1½ miles. (2.4 km)
- *Football Field:*
  (a) Length : 100 – 120 yards.
  Breadth: 50 – 56 yards.
  (b) Rugby : 100 yards by 75 yards
- *Hockey Ground:* 100 yards by 55 to 60 yards
- *Lawn Tennis Court:* 78 ft. by 36 ft. (double), 78 ft. by 28 ft. (single)
- *Marathon Race:* 26 miles, 385 yards
- *Polo Ground:* 300 yards by 200 yards (if boarded)
- *Golf:* Hole 4½ inches in diameter.

## Sports Terms

- **Badminton:** Mixed doubles; Deuce; Drop; Smash; Let; Foot work; Setting.
- **Base Ball:** Pitcher; Put out, Strike; Home; Bunt.
- **Billiards:** Cue; Jigger; Pot; Break; In Baulk; In Off; Cannons.
- **Boxing:** Upper cut; Round; Punch; Bout; Knock down; Hitting below the belt; Ring.
- **Bridge:** Finesse; Dummy; Revoke; Grand Slam; Little Slam; No Trump; Rubber.
- **Chess:** Bishop, Gambit; Checkmate; Stalemate.
- **Cricket:** L.B.W. *(leg before wicket)*; Creases, Popping-creases; Stumped; Bye; Leg-Bye; Googly; Hattrick; Maiden over; Drive; Bowling; Duck; Follow-on; No ball; Leg Break; Silly point; Cover point; Hit-wicket; Late-cut; Slip; Off-spinner; In-swing.

- **Football:** Off Side; Block; Drop-kick; Penalty-kick (or *goal kick*); Corner-kick; Free-kick; Dribble; Thrown-in; Foul.
- **Golf:** Boggy; Foursome; Stymic; Tee; Put; Hole; Niblic; Caddie; Links; The green; Bunker.
- **Hockey:** Carried; Short Corner; Bully; Sticks; Off side; Roll in; Striking Circle; Under-cutting; Dribble.
- **Horse racing:** Jockey; Punter.
- **Polo:** Bunker; Chukker; Mallet.
- **Tennis:** Back hand drive; Volley; Smash; Half-volley; Deuce; Service; Let; Grand Slam.

## Name of Playing Compound of Different Games

| *Name of Compound* | *Related Sports* | *Name of Compound* | *Related Sports* |
|---|---|---|---|
| Court | Lawn Tennis, Badminton, Netball, Hand ball, Volleyball, Squash, Kho-Kho, Kabaddi | Pool | Swimming |
| | | Alley | Bowling |
| | | Mat | Judo, Karate II |
| Diamond | Baseball | Arena | Horse Riding |
| | | Vellodrum | Cycling |
| Ring | Boxing, Skating, Wrestling, Circus, Riding display | Field | Polo, Football, Hockey |
| | | Track | Athletics |
| Course | Golf | Pitch | Cricket, Rugby |
| Board | Table Tennis | Rink | Ice Hockey |

## National Sports and Games of Some Countries

| | | | |
|---|---|---|---|
| Australia | Cricket | Spain | Bull Fighting |
| Canada | Ice Hockey | USA | Baseball |
| England | Cricket and Rugby Football | China | Table Tennis |
| Russia | Chess | Malaysia | Badminton |
| Scotland | Rugby Football | Pakistan | Hockey |

## Number of Players in each side (each team) in Some Games/Sports

| *Sports* | *No. of Players* | *Sports* | *No. of Players* |
|---|---|---|---|
| Badminton | 1 or 2 | Hockey | 11 |
| Baseball | 9 | Lacrosse | 12 |
| Basketball | 5 | Netball | 7 |
| Billiards (Snooker) | 1 | Polo Rugby | 4 |
| Boxing | 1 | Football (Rugby) | 15 |
| Bridge | 2 | Table Tennis | 1 or 2 |
| Chess | 1 | Lawn Tennis | 1 or 2 |
| Cricket | 11 | Volleyball | 6 |
| Croquest | 13 or 15 | Water Polo | 7 |
| Football (Soccer) | 11 | | |

## OLYMPIC GAMES

First of all these games were held by the Greeks in 776 B.C. on Mount Olympus in honour of the Greek God Zeus. In this way, the history of Olympic Games is about twenty eight hundred years old. These games continued to be held every four years until 394 A.D. When these games were stopped by a royal order of the emperor of Rome. The modern Olympic Games which started in Athens in 1896, are the result of the devotion and dedication of a French educator Baron Pierre de Coubertin and the first Olympic meet in the modern series was held in 1896 in Athens, the Capital of Greece. Since then, they are being held every four years except for breaks during world wars. The Olympic flag is white in colour with five coloured rings, each ring symbolic of a continent. Summer as well as winter Olympics are held in the same year.

### Olympic Games (Venues & Dates)

| *Year* | *Venue* | *Organising* | *Participating Countries* |
|---|---|---|---|
| 1896 | Athens | 6–15 April | 13 |
| 1900 | Paris | 20th May to 28th Oct. | 22 |
| 1904 | St. Louis | 1st July to 23rd Nov. | 13 |
| 1908 | London | 27th April to 31st Oct. | 22 |
| 1912 | Stockholm | 5th May to 22nd July | 28 |
| 1916 | Berlin | Cancelled due to World War | — |
| 1920 | Antwerp | 20th April to 12th Sept. | 29 |
| 1924 | Paris | 4th May to 27th July | 44 |
| 1928 | Amsterdam | 17th May to 12 Aug. | 46 |
| 1932 | Los Angeles | 30th July to 14th Aug. | 47 |
| 1936 | Berlin | 1st May to 16th Aug. | 49 |
| 1940 | Tokyo (Helsinki) | Cancelled due to Wold War | — |
| 1944 | London | Cancelled due to World War | — |
| 1948 | London | 29th July to 14th Aug. | 59 |
| 1952 | Helsinki | 19th July to 3rd Aug. | 69 |
| 1956 | Melbourne | 22nd November to 8th December | 71 |
| 1960 | Rome | 25th Aug. to 11th Sept. | 83 |
| 1964 | Tokyo | 10th to 24th October | 93 |
| 1968 | Mexico City | 12th to 27th October | 112 |
| 1972 | Munich | 26th August to 10 September | 122 |
| 1976 | Montreal | 17th July to 1st Sep- | 88 |
| 1980 | Moscow | 19th July to 3rd Aug. | 81 |
| 1984 | Los Angeles | 28th July to 12th Aug. | 140 |
| 1988 | Seoul | 17th Sept. to 2nd Oct. | 160 |
| 1992 | Barcelona | 25th July to 9th Aug. | 170 |
| 1996 | Atlanta | 19th July to 4th Aug. | 197 |
| 2000 | Sydney | 15th Sept. to 1st Oct. | 199 |
| 2004 | Athens | 14th to 29th August | 202 |
| 2008 | Beijing | 8th to 24th August | 204 |
| 2012 | London | 27th July to 12 August | 204 |
| 2016 | Rio de Janeiro | 5th to 21st August | 207 |
| 2020 | Tokyo | 23rd July to 8th August 2021 | 206 |

**Note:** Games not held in 1916, 1940, and 1944.

## ASIAN GAMES

After the Second World War, most of the Asian Countries gained independence. On the lines of Olympic Games, Asian Games were planned every four years. India hosted the first Asian Games in 1951.

### Asian Games: An Overview

| *Year* | *Venues* | *Participating Countries* | *No. of Games* | *First Position* |
|---|---|---|---|---|
| 1951 | New Delhi | 11 | 6 | Japan |
| 1954 | Manila | 18 | 7 | Japan |
| 1958 | Tokyo | 20 | 13 | Japan |
| 1962 | Jakarta | 16 | 13 | Japan |
| 1966 | Bangkok | 18 | 14 | Japan |
| 1970 | Bangkok | 18 | 13 | Japan |
| 1974 | Teheran | 25 | 16 | Japan |
| 1978 | Bangkok | 25 | 19 | Japan |
| 1982 | New Delhi | 33 | 21 | China |
| 1986 | Seoul | 34 | 25 | China |
| 1990 | Beijing | 37 | 27 | China |
| 1994 | Hiroshima | 42 | 34 | China |
| 1998 | Bangkok | 41 | 36 | China |
| 2002 | Busan | 44 | 38 | China |
| 2006 | Doha | 46 | 43 | China |
| 2010 | Guangzhou | 45 | 42 | China |
| 2014 | Incheon | 45 | 36 | China |
| 2018 | Jakarta | 45 | 40 | China |
| 2022 | Hangzhou (Held in 2023) | 45 | 40 | China |

# COMMONWEALTH GAMES

The Commonwealth Games are held every four years, in the year in which Asian Games are held. All the Commonwealth Countries (former colonies of Britain) can take part in it. The first Commonwealth Games were held in 1930 at Hamilton (Canada).

## Venues of Commonwealth Games

| Venues | Year | CGA | Sports | Venues | Year | CGA | Sports |
|---|---|---|---|---|---|---|---|
| Hamilton, (Canada) | 1930 | 11 | 6 | Brisbane, (Australia) | 1982 | 47 | 10 |
| London, (U.K.) | 1934 | 16 | 6 | Edinburgh, (U.K.) | 1986 | 26 | 10 |
| Sydney, (Australia) | 1938 | 15 | 7 | Auckland, (New Zealand) | 1990 | 55 | 10 |
| Auckland, (New Zealand) | 1950 | 12 | 7 | Victoria, (Canada) | 1994 | 64 | |
| Vancouver, (Canada) | 1954 | 24 | 9 | Kuala Lumpur, (Malaysia) | 1998 | 70 | 16 |
| Cardiff, (U.K.) | 1958 | 35 | 9 | Manchester, (U.K.) | 2002 | 72 | 17 |
| Perth, (Australia) | 1962 | 35 | 9 | Melbourne, (Australia) | 2006 | 71 | 16 |
| Jamaica, (West Indies) | 1966 | 34 | 9 | Delhi, (India) | 2010 | 71 | 17 |
| Edinburgh, (U.K.) | 1970 | 42 | 9 | Glasgow, (Scotland) | 2014 | 71 | 18 |
| Christchurch, (New Zealand) | 1974 | 39 | 9 | Gold Coast (Aus.) | 2018 | 71 | 19 |
| Edmonton, (Canada) | 1978 | 48 | 10 | Birmingham (U.K.) | 2022 | 72 | 19 |

## World Cup Football

| Year | Winner | Runners-Up | Year | Winner | Runners-Up |
|---|---|---|---|---|---|
| 1930 | Uruguay | Argentina | 1982 | Italy | W. Germany |
| 1934 | Italy | Czechoslovakia | 1986 | Argentina | W. Germany |
| 1938 | Italy | Hungary | 1990 | W. Germany | Argentina |
| 1950 | Uruguay | Brazil | 1994 | Brazil | Italy |
| 1954 | West Germany | Hungary | 1998 | France | Brazil |
| 1958 | Brazil | Sweden | 2002 | Brazil | Germany |
| 1962 | Brazil | Czechoslovakia | 2006 | Italy | France |
| 1966 | England | West Germany | 2010 | Spain | Netherlands |
| 1970 | Brazil | Italy | 2014 | Germany | Argentina |
| 1974 | W. Germany | Poland | 2018 | France | Croatia |
| 1978 | Argentina | Holland | 2022 | Argentina | France |

## World Cup Cricket

| Year | Venue | Winner/Runner | Year | Venue | Winner/Runner |
|---|---|---|---|---|---|
| 1975 | U.K. | West Indies beat Australia | 2003 | South Africa | Australia beat India |
| 1979 | U.K. | West Indies beat England | 2007 | West Indies | Australia beat Sri Lanka |
| 1983 | U.K. | India beat West Indies | 2011 | India, Sri Lanka, Bangladesh | India beat Sri Lanka |
| 1987 | India & Pakistan | Australia beat England | 2015 | Australia, New Zealand | Australia beat New Zealand |
| 1992 | Australia | Pakistan beat England | 2019 | England | England beat New Zealand |
| 1996 | India, Pakistan & Sri Lanka | Sri Lanka beat Australia | 2023 | India | Australia beat India |
| 1999 | U.K. | Australia beat Pakistan | | | |

* * * * *

# 15. National/ International Days

**JANUARY**

| | |
|---|---|
| **Infant Protection Day** | : January 7 |
| **African National Congress Foundation Day** | : January 8 |
| **NRI Day (India)** | : January 9 |
| **World Laughter Day** | : January 10 |
| **National Youth Day (India)** | : January 12 |
| **Army Day (India)** | : January 15 |
| **Indian Tourism Day** | : January 25 |
| **Republic Day (India); International Customs Day** | : January 26 |
| **Martyrs' Day (India); World Leprosy Eradication Day** | : January 30 |

**FEBRUARY**

| | |
|---|---|
| **World Wetlands Day** | : February 2 |
| **World Marriage Day** | : Second Sunday of February |
| **Valentine Day (World)** | : February 14 |
| **Mother Tongue Day (World)** | : February 21 |
| **National Science Day (India)** | : February 28 |

**MARCH**

| | |
|---|---|
| **International Women's Day;** | : March 8 |
| **World Disabled Day : World Consumer Rights Day** | : March 15 |
| **World Forestry Day; International Day for Elimination of Racial Discrimination** | : March 21 |
| **World Day for Water** | : March 22 |
| **World Meteorological Day** | : March 23 |
| **World TB Day** | : March 24 |

**APRIL**

| | |
|---|---|
| **National Maritime Day (India)** | : April 5 |
| **World Health Day** | : April 7 |
| **World Aviation and Cosmonautics Day** | : April 12 |
| **World Haemophilia Day** | : April 17 |
| **World Heritage Day,** | : April 18 |
| **Earth Day (World)** | : April 22 |
| **World Book and Copyright Day** | : April 23 |

**MAY**

| | |
|---|---|
| **Workers' Day (International Labour Day)** | : May 1 |
| **Press Freedom Day; World Asthma Day** | : May 3 |
| **World Red Cross Day** | : May 8 |
| **World Mother's Day (2nd Sunday of May)** | : May 8 |
| **World Thalassaemia Day** | : May 9 |
| **National Technology Day** | : May 11 |
| **International Nurses Day** | : May 12 |
| **International Day of the Family** | : May 15 |
| **World Telecommunication Day** | : May 17 |
| **Anti-Terrorism Day** | : May 21 |
| **Commonwealth Day** | : May 24 |
| **Anti-Tobacco Day** | : May 31 |

**JUNE**

| | |
|---|---|
| **International Day of Innocent Children Victims of Aggression** | : June 4 |
| **World Environment Day** | : June 5 |
| **Father's Day (3rd Sunday of June)** | : June 19 |
| **International Yoga Day** | : June 21 |
| **International Day Against Drug Abuse & Illicit Trafficking** | : June 26 |

## JULY

Doctors' Day : July 1
American Independence Day : July 4
World Zoonosis Day : July 6
World Population Day : July 11

## AUGUST

World Breast Feeding Week : August 1-7
International Friendship Day : August 3
Hiroshima Day : August 6
World Senior Citizen's Day : August 8
Quit India Day; Nagasaki Day : August 9
Indian Independence Day : August 15
International Day of the World's Indigenous People : August 18
Sadbhavna Divas (India) : August 20
National Sports Day (India) : August 29

## SEPTEMBER

Teachers' Day : September 5
World (International) Literacy Day : September 8
Hindi Day (India) : September 14
All India Flag Day : September 15
World Ozone Day : September 16
Alzheimer's Day (World) : September 21
Day for Peace & Non-Violence (UN) : September 21
Rose Day (Welfare of Cancer Patients) World Heart Day : September 22
International Tiger Day : September 25
World Tourism Day : September 27

## OCTOBER

International Day for the Elderly People : October 1
Gandhi Jayanti, International Day of Non-Violence : October 2
World Animal Day : October 2
World Vegetarian Day : October 2
World Habitat Day : October 3
World Animal Welfare Day : October 4
World Post Office Day : October 9
National Post Day (India) : October 10
World Allergy Awareness Day : October 11
UN International Day for Natural Disaster Reduction : October 13
World Standards Day : October 14
World Food Day : October 16
International Day for the Eradication of Poverty : October 17
UN Day : October 24
World Development Information Day : October 24
Infants Day : October 27
World Thrift Day : October 30
National Integration Day (India) : October 31

## NOVEMBER

Legal Services Day : November 9
Children's Day (India) : November 14
Diabetes Day : November 14
National Epilepsy Day : November 17

## DECEMBER

World AIDS Day : December 1
World Disabled Day : December 3
International Volunteer Develompent Day : December 5
Armed Forces Flag Day (India) : December 7
Human Rights Day (World) : December 10
National Energy Conservation Day : December 14
Farmer's Day : December 23

* * * * *

# MULTIPLE CHOICE QUESTIONS

**1.** The part of the Sun, which is visible during eclipses only, is known as
A. photosphere
B. chromosphere
C. corona
D. all the parts are visible with naked eye

**2.** Sphygmomanometer is used for
A. measuring the brain pulse of a patient
B. measuring the systolic and diastolic blood pressures of man
C. measuring the amount of blood in a human body
D. measuring the haemoglobin count in a human body

**3.** The most abundant gas in air is
A. nitrogen B. hydrogen
C. oxygen D. ozone

**4.** The most commonly found acid in nature is
A. hydrochloric acid
B. sulphuric acid
C. lactic acid
D. acetic acid

**5.** This bomb is used to destroy living beings but would not damage the buildings and other property
A. napalm bomb
B. neutron bomb
C. hydrogen bomb
D. None of the above

**6.** Electrical energy is measured in terms of units which are also termed as
A. KW B. KWH
C. WH D. KVAR

**7.** In cold countries, the radiator water of cars is mixed with glycerol. This is done to
A. increase the specific heat of water
B. reduce the freezing point of water
C. improve the engine efficiency
D. glycerol is not added in radiator water

**8.** If the Richter scale shows a value of 7.2, then the seismograph indicates
A. an earthquake of low intensity
B. an earthquake of very high intensity
C. an earthquake of moderate intensity
D. either A or C

**9.** The theory of origin of species is based primarily on
A. the process of biological evolution
B. the process of natural selection
C. the evolution of life from the oceans
D. the evolution of man from apes

**10.** Common coal used in our households is
A. Anthracite B. Bituminous coal
C. Lignite D. All of the above

**11.** Some recent findings on moon, which point out towards the possibility of settlement of man on moon, include
A. nil atmospheric gases
B. ice reserves on the poles
C. micro-organisms
D. None of the above

**12.** Viagra is a medicine for
A. treatment of AIDS
B. treatment of female fertility
C. treatment of male impotency
D. treatment of Lukaemia

**13.** Rickets is a disease which is caused by the deficiency of
A. Vitamin A B. Riboflavin
C. Vitamin C D. Vitamin D

**14.** When a ship enters waters of the sea from a river, then its level
A. rises as the sea water is saline and hence bouyancy force is more

B. decreases as ocean is a large mass of water
C. remains the same as water is the same for the river and the sea
D. None of the above

**15.** The major constituent of pearl is
A. calcium carbonate
B. calcium oxide and ammonium chloride
C. organic mass
D. calcium carbonate and silica

**16.** A healthy person needs ..... calories per day.
A. 2200 B. 2400
C. 2500 D. 1800

**17.** The value of one (marine) Naut is
A. 1951 metre per hour
B. 1852 metre per hour
C. 2305 metre per hour
D. 1860 metre per hour

**18.** Acid and base combine to form
A. salt and nitrogen
B. nitrogen and oxygen
C. salt and water
D. acid and alkali

**19.** Cellulose could be obtained from
A. wood and cotton B. silk and cotton
C. paper and silk D. wood and silk

**20.** ELISA test is done for the detection of
A. cancer B. AIDS
C. diabetes D. None of the above

**21.** Triple Antigen, prevents
A. small pox, malaria, whooping cough
B. tetanus, diphtheria, small pox
C. whooping cough, tetanus, polio
D. diphtheria, tetanus, whooping cough

**22.** A freely falling body
A. would fall towards the surface of the earth
B. would have no weight
C. would have one half of its original weight
D. None of the above

**23.** If the motor neurons of the spinal cord of a child are damaged, then he would develop the following disease.
A. Rickets B. Polio
C. Diphtheria D. Jaundice

**24.** Which one of the following is not a part of the balanced diet?
A. Vitamins B. Carbohydrate
C. Proteins D. Alcohol

**25.** Which statement is not correct in connection with human physiology?
A. The length of the small intestine is 7 metres and its diameter is 2.5 cm.
B. There are 639 muscles in a human body
C. An infant breathes 45 times per minute whereas a six year old child breathes 25 times per minute
D. The weight of the adult human brain is nearly 700 gms

**26.** The bottles of beer are not kept in the deep freezer because
A. beer is an alcohol which could burst under conditions of low temperature
B. alcohol could damage the deep freezer due to its corrosive action if the bottles break accidently
C. water content in beer gets converted into ice which expends (after change of state from water to ice) and this could lead to bursting of beer bottles
D. the low temperature could degrade the beer and hence, it may not good remain for consumption

**27.** Rocket works on the basis of
A. principle of conservation of momentum
B. principle of relativity
C. principle of conservation of mass
D. principle of conservation of energy

**28.** Which one of the following groups is more closely related from the viewpoint of taxonomy?
A. silverfish, starfish, cuttlefish
B. earthworm, seahorse, hookworm
C. housefly, dragonfly, butterfly
D. None of the above

**29.** Red blood corpuscles are produced in
A. liver B. spleen
C. bone marrow D. kidneys

**30.** The disease for which the first oral drug has been developed for treatment.
A. Cancer B. Pneumonid
C. Small pox D. Plauge

**31.** E-comm is a short form of
A. Engineering Commercial
B. Electronic Commercial
C. Electronic Commerce
D. None of the above

**32.** High AC voltages are used for transmitting electric power because
A. at high voltages, current is low and hence, losses are low
B. the transmission of power is quicker
C. the high voltages a consume lesser materials for transmission
D. None of the above

**33.** There is a hole in the boat through which, water is seeping into the boat. Just before the boat capsizes
A. water level would decrease
B. water level would increase
C. water level would remain the same
D. None of the above

**34.** During which month, the rate of rotation of the earth on its axis is the fastest?
A. December
B. May
C. the rate of rotation is fixed
D. It is fastest when the earth is closest to the Sun.

**35.** The time taken by the Sun rays to reach the earth is
A. 9 minutes B. 10 minutes
C. 7 minutes D. 8 minutes

**36.** The outer planets are
A. Moon, Earth, Mercury, Venus
B. Jupiter, Saturn, Uranus, Earth, Mars
C. Jupiter, Uranus, Saturn, Neptune
D. None of the above

**37.** According to the astrophysicists
A. the universe is mobile and expanding
B. the universe is heading for a collision with another universe
C. the universe is stationary
D. the doomsday of universe is near due to the formation of many new black holes

**38.** Which is popular as the White City?
A. New York B. Belgrade
C. Bangalore D. Bab-el-mandab

**39.** The national currency of Haiti is
A. Rupiah B. Gourde
C. Quetzal D. Dong

**40.** Which one is not a news agency of India?
A. UNI
B. PTI
C. Hindustan Samachar
D. Reuters

**41.** The abundant element of the earth's atmosphere is:
A. Oxygen B. nitrogen
C. hydrogen D. $CO_2$

**42.** The first talking movie of India was ..... and the first silent movie of India was .....
A. Aan, Aawara
B. Raja Harish Chandra, Alamara
C. Alamara, Raja Harish Chandra
D. Purana Mandir, Raja Harish Chandra

**43.** Hair becomes grey because
A. rays of the Sun force it to become grey
B. the quantity of melanin is reduced in human body with growing age
C. there is a lack of vitamins in the body due to growing age
D. None of the above

**44.** Salaries of Supreme Court judges are drawn from:
A. Law Ministry Grants
B. Consolidated Fund of India
C. Home Ministry Grants
D. Parliamentary Grants

**45.** The term "Paper-gold" is associated with
A. deficit budgeting
B. loans from the World Bank
C. Special Drawing Rights (SDRs) from the IMF
D. None of the above

**46.** TRAI refers to
A. Terresteral Remote Sensing Authority of India
B. Telecommunication Research Authority of India
C. Transport Regulatory Authority of India
D. Telecom Regulatory Authority of India

**47.** NSDL is an organisation in India which
A. provides security to depositors
B. accepts deposits from recognised bodies

C. provides data security for on-line computer systems
D. None of the above

**48.** The enzyme pepsin converts
A. proteins into peptones
B. fats to amino acids
C. carbohydrates to sugars
D. proteins to amino acids

**49.** Who among the following is not a winner of the PVC?
A. Bana Singh
B. Nirmal Jeet Singh Sekhon
C. Somnath Sharma
D. Shanti Swaroop Rana

**50.** Which one of the following pairs is not correct?
A. Narmada – Betul district
B. Krishna – near Mahabaleshwar
C. Chambal – near Mhow
D. Godavari – Nashik district

**51.** The Japanese art of flower arrangement is known as
A. Bonsai
B. Ongami
C. Ikebota
D. None of the above

**52.** The meaning of the Latin word *Vive Rex* is
A. Long live the king!
B. Let the Nation Live
C. A middle course
D. Nothing wrong here

**53.** The permanent station of India in Antarctica is known as
A. *Vikalp*
B. Antarctica India Station
C. *Maitri*
D. *Dakshin Yamunotri*

**54.** A man dies due to electrocution because
A. electric current passes through his body to earth which leads to sudden contraction and expansion of muscles (including heart muscles) and this, alongwith development of heat in the body, leads to heart failure.
B. there is no resistance offered by the body
C. the body allows the current to flow through the blood which cannot circulate any longer
D. None of the above

**55.** "Blue Dwarfs" are
A. members of the Russian circus
B. warriors of Mongolia
C. young stars of the universe
D. naval officers in the high seas

**56.** What is a fly leaf?
A. thin paper sheet for making packaging material
B. a blank page at the beginning or end of a book
C. a marker in a book
D. a sheet of paper next to the main title of the book

**57.** Who is associated with the theory of inheritance of acquired characters?
A. Spencer
B. Mandeleev
C. Lamarck
D. All of the above

**58.** Ligaments and tendons in the body are made up of
A. skeletal tissue
B. muscular tissue
C. connective tissue
D. epithelial tissue

**59.** A cell membrane is
A. completely permeable
B. impermeable
C. semi-permeable
D. None of the above

**60.** The tenure of the non-permanent members of the UN Security Council is
A. one year
B. three years
C. two years
D. there is no fixed tenure

**61.** Why proper earthing is necessary?
A. It reduces the consumption of electricity
B. It allows the current to flow through the earth wire and into the earth, thus protecting the person
C. It allows the appliance to operate efficiently
D. None of the above

**62.** Which one of the following items has not been included in the minimum needs programme?
A. unemployment allowance
B. rural water supply
C. rural electrification
D. adult education

**63.** This is not the principle organ of digestion and absorption in the human body.
A. small intestine B. stomach
C. large intestine D. Both A and B

**64.** Which are the two stars which appear as morning stars in the Eastern sky and evening stars in the Western sky?
A. Jupiter and Mars
B. Mars and Venus
C. Saturn and Mercury
D. Mercury and Venus

**65.** Which planet rotates on its axis from East to West?
A. Mercury B. Jupiter
C. Earth D. Venus

**66.** The chemical compound present in the stone of human kidney is
A. calcium phosphate
B. calcium carbonate
C. silica
D. calcium oxalate

**67.** Which one of the following diseases would be caused by bacterial infection?
A. tetanus B. rabies
C. cancer D. malaria

**68.** India On-line Limited is
A. an advertising agency
B. a reservation office
C. an information service
D. an internet services provider

**69.** CTBT is related to
A. economic sanctions imposed by the USA on India
B. the codename of Pokharan-II blasts
C. the nuclear test ban treaty which India is being forced to adhere to
D. codename of Pakistani nuclear arsenal

**70.** The disagreement between Lok Sabha and Rajya Sabha is solved by:
A. setting up Joint Select Committee
B. dissolving Lok Sabha
C. setting up adjudication committee
D. calling a joint session

**71.** The national anthem was written by ..... and was translated into English by .....
A. Bankim Chandra Chatterji, Aurobindo Ghosh
B. Rabindra Nath Tagore, Aurobindo Ghosh
C. Bankim Chandra Chatterji, Rabindra Nath Tagore
D. the national anthem was originally written in English and was translated later

**72.** The tear in human body is a solution of :
A. Sodium hydroxide and sodium chloride
B. Calcium bicarbonate and sodium chloride
C. Magnesium bicarbonate and sodium hydroxide
D. Sodium bicarbonate and Magnesium chloride

**73.** The drug seroxat is
A. a new medicine for treating the lepers.
B. a new medicine developed by British scientists and is used for the treatment of shyness and social phobia
C. is anti-AIDS therapy developed by France
D. is an antacid developed in India under guidance of WHO

**74.** What is "Bermuda Triangle" sometimes referred to as the "Grakeyard of ships", located?
A. in the South Pacific ocean
B. in the North Atlantic ocean
C. in the Indian ocean
D. in the Arctic ocean

**75.** The theory propounded by Nobel laurate Professor Amartya Sen–is commonly known as
A. The Famine Economics
B. The Theory of Economic Divide
C. The Amartya Sen Shift
D. The Amartya Sen Divide

**76.** Which is known as the Electronics City of India?
A. Tumkoor B. Secunderabad
C. Bhopal D. None of the above

**77.** The main objective behind the creation of concept of *Navratnas* in the public sector was

A. to increase the control of the PSUs over economy
B. to boost local manufacturing and exports in the core sectors
C. to improve the functional autonomy
D. to improve their image and efficiency by giving them high status

**78.** The North American seaport on the Pacific side is
A. Baltimore B. Boston
C. New York D. Seattle

**79.** The old name of Harare was
A. Sam B. Rhodesia
C. Salisbury D. Batavia

**80.** The famous Prince of Wales Museum is located in
A. Mumbai B. Kolkata
C. Vadodara D. Bangalore

**81.** Who invented Atom Bomb (Uranium Fission)?
A. A W Haffmann
B. Otto Hahn
C. A Einstein
D. None of the above

**82.** The first ever woman to go into space was
A. Kalpana Chawla
B. Valentina Tereshkova
C. Mary Pierce
D. None of the above

**83.** The highest mountain peak in India is
A. K-2 B. Everest
C. Kanchanjunga D. Makalu-I

**84.** The "Garden City" of England is
A. Portsmouth B. Manchester
C. Kent D. Warwickshire

**85.** *Habeas Corpus* is
A. an order of the International Court of Justice
B. a type of writ issued by a High Court or Supreme Court against illegal detention of a person.
C. the petition of a lawyer in the Supreme Court on behalf of his client for bail against the orders of any other court in India
D. None of the above

**86.** If impeachment motion is passed by the American Senate against the US President, he would have to
A. leave office and all his assets created by him during Presidency
B. leave office, lose his pensions, security cover and all those benefits that are accorded to a retired US President
C. jailed for five years and will not get any benefits.
D. retire honourably with all his benefits, compensations, assets and pensions remaining intact

**87.** Who appoints the non-permanent members of the UN Security Council?
A. the permanent members
B. the General Assembly
C. the International Court of Justice
D. None of the above

**88.** The Preamble of the Constitution was amended by:
A. 1st amendment B. 26th amendment
C. 42nd amendment D. 44th amendment

**89.** NNP is equal to
A. GNP + Depreciation
B. GNP – Depreciation
C. GNP + Exports
D. GNP – Exports

**90.** The official airline of Australia is
A. SIA B. Lufthansa
C. Modiluft D. None of the above

**91.** Which one of the following types of coal contains a higher percentage of carbon than the rest?
A. Bituminous Coal B. Lignite
C. Anthracite D. Peat

**92.** Ten Commandments were revealed by God to:
A. Abraham B. Moses
C. Jesus D. Peter

**93.** Kalinga in older days, is now known as:
A. Odisha B. Kohima
C. Karnataka D. Maharashtra

**94.** Bihu festival is celebrated in:
A. Gujarat B. Assam
C. Bihar D. West Bengal

**95.** Milk is an example of

A. gel B. emulsion

C. suspension D. mixture

**96.** The President can dissolve the Lok Sabha before expiry of its term, on the advice of:

A. Prime Minister

B. Speaker

C. Vice-President

D. Election Commissioner

**97.** In a landmark judgement, the Allahabad High Court ruled that

A. Capital Sentence is not to be imposed upon the rapists

B. pension is the fundamental right of the government employees

C. the Supreme Court should not be bothered for cases of financial compensation

D. None of the above

**98.** Tughlaq dynasty occupied Delhi throne after decline of:

A. Suri dynasty B. Slave dynasty

C. Lodhi dynasty D. Khilji dynasty

**99.** Governors of states are:

A. appointed by Chief Ministers

B. appointed by the President

C. elected by members of Legislative Assembly

D. elected by people

**100.** The partition of Bengal was carried out by:

A. Lord Curzon B. Lord Minto

C. Lord Canning D. Lord Ripon

**101.** The Air Force Day falls on

A. October 10 B. October 9

C. September 5 D. October 8

**102.** MAD stands for

A. Most Active Disease

B. Mica Aluminium Duo

C. Mutually Assured Death

D. Mutually Assured Destruction

**103.** "Disguised Unemployment" means

A. more persons employed for a job that only a few could accomplish

B. people without any technical jobs

C. woman without jobs in rural areas

D. employment of children in factories

**104.** In India, an active volcano is situated at

A. Lakshadweep

B. Chhotanagpur Plateau

C. Andaman and Nicobar

D. Malawa Plateau

**105.** The first country to establish trade relationships with India was

A. England B. France

C. Holland D. Portugal

**106.** Which has the highest share of electrical power generation in India?

A. thermal power

B. nuclear power

C. hydro-power

D. naphtha-based and gas-based power

**107.** The great ocean liner, known to be the best and luxurious during her times, sank in the year

A. 1902 B. 1912

C. 1908 D. 1889

**108.** Who among the following is known as the Indian Napoleon?

A. Chandra Gupta Maurya

B. Bindusar

C. Samudra Gupta

D. Harshvardhana

**109.** Time gap between two sessions of Parliament cannot exceed:

A. 3 months B. 6 months

C. 1 year D. no fixed gap

**110.** In which state, Panchayati Raj was introduced for the first time?

A. Bihar

B. Punjab

C. Rajasthan

D. Andhra Pradesh

**111.** Which one is not a national duty?

A. Respect the Constitution

B. Respect the President

C. Defend the country

D. Protect natural environment

**112.** Treaty of Seringapatam was signed between:

A. Tipu Sultan and Nawab of Hyderabad

B. Tipu Sultan and English

C. Tipu Sultan & Rani of Jhansi

D. Tipu Sultan and French

**113.** NHRC stands for
A. National Hydro Research Committee
B. National Handicapped Rahabilitation Council
C. National Human Rights Commission
D. None of the above

**114.** "Water water everywhere but not a drop to drink" who stated these lines in a poem?
A. John Milton
B. Samuel Taylor Coleridge
C. Lord Byron
D. P.B. Shelley

**115.** Rabindranath Tagore gave up his knighthood after:
A. Jallianwala Bagh Tragedy
B. Introduction of separate electorates
C. Bengal faminine
D. Bengal Partition

**116.** Which country is known as the land of golden wool?
A. India B. Turkiye
C. Australia D. Myanmar

**117.** BIFR stands for
A. Bilateral and International Foreign Regulation
B. Board of Industrial Financial Resurrection
C. Board of Industrial and Financial Reconstruction
D. None of the above

**118.** Pinaca is a
A. drug for curing AIDS
B. multi-barrel rocket system
C. fighter aircraft developed by HAL
D. codename of the nuclear test operation carried out on May 11, 1998

**119.** Vice-President is ex-officio:
A. Member of Rajya Sabha
B. Chairman of Rajya Sabha
C. Member of Lok Sabha
D. Speaker of Lok Sabha

**120.** Vitamin C is not available in this food in sufficiently large quantities.
A. lemon B. tomato
C. cod liver oil D. fresh fruits

**121.** This book was not written in a jail
A. *Glimpses of World History* – J L Nehru
B. *The Bible* (German) – Martin Luther
C. *Les Miserables* – Victor Hugo
D. *Yama* – Mahadevi Verma

**122.** Who among the following can be removed from office through impeachment by Parliament?
A. Speaker of Lok Sabha
B. Prime Minister
C. President of India
D. Vice-President of India

**123.** The following is not the function of the liver.
A. to store excesssive sugar in the form of glycogen
B. the produce an antidote for neutralising poison
C. to manufacture red blood corpuscles
D. to purify the blood through bile

**124.** A fascist is a person whose views are extremely
A. left-winged B. rational
C. right-winged D. liberal

**125.** The famous mathematician and a professor of Astronomy designed this building in London
A. Westminister Abbey
B. St Paul's Cathedral
C. Stock Exchange
D. Tower of London

**126.** Which one of the following sounds cannot be heard by a human ear?
A. 30,000 vibrations per second
B. 10,000 vibrations per second
C. 1,000 vibrations per second
D. 300 vibrations per second

**127.** A weather balloon may not be inflated completely on the ground because
A. it cannot withstand the atmospheric pressure if inflated fully
B. if the balloon is inflated fully on ground, fuel consumption would be higher
C. the air inside the balloon expands as it rises and hence, the balloon could get burst
D. None of the above

**128.** Which one of the following vitamins is stored in the liver?
A. Vitamin C

B. Vitamin $B_{12}$
C. Vitamin A
D. Vitamin K and Vitamin A

**129.** All of the following are plant products except
A. silk B. cork
C. hemp D. linen

**130.** Which one of the following organs in the human body is known as "Adam's Apple"?
A. thyroid B. liver
C. thymus D. adrenal

**131.** Insecticides or medicines could be harmful
A. to the insects and weeds as they kill them instantaneously upon consumption
B. to the habitat as the environment could become polluted due to excessive usage of chemicals in our crop management processes
C. to the human beings and animals who consume the food adulterated by the insecticides and weedicides
D. to the transporters and movers of the crops who could inhale noxious fumes of insecticides and weedicides

**132.** Name the assassin of John Lennon
A. Art Buchwald
B. Lee Oswald
C. Mark David Chapman
D. None of the above

**133.** Which one of the following is not a sprinter?
A. Marion Jones
B. Florence Griffith Joyner
C. Ben Johnson
D. Susie O' Neill

**134.** Which of the following is called the "Gateway to the Pacific"?
A. Suez Canal
B. Bering Sea
C. Panama Canal
D. Gulf of Alaska

**135.** Which one of the following statements is true regarding the treaty on banning the landmines?
A. the USA does not want to sign the CTBT
B. the treaty was kept open for signatures in Ottawa in December, 1997.
C. India has already signed it
D. A and B are true

**136.** The General Assembly of the UNO has declined to reduce the budgetary contribution of this country as she has refused to pay her pending arrears.
A. the UK B. Iraq
C. Japan D. the USA

**137.** The famous Gandhian, who was also known as the "Frontier Gandhi," is
A. Liaqat Ali Khan
B. Yusuf Khan
C. Khan Abdul Ghaffar Khan
D. Abdul Wali Khan

**138.** Which one of the following is an alloy?
A. copper B. lanthanum
C. bronze D. uranium

**139.** World Environment Day is celebrated on
A. June 4 B. June 5
C. June 7 D. March 5

**140.** This country is the largest producer of cotton in the world.
A. India B. China
C. Egypt D. the USA

**141.** Which tax can be levied by Gram Panchayat?
A. Sales Tax B. Custom Duty
C. Tax on local fairs D. Land Revenue

**142.** The temples of Khajuraho were built by
A. Chalukyas B. Pallavas
C. Rashtrakutas D. Chandelas

**143.** National Remote Sensing Agency (NRSA) is located at:
A. Hyderabad
B. Bangalore
C. Thiruvananthapuram
D. Gadanki, near Tirupati

**144.** The clones for .... and .... have been developed.
A. man, cow B. crow, sheep
C. rat, cat D. sheep, rat

**145.** AWWA stands for
A. All Women Welfare Association
B. Army Wives Welfare Association
C. Airport Weather and Welfare Authority
D. None of the above

**146.** The popular book *The Gift of Time* by Jonathan Schell, deals with

A. the lewid affair of Bill Clinton and Monica Lewinsky
B. the elimination of nuclear weapons from the world
C. Indo-US relationships
D. the deteriorating environment in industrial America

**147.** How can a person move on a hard icy surface?
A. he should use roller skates
B. he should hop, sneeze, jump and step in the direction which is opposite to the direction of his required movement
C. he should hop, sneeze, jump and step in the direction in which the movement is required
D. he should skid on his knees and hands

**148.** Which states are deriving benefits from the Tungbhadra project?
A. Tamil Nadu, Karnataka, Kerala
B. Tamil Nadu only
C. Andhra Pradesh and Tamil Nadu
D. Tamil Nadu, Andhra Pradesh, Karnataka

**149.** Where did Mahatma Buddha's 'Mahaparinirvan' take place?
A. Lumbani B. Kushinagar
C. Bodh Gaya D. Kapilavastu

**150.** Pyroclastics are
A. non-toxic gases
B. lava flows
C. fragments of hot rock and spattering lava
D. pollutant chemicals from a leather factory

**151.** Which one of the following is not a sedimentary rock?
A. slate B. limestone
C. clay D. sandstone

**152.** Oketa is
A. used to define human-induced climatic changes
B. used to describe increasing drought periods of high magnitudes
C. a unit to describe the prevailing cloudiness
D. None of the above

**153.** The following state produces the maximum quantities (85 per cent) of raw silk in India
A. Kerala
B. Jammu and Kashmir
C. Karnataka
D. Tamil Nadu

**154.** Salal Hydro Electric Project is situated on the river
A. Beas B. Jhelum
C. Chenab D. Sutlej

**155.** Which is the largest island sea in the world?
A. Caribbean Sea B. Mediterranean Sea
C. Red Sea D. Beaufort Sea

**156.** What is the name of the bell used at the Lloyds in London?
A. The Great Bell B. The Charmer
C. The Tower Bell D. Lutine

**157.** What are "The Hagiographs?"
A. These are the poems written by Lord Byron
B. These are the holy writings of Jewish scriptures
C. These are the geographical lines representing same rainfall levels
D. None of the above

**158.** Which one of the following forms would provide the lowest protection?
A. Patent B. Trademark
C. Copyright D. Logo

**159.** Ladakh become a Union Territory in:
A. 2019 B. 2018
C. 2017 D. 2016

**160.** What does the 17th Parallel line separate?
A. South and North America
B. North and South Korea
C. South and North Yemen
D. South and North Vietnam

**161.** Operation Flood-II, the prestigious milk products revolution of India, was initiated on
A. October 1, 1979 B. October 2, 1979
C. January 26, 1979 D. October 2, 1978

**162.** After World War I, the peace treaty was signed in:
A. Geneva B. Versailles
C. Paris D. Venice

**163.** Potassium chloride is given to the patient for
A. curing his bleeding gums
B. reducing his cholestrol level
C. reducing his blood pressure
D. alleviating his arthiritis pain

**164.** What is notation?

A. It is another word for "Mutually Assured Destruction"

B. It is the Latin deformation of the phrase "to swim"

C. It is a term used to denote the growth of illeterate masses

D. None of the above

**165.** The hideout of Adolf Hitler in the mountains was

A. Stuttgart B. Heidelberg

C. Berchtesgaden D. Both A and C

**166.** Who stated, "Where wealth accumulates decay?"

A. J M Keynes B. Adam Smith

C. Frederic Engels D. Oliver Goldsmith

**167.** Who was the national leader who wrote History of India on the walls of the Andaman Cellular Jail?

A. Ambedkar B. Vir Savarkar

C. Nandlal Bose D. Jyotiba Phule

**168.** The USA does not possess the following space shuttle

A. Columbia B. Atlantis

C. Challenger D. Discovery

**169.** The term "White Elephant" is used to denote

A. very bright and white item

B. very costly and expensive item

C. an item or a head that is very costly to maintain

D. an item or a head that is a part of the national economic budget of a country

**170.** Kolar Gold Mines are in this state.

A. Karnataka B. Bihar

C. Odisha D. Madhya Pradesh

**171.** Which is the morning star?

A. Pluto

B. Venus

C. Neptune

D. None of the above

**172.** Which one of the following is not an alkali?

A. sodium hydroxide

B. calcium carbonate

C. magnesium hydroxide

D. sodium sulphate

**173.** Polar ice is melting due to greenhouse effect. This would lead to

A. more melting of the polar glaciers and hence, subsequent submerging of land areas of earth

B. increasing temperatures on polar caps

C. reduction in temperature of ocean waters and rise in temperature of the Arctic circle waters as well as those of the Antartic circle waters

D. no impact

**174.** *India 2020* is a book written by

A. Trilok Gurtu

B. Khushwant Singh

C. P Chidambaram

D. A P J Abdul Kalaam

**175.** The Panama Canal connects:

A. The Pacific and Atlantic Oceans

B. The Pacific and Arctic Oceans

C. The Atlantic and Arctic Oceans

D. The Atlantic and Indian Oceans

**176.** The following are single cell structures

A. Paramaecium B. Amoebia

C. Both A and B D. None of A or B

**177.** 'The Last Supper' was painted by:

A. Picasso B. Francis Bacon

C. Michaelangelo D. Raphael

**178.** The plants, which can resist high temperatures, are known as

A. thermophilic B. thermophobic

C. thermoduric D. Both A and B

**179.** Which one of the following vaccines is used for controlling tuberculosis among the cattle?

A. Cell Culture Vaccine

B. Goat Tissue Adapted Vaccine

C. Adjuvant Vaccine

D. BCG Vaccine

**180.** Which one of the following chemicals is carcinogenic if inhaled?

A. carbon dioxide

B. suspended particulate matter

C. lead oxide

D. sulphur dioxide

**181.** What is a "Tenurial System?"

A. It is a system that identifies the ownership of land and the relationship of the land owner with the actual cultivator

B. It identities the land size and the *modus-operandi* of its usage
C. It identifies the ownership of the land
D. None of the above

**182.** Pulses are deficient in
A. methionine B. lysine
C. leusine D. iso-leusine

**183.** Which types of roses are grown in India for industrial applications?
A. R Centripetala and Bushra Rose
B. R Damascena Var Bifera
C. Rosa Damascena
D. A, B and C

**184.** Why sprinkler irrigation is preferred over other methods of irrigation?
A. It is a cheap method and does not require canal-digging and canal maintenance
B. It uses water effectively and water resolves are optimally utilised
C. It does not require well-digging measures which are costly
D. It supplies water only to those fields where the same is required

**185.** The size of clay particles is
A. greater than 0.2 mm
B. 0.02 mm – 0.2 mm
C. 0.002 mm – 0.02 mm
D. less than 0.002 mm

**186.** Which one of the following plants is of great medicinal value?
A. Ranwolfia Serpentiana
B. Thea Sinesis
C. Coffea Robusta
D. Ficus Religiosa

**187.** Biological control agents of soil borne plant pathogens act by
A. rapidly repleting nutrients and thereby, causing starvation and death of the pathogen
B. secreting toxic metabolitics
C. direct parastism or predation on the pathogens
D. All of the above

**188.** Nearly 80 percent of sugarcane in India is planted during
A. July – December B. May – August
C. June – August D. December – April

**189.** Soluble salt content of soil is determined by measuring its
A. pH Value
B. organic matter content
C. Sulphur content
D. electrical conductivity

**190.** Operation Flood is related to ..... whereas development of fisheries is related to .....
A. white revolution, black revolution
B. white revolution, blue revolution
C. green revolution, blue revolution
D. blue revolution, green revolution

**191.** An upper air wind system with very high velocities in certain parts of the atmosphere is called
A. Cyclone B. Anticyclone
C. Jet stream D. Tsunami

**192.** "Mixed Farming" refers to
A. farming by traditional and modern methods
B. agriculture and dairy farming clubbed together
C. farming without synthetic fertilisers but with traditional manure
D. farming with synthetic fertilisers and with traditional manure

**193.** The main constituent of *Gobar Gas* is
A. butane B. carbon monoxide
C. methane D. octane

**194.** Speed of sound waves is maximum in
A. solids B. liquids
C. gases D. vacuum

**195.** When a body gets positively charged, it actually
A. gains electrons
B. loses electrons
C. becomes a donor of ions
D. becomes a receptor of ions

**196.** Which type of nerves carries impulses from the sense organs in response to the stimulus?
A. sensory B. motor
C. secretory D. None of the above

**197.** Which gas does not pollute air (for human and animal consumption)?
A. carbon monoxide B. nitrogen dioxide
C. sulphur dioxide D. carbon dioxide

**198.** The human brain sends and receives signals as

A. electrical impulses
B. chemical impulses
C. motor movements
D. either A or B

**199.** "Foot and Mouth" disease attacks

A. cattle
B. pigs and cattle
C. sheep and pigs
D. cattle, sheep and pigs

**200.** While returning to earth, the spacecraft has a total communication blackout. The reason is

A. during the re-entry period, the density of the plasma generated by the intense functional heat is so high that the operational frequencies used for communication become much lesser than the plasma cut-off frequency, thus resulting in a total blackout
B. the electromagnetic waves present in the space above the earth temporarily over-power the communication system of the aircraft, thus completely crippling its operation and transmission
C. the force of gravity counters the radiowaves emitted by the aircraft
D. None of the above

**201.** The first winning stroke in Lawn Tennis gives the player:

A. 2 points B. 1 point
C. 10 points D. 15 points

**202.** Which of the following game is played for stipulated period of 70 minutes?

A. Hockey B. Football
C. Rugby D. Basketball

**203.** Who among the following was the Constitutional adviser to the Constituent Assembly of India?

A. Dr. B.R. Ambedkar B. Dr. B.N. Rao
C. K.M. Munshi D. M.C. Setalvad

**204.** Arjuna Award has been instituted for outstanding contribution in the field of

A. Social Service
B. Games and Sports
C. Literature
D. Art and Music

**205.** Murugappa Gold Cup is associated with:

A. Football B. Polo
C. Hockey D. Bridge

**206.** Jimmy Connors and Geoff Boycott are related with following games respectively:

A. Tennis, Football B. Tennis, Cricket
C. Chess, Cricket D. Football, Hockey

**207.** 'AVAHAN', the Indian segment of 'Bill and Melinda Gates Foundation', is engaged in the prevention of:

A. dengue B. polio
C. HIV/AIDS D. None of the above

**208.** The Constituent Assembly which framed the Constitution for Independent India was set up in:

A. 1945 B. 1946
C. 1947 D. 1949

**209.** The term 'Steeple Chase' is associated with which of the following games

A. Polo B. Tennis
C. Horse Racing D. Cricket

**210.** Who is known as Father of India's "White Revolution" and "Operation Flood"?

A. Dr. Verghese Kurien
B. J.B. Kripalani
C. Baba Amte
D. Har Gobind Khorana

**211.** The first Olympic games were revived by ..... in 1896 at Athens

A. Lord Welsley
B. Queen Elizabeth-I
C. Baron Piere de Cubertin
D. None of the above

**212.** The national game of the USA is

A. swimming B. baseball
C. athletics D. None of the above

**213.** Jules Rimmet Cup is associated with

A. hockey B. archery
C. football D. table tennis

**214.** The approximate weight of a cricket ball is

A. 5.25 Oz B. 6.30 Oz
C. 7.20 Oz D. 8.25 Oz

**215.** The number of players on each side in a basketball match is
A. 10 B. 6
C. 5 D. 8

**216.** The first woman in the history of US open Championship to have played 100 matches, is:
A. Martina Navaratilova
B. Chris Evert
C. Steffi Graf
D. Helena Sukova

**217.** Swaythling Cup is associated with
A. World Table Tennis Tournament (men)
B. World Table Tennis Tournament (university)
C. World Table Tennis tournament (women)
D. World Hockey Tournament (university)

**218.** Which one of the following is not a cricket - playing nation?
A. West Indies B. Zimbabwe
C. Kenya D. Columbia

**219.** The first recipient of *Rajiv Gandhi Khel Ratna Award* (1991-92) (Now Major Dhyan Chand Khel Ratna Award) was:
A. Geet Sethi B. N Kunjurani Devi
C. V Anand D. P K Garg

**220.** The first Olympic Games were held at Olympia (Greece) in the year:
A. 300 BC B. 776 BC
C. 500 BC D. 394 AD

**221.** Which of the following is the National Game of Spain?
A. Bull fighting B. Baseball
C. Rugby D. Golf

**222.** 'Ashes' is the name of a series between ..... and ..... and it relates to .....
A. Pakistan, Australia, Hockey
B. India, England, Cricket
C. England, Australia, Cricket
D. New Zealand, Australia, Cricket

**223.** The term "Butterfly Stroke" is associated with
A. Kabaddi B. Wrestling
C. Polo D. Swimming

**224.** The Australian Open Tennis Women's Championship (2023) was won by
A. C. Martinez
B. Lindsay Davenport
C. Aryna Sabalenka
D. Monica Seles

**225.** 'Gambit' is a term normally associated with
A. Bridge B. Chess
C. Billiards D. Polo

**226.** 'Bunker' and 'Chukker' are the two terms associated with
A. Polo B. Rowing
C. Bungey Jumping D. Ice Hockey

**227.** A Lawn Tennis court measures.
A. 78 feet by 28 feet B. 79 feet by 29 feet
C. 76 feet by 26 feet D. 70 feet by 24 feet

**228.** Vyas Samman is given for excellence in the field of:
A. Science B. Dance
C. Economics D. Literature

**229.** Which one of the following has been entrusted with the responsibility of training coaches in various disciplines of sports?
A. Tata Football Academy
B. Ministry of Human Resource Development
C. Netaji Subhash Institute of Sports
D. Lakshmibai National College of Physical Education

**230.** Name the city in which Golden Temple is located:
A. Ludhiana B. Chandigarh
C. Amritsar D. Delhi

**231.** Governor will act on the advice of Council of Ministers while
A. Dissolving the Legislative Assembly
B. Appointing the Chairman of the State Public Service Commission
C. Recommending for President's Rule in the State
D. Returning a bill for reconsideration

**232.** Who was the first deaf & dumb swimmer in the world to swim 30 km Gibralter strait?
A. Des Renford B. Mihir Sen
C. Arti Pradhan D. Taranath Shenoy

**233.** The height of the net in the centre of the tennis court is
A. 3 feet, 5 inches B. 3 feet, 2 inches
C. 2 feet, 8 inches D. 2 feet, 6 inches

**234.** 'Canon' is a sports term associated with the following game.
A. Billiards B. Volleyball
C. Shot-Put D. Table Tennis

**235.** The Himalayan Mountaineering Institute is located in
A. Leh B. Darjeeling
C. Kohima D. Dispur

**236.** The diameter of a golf hole is
A. 4.36 inches B. 4.50 inches
C. 5.63 inches D. 4.75 inches

**237.** The total distance of a Marathon Race is ..... miles and ..... yards.
A. 29, 388 B. 26, 380
C. 26, 385 D. 25, 372

**238.** The first woman, who won six gold medals in a single Olympics tournament, was
A. Evelyn Ashford
B. Florence Griffth Joyner
C. Kristin Otto
D. Susi Susanti

**239.** In which year on account of a decree issued by Roman Emperor the Olympic Games were ceased to be played?
A. 350 AD B. 394 AD
C. 300 BC D. 384 AD

**240.** Putney (UK) is a place most frequently associated with
A. swimming B. horse racing
C. boat rowing D. polo

**241.** The World Pole Vault Champion, from Ukraine, is
A. Sergei Bubka
B. Mikael Tillstrom
C. Todd Woodbridge
D. None of the above

**242.** The term 'Finesse' is normally associated with this game.
A. Chess B. Bridge
C. Snooker D. Rowing

**243.** The following trophy is not associated with cricket.
A. Ranji Trophy
B. Rohintan Baria Trophy
C. Ashes
D. Wimbledon Trophy

**244.** P.V. Sindhu is associated with which game?
A. Rowing B. Table Tennis
C. Badminton D. Boxing

**245.** When and where the first Asian Games were held?
A. 1955, Seoul B. 1951, New Delhi
C. 1954, Manila D. 1970, Bangkok

**246.** Music legend Bob Dylan became the first song-writer to win the Nobel Prize for Literature 2016. He belongs to which country?
A. France B. USA
C. Italy D. Britain

**247.** What is the measurement of a Golf Hole?
A. 3½ inch in diameter
B. 4½ inch in diameter
C. 7½ centimeter in diameter
D. 10 inch in diameter

**248.** The Supreme Court of India was set up by the
A. Regulating Act, 1773
B. Pitts India Act, 1784
C. Charter Act, 1813
D. Charter Act, 1833

**249.** K Sasikaran is well known as a
A. table tennis player
B. swimmer
C. chess player
D. football player

**250.** Which one of the following pairs is correctly matched?
A. Plimsoll Line : India and Afghanistan
B. Durand Line : India and Myanmar
C. Radcliff Line : India and Pakistan
D. Macmohan Line : India and Nepal

**251.** In which of the following years 'Nobel Prizes' were instituted?
A. 1910 B. 1905
C. 1901 D. 1911

**252.** The writer who refused the Nobel Prize for Literature was:
A. Winston Churchill B. Prem Chand
C. Jean Paul Sartre D. None of the above

**253.** Which country awards the Noble Prize?
A. USA B. India
C. Russia D. Sweden

**254.** In which of the following years Arjuna Awards were instituted
A. 1951 B. 1971
C. 1961 D. 1965

**255.** National Awards for Popularising Science was instituted in the year
A. 1981 B. 1985
C. 1987 D. 1988

**256.** The Government of which state has instituted the 'Tansen Samman'?
A. Madhya Pradesh
B. Uttar Pradesh
C. Gujarat
D. Maharashtra

**257.** Nobel Prizes are not given for which of the following fields?
A. Physics B. Music
C. Chemistry D. Peace

**258.** Who returned the award of 'Sir' given by the British government in protest against the "Jallianwala Bagh Massacre" on April 13, 1919?
A. Prem Chand
B. Thomas Roe
C. Rabindra Nath Tagore
D. Dada Bhai Nauroji

**259.** Nobel Prize is not awarded in the following disciplines
A. Chemistry and Physics
B. Literature and Peace
C. Economics and Medicine
D. Geography and Space Research

**260.** In which year Nehru Award for International Understanding instituted
A. 1965 B. 1969
C. 1974 D. 1964

**261.** Which of the following Indians was awarded Legion D award, the highest civilian awards of France
A. Jawahar Lal Nehru
B. Satyajit Ray
C. Mother Teresa
D. Shahrukh Khan

**262.** 'Pulitzer' prizes are awarded to Americans for excellence in
A. Films B. Journalism
C. Medicine D. Social Work

**263.** C.V. Raman received Nobel Prize in the year
A. 1934 B. 1931
C. 1932 D. 1930

**264.** Saraswati Samman is awarded by
A. Government of India
B. Sahitya Academy
C. K.K. Birla Foundation
D. Lalit Kala Akademi

**265.** On which day every year National Awards for Teachers are announced?
A. August 15 B. September 5
C. November 19 D. November 14

**266.** The National Award given to the distinguished sportsmen/women in India is known as
A. Dronacharya Award
B. Param Vir Chakra
C. Arjun Award
D. Nehru Award

**267.** The prestigious Ramon Magsaysay Award was instituted in the memory of Mr Ramon Magsaysay who was
A. the Secretary – General of UN
B. the Commander of NATO in Europe
C. the President of the Philippines
D. the President of Cambodia

**268.** The Kalinga Prize is awarded by UNESCO but it was founded by an Indian. His name is
A. Biju Patnaik B. Sharad Pawar
C. C V Raman D. Piloo Modi

**269.** Who was the first Indian to receive the World Food Prize
A. Dr. M.S. Swaminathan
B. Dr. Amrita Patel
C. Dr. Verghese Kurien
D. None of these

**270.** Jesse Owens Global award is given in the field of:
A. Literature B. Sports
C. Science D. Journalism

**271.** Nobel Alfred Bernhard after whom Nobel Prizes are given was:
A. Engineer B. Doctor
C. Chemist D. Pilot

**272.** Grammy Awards are given in the field of
A. painting B. architecture
C. music D. rock dance

**273.** The highest civilian award of India is
A. *Padma Vibhushan*
B. *Padma Shri*
C. *Bharat Ratna*
D. *Param Vir Chakra*

**274.** The highest military award of India is
A. Shaurya Chakra
B. Param Vishisht Sewa Medal
C. Param Vir Chakra
D. Kirti Chakra

**275.** The first ever B R Ambedkar National Award was given to
A. Baba Amte
B. T Shiv Shankar Pillai
C. International Red Cross
D. National Institute for Social Work and Social Sciences

**276.** 'Victory Medal' is awarded in:
A. UK B. USA
C. Russia D. France

**277.** Which one of the following is not a Shram Award
A. Shram Bhushan B. Shram Dev
C. Shram Devi D. Shram Vir

**278.** Dr Shanti Swaroop Bhatnagar Awards are given in any field of science by
A. Indian Council of Applied Economic Research
B. Defence Research and Development Organisation
C. National Institute for Social Work and Social Sciences
D. Tata Institute of Fundamental Research

**279.** Veda Samaj founded under the initiative of Kesab Chandra Sen in 1864 in Madras was renamed as the Brahmo Samaj of South India in 1871 by:
A. Sir R. Venkataratnam Naidu
B. K. Sreedharalu Naidu
C. Subbarayala Chetti
D. Rajagopala Naidu

**280.** First Miss World Competition was established by 'Miss World Incorporation' in the year
A. 1941 B. 1950
C. 1951 D. 1957

**281.** The size of an Olympic medal is ..... mm and thickness is ..... mm.
A. 50, 2.5 B. 60, 3.0
C. 60.5, 3.5 D. 55.2, 2.5

**282.** "Dhanwantari Award" is given in the field of
A. swimming B. Bharata Natyam
C. cinema D. medicine

**283.** Duncan Passage is situated betwee:
A. Minicoy and Amindiv
B. Minicoy and Maldives
C. South Andaman and Little Andaman
D. Little Andaman and Car Nicobar

**284.** Which is the second Highest Civilian award in India?
A. Padam Vibushan B. Padam Shri
C. Bharat Ratna D. Ashok Chakra

**285.** Gandhiji started the Dandi March for
A. Poorna Swaraj
B. Home-rule
C. Protest against the imposition of Salt Tax
D. Responsible Government

**286.** The second highest gallantry award in India is:
A. Padam Bhushan B. Vir Chakra
C. Mahavir Chakra D. Ashok Chakra

**287.** 'Mubarak-Al-Kabir' medal is the highest honour of
A. Kuwait B. Iran
C. Afghanistan D. Iraq

**288.** Bharatendu Harish Chandra awards are given annually for:
A. best local self administration
B. showing kindness and generosity of unusual kind
C. promoting original writing in Hindi
D. None of the above

**289.** Who replaced Planning Commission in 2015?
A. NITI Aayog B. NIYAM Aayog
C. NIYANTA Aayog D. PRITI Aayog

**290.** Who has been selected for the prestigious Jnanpith award for the year 2021?
A. Alok Puranik
B. Damodar Mauzo
C. Mrinal Pandey
D. Vishwanath Tiwari

**291.** Neeraj Chopra is associated with which sports?
A. Weighlifting  B. Boxing
C. Hockey  D. Javelin Throw

**292.** Oscar award is related to
A. books
B. politics
C. European Community
D. films

**293.** USB stands for
A. Unique Serial Bus
B. Universal Serial Bus
C. Unary Serial Bus
D. Universal Secondary Bus

**294.** Out of the Gallantry awards — PVSM, AVSM and VSM — the most exceptional medal is
A. PVSM
B. AVSM
C. VSM
D. All have equal recognition status

**295.** *Jeewan Raksha Padak* is awarded for
A. bravery in the battle front
B. fine display of vocal music skills
C. saving the life of human beings
D. None of the above

**296.** Who is not eligible for Bharat Ratna?
A. A government official
B. A sportsperson
C. A film actress
D. A Prime Minister

**297.** Jamnalal Bajaj award is given in the field of
I. Social Work
II. Fine Arts
III. Application of Science and Technology
IV. Literature
A. I and II  B. I, II and III
C. II and IV  D. I and III

**298.** In which year Indira Gandhi Peace Prize was instituted?
A. 1985  B. 1984
C. 1986  D. 1987

**299.** Borlaug Award was instituted for recognising outstanding contribution in the field of:
A. Ecology  B. Medicine
C. Agriculture  D. Journalism

**300.** Except Dr. Nelson Mandela, who is the other non-Indian so far honoured with Bharat Ratna
A. Dr. Julius Nyerere
B. Helen Hint
C. Hideki Yuka
D. Khan Abdul Ghaffar Khan

**301.** The book "*The Insider*" is written by
A. Madhav Rao Scindia
B. Nana Patekar
C. Shobha De
D. P V Narasimha Rao

**302.** *India Wins Freedom* was written by
A. Dadabhai Nauroji
B. Ashfaqulla Khan
C. Sarojini Naidu
D. Maulana Abul Kalam Azad

**303.** *A Tale of Two Cities* is, in fact, the story of two famous cities. Those cities are
A. Paris and New York
B. London and New York
C. London and Paris
D. Stockholm and New York

**304.** *Ben Hur* was penned by
A. Lewis Wallace
B. Lord Byron
C. William Shakespeare
D. None of the above

**305.** *Panchatantra* was written by
A. R K Narayan  B. R K Laxman
C. Vishnu Sharma  D. None of the above

**306.** Arundhati Roy has been awarded the prestigious
A. Booker's Prize – 1997
B. Jnanpeeth Award – 1997
C. Sahitya Akademi Award – 1998
D. None of the above

**307.** Who wrote *Odyssey?*
A. George Orwell
B. Homer
C. Dom Moraes
D. None of the above

**308.** Which one of the following was not written by Shakespeare?
A. *As You Like It*
B. *Mcbeth*

C. *Hamlet*
D. *A Farewell to Arms*

**309.** Lewis Carol wrote a masterpiece. What is its name?
A. *Don Quixote*
B. *Alice in Wonderland*
C. *Adventures of Robinson Crusoe*
D. *Great Expectations*

**310.** The *Tamil Ramayana* is the work of
A. Tulsidas B. Jayangondar
C. Kambar D. Veda Vyas

**311.** In *Shrimad Bhagwat Geeta,* Lord Krishna teaches his disciple Arjuna to
A. rise to the occasion and fight with his near and dear ones
B. withdraw from the battlefield
C. do his duty and not to expect anything in return
D. attack the enemy in a planned and meticulous approach

**312.** Who wrote *Origin of Species?*
A. Charles Darwin
B. Alexander Flaming
C. G.B. Shaw
D. D.H. Lawrence

**313.** The poet and the well-known friend of Prithvi Raj Chauhan, who wrote *Prithvi Raj Raso,* was
A. Harisena B. Vishnu Datt
C. Chand Bardai D. None of the above

**314.** The first book was printed in India in the year 1561. Its name was
A. *The spiritual Compendium of the Christian Life*
B. *Aain-e-Akbari*
C. *Babur Nama*
D. *Ram Charit Manas*

**315.** The famous book *Runs and Ruins* was written by
A. Sir Donald Bradman
B. Sunil Gavaskar
C. Kapil Dev
D. Richard Hadlee

**316.** Adam Smith wrote the following famous book
A. The Wreck
B. Dr Zhivago
C. The Wealth of Nations
D. Tarzan of the Apes

**317.** H G Wells is known as a
A. poet
B. science-fiction writer
C. thriller-fiction writer
D. essay writer and critic

**318.** Tukaram wrote his devotional songs in this language
A. Urdu B. Gujarati
C. Hindi D. Marathi

**319.** Our ancient scholars and writers used this language for their social, religious and political books and works
A. Tamil
B. Sanskrit
C. Urdu
D. Hindi *(Devanagari)*

**320.** *Gora* is the hero of a book written by Rabindra Nath Tagore. What is the name of the book?
A. *Geetanjali* B. *Patanjali*
C. *Gora* D. *Twelfth Night*

**321.** Shylock is
A. the villain *in A Pound of Flesh* by William Shakespeare
B. an old Jew who is a famous hero of the Israeli nation
C. the hero of *Miranda,* written by William Shakespeare
D. the comic character of *Alice In the Wonderland* by Lewis Caroll

**322.** The following was a famous Hindi author and story-writer
A. Shobha De B. Aruna Asaf Ali
C. Mahadevi Verma D. Amrita Pritam

**323.** *Mudrarakshasa* was composed by
A. Vishakhadatta B. Bhavabhuti
C. Sivananda D. Jayadeva

**324.** *Razor's Edge* was written by
A. Toni Morrison
B. Saul Bellow
C. W Somerset Maugham
D. None of the above

**325.** *Sakharam Binder* is a famous play written by
A. Anil Barve B. Vijay Tendulkar
C. V S Naipaul D. Tasleema Nasreen

**326.** The major work of Sir Isaac Newton is
A. *Principia*
B. *Heritage*
C. *Human knowledge*
D. *I Dare*

**327.** The hero of *The Jungle Book,* written by Rudyard Kipling, is
A. the lion
B. Mowghuli
C. the father of Mowghuli
D. there is no hero

**328.** Who stated, "Peace hath her victories, no less renowned than war?"
A. Alfred Lord Tennyson
B. William Shakespeare
C. John Milton
D. None of the above

**329.** Macawber is a character who was created by
A. Thomas Hardy
B. P G Wodehouse
C. Charles Dickens
D. J W Von Goethe

**330.** *Pride and Prejudice* was written by
A. Anton Chekhov B. Maxim Gorky
C. Jane Austen D. Anthony West

**331.** *In the Afternoon Time* is the English translation of the autobiography of the famous poet, Harivansh Rai Bachchan. The autobiography was translated into English by
A. Vikram Seth
B. Dr Rupert Snell
C. William Faulkner
D. P D Tandon

**332.** Who is the author of the book *The Celestine Vision?*
A. Paul Hockins B. Salman Rushdie
C. Joseph Conrad D. James Redfield

**333.** The author of the famous book *Blue Mountain Revisited* is
A. Charles Kingsley B. Virginia Woolf
C. Arthur Koestler D. Peter Topkins

**334.** Homer was the great poet of the following language
A. Italian B. Greek
C. Arabic D. French

**335.** A factor which would strongly influence a business person to adopt a computer is its:
A. Accuracy
B. Reliability
C. Speed
D. All of these

**336.** *Godaan* was written by Munshi Prem Chand and it depicts
A. the methodology for taking adequate care of the cows
B. exploitation of simple rural folk by the rich landlords of rural India
C. the mutiny of 1857 in which, Indians refused to bite the *Kartoos* made with cow beef
D. None of the above

**337.** Manu wrote a book during ancient times in which, he divided the Aryan society into four distinct classes. What was the name of the book?
A. *Arthashastra* B. *Manusmriti*
C. *Moti Mahal* D. *My Truth*

**338.** R. Venkataraman wrote *My Presidential Years.* What was the main theme of the book?
A. It described the aristocratic procedures being followed in the *Rashtrapati Bhawan* during his tenure as President
B. It described the power equations and ploys in the centre and in the states during his term
C. It described how he felt caged while he was President due to a load of procedures and formalities
D. It explained the machinations of the political party which was in power during his tenure as President

**339.** The hero of the play cried in the end, "Et Tu, Brute!" and died. Which is the play and who is the author?
A. The Wealth of Nations — Adam Smith
B. Mein Kempf — Adolf Hitler
C. Julius Caesar — William Shakespeare
D. None of the above

**340.** Don Veto Corleone was the undisputed king of the underworld in this novel. This masterpiece was also converted into a film in which Al Pacino played the role of the Don. What is the name of the novel and that of the author?

A. *A Farewell to Arms* — E Hemingway
B. *The Godfather* — Mario Puzo
C. *From Here to Eternity* — James Jones
D. *Dialogue with Death* — Arthur Koestler

**341.** *Gypsy Camp Vanishes Into the Blue* was a famous blockbuster movie made by the erstwhile USSR. The original story was written by a famous author. His name is

A. Leo Tolstoy
B. Anton Chekhov
C. Maxim Gorky
D. Leon Uris

**342.** The total number of *Puranas* written during the Vedic age is

A. 22
B. 9
C. 18
D. 25

**343.** In computer network terminology. WAN stands for

A. World area network
B. Wide area network
C. Wide array net
D. Wireless area network

**344.** The first woman in the world to have climbed Mt. Everest twice is

A. Bachendri Pal
B. Molly Chacko
C. Santosh Yadav
D. Theresia Kiesl

**345.** According to *The Ramayana,* who received the last teaching lessons from the knowledgeable Ravana while he was on his death-bed?

A. Rama
B. Sugreeva
C. Laxmana
D. Both A and C

**346.** He was a German but hc saved many a Jew from the cruel hands of the Nazis. A movie was made on this theme which won the coveted Oscar Prize. The book and the author are

A. *Operation Shylock* — Philip Roth
B. *Schindler's List* — Thomas Keneally
C. *The Rescue* — Joseph Conrad
D. *The Slave* — Isaac Bashevis Singer

**347.** He was the favourite assistant of Sherlock Holmes, the famous character created by Arthur Conan Doyle. His name is

A. Zhivago B. Watson
C. Hawkins D. Hector

**348.** He was a former member of British Parliament. He has written many hit fiction novels. One of his novels is

A. Shall We Tell the President?
B. The Rape of the Lock
C. Snow Country
D. Small Land

**349.** He wrote *Sharmili*, *Gaylord* and *Kati Patang*. His novels were written in Hindi and some of them have been converted into films also. His name is

A. Gita Mehta
B. B N Mullick
C. Nirad C Chaudhary
D. Gulshan Nanda

**350.** The oldest mountains in India according to geographical history are:

A. Satpuras B. Nilgiris
C. Vindhyas D. Aravallis

## ANSWERS

| 1 | 2 | 3 | 4 | 5 | 6 | 7 | 8 | 9 | 10 |
|---|---|---|---|---|---|---|---|---|---|
| C | B | A | D | B | B | B | B | B | A |
| **11** | **12** | **13** | **14** | **15** | **16** | **17** | **18** | **19** | **20** |
| B | C | D | A | A | C | B | C | A | B |

| 21 | 22 | 23 | 24 | 25 | 26 | 27 | 28 | 29 | 30 |
|---|---|---|---|---|---|---|---|---|---|
| D | B | B | D | D | C | A | C | C | C |
| **31** | **32** | **33** | **34** | **35** | **36** | **37** | **38** | **39** | **40** |
| C | A | A | C | D | C | A | B | B | D |
| **41** | **42** | **43** | **44** | **45** | **46** | **47** | **48** | **49** | **50** |
| B | C | B | B | C | D | A | A | D | A |
| **51** | **52** | **53** | **54** | **55** | **56** | **57** | **58** | **59** | **60** |
| D | A | C | A | C | B | C | A | C | C |
| **61** | **62** | **63** | **64** | **65** | **66** | **67** | **68** | **69** | **70** |
| B | A | C | B | D | D | A | C | C | D |
| **71** | **72** | **73** | **74** | **75** | **76** | **77** | **78** | **79** | **80** |
| B | B | B | B | C | D | C | D | C | A |
| **81** | **82** | **83** | **84** | **85** | **86** | **87** | **88** | **89** | **90** |
| B | B | A | C | B | B | B | C | B | D |
| **91** | **92** | **93** | **94** | **95** | **96** | **97** | **98** | **99** | **100** |
| C | B | A | B | B | A | B | D | B | A |
| **101** | **102** | **103** | **104** | **105** | **106** | **107** | **108** | **109** | **110** |
| D | D | A | C | D | A | B | C | B | C |
| **111** | **112** | **113** | **114** | **115** | **116** | **117** | **118** | **119** | **120** |
| B | B | C | B | A | C | C | B | B | C |
| **121** | **122** | **123** | **124** | **125** | **126** | **127** | **128** | **129** | **130** |
| D | C | D | C | B | A | C | C | A | A |
| **131** | **132** | **133** | **134** | **135** | **136** | **137** | **138** | **139** | **140** |
| C | C | D | C | D | D | C | C | B | B |
| **141** | **142** | **143** | **144** | **145** | **146** | **147** | **148** | **149** | **150** |
| C | D | A | D | B | B | B | D | B | C |
| **151** | **152** | **153** | **154** | **155** | **156** | **157** | **158** | **159** | **160** |
| A | C | C | C | B | D | B | A | A | D |
| **161** | **162** | **163** | **164** | **165** | **166** | **167** | **168** | **169** | **170** |
| B | B | C | B | C | D | B | C | C | A |
| **171** | **172** | **173** | **174** | **175** | **176** | **177** | **178** | **179** | **180** |
| B | D | A | D | A | C | C | C | D | C |
| **181** | **182** | **183** | **184** | **185** | **186** | **187** | **188** | **189** | **190** |
| A | A | D | B | D | A | D | D | D | B |
| **191** | **192** | **193** | **194** | **195** | **196** | **197** | **198** | **199** | **200** |
| C | B | C | A | B | A | D | B | D | A |
| **201** | **202** | **203** | **204** | **205** | **206** | **207** | **208** | **209** | **210** |
| D | A | B | B | C | B | C | B | C | A |
| **211** | **212** | **213** | **214** | **215** | **216** | **217** | **218** | **219** | **220** |
| C | B | C | A | C | B | A | D | C | B |
| **221** | **222** | **223** | **224** | **225** | **226** | **227** | **228** | **229** | **230** |
| A | C | D | C | B | A | A | D | C | C |
| **231** | **232** | **233** | **234** | **235** | **236** | **237** | **238** | **239** | **240** |
| A | D | B | A | B | B | C | C | B | C |
| **241** | **242** | **243** | **244** | **245** | **246** | **247** | **248** | **249** | **250** |
| A | B | D | C | B | B | B | A | C | C |

| 251 | 252 | 253 | 254 | 255 | 256 | 257 | 258 | 259 | 260 |
|---|---|---|---|---|---|---|---|---|---|
| C | C | D | C | C | A | B | C | D | D |
| **261** | **262** | **263** | **264** | **265** | **266** | **267** | **268** | **269** | **270** |
| B | B | D | C | B | C | C | A | C | B |
| **271** | **272** | **273** | **274** | **275** | **276** | **277** | **278** | **279** | **280** |
| C | C | C | C | D | B | B | C | B | C |
| **281** | **282** | **283** | **284** | **285** | **286** | **287** | **288** | **289** | **290** |
| B | D | C | A | C | C | A | C | A | B |
| **291** | **292** | **293** | **294** | **295** | **296** | **297** | **298** | **299** | **300** |
| D | D | B | A | C | A | D | C | C | D |
| **301** | **302** | **303** | **304** | **305** | **306** | **307** | **308** | **309** | **310** |
| D | D | C | A | C | A | B | D | B | C |
| **311** | **312** | **313** | **314** | **315** | **316** | **317** | **318** | **319** | **320** |
| C | A | C | A | B | C | B | D | B | C |
| **321** | **322** | **323** | **324** | **325** | **326** | **327** | **328** | **329** | **330** |
| A | C | A | C | B | A | B | C | C | C |
| **331** | **332** | **333** | **334** | **335** | **336** | **337** | **338** | **339** | **340** |
| B | D | D | B | D | B | B | C | C | B |
| **341** | **342** | **343** | **344** | **345** | **346** | **347** | **348** | **349** | **350** |
| C | C | B | C | C | B | B | A | D | D |

✸ ✸ ✸ ✸ ✸

# HIGHLIGHTS OF COMPANIES ACT, 2013

## INTRODUCTION

### Background

Companies Bill, 2012 was passed by the Lok Sabha on 18th December, 2012 and by the Rajya Sabha on 8th August, 2013. On receiving the assent of the Hon'ble President of India on August 29, 2013, it was notified on **August 30, 2013** as the Companies Act, 2013.

It may be noted that **only Section 1** of the Companies Act, 2013 has come into force with effect from 30th August, 2013. As far as the remaining provisions of this Act is concerned, they shall come into force on such date as the **Central Government (Ministry of Corporate Affairs)** may, by notification in the Official Gazette, appoint and different dates may be appointed for bringing into force different provisions of the Companies Act, 2013. For instance, Central Government has made, **98 Sections and part thereof** of the Companies Act, 2013, **effective from 12th September, 2013.**

Thus, Companies Act, 2013 is all set to replace the existing 56 year old company law, i.e., Companies Act, 1956, very soon. It moves from the regime of control to that of liberalisation or self-regulation.

### Structure of the Act

The Companies Act, 2013 has **470 Sections (covered in 29 Chapters) and 7 Schedules** as against 658 Sections (covered in 13 Parts) and 15 Schedules of the Companies Act, 1956.

It may be noted that the number of Sections has been drastically reduced, but at the same time the Central Government has been empowered, in number of Sections, to prescribe various aspects in the form of **Rules,** thereby recognizing the more importance of **delegated legislation.** It can be said Companies Act, 2013 has been structured on **skeleton approach.** This has been done for ensuring that the law remains relevant at all times in the changing economic environment.

### Applicability of the Act

Section 1 provides that the Companies Act, 2013 applies on whole of India.

Companies Act, 1956 also applies on whole of India. However, proviso to Section 1(3) of the Companies Act, 1956 empowers the Central Government to modify the provisions of the Act, while applying this Act on the State of Nagaland. Similarly, Sections 620B and 620C of the Companies Act, 1956 empowers the Central Government to, modify, or exempt from, the provisions of the Act, while applying this Act on the States of Goa, Daman, Diu and Jammu & Kashmir respectively. These kinds of powers of the Central Government have been taken away by the Companies Act, 2013.

Thus, the 2013 Act puts an end to the power of the Central Government under the 1956 Act to exempt companies from provisions of Companies Act based on regional considerations.

## IMPORTANT HIGHLIGHTS

Following are the important highlights of Companies Act, 2013 :

### Preliminary

- ☞ New definitions have been introduced, some of which are auditing standards, associate company, CEO, CFO, control, employee stock option, financial statement, global depository receipt, Indian depository receipt, independent director, interested director, key managerial personnel, promoter, one person company, small company, turnover, voting right, etc.
- ☞ Number of existing definitions have been modified, for example, definitions of abridged prospectus, body corporate, director, expert, managing director, officer in default, etc.
- ☞ Definition of private company changed - the limit on maximum number of members increased from 50 to 200.
- ☞ The concept of One Person Company introduced. It will be a private limited company.
- ☞ The concept of Small Company introduced. It will be subject to lesser stringent regulatory framework.

### Capital Raising

- ☞ Money raised through a prospectus cannot be used for dealing in equity shares of another company. If a company changes terms of the prospectus or objects for which money is raised, it shall provide dissenting shareholders an exit opportunity.
- ☞ Shares, other than Sweat Equity Shares, cannot be issued at a discount. It means the practice of issuing shares at a discount with the approval of CLB, as provided in Section 79 of Companies Act, 1956, has been discontinued.
- ☞ Public companies can accept deposit from public on complying with certain conditions like credit rating.

## Management & Administration

- All companies to follow uniform financial year, running from April to March. Exceptions to be made only for certain companies with the approval of NCLT.
- First Annual General Meeting of the Company shall be held within 9 months from the closure of its first financial year instead of 18 months from the date of incorporation, as provided in the Companies Act, 1956.
- Quorum of general meeting for a **public company** will now depend upon the numbers of the company. For companies with up to 1000 members, 5 members personally present; for companies with members more than 1000 but up to 5000, 15 members personally present; and for companies with more than 5000 members, 30 members personally present, shall be the quorum. The Companies Act, 1956 prescribes a fixed quorum of 5 members personally present.
- Postal Ballot to be applicable to all the companies, whether listed or unlisted.
- The National Advisory Committee on Accounting Standards renamed as The National Financial Reporting Authority (NFRA).

## Auditors & Financial Statements

- Every company is required at its first annual general meeting (AGM) to appoint an individual or a firm as an auditor. The auditor shall hold office from the conclusion of that meeting till the conclusion of its 6th AGM and thereafter till the conclusion of every 6th meeting. The appointment of the auditor is to be ratified at every AGM.
- Individual auditors are to be compulsorily rotated every 5 years and audit firm every 10 years in listed companies & certain other classes of companies, as may be prescribed.
- A company's auditor shall not provide, directly or indirectly, the specified services to the company, its holding and subsidiary company.

## Directors

- Prescribed class or classes of companies are required to appoint at least one woman director **(Woman Director)**.
- At least one director should be a person who has stayed in India for a total period of not less than 182 days in the previous calendar year **(Resident Director)**.
- At least one-third of the total number of director of a listed public company should be independent directors. Government may prescribe requirement of Independent Directors for certain unlisted public companies also.
- Liability of independent directors and non-executive directors not being promoter or key managerial personnel to be limited.
- A person can hold directorship of up to 20 companies, of which not more than 10 can be public companies.
- Companies can have maximum of 15 directors. More can be appointed after passing a special resolution.

## Governance

- Companies with more than 1,000 shareholders, debenture-holders, and any other security holders at any time during a financial year to constitute a Stakeholder's Relationship Committee, with a non-executive director as a chairperson.
- The provisions on inter-corporate loans and investment (372A of Companies Act, 1956) extended to include loan and investment to any person.
- A company cannot, unless otherwise prescribed, make investment through more than 2 layers of investment companies.
- No central government approval required for entering into any related party transactions.
- No central government approval required for appointment of any director or any other person to any office or place of profit in the company or its subsidiary.
- The Act makes provision for cross border amalgamation between Indian Companies and companies incorporated in the jurisdictions of such countries as may be notified from time to time by the central government.
- The authority CLB is being replaced by National Company Law Tribunal (NCLT).

## Miscellaneous

- The Act provides provisions related to Corporate Social Responsibility (CSR).
- The Act provides for class action suit by specified number of members or depositors against the company except the banking company, which is prevalent in developed countries.
- Where any valuation is required to made of any property, stocks, shares, debentures, securities or goodwill or any other assets or net worth of a company or its liabilities under the Act, it shall be valued by a registered valuer.

# CONCEPTS OMITTED

## Major Omission/Deletions

| S.No. | Section of Companies Act, 1956 | Provisions of the Companies Act, 1956 which have been deleted in the Companies Act, 2013 |
|---|---|---|
| 1. | 43A | Private company to become public company in certain cases. |
| 2. | 44 | Filing of Prospectus or statement in lieu of prospectus by private company on ceasing to be private company. |
| 3. | 58AA | The provisions of section 58AA relating to acceptance of deposits from small depositors and intimation of default in repayment of deposits thereof has been dropped. |
| 4. | 58AAA | Section 58AAA which makes any offence connected with or arising out of acceptance of deposits u/s 58A or 58AA as cognizable has been done away with. |
| 5. | 120 | The concept of perpetual debentures has been omitted. |
| 6. | 121 | The concept of re-issue of redeemed debentures has been omitted. |
| 7. | 153A | Appointment of public trustee. |
| 8. | 165 | Statutory meeting and statutory report of company. |
| 9. | 224A | Auditor not to be appointed except with the approval of the company by special resolution in certain cases. |
| 10. | 233A | Power of Central Government to direct special audit in certain cases. |
| 11. | 258 | Right of company to increase or reduce the number of directors. |
| 12. | 270 | Time within which share qualification is to be obtained and maximum amount thereof. |
| 13. | 294AA | Power of Central Government to prohibit the appointment of sole selling agents in certain cases. |
| 14. | 417 | Employees' securities to be deposited in post office/savings bank or Scheduled Bank. |

# IMPORTANT POINTS OF COMPANIES ACT 2013

## New Concepts and Definitions

2013 Act has introduced several new concepts and definitions. Few of them which we believe to be the most crucial are analyzed below:

## Companies

- **One Person Company:** 2013 Act now allows one person to form a company vis-à-vis the earlier position where a minimum of two persons were required to form a company (private). This new concept will be beneficial as entrepreneurs will be able to singly set up a corporate entity, restrict the liability of business and reduce compliances. Further, it will now be easier for foreign companies to set up wholly owned private subsidiaries in India, as it will not require divesting any part of stake in such subsidiaries to its group or subsidiary companies unlike under the 1956 Act wherein such divestment was required to meet the minimum two person rule to set up a company. [Section 2(62) and Section 3(1)(c)].
- **Small Company:** 2013 Act introduces this new concept of a small company, which means a company other than a public company having paid up share capital not exceeding INR 50,00,000 (or such higher amount as may be prescribed which shall not be more than INR 5,00,00,000) or turnover of which as per its last profit and loss account does not exceed INR 2,00,00,000 (or such higher amount as may be prescribed which shall not be more than INR 20,00,00,000). However, this section of small company will not be applicable to (a) holding or subsidiary company; (b) company registered under Section 8 of 2013 Act (i.e. companies form with the charitable object); or (c) company or a body corporate formed under the special Act. [Section 2(85)].
- **Dormant Company:** 2013 Act now allows a company to be formed and classified as a dormant company

for holding assets or intellectual property subject to the company not having any significant accounting transaction. Further, an inactive company can also make an application to the Registrar in such manner as may be prescribed for obtaining the status of a dormant company. [Section 455]

- **Associate Company:** 2013 Act now defines the much controversial Associate Company to mean a company which has 'Significant Influence' over the other company and which is not a subsidiary company but includes a joint venture company. Further it has been explained that 'Significant Influence' shall mean control of at least having 20% of total share capital or control of the business decision under an agreement. [Section 2(6)]
- **Private Company:** 2013 Act has now increased the total limit of number of members / shareholders in private company from 50 to 200. [Section 2(68)(ii)]
- **Investments Companies:** 2013 Act provides that any company (unless otherwise prescribed) shall not make investment through more than two layers of investment companies. However, this section has not been made applicable to a company acquiring any other company incorporated outside India, if such other company has investment subsidiaries beyond two layers as per the laws of such country. This Section may considerably restrict the flexibility of Indian companies in structuring their transactions. [Section 186]

**Object Clause :** 1956 Act required the object clause (which is stated in the memorandum of association of a company) to be classified into (a) main object; (b) objects incidental or ancillary to the attainment of the main objects; and (c) other objects of the company. The reason for having such classification in the object clause was to restrict the company from commencing any other business unless it complies with certain requirements. However, this requirement of such classification has been done away with by the 2013 Act, i.e. all objects will now be the main objects of the company. [Section 4(1)]

**Key Managerial Personnel (KMP):** KMP is commonly used in investment agreements and now finds a place in the 2013 Act. KMP includes (a) Managing Director (MD) or Chief Executive Officer (CEO); (b) Whole time director; (c) Chief Financial Officer (CFO); (d) Company Secretary (CS) and; (e) such other officer as may be prescribed. 2013 Act requires certain companies to appoint KMPs which will be notified in the Rules. [Section 2(51)]

**Promoter:** The term Promoter was not defined in the 1956 Act. However, it was extensively used through company law. 2013 Act now specifically defines Promoter, which includes (a) a person who has been named as such in the prospectus or is identified as such in the annual return; or (b) who has control over the affairs of the company (other than in a professional capacity), as a shareholder or a director or otherwise; or (c) in accordance with whose advice or directions the Board is accustomed to Act. [Section 2(69)]

**Class Action Suits:** 2013 Act introduces the western concept of class action suits which allows requisite number of members, depositors or any class of them file a suit against the company, its directors, auditors and/or other experts or consultants or advisors, if they believe that affairs of the company are conducted in a manner prejudice to the company or its members or depositors. [Section 245]

**Buy back of Securities:** 2013 Act provides that no buy back will be done by a company within one year from date of closure of previous buy back. Based on this provision, each company will now require having a cooling off period of one year between the two buy backs. Further, if a company has defaulted in repayment of its loans, deposits or interests payable then the company shall compulsorily have to wait for a period of three years after repayment of all such outstanding amount and rectifying such breach. [Section 68]

## Management and Administration

2013 Act provides detailed role of the management by incorporating sections enunciating powers, duties and responsibilities of board of directors, KMP, etc. Following are some of the important changes in the 2013 Act vis-à-vis 1956 Act:

### *Directors*

- **Maximum Number of Directors:** The maximum number of directors for a public company has been increased from 12 to 15. In case, the company desires to further increase the board size, it may do so by passing a special resolution. The requirement of taking permission of the Central Government as provided in 1956 Act is done away within 2013 Act [Section 149(1)]
- **Number of Directorships:** A person cannot be a director (including alternate director) in more than 20 companies out of which he or she cannot be a director of more than 10 public companies. 2013 Act now restricts over all directorship of any individual as compared to 1956 Act which allowed 1[illegible] directorships of any person in a public company and any number of directorships in a private company [Section 165]

- **Resident Director:** At least one director of the company is required to fulfill the residency test i.e. stay for not less than 182 days in India in the previous calendar year. [Section 149(3)]
- **Woman Director:** Certain class of the companies (which will be notified in the Rules) must have at least one woman director on the board. [Section 149(1)]
- **Small Shareholder Director:** A listed company may have one director elected by small shareholders. Small shareholder means a shareholder holding shares of nominal value of not more than INR 20,000 or such other sum as may be prescribed.
- **Independent Directors:** To align the company law with Clause 49 of Equity Listing Agreement **(Clause 49),** 2013 Act has introduced the concept of Independent Directors. In this respect, few of our general observations are as follows:

(a) The term independent director has been defined with certain prescribed qualification and disqualification. [Section 149(6)]

(b) Every listed company is required to have at-least one-third of the total number of directors as independent directors. Independent directors shall be entitled to sitting fees, commission from the profit and reimbursement of expenses. However, they will not be entitled to stock options. [Section 149(9)]

(c) The appointment of the independent director shall be approved by the members in a general meeting and they will not be required to retire by rotation. [Section 149(13)]

(d) An independent director can hold the office for consecutive two terms of five years each following which there should be three years break before he or she is reappointed as an independent director. [Section 149(11)]

(e) Nominee director shall not be considered as an independent director. [Section 149(6)]

(f) While the intention of 2013 Act is to align itself with Clause 49, there are few aspects which are different. All listed companies will now have to comply with Clause 49 and 2013 Act which will make the compliance process more cumbersome.

(g) Independent director shall only be liable for such act of omission, commission by a company which had occurred with his or her knowledge, attributable through Board processes, and with his/her consent or connivance or where he or she had not acted diligently. [Section 149(12)]

**Duties of the Director:** 2013 Act attempts to codify the duties of directors, including but not limited to the following, they are required to (a) act in good faith and in the best interest of the company; (b) not to have direct or indirect conflict of interest with the interest of the company; and (c) exercise duties with diligence and reasonable care and declares that it would be punishable offence to commit a breach of those duties. The liability of the director in default for contravention, for which no specific penalty is prescribed, has been increased from INR 50,000 to INR 500,000. [Section 166)]

## Board Meetings:

- The first board meeting is required to be held within 30 days of incorporation of a company and a minimum of four meetings are required to be held every year in such a manner that there are not more than 120 days between two meetings. [Section 173 (1)]
- A notice of minimum seven days is required to be given for convening a board meeting. The company can hold board meetings at a shorter notice to transact urgent business subject an independent director, if any shall be present in the meeting. In case of absence of independent directors from such a meeting, the decisions taken at such a meeting shall be circulated to all the directors and shall be final only upon the ratification thereof by at least one independent director, if any. [Section 173 (3)]
- The board meeting can be attended by the directors through video conferencing or other audio-visual modes, and such presence will be counted as quorum for the meeting, subject to the condition that they can be recorded and stored. [Section 173 (2)]

**Committees:** Besides the Audit Committee, the 2013 Act requires listed and such other class of companies as may be prescribed to form Nomination and Remuneration Committee, Corporate Social Responsibility Committee and Stakeholders Relationship Committee. [Section 178]

## Corporate Social Responsibility (CSR)

The Ministry of Corporate Affair had introduced CSR Voluntary Guidelines in 2009. These guidelines are now part of the 2013 Act and mandates following companies with the CSR activities:

Every company having net worth of INR 500,00,00,000 or more, or turnover of INR 1000,00,00,000 or more or a net profit of INR 5,00,00,000 or more during any financial year shall constitute a CSR Committee of the Board consisting of three or more directors, out of which at least one director shall be an independent director.

CSR Committee shall formulate the policy for activities specified in Schedule VII of the 2013 Act which broadly includes (a) eradicating extreme hunger and poverty; (b) promotion of education; (c) promoting gender equality and empowering women; (d) reducing child mortality and improving maternal health; (e) combating human immunodeficiency virus, acquired immune deficiency syndrome, malaria and other diseases; (f) ensuring environmental sustainability; (g) employment enhancing vocational skills; (h) social business projects; (i) contribution to the Prime Minister's National Relief Fund or any other fund set up by the Central Government or the State Governments for socio-economic development and relief and funds for the welfare of the Scheduled Castes, the Scheduled Tribes, other backward classes, minorities and women; (j) such other matters as may be prescribed.

2013 Act mandates companies to spent at least two percent of the average net-profits of immediately preceding three years on CSR activities, and if not spent, an explanation with the reasons thereof shall be required to be given in the Director's Report. [Section 135]

## Shareholders Meeting

**Notice:** A notice of clear 21 days is required to be given to each shareholder. 2013 Act now permits notice to be sent through electronic mode and should also be given to all the directors.

**Quorum:** 2013 Act has revised the quorum requirement for a general meeting of public company. The new requirements are broadly linked to the total number of shareholders of the particular company. Quorum for the meeting will be as follows:

***Public Company***

(a) Five members personally present shall be the quorum for the meeting, if the total number of members does not exceed 1000;

(b) 15 members personally present shall be the quorum for the meeting, if the total number of members are up to 5000; and

(c) 30 members personally present shall be the quorum for the meeting, if the total number of members exceeds 5000. [Section 103]

***Private Company:*** Two members personally present shall form the quorum for the meeting.

**Electronic Voting:** Central Government shall prescribe class or classes of companies and the manner in which members may exercise his/her rights to vote by electronic means. [Section 108]

**Demand for Poll:** A member having not less than 1/10th of the total voting power or holding shares of an aggregate of not less than INR 500,000 can demand poll. Further, 2013 Act removes the distinction between the private or public company in terms of eligibility of members for making demand for poll. [Section 109]

**Postal Ballot:** Unlike 1956 Act wherein postal ballot was only applicable to listed companies, it appears that 2013 Act has extended postal ballot requirement to all the companies which includes pubic unlisted and private companies as well. Central Government has yet to provide what specific items would require members' resolutions passed through postal ballot. [Section 110]

## Mergers and Amalgamation

2013 Act introduces some new provisions with regard to mergers and acquisitions, apart from incorporating changes to the existing provisions in the 1956 Act. The objective of bringing these changes is to simplify the procedures involved and ensure higher standards of accountability. Some of the key new provisions in this respect are:

**Holding and subsidiary:** A fast track procedure has been introduced for merger and amalgamation of holding company and its fully owned subsidiary. An approval of the court is not required as long as the Registrar of Companies **(ROC)** and official liquidator have no objection and the Central Government has granted its consent. [Section 233]

**Cross Border Mergers:** 1956 Act did not permit Indian companies to merge with foreign companies. 2013 Act now allows Indian companies to merge with foreign companies subject to an approval of the Reserve Bank of India and foreign company being incorporated in the jurisdiction notified by Central Government. [Section 234]

**Listed to Unlisted:** In the event of an arrangement between a listed transferor company and an unlisted transferee company, 2013 Act now permits for the (subject to consent of the tribunal) unlisted company to stay unlisted until it becomes listed. Further, if the shareholders of the transferor company decide to exit, the exit price cannot be less than the price as provided under Securities Exchange Board of India Regulations.

**Squeeze out of minority shareholding:** 2013 Ac now allows 90% majority shareholders of a company t squeeze out the minority shareholders at a price determine on the bases of value determined by the registered value [Section 236]

## Audit and Auditors

With the background of Satyam corporate scandal India, 2013 Act extensively enhances accountability of th auditors. The key changes in this respect are as follow

**Appointment of Auditors:** Auditors will now b appointed for a term of five years. However, their term w be ratified at each annual general meeting. [Section 139(

**Mandatory Rotation:** Auditors for listed companies (and other class(es) of companies as may be prescribed) are now required to mandatorily rotate their auditors – every five years in case of the appointment of an individual as auditor and every 10 years in case of appointment of an audit firm with a uniform cooling off period of five years in both cases. Further, firms with common partners in the outgoing audit firm will also be ineligible for appointment as auditor during the cooling off period. [Section 139(3)]

**Non-audit Service:** Any services to be rendered by an auditor of a company should be approved by the Audit Committee or the board of the company. Additionally, the auditor is restricted directly or indirectly from providing certain specific services, which include (a) accounting and book keeping services; (b) internal audit; (c) design and implementation of any financial information system; (d) actuarial services; (e) investment advisory services; (f) investment banking services; (g) rendering of outsourced financial services; (h) management services, and any other services which may be prescribed. [Section 144].

**Secretarial Audit:** 2013 Act provides for a mandatory requirement to have secretarial audit which is required to form a part of the director's report for all listed companies and other classes of companies that may be prescribed. [Section 204]

## Financial Statement and Dividend

**Financial Year:** Under the 1956 Act, companies were permitted to decide their own financial year. 2013 Act has taken away this liberty and requires all the companies to have a financial year ending as on the 31st of March. If any company desires to follow a different financial year because the holding company or subsidiary company requires following of different financial year for consolidation of its accounts, it will have to make an application to Tribunal. Tribunal, if satisfied, shall grant such an exemption. [Section 2(41)]

**Consolidated Statement:** 2013 Act requires consolidation of certain financial statements of any company having subsidiary, associate or joint venture company to prepare and present in addition to stand alone financial statements.

**Dividend:** Unlike the 1956 Act, the 2013 Act does not require certain percentage of profit to be transferred to the reserves before declaring the dividend. Further, a company which has incurred any loss during the current financial year upto to the end of the quarter immediately preceding the date of declaration of interim dividend, shall not be required to declare such interim dividend at a rate higher than the average dividends declared by the company during the immediately preceding three financial years. [Section 123]

## Regulators

**National Company Law Tribunal (NCLT or Tribunal):** 2013 Act provides for constitution of Tribunal and Appellate Tribunal with the objective of facilitating expeditious disposal of proceedings. All the matters, issues and disputes falling within the ambit of 2013 Act will now be referred to NCLT. Appeal would lie before the Appellate Tribunal and thereafter can be challenged before the Supreme Court. High Courts will now have no jurisdiction in matters related to company law. [Section 407 to 434]

**National Financial Reporting Authority (NFRA):** 2013 Act also provides for constitution of NFRA which will substitute the National Advisory Committee on Accounting and Auditing Standards. NFRA will supervise and regulate the activities of auditors and companies and see that they are in compliance with accounting and auditing standards. [Section 132]

**Serious Fraud Investigation Office (SFIO):** SFIO is an expert body established by Central Government in 2003 as a special organization to examine serious cases of fraud and scams received from MCA. The body was formed to carry out investigations under the provisions of the 1956 Act and was formed in light of the rise in white collar crimes and stock market scams. 2013 Act now itself incorporates within its folds the mandate for setting up an investigative body and recognizes the already existing SFIO as the investigative body. [Section 211]

## Revival and Rehabilitation of Sick Company

The existing provisions for revival and rehabilitation of sick companies have been substantially altered. 2013 Act now permits 'any' company and not just an 'industrial' company to be declared as sick company and avail benefits of this scheme.

The determination of whether a company is a sick company or not has moved from the concept of 'erosion of net worth' to 'inability to pay debt'. If a company fails to repay its debt within 30 days from receipt of a demand from the secured creditor representing 50% or more in value of the outstanding debt of the company, the company would be considered as a sick company.

A secured creditor whose debt has not been repaid can apply to the Tribunal for declaration of the company to be sick. If the said company is unable to provide a scheme to the Tribunal for its revival, an interim administrator may be appointed by the Tribunal to take over the management of the sick company. The Tribunal may consider various options for the revival of the sick company including its acquisition by a solvent company, restructuring of its assets, etc. If the Tribunal is satisfied that revival is not possible, it will pass an order for winding up of the company. [Chapter XIX]

## Winding-up

1956 Act provided three modes of winding-up of a company i.e. (a) Compulsory Winding-up ordered by the court; (b) Voluntary Winding-up by members; and (c) Winding-up under supervision of the court. 2013 Act now prescribes only two modes i.e. (a) Winding-up by the Tribunal and (b) Voluntary Winding-up. Further, 2013 Act does not acknowledge the distinction between member voluntary winding-up and creditor voluntary winding-up vis-à-vis the position in the 1956 Act.

2013 Act adds following new grounds for winding-up of a company by NCLT:

- If the company has acted against the interests of the sovereignty and integrity of India, the security of the State, friendly relations with foreign States, public order, decency or morality;
- If order has been made by NCTL under Chapter XIX (Revival and Rehabilitation of Sick Companies);
- If on an application made by the ROC or any other person authorised by the Central Government by notification under 2013 Act and NCLT is of the opinion that the affairs of a company have been conducted in a fraudulent manner or the company was formed for fraudulent and unlawful purpose or the persons concerned in the formation or management of its affairs have been guilty of fraud, misfeasance or misconduct in connection therewith and that it is proper that the company be wound-up;
- If the company has made a default in filing with the ROC its financial statements or annual returns for immediately preceding five consecutive financial years; or
- If NCLT is of the opinion that it is just and equitable that the company should be wound-up. [Section 270 to 365]

# The Companies (Amendment) Act, 2015

The Companies (Amendment) Bill, 2014, a bill to amend the Companies Act, 2013 (“**Act**”), has now been passed by both the houses of the Parliament and has received the assent of the President of India on May 25, 2015 making it the Companies (Amendment) Act, 2015 (“**Amendment Act**”). The provisions of the Amendment Act have come into force from May 29, 2015.

## ANALYSIS AND IMPACT OF THE KEY AMENDMENTS

## I. Related Party Transactions (“RPTs”)

Section 297 of the erstwhile Companies Act, 1956 set out the requirement for procuring Central Government approval for RPTs while the Act required a special resolution for RPTs where a shareholder who was a related party was not allowed to vote on such special resolution. Now, the Amendment Act further relaxes this provision and allows companies to enter into RPTs after passing an ordinary resolution for the same. This will enable group companies in transacting *inter se* business. Further, the requirement of shareholder's approval in case of RPT between holding company and wholly owned subsidiary (“**WOS**”) has been dispensed with. This exception was earlier present under the Companies (Meetings of Board and its Powers) Rules, 2014 (“**Rules**”) and now has been incorporated in the substantive law itself.

## II. Omnibus approval for RPTs

In addition to the amendment of allowing companies to undertake RPTs through an ordinary resolution; the Amendment Act amends Section 177 whereby a new proviso to Section 177 (4) has been inserted which reads as follows *“provided that the Audit Committee may make omnibus approval for related party transactions proposed to be entered into by the company, subject to such conditions as may be prescribed.”* Thus, for ease in doing business, now the audit committee will be empowered to give omnibus approvals for related party transactions to be entered into by the company.

This amendment seems to be in line with the provisions of the recently amended Clause 49 of the Listing Agreement as regards omnibus approval of related party transactions by the audit committee constituted under the Board of the company. This amendment may also result in defeating the principles of healthy corporate governance practices to be followed by companies whereby they are required to inform the shareholder of all pertinent details in relation to a related party transaction so as to enable him to take an informed decision. The conditions for the omnibus approval are yet to be notified and are expected to bring in more clarity on the subject.

## III. Minimum Capital Requirement

The requirement for having a minimum paid-up capital of ₹ 1,00,000 for private limited companies and ₹ 5,00,000 for public limited companies has now been done away with. This amendment is expected to reduce registration costs for incorporation of new companies. However, the minimum capital requirements generally acted as filters and, to an extent, ensured the formation of companies for bonafide and genuine purposes. This amendment may now encourage formation of bogus shell companies.

## IV. Loan to WOS

Section 185 of Act prohibits a company from:

(i) advancing any loan, including a loan represented by a book debt, to its director or to any other person in whom the said director is interested; and/or

(ii) giving any guarantee or providing any security in connection with any loan taken by the director or any other person in whom the director is interested.

Transactions in the nature of loans and guarantees between a holding company and its WOS were exempted from the applicability of Section 185. This exemption was already provided for in the Rules and now it has been incorporated in the substantive law itself.

## V. Restriction on inspection of Board Resolutions

Section 117 of the Act required a company to file certain specified resolutions with the Registrar of Companies and permitted public inspection of such resolutions, thus raising concerns of breach of confidentiality. This provision under the Act was not well received by the stakeholders. The Amendment Act now inserts a new proviso to clause (g) of Section 117 of the Act, which states that *"provided that no person shall be entitled under section 399 to inspect or obtain copies of such resolutions"* thus ensuring confidentiality of such resolutions.

## VI. Common Seal

The Amendment Act has omitted the words 'and a common seal' appearing under Section 9 of the Act which means it shall not be mandatory for a company to have a common seal. This is not a major change yet it is a welcome change. In the era of digital signatures and documents being maintained in the electronic form, common seal was an obsolete requirement of the law.

## VII. Deposits

Section 76(A) has been inserted by the Amendment Act whereby a minimum penalty of ₹ 1 Crore is sought to be imposed on companies which *"accept or invite or allow or cause any other person to accept or invite on its behalf"* deposit in contravention of provisions of Section 73 of the Act or *"fails to repay the deposit and interest thereon"*. This insertion seeks to protect the interests of the funds of the investors and imposes a harsh fine and punishment on the company as well as every other officer who is in default in relation to such non-compliance.

## VIII. No dividend, without depreciation

The Companies (Declaration and Payment of Dividend) Rules, 2014 were amended by the Companies (Declaration and Payment of Dividend) Amendment Rules, 2014 whereby companies were prohibited from declaring dividend unless the previous year or years' losses and unabsorbed depreciation which had not been provided for by the company were set off against current year's profits. This provision has been incorporated in the substantive law by amendment of Section 123 of the Act. This is a welcome move for ensuring financial health of a company.

## IX. Fraud Reporting-threshold limits

The Act required an auditor, who believes that an offence involving a fraud is being or has been committed in a company, to report the same to the Central Government. The existing Section 143 (12) has been substituted by a new clause which stipulates that if the auditor, during the course of his audit, discovers or suspects a fraud, he has to report it to the Central Government when the amount of the fraud crosses the threshold limit to be prescribed by the Central Government and in respect of other frauds/ suspected frauds below the threshold limit, the same needs to be reported by the auditor to the audit committee constituted under the Board of the company and in cases where the company does not have an audit committee, the same may be reported to the Board of the company. Whether or not the amendment is a welcome change can be more affirmatively ascertained upon notification of the threshold limits.

## X. Special Courts

The Amendment Act amends the provisions of Section 435 whereby the Special Courts constituted under the Act shall try only those offences which are punishable by an imprisonment of two years or more. All other offences may be tried by the Metropolitan Magistrate or Judicial Magistrate First Class.

## XI. Bail restrictions to apply only for offence relating to fraud

Section 212 of the Act specified the offences under specific Sections of the Act which attracted the punishment for fraud under Section 447 and which were to be cognizable offences and in respect of which, bail restrictions as specified in Section 212 (6) (i) and (ii) would apply. The Amendment Act now widens the ambit of Section 212 to remove the specific list of offences and specifies that any offence which falls within the definition of 'fraud' under Section 447 shall be considered as a cognizable offence and the bail restrictions as specified in Section 212 (6) (i) and (ii) would apply to any such offence.

## SECTION-WISE SUMMARY OF AMENDMENTS

| SECTION | EARLIER PROVISION | PROVISIONS AFTER AMENDMENT |
|---|---|---|
| 2 (68) | Private Company required "Minimum Paid up Share Capital of ₹ 100,000" | No requirement of Minimum Paid Up Capital. |
| 2 (71) | Public Company required "Minimum Paid up Share Capital of ₹ 500,000" | No requirement of Minimum Paid Up Capital. |
| 9, 12 and 223 | Affixation of Common Seal is Mandatory | Use of Common Seal is now optional. (Not Mandatory) |
| 11 | Commencement of Business | No requirement of Commencement of Business Certificate. Such section shall be omitted. |
| 22 | Execution of Bills of Exchange | Use of Common Seal is now optional. (Not Mandatory)If company doesn't have common seal the authorization under sub section (2) of Section 22 shall be made by two directors or by a director and the Company Secretary, wherever the company has appointed a Company Secretary. |
| 46 | Issue of Share Certificate(46(1): A share certificate issue under the common seal of Company{Clause substituted) | Use of Common Seal is now optional. (Not Mandatory) If company doesn't have common seal then signed by two Directors or by a director and Company secretary (if any) |
| 76A | This was not in the Act. | New Section 76A inserted after Section 76 for punishment for deposits accepted in violation of the provisions of the said Act. |
| 117(3)(g) | Public can inspect the form MGT-14 filed by the Companies as per section 179(3) for the Board Resolution. | Public can't inspects form MGT-14 filed for the purposes mention in section 179(3). {MGT-14 (filed for purpose of Section 179(3), Board Resolution) will not available for public inspection on MCA portal.} |
| 123(1) | This was not in the Act. | After the third proviso of 123(1), the following proviso is inserted. Proviso, No company shall declare dividend unless carried over previous losses and depreciation not provided in previous year or years are set off against profit of the company for the current year. |

| SECTION | EARLIER PROVISION | PROVISIONS AFTER AMENDMENT |
|---|---|---|
| 124(6) | Unpaid or unclaimed dividend has been transferred under sub-section (5) Substituted | (i) For the words, brackets and figure "unpaid or unclaimed dividend has been transferred under sub-section (5) shall also be", the words "dividend has not been paid or claimed for seven consecutive years or more (ii) After the proviso, the following explanation shall be inserted", namely: — "Explanation— In case any dividend is paid or claimed for any year during the said period of seven consecutive years, the share shall not be transferred to Investor Education and Protection Fund." |
| 134(3) | Not Earlier in the Act. | After Clause "c" following clause (ca) is inserted: Details in respect of frauds reported by auditors under sub-section (12) of section 143 **"other than those which are reportable to the Central Government"** |
| 143(12) | The Act requires that if the auditor of a company has reason to believe that an offence of fraud has been committed against the company, by its employees, he must report the matter to the central government within a time period and in a manner prescribed. | Notwithstanding anything contained in this section, if any auditor of a company in the course of the performance of his duties as auditor, has reason to believe that an offence of fraud involving such amount or amounts as may be prescribed, is being or has been committed in the company by its officers or employees, the auditor shall report the matter to the central government within such time and in such manner as may be prescribed: Provided that in case of a fraud involving lesser than the specified amount, the auditor shall report the matter to the audit committee constituted under section 177 or to the Board in other cases within such time and in such manner as may be prescribed: Provided further that the companies whose auditors have reported frauds under subsection 12 to the Audit Committee or the Board but not reported to the Central Government, shall disclosed details about such frauds in the Board Report in such manner as may be prescribed. |
| 117(4)(iv) | Every Audit Committee shall act in accordance with the terms of reference specified in writing by the Board which shall inter alia include (iv) approval or any subsequent modification of transaction of the Company with Related Party. | After 117(4)(iv) following proviso added: Provided that the Audit Committee may make omnibus approval for related party transaction proposed to be entered into by the company subject to such conditions as may be prescribed. |
| 185 | Not Earlier in the Act. Bare Act Language of Section 185(1)(b) : A company which in the ordinary course of its business provides loans or gives guarantees or securities for the due repayment of any loan and | After clause (b) Sub Section (1) of Section 185 following clause and proviso added: (c) Any loan made by a Holding Company to its Wholly own Subsidiary Company or any guarantee given or security provided by a Holding Company in respect of any loan made to its wholly own subsidiary |

| SECTION | EARLIER PROVISION | PROVISIONS AFTER AMENDMENT |
|---|---|---|
| | in respect of such loan an interest in charged at a rate not less than the bank rate declared by the RBI. | Company, (d) Any guarantee given or security provided by a Holding Company in respect of Loan made by any Bank or financial institution to its subsidiary Company provided that the loan made under clauses (c) and (d) are utilized by the subsidiary company for its **principal business activity.** |
| 188(1) | Earlier Special Resolution was required.(As per the previous system, the companies with a paid up capital of Rs 10 crore or more were required to get shareholders' nod through a special resolution in case of related party transactions) | For the word "Special Resolution" the word "Resolution" is substituted under the Act. Now Ordinary resolution will work. |
| 188(1) | Not Earlier in the Act. | Not required to follow provision of Section 188. After the third proviso of Section 188(1) the following proviso inserted: Provided also that the requirement of passing the resolution under the first proviso shall not be applicable for transactions entered between a holding company and its wholly owned subsidiary whose accounts are consolidated with such holding company and have been placed before the shareholders for their approval. |
| 212(6) | Investigation into affairs of Company by Serious Fraud Investigation Office. Here, provided Bail restriction for many sections. | The bail restrictions to apply only for offence relating to fraud u/s 447. |
| 419(4) | In Section 419(4) winding up was mentioned. | The word WINDING UP shall be omitted. |
| 435 | Establishment of Special Courts. The Central Govt. may for the purpose of providing speedy (Trial of offences under this Act), established or designate as many Special Courts as may be necessary. | For the Words "Trial of Offences under This Act", The words "Trial of offences punishable under this Act with imprisonment with 2 years or more" is substituted. After Sub Clause (1) the following proviso is inserted: "Provided that all other offences shall be tried, as the case may be by a metropolitan Magistrate or a Judicial Magistrate of the first class having jurisdiction to try any offence under this Act or under any pervious Company Law. |
| 436 | Offence Triable by special courts Section 436(1)(a) | For the words "all offences under this Act", the words, brackets and figures "all offences specified under sub-section (1) of section 435" shall be substituted Section 435(1) given below. |
| 462 | Sub-section {2,3 and 4 of Section 462) shall be substituted. | Substituted language of Section 462(2),(3) and (4). |

# HIGHLIGHTS OF COMPANIES (Amendment) ACT, 2017

Companies (Amendment) Bill, 2017 was introduced in Lok Sabha on March 16, 2016 then the Bill was referred to the Standing Committee on Finance on 12 April, 2016 and Committee after hearing the views of different representatives and professionals adopted its report on 30th November, 2016.

- Lok Sabha passed this bill on July 27, 2017,
- Rajya Sabha passed this bill on December 19, 2017
- Received assent of President of India on the January 3rd, 2018 and it was published in the "Official Gazette of India" on the same date i.e., WEDNESDAY, JANUARY, 3, 2018, and the Bill becomes the Companies (Amendment) Act, 2017 from this date and is applicable from the same date.

The Companies (Amendment) Act, 2017 introduces several amendments to the Companies Act 2013, realigning provisions to improve corporate governance and ease of doing business in India while continuing to strengthen compliance and investor protection. This is the second round of amendments made to the Companies Act, 2013, with the first are being made in 2015.

The major amendments include simplification of the private placement process, rationalization of provisions related to loan to directors, omission of provisions relating to forward dealing and insider trading, doing away with the requirement of approval of the Central Government for managerial remuneration above prescribed limits, aligning disclosure requirements in the prospectus with the regulations to be made by SEBI, providing for maintenance of register of significant beneficial owners and filing of returns in this regard to the ROC and removal of requirement for annual ratification of appointment or continuance of auditor.

The major official amendments subsequently introduced include continuing with the provisions relating to layers of subsidiaries, continuing with the earlier provisions with respect of memorandum, making offence for contravention of provisions relating to deposits as non-compoundable, requiring attaching of financial statement of associate companies, stringent additional fees of ₹ 100 per day in case of delay in filing of annual return and financial statement etc.

## The Companies (Amendment) Act, 2017. Key Changes and Highlights

| S. No. | Section | AMENDMENT |
|---|---|---|
| 1. | Section 2(6)- Definition of 'associate company' | • Change in explanation of the term 'significant influence' under the definition of Associate Company has been proposed.<br>Significant influence is proposed to mean control of at least 20% of the voting power or control or participation in business decision under an agreement.<br>Currently the Act provides for control of at least 20% total share capital. |
| | | • Further the term 'Joint Venture' has also been defined to mean a joint arrangement whereby the parties that have joint control of the arrangement have rights to the net assets of the arrangement. |
| 2. | Section 2(28)- Definition of 'cost accountant' | Change in definition of 'cost accountant' is proposed.<br>"Cost Accountant" means a person who is a member of the Institute of Cost and Works Accountants of India and who holds a valid certificate of practice. |
| 3. | Section 2(30)- Definition of 'Debenture' | Under the definition of the term "debenture", it is proposed to exclude instruments referred to in Chapter III-D of the Reserve Bank of India Act 1934 and such other instruments prescribed by the Central Government in consultation with the RBI. |
| 4. | Section 2(41)- Definition of 'Financial year' | It is proposed that associate company of a company incorporated outside India can also apply to the Tribunal for a different financial year. |

| S. No. | Section | AMENDMENT |
|---|---|---|
| 5. | Section 2(46)-Definition of 'Holding Company' | It is proposed that for the purpose of definition of the term 'holding company', the expression "company" will include any body corporate. |
| 6. | Section 2(49)-Definition of 'Interested director' | It is proposed to delete the definition of the term 'Interested director'. |
| 7. | Section 2(51)-Definition of 'Key Managerial Personnel' | Under the definition of the term "Key Managerial Personnel", such other officer not more than one level below the directors who is in whole time employment and designated as KMP by the Board, is proposed to be included. |
| 8. | Section 2(57)-Definition of 'net worth' | It is proposed to include the debit or credit balance of profit and loss account in the calculation of net worth. |
| 9. | Section 2(71)-Definition of 'public company' | Including the word 'and' in the definition for more clarity is proposed to clarify that a public company must satisfy both the conditions mentioned in the subsection. |
| 10. | Section 2(72)-Definition of 'public financial institution' | It is proposed that the Central Government may notify other institution which has been established or constituted by or under any Central or State Act other than the Companies Act, 2013 or previous Company Law after consultation with the RBI as "public financial institution". |
| 11. | Section 2(76)-Definition of 'Related Party' | Following two amendments are proposed:<br>• Instead of only a company, anybody corporate which is holding, subsidiary or an associate company of such company or a subsidiary of a holding company to which it is also a subsidiary or an investing company or venture of the Company, shall be considered as a related party. |
| | | • "An investing company or the venturer of the company" will mean a body corporate whose investment in the company would result in the company becoming an associate company of the body corporate. |
| 12. | Section 2(85)-Definition of 'small company' | • It is proposed to increase the maximum paid-up share capital amount which can be prescribed for the purpose of determining a company as a small company from five crore rupees to ten crore rupees and prescribed turnover amount from twenty crore rupees to one hundred crore rupees. |
| | | • Further turnover should be as per profit and loss account for the immediately preceding financial year and not as per its last financial year. |
| 13. | Section 2(87)-Definition of 'subsidiary company' | It is proposed that a company will be treated as subsidiary in case the holding company exercises or controls more than one-half of the total voting power either at its own or together with one or more of its subsidiary companies. Currently the Act provides for exercise or control of more than half of the total share capital. |

| S. No. | Section | AMENDMENT |
|---|---|---|
| **14.** | Section 2(91)-Definition of 'Turnover' | It is proposed to change the definition of turnover to mean the gross amount of revenue recognised in the profit and loss account from the sale, supply, or distribution of goods or on account of services rendered, or both, by a company during a financial year. |
| **15.** | Section 3A-Members severally liable certain cases | It is proposed to insert a new section regarding liability of members in case number of members is reduced from statutory minimum, i.e. seven in the case of public company or two in case of a private company. This section was there in the Companies Act 1956 but was missing from the Companies Act 2013. |
| **16.** | Section 4-Memorandum | • It is proposed that in case of incorporation, name reserved by the RoC shall be valid for 20 days from date of the approval or such other period as may be prescribed instead of 60 days from the date of application, as currently provided; |
| | | • in case of change in name by an existing company, name reserved by the RoC shall be valid for 60 days from the date of approval. |
| **17.** | Section 7-Incorporation of company | At the time of incorporation of the company, declaration by each subscriber will be required to be attached instead of an affidavit, as currently provided. |
| **18.** | Section 12-Registered office of company | • It is proposed that the company shall within 30 of its incorporation have registered office instead of current requirement to have registered office on and from the fifteenth day of its incorporation. |
| | | • It is proposed that notice of every change of the situation of the registered office, shall be given to the Registrar within 30 days instead of 15 days, as currently provided. |
| **19.** | Section 21-Authentication of documents, proceedings and contracts | Apart from KMP and any officer of the company, it is proposed that an employee can also be authorized to authenticate documents on behalf of the company. |
| **20.** | Section 26-Matters to be stated in Prospectus | Instead of detailed list of contents of the Prospectus, it is proposed that the prospectus shall state such information and set out such reports on financial information as may be specified by SEBI in consultation with the Central Government.<br>Till the time SEBI specifies the information and reports on financial information, the regulations made by it under the SEBI Act, 1992, in respect of such financial information or reports on financial information shall apply. |
| **21.** | Section 35-Civil liability for Misstatements in prospectus | It is proposed to amend section 35 of the Act to relieve the Director, promoter etc. from any civil liability if such person(s) has relied on a misleading statement made by an expert and he had reasonable ground to believe and did up to the time of the issue of the prospectus believe, that the person making the statement was competent to make it and that the said person had given the consent required and had not withdrawn it. |

| S. No. | Section | AMENDMENT |
|---|---|---|
| 22. | Section 42-Private placement | Though the entire section is proposed to be substituted but major changes proposed are: –<br>• Return of allotment has to be filed within 15 days instead of 30 days. |
| | | • Money received under the private placement shall not be utilized unless the return of allotment is filed with the ROC. |
| | | • Private Placement offer letter shall not contain any right of renunciation. |
| 23. | Section 47-Voting rights | Since a member who is a related party cannot vote on a resolution to be passed under section 188 of the Companies Act 2013, it is proposed to clarify that the right of every member holding equity shares to vote on all resolutions placed before the meeting would be subject to sub-section (1) of section 188 of the Act. |
| 24. | Section 53-Prohibition on issue of shares at discount | • It is proposed to replace the words "discounted price" with the word "discount". |
| | | • Further it is proposed to allow companies to issue shares at a discount to its creditors when its debt is converted into shares in pursuance of any statutory resolution plan or debt restructuring scheme in accordance with any guidelines or directions or regulations specified by Reserve Bank of India under the Banking Regulation Act, 1949 or the Reserve Bank of India Act 1934. |
| 25. | Section 54-Issue of Sweat Equity Shares | It is proposed to allow issue of sweat equity shares at any time after registration of the company. Currently such shares can be issued only after the expiry of one year from the date of commencement of business. |
| 26. | Section 62-Further issue of share capital | • It is proposed to bring the requirement of compliance with section 42 in respect of the preferential offer in the section itself. Currently the applicability of section 42 is provided by the rules. |
| | | • It is proposed that right issue offer letter can be sent through courier also. |
| 27. | Section 73-Prohibition on acceptance of deposits from public | • It is proposed that an amount being not less than 20% of the amount of deposits, maturing during the following financial year be deposited on or before the 30th day of April each year and kept in a scheduled bank in a separate bank account to be called deposit repayment reserve account. Currently at least 15% of such amount is required to be deposited and that is also of amount of deposits maturing during a financial year and the financial year next following. |
| | | • Further it is proposed to omit the requirement of providing deposit insurance. |
| | | • It is also proposed that companies which had defaulted in repayment of deposits, can also accept deposits after a period of 5 years from the date of making good the default. |

| S. No. | Section | AMENDMENT |
|---|---|---|
| **28.** | Section 74-Repayment of Deposits, etc., accepted before commencement of this act | Where any amount of deposit or part thereof or interest thereof remains unpaid on the commencement of the Companies Act 2013, it is proposed that such amount shall be repaid within 3 years from the date of commencement or before the expiry of the period for which the deposit was accepted, whichever is earlier. Currently the amount was to be repaid within 1 year or before the expiry of the period for which the deposit was accepted, whichever is earlier. |
| **29.** | Section 76A-Punishment for Contravention of Section 73 or Section 76 | • It is proposed to change the penalty from a fine not less than rupees one crore to rupees one crore or twice the amount of deposits accepted by the company, whichever is lower. |
| | | • Further it is proposed that an officer of the company who is in default shall be punishable with imprisonment and fine. Earlier it was imprisonment or fine. In the process, the offence has been made non-compoundable. |
| **30.** | Section 77-Duty to register charges, etc. | It is proposed that this section shall not apply to certain charges, as may be prescribed by the Central Government in consultation with the Reserve Bank of India. |
| **31.** | Section 78-Application for Registration of charge | It is proposed that the person in whose favour the charge has been created can file the charge on the expiry of 30 days from the creation of charge where a company fails to file so. Currently the charge holder can register the charge only in case the company fails to do so within the period specified under section 77, which is 300 days. |
| **32.** | Section 82-Company to report satisfaction of charge | Timeline for filing of satisfaction of charge is proposed to be increased to 300 days on payment of additional fee. |
| **33.** | Section 89-Declaration in respect of beneficial interest in any share | As per the current law, return of beneficial interest declaration can also be filed on payment of additional fee within 270 days from the date by which it should have been filed. It is proposed to do away with the time limit of 270 days and the return can be filed at any time on payment of prescribed additional fee.<br>For the purpose of declaration of beneficial interest, it is proposed that beneficial interest in a share includes, directly or indirectly, through any contract, arrangement or otherwise, the right or entitlement of a person alone or together with any other person to—<br>• exercise or cause to be exercised any or all of the rights attached to such share; or |
| | | • receive or participate in any dividend or other distribution in respect of such share. |
| **34.** | Section 90-Investigation of beneficial ownership of shares in certain cases | The provisions are proposed to be revamped. Key changes proposed are as under:<br>• Every individual, who acting alone or together, or through one or more persons or trust, including a trust and persons resident outside India, holds beneficial interests, of not less than twenty-five per cent. or such |

| S. No. | Section | AMENDMENT |
|---|---|---|
| | | other percentage as may be prescribed, in shares of a company or the right to exercise, or the actual exercising of significant influence or control as defined in clause (27) of section 2, over the company shall make a declaration to the company. The Central Government may however, prescribe class(es) of persons who shall not be required to make declaration. |
| | | • Every company shall maintain a register of the interest declared by individuals as aforesaid and such register shall be open to inspection of members. |
| | | • Every company shall file a return of significant beneficial owners of the company and changes therein with the Registrar. |
| | | • Obligation is cast on the company to give notice, in the prescribed manner, to any person whom the company knows or has reasonable cause to believe to be a significant beneficial owner of the company who is not registered as a significant beneficial owner with the company as required under this section. |
| | | • In case information asked is not provided, the Company shall apply to the Tribunal for an order directing that the shares in question be subject to restrictions with regard to transfer of interest, suspension of all rights attached to the shares. |
| | | • Stringent penalties have been provided for default of this section including liability for fraud u/s 447. |
| **35.** | Section 92-Annual Return | • It is proposed to omit the requirement of MGT-9 i.e. extract of annual return to form part of the Board's Report. Instead, the copy of annual return shall be uploaded on the website of the company, if any, and its link shall be disclosed in the Board's report. |
| | | • The Central Government may prescribe abridged form of annual return for One Person Company ('OPC'), Small Company and such other class or classes of companies as may be prescribed. |
| | | • It is also proposed to omit the requirement related to disclosing indebtedness and details with respect to name, address, country of incorporation etc. of FII in the annual return of the company. |
| | | • Time limit of 270 days within which annual return could be filed on payment of additional fee has been done away with. It is proposed that a company can file the annual return with ROC at any time on payment of prescribed additional fee. |
| **36.** | Section 93-Return to be filed with Registrar in case Promoters' stake changes | It is proposed to omit section 93 relating to return to be filed with respect to changes in promoters' and top ten shareholders' stake. |
| **37.** | Section 94-Place of keeping and inspection of | • It is proposed to omit the requirement of filing of special resolution in advance with the Registrar of Companies for keeping of the registers and returns at a place other than the registered office of the company. |

| S. No. | Section | AMENDMENT |
|---|---|---|
| | registers, returns, etc. | • Further it is proposed that certain prescribed particulars in the return, register or index referred to in this section shall not be available for inspection or for taking extracts or copies. |
| 38. | Section 96- Annual General Meeting | It is proposed that Annual General Meeting ('AGM') of unlisted company may be held at anyplace in India if consent is given is writing or by electronic mode by all the members in advance. |
| 39. | Section 100- Calling of Extraordinary General Meeting | It is proposed that Extraordinary General Meeting ('EGM') of wholly owned subsidiary of a company incorporated outside India can be held outside India. A company other than wholly owned subsidiary of a company incorporated outside India must hold EGM at a place within India. |
| 40. | Section 101- Notice of meeting | • It is proposed that a general meeting may be held at a shorter notice if in case of an Annual General Meeting consent in writing or by electronic mode is given by not less than 95% of the members entitled to vote and in case of other general meetings consent is given by majority in number of members entitled to vote and who represent not less than 95% of paid-up share capital (in case of company having share capital) or total voting power exercisable at the meeting (in case of company not having share capital). |
| | | • Where any member of a company is entitled to vote only on some resolution or resolutions to be moved at a meeting and not on the others, then his vote with respect to shorter notice shall only be counted for the purpose of the resolution on which he can vote. |
| | | • Currently for calling both AGM and EGM at shorter notice, consent of 95% of members entitled to vote at the meeting is required. |
| 41. | Section 110- Postal Ballot | It is proposed to allow companies which are mandatorily required to provide electronic voting facility, to transact items in general which, which are mandatorily required to be transacted through postal ballot. |
| 42. | Section 117- Resolutions and Agreements to be filed. | • It is proposed to provide exemption to banking companies from filing resolutions with respect to grant of loans, giving of guarantee or providing of security in respect of loans in the ordinary course of its business. |
| | | • It is proposed to omit clause (e) of sub-section (3) of the section as the requirement under the clause is already covered in clause (a). |
| | | • The minimum fine for non-filing under this section for company and officer in default is proposed to be reduced from rupees five lakh to one lakh rupees and from rupees one lakh to rupees fifty thousand. |
| | | • Time limit of 270 days within which resolutions and agreements could be filed on payment of additional fee has been done away with. It is proposed that a company can file the resolutions and agreements with ROC at any time on payment of prescribed additional fee. |

| S. No. | Section | AMENDMENT |
|---|---|---|
| 43. | Section 121- Report on annual general meeting | Time limit of 270 days within which report on annual general meeting could be filed on payment of additional fee has been done away with. It is proposed that a company can file the report on annual general meeting with ROC at any time on payment of prescribed additional fee. |
| 44. | Section 123- Declaration of dividend | • It is proposed that in computing profits any amount representing unrealized gains, notional gains or revaluation of assets and any change in carrying of an asset or of a liability on measurement of the asset or the liability at fair value shall be excluded |
| | | • In the case of inadequate or absence of profits, dividend can be declared out of accumulated profits earned by the company in previous years and transferred by the company to free reserves (instead of reserves). |
| | | • It is also proposed that the Board of Directors of a company may declare interim dividend during any financial year or at any time during the period from closure of financial year till holding of the annual general meeting out of the surplus in the profit and loss account or out of profits of the financial year for which such interim dividend is sought to be declared or out of profits generated in the financial year till the quarter preceding the date of declaration of the interim dividend.<br>In case the company has incurred loss during the current financial year up to the end of the quarter immediately preceding the date of declaration of interim dividend, such interim dividend shall not be declared at a rate higher than the average dividends declared by the company during immediately preceding three financial years. |
| 45. | Section 129- Financial Statement | • The explanation providing that subsidiary includes associate company and joint venture has been deleted. The section has been amended to provide for consolidation of the accounts of associate companies in addition to its subsidiaries in the same form and manner as that of its own in accordance with applicable accounting standards. |
| | | • The company shall also attach along with its financial statement, a separate statement containing the salient features of the subsidiary and associate companies. |
| 46. | Section 130- Reopening of accounts on court's or tribunal's orders | • It is proposed that in addition to authorities already specified, any other person concerned shall be given notice before passing an order for re-opening of accounts and the court or the Tribunal shall also take into consideration the representations made by the other person. |
| | | • It is also proposed that order for reopening of accounts can be made upto eight financial years preceding the current financial year unless there is a specific direction under section 128(5) from the Central Government that the books of accounts may be kept for longer period in which case the books of account may be ordered to be reopened for a longer period |
| 47. | Section 132- Constitution of National Financial Reporting Authority | • It is proposed to reduce the minimum fine in respect of professional or other misconduct from ten lakh rupees to five lakh rupees. |
| | | • It is proposed to omit the provisions regarding constitution of separate Appellate Authority under this section and appeal against any order of NFRA shall lie before the National Company Law Appellate Tribunal in the prescribed manner. |

| S. No. | Section | AMENDMENT |
|---|---|---|
| **48.** | Section 134-Financial Statement, Board's report, etc. | • It is proposed that CEO whether appointed as a Director or not, will sign the financial statement, in case there is no chairperson of the Company. Currently CEO is required to sign, only if he is also acting as a director. |
| | | • In case of Board report, it is proposed that disclosures which have been provided in the financial statement shall not be required to be reproduced in the report again. |
| | | • It is proposed that in place of extract of the annual return, only the web address, if any, where annual return has been placed shall be mentioned. |
| | | • It is proposed that instead of exact text of the policies, key feature of policies along with its web link shall be disclosed in Board report. |
| | | • In respect to performance evaluation, it is proposed to omit the responsibility of the Board for carrying the performance evaluation of Board, Directors and Committee. It is now required to include in the Board's report of listed companies and other prescribed public companies that annual evaluation of the performance of the Board, its Committees and of individual directors has been made. |
| | | • Central Government may prescribe abridged Board Report for small and one person companies. |
| **49.** | Section 135-Corporate Social Responsibility | • Eligibility criteria for the purpose of constituting the corporate social responsibility committee and incurring expenditure towards CSR is proposed to be calculated based on immediately preceding financial year. Currently this eligibility is decided based on preceding three financial years. |
| | | • Further it is proposed that where a company is not required to appoint an independent director, it shall have in its Corporate Social Responsibility Committee two or more directors. |
| | | • It also proposed to empower the Central Government to prescribe sums which shall not be included for calculating 'net profit' of a company under section 135. |
| **50.** | Section 136-Right of member to copies of audited financial statement | • It is proposed that copies of audited financial statements and other documents can be sent at shorter notice if it is so agreed by members-<br>(a) holding, if the company has a share capital, majority in number entitled to vote and who represent not less than ninety-five per cent of such part of the paid-up share capital of the company as gives a right to vote at the meeting; or<br>(b) having, if the company has no share capital, not less than ninety-five per cent of the total voting power exercisable at the meeting. |
| | | • It is proposed that only listed companies shall place on its website, if any the separate audited accounts of its subsidiary or subsidiaries. Currently all companies required to comply this. |
| | | • If the foreign subsidiary is statutorily required to prepare consolidated financial statement under any law of the country of its incorporation, it is proposed that the requirement of posting audited accounts of subsidiary shall be met if consolidated financial statement of such foreign subsidiary is placed on the website of the listed company. |

| S. No. | Section | AMENDMENT |
|---|---|---|
| | | • If the foreign subsidiary is not required to get its financial statement audited, it is proposed that the holding listed company may place such unaudited financial statement on its website and where such financial statement is in a language other than English, a translated copy of the financial statement in English shall also be placed on the website. |
| | | • It is proposed that every company having a subsidiary or subsidiaries shall provide a copy of separate audited or unaudited financial statements, as the case may be, as prepared in respect of each of its subsidiary to any member who asks for it. |
| **51.** | Section 137- Copy of Financial Statement to be filed with Registrar | • It is proposed to allow the filing of unaudited financial statements of foreign subsidiary which is not required to get its accounts audited along with a declaration to that effect. |
| | | • Time limit of 270 days within which financial statement could be filed on payment of additional fee has been done away with under all the sub-sections. It is proposed that a company can file the financial statement with ROC at any time on payment of prescribed additional fee. |
| **52.** | Section 139-Appointment of Auditors | It is proposed to omit the requirement related to ratification of appointment of auditors by members at every annual general meeting. |
| **53.** | Section 140-Removal, Resignation of Auditor and giving of special notice | It is proposed to reduce the fine in case of failure to file resignation by auditor in Form ADT-3 to fifty thousand rupees or the remuneration of auditor whichever is less. |
| **54.** | Section 141- Eligibility, Qualification and Disqualifications of Auditors | It is proposed that a person who, directly or indirectly, renders any service referred to in section 144 to the company or its holding company or its subsidiary company will not be eligible for appointment as Auditor. Currently the restriction is only on the person, whose subsidiary, associate company or any other form of entity is engaged as on the date of appointment in consulting and specialized services as provided in section 144. |
| **55.** | Section 143- Powers and duties of auditors and auditing standards | • It is proposed to cover associate companies along with subsidiary companies with respect to right of auditors to have access to accounts and records. |
| | | • The auditor's report is to include whether internal financial controls with reference to financial statement are in place and not in respect of internal financial control system. |
| **56.** | Section 147- Punishment for contravention | • The maximum fine which can be imposed on an auditor has been revised from rupees five lakh to rupees five lakh or four times the remuneration of the auditor, whichever is less. If the auditor has contravened provisions knowingly or wilfully with the intention to deceive the company etc., the amount of fine has been reduced to minimum of fifty thousand rupees but which may extend to twenty-five lakh rupees or eight times the remuneration of the auditor, whichever is less. |

| S. No. | Section | AMENDMENT |
|---|---|---|
| | | • It is proposed to restrict the liability of auditor who is convicted of any default, to pay the damages to any person for loss arising out of incorrect or misleading statements made in the audit report, to only members and creditors of the company. Currently the Auditor is liable to pay damages to any person concerned. |
| | | • It is proposed that criminal liability of an audit firm, in respect of liability other than fine, the concerned partner or partners, who acted in a fraudulent manner or abetted or, as the case may be, colluded in any fraud shall only be liable. Currently the criminal liability is of the partner or partners concerned of the audit firm and the firm, jointly and severally. |
| **57.** | Section 148-Central Government to specify audit of items of Cost in respect of Certain Companies | It is proposed to substitute the words 'cost accountant in practice' with the words 'cost accountant' and also to substitute the words 'Institute of Cost and Works Accountants of India' with the words 'Institute of Cost. |
| **58.** | Section 149-Company to have Board of Directors | • It is proposed that 182 days for determining whether a director is resident in India shall be computed with reference to the financial year. Currently it is calculated in reference to previous calendar year. |
| | | • Further it is proposed that in case of new companies, the requirement of period of 182 days shall apply proportionately at the end of the financial year in which it is incorporated. |
| | | • In the definition of Independent Director, the words 'pecuniary interest' is proposed to be substituted by pecuniary relationship, other than remuneration as such director or having transaction not exceeding ten per cent, of his total income or such amount as may be prescribed. |
| | | • While determining the eligibility for appointment as Independent director, it is proposed to extend the restriction related to pecuniary relationships with respect to relative of a director to include the following:<br>(i) is holding any security of or interest in the company, its holding, subsidiary or associate company during the two immediately preceding financial years or during the current financial year. Provided that the relative may hold security or interest in the company of face value not exceeding fifty lakh rupees or two per cent of the paid-up capital of the company, its holding, subsidiary or associate company or such higher sum as may be prescribed;<br>(ii) is indebted to the company, its holding, subsidiary or associate company or their promoters, or directors, in excess of such amount as may be prescribed during the two immediately preceding financial years or during the current financial year;<br>(iii) has given a guarantee or provided any security in connection with the indebtedness of any third person to the company, its holding, subsidiary or associate company or their promoters, or directors of such holding company, for such amount as may be prescribed during the two immediately preceding financial years or during the current financial year; or |

| S. No. | Section | AMENDMENT |
|---|---|---|
| | | (iv) has any other pecuniary transaction or relationship with the company, or its subsidiary, or its holding or associate company amounting to two per cent or more of its gross turnover or total income singly or in combination with the transactions referred to in subclause (i), (ii) or (iii) above. |
| | | • It is proposed to allow the appointment of person as an independent director, whose relative is an employee during the three financial years immediately preceding the financial year, in which the person is proposed to be appointed as Independent Director. |
| **59.** | Section 152-Appointment of directors | It is proposed to make necessary provisions to provide that in addition to DIN, a director may hold any other identification as may be prescribed by the Central Government under section 153. |
| **60.** | Section 153-Application for allotment of Director Identification Number | It is proposed to empower the Central Government to recognize any other identification number to be treated as director identification number. It is expected that Central Government will notify either PAN or Aadhar as DIN. |
| **61.** | Section 157-Company to inform Director Identification Number to Registrar | Time limit of 270 days within which a company could furnish DIN of all its directors on payment of additional fee has been done away with. It is proposed that a company can furnish DIN of all directors to ROC at any time on payment of prescribed additional fee. |
| **62.** | Section 160-Right of persons other than retiring directors to stand for directorship | It is proposed that the requirement of deposit of rupees one lakh with respect to nomination of directors shall not be applicable in case of appointment of independent directors or directors nominated by nomination and remuneration committee or a director recommended by the Board of Directors of the Company, in the case of a company not required to constitute Nomination and Remuneration Committee. |
| **63.** | Section 161-Appointment of Additional director, Alternate director and Nominee director | • It is proposed to restrict a person from being appointed as an alternate director if he is holding directorship in the same company. |
| | | • It is also proposed that all companies including a private company may fill up the causal vacancy by the board and casual vacancy filled by the Board shall be subsequently approved in the immediate next general meeting. |
| **64.** | Section 164-Disqualifications for appointment of director | • It is proposed that when a director is appointed in company which is in default of filing of financial statements or annual return or repayment of deposits or pay interest or redemption of debentures or payment of interest thereon or payment of dividend then such director shall not incur the disqualification for a period of six months from the date of his appointment.<br>It is also proposed to be clarified that disqualification arising due to conviction by court or order passed by court or tribunal or conviction related to section 188, shall continue to exist even if appeal or petition has been filed against the order of conviction or disqualification. |

| S. No. | Section | AMENDMENT |
|---|---|---|
| **65.** | Section 165-Number of Directorship | It is proposed that the directorship in a dormant company shall not be included in the limit of directorships of 20 companies. |
| **66.** | Section 167-Vacation of office of director | • It is proposed that in case a director incurs any of disqualifications under section 164 (2) due to default of filing of financial statements or annual return or repayment of deposits or pay interest or redemption of debentures or payment of interest thereon or payment of dividend, then he shall vacate office in all the companies other than the company which is in default. |
| | | • It is also proposed that the director will not vacate office in certain cases where an appeal is preferred. |
| **67.** | Section 168-Resignation of director | It is proposed to make filing of Form DIR-11 regarding forwarding of copy of resignation by director to the Registrar optional. |
| **68.** | Section 173-Meetings of Board | It is proposed to allow participation of directors on restricted items at Board meetings through video conferencing or other audio-visual means if there is quorum through physical presence of directors. |
| **69.** | Section 177-Audit Committee | • It is proposed that instead of every listed company, every listed public company shall constitute an audit committee. |
| | | • It is proposed that related party transactions other than those prescribed under section 188, if not approved by Audit committee, will require the approval of Board of Directors. |
| | | • In case any transaction involving any amount not exceeding one crore rupees is entered into by a director or officer of the company without obtaining the approval of the Audit Committee and it is not ratified by the Audit Committee within three months from the date of the transaction, such transaction shall be voidable at the option of the Audit Committee and if the transaction is with the related party to any director or is authorised by any other director, the director concerned shall indemnify the company against any loss incurred by it. |
| | | • It is also proposed that approval of audit committee with respect to transactions between a holding company and its wholly owned subsidiary company will only be required, if the transactions falls under section 188. |
| **70.** | Section 178-Nomination and remuneration Committee and Stakeholders Relationship Committee | • It is proposed that instead of every listed company, every listed public company shall constitute a Nomination and Remuneration Committee ('NRC'). |
| | | • It is proposed that committee will specify methodology for effective evaluation of performance of Board and committees and individual directors either by the Board, NRC or an independent external agency and NRC can review the implementation of evaluation system. |
| | | • It is further proposed that instead of disclosing the policy in the Board's report, such policy shall be placed on the website of the company, if any and only the salient features of the policy and the changes therein need to be disclosed in the Board's report. |

| S. No. | Section | AMENDMENT |
|---|---|---|
| **71.** | Section 180-Restrictions on powers of board | It is proposed to include securities premium along with paid-up share capital and free reserves for calculation of maximum limits on borrowing powers of the Board. |
| **72.** | Section 184-Disclosure of interest by directors | • It is proposed to omit the minimum penalty with respect to failure by directors to disclose interest. |
| | | • It is also proposed to exempt body corporate where any director or two or more of them holds or hold not more than 2% of the paid-up share capital, from the purview of section 184. |
| **73.** | Section 185-Loan to directors, etc. | A completely new section 185 is proposed. Some of the key changes are:<br>• Complete restriction on providing loan, guarantee or security in connection with loan to any director, director of the holding company or any partner or relative of any such director or any firm in which any such director or relative in a partner. |
| | | • Loan to following parties is allowed subject to special resolution of shareholders and certain other prescribed conditions<br>(i) any private company of which any such director is a director or member;<br>(ii) any body corporate at a general meeting of which not less than twenty-five per cent of the total voting power may be exercised or controlled by any such director, or by two or more such directors, together; or<br>(iii) any body corporate, the Board of directors, managing director or manager, whereof is accustomed to act in accordance with the directions or instructions of the Board, or of any director or directors, of the lending company.<br>Currently transactions with aforesaid categories is prohibited<br>• Current exemption provided under section 185(1) continues to remain except that when company which in the ordinary course of its business provides loans or gives guarantees or securities for the due repayment of any loan and in respect of such loans an interest is charged at a rate not less than the rate of prevailing yield of one year, three year, five year or ten year Government security closest to the tenure of the loan. The rate of interest is clarified |
| | | • It is also proposed to penalize defaulting officer in the company along with the company and director or the other person to whom any loan is advanced or guarantee or security is given. |
| **74.** | Section 186-Loan and Investment by company | • It also proposed to exclude employees from the ambit of this section. |
| | | • It is proposed that shareholders' approval will not be required where a loan or guarantee is given or where a security has been provided by a company to its wholly owned subsidiary company or a joint venture company, or acquisition is made by a holding company, by way of subscription, purchase or otherwise of, the securities of its wholly owned subsidiary company. |

| S. No. | Section | AMENDMENT |
|---|---|---|
| **75.** | Section 188-Related Party Transactions | • It is proposed that the requirement related to restriction on voting by relatives in the general meeting shall not apply to a company in which ninety per cent or more members in numbers are relatives of promoters or related parties. |
| | | • It is also proposed to provide that non-ratification of transaction shall be voidable at the option of the Board or shareholders, as the case may be. This amendment aims at bringing clarity since currently though ratification is allowed both by Board or Shareholders but transaction was only voidable at the option of the Board. |
| **76.** | Section 194-Prohibition on Forward dealings in securities of company by director or Key Managerial Personnel | It is proposed to omit this section. |
| **77.** | Section 195-Prohibition on Insider trading of securities | It is proposed to omit this section. |
| **78.** | Section 196-Appointment of Managing Director, Wholetime director or Manager | • It is proposed that a person beyond the age of seventy years can be appointed as managing director or whole time director or manager even when such appointment has not been approved by special resolution provided that the resolution for such appointment is passed with votes cast in favour of the motion exceed the votes, if any, cast against the motion and the Central Government is satisfied, on an application made by the Board, that such appointment is most beneficial to the company, the appointment of the person who has attained the age of seventy years may be made. |
| | | • Further it is proposed that in respect of appointment of managing director, whole time director or manager, approval of Central Government shall only be required in case the appointment is not in accordance with the matters specified in Part I of Schedule V. |
| **79.** | Section 197-Overall maximum managerial remuneration and managerial remuneration in case of absence or inadequacy of profits | • It is proposed that the approval of the Central Government shall not be required at the time of the payment of remuneration exceeding 11% of the net profits of the company. |
| | | • It is proposed that company with the approval of shareholders by way of special resolution can pay the remuneration in excess of individual limits provided for payment of remuneration to executive or non-executive directors. Further where the company has defaulted in payment of dues to any bank or public financial institution or non-convertible debenture holders or any other secured creditor, the prior approval of the bank or public financial institution concerned or the non-convertible debenture holders or other secured creditor, as the case may be, shall be obtained by the company before obtaining the approval in the general meeting. Currently requirement is of ordinary resolution and no provision is there for approval of financial institutions etc. |

| S. No. | Section | AMENDMENT |
|---|---|---|
| | | • It is also proposed that in case of loss or inadequacy of profits, remuneration can only be paid in accordance with Schedule V. This is very important amendment because currently in case where remuneration is not paid in accordance with Schedule V, then approval of Central Government can be obtained but by way of amendment, the provision of approval is proposed to be omitted. |
| | | • It is also proposed to provide relief to director to refund the excess remuneration received by providing a timeline of two years or such lesser period as may be allowed by the company. Further until such sum is refunded, the director shall hold it in trust for the company. Consequently it is proposed to delete the provisions related to waiver of excess remuneration paid to directors with the approval of Central Government. |
| | | • It is also proposed to make a provision which empowers the Company to waive the recovery of excess remuneration paid to directors provided approval of company by special resolution within two years from the date the sum becomes refundable is obtained. Further where any term loan of any bank or public financial institution is subsisting or the company has defaulted in payment of dues to any bank or public financial institution or non-convertible debenture holders or any other secured creditor, the prior approval of the bank or public financial institution concerned or the non-convertible debenture holders or other secured creditor, as the case may be, shall be obtained by the company before obtaining the approval in the general meeting. |
| | | • It is also proposed that the auditor of the company shall, in his report under section 143, make a statement as to whether the remuneration paid by the company to its directors is in accordance with the provisions of this section, whether remuneration paid to any director is in excess of the limit laid down under this section and give such other details as may be prescribed. |
| | | • It is also proposed to provide relief to the company whose application is pending for approval before the Central Government under section 197 by making a provision under which on and from the commencement of the Companies (Amendment) Act, 2017, any application made to the Central Government under the provisions of this section as it stood before such commencement, which is pending with that Government shall abate, and the company shall, within one year of such commencement, obtain the approval in accordance with the provisions of this section, as so amended. |
| **80.** | Section 198- Calculation of profits | It is proposed that credit for profit arising by way of premium on shares or debentures of the company which are issued or sold by an investment company as referred to in clause (a) of the explanation to section 186 shall be allowed as credit to the profit and loss account. Currently such credit is not allowed in case of all companies including investment companies.<br>• It is also proposed that at the time of calculation of profits, credit shall not be given for any amount representing unrealized gains, notional gains or revaluation of assets. |
| | | • It is further proposed that sums related to excess of expenditure over income, which had arisen in computing the net profits in accordance with this section in any year, in so far as such excess has not been deducted in any subsequent year preceding the year in respect of which the net profits have to be ascertained, shall be allowed as a deduction. |

| S. No. | Section | AMENDMENT |
|---|---|---|
| 81. | Section 200-Central Government or company to fix limits with regard to remuneration | It is proposed to omit the power of the Central Government to fix the remuneration within the limits specified in the Act, at such amount or percentage of profits as it may deems fit. |
| 82. | Section 201-Forms of, and procedure in relation to, certain applications | It is proposed to amend the section as a consequential change to amendment in section 196. |
| 83. | Section 216-Investigation of ownership of company | It is proposed to empower the Central Government to appoint inspectors for determining true persons who have or had beneficial interest in shares of a company or who are or have been beneficial owners or significant beneficial owner of the company. |
| 84. | Section 223-Inspector's report | It is proposed that a copy of inspectors report shall be made available only to members, creditors or any other person whose interest is likely to be affected, on their request. Currently any person can request for the copy. |
| 85. | Section 236-Purchase of Minority Shareholding | It is proposed to substitute the words 'transferor company' with the words 'company whose shares are being transferred' for providing clarity in sub-sections (4), (5) and (6). |
| 86. | Section 247-Valuation by Registered Valuers | It is proposed to dilute the restriction on appointment of a registered valuer by providing that registered valuer can be appointed for valuation of an asset in which he has a direct or indirect interest or becomes so interested during a period of three years prior to appointment as valuer or three years after valuation of assets.<br>Currently restriction on appointment of registered valuer for undertaking valuation of any assets in which he has a direct or indirect interest or becomes so interested is without any limitation on time. |
| 87. | Section 366-Companies capable of being registered | It is proposed to allow conversions of partnership firms, LLP, etc. with two or more partners into private companies. Currently they must have seven partners. |
| 88. | Section 374-Obligations of companies registering under this Part | It is proposed to bring the clarity that upon registration as a company under the Part-I of Chapter-XXI, a limited liability partnership incorporated under the Limited Liability Partnership Act, 2008 shall be deemed to have been dissolved under that Act without any further act or deed. |
| 89. | Section 379-Application of Act to foreign companies | • It is proposed to bring clarity with respect to applicability of provisions of the Act to foreign companies by providing that sections 380 to 386 and 392 and 393 shall apply to foreign companies.<br>• It is also proposed to empower the Central Government to exempt any class of foreign companies from complying with the aforesaid provisions. |

| S. No. | Section | AMENDMENT |
|---|---|---|
| 90. | Section 384-Debentures, Annual Return, Registration of charges, books of account and their Inspection | It is proposed to amend the section for providing applicability of section 135 on foreign companies. |
| 91. | Section 391-Application of sections 34 to 36 and Chapter XX | It is proposed that the provisions relating to winding up contained in Chapter XX shall apply for closure of place of business of a foreign company in India as if it were a company incorporated in India in case such foreign company has raised monies through offer or issue of securities which have not been repaid or redeemed. In other words, if a foreign company has not raised monies, the provisions relating to winding up will not be applicable. |
| 92. | Section 403-Fee for Filings, etc. | • It is proposed that only document, fact or information required to be submitted under section 92 (Annual Return) or 137 (Copy of financial statement to be filed with registrar) may be submitted, after expiry of the period so provided in those sections, on payment of such additional fee as may be prescribed which shall not be less than ₹ 100 per day and different amounts may be prescribed for different classes of companies. |
| | | • Further it is proposed that where the document, fact or information, in cases other than sections 92 or 137, is not submitted, within the period provided in the relevant section, it may, without prejudice to any other legal action or liability under this Act, be submitted, filed, registered or recorded, on payment of such additional fee as may be prescribed and different fees may be prescribed for different classes of companies. |
| | | • It is also proposed that where there is default on two or more occasions in submitting, filing, registering or recording of the document, fact or information, it may, without prejudice to any other legal action or liability under this Act, be submitted, filed, registered or recorded, on payment of a higher additional fee, as may be prescribed and which shall not be lesser than twice the additional fee provided under the first or the second proviso as applicable. |
| | | • Further it is proposed that where a company fails or commits any default to submit, file, register or record any document, fact or information before the expiry of the period specified in the relevant section, the company and the officers of the company who are in default, shall, without prejudice to the liability for the payment of fee and additional fee, be liable for the penalty or punishment provided under this Act for such failure or default. |
| 93. | Section 406-Power to modify act in its application to 'Nidhis' | • It is proposed to provide that Nidhi" or "Mutual Benefit Society" means a company which the Central Government may, by notification in the Official Gazette, declare to be a Nidhi or Mutual Benefit Society, as the case may be. Currently mutual benefit society is not covered. |
| | | • Further exhaustive definition of Nidhi company has been deleted and it is left to the Government to declare a company to be a Nidhi or Mutual Benefit Society by notification in the Official Gazette. |
| | | • It is also proposed to modify the requirements relating to laying of copy of exemption notification before both Houses of Parliament. |

| S. No. | Section | AMENDMENT |
|---|---|---|
| 94. | Section 409-Qualification of President and Members of Tribunal | Following changes are proposed with respect to eligibility for technical members with respect to the constitution of the National Company Law Tribunal:<br>• Instead of Joint Secretary to the Government of India, person who has been holding the rank of Secretary or Additional Secretary to the Government of India, will be eligible. |
| | | • A person of proven ability, integrity and standing having special knowledge and professional experience of not less than fifteen years in industrial finance, industrial management, industrial reconstruction, investment and accountancy will be eligible. Expertise in other disciplines like law, labour laws, and disciplines related to management, conduct of affairs, revival, rehabilitation and winding-up of companies are proposed to be deleted. |
| 95. | Section 410-Constitution of Appellate Tribunal | In addition to the order of the Tribunal, it is proposed to bring out the order of the National Financial Reporting Authority also for appeal before the National Company Law Appellate Tribunal. |
| 96. | Section 411-Qualifications of Chairperson and Members of Appellate Tribunal | Eligibility for appointment as Technical member is proposed to be brought in sync with the amendment proposed in section 409. |
| 97. | Section 412-Selection of Members of Tribunal and Appellate Tribunal | It is proposed to align with Supreme Court directions with respect to constitution of Selection Committee. |
| 98. | Section 435-Establishment of Special Courts | • It is proposed to authorize Central Government to establish Special Courts for the purpose of speedy trials of offences under the Act. Currently Special Court can be established for trying offences punishable with imprisonment of two years or more. |
| | | • The constitution of Special Court has been changed and will depend upon the nature of offence. |
| 99. | Section 438-Application of Code to proceedings before Special Court | It is proposed to amend section 438 of the Act as a consequence of amendments to section 435. |
| 100. | Section 439-Offences to be non-cognizable | It is proposed to include member along with shareholders in respect of complaint with respect to taking cognizance of offences under the Act by the Court. |
| 101. | Section 440-Transitional provisions | It is proposed to provide that till the time a Special Court is established, the trial of offences shall be continued with Court of Session or Court of Metropolitan Magistrate or a Judicial Magistrate of the First Class. |
| 102. | Section 441-Compounding of certain offences | It is proposed to enable the Tribunal to compound offences punishable with fine only as well as offences punishable with fine or imprisonment. The provision has now been brought in line with section 621A of the 1956 Act. |

| S. No. | Section | AMENDMENT |
|---|---|---|
| 103. | Section 446A-Factors for determining level of punishment | It is proposed to insert a new section providing for the following factors which the court or special court will consider while determining level of punishment:<br>(a) Size of the company;<br>(b) Nature of business carried on by the company;<br>(c) Injury to public interest;<br>(d) Nature of the default; and<br>(e) Repetition of the default. |
| 104. | Section 446B-Lesser penalties for One Person Companies or small companies | It is proposed to provide relief to OPC and Small Co., in case of failure to comply with the provisions of sub-section (5) of section 92 (Annual Return), clause (c) of sub-section (2) of section 117 (Resolutions and agreements to be filed), sub-section (3) of section 137 (Copy of financial statement to be filed with Registrar). In case of default, such company and officer in default of such company shall be punishable with fine or imprisonment or fine and imprisonment, as the case may be, which shall not be more than one-half of the fine or imprisonment or fine and imprisonment, as the case may be, of the minimum or maximum fine or imprisonment or fine and imprisonment, as the case may be, specified in such sections. |
| 105. | Section 447-Punishment for Fraud | • It is proposed that only person guilty of fraud involving an amount of at least ten lakh rupees or one per cent of the turnover of the company, whichever is lower shall be punishable with imprisonment for a term which shall not be less than 6 months but which may extend to ten years and shall also be liable to a fine which shall not less than the amount involved in the fraud but which may extend to three times the amount involved in the fraud. |
| | | • Further that where the fraud involves an amount less than ten lakh rupees or one per cent of the turnover of the company, whichever is lower and does not involve public interest, any person guilty of such fraud shall be punishable with imprisonment for a term which may extend to five years or with fine which may extend to twenty lakh rupees or with both. |
| 106. | Section 458 Delegation by Central Government of its powers and functions | Consequent upon omission of sections 194 (Forward dealings) and 195 (Insider trading), the proviso to sub-section (1) of section 458 is proposed to be omitted. |